Innovations in Client-Centered Therapy
by David A. Wexler and Laura North Rice

The Rorschach: A Comprehensive System, in two volumes
by John E. Exner

Theory and Practice in Behavior Therapy
by Aubrey J. Yates

Principles of Psychotherapy
by Irving B. Weiner

Psychoactive Drugs and Social Judgment: Theory and Research
edited by Kenneth Hammond and C. R. B. Joyce

Clinical Methods in Psychology
edited by Irving B. Weiner

Human Resources for Troubled Children
by Werner I. Halpern and Stanley Kissel

Hyperactivity
by Dorothea M. Ross and Sheila A. Ross

Heroin Addiction: Theory, Research, and Treatment
by Jerome J. Platt and Christina Labate

Children's Rights and the Mental Health Profession
edited by Gerald P. Koocher

The Role of the Father in Child Development
edited by Michael E. Lamb

Handbook of Behavioral Assessment
edited by Anthony R. Ciminero, Karen S. Calhoun, and Henry E. Adams

Counseling and Psychotherapy: A Behavioral Approach
by E. Lakin Phillips

Dimensions of Personality
edited by Harvey London and John E. Exner, Jr.

The Mental Health Industry: A Cultural Phenomenon
by Peter A. Magaro, Robert Gripp, David McDowell, and Ivan W. Miller III

Nonverbal Communication: The State of the Art
by Robert G. Harper, Arthur N. Wiens, and Joseph D. Matarazzo

Alcoholism and Treatment
by David J. Armor, J. Michael Polich, and Harriet B. Stambul

Cognitive Style: Five Approaches and Relevant Research
by Kenneth M. Goldstein and Sheldon Blackman

A Biodevelopmental Approach to Clinical Child Psychology: Cognitive Controls and Cognitive Control Theory
by Sebastiano Santostefano

Handbook of Infant Development
edited by Joy D. Osofsky

Understanding the Rape Victim: A Synthesis of Research Findings
by Sedelle Katz and Mary Ann Mazur

Childhood Pathology and Later Adjustment: The Question of Prediction
by Loretta K. Cass and Carolyn B. Thomas

Handbook of Minimal Brain Dysfunctions
edited by Herbert E. Rie and Ellen D. Rie

Intelligent Testing with the WISC-R
by Alan S. Kaufman

Handbook of Adolescent Psychology
edited by Joseph Adelson

About the author

JOSEPH ADELSON is concurrently Professor of Psychology at the University of Michigan in Ann Arbor, and Director of both the Psychological Clinic at the University of Michigan and the Center for the Clinical Study of Personality. He received his Ph.D. from the University of California, Berkeley, and has held the positions of psychologist and psychotherapist in both public and private practice. A former Consultant to the Ford Foundation Behavioral Science Project at Bennington College and a research consultant to the Institute of Social Research. Dr. Adelson was also a consulting editor to various journals. At present, he is the consulting editor of the Merrill-Palmer Quarterly, the associate editor of the Journal of Youth and Adolescence, and is a Fellow of the American Psychological Association.

HANDBOOK OF
ADOLESCENT PSYCHOLOGY

HANDBOOK OF ADOLESCENT PSYCHOLOGY

Edited by

JOSEPH ADELSON

A WILEY–INTERSCIENCE PUBLICATION

JOHN WILEY & SONS, New York • Chichester • Brisbane • Toronto

Copyright © 1980 by John Wiley & Sons, Inc.

All rights reserved. Published simultaneously in Canada.

Library of Congress Cataloging in Publication Data

Main entry under title:

Handbook of adolescent psychology.

   (Wiley series on personality processes)
   "A Wiley-Interscience publication."
   Includes index.
   1. Adolescent psychology—Addresses, essays,
lectures.   I. Adelson, Joseph.   [DNLM:
1. Adolescent psychology. WS462.3 H236]

BF724.H33   155.5   79-21927
ISBN 0-471-03793-1

Printed in the United States of America

10 9 8 7 6 5 4 3 2 1

Contributors

JOSEPH ADELSON, Psychological Clinic, University of Michigan.

RICHARD BRAUNGART, Department of Sociology, Syracuse University.

J. C. COLEMAN, Psychiatric Department, The London Hospital Medical College, London, England.

MARGERY DOEHRMAN, Psychological Clinic, University of Michigan.

GLEN ELDER, Center for the Study of Youth, Omaha, Nebraska.

DAVID ELKIND, Department of Psychology, University of Rochester.

NORMAN FEATHER, School of Social Sciences, The Flinders University of South Australia, Bedford Park, South Australia.

JUDITH GALLATIN, Portland, Oregon.

MARTIN GOLD, Institute for Social Research, University of Michigan.

EILEEN HIGHAM, Baltimore, Maryland.

MARTIN HOFFMAN, Department of Psychology, University of Michigan.

ROBERT HOGAN, Department of Psychology, Johns Hopkins University.

RUTHELLEN JOSSELSON, Baltimore, Maryland.

DANIEL KEATING, Institute of Child Development, Minneapolis, Minnesota.

NORMAN LIVSON, Institute of Human Development, University of California, Berkeley.

JAMES MARCIA, Department of Psychology, Simon Fraser University, Burnaby, British Columbia, Canada.

PATRICIA MILLER, Institute for Urban Studies, University of Houston.

HARVEY PESKIN, Institute of Human Development, University of California, Berkeley.

ANNE PETERSEN, Department of Psychiatry, Michael Reese Hospital, Chicago.

RICHARD PETRONIO, Institute for Social Research, University of Michigan.

WILLIAM SIMON, Institute for Urban Studies, University of Houston.

BRANDON TAYLOR, Department of Psychiatry, Michael Reese Hospital, Chicago.

IRVING WEINER, Department of Psychology, University of Denver.

Series Preface

This series of books is addressed to behavioral scientists interested in the nature of human personality. Its scope should prove pertinent to personality theorists and researchers as well as to clinicians concerned with applying an understanding of personality processes to the amelioration of emotional difficulties in living. To this end, the series provides a scholarly integration of theoretical formulations, empirical data, and practical recommendations.

Six major aspects of studying and learning about human personality can be designated: personality theory, personality structure and dynamics, personality development, personality assessment, personality change, and personality adjustment. In exploring these aspects of personality, the books in the series discuss a number of distinct but related subject areas: the nature and implications of various theories of personality; personality characteristics that account for consistencies and variations in human behavior; the emergence of personality processes in children and adolescents; the use of interviewing and testing procedures to evaluate individual differences in personality; efforts to modify personality styles through psychotherapy, counseling, behavior therapy, and other methods of influence; and patterns of abnormal personality functioning that impair individual competence.

IRVING B. WEINER

University of Denver
Denver, Colorado

Preface

After a long, long period of intellectual sleepiness the study of adolescence has begun to stir itself awake. During the last decade genuinely new ideas and findings have made their appearance in the scientific literature; yet the revival has gone virtually unnoticed, except among specialists. Hence this book is an attempt to bring that new material to a larger audience of scholars and students.

We begin with a group of conceptual essays, chapters devoted to adumbrating some of the important current perspectives in adolescent psychology—the historical, longitudinal, psychodynamic, and biological approaches. We have omitted a chapter on the cognitive perspective because it is abundantly represented in other essays—indeed, it is probably the dominant approach in adolescence research today. The second major section of the Handbook concentrates upon some of the central processes common to adolescence in general—personality development; the growth of thinking, and of ideas and ideals; social and sexual maturation. We conclude with a set of essays exploring significant variations in adolescence, e.g., disturbed and delinquent behavior, the psychology of the gifted, biological anomalies, political activism. In selecting chapter topics, our intention was to look ahead, trying to discern those themes and tendencies likely to show substantial advances in the immediate future, and perhaps beyond.

A book of this sort is generally a collaboration between the editor and the contributors. The editor proposes; the author counter-proposes; a dialogue ensues; and the chapter is shaped. So my first debt of gratitude is to that silent editorial board of contributors, who gently but firmly told me what I ought to be asking them to do. Throughout the process, but especially in its early phases, I relied on the advice and immense erudition of Daniel Offer. I am particularly grateful for the climate of wit and intellectual seriousness provided by the Psychological Clinic; for the support given by my colleagues, and above all my collaborator Margery Doehrman; and for the presence of my marvelous secretary Deborah Wissner.

JOSEPH ADELSON
Ann Arbor, June 1979

Dedication

This book is dedicated to the memory of my loving and beloved father.

Contents

PART ONE   NEW PERSPECTIVES ON ADOLESCENCE

1. Adolescence in Historical Perspective   3
   Glen H. Elder, Jr.

2. Perspectives on Adolescence from Longitudinal Research   47
   Norman Livson and Harvey Peskin

3. The Psychodynamic Approach to Adolescence   99
   Joseph Adelson and Margery J. Doehrman

4. The Biological Approach to Adolescence   117
   Anne C. Petersen and Brandon Taylor

PART TWO   THE PROCESSES OF ADOLESCENCE

5. Identity in Adolescence   159
   James E. Marcia

6. Ego Development in Adolescence   188
   Ruthellen Josselson

7. Thinking Processes in Adolescence   211
   Daniel P. Keating

8. Values in Adolescence   247
   Norman T. Feather

9. Moral Development in Adolescence   295
   Martin L. Hoffman

10. Political Thinking in Adolescence   344
    Judith Gallatin

11. The Development of Sexuality in Adolescence   383
    Patricia Y. Miller and William Simon

12. Friendship and the Peer Group in Adolescence   408
    John C. Coleman

13. Strategic Interactions in Early Adolescence   432
    David Elkind

PART THREE   VARIATIONS IN ADOLESCENCE

14. Psychopathology in Adolescence   447
    Irving B. Weiner

15. Variations in Adolescent Psychohormonal Development   472
    Eileen Higham

16. Delinquent Behavior in Adolescence   495
    Martin Gold and Richard J. Petronio

17. The Gifted Adolescent   536
    Robert Hogan

18. Youth Movements   560
    Richard G. Braungart

NAME INDEX   599

SUBJECT INDEX

HANDBOOK OF
ADOLESCENT PSYCHOLOGY

PART ONE

New Perspectives on Adolescence

CHAPTER 1

Adolescence in Historical Perspective

Glen H. Elder, Jr.

Adolescence is intimately linked to matters historical: the evolution of social age categories, the emergence of youth-related institutions, the impact of social change in lives. The developmental foci of all these involve the relationship between historical variation and life patterns. Adolescent experience may be shaped directly by historical events, as in the 1960s, and indirectly through the life histories that young people bring to this stage. After years of neglect, this perspective is beginning to appear not only on the agenda of those involved in developmental research[1], but also in the promising outline of a life-course framework that relates history and social structure in the human biography. Fruitful applications of this framework are seen in the notable growth since the 1960s of genuine archival studies on youth in history, a scope of inquiry that extends from the preindustrial age to the present. This chapter examines these developments in terms of their contribution to an analytical perspective that locates adolescence and young people in historical time, in the social order, and in the life span.

These developments began to crystallize in the troubled decade of the 1960s; and reflect the intellectual currents and problematic issues of these years. In combination, they represent a line of demarcation between the atemporal theme of postwar research on youth and an expanding recognition of the interdependence between social history and life history. Though historical change has long been noted as a determinant of life patterns (Thomas & Znaniecki, 1918–1920; Kuhlen, 1940), this observation left no enduring imprint on research until the 1960s. At this point, we see thoughtful efforts across disciplines that suggest ways of viewing social change in lives. Warner Schaie (1965) proposed a methodology for assessing the effect of historical change on development; Norman Ryder (1965), in social demography, outlined a cohort historical perspective on

---

[1] Two developments in psychology warrant special notice: (1) the increasing emphasis on developmental studies that investigate transactions between the growing human organism and its changing environment, as expressed by the writings of Urie Bronfenbrenner in particular (1977); and (2) the evolution of a life-span developmental psychology that is focused on the assessment of antecedent-consequent relations in behavioral development from birth to death (Baltes & Schaie, 1973). Though both developments have much in common, including a life-span orientation, they represent outgrowths of issues and problem foci that are located at opposite ends of the life-span continuum — childhood in the case of Bronfenbrenner and the adult years or old age in the case of Baltes and Schaie. Greater sociological interest in historical and social influences on human development is associated with the emergence of a life-course perspective from the study of age (see Riley, Johnson, and Foner, 1972; Elder, 1975).

Preparation of this chapter was supported by Grant MH-25834 from the National Institute of Mental Health (Glen H. Elder, Jr., principal investigator).

social change in the life course; and historians (see Thernstrom, 1965) specified the potential interpretative errors in research that ignores historical facts. Intergenerational tensions also posed questions that could only be answered from an understanding of the diverse historical origins of parents and offspring, a problem identified many years ago by Kingsley Davis (1940).

Though path-breaking in many respects, these analytic ventures toward history have only recently made a difference in the actual study of adolescence and youth (Nesselroade & Baltes, 1974; Elder, 1974; Gillis, 1974). By and large, the contemporary literature on adolescence is distinguished by the absence of historical facts and considerations. Adolescents are seldom viewed within the life course and historical context; longitudinal studies pay little attention to the implications of social change (Elder, 1975a). These deficiencies stand out among contemporary textbooks on adolescence. For example, Muus's *Theories of Adolescence* (1975) includes only one section that bears on adolescence as a socially defined age division, and it makes no reference to analytical developments that place this stage within the life course and historical time. However rudimentary, these developments raise questions of critical importance for any study of human development. In what sense can we presume to understand the psychosocial development of youth without systematic knowledge of their life course and collective experience in specific historical times?

As a point of departure, I begin the chapter with a brief overview of its two central themes: (1) the life course as an emergent perspective that incorporates the historical dimension and (2) the burgeoning field of historical research on youth. With this as background, I turn to various age-based concepts of adolescence and their distinctive features. These concepts and the problem foci of historical periods have shaped the study of American adolescence and young people since the 1920s. This development is portrayed in terms of key studies, their strengths and limitations, and three age concepts (developmental, social, and historical) in the life-course framework. I conclude by reviewing selected themes in historical research, findings, and analytical contributions. The objective is not to provide a survey of research and knowledge on youth in history, which is available in other sources (Gillis, 1974; Kett, 1977), but to suggest something of the possibilities of an analytical perspective on the life course that brings historical considerations to the study of adolescence.

THE LIFE COURSE AND HISTORICAL RESEARCH

The life-course perspective represents developments over the past decade in understanding the bond between age and time (Riley, Johnson, and Foner, 1972; Elder, 1975b). Three temporal modalities have been identified:

1. The lifetime of the individual — chronological or developmental age as a rudimentary index of stage in the aging process.
2. Social time in the age-patterning of events and roles throughout life (e.g., entry into formal schooling, departure from home, first job, and marriage) — a pattern structured by age criteria in norms, roles, and institutions.
3. Historical time in the process of social change — birth-year, or entry into the system, as an index of historical location and membership in a specific cohort.

The lifetime perspective focuses on the inevitable and irreversible process of aging; social time, on age differentiation in the sequence and arrangement of life events and roles; and historical time, on cohort membership, differentiation, and succession, with their implications for life patterns. We derive the meaning of each temporal dimension from correlated variables; in the case of historical time, from knowledge of events, circumstances, and mentalities of the period.

Each temporal perspective is associated with a distinctive tradition of research and theory:

1. Lifetime — John Dollard's (1949, p. 3) use of life histories to assess the growth of a person in a cultural setting; Charlotte Bühler's (1935) concept of the biological cycle of life; and the general field of life-span development (Goulet & Baltes, 1970).

2. Social time — analyses of age strata and hierarchies by Ralph Linton (1942) and Talcott Parsons (1942), as well as S. N. Eisenstadt's (1956) pioneering synthesis of ethnographic materials on age-based differentiation and youth groups.

3. Historical time — most notably Karl Mannheim's (1928/1952) influential essay on the emergent mentalities of generations (age cohorts in conventional terminology) and generation units or subgroups.

Important continuities within the framework of social time are illustrated by assessments of the "traditions of youth," from Willard Waller's (1932/1965) insightful essay on age-graded student traditions to David Matza's (1964) thoughtful essay on American youth and John Gillis's (1974) historical exploration of European age relations. Life transitions constitute another prominent theme across time, from Leonard Cottrell's (1942) propositional inventory on age-status adjustments to Modell, Furstenberg, and Hershberg's (1976) study of social change in the transition to adult roles. On historical time, a number of Mannheim's conceptual distinctions ("fresh contact with social change," stratification of experience, and the psychology of subgroups) influenced theoretical approaches in studies of student unrest and movements in the 1960s (Bengtson & Laufer, 1974; Braungart, 1975, pp. 255–289).

More than ever before, the life span defines the analytic scope of these areas of inquiry. Socialization, behavioral adaptation, and development are represented as lifelong processes that relate life stages in the human biography, from childhood to old age. Thus in the study of aging, life-span theoretical interests have fostered studies that extend beyond such age categories as adolescence (Baltes & Schaie, 1973; Baltes, 1977; Huston-Stein & Baltes, 1976). According to programmatic statements, the objective of these studies is to describe and explain age-related behavior change from birth to death as well as to specify temporal linkages through the identification of antecedent-consequent relations. For the most part, this explanatory aim remains an ideal. It has not been implemented by research on diverse life paths through the dependency years and their psychological effects.

Life-span issues in the sociocultural tradition (social time) are expressed in the literature on careers and by studies of orientations toward adult careers — marriage, parenthood, work — in the field of adolescence. But only in the past decade have career orientations and paths been viewed in terms of temporal distinctions from an articulation of social age (Clausen, 1972), the timing of events and their synchronization across multiple careers, and the role of age standards in self-assessments of career progress. Norman Ryder (1965) and Riley, Johnson, and Foner (1972) have linked historical change to the life course, a connection not developed in Mannheim's essay, "The Problem of Generations." The current trend is toward a more inclusive perspective on the life course, one that builds on all three temporal foci; locates individuals in age cohorts and thus, according to historical time, depicts their age-differentiated life pattern in relation to historical context; and represents the interplay between life paths and development. Evidence of this development is seen in the establishment in October 1977 of an Social Science Research Council Committee on the Life Course.

According to this perspective, adolescence (or the broader category of youth) can be fully understood only when viewed within the life course and its historical setting. Each generalized stage, or age category, is constructed from norms and institutional constraints that establish a basis for identity and specify appropriate behavior, roles, and timetables. Cultural norms that differentiate age categories also structure modes of interdependence among them; one's rights implies another's obligations in cross-age (e.g., children vs. adolescents) and intergenerational relationships. The interlocking careers of parents and offspring relate young-adult status and childhood, middle age and adolescence, old age and maturity. The experience of adolescence is shaped by what one has been and by what is foreseen, by the problems of middle-aged parents and by those of the very young. Cross-age linkages are basic elements of an evolving life course.

A normative model of the life course includes event schedules that serve as guidelines for the life course, alerting individuals or cohorts to the appropriate timing and sequencing of social transitions. In theory, these schedules define appropriate times for school entry and departure; for leaving home and establishing an independent domicile; for economic independence, marriage, and parenthood. An informal system of rewards and negative sanctions ensures, for example, consciousness of the relationships between age and status or the consequences associated with being early, on time, or late in role performance and accomplishments. Referring to preindustrial Europe, Gillis (1974, p. 4) notes that despite the apparent disarray of age norms ''premature entry into the marriage market was bound to provoke public censure, while remaining unmarried past a certain age made 'old maids' of girls and confirmed bachelors of boys.'' During the 1960s in midwestern America, Neugarten, Moore, and Lowe (1965) observed a high level of consensus among middle-class adults on age norms (usually above 80%) across some 15 age-related characteristics, including the timing of marriage. This study and a partial replication in a Japanese city (Plath & Ikeda, 1975) show generalized agreement on the major phases of the life course and a pattern of increasing sensitivity to age norms from early adulthood to old age. However, age norms and perceptions of age status constitute an undeveloped field of inquiry. Normative assertions are frequently made without adequate empirical evidence.

Beyond generalized age categories, the life course reflects the degree of social differentiation in complex societies, their plural age structures, timetables, and constraints across institutional domains — family, education, workplace, military. Status passage over the life course entails the assumption of concurrent multiple roles — from those of son or daughter, age-mate, and student during years of dependency to adult lines of activity in major institutional sectors. One's life course thus takes the form of interlocking career lines, each defined by a particular event sequence and timetable, for example, the temporal pattern of events and transitions in schooling and its relation to the timetable of family life and to the anticipated claims of military service, marriage, and work. Problems of life management arise in large measure from the competing demands of multiple careers.

Relevant to this point is Goode's observation that an individual's set of obligations is ''unique and overdemanding'' (1960). Since all demands cannot be met within the same time frame, a manageable course requires strategies that minimize conflicts and strain, for example, the selection of compatible lines of action, the scheduling and deferring of obligations, or appeals to shared values or authorities to rationalize priorities. The pressures of these demands, most notable when youth are entering lines of adult activity, bring to mind Erikson's observations on role confusion. This psychic state becomes most acute, according to Erikson (1959), when the adolescent is exposed to a ''combination of experiences which demand his simultaneous commitment to *physical intimacy* (not by any means overtly sexual), to decisive *occupational choice,* to energetic *competition,* and to *psychosocial self-definition''* (p. 123).

With a multi-dimensional concept of the life course, we are able to represent the diverse pathways that link childhood to the adult years and explore developmental problems and processes that arise from their interdependence. This concept parallels the organismic concept of ''developmental lines,'' such as intellectual, moral, and sexual, ''each of which may be in or out of phase with the others'' (Keniston, 1970, p. 636; see also 1971). Variations in the timing and sequencing of events and decisions during late adolescence acquire psychological significance through investigation of their implications for coherent or discordant patterns of development. Completion of education, marriage, and economic independence are commonly viewed as indications of the lower boundary of adulthood, yet the timing of these events spans a wide age range, up to 10 years or more. Leaving school, departing from home, marriage, and economic independence come early for some young people and relatively late for others (Modell, Furstenberg, & Hershberg, 1976). The order and spacing of these events also vary widely. Marriage may occur before the completion of formal education, especially when schooling is prolonged, whereas early teen-age pregnancy typically precedes marriage and economic independence. For the individual, such variations pose important implications for social identity, personal integration, and life chances. The full meaning of a transition is derived from knowledge of this life course and related situational change.

Historical placement of adolescence and young people inevitably generates questions regarding the social and cultural milieu of time and place. What are the historical events and forces that have relevance for life chances and psychosocial development? How were generalized trends in demographic, economic, and cultural change expressed in this setting, giving form and substance to the biographies of youth, their life stage, collective experience, and future? The birth-year of youth directs inquiry toward their historical origins and experiences as they move through time in an age cohort. At points of rapid change, the historical experience of successive cohorts varies through exposure to different events (such as wartime mobilization for persons born before and after World War II) and by exposure to the same event at different points in the life course.

Cohort differences in life stage at times of drastic change suggest variations in adaptive options relative to the event, in resulting experience, and thus in the process by which the event is expressed in life patterns. World War II entailed military obligations for American males who were born in the early 1920s and experienced adolescence in the depressed 1930s. By contrast, younger men, who were born at the end of the 1920s, experienced this war as adolescents on the home front, following a childhood shaped by the Great Depression. We derive the psychosocial meaning of cohort membership and of particular cohort attributes from knowledge of this differential experience. Cohort attributes (e.g., relative size and composition) are themselves a product of historical change, business cycles, institutional change, mass migration.

From this vantage point, youth cohorts represent a connection between social change and life-course patterns, historical time and lifetime. Within each cohort, processes of socialization and role allocation (via schools, etc.) serve as linkages between the young and social options — the labor requirements of industry, citizenship obligations in war and peace. Social change threatens the fragile character of these linkages as disparities emerge between youth characteristics and available options, for example, large cohorts who have come of age in a period of declining opportunities. Some analysts, for example, have viewed the rise of National Socialism in terms of the large German youth cohorts that encountered depressed opportunities in the 1930s after a history of wartime deprivations (Loewenberg, 1972; cf. Merkl, 1975). Likewise, a mood of fear (Scully, 1977) has been noted among the large postwar cohorts of university students in Europe who face declining opportunities for commensurate employment. American student unrest and protests in the 1960s, a decade of extraordinary growth of the youth population, generally support Herbert Moller's historical assessment (1968) over three centuries — that periods of social and revolutionary change are characterized by youth cohorts of ascending size. The historical dialectic between successive cohort flows and the social order tells us much about the socialization, opportunities, and actions of young people in concrete situations. It is this interplay that underscores the inadequacy of approaches that have focused on the age structure without attention to demographic factors or that have theorized about adolescent development in an historical vacuum.

A cohort is said to be distinctively marked by the life stage it occupies when historical events impinge on it (Ryder, 1965), but exposure to an event is not likely to be uniform among its members. For example, father-absence represents an important connection between World War II and the lives of young people; military service altered the socialization of children by removing fathers from the family over a two-to three-year period. However, deferments of one kind or another kept some fathers at home throughout this conflict. With such variation, the war's impact on a cohort of youth can be assessed by comparing psychological development under conditions of father-absence and father-presence (see Carlsmith, 1973). The hypothesis of life-stage variation (change has differential consequences for persons of unlike age) cautions against generalization from this comparison to other groups and favors a comparative design in which the developmental effects of war-caused father-absence are assessed in successive cohorts, for example, birthdates of 1930–1933, 1934–1937, 1938–1941.

This intracohort approach permits direct analysis of historical factors and explication of the process by which they are expressed in the lives of youth. The process is shaped in part by what families and offspring bring to events, their cultural heritage and expectations, their material resources and social position. Class, ethnic, and residential variations may identify subgroups that differ in how they "work up" historically relevant experience. Thus middle- and working-class families brought different resources to the Great Depression, resources that shaped both their response to economic misfortunes and the effect of the Depression on their children (Elder, 1974). Likewise, father-absence in World War II occurred in contexts (defined by marital harmony or conflict, financial security or strain) that influenced the meaning of the event and its impact on the welfare of family members (Hill, 1949). More recent examples include differences between college and noncollege youth of the 1960s in attitudes and actions relative to the Vietnam War (Braungart, 1975). As stressed by Mannheim's essay (1928/1952), historical differentiation within cohorts may stem from three sources of variation: exposure to events, interpretations of them, and subsequent modes of response.

Up to this point, we have emphasized historical facts that differentiate and explain the experience of youth cohorts or subgroups. Instead of asking whether there are behavioral variations across successive cohorts, investigation is guided by the rationale that expects such variation in the first place. Given known variations among and within cohorts, the research problem concerns their relevance for life experience. Developmental questions are posed by an understanding of historical realities and their plausible life-course effects, proximal and enduring. This approach is not synonomous with cohort studies and a large number bear only superficial resemblance to historical analysis — to the assessment of historical facts that give explicit meaning to the life experience of youth cohorts (for a review, see Bengtson & Starr, 1975). Estimates of developmental variation across cohorts point to the influence of social change (Baltes, Cornelius, & Nesselroade, 1977), but global reference to change leaves unspecified what aspects of change produced this outcome and the processes involved.

Without any doubt, the most notable advance on knowledge of social change in youth experience has come from the work of social historians, especially those of the new generation who have applied the procedures and techniques of social science to studies of the "inarticulate" — the ordinary folk who left no personal record of their lives, for example, letters, diaries, genealogies, and so on. Archival data for this research is largely based on institutional records – government censuses, welfare and property lists, marriage certificates, parish registers, school censuses, employment rolls. From Newark, New Jersey of the mid-nineteenth century (Bloomberg, 1974) to Manchester, New Hampshire of 1900–1930 (Hareven, 1975), the studies of historians show an attention to historical facts that warrants emulation if historical time is to acquire substantive and theoretical meaning in research on youth.

A major turning point toward historical research on youth occurred with the publication of Philipe Ariès's impressionistic history of childhood and youth in France *(Centuries of Childhood,* 1965) and Bernard Bailyn's *Education in the Forming of American Society* (1960). Due to research limitations at the time, both volumes could offer only tentative characterizations of institutional, ideological, and demographic changes in life stages, timetables, and pathways from birth to adult status. Among other issues Ariès's dating of male adolescence in the late eighteenth century, according to military conscription and advanced schooling, has been challenged by more recent work (see N. Z. Davis, 1975, pp. 97–123). Nonetheless, his path-breaking study and the research agenda outlined by Bailyn identified questions and unknowns that have influenced the course of subsequent inquiry, for example, on the emergence of mass schooling or the interaction of family, educational, and industrial change. Since the early 1960s the historical literature on youth has grown exponentially, with a scope that extends from the colonial era (Demos, 1970; Greven, 1970; Smith, 1973) into the twentieth century (Modell, Furstenberg, & Hershberg, 1976). Robert Bremner's multivolume anthology (1970–1974) of documents on American children and youth also spans this time frame. Two synthetic works on youth in history provide extensive bibliographies of American and European research: (1) Joseph Kett's survey (1977) of American youth, which is based largely on the social commentaries of upper-class adults; (2) John Gillis's (1974) analytical study of historical change in the position and traditions of youth in England and Germany.

In historical settings, the life experience of American youth has been depicted through assessments of family and kinship (Hareven, 1978), the most rapidly expanding field in social history; by studies of educational change and reform in the nineteenth century and their interplay with family patterns, demographic and economic change, and ideologies (Tyack, 1975; Kaestle & Vinovskis, 1976); and by studies of "child-saving" ideology and institutional realities (the juvenile court) through the progressive era (Platt, 1969;

Schlossman, 1977). With skillful use of archival data and methodologies, historians have moved beyond social concepts of youth and age vocabulary to the actual structure and content of the transition from childhood to full adult status. Their studies have enlarged our perspective on adolescence and its emergence as a concept in late nineteenth-century America by stressing the variable properties of the stage of youth across time and place, a view consistent with Eisenstadt's (1956) observation that a period of youth between childhood and adulthood exists to some extent in all known societies and historical periods. Its variation reflects the degree to which roles are assigned on the basis of age criteria, the prevalence of groups based on age, and the exigencies of demographic/economic conditions.

As in sociology, intensive study of age by historians has led to conceptual distinctions that are part of a life-course framework — the social timetable of events and roles, multiple career lines and transitions, the relation between age cohorts and age strata. Research themes include the changing normative and demographic properties of childhood and youth from the preindustrial age to the twentieth century (Gillis, 1974); nineteenth-century institutional change in life-course differentiation and the extension of age-graded schooling (Meyer et al., 1977); strain arising from change toward a broader social base in the composition of student cohorts among early nineteenth-century colleges (Allmendinger, 1975); change since 1860 in the timing of marriage and its life-course implications (Modell, Furstenberg, and Strong, 1978); and age patterns in the life course and psychological development in Plymouth Colony (Demos, 1970). Examples of this historical research will be discussed in a later section of the chapter.

Since the writings of G. Stanley Hall, *Adolescence* (1904), concepts of adolescence and its study have reflected the various lines of inquiry that come together on the life course — developmental, social-structural, historical. As a life stage, adolescence has been defined in terms of observed or attributed characteristics of the developing organism — the physical and physiological changes during puberty, the stage of formal operations in cognitive development and moral judgment. Hall used late nineteenth-century knowledge of man's evolution in formulating his developmental concept of adolescence and life stages generally — law of recapitulation, saltatory rather than continuous development (Grinder, 1969; Ross, 1972); Harold Jones (1939), Director of the well-known Oakland Growth Study of Adolescents, emphasized the biological parameters of adolescence; and, more recently, Jerome Kagan (1971) has argued that developmental knowledge warrants postulation of a psychological stage called "early adolescence," a stage defined by the emergence of a new cognitive competence among 12-year-olds in the ability to "examine the logic and consistency of existing beliefs" (p. 998).

Historically, developmental concepts of life stages have provided rationales for corresponding social timetables and mechanisms of socialization (Demos & Demos, 1969; Skolnick, 1975; Lüscher, 1975). But the problematic record of their social expression — for example, from the Judge Lindsay doctrine of love-oriented treatment to the punitive realities of the juvenile court (Schlossman, 1977) — offers a valuable reminder of the distance between a concept and its implementation. In this regard, Rothman (1971) correctly warns that just because the concept of adolescence as a developmental stage "was invented only at the end of the nineteenth century is no indication that the *actual* experience of the young had changed" (p. 367).

Developmental variations and social attributes on the individual level may generate different status classifications as to life stage. Thus Keniston's (1970) observations on an emerging category of youth in postwar America refer to a psychological stage that "cannot be equated with a particular age-range." The developmental themes of this stage (e.g., vacillating moods of estrangement and power, ambivalence toward self and social institutions) identify young people who do not "necessarily join together in identifiable groups, nor do they share a common social position" (pp. 648–649). By making explicit the distinction between youth as a developmental age and a social age, Keniston's essay leads beyond aspects of each domain to problems involving their relationship, to the social and developmental implications of inconsistent placement on psychological and social criteria, for example, the "youthful" person who is socially defined as an adult. Problems of this sort have been explored by Erikson (1964) and by Berger (1971) in a study of life styles.

The literature on adolescence over the past half century is distinguished by relatively separate lines of research on the developmental and social properties of adolescence. The former typically viewed adolescent experience in terms of ontogenetic development with minimal attention to sociocultural influences, whereas sociological research neglected developmental facts in the study of age categories, subcultures, generational relations, and youth movements. Despite the separation, there has always been a degree of interchange and debate between proponents of each perspective. Thus the presumed turmoil and conflicts of adolescence in the developmental perspective of G. Stanley Hall were challenged: (1) by evidence of cross-cultural variation through the anthropological studies of Margaret Mead (1928) and (2) by historical specification in Kingsley Davis's (1940) analysis of rapid change in generational conflict. Some lessons from this interplay are manifested in the life-course approach of the 1960s and 1970s. Social conditions and issues at the time gave visibility to the historical dimension of lives, institutions, and their temporal interdependence. In addition to its developmental and social features, the study of adolescence slowly acquired an historical feature, one shaped by matters of time, place, and by the life histories of its members.

One way to view this development is through an examination of studies that reveal the strengths and limitations of a single concept of adolescence, whether developmental, social, or historical. We begin with a brief consideration of historical times in research themes from the 1920s to the 1970s and pursue this topic in greater depth from the vantage point of concepts of adolescence and their problem foci. Then we cover developmental and social themes through the 1940s, the 1950s' perspective on adolescence in the course of societal development, and the introduction of historical questions to the study of adolescence and youth in the 1960s. This brings us to specific examples of life-course analysis in historical research on youth.

HISTORICAL TIMES AND THE STUDY OF ADOLESCENCE: 1920S TO THE 1970S

Child development emerged as a scientific field of inquiry in the United States during the 1920s, and we see a pale shadow of this beginning in the accumulation of studies of adolescents by the 1930s (Hollingsworth, 1928). Social needs or concerns were prominent in the development of research on children (Sears, 1975, p. 4) and in the study of adolescents, especially among sociologists. In the 1920s, rapid change through urbanization and immigration focused attention on the costs of social disorganization; the sociological research of Clifford Shaw and his colleagues depicted the juvenile delinquent as disaffiliated, lacking social bonds, supports, and controls (Finestone, 1976). Problems of employment and family disorganization gained prominence in the 1930s (Elder, 1974) in addition to questions regarding the impact of movie attendance and the radio on young people. Between the Depression and the 1970s, research on families and youth continued to reflect public issues of the times (Elder, 1978), from social change in World War II (rural to urban migration, absent fathers, employed mothers) to massive population and institutional growth in the postwar era and the civil strife of the 1960s.

Educational developments since the turn of the century stand out in the evolution of adolescence and its extension to a category of older youth: the rapidly expanding enrollment of young people (ages 14 to 17) in the high-school grades up to 1940 and a pronounced increase during the postwar era in the proportion of youth (ages 18 to 21) enrolled in higher education (Figure 1). Only one-third of American youth, ages 14 to 17, were attending high school by 1920, but this figure is six times the rate of 1890. In the city of Middletown, the Lynds' (1929) found that the high school had become the locus of youth activity and peer association: "The high school, with its athletics, clubs, sororities and fraternities, dances and parties, and other 'extracurricular' activities, is a fairly complete social cosmos in itself — a city within a city" (p. 211). The first major assessment of the social world of high school was authored by Willard Waller (1932/1965) in the 1930s,[2] followed some 10 years later by another classic, August Hollingshead's (1949) empirical investigation of high-school youth in Elmtown. With the proportion of youth in high school climbing above 80% in the 1950s, it is not surprising that the literature of the decade includes major studies of adolescent subcultures and peer influence, such as James Coleman's *The Adolescent Society* (1961).

Two important implications emerge from the trend toward universal high-school education, and both are represented in the literature on adolescents: (1) increasing age segregation and (2) social inequality in student access to school rewards and life opportunities. From Hollingshead to Coleman and the Presidential Science Advisory Commission's report, *Youth* (1973), we see emphasis on the forms and dysfunctions of age segregation relative to the transition between childhood and adult life. Hollingshead's *Elmtown's Youth* (1949) focused on class origins in the collective experience and life chances of youth at a time when the high-school student body was still heavily weighted toward the sons and daughters of the middle class. This problem gained significance in the postwar era as successive high-school cohorts recruited even larger proportions of students from the lower strata, accentuating issues of social privilege and status deprivation in the school environment (Trow, 1961). During this era, theory viewed juvenile delinquency as an adaptation to the disparity between the "American dream" and the constraints of social position. The image of the juvenile delinquent was that of a young male who had been sold a bill of goods, but lacked the approved means of acquiring those goods; in Finestone's words, (1976) the image of a "frustrated social climber" (p. 12). Arthur Stinchcombe (1964) provides a superior example of this conceptual approach in his study, *Rebellion in a High School*.

---

[2]At the time, family sociologists were preoccupied with the evolution of the family as a more specialized unit in the social structure and with the intrafamilial consequences of this change for members. In conjunction with the 1930 White House Conference on Child Health and Protection, a survey of adolescents, *(The Adolescent in the Family,* 1934), obtained evidence (more favorable personality adjustment of urban than rural youth) that was used to support the assumption that "loss of certain economic and other functions from the home makes possible the more harmonious organization of family life upon a cultural and affectional basis" (p. 7). The data were too superficially analyzed to support confidence in this finding; the assumption itself is suggestive of the limitations that grand theory on family change has for understanding the dynamics of family life.

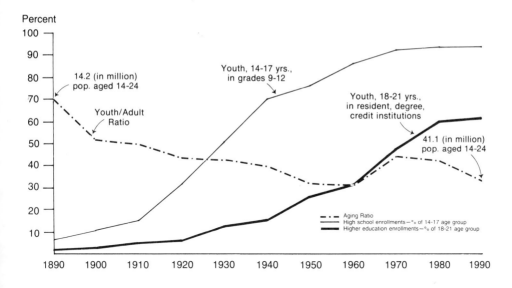

Enrollment statistics, by decade:
    Digest of Education Statistics, 1975 Edition, DHEW, Education Division, National Center for Education Statistics, U.S. Government Printing Office, 1976.
    Table 30, p. 37; Table 80, p. 80. Historical Statistics of the United States, Bureau of the Census, 1975, p. 383. Projections of Education Statistics to
    1984-85, National Center for Education Statistics, 1976. Table 3, p. 18; Table 5, p. 21; Table B-2, p. 154; and Table B-3, p. 155.

Aging ratio:
    Ratio of population, 14-24 to population aged 25-64 from Table 2, Chapter 3 of PSAC report, 1973; Chapter 3 prepared by Norman Ryder.

Figure 1.   Secular trends in population aging and enrollment rates for secondary and higher education, United States, 1890–1990.

Though far more numerous in the 1950s than at the turn of the century, American youth had become a smaller proportion of the adult population, an aging trend characteristic of modernizing societies. There were more adults per youth to serve as *socializers* in the 1950s than in 1900, thus indicating a decline in the burden of *socialization* and status placement. This trend reversed dramatically in the 1960s, owing to the postwar baby boom, and coincided with a noteworthy increase in the proportion of older youth in schools of higher learning. The size and broader composition of college cohorts in this decade implies an emerging life stage beyond traditional adolescence — a stage of youth or studentry (Parsons & Platt, 1972, pp. 236–291). Problems once identified with early adolescence and high school — age segregation and status deprivation — acquired prominence on the college campus through student mobilization and protests on civil-rights issues (Braungart, 1975). This development suggested to some (Gillis, 1974) the beginning of the end of an insular, protracted stage (adolescence?) of semidependency and social disability. Youth problems among older adolescents and college students in the 1960s focused attention on the transition to adulthood[3] (PSAC, 1973; Heyneman, 1976),

[3]Symptomatic of the concern over problems in the transition to adult status is the formation of the National Commission on Resources for Youth. The commission was established in 1967 by a small group of professionals who had "long been concerned with the well-being of youth. The decision to form a small organization was made as they discussed the difficulties young people face in making a constructive transition to adult life" (Ralph Tyler in "Foreword," *New Roles for Youth in the School and Community,* National Commission on Resources for Youth, 1974, p. viii). The role of schooling in this transition has been appraised by several independent reports, including that of the Presidential Science Advisory Commission (PSAC, 1973). In *Youth Policy in Transition* (1976), Michael Timpane and associates provide a thoughtful assessment of policy recommendations from the above reports in terms of available social science evidence, its knowledge base, limitations, and unknowns.

placing early adolescence in the shadows. Joan Lipsitz (1977) aptly refers to younger adolescents in the 1970s as "growing up forgotten," a theme also stressed by a recent National Institute of Mental Health (NIMH) Conference on Early Adolescence, (May 1976).

Despite the imprint of historical conditions on research foci over the past decades, these conditions seldom became variables in the study of adolescence and youth. Indeed, by far the largest share of research through the 1940s centered on the developmental perspective of adolescence and paid little attention to the social and historical contexts of young people. Critiques of this literature by sociologists and anthropologists offered correctives by stressing the social character of life stages, but they often did so without regard for developmental variations, their interaction with the social environment, and historical forces. In retrospect, one gains some appreciation of these conceptual limitations from the incompleteness of the work and thus of analytical distinctions that are now part of a life-course perspective on adolescence. We shall illustrate this point by reference to *Adolescence* (1944) the 43rd Yearbook of the NSSE — National Society for the Study of Education — (see also Dennis, 1946, pp. 633–666); Hollingshead's Elmtown study (1949); and prominent social views of adolescence in the 1950s.

Developmental and Social Themes in the Study of Adolescence

Adolescence as a "biological phenomenon" defines a primary theme of contributions to *Adolescence* (1944), a perspective that reflects research priorities at the time as well as the influence of Harold Jones (Chairman of the NSSE 43rd Yearbook Committee) and his pioneering, longitudinal study of physical growth and development at the Institute of Child Welfare (now Human Development), Berkeley, California. Half of the contributions portray the course of physical and physiological change; the development of physical, motor, and mental skills; and asynchronies across developmental lines. But even in these chapters, assumptions about age-graded expectations informed assessments of the psychosocial implications of physical growth, for example, in the case of maturation rates that depart from social expectations. Lack of time-series data ruled out consideration of one of the most important biological developments viewed in relation to the age structure: a pronounced upward trend in the height and weight of youth since at least the 1850s and a decline in the average age of menarche — approximately four months per decade over this period (Tanner, 1962, p. 152; Laslett, 1971). Nevertheless, the lag between developmental maturity and commensurate options was commonly acknowledged by analysts of the 1930s and 1940s as a prime source of adolescent emotional and social problems (K. Davis, 1944). In their classic monograph, *Frustration and Aggression* (1939), John Dollard and associates viewed this lag in terms of sources of adolescent frustration — the taboo on sexual activity, constraints on employment. The adolescent "gives every indication of being strongly instigated to perform the varied goal-responses appropriate to his new capacities, but tends to find that these responses are interfered with by adult restrictions" (pp. 96–97).

The biological theme of the yearbook exemplified a view of adolescence that August Hollingshead (1949) challenged through his investigation of adolescents in the class structure of Elmtown, a midwestern community studied in 1941–1942. After sorting through the available literature, heavily biased toward physical manifestations, Hollingshead stressed the primacy of environments that give meaning to physical facts (see also Mead, 1928). Whatever the connection of physical and physiological facts to adolescence and behavior, Hollingshead (1949) argued that "their functional importance for the maturing individual is defined by the culture" (p. 6). In social terms, the noteworthy feature of the adolescent years is not puberty, the growth spurt, or maturational processes in general, but rather how society views the maturing individual. Adolescence represents a social stage in which the individual is regarded as neither a child nor an adult in status, roles, or functions.

A full understanding of these facts in lives entails knowledge of the culture and social structure, but the underlying assumption throughout *Elmtown's Youth* is that adolescent behavior is far more contingent on position in the social structure than upon age-related biopsychological phenomena. Just as psychologists had ignored or oversimplified the cultural environment relative to developmental processes, Hollingshead excluded physical characteristics from analysis in relation to age-expectations and class subcultures. The questions he posed on cultural variation in causal linkages between pubertal growth phenomena and adolescent behavior were not subjected to empirical test. Nevertheless, a number of implicit premises on development informed the study. As the gap between development and social options suggests, the social character of adolescence also acquires meaning from knowledge of the human organism, its developmental timetable and processes.

Elmtown's Youth offers a vivid portrait of social stratification (age, sex, and class) in the life experience and chances of young people. It documents the control functions of age and class patterns in adolescent behavior and provides a firm reminder of adolescence as a variable in social and physical space within the course of lives. Four social properties of adolescence were singled out for special attention:

- The social ambiguity and status contradictions of this life stage ("an ill-defined no man's land").
- Competition and conflicts among youth-training institutions.
- Age segregation as a social control mechanism.
- Class variations in the transition to adult status.

Field work in the community disclosed few widely shared concepts regarding the lower or upper boundaries of adolescence, other than the span of years encompassed by secondary school and the assumption of adult roles. Inconsistent age norms in legal codes, from employment to matrimony and criminal law, underscored the ambiguous position of young people who were neither children nor adults; a "contrast" category defined by what it is not. Expressions of general developmental trends (institutional differentiation and specialization) took the form of: (1) multiple, youth-training agencies with competing claims on the adolescent's time and commitments and (2) an elaborate system of age segregation that sought to ensure "proper" development by isolating youth from the adult world of their parents — an isolation most typical of the middle-class student in school. On a theme that reappears in the 1950s and 1960s, Hollingshead (1949) cites the essentially negative character of a system that turned youth away from adult realities; "by trying to keep the maturing child ignorant of this world of conflict and contradictions, adults think they are keeping him 'pure' " (p. 108).

Hollingshead's study provides only a small sample of the wide variation in American youth experience at the time of World War II, but it offers a uniquely valuable picture of the institutional changes that have shaped adolescence as a social stage, in particular, the extension of schooling and its pronounced class variation among youth. As a category of dependents set apart from the adult world and childhood, adolescence had relevance mainly to the sons and daughters of middle- and upper-middle-class families. They were most likely to be members of the student body of the local high school (with its youth culture) and to pursue a college education and delay marriage. Offspring of the lower strata typically left school before the ninth grade with the prospect of unstable, menial employment as well as early marriage and childbearing. The harsh realities of adult disadvantage came early to the experience of these young people.

But other realities, World War II and a background in the Great Depression, also impinged on the life chances of youth in all class strata in Elmtown. Hard times in the 1930s generally encouraged school persistence and led to the postponement of adult entry (marriage, full-time employment) among older youth, but it also brought younger adolescents into the world of adultlike tasks through the labor-intensive and financial needs of deprived households (Elder, 1974). World War II produced a striking contrast in the balance of young labor supply and demand; military service and work absorbed the older segment of youth and a substantial number of adolescents of high-school age left school early for lucrative jobs (Magee, 1944). These historical conditions did not enter the analysis of Elmtown's youth. Civilian mobilization and the likelihood of military service were not part of the wartime experience of these adolescents, as we see it described; nor was any assessment made of their Depression experience as children. In these respects, at least, the youth of Elmtown appear in a "timeless" realm. Though Hollingshead effectively placed adolescents in the social structure, he failed to locate them in historical time and thus according to events that may have shaped their developmental course and life chances.

Adolescence in Societal Development

Social views of adolescence in the 1950s generally correspond to that of *Elmtown's Youth:* we see historical change in the social position of adolescents, but not in the particular events of life histories. The general theme is long-term structural change, especially its contemporary manifestations (Eisenstadt, 1956; Coleman, 1961; Parsons, 1964), that is, the expanding role of formal education, adult-directed youth groups, and peer groups in socialization. These reflect structural change that diminished the family's role in upbringing and enlarged the gap between family experience and the requirements of adult life.

Discontinuities between family experience and adult life generate problems for the adult community and young people. The problem for adults and social institutions is to link youth to adult roles through appropriate socialization and mechanisms of role allocation, such as the schools. For young people, the problem entails matters of independence, sexual relations, decisions on future options, and the establishment of their identity. These conditions give rise to organized, adult-directed agencies or groups that presumably serve the collective interests of society and also generate a propensity for peer association among youth. Functional specialization of the family is thus expressed in a more differentiated socialization environment.

As suggested by Hollingshead's study of Elmtown, the family of small-town America represented a major force in this multifaceted environment. However, postwar change suggested a shift in relative contributions to socialization, from family to school and peers. Two related developments, in particular, gave a sense of reality to the image of "adolescents in a world of their own": (1) increasing school size and (2) functional differentiation, for example, the growth of junior high schools. The major demographic change between 1940 and 1960 occurred in the average size of student cohorts, not in the proportion of youth enrolled in high school. Between the 1930s and 1960s, the estimated average size of high schools more than doubled — from 682 to 1539 in 1967. Small student bodies (less than 400) could still be found in the 1950s among towns with less than 10,000 residents, but these urban places were far less numerous than before the war. During the 1950s, the average high school in large suburbs (10,000+) and large cities (50,000+) ranged above 1000 students (Garbarino, 1977). This figure was, of course, much higher in metropolitan centers, often exceeding 3000 in places such as Chicago and New York. If large schools enhanced the power of youth groups, they may have done so in part by offering less to the individual student in social rewards, such as less recognition from peers, that is greater anonymity, (Barker & Gump, 1964) or less opportunity, when compared to students in small schools, to assume leadership or responsible positions.

The large school phenomenon was coupled with noteworthy structural and functional changes in educational environment. Both the lower and upper reaches of secondary education were in transition to new forms and functions: the lower grades through physical separation of sixth and seventh graders (Blyth, Simmons, & Bush, 1977); the upper grades of high school through functional ties to higher education (Trow, 1961). Though junior high schools date back to 1918, it was only in the early 1950s that separate or combined junior and senior high schools became more prominent as an organizational type than the eight-year elementary school and the four-year high school. The tipping point between these organizational types, either as an historical development or as a change with profound social implications, arrived with little notice. The emerging school structure established a more standard marker for the lower boundary of adolescence and linked early adolescence, with its developmental changes, to an age-segregated phase of schooling. The transition to secondary school in this new system placed students in a larger, more heterogeneous setting at an earlier age, posing issues of social acceleration and the erosion of parental control.

Analytic themes on youth of the 1950s generally mirror some implications of this change, in particular the ascendance of the peer group in an age-segregated society. Major appraisals of peer influence were published or initiated during this decade, including David Riesman's *The Lonely Crowd* (1950), which depicts the emergence of other-directed peer groups in the upper middle class; S. N. Eisenstadt's *From Generation to Generation* (1956), a scholarly analysis of ethnographic materials on age groups and relationships; Albert Cohen's influential treatise on delinquent subcultures, 1955; Calvin Gordon's study, *The Social System of the High School* (1957); James Coleman's major work on youth in 10 midwestern high schools, *The Adolescent Society* (1961); and Ralph Turner's research on adolescent ambition in the subcultures of high schools, *The Social Context of Ambition,* 1964. In combination, these studies brought fresh awareness to the dysfunctions of age segregation and social inequality in the transition of youth to adult roles.

The transfer of control over socialization from family to school and peers is most vividly described in Riesman's provocative essay, which some (Lipset & Lowenthal, 1961) regard as "one of the most significant and successful sociological contributions of our time" (p. v). The essay covers an exceedingly broad canvass on relations among historical change, social structure, and character, but considerable attention is given to the emergence of other-directed peer groups in the upper middle class. Bureaucratization and growth of a service-oriented economy are linked to an other-directed personality among the young through adaptations of socialization to structural requirements, in particular the emergence of prolonged schooling and youth groups.

Affluent parents may select appropriate environments for their offspring by choice of residence, but control over what is "best" resides with school and peers, who help locate the young in the social order. Parents in this stratum function mainly as stage managers or facilitators for their child's experience. Lacking clear standards on upbringing, they seek the counsel of magazines, other parents, and the peer groups of their sons or daughters. The young learn how the parental role should be played from television and peers and use this knowledge to achieve their ends. In postwar America, children of the upper middle class may have been "loved" toward maturity, but they were no longer "brought up" as were the products of inner-directed homes.

For parents and offspring, success is being popular, accepted, making friends — a standard that enhances the peer group's control over valued rewards and its power to enforce conformity. Through group sanctions, competition for individual prominence is replaced by competition for peer acceptance. Social pressures enforce taste standardization and fashion skills in consumption, defining peers as the behavioral model and measuring rod for all endeavors. In the world of the other-directed, parents have abdicated their responsibilities and authority to their children's peer group. As Riesman (1961) puts it, "if adults are the judge, these peers are the jury, and as in America, the judge is hemmed in by rules which give the jury a power it has in no other common-law land, so the American peer-group, too, cannot be matched for power throughout the middle-class world" (pp. 70–71).

However insightful, this characterization has been faulted on a number of grounds, from its simplistic image of parent-youth relations to the lack of empirical support from studies carried out in the 1950s. In Parsons's judgment (1964), the major weakness of Riesman's depiction of peer influence is that he "tends to 'reify' the peer group, as if it were the overwhelmingly predominant factor in socialization and constituted a kind of microcosm of the emerging adult 'other-directed' society" (p. 221). Empirical studies of the 1950s (Bowerman & Kinch, 1959; Douvan & Adelson, 1966) show a more differentiated picture in which adolescent orientations to parents and peers vary according to issues and family patterns. Strong ties to peers do not necessarily imply weak ties to parents. The task is to specify situations and areas in which peers are most likely to function as allies or adversaries of parents in youth socialization. Thus Bowerman and Kinch observed that greater dependence on peers than parents for support and guidance was most probable under conditions of parental indifference; rejection, and lack of understanding. Important studies from the 1950s to the present (Kandel & Lesser, 1972; Jennings, Allerbeck, & Rosenmayr, 1976) have consistently documented the central role of family in the lives of young people.

The disparity between Riesman's assessment and empirical work reflects in part a common tendency in the postwar years of social change: that of describing youth behavior in terms of inferences that are based on institutional change, as in schooling. Though postwar change indicates constraints and options relative to parent and youth behavior, it does not specify actual patterns of behavior. A differentiated environment of socialization does not tell us how parents and youth work out relationships and choices within this setting. Moreover, the self-reports of youth do not enable us to determine the character of generational patterns; perceptions of parents are not a reliable gauge of parental values, attitudes, and behavior. Dependence on this data source represents a major limitation of

James Coleman's (1961) study of the presumed cleavage between the adult world and the isolated cultural setting of adolescents in high school: that the adolescent in high school is "cut off" from the rest of society and maintains only "a few threads of connection" with significant others and realities in the adult community.

Across 10 high schools in the Chicago area, Coleman (1961) found that a sizable percentage of adolescents were more reluctant to break with a friend than to receive parental or teacher disapproval; that student leaders, in the liberated climate of large high schools, were more inclined than followers to side with peers (against the perceived wishes of parents) on issues involving social participation and club membership; that students placed greater emphasis on popularity, social leadership, and athletics than on academic excellence; and that the anti-intellectual climate of youth groups generally discouraged intellectual accomplishment. The overall impression seems to be one of stronger peer than parental influence and a cultural cleavage between the adolescent and adult communities. However Coleman's questions frequently set up a forced opposition between parents and peers (with no option to favor both), and he did not have parent information from which to assess value differences between the generations. The leading student groups may not have prized "academic brilliance" above all else, but they were headed, in large measure, for the rewards of higher education.

Judging from the literature, distinctive features of adolescence in the 1950s were not perceived in organismic development, which had changed little since the 1930s, but rather in emerging social form and content. Countless pubertal youth, who would have been grouped with younger children in past times, were identified with secondary school; a large proportion found themselves segregated in physical space from both older and younger students. With steadily expanding numbers of adolescents continuing their education beyond high school, a more prolonged stage of semi-independence acquired generalized significance. The correspondence between these social changes and problem foci is striking. Equally apparent is the inattention to demographic processes and historical facts in lives: the ascending size and changing composition of youth cohorts, from Depression births to the postwar baby boom; specific historical experiences that varied across these cohorts and may have differentiated their developmental course and life chances. High-school cohorts around 1950 were smaller than those at the end of the decade and encountered major historical events (depression, war, recovery) at different points in their lives. Neither studies of adolescent development nor research on adolescent subcultures or generational relations considered the potential implications of such variation for the explanation, interpretation, and generalization of findings.

The skeptic may question the utility of a research strategy that takes demographic or historical factors into account (Do such differences make a difference?), and one finds little hard evidence to support a convincing response. Nevertheless, an historical perspective would have sensitized James Coleman to factors that distinguished his adolescent sample of 1957 from older and younger cohorts. Most of the students in Coleman's "adolescent society" were born in the early 1940s (World War II) and thus were exposed in large numbers to the deprivations of father-absence and the stress of family readjustments on father's return. Though socially accepted, the temporary absence of fathers (two or more years) markedly altered family relationships, placing mothers in a dominant, instrumental role, and establishing fertile conditions for conflict when the returning veteran attempted to resume old family roles (Hill, 1949). Especially relevant to Coleman's generational theme are Lois Stolz's (1954) empirical observations on the father-son relations of war-born children: that sons born during the war experienced a more stressful relation with fathers who served in the military than those born after the war to veterans. Even several years after the father's return to the family, their relations with war-born sons were characterized by greater emotional distance and strain.

No one knows whether such effects persisted into the high-school years, though Carlsmith's study (1973) of Harvard students is suggestive along this line. Carlsmith compared students born during the war with a control group of men from homes in which the father was present, and found that men who experienced father-absence during the war were more likely to describe their ideal self as more like mother. They also shared fewer interests with males in general, displayed a more feminine cognitive style (see also Nelson & Maccoby, 1966), and projected a more delayed pattern of career establishment after college. Although the father-absent students appeared well adjusted to the college environment, Carlsmith concluded that they "feel somewhat less secure about their future roles as adult men." In combination, these studies are much too fragmentary to warrant generalizations regarding war-caused father-absence, but their findings obviously bear on the generational concerns of Coleman. They are also at least suggestive of the developmental implications of one historical event in the lives of males in this cohort.

From Generation to Cohort and History

I have suggested that developments in the 1960s marked a turning point toward historical considerations in the study of adolescence and youth, from the emergence of a life-course perspective that placed lives in historical context to the growth of genuine historical research on young people, their families, and settings. However, other analysts have detected no appreciable change in this direction. As recently as the early 1970s, Seeley (1973) claimed that the literature on adolescence is devoid of a "sense of society and a sense of history," of recognition that adolescence represents "a crucial articulation point or period in the historic as well as the ontogenetic process," a period that spans "the stage of the acted-upon-by history (the child) and the actor in and upon history (the adult)" (pp. 21, 23). Seeley provides numerous examples of these deficiencies, and concludes with a special plea for "the study of what is to be seen in the simultaneously dual perspective of history and life history" (p. 28).

Seeley's criticism is well supported by even a casual search of the literature, but so also is the thesis of a turning point in the 1960s toward the dual perspective he advocates; periods of change are generally characterized by a mixture of old and new and by a lag between innovation and implementation. Analytic themes in the turbulent 1960s reflect a mixture of continuity and change relative to the prior decade; continuity in the prevalence of generational analysis from a social age perspective; and change through greater awareness of historical, demographic, and cultural variations in adolescent experience. New questions were posed by the public issues and problems of this extraordinary decade, its tensions, outbursts, and social movements along racial-ethnic, class, and generational lines. Queries as to the timing of youth unrest (Why the 1960s rather than the 1950s?) focused attention on the diverse historical childhoods of young and old—on Depression hardship in parental lives and postwar affluence among the young.

Studies during the 1960s more frequently identified adolescents and college youth by their membership in a particular age cohort and its subgroups, with guidance from Karl Mannheim's essay on "The Problem of Generations" (Bengtson & Laufer, 1974) and a perspective on age patterns in the life course. Historical analysis and cultural diversity in *Youth* (1975), the 74th NSSE Yearbook, provide a noteworthy record of these developments and the change that has occurred in the study of young people since *Adolescence* (1944), the 43rd NSSE Yearbook. In contrast to the latter's emphasis on physical development, *Youth* is characterized by historical, institutional, and cultural themes; historical change in sex roles; the psychohistory of college youth; comparisons of youth cohorts; demographic and institutional change; cultural differentiation (black, Mexican-American, rural youth); and class or income strata.

In addition to advances in the sociological study of age, some developmentalists began to question research designs that were uninformed by matters of social change and that dealt only with a segment of the life span. Path-breaking essays by Warner Schaie (1965) and Paul Baltes (1968) gave visibility to: (1) the lifelong character of behavioral development, its multidimensionality and plasticity relative to environmental change and (2) the interpretive problems that arise from the ambiguous meaning of age differences, as an outcome of historical change, life situation, or both. These early insights of what is now recognized as life-span developmental psychology (Baltes & Schaie, 1973), along with methodological strategies for disentangling the multiple properties of age, constitute an important step toward placing adolescence within the intersection of social and life history. In sociology and psychology, such efforts to articulate the relation between age and time gradually linked three age concepts — developmental, social, and historical — in a perspective that places adolescence in the life course and history.

To some extent, this perspective can be viewed as a critique of theoretical models that prevailed in the 1950s and continued to shape questions and research on youth unrest in the 1960s. Whether developmental or sociological, age-specific analyses were ill suited to an understanding of the antecedents and outcomes of youth behavior. Theory on adolescence in societal development linked generational strains to periods of rapid change and directed inquiry away from the discordance between youth, as a collective or cohort, and the larger social, economic, and political system. A large number of studies in the 1960s were guided by the *expectation* of parent-youth conflict and value differences in student unrest, an expectation that received little empirical support (Andersson, 1969; Kandel & Lesser, 1972; Bengtson & Laufer, 1974). One overview of the literature concludes that "any major differences that might exist between youth and older generations are more apt to be differences *within* the adult group, which are being manifested in the youth group, than between parents and their adolescent children" (Timpane et al., 1976 p. 48). Observed variations in generational relations and social transmission proved wholly insufficient for explaining the emergence of collective patterns among youth, their timing, location, and diversity in form and substance.

This orientation to youth behavior in the 1960s was influenced by Kingsley Davis's theory of parent-youth conflict (1940), a theory that is based on a comparative analysis of societies at different stages of development. Davis sought an answer to the question of why modern industrial societies were characterized by "an extraordinary amount of parent-adolescent conflict," when compared to premodern societies. Against the background of certain universals (e.g., differential upbringing, status, and aging patterns between parents and youth), Davis identified four major sets of variables that seemed to accentuate the likelihood of generational conflict and also distinguished between historical societies and regions at varying levels of development:

- Rate of social change.
- Degree of structural differentiation and complexity.
- Level and form of cultural variation.
- Mobility, both social and geographic.

Though not meant to account for generational variations in modern societies, Davis's theory did serve as a point of departure for analysts who questioned the explanatory value of rapid change for an understanding of youth behavior in the 1960s. For example, Seymour Lipset (1976) concludes that Davis's account is unsatisfactory because it does not "explain why certain epochs of rapid change lead to student activism, while others do not" (p. 15). In part, the theory fails because it conceptualizes change within the framework of long-range development; it is too global to specify modes of change and their consequences in specific historical settings of modern societies. Theoretical requirements in the modern setting require a more differentiated concept of social change in type, rate, and configuration, as well as assessments of the process by which change finds expression in lives.

In drawing upon Davis's essay, Lipset implicitly assumes a generalized model of causal chains that lacks conceptual precision and verification within industrial societies:

rapid change $\rightarrow$ parent-youth conflict $\rightarrow$ student activism

Very little is known about the process that links types of rapid change to specific youth outcomes, but it is clear that an understanding of this process requires knowledge of the change and its implications for adaptations in concrete situations (Elder, 1974). Even more uncertain is the presumed link between generational conflict and student activism; as noted, the literature of the 1960s provides little empirical support for this connection. Generational conflict may take a variety of forms under different circumstances; it represents only one potential link between rapid change and youth behavior.

In retrospect, the emerging life-course approach of the 1960s identifies at least three problems or limitations in a purely generational approach to social change in youth experience:

1. The ambiguous meaning of generational differences.
2. The imprecision of generational membership as an index of historical location.
3. Neglect of the relationship between youth and options, cohorts and the social order.

Generational differences in values may reflect the disparity in life stage between parents and offspring, since values are shaped by the imperatives of life situations, or they may indicate socialization differences that are linked to cohort membership and historical times (Bengtson, 1975). Since historical location and life stage are jointly determined by age, both factors and related experience could account for parent-adolescent conflicts over sexual behavior, material concerns, financial responsibility, and so on.

This point is illustrated by one result from a study of three generations in the Los Angeles area (Bengtson & Lovejoy, 1973). Financial support was ranked more highly as a value by the parent and grandparent generations than by the younger generation. Life-stage differences between the generations are suggested as a plausible explanation: that financial constraints and pressures enhanced the importance of this item among the older generations. However, an equally plausible case could be made for a historical explanation, with special reference to experiences in the Great Depression. One solution to this interpretational problem stems from the premise that social change differentiates the experience of persons who share a common historical location. For example, not all families in the Depression suffered heavy income losses. When historical experience is not uniform among lineages with the same age differential, it represents a testable explanation for differences between parents and offspring.

A search for historical factors that account for generational differences requires knowledge of each generation's historical location relative to events and change. However, members of a generation do not occupy anything resembling a common location in the historical process, owing to variations in the timing of births. An age range of 20 years, as in Bengtson and Lovejoy's (1975) sample of parents and grandparents, is far too broad to permit analysis that relates events to lives. The oft mentioned Depression-background of parents of youth in the 1960s was in fact highly differentiated. Some parents encountered the Depression as adolescents, others as young children; a large number were spared hardships altogether. By dividing the age range of a parent generation into birth cohorts and thus across descending generations, generational membership acquires historical precision and enables study of the social transmission of historical experience. *Generational cohorts* facilitate contemporary explorations of Kingsley Davis's research problem—that of rapid change in parent-offspring relations. Consider, for example, the differential experience of two generational cohorts with birth dates before the Great Depression (1920, 1929). Members of the oldest cohort (1920) entered the depression as preadolescents, were old enough to play a major role in the economy of deprived households, and left high school during the early phase of war mobilization. By contrast, some members of the younger cohort (1929) experienced a more prolonged phase of family hardship, beginning in the early years of childhood and extending to the 1940s. These differences, among others, suggest a number of implications for the parental values of these cohorts in the postwar era.

Whether placed in historical context or not, the microenvironment of generational relations had little to offer for understanding the distinctive collective features of adolescence and youth in the 1960s, in particular, the ascending size of youth cohorts, with their institutional consequences and impact on youth experience. As noted in Figure 1, young Americans, ages 14 to 24, increased by an unparalleled 52% between 1960 and 1970. Most of the increase was absorbed by the military and schools, transforming college campuses into a more conducive environment for student mobilization against the Vietnam War. Change of this sort began to inform studies of youth in the mid-1960s (Musgrove, 1965; Moller, 1968) and brought a neglected dimension to the familiar concept of institutional change when there is social discontinuity between family experience and adult life. The nature of this discontinuity, and the resulting problems for institutions and youth, vary according to economic and demographic conditions. This principle is illustrated by the contrasting institutional problems and life chances associated with the small cohort of Depression-born youth who came of age in the early 1950s and the relatively large cohort that entered a depressed labor market in the early 1970s. Musgrove's historical analysis (1965) suggests that the status and rewards of youth have varied with their relative size in the population, and he concludes that youth in the 1960s, as in the 1970s, are likely to pay a price for their "comparative abundance in the previous twenty years" (p. 81). Large youth cohorts in the 1960s and the prevalence of student protests on large university campuses (Scott & El-Assal, 1969) generally conform to Herbert Moller's historical thesis (1968): that periods of social change and youth unrest are characterized by cohorts of ascending size.

Some developmental implications of membership in a large youth cohort are suggested by Roger Barker's concept of an "overmanned behavior setting" (1968), a setting in which people far outnumber options and only a small number (the elite in background and talent) have access to challenging parts in the drama. This is a setting that exaggerates traits commonly attributed to adolescence as a social category — a no-man's-land without self-defining, productive roles; a position of marginality and low integration relative to the larger community. Observing a historical decline in the prevalence of undermanned settings for Americans, Barker (1968) points out the broader implications of the trend through an idea that links this type of environment to a way of life — the free frontier, people of abundance, a land of opportunity. It is the idea that "there has been a superabundance of goals to be achieved and an excess of tasks to be done in relation to the nation's inhabitants, and that these have been important influences in the American society and people" (p. 189). This idea may still have a future with the pronounced decline in fertility since the 1960s, though much depends on the economy.

Apart from the effect of cohort size, youth unrest in the 1960s was also viewed in terms of a mismatch between the social and developmental characteristics of cohorts and available options. Strains may arise when change provides options and demands that do not correspond with the modal dispositions or skills of particular cohorts, or when developmental change through socialization is not coupled with parallel change in the social order. Consistent with Mannheim's writings on the mentalities of generation or cohort units, variations in life history among members of cohorts in the 1960s were associated with variations in exposure to specific events (e.g., an administrative decision on a college campus), in the personal meaning or relevance of the events, and in responses to the events, collective and otherwise. Thus studies found differences in social and political attitudes between segments of the youth cohort, for example, non-college versus college (Lipset, 1976), to be as large or larger than those observed between youth and older-age groups. Conflict between the development of youth and social institutions is suggested by research that characterized youth of the counterculture as products of socialization within the upper middle class (see Flacks, 1971). Relevant to this point is Hampden-Turner's (1970) observations on coming to this country from England. He was struck by the contrasting position of developmental and humanistic themes in American education and childrearing, on the one hand, and in the commercial-political world, on the other. "It has long seemed to me only a matter of time before the developmental themes in American life confronted the repressive themes, and before those students nurtured in the better homes and schools came to regard the opportunities offered by business and government as an insult to their actual levels of psychosocial development" (Hampden-Turner, p. 364).

Cohort research on youth and social institutions depicted the young as actors responding to and shaping their life situations, not merely as products of institutional change and socialization. Though Gillis (1974) is correct in noting an underrepresentation of youth's own "response to change," compared to the molding influence of institutions (p. ix), such bias was far less apparent in the literature of the 1960s than in prior decades. Youth behavior in the 1960s had much in common with W. I. Thomas's (Elder, 1978) account of responses to situational change: that of persons "working out adaptations to the times that find meaning, if not a plan of action, in customary understanding and values" (p. 519). The actions of young people in this decade were less an outgrowth of new ideas than of old ideas (e.g., civil rights) operating in new or changing situations. From surveys of age groups in Western Europe during the early 1970s, Inglehart (1977) identified postwar economic growth and rising levels of education among successive youth cohorts as prominent factors in the shift from interests centered on "material consumption and security toward greater concern with the quality of life" (p. 363). However, such preferences are subject to the imperatives of changing historical circumstances. Yankelovich's (1974) surveys of American college students between 1969 and the recession year of 1973 show a significant increase among the cohorts in the priority assigned to economic security as a job criterion and to continued support for sexual freedom and civil liberties, but there is a decline in regard for patriotism and religion as central values. Both historical change and cohort properties may account for this change; determination of its meaning and consequences in lives and institutions awaits thorough study in longitudinal samples (see Fendrich, 1974) and cohort comparisons over multiple data points.

Up to now, we have identified research themes in the 1960s that represent both continuity and change relative to prior decades in studies of adolescence and youth; continuity through generational analysis and its limitations for historical research; and change through the study of youth cohorts, their characteristics, historical settings, and relation to institutions and social options. In generational analysis, the family constitutes a link between historical change and the lives of young people; the impact of change may occur through social transmission or through a breakdown in this process. However, generational status (parent or child) does not place individuals in a precise historical setting, nor does it confer membership in an age group that encounters historical events at the same point in the life span. Youth are characterized as individuals without shared experience in specific historical times. The focal point of generational analysis — parent-youth relations — tended to shift inquiry away from the problematic interplay between youth cohorts and social institutions and the relation of this interplay to both continuity and discontinuity between the generations. Though modest in number and accomplishments, studies of youth cohorts drew attention to this interplay and, with efforts to elaborate the bond between age and time, introduced a temporal and processual dimension to views of adolescence and youth, a perspective that depicts adolescent experience in terms of interactions between historically defined cohorts, their developmental histories, and life stage in the social structure.

This view of adolescence suggests a number of unexplored questions on change or continuity both in the cultural properties of this life stage as well as their consequences for the life course of youth. Consider, for example, the hypothesis that structural features of adolescence (dependency, status uncertainty, loose integration) are expressed in identities or life styles that have persisted across successive youth cohorts. Matza (1964) refers to a set of conventional life styles (academic, sports, moral scrupulosity) and rebel identities (delinquency, bohemianism, radicalism) as "traditions" of youth that have "grown into traditional styles which have been assumed and put aside by one cohort after another" (p. 199). With counterparts and carriers in the larger society, these "traditions" are said to represent adaptations of youth to an emerging social position. The nature of this position would of course vary according to the particular history and characteristics of youth cohorts under changing conditions; this variation implies differing adaptive requirements, for example, cohorts in the Great Depression and the postwar years of prosperity. Sources of "life-style" continuity and change from cohort to cohort are poorly understood, and little is known about the expression of traditional identities in new forms (but see Gillis, 1974) that are more responsive to the times.

Another question concerns normative variation by demographic and economic change in age-graded expectations and the phenomenology of age status. Within the family these expectations may be thought of in terms of independence standards or guidelines — the ages at which the young are expected or permitted to engage in certain behavior. What factors account for change in these standards from one parent cohort to another? Are they subject to change as material conditions vary from good to hard times? Behavioral observations tend to produce more questions than answers along this line. For example, adolescents in the Great Depression frequently assumed positions of family responsibility, suggesting a downward extension of adult expectations, but the depressed labor market also encouraged school persistence and delayed marriage and childbearing (Zachry, 1944, pp. 336–337). The postwar years offer a similar contradiction. They have been described as a period when youth dependency was prolonged, and the extension of formal education generally supports this interpretation. However, this period was also marked by a substantial decline in age at first marriage (Modell, Furstenberg, & Strong, 1978), an event that many regard as the prime indicator of adult status. In the 1960s, we see an increasing tendency to delay marriage and childbearing within a continuing upward trend in the proportion of youth in higher education. The normative meaning of this change is largely unknown (see Jordan, 1976; Goldstein, 1976).

Apart from these unknowns, research on demographic change in the 1960s suggested one noteworthy connection between cohort size and normative factors in the lives of adolescents — by increasing membership in all categories, expanding youth cohorts heightened the visibility of adolescent deviance and its problematic aspects, raising public concern and the likelihood of social intervention. The sheer numerical increase of youth relative to adults had much to do with public concern over juvenile delinquency, deprived youth, student radicals, and teen-age parenthood. Furstenberg (1976) observes that it was only in the 1960s that "public concern about the problem of teenage parenthood became manifest" (p. 8), as seen in the popular literature, government programs, and clinics for young mothers. He attributes this normative change to a convergence of developments, including the large adolescent cohorts of the 1960s and the general issue of overpopulation. There were more adolescent girls of childbearing age than ever before. An increasing proportion of teen-age births were children born out of wedlock (from 15 to 30%, 1960–1970), owing partly to the pregnancy risks of a trend toward earlier sexual experience and a rising pattern of later marriage. Throughout the decade, concern over unplanned childbearing and its social disadvantage led to a broad range of intervention programs; well over 100 programs offering educational and health services were in operation by 1970.

Demographic and normative factors are well represented in Furstenberg's important study of adolescent childbearing; one of the clearest examples of how analytic developments on historical time and the life course began to shape problem foci in adolescent research during the 1960s. The project was launched in 1966 as a traditional, short-term evaluation of a service program for teen-age mothers (before age 18, $N = 323$) in predominantly low-income, black neighborhoods of Baltimore. Like other research on the subject, this initial study focused on the causes of adolescent parenthood and births out of wedlock and paid no attention to historical trends, demographic trends, or to the differentiated life course of the young mother. But events (lack of funds, etc.) soon offered Furstenberg a chance to rethink the study in the light of emerging ideas on the life course and to recast it as a longitudinal investigation of the career of early parenthood and of adaptations to an ill-timed event. Apart from the approved timing of parenthood, early parenthood is "off schedule" in relation to the young mother's social maturation, schooling, and prospects for economic support. Marital postponement, kin support in childcare, the rescheduling of schooling and work, and fertility control represented potential options for managing the deprivations, tensions, and disorder associated with an unplanned birth at an early age. In order to carry out this study, Furstenberg selected a matched sample of the former classmates of the teen-age mothers who had not become pregnant in adolescence. Interviews were conducted with both groups in 1970 and 1972.

Furstenberg located the adolescent girls in his study within the course of postwar developments (rising levels of teen-age childbearing, births out of wedlock). In doing so, he placed the analysis in a context that suggests broader implications, that is, What are the life outcomes and social consequences of the trend in illegitimate births? At the same time, he properly notes distinctive features of his cohort and its historical time, which limit generalizations to other cohorts and times, such as change in the availability of birth-control devices for adolescents. However, the major contribution of the study is seen in its concept of multiple, interlocking career lines and its creative application to the adaptations of unwed adolescent mothers. A specific sequence of events leads to an illegitimate birth, and at each decision point the outcome can be averted: premarital sexual experience or not, contraceptive use or not, pregnancy or not, birth or abortion or marriage. Birth of a child out of wedlock is followed by a number of potential options: abandonment of the child or putting the child up for adoption; marriage or single parenthood; more illegitimate births; educational and vocational decisions; entry into the welfare system or economic independence. Decisions at each stage of the career entail different explanatory processes. Variables that influence early sexual experience differ from those that bear on the use of contraceptives. A full model of unwed motherhood links these separate explanations into a life-course perspective.

The consequences of unplanned parenthood vary according to the form of this career and its relation to other career lines — marital, occupational, and educational. Problems of synchronization and life management stem from this event, and are expressed in coping strategies; judicious planning and use of resources, the rearrangement of event schedules, and educational aspirations play a key role in enabling some adolescent mothers to minimize the disadvantage of an early birth in their life chances and in the development of their children. By following the young mothers into their early 20s, we discover how erroneous some popular impressions of early parenthood have been; in particular, the belief that it leads inevitably to a life of deprivation. On the contrary, diversity in life pattern and prospects stands out as the more prominent theme in their experiences. Though most of the women grew up in disadvantaged homes, their life situations some five years after the birth of their first child reflect a wide range of advantage and hardship. Many questions are left unanswered, as one might expect, and provide an agenda for subsequent work. But most importantly, this study of the life paths of teen-age mothers suggests a fruitful way to investigate the historical, social, and developmental features of adolescence in the life course.

YOUTH IN HISTORICAL TIME AND SOCIAL CHANGE

Historical considerations during the 1960s appear in theoretical formulations and methodological designs, in the reformulation of old questions, and in the appraisal of puzzling findings. The use of archival resources to trace out the effects of historical change in lives, cohorts, and institutions is largely missing from this picture. Indeed, questions regarding such effects serve to underline the scarcity of firm knowledge on the past and on the causal processes linking Depression, War, and postwar developments to life situations during the 1960s. In retrospect, this deficiency represents one consequence of a strategy long prominent in sociological work on change: the objective, as Abrams points out (1972), "was not to *know* (italics added) the past but to establish an idea of the past which could be used as a comparative base for the understanding of the present" (p. 28). In the absence of reliable knowledge on the historical record, such ideas often told us more about concepts of the present and the limitations of global theories and grand designs.

Over the past decade, genuine archival research on young people has made us more aware that limited understanding of the present has roots in countless unknowns of the past[4] and that many presumptions regarding social change have been misleading or false. Consider a popular account of family change that has influenced interpretations of youth socialization since the 1920s: a "decline version" that stressed "the great withering away of functions," resulting from urbanization and industrialization (Elder, 1978). Separation of the productive activities from households and the general process of functional specialization (in education, etc.) diminished the family's role in upbringing, hence the conclusion regarding a long-term decline in parental control. The insights of historical research (Smith & Hindus, 1975; Lipschutz, 1977) yield a far more complex picture of fluctuating trends and patterns of time and place, social stratum, mode of control, and life stage.

Well before industrialization, in the agrarian world of seventeenth- and eighteenth-century Andover, Mass., Philip Greven's (1970) study documents a substantial change, from father to son across four generations, in the son's control over his own life course of marriage and work. By and large, yeoman fathers in the first generation exercised firm control over the time of adult independence through the division of their estate. The division occurred relatively late in the father's life, thereby delaying the son's marriage and financial autonomy. By the third and fourth generations, we see a decline in paternal control and greater willingness to assist sons in making their own way, a change stemming from the increasing scarcity of land (favoring impartible inheritance) and greater economic opportunities away from homestead and kin, especially in neighboring towns and villages. Men of the fourth generation were most likely to launch families and an independent worklife at a relatively early age. During the same time period, another study of a New England community (Smith, 1973) has described a shift in control over marriage from parents to offspring by the mid-nineteenth century.

Further erosion in parental control is commonly attributed to industrialization, with special reference to the removal of work and father from household. But a contrary view is suggested by an increasing tendency during the last half of the nineteenth century for young people to remain in the family well beyond puberty (Katz, 1975): a noteworthy reversal of a long-standing parental practice in preindustrial society of sending children out to live as a member of another household between puberty and marriage. This change, which began to equate adolescent dependency with family residence, has been attributed to a number of factors that converged at the time — the decline of apprenticeship training, extension of mass schooling to the secondary years, the rise of domestic sentiments, and the appeal of homelife. Whatever the cause in residential change, its potential implications

---

[4]After reviewing the distorted knowledge on society that we have gained from synchronic social science, Peter Laslett (1977) — concludes that, "we do not understand ourselves because we do not yet know what we have been and hence what we may be becoming" (p. 5). Something of this appraisal is reflected in the deliberations of an international colloquium that was convened in September 1975, on the topic of adolescence in the year 2000 (Hill & Monks, 1977). At the outset of the colloquium, the severe lag in scientific knowledge on adolescence, past and present, was recognized and the participants dealt more with preferred models of the future than with specific predictions.

include a strengthening of generational ties. Indeed, Bloomberg (1974) concludes that perhaps "the most pronounced change in family roles caused by industrialization was in enhancing the powers of parents and decreasing the independence of teenage boys." (p. 13).

Parental control is merely one aspect of a more general historical question on social change in the life course of youth. Historians and sociologists have begun to explore this question from the vantage point of constraints (institutional, demographic, and economic) and their implications for the life course, especially the timing and configuration of events in the transition to adult status. Three studies illustrate different applications of this approach: Michael Katz's intensive study (1975; Katz & Davey, 1978) of youth and their life paths to adulthood before and during early industrialization (1851–1971) in the city of Hamilton, Canada; a comparative study (Modell, Furstenberg, & Hershberg, 1976) of the changing pattern of events in the transition to adult status between late nineteenth-century America and 1970; and a longitudinal investigation of one historical event, economic deprivation during the 1930s in the life patterns of predepression birth cohorts—an Oakland, California cohort with birthdates of 1920–1921 (Elder, 1974) and a Berkeley cohort, 1928–1929 (Elder & Rockwell, 1979). The problem foci of these studies imply a processual view of lives, though only the Depression project is based on a longitudinal-data archive. Even so, Modell and associates employ their cross-sectional data (mainly based on census schedules) to good effect in suggesting implications for individual life patterns. Katz has linked some data at different points (1851 and 1861) to form life records on individuals, but his analysis relies primarily on cross-sectional information.

The time frame of the Hamilton study is uniquely suited for an examination of how the lives of youth — middle and working class, native and foreign born — were altered by events during the early stage of industrialization. Between 1851 and 1871, Hamilton was transformed from a small commercial center of 14,000 (hit hard by a depression in the late 1850s) to an industrial-commercial center of 26,000. In this period, the city fathers modernized the school system, segregating youth from children; improved local transportation and public services; and witnessed a threefold increase in the number of large firms (10 or more employees). Hamilton's industrialization (from heavy industry to apparel firms) did not include the development of textile mills, with their opportunities for the employment of women and children. Quantifiable data on youth and families were obtained from census manuscripts in 1851, 1861, and 1871. To explore the life-course changes among youth across these points, Katz focused on the temporal configuration of residence, education, work, and marriage. These events, he suggests (1975), "interacted with one another in a way that gave to the experience of people whom today we would call adolescents a distinctly different pattern from that which it has since assumed" (p. 156).

For many years, an image of early nineteenth-century youth depicted an early and abrupt transition to adulthood; complete independence followed a relatively short period of dependency as boys left home at ages of 15 or younger and entered the world of adults. Both Katz (1975) and Joseph Kett (1977) challenge this belief with evidence suggesting an intervening stage of semi-independence or partial autonomy. According to Kett, this state is characterized by a disorderly pattern of events in which age is only loosely correlated with status; boys moved back and forth between school, where they were defined as children, and work, which offered adult status. Preindustrial youth "grew up on a series of separate timetables" (Kett, 1977, p. 42) that were largely influenced by family or household needs and resources. From data on Hamilton youth before industrialization,

Katz observed greater uniformity in life pattern, relative to Kett's description, and a stage of semiautonomy between leaving home and marriage, one based on both employment and place of residence. "Young men and women frequently worked and lived as members of a household other than that of their parents" (Katz, 1975, p. 257) — generally households in the higher socioeconomic strata of the community. This stage of the early life course has been documented by other studies (see Little & Laslett, 1977; Bloomberg, 1974) on nineteenth-century communities in America.

Katz and Davey (1978) refer to the stage of semiautonomy as the "lost phase" of the life course, for it was gradually replaced in the course of industrialization by more prolonged residence in the parental home. A slight majority of Hamilton youth (aged 15 to 19 years) were living in nonparental residences as of 1851; 20 years later, this figure had declined to one-fourth of the males and one-third of the females. The median age at leaving home increased for young men from 17 to 22; for women, from 17 to 20. The practice of resident domestic service, which continued until late in the nineteenth century, accounts for the smaller change among young women. Four strands of evidence generally support Katz's (1975) claim that young men who boarded out experienced greater autonomy than those who remained in the family of origin:

- The more contractual basis of boarding, in contrast to the diffuse obligations of family life and parental surveillance.
- The link between boarding and employment — less than 10% of the boarders were employed by the household head.
- The concentration of school attendance and work for father among youth who resided at home, implying dependence on parental resources.
- A pattern of earlier marriage among boarders, when compared to family residents.

Overall, the stage of partial autonomy seemed to ease the transition between dependency and the obligations of adulthood (Katz, 1975): "Those men who left home were readier than those who remained to cross the boundary between child and adult" (p. 268).

Despite the change in residence between 1851 and 1871, little change occurred in age at entry into the labor market among boys and in the timing of marriage; women generally married by the age of 23, men by the age of 27. But with the extension of family residence, we see a pronounced decline in the prevalence of what might be called "idle" youth, those who were neither in school nor employed, a change reflecting increasing educational and economic opportunities. Nearly half of the 11- to 15-year-olds in 1851 and one-fourth of the 16- to 20-year-olds were neither enrolled in school nor working; the percentages were even greater among girls, leading Katz (1975) to conclude that,

> many adolescents must have roamed the city with little or nothing to do, a situation which provides an objective underpinning for the desire felt by adults in this period to devise institutions that would take adolescents off the streets. [P. 262]

Rising school enrollment markedly reduced this pool of youth during the first decade of educational expansion, followed by the impact of increasing job opportunities. Among 13- to 16-year-olds who were living at home (Figure 2), school and work recruited a larger proportion of boys in 1871 than in 1851; school attendance accounted for the major change in the status of girls. For this age group of girls, domestic service in other households represented the primary job opportunity.

During the early phase of industrialization in Hamilton, family rank or class became a more potent source of life-course differentiation in relation to residence, extended

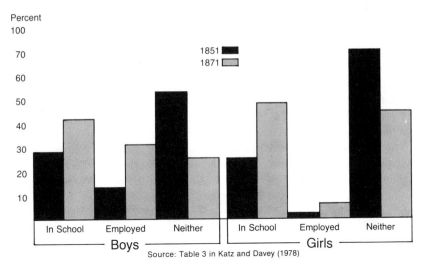

Figure 2. Work and school status among 13 to 16-year-olds living at home in Hamilton, Ontario, 1851 and 1971.

schooling, employment, and marriage. The sons and daughters of higher-status families remained at home for a longer period of time than youth from the lower strata (Katz & Davey, 1978). They were also more likely to continue their education through secondary school and to delay employment and marriage. Lower-status youth generally attended school on a more irregular basis, owing partly to family transience and needs. In leaving school for work at an early age, a good many of these youth undoubtedly played an important role in the economy of their families. Class differentials in schooling thus linked age-grading and class segregation; the world of secondary school was that of the sons and, to a lesser extent, the daughters of middle-class families.

This portrait of Hamilton youth shows (1) the decline of a life phase and practice that extended across class strata — that of young people between puberty and marriage living as members of other households and (2) an accentuation of class differentiation in the social worlds and life chances of youth. Many of the conditions we now ascribe to adolescence — features of institutionalized dependency — were emerging in the middle class of late-nineteenth-century Hamilton and other industrial communities. With workplace separated from the domestic unit and urban schools largely staffed by female teachers, prolonged family residence and education in the middle class placed male youth in a socialization environment managed by women — an environment too sheltered, some believed, from the male influences and real-world disciplines that make "big men of little boys" (Hantover, 1976, p. 117). This climate of "masculine anxiety" converged with the perceived dangers of idle, unruly youth in the lower classes as a stimulus to middle-class support for adult-led organizations—Boys Clubs, YMCA, the Boy Scouts.

The Hamilton study brings us to the latter decades of the nineteenth century and to the question of how the transition to adulthood was altered by social changes of the twentieth century. If we think in terms of departure from home and the completion of schooling, educational upgrading over the twentieth century seems to indicate a more extended transition among contemporary youth cohorts when compared to the experience of youth in the nineteenth century. And yet, the downward trend in age at first marriage between

1900 and postwar America supports a different conclusion and even suggests a resemblance to Kett's description of preindustrial youth, straddling multiple timetables that varied greatly from one youth to another. Modell, Furstenberg, and Hershberg (1976) explored life-course change across this period through a comparison of two widely separated cohorts — white youth (male and female) in Philadelphia of 1880 (data from census manuscripts) and an all U.S. Census sample for 1970. A comparison of cohorts in different social units leaves much to be desired, but the authors concluded from available evidence that the transition of adulthood among Philadelphia youth generally resembled a common pattern of late-nineteenth-century America. The rich contextual detail of the Hamilton study is necessarily absent from this broad ''then-and-now'' contrast. However, the study constitutes a pioneering effort to identify gross changes in the early life course of youth and provides an empirical point of departure for more focused explanatory research.

At both time periods, data were available on five life events or transitions:

- Exit from school.
- Entry into the labor market.
- Departure from home.
- First marriage.
- The establishment of an independent domicile.

Instead of dealing with the average timing of these events, Modell and associates (1976) focused on their dispersion across age categories in the following concepts and operations:

- Prevalence — the proportion of a cohort that experiences a given transition in specific age categories.
- Timing — typical points of transition, such as when half a cohort has experienced an event.
- Spread — the span of time required for a given proportion of a cohort to pass through a transition.
- Age congruity — the degree to which the spread of transitions overlap.

All of the concepts are meaningful only on the aggregate or cohort level.

The concept of prevalence is based on the assumption that some individuals will not experience a particular event, such as marriage. As one might expect, schooling shows the greatest increase in prevalence, but contemporary youth more uniformly encounter all of the transitions (except for work among females) when compared to the Philadelphia population. On spread, or duration, of the transition within a cohort, the data show that young men and women today generally take longer to complete their schooling, but they also pass more quickly through the family transitions. Moving out of the parental household, marrying, and setting up an independent household occurs more rapidly now than among late-nineteenth-century youth. With matters of timing in the picture, the early life course of nineteenth-century youth differs from that of youth today in two major respects: (1) leaving school and work entry started earlier and required less time to complete and (2) the familial transitions were experienced later and consumed a larger portion of the life span.

Over the past century, the combination of change in timing and spread has resulted in a greater prevalence of overlapping transitions. Unlike the nineteenth-century pattern in which members of a cohort typically left one status before entering another, the contemporary pattern shows a mixture of familial and non familial transitions. ''A far larger proportion of a cohort growing up today is faced with choices about sequencing and combining statuses'' (Modell, Furstenberg, and Hershberg, 1976, p. 29). But the compression of transitions has not resulted in a helter-skelter response with the order of events following a near-random pattern. The range of choice and action in the lives of late-nineteenth-century youth has been replaced by a more tightly organized schedule of contingent transitions to adult status. Early life transitions are more compressed and contingent because they are more constrained by the scheduling imperatives of formal institutions. Control over these transitions has shifted from the family of origin, which allowed a wide measure of flexibility, to young people themselves and the generalized requirements of school and workplace. '' 'Timely' action to nineteenth century families consisted of helpful responses in times of trouble; in the twentieth century, 'timeliness' connotes adherence to a schedule'' (Modell, Furstenberg, and Hershberg, 1976, p. 30).

Missing from this analysis and interpretation is an explicit account of social change in the transitions of urban boys and girls from the middle and lower classes. Though working-class youth played an important role in family support within the uncontrolled economy of nineteenth-century America, this role bears little resemblance to that of the sons and daughters of upper-middle-class families at the time. Twentieth-century affluence increased the prevalence of this ''favored'' life situation among youth, liberating an expanding number from the pressing demands of family survival. It is this global change through multiple institutions that is most vividly described by the life-course changes reported by Modell, Furstenberg, and Hershberg (1976). The impact of major historical transformations that occurred between late-nineteenth-century America and the 1970s — especially the Great Depression and the two World Wars — as well as class and ethnic differences in life-course change have yet to be explored in detail. Winsborough (1975, 1976), for example, has observed the same historical trend toward overlapping transitions in the early life course of male cohorts from 1911 to 1941. He suggests that the anticipation of life disruptions associated with military service (see Hogan, 1976), especially during the post-1940 era of the draft, may have fostered greater ''calculation about how to make the component transitions, an overcompensation for the time which may be lost, and a pressure to get on with the business of getting started in life before the ax falls'' (Winsborough, 1975, p. 37).

Demographic records on events in the course to adulthood describe the patterning of one segment of the life span at different times and places, but they do not, in themselves, tell us what specific life paths or events meant to youth and the larger community. We can be certain that an extension of family residence and schooling in the latter half of the nineteenth century profoundly altered the social environment of young people, but a precise understanding of this environment and its developmental effects eludes our grasp with the historical documents at hand. Nevertheless, it is knowledge of these developmental outcomes that some historians regard as the ultimate objective of historical research on the family: to seek an understanding of family change and continuity in the lives of individuals (Greven, 1973, p. 11). Though folk literature (diaries, etc.) may offer valuable insights on the psychosocial dimensions of family life, its selective representations bear a highly problematic relation to the general population and to actual situations or behavior. Apart from this constraint, widely separated data points leave much to the imagination, as in the Hamilton study. We see Hamilton youth in 1851 and in 1861, but not the differential experience of their families in the depression of the 1850s and its consequences on their upbringing. These observations illustrate some common data constraints that limit the possibilities of a life-course approach to the study of youth in historical times.

The impact of social change on youth is mediated by their proximal environments (family, school, peer groups, etc.), and one of the best opportunities to investigate this process is found in longitudinal archives that were initiated by child-study centers during the 1920s and 1930s. At the Berkeley Institute of Child Welfare (Now Human Development, California), we see this development in the establishment of three longitudinal studies (Jones et al., 1971): the Oakland Growth Study—launched in 1930–1931, it followed children from northeastern Oakland, California, through the 1930s and up to the middle years of life (N= 145); the Guidance Study—selected infants who were born in Berkeley during 1928–1929 and investigated their course of development through annual measurements up to the end of World War II, approximately 180 members of the original core sample (N= 214) have participated in at least two adult follow-ups through 1970; and the Berkeley Growth Study—a small, intensively studied sample of children that corresponds in time frame with the Berkeley Guidance Study.

Over the past half century, these longitudinal projects have generated an impressive body of information on life-span development, though limited by neglect of life-course and historical experience. During the early 1960s, initial surveys of the Oakland archive alerted the author to the profound impact of the Depression on families and their offspring, to substantial variation in economic loss and adaptations, and, subsequently, to the design of a study on Depression hardship in the life experience of adolescents who entered the 1930s from the middle and the working classes (Elder, 1974). Research questions focused on the psychosocial effects of the Depression experience. Specification of this experience thus represented a first step toward identifying and explaining life outcomes of family deprivation during the 1930s. To what extent and in what ways did economic loss differentiate the social worlds of the Oakland adolescents? What were the social and psychological consequences of such variation? How were these early outcomes of Depression hardship expressed in the life course and in the adult personality? These questions established contexts in which to formulate models, using available theory and observation—models that specified plausible linkages between a family's deprivational status in the 1930s and its offspring's development. Notions of an event-structured life course acquired significance through efforts to sketch these interconnections between economic events of the 1930s and adolescent experience and between the latter and the adult years.

Prior to the Depression, middle- and working-class families in the sample were characterized by values and resources that had implications for their interpretation and response to economic deprivation. Middle-class families entered the 1930s with claims that placed them in a more vulnerable "psychic position" relative to income loss when compared to families in the lower strata, but they also occupied a position of relative advantage on problem-solving resources — knowledge, technical skills, material assets. Class position (as of 1929) entered the analysis by defining the cultural and economic context in which families worked out lines of adaptation to economic loss. Within the middle and working classes, the study compared families that differed in economic loss — the relatively nondeprived (less than 35% loss, 1929–1933) and the deprived (a classification that made allowances for a one-fourth drop in the cost of living at the time). The effects of deprivation were assessed within each class stratum according to a model that depicted the socioeconomic and psychological adaptations of the family to Depression hardship as the primary link between economic change, on the one hand, and the life experience and personality of the Oakland Study members, on the other.

With economic deprivation as the focal point, the investigation necessarily led to a variety of outcomes in the life course of the Oakland cohorts, a mode of inquiry that is well described as a ''branching tree.'' Three hypothesized connections between family hardship and the adolescent emerged from the analysis:

1. *Change in the household economy* — drastic loss of income required new modes of economic maintenance, which altered the domestic and economic roles of family members, shifting responsibilities to mother (via employment, budgetary management) and the older children. Girls played a major role in household operations; boys contributed earnings from paid jobs.

2. *Change in family relationships* — father's loss of earnings and resulting adaptations in family support increased the relative power of mother, reduced the level and effectiveness of parental control, and diminished the attractiveness of father as a model.

3. *Social strains in the family* — resource losses, parental impairment, and status inconsistency enhanced the degree of social ambiguity, conflict, and emotional strain in the lives of family members.

These family conditions were associated with Depression hardship in both social classes and acquired developmental meaning in terms of the Oakland cohort's life stage. Members of the cohort were beyond the critical early stage of development and dependency when family losses occurred; they left high school in the late 1930s during economic recovery and the initial phase of wartime mobilization. Unlike younger children, they were old enough to play important roles in the household economy and to confront future prospects within the context of Depression realities. In the lives of youth from deprived families, hard times generally lowered the social boundary of adulthood when compared to the life situation of youth from more privileged homes. Deprived youth, middle and working class, were more likely to be involved in adultlike tasks within the family economy, to aspire to grown-up status, and to enter the adult roles of marriage and/or work at an early age. Common psychic states observed in the course of adolescent development (e.g., self-consciousness, emotional vulnerability, desire for social acceptance) were more characteristic of boys and girls from hard-pressed families in both social classes, but we find little evidence of an enduring social or psychological disadvantage by the end of the 1930s. Family deprivation did not impair attainment in secondary school or lessen ambition, though it reduced prospects for education beyond high school among youth from the working class.

Soon after the Oakland boys left high school, they were called to military duty in World War II; all but a handful served two or more years. Though military service uniformly interrupted career beginnings in the cohort, the long arm of the Depression made a difference in event schedules and in the patterning of worklife, apart from the influence of class origin. Compared to the nondeprived, young men from hard-pressed families entered adulthood with a more crystallized idea of their occupational goals; they were more likely to delay parenthood, to establish their worklife at an early age, and, despite some handicap in formal education, managed to end up at midlife with a slightly higher occupational rank. Job security was uniquely important to men with a deprived background only under conditions of economic pressure and worklife problems. Despite the significance of work to men from deprived homes, they were more inclined than the nondeprived to stress family activity, to consider children the most important aspect of marriage, to emphasize the responsibilities of parenthood, and to stress the value of dependability in children. Personal aspects of Depression life are reflected in these preferences — the role of children in helping out, the importance of family support in time of crisis. From the vantage point of midlife, clinical ratings of health and self-evaluations show no adverse signs of growing up in the Great Depression, except perhaps among the offspring of working-class parents. On the whole, adulthood offered abundant gratification for men from deprived homes, and they were more likely than the nondeprived to regard these years as the best time of their life.

In life course and values, the Oakland women resemble the "ultradomestic" climate of the postwar years. However, a domestic life style is most pronounced among those women who grew up in deprived, mother-dominated families where they were involved in household responsibilities. During adolescence, these women were more inclined to favor marriage and family over a career when compared to women who were spared family hardships; they tended to enter marriage at an earlier age in the middle class; and they most frequently dropped out of the labor force after marriage or before the birth of their first child. Despite an educational disadvantage, the deprived were no less successful than other women in marrying college-educated men who made their way to the upper echelons of business and the professions. At midlife, family, children, and homemaking distinguished their priorities from those of the nondeprived, regardless of educational level or social position. From these gratifications to sound health, the adult years represented the best time of their lives, more satisfying by far than adolescence in the depressed 1930s and their memories of social exclusion, family burdens, and a controlling mother.

The full array of findings from this study inevitably raise questions concerning their generality, both in terms of a broader sample of Americans in the 1920–1921 cohort and the Depression's impact on other cohorts. The Oakland sample is small and its members were selected by criteria (e.g., permanence in the area) that ensured some degree of bias. The city of Oakland, its economic base, cultural institutions, and Bay Area locale, place other constraints on generalizations from the study. Generality is even more of a question when we turn to cohort variation. Successive cohorts encounter historical events at different points in the life course, which implies variations in adaptive potential and developmental outcomes. One might argue that the Oakland cohort occupied a "favored" position relative to events of the 1930s; in developmental age at the time of the economic crisis and in opportunities at the end of the decade. By contrast, younger cohorts experienced the crisis when they were more dependent on family nurturance and, consequently, were more vulnerable to family instability, emotional strain, and conflict. Family hardship came early in their lives and thus entailed a more prolonged experience, from the economic trough to the war years or departure from home. Issues of this sort led to the initiation of another longitudinal study of Depression hardship, one based on data from the Guidance archive at Berkeley—a study designed to parallel the Oakland project in analytic model, measurements (e.g., economic deprivation), and research foci. Members of the Berkeley Guidance Study were born in 1928–1929 and thus provide a sharp contrast with the Oakland cohort on life stage. Childhood in the prosperous 1920s preceded the Depression adolescence of the Oakland subjects, whereas the Berkeley children entered adolescence in the affluent and unsettled years of World War II, after a childhood shaped by economic deprivation and insecurity.

According to life-stage considerations, one would expect more adverse consequences from Depression hardship in the Berkeley cohort; preliminary analyses generally support this hypothesis on males (Elder & Rockwell, 1979). In the middle and working classes, Berkeley youth from deprived families held lower aspirations during wartime adolescence than members of nondeprived families (no difference in IQ); their scholastic performance turned sharply downward at this point, falling well below that of adolescents in more affluent homes. Despite expanding opportunities during the war, deprived boys were least likely to be hopeful, self-directed, and confident about their future, a dysphoric outlook most prevalent in the formerly hard-pressed middle class. This outlook is one element of a ''dependency'' syndrome that emerged from personality ratings in adolescence — personal and social inadequacy, a passive mode of responding to life situations, feelings of victimization, withdrawal from adversity, and self-defeating behavior. Aspects of this syndrome distinguished the behavioral course of adolescents who grew up in deprived families from that of youth who were spared such hardship, regardless of class origin.

The causal link between family deprivation in the early 1930s and adolescent personality included a continuing pattern of socioeconomic instability, with its distorting influence on family life — the emotional strain of resource exhaustion; loss of an effective, nurturant father; and an overburdened, dominant mother, anxiously preoccupied with matters of status and mere survival. The connection is most striking among deprived households in the middle class, especially when mothers sought gratification through the accomplishments of their sons. As of the 1930s, these mothers were most likely to have had a nonsupportive or impaired husband, a conflicted marriage, and lofty material aspirations. In fateful ways, wartime adolescence clearly bore the imprint of Depression experiences among some Berkeley youth.

The disadvantage of growing up in a deprived household continued into the postwar years, limiting formal education among the sons of both middle- and working-class parents and shaping a life course of relatively early work, late marriage, and military service. But records show a striking reversal in life experience by the middle years. Deprived men were likely to do far better in worklife than predictions based on their education. At midlife, their occupational attainment closely resembled that of men from nondeprived families. Marriage, work, and especially the ''time out'' provided by military service constitute plausible turning points in the lives of deprived men. These events offered a relatively independent, maturing experience, a chance to establish their own life course with minimal intrusion by parents. Between adolescence and midlife, deprived men achieved notable developmental gains (in self-esteem, assertiveness), though not sufficient to erase completely the inadequacies of the early years. Nevertheless, life had clearly improved since childhood and adolescence. From the vantage point of middle age, deprived men were most likely to regard adolescence as the very worst time of life and the years after 30 as a high point in their life.

Comparison of the Berkeley and Oakland men is risky at best, owing to differences in sample and locale. Nevertheless, the results to date identify suggestive cohort variations in the developmental and life-course effects of Depression hardship. In both cohorts, economic deprivation produced similar changes in the family (division of labor, family relationships, social strains), but their developmental effects vary in ways that generally conform to differences in life stage relative to Depression and war. By encountering such times at different points in life, the Berkeley and Oakland men have different stories to tell about childhood, adolescence, and adulthood. Worklife played a major role in enabling men in both cohorts to surmount at least some of the handicaps associated with family deprivation. Correlated developmental gains in the Berkeley cohort provide some clues to Jean Macfarlane's observation (1963) that nearly half of the ''Guidance'' men turned out to be more "stable and effective adults than any of us with our differing theoretical biases would have predicted. . ." (p. 338). A large proportion of the "most outstandingly mature adults in our entire group. . . are recruited from those who were confronted with very difficult situations and whose characteristic responses during childhood and adolescence seemed to us to compound their problems" (Macfarlane, 1964, p. 121). In retrospect, Macfarlane (1963) cites two sources of error in the early predictions:

1. Overweighting the presumed negative influence of pathogenic aspects of development at the expense of recognizing the maturing benefits of hardship.
2. Insufficient awareness of the potential of adult independence and late development for changing the course of lives.

Needless to say, childhood and adolescence do not make a life.

Consistent with a "perspectives" theme, we have focused this concluding section on studies that illustrate the use of archival resources for tracing the effects of historical setting and change to the life course of youth. Breadth of coverage on historical times and topics [now available in book-length surveys (Gillis, 1974; Kett, 1977)] was sacrificed for a more intensive examination of studies that have applied a life-course perspective to aspects of social change in youth experience: early industrialization and institutional change — the Hamilton study of Canadian youth between 1851 and 1871; institutional change between late-nineteenth-century America and 1970 — the study by Modell and associates of change in the transition of adulthood; and the Great Depression — a longitudinal investigation of family deprivation in the life course of development of two cohorts, with birthdates in the 1920s. However flawed, these studies constitute a new venture in the historical study of youth; their publication dates (1974–1976) bear witness to the early stage of development of this approach. Knowledge cumulation is beginning to occur on youth in nineteenth-century America and earlier times, but not in the twentieth century. We have learned very little about historical forces in lives, cohorts, and institutions since the 1920s. The archives of older longitudinal studies (e.g., the Terman gifted sample, the Fels Institute sample, and Grant samples, Harvard University) remain largely untapped by efforts to assess the impact of historical times and change in the course of adolescent and life-span development. Nevertheless, even a casual glance at the literature of recent decades indicates that much has been accomplished in bringing history to the study of youth.

OVERVIEW

Dominant and emerging perspectives offer a useful base from which to view the course of inquiry on adolescence and young people since the early decades of the twentieth century. Over this time period, two perspectives, developmental and social, have shaped perceptions of adolescence, theoretical concerns, and research. Adolescence has been defined by characteristics of the maturing organism (physical, cognitive, moral); by social criteria that specify the meaning of age categories and roles; and by the relation between developmental and social timetables. By the mid to late 1960s, we see evidence of a third perspective that viewed these timetables according to historical time and change, a perspective influenced by concepts of life-span development, greater understanding of age patterns in the life course, and the growth of archival studies on social change in youth experience. Two related developments emerged from this shift toward historical considerations and constitute central themes of this chapter: (1) the integration of three traditions of research and theory (developmental, social, and historical) in a life-course framework and (2) its application to studies of youth.

As a theoretical orientation, the life course is informed by three strands of theory and research that link age and time and, by association, life history and social history:

1. Life, or developmental time, and its focus on the process of aging from birth to death — chronological or developmental age as an index of position in the aging process.

2. Social time in the age-patterning of social roles and events across multiple, interlocking career lines, which constitute the social life course.

3. Historical time, with birth-year defining location in the historical process and membership in cohorts that may vary according to composition (social, cultural, psychological), size, and ecological setting.

Renewed attention to the latter dimension in the 1960s gave fresh visibility to the interdependence of life history and social history as well as to the variable nature of psychosocial development and institutions in the course of social change. Three general premises in the life-course approach illustrate this perception in current research:

1. The implications of historical change vary according to the developmental and social age of individuals and cohorts at the point of change.

2. The meaning of an historical event is derived in part from the life histories that individuals and cohorts bring to the situation — from life histories influenced by social change and differential location in class, ethnic, and residential subgroups.

3. Historical conditions are variable at points in time and in whether and how they are experienced by particular individuals and cohorts.

The remarkable growth of historical studies of youth since the 1960s represents one aspect of what some have called the ''new social history'' on the lives of ordinary people. This work has played a major role in the evolution of a life-course perspective through documentation of historical variations and their implications for the lives of young people. Moreover, some historical research has addressed issues and employed concepts that are part of a life-course approach: the interplay of youth cohorts and social institutions under conditions of economic and demographic change; youth cohorts as both consequence and vehicle of social change; life patterns among youth in relation to family, education, and economic change; and the timing and sequencing of events in the transition from childhood to adult status. For reasons of space and theme, only a small fraction of this research has been cited or reviewed, but even such limited coverage indicates something of the utility and necessity of an approach that links social history and the life course. From research on nineteenth-century American youth, we now have a clearer notion of what is distinctive of modern adolescence; for example, the lag between physical maturity and adult independence, long attributed to modern adolescence, was at least as characteristic of late-nineteenth-century youth. Though few studies have actually traced the effects of social change on the life course of youth, the evidence at hand tends to shift the burden of proof on assumptions of ''developmental invariance'' to the investigator.

In closing, it is fitting to return to John Seeley's trenchant criticism of the literature on adolescence as he perceived it during the early 1970s: the absence of a ''sense of history'' in which adolescence constitutes a point of articulation between historical time and the ontogenetic process. This criticism is well deserved by the literature through the mid-1960s as reviewed by Elder (1968); and one might be tempted to claim that it applies to contemporary research as well — historical considerations still rarely appear in studies of youth development and groups, life styles and status attainment (see Dragastin & Elder, 1975). However, significant change toward a historical perspective has occurred since the 1960s, even apart from developments in the field of history. We now have conceptual and methodological tools for studying youth according to historical time and the life span; in addition we have an expanding body of research that has put these tools to work on data archives. In potential, if not accomplishment, these developments suggest the possibilities of a historical perspective on adolescence.

REFERENCES

Abrams, P. The sense of the past and the origins of sociology. *Past and Present* 1972, *55,* 18–32.

Allmendinger, D. F., Jr. *Paupers and scholars: The transformation of student life in nineteenth-century New England.* New York: St. Martin's Press, 1975.

Andersson, B. E. *Studies in adolescent behavior.* Stockholm: Almquist & Wiksell, 1969.

Ariès, P. *Centuries of childhood,* trans. R. Baldick. New York: Vintage, 1965.

Bailyn, B. *Education in the forming of American society.* Chapel Hill: University of North Carolina Press, 1960.

Baltes, P. B. Longitudinal and cross-sectional sequences in the study of age and generation effects. *Human Development,* 1968, *11,* 145–171.

————. Life-span developmental psychology: Some observations on history and theory. Presidential Address, Division 20 (Adult Development and Aging), American Psychological Association, San Francisco, August 1977.

Baltes, P. B. and Schaie, K. W. *Life-span developmental psychology: Personality and socialization.* New York: Academic, 1973.

Baltes, P. B., Cornelius, S. W., and Nesselroade, J. R. Cohort effects in developmental psychology: Theoretical and methodological perspectives. In W. A. Collins (Ed.), *Minnesota Symposium on Child Psychology* (Vol. 11). Minneapolis: University of Minnesota 1977.

Barker, G. and Gump, V. *Big school, small school: High school size and student behavior.* Stanford, Calif.: Stanford University Press, 1964.

Barker, R. *Ecological psychology.* Stanford, Calif.: Stanford University Press, 1968.

Bengtson, V. L. and Laufer, R. S. (Eds.) Youth, generations, and social change (Parts 1 and 2). *Journal of Social Issues,* 1974, *30* (2), (3).

Bengtson, V. L. and Laufer, R. S. Youth, generations, and social change (Parts 1 and 2). *Journal of Social Issues,* 1974, *30* (2), 000–000; 1974, *30* (3), 000–000.

Bengtson, V. L. and Lovejoy, M. C. Values, personality, and social structure: an intergenerational analysis. *American Behavioral Scientist,* 1973, *16,* 880–912.

Bengtson, V. L. and Starr, J. M. Contrast and consensus: A generational analysis of youth in the 1970s. In R. J. Havighurst and P. H. Dreyer (Eds.), *Youth.* (74th Yearbook, National Society for the Study of Education.) Chicago: University of Chicago Press, 1975.

Berger, B. M. *Looking for America.* Englewood Cliffs, N.J.: Prentice-Hall, 1971.

Bloomberg, S. H. The household and the family: The effects of industrialization on skilled workers in Newark, 1840–1860. Paper presented at the Organization of American Historians, Denver, 1974.

Blyth, D. A., Simmons, R. G., and Bush, D. The transition into early adolescence: A longitudinal comparison of youth in two educational contexts. Revision of paper presented at the Biennial Meeting of the Society for Research in Child Development, New Orleans, March 1977.

Bowerman, C. E. and Kinch, J. W. Changes in family and peer orientation of children between the fourth and tenth grades. *Social Forces,* 1959, *57,* 206–211.

Braungart, R. G. Youth and social movements. In S. Dragastin and G. H. Elder, Jr. (Eds.), *Adolescence in the life cycle.* Washington, D.C.: Hemisphere, 1975.

Bremner, R. (Ed.). *Children and youth in America:* A documentary history (3 vols.). Cambridge: Harvard University Press, 1970–1974.

Bronfenbrenner, U. Toward an experimental ecology of human development. *American Psychologist,* 1977, *32,* 513–531.

Bühler, C. The curve of life as studied in biographies. *Journal of Applied Psychology,* 1935 *19,* 405–409.

Carlsmith, L. Some personality characteristics of boys separated from their fathers during World War II. *Ethos,* Winter 1973, *1,* 467–477.

Clausen, J. A. The life course of individuals. In M. W. Riley, M. Johnson, and A. Foner (Eds.), *Aging and society: A sociology of age stratification.* New York: Russell Sage, 1972.

Cohen, A. K. *Delinquent boys: The culture of the gang.* Glencoe, Ill.: Free Press, 1955.

Coleman, J. S. *The adolescent society.* New York: Free Press, 1961.

Cottrell, L. S. The adjustment of the individual to his age and sex roles. *American Sociological Review,* 1942, *7,* 617–620.

Davis, K. Sociology of parent-youth conflict. *American Sociological Review,* 1940, *1,* 523–535.

———. Adolescence and the social structure. *The Annals of the American Academy of Political and Social Science,* 1944, *236,* 8–16.

Davis, N. Z. The reasons of misrule. In *Society and Culture in Early Modern France.* Stanford, Calif.: Stanford University Press, 1975.

Demos, J. *A little commonwealth: Family life in Plymouth Colony.* New York: Oxford University Press, 1970.

Demos, J. and Demos, V. Adolescence in historical perspective. *Journal of Marriage and the Family,* 1969, *31,* 632–638.

Dennis, W. The adolescent. In Leonard Carmichael (Ed.), *Manual of child psychology.* New York: Wiley, 1946.

Dollard, J. *Criteria for the life history.* New York: Peter Smith, 1949.

Dollard, J., Doob, L. W., Miller, N. E., Mowrer, O. H., and Sears, R. R. *Frustration and aggression.* New Haven, Conn.: Yale University Press, 1939.

Douvan, E. and Adelson, J. *The adolescent experience.* New York: Wiley, 1966.

Dragastin, S. E. and Elder, G. H., Jr. *Adolescence in the life cycle.* Washington, D.C.: Hemisphere, 1975.

Eisenstadt, S. N. *From generation to generation.* Glencoe, Ill.: Free Press, 1956.

Elder, G. H., Jr. *Adolescent socialization and personality development.* Chicago: Rand McNally, 1968.

———. *Children of the Great Depression.* University of Chicago Press, 1974.

———. Adolescence in the life cycle. In S. Dragastin and G. H. Elder, Jr. (Eds.), *Adolescence in the life cycle.* Washington, D.C.: Hemisphere, 1975a.

———. Age differentiation and the life course. In A. Inkeles (Ed.), *Annual Review of Sociology,* Palo Alto, Calif.: Annual Reviews, 1975b.

————. Approaches to social change and the family. *American Journal of Sociology,* 1978, *84.* (Special supplement)

Elder G. H., Jr. and Rockwell, R. W. Economic depression and postwar opportunity in men's lives: A study of life patterns and health. In R. G. Simmons (Ed.), *Research in community and mental health.* Greenwich, Conn.: JAI Press, 1979.

Erikson, E. H. Identity and the life cycle. *Psychological Issues,* 1959, *1.*

————. *Insight and responsibility.* New York: Norton, 1964.

Fendrich, J. M. Activities ten years later: A test of generational unit continuity. *Journal of Social Issues,* 1974, *30,* 95–118.

Finestone, H. *Victims of change: Juvenile delinquents in American society.* Westport, Conn.: Greenwood Press, 1976.

Flacks, R. *Youth and social change.* Chicago: Markham, 1971.

Furstenberg, F. F., Jr. *Unplanned parenthood: The social consequences of teenage childbearing.* New York: Free Press, 1976.

Garbarino, J. The historical and ecological correlates of school size: Shaping the adolescent experience. Unpublished manuscript, 1977.

Gillis, J. R. *Youth and history: Tradition and change in European age relations, 1770–present.* New York: Academic, 1974.

Goldstein, J. On being an adult in secular law. *Daedalus,* Fall 1976, *105,* 69–87.

Goode, W. J. A theory of role strain. *American Sociological Review,* 1960, *25,* 483–496.

Gordon, C. *The social system of the high school.* Glencoe, Ill.: Free Press, 1957.

Goulet, L. R. and Baltes, P. B. *Life-span developmental psychology: Research and theory.* New York: Academic, 1970.

Greven, P. J., Jr. *Four generations: Population, land, and family in colonial Andover, Massachusetts.* Ithaca, N.Y.: Cornell University Press, 1970.

————. Comments for the panel discussion on "Change and continuity in family structure." *The Family in Historical Perspective, An International Newsletter,* No. 5, Autumn 1973, 9–11.

Grinder, R. E. The concept of adolescence in the genetic psychology of G. Stanley Hall. *Child Development,* 1969, *40,* 355–369.

Hall, G. S. *Adolescence: Its psychology and its relations to physiology, anthropology, sociology, sex, crime, religion, and education.* New York: Appleton, 1904.

Hampden-Turner, C. *Radical men.* Cambridge, Mass.: Schenkman, 1970.

Hantover, J. P. Sex role, sexuality, and social status: The early years of the Boy Scouts of America. Unpublished doctoral dissertation, University of Chicago, 1976.

Hareven, T. K. Family time and industrial time: Family and work in a planned corporation town, 1900–1924. *Journal of Urban History,* 1975, *1,* 365–389.

————. *Transitions: The family and the life course in historical perspective.* New York: Academic, 1978.

Heyneman, S. P. Continuing issues in adolescence: A summary of current transition to adulthood debates. *Journal of Youth and Adolescence,* 1976, *5,* 309–323.

Hill, J. P. and Monks, F. J. *Adolescence and youth in prospect.* Guildford, Surrey, England: IPC Science and Technology Press, 1977.

Hill, R. *Families under stress.* New York: Harper & Brs., 1949.

Hogan, D. P. The passage of American men from family of orientation to family of procreation: Pattern, timing, and determinants. Doctoral dissertation, University of Wisconsin, 1976.

Hollingshead, A. *Elmtown's youth.* New York: Wiley, 1949.

Hollingworth, L. S. *The psychology of the adolescent*. New York: Appleton, 1928.

Huston-Stein, A. and Baltes, P. B. Theory and method in life-span developmental psychology: Implications for child development. In H. W. Reese (Ed.), *Advances in child development and behavior*. New York: Academic, 1976.

Inglehart, R. *The silent revolution: Changing values and political styles among Western publics*. Princeton, N.J.: Princeton University Press, 1977.

Jennings, K. M., Allerbeck, K., and Rosenmayr, L. Value orientations and political socialization in five countries. Paper presented at the Workshop on Political Behavior, Dissatisfaction, and Protest, Louvain-La-Nueve, April 8–14, 1976.

Jones, H. E. The adolescent growth study: I. Principles and methods, II. Procedures. *Journal of Consulting Psychology*, 1939, *3*, 157–159; 177–180.

Jones, M. C., Bayley, N., Macfarlane, J. W., and Honzik, M. P. *The course of human development*. Waltham, Mass.: Xerox, 1971.

Jordan, W. D. Searching for adulthood in America. *Daedalus*, Fall 1976, *105*, 1–11.

Kaestle, C. F. and Vinovskis, M. A. Education and social change in nineteenth-century Massachusetts: Quantitative studies. Final Research Report, National Institute of Education, December 1976.

Kagan, J. A conception of early adolescence. *Daedalus*, Fall 1971, *100*, 997–1012.

Kandel, D. B. and Lesser, G. S. *Youth in two worlds: United States and Denmark*. San Francisco: Jossey-Bass, 1972.

Katz, M. B. *The people of Hamilton, Canada West: Family and class in a mid-nineteenth-century city*. Cambridge: Harvard University Press, 1975.

Katz, M. B. and Davey, I. F. Youth and early industrialization in a Canadian city. *American Journal of Sociology*, 1978, *84*. (Special supplement)

Keniston, K. Youth as a stage of life. *American Scholar*, 1970, *39*, 631–654.

———. Psychological development and historical change. *The Journal of Interdisciplinary History*, Autumn 1971, *2*, 329–345.

Kett, J. F. *Rites of passage*. New York: Basic Books, 1977.

Kuhlen, R. G. Social change: A neglected factor in psychological studies of the life span. *School and Society*, 1940, *52*, 14–16.

Laslett, P. Age at menarche in Europe since the eighteenth century. *The Journal of Interdisciplinary History*, 1971, *2*, 221–236.

———. *Family life and illicit love in earlier generations*. New York: Cambridge University Press, 1977.

Linton, R. Age and sex categories. *American Sociological Review*, 1942, *7*, 589–603.

Lipschutz, M. R. Runaways in history. *Crime and Delinquency*, 1977, *23*, 321–332.

Lipset, S. M. *Rebellion in the university* (Rev. ed.). Chicago: University of Chicago Press, 1976.

Lipset S. M. and Lowenthal, L. *Culture and social character*. New York: Free Press, 1961.

Lipsitz, J. *Growing up forgotten*. Lexington, Mass.: Lexington Books, 1977.

Little, M. and Laslett, B. Adolescence in historical perspective: The decline of boarding in 19th century Los Angeles. Paper presented at the American Sociological Meetings, Chicago, September 6, 1977.

Loewenberg, P. The psychohistorical origins of the Nazi youth cohort. *American Historical Review*, 1972, *76*, 1457–1502.

Lüscher, K. Perspektiven einer soziologie der sozialisation — Die entwicklung der rolle des kindes [Towards a sociology of socialization — The development of the child's role], *Zeitschrift für Soziologie*, 1975, *4*, 359–379.

Lynd, R. S. and Lynd, H. M. *Middletown*. New York: Harcourt, Brace and World, 1929.

Macfarlane, J. W. From infancy to childhood. *Childhood Education*, 1963, *39*, 336–342.

———. Perspectives on personality consistency and change from the "Guidance Study". *Vita Humana*, 1964, *7*, 115–126.

Magee, E. S. Impact of the war on child labor. *The Annals of the American Academy of Political and Social Science*, 1944, *236*, 101–109.

Mannheim, K. The problem of generations. In P. Keckskemeti (Ed.) *Essays on the sociology of knowledge*. New York: Oxford University Press, 1952. (Originally published, 1928).

Matza, D. Position and behavior patterns of youth. In R. Faris (Ed.), *Handbook of modern sociology*. Chicago: Rand McNally, 1964.

Mead, M. *Coming of age in Samoa*. Ann Arbor, Mich.: Morrow, 1928.

Merkl, P. H. *Political violence under the swastika*. Princeton, N.J.: Princeton University Press, 1975.

Meyer, J. W., Tyack, D., Nagel, J., and Gordon, A. Education as nation-building in America: Enrollments and bureaucratization in the American States, 1870–1930. Unpublished research paper, Boys Town Center, Stanford University, 1977.

Modell, J., Furstenberg, F. F., Jr., and Hershberg, T. Social change and the transition to adulthood in historical perspective. *Journal of Family History*, Autumn 1976, *1*, 7–32.

Modell, J., Furstenberg, F. F., Jr., and Strong, D. The timing of marriage in the transition to adulthood: Continuity and change, 1860–1975. *American Journal of Sociology*, 1978, *84*. (Special supplement)

Moller, H. Youth as a force in the modern world, *Comparative Studies in Society and History*, 1968, *10*, 237–260.

Musgrove, F. *Youth and the social order*. Bloomington: Indiana University Press, 1965.

Muus, R. *Theories of Adolescence* (3rd ed.). New York: Random House, 1975.

National Commission on Resources for Youth. *New roles for youth in the school and community*. New York: Citation Press, 1974.

National Society for the Study of Education (NSSE). *Adolescence*. (43rd Yearbook, National Society for the Study of Education.) Chicago: University of Chicago Press, 1944.

———. In R. J. Havighurst and P. H. Dreyer (Eds.), *Youth*. (74th Yearbook, National Society for the Study of Education.) Chicago: University of Chicago Press, 1975.

Nelson, E. A. and Maccoby, E. E. The relationships between social development and differential abilities on the Scholastic Aptitude Test. *Merrill-Palmer Quarterly*, 1966, *12*, 269–284.

Nesselroade, J. R. and Baltes, P. B. Adolescent personality development and historical change: 1970–1972. *Monographs of the Society for Research in Child Development*, 1974, *39* (1, Serial No. 154).

Neugarten, B. L., Moore, J. W., and Lowe, J. C. Age norms, age constraints, and adult socialization. *American Journal of Sociology*, 1965, *70*, 710–717.

Parsons, T. Age and sex in the social structure of the United States. *American Sociological Review*, 1942, *7*, 604–616.

———. *Social structure and personality*. New York: Free Press, 1964.

Parsons, T. and Platt, G. M. Higher education and changing socialization. In M. W. Riley, M. E. Johnson, and A. Foner (Eds.), *Aging and society: A sociology of age stratification*. New York: Russell Sage, 1972.

Plath, D. W. and Ikeda, K. After coming of age: Adult awareness of age norms. In T. R. Williams (Ed.), *Socialization and communication in primary groups*. The Hague: Mouton, 1975.

Platt, A. *The child-savers: The invention of delinquency.* Chicago: University of Chicago Press, 1969.

Presidential Science Advisory Commission, Panel on Youth. *Youth: transition to adulthood.* Washington, D. C.: U.S. Government Printing Office, 1973.

Riesman, D. (with Glazer, N. and Denney, R.). *The lonely crowd.* New Haven, Conn.: Yale University Press, 1950.

——. *The lonely crowd.* New Haven, Conn.: Yale University Press, 1961, [Abridged edition with new preface]

Riley, M. W., Johnson, M. E., and Foner, A. *Aging and society: A sociology of age stratification.* New York: Russell Sage, 1972.

Ross, D. *G. Stanley Hall: The psychologist as prophet.* Chicago: University of Chicago Press, 1972.

Rothman, D. J. Documents in search of a historian: Toward a history of childhood and youth in America. (Review of *Children and youth in America: A documentary history,* R. H. Bremner, Ed.). *The Journal of Interdisciplinary History,* Autumn 1971, *2,* 367–377.

Ryder, N. B. The cohort as a concept in the study of social change. *American Sociological Review,* 1965, *30,* 843–861.

Schaie, K. W. A general model for the study of developmental problems. *Psychological Bulletin,* 1965, *64,* 92–107.

Schlossman, S. L. *Love and the American delinquent.* Chicago: University of Chicago Press, 1977.

Scott, J. W. and El-Assal, M. Multiversity, university size, university quality, and student protest: An empirical study. *American Sociological Review,* 1969, *34,* 202–209.

Scully, M. G. Student protest in Europe: The motive is 'fear'. *The Chronicle of Higher Education,* April 4, 1977, p. 9.

Sears, R. R. Your ancients revisited: A history of child development. In E. Mavis Hetherington (Ed.), *Review of child development research.* Chicago: University of Chicago Press, 1975.

Seeley, J. R. Adolescence: The management of emancipation in history and life history. H. Silverstein (Ed.), *The sociology of youth.* New York: Macmillan, 1973.

Skolnick, A. The limits of childhood: Conceptions of child development and social context. *Law and Contemporary Problems,* Summer 1975, *39,* 38–77.

Smith, D. S. Parental power and marriage patterns: An analysis of historical trends in Hingham, Mass. *Journal of Marriage and the Family,* 1973, *35,* 419–428.

Smith, D. S. and Hindus, M. S. Premarital pregnancy in America 1640–1971: An overview and interpretation. *Journal of Interdisciplinary History,* Spring 1975, *5,* 537–570.

Stinchcombe, A. L. *Rebellion in a high school.* Chicago: Quadrangle, 1964.

Stolz, L. *Father relations of war-born children.* Stanford, Calif.: Stanford University Press, 1954.

Tanner, J. M. *Growth and adolescence* (2nd ed.). Springfield, Ill.: Thomas, 1962.

Thernstrom, S. Yankee city revisited: The perils of historical naivete. *American Sociological Review,* 1965, *30,* 234–242.

Thomas, W. I. and Znaniecki, F. *The Polish peasant in Europe and America* (Vols. 1 and 2). Chicago: University of Chicago Press, 1918–1920.

Timpane, M., Abramowitz, S., Bobrow, S. B., and Pascal, A. *Youth policy in transition.* Santa Monica, Calif.: Rand Corporation, 1976.

Trow, M. The second transformation of American secondary education. *International Journal of Comparative Sociology,* 1961, *2,* 144–166.

Turner, R. H. *The social context of ambition.* San Francisco: Chandler, 1964.

Tyack, D. B. *The one best system: A history of American urban education,* Cambridge: Harvard University Press, 1975.

Waller, W. *The sociology of teaching.* New York: Wiley, 1965. (Originally published, 1932.)

White House Conference on Child Health and Protection. *The adolescent in the family.* New York: Appleton-Century, 1934.

Winsborough, H. H. Statistical histories of the life cycle of birth cohorts: The transition from schoolboy to adult male. Paper presented at the Conference on Social Demography, University of Wisconsin, Madison, July 15–16, 1975.

————. The transition from schoolboy to adult: Accounting for change in the process. Paper presented to a Seminar on "The Life Cycle as a Demographic Perspective," at the Annual Meeting of the Population Association of America, Montreal, Canada, April 1976.

Yankelovich, D. *The new morality: A profile of American youth in the 70s.* New York: McGraw-Hill, 1974.

Zachry, C. Preparing youth to be adults. In *Adolescence.* (43rd Yearbook of the National Society for the Study of Education (Part I). Chicago: University of Chicago Press, 1944.

CHAPTER 2

Perspectives on Adolescence from Longitudinal Research

Norman Livson and Harvey Peskin

THE LONGITUDINAL PERSPECTIVE: ITS PROMISE AND PROBLEMS AS A GENERAL APPROACH

Some Historical Notes

"The longitudinal approach is the *only* approach which gives a complete description of the growth phenomenon . . . . The cross-sectional approach can never satisfy the objective of a study which requires the measurement of the change in a trait through time in a given individual'' (Kodlin & Thompson, 1958, p.8 — italics in original). This monograph, which presents a painstaking and lucid appraisal of the longitudinal method, is "old," in that the past two decades have seen substantial innovations in methods of data-collection and analysis within the longitudinal perspective. Yet it is in no sense dated since the truism it asserts remains a relevant reminder for contemporary studies that the sufficient study of development insists on certain irreplaceable contributions from the longitudinal method. Wohlwill (1973) agrees that such reminding is still necessary and suggests why. He observes that "perhaps in the belief that the advocacy of the longitudinal method in studying development needs no defense, its proponents have rarely been very explicit in specifying precisely what sort of information it was expected to yield, or in what situations it was either required or strongly preferred over the cross-sectional alternative'' (p. 140). In his comprehensive volume, *The Study of Behavioral Development* (1973), Wohlwill distinguishes among four kinds of goals for which longitudinal data are essential:

(1) to preserve information as to the shape of the developmental function; (2) to provide information on change and patterning of change; (3) to relate earlier behavior to later, and (4) to relate earlier conditions of life to subsequent behavior. . . . [For these] longitudinal data are either absolutely required, or substitutable only at a considerable sacrifice. [p. 140]

The preparation of this chapter was in part supported by Grant AG-00365 from the National Institute of Aging to the Institute of Human Development. We are deeply grateful to the dozens of researchers in the area of longitudinal studies of adolescence who responded to our survey of ongoing work. Although it has not been possible to refer directly to all of the material they so generously provided to us, each of them has contributed significantly to our understanding. To Joanne Bjerke, our superb typist, who in some magical manner transformed our mounds of copy into an actual chapter manuscript, we owe — and happily pay — our considerable debt of appreciation.

In the 1950s, the longitudinal perspective on developmental research generally had just managed to stay alive through some lean years. Nor had the siege been totally lifted by then; Baldwin (1960) in his influential overview of research methodology in child development noted that "longitudinal studies, as they were originally conceived, seemed to have gambled on the existence of clear developmental trends that would shine through the welter of influences of uncontrolled events" (p. 25). If by "clear developmental trends" he meant (as he seemed to) that finding clean-cut continuities of single characteristics would add important depth to our understanding of human development, then his verdict that the bet had been largely lost was a supportable one, especially in the arena of personality development. He forecast a time when developmental theories would become more "genuinely multivariate." He appeared to offer longitudinal researchers the consolation that their arduously gathered long-term data would by that time finally prove valuable, but only as individual case studies. He was both right and wrong. Theories have become more "multivariate," but so have the techniques used for analyzing longitudinal data. Their utilization is still quite limited, however, when what has already been done is considered in the context of the enormous potential power of multivariate statistical methods for mining the rich ore of repeated assessments of the same developing individuals over time. This is so, whether the data are from the current crop of short-term longitudinal studies or from the archives of the "classic" long-term ones. On this point, more later.

During the years of its lapsing popularity, longitudinal researchers were often as mystified as they were threatened by its fall from grace. Longitudinal studies, from their beginnings in the late 1920s and early 1930s (not many years after the birth of developmental psychology itself) had been doing quite well. These studies had managed to maintain data collection and analysis through the years of the Great Depression, emerging into what seemed their heyday in the years after World War II. It was a time of payoff; the relatively long developmental span achieved by these studies began to yield some surprising results. At Berkeley's Institute of Human Development, alone, two longitudinal investigations (the Berkeley Growth Study and the Guidance Study) had documented the variety of individual patterns of mental development as well as the unexpectedly modest predictability of IQ, especially from the preschool to the adolescent years (Bayley, 1949; Honzik, Macfarlane, & Allen, 1948). Such findings were uniquely accessible to longitudinal study. Perhaps even more important, several similar investigations were beginning to replicate findings. On this result — of widely divergent IQ growth patterns — censensus was to be found in research reports from studies at Fels and at Harvard, as well as with longitudinally followed samples of children in Chicago, Cleveland, and Denver.

The longitudinal perspective was thriving then, and adolescent growth phenomena were coming in for a substantial share of research attention. Biological and morphological changes during adolescence, which also demonstrated enormous individual variation in growth rates, were being reported — and again with multistudy replication. Adolescent shifts in personality characteristics and in social behavior were being related to such biological changes (Jones & Bayley, 1950) as well as to a broad range of data that had been gathered on family environment and the child's earlier development. This productivity plus the new postwar availability of federal monies for developmental research seemed to hold a bright promise for the longitudinal perspective. Yet, it was just about then that longitudinal research stood on the threshold of its wane, a period of forgetfulness of its methodological necessity.

The Politics of Longitudinal Research

What accounted for this lapse? For one thing, it had become clear that longitudinal research was difficult, costly, and beset by myriad problems. Perhaps the ardor generated in the search for different approaches to developmental issues led to losing sight of the absolute indispensability of longitudinal research for certain questions. Perhaps the relatively large cost of such research caused it to be seen as a wasteful (even greedy) consumer of grant-funding resources, although (as we shall argue and hope to demonstrate later on) it makes extraordinarily efficient use of data. The funding resources had certainly increased, but so had the developmental field. And its face had begun to change in a critical way: it was turning "experimental." Whereas in its earlier years, the field had been populated largely by investigators of diverse training and experience (but rarely of an experimental bent), the new breed seemed dedicated to the proposition that developmental psychology should at long last join the ranks of "true science."

This last consideration is more subtle than the others, more elusive, and, we strongly suspect, most persistent of all. In our view, it continues to dog the path of the longitudinal researcher. By its very nature, the longitudinal perspective rarely, if ever, permits using classical experimental paradigms. It would be "nice" (though not at all feasible or ethical), for example, to assign infants at random to systematically different parental "treatments" or to prescribed categories of family environments. This is of course a limitation that is as obvious as it is inevitable. In longitudinal research, with rare and minor exceptions, we can only observe — never intervene. The perspective therefore insists on a "correlational" approach, in its broadest sense, since we can only relate naturally occurring variations in "treatments" to outcome measures over whatever time span we study. Furthermore, and typically, the "independent variables" studied by longitudinalists are "artificially tied," in Egon Brunswik's (1956) sense of the term; that is, they necessarily covary in the natural world. How parents treat their adolescent children is related to their individual personalities; the nature of their marriage; the values and expectations of their community; and (more generally) their social class, the number (and age and sex) of their other children, and so on. It would indeed be nice if we could set up a factorial design that would assign adolescents randomly and in equal numbers to each of the cells generated by such a design. Failing in this, as we must, we can only hold out the hope that the untampered-with world will approximate this condition for us but, without fail, it does not. These "independent variables" are simply not independent.

This rebuttal implies criticism. Is such an apologia necessary? Those who have worked and published from the longitudinal perspective frequently encounter critiques that suggest it is. It has always been thus since longitudinal investigations have never been quite within the mainstream of psychological research generally, nor even that of developmental psychology. But it seems to us that the tendency to fault longitudinal research for not measuring up to "experimental" standards has grown (and understandably so) as developmental studies have increasingly moved toward the experimental pole in the postwar years. The "new breed" mentioned earlier both reflects and furthers this trend and, we believe, graduate training today almost always neglects adequate exposure to the longitudinal perspective. In short, the socialization experiences of the developmental investigator contribute generally to a scientific environment that is less than optimally nourishing of longitudinal research. The fact that the longitudinal perspective appears now to be entering a renaissance — particularly in the study of adolescence — may promise some drop in the proportion of the longitudinalist's work load devoted to rebuttal, but it is too early to tell.

All this is not an appeal for a general pardon for all methodological sins of the longitudinal perspective — past, present, and future. There is, of course, some sloppy research within this perspective beyond the sloppiness born of the intrinsic limitations of the approach. But even the best of this kind of research is blemished by such limitations, and it is these limitations that we shall now outline. The problems with which this approach is beset are by no means peculiar to its use in studies of adolescent phenomena, except that the problems are somewhat ameliorated in short-term studies which are restricted to the adolescent period itself. An understanding of the longitudinal perspective requires that it be considered in its most general form.

Some Real and Some Imagined Problems for the Longitudinal Perspective

Longitudinal-research studies in general, and in particular those that are long-term ones, have since their inception been faulted for what is by now a "standard" inventory of shortcomings. Some of these, we believe, are illusory. Rather than being "problems," they are in fact advantages. Some are intrinsic to the longitudinal perspective, but they are well worth the price since no other adequate choices exist. For some of these flaws remedies exist, and they have begun to be put into practice. Whether or not the reader accepts our evaluation of these problems, at the very least our discussion should provide an informative inventory of what has been said (and is still being said) of the limitations of the longitudinal perspective. These limitations, be they real or imagined, have been obvious from the start; they have been so long with us that they are by now almost classic in stature. For this reason, we shall be drawing on literature that, considering the relatively short history (and rapid growth) of developmental psychology, will seem to be "old." But this is appropriate because the early debates were perhaps the most articulate ones; their current forms are necessarily derivative and often seem to us to be less focused and less eloquent. Now to the limitations.

Is Longitudinal Research Atheoretical?

Yes, it generally has been and (though to a somewhat lesser extent) it still is, especially in the longer-term longitudinal investigations. But is this a limitation, a problem? A pioneer of one such investigation (the Berkeley Growth Study) provides a spirited denial that it is:

> The horrible example of the longitudinal study described by its critics is one in which the investigators rushed into a long-term project with no research design: they just started measuring everything they could think of in the hope of finding some significant relations. This I consider to be an irresponsible criticism, usually made by young persons who forget that many of the hypotheses to be tested thirty or forty years ago have long since been proved (or disproved) and are now in the textbooks as common knowledge. Also, these earlier hypotheses were not formulated in the words of the current ritual, which gives at least a semblance of scientific exactitude. What the earlier investigators did was to ask questions that were relevant for testing accepted beliefs, partially verified theories, or even sometimes mere hunches. There is nothing the matter with this procedure in its proper place. When a field of investigation is new, it is necessary to be more exploratory, to make a crude map of the territory in order to get one's bearings, before an exact and detailed map is possible (Bayley, 1965, p. 186).

Is criticism "irresponsible" when it states that longitudinal investigations, at least the earlier ones, were deficient in design because they typically did not specify clearly stated hypotheses?

Bayley goes on to cite several instances where the "let's-just-look-and-see" approach paid off handsomely; a vivid example comes from her own work that laid to rest the then-current notion that IQ remained essentially constant during the first few years of life. This finding, since and often convincingly replicated, is by now "common knowledge." It is easily forgotten today (by persons of any age) that the converse was an accepted truth, and one with serious societal implications. For example, placement of infants for adoption was in part determined by their tested IQ's and, what we now know was an even worse effect, their institutionalization was occasionally prolonged in order to permit a "valid" assessment of their intelligence before they were made available for adoption.

Harold Jones, founder of the Adolescent Growth Study, observed in 1958 that such "accidental [findings can be] very annoying to the investigator who deals only with short-term situational research, and who believes that all scientific inquiry should be theoretically pinpointed — if they are to be respectable, research findings should be deduced from theory and predicted in advance" (p. 95). One instance of such a finding (Ames, 1957) and, again, one which has stood the test of replication — is that leadership qualities and occupational success in adulthood can be better predicted by rate of skeletal maturing in adolescence than by such apparently and "theoretically" more promising predictors, such as adolescent peer-group leadership itself. Harold Jones observes that since "we do not know enough about development to make all of the relevant predictions, the research worker in this [longitudinal] field must be willing to explore frontiers and tolerate unforeseen outcomes," a challenge (or a hazard) inevitably arising from the "many-faceted nature of growth studies, which are too complex to fit into any of the major systems of theory" (p. 96). Perhaps today's developmental researcher will wish to demur from this indictment of "not knowing enough" and of the inadequacy of "major systems of theory"; after all, more than 20 years have gone by since it was filed. This is not the place to debate the issue of the greater power of current knowledge and theory in developmental psychology, but we will permit Harold Jones to record his wry (and likely still true) assessment of theoretical currency:

It is clear that longitudinal research requires a certain doggedness which cannot quickly reflect popular turns of interest. It encounters the status-hazard of being sometimes in vogue and sometimes out of step. It may be both too far ahead and too far behind the contemporary preoccupations. If we recognize this as one of our calculated risks, it need not disturb us nor deflect us from what we have set out to do. Moreover, it has often been noted that when an area in psychology achieves high prestige it is already beginning to decay, and the longitudinal investigator who resolutely stays with his design need have no difficulty outlasting any given turn of fashion among his more denominational colleagues. [1958, p. 96]

All this is not to deny that longitudinal investigations, even long-term ones, that are rigorously focused on testing particular hypotheses derived from particular theories are possible — or, less stringently, that the design of a study and the battery of measurements periodically applied can be largely shaped and guided by specific theoretical consid- erations. This, of course, has been done. One recent example is the large-scale study by Jessor and Jessor (1977). They carried out an investigation of psychological development during adolescence focusing exclusively on testing their "problem-behavior" theory of development. There are others of this genre (discussed later), but they tend to be short-term studies, a state of affairs that we suspect is not a chance outcome. Even though short-term longitudinal research requires a considerable investment, it is nevertheless a relatively limited one which, in turn, justifies (in our opinion) what we consider the restrictiveness of a theory-guided investigation in these instances.

To suggest that theoretically based longitudinal research requires justification may appear to be a curious, even cavalier, point of view. But it is not a disdain of theory that underlies such an attitude. Rather, it follows from our belief that to plan and conduct a long-term longitudinal study wholly within the strict confines of a particular conceptual orientation borders on the impossible rather than the irresponsible. Such studies can and have been planned, but only the most blindly doctrinaire researches could continue to conduct their work in an iron-clad framework undaunted and untouched by the new hunches they inevitably pick up from their data over the years. Furthermore, while the study is going on, theoretical innovations, elaborations, and alternatives are being proposed. For just these reasons, we would argue that even the most theoretically committed investigators (if they be wise) will intentionally build into their research design and data-collection inventory as wide a range of observations and measurements as their patience (and budget) permit. Why? Because in no other way will their accumulation of data come to serve the critical archival function of a longitudinal study, especially a long-term one. That function is to permit a testing, at some time in the future, of new hypotheses that derive from theory and data that arise within developmental psychology and allied disciplines during the course of the research. Indeed, after-the-fact longitudinal research within a precise theoretical framework has been carried out, both from a psychoanalytic orientation (Peskin & Livson, 1972; Peskin, 1972) and from a Piagetian psychodynamic perspective (Haan, 1977).

Such testing of new hypotheses data, of course, is for the most part a product of nonlongitudinal approaches — cross-sectional studies, experimental investigations, and clinical observations — a fact of life that is as understandable as it is fortunate. A major forte of longitudinal study is its rather special hypothesis-generating power. But, since longitudinal studies can and should lay claim to only a relatively minor portion of developmental research resources, it is understandable and fortunate that other kinds of efforts carry the primary burden for providing the necessary nutrients for continual growth in understanding within this area of human concern. Nevertheless, relatively few as they are, each comprehensive longitudinal investigation represents a major scientific undertaking that requires major societal support. For this very reason we believe it essential that such investigations forego the luxury of a precise conceptual focus and, instead, choose the eclectic path that we believe is more likely to maximize the archival utility of their data.

One addendum to this argument may help to support it: a by-product of a comprehensive and wide-ranging assessment strategy in longitudinal studies is that frequently (if not perhaps typically) unexpected and useful findings insinuate themselves into research reports *only* because "irrelevant" data just happen to be available. Such reports start by asking questions in the traditional mode of "What is the relationship of X to Y?" But the ready availability of additional data on the same persons tempts the investigator to consider the possible mediating influences of variables, which seem, at least initially, of little or no relevance to the main question. Yielding to this temptation, once a laborious and costly diversion, has increasingly become almost standard practice as computerized multivariate data analysis becomes easier, cheaper, and faster. Thus the main question may concern the relationship between styles of parental discipline and adolescent rebelliousness. But (however unpromising it seems), why not check out whether the adolescent's IQ or physical maturation rate strengthens (though it may complicate) the main predictive relationship?

This example is hypothetical, but there are real ones; one of these will illustrate the point. It is an early one that, in fact, exactly followed this "little-resistance-to-temptation'' paradigm and was entitled, ''An Exploration of Patterns of Impulse Control in Early Adolescence'' (Livson & Bronson, 1961). The main question in this instance was ''to explore the linkages of the ways in which early adolescent boys and girls handle their impulses with other aspects of their behavior and personality organization. . . .'' (p. 75). The basic data for this study were comprehensive clinical assessments of these children (participants in the longitudinal Guidance Study) prepared by Erik Erikson and later made available for quantitative analysis by being ''translated'' through a specially tailored Q-sorting procedure. One of the findings was that of substantial sex differences in the correlates of different patterns of impulse control, but the answers to the main question are off the point here. What does serve to make our point was an unexpected finding arising directly from a ''why-not-look-and-see'' expedition into easily accessible ''irrelevant'' data — in this case, thorough and multifaceted assessments of physical maturation rate during adolescence.

It was discovered that *both* girls whose growth spurt (year of maximum height increase) is relatively early and those whose menarche occurs relatively late tend toward extreme overcontrol of impulses during this early adolescent period. This led to testing the relationship of the *interval* between these two maturation-rate indices to impulse overcontrol. Despite the substantial positive association of these measures ($r = .71$), there remained sufficient unshared variance to permit the surprising finding that the length of the interval was indeed related to overcontrol so that, ''a relatively tall and sexually immature girl [tends] toward greater inflexibility in handling her impulses during early adolescence than one who is small and relatively mature'' (Livson & Bronson, 1961, p. 87).

This happening upon a link between an asynchrony in adolescent physical development and impulse control could have only been a serendipitous event; it is certainly not a relationship that could have been hypothesized from any then (or now) available theory. Its detection is a uniquely longitudinal phenomenon, if only a peripheral spinoff from the major thrust of this methodological perspective. Its intrinsic importance is not at issue here, but its hypothesis-generating nature should be readily apparent. It shows that the largely atheoretical, militantly eclectic, and seemingly rambling nature of much research design and data-collection within the longitudinal perspective is part of its promise and is essential to its payoff — and is not one of its flaws.

Is Longitudinal Research Inefficient?

Does it cost too much money? Does it take too sustained an effort from the investigator? Does it take too much time to get results? All serious questions. However, these can be easily answered if one accepts what we have asserted earlier: that certain developmental questions can only be addressed from the longitudinal perspective and, perhaps more critically, that these questions need to be asked if our study of the process of human development is to aspire to sufficiency. Seen in this light, the issue of ''too much'' money, effort, and time becomes no longer moot; no matter the price, it must be paid if we cannot afford to be without the product. We have already given the particulars of what we consider to be the unique and indispensable contributions that flow from the longitudinal perspective. The merit of our argument is, at the moment, an individual value judgment, although we believe that, ultimately, its validity will depend on (and be confirmed by) the eventual full story that will emerge from the continuing psychological study of development. But the ''cost'' issues deserve some discussion.

That the "costs" remain issues currently is attested by Wohlwill's (1973) observation that "neither psychologically nor socioculturally is the research enterprise fitted to support and encourage research extending far into the future. The problems to be faced range from the primary one of financial support, to the impermanence of staff and facilities, to the slow rate of return from investment to time, effort, and money" (p. 145). We have commented on some of these problems, but something more can usefully be said.

First, the research staff of long-term longitudinal studies should themselves be a special breed if the investigations are to achieve their goals. "Rapport" is something that any researcher acknowledges to be necessary if valid data are to be obtained. Even for the one-session experimental investigation, it is now recognized that the "subject" must be a willing and (so far as is possible) an informed participant. The reasons for this are both scientific and ethical, and it is fortunate indeed that these two desiderata are not only compatible, but even synergistic. This truth is writ large on the life-size screen of a long-term longitudinal study, and it has always been an article of faith for any longitudinal researcher, to be ignored at the peril of failure. To maintain the active cooperation of the study participants and their families (and of the community itself) does require of the research staff a quality of rapport far more sensitive and enduring than is necessary for the developmental researcher generally. Those who find the effort "too much" may turn to other arenas, and some do. But, on the whole, the turnover of longitudinal staff, when considered against the base line of the duration of such studies, is surprisingly low. The surprise is heightened when one considers that funding uncertainties translate into job insecurity and that major publications generally must await coming to the end of the time span being investigated. What is sometimes overlooked, however, is that longitudinal studies typically produce numerous research reports — both cross-sectional and short-term longitudinal — while accumulating data for their primary research goals. Furthermore (and this is a necessary chore for longitudinal staffs) such sheer "housekeeping" functions as insuring precise scheduling of recurrent data-collection and continuously maintaining extensive, and easily accessible, cumulative-data archives are critical, though hardly immediately satisfying, aspects of their work loads.

What should be clear is that the business of long-term longitudinal research is not for those who are uncomfortable with delay of gratification. In any case, when the history of developmental psychology is written, it will then be clear whether the longitudinal perspective has been "inefficient" or, instead, necessarily demanding of time and effort toward a worthwhile goal.

Is Longitudinal Research Wasteful of Data?

There are at least three aspects to this question:

1. Many data are in fact gathered in longitudinal studies for which a clear purpose does not initially exist, in the sense of their not being specifically focused on a precise research question. This may appear wasteful. But, as we noted earlier, seemingly "irrelevant" data often come to have substantial value. Some perhaps will never be put to good use, but such an outcome is the price to be paid for adhering to a "get-it-while-you-can" data-gathering strategy. Longitudinal researchers are cast into the role of gatekeeper, and those who pretend to prescience are likely to deny — irretrievably — essential data to future researchers. Data which have not yet been put to good use, may still be — or may never be. This

may seem wasteful, but so also would be a failure to have made observations (often at trivial increments of cost) that later come to be needed.

2. The nature of the data gathered at any given point along the span of a longitudinal study necessarily reflects the then-current state of the art. The questions asked, the observations made, the tests administered, the characteristics quantified — all these are in a sense inevitably dated. This opens up the possibility that newer conceptions and instruments will require a discarding of earlier data. But experience has demonstrated that longitudinal data, *if sufficiently detailed and comprehensive,* are akin to Lazarus. "Dead" data are easily resurrected by translation of old texts into new forms. Examples of this abound. Scores on newly developed scales for already administered personality inventories require only recourse to the original-item responses; new skeletal age standards can be applied to stored bone X-ray records; mental tests can be rescored according to revised norms and new scores computed for newly derived, factor-based intellective subtest dimensions. Recovery of data is commonplace in longitudinal studies; perhaps the most frequent instances involve application of new rating scales and Q sorts to raw transcripts of interview and observational data (e.g., Block with Haan, 1971; Schaefer & Bayley, 1963). Little is wasted and much is usefully transformed to modern parlance.

3. This last facet of the "wasteful-of-data" question is a curious one. Longitudinal study samples are indeed typically small, as they must be, if the already high costs of such research are to remain within the bounds of possibility. It is this fact of relatively small sample size that has led to the charge that gathering so enormous a pool of information on so few cases is a wasteful procedure. Quite the contrary is the case. Repeated measures on the same individuals provide substantially more statistical power for the detection of time-related changes than is possible from cross-sectional data involving the identical total number of observations. To the extent that the repeated measures are correlated over occasions, the error term against which age differences are evaluated becomes smaller. When the differences are small ones, repeated measurements are likely to offer greater sensitivity to such subtle developmental changes. The case for the greater statistical power of longitudinal over cross-sectional data has long been recognized. In *A Handbook of Methods for the Study of Adolescent Children,* Greulich et al. (1938) made the point dramatically long ago. In the context of discussing physical growth measurements from the Harvard Growth Study, they were able to demonstrate that measurements repeated annually for ten years on only 100 cases will serve as well (for establishing growth trends) as cross-sectional measurements on 60,600 cases. For less reliable data, such as from personality assessments, the advantage is somewhat reduced, but remains nonetheless quite substantial.

"Wasteful of data?" No!

Are There Sampling Problems in Longitudinal Research?

Aside from the sample-size issue we have just touched on, there are two related potential problems associated with typical longitudinal samples: (1) initial sampling bias and (2) sample attrition. Of course, no study, whether longitudinal or cross-sectional, even approaches the ideal of sampling randomly from the population to which the results are to be generalized. National-opinion surveys perhaps come closest to this goal, but they can do so only because their brief one-shot procedures are more transportable and acceptable. Any developmental study almost inevitably draws its voluntary participants from within its local community, which necessarily restricts the possible range of sample characteristics and imposes certain (and often unknown) selective factors. Range restriction implies a likely attenuation of relationships, but seems not in itself a serious problem; selection, however, is potentially biasing, whether it be on sociocultural, intellective or even genetic parameters. But is the problem worse for longitudinal samples? Probably not, since they have typically extended themselves more than cross-sectional studies in seeking at least representativeness for their geographic locality. (Berkeley's Guidance Study, for example, began with a serially drawn subsample of every third child born in that community over an 18-month period in 1928–1929.) Furthermore, lack of representativeness seems more likely to be reflected in biased estimates of *levels* of the measured variables than in *relationships* over time, which are the very essence of the longitudinal-research product. Be that as it may, we do not yet know (and may never know) the truly relevant criteria for evaluating the representativeness for a given sample *generally*.

In the final analysis all that can be done is to define, in as precise terms as possible, the nature of the procedures of sample selection; longitudinal studies have been particularly careful in this respect. As researchers attempt to verify one another's findings, the magnitude of the problem will come into clearer focus; thus far, the results have been heartening. Much the same prescription can be made for handling the inevitable attrition of longitudinal samples: describe the process as fully as possible and attempt to evaluate its impact. In one such attempt (Haan, 1962) it was found that participants in the Oakland Growth Study who were lost to the sample during their adolescent years did not differ significantly two decades later from those who were available for study — on their adolescent intelligence and personality, their family socioeconomic status and family size. But, apart from the issue of possible bias attributable to attrition, sample shrinkage has the potential of eroding seriously the power of the long-term longitudinal study. For this very reason such studies have placed enormous emphasis on maintaining the cooperativeness of their participants and a current knowledge of their whereabouts, as well as visiting them far afield when follow-up data are to be collected, if that becomes necessary.

In short, sample restriction and sample attrition are both problems for longitudinal studies; some things can and have been done to define and circumscribe their effects. The result is that the longitudinal perspective does not have the full power it might have, given an "ideal" world in which sample representativeness and maintenance could be somehow guaranteed. Given the nature of the real world, it is as powerful as it can be — and adequately so, given that it has no true competitors for answering its special questions. But is this a "given"?

Are There Shortcuts to Longitudinal Data?

It is tempting to answer this question tersely, and then go on to other matters. No, there are no shortcuts that are adequate, if by adequacy we mean an ability of such other methodologies to provide data that are appropriate substitutes for longitudinal data. There have been other methods proposed and used. We shall say a little about these. But, to put the conclusion before the critique, no other research technique can do such things as document *individual* developmental functions or determine predictive relationships over substantial periods of development.

The choice essentially falls into two types: (1) employing retrospective reports and (2) accelerating the acquisition of developmental data over long time spans by a combination of cross-sectional and short-term longitudinal methods. Each have their important limitations.

RETROSPECTIVE REPORTS

It would be fortunate indeed if retrospective reports of past developmental events could be trusted to provide sufficiently precise estimates of contemporaneously obtained data. But they cannot, even over very short intervals; Bartlett's (1932) classic experimental study, *Remembering,* should by itself provide sufficient evidence to discard retrospection as a method promising even passable validity. Since both "sharpening" and "leveling" (both highly distorting of initial stimuli) pervade even very short-term recall of affectively neutral material, how can we expect persons to be able to report accurately long-ago, personal data viewed through a screen of years of eventful living?

However, we need not rely on such indirect evidence when we have available a number of systematic investigations of the validity of retrospective reports of developmental data. This is not the place to present their findings in detail. Several comprehensive evaluative summaries can be found elsewhere, among these are Wenar and Coulter (1962), Mednick and Shaffer (1963), and Yarrow, Campbell, and Burton (1970). Although the predominant focus of such research has been on the recall of childhood developmental data (typically by mothers), the data reviewed extend into other age ranges and deal with other types of developmental information. Although the validity of retrospection varies with age of the event and of its recall, with personal characteristics of the respondent, and with the nature of the data solicited, the verdict is a unanimous one: retrospective reports fall far short of their goal of portraying development with sufficient accuracy to substitute for contemporaneous, longitudinally gathered information. The discrepancy between the two methods is even large enough to allow for the detection of substantial systematic correlates of retrospective distortion, and it should not be surprising to learn that some of these are to be found in the personal characteristics of the reporter. For example, Brekstad (1966) found that mothers' anxiety levels significantly affected the reliability of their recall of events surrounding the births of their children, even after an interval of only six months.

With particular relevance to adolescence, Rosenthal (1963), in an investigation assessing the accuracy of adult (age 40) memories of adolescent relations with parents and of adolescent social and personality measures, found it necessary to partial out adult personality characteristics, which did relate to accuracy. Having done this, she did find some useful consistency for men, although their validity coefficients account for no more than a quarter of the variance. Recall is considerably less accurate for women, especially in their reports of their adolescent interactions with their parents. She further reports that in some cases, the women's memories were more likely related to the present (age 40) than the past, and in others they were associated with adolescent items other than the corresponding measures. This is a provocative finding since it suggests, most generally, that retrospection better serves a projective technique function and reflects selective rather than inaccurate recall: something may be going on in recall at age 40 that involves a possibly systematic "reconstruction" of the adolescent past by adults in line with, and in the service of, their present personal reality. We shall be saying much more about this when we discuss our notion of the "uses of the past" as presenting a radical new opening into the understanding of adolescence.

We cannot but agree with Wohlwill's (1970) conclusion, in evaluating retrospection as a developmental method, that as a substitute for the longitudinal approach for obtaining information on age changes in behavior the retrospective approach appears to be of very limited value. It does, however, promise considerable value, but for a purpose considerably removed from its hoped-for substitutive function. Certainly, studying the individuals' *perceptions*, at any given age, of their earlier years can be highly useful for the understanding of developmental phenomena, and we can easily agree with the observation by Abhammer and Baltes (1972) that for phenomenologically oriented developmental theory, research on perceived age changes is interesting in its own right. Accepting this assertion in no way weakens our conclusion that the retrospective method does not provide a shortcut to obtaining the equivalent of longitudinal data.

ACCELERATING THE ACQUISITION OF DEVELOPMENTAL DATA

What about the shortcut of approximating long-term developmental functions by a combination of cross-sectional and short-term longitudinal methods? The general strategy of this approach is to work with different samples over different age ranges, studying each one longitudinally over relatively short, partially overlapping time spans. An early example is Bell's (1953) "convergence" method, which can yield an estimate of long-term developmental functions by stringing together successive and overlapping longitudinal series. This approach, which obviously accelerates data collection, can provide us with *group-averaged* pictures of such functions, but apparently at the cost of assuming that the function in question is not susceptible to the influences of any secular trend. Bell believes his method can be made to yield *individual* developmental functions through a sophisticated procedure of matching different individuals across the combined longitudinal series, thus providing a sketch of the "same" person over a long-time span. The validity of such a matching procedure is of course the essential test of the usefulness of the convergence approach and, for psychological characteristics, it has yet to be evaluated. Its promise, therefore, remains a matter for speculation and for focused research.

The convergence approach is essentially one facet of a later comprehensive challenge to the traditional longitudinal perspective initiated by Schaie's (1965) proposal of three complementary methodologies for developmental research. It would require a chapter in itself to present, even in reasonable detail, the full complexities of Schaie's General Developmental Model; to trace its subsequent (and still ongoing) modifications and elaborations in the published literature; and to summarize the numerous empirical applications and tests that have flowed from it. Baltes, Cornelius, and Nesselroade (1977) have done essentially just this, and in a thorough and masterful manner. But for our purpose of presenting the longitudinal perspective as a general approach, there seems no need to expound on the substantial methodological intricacies that are involved. However, it may be useful to present a brief overview of this body of work, especially since it raises important issues regarding the possible limitations of the single-sample longitudinal design on which we have been focusing.

Schaie's (1965) basic purpose is to suggest designs that at least partially permit the unconfounding of three components that inevitably affect the study of any developmental function: the *age* of subjects at the time of measurement, the *cohort* (time of birth) from which they were drawn, and the actual (historical) *time of measurement* itself. Towards this end he distinguishes three major types of developmental methodologies:

1. The *cohort-sequential* method, which involves repeated assessments over time of two or more cohorts; the traditional single-sample longitudinal study can be seen

as a limited case within this method. The cohort-sequential strategy does permit independent evaluations of age differences (not confounded by cohort differences) and of cohort differences (unaffected by age differences), but necessarily the third factor, time of measurement, remains a confounding factor.

2. The *time-sequential* method, which involves assessing independent samples at different ages over two or more times of measurement. (Here, the standard cross-sectional design is the limited case.) By this method both age and time of measurement effects may be independently determined, but in this instance cohort differences remain as a potentially confounding factor.

3. The *cross-sequential* method, which involves assessing different cohorts at two or more times of measurement. This method is sensitive to "time-lag" phenomena, that is, to changes related to historical time itself. Here the variance attributable to cohort and time of measurement are separable, but age variance remains uncontrolled, and possibly confounding.

Baltes (1968) has argued that, since Schaie's (1965) three components are inescapably interdependent, a two-component formulation would do as well and have an obvious parsimonious advantage. His preference is for selecting age and cohort as the two components, based on his assumption that time of measurement is of lesser interest for typical developmental psychology research. In countering this argument, Schaie (1970) makes the point that, insofar as his three components can have independent conceptual status, they remain viable, despite their statistical interdependence. He goes on to propose a "most efficient" design that requires data at two or more age levels, for two or more cohorts, collected at two or more times of measurement — plus an additional cohort assessed at the same age as the youngest cohort at its first time of measurement. This design has the distinct advantage of providing unconfounded estimates of the variance due to age changes (in the longitudinal sense), to age differences (in the cross-sectional sense), and to historical (or "time-lag") changes. An in-progress application of this design is the Nijmegen Growth Study, in which the sample was 900 Dutch children — comprised of six overlapping cohorts, each to be studied over a five-year period — ranging in age from 4 to 14 years (Mönks et al., 1975).

What should concern us most here is the challenge to the traditional longitudinal-study design, in which only a single cohort is assessed and where each assessment-age corresponds to a particular point in historical time. The basic issue to be addressed, then, is the generality of the body of results we have from decades of research in the traditional, single-sample, long-term perspective. If we can agree with Baltes (1968) that time of measurement, per se, is a subordinate consideration, then the question asked is that posed in the following section.

Are Single-Sample Longitudinal Results Cohort-Specific?

Baltes, Cornelius, and Nesselroade (1977) observe that attention to cohort effects, whether empirical or theoretical, is a relatively recent phenomenon. They note that it has been "generally a common assumption among developmental psychologists that — within a given cultural entity such as the United States — information about behavioral development would be relatively robust and that ontogenetic patterns could be generalized to subsequent decades." We agree, and perhaps long-term longitudinal researchers have been wed to this assumption more than most. This would be easily understandable since it would seem that a belief in the enduring robustness of their findings would be for them an almost inescapable article of faith, justifying their decades of work investigating a single sample. In the absence of polling data, we cannot say whether or not this is so; what we do know is that longitudinal researchers have not altogether had their heads buried in the sands of denial. Consideration and concern regarding the cross-cohort generality of their findings is apparent throughout their publications. These frequently conclude on a note of caution with respect to the risks of overgeneralizing from their single-cohort results, and with a call for replication with data from other cohorts. This may seem like lip service (and to an extent it may have been) since there have been few, if any, sufficiently long-term longitudinal studies with sufficiently comparable data to permit frequent heeding of this call. Occasionally replication has been possible, as noted earlier, for the finding of the predictive uselessness of very early mental test scores. We expect more of this will be done as some of the long-term studies have recently begun efforts, perhaps long overdue, at pooling their data for cross-validation purposes. Thus far, however, little has been done along these lines so that such works as Elder (1979) and Elder and Rockwell (1978), which contrast the adolescent development of the Oakland Growth Study and Berkeley Guidance Study cohorts, represent a rare and highly productive effort. Their research (discussed in detail below) focuses on the occurrence of the Great Depression during the adolescence of one sample and during the childhood of the other sample, and does point to cohort effects.

These findings provide one hint as to one type of condition that should alert us to be on the watch for such an effect. Periods of extreme, if transient, societal stress — whether because of economic deprivation, wartime trauma, natural catastrophes, and the like — can well lead to some distortion of what might nevertheless be regarded as the ''normal'' course of a given developmental process. But to speak of a ''normal'' course is to betray a belief that single-cohort data may indeed provide reasonably valid depictions of developmental phenomena, unless one has been so unlucky as to have worked with an atypical cohort. However, there is in fact another type of condition that is suggestive of cohort differences, a condition that is far more gradual in its impact on development and by no means transient in its possible effects. Included here are such potentially development-relevant factors as progressive changes in a society's educational policies, its health delivery systems, its dietary resources and habits, and its cultural values. These factors can modify a population's characteristics in manners likely to be significant for ''normal'' courses of development and can range from altering its genetic pool to transforming its pervasive social climate.

Having identified some of the conditions that appear likely to impugn any claims of cross-cohort generality for single-cohort longitudinal results, we can hardly argue that such results are never (well, hardly ever) cohort-specific. We cannot, and we do not. Baltes, Cornelius, and Nesselroade (1977) definitively review the current literature on cohort effects in behavioral development and identify such effects for a number of developmental processes and within a number of developmental periods, ranging from infancy to adulthood. One of their own studies (Nesselroade & Baltes, 1974), entitled ''Adolescent Personality Development and Historical Change: 1970–1972,'' provides a singularly appropriate example of their general point. Birth cohorts 1955, 1956, 1957, and 1958 were studied for two years (1970–1972), involving the age range 12 to 17 years. In part, they report cohort effects over the two-year interval for independence (which increased) and for achievement and superego strength (which decreased). To illustrate: in 1970, 14-year-olds were highest on achievement of all age groups while, in 1972, adolescents of this age were lowest of all on this characteristic. They go on to speculate that the impact of the Vietnam war with its associated focus on aggressive behavior and youth activism might very well have represented the key elements of change towards less achievement, more independence, and less superego strength during the 1970–72 period. They admit that these cohort effects could not be attributed to a specific set of antecedent or concomitant factors with the data they had available. Nonetheless, their interpretation of these results show a sensitivity to the prevailing social climate and are certainly not unreasonable. More importantly, they are hypothesis-generating, although not specifically replicable by future investigations since that time in our history is now past.

It is just this sort of sensitivity to social climates that supplies, paradoxically, a powerful defense against the charge that single-sample longitudinal results are cohort-specific. Such results are, if taken literally and promulgated as providing once-and-for-all answers to developmental questions. They are not, if they are interpreted in such a fashion as explicitly to take into account the comparative social climates prevailing during the lifetimes of the cohort on which the results are based and the cohort to which one wishes to generalize them. Another research illustration should help: working with samples of women from the Oakland Growth Study and the Berkeley Guidance Study (born respectively in the early and late 1920s), Livson and Day (1977) found, in part, that "intellectual competence" (a highly reliable dimension deriving from a cluster analysis of Q-sort data) was a highly significant predictor of actual completed family size — this was true for independent personality assessments carried out in early and late adolescence separately, and for both cohorts. All four regressions were linear and *positive* in slope. This finding seemed distinctly counterintuitive; today's social climate certainly would not suggest that the more competent the girl during her adolescence, the larger the family she would go on to rear. This is not a result which could stake an undisputed claim to eternal verity, and this was not done. What was done was to use the result as a springboard for the generation of two competing hypotheses and to propose new analyses of data *from the same longitudinal samples* whose outcomes could at least suggest how competence and family size might be expected to relate in the future for a *contemporary* cohort of adolescent girls. We quote at length from this research report by Livson and Day since it attempts to supply a convincing response to the critical question posed in this section:

> One hypothesis is that . . . competence, so clearly present in adolescence, later finds expression in an indirect manner. Perhaps at some level of awareness . . . the intellectually motivated and competent adolescent girl recognized that the "real world" of her generation held little promise for direct satisfaction and use of these propensities. Instead, she may have redirected these energies into channels then more accessible and appropriate — specifically the successful rearing of large numbers of children. The drive to become an effective adult thereby may have been transformed — in the psychoanalytic sense, perhaps sublimated. What would follow from such a transformation would be a fundamental restructuring of personality organization in the course of adult development. . . . We might expect this kind of woman to limit her educational career; to marry a dominant man who has and manifests high competence; to do little in terms for a working career; and, perhaps, even to show a reduction in IQ level. We would also expect her to be involved deeply with her family, particularly with her children; and this involvement, in turn, might permit active and competent participation in *family-related* community activities. . . .

> An alternative hypothesis requires no redirection or distortion of early competence. . . . In this view, the intellectually competent woman will rear a large family as one of many direct manifestations of a generalized competence/effectance drive. Furthermore, she might continue to pursue her intellectual interests through continuing formal or informal education and, so far as the responsibility of a large family permits, even to find some challenging employment. Again, because

she is generally an active and effective person, she would not only participate vigorously in community affairs but also possibly assume leadership roles in such activities. Her choice of a husband is difficult to anticipate, except that she is unlikely to choose a man to whom she would be a subservient shadow. Should this "generalized competence" hypothesis prove the more accurate one, our guess is that such women will have satisfying marriages and enjoy good health, both psychologically and physically.

In evaluating alternative hypotheses and extending the results to the contemporary scene, we must not lose sight of the profound cultural changes of the past few decades. If our hypotheses and results were to be interpreted in a direct cause-and-effect fashion, the further investigation proposed here would be of little value. Our subjects were born during the decade 1920–1930 and produced most of their offspring in the 1940s and 1950s. Most of these children were conceived before the alarm regarding overpopulation became widespread, and before the large-scale availability of such effective means of contraception as "the pill" and intrauterine devices. And these children came into existence before the currently ongoing evolution of new definitions of appropriate sex roles, which has generated pervasive social changes in most postindustrial societies. . . .

With these considerations in mind it should be clear that our results remain useful for the understanding and prediction of family size outcomes only if they are interpreted not as direct if-then relationships, but as providing an understanding of the intrapsychic and interpersonal characteristics that mediate one's child-bearing response to a social context prevailing *during the period in which fertility decisions were made*. With an appropriate appreciation of the nature of such contextual determinants affecting decisions about family size, we may become able to predict how these person-centered characteristics will be expressed in other, and perhaps future, cultural settings.

What of the intellectually competent adolescent girl of the 1970s? Here the implications of our alternative hypotheses lead to critically different conclusions. If the "redirection" hypothesis proves most supportable, then we would not expect a highly competent contemporary adolescent girl to rear a large family. The "real world" has indeed opened up to her (e.g., employment and higher educational opportunities) and will contine to do so. What need, then, does she have to channel her energies and drive to be effective into childrearing. . . ? Perhaps the opposite direction will be taken and motherhood (and even marriage) will become a far less attractive developmental route. If this be the case, then early adolescent competence today would predict small families tomorrow.

What is the prediction from the "generalized competence" hypotheses? Quite the opposite, we believe. Or, rather, we would expect high competence in an adolescent girl to continue to lead her to have a large family. If the challenge of rearing many children is what attracts her to such a course, then the challenge today should be no less, and the expected adult outcome therefore the same.

Clearly, if we heed our cautions, we can petition for absolution from the chronic sin of long-term longitudinal research — that it tells something only about the lifetime development of an ancient cohort. We believe that our work with these data in further research, which will remain alert to cultural change, will contribute an enduring increment to the understanding and prediction of family size in population reserach. [Livson & Day, 1977, pp. 320–323]

This "future research" is underway and, at a very early stage, the "generalized competence" hypothesis seems to have the edge. Also planned is a study of the daughters of these same subjects — of their contemporaneously assessed adolescent competence and their desired family size. Whatever the outcome of this work, perhaps its rationale has provided some insight into the potential of single-cohort longitudinal data, and some optimism that, properly interpreted, they are something more than cohort-specific.

ADOLESCENCE IN CHILD-CENTERED LONGITUDINAL STUDY

Just as the preacher who complained that the most able of his flock were the least willing, the longitudinal study of adolescence has, until recently, been beset by the paradox that the best data are often the least forthcoming. Finding adolescence within archives of longitudinal data requires something like the Freudian ardor of reconstructing childhood, namely, breaking through the husk of time and already-lived experience, albeit with uncovering techniques that are statistical rather than verbal. Once the nature of the reconstructive task is realized, perhaps the least noticed of all the unique advantages of the birth-to-maturity longitudinal method then becomes apparent: to enable the study of stage transitions, in general, and transition to and from adolescence, in particular. Adolescence embedded within, but not confounded by, the context of earlier stages is the special province of birth-to-maturity research. How adolescence elaborates, widens, and otherwise collaborates with prior development in creating modes of adult adaptation cannot, as far as we know, be retrieved by other than the longitudinal approach of research design and certainly not by therapeutic recall. The scarcity of birth-to-maturity studies that encompass adolescence corresponds, then, to the scarcity of theoretical concepts — even in stage theories of personality development — that pertain to how phases transform each other and work jointly together.

The major thrust of the birth-to-maturity longitudinal studies in America has not, however, been toward studying the differences and transformations of behavior between stages, but toward long-term stabilities of behavior. In this tradition, "unstable" behaviors, lacking obvious (phenotypic) identity over time, have been treated somewhat like discarded chaff in a harvest seeking only behavioral permanence. Yet these discards may contain the very clues for establishing stage *boundaries* if one had the conceptual mind-set for drawing them. Given the slow emergence of adolescence in longitudinal study, this mind-set may amount to assuming for a time, at least at the starting line, the critical and prodding stance of an advocate of stage-specific and stage-transitional study, that is, how developmental phases make their separate contribution and obey differential processes. For so much has a "psychology of the permanent" dominated research in the birth-to-maturity studies, such as the Fels Study (Kagan & Moss, 1962), and the Berkeley Growth (Schaefer & Bayley, 1963), and Guidance Study, that alternative approaches to recognizing and understanding the adolescent era have seemed less probable and less parsimonious, rather than being merely less established. The concern with behavioral permanence from childhood on has meant that developmental characteristics are chosen for study that can be assessed from earlier childhood onward rather than newly added in adolescence. This Procrustean insistence on uniform methods and inventories of data collection has as its consequence the relative disregard of new procedures and measurements that might have allowed for the emergent phenomena of adolescence. Hence, permanence, or phenotypic continuity (which we discuss later) tends to favor child-centered and neglects adolescent-centered dimensions, such as pubertal-induced behavioral change, identity formation, parent–offspring separation processes, group process of youth culture, career choice, and other phenomena recognized as peaking in, or peculiar to, adolescence. Obviously neglected, then, are the childhood precursors or adult outcomes of such adolescent processes. The report by Moriarty and Toussieng (1975) — on the childhood antecedents of adolescent coping styles of *censors* and *sensers* in the birth cohort of the Coping Studies of Murphy and Moriarty (1976) — is one of few exceptions in birth-to-maturity studies. Study of the adolescent processes has, of course, been much better served within adolescent and adolescent-to-maturity designs. Table 1 organizes these studies under a series of headings that identify the several foci of such research. These studies (as well as those with birth-to-maturity designs) vary, however, in their intended or unintended contribution to establishing adolescence as a distinct developmental era. Hence, only those studies most pertinent to our own intent to

Table 1   Adolescent-to-Adolescent and Adolescent-to-Maturity Longitudinal Studies

Pubertal-induced behavior.   Ames, 1957; Boutourline Young, 1973; Clausen, 1975; H. E. Jones, 1946, 1949; M. C. Jones, 1957, 1958, 1965; M. C. Jones & Bayley, 1950; More, 1953; Mussen & Boutourline Young, 1964; Mussen & M. C. Jones, 1957, 1958; Schmidt, 1965; Simmons, et al., 1977; Steinberg, 1978.

Consistency and change.   Bachman, O'Malley, & Johnston, 1978; Block with Haan, 1971; Frenkel-Brunswik, 1942; Haan & Day, 1974; Hertz & Baker, 1941; F. Livson, in press; Nawas, 1971; Nesselroade & Baltes, 1974; Offer, 1969; Offer & Offer, 1975; Peck & Havighurst, 1960; Skolnick, 1966a, 1966b; Tuddenham, 1959.

Prediction of adaptation, psychopathology, and social deviance.   Anthony, 1978; Bower & Shellhamer, 1960; Goldstein, et al., 1976; Haan, 1974; Hafner, Quast, & Shea, 1975; Jessor & Jessor, 1977; F. Jones, 1974; Kandel, 1975; Lief & Thompson, 1961; Masterson, 1958; Nameche, Waring, & Ricks, 1964; Robins, 1966; Stewart, 1962; Symonds & Jensen, 1961; Vlach, 1977; Watt, 1974; Watt & Lubensky, 1976.

Youth and school culture.   Blyth, Simmons, & Bush, 1978; Jessor & Jessor, 1977; Moore & Clautour, 1977; Savin-Williams, 1976; Tryon, 1939; Tuddenham, 1951.

Identity-formation, sex-role identification, and vocational planning.   Constantinople, 1969; Hauser, 1971; Jordaan & Super, 1974; Milner, 1949; Mussen, 1961; Trent & Medsker, 1967.

Later separation and autonomy.   Lowenthal, Thurnher, & Chiriboga, 1975; E. Murphey et al., 1963; Robinson, 1978; Tindall, 1978; Vaillant & McArthur, 1972.

Environmental and family stress.   Blyth, Simmons, & Bush, 1978; Elder, 1974; Haan, 1977; Peck & Havighurst, 1960; Wallerstein & Kelly, 1974.

Retrospection.   Elder, 1974; Rosenthal, 1963.

establish this viewpoint will be cited in this chapter. The comprehensive cataloging of Table 1 will be of use to those who intend to work within the longitudinal perspective for adolescent-oriented study.

Reconstructing Adolescence from Longitudinal Data

In both the theoretical and empirical underpinnings of birth-to-maturity longitudinal study, the adolescent years may have been unduly hidden or homogenized in the grist of consistencies over time, weakening their psychosocial and psychobiological claim to status as a separate phase. Notwithstanding its inclination to theoretical neutrality, such longitudinal research has importantly contributed to the tradition of early American developmental and European psychoanalytic psychologies of seeking for ingrained behavior tendencies and for early labeling of fixed cause-and-effect relationships. Indeed, the "science of the permanent" is Piaget's (1962) ironic critique of the early Freudian neglect of development and change.

From its empirical and atheoretical side, longitudinal research in the birth-to-maturity genre has fashioned an image of evenhandedness — choosing methods that give the appearance of equal appropriateness for all age periods — and strives to establish the persistence of psychological dimensions over the course of childhood, adolescence, and adulthood. But such treatment may have inordinately dulled rather than revealed the timing and processes of adolescence, while inadvertently sharpening those of childhood years. This is because, in the prospective gathering of data, the material from the early periods is the most reliable, whereas adolescence, disadvantaged by the crust of intervening time, needs statistical reconstruction to gain the same reliability. On first thought, this situation is exactly the reverse of retrospection, where the earliest years are dimmest and least reliably recalled. However, as an addendum to our earlier discussion of retrospective accuracy, there are an increasing number of clinical reports warning that recall of one's adolescence also undergoes distortion and is in need of careful reconstruction too (Spiegel, 1958; Deutsch, 1967; Feigelson, 1976). The clinician, in his child-centered therapies, gives short shrift to adolescence as being no more than a way station between childhood and adulthood whose processes are too fluid to allow for structured memories.

The handicap under which adolescence may labor in birth-to-maturity studies contradicts the obvious argument that its nearness to adulthood should inflate, rather than obscure, the importance of adolescence, that is, adolescent characteristics should be expected to show larger correlations than childhood ones with adult outcome. But when, in spite of this apparent advantage, an adolescent effect still fails to materialize, while a childhood effect does indeed emerge, the formulation is likely to implicate the random action of adolescent turmoil rather than the potential handicap of data-gathering procedures or statistical analysis. The term "sleeper effect" has been aptly coined by Kagan and Moss (1962) to describe just such outcomes in the Fels Study where a childhood behavior correlates more highly with adult outcome than the same behavior in adolescence. Such a pattern of findings is not unfamiliar in published tables of simple, zero-order correlations between childhood and adolescence, on the one hand, and adulthood, on the other. For example, Crandall and Battle (1970), on Fels data, report for males and females an abundance of significant predictors of adult "academic effort" (ages 18 to 26) from three periods of childhood, but virtually none from adolescence (ages 13 to 17); similarly Bronson (1967) and Livson and Peskin (1967) on Berkeley Guidance data report lower adult prediction (age 30) from ages 14 to 16 than from the prior period of ages 11 to 13.

A less child-centered psychology might discern that the "sleeper effect" can as well describe the masking of adolescence by childhood as the reverse. For the very prominence of a significant childhood predictor can be shown to hide the impact of adolescence under certain conditions: when the effect of a stable behavioral variable is hidden during adolescence because of its *opposite* effect in childhood. Where a stable behavior at two periods actually predicts to adulthood in opposite directions, the prediction of the later period will appear reduced or washed away since simple correlations from a later time period necessarily sum and confound effects of the early period. If, however, the significant earlier prediction has been removed, then the later one will be free to emerge with reversed sign. This removal can be easily accomplished with multivariate correlational techniques, such as partial correlation, which can establish the adolescent effect after significant childhood predictors have thereby been held constant.

By failing to take account of such masking artifacts, the importance of adolescent functioning for adult outcome may have been appreciably underestimated in certain sectors of personality development:

1. For the correlations in the Fels Study that prompted the sleeper-effect label, partialing out the significant childhood effect markedly increases the original low adolescent predictor: for example, as tabled in Kagan and Moss, the zero-order correlation of *hyperkinesis* (activity level) at ages 10 to 14 and adult *dependency on love object* for males is $+.02$; this prediction increases to $+.58$ after partialing out the correlation of *hyperkinesis* at ages 3 to 6 with adulthood ($r = -.61$). The correlation is .58 between *hyperkinesis* at ages 3 to 6 and 10 to 14. The

recalculated, highly significant finding should now read that *low* activity level in early childhood *and high* activity in pre- and early adolescence predict adult dependency. Rather than being permanently fixed in early childhood, our reanalysis reveals an instance of stage reversal, when a developmental line (here, dependency) is likely to draw on opposite behavioral dispositions in its passage from early childhood to adolescence.

2. Our own research in the Berkeley Guidance Study on the prediction of adult psychological health from behavior in four periods of development — early and late childhood, preadolescence and adolescence (Livson & Peskin, 1967) — reported significant prediction for males and females from preadolescence (ages 11 to 13), but not from the two childhood periods nor from the adolescent period (ages 14 to 16). Recalculation revealed, however, that significant adolescent effects emerged when the earlier reported (and *opposite*) effects from preadolescence were held constant (Peskin, 1972). Thus, for girls, the stage sequence of behavioral change that *maximized* adult psychological health was one that involved preadolescent *independence, self-confidence, controlled temper, and rare whining* turning to adolescent *dependence, low self-confidence, explosive temper, and frequent whining,* respectively. Boys showed stage reversals predictive of adult psychological health from preadolescent *stolidness and hearty appetite* to adolescent *irritability and poor appetite.* For boys, the effect of adolescence for adult health was, however, more often a cumulative one, adding to the preadolescent effect rather than reversing it. Thus, if the boy remained expressive, socially comfortable, and cheerful over preadolescence *and* adolescence, he would more likely enjoy a healthier adulthood at age 30. Although an increase in apparent stress on entry into adolescence is evident for the healthier members of our adult sample for both sexes, it is clearly more abrupt, disquieting, and pervasive for the girls. The turmoil of adolescence, first implied by lack of any statistical evidence prior to statistical partialling, appears now with more substance and more salutary effect. Since they suggest that preadolescent and adolescent turmoil have disparate meanings and adult outcomes, these findings accord with psychoanalytic formulations that turmoil in adolescence signifies the readiness of a stable preadolescent ego to allow for pubertal changes (A. Freud, 1958; Deutsch, 1967). From the side of method, the findings call for modification in longitudinal statistical analysis, to allow adolescent processes to shine through the masking effects of contiguous stages.

3. It follows that longitudinal studies lacking childhood or preadolescent data will be inconclusive on issues, such as psychosocial stresses, affected by cross-stage confounding. The best known of such longitudinal studies is the Offers' research on middle-class adolescent males followed from ages 14 to 22 (Offer & Offer, 1975). The participants were selected for their "modal" placement on psychological and academic dimensions in a school population. Over the eight years of followup, the authors concluded that turmoil is not the universal state of adolescence nor a healthy component of adolescent ego development. On the contrary, overall experienced stress was associated with overall difficulty in psychological adaptation during this developmental period. Three groupings of subjects, statistically identified by person-clustering technique, showed concomitant coping difficulties and emotional distress in their distinctive "developmental

routes'' over eight years of study in the order: *continuous growth group, surgent growth group,* and *tumultuous growth group.* The study nicely validates both the ''common sense'' intuition that the range of individual differences among adolescents is large indeed and the finding elsewhere (Block with Haan, 1971) that both males and females show increasing variance in their personalities between early adolescence and late adolescence.

So far as the issue of the specificity of adolescent turmoil is concerned, however, the Offers' study does not start until age 14, more than one year past the average age of initial secondary sex changes, so that preadolescent and pubertal sources of stress cannot be separated. Beyond this, the observer would be hard pressed to disentangle emotional adaptations newly constructed from old ones to which the subjects returned. Indeed, as the Offers state, it is likely that the individuals in each of the three groupings, and adolescents generally, maintain their prior levels of mental health. Thus tumultuous growth is more likely a continuous, persistent quality of personality rather than a transitory or a developmental (emergent) one. Other longitudinal studies of normal and clinic samples followed from middle or late adolescence that also report such long-term consistency (Bachman, O'Malley, & Johnston, 1978; Hafner, Quast, & Shea, 1975; Masterson, 1958; Robins, 1966; Vaillant & McArthur, 1972) have lacked the necessary prior data to establish turmoil as distinctive to adolescence rather than carried over from earlier personality functioning.

Not only the late onset age, but also the statistical method of classifying participants in the Offers' study, likely confounds developmental routes with permanent patterns of adjustment prior to the adolescent era, so that persistent and stage-specific sources of stress cannot be told apart.

The Offers call on a method of person-groupings (typal analysis) based on 10 factored dimensions of 55 ratings and scores selected from a larger pool over the eight years of study. Although the rationale for selecting from the pool is not given, its result makes it clear that the researchers wish to avoid duplication of ratings over time. Thus the developmental course of a particular dimension cannot be followed to evaluate for change or persistence. The selected measures are sometimes specifically tied to a single age and (sometimes) characteristic of the whole study period, so that permanence and development seem to be more arbitrarily than systematically sampled. Moreover, the heavy emphasis on ''good/bad'' mental-health content makes for groupings of personal integration, regardless of age or stage, rather than the intended identification of developmental routes. The inclusion in this set of general variables of environmental advantage and disadvantage, such as parental education, does help further to delineate person-groupings of degree of adolescent stress, but in the process obscures the construct of turmoil. It is indeed just these overall differentials in stressful living and general personality adjustment that need to be partialled out in order to discern the *processes* of adolescence that may be hidden beneath. It would be good to have, *within* person-groupings, the quality and direction of stress and behavioral change systematically described over time and over adolescent transitions, for example, from junior high to senior high school, from senior high school graduation to first job, leaving home for college, and so on. As skillful clinicians and theoreticians, the Offers attempt to do just this, but at the price of abandoning statistical analysis, just when it might finally prove its capacity to reconstruct adolescence and to contribute to a taxonomy of behavioral stress in adolescence. The Offers' conclusion that their findings dispute the psychoanalytic theory of adolescent upheaval implicitly supports the child-centered classical theory that adolescent response is predetermined long before — an ironic twist perhaps, in light of the Offers' clear willingness generally to dispute ironclad orthodox thinking of whatever theoretical bent.

Stage Transitions in Adolescence

Starting data-collection close to, or within, adolescence — as in the late-elementary-school grades in the Oakland Growth Study or at age 14 in the Offers' sample — does not, of course, necessarily preclude study of turmoil (or other constructs) as phenomena of adolescence. But such study, having forfeited direct observation of the transition *to* adolescence, is necessarily narrowed to behavioral or attitudinal changes within appropriate subphases, passages, or transitions. Minimally, such study requires more than coincidental or arbitrary choice of an adolescent age for classifying antecedents or outcomes. Therefore, not any longitudinal study involving adolescence will do; the before/after designs that relate global or one-time adolescent status to an adult outcome are most probably measuring permanence over time and cannot establish an effect as phase-specifically adolescent. Longitudinal studies of psychopathology are typically focused on such one-time prediction or postdiction (Symonds, 1961; Robins, 1966; Hafner, Quast, & Shea, 1975; Masterson, 1958; Lief & Thompson, 1961; see Werner & Smith, 1977, for a review of follow-up studies of behavioral disorders to and from adolescence).

The problem of overtime permanence refers, of course, not only to the carryover of childhood behavior into adolescence but to adolescent behavior carried into adulthood. Distinguishing between effects that belong to late adolescence and to the sheer persistence or continuity of behavior is made more difficult where, as in several major longitudinal studies, there exists a long hiatus in data collection between late adolescence and adulthood. Without observation across the adult threshold, the effects belonging to adolescence cannot be recovered by the convenient partialling of contiguous adult years.

Several studies in the prediction or prognosis of psychopathology are noteworthy for displaying more than the marginal interest in adolescence usual in this area of longitudinal research. In their several ways, they have sought to recover adolescence either by assessing its differential effectiveness against the power of adjacent eras or by searching for within-stage transitions through charting change over the adolescent duration.

Werner and Smith (1977) followed a stable multiethnic cohort of more than 600 youth born on the island of Kauai, Hawaii, at birth, and at ages 2, 10, and 18. The late-adolescent followup in 1972–74 was to assess the long-term consequences of learning and behavior disorders identified in early and middle childhood and to discover new problems that arose in adolescence. For the latter, low socioeconomic status and low educational stimulation are reported to be the infrequent early predictors from among a large battery of physical, aptitude, educational achievement, behavioral, and home assessments at birth, age 2, and age 10. Conversely, high socioeconomic status was associated with spontaneous improvement in adolescence among those at age 10 who had been considered in need of short-term mental health services. Corresponding differences in adolescent locus-of-control were found: a low sense of personal efficacy for the new problem youth in adolescence, and a high sense of personal control, hard work, and persistence among those who improved since childhood. Although the stage-specific role of socioeconomic status for adaptation is not established in this report, the weave of such statistical findings suggests that middle-class modeling may selectively shape an ethic of industry and work (or lack thereof) in the vocational rehearsals of adolescence which lends itself to believing in the efficacy of one's own actions.

The "follow-back" longitudinal study by Watt (1974) is another exception. Here, the school records of diagnosed adult schizophrenics were retrieved over several years, from elementary school through high school, in order to find the optimum time to begin screening for behavioral signs of risk. Another important departure from the before/after design in the study of psychopathology is a study by Stewart (1962) that reports the course of interpersonal adjustment during adolescence for members of the Oakland Growth Study who will develop psychosomatic symptoms as adults. Compared to symptom-free and behavior-maladjusted adults, psychosomatic men and women showed the largest rise on scales of interpersonal adjustment between the ages of 11 to 12 and 17. Stewart interprets this change as a growing preoccupation by psychosomatic-prone individuals with sustaining good relationships to offset the feared loss of affection brought on by an underlying sense of unworthiness. Stewart's focus on the adolescent period for emerging mechanisms of coping and defense of lasting import for adult adjustment brings us again to a core conceptual issue of the meaning of adolescent change that will guide the next sections of our chapter: change as transient turmoil or as nutriment for new constructions of basic personality dispositions.

A common search for developmental *discontinuities* can be discerned in just such studies, in which adolescence is made prominent in the nexus of the formative years. Where research findings indicate certain changing patterns of over-time predictions that cannot be attributed to behavioral consistency, adolescence is well-served. Findings of (1) new adolescent predictors of adulthood unreported for earlier stages, (2) adolescent predictors that reverse the direction of earlier or later predictors, or (3) declining predictions *after* adolescence (sleeper effect) — all attest to the specificity of adolescent effects and will be given higher priority in this chapter's review. Where longitudinal data are sufficiently reliable for subphase analysis (such as early vs. late adolescence, pubertal vs. postpubertal, junior high school vs. senior high school), the opportunity to discern changing predictive patterns across subphases increases. With the thrice-repeated Q-sort procedure in the Oakland Growth Study and Berkeley Guidance Study for junior high school, senior high school, and mid-adulthood, Block with Haan (1971) generate several research strategies for discovering the properties of adolescent subphases, such as changes between junior high school and senior high school (1) for the full sample, and (2) for subgroups of respondents who (via inverse factor analysis) are commonly described on Q-sorts for junior high *and* mid-adulthood. Although excluded from the original factor analysis, the Q-sort ratings at senior high school come into play to chart the behavioral changes over adolescence for these person-typologies defined by personality status over widely separated points in time. The assessments at senior high school serve then as a vantage midpoint, as it were, to monitor and evaluate behavioral transformations and thus guard against overdoing the "psychology of the permanent" to account for the years of missing data. In effect, a phase-specific adolescence can still be identified if discontinuity can be demonstrated, even with breaks in the flow of longitudinal data. Thus, if junior high school (or a change between junior high school and senior high school) predicts to adulthood, whereas senior high alone does not (even after appropriate partialling), then a discontinuous sleeper effect has been found that clearly indicates an early-adolescent contribution. Such a finding cannot be accounted to the presumption of over-time permanence in the non-studied years. Another sleeper effect that would help confirm the adolescent era would be the larger yield of adolescent predictors of later rather than earlier adult periods.

In sum, a strong case for adolescence must deal squarely with the two-sided contention that adolescence makes no specific or lasting contribution to personality, because, first, it is weak against the much larger thrust of behavioral stabilities over the early life span; second, the sound and fury that distinguish it also extinguish it, leaving little of conceptual importance.

Our case for reconstructing adolescence implies, of course, a larger viewpoint, to which we now turn: that adolescent personality is no longer to be construed as inherently unchartable, but rather as relatively uncharted. The turmoil and flux of the adolescent condition have too long served as a deterrent to a closer scientific scrutiny on the nature and types of adolescent perturbation and the longitudinal outcomes that they help create and shape. Once these possibilities have been recognized, the longitudinal study of adolescence can be seen as providing a most auspicious field for empirical personality study. It is then that palpable psychophysiological changes and the obvious psychosocial transitions come together to provide, as perhaps at no other time in the formative years, clearly discriminating measurements with a functional and theoretical relevance of what is measured. The potential offered by adolescent longitudinal study for relatively precise naturalistic research in personality-theory construction is just beginning to become apparent; such research is richly possible indeed. Although currently a patchwork quilt rather than a well-designed tapestry, the promising finer weave may be imagined from a detailed and evaluative survey of longitudinal research on two facets of transition: in adolescent psychophysiological pubertal growth and in psychosocial development.

Adolescence as Pubertal Growth and Development

Early and Late Maturation

The flux and asynchrony of adolescence was perhaps first demystified in the most visible sector of transition and change, the pubertal growth spurt. The remarkable regularity and predictability of growth both within and between physical parameters, such as status and rates of change in height, skeletal, and secondary sex characteristics (Stolz & Stolz, 1951; Nicolson & Hanley, 1953; Tanner, 1962), became the basis for the initial concentration of pubertal longitudinal study on the "psychology of the permanent." The focus was on the classification and comparison in the Oakland Growth Study sample of adolescents who consistently maintain early or late physical maturation throughout adolescence (Ames, 1957; M. C. Jones, 1957, 1958, 1965; M. C. Jones & Bayley, 1950; Mussen & M. C. Jones, 1957, 1958).

It was reasonably assumed and empirically supported that the early-maturing male's greater nearness to physical maturity and adult appearance would draw a favorable reception from the adult world and, eventually, would shape a self-image of positive esteem and behavioral confidence, social maturity, and the like. The energetic, bouncy, and bossy late-maturing male, by contrast, was seen as leaping immaturely into behavioral styles of bravado and activity to compensate for, yet betray, his sense of physical inferiority. Most impressively, the effects of greater prestige accorded the early-maturing male in social and occupational spheres was still apparent in adulthood (age 33), long after growth differentials between the groups had vanished. Thus, far from triggering universal turmoil, pubertal growth led to new lines of predictable development. Turmoil itself was first considered to express the late maturer's social frustration at being a mediocre contender whose reach for social participation exceeded the promise of his physical image. But a later and far-ranging follow-up at age 38 (M. C. Jones, 1965) brought an important change in understanding the nature of adolescent stress in the context of maturational timing. The early maturer's social ease and success and the late maturer's social distress and thwarted ambition in adolescence do indeed carry over into adulthood. The early-maturing males as adults are more responsible, cooperative, sociable, and self-controlled, *but also* more rigid, moralistic, humorless, and conforming; the late maturers as adults remain more impulsive and assertive, *but also* are more insightful, perceptive, creatively playful and able to cope with the ambiguity of new situations. The original one-dimensional view that a becalmed social maturity, modeled after an early identification with adult models, was indisputably favorable for an adolescent male was thus significantly altered to imply eventual role inflexibility and a failure to allow for and cope with the unexpected, the untoward, the ambiguous, and the private. This revised view, however, did not extend this weakness in coping to the internal events of puberty itself, that is, the upsurge of new affect associated with pubertal onset. As you will see, our own research promulgated a further revision, one that gave decisive importance to the pubertal transition in establishing the new developmental trends and adult outcomes that the Oakland studies revealed.

Whereas the initial view betrayed the now-waning image of adolescence as mere passive repository for adult rehearsals and socialization, the revised view by M. C. Jones (1965) began to credit the adolescent with being a constructive actor in creating new situations to explore his own capacities to survive and develop. As we shall discuss elsewhere, this view of the self-constructive adolescent (Haan, 1977) has since become more full bodied as a result of longitudinal study, especially in the salutary outcomes for the adolescent facing environmental stresses of divorce, economic deprivation, and family discord. For the stressed adolescent, rather than a preadolescent child under similar stress or a nonstressed adolescent, an advance in ego development is likely to occur under manageable conditions of disequilibrium — a disequilibrium between who he has been and who he must become in order to continue his sense of self-continuity under such untoward circumstances. Returning to early/late maturation, it is important to note that the stress befalling the late-maturer makes him not so much a tougher being than one who is cognitively more flexible and independent in pursuing life's problem-solving. It is especially in the arena of maintaining or increasing cognitive competence and exploration that the effectiveness of management of stress is most significantly implicated.

Comparison of early- and late-maturing females in the Oakland Study has been reported for the adolescent years (H. E. Jones, 1949), but not thereafter in adult follow-ups. Briefly, the early-maturing girl, much as the late-maturing boy, is expected to be psychologically and socially out of step with her age-peers — with valued mores and standards of American culture pertaining to beauty, heterosexual interests, and sexual conspicuousness generally. Indeed, the early-maturing girl is rated as less popular, less poised, less expressive, and more submissive, withdrawn, and unassured than her age-mates. The late-maturing girl — whose growth is less abrupt, whose stature is more petite (in line with standards of femininity) and more in synchrony with the maturational rate of boys in her age group — is assumed to be in step socially and psychologically. Indeed she is rated more favorably in personal appearance and attractiveness, in expressiveness and activity, and in sociability, leadership, and prestige. These results are appreciably replicated in a study by Peskin (1973) with the Berkeley Guidance Study sample. The early-maturing girl in adolescence is again cheerless, ill poised, socially vulnerable, easily disorganized under stress, and preoccupied with her early sexual image; the late-maturing girl is gregarious, socially poised and aware, as well as assertive and active.

Peskin's (1973) study also includes findings from age 30 follow-up data that impressively correspond to the male's personality transformation between adolescence and adulthood. The stress-ridden early-maturing girl in adulthood has become clearly a more coping, self-possessed, and self-directed person than the late-maturing female in the cognitive and social as well as emotional sectors. The intellectual and philosophical values that were detectable in her introverted adolescence seem to have flowered into a self-assured sense of problem-solving competence and cognitive purpose in adulthood. By contrast it is the late-maturing female, carefree and unchallenged in adolescence, who faces adversity maladaptively in adulthood. Perhaps the most conspicuous and theoretically important change — for it underscores even more sharply a similar thrust toward cognitive mastery in the late-maturing male groups — is the widened cognitive grasp in adulthood of the early-maturing females who had apparently been beset by the dissonances between self and society during adolescence.

Pubertal Onset and Ego Development

The remarkable changes, even reversals, of behaviors between the adolescence and adulthood of early and late maturers demonstrate the underestimated power of longitudinal studies to establish that behavior not only persists, but also transforms itself. Yet, although the later papers from the Oakland Growth Study allowed for these reversals, their original social-learning model stayed intact, positing that the individual is basically and gradually bestirred only when nurture calls, programmed by gender-role assignments made to the measure of what an adolescent is supposed to become as an adult. Unaccounted for in the social-learning model was the experience of the onset of puberty as an internal event of affective and maturational change for which early and late maturers might be differently prepared. That early and late maturers might experience differently the internal side of puberty is a reasonable inference from the shorter and longer lengths of time they had to prepare for their respective pubertal spurts. Younger at the start of puberty, the early maturer has had less time than the late maturer unexposed to hormonal change. But, having started data-collection in early adolescence, the Oakland Growth Study could not deal with this or any other factor affecting preparation for adolescence that required information from childhood and preadolescence.

Where an individual falls on the continuum of early/late maturation could also tell the relative timing of his pubertal spurt and the duration of the prior prepubertal period. Cannot the Oakland findings rather be attributed to the differential timing of puberty, hence the length of the prior period for early and late maturers? This issue may be recognized as a specific case of the by now familiar question for which longitudinal design is uniquely suited: How is one able to unconfound and separate behaviors of long standing from those emerging with new stage transitions? The lack of Oakland prepubertal data precluded inquiry into the role possibly played by differing pubertal onsets in bringing about the reported differences between early and late maturers. The birth-to-maturity breadth of the Berkeley Guidance Study does, however, provide the necessary prepubertal material for pursuing the effects of pubertal onset and preparation for puberty. Indeed, birth-to-maturity designs could perform the double duty of pinpointing onset of stage effects and readiness for entry into new stages.

Peskin (1967) replicated the Oakland procedure of classifying early/late maturation in the male sample of the Guidance Study and thereafter proceeded to compare groups at their respective ages of pubertal onset and at yearly intervals before and after pubertal onset. Comparing groups in this manner at similar *maturational* (rather than chronological) age points could separate findings into those to be attributed to prepubertal differences, to pubertal timing, and to the pubertal period itself. Peskin was especially interested in the effects of pubertal timing that might reflect differential preparation for the pubertal spurt: with a briefer prelude to the pubertal changes, the early maturer would be expected initially to experience these effects as relatively more intense and less tolerable. In psychoanalytic developmental terms, the early maturer would be said to undergo a shorter latency period, the late maturer a longer one. The usual developmental advances in mastery of impulse and cognitive functioning during the latency phase would be supposed to be greater for the late maturer, who has had a longer time to exercise and integrate new ego mechanisms tied to expanded intellectual and motor skills. The greater coping and cognitive skills of the late maturer, reported in the later Oakland findings, are expected then to be identified at the very start of puberty as he confronts the increased psychosexual and physical changes with more confidence and safety, rather than (as the revised view of the Oakland findings maintained) as gradual victory over his disadvantaged social position. Yet, the Oakland findings doubtless point to the important role of the early maturer's rapid ascent toward adulthood and to the attraction of the perceptible rewards, serious responsibilities, and firm images readily offered him by the community at an earlier time. The early maturer then could be said to live between a diffuse internal state and a well-ordered external one, a disparity that would overdetermine his acceptance of the community's recognition since it offers a flight from the hazardous internal experience at the same time that such flight — on the model of avoidance learning — self-fulfillingly heightens and proves the inner danger of pubertal affect. The late-maturing boy, on the other hand, feels less endangered by an internal state for which he has had time to prepare; additionally, the relative social neglect he suffers may increase the actuality of the internal state and promote a more vivid confrontation of its affects and affect-laden thoughts. In terms of cognitive and problem-solving strategies, the disparity between the internal and external states of the early maturer would lead him to seek and find rapid solutions after minimal exploration; the late maturer, expecting to find neither an easy niche nor an *ersatz* adult-styled role, creates new possibilities from his larger tolerance for the pubertal change.

Several behaviors suggestive of these hypothesized differences did indeed statistically discriminate early and late maturers only at and after the onset of puberty, but *not* before. The late maturer showed significantly higher ratings on behaviors of intellectual curiosity, exploratory behavior, social initiative, and activity level, whereas the early maturer tended to avoid problem-solving or new situations unless urged or helped. The early maturer appeared to approach cognitive tasks cautiously and timidly, with a preference for rules, routines, and imitative action. Far from complacent or comfortable conformity, as the Oakland findings in adulthood had suggested, it was the early maturer at pubertal onset who had experienced more disorganizing stress and tension-discharge in his manifest anxiety and more frequent and intense temper tantrums. This poorer management of stress close to the onset of puberty is taken to reflect the early maturer's relatively more inflexible defenses and sense of instinctual danger arising from his foreshortened time to prepare for the internal processes of adolescence.

For girls, Peskin (1973) expected that pubertal timing would lead to very different assimilations of the internal and external experiences of the soma. As H. E. Jones (1949) pointed out in accounting for the greater unhappiness of the early-maturing girl in the Oakland Growth Study sample, early maturation in girls does not invite the same straightforward or approving response that boys receive, and so it is less likely that early-maturing girls have available the same adaptive retreat to the community from a more intense internal state. Thus we conceived of the early-maturing girls in the unique situation of having to confront an internal-drive state for which an early pubertal onset has ill prepared her. Findings reflect both poorer preparation *and* greater confrontation: rating scales that significantly discriminated early and late maturers at or after puberty indicated that pubertal onset is indeed more stressful, disorganizing, and abrupt for the early maturer, *but* also more comprehended and experienced rather than withdrawn from and denied. The early-maturing adolescent girl seems tuned to the internal happenings of puberty, as revealed by more extensive dream recall and higher ratings of introversion. Conversely, the late maturer seems more in compliance with the demands of external situations and less challenged by or actively struggling with either internal or outer worlds. For the late maturer, the longer preparation for the pubertal changes together with the less hazardous sense of sexuality in social relationships may add up to psychological climates all too safe, facile, and lacking the sense of real mastery that presupposes challenge and disequilibrium. The cognitive strength of the early-maturing female is already incipient in early puberty (in capacity to recall dreams and in interest in philosophical problems), which suggests the construction of coping resources when pubertal changes are first confronted. Yet further confrontations may serve as nutriment for further coping. By adulthood, as we reviewed earlier, the cognitive strength of the early-maturing female is impressive indeed.

Childhood Factors in the Response to Puberty

As we have seen so far, the long-term longitudinal outcome provides definitive evidence for the adaptive or maladaptive, coping or defensive, significance of prior adolescent behavior. The import of considering adult outcome has so far been to trim our overestimation of phase-specific adolescent tranquility, compliance, and social adjustment as well as to correct our underestimation of adolescent struggle and stress, especially in the context of emerging cognitive skills and personal autonomy. The longitudinal perspective here frees us from having to overvalue phenomenological experience in the adolescent's here-and-now and thus permits us to disentangle yet another confounded issue: how to separate the adolescent's present discomfort from his capacity to learn to manage, that is, to maintain, sublimate, or make direct use of tension and stress. Neither adolescent turmoil nor tranquility alone paves a longitudinal road to adult adaptation.

The understanding of adolescent stress (and adolescent experience generally) may also be appreciably advanced when the individual's *earlier* history permits us to predict whether the rapid sensory inputs of adolescent maturation and development will be experienced as nutriment or detriment to ego control and mastery as well as to cognitive learning and performance. Such use of developmental history is illustrated in our above study, which formulates response to the pubertal onset as a function of length of the prior latency period.

Birth-to-maturity studies permit, of course, unlimited inquiry into early developmental factors that might help shape a safe or risk-laden response to puberty. Outcomes of the dissonant or harmonious interplay between early childhood temperament and adolescent environment are presented by Chess and Thomas (1977), using selected case histories from the New York Longitudinal Study and from the Coping Studies by Murphy and Moriarty (1976), both starting at birth. These are exceptions; otherwise, the sway of the "psychology of the permanent" over longitudinal research has delayed research programs in phase-specific processes, including their antecedents and remote temporal outcomes.

The stage-developmental theory of psychoanalysis, as it bears on adolescence, offers rich leads into just such longitudinal study of childhood determinants of the pubertal response that have remained largely unexplored. The operational criteria for such research, however, are clearly more demanding than the simpler standards for defining key independent variables regulating the oral and anal phase, as witnessed by the perhaps excessive number of studies on nursing and toilet training in the before/after genre of longitudinal design. The theory of adolescence, broadly stated so as to embody classical and contemporary aspects of Freud, Anna Freud, and Erikson, concerns the renewal of the psychosexual and psychosocial issues of childhood with the arousal of sexual and aggressive affect and motivation of puberty. But, as we have emphasized, before/after predictions from childhood to adolescence would not separate findings as phase-specific from those that remain consistent across phases. Ideally, longitudinal study therefore calls for evaluating behavioral change over the full range of years from childhood to adolescence to discern the unique interactions of childhood disposition and puberty.

In this framework, Peskin (1973) studied changes in response to puberty as a function of differential psychosexual arousal during early childhood. The research consisted of assessing the prepubertal and pubertal outcomes of two early-childhood environments in which boys of the Berkeley Guidance Study were exposed to a greater or lesser amount of psychosexual stimulation. The greater amount was assumed to be the outcome of a family setting where the mother was rated as expressing more love to her son than to her spouse. This group of 11 boys, between the ages of 3 to 5 years, was designated as "strong oedipal" to indicate a family context that validated the oedipal fantasy of maternal possession and paternal competition. The lesser amount of stimulation was assumed in a family system where the mother was rated as expressing as much love to son as to spouse. This group of 16 boys was designated "normal oedipal" to reflect the developmental wane of parental possession and rivalry. On psychoanalytic grounds, puberty should be a more disruptive time for the "strong oedipal" boys. The implicit sexualization of feelings and social relationships in their family interaction, when the child was ill prepared, makes the overt sexualization of puberty yet more difficult to assimilate, less manageable consciously, and more likely to be dealt with by denial and withdrawal. Again, such an hypothesis calls for group differences at or after pubertal onset, but not before. Findings indicated that the "strong oedipal" boys indeed sharply retreat from internal and social derivatives of psychosexual stimulation between the latency and pubertal periods, for example, their greater recall of dreams and emotional dependence on mother before puberty are markedly reduced once puberty has begun.

Under the new press of the adolescent's attempts to manage the maturational and developmental thrusts of puberty, the family too may generally alter its prior organization of affectional relationships and dominance hierarchies. Such normative family change with the growing child's move into adolescence is especially suited to longitudinal study, although barely undertaken. Our own research (Peskin, 1963) shows that such family transformations are most likely when the early-childhood organization of parent–child closeness would appreciably escalate the psychosexual vulnerability of the adolescent and further reduce normative allowance for pubertal affect. Thus the mother who (relatively) withdraws from her son when he enters puberty (from the year before puberty to the year after) had in childhood favored him over a spouse who was assessed as psychologically distant from the family. The decreasing relatedness at puberty between mother and son in such a family system might well be seen as an interactive effort to reduce the heightened pubertal stress of a relatively more intense and prolonged oedipal fantasy and actuality.

Interestingly, the male adolescents in these family circumstances are among the earliest physical maturers in the Berkeley Guidance Study. The potential importance of psychological factors as determinants of differential physical growth rates requires longitudinal design to separate *cause* from *effect,* that is, psychosomatic from somato-psychic (Boutourline Young, 1973; Tanner, 1962; Peskin, 1963, 1968, 1973; Widdowson, 1951). The rich diversity of somatic growth variations surrounding the pubertal spurt, described further below, offers an obvious, yet still untapped testing ground for such study.

Regardless of theoretical predilection, behavioral change over the pubertal threshold, we suggest, constitutes a potentially powerful research vantage point for uncovering the latent vulnerabilities and strengths of earlier childhood-rearing schedules or nonnormative stress. Exposure to pubertal stimulation becomes a naturalistic challenge for testing the growth-retarding or growth-promoting aspects of such events as divorce, family disloca-tion, physical illness, economic deprivation, and so on.

Development between Substages of Physical Maturation

Beyond the pubertal transition, there is a lack of longitudinal research on the diverse patterns of physical growth and their psychological sequelae. Under the sway of the ''psychology of the permanent,'' the consistency of adolescent growth has mistakenly led to the neglect of sizable growth asynchronies (Livson & Bronson, 1961; Eichorn, 1975) between positively correlated growth systems. The same tendency to reduce growth to single-factor mediation has also obscured the possibility of yet other growth regularities, for example, *rate* of physical change in contrast to *timing* of stage completion. In secondary sexual characteristics, as a case in point, the *early* maturer is taken to be the *fast* maturer. In terms of number of years to complete such growth, the early maturer is, in fact, also the *slow* maturer, notwithstanding his still-earlier completion of puberty (Schmidt, 1965; Peskin, 1973). Designating growth by overall early/late maturation is likely then to confound timing and rate (e.g., velocity, duration) under which the growth process unfolds. Obviously, longitudinal data are crucial for separating pubertal timing and rate, and for studying their distinctive and interactive effects. The confounding of timing and rate in cross-sectional and very brief longitudinal designs calls into question the usual empirical claim of a positive association between maturation and cognitive or psychosocial developments (e.g., Tanner, 1962; Kiernan, 1977). Our own analysis, in which timing and rate of secondary sexual development are partialled out from the other, indicates that cognitive skill is attributable to slow growth rate rather than to early timing.

Homogeneity of growth means as well that the researcher can expect broadly predictable patterns of physical change and reasonable ease in finding samples whose psychological development can be followed from one definable substage of pubertal growth to another. The able study of Steinberg (1978) in this mode breaks new ground in adolescent longitudinal research on physical growth, even with its relatively brief, one-year span. The study follows the changes in family relations as a function of progression in the male pubertal cycle. Transformations in the decision-making interaction patterns of 29 middle-class early adolescent boys and their parents were analyzed in relation to passage through the stages of puberty, from prepubertal to termination of puberty. The overall pattern of change on repeated performance of a family decision-making task suggested a conflict between the adolescent and his mother, which erupts at the time of the adolescent's pubertal onset, peaks near the pubertal apex, and tapers off during the postapex period. This conflict is accompanied by a gain in influence on the part of the physically mature adolescent, primarily at the expense of his mother.

Steinberg's study constitutes an infrequent look into the longitudinal study of family organization in contrast to the usual focus on individual behaviors and is the lone study, so far as we know, in repeated measurement of such family interaction pertaining to normal adolescent development. It is, therefore, an important contribution to, and model for, normative study of how the family reorganizes and redefines itself as the adolescent struggles to have the family validate changes in the self. Steinberg's study grasps the essential disequilibrating nature of adolescence when the accustomed problem-solving structures of the family are inherently out of phase with the changing state of the adolescent's new skills and aspirations. The conflict between adolescents and parents, which Steinberg reports, can then be regarded as leading to purposeful transformations of family structure for further individual and family development. The process indeed draws on adolescent turmoil and, as Steinberg suggests, perhaps also on revived oedipal conflict. But these elements by themselves cannot account for the new forms of reciprocity in the family that give new actuality to the adolescent's attempt to expand the boundaries of the self, as Erikson has described (1970).

Differential rate of substage maturation is virtually an untapped area of growth asynchronies, yet one that lends itself to the study of certain social vicissitudes in adolescence. If concordance among adolescents in their growth rates and stature is an important determinant of friendship choices, then — as Sullivan (1953) contended — friendships are vulnerable to breakup and to being reconstituted as the growth paces of the partners diverge. Longitudinal study here would be well served by growth data of friendship pairs. But even the usual single-person orientation of longitudinal study can pursue such issues by implication. For example, sharp changes in an adolescent's growth over brief periods, relative to the sample norm, imply such interpersonal flux. Since, according to Nicolson and Hanley (1953), skeletal growth between preadolescence and early adolescence is less consistent in males, the intriguing question is raised of sex differences in the stability of social networks. In any event, we are drawn again to the preadolescent/adolescent transition and recognize afresh that its longitudinal study offers an important heuristic and testing ground for a wide range of social and maturational issues. The longitudinal work-in-progress of Offer's research group with a new sixth-grade sample of males and females (Report of the Laboratory for the Study of Adolescence, 1978) is a welcome indication that the adolescent threshold will be increasingly noticed as an unusually versatile terminus for understanding human development.

Institutionalized Psychosocial Transitions

Studies here explore the adolescent's capacity to master normative, institutionally arranged transitions from one social network to another. Insofar as personality development may be effected, such passages involve assumption of new responsibilities and privileges, on the one hand, and loss of and separation from the familiar, on the other.

Between Elementary and Junior High School

A familiar warning against overestimating the ill effects of a stressful adolescent transition is sounded by Blyth, Simmons, and Bush (1978), who report several personality-connected effects in school change and preparation for change between the sixth and seventh grades in two types of school organization. The empirical research with over 250 sixth graders followed for one year into the seventh grade seeks to determine whether type of school structure — kindergarten through eighth grade (K through 8) or kindergarten through sixth grade (K through 6) and an associated junior high school — leads to differential change in self-esteem and other aspects of interpersonal and academic behavior. Findings indicate that those who have moved to junior high school show lowered self-esteem (especially girls) and feel more anonymous and victimized (especially boys) in their new school environment than those who remain in the same K-through-8 school between sixth and seventh grades. Prior to the changeover, sixth graders in K-through-6 schools are reported to have internalized a greater sense of responsibility, to want more independence from parents, and to be more academically oriented, reflecting their preparation for the transition to junior high.

Blyth, Simmons, and their colleagues are now following the samples between the ninth and tenth grades, the first transition for K-through-8 students and the second transition for the junior-high students. The larger question here is, of course, readiness for environmental change and optimal timing for such enforced change, where such a change may not only come too soon, but also too late. For the increased stress of the K-through-6 students who move to junior high school, the question then remains open for longer-term longitudinal follow-up as to whether the transition is too early to facilitate ego development (drawing off energy to control anxiety) or well timed to create the growth-promoting disequilibrium that challenges adolescents to reach beyond their grasp. Interestingly, the distress and discomfort of the K-through-6 students in their new junior high schools had been preceded by cognitive competence and personal autonomy, a sequence which, for girls in the Berkeley Guidance Study, was predictive of adult psychological health (Peskin, 1972). Indeed, as our literature survey shows, the availability of cognitive capacities increases the likelihood that adolescent stress is nutriment for self-constructive processes of ego control and mastery.

The studies of Blyth, Simmons, and their colleagues are important reminders that adolescent personality emerges over subtransitions in socialization, such as the moves from elementary school to junior high school and senior high school. In the virtual uniformity of school environments (from elementary to junior high school), such subtransitions are simply easy to forget as determinants of adolescent development. Waning as the K-through-8 environment is, its differential effects strongly suggest that adolescent development is tied to and presupposes the impact of social–educational structures and warn us against exclusive maturational or chronological formulations.

Planned change is never as well wrought as one might want and, as we pointed out earlier, naturalistic observation in much longitudinal study makes for confoundings that are more in the nature of life complexities than experimental artifact. School change, for example, necessarily presumes differential opportunities and stresses for select subgroups so that a planned transition releases others that are unplanned and varying with sociological, economic, sex-role, and racial contexts. Indeed, the very flux of physical development is enough to doubt homogenous outcomes that one expects from age-graded criteria only. Findings by Simmons et al. (1977) support the greater tendency for early-maturing girls to date; the larger opportunity to date for those sixth graders moving to junior high school suggests that they comprise a particular subgroup at risk in the multiple transitions of school, pubertal, and sex-role expectations. For the sample studied over one year in the K-through-6 and K-through-8 environments, Simmons et al. report that such a subgroup of early maturing girls who date in their first year of junior high has an increased vulnerability in terms of diminished self-esteem.

From Junior High School to Senior High School

Assessment of behavior in junior high and senior high school has been undertaken for a combined sample from the Oakland Growth and Berkeley Guidance studies. These assessments were not specifically designed for studying the transition between these environments, but rather to describe personality separately at the junior- and senior-high-school levels (Block with Haan, 1971; Haan, 1974; Haan & Day, 1974) — these two educational levels essentially correspond to early and late adolescence.

Block with Haan (1971) used a panoply of relatively simple statistical techniques to describe behavioral consistency and change between early and late adolescence. Applied in the ipsative mode of Q-sort methodology, where each person is his own frame of reference, these techniques describe behaviors according to whether they maintain their:

1. Order over time (correlation).
2. Salience (mean change over time).
3. Diversity (convergence or divergence of variance over time).

No attempt, however, is made to separate the *sub*stage-specific effects of early/late adolescence by partialling one from the other, as in our earlier discussion. Hence, reversals of statistical effects between substages for the same behaviors necessarily go unreported. Otherwise, these statistical techniques of Block with Haan (1971) are nicely tailored to the structural definition and task of adolescence in either Eriksonian or Piagetian modalities: the preservation of continuity with the integration of change. The items of the California Q sort, independently sorted for junior high and senior high school and analyzed by the above techniques, reveal sex-differential patterns of change between early and late adolescence: females show increasing turbulence in terms of hostility, affectation, lack of frankness, and also declining likeability. However, such stress does not impair their intellectual, aesthetic, and interpersonal competence. Indeed, such skills not only maintain their order but some even increase their salience between substages. The authors bring these apparently disparate findings together under a broad psychodynamic interpretation that posits the turbulence to be ''a screen behind which the adolescent girl can privately work over and assimilate or reject the consequences of her experience'' (p. 72). Boys, in contrast, ''generally decreased their affective vulnerabilities and their dependence and have clearly become composed and better able to cope with the world for which they are beginning to plan'' (p. 72).

These reported significant findings are open, of course, to a variety of interpretations within any one of several theoretical frameworks pertaining to adolescent development. Without statistical connections to adult outcomes in conceptual or functional terms (adaptation, coping, psychological health, etc.), interpretation is likely to be gratuitous, even if descriptively rich, since it answers to no clear developmental process or structure. Why, for example, does the girl need a screen (and one of turbulence) behind which she can privately work? Cannot turbulence and assimilation of experience be different sides — psychosocial and cognitive — of a common process of the expanding and reorganizing self during adolescence? Haan (1974, 1977) proceeds in such a direction in reanalyzing the Q sorts of the Oakland Growth sample by predicting to adult outcomes from a conceptual model of ego coping and defense. Haan's model draws heavily, rigorously, and imaginatively on the structural concepts of Piaget and modern psychoanalysis (especially Erikson) pertaining to stage reorganization, cognitive capability, and ego expansion. Applied to adolescent behavioral change as predictors of adult styles of coping and defense, this model offers a deliberate theoretical focus and verifiable hypotheses on adolescent development that have been typically lacking in the descriptive level of much longitudinal study. Briefly, adults are rated higher on capacity to cope if they are open to experience, able to synthesize new information, and are solving problems effectively. In adolescence, one would be expected to address, therefore, the psychosocial questions posed by one's emerging capabilities, society, and the imbalances between self and society. Such psychosocial and cognitive initiative, says Haan, entails some confusion, disequilibrium, and personal–social disarray — signs not of regression, but of the reorganizing processes that will lead the adolescent progressively to an enlarged self in adulthood. Adult defenders, on the other hand, protect themselves from disquieting information; in adolescence, therefore, they would be expected to reject the psychosocial questions of adolescence and veer away from new definitions of the self. For adult men and women classified as primarily coping individuals, there is a larger increase in cognitive capabilities over adolescence, or between adolescence and adulthood, than for other adult groups favoring defensive or mixed styles. For psychosocial aspects of reorganization, it is the coping adults again who, as late adolescents, were the most autonomous, self-questing and psychologically minded.

The progressive increase in cognitive and autonomous capabilities for both men and women over adolescence and adulthood in Haan's (1974) study does much to dispel the claims or ambiguities that have pointed to apparent emotional regression in females as a requisite for adult adaptation. Sex differences have tended to predominate in reports and in conceptualization of findings, usually along social-learning lines, where differential gender roles are obviously telling. Haan's results of reasonably similar adolescent antecedents for men and women with the same modes of ego adaptation underscore the commonalities in other studies that may exist between the sexes, even when manifest differences are plentiful. Thus, as discussed earlier, common themes of stage reorganization may be discerned in both early-maturing girls and late-maturing boys, notwithstanding disparate specific findings. This caveat, of course, offers no clear guidelines for setting forth the conditions under which regression and disequilibrium can be told apart. The question is theoretically important, for on it rests, for example, the difference between two incompatible theories, the Piagetian and the classical Freudian, the latter propounding the necessity of a regressive turn in the female's adolescent development to achieve healthy femininity.

Emotional regression that is poorly or insufficiently balanced by stability or by progressive changes toward increased competence and autonomy calls into serious question the adequacy of the adult criterion of adaptive psychological functioning. Conversely, stability or progressive changes (in cognitive capabilities and personal autonomy) within adolescence without behavioral regression may also raise doubt about the properties of our adult standard. Indeed, there may be more empirical and theoretical consensus about the preconditions of low psychological health, defensiveness, and the like, than of optimal health, ego coping, and so on. Psychoanalytic theory on adolescent turmoil (A. Freud, 1958) is rather more cautious than is usually thought on this issue since it is not inner turmoil that is "required" for healthy development so much as it is the need for "upholding a steady equilibrium" that is pathogenic. In Peskin's (1972) predictive study of adult psychological health, it is the least healthy women who protect the steady state or have actually moved toward increased control and competence from preadolescence to adolescence, rather than the healthiest abandoning themselves to inner unrest. The healthiest women did not rampantly "regress" on all predictive behaviors, but showed a pattern of intensified emotionality ("regression") coexisting with enhanced coping. Haan's (1974) findings, on a different female sample, accord with a view of balance between regressive and progressive forces: the coping women become increasingly more self-indulgent, socially labile, and self-defeating, as well as cognitively capable and personally autonomous over adolescence. Thus both Peskin's and Haan's results also well fit a formulation leaning toward the ego-psychology mode of stage reorganization, yet are compatible with the coping model of Haan, namely, that the firm sense of personal and cognitive competence in preadolescence or early adolescence makes it safe for the girl to venture out to new boundaries of selfhood, especially in affective spheres. It is most interesting to note unusual support for this viewpoint in the finding that preschizophrenic girls, in adolescence, were reported in the follow-back study of Watt (1974) to be *higher* than normal controls in industry and responsibility, indeed, to display a pattern of "extreme conscientiousness." The control girls are *more* nervous, restless, and worried.

Beyond Senior High School

The psychosocial terminus of adolescence begins in the transition from senior high school to college, first job, or leaving home (Lowenthal, Thurnher, & Chiriboga, 1975; Murphey et al., 1963; Trent & Medsker, 1967). Coterminous with early adulthood, this transition is likely to draw increasing attention from the growing discipline of adult development, on the one hand, and the expanding attention being paid to separation and individuation in the Eriksonian ambiance of identity formation, on the other. Under the adult-development approach, longitudinal study of this last adolescent transition has been launched in the Transitions Study of the Human Development and Aging Program (University of California, San Francisco), which has followed a senior-high cohort from the last year of high school to several years beyond. Findings of the sample at the initial high-school round along with other samples undergoing later adult transitions are reported in *Four Stages of Life* (Lowenthal, Thurnher, & Chiriboga, 1975). Also relevant here, but discussed in detail earlier in this chapter, is the work of Offer and Offer (1975).

The clinical study by Murphey and her colleagues (1963), based on parent and adolescent interviews, focuses on the varieties of parent-offspring management of the gains and losses over one year involved in separation from the home among freshman college students during the transition from high school. The authors demonstrate the characteristic respect of the longitudinal researcher for developmental change by drawing no final conclusions after only one year of study about preferred parent-offspring patterns of regulating separation. They warn both against dismissing as less desirable the more stress-ridden pattern (in which the offspring are high in autonomous behavior, *but* low in parental relatedness) or accepting as more benign the less stressful pattern (in which the offspring are high in autonomous behavior *and* high in parental relatedness). Murphey and her colleagues say:

> Perhaps those students who achieved autonomy while maintaining distance in relation to their parents may be in a growth-stimulating situation where continued development of autonomy and further changes in family relationships are possible . . . perhaps, unsure of their newly exercised autonomy, it is necessary for them to maintain distance from their parents until a sense of consolidation and mastery is achieved. Similarly, there is a possibility that some of those who show an unusual spurt of autonomy, while maintaining a close relationship with their parents, may be restricted in their further development if they are deeply concerned about maintaining the status quo in relationships with their parents. [p. 652]

This caveat is insightful indeed, adumbrating the more recent recognition that the adolescent's separation from the home may constitute a life-span transition (the "empty nest") for the parents as well (Lowenthal, Thurnher, & Chiriboga, 1975). These interlocking losses, in fact, call for interlocking longitudinal study of adolescent and parent, hence rapprochement between longitudinal studies in child development and adult development. We suggest that the simultaneous study of parent and separating adolescent will contribute significantly to formulating the conditions for telling adolescent regression apart from disequilibrium.

Environmental Stress in Adolescence

Reconstructing adolescence has recently been appreciably advanced by several studies contrasting the effects of differential timing of the same environmental crisis and unplanned dislocation — divorce, parental conflict, and economic deprivation — in adolescence or childhood eras. The studies of Wallerstein and Kelly on divorce (1974, 1975, 1976), Weinstock on parental conflict (1967a, 1967b), Elder (1974, 1979) and Elder and Rockwell (1978) on economic deprivation in the Great Depression have commonly presumed that such hardships in early childhood retard psychological mastery, but in adolescence become grist for coping and for constructing a sense of competence and worth. For the studies of divorce and economic deprivation, the longitudinal outcomes of different samples that have undergone the same stress in childhood and adolescence are compared; for Weinstock's studies the impact of family stress on the male sample of the Berkeley Guidance Study is compared in childhood and adolescence.

The clinical report on the experience of parental divorce for 21 adolescents is based on interviews by Wallerstein and Kelly (1974) conducted at the height of the divorce decision or crisis and subsequently over a lapse of 12 months to 18 months, "when relationships had presumably had a chance to achieve a more stable equilibrium" (p. 481). (Data from further follow-ups 5 years are reported in Wallerstein & Kelly, 1980.) In contrast to children in preschool and early latency who were essentially inconsolable or overwhelmed, the divorce process for adolescents can be toward

> an earlier, more realistic acceptance of personality differences, a greater sense of closure about the divorce, and a smoother process of their identity formation. For some this contributes to a more mature look at the hazards and potentialities of marital interactions. The abrupt individuation of the parents forced by the divorce may at the same time serve a defensive function by transforming feelings of helplessness into a sense of control via active mastery. [pp. 491–492]

In Weinstock's study (1967a and b), a family stressed during the subject's adolescence was an antecedent of several coping styles [in Haan's model], especially tolerance of ambiguity and regression of the service of the ego. Haan (1977) suggests that the occasion for the parental disagreement may well have been the disequilibrium created by the adolescent in his or her self-constructive development, whereas, in childhood, parental disagreement may have had no connection to the child's initiative to master the self and environment. The self-constructive outcome of even emotionally disturbed adolescents from "high-emotional-involvement" homes underscores the coping thrust of the adolescent years. Anthony (1978), in a longitudinal report on breakdown in adolescents at high risk for psychosis, remarks that the adolescent experiences not only a sense of alienation following breakdown, but also takes a step forward in the process of emancipation from the premorbid relationship with parents.

The adolescent's relative capacity to separate and move toward increased autonomy under hardships that retard ego development at a younger age is also reflected in Elder (1979) and Elder and Rockwell (1978). These involved impressive separate analyses of two different birth cohorts, whose families experienced the Depression when the offspring were of preschool age (Berkeley Guidance Study) and during adolescence (Oakland Growth Study) when the children were old enough to contribute to the household economy. Within middle- and working-class families of both samples, offspring in families deprived and nondeprived during the Great Depression were compared in adulthood on personality functioning and family, work, and educational histories. Especially in the middle-class subjects, differential timing of economic stress led to greater mobilization of effort and ambition for adult work, family security, and educational advancement when deprivation came in adolescence; such family hardships experienced in early childhood led to lowered expectations and achievements in these adult outcomes. Further comparisons by Elder (1979) reveal intercohort sex differences such that the earlier occurrence of severe economic loss in the Berkeley Guidance Study took a much heavier psychic toll on the male, whereas later deprivation in the Oakland cohort was somewhat more costly to the female, obligated too soon to undertake domestic work. Notwithstanding certain sampling differences between these two studies, Elder's studies stand as a model within longitudinal perspective on the social-historical context of the life course and is a significant, nonbanal example of the sequential longitudinal design where historical change can be isolated from life-course change (Schaie, 1965; Nesselroade & Baltes, 1974). We have here, however, focused on Elder's work within the larger arena of the timing of stressful experiences in order to reveal the stage-specific capacities of adolescence. Elder's design of comparing historically different adolescent cohorts permits the reasonable assumption that adolescent effects have been isolated, notwithstanding the lack of childhood data.

NEW PERSPECTIVES ON THE LONGITUDINAL PERSPECTIVE

Uses of the Past: From Adolescence to Adulthood

The more time that is spent following the adulthood of a longitudinal sample, the less the researcher is likely to equate *becoming adult* with *completing development*. The "mythical plateau of adulthood" (Brim, 1976) with its corollary of an inevitable sequence of events leading to it, gives way to alternative models of past-present relationships as the longitudinal researcher journeys with the same samples. So long as the researcher contends with one adult criterion age only, the most parsimonious line to be drawn between the two points of youth and adulthood is the straight one of cause and effect. But with additional adult ages, cause and effect is neither the more supportable nor parsimonious connection between past and present. The conceptualization of past time that satisfactorily accounted for the earlier adult outcome now seems ill fitted for the lives of our participants later in adulthood. For the age at which a longitudinal study expects to come of age seems to recede as the next follow-up yields new connections with the "same, permanent" past that were unsuspected in the conceptual framework of the one before.

Adult development, in our view, transforms the individual's particular past into a well of resources to be drawn from to meet the ever-changing demands of the present. By this view, neither past nor present, neither childhood nor adolescence, nor any era of adulthood is fixed in its effects or of higher priority in its contribution. Rather, experience of the past and the present couple, uncouple, and recouple in ways that cause the usual lines of cause and effect to blur and even to reverse. The expanding past thus brings with it the potential for new combinations and emerging capacities for later life change. We expect, then, to find changing organizations of the past as the adult moves into new developmental tasks and life structures of new times (Peskin & Gigy, 1977; Peskin & Livson, in press). Conceptually, we are then dealing neither with a single "authentic" past nor with a single, once-and-for-all adulthood, but rather with ongoing states of adult development that differentially recruit and actively combine material from the past for present adaptive and creative functioning.

Our approach contrasts with the psychoanalytic method, in which reconstruction of the past is keyed to a timeless adult "plateau." Accordingly, the psychoanalytic view of reconstruction essentially deals with the person's retrieval of a once-given, fixed past, the basis for Piaget's apt criticism that psychoanalysis has been too much a science of the permanent. In the work of Piaget on the constructive activity of consciousness in children, we find a notable exception to the divisiveness between child-centered (e.g., psychoanalysis) and adult-centered theories of personality (where the remote past is simply irrelevant). Our view that the past is continually reorganized around the evolving adult tasks of the present is largely consistent with Piaget's position that the "living aspects of the past" are preserved by continual accommodation "to the manifold and irreducible present" (Piaget, 1962, p. 208).

Cognitively and psychosocially, the adolescence of the Berkeley Guidance and Oakland samples is well suited to demonstrate the accessibility of past resources for psychological health at later adult eras. Cognitively, the emergence of formal operations in adolescence means that the young man and young woman have become reliably capable of thinking in terms of life-span possibilities and alternatives (Cottle & Klineberg, 1974; Flavell, 1963) remote from the here and now, giving behavior an intentional quality of rehearsal for the psychosocial tasks of adulthood. These rehearsals or anticipations, we suppose, are long acting and stored, as it were, for nutriment in later eras of adulthood. Adolescent behavior, organized around a strengthened personal identity, takes on the quality of belonging and being accountable to the self and thus available for its own later revisions and elaborations. An aspect of this self-possession, and of identity formation in Erikson's terms (1959), is the more inward, assimilative work by adolescents of taking new charge of their own past. Adolescents become able, according to Erikson, of thinking about possibilities in reference to the past as well as the future — indeed, to coordinate the earlier identifications they wish to carry forward from the past with the upcoming goals they have identified for themselves. Such a constructionist view of their own past may help adolescents expand their sense of where new resources for definition of the self can be found. Making use of the past, then, is an obvious advance over less self-directed and more short-term functions to which the past has been put before adolescence, for example, for defensive reconstructions or for modeling of specific role assignments.

If adolescence provides resources for adulthood, life-span theory suggests that the specific nutriment drawn on will reflect the changing purposes of adult eras (Gutmann, 1976; Jung, 1933/1971; Levinson, et al., 1974; Neugarten, 1969). Thus for young adults whose selfhood and individuation must be constructed in life contexts of becoming established in the outer world, adolescence should provide the instrumental and expressive resources connected with family and occupational achievements. Such resources, we expect, would be attached to traditional sex-role and age-role expectations pertaining to parenting and occupation. For later adulthood, when personal control of the outside world has subsided as a central orientation of living, resources from the past for the development of the self should more likely consist of behaviors freed from the constraints of sex- and age-appropriate roles and functions.

The changeover of resources from early to later adulthood does not necessarily imply any lessening of access to the adolescent past with advancing years, but rather changing patterns of access suitable to the integration of the self along the life span of psychosocial transitions.

Establishing adolescence by its selective usefulness for adult eras requires research strategies that predict to adult functioning at specified ages or around particular psychosocial tasks. Lumping together disparate age groups in the adult criteria would very likely attenuate evidence that adult stages could be drawing upon different, even opposite, adolescent resources. Even in the later life-span seemingly so far from adolescence, its effects may then still be masked by confounding — now from among adult stages. The longitudinal study of adolescence will contribute to life-span models whenever adult ages or stages are differentially formulated and separately treated to safeguard their properties from being hidden by inappropriate reductions. A positive case is F. Livson's study (1979) of the adolescent antecedents of consistency and change in psychological health between the ages of 37 and 47 in the Oakland Growth Study. A subgroup of women at age 37, selected for showing increasing psychological health over the next ten years, revealed little of their considerable adolescent cognitive strengths. Ten years later, at age 47, such early strengths are evident again, when the decline of mothering, F. Livson speculates, may have freed these women to return to a detoured developmental course of self-assertion and intellectual mastery. The notion of women's return to detoured personal resources is suggested by T. Peskin (1975) to account for adolescent behavioral differences among married, divorced, and remarried women at the Berkeley Guidance Study. In their adolescence, divorced women at age 40 had been rated as more autonomous than those who stayed married. Among the divorced, those who did not remarry had been more autonomous in adolescence, presumably regaining the personal mastery lost in the female's socialized obligations to achieve for the marriage, not for the self.

A negative case for advancing life-span models for adolescence is the adolescent/adult factor typologies of Block with Haan (1971) based on an adult sample of mixed ages, namely, Guidance Study participants near age 30 and Oakland members near age 40. Block's rationale — that at either age ''you are pretty much the kind of person you are going to be'' (p. 112) — falls squarely in the genre of the ''adult-plateau'' rather than life-span research concerned with differential tasks of early and middle adulthood.

Some Hypotheses and Findings from a Uses-of-the-Past Perspective

Specifically, we hypothesized that differences in early preparation for phases of building a family will create differential access to the adolescent past between eras and sexes for the Berkeley Guidance and Oakland samples in two adult follow-ups. Guidance subjects were evaluated at age 30 and 40, Oakland Growth Study subjects at age 37 and 47.

Women are long prepared for marriage and motherhood, but little at all for disengaging from parenting when the last child is no longer in infancy or preschool (Pearlin, 1975; Lowenthal, Thurnher, & Chiriboga, 1975). When women are engaged in early childrearing, we would then expect larger access to the past than when they are nearer to disengagement from parenting. Specifically, such declining access should be evident between ages 30 and 40 when the oldest child of the Berkeley Guidance mothers has grown from early school age to near the senior year of high school and the youngest child from preschool to middle elementary school.

Men are socialized in youth to reach for goals in the adult world considerably beyond marriage and early parenting. Being established and settled in the adult world means that men plan for their lives over significantly longer distances than females (Brim & Forer, 1956; Douvan & Adelson, 1966; Ezekiel, 1968; Lessing, 1968). Accordingly, we should expect that men at age 40, drawing close to, or already settled down in, the adult world (Levinson, et al., 1974), will also draw amply from the adolescent past, where such long-term goals had been assimilated. Although research in time-perspective does not report whether adolescent males envision age 30 with as much clarity as females, one can imagine that males' longer view of their development is matched by considerable ambiguity about the less distant future of young manhood. Adult models for "being thirty" are not in abundance for the adolescent male, whose father is older and siblings and friends younger than age 30. Socialization for marriage and parenting, of course, is also less defined for the young man. We expected then that Berkeley Guidance men between the ages of 30 and 40 would show increasing access to the past.

Relative release from the constraints of sex and age roles in yet later stages of family organization should be reflected in access to past resources, which had been bypassed because irrelevant for earlier adult stages. Drawing on adolescent behaviors freed of such restraints should become more prominent between ages 37 and 47 for the Oakland Growth Study samples of men and women whose youngest children are well along in adolescence.

Operationally, degree of access to the past consisted of the sheer count of significant statistical associations between personality traits over early and late adolescence (evaluated by Q sort in junior and senior high school) and psychological health (Livson & Peskin, 1967) at each adult age. Psychological health, thus assessed, is taken to reflect overall adaptation to living at each adult age.

Results show that access to the adolescent past (in terms of numbers of significant adolescent-adult correlations) between ages 30 and 40 increases for Berkeley Guidance men and decreases for Berkeley Guidance women. At age 30, men draw far less from adolescence than they will at age 40; women reverse this trend, drawing more from the past at age 30 than age 40. Women's diminishing access is consistent with our view of their relatively greater preparation in youth for the early-adult tasks of family building and childrearing. The contrary finding for men is also consistent with our expectation that men at age 30 will turn little to the relatively closer adolescent past, but will do so once they may feel irrevocably established as an adult by age 40.

The specific content of the drawn-upon adolescent personality traits also supports the uses-of-the-past model at progressive adult eras. The relatively larger access by Berkeley Guidance women at age 30 pertains to adolescent traits reflecting both inner strength and a realistic orientation to the outer world: healthy women at age 30 draw on their earlier responsibility, insightfulness, intellectual competence, nurturance, and their earlier low power-orientation and lack of repression. (That these resources are drawn upon for the mothering role is supported also by similar findings only for the subgroup of women at age 40 with a preschool child). Men at age 40 draw on adolescent behaviors that reflect the sense of being established in the external world: healthy men at age 40 draw on their earlier sociability, sex-appropriate behavior, power-orientation, decisiveness, nurturance, and taking of responsibility.

Between ages 37 and 47 for both the men and women of the Oakland sample, access to the past actually increases. For men, this larger access draws on specific adolescent behaviors in the arena of sex-role expectations: healthy men at age 47 show use of their adolescent nurturance, sex-inappropriate behavior, lack of power-orientation, and esthetic reactivity. For women, a corresponding changeover is not so clearly on sex-role lines. Rather, healthy women at age 47 differentially draw on earlier cognitive competence and personal decisiveness.

The same behaviors in early and late adolescence had different, sometimes opposite, properties as resources for adult psychological health. For example, healthy men at age 30 draw on both early-adolescent irresponsibility and late-adolescent responsibility; healthy men at age 40 draw on both early-adolescent need-to-seek-reassurance and late-adolescent giving up of reassurance. Such findings point to the complex makeup of past resources. Moreover, directional behavioral reversals from early to late adolescence suggest that the healthy adult draws on whole *sequences* of earlier behavior that embody mastery or conflict-resolution (e.g., from seeking *to* foregoing reassurance) (see Peskin, 1972). It should be apparent from the discussion of our ''uses-of-the-past'' formulation that some fundamental redefinition of continuity within personality development between adolescence and its surrounding developmental stretches is not only implied, but required. The findings rather make a reasonable case for discontinuity in the sense, discussed earlier, that adolescent effects stand out more prominently than the over-time persistence of behaviors. First, predictive reversals were in evidence. Next, sleeper-effects occured beyond their statistical likelihood, both in the larger yield of early-adolescent than late-adolescent predictors, and in the larger number of adolescent predictors of later than earlier adulthood.

Toward a New Definition of Continuity in the Longitudinal Perspective

From our examination of the adolescent antecedents that contributed to adult psychological health, we clearly find that not only do different adult stages draw on different adolescent resources, but also (and more importantly for the present point) the general predictive picture is certainly not one of health predicting health. This should not come as a surprise, yet, it seems to us, that this sort of result has been long regarded as a negative one since it is taken to imply that the search for continuities in personality development within longitudinal studies, especially over long time spans, has questionable utility. This is so only from a particular — and, for us, narrow — view of continuity, one that looks only at regularities over time within the same characteristic. This view has long been with us, and has exerted a powerful influence both on how longitudinal researchers analyzed their data and how critics evaluated their results. Labeling this orientation as the ''stability template,'' Gergen (1977) observes that ''for many years the dominant theoretical form within developmental psychology placed greatest emphasis on the stability of behavior patterns over time'' and involves the assumption that ''without massive intervention . . . the same psychobehavioral patterns will relentlessly repeat throughout the life cycle'' (pp. 140–141).

We believe that investigations of personality development, and especially long-term, longitudinal studies, have been fundamentally and unnecessarily hampered by an almost exclusive focus on assessing the developmental stability of personality characteristics over time. Anyone who has done a longitudinal study over whatever time span in which the ''same'' personality characteristics were assessed for at least two developmental points has had something to say about their stability. Not only are the data varied on this question but so are the labels for this approach: ''isomorphic continuity'' (Bell, Weller, & Waldrop, 1971); ''individual stability'' (Emmerich, 1964); ''phenotypic persistence'' (Livson, 1973).

It would be inappropriate here to attempt a synthesis of studies of this sort, nor would such an attempt be particularly useful. Not only are the personality characteristics thus studied not defined identically, but also the methods and settings of their measurement are highly diverse. However, others have made such attempts. Yarrow and Yarrow (1964) present a good sketch of what they call ''phenotypic consistency'' within the earlier years; several useful summaries for the same period can be found in Iscoe and Stevenson (1960). Stone and Onqué's (1959) abstracts of longitudinal studies of child personality, while less convenient to use, can also be a valuable source. Neugarten (1964) overviews the middle years; she has also edited a selection of original reports for this time span (Neugarten, 1968). Kuhlen (1964) and Chown (1968) provide good reviews of data on later life. Bloom's (1964) *Stability and Change in Human Characteristics* attempts to cover infancy to adulthood and therefore is perhaps most relevant, if not up to date for adolescent data.

Cohen (1977) regards this latter review as providing ''consistent support for the stability model,'' but our assessment is less sanguine. By and large, one is not struck by inescapable regularities within the data on phenotypic persistence. Certainly there are no hard data on the long-term persistence of specific personality characteristics throughout development because longitudinal studies of entire lives have not yet been completed. The mass of rather chaotic data on this topic leaves the impression that, although some bits and pieces of personality do seem to persist over limited periods of development, few persuasive themes are yet evident. [In her succinct summary of continuities found in Berkeley's three longitudinal studies, Eichorn (1973) identifies some of these: introversion, warmth, expressiveness, and explosiveness.] Most data, however, refer to the persistence of specific traits, not to general dimensions defined in multivariate terms. Furthermore, such data are extraordinarily difficult to tie in with any full-blown theories of personality development. To be confined to, or even to focus on, overtime persistence of the ''same'' personality characteristics seems a foredoomed enterprise. Even if it were not risky to assume, for example, that the dependency of a two-year-old is psychologically identical with that of an adolescent, or of a middle-aged adult, it seems at best a curiously limiting strategy for exploiting longitudinal data. Why not extend the approach to looking at correlations among *phenotypically dissimilar* traits over time?

The so-called sleeper effect (Kagan & Moss, 1962), which we discussed earlier, seems a by-product of this unnecessary restriction to phenotypically defined channels of development. At least this appears to be the case in one of their examples of the effect — the greater predictability of "love-object dependency" in adult men from phenotypically, somewhat similar characteristics (passivity and fear of bodily harm) in the preschool period than from the same characteristics in later childhood and early adolescence. The sleeper effect, in this instance, refers to the lack of predictability and continuity within these later (and closer to adulthood) periods. Kagan and Moss (1962) suggest here only that "a covert disposition to passivity may be present during the school years and may find expression in adolescent and adult derivative reactions" (p. 278). This hypothesis may well be true, but it is hardly an explanation of the phenomenon. One might guess that this gap in phenotypic continuity could have been bridged by looking into what characteristics, other than some obvious variant of dependency, might have emerged during this apparent breakdown in continuity that might have been predicted from preschool passivity. These mediating characteristics might then, in turn, have predicted adult dependency.

The point of this too abbreviated history is to set the stage for another kind of definition of continuity — "genotypic continuity" (Livson, 1973). The definition follows immediately from a belief that personality is indeed a substantially predictable multidimensional construct throughout the life span if, *and only if,* we abandon the search for simple persistence or phenotypic continuity of specific personality characteristics over time. We feel confident that we can establish an underlying set of predictable patterns if, instead, we seek for genotypic continuity. To take one example from a recent paper (Livson, 1977): a conventionally socialized, very "nice" adolescent girl is likely to develop into an age-40 woman of considerable depth, strength, and interpersonal attractiveness. The two sets of characteristics, being "nice" and being interesting, bear no resemblance whatsoever to one another, yet it is possible to posit a reasonable theoretical basis for expecting such a developmental transformation.

If we are to permit our longitudinal data to detect unexpected relationships such as this one, we must employ multivariate techniques that are not intrinsically blind to other than phenotypic consistencies. By this we mean analyzing longitudinal data in a manner that assigns no priority to specific-trait stability and, instead, permits the data to reveal whatever threads of predictability do exist, whether or not these threads involve the same or different personality characteristics at the predicting and outcome ages. These threads *are* what Livson (1973) calls "developmental dimensions." Genotypic continuity, therefore, is the necessary assumption for expecting to detect such developmental dimensions.

We regard it as more than an assumption, however, because it seems for us to be an inevitable axiom for the life-span study of personality development. In this context (although it can be defined more broadly), it refers to the predictability (and postdictability), *in whatever form,* of personality organization between developmental points all along the life span. Put another way, genotypic continuity subsumes any and all evidence for an unbroken chain of causation, or at least connectedness (in the uses-of-the-past sense), linking all occasions at which personality organization is assessed. Phenotypic regularities may provide some of the links in this chain, but, insofar as these exist, they will be subsumed within the more general definition. Such genotypic continuity, we propose, does exist throughout personality development, and our methodology should permit its detection. The converse of this view, at the extreme, is the "situationist" conception of personality within which continuity is not to be expected at all, an approach which has been well presented and critiqued by Bowers (1973). A middle-ground orientation is the "aleatory-change" model proposed by Gergen (1977), which appears to allow for both genotypic continuity and situation-determined influences, and their interaction.

The methodology for extracting developmental dimensions from longitudinal data — canonical correlation — has been waiting in the wings for some time. Hotelling (1935, 1936) introduced canonical correlation as a method for analyzing the relationships between two sets of measurements. He regards the method as "predicting the most predictable criterion" in the sense that the canonical correlation is the maximum correlation that can possibly be obtained between linear combinations of variables within each of the two sets. In other words, the result of this procedure is a weighted composite score (or canonical variate) from each set which, when these two sets of scores are intercorrelated, the obtained correlation is the maximum attainable. Each analysis can yield additional canonical correlations with their accompanying pair of canonical variates since the procedure can be reapplied to residual covariance matrices. The only restriction is that successive variates are orthogonal to all preceding ones.

It is essential to realize that canonical variates do not define the dimensional structure of a set of personality measures *within* a given age level, as traditional factor analysis would do. Their natural focus, rather, is on the gap between ages, and it is precisely there that developmental dimensions — which tell us "what" from a given age predicts "what" at a later age — are necessarily to be found. And, operationally, these canonical variates *are* the developmental dimensions we have been discussing. Their function is to suggest how to dimensionalize personality to exploit the maximum predictability possible between developmental periods and to do so with no preference whatsoever given to phenotypic resemblance. Of course, it may turn out in a given analysis that an assortment of specific traits at one age yields the maximum possible correlation with a very similar assortment at another. But this outcome would be the "special case" because the normal course of personality development probably does not follow such neat channels.

To conclude this background, a brief example of empirical application of canonical correlation to longitudinal data will, perhaps, best clarify the presentation. It is taken from the first instance we know of involving the application of the method to personality development (Livson, 1965). The raw data were personality ratings of subjects in the Berkeley Guidance Study and consisted of sets of cluster scores derived separately from these ratings for the two sexes and for five age periods (early childhood, late childhood, early adolescence, late adolescence, and age 30). Although the cluster solutions were somewhat similar at each of these periods, they varied in numbers of clusters found and, in each instance, involved some clusters unique to a particular age period. Certain clusters did indicate substantial phenotypic persistence over all of the age periods (e.g., introversion) and other single clusters were predictable by multiple-regression techniques from combinations of cluster scores from earlier periods. For the present purpose, however, one of the results from two-set canonical correlation analyses carried out between all possible combinations of the five age periods will serve to illustrate the nature of the technique. Relating personality cluster dimensions from age-30 assessments to those from early adolescence, a significant canonical correlation ($p < .05$) was found for males, *although not one of the first-order correlations between the clusters at the two ages was itself significant.* The canonical factor or developmental dimension, which can be interpreted from the pattern of weights of individual variables (in this case, clusters) on the two canonical variates, can be read as follows: a boy who in early adolescence is quite independent, even cocky, and given to frequent explosive rages turns out (at age 30) to present a pattern of irresponsibility and a lack of warmth and generosity. No phenotypic continuity seems immediately evident here, but there is the suggestion of a developmental dimension connecting early adolescence and age 30. A possible interpretation of this dimension is that it involves a thread of unresolved adolescent rebellion. The specific behavioral form taken by this rebelliousness is, in a sense, appropriate in its expression — and therefore different in form — at the two age levels.

This result, of itself, is of course not a substantial one; its presentation has only the purpose of exemplifying the particular statistical technique being promoted, one which seems to have been bypassed in developmental psychology. There are other multivariate methods, such as multiple-regression and multiple-discriminant analysis, that have been used and that are also able to detect genotypic continuities, although with somewhat lesser sensitivity. These methods, taken together, constitute no panacea. They do, nevertheless, represent approaches that are far more finely tuned to those bands within developmental psychology's theoretical spectrum than are simple "persistence" correlations computed between time 1 and time 2. However, they require a diet rich in degrees of freedom if they are to bear statistically reliable fruit and, even then, still cry out for cross validation on new samples. Since longitudinal studies of development are typically on samples of modest size and since their data-overlap is also modest, these conditions are not easy to meet. Sterns and Alexander (1977) raise essentially these problems and question the appropriateness of available multivariate techniques generally for evaluating these kinds of relationships within developmental psychology. They recommend that "the field might be well advised to spend less effort contorting the interrelationships of human behavior to 'fit' existing statistical (particularly linear additive) models and begin the search for models that better fit the empirical and theoretical relationships of interest" (p. 116). They may be right but, at the moment, existing multivariate techniques, despite their drawbacks, seem to us to be the best game in town. When they can be used appropriately on longitudinal data, we suggest that such techniques hold out a promise for yielding, at the very least, fresh insights and hypotheses toward furthering our understanding of human development.

REFERENCES

Abhammer, I. M., and Baltes, P. B. Objective versus perceived age differences in personality: How do adolescents, adults, and older people view themselves and each other? *Journal of Gerontology, 1972, 27,* 46–51.

Ames, R. Physical maturing among boys as related to adult social behavior. *California Journal of Educational Research, 1957, 8,* 69–75.

Anthony, E. J. From birth to breakdown: A prospective study of vulnerability. In E. J. Anthony, C. Koupernik, and C. Chiland (Eds.), *The child in his family: Vulnerable children. Yearbook of the International Association for Child Psychiatry and Allied Professions,* Vol. 4. New York: Wiley, 1978.

Bachman, J. G., O'Malley, P. M., and Johnston, J. *Adolescence to adulthood — Change and stability in the lives of young men.* Ann Arbor: Institute for Social Research, University of Michigan, 1978.

Baldwin, A. L. The study of child behavior and development. In P. H. Mussen (Ed.), *Handbook of research methods in child development.* New York: Wiley, 1960.

Baltes, P. B. Longitudinal and cross-sectional sequences in the study of age and generation effects. *Human Development,* 1968, *11,* 145–171.

Baltes, P. B., Cornelius, S. W., and Nesselroade, J. R. Cohort effects in behavioral development: Theoretical and methodological perspectives. In W. A. Collins (Ed.), *Minnesota Symposium on Child Psychology* (Vol. 11). New York: T. R. Crowell, 1977.

Bartlett, F. C. *Remembering.* Cambridge: Cambridge University Press, 1932.

Bayley, N. Consistency and variability in the growth of intelligence from birth to eighteen years. *Journal of Genetic Psychology,* 1949, *75,* 165–196.

———. Research in child development: A longitudinal perspective. *Merrill-Palmer Quarterly,* 1965, *11,* 183–208.

Bell, R. Q. Convergence: An accelerated longitudinal approach. *Child Development,* 1953, *24,* 145–152.

Bell, R. Q., Weller, G. M., and Waldrop, M. F. Newborn and preschooler: Organization of behavior and relation between periods. *Monographs of the Society for Research in Child Development,* 1971, *36* (2, Serial No. 142).

Block, J. (in collaboration with Haan, N.). *Lives through time.* Berkeley, Calif.: Bancroft Books, 1971.

Bloom, B. S. *Stability and change in human characteristics.* New York: Wiley, 1964.

Blyth, D., Simmons, R., and Bush, D. The transition into early adolescence: A longitudinal comparison of youth in two educational contexts. *Sociology of Education,* 1978, *51,* 149–162.

Boutourline Young, H. Environmental influences upon time of arrival at puberty. *Rhode Island Journal of Medicine,* 1973, *56,* 265–273.

Bower, E., and Shellhamer, T. School characteristics of male adolescents who later become schizophrenic. *American Journal of Orthopsychiatry,* 1960, *30,* 712–729.

Bowers, K. S. Situationism in psychology: An analysis and a critique. *Psychological Review,* 1973, *80,* 307–336.

Brekstad, A. Factors influencing the reliability of anamnestic recall. *Child Development,* 1966, *37,* 603–612.

Brim, O. Life-span development of the theory of oneself: Implications for child development. In H. Reese (Ed.), *Advances in child development and behavior* (Vol. 11). New York: Academic, 1976.

Brim, O., and Forer, R. A note on the relation of values and social structure to life planning. *Sociometry,* 1956, *19,* 54–60.

Bronson, W. C. Adult derivatives of emotional expressiveness and reactivity-control: Developmental continuities from childhood to adulthood. *Child Development,* 1967, *38,* 801–817.

Brunswik, E. *Perception and the representative design of psychological experiments.* Berkeley, Calif.: University of California Press, 1956.

Chess, S., and Thomas, A. Temperamental individuality from childhood to adolescence. *Journal of the American Academy of Child Psychiatry,* 1977, *16,* 218–226.

Chown, S. M. Personality and aging. In K. W. Schaie (Ed.), *Theory and methods of research on aging.* Morgantown: West Virginia University Library, 1968.

Clausen, J. The social meaning of differential physical and sexual maturation. In S. Dragastin and G. H. Elder, Jr. (Eds.), *Adolescence in the life cycle.* New York: Wiley, 1975.

Cohen, S. H. Another look at the issue of continuity versus change in models of human development. In H. Datan and H. W. Reese (Eds.), *Life-span developmental psychology: Dialectical perspectives on experimental research.* New York: Academic, 1977.

Constantinople, A. An Eriksonian measure of personality development in college students. *Developmental Psychology,* 1969, *1,* 357–372.

Cottle, T., and Klineberg, S. *The present of things future*. New York: Free Press, 1974.

Crandall, V., and Battle, E. The antecedents and adult correlates of academic and intellectual achievement effort. In J. Hill (Ed.), *Minnesota Symposium on Child Psychology* (Vol. 4). Minneapolis: University of Minnesota Press, 1970.

Deutsch, H. *Selected problems of adolescence*. New York: International Universities Press, 1967.

Douvan, E., and Adelson, J. *The adolescent experience*. New York: Wiley, 1966.

Eichorn, D. The Berkeley longitudinal studies: Continuities and correlates of behaviour. *Canadian Journal of the Behavioural Sciences*, 1973, *5*, 297–320.

————. Asynchronizations in adolescent development. In S. Dragastin and G. H. Elder, Jr. (Eds.), *Adolescence in the life cycle*. New York: Wiley, 1975.

Elder, G. H., Jr. *Children of the Great Depression*. Chicago: The University of Chicago Press, 1974.

Elder, G. H., Jr. Historical change in life patterns and personality. In P. B. Baltes and O. G. Brim (Eds.), *Life-span development and behavior* (Vol. 2). New York: Academic Press, 1979.

Elder, G. H., Jr. and Rockwell, R. W. Economic depression and postwar opportunity in men's lives: A study of life patterns and health. In R. G. Simmons (Ed.), *Research in community and mental health: An annual compilation of research*. Greenwich, Conn.: JAI Press, 1978.

Emmerich, W. Continuity and stability in early social development. *Child Development*, 1964, *35*, 311–332.

Erikson, E. H. Identity and the life cycle: Selected papers. In *Psychological Issues* (Vol. 1). New York: International Universities Press, 1959.

————. Reflections on the dissent of contemporary youth. *Daedalus*, 1970, *99*, 154–176.

Ezekiel, R. The personal future and peace corps competence. *Journal of Personality and Social Psychology Monograph*, 1968, *8*(2, Pt. 2). (Supplement)

Feigelson, C. Reconstruction of adolescence (and early latency) in the analysis of an adult woman. In R. Eissler et al. (Eds.), *The psychoanalytic study of the child* (Vol. 31). New York: International Universities Press, 1976.

Flavell, J. H. *The developmental psychology of Jean Piaget*. Princeton, N. J.: Van Nostrand, 1963.

Frenkel-Brunswik, E. Motivation and behavior. *Genetic Psychology Monographs*, 1942, *26*, 121–265.

Freud, A. Adolescence. In R. S. Eissler et al. (Eds.), *The psychoanalytic study of the child* (Vol. 13). New York: International Universities Press, 1958.

Gergen, K. J. Stability, change, and chance in understanding human development. In H. Datan and H. W. Reese (Eds.), *Life-span developmental psychology: Dialectical perspectives on experimental research*. New York: Academic, 1977.

Goldstein, M., Rodnick, E., Jones, J., McPherson, S., and West, K. *Familial precursors of schizophrenia: Spectrum disorders*. Paper presented at the Second Rochester International Conference on Schizophrenia, Rochester, New York, May 1976.

Greulich, W. W., Day, H. G., Lachman, S. E., Wolfe, J. B., and Shuttleworth, F. K. A handbook of methods for the study of adolescent children. *Monographs of the Society for Research in Child Development*, 1938, *3*(2, Serial No. 15).

Gutmann, D. Developmental issues in the masculine mid-life crisis. *Journal of Geriatric Psychiatry*, 1976, *9*, 41–59.

Haan, N. *Some comparisons of various Oakland Growth Study subsamples on selected variables*. Unpublished manuscript. Berkeley: Institute of Human Development, University of California, 1962.

————. The adolescent antecedents of an ego model of coping and defense and comparisons with Q-sorted ideal personalities. *Genetic Psychology Monographs,* 1974, *89,* 273–306.

————. *Coping and defending: Processes of self-environment organization.* New York: Academic, 1977.

Haan, N., and Day, D. A longitudinal study of change and sameness in personality development: Adolescence to later adulthood. *International Journal of Aging and Human Development,* 1974, *5,* 11–39.

Hafner, A., Quast, W., and Shea, M. The adult adjustment of one thousand psychiatric and pediatric patients: Initial findings from a twenty-five year follow-up. In R. Wirt et al. (Eds.), *Life history research in psychopathology* (Vol. 4). Minneapolis: University of Minnesota Press, 1975.

Hauser, S. *Black and white identity formation.* New York: Wiley, 1971.

Hertz, M. R., and Baker, E. Personality changes in adolescence. *Rorschach Research Exchange,* 1941, *5,* 30–34.

Honzik, M. P., Macfarlane, J. W., and Allen, L. The stability of mental test performance between two and eighteen years. *Journal of Experimental Education,* 1948, *17,* 309–324.

Hotelling, H. The most predictable criterion. *Journal of Educational Psychology,* 1935, *26,* 139–142.

————. Relations between two sets of variates. *Biometrika,* 1936, *28,* 321–377.

Iscoe, I., and Stevenson, H. W. (Eds.). *Personality development in children.* Austin: University of Texas Press, 1960.

Jessor, R., and Jessor, S. *Problem behavior and psychosocial development.* New York: Academic, 1977.

Jones, F. A four-year follow-up of vulnerable adolescents: The prediction of outcomes in early adulthood from measures of social competence, coping style, and overall level of psychopathology. *Journal of Nervous and Mental Disease,* 1974, *159,* 20–39.

Jones, H. E. Physical ability as a factor in social adjustment in adolescence. *Journal of Educational Research,* 1946, *39,* 287–301.

————. Adolescence in our society. In *The family in a democratic society.* Anniversary papers of The Community Service Society of New York. New York: Columbia University Press, 1949.

————. Problems of method in longitudinal research. *Vita Humana,* 1958, *1,* 93–99.

Jones, M. C. The later careers of boys who were early- or late-maturing. *Child Development,* 1957, *28,* 113–128.

————. A study of socialization patterns at the high school level. *Journal of Genetic Psychology,* 1958, *93,* 87–111.

————. Psychological correlates of somatic development. *Child Development,* 1965, *36,* 899–911.

Jones, M. C., and Bayley, N. Physical maturing among boys as related to behavior. *Journal of Educational Psychology,* 1950, *41,* 129–148.

Jordaan, J., and Super, D. The prediction of early adult vocational behavior. In D. Ricks et al. (Eds), *Life history research in psychopathology* (Vol. 3). Minneapolis: University of Minnesota Press, 1974.

Jung, C. The stages of life. In J. Campbell (Ed.), *The portable Jung.* New York: Viking, 1971. (Originally published, 1933.)

Kagan, J., and Moss, H. *Birth to maturity.* New York: Wiley, 1962.

Kandel, D. Stages in adolescent involvement in drug use. *Science,* 1975, *190,* 912–914.

Kiernan, K. Age at puberty in relation to age at marriage and parenthood: A national longitudinal study. *Annals of Human Biology,* 1977, *4,* 301–308.

Kodlin, D., and Thompson, D. J. An appraisal of the longitudinal approach to studies of growth and development. *Monographs of the Society for Research in Child Development,* 1958, *23*(1, Serial No. 67).

Kuhlen, R. G. Personality change with age. In P. Worchel and D. Byrne (Eds.), *Personality change.* New York: Wiley, 1964.

Lessing, E. Demographic, developmental, and personality correlates of length of future time perspective. *Journal of Personality,* 1968, *36,* 183–201.

Levinson, D., Darrow, C., Klein, E., Levinson, M., and McKee, B. The psychosocial development of men in early adulthood and the mid-life transitions. In D. Ricks et al. (Eds.), *Life history research in psychopathology* (Vol. 3). Minneapolis: University of Minnesota Press, 1974.

Lief, H., and Thompson, J. The prediction of behavior from adolescence to adulthood. *Psychiatry,* 1961, *24,* 32–38.

Livson, F. Paths to psychological health in the middle years: Sex differences. In D. H. Eichorn et al. (Eds.), *Present and past in middle life.* New York: Academic Press, in press.

Livson, N. Developmental dimensions of personality: A longitudinal analysis. In R. C. Tryon (Chair), *Personality dimensions and typologies revealed by modern cluster analysis.* Symposium presented at the Western Psychological Association, Honolulu, 1965.

————. Developmental dimensions of personality: A life-span formulation. In P. B. Baltes and K. W. Schaie (Eds.), *Life-span developmental psychology: Personality and socialization.* New York: Academic, 1973.

————. *The physically attractive woman at age 40: Precursors in adolescent personality and adult correlates from a longitudinal study.* Paper presented at the International Conference on Love and Attraction, University of Swansea, Wales, September 1977.

Livson, N., and Bronson, W. C. An exploration of patterns of impulse control in early adolescence. *Child Development,* 1961, *32,* 75–88.

Livson, N., and Day, D. Adolescent personality antecedents of completed family size: A longitudinal study. *Journal of Youth and Adolescence,* 1977, *6,* 311–324.

Livson, N., and Peskin, H. Prediction of adult psychological health in a longitudinal study. *Journal of Abnormal Psychology,* 1967, *72,* 509–518.

Lowenthal, M., Thurnher, M., and Chiriboga, D. *Four stages of life.* San Francisco: Jossey-Bass, 1975.

Masterson, J. Prognosis in adolescent disorders. *American Journal of Psychiatry,* 1958, *114,* 1097–1103.

Mednick, S. A., and Shaffer, B. P. Mothers' retrospective reports in child-rearing research. *American Journal of Orthopsychiatry,* 1963, *33,* 457–461.

Milner, E. Effects of sex role and social status on the early adolescent personality. *Genetic Psychology Monographs,* 1949, *40,* 231–325.

Mönks, F. J., van den Munckhof, H. C. P., Wels, P. M. A., and Kowalski, C. J. Application of Schaie's most efficient design in a study of the development of Dutch children. *Human Development,* 1975, *18,* 466–475.

Moore, T., and Clautour, S. Attitudes of life in children and young adolescents. *Scandinavian Journal of Psychology,* 1977, *18,* 10–20.

More, D. M. Developmental concordance and discordance during puberty and early adolescence. *Monographs of the Society for Research in Child Development,* 1953, *18*(1, Serial No. 56).

Moriarty, A., and Toussieng, P. Adolescence in a time of transition. *Bulletin of the Menninger Clinic,* 1975, *39,* 391–408.

Murphey, E., Silber, E., Coelho, G., Hamburg, D., and Greenberg, I. Development of autonomy and parent-child interaction in late adolescence. *American Journal of Orthopsychiatry,* 1963, *33,* 643–652.

Murphy, L., and Moriarty, A. *Vulnerability, coping and growth.* New Haven, Conn.: Yale University Press, 1976.

Mussen, P. H. Some antecedents and consequents of masculine sex typing in adolescent boys. *Psychological Monographs,* 1961, *75*(9, Whole No. 506).

Mussen, P. H., and Boutourline Young, H. Personality characteristics of physically advanced and retarded adolescents in Italy and the United States. *Vita Humana,* 1964, *7,* 186–200.

Mussen, P. H., and Jones, M. C. Self-conceptions, motivations, and interpersonal attitudes of late- and early-maturing boys. *Child Development,* 1957, *28,* 243–256.

————. The behavior-inferred motivations of late- and early-maturing boys. *Child Development,* 1958, *29,* 61–67.

Nameche, G., Waring, M., and Ricks, D. Early indicators of outcome in schizophrenia. *Journal of Nervous and Mental Disease,* 1964, *139,* 232–240.

Nawas, M. Change in efficiency of ego functioning and complexity from adolescence to young adulthood. *Developmental Psychology,* 1971, *4,* 412–415.

Nesselroade, J., and Baltes, P. B. Adolescent personality development and historical change: 1970–1972. *Monographs of the Society for Research in Child Development,* 1974, *39*(1, Serial No. 154).

Neugarten, B. L. *Personality in middle and late life.* New York: Atherton, 1964.

————. *Middle age and aging: A reader in social psychology.* Chicago: University of Chicago Press, 1968.

————. Continuities and discontinuities of psychological issues into adult life. *Human Development,* 1969, *12,* 121–130.

Nicolson, A. B., and Hanley, C. Indices of physiological maturity: Derivation and interrelationships. *Child Development,* 1953, *24,* 3–38.

Offer, D. *The psychological world of the teen-ager.* New York: Basic Books, 1969.

Offer, D., and Offer, J. *From teenage to young manhood.* New York: Basic Books, 1975.

Pearlin, L. Sex roles and depression. In N. Datan and L. Ginsberg (Eds.), *Life-span developmental psychology.* New York: Academic, 1975.

Peck, R., and Havighurst, R. *The psychology of character development.* New York: Wiley, 1960.

Peskin, H. Possible relations of growth and maturity to early psychic experiences. In H. Boutourline Young (Chair), *Biological Time.* Symposium presented at the meeting of the Society for Research in Child Development, Berkeley, California, April 1963.

————. Pubertal onset and ego functioning: A psychoanalytic approach. *Journal of Abnormal Psychology,* 1967, *72,* 1–15.

————. The duration of normal menses as a psychosomatic phenomenon. *Psychosomatic Medicine,* 1968, *30,* 378–389.

————. Multiple prediction of adult psychological health from preadolescent and adolescent behaviors. *Journal of Consulting and Clinical Psychology,* 1972, *38,* 155–160.

————. Influence of the developmental schedule of puberty on learning and ego functioning. *Journal of Youth and Adolescence,* 1973, *2,* 273–290.

Peskin, H., and Gigy, L. Time perspective in adult transitions. Paper presented at the Gerontology Society, San Francisco, November 1977.

Peskin, H., and Livson, N. Pre- and post-pubertal personality and adult psychologic functioning. *Seminars in Psychiatry,* 1972, *4,* 343–353.

Peskin, H., and Livson, N. Uses of the past in adult psychological health. In D. H. Eichorn et al. (Eds.), *Present and past in middle life*. New York: Academic Press, in press.

Peskin, T. *Personality antecedents of marital careers*. Paper presented at the Gerontology Society, Louisville, October 1975.

Piaget, J. *Play, dreams, and imitation in childhood*. New York: Norton, 1962.

Report of the Laboratory for the Study of Adolescence. Chicago: Institute for Psychosomatic and Psychiatric Research and Training, Michael Reese Hospital and Medical Center, 1978.

Robins, L. *Deviant children grow up: A sociological and psychiatric study of sociopathic personality*. Baltimore: Williams & Wilkins, 1966.

Robinson, B. *Centering and the passage to adulthood*. Unpublished doctoral dissertation, University of California, San Francisco, 1978.

Rosenthal, I. Reliability of retrospective reports of adolescence. *Journal of Consulting Psychology*, 1963, *27*, 189–198.

Savin-Williams, R. An ethological study of dominance formation and maintenance in a group of human adolescents. *Child Development*, 1976, *47*, 972–979.

Schaefer, E. S., and Bayley, N. Maternal behavior, child behavior, and their intercorrelations from infancy through adolescence. *Monographs of the Society for Research in Child Development*, 1963, *28*(3, Serial No. 87).

Schaie, K. W. A general model for the study of developmental problems. *Psychological Bulletin*, 1965, *64*, 92–107.

———. A reinterpretation of age related changes in cognitive structure and functioning. In L. R. Goulet and P. B. Baltes (Eds.), *Life-span developmental psychology: Research and theory*. New York: Academic, 1970.

Schmidt, M. *Somatische und psychische Faktoren der Reifeentwicklung*. Munich: Johann Amrosium Barth, 1965.

Simmons, R., Blyth, D., Van Cleave, E., and Bush, D. *The impact of school structure and puberty upon the self-esteem of early adolescents*. Paper presented at the meeting of the Society for Research in Child Development, New Orleans, March 1977.

Skolnick, A. Motivational imagery and behavior over twenty years. *Journal of Consulting Psychology*, 1966a, *30*, 463–478.

———. Stability and interrelationships of thematic test imagery over twenty years. *Child Development*, 1966b, *37*, 389–396.

Spiegel, L. Comments on the psychoanalytic psychology of adolescence. In R. S. Eissler et al. (Eds.), *The psychoanalytic study of the child* (Vol. 13). New York: International Universities Press, 1958.

Steinberg, L. *Transformations in family relations over the male pubertal cycle*. Unpublished manuscript, Cornell University, 1978.

Sterns, H. L., and Alexander, R. A. Cohort, age, and time of measurement: Biomorphic considerations. In H. Datan and H. W. Reese (Eds.), *Life-span developmental psychology: Dialectical perspectives on experimental research*. New York: Academic, 1977.

Stewart, L. H. Social and emotional adjustment during adolescence as related to the development of psychosomatic illness in adulthood. *Genetic Psychology Monographs*, 1962, *65*, 175–215.

Stolz, H. R., and Stolz, L. M. *Somatic development of adolescent boys*. New York: Macmillan, 1951.

Stone, A., and Onqué, G. *Longitudinal studies of child personality*. Cambridge: Harvard University Press, 1959.

Sullivan, H. S. *The interpersonal theory of psychiatry*. New York: Norton, 1953.

Symonds, P., and Jensen, A. *From adolescent to adult*. New York: Columbia University Press, 1961.

Tanner, J. *Growth at adolescence*. Springfield, Ill.: Thomas, 1962.

Tindall, R. H. The male adolescent involved with a pederast becomes an adult. *Journal of Homosexuality,* 1978, *3,* 374–382.

Trent, J., and Medsker, L. *Beyond high school*. Center for Research and Development in Higher Education, University of California, Berkeley, 1967.

Tryon, C. Evaluations of adolescent personality by adolescents. *Monographs of the Society for Research in Child Development,* 1939, *4*(4, Serial No. 23).

Tuddenham, R. D. Studies in reputation. III: Correlates of popularity among elementary school children. *Journal of Educational Psychology,* 1951, *42,* 257–276.

———. The constancy of personality ratings over two decades. *Genetic Psychology Monographs,* 1959, *60,* 3–29.

Vaillant, G., and McArthur, C. Natural history of male psychologic health. I: The adult life cycle from 18–50. *Seminars in Psychiatry,* 1972, *4,* 415–427.

Vlach, W. *Young adult life style and substance use: A study of working class males*. Unpublished doctoral dissertation, California School of Professional Psychology, San Francisco, 1977.

Wallerstein, J., and Kelly, J. The effects of parental divorce: The adolescent experience. In E. Anthony and C. Koupernik (Eds.), *The child in his family: Children at psychiatric risk* (Vol. 3). New York: Wiley, 1974.

———. The effects of parental divorce: Experiences of the preschool child. *Journal of the American Academy of Child Psychiatry,* 1975, *14,* 600–616.

———. The effects of parental divorce: Experiences of the child in later latency. *American Journal of Orthopsychiatry,* 1976, *46,* 256–269.

———. *Divorcing with children: The first five years*. New York: Basic Books, 1980.

Watt, N. Childhood and adolescent routes to schizophrenia. In D. Ricks et al. (Eds.), *Life history research in psychopathology* (Vol. 3). Minneapolis: University of Minnesota Press, 1974.

Watt, N., and Lubensky, A. Childhood roots of schizophrenia. *Journal of Consulting and Clinical Psychology,* 1976, *44,* 363–375.

Weinstock, A. Family environment and the development of defense and coping mechanisms. *Journal of Personality and Social Psychology,* 1967a, *5,* 67–75.

———. Longitudinal study of social class and defense preferences. *Journal of Consulting Psychology,* 1967b, *31,* 539–541.

Wenar, C., and Coulter, J. B. A reliability study of developmental histories. *Child Development,* 1962, *33,* 453–462.

Werner, E. E., and Smith, R. S. *Kauai's children come of age*. Honolulu: University Press of Hawaii, 1977.

Widdowson, E. Mental contentment and physical growth. *Lancet,* 1951, *1,* 1316–1318.

Wohlwill, J. F. The age variable in psychological research. *Psychological Review,* 1970, *77,* 49–64.

———. *The study of behavioral development*. New York: Academic, 1973.

Yarrow, M. R., Campbell, J. D., and Burton, R. V. Recollections of childhood: A study of the retrospective method. *Monographs of the Society for Research in Child Development,* 1970, *35*(5, Serial No. 138).

Yarrow, L. J., and Yarrow, M. R. Personality continuity and change in the family context. In P. Worchel and D. Byrne (Eds.), *Personality change*. New York: Wiley, 1964.

CHAPTER 3

The Psychodynamic Approach to Adolescence

Joseph Adelson and Margery J. Doehrman

In his famous poem in memory of Sigmund Freud, W. H. Auden writes:

> To us he is no more a person
> Now but a whole climate of opinion.

That is even more the case today than it was when the poem was written, shortly after Freud's death in 1939: the psychodynamic point of view has penetrated the common consciousness in almost all strata of American society. Several years ago, in the course of interviewing adolescents on their political ideas, it came as a surprise to note the ease and degree with which youngsters made use of ideas and language stemming from the psychodynamic tradition — the idea, for example, that the springs of motivation are often hidden from the self or the idea that the family is often the crucible within which character and behavior are forced (Adelson, 1972). In that sense all of us now dwell within the Freudian climate and, that being so, it is difficult to isolate the psychodynamic approach from common parlance. This chapter will therefore spare the reader an extended treatment of the more widely understood psychodynamic doctrines.

A second preliminary caveat: the commonplaceness of psychodynamic ideas is also reflected within this volume. Some of the chapters are largely and directly within that tradition (e.g., Chapter 5 by Marcia and Chapter 6 by Josselson) and several more either discuss or draw on it significantly (Chapter 4 by Petersen and Taylor, Chapter 9 by Hoffman, and Chapter 14 by Weiner, among others). One might even make the case that our chapter is superfluous, given the degree to which many of the essential notions of psychodynamic thinking have already penetrated specific topics within this collection; we have ourselves been tempted, more than once, to abandon our chapter on grounds of redundancy. We have persuaded ourselves not to do so for two rather separate reasons: (1) it is useful for the reader to have at hand in one place the essentials of the psychodynamic theory taken in toto and (2) to allow a *critical* consideration of the approach.

A few words about why our stance will be critical. This essay began as a more or less conventional handbook chapter, in both tone and format. In tone, it was to be evenhanded; in format, expository. To some degree, these earlier intentions persist. But as we searched the recent literature, we found ourselves increasingly troubled at what seems to us to be a continuing failure to realize the potentials of the psychodynamic approach. In an oft-quoted statement made about two decades ago, Anna Freud termed the study of adolescence a "stepchild" in psychoanalytic theory (A. Freud, 1958, pp. 255–278). She meant that the period had not received the full attention of psychoanalytic writers, that it was victimized by neglect.

Since that time, the degree of neglect is no longer quite so considerable. If one surveys sequentially the volumes of *The Psychoanalytic Study of the Child,* one finds a modest, but steady, increase in the number of papers devoted to adolescence. There is an organization devoted exclusively to adolescent psychiatry. It publishes an annual volume of papers, entitled *Adolescent Psychiatry,* covering the widest range of topics. In addition, developmental psychology journals have begun to apply "affirmative-action" principles on behalf of manuscripts on adolescence, so that papers dealing with the period are given something of an edge in the editorial process. All of this suggests that the unsatisfactory state of writing in adolescent psychodynamic psychology is no longer due to neglect, and that we ought to look elsewhere for an explanation. Our examination of the literature led us to believe that the problems are due to some unfortunate intellectual habits, specifically, a restricted methodology, a narrowness of range in the populations studied, and an overall parochialism in theory.

It was this dolorous recognition that led, slowly but implacably, to our decision to attempt a critical analysis of the psychodynamic doctrine, with less attention given to explicating who said what, when, rather more given to analyzing these tendencies. The loss is rather less than one might imagine, since there is a remarkable degree of redundancy in the literature, with "B" merely repeating what "A" said many years before or, even more commonly, "B" repeating himself ad infinitum, and adding very little new to our understanding. Hence this chapter is organized in three major sections: we begin with an exposition of the core ideas of the psychodynamic approach, that is, what we take to be the central conceptions by which those of us who are psychodynamically oriented attempt to understand and organize the events of the adolescent period; we then continue on to a discussion (rather briefer because parts of it are considered more fully in other sections of this volume) of some new directions in the canon; and finally, we offer some comments on the intellectual constrictions that to our mind inhibit more rapid conceptual progress in this tradition.

THE CORE IDEAS

Regression

It is by now generally understood that most psychodynamic theories are *historical,* that is, they hold that the person's experience of the present can be grasped fully only by some reference to his or her past. It is not an inflexible historicism since it is recognized that the burden of the past is at times so light as to be nearly nonexistent, that in many situations the person responds mainly to the exigencies or the clamor of the moment. Nevertheless, in comparison with almost all competing theories, the psychodynamic is distinctive in its emphasis on personal history. It holds that in truly important moments of one's life one is unwittingly held captive by the past. Whom we marry and how the marriage fares; the work we choose and how well we do it; whether we have children and when and how we raise them and feel about them; when we become ill and how we survive or fail to — all these and other vital events of the life course can be understood in depth only after we have a sufficient understanding of the personal past.

To say this may seem merely to repeat a psychodynamic truism, but what is not fully sensed is the seriousness with which this assumption is held and maintained. Suppose, for example, that having a "natural" bent for the sciences and hence being free to choose among a variety of vocations — medicine, physics, mathematics, biology, and so on — the specific choice one makes is physics. In that case the psychodynamic theorist or practitioner would feel constrained to ask, Why physics and why not something else? — raising that question in relation to the childhood history. Merely raising the question does not suggest that the answer will be found through a study of one's personal history; it may well be that one chooses physics simply because it is at the moment prestigious or lavishly funded, or what have you. Nevertheless the psychodynamic theorist would certainly earnestly scrutinize the possibility that the choice is neither "free" nor "objective," that it is in some way conditioned by unknown circumstances in one's personal history, for example, that the personal or collective imagery of physics has some particular appeal rooted in the past or that a significant teacher is linked psychologically to a significant family figure. The reverberations from the past are of course felt even more forcefully in such spheres as the erotic, love, and childrearing.

All this may seem sweeping enough, yet in relation to adolescence the psychodynamic approach places an even greater degree of emphasis on personal history, for it holds that the recrudescence of the past is essential to *normal* development in the adolescent years. Here is Peter Blos, in the course of a highly influential article:

> Adolescent regression, which is not defensive in nature, constitutes an integral part of development at puberty. This regression, nevertheless, induces anxiety more often than not. Should this anxiety become unmanageable, then, secondarily, defensive measures become mobilized. Regression in adolescence is not, in and by itself, a defense, but it constitutes an essential psychic process that, despite the anxiety it engenders, must take its course. Only then can the task be fulfilled that is implicit in adolescent development.

[Blos, 1967, p. 173] Note that the adolescent regression in normal development is taken not merely as frequent and acceptable, but as universal and necessary; as a corollary, it is held that the absence of a sufficient degree of regression is prima facie evidence of a fault in development.

As we shall see in a moment, the theory of regression as currently formulated leaves us with many unanswered questions: Which systems of personality undergo regression, to what degree, and under what circumstances? One sometimes has the feeling in reading the literature that the term is used in an almost incantatory fashion to explain any and all adolescent phenomena. Yet that should not dissuade us from recognizing the presence and power of regressive phenomena at critical moments in adolescence. Perhaps the most visible (though not necessarily the most profound) expressions of regression are to be seen during the middle years of the period, between 14 and 17 (the dates are to be taken as approximate), wherein it is not at all difficult to discern a striking reappearance of the oedipal drama. The boy may suddenly turn surly or sullen or cocky or competitive or scornful vis à vis his father; the girl may treat her mother with withering scorn or her most patronizing, brittle "friendliness," or may be overcome with dark, inexplicable rages. With respect to the opposite-sex parent, the oedipal revival is generally more decorous or more disguised. Yet even so it is not uncommon to see fairly clear signs of it: the boy displaying his muscles to his mother or the girl reacting to her father with an exaggerated embarrassment or provocativeness, calling attention to the otherwise unspoken sexual dialogue between them.

Still, these are only the most direct, least complex reflections of the oedipal revival (which is, in turn, the most easily perceived aspect of adolescent regressiveness). Much of the time oedipal motifs are expressed indirectly, for example, in erotic or love fantasies or in collective fantasy (responding to films or novels). In other instances the significant expression of oedipal feeling may involve displacement via the choice of love objects (or adversaries) who represent the parents and with or towards whom acts of defiance or conquest or rivalry are carried out. Instances of this are seen quite commonly in clinical practice with youngsters, and there is no reason to believe it will not be possible to explore these phenomena in other populations as well. Sherry Hatcher (1973), for example, has provided some revealing examples of the oedipal regression in her study of out-of-wedlock pregnancy among adolescent and young adult women. She found that those who were in the middle-adolescent phase of psychosocial growth — as measured by psychological tests — showed patterns that reflected clearly the presence of oedipal motifs both in what led up to the pregnancy and the response to it, for example, the babies' fathers were more often married men; the conception more often took place in the parental home; it was the mother (rather than a friend or the lover) who was first told about the pregnancy; and so on. Hence the pregnancy seemed to represent an unconscious effort to live out the oedipal drama, conceiving and bearing a child by a paternal surrogate.

The most recent psychoanalytic theories of adolescence give an even greater role to regressive processes than earlier ones did, in particular, Peter Blos's phase theory (1962) postulates a sequence from early to midadolescence that involves the sequential recapitulation of preoedipal and oedipal experiences. That drive, ego, and superego regressions are frequent in adolescence seems well supported by the almost universal testimony of clinicians and supported to a lesser degree, by more carefully controlled observation, see the suggestive evidence from longitudinal studies compiled by Livson and Peskin in Chapter 2, particularly their discussion of work by Peskin (1972) and Haan (1974).

Nevertheless, the theory of regression, when examined closely, raises a great many questions still largely unanswered. Like much else in psychoanalytic theory, the idea of regression arises at a specific observation made in specific cases — and is then universalized. That sequence, from the particular to the universal, tends in its very nature to omit variations and differentiations. Hence the theory does not yet tell us as much as we need to know about patterns and tendencies in regression: Which systems of the personality are vulnerable to regression, and when, and under what circumstances? Until we take some further steps toward achieving that specificity, the theory of regression — and with it psychodynamic theory — will remain radically incomplete. A colleague, a shrewd woman with long clinical experience with adolescents, told us recently that when she undertakes clinical work with a teenager, she knows that she will uncover a significant regression or recapitulation, but that she does not know what it will be. That is, she knows that the neurotic crisis of adolescence will have been brought on by a regressive episode, but it remains unclear initially whether the crisis will relate to an earlier problem in separation; with the oedipal conflict, negative or positive; or whatever. Clinical testimony of this sort reminds us that adolescence is regression-prone, probably more than any other era of the life cycle, but it does not as yet tell us much more than that.

The Drives and Emotions

Here, too, we have an emphasis in the psychodynamic approach that is understood widely, but often not too well. One need not belabor the point that psychoanalysis traditionally has been rooted in instinct theory and that its conception of adolescence has placed the drives and their destiny at the center. Adolescence seemed to involve a powerful resurgence of the drives, so much so that their control (via the defenses) and their transformation (via displacements and sublimation) has been the essential formula for the psychoanalytic view of the adolescent period. To be sure, the drive theory has in recent years been removed from the center of concern, but this is so only because it is deemed so well established that it need no longer be argued. Thus in current writing more attention is given to such topics as: object-attachment (the relationship to others); to the self and its vicissitudes (identity, narcissism, and the like); and to internalized structures of the personality (the superego, the ego ideals).

When we speak of the resurgence of drives in adolescence we generally intend to connote more than the appearance of conscious sexual urges. Although these can represent acute problems, especially for boys, they are only part of the picture and in most respects the least important part. The boy coping with *recognized* sexuality — with erections, prurience, "insane" impulses, and the like — is certainly subject to periods of profound distress, because of anxiety, shame, guilt, embarrassment, and so on. Yet as painful as these feelings may sometimes be, they are probably not quite as troublesome for the youngster's adjustment as are drives and derivatives not so easily recognized, in particular, dependency and sadism. Here again it is the regressive aspect of these drives with which the child finds it most difficult to deal, in that the instinctual upsurge threatens to revive atavistic elements of the personality, in particular, primitive oral dependencies and yearnings, anal cruelties and rages, and the like. As we shall see in the next section, the task of *defending* against the emergence of these drives has for some years been understood as the central intrapsychic problem of adolescence in the psychoanalytic view of things.

The emphasis on instincts — and latterly on object attachments — has so tended to dominate discourse that the emotions, intensely felt at adolescence, have been somewhat neglected as an object of study. Of course, most writers do make note of the emotional volatility of the period — it is far too conspicuous to overlook. There has been less attention given to a particularized understanding of the affects, to their sources, their effects, their vicissitudes, the defenses against them, the strategies the social order develops for controlling and channelling them. For example, no one who has worked with adolescents clinically can fail to be impressed by the importance of shame and defenses against shame in the social transactions of adolescence — the ways in which rumor and gossip and the expectation of shame govern the way adolescents deal with each other. The vicissitudes of shame — pride, "shamelessness," display, mortification, morbid shyness — are central in the phenomenology of adolescence. Indeed, we are fairly certain that shyness is the most common "symptom" normal adolescents complain about; one is also struck by the frequency with which youngsters who seem to be free of shyness are envied by their peers. Beyond that, the social system (the family, the peer group, and such institutions as church and school) uses these and other exfoliations of shame in the course of socializing youngsters toward "larger" social goals or in the aim of containing and channelling the potentially explosive energies of the young.

The Ego and the Defenses

In our view, the definitive account of the psychodynamics of adolescence, both for better and for worse, is Anna Freud's characteristically lucid, succinct treatment of the topic written in 1958. It is worth noting that the paper places at its forefront of concern the role of the defense mechanisms in adolescent adjustment. In so doing, Anna Freud was, a generation later, continuing the emphasis of her earliest contributions to this field. She was able to illustrate both the defensive sides of adolescent psychology and the pathological variations of ego functioning by close and revealing examination of the ego's defensive operations in the adolescent years (A. Freud, 1966).

In the earlier discussion, Anna Freud was concerned to demonstrate that the increased urgency of the instincts produced, in turn, a heightened vigilance of defense. Hence many of the peculiar aspects of adolescent behavior ought to be understood as ways of taming the instinctual beast: children who become "ascetic," who turn away from the temptations of the flesh and, in the course of doing so, seem to abandon or lose the usual animal spirits of adolescence; or children who lose themselves in the pursuit of interests that soon take on an obsessive, even magical meaning (these days one is particularly apt to see this among those youngsters who become transfixed by computers); or youngsters who give themselves over to one or another form of fanaticism.

In these and similar instances, the most efficient formula for some years had seemed to be along id versus ego-superego lines. In time, that formula began to seem both thin and a bit mechanical, especially so as we began to grasp the importance of object attachments. It was gradually understood that the child's attachment to his parents and the revival of archaic feelings towards them was the source of many of the anomalies of adolescent experience. Here is Anna Freud:

. . . the danger is felt to be located not in the id impulses and fantasies but in the very existence of the love objects of the individual's oedipal and preoedipal past. The libidinal cathexis to them has been carried forward from the infantile phases, merely toned down or inhibited during latency. Therefore the reawakened pregenital urges or — worst still — the newly acquired genital ones, are in danger of making contact with them, lending a new and threatening reality to fantasies which had seemed extinct but are, in fact, merely under repression. [A. Freud, 1958, p. 268]

In a penetrating and brilliant analysis of psychopathology from this standpoint — it cannot be done justice in brief compass — Anna Freud describes central forms of defense against infantile object ties. Youngsters may withdraw libido suddenly from the parents and transfer it to others: to parent substitutes, to leaders who represent "ideals," or to peers. Or children may defend themselves not by the displacement of libido, but rather through a reversal of affect — from love to hate or from dependence to revolt. Or the instinctual fears may produce genuinely ominous defensive solutions: a withdrawal of libido to the self, culminating in grandiose ideas of triumph or persecution; or regression, in which there is a grave loss of ego boundaries.

The detailed scrutiny of defensive functions does not have a counterpart in an equally careful study of ego growth during adolescence. As other chapters in this Handbook will make clear, it is a period of remarkable maturation in thinking and cognitive grasp in general, and there has been an impressive increase in our understanding of these processes. Yet little of this is evident in the psychodynamic literature. One sees some lip service given to the idea that the child's development in this period is progressive, adaptive, functional, as well as regressive; nowadays one will see the name Piaget mentioned, though a bit uncomfortably, mechanically. But the emphasis remains on psychopathology and on the psychic system under stress; little productive attention has been given to the interaction between progressive and regressive ego capacities.

How this is to be done is quite unclear, given the few opportunities clinicians have to examine adaptive functioning among adolescents (or for that matter, anyone else). Both the methods and the situs (couch, clinic) of the clinician encourage regression and the emergence of the irrational, in much the same way as method and situs (classroom, laboratory) among academic developmentalists encourage an overemphasis on the rational. A division of labor has developed that is pernicious in its effect, in that the study of particular functions, such as thinking or moral cognition, tacitly tends to generate a model of that adolescent in which that function is dominant. Hence the picture of the adolescent we construe from a steady reading of *Child Development* is of a youngster engaged in an implacable expansion of intellectual and moral capacity, whereas the one we will develop from a regular diet of *Adolescent Psychiatry* is of a youngster miraculously holding on to his sanity, but doing so only by undertaking prodigies of defense. In truth we may be observing the same youngster through separate perspectives. Any clinician working with adolescents soon becomes aware that some deeply disturbed youngsters show no signs of difficulty in other realms of functioning, and that the conflict-free sphere of the ego can maintain itself and, indeed, expand during periods of intense personal disorder. This is true not merely in the realm of special skills, such as mathematics, music, or chess, but also in areas where one would expect to observe intrusions of the personal conflict, such areas as judgment and personal sensitivity. Such discrepancies are to be found in other stages of the life cycle, but they are particularly striking when seen in adolescence, simply because at that time one can so easily observe periods of emotional perturbation along with astonishing growth in the acquisition and refinement of complex ego function.

Family and Friends

The psychodynamic theory is also distinctive in both the degree and nature of its emphasis on the family. Other approaches seem to see the family as one institution among several, and indeed a declining one during this period when the family finds itself competing with other sources of influence. That tends to a decathected view of the family; in some textbooks on adolescence, much of the material is organized under the rubric ''parent versus peer influence,'' as though an arithmetic calculation of influence could capture the complex dynamics at work in the child's struggle to disengage.

To its credit, the psychodynamic view avoids such superficiality. It holds that the family by no means moves from the center. To the contrary, all of the regressive forces of the era draw the child closer to the family, dangerously close, so much so that much of the adolescent's psychological life is given over to oscillation between closeness and flight. As we have seen, youngsters find themselves beset by atavistic images of their parents and archaic feelings toward them, both of these being essentially unconscious. That the inner world is once again so highly charged is troubling enough in itself, yet the child must also reckon with the all-too-palpable presence of those very persons who are the original source and target of those feelings. We have heard it remarked that for some adolescents life in the family is akin to life lived on the psychoanalytic couch in the midst of a transference neurosis. One is in the grip of erratic and, at times, uncanny emotions, subject to storms of affect — rages, depressions, enthusiasms, and the like — which seem to possess a life of their own.

We must now mention another important element: that the child's coming into maturity will often evoke equally strong regressive feelings in the parents. The child's nubility may awaken conflicted, unconscious emotions of rivalry and desire along with a sense of time's passing and the waning of one's own power and beauty. One will often discern, even in households characterized by self-control, a certain amount of semiconscious, semierotic ''gesturing'' between parents and their adolescent children. How common and how significant such displays are is hard to say, we would guess that more or less ''unconscious'' sexual signaling between parents and children is more the norm than otherwise. We would even argue that the child's sense of himself as sexually valuable is attendant upon a certain degree of such gesturing or signaling from the opposite-sex parents. But in adolescence such display may loom larger, may seem more dangerous, may threaten to get out of hand because of the sexual maturity of the adolescent children. If that is commonly the case in "normal" households, then one can easily imagine the hothouse quality of life in more disorganized or ideologically atypical families. We have ourselves been startled, and more than once, by the degree of sexualization reported by adolescents and young adults in their families; it may be worth remembering that the first adolescent seen in psychoanalysis, the celebrated Dora, found herself entangled in her father's erotic affairs.

Sexual nubility and its complications are only part of the problems of the adolescent family, in many respects a minor part. Many of the more difficult transactions between parents and their adolescent youngsters stem from the repetition (through the regression) of earlier, presumably "settled" areas of conflict. The anal struggles of childhood over autonomy, compliance, cleanliness, and the like, may be revived, or the child may be overcome by a sudden descent into passivity, and so on. It is very nearly impossible to generalize about patterns and outcomes, so various, indeed so protean, are the forms of adolescent regression and the familial responses to them. In fact, it has often seemed to us that one of the common errors of clinical writing has been the tendency to generalize too boldly from the clinical observation of particular patterns of regression and response.

Nevertheless, certain general observations may be of value. First, the areas of conflict that appear in adolescence are likely to be precisely those that are, in fact, "unsettled" (appearance to the contrary notwithstanding). A struggle about, say, power and control between the child and the parents (whether or not oedipal in origin and meaning) will suggest to us that the earlier solution was either thin or false — an accommodation or an uneasy truce. In this sense the intrafamiliar struggles of adolescence can be said to expose (often by amplifying) the unresolved issues of childhood. Second, it is important to bear in mind that although we tend to see these conflicts as belonging to or stemming from the adolescents themselves, they almost always also involve the family — indeed, the family "system." As we have learned more about family dynamics through psychotherapies devoted to them, we have become acutely aware how nearly seamless is the web joining children and parents so far as psychopathology is concerned. Third, here as elsewhere appearances can deceive, in that the issues that ostensibly divide child and parents will often serve to conceal latent issues of far greater significance. In particular, adolescent conflicts often tend to center on the question of autonomy, the youngster's need to establish independence. That motif may in fact disguise entirely different conflicts, particularly the revival of archaic longings for fusion with the mother. Finally, it may be noted that in recent psychodynamic writing on adolescence it has been the recrudescence of those dangerous preoedipal attachments that has been at the forefront of attention, just as in psychodynamic theory in general we have seen a shift in interest from the oedipal to preoedipal sources of action and character.

Since much of what we have said may seem abstract, it may be of use to offer a very brief case account, which perhaps will illustrate some of these issues. We first met John when he was 16, on his entry into a therapy group for adolescents we were initiating. He was then recovering from an acute depression he had suffered following the breakup of a love affair. It was the girl's mother who in fact made the referral to us; she sensed that both the depth and duration of John's depression were excessive, just as she had earlier sensed that his dependency on her daughter was extreme. John turned out to be a handsome, highly intelligent, articulate boy, a leader at school and quite attractive to girls — hardly what we had imagined on having been told that he was both depressed and given to a slavish dependency. In the course of our work with him (some of which continued in later years) the apparent contradictions could be understood. He tended to keep most girls at a distance, especially so when they seemed intent on intimacy or on "mothering" him; he was, on the other hand, drawn to girls who were either aloof or boyish. It became clear in time that his relationships to girls were dominated by the wish to reestablish a symbiotic union and an intense fear of that very wish. He was drawn to girls whose boundaries seemed firm, yet having once established a connection to them, he would find himself sinking into an uncontrollable dependency, into a kind of enthrallment.

To some considerable degree these attachments to girls were an effort to come to terms with a dangerously heightened wish to fuse with his mother. He would become quite abusive to her, at times driving her to tears through mockery and ridicule; on one occasion his father became so enraged by the savagery of John's contempt for his mother that he lost control and struck him, an unparalleled event in what was a gentle and genteel academic household. John's complaint was that his mother nagged him, but in truth he was intensely frightened by his regressive feelings toward her, his impulse toward union. We could see this quite clearly in the therapy group, where his ordinarily intelligent and helpful participation would give way to sharpness, then to sarcasm, then to withering scorn, whenever he felt drawn to the "maternal" females of the group, particularly the woman therapist, who was seen as the group mother.

This vignette may also serve to say something about the psychodynamic approach to friendship and other peer relationships. Note that we have viewed John's feelings toward girls as ancillary to — and indeed as a displacement from — the more central intrapsychic task of adolescence, the resolution of residual and revived infantile ties to the parents. In doing so, we have spoken volumes about both the strengths and weaknesses of the psychodynamic approach to peer relationships. Its strength is in its depth, its ability to look beneath the surface and to perceive the murk and complication that may inform the most quotidian of human relationships — friendship. Its weakness is in its tendency to see friendship as merely the shadow or reflection of something else, something deeper and earlier, and thus presumably more important. The reductionist bias in the psychodynamic approach is nowhere more evident than in its essentially dismissive attitude toward the adaptive function of adolescent friendship. Our survey of the literature has uncovered only a handful of studies rooted in the psychodynamic tradition that give serious attention to the role of friendship in adolescent life, and there are fewer still (e.g., Douvan and Adelson, 1966) that concentrate on friendship as a means through which the ego's capacities are nourished and enhanced. On the other hand, it is in this respect like all other theories of adolescence. Friendship, which looms so large in the life of the teenager both in its presence and in its absence, remains essentially unexplored by psychology.

SOME NEW IDEAS

The Reorganization of Personality

During the last two decades or so, much of the intellectual energy of psychodynamic theory has had as its target an understanding of character change and consolidation in adolescence. There has been no agreement reached as to the best way to formulate the processes, nor is any visible. The idea of ego identity represents one effort to come to grips with the question; another, still largely nascent, is in the attempt to develop an extended theory of the self; a third — the mainstream effort — involved the extension or reworking of such structural concepts as the superego or the ego ideal. Because these writings are discussed elsewhere in this volume (Marcia in Chapter 5 on ego identity; Josselson in Chapter 6 on ego development; Hoffman in Chapter 9 on moral development) we shall make no effort to provide a detailed account. Instead we want to call attention, in general terms, to what seems to us to be the opportunities and problems facing this aspect of psychodynamic theory.

Perhaps we can best begin by discussing a specific phenomenon in adolescent psychology — "adolescent asceticism." It is one of the clinical problems discussed by Anna Freud in her earliest observations on adolescent psychopathology, *The Ego and Mechanisms of Defense* (1966), and it is a topic she returned to in what seems to have been her last major article on adolescence (A. Freud, 1958, pp. 255–278). It is not hard to see why. Although it is not, in our view, a common adolescent syndrome, it is hard to imagine a better example for illustrating the instinct-defense paradigm, which remains at the center of traditional psychoanalytic thinking: "Total war is waged against the pursuit of pleasure as such. Accordingly, most of the normal processes of instinct and need satisfaction are interfered with and become paralyzed" (A. Freud, 1958, p. 274). The ascetic adolescent will not only abjure sex as such, but the activities normally propaedeutic to it as well: dating, dancing, drinking, and the like. He may, in fact, turn away from all sources of gratification.

Yet once we begin pondering the matter, it becomes evident that the ego-id formulation, though necessary, is not by itself a sufficient explanation of what is involved. The choice of the *ascetic moment* is itself a reflection of a larger cultural or spiritual ideal. The transformation of that moment into permanence, as in the choice of the ascetic vocation (religious or political, these days), requires more, conceptually speaking, than the theory of instinct and defense can provide. It would not help us to understand St. Francis (or, for that matter, Cromwell or Lenin or Gandhi) or dozens of other personalities whose lives are or were ascetic in intention and practice. Here we find asceticism at or near the center of being; it is either the essential value of being or directly instrumental to the achievement of some central value. It organizes character. It organizes the perception and interpretation of reality. Beyond that it persists, amplifies, and becomes permanent. Hence a full account of asceticism, or any other important tendency or constellation of character, must venture beyond an id-ego paradigm to consider those forces and structures involved in its becoming an integral and enduring feature of the personality. Furthermore, adolescence has seemed to be a particularly fruitful moment for studying the organization of personality since it is a time when old structures appear to be dissolving and new ones taking their place.

Thus in the last several decades the thrust of psychodynamic theory has to some degree moved from the explication of conflict in adolescence to the study of the origins of adult personality structure. One can discern this simply enough by examining titles in the influential journals and reviews, where we may note, inter alia, such efforts as Peter Blos's (1972, pp. 93–97; 1974, pp. 43–88) papers on the ego ideal. The task is intrinsically difficult, of course, but has not been made easier by certain inclinations within the psychodynamic theory — above all its uneasy relationship to the concept of the self. The essential genius of Freudian theory at its inception involved a bypassing of the self, that is, the theory set itself against a tendency to give an undue weight to consciousness and its agencies (will, intention) as motivators of action. Until quite recently, it has been more comfortable in seeing the self and consciousness as exiguous in their impact on conduct — the theory is at its heart epiphenomenalistic, that is, holding to "the doctrine of consciousness as merely an epiphenomenon of physiological processes" (*Random House Dictionary*). As the limits of that tendency became evident, in the study of adolescence and elsewhere, psychodynamic theory began to reach out to the self, at first through extensions of the ego concept; later in the development of Erikson's ideas on ego-identity (1959); and still later in an increased concern with the sources and pathologies of self-regard, as in the work of Kohut and his collaborators (Kohut 1971, Goldberg & Kohut, 1978).

Yet the inner conflict between what we may term — crudely — the dynamic and the structural modes of formulation have persisted, albeit unwittingly. It is of some interest to note that despite Erik Erikson's enormous prestige in the intellectual culture at large, very little of his thinking on ego identity has as yet been absorbed into mainstream psychoanalytic theory. To some degree this is due to the protean and, at times, diffuse nature of the concept itself; we suspect it is also due to the problems inherent in phrasing identity itself as a source of conduct. An even more troubling and revealing event, along these lines, is that Heinz Kohut, who has developed a considerable body of doctrine on the self and its vicissitudes, has recently been rebuffed by his colleagues at the Chicago Institute, the gravamen of the charge being the departure of his theory from orthodoxy. Leaving the Byzantine, not to say Torquemadan politics of the psychoanalytic movement aside, that action reflects a genuine, though largely unrecognized, intellectual dilemma: How can we revise the philosophical vocabulary of psychodynamic theories to include an adequate recognition of the self or, at least, the events that the self theory has been developed to explain?[1]

The absence of that vocabulary and of an adequate theory of the self in action are, we feel, especially limiting when the object of attention is the adolescent. In no other phase of the life cycle do we find a more heightened awareness of self (in self-consciousness, embarrassment, shyness, shame); at no other time do we find quite so acute a concern about questions of self-regard. The most promising attempt to address these questions is in the work of Kohut. It has not yet been applied systematically and in detail to adolescence itself, though we can piece together from occasional comments and writings how the application would be made.

It is the Kohutian view that the reorganization of the self is the essential task of adolescence. Specifically, it is not the onset of puberty but rather a change in the self caused by a transformation of the ego ideal that sets the adolescent process in motion. The restructuring of the self is discussed in an important, yet little-known, paper by Wolf, Gedo, and Terman (1972) who describe adolescence as a period wherein the ego ideal established in childhood is discredited and a new ideal constructed. This period of change can and often does constitute a narcissistic peril, especially where there were defects in the original consolidation of the self in early childhood. The structural and psychosocial changes of adolescence may result in some regressive shifts to an earlier narcissistic position, and thus threaten the cohesiveness of the entire personality. The vulnerability of this period is to be seen in the frequent oscillations of self-esteem so often manifest during adolescence. According to Wolf, Gedo, and Terman (1972), friendships and peer

---

[1]Some of these issues are taken up in an interesting exchange between Marohn (1977), offering a Kohutian discussion of several adolescent delinquents, and Giovacchini (1977) who criticizes the discussion from an orthodox standpoint. Roy Schafer's recent work (1976, 1978) represents another attempt to treat these problems.

relationships are especially vital in easing the adolescent transition. As the old idealized parental models are deidealized and replaced by newly internalized ideals, the use of ''an intense peer relationship'' helps the youngster maintain a cohesion of the self as well as sufficient narcissistic balance until such time as a new ego ideal can be established. Once this new structure is formed, the alter-ego is no longer needed and is either discarded or transmuted into ordinary friendship.

In general, the developmental sequence in the Kohutian view runs somewhat as follows. A disillusionment with the parents leads to a dissolution of the child's ego ideal. In pursuit of a new ideal, transformations of the self occur. The adolescent group encourages the process of deidealization of earlier parental imagos through the espousing of new values. The group also offers cohesion to the self in that period prior to the formation of new guiding ideals. Since such changes in the ideal system can occur anywhere from the age of 11 until sometime after the age of 20, Wolf, Gedo, and Terman (1972) state ''This woutd suggest adolescence is not the consequence of sexual maturation. The essential requirement for its occurrence seems to be the emergence of an inner necessity for new ideals, accompanied by opportunities encountered for such a transformation of the self'' (p.269).

The Phases of Adolescence

Without question the most influential contemporary writer in the psychodynamic tradition is Peter Blos (1962, 1967, 1972, 1974). His most important contribution, in our view, has been his account of adolescence as a temporal process, extending from the latency period to young adulthood, and his patient, searching exploration of the phases within those years. It has been on the whole an admirable effort, particularly so since there has been so little intellectual support from other writers; almost all we know — or think we know — about the internal history of adolescence derives from Blos. Having said that, let us also confess to some reservations about some aspects of his work. The writing is labored (which might be putting it gently) and hence not easily accessible, except to the most devoted reader. As a whole, the Blosian canon is redundant, with far too much attention given to explications of minor variations and nuances of doctrine. Above all, one is troubled by the elaborateness of the theoretical system, in view of the limited observations on which it is based; in particular one is disturbed by the facile extension of clinical observations to other populations, although in this respect Blos is very much like all other writers discussed in this chapter.

Blos begins his account of the adolescent period with a discussion of latency, since he feels that the consolidation so marked during this phase is a prerequisite for the more turbulent phases that follow. Latency is characterized by sexual inhibition and by a considerable increase in control of ego and superego over the instinctual life. Ego functions and skills are enhanced, as are the child's resources. On the whole, affect and mood are stable. This period of relative quiescence is brought to an end by the instinctual upsurge that characterizes puberty. It is here that we see the struggle between a resurgent id and reactive defenses that were discussed earlier in this chapter. In this phase the child is so intent on warding off instinctual dangers that he becomes difficult to reach, to teach, and to control.

In the boy, castration anxiety reappears in relation to the archaic phallic mother so that the male preadolescent's central conflict involves a fear and envy of the female, feelings often defended against by a homosexual defense. (It might be remarked here that this differs from the second homosexual phase in early adolescence, wherein the same sex is taken as a love object; the homosexual defense in preadolescence lacks the erotic component that it takes on in the later period.) Whereas the boy in preadolescence is struggling with his anxieties about the phallic mother, the girl is defending herself against a regressive pull toward the preoedipal mother by a forceful turning toward heterosexuality. It is she, therefore, who tends to become the aggressor and seducer. The tendency is reinforced by the fact that the girl at this stage (between 11 and 13 approximately) is generally taller than the boy.

In the next two phases — early adolescence and adolescence proper — the central concern is the problem of object relations. In the first of these stages we see the first sign of the youngster's turning away from the primary incestuous love object in the relationship to the friend, who is then idealized. Characteristically, a series of close, idealizing friendships occur with same-sex peers. At the same time a sustained interest in creativity tends to diminish as the child begins to grope for values that are in opposition to those of his parents. The parents' internalized moral injunctions are decathected so that the superego weakens and tends to leave the ego weak and self-control inadequate. In extreme cases, we see a delinquent development.

The end of early adolescence and the entry into adolescence proper is marked by heterosexual object-finding; this signals the final renunciation of the incestuous object and a decisive break from childhood. Now the adolescent abandons the bisexuality of the earlier stage along with earlier preoedipal and oedipal attachments, turns to genitality, and chooses a nonincestuous heterosexual object. In this phase (also referred to as middle adolescence), we see an object-hunger developing as the youngster disengages himself from the primary love objects. The adolescent is now, as it were, in a state of "mourning." That the first heterosexual love choice is really an attempt at displacement from the primary love object is to be seen in the fact that these choices are quite frequently determined by some physical or mental similarity or dissimilarity to the parent of the opposite sex. Yet the actual parent, at one time idealized, is now devalued — a fallen idol.

During adolescence proper one also sees an increase in narcissism, reflected in the self-absorption, extreme touchiness, and self-aggrandizement so often observable in youngsters at this time. Though on the whole the child's movement is progressive, toward greater emotional maturity, the subordination of pregenital drives to genital primacy tends to produce instinctual anxiety, thus calling into play the rather stringent defenses characteristic of this phase — asceticism and intellectualization among others. However, at the same time we see some considerable growth of the adaptive ego processes. Cognition becomes increasingly objective and analytical; the reality principle assumes increasing dominance. The adolescent begins to think in terms of the future, though it is not until the late adolescent period that the larger questions of ego-identity and futurity come to the fore.

In late adolescence, the anxious question "Who am I?" is on its way toward resolution, as a positive awareness and acceptance of the self gradually emerges. Self-esteem becomes stabilized, emotions become more even and predictable, and a firm sexual identity is established. Thus, late adolescence is primarily a phase of consolidation, as the ego becomes increasingly unified in expressing itself through stable manifestations in work, love, and ideology. In terms of sexual identity, by the ages of 18 to 20, the final overt sexual choice has by and large been made, and the predisposition to a specific type of love relationship is established. The result is a new stability in the personality of the young adult.

The final phase described by Blos is postadolescence, which involves the implementation of the goals set forth as life tasks during late adolescence. Permanent relationships, expressed ultimately in courtship, marriage, and parenthood, are defined and achieved. The young male must come to terms with his father image and the young woman with her mother image before each of them is able finally to move into adulthood and maturity. Strengthened by the diminution of earlier instinctual conflicts, the ego becomes totally absorbed in these life tasks. In short, the ego activity of the young adult in postadolescence is essentially involved in the final task of settling down.

A CRITICAL OVERVIEW

In a chapter already suffused with critique, it may seem gratuitous to end with a section devoted entirely to critique. Yet we believe that anyone reading the psychodynamic literature carefully will conclude that its growth is painfully slow, especially so in view of its potential intellectual power. To be sure, that sluggishness represents a more general state of affairs in adolescent psychology as a whole; nevertheless, other approaches have shown far greater vitality — the cognitive orientation being one example, as the chapters by Keating (Chapter 7), Hoffman (Chapter 9), Gallatin (Chapter 10), and Elkind (Chapter 13) in this handbook will attest. What we see in the cognitive schools is a continuing interaction between theory and research, each reinforcing the other; that is precisely what we now seem to lack in the psychodynamic school. There are some noteworthy exceptions — the many studies conducted by Daniel Offer and his associates at Michael Reese Hospital (inter alia) Offer 1969; Offer and Offer 1975); the work on ego identity by James Marcia and others, reported in this volume. But, by and large, it is difficult to find cases wherein sustained programs of research were inspired by psychodynamic thinking and — even more important — instances in which the findings of such studies have had much impact on the theory itself. The realm of theory and the realm of empirical inquiry exist separately and fail to recognize or support each other.

To some degree this is due to the notorious insularity of the psychoanalytic movement, which has until now provided most of the theory we term "psychodynamic." Yet that insularity, though characteristic, need not be inevitable. We find an instructive contrast in the one area where the psychodynamic approach in developmental psychology has made significant progress in recent years — the study of early childhood. The work of Mahler, Fraiberg, Escalona, Provence and others has entirely transformed our understanding of the experience of young children in the first two to three years of life. There are several reasons in our view that this has happened. There has been an openness to new and more appropriate methods of observation and inference — involving essentially a shift to ingenious in situ methods of direct observation (as against earlier methods, which relied heavily on retrospective accounts from older samples or from tortured inferences derived from studies of acutely disturbed individuals). There has been a willingness to study normal along with troubled populations. There has been an eagerness to absorb findings and theory from other schools, in particular, from Piaget and those influenced by him. There has been a readiness to rely on experimentation and other nonclinical methods — the exemplary instance here being Mary Ainsworth's work on attachment (Ainsworth, Blehar, Walters, and Wall, 1978).

In all vital respects, the situation has been entirely different in the psychodynamic study of adolescence, where we find, on the whole, a striking conservativism of method compounded by a concentration on fairly narrow segments of the population. The primary method is the one-on-one therapeutic or diagnostic interview — a superb instrument of inquiry in and of itself, but limited and to some degree distorting unless supplemented by other methods. Even more troubling is the reliance on inferences drawn from the study of atypical portions of the total population of the young. It is obvious enough that we find an excessive degree of attention given to clinical populations (youngsters seen in psychotherapy or youngsters whose disturbances strain the tolerance of the total community), those who are delinquent, or addicted to drugs or alcohol. What may be less obvious is the skewing with respect to social class — most of our observations being made in work with: (1) the New Class strata (professional, managerial, public-sector) of the upper-middle-class (whose children form the largest group of those undertaking extended psychotherapy) and (2) from the more impoverished and disorganized strata, who are drawn substantially from the underclass or from disorganized and downwardly mobile families. What may be least obvious of all is the degree (precisely unknown but we suspect considerable) to which the reliance on clinical population has meant *eo ipso* a reliance on the study of males, leading to a psychology that is tacitly, unwittingly masculine in its formulations.

This skewing in the populations observed or studied has resulted in some considerable error in the theory itself. The most striking illustration is to be found in relation to the issue of adolescent turmoil. The controversy is by now fairly familiar to those having any interest at all in adolescent psychology, but it very much warrants some brief discussion here since it exemplifies the current rigidities of psychodynamic doctrine and some of their sources. From the beginning, the psychoanalytic view of adolescence has seen it as an era marked by extreme inner turbulence. Although this conception has earlier roots — in the seminal work of G. Stanley Hall — its preeminence today undoubtedly rests on the highly influential work of Anna Freud, dating from 1936, and discussed earlier in this chapter. That view has since held and has become dogma — unquestioned in its essentials by any of the influential writers in the psychoanalytic tradition. One characteristic statement of the position holds that the five qualities that distinguish adolescence are: emotional volatility, need for immediate gratification, impaired reality testing, failure of self-criticism, and indifference to the world at large (Fountain, 1961). That phrasing suggests that youngsters of this age are all impulse and feeling, very little ego or superego.

From where can such a view derive? What observations shape it? It is clear from the most cursory perusal of the literature that the formulations are achieved through the study of disturbed youngsters. Once we turn to more ordinary groups, we get an entirely different sense of the adolescent process. The turmoil theory has been disputed by each and every study that has based itself on a representative sampling of adolescents (e.g., Block, 1971; Douvan and Adelson, 1966; Elkin and Westley, 1955; Offer, 1969; Offer and Offer, 1975; Vaillant, 1977). That this is not due to a difference in theory is suggested by the fact that most of those studies are based explicitly on psychoanalytic assumptions. It has made little difference; the steady accumulation of contrary evidence seems to have had almost no effect on the doctrinal orthodoxy.

When the psychodynamic theorist turns away from the study of the disturbed and looks about him for examples of "normality," his eye is likely to fall on those most near and dear — his own children and those of his friends and neighbors or, if he is connected to a university, his students. In short, he will tend to understand the "ordinary" adolescent through the observation of a narrow social enclave, one which tends to emphasize for its youngsters the values of expressiveness (as against inner restraint), of rebelliousness (as against conformity), and of adversarial indignation (as against the acceptance of social givens). Hence we find a continuing failure to give sufficient weight to those habitual strategies of coping found among many and perhaps most adolescents — strategies that involve ego restriction and an identification with the values and standards of the family and dominant social institutions. The emphasis, instead, is given to traits and qualities well represented in the upper-middle-class — for example, the intellectualizing strategy or the stress placed on ideals, values, and the taking of moral positions on social questions. The issue here is not the importance of these qualities for understanding the common adolescent experiences of the youngsters of modernity, rather it is the ready tendency to universalize what is specific to a particular social cadre in a particular historical era. One well-known psychoanalyst has written that, "developing a social conscience is a universal need" (Solnit, 1972, p. 98). One may doubt that it is a need; one may be certain that it is not universal. In the sense in which it is employed, "social conscience" is an attitude rare or unknown during most of human history and throughout most of the world today. But it is an attitude frequently seen in the morally uneasy youngsters of a moralizing class in a historically moralistic nation — and it is those youngsters, that class, that nation that provide the social and historical milieu occupied by most writers in the psychodynamic tradition. In the absence of methods that would expose them to more diverse strata, the result is a social and historical parochialism.

The masculine bias in psychodynamic theory — and elsewhere in the study of adolescence — is rather more subtle, more difficult to document as to its specific effects, but there should be no question about its reality. Adolescent girls have simply not been much studied. One example: in the preparation of this Handbook, a distinguished scholar in women's psychology was asked to write a chapter on feminine adolescent development. After a careful survey of the literature, she concluded that there was not enough good recent material to warrant a separate chapter. Much the same conclusion on our state of knowledge has been reached by other students of adolescence.[2]

This neglect of female adolescents almost certainly reflects an inattention to women in psychology as a whole, at least until quite recently. But to some degree it may also reflect the fact that adolescent boys are more troublesome to society, hence more visible to the caretakers and theorists of disorder. Many adolescent boys manage internal conflict by acting out — through delinquency, vandalism, and the like. One also suspects that even the more ordinary pathologies are thought to be more troublesome when seen in boys than in girls, perhaps because life chances are felt to be more directly endangered. At any rate, one is struck by the disproportionate representation of boys over girls in the clinical literature, even when we leave aside youngsters seen for acting-out disorders. Our own informal count of psychoanalytic case studies reveals that boys are written about more frequently in a two-to-one ratio.

How this has affected the theory is hard to say with any certainty; all we can know is the state of the doctrine as it now exists and not what it might otherwise be. But we are willing to venture the opinion that the inattention to girls, and to the processes of feminine development in adolescence has meant undue attention to such problems as impulse control, rebelliousness, superego struggles, ideology, and achievement, along with a corresponding neglect of such issues as intimacy, nurturance, and affiliation. To read the psychodynamic literature on adolescence has, until very recently, meant reading about the psychodynamics of the male youngster writ large. What is particularly troubling is that the

---

[2] Anne Petersen 1978: personal communication.

biases reinforce each other: the separate, though interacting, emphases on pathology; on the more ideologized, least conformist social strata; and on males has produced a psychodynamic theory of adolescence that is both one-sided and distorted.

It is hard to imagine a satisfying theory of adolescence without the strongest contribution from psychodynamic theory. No other approach can offer, potentially, a comparable depth and range of observation; no other approach is as well suited — again, potentially — to pull together evidence drawn from other sources. Yet it is even harder to imagine that happening today, given the sad state of the art. It is at the moment a fossilized doctrine, resisting innovation in method, unshakably parochial in outlook. The illusion of being up to date is occasionally provided by the attention (excessive, in our view) given to fashionable topics: the politically active young or new modes of pathology. That work is rarely illuminating, given an insular theory and tired, overemployed concepts — above all, the idea of regression, which is used as a universal solvent for all conceptual difficulties. We have tried in the course of this essay to suggest that what is needed is a vastly increased pluralism, an openness to new research methods, diverse populations, competing ideas. We have already seen this take place in the study of infancy and early childhood, despite far greater formal difficulties in research methodology. There is no reason to believe a similar evolution is beyond the reach of those of us committed to the study of adolescence.

REFERENCES

Adelson, J. The political imagination of the young adolescent. In J. Kagan and R. Coles (Eds.), *12 to 16: early adolescence*. New York: Norton, 1972.

Ainsworth, M., Blehar, M., Waters, E. and Wall, S. *Patterns of attachment*. Hillsdale, N.J.: Lawrence Erlbaum Assoc., 1978.

Block, J. *Lives through time*. Berkeley, Calif.: Bancroft Books, 1971.

Blos, P. *On adolescence*. New York: Free Press, 1962.

———. The second individuation process of adolescence. In R. S. Eissler et al. (Eds.), *Psychoanalytic study of the child*, (Vol. 22). New York: International Universities Press, 1967.

———. The function of the ego ideal in late adolescence. In R. S. Eissler et al. (Eds.), *Psychoanalytic study of the child*, (Vol. 27). New York: International Universities Press, 1972.

———. The genealogy of the ego ideal. In R. S. Eissler et al. (Eds.), *Psychoanalytic study of the child*, (Vol. 29). New Haven, Conn.: Yale University Press, 1974.

Douvan, E. and Adelson, J. *The adolescent experience*. New York: Wiley, 1966.

Elkin, F., and Westley, W. A. The myth of the adolescent peer culture. *American Sociological Review*, 1955, *20* 680–684.

Erikson, E. H. Identity and the life cycle. *Psychological Issues*, 1959, *1*, 1–171.

Fountain, G. Adolescent into adult: An inquiry. *Journal of the American Psychoanalytic Association*, 1961, *9*, 417–433.

Freud, A. Instinctual anxiety during puberty. In *The writings of Anna Freud: The ego and the mechanisms of defense* (Rev. Ed.) New York: International Universities Press, 1966.

Freud, A. Adolescence. In R. S. Eissler et al. (Eds.), *Psychoanalytic study of the child*, (Vol. 13). New York: International Universities Press, 1958.

Giovacchini, P. Discussion of Dr. Richard Marohn's chapter: A critique of Kohut's theory of narcissism. In S. Feinstein and P. Giovacchini, (Eds.), *Adolescent psychiatry* (Vol. 5). New York: Jason Aronson, 1977.

Goldberg, A., and Kohut, H. *The psychology of the self: A casebook*. New York: International Universities Press, 1978.

Haan, N. The adolescent antecedents of an ego model of coping and defense and comparisons with Q-sorted ideal personalities. *Genetic Psychology Monographs*, 1974, *89*, 273–306.

Hatcher, S. The adolescent experience of pregnancy and abortion: A developmental analysis. *Journal of Youth and Adolescence*, 1973, *2*, 53–102.

Kohut, H. *The analysis of the self*. New York: International Universities Press, 1971.

Marohn, R. The juvenile imposter: Some thoughts on narcissism and the delinquent. In S. Feinstein and P. Giovacchini (Eds.), *Adolescent psychiatry* (Vol. 5). New York: Jason Aronson, 1977.

Offer, D. *The psychological world of the teenager*. New York: Basic Books, 1969.

Offer, D. and Offer, J. *From teenage to young manhood*. New York: Basic Books, 1975.

Peskin, H. Multiple prediction of adult psychological health from preadolescent and adolescent behaviors. *Journal of Consulting and Clinical Psychology*, 1972, *38*, 155–160.

Schafer, R. *A new language for psychoanalysis*. New York and London: Yale University Press, 1976.

———. *Language and insight*. New Haven, Conn., and London: Yale University Press, 1978.

Solnit, A. Youth and the campus: The search for social conscience. In R. S. Eissler et al. (Eds.), *Psychoanalytic study of the child*, (Vol. 27). New York: International Universities Press, 1972.

Vaillant, G. *Adaptation to life*. Boston: Little, Brown, 1977.

Wolf, E., Gedo, J., and Terman, D. On the adolescent process as a transformation of the self. *Journal of Youth and Adolescence*, 1972, *1*, 257–272.

CHAPTER 4

The Biological Approach to Adolescence:
Biological Change and Psychological Adaptation

Anne C. Petersen and Brandon Taylor

Why is biological development presented in a psychological volume? It has long been assumed that puberty plays a critical role in the psychological events of adolescence[1] (Blos, 1962; A. Freud, 1946, 1958; S. Freud, 1905/1953). We shall critically review the evidence for this relationship and attempt to place the hypothesis for biological influence in a broader theoretical framework.

More than development in other phases of the life cycle, many aspects of adolescent development have been thought to have biological determinants. It is only with particular life events for women (e.g., postpartum, menopause) that psychological variables have been so strongly linked to biological change. The biological changes at puberty *are* dramatic and relatively rapid. However, there are also important sociocultural factors that strongly influence adolescent development. In our society at least, we may have been overestimating the significance of biological factors because of the difficulty of dealing with some problems associated with adolescence. We tend misguidedly to equate "biological" with "immutable." By assuming that some adolescent behavior results from pubertal changes, such behavior is sometimes considered inevitable and resistant to intervention. It is possible that these assumptions about biological determinants of so-called adolescent phenomena, such as delinquency or acting out, may prove to be correct, though no evidence currently exists. Nevertheless, the rationale for such assumptions should be questioned and the hypotheses submitted to empirical test. We shall return to the psychosocial correlates of puberty later in this chapter.

PUBERTAL DEVELOPMENT

The Process of Puberty

It is now known that puberty is a process that takes place within an existing biological system, that is, no new system is suddenly created at puberty. All of the components required for sexual functioning are present prenatally in normal individuals, though some

---

[1]The process of puberty is differentiated from the stage of life called adolescence. Puberty is frequently considered the beginning of adolescence, though usually in terms of markers, such as menarche, a relatively late pubertal event. The end of adolescence is defined with even less clarity than its beginning point. In any case, puberty in most individuals has generally been completed long before most definitions of the end of adolescence. Hence, this chapter describes a phenomenon characteristic of early adolescence for most individuals.

are immature. The development of reproductive capacity, both in terms of function and somatic features, begins at conception. What we call puberty is a part of this longer process.

Puberty is usually considered as the period of rapid change to maturation. Figure 1 roughly portrays the achievement of sexual maturation and decline in terms of evidence about sex-hormone levels. Current evidence is primarily based on cross-sectional studies, the vast majority using male subjects (e.g., Horst, Bartsch, & Dirksen-Thedens, 1977; Marcus & Korenman, 1976). If this representation is proven accurate with longitudinal investigation, it suggests that the primary factor distinguishing puberty from the rest of the biological life cycle is the *rate* of change, though the *magnitude* of somatic change is also dramatic at puberty. Growth and development in infancy is more rapid than that at puberty, but many (e.g., Tanner, 1972) have suggested that it is less important because the infant cannot experience change as an older child can. Changes also occur with aging, though most are slow and gradual.

Basic Endocrinology

Before we discuss the onset of puberty, it is necessary to provide some basic endocrine terminology and concepts. Hormones are powerful and highly specialized chemical substances that interact with cells. The cells have differentiated in such a way that they are able to receive the hormonal "message" and to act on it. The endocrine system consists of endocrine glands (hormone-producing cells); their secretory products; intracellular mechanisms, which permit cells to respond to such products; and auxiliary tissues, which participate in regulating the function of the glands. The endocrine glands are ductless and use blood vessels for transporting hormones.

There are several endocrine systems. In puberty, the gonadal, adrenal, and hypothalamo-hypophyseal (hypothalamus and pituitary) systems are of central importance. Other systems and their hormones will be mentioned where relevant. The endocrine systems are distinct though interrelated.

The glands of the reproductive system are the testes (male) and the ovaries (female). Though glandular function is of some interest, what is usually measured are the hormones produced by the glands. The "sex" hormones, primarily androgens and estrogens, are not, however, solely produced by the gonads. In addition, though the gonads have

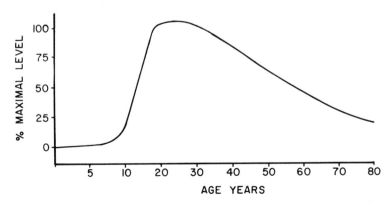

Figure 1   Hypothetical representation of sexual development in terms of sex hormone levels.

sex-specific functions, very few hormones are restricted to one sex. Androgens are thought of as "male" hormones, while estrogens are frequently considered "female" hormones. Both types of hormones are produced by both sexes, though the average mature female produces more estrogens than androgens and the average mature male produces more androgens than estrogens.

Hormones are not only produced at glandular sites, but they may also be produced in other body tissues. Furthermore, many forms of the sex hormones can be biochemically transformed into one another. A common enzymatic pattern is the peripheral (i.e., in tissue) conversion pathway from cholesterol to progesterone to testosterone (an androgen) to estradiol (an estrogen) or cortisol (Tepperman, 1968).

The circulating active level of a hormone (i.e., unbound or free hormone) is only one component of the process by which a hormone has influence. The receptivity of the target tissue is also an important factor. Evidence for the role of tissue responsivity is given by the androgen insensitivity syndrome, in which genetic males become phenotypic females due to a deficiency of cellular androgen-binding capacity (Faiman & Winter, 1974, pp. 32–55). There also appear to be individual differences in hormone responsivity among normal persons.

Related to tissue responsivity, or tissue (cellular) capacity to use or bind hormones, is the capacity of hormones to bind each other. Only unbound hormones can function actively (Rosenfield, 1971). For example, there is a dynamic antagonism between androgens and estrogens, such that the biological effects of one may be inhibited by the presence of the other. The precise biochemical mechanism here is unknown, though testosterone-estrogen binding globulin (TEBG), induced by estrogen and suppressed by androgen (Marcus & Korenman, 1976), may play a role. The development of this binding globulin is also thought to be the most important factor in the onset of puberty (Horst, Bartsch, & Dirksen-Thedens, 1977).

The flow of sex hormones is controlled by a negative feedback system. The pituitary gland controls endocrine levels, but is itself under the control of the hypothalamus, a portion of the upper brain stem. The pituitary sends a message via a gonadotropin to the gland to manufacture hormone. Then the pituitary, through the hypothalamus, senses when an optimum hormone level is attained and responds by maintaining gonadotropin and sex hormone production at this level.

Methodological Issues

The reader should, by now, have an appreciation for the complexities of endocrinology. Psychologists sometimes presume that the physical and biological sciences present neater problems, which are more easily addressed than those in the social or behavioral sciences. On the contrary, in endocrinological studies reliability and validity of measurement are quite problematic. For example, there is the question of what to look at: Which form of hormone? In urine or serum? If the purpose of hormone measurement is to gain an assessment of functioning, blood hormone levels obtained at a single point in time may not provide an accurate picture. Clearance rate, indicating hormone utilization, may also be important. In addition, hormone levels fluctuate with various types of cycles now apparent. There are monthly cycles in women and some men (Doering et al., 1975), diurnal cycles (Resko & Eik-Nes, 1966), and hourly cycles with some hormones (Santen & Bardin, 1973; Seyler & Reichlin, 1974). Furthermore, external factors, such as stress, sleep, food intake, drug intake, and activity, can also alter hormone levels (West et al.,

1973). In short, the endocrine system is an open system, interacting with many influences. Reliability and validity of measurement present complex and difficult problems.

The Onset of Puberty

A recent conference was convened to integrate extant information on the control of the onset of puberty (Grumbach, Grave, & Mayer, 1974). In the introduction to the proceedings of the conference, Grave (1974) states, "We know a good deal about hormone events that accompany puberty but very little about the control of its onset. For too long we have accepted concomitance as causality" (p. xxiii).

Our current knowledge of the mechanisms related to the onset of puberty has been summarized by Grumbach et al. (1974) and is reproduced in Figure 2 and Table 1. Note that endocrinologists trace sexual maturation from conception rather than beginning with puberty. The dramatic prenatal endocrine changes are linked to the "sexing of neural tissues" (Faiman & Winter, 1974, p. 52).

By the third trimester of pregnancy, the negative feedback system is established with clear sex differences apparent. There is now evidence that sex differences in fetal hormones are due to the fetal testis and perhaps the fetal ovary, though maturational differences between the sexes may play a role as well (Robinson et al., 1977; Warne et al., 1977).

In infant girls, levels of follicle-stimulating hormone (FSH) are elevated, sometimes to adult levels (Faiman & Winter, 1974; Winter & Faiman, 1973b). Then the hypothalamic gonadotropin regulating mechanism is "set" at a low level, highly sensitive to the negative feedback cycle that maintains endocrine levels at a low point throughout the prepubertal period. The pubertal change in sensitivity, however, is a gradual rather than a sudden event.

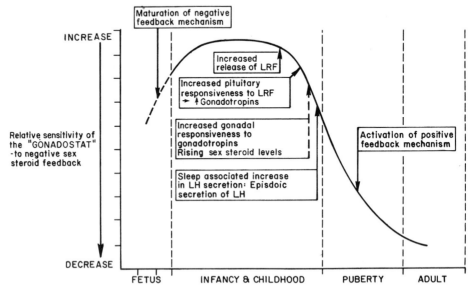

Figure 2 Schematic illustration of the hypothalamic changes and the maturation of feedback mechanisms from fetal life to adulthood in relation to pubertal endocrine changes. (Reproduced with permission from Grumbach, Roth, Kaplan, and Kelch, 1974.)

Table 1   Postulated ontogeny of hypothalamic-pituitary gonadotropin-gonadal circuit

Fetus

(a)   Secretion of pituitary gonadotropins (FSH and LH) by 80 days gestation

(b)   "Unrestrained" secretion of luteinizing hormone-releasing factor (LRF)

(c)   Maturation of negative sex-steroid-feedback mechanism after 150 days gestation — sex difference

(d)   Low level of LRF secretion at term

Infancy

(a)   Negative feedback control of FSH and LH secretion highly sensitive to sex steroids (low set point)

(b)   Higher mean serum FSH and LH levels in females

Late prepubertal period

(a)   Decreasing sensitivity of hypothalamic gonadostat to sex steroids (increased set point)

(b)   Increased secretion of LRF

(c)   Increased responsiveness of gonadotropes to LRF

(d)   Increased secretion of FSH and LH

(e)   Increased responsiveness of gonad to FSH and LH

(f)   Increased secretion of gonadal hormones

Puberty

(a)   Further decrease in sensitivity of negative feedback mechanism to sex steroids

(b)   Sleep-associated increase in episodic secretion of LH

(c)   Progressive development of secondary characteristics

(d)   Mid to late puberty — maturation of positive feedback mechanism and capacity to exhibit an
          estrogen-induced LH surge

(e)   Spermatogenesis in male; ovulation in female

Source: Grumbach et al., 1974, p. 159.

In the late prepubertal period, the hypothalamic gonadostat decreases in sensitivity (Kulin, Grumbach, & Kaplau, 1969) with increasing levels of luteinizing hormone-releasing factor (LRF) and gonadotropins (LH and FSH), but especially follicle-stimulating hormone (FSH) and sex steroids. The cause of decreasing sensitivity is still insufficiently understood, though recent research suggests that the adrenal may play a central role (Ducharme et al., 1976; Sizonenko & Paunier, 1975).

At puberty, there is an increase in the amplitude of episodic or pulsatile discharges of luteinizing hormone (LH) with minor fluctuations in follicle-stimulating hormone (FSH) (Penny, Olambiwonnu, & Frasier, 1977). During sleep, pubertal subjects show increased LH secretory activity (Boyar et al., 1972; Judd, Parker, & Yen, 1977; Kapen et al., 1974).

Another pubertal endocrine phenomenon is the maturation of the positive feedback system typical of mature females in which estrogen induces the preovulatory gonadotropin surge related to ovulation (Kulin, Grumbach, & Kaplan, 1972). Grumbach et al. (1974) further suggest, based on preliminary evidence, that the positive feedback action of estrogen is not sex specific and also occurs with males.

Critical Weight at Menarche

An additional factor related to the onset of puberty has been suggested by Frisch (1974, pp. 403–423). Frisch and Revelle (1969a) found that the time of fastest weight gain during the adolescent growth spurt occurred at roughly the same mean weight but at differing ages across subjects. Subsequent studies (e.g., Frisch & Revelle, 1969b, 1970, 1971) confirmed the significance of mean weight in relation to pubertal events, for boys as well as girls. This research, suggesting some importance of a critical weight (or weight range), further serves to link the secular trend toward earlier menarche (Tanner, 1969, pp. 19–20; 1972) to nutritional adequacy. While Frisch (1974, pp. 403–423) attempts to argue that metabolic size is a pubertal "trigger," an argument also made by Cheek (1974, pp. 424–442), most biologists (e.g., Donovan, 1974, pp. 473–476) prefer to consider critical weight a manifestation rather than a cause of puberty.

The Termination of Puberty

Before describing the endocrine and somatic manifestations of puberty, we wish to comment on the termination of puberty. We could find no literature on this topic. As meager as our understanding of the onset of puberty is, we seem to know even less about the termination of this process. The rapid stimulation of growth in the long bones is also associated with the eventual closure of the bony epiphyses, thus terminating growth. But what causes the endocrine system to stabilize once it reaches mature levels? Even descriptive studies of endocrine levels across the life span are lacking. There is some evidence, however, that there is only a relatively brief plateau upon maturity, followed by decline in hormone levels and other biological factors. This developmental process is surely related to the reproductive cycle with the duration of maximal fecundity dependent on the fitness of the individual (Frisch, 1978).

Endocrine Changes at Puberty

It has long been assumed that pubertal changes in sex-steroid level are responsible for the observed differences between children and adults as well as between mature males and females. Only relatively recently, however, have such changes been documented with newer methods of endocrine assay. Indeed, these radioimmunoassay methods have detected differences in hormone level due to such factors as sleep, circadian rhythms, food ingestion, and sexual activity, hence raising new problems with interpretation of hormone measurements. In short, the new methods have verified gross discriminations but are so powerful that they have introduced a new set of factors that complicate the assessment of endocrine status.

Since the origin of hormone measured in plasma or urine is difficult, though not impossible, to determine, we shall organize our discussion of pubertal endocrine changes by type of hormone (e.g., androgens and estrogens) rather than glandular site (e.g., gonadal or adrenal).

Figures 3, 4, and 5 present data from Gupta, Attanasio, and Raaf (1975). Their cross-sectional study included 44 boys and 43 girls from ages 7 to 18 as well as 13 adults for comparison. Though these data are fairly typical, issues of comparability will be discussed later.

Figure 3 shows the mean trends in plasma concentrations of dihydrotestosterone and testosterone in relation to Tanner's (1962) pubertal developmental stages. Note the

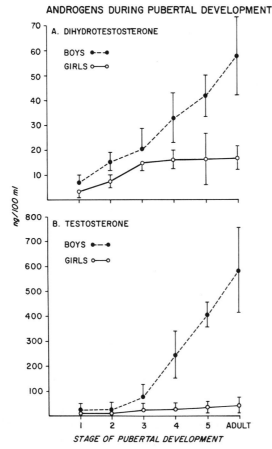

ANDROGENS DURING PUBERTAL DEVELOPMENT

Figure 3   Mean trends in plasma concentrations of (a) dihydrotestosterone and (b) testosterone related to pubertal developmental stages. (Reproduced with permission from Gupta, Attanasio, and Raaf, 1975.)

stage-related increases, which are especially dramatic for males. Testosterone is the more potent androgen of the two and barely increases in these data for females.

In Figure 4 are shown the mean trends in estrone and estradiol levels in relation to pubertal stages. Again, increases are apparent, especially with estradiol for girls.

Sex differences are dramatically highlighted in Figure 5, showing the ratios of estradiol and estrone to testosterone across the pubertal stages. The divergence between the sexes begins at stage 3, the second stage for pubertal changes. The ratio including estradiol differentiates between the sexes more than that including estrone. Estradiol is generally considered a more potent form of estrogen.

The data just presented are quite similar to those of other cross-sectional studies (Angsusingha et al., 1974; Korth-Schutz, Levine, & New, 1976; Sizonenko & Paunier, 1975; Winter & Faiman, 1973b). One difference seen in other studies is a clearer increase in testosterone in females (Apter & Vihko, 1977; Faiman & Winter, 1974, pp. 32–55). Some cross-sectional studies have used age as the time dimension (Ducharme et al., 1976; Horst, Bartsch, & Dirksen-Thedens, 1977). Tanner (1962) and Gupta (1975) present data that clearly show the deficiencies in this approach. Although trends can be observed with increasing chronological age, variability is dramatically reduced when the same data are related to the pubertal developmental stage. A group of 14-year-old boys may contain

ESTROGENS DURING PUBERTAL DEVELOPMENT

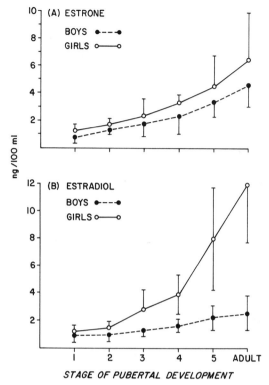

Figure 4 Mean trends in plasma concentrations of (a) estrone and (b) estradiol related to pubertal developmental stages. (Reproduced with permission from Gupta, Attanasio, and Raaf, 1975.)

individuals at all stages of development, from undeveloped to fully mature. Bone age, a more continuous and precisely defined measure of development, has also been used in endocrine studies (Apter & Vihko, 1977; Sizonenko & Paunier, 1975).

Other hormones, besides those just discussed, increase during puberty. For example, the gonadotropins increase; the increase in follicle-stimulating hormone (FSH) precedes that of luteinizing hormone (LH). This pattern led Faiman and Winter (1974) to suggest that FSH plays a primary role in the development of secondary sex characteristics, while LH is important to Leydig cell function in males and ovulation in females.

Adrenal hormones — including dihydroepiandrosterone, its sulfate, and androsterone — also increase during puberty (dePeretti & Forest, 1976; Ducharme et al., 1976; Hopper & Yen, 1975; Korth-Schultz, Levine, & New, 1976; Sizonenko & Paunier, 1975). Progesterone and other progestins, produced by the corpus luteum during the luteal phase of the menstrual cycle as well as by the adrenal, show steady increases across pubertal stages (Apter & Vihko, 1977).

Longitudinal studies of pubertal endocrine changes are just beginning to appear. Pubertal stage and even bone age provide only rough approximations to maturational level and rapid intraindividual incremental changes may yet be obscured (Tanner, 1962). Gupta (1975) has reported preliminary longitudinal data using urinary measures with boys. Lee and colleagues (Lee, Jaffe, & Midgley, 1974; Lee & Migeon, 1975) have reported longitudinal data, again with boys, using serum measures. Faiman and Winter (1974, pp.

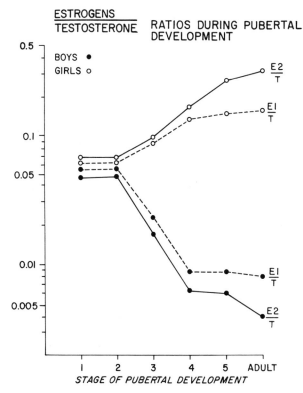

Figure 5 Mean trends in estrone/testosterone and estradiol/testosterone during pubertal development. (Reproduced with permission from Gupta, Attanasio, and Raaf, 1975.)

32–55) studied both boys and girls using serum measures. The results of these longitudinal studies are generally in agreement; in addition, they roughly compare to cross-sectional research. There is still controversy, however, as to the best way to measure hormones in such studies (Faiman & Winter, 1974, pp. 32–55). Furthermore, the timing of fertility in relation to endocrine changes is basically unknown.

Female Puberty

Mature reproductive capacity in the female involves an additional process not yet discussed: approximately monthly fluctuations in hormones with menstrual bleeding. As with puberty in general, the development of the mature menstrual cycle is a relatively long process, extending several years both before and after menarche. Prior to the onset of menses, marked fluctuations in FSH and LH become apparent (Hayes & Johanson, 1972; Penny et al., 1977; Winter & Faiman, 1973a). Hansen, Hoffman, and Ross (1975) found 20- to 40-day cycles in urinary gonadotropin secretion in premenarcheal girls, though peaks comparable to those producing ovulation were only occasionally observed. Similarly, estradiol shows large day-to-day fluctuations premenarcheally but not prepubertally (Boyar et al., 1976; Penny et al., 1977; Winter & Faiman, 1973a). Only after menarche, however, do estrogen and gonadotropin peaks become synchronized.

Although endocrine patterns begin stabilizing with menarche, ovulation may not occur for several years, particularly on a regular basis (Apter & Vihko, 1977; Penny et al., 1977;

Winter & Faiman, 1973a). In a recent Finnish study, which included 200 normal girls, Apter and Vihko (1977) found that at least 55% of the cycles were anovulatory in the first two postmenarcheal years; by five years postmenarche, 20% or less were anovulatory. Ovulatory and anovulatory cycles probably co-occur immediately after menarche, thus permitting fertility even though a regular cycle has not yet been established.[2]

Somatic Development

The most obvious manifestations of puberty are the changes in somatic characteristics. Within a few years, four on the average, the child is transformed into an adult, at least an adult in terms of physical appearance. Tanner (1962) has described these changes in terms of a series of pubertal stages. Pubertal stages are described in terms of genital development (boys only), breast-development stages (girls only), and pubic-hair development (both sexes). These three sets of stages are described in Table 2.

In general, the stages of each of these three secondary sex characteristics proceed in an invariant sequence. The relations among these sequences vary considerably within and between individuals. [See Eichorn (1975) for a general discussion of asynchronies in pubertal development.] For example, a boy may be in stage 2 of genital development and stage 5 of pubic-hair development. And a second boy may show the reverse sequence for the stages. Marshall and Tanner (1969, 1970) have presented data from boys and girls in the Harpenden Growth Study that show the average ages for each pubertal stage.

Growth in some pubertal characteristics is shown in Figure 6. The figure shows that, while pubic-hair development is about two years later for males than for females, as expected, breast and genital development only differ by about six months. Similarly, the lag between pubic-hair and breast development is greater in girls than is the time difference between genital and pubic-hair development in boys. This is undoubtedly due in part to the different hormones responsible for these processes. Estrogens are primarily responsible for mammary development, while androgens influence pubic-hair and genital development.

Tanner (1969) describes (without presenting data) aspects of pubertal development in addition to the major characteristics. Axillary hair (i.e., underarm hair) generally develops about two years after pubic hair. Circumanal hair most frequently appears just prior to the growth of axillary hair. Facial hair is usually coincident with axillary hair and develops in particular sequence: hair first appears at the corners of the upper lip, then all across the upper lip; next at the upper part of the cheeks and at the midline below the lower lip; the sides and lower border of the chin are the last sites of hair growth. Facial hair growth in males is seldom completed before stage 5 in genital and pubic-hair development have been attained. Other body hair begins to appear at about the same time as axillary hair and may continue developing well into the third decade of life.

The change in voice pitch is a major pubertal process in males. This is a relatively late occurrence that develops only gradually. The pitch of the female voice also deepens with puberty. In addition, there is a change in quality, or timbre, of the voice in both sexes.

The time of the first ejaculation of seminal fluid is frequently proposed as a male pubertal analog to menarche. It generally occurs about a year after the beginning of accelerated penis growth, though with great variation, perhaps due to reporting bias.

---

[2]This discussion of fertility in girls raises the question of the same capacity in pubertal boys. Unfortunately, systematic studies of this are lacking. First emission is frequently mentioned as the male analog to menarche, but whether sperm are consistently viable from the outset is unknown.

Table 2   Pubertal Stages

Stage	Genital Development[a]	Pubic-Hair Development[a,b]	Breast Development[b]
		Characteristic	
1	Testes, scrotum, and penis are about the same size and shape as in early childhood.	The vellus over the pubes is not further developed than over the abdominal wall, i.e., no pubic hair.	There is elevation of the papilla only.
2	Scrotum and testes are slightly enlarged. The skin of the scrotum is reddened and changed in texture. There is little or no enlargement of the penis at this stage.	There is sparse growth of long, slightly pigmented, tawny hair, straight or slightly curled, chiefly at the base of the penis or along the labia.	Breast bud stage. There is elevation of the breast and the papilla as a small mound. Areolar diameter is enlarged over that of stage 1.
3	Penis is slightly enlarged, at first mainly in length. Testes and scrotum are further enlarged than in stage 2.	The hair is considerably darker, coarser, and more curled. It spreads sparsely over the function of the pubes.	Breast and areola are both enlarged and elevated more than in stage 2 but with no separation of their contours.
4	Penis is further enlarged, with growth in breadth and development of glans. Testes and scrotum are further enlarged than in stage 3; scrotum skin is darker than in earlier stages.	Hair is now adult in type, but the area covered is still considerably smaller than in the adult. There is no spread to the medial surface of the thighs.	The areola and papilla form a secondary mound projecting above the contour of the breast.
5	Genitalia are adult in size and shape.	The hair is adult in quantity and type with distribution of the horizontal (or classically "feminine") pattern. Spread is to the medial surface of the thighs but not up the linea alba or elsewhere above the base of the inverse triangle.	Mature stage. The papilla only projects with the areola recessed to the general contour of the breast.

[a]For boys.
[b]For girls.

Tanner (1969) notes that cultural factors influence the timing of first ejaculation. It is possible, however, that first ejaculation is no more influenced by cultural factors than is menarche and that both are equally susceptible to reporting bias, especially to those who have no firsthand evidence. Cultural influences have been more extensively investigated with menarche. It is possible that similar factors operate with first ejaculation.

Accompanying penis growth in males is the development of the seminal vesicles, the prostate, and bulbourethral glands. The prostate, in particular, increases greatly in size. Similarly, in girls the development of the uterus, vagina, labia, and clitoris proceeds simultaneously with the breasts.

Several changes are also seen in the skin at puberty. The sebaceous and apocrine sweat glands, particularly of the axillary, genital, and anal regions, develop rapidly during puberty. Their characteristic odor, more marked in the male than the female, may be related to pheromonal sensitivity, perhaps once important for sexual timing.

Acne and other skin eruptions due to enlarged pores and increased oiliness are also characteristic of puberty. These problems occur more frequently in boys than girls. The

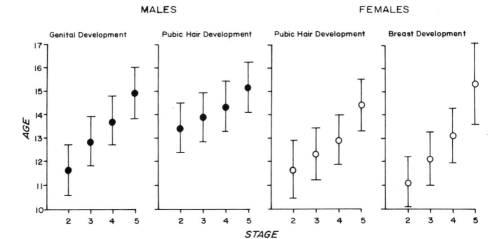

Figure 6   Tanner stages of secondary sex characteristic development for males and females.

skin becomes rougher, especially on the outer thighs and upper arms, again with greater roughness seen in boys.

A major change in puberty is the rapid increase in height and weight. Growth in stature has been more rigorously investigated than weight, partly because height is less susceptible to such environmental influences as eating habits and exercise. Tanner (1962) has reported his investigation of growth in stature based on subjects in the Harpenden Growth Study. His method was primarily descriptive and various parameters of growth were determined by fitting the curve "by eye." Because of the possibility of measurement error with these methods and because these data have already been widely disseminated, the present review will focus on the results presented by Bock and colleagues (Bock et al., 1973; Thissen et al., 1976), who used subjects from four American growth studies. Differences between these results and Tanner's will be noted.

Bock et al. (1973) used a statistical procedure for estimating the growth parameters. A two-component logistic model was fitted to stature data from age one to maturity. Although it is possible that this procedure artifactually induces relationships between some of the parameters (see Petersen, 1979), such bias, if it exists, is uniform across subjects. On the other hand, the procedure enables us to test the goodness of fit by comparing estimated with observed growth curves.

Thissen et al. (1976) concluded that the prepubertal component of height is about 149 centimeters in males and 139 centimeters in females. The pubertal component is more similar for the sexes averaging 30.80 centimeters in males and 28.05 centimeters in females. Though this difference is statistically significant (and its magnitude varies across the four studies), it is small compared to the large prepubertal difference. Hence we may conclude that most of the difference between males and females in mature stature is due to the fact the pubertal growth spurt begins *earlier* in females (11.03 years) than males (13.07 years) rather than to a larger pubertal component among males, as had been commonly believed (e.g., Tanner, 1962).[3] A similar result is that the prepubertal

---

[3]Tanner (1962) as well as Blizzard et al., (1974, pp. 342–359) claim that boys grow more than girls during puberty because of stronger testosterone effects. As we have noted, the sex differences are small. Furthermore, Rosenfield (1974) suggests that estrogen also influences growth.

component of growth is more strongly related to mature stature (r = .67) than is the pubertal component (r = .22). Tanner (1974, pp. 448–470) reports a correlation of .80 between adult and prespurt height. The time at onset is unrelated to the rate and duration of puberty as well as adult height (Faust, 1977; Tanner, 1962).

The pubertal spurt in stature is primarily due to acceleration of trunk length, though leg length reaches its peak growth first (Tanner, 1974). Muscle growth parallels the development of skeletal growth and is associated with a deceleration of fat accumulation, resulting in a loss for boys. Figure 7, based on data from Cheek (1974), shows muscle and fat development across bone age for males and females. Sex differences in these processes are apparent.

Tanner (1974, pp. 448–470) attributes the appearance by the end of puberty of a sex difference in strength to the marked pubertal increase in muscle size in boys. Boys also develop more force per gram of muscle, larger hearts and lungs relative to their size, a higher systolic blood pressure, a lower resting heart rate, a greater capacity for carrying oxygen in the blood, and a greater power for neutralizing the chemical products of muscular exercise, such as lactic acid (Tanner, 1962). Blood hemaglobin and the number of red blood cells also increase far more markedly in males than females (Young, 1971). The effect of the increased physical exercise and activity manifested by adolescent boys relative to their female peers, however, may be influencing at least some of these sex differences. Until recently, there have been strong sociocultural pressures on girls to cease such ''masculine'' activity at adolescence. Studies are needed that control for physical exercise. Tanner (1974, pp. 448–470) concludes that the increase in athletic ability among adolescent boys is due to the anatomical and physiological changes. Although such changes may *enable* athletic prowess, it is possible that they are much less dramatic without exercise.

Figure 8 summarizes the major pubertal changes for males and females. The sequence of these events is quite regular, though the timing for different individuals is highly variable (Faust, 1977; Tanner, 1962, 1969, pp. 19–20; 1974, pp. 448–470).

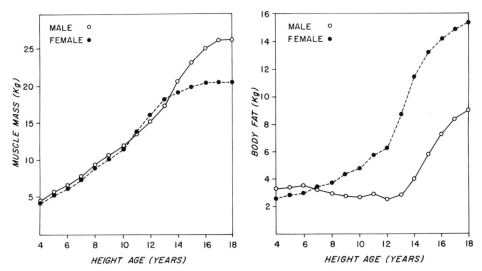

Figure 7 Muscle mass and body fat by height age for males and females. (Reproduced with permission from Cheek, 1974.)

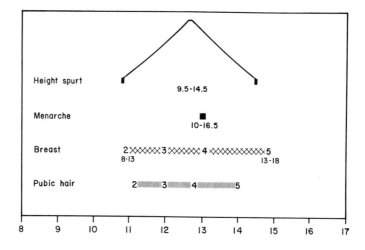

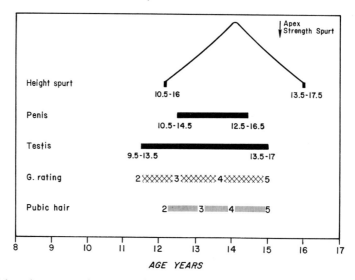

Figure 8 Schematic sequence of events at puberty. An average girl (upper) and boy (lower) are represented. The range of ages within which each event charted may begin and end is given by the figures placed directly below its start and finish. (Reproduced with permission from Tanner, 1974.)

The body shape of males and females also changes in puberty (Faust, 1977; Petersen, 1973). The major developmental change is with shoulder width relative to hip width. Both of these characteristics increase in males and females, but shoulders grow more in males and hips grow more in females. Prepubertally females have a larger shoulder/hip ratio; after puberty males have a larger ratio (Faust, 1977).

Summary of the Process of Puberty

Before discussing the psychosocial correlates of puberty, we shall summarize the important aspects of the biological process. We have selected aspects, not from the biological perspective, but by considering the biological factors that *might* be important for psychosocial development.

Current research clearly indicates that puberty is not a sudden new development, but it is part of a gradual process that begins at conception. We might think of puberty as the final, most rapid phase of the development of mature reproductive capability. Puberty has different characteristics for males and females since the mature outcomes differ, but there are also many similarities. Among the similarities in puberty for males and females are the negative feedback system, which regulates endocrine functioning, the episodic secretion of luteinizing hormone during sleep in early puberty, growth to an adult size and development of secondary sex characteristics (though some characteristics differ by sex), rapidly increasing levels of several hormones, and the maturation of the positive feedback system. Now for the differences. Puberty is typically two years later for boys than for girls. Boys generally end up taller and heavier than girls with more facial and body hair, a different basic body shape, and develop a mature penis and testicles with sperm production. Girls develop breasts and a mature vagina-labia region with a mensual cycle of hormone production, including a menstrual flow of blood. In addition, muscle development is typically more extensive in males than females, though more similar exercise patterns, only now becoming prevalent, may change these data.

PSYCHOLOGICAL ADAPTATION TO PUBERTY

In theories of adolescent psychological development, the biological changes of puberty are frequently assumed to present a major adaptive task to the personality (Blos, 1962; A. Freud, 1946, 1958; S. Freud, 1905/1953; Hamburg, 1974; Kestenberg, 1967a, 1967b, 1968). Initial theoretical formulations of these adaptive processes were developed primarily within the psychoanalytic paradigm, which provided the first, and perhaps only, sustained theoretical examination of puberty from the perspective of its implications for personality development.

Early theoretical formulations placed virtually exclusive emphasis on psychological adaptation to an upsurge in the "drives." Sigmund Freud (1905/1953) postulated that the central stimulus to development in adolescence stems from a marked increase in the sexual drive at puberty. Anna Freud (1946, 1958) was influential in consolidating the orthodox psychoanalytic assumption that psychological upheaval in adolescence was the universal and inevitable consequence of drive development at puberty. Adolescence was viewed as a period when "a relatively strong id confronts a relatively weak ego," resulting in increased instinctual anxiety, heightened conflict over impulse expression, intensified defenses against impulse, greater affective lability, and psychologically regressive behavior (A. Freud, 1946). It was assumed that this process necessarily engendered a high degree of psychological conflict and stress throughout adolescent populations and represented an invariant feature of psychological development. A recent analogous position was adopted by Kestenberg (1967a, 1967b, 1968), who hypothesized direct relationships between pubertal changes in hormone production and phases of psychological development.

A second formulation provided a somewhat expanded theoretical focus — related to the adolescent's attachments. Pubertal maturation was seen as initiating a revolution in the adolescent's primary emotional investments and altering psychological ties to the parents. It was proposed that an intensified sexualization of parental affectional bonds occured, reactivating unresolved oedipal fantasies. The anxiety aroused by this development was seen to result in defenses against the emotional ties to the parents and eventual reinvestment of primary sexual and affectional needs outside the family (Blos, 1962; A. Freud, 1958; S. Freud, 1905/1953).

A third theoretical perspective shifted emphasis to an analysis of the effects of pubertal changes in physical appearance on gender identity and on the adolescent's body image (Blos, 1962; Kestenberg, 1967a, 1967b, 1968; Schonfeld, 1963, 1966, 1969, 1971).

Research on psyche/soma relationships at puberty is in a preliminary stage and has not kept pace with biological studies. Findings are sparse and scattered, with the exception of substantial, growing literatures on the psychological effects of early and late maturation (Clausen, 1975; Jones, 1965; Jones & Bayley, 1950; Jones & Mussen, 1958; Peskin, 1967, 1973; Peskin & Livson, 1972) and on adolescent sexual attitudes and behavior (Jessor & Jessor, 1975; Sorensen, 1973; Zelnik & Kantner, 1977). Consequently, despite a proliferation of theoretical positions hypothesizing causal connections between physiological and psychological changes in early adolescence, much of our thinking in this area remains in the realm of assertion and belief.

At a formal level, theory-building concerning processes of accomodation to pubertal change remains disappointingly unsystematic, particularly within the psychoanalytic paradigm. In particular, formulations and classifications of variables affecting these processes remain poorly systematized. Undoubtedly part of the problem lies in the enormous conceptual difficulties of articulating relationships among variables in three systems: biological, sociocultural, and psychological.

This section will examine models of psychological adaptation to puberty. This focus provides a context for a more organized scrutiny of the relationships among biological change, the modification of psychological systems in the individual, and the effects of variations in socialization and sociocultural factors on this process of modification.

Conceptual Models of Psychological Adaptation to Puberty

For heuristic purposes it is fruitful to group propositions about the relationships between pubertal maturation and psychological development into two broad categories: (1) *direct effects models,* which attribute certain psychological effects to direct physiological sources and (2) *mediated effects models,* which stress that the psychological effects of puberty are mediated by complex causal chains of intervening variables (such as culturally influenced ideational processes or patterns of social controls). We recognize that such a dichotomy represents an abstraction of what is more likely a continuum of models, ranging from models for biological direct effects, through mediated (or interactive) models, to models for direct sociocultural effects. Furthermore, our focus on psychological adaptation to puberty necessarily implies consideration of causal sequences from biological to psychological development. In fact, the reverse sequence may obtain. For example, as in the case of anorexia nervosa, an extreme psychological state may postpone or reverse aspects of the pubertal sequence. In this chapter, however, we are limiting discussion of the interactive biological, sociocultural, and psychological systems to the perspective of psychological adaptation to pubertal events.

Direct-Effect Models

These formulations propose that pubertal changes exercise a direct, unmediated effect on psychological development. That is, direct causal linkages are proposed between physiological (e.g., neuroendocrine) changes as antecedent variables and certain psychological phenomena of adolescence as the dependent variables. Because primary importance is attributed to physiological causes, other causal, intervening variables (such as psychological structures, cognitive processes, or sociocultural influences) are not included as significant features of this model. Schematically:

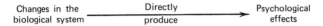

Changes in the — Directly produce → Psychological
biological system — Directly produce → effects

The formulations of psychoanalytic theorists often fall into the category of direct-effect models. Two distinguishable hypotheses are frequently advanced simultaneously. First, there is the *hypothesis of direct hormone/mood state linkages*. Kestenberg (1967a, 1967b, 1968), for example, proposes direct linkages between pubertal changes in hormone levels and changes in psychological states and phases of psychological development. Second, there is the *drive hypothesis,* which postulates biologically based motivational changes, consisting of dramatic quantitative increases in sexual and aggressive impulses. These primary psychobiological disequilibria are commonly linked in theory to a variety of secondary psychological effects and adaptations, including transient psychological turmoil and eventual development of further regulatory controls over impulses and affects.

Any model of the effects of puberty on personality must be able to provide an effective explanation for individual variations in the psychological phenomena and adaptations under discussion. Direct-effect models usually entail a priori assumptions about the limits of variation in the dependent variable (psychological effects) and are relatively limited in their effectiveness in accounting for these variations. Individual differences in adaptation to puberty, for example, are largely discounted. It is frequently assumed that a high degree of psychological conflict and stress are the inescapable consequence of hormonal and drive developments, which are presumed to be inherently disruptive to personality functioning. This emotional stress is assumed to occur throughout adolescent populations and to represent an invariant and universal feature of psychological development at this phase of the life cycle. Such individual differences in adaptation to puberty that *are* observed to occur are frequently attributed to variation within antecedent biological variables, for example, "the quantity of instinct" or "the strength of the drives" (A. Freud, 1946, 1958). Although certain "direct-effect" theorists are not strict biological determinists and make concessions to nonbiological influences on the adolescent's adaptation to puberty, these factors are often given superficial elaboration and do not occupy a significant causal role in the model.

Research Evidence for Direct Effects

What evidence is there for a direct effect of puberty on adolescent psychological development? Though the connection between gonadal function and behavior has been recognized since the time of Aristotle (Tepperman, 1968), the scientific study of behavioral endocrinology is relatively recent (Beach, 1975) due in part to the recency of adequate endocrine methodology. Most of this research has focused on sexual behavior with animal subjects; relatively little attention has been devoted to the influence of hormones on nonsexual behaviors or moods in humans. No studies exist of the relation between endocrine and psychological changes in puberty. This lack of striking — in contrast to the prevalent beliefs about hormonal influence.

A review of the research on hormone-behavior relationships suggests that there is some evidence for hormone effects, though this evidence is weaker than popularly believed.

The research linking hormones to psychological variables may be categorized in three areas:

1. Prenatal effects.
2. Hormones in women at menarche, postpartum, menopause, as well as during the menstrual cycle.
3. Other general effects.

Though Money and Ehrhardt (1972) concluded that prenatal hormones influence some ''sex-appropriate'' behavior later in life, sociocultural factors remain confounded with genetic and endocrine status in these studies. Studies of individuals lacking pubertal hormones (due to prenatal effects) suggest that adolescent sexual motivation is not dependent on hormones, though it may be intensified by them (Money, 1967). The studies of hormone-behavior relations in women[4] have shown that although hormone changes may be partly involved, sociocultural expectations and other factors are probably more important (see Melges & Hamburg, 1977, for a review).

In summary, the evidence for direct hormonal effects is less than overwhelming. We must note, however, that the previously inadequate state of endocrine methodology has made it impossible until recently to obtain hormone measurements precise enough to relate to psychological variables. Future research may demonstrate more relationships.

Mediated-Effect Models

These formulations propose that the effects of pubertal changes on psychological development are mediated by intervening variables, or moderated by other exogenous or contextual factors. Causal pathways might be depicted schematically as follows:

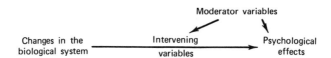

In this schema, intervening variables represent internalized psychological factors, for example, fantasies about bodily developments. These factors directly mediate, at a process level, adolescent adaption to puberty. Moderator variables may be thought of as factors exogenous to the personality (e.g., sociocultural contexts and socialization practices). These factors influence intervening psychological variables or otherwise modify psychological adaptations. Mediated-effect models posit more complex causal pathways between physiological development and psychological adaptation than do direct-effect models. In particular, these models give more systematic attention to the influence on individual development of contextual variables, especially in the realm of enculturation and socialization. Mediated-effect models also permit examination of how the social management of puberty affects basic psychological processes in development. Given the unsystematic nature of much theory and research inferring causal relationship between pubertal maturation and adolescent personality change, a preliminary, more

---

[4]Until recently (Doering et al., 1974; Parlee, 1977), it has been assumed that hormone levels in males were stable, and hence unrelated to psychological variations.

methodical classification of variables may prove useful to future thinking. At a formal level, a systematic elaboration of the various components of an explanatory model should include the following taxonomies of variables.

A Taxonomy of Antecedent Biological Variables

Puberty is sometimes superficially treated as a unitary maturational phenomenon by theorists concerned with its implications for psychological development. Alternatively, one feature of puberty is singled out for emphasis, to the relative neglect of other important features of this process. As can be seen from the first section of this chapter, puberty has many aspects and it is not a unitary phenomenon. Hence a systematic developmental analysis of psyche/soma relationships during this period requires consideration of the various pubertal processes. These would include:

1. Neuroendocrine changes, including increases in levels of the major gonadotrophic and sex hormones as well as the related changes in the central nervous system, particularly in the hypothalamus.

2. Morphological changes, including visible development of secondary sex characteristics and changes in height, body-mass and shape.

3. The development of adult reproductive capacity, including the onset of menses for females and seminal emissions for males as well as alterations in levels of sexual arousability or responsivity.

4. The timing of pubertal changes.

For analytical purposes distinctions among these processes are essential since they provide functionally different forms of stimuli to the personality and social system. That is, they constitute distinct factors that may interact with personality and sociocultural variables differently. For example, external, morphological changes (which are relatively visible and have more immediate social-stimulus value) are likely to have different significance to the individual and to his or her social network than would internal changes in hormone levels. Note that the model of direct effects refers primarily to the first of these biological variables.

A Taxonomy of Intervening or Moderating Variables

The process of psychological accommodation to pubertal changes may be mediated by contextual factors endogenous or exogenous to the personality. Endogenous personality characteristics might include:

1. Internalized patterns of thought and feeling (beliefs, fantasies, attitudes, or concerns) about the body, body processes, and the meanings of pubertal changes.

2. Preferred or internally prohibited modes of tension reduction, including presence or absence of conflict over genital stimulation and gratification.

3. Attitudes toward growing up and adulthood, the acceptance of biological gender, and the extent to which parental identifications have become associated with psychological conflict.

4. Self-esteem, anxieties about acceptability, degree of autonomy from need for external approval.

Exogenous variables at the level of peer and family groups might include such factors as:

1. Degree of parental conflict or anxiety around various aspects of the adolescent's pubertal developments.
2. Overt or covert communication of positive or negative evaluations of these developments.

Exogenous influences at the sociocultural levels would subsume such factors as:

1. Ideational contexts surrounding pubertal developments, including not only cultural standards of attractiveness and notions of the desirable and undesirable in physical development, but also culturally shared beliefs, attitudes, or perceptions concerning such matters as early or late maturation, menarche and menstruation, and masturbation.
2. Overt pre- and postpubertal socialization pressures associated with normatively expected or inappropriate forms of behavior, particularly in the realm of sexual behavior.

A Classification of Psychological Systems or Processes Potentially Modified in Conjunction with Puberty

In models of psychological adaptation to puberty, psychological effects represent the dependent or consequent variables in the formulation. The literature had focused on various processes, such as:

1. Changes in the regulation of affect states or mood, including increases or decreases in subjectively experienced feelings of depression, guilt, stress or anxiety, irritability, shame, erotic arousability, pleasure, pride, and so forth.
2. Modifications in representations, perceptions, fantasies, or attributions about the self (or, more broadly, in self-concept, identity, or body-image).
3. Changes in regulation of the self-esteem system; modifications in positive or negative evaluations of the self.
4. Alterations in psychological defenses and drive-regulatory capacities.
5. Behavioral changes, particularly in the realm of heterosexual behavior.
6. Alterations of psychological ties to, and interpersonal behavior with, parental figures.
7. Development of specific areas of psychological conflict around sexual motives, masturbation, menstruation, body-appearance, and the like.

Temporal duration must also be considered a variable feature of psychological effects. Psychological changes associated with puberty may be relatively transient, as with certain fluctuations of affect states, or represent more lasting alterations in patterns of behavior or thought and feeling about the self.

Cognitive Mediation of Psychological Adaptation to Puberty

In a mediated-effects model of adaptation to puberty, one intervening personality variable that hypothetically may mediate reactions to pubertal changes is the inner representational world of the adolescent. From this perspective, biological developments are received into an adolescent's ideational, attributional, or representational contexts and may be imbued with various affective meanings. The presumption is that it is not the biological acquisitions of puberty, per se, that determine the psychological effect on the adolescent, but their subjective stimulus value, that is, how the changes are experientially encoded and the significance attributed to them. In its formal properties, this formulation resembles attributional models of the processes whereby changes in physiological states are labeled (Bem, 1974; London & Nisbett, 1974; Nisbett & Schachter, 1966; Schachter, 1964; Schachter & Singer, 1962). The attribution model posits a typical sequence in which a change in bodily state arouses evaluative needs in the individual, which result in an interpretation of the meaning of the change. The process of interpretation is based on either situational cues derived from the immediate circumstances of the subject or derived from the subject's own overt behavior. It is the meaning attributed to the physiological change that results in a particular emotional reaction. Research in this paradigm suggests that, with variations in situational cues or the subject's own behavioral cues, the labeling of physiological changes and subsequent reactions are highly manipulable.

Hence it becomes important to codify the potential variables that influence the adolescent's ideation about his or her own biological changes and the subjective meaning or affective significance attributed to them. These variables would include: (1) childhood patterns of thought and feeling, (2) parental and peer attributions, and (3) publicly shared ideas about, or the symbolic significance of, pubertal events.

Childhood Patterns of Thought and Feeling

It is important to assess the extent to which the adolescent's ideational context for puberty may stem from phases of development prior to puberty itself. For example, prior learning from early socialization experiences connected with parental and cultural attitudes toward the genitals, internalized taboos or prohibitions relating to the management of physical tensions, and the nature of prior exposure to adult sexual behavior — all may result in motivational residues and affectively charged patterns of thought and feeling that influence contemporaneous patterns of adaptation to puberty. Psychoanalytic theory (Blos, 1965; Kestenberg, 1967a, 1967b, 1968) places particular emphasis on the degree to which the adolescent may rely on cues from an idiosyncratic inner world of early fantasies, beliefs, and fears to interpret the significance of pubertal developments. Evidence for this perspective is predominantly idiographic in character and is based largely on clinical inference from intensive, individual case studies (Blos, 1970).

Parental and Peer Attributions

The subjective evaluation by adolescents of their pubertal developments may partially derive from cues from their immediate social environment. The literatures on adolescent body-image (Bruch, 1943; Schonfeld, 1966) and on the psychological consequences of early or late maturation (Clausen, 1975; Jones & Mussen, 1958) indicate the importance of parental and peer environments as influential variables in the adolescent's acceptance or satisfaction with body change. Change in height, weight, complexion, and secondary sex characteristics have significant social stimulus value (Clausen, 1975; Lerner, 1969; Staffieri, 1967). Parents and peers may communicate positive or negative evaluations of the adolescent's appearance by many overt or covert means. Perceived parental tensions or anxious preoccupation with the course and outcome of the adolescent's physical development may have a significant effect on the adolescent's subjective experience of these bodily events (Schonfeld, 1966).

Sociocultural Interpretations of Pubertal Maturation

It is important to consider the extent to which the subjective meaning or significance of pubertal developments for the individual is influenced by meaning contexts operative at the cultural level. Pubertal changes frequently have a generalized symbolic or social-stimulus value and are encoded into a current system of cultural interpretations and meanings.

LeVine (1973) and Fabrega (1972) have recently directed theoretical attention to the ways in which individuals incorporate the culturally shared, normative meanings assigned to perturbations or changes in bodily functioning into their personal ideational contexts, with which they monitor bodily processes. Fabrega (1972) assembles a substantial body of evidence illustrative of the fact that: (1) cultural groups differ considerably in the significance they attribute to bodily events and (2) these normative evaluations may influence both how these biological events are noticed and encoded into subjective experience and whether these categorizations give rise to experiences of anxiety or conflict.

Hence one line of analysis in the elaboration of a ''cognitive-mediation'' model of adaptation to puberty should concern variations in cultural modes of managing or responding to this maturational phase and the possible consequence of these responses for the experience and personality development of the youth involved. The range of cultural variation in the normative meanings assigned to these biological developments is enormous, as Mead (1958) as well as Ford and Beach (1951) have pointed out. Among the Samoans of the South Pacific and the Dobuans of the Solomon Sea, for example, puberty may go largely unremarked. In other instances, these changes may be stressed and become the stimulus for a variety of cultural ideas and ritual observances.

Psychological Consequences of Cultural Interpretations of Pubertal Maturation

Unfortunately, with the exception of the early work of Mead (1928), there has been virtually no systematic investigation of the relationship between these variations at a cultural level and adolescents' subjective experiences of their pubertal development. The psychological effects on adolescents of these variations in cultural-meaning systems cannot be determined on a strictly a priori basis and have not been systematically investigated. Although there are good reasons to suggest that adolescents' subjective experience of bodily changes may vary considerably with ideational contexts supplied by the culture, as theorists we are not entitled to assume absolute congruence between normative meanings and individual experience of these changes. The issue involves the extent to which shared cultural interpretations of the significance of puberty interpene-trates and provides the content of adolescents' *perceptions* of these developments. Related to this is the issue of psychological effect, that is, of the extent to which the content of these perceptions facilitates a relatively nonstressful adaptation to puberty or results in stressful disruptions to psychological equilibrium, in the form of experiences of anxiety, shame, or depression.

Patterns of Social Control as Moderating Variables in Psychological Adaptation to Puberty

It is our contention that formulations of pubertal adaptation must recognize that the adolescent must accommodate psychologically to the *adaptive context* of puberty (the social environment's response to this maturation) as well as to the maturational changes themselves. This adaptive ecology, or setting, consists not only of an ideational context of cultural beliefs and attitudes concerning puberty, but also of a normative context of pressures and controls associated with socially prohibited, permitted, and expected behaviors. At puberty the adaptive process exhibits a *dual responsiveness* to both internal maturational factors and these external normative pressures.

This dual responsiveness of adaptation becomes particularly evident in an analysis of the maturation and social regulation of the adolescent's reproductive capacity and sexual motivations.

Puberty typically brings with it two developments of singular social import, developments that inevitably implicate the young person's social context, these are: (1) the development of reproductive capacity and, possibly, (2) the intensification of a powerful motivational system, the sexual drive. As Goethals (1971) has pointed out, all societies structure to some degree the sexual activities of the unmarried adolescent to insure the maintenance and continued functioning of certain forms of social organization and adaptation. With regard to the nature of these controls, there are remarkable variations among cultures both in the amount and type of sexual behavior that is socially permissible and in the consistency of a society's standards as development proceeds (and thus in the developmental continuities and discontinuities imposed on the individual).

Social Organization and the Regulation of Adolescent Sexual Behavior

Attempts to account for the tremendous variations of patterns of control, from permissive to severely restrictive, in terms of social-structural variables have yielded a number of very intriguing findings (Goethals, 1971; Murdock, 1964; Whiting, 1953). The functions of various patterns of control have been associated with the problems that unwanted pregnancy creates for considerations of inheritance, the maintenance of clear lines of descent, and the responsibility for offspring. Other associations have involved the protection of family status against hypogamy (marrying down); financial considerations, as in bride-price cultures: the continued maintenance of parental control (Kenyatta, 1968); and the control of sexual access in polygamous cultures. Strict regulation (prohibition) of unmarried, adolescent sexual behavior has been correlated highly with agricultural economics in which the orderly transfer and inheritance of property is emphasized and with societies characterized by complex and highly delineated social-class structures combined with achievable rather than ascribed social positions (Goethals, 1971). Hence social-structural factors may be seen to act as distal, moderator variables or constraints affecting the more proximal system of training, controls, and sanctions that limit or channel the expression of adolescent sexual behavior.

Continuities and Discontinuities in the Social Regulation of Pre- and Postpubertal Sexual Behavior

In addition to variations in the amount and type of sexual behavior that is culturally appropriate for the adolescent, a further factor of potential psychological relevance has to do with the consistency of cultural norms and controls to which the adolescent must adapt. Patterns of social controls may be *sequentially consistent,* that is, continuously restrictive or permissive with regards to sexual behavior throughout childhood and the postpubertal period. Alternatively the controls may be *sequentially inconsistent,* that is, they may restrict the sexual explorations of the young and provide external pressure for sexual activity after puberty — or precisely the reverse discontinuity may obtain. Such radical discontinuities in socialization are institutionalized in certain cultures. The children of Alor (Indonesia) enjoy significant sexual freedom. Infants are masturbated during nursing and, later, free masturbation is permitted. Much sex play is allowed between boys and girls, including attempts at intercourse. Later, "sexual activity is frowned upon and during late childhood such behavior is forbidden to both boy and girl" (Ford & Beach, 1951, p. 189). Alternatively, among the Siriono of South America, the Chukchee (Northeast Asia), the Ashanti (Ghana) and the Ao (Assam, India), the girl is permitted no sex play before puberty, but intercourse is customary once she has menstruated (Ford & Beach, 1951). In addition, in social settings characterized by normative pluralism, the adaptive context of the adolescent may reflect a *concurrent inconsistency* among contradictory or competing social pressures and expectations. Ford and Beach (1951) provide an excellent survey of cross-cultural differences in the regulation of sexual behaviors.

Potential Constraints on Adolescent's Psychological and Behavioral Adaptation to Social Regulations of Sexual Behavior

In assessing the psychological consequences of various patterns of social control it must be kept in mind that actual conformity with social norms cannot be taken for granted. LeVine (1973) for example, has noted that restrictions or sanctions may be ineffective in controlling behavior and that covert rule-breaking may be a common mode of individual adaptation to social constraints or expectations. Ford and Beach (1951) provide numerous examples of covert sexual activity among adolescents despite severe social prohibitions and sanctions.

However, to the extent that it is necessary for adolescents to adapt to particular social constraints or pressures regarding sexual activity, the psychological consequences of a sequentially discontinuous or an inconsistent pattern of socialization will depend on the plasticity of prior psychological adaptations. The issue of the malleability of previous psychological accommodations is raised when, for example, the adolescent encounters an external cultural pressure to engage in sexual behaviors that were previously prohibited, punished, or made a source of anxiety; or, alternatively, when the adolescent is expected to suppress sexual motives, interests, and sources of gratification that were previously allowed expression.

It is plausible that accommodation to current social expectations may occur at a *behavioral level,* while limits may exist on accommodation at an intrapsychic or *psychological level.* Consequently, in examining the effects of discontinuities in socialization on the functioning of personality, it is important to explore how impervious to modification are prior psychological accommodations to earlier environmental constraints. In some instances early internalization of sex training may prove to be a greater predictor of later adaptation at puberty than socialization pressures operative at the time of puberty. This form of "sleeper effect" emerges, for example, in findings of Simon and Gagnon (1967) that the crucial operating influence in the development of female homosexual adaptations appears to be prepubertal sex-role learning rather than later socialization experiences (not measurably distinguishable from those of heterosexual controls) associated with the entry into actual sexual behavior.

Adequate investigation of the psychological level of adaptation to discontinuous patterns of socialization would attempt to assess whether the effects of early modes of socialization continue to persist or exert influence on later adaptations. The conflict between early modes of psychological adaptation and later behavioral accommodations could be expected to emerge in the form of disturbance in the sense of self and in the subjective sense of well being. This disturbance should manifest itself in the persistence of feelings of shame, anxiety, guilt, frustration, tension, discomfort, and avoidance measures in connection with the newer behavioral adaptations. LeVine (1973), Spiro (1961), and Whiting (1966) have suggested adopting such a cost-benefit perspective on psychological adjustment to social constraints, focusing on subjective experiences of gratification or frustration.

Cross-Cultural Comparisons of Psychological Adaptations to Social Control

The cross-cultural approach provides a particularly useful strategy for assessing the effects of varied socialization patterns on psychological adaptations to puberty. Despite extensive cross-cultural investigations of socialization practices related to puberty and adolescent sexual behavior, there has been little in-depth research on the psychological issue of how varied cultural norms, regulations, and responses are experienced. The question of precisely how these social arrangements influence the extent to which individuals experience the management of biological drives and the adjustment to bodily change — as conflictual and disruptive or as relatively unstressful — has not been extensively investigated. Mead (1928) has presented impressionistic data suggesting that the consistency of Samoan permissiveness and openness in the sexual realm contributed to a smooth and unconflicted adaptation to pubertal change. Christensen and Carpenter (1972), in a study of three sociocultural settings, report that significant psychological conflict and stress increases among adolescents when there is increased restrictiveness of sexual norms. By and large, however, the comparative literature is disappointingly scanty. The collection of data providing access to the intrapsychical costs and benefits of adaptation to puberty in varied social contexts has not kept pace with the description of the objective features of sociocultural correlates of these changes.

Adolescent Sexual Adaptations at the Behavioral Level: Current U.S. Research

It has already been mentioned that social-structural variables (e.g., socioeconomic status, ethnic background, cohort) appear to act as distal moderator variables affecting the process of adaptation to puberty. For example, the timing of entry into actual coital sexual behavior has been strongly related to social class for males, with the age of first intercourse varying inversely with class (Kinsey, Pomeroy, & Martin, 1948). For females, the age of first intercourse is more resistant to class variation (Kinsey, Pomeroy, & Martin, 1953; Simon & Gagnon, 1969).

There is a considerable body of accumulating evidence to suggest that the incidence of, and the age of entry into, active sexual (coital) behavior has been particularly affected by recent age cohorts (Udry, Bauman, & Morris, 1975; Vener & Stewart, 1974). Zelnik and Kantner (1977), using longitudinal findings from a national probability sample of women aged 15 to 19, report a 30% increase in the prevalence of premarital intercourse behavior between 1971 and 1976. An earlier index of these cohort effects is provided by Christensen and Gregg (1970) who report that the percentage of unmarried women engaging in intercourse rose from 21 to 34% between 1958 and 1968, when corrected for shifts in the age of first marriage.

Empirical findings suggest that premarital sexual behavior is becoming behaviorally normative rather than representing a deviant behavior. Sorensen (1973), in a cross-sectional study based on a national probability sample of adolescents, reports that: (1) among boys aged 13 to 15, 44% have had intercourse; for boys aged 16 to 19, the prevalence is 72% and (2) for girls aged 13 to 15, the prevalence is 30%, which rises to 57% for those aged 16 to 19. However, these figures may be somewhat inflated by biases introduced in the sampling procedure (Ryser, 1974; Vener & Stewart, 1974). Zelnik and Kantner's (1977) findings for girls suggest a somewhat lower prevalence of 18% for girls by age 15, but similar prevalence (55%) by age 19, with a median age for first intercourse of 16.2 years. Jessor and Jessor (1975) present comparable prevalence rates for girls, but somewhat lower rates for boys. Findings on the age of entry into coital behavior suggest that among all nonvirgins aged 13 to 19, 71% of boys and 56% of girls had intercourse by the age of 15 (Sorensen, 1973).

Psychological Correlates of Postpubertal Sexual Adaptations

As with cross-cultural research, research on social-structural variables and adolescent adaptations to puberty typically address differences in behavioral accommodations (e.g., age of first intercourse), but have rarely investigated the psychological concomitants of those adaptations. However, recent research concentrating on American adolescents has begun to provide initial findings concerning psychological reactions around sexual issues. Offer (1969) reports findings from his longitudinal study of adolescent boys suggesting general anxiety about and avoidance of sexual relations. Sorensen (1973) reports pronounced sex differences in psychological experiences related to early sexual behavior. Masturbation appears to be a particularly conflictual area for young adolescents. Among 13- to 15-year-old girls, the level of guilt and anxiety (experienced "often" or "sometimes") over masturbation is very high (76%), although this conflict appears to moderate among 16- to 19-year-olds (43%). For boys 13 to 19, the level of anxiety and guilt appear to persist over time between 43 and 47% (Sorensen, 1973). There are similar sex differences in psychological reactions to first intercourse. Girls more frequently report negative affects, such as "afraid" (girls: 63%; boys: 17%), "guilty" (girls: 36%; boys: 3%), or "embarrassed" (girls: 31%; boys: 7%). Boys more frequently report positive experiences, such as "happy" (boys: 42%; girls, 26%) or "satisfied" (boys: 43%; girls: 20%).

Psychological Adaptations to Specific Biological Changes

We have just described two ways in which mediation of psychological adaptation to puberty occurs: (1) through intervening cognitive mediation and (2) through moderation by social control. Returning to the set of four groups of pubertal changes, we shall now review the evidence for the related psychological adaptations. As we mentioned, almost no research has investigated psychological correlates of endocrine changes. Psychological reactions to changes in reproductive status have been reviewed above. So we shall discuss adaptation to the timing of the onset of puberty and to the morphological changes.

Psychological Correlates of the Timing of the Onset of Puberty

The timing of pubertal onset shows considerable latitude, both for males and females (Faust, 1977; Marshall & Tanner, 1969, 1970). As a maturational variable, timing of pubertal onset is associated with both persistent psychological effects and other transient effects, which appear to "wash out" by late adolescence. Explanations of the differential consequences of early or late maturation take two broad forms. The first of these we shall call a *status* or *deviance hypothesis*. From this perspective early or late maturation places the adolescent in a socially "deviant" category, which may confer either social advantages or disadvantages. Differential psychosocial effects are interpreted as a function of the social-stimulus value of early versus late maturation. Stereotypic expectations associated with maturational timing are viewed as influencing the adolescent's social prestige, social adaptation, and self-concept.

A second position, which we shall call the *stage termination hypothesis,* argues that differences between early and late maturers may be a function of the amount of time available for continued ego development prior to the onset of puberty. From this perspective, early maturation interrupts the stabilizing acquisition and consolidation of adaptive skills that characterize the latency years. For girls, the detrimental effects of an early interruption may be offset, according to this theory, by the additional time provided for the developmental tasks of adolescence (Peskin, 1973; Peskin & Livson, 1972).

Research on the psychosocial effects of the timing of pubertal onset has focused on comparisons of the two "deviant" populations of early and late maturers. There is substantial inconsistency between the results of various studies, for reasons that are not altogether clear. The sex of the adolescents studied exercises a clear differential effect on findings. In addition, social-class differences as well as probable cohort and population differences appear to contribute to inconsistency of results (Clausen, 1975).

Earlier studies of pubertal onset in boys stress the desirable effects of early maturation. Based on data from the longitudinal Oakland Growth Study, early maturing boys were seen as more relaxed and attractive to adults (Jones & Bayley, 1950) and more attractive and popular with their peers than were the late maturers (Jones, 1965). At 17 years of age they displayed less dependency, greater self-confidence, and more "adult" behavior in interpersonal situations (Mussen & Jones, 1957). In the senior-high-school-years, early maturing was predictive of leadership, although this relationship was more powerful in the working class than in the middle class (Clausen, 1975). Jones (1965) found that, at age 30, late maturers scored significantly higher on the psychoneurotic scale of the California Psychological Inventory, while early maturers scored significantly higher on scales for socialization (indicating greater conformity), dominance, and good impression. Many of these effects appear to be transient. Later comparison of these groups at age 38 reveal only two differentiating characteristics: early maturers were seen as more conventional and took pride in seeing themselves as objective (Clausen, 1975).

Data on boys from the longitudinal Berkeley Guidance Study reveal somewhat different consequences of early and late maturation. The findings suggest that early maturation may also involve detrimental features, when conventional social criteria are not used as the primary focus of comparison. Peskin (1967) reports that early maturers become significantly more somber, temporarily more anxious, more submissive, less exploratory, less intellectually curious, and less active. With the onset of puberty, the late maturers displayed no consistent changes on these dimensions.

Studies of early- and late-maturing girls have produced somewhat divergent and confusing findings. Early maturers appear to suffer psychologically, but may enjoy enhanced social prestige. In an early study, Stolz and Stolz (1944) reported that early-maturing girls felt particularly conspicuous because of their size, frequently poor complexion, and menstrual status. Faust (1960) found that advanced physical development was related to greater social prestige in grades seven to nine, while being average for age was most desirable in grade six. In contrast, Jones and Mussen (1958) found that early-maturing girls in the Oakland Growth Study had "little influence on the group and seldom attained a high degree of popularity, prestige, or leadership" (p. 492). They were seen as "submissive, listless, or indifferent in social situations and lacking in poise" (p. 492). Late-maturing girls, in contrast to the boys as well as early-maturing girls, were described as significantly more outgoing, confident, assured, and having greater leadership ability. Clausen (1975) in a later analysis of the same sample reported that social-class variables mediated this relationship. For middle-class girls, early maturation was positively related to self-confidence on California Personality Inventory Scale, while for working-class girls there was a negative relationship between early maturation and confidence.

Peskin (1973), using the Berkeley Guidance Study sample, found that early-maturing girls displayed significantly greater undisguised crisis, loss of control, and unrest in adolescence, with greater explosiveness of temper, increased introversion, diminished sociability, and more whiney behavior. These negative effects appear to represent transient stress reactions because by age 30 the early maturers surpassed the late maturers in overall psychological health.

Body Satisfaction and Alteration of Body-Image in Puberty

The adolescent's system of cognitive self representations, referred to as body-image or body-schema, changes in response to the dramatic morphological changes of puberty. These changes in body image are frequently viewed as a major psychological task of early adolescence (Clifford, 1971; Hamburg, 1974; Kestenberg, 1967a and b, 1968; Schonfeld 1966, 1969, 1971). Surveys of young adolescents confirm high degrees of anxious body preoccupation and dissatisfaction (Hamburg, 1974). Junior-high-school students, in contrast to older adolescents, more frequently cited physical characteristics as what they most disliked about themselves (Frazier & Lisonbee, 1950; Jersild, 1952).

Although research on this issue remains unsystematic, a variety of intervening or contextual variables appear to mediate the adolescent's emotional evaluation of, and adaptation to, his or her changing physique. We have identified three such sets of variables.

First, the evaluations, reactions, and impressions imparted by parents and others concerning the adolescent's physical transformation appear to play a causal role. Bruch (1943) observes, for example, that parental attitudes of acceptance or depreciation concerning children's physical abnormalities are frequently more important in determining subjective attitudes toward the body than the actual bodily deviations themselves. Schonfeld (1966) reports that adolescents from families placing a high degree of value on physical attractiveness exhibit particular difficulty with perceived deviations from family norms.

Second, personality variables also mediate subjectively experienced stress or satisfaction associated with body developments. Schonfeld (1971) notes, for example, that repeated studies indicate that among adolescents well within the range of normal physical development, those who suffer from low self-esteem and general feelings of unacceptability are more likely to become disturbed, anxious about, and disapproving of, the appearance of their own bodies (Curran & Frosch, 1942; Levy, 1932; Stolz & Stolz, 1951). Jacobson (1964) observes that acceptance of changes in physique are also frequently complicated (or facilitated) by the extent to which the adolescent accepts the same-sex parent as a role model, in other terms, attitudes toward the morphological transition to adulthood may become colored by a broader struggle against identification (Greenson, 1954).

Third, sociocultural factors, including cultural standards of attractiveness, may also mediate psychological accommodations to morphological change. Research by Lerner (1969) and Staffieri (1967) document clear preferences for types of physique among children and adolescents with mesomorphy positively valued and endomorphy and ectomorphy negatively viewed. Clausen (1975) reports that the body-build of adolescents correlates with actual positive and negative evaluations by peers as well as with peer relationships and prestige. The nature of these correlations is significantly affected by social class (Clausen, 1975) as well as by cultural context (Mussen & Young, 1964). Although Clausen does not report relationships between these peer evaluations and the degree of subjectively reported conflict or satisfaction with body-development, it would be quite useful to determine whether such a correlation exists.

BIOPSYCHOSOCIAL DEVELOPMENT

We have reviewed the various biological aspects of puberty as well as the extant theories and data concerning psychological adaptation to puberty. This review reveals a recently expanding body of research on the biological changes but points out the serious deficiencies in theories and research examining psyche/soma relationships during puberty. At the theoretical level, formulations of the variables affecting this relationship are frequently unsystematic. At the research level, despite the long-standing theoretical assumptions about the psychological effects of pubertal changes, data are virtually lacking. Others (e.g., Lipsitz, 1977; Melges & Hamburg, 1977) have also remarked on the paucity of such investigations.

In the preceding section, we have organized our discussion of psychological adaptation to puberty by presenting two basic models for this process: direct-effect models and mediated-effect models. The consideration of these two models dichotomizes the continuous spectrum of ways that pubertal development might relate to psychological development. Petersen's (in press) model for biopsyschosocial development provides a starting point for the consideration of the various sources of influence on psychological development over the life span (Figure 8). These influences interact with each other and with psychological development.

Figure 10 shows how several biological factors might interact with sociocultural influences to affect psychological adaptation to pubertal changes. (Recall that though we recognize the reciprocal influence of psychological and sociocultural variables on physical change, we are here only focusing on paths from biological to psychological development.) Undoubtedly, genetic potentials underlie the timing and nature of pubertal events, particularly the endocrine changes. Hormonal changes, in turn, lead to secondary sex characteristic development. The timing of puberty and the nature of the morphological

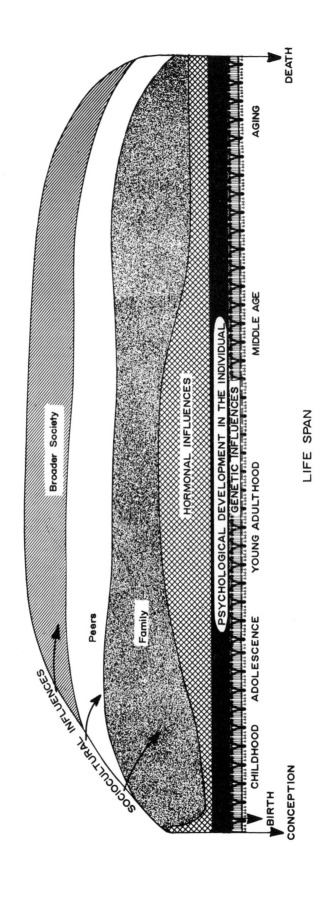

Figure 9 Hypothetical model for biopsychosocial development over the life cycle.

146

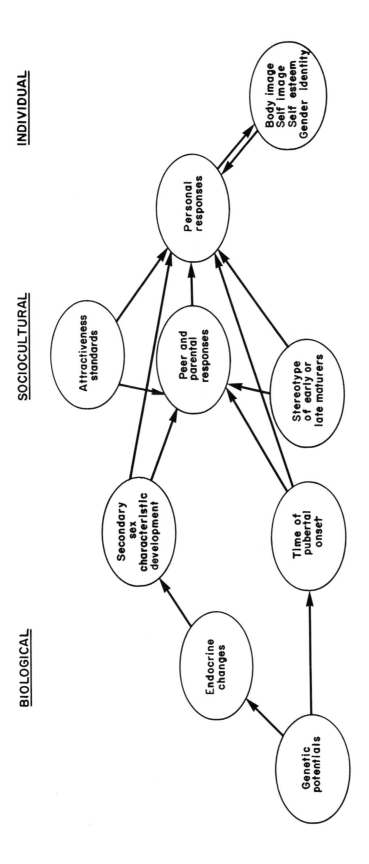

BIOLOGICAL

SOCIOCULTURAL

INDIVIDUAL

Figure 10 Hypothetically important paths between pubertal changes and psychological responses.

changes then interact with such sociocultural variables as standards of attractiveness and stereotypes of early and late maturers. These influence the individual directly as well as through parents and peers. The individual's integration of these influences, then, has an impact on such psychological factors as body-image, self-image, self-esteem, and gender identity.

In lieu of adequate data on this, Figure 11 depicts a hypothetical causal pathway between changes in pubertal hormones and psychological development. The steadily increasing levels of gonadal hormones lead to the development of secondary sex characteristics and increasing sexual dimorphism. This morphological change requires a change in the body image, a change that is mediated by sociocultural standards of attractiveness. For example, sociocultural ideals of a slender versus a Rubenesque shape may affect the feelings girls have about their own shapes. Body-image, in turn, is likely to be related to gender identity, self-image and self-esteem.

A second possible pathway for the influence of pubertal hormones might be a more direct one. It is possible that the erratically fluctuating levels of gonadotropins in early puberty might lead to a moodiness in these youth. Presumably, any such effect would be mediated by sociocultural norms for appropriate behavior for youth at this stage of life. It is further possible that moody behavior might produce negative responses from others, particularly parents, tending to lead to psychological turmoil. Such a pathway remains purely hypothetical at this point; no direct evidence exists for it.

We have stressed the need for more research on early adolescence, the pubertal years. The neglect of youth at this age (see Lipsitz, 1977) is puzzling. Early adolescents may be baffling to adults, because of acting out, moodiness, or whatever, but there is some hint that adults have a particular problem responding to these young people. Pubescent youth

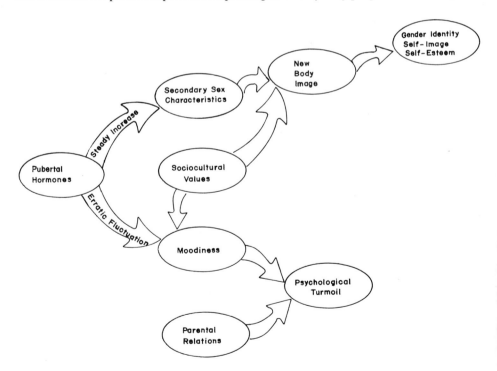

Figure 11   Possible pathways for influences of pubertal hormones.

seem to elicit anxiety in adults, perhaps due to remembrances of the adult's own puberty or to new sexual feelings in parents toward their pubertal children. Similarly, people seem to have a peculiar amnesia about their own puberty. Sommer (1978) reported that college students could remember events and feelings from the previous years, except for the pubertal years. A. Freud (1958) reported that patients in psychoanalysis recall events — but rarely recall any affect related to the pubertal years. What might be responsible for this forgetting?

Grave (1974), an endocrinologist, suggested that the significant aspect of pubertal growth, relative to other equally dramatic periods of growth occurring earlier in life, is that young people can see themselves changing. Perhaps the experience is too stressful to integrate easily. The psychological meaning of the pubertal experience is currently unknown. Discovering its meaning will require simultaneous consideration of the various factors known to mediate the psychological experience of biological change.

REFERENCES

Angsusingha, K., Kenny, F. M., Nankin, H. R., and Taylor, F. H. Unconjugated estrone, estradiol, and FSH and LH in prepubertal and pubertal males and females. *Journal of Clinical Endocrinology and Metabolism*, 1974, *39*, 63–68.

Apter, D. and Vihko, R. Serum pregnenolone, progesterone, 17-hydroxyprogesterone, testosterone, and 5-dehydrotestosterone during female puberty. *Journal of Clinical Endocrinology and Metabolism*, 1977, *45*, 1039–1048.

Beach, F. A. Behavioral endocrinology: An emerging discipline. *American Scientist*, 1975, *63*, 178–187.

Bem, D. J. Cognitive alteration of feeling states. In H. London and R. E. Nisbett (Eds.), *Thought and feeling*. Chicago: Aldine, 1974.

Blizzard, R. M., Thompson, R. G., Baghdassarian, A., Kowarski, A., Migeon, C. J., and Rodriguez, A. The interrelationship of steroids, growth hormone, and other hormones in pubertal growth. In M. M. Grumbach, G. D. Grave, and F. E. Mayer (Eds.), *Control of the onset of puberty*. New York: Wiley, 1974.

Blos, P. *On adolescence: A psychoanalytic interpretation*. New York: Free Press, 1962.

———. The initial stage of male adolescence. In *The Psychoanalytic Study of the Child* (Vol. 22). New York: International Universities Press, 1965.

———. *The young adolescent*. New York: Free Press, 1970.

Bock, R. D., Wainer, H., Petersen, A., Thissen, D., Murray, J., and Roche, A. F. A parameterization for individual human growth curves. *Human Biology*, 1973, *45*, 63–80.

Boyar, R. M., Finkelstein, J. W., Roffwarg, H., Kapen, S., Weitzman, E. D., and Hellman, L. Synchronization of augmented luteinizing hormone-secretion with sleep during puberty. *The New England Journal of Medicine*, 1972, *287*, 582–586.

Boyar, R. M., Wu, R. H. K., Roffwarg, H., Kapen, S., Weitzman, E. D., Hellman, L., and Finkelstein, J. W. Human puberty: 24-hour estradiol patterns in pubertal girls. *Journal of Clinical Endocrinology and Metabolism*, 1976, *43*, 1418–1420.

Bruch, H., Psychiatric aspects of obesity in children. *American Journal of Psychiatry*, 1943, *99*, 752–757.

Cheek, D. B. Body composition, nutrition, and adolescent growth. In M. M. Grumbach, G. D. Grave, and F. E. Mayer (Eds.), *Control of the onset of puberty*. New York: Wiley, 1974.

Christensen, H. T. and Carpenter, G. Value-behavior discrepancies regarding premarital coitus in three western cultures. *American Sociological Review,* 1972, *27,* 66–74.

Christensen, H. T. and Gregg, C. F. Changing sex norms in America and Scandinavia. *Journal of Marriage and the Family,* 1970, *32,* 616–627.

Clausen, J. A. The social meaning of differential physical and sexual maturation. In S. E. Dragastin and G. H. Elder, Jr. (Eds.), *Adolescence in the life cycle.* New York: Halsted, 1975.

Clifford, E. Body satisfaction in adolescence. *Journal of Perceptual and Motor Skills,* 1971, *33,* 119–125.

Curran, F. J. and Frosch, J. The body image in adolescent boys. *Journal of Genetic Psychology,* 1942, *60,* 37–60.

dePeretti, E., and Forest, M. C. Unconjugated dehydroepiandrosterone plasma levels in normal subjects from birth to adolescence in humans: The use of a sensitive radioimmunoassay. *Journal of Clinical Endocrinology and Metabolism,* 1976, *43,* 982–991.

Doering, C. H., Brodie, H. K. H., Kraemer, H., Becker, H., and Hamburg, D. A. Plasma testosterone levels and psychologic measures in men over a 2-month period. In R. C. Friedman, R. M. Richard, and R. L. VandeWiele, (Eds.), *Sex differences in behavior.* New York: Wiley, 1974.

Doering, C. H., Kraemer, H. C., Brodie, H. K. H., and Hamburg, D. A. A cycle of plasma testosterone in the human male. *Journal of Clinical Endocrinology and Metabolism,* 1975, *40,* 492–500.

Donovan, B. T. Concluding comments. In M. M. Grumbach, G. D. Grave, F. E. Mayer (Eds.), *Control of the onset of puberty.* New York: Wiley, 1974.

Ducharme, H. R., Forest, M. O. dePeretti, E., Sempé, M., Collu, R., and Bertrand, J. Plasma adrenal and gonadal sex steroids in human pubertal development. *Journal of Clinical Endocrinology and Metabolism,* 1976, *42,* 468–476.

Eichorn, D. H. Asynchronizations in adolescent development. In S. E. Dragastin and G. H. Elder, Jr. (Eds.), *Adolescence in the life cycle.* New York: Halsted, 1975.

Fabrega, H. The study of disease in relation to culture. *Behavioral Science,* 1972, *12,* 183–203.

Faiman, C. and Winter, J. S. D. Gonadotropins and sex hormone patterns in puberty: Clinical data. In M. M. Grumbach, G. D. Grave, and F. E. Mayer (Eds.), *Control of the onset of puberty.* New York: Wiley, 1974.

Faust, M. S. Developmental maturity as a determinant of prestige in adolescent girls. *Child Development,* 1960, *31,* 173–184.

———. Somatic development of adolescent girls. *Monographs of the Society for Research in Child Development,* 1977, (1, Serial No. 169).

Ford, C. and Beach, F. *Patterns of sexual behavior.* New York: Harper-Hoeber, 1951.

Frasier, A. and Lisonbee, L. K. Adolescent concerns with physique. *School Review,* 1950, *58,* 397–405.

Freud, A. *The ego and the mechanisms of defense.* New York: International Universities Press, 1946.

Freud, A. Adolescence. In R. S. Eissler et al. (Eds.), *Psychoanalytic study of the child* (Vol. 13). New York: International Universities Press, 1958.

Freud, S. The transformation of puberty. In J. Strachey (Ed.), *The standard edition of the complete psychological works of Sigmund Freud* (Vol. 7). London: Hogarth, 1953. (Originally published, 1905).

Frisch, R. E. Critical weight at menarche, initiation of the adolescent growth spurt, and control of puberty. In M. M. Grumbach, G. D. Grave, and F. E. Mayer (Eds.), *Control of the onset of puberty.* New York: Wiley, 1974.

————. Population, food intake, and fertility. *Science,* 1978, *199,* 22–30.

Frisch, R. E. and Revelle, R. Variations in body weights and the age of the adolescent growth spurt among Latin American and Asian populations in relation to caloric supplies. *Human Biology,* 1969a, *41,* 185–212.

————. Height and weight of adolescent boys and girls at the time of peak velocity of growth in height and weight: Longitudinal data. *Human Biology,* 1969b, *41,* 536–559.

————. Height and weight at menarche and a hypothesis of critical body weights and adolescent events. *Science,* 1970, *169,* 397–399.

————. The height and weight of girls and boys at the time of initiation of the adolescent growth spurt in height and weight and the relationship to menarche. *Human Biology,* 1971, *43,* 140–159.

Goethals, G. W. Factors affecting permissive and nonpermissive rules regarding premarital sex. In J. M. Henslin (Ed.), *The sociology of sex: A book of readings.* New York, Appleton-Century-Crofts, 1971.

Grave, G. D. Introduction. In M. M. Grumbach, G. D. Grave, and F. E. Mayer (Eds.), *The control of the onset of puberty.* New York: Wiley, 1974.

Greenson, R. The struggle against identification. *Journal of the American Psychoanalytic Association,* 1954, *2,* 200–217.

Grumbach, M. M., Grave, G. D. and Mayer, F. E. (Eds.), *Control of the onset of puberty.* New York: Wiley, 1974.

Grumbach, M. M., Roth, J. C., Kaplan, S. L., and Kelch, R. P. Hypothalamic-pituitary regulation of puberty: Evidence and concepts derived from clincial research. In M. M. Grumbach, G. D. Grave, and F. E. Mayer (Eds.), *Control of the onset of puberty.* New York: Wiley, 1974.

Gupta, D. Changes in the gonadal and adrenal steroid patterns during puberty. *Clinics in Endocrinology and Metabolism,* 1975, *4,* 27–56.

Gupta, D., Attanasio, A., and Raaf, S. Plasma estrogen and androgen concentrations in children during adolescence. *Journal of Clinical Endocrinology and Metabolism,* 1975, *40,* 636–643.

Hamburg, B. Early adolescence: A specific and stressful stage of the life cycle. In G. Coelho, D. A. Hamburg, and J. E. Adams (Eds.), *Coping and adaption.* New York: Basic Books, 1974.

Hansen, S. W., Hoffman, H. J., and Ross, G. T. Monthly gonadotropin cycles in premenarcheal girls. *Science,* 1975, *190,* 161–163.

Hayes, A. and Johanson, A. Excretion of follicle stimulating hormone (FSH) and luteinizing hormone (LH) in urine of pubertal girls. *Pediatric Research,* 1972, *6,* 18–25.

Hopper, B. R., and Yen, S. S. C. Circulating concentrations of dehydroepiandrosterone and dehydroepiandrosterone sulfate during puberty. *Journal of Clinical Endocrinology and Metabolism,* 1975, *40,* 458–461.

Horst, H. J., Bartsch, W., and Dirksen-Thedens, I. Plasma testosterone, sex hormone binding globulin binding capacity and percent binding of testosterone and 5a-dihydrotesterone in prepubertal, pubertal, and adult males. *Journal of Clinical Endocrinology and Metabolism,* 1977, *45,* 522–527.

Jacobson, E. *The self and the object world.* New York: International Universities Press, 1964.

Jersild, A. I. *In search of self.* New York: Columbia University Press, 1952.

Jessor, S. L. and Jessor, R. Transition from virginity to nonvirginity among youth: A social-psychological study over time. *Developmental Psychology,* 1975, *11,* 473–484.

Jones, M. C. Psychological correlates of somatic development. *Child Development,* 1965, *36,* 899–911.

Jones, M. C. and Bayley, N. Physical maturing among boys as related to behavior. *Journal of Educational Psychology*, 1950, *41*, 129–148.

Jones, M. C. and Mussen, P. H. Self-conceptions, motivations, and interpersonal attitudes of early- and late-maturing girls. *Child Development*, 1958, *29*, 491–501.

Judd, H. L., Parker, D. C., and Yen, S. S. C. Sleep-wake patterns of LH and testosterone release in prepubertal boys. *Journal of Clinical Endocrinology and Metabolism*, 1977, *44*, 865–869.

Kapen, S., Boyar, R. M., Finkelstein, J. W., Hellman, L., and Weitzman, E. D. Effect of sleep-wake cycle reversal on luteinizing hormone-secretory pattern in puberty. *Journal of Clinical Endocrinology and Metabolism*, 1974, *39*, 293–299.

Kenyatta, J. *Facing Mt. Kenya*. New York: Random House, 1968.

Kestenberg, J. Phases of adolescence with suggestions for a correlation of psychic and hormonal organization. Part I: Antecedents of adolescent organizations in childhood. *Journal of the American Academy of Child Psychiatry*, 1967a, *6*, 426–463.

———. Phases of adolescence with suggestions for correlation of psychic and hormonal organizations. Part II: Prepuberty, diffusion, and reintegration. *Journal of the American Academy of Child Psychiatry*, 1967b, *6*, 577–614.

———. Phases of adolescence with suggestions for a correlation of psychic and hormonal organizations. Part III: Puberty growth, differentiation, and consolidation. *Journal of the American Academy of Child Psychiatry*, 1968, *7*, 108–151.

Kinsey, A. C., Pomeroy, W. B., and Martin, C. E. *Sexual behavior in the human male*. Philadelphia: Saunders, 1948.

———. *Sexual behavior in the human female*. Philadelphia: Saunders, 1953.

Korth-Schultz, S., Levine, L. S. and New, M. I. Serum androgens in normal prepubertal and pubertal children and in children with precocious adrenarche. *Journal of Clinical Endocrinology and Metabolism*, 1976, *42*, 117–124.

Kulin, H. E., Grumbach, M. M. and Kaplan, S. L. Changing sensitivity of the pubertal gonadal hypothalamic feedback mechanism in man. *Science*, 1969, *166*, 1012–1013.

———. Gonadal-hypothalamic interaction in prepubertal and pubertal man: Effect of clomiphene citrate on urinary follicle — stimulating hormone and luteinizing hormone and plasma testosterone. *Pediatric Research*, 1972, *6*, 162–171.

Lee, P. A., Jaffe, R. B. and Midgley, A. R., Jr. Serum gonadotropin, testosterone, and prolactin concentrations throughout puberty in boys: A longitudinal study. *Journal of Clinical Endocrinology and Metabolism*, 1974, *39*, 664–672.

Lee, P. A. and Migeon, C. J. Puberty in boys: Correlation of plasma levels of gonadotropins (LH, FSH), androgens (testosterone, androstenedione, dehydroepiandrosterone and its sulfate), estrogens (estrone and estradiol) and progestins (progesterone and 17-hydroxyprogesterone) *Journal of Clinical Endocrinology and Metabolism*, 1975, *41*, 556–562.

Lerner, R. M. The development of stereotyped expectancies of body build-behavior relations. *Child Development*, 1969, *40*, 137–141.

LeVine, R. *Culture, behavior, and personality*. Chicago: Aldine, 1973.

Levy, D. M. Body interest in children and hypochondriasis. *American Journal of Psychiatry*, 1932, *12*, 295–315.

Lipsitz, J. *Growing up forgotten*. Lexington, Mass.: Lexington Books, 1977.

London, H. and Nisbett, R. E. (Eds.), *Thought and feeling*. Chicago: Aldine. 1974.

Marcus, R. and Korenman, S. G. Estrogens and the human male. *Annual Review of Medicine*, 1976, *27*, 357–370.

Marshall, W. A. and Tanner, J. M. Variations in the pattern of pubertal changes in girls. *Archives of Disease in Childhood,* 1969, *44,* 291–303.

――――. Variations in the pattern of pubertal changes in boys. *Archives of Disease in Childhood,* 1970, *45,* 13–23.

Mead, M. *Coming of age in Samoa.* New York: Morrow, 1928.

Mead, M. Adolescence in primitive and modern society. In G. E. Swanson, T. M. Newcomb, and E. K. Hartley (Eds.), *Readings in social psychology.* New York: Holt, 1958.

Melges, F. T. and Hamburg, D. A. Psychological effects of hormonal changes in women. In F. A. Beach (Ed.), *Human sexuality in four perspectives.* Baltimore: The Johns Hopkins University Press, 1977.

Money, J. Adolescent psychohormonal development. *Southwestern Medicine,* 1967, *48,* 182–186.

Money, J. and Ehrhardt, A. A. *Man and woman, boy and girl.* Baltimore: The Johns Hopkins University Press, 1972.

Murdock, G. P. Cultural correlates of the regulation of premarital sex behavior. In R. A. Manners (Ed.), *Process and pattern in culture: Essays in honor of Julian B. Steward.* Chicago: Aldine, 1964.

Mussen, P. H. and Jones, M. C. Self-conceptions, motivations and interpersonal attitudes of late- and early-maturing boys. *Child Development,* 1957, *28,* 243–256.

Mussen, P. H. and Young, H. B. Relationships between rate of physical maturing and personality among boys of Italian descent. *Vita Humana,* 1964, *7,* 186–200.

Nisbett, R. E. and Schachter, S. The cognitive manipulation of pain. *Journal of Experimental Social Psychology,* 1966, *2,* 227–236.

Offer, D. *The psychological world of the teenager,* New York: Basic Books, 1969.

Parlee, M. B. Time series analysis of infradian rhythms in human beings. Paper presented in a Symposium at the American Psychological Association Annual Meeting, San Francisco, 1977.

Penny, R., Olambiwonnu, N. O., & Frasier, S. D. Episodic fluctuations of serum gonadotropins in pre- and postpubertal girls and boys. *Journal of Clinical Endocrinology and Metabolism,* 1977, *45,* 307–311.

Penny, R., Parlow, A. G., Olambiwonnu, N. O., and Frasier, S. D. Evolution of the menstrual pattern of gonadotrophin and sex-steroid concentrations in serum. *Acta Endocrinologica,* 1977, *84,* 729–737.

Peskin, H. Pubertal onset and ego functioning. *Journal of Abnormal Psychology,* 1967, *72,* 1–15.

Peskin, H. Influence of the developmental schedule of puberty on learning and ego development. *Journal of Youth and Adolescence,* 1973, *2,* 273–290.

Peskin, H. and Livson, M. Pre- and postpubertal personality and adult psychological functioning. *Seminars in Psychiatry,* 1972, *4,* 343–353.

Petersen, A. C. *The relationship of androgenicity in males and females to spatial ability and fluent production.* Unpublished doctoral dissertation, University of Chicago, 1973.

――――. Female pubertal development. In M. Sugar (Ed.), *Female adolescent development,* New York: Brunner/Mazel, 1979, pp. 23–46.

――――. Biopsychosocial development of sex-related differences. In J. Parsons (Ed.), *Psychobiological bases of sex-role related behaviors.* Washington, D.C.: Hemisphere Publishing Co., in press.

Resko, J. A. and Eik-Nes, K. B. Diurnal testosterone levels in peripheral plasma of human male subjects. *Journal of Clinical Endocrinology and Metabolism,* 1966, *26,* 573–576.

Robinson, J. D., Judd, H. L., Young, P. E., Jones, O. W., and Yen, S. S. C. Amniotic fluid androgens and estrogens in midgestation. *Journal of Clinical Endocrinology and Metabolism,* 1977, *45,* 755–761.

Rosenfield, R. L. Plasma testosterone binding globulin and indexes of the concentration of unbound plasma androgens in normal and hirsute subjects. *Journal of Clinical Endocrinology and Metabolism,* 1971, *32,* 717–728.

Ryser, P. E. *Review of "Adolescent sexuality in contemporary America."* by R. Sorenson. *Journal of Marriage and the Family,* 1974, *34,* 637–641.

Santen, R. J. and Bardin, C. W. Episodic luteinizing hormone secretion in man. *Journal of Clinical Investigation,* 1973, *52,* 2617–2628.

Schachter, S. The interaction of cognitive and physiological determinants of emotional state. In L. Berkowitz (Ed.), *Advances in experimental social psychology* (Vol. 1). New York: Academic, 1964.

Schachter, S. and Singer, J. E. Cognitive, social, and physiological determinants of emotional state. *Psychological Review,* 1962, *69,* 379–399.

Schonfeld, W. Body-image in adolescents: A psychiatric concept for the pediatrician. *Pediatrics,* 1963, *31,* 845–855.

———. Body-image disturbances in adolescents: Influence of family attitudes and psychopathology. *Archives of General Psychiatry,* 1966, *15,* 16–21.

———. The body and body image. In G. Caplan and S. Leibovici (Eds.), *Adolescence: Psychosocial perspectives.* New York: Basic Books, 1969.

———. Adolescent development: Biological, psychological, and sociological determinants. In S. Feinstein, P. Giovacchini, and A. Miller (Eds.), *Adolescent psychiatry* (Vol. 1). New York: Basic Books, 1971.

Seyler, L. E. and Reichlin, S. Episodic secretion of luteinizing hormone-releasing factor (LRF) in the human. *Journal of Clinical Endocrinology and Metabolism,* 1974, *39,* 471–498.

Simon, W. and Gagnon, J. H. The lesbians: A preliminary overview. In J. H. Gagnon and W. Simon (Eds.), *Sexual deviance.* New York: Harper & Row, 1967.

———. On psychosexual development. In D. A. Goslin (Ed.), *Handbook of socialization theory and research.* Chicago: Rand McNally, 1969.

Sizonenko, P. C., and Paunier, L. Hormonal changes in puberty. III: Correlation of plasma dehydroepiandrosterone, testosterone, FSH, and LH with stages of puberty and bone age in normal boys and girls and in patients with Addison's disease and hypogonadism or with premature or late adrenarche. *Journal of Clinical Endocrinology and Metabolism,* 1975, *41,* 894–904.

Sommer, B. *Puberty and adolescence.* New York: Oxford University Press, 1978.

Sorensen, R. C. *Adolescent sexuality in contemporary America.* New York: World, 1973.

Spiro, M. E. Social systems, personality, and functional analysis. In B. Kaplan (Ed.), *Studying personality cross-culturally.* Evanston, Ill: Row, Petersen, 1961.

Staffieri, J. R. A study of social stereotype of body-image in children. *Journal of Personality and Social Psychology,* 1967, *7,* 101–104.

H. R. Stolz and L. M. Stolz (Eds.), National Society for the Study of Education (NSSE). In *Adolescence* (Part I) (43rd Yearbook, National Society for the Study of Education.) Chicago: University of Chicago Press, 1944.

Stolz, H. R. and Stolz, L. M. *Somatic development of adolescent boys.* New York: Macmillan, 1951.

Tanner, J. M. *Growth at adolescence.* Springfield, Ill.: Thomas, 1962.

————. Growth and endocrinology of the adolescent. In L. I. Gardner (Ed.), *Endocrine and genetic diseases of childhood*. Philadelphia: Saunders, 1969.

————. Sequence, tempo, and individual variation in growth and development of boys and aged twelve to sixteen. In J. Kagan and R. Coles (Eds.), *Twelve to sixteen: Early adolescence*. New York: Norton, 1972.

————. Sequence and tempo in the somatic changes in puberty. In M. M. Grumbach, G. D. Grave, and F. E. Mayer (Eds.), *Control of the onset of puberty*. New York: Wiley, 1974.

Tepperman, J. *Metabolic and endocrine physiology*. Chicago: Year Book Medical Publishers, 1968.

Thissen, D., Bock, R. D., Wainer, H., and Roche, A. F. Individual growth in stature: A comparison of four growth studies in the USA. *Annals of Human Biology*, 1976, *3*, 529–542.

Udry, J. R., Bauman, K. E., and Morris, N. M. Changes in premarital coital experience of recent decade-of-birth cohorts of urban American women. *Journal of Marriage and the Family*, 1975, *37*, 783–787.

Vener, A. M. and Stewart, C. S. Adolescent sexual behavior in middle America revisted: 1970–1973. *Journal of Marriage and the Family;* 1974, *36*, 728–735.

Warne, G. L., Faiman, C., Reyes, F. I., and Winter, J. S. D. Studies on human sexual development: V. Concentrations of testosterone, 17-hydroxyprogesterone and progesterone in human amniotic fluid throughout gestation. *Journal of Clinical Endocrinology and Metabolism*, 1977, *44*, 934–938.

West, C. D., Mahajan, D. K., Chavre, V. J., Nabors, C. J., and Tyler, F. H. Simultaneous measurement of multiple plasma steroids by radio-immunoassay demonstrating episodic secretion. *Journal of Clinical Endocrinology and Metabolism*, 1973, *36*, 1230–1236.

Whiting, J. W. and Child, I. L. *Child training and personality*. New Haven, Conn.: Yale University Press, 1953.

————. *Field guide for the study of socialization*. New York: Wiley, 1966.

Winter, J. S. D. and Faiman, C. The development of cyclic pituitary-gonadal function in adolescent females. *Journal of Clinical Endocrinology and Metabolism*, 1973a, *37*, 714–718.

————. Pituitary-gonadal relations in female children and adolescents. *Pediatric Research*, 1973b, *7*, 948–953.

Young, H. B. The physiology of adolescence. In J. G. Howells (Ed.), *Modern perspectives in adolescent psychiatry*. New York: Brunner/Mazel, 1971.

Zelnik, M. and Kantner, J. F. Sexual and contraceptive experience of young unmarried women in the United States, 1976 and 1971. *Family Planning Perspectives*, 1977, *9*, 55–71.

PART TWO

The Processes of Adolescence

CHAPTER 5

Identity in Adolescence

James E. Marcia

INTRODUCTION

One difficulty in studying adolescence is the definition of the period itself. It is somewhat variable but specific in its beginnings with the physiological changes of puberty; it is highly variable and nonspecific in its end. If the termination of adolescence were to depend on the attainment of a certain psychosocial position, the formation of an identity, then, for some, it would never end. Moreover, identity is an even more difficult term to delimit than is adolescence. Identity refers to an existential position, to an inner organization of needs, abilities, and self-perceptions as well as to a sociopolitical stance. Studying identity in adolescence is not a task for the methodologically hypersensitive.

In this chapter, I shall not try to cover every bit of research done on identity in adolescence. What I shall do is take a theoretical position, ego psychoanalytic, discuss research conducted within that theoretical framework, and suggest some directions for future investigation. Erik Erikson (1959, 1963, 1968) has been the most influential writer on identity in the past two decades. He places identity within the context of ego-psychoanalytic theory, viewing it as the epigenetically based psychosocial task distinctive, but not exclusive, to adolescence.

IDENTITY

Identity has been called a ''sense,'' an ''attitude,'' a ''resolution,'' and so on. I would like to propose another way of construing identity: as a self-structure — an internal, self-constructed, dynamic organization of drives, abilities, beliefs, and individual history. The better developed this structure is, the more aware individuals appear to be of their own uniqueness and similarity to others and of their own strengths and weaknesses in making their way in the world. The less developed this structure is, the more confused individuals seem about their own distinctiveness from others and the more they have to rely on external sources to evaluate themselves. The identity structure is dynamic, not static. Elements are continually being added and discarded. Over a period of time, the entire gestalt may shift. Although the content of individual identities may be interesting, the most crucial area for study is the underlying process: the patterning of more or less disparate parts into a flexible unity.

Viewed in this way, it is not entirely accurate to say that one ''has'' an identity, any more than one ''has'' formal operations, or ''has'' postconventional moral reasoning. All three of these are inferred, underlying, and fairly stable structures whose referents are

159

observable sets of problem-solving responses. These organizations, or structures, change gradually. The material to which they give form, the forms evolved, and the responses that proceed from them change with age and experience. There are some periods in individuals' lives that are more crucial than others for change in structural form. Adolescence seems to be one of these. It is a period of transition in approach to cognitive tasks — from concrete to formal operations; in approach to moral issues — from law-and-order ("duty") reasoning to transcendent human values; in approach to psychosocial concerns — from others' expectations and directives to one's own unique organization of one's history, skills, shortcomings, and goals.

The most proximate psychosocial forerunner to identity in adolescence is the sense of industry attained in latency. Identity's most immediate heir is intimacy, the predominant issue of young adulthood. Although there are good social and physiological reasons for this industry-identity-intimacy progression, there are even more compelling psychological ones. The dependence of identity achievement on a sense of industry results from the importance of vocational[1] commitment in identity formation. A successful outcome of the industry period leaves one with a set of specific skills and confidence in one's capacity for worthwhile work. It is this generally positive attitude toward work and the secure possession of skills that form the basis for vocational direction. Identity contributes to intimacy that sense of a secure self necessary to enable one to risk the vulnerability inherent in temporary merger with another. It is the paradox of intimacy that it is a strength that can be acquired only through vulnerability; and vulnerability is possible only with the internal assurance of a firm identity.

The identity process neither begins nor ends with adolescence. It begins with the self-object differentiation at infancy and reaches its final phase with the self-mankind integration at old age. What is important about identity in adolescence, particularly late adolescence, is that this is the first time that physical development, cognitive skills, and social expectations coincide to enable young persons to sort through and synthesize their childhood identifications in order to construct a viable pathway toward their adulthood. Resolution of the identity issue at adolescence guarantees only that one will be faced with subsequent identity "crises." A well-developed identity structure, like a well-developed superego, is flexible. It is open to changes in society and to changes in relationships. This openness assures numerous reorganizations of identity *contents* throughout the "identity-achieved" person's life, although the essential identity *process* remains the same, growing stronger through each crisis.

Identity formation does not happen neatly. At the bare minimum, it involves commitment to a sexual orientation, an ideological stance, and a vocational direction. Synthesizing the identity components is as much a process of negation as affirmation. One must relinquish one's parents as psychosexual objects, relinquish childhood ideology based on one's position as a "taker," and relinquish the fantasized possibilities of multiple, glamorous life styles. In the ongoing construction of an identity, that which one negates is known; what one affirms and chooses contains an element of the unknown. That is one of the reasons why some young people either do not form an identity or form only a partial one. They cannot risk saying "no" to elements of their past of which they are certain and make the affirmative leap into an uncertain future.

Although some identity crises are cataclysmic and totally preoccupying, identity

---

[1] "Vocation" has been used here instead of "occupation" in order to provide as broad a term as possible for one's "work in the world." So long as only occupation, specifically, is considered, a predominant mode of identity formation for many women, the development and maintenance of interpersonal relationships, is overlooked or inadvertently disparaged. This issue will be discussed later in the chapter.

formation usually proceeds in a much more gradual and nonconscious way. It gets done by bits and pieces. Decisions are not made once and for all, but have to be made again and again. And the decisions may seem trivial at the time: whom to date, whether or not to break up, having intercourse, taking drugs, going to college or working, which college, what major, studying or playing, being politically active, and so on. Each of these decisions has identity-forming implications. The decisions and the bases on which one decides begin to form themselves into a more or less consistent core or structure. Of course, there are ways in which one can circumvent the decision-making process: one can let previously incorporated, parentally based values determine one's actions; one can permit oneself to be pushed one way or the other by external pressures; or one can become mired in indecision. The origins and natures of some of these pathways toward identity in adolescence have been described by Douvan and Adelson (1966), Offer and Offer (1975) and Waterman (in press). What I shall discuss now are some styles of resolution of the identity issue observable in late adolescence: the identity statuses.

IDENTITY STATUSES

The identity statuses were developed as a methodological device by means of which Erikson's theoretical notions about identity might be subjected to empirical study. They seem now to have become a part of identity theory. The identity statuses are four modes of dealing with the identity issue characteristic of late adolescents:

- Identity Achievement
- Foreclosure
- Identity Diffusion
- Moratorium

Those classified by these modes are defined in terms of the presence or absence of a decision-making period (crisis) and the extent of personal investment (commitment) in two areas: occupation and ideology. *Identity Achievements* are individuals who have experienced a decision-making period and are pursuing self-chosen occupation and ideological goals. *Foreclosures* are persons who are also committed to occupational and ideological positions, but these have been parentally chosen rather than self-chosen. They show little or no evidence of "crisis."[2] *Identity Diffusions* are young people who have no set occupational or ideological direction, regardless of whether or not they may have experienced a decision-making period. *Moratoriums* are individuals who are currently struggling with occupational and/or ideological issues; they are *in* an identity crisis. The criteria for the identity statuses are summarized in Table 1.

There are two clear advantages of the identity statuses as an approach to research on ego identity. The first is that they provide for a greater variety of styles in dealing with the identity issue than does Erikson's simple dichotomy of identity versus identity confusion. Secondly, there are *both* healthy and pathological aspects to each of the styles, save perhaps the Identity Achievement status. For example, Foreclosures may be seen either as steadfast or rigid, committed or dogmatic, cooperative or conforming; Moratoriums may be viewed either as sensitive or anxiety-ridden, highly ethical or self-righteous, flexible or vacillating; Identity Diffusions may be considered either carefree or careless, charming or psychopathic, independent or schizoid. Identity Achievements, for the most part, are seen as strong, self-directed, and highly adaptive. Even here, however, there is a kind of pre-

[2]This status is similar to what Blos (1962) refers to as "abbreviated adolescence."

Table 1   Criteria for the Identity Statuses

Position on Occupation and Ideology	Identity Status			
	Identity Achievement	Foreclosure	Identity Diffusion	Moratorium
Crisis	present	absent	present or absent	in crisis
Commitment	present	present	absent	present but vague

mature identity achievement that may limit one's ultimate adaptiveness by fixing too early on occupational and ideological commitments. Another advantage of the identity statuses is that, at least in comparison with Erikson's theoretical writings, they are relatively objective. They can be determined with a fair degree of interobserver reliability, usually around 80% (Marcia, 1976b).

Whether it is for the above or other reasons, much of the psychological research on identity in the past 10 years has utilized the identity statuses. In the sections that follow, I shall discuss identity and identity-status research in four general areas: individual personality characteristics; patterns of interactions with others; developmental antecedents and consequents; and identity in women. The latter constitutes a separate area for two reasons: (1) the same variables have seldom been explored with both males and females and (2) the findings obtained with females have been sufficiently different and problematical to justify a separate discussion. It should be kept in mind that the descriptions that follow apply only to males unless specifically noted otherwise. The chapter will close with a discussion of implications of the research and some suggestions for future directions.

PERSONALITY CHARACTERISTICS

Much of the early research on identity and identity status was concerned with establishing some validity for the construct itself. These initial studies as well as some later ones yielded a number of personality correlates of identity and established the identity statuses as discriminable modes of identity resolution. The research reported in this section is addressed especially to the question: What are characteristics of late-adolescent males who pursue different modes of identity resolution?

Anxiety

Moratoriums, as might be expected from their "in-crisis" position, are the most anxious of the statuses, and Foreclosures, perhaps for defensive reasons, are the least anxious (Marcia, 1967). Closely related to anxiety is the represser-sensitizer dimension developed by Byrne (1961). Employing this measure, Mahler (1969) found Moratoriums to score in the sensitizer direction and Foreclosures to score in the represser section. Podd, Marcia, and Rubin (1970) also interpreted Moratoriums' unusually long response latencies in a prisoners' dilemma game as indicative of high anxiety. Oshman and Manosevitz (1974) found that Moratoriums, together with Foreclosures, had conflict patterns on the

Minnesota Multiphasic Personality Inventory (MMPI), as contrasted with normal patterns for Identity Achievements and Identity Diffusions. Stark and Traxler (1974) obtained a negative correlation between identity- and anxiety-scale scores.

Self-esteem

Cabin (1966) found that high-identity college males rated themselves more positively in an ambiguous social situation than did low-identity males. College males high in identity reported greater self-ideal similarity with self than did those low in identity (Rosenfeld, 1972); correspondingly, identity-diffuse high-school boys had a greater discrepancey between their self-concept and their concept of how others perceived them than did boys who were attaining an identity (Bunt, 1968). According to Breuer (1973), Identity Achievements and Moratoriums obtained higher self-esteem scores than did Foreclosures and Identity Diffusions. Marcia (1967) found that Foreclosures and Identity Diffusions were more liable to change their evaluations of themselves, both positively and negatively, in response to external feedback than were Identity Achievements and Moratoriums. Moreover, Foreclosures showed the greatest susceptibility to self-esteem change when the situational demands were clear that they "should" do so. These findings are consistent with Gruen's (1960) definition of low-identity attainment as an individual's willingness to accept a personality description of himself given to him by a stranger.

Authoritarianism

Foreclosures, both male and female, are the most endorsing of authoritarian values among the identity statuses (Breuer, 1973; Marcia, 1966, 1967; Marcia and Friedman, 1970; Matteson, 1974[3]; Schenkel and Marcia, 1972). What is, perhaps, one of the consequences of this attitude is a somewhat chilling finding by Podd (1972). Among subjects in all statuses who had delivered what they thought to be maximum electrical shock to a "victim" in a Milgram obedience task, only Foreclosures showed a significant willingness to do so again; in fact, all Foreclosures who had delivered maximum shock were willing to do it again.

Using an ego-identity measure derived from those of Rasmussen (1964) and Constantinople (1969), Tzuriel and Klein (1977) found that among Western and Oriental Israelis ego identity was negatively associated with ethnocentricity, while being positively related to ethnic-group identification.

Moral Reasoning

Development of moral reasoning seems to accompany the development of identity. Individuals high in identity (Identity Achievements and Moratoriums) tend to be functioning at postconventional levels of moral reasoning, while subjects lower in identity (Foreclosures and Identity Diffusions) are found to be at preconventional and conventional levels (Podd, 1972; Poppen, 1974). Although this is disputed in a study by Cauble (1976), there are sufficient methodological questions about this research to retain confidence in the original findings, particularly in view of a recent direct replication of the identity status/moral reasoning relationship by Rowe (1979). In addition, Hayes (1977), using

[3]Matteson's research was conducted with Danish high-school students (17 to 18 years old).

measures of moral attitudes developed by Hogan (1973) found that high-identity individuals were more highly ethical, empathetic, and socialized than were low-identity persons.

Autonomy

Foreclosures and Identity Diffusions are low on various measures of self-directedness. Orlofsky, Marcia, and Lesser (1973) found Foreclosures lowest on the (EPPS) autonomy scale and highest on need for social approval. Matteson (1974) reported that his Danish Foreclosures and Identity Diffusions had lower autonomy scores than did Identity Achievements and Moratoriums. Waterman, Buebel, and Waterman (1970), investigating differences among the identity statuses on locus of control, found Foreclosures and Identity Diffusions more externally oriented and Identity Achievements and Moratoriums more internally oriented. Similarly, Waterman and Waterman (1971) and Waterman and Goldman (in press) noted that Foreclosures showed the greatest willingness among the statuses to involve their families in making their own life decisions, while Neuber and Genthner (1977) noted that Identity Achievement and Moratorium men and women, as contrasted particularly with Identity Diffusions, tended to take more personal responsibility for their own lives. In an investigation of both instrumental and terminal values, Andrews (1973) reported an orientation pattern of independence and active achievement for college males high in identity, while those low in identity were more passive and affective.

Styles of Cognition

A number of studies have demonstrated no differences in intelligence among the identity statuses for both males and females (Bob, 1968; Cross and Allen, 1970; Jordan, 1971; Marcia, 1966; Marcia and Friedman, 1970; and Schenkel, 1975). However, when social interactional variables were combined with cognitive performance, differences were apparent. Marcia (1966) found that Identity Achievements did the best and Foreclosures did the poorest on a concept-attainment task administered under stressful conditions. Although failing directly to replicate Marcia's findings, Bob (1968) reported that when faced with a difficult cognitive task, Foreclosures tended to become constricted and Identity Diffusions tended to withdraw. The addition of stress to a cognitive task actually improved the performance of Identity Achievements.

Looking at the impulsivity-reflectivity dimension of cognitive style, Waterman and Waterman (1974) reported that Foreclosures and Identity Diffusions were more impulsive (responded quickly, made more errors) and that Identity Achievements and Moratoriums were more reflective. Chapman and Nicholls (1976) reported that among Pakeha and Maori boys in New Zealand, those individuals in the identity-achievement status were more field-independent than those in other statuses. Support for this finding in North America was provided in a study by Davidson (1978) who, in comparing Identity Achievements and Foreclosures, found the former to have a more highly differentiated level of ego functioning. Protter (1973), studying identity status and temporal perspective, reported that Identity Achievement and Foreclosure males had a more future-oriented time perspective than did the other statuses.

One cognitive dimension on which there seems to be some degree of agreement is that of complexity. Tzuriel and Klein (1977), studying Oriental and Western settlers in Israel, found a curvilinear relationship between identity and cognitive complexity: high identity was associated with *moderate* complexity. Similarly, Côté (1977) reported that Identity Diffusions, as contrasted with Identity Achievements and Moratoriums, had complex cognitive systems; he interpreted this as reflective of Identity Diffusions' difficulties in maintaining a "tight construct system" (Kelly, 1955). Finally, Kirby (1977) found cognitive simplicity to be associated with Foreclosures and complexity to be more characteristic of Identity Diffusions. Although one has to extrapolate somewhat from among these three studies, the tentative conclusion may be drawn that Foreclosures are characterized by cognitive simplicity, Identity Achievements and Moratoriums by complexity, and Identity Diffusions by extreme complexity (disorganization?). A definitive study addressed directly to this issue would be useful.

Another area of investigation has been the quality and nature of intellectual performance of the identity statuses in college. Cross and Allen (1970) showed that Identity Achievements obtained higher grades; and Waterman (1970) demonstrated that, as college freshmen, they had better study habits than did individuals in the other statuses. Identity Achievements and Moratoriums showed greater cultural sophistication (interest in art, music and literature) than did Foreclosures and Identity Diffusions (Waterman and Waterman, 1971; Waterman and Goldman, in press). This finding recalls a previous one by Hershenson (1967) of greater enculturation on the part of high-identity college males. Similarly, Waterman, Kohutis, and Pulone (1977) found that both men and women who wrote poetry in college were more likely to be in the Identity Achievement status than those who did not. Underlying this may be the greater ability of high-identity subjects to "regress in the service of the ego" (Gombosi, 1972).

College Behavior Patterns

Part of the research strategy of Waterman and Waterman has been to look at the identity statuses in terms of the separate components of the identity status interview: occupation, religion, and politics.[4] Investigating satisfaction with college, they found that individuals who were Moratoriums in occupation were most dissatisfied with their college experience (1970), while occupational Foreclosures were most satisfied. Another study by Waterman and Waterman (1972) showed that Moratoriums changed college majors more frequently than did individuals in other statuses. They also reported that when Foreclosures and Identity Diffusions left school, they tended to do so in the face of negative external pressure (e.g., low grades), while those Identity Achievements who left did so for more self-initiated reasons.

Studying the frequency of nonprescription drug use among college students, Dufresne and Cross (1972) reported that Foreclosures were predominant in the "adamant non-drug-user" category and that Moratoriums were notably absent here. This finding is consistent with Matteson's (1974) description of Danish Identity Achievement and Moratorium youth as freer in impulse expression than Foreclosures and Identity Diffusions. Looking only at marijuana use, Pack, Brill, and Christie (1976) found that there was a relationship between the ability to stop using marijuana and firm occupational and ideological commitment: more Identity Achievements and Foreclosures had stopped using marijuana, while more Moratoriums and Identity Diffusions had either never used it or were continuing to use it.

---

[4]Both Matteson (1977) and Rothman (1978) have used and advocated this method of investigating identity status areas separately rather than using summary ratings.

Alternative Measures of Eriksonian Identity

In establishing validity for the identity statuses, Marcia (1966) found Identity Achievements scoring highest and Identity Diffusions scoring lowest on a measure of overall ego identity, the Ego Identity Incomplete Sentence Blank (EI-ISB). Gregoire (1976) used this measure to assess a treatment program for juvenile delinquents. Simmons (1970, 1973) developed a forced-choice measure of identity, the Identity Achievement Scale (IAS), based on the EI-ISB. Although this scale, like the EI-ISB does not allow for the differentiation of identity statuses, it is easily administered and scored and is psychometrically sound. Some cross-cultural validity for the IAS has also been established. Jegede (1976) obtained essentially the same distribution of scores for male and female college students in Nigeria as Simmons did in the United States. One criticism of any overall ego identity measure is that it may mix in Foreclosures with Identity Achievements at the high end of the continuum because of the high commitment of Foreclosures. An apparently successful attempt to develop an identity scale free from this possible contamination has been made by Tan et al. (1977), who constructed and partially validated a 12-item scale.

Measures of identity developed by Rasmussen (1964) and Constantinople (1969) include scales tapping the resolution of other psychosocial crises, so that they are useful in assessing the relationship between identity and previous and subsequent psychosocial stages. Hauser (1971) used a Q-sort technique in studying identity formation in black and white adolescents. Other ego identity measures have been constructed by Dignan (1965) and Baker (1971). Although little comparative work has been done on these measures, Miller (in progress) has established a significant relationship between Constantinople's questionnaire measure and the identity statuses.

PATTERNS OF INTERACTIONS

Although the preceding section deals primarily with the individual personality characteristics of males in the identity statuses, this one contains descriptions of research on the interactional styles of individuals with differing modes of identity resolution: how they relate to their peers in both laboratory and real-life situations.

Cooperation and Competition

Using a prisoners' dilemma game in which participants played against preplanned strategies, Podd, Marcia, and Rubin (1970) found behavioral evidence for the hypothesized ambivalence of Moratoriums. These individuals were less cooperative with authorities than with peers, yet showed a tendency to match their responses to the responses of all of their opponents, reflecting needs for both rebellion and conformity.

Intimacy

The Eriksonian hypothesis that identity is a precursor to intimacy has been supported in three studies. Kinsler (1972) found Identity Diffusions to be lowest of the statuses on Yufit's (1956) paper-and-pencil measure of intimacy and least self-revealing in a situational intimacy task. Constantinople (1969), investigating the effects of resolution or nonresolution of the different psychosocial stages in college students, found some support for a relationship between the attainment of a sense of identity and intimacy. Probably the most thoroughgoing approach to the investigation of the relationship between these two psychosocial stages was undertaken by Orlofsky, Marcia, and Lesser (1973). They constructed five intimacy statuses, condensed into three for the data analysis. These intimacy statuses, based on criteria of depth and mutuality of interpersonal relationships were:

- Intimate
- Stereotyped Relationships
- Isolate

Identity Achievements and Moratoriums tended to be in the Intimate category; Foreclosures and Identity Diffusions were predominant in the category of Stereotyped Relationships; and there were more Identity Diffusions in the Isolate category than other identity statuses. No Identity Diffusions and only 18% of the Foreclosures were in the Intimate category.

The Counseling and Teaching Settings

Shaffer (1976) explored the relationship between ego identity status and the progress of university counseling center clients in human potential seminars. She found that Identity Achievements and Moratoriums were more favorably perceived by other participants and experienced more positive personal outcomes than individuals in other statuses. These positive changes were corroborated by friends and associates outside of the group. Looking at graduate-level (M.A.) students in clinical psychology, Genthner and Neuber (1975) and Neuber and Genthner (1977) found that Identity Achievements had more facilitative counseling styles than did non-Identity Achievements. Treating identity as a dependent variable, Stark (1976) found that training graduate-level (M.A.) counseling students in techniques of nonverbal communication decreased their identity-diffusion scores on the Dignan scale. Walters (1975) found high scores on the Constantinople identity measure to be associated with the effective classroom performance of student teachers; she also found that the identity measure predicted quality of teaching better than did several cognitive measures.

Interpersonal Style and Object-Relatedness

James Donovan (1975) completed a doctoral dissertation that provides us with an extensive, in-depth view of the identity statuses. His subjects, 13 males and 9 females, were observed and tape-recorded in 39 group sessions. They each completed a Thematic Appreciation Test (TAT), a Rorschach, an Early Memories inventory, a 10- to 20-page autobiography, and a week-long log.[5] He found Identity Diffusions to be generally withdrawn, feeling out of place in the world, and keeping rather odd hours. They described their parents as distant and misunderstanding. A bit wary of both peers and authorities, they tended to project their aggressive feelings and then to retreat into fantasy. Donovan described their general level of object-relatedness as preoedipal. Foreclosures were the ''best behaved'' of the statuses. They studied diligently, kept regular hours, and

---

[5]No brief summary can do justice to the wealth of description found either in this study or in Josselson's (1972) to be discussed later. Interested readers are directed to the original sources referenced at the end of this chapter.

seemed happy — even in the face of upsetting circumstances. They described their homes as loving and affectionate and seemed bent on recreating a similar situation for themselves as adults. They appreciated structure and eschewed expression of any strong feelings, positive or negative. Donovan noted that their main defense mechanism was repression and described them as being on an unconflicted oedipal level of object-relatedness. The Moratoriums were as volatile as the Foreclosures were placid. They seemed to have a stake in being attractive, visible people. They experienced and expressed their feelings in clear, immediate ways. They seemed to thrive on intense relationships, depth of self-knowledge, and exploration of their world. Interactions with others were characterized by ambivalence, competitiveness, and intense engagement and disengagement. As contrasted with Foreclosures, who seemed to be luxuriating in the oedipal position, Donovan described the Moratoriums as struggling with oedipal issues and attempting to free themselves from parental introjects. Only two Identity Achievements were discussed in this study, both were women in their mid-to-late forties. Donovan described them as demonstrating nondefensive strength and with a capacity to care for others in a noncompulsive, nonbinding way.

DEVELOPMENTAL ASPECTS OF IDENTITY

This section will be divided into three parts: a description of conditions prior to college age that are related to the formation of identity, a discussion of the development of identity within the college years, and some brief notes on postadolescent outcomes of the identity statuses.

Quasi-Longitudinal Studies

Thus far there have been no true longitudinal investigations of identity development. The nearest approach to this is a study by Meilman (1977). He investigated the formation of identity in five age groups of males: 12, 15, 18, 21, and 24. His data indicate that most males begin as Identity Diffusions or Foreclosures and that the greatest change in identity status occurs between 18 and 21 years of age. The modal shift is from Identity Diffusion and Foreclosure to Identity Achievement status.[6] Similar findings were obtained by Stark and Traxler (1974). In a large-scale study using the Dignan measure with male and female college students divided into two age groups, 17 to 20 and 21 to 24, they found that the 21- to 24-year-old group had significantly higher ego identity scores than did the 17- to 20-year-old group. Also, freshman subjects were more diffuse than senior ones, and, interestingly, females scored higher than males. Additional support for the crucial nature of the late-adolescent period (18 to 21) in identity formation is found in research by Offer, Marcus, and Offer (1970) who reported that the 19- to 20-year-old males in their longitudinal study had not yet "achieved" an identity, but were in the process of consolidating identity-related areas of their lives and appeared about to resolve the issue.

Whether most males enter adolescence as Identity Diffusions or as Foreclosures is not known. Meilman's data are mixed and Matteson's (1974) research covers only late adolescents. Wagner (1976) found significant age trends in overall identity development

---

[6]This finding is consistent with theoretical speculations of A. S. Waterman (in press) concerning sequential patterns of identity development.

for males and females aged 10 to 18. Constantinople (1969) also found consistent increases in identity attainment over the four college years. The following seems to be the safest generalization: identity increases from early adolescence (age 12) until late adolescence (18 to 21); at the earlier ages one may expect a predominance of (temporary) Foreclosures and Identity Diffusions, many of whom will begin crossing over into the Moratorium and Identity Achievement statuses around age 18. By age 21, the highest proportion of individuals will be Identity Achievements. A limit to this generalization is that it applies primarily to white males. Constantinople (1969) and Matteson (1974) found more ambiguous patterns for females; Hauser (1971) reported a predominant pattern of identity foreclosure for black high-school students.

The hypothesized relationship between the attainment of a sense of industry and the development of identity has been explored retrospectively in three studies. Gilmore (1971), studying high-school boys, found that feelings of competence were related to the attainment of identity and that both of these were related to exploratory behavior. Employing a TAT to measure a sense of industry (achievement), Bauer and Snyder (1972) reported that college students high on Rasmussen's identity measure were also high in achievement imagery. In a multivariate analysis of psychosocial crisis variables related to identity status, Rothman (1978) found that the autonomy and industry stages were the most important predecessors to identity resolution.

The factors contributing to a growing sense of identity in high-school students have been explored in several studies. Bell (1969) found that high-school boys who were occupationally committed were also high on a measure of identity. The importance of a father or father surrogate for the identity development of males was established in a study by Oshman (1975). Similarly, in investigating differences between identity achievement and moratorium men and women who were college seniors, Jacobson (1977) reported that Identity Achievement men had a higher frequency of supportive paternal relationships and more harmonious authority relationships, in general, than did Moratorium men. These findings support Jordan's (1970) and Donovan's (1975) hypothesis about the oedipal involvement of Moratoriums. In neither the Oshman nor the Jacobson study were father factors found to be important to women's identity development.

Josselson, Greenberger, and McConochie (1977a, b) have been conducting an especially valuable series of studies on psychosocial maturity. Looking at identity development in high-school boys, they found that involvement in heterosexual behavior was not necessarily related to identity development. Low-maturity boys were often found to be preoccupied with heterosexual contacts, whereas high-maturity boys seemed more able to "take it or leave it." These latter appeared more concerned with the meaning and future direction of their lives. LaVoie (1976), in an investigation of identity formation in middle adolescence, used several personality inventories, including both the Constantinople measure and the EI-ISB. In general, he found that high-identity males and females were confident of their sexual identity, had a sense of basic trust and of industry, perceived themselves positively across a number of dimensions (e.g., moral, physical, personal, etc.), and used adaptive-positive defenses. Low-identity subjects showed a lack of personality integration and general maladjustment.

Identity Development in College

Most of the work on identity formation has been done with college students. This may bias the age at which identity status is seen to "solidify." However, Meilman's (1977) study using precollege-age subjects, Munro and Adams's (1977) research with noncollege youth, and Howard's (1960), and LaVoie's (1976) studies with high-school students all support the critical nature of the 18- to 21-year-old period. Munro and Adams (1977) found that individuals who go to work following high school are more likely to be in the Identity Achievement status than those who go on to college, presumably because of the encouragement of a "psychosocial moratorium" provided by college.

The most extensive work on identity development within the college years has been completed by Waterman and Waterman (1971), Waterman, Geary, and Waterman (1974), and Waterman and Goldman (1976). Individuals in these studies were interviewed at the beginning of their freshman year and at the end of their senior year in college. The research took place at both a polytechnic institute and a liberal arts college. This series of studies investigated identity status separately for the three interview areas of occupation, religion, and politics.[7] In occupation, there was an increase in the Identity Achievement status and a decrease in the Moratorium status over the four college years at both schools with a decrease in the Identity Diffusion status found only at the liberal arts school. In religion, there was a decrease in Foreclosures and an increase in Identity Diffusions at the polytechnic school. Notably, there was no increase in identity within the religious area during the four years at either institution. In politics, there was an increase in Identity Achievements and a decrease in Foreclosures only at the polytechnic school. Hence, while college attendance seems to facilitate identity growth in the occupational area, its effects on ideology are mixed, at least it does not facilitate Foreclosures. A. S. Waterman (in press b) in reviewing these data stresses the importance of the experience of undergoing an identity crisis period, and, by implication, the importance of the college atmosphere in initiating such crises:

> [If a crisis occurred] the average probabilities of successfully resolving the identity crisis in the various areas of concern were: vocational plans — 83%, religious beliefs — 83%, political ideology — 75%. [Chapter 5.]

Matteson (1975) presents a thoughtful integration of the work of Kohlberg and Kramer (1969) and Perry (1968) on the development of values during the college years. His conclusions are that, as with identity, the variables of crisis and commitment are applicable to the developmental models of these investigators also. He sees "the move away from home" as a key crisis-inducing factor and views college as providing a period of limited societal disengagement in an atmosphere that encourages commitment to postconventional values. How successful this "encouragement" is, is questionable in light of the Waterman studies.[8]

A number of investigators, besides those previously mentioned, have studied the importance of the resolution of earlier psychosocial stages on the achievement of identity during the college years (Boyd and Koskela, 1970; Constantinople, 1969; Waterman and Goldman, in press; Waterman, Buebel, and Waterman, 1970; and Whitbourne and Waterman, in press). In general, significant positive relationships have been found. However, all of these data remain only suggestive of an epigenetic sequence. Observa-

---

[7]The findings discussed here are paraphrased from summaries found in A. S. Waterman's text (in press b).

[8]Paranjpe (1976) has taken an approach to identity somewhat unique among the sources mentioned here, save for Erikson himself. He has published a set of case studies of the identity development of youth in India. These are construed in Eriksonian terms and together with the historical, theoretical, and philosophical background presented in the beginning of his book provide interesting, albeit nonexperimental, insights into identity formation.

tional, longitudinal data on the same subjects over a period of time are required to establish the causal nature of the relationship of one stage to the next, if such exists. Looking only at the psychosocial antecedents of identity formation, this would mean about a 20- to 25-year study.

Parental Patterns and Their Relationship to Styles of Identity

The descriptions presented here of parents of individuals in the different identity statuses are based primarily on three studies. The first two were conducted by Jordan (1970, 1971) and involved the completion by parents and their offspring of questionnaires on perceptions of child-rearing practices. The third study was conducted in Denmark by Matteson (1974) and also employed a triadic method. However, rather than obtaining retrospective accounts, he collected ratings and descriptions of the participation of three family members in a standardized laboratory situation: the construction of endings to short stories. The three studies taken together provide pictures of both past and present interactions of individuals in the various identity statuses with their parents.

Foreclosures were described by Jordan (1970, 1971) as "participating in a love affair" with their families. The offspring saw his parents as accepting and encouraging; his parents saw themselves as child-centered and protective. Matteson (1974) found Foreclosure families to be the most task-oriented of the statuses. Fathers seemed to dominate their sons and emotional expression was not encouraged. Within the context of father-son conflict, however, some assumption of leadership on the part of the youth was accepted. Taken together, the Jordan (1970, 1971) and Matteson (1974) studies suggest that there is considerable pressure and support for adolescent conformity to family values among Foreclosure families and that this is perceived positively by the male offspring.

Identity Diffusion youth were seen by Jordan (1970, 1971) as experiencing "rejection and detachment" from their parents, particularly from the father.[9] Among Danish youth, Matteson (1974) noted that fathers of Identity Diffusion males also seemed particularly inactive; this contrasted sharply with the somewhat coercive involvement of Foreclosure fathers.

Moratorium individuals seem to have an ambivalent relationship with their parents, according to Jordan (1970, 1971). Moratorium sons appear to be engaged in a struggle to free themselves from their mothers. Schilling (1975) reported that Moratoriums tended to see their parents as disappointed in them or as disapproving of them. Matteson (1974) found Moratoriums giving in less to their parents than individuals in other statuses. Autonomy, activity, and self-expression characterized the interaction of the Moratorium families. Jordan (1970, 1971), like Donovan (1975), commented on the oedipal quality of the ambivalent relationships Moratoriums have with their parents.

Identity Achievement persons in the Jordan study were fairly balanced in their views of their parents. Father, mother, and offspring all reported a positive, though moderately ambivalent, relationship with each other. There was some ambivalence expressed by the son toward the father, but this had neither the highly charged aspect of the Moratoriums nor the feelings of abandonment characterizing the Identity Diffusions.[10]

---

[9]Further evidence for this sense of distance from parents was presented by Schilling (1975) who found that Diffusions saw more differentiation between their own roles and those of their mothers than did subjects in other statuses.

[10]There are no Matteson (1974) data for Identity Achievements in this area.

A finding cutting across these Jordan and Matteson studies as well as those of Cross and Allen (1971), and LaVoie (1976) is the importance of the father in male identity status. All significant results in the Cross and Allen study involved father factors. Deldin (1976) reported that the most important influence on male Identity Achievement was the level of perceived sex-role typing in the adolescent's father. Those males with highly masculine, stereotyped fathers had higher identity scores.[11] LaVoie found that high-identity males reported less parental control and more praise from their fathers than did low-identity males. However, the influence of the father on his son's identity does not seem to be related to the father's identity status (Waterman and Waterman, 1975), nor, necessarily, to his actual presence (Oshman and Manosevitz, 1974). What does seem important about the father is his style and the amount of his interaction with his son if he is present in the home.

Consequences of Identity Status

Only one follow-up study has been completed investigating the effects of different styles of identity formation in college on later personality development. Marcia (1976a) reinterviewed males 6 to 7 years following the initial identity status interviews given when they were juniors or seniors in college. In addition to information on the life styles of the different statuses, two important findings emerged. The first was longitudinal support for the Orlofsky, Marcia, and Lesser (1973) report of a relationship between identity and intimacy; the second was more evidence for the crucial nature of the college years for identity formation. If an individual was high in identity status (Achievement or Moratorium) during college, chances were about even (43%) that he would be found subsequently in either the Identity Achievement or Moratorium status. However, if he was a Foreclosure or an Identity Diffusion when interviewed in college, chances were very good (84%) that he would be a Foreclosure or Identity Diffusion 6 to 7 years later.

IDENTITY IN WOMEN

Both because of the differences in criteria used to establish the identity statuses in women and because the results of studies with them differ from those with men, identity and identity status in women constitutes a separate section in this chapter. There have been some problems with the identity status approach to women; these problems and possible remedies will be discussed in the next section. Here, only the findings of the various studies will be reported.

The early identity status research was conducted primarily with males, the one exception being the Podd, Marcia, and Rubin (1970) study in which no sex differences were found. In approaching identity research with females, it was thought that the process of identity formation would likely be the same as that for males, but that it would center around different content areas. When "career-marriage conflict" failed to be a discriminating issue, the area of "attitudes toward pre-marital intercourse" was chosen to complement the other identity status interview areas of occupation and ideology. Hence the women's identity status interview differed from the men's by virtue of this additional area. The value of this addition was demonstrated by Schenkel and Marcia (1972) who

---

[11]This finding may be due in part to the effect of using a measure like the EI–ISB, which does not discriminate well between the Identity Achievement and Foreclosure statuses.

found that a combination of the sex and religion interview areas provided greater predictive utility than any other combination of interview areas. More tangential evidence for the importance of the sexual area in women's identity comes from studies by Poppen (1974) and Waterman and Nevid (1977). They reported that more females than males had gone through a crisis period and made commitments in this area. Some investigators have extended the sexual area to include "life style orientation" (Howard, 1975; Josselson, 1972, 1973; Lacks[12]; Morse, 1973; and Schenkel, 1975). Still other researchers have advocated using the same interview for men and women, expanding the men's interview to include the sexuality/sex roles area. Matteson (1977) states:

> The clear conclusion from our Danish population is that the two areas of value and sex roles are central to the identity process regardless of sex. [P. 371]

Further support for the use of a common interview for men and women comes from a study by Hopkins (1977) who found that an "inner-space" interview developed for women yielded about the same findings as the standard identity status interview.

Personality Characteristics and Patterns of College Behavior

Foreclosure women tend to score high on self-esteem and low on anxiety scales; women who are Moratoriums and Identity Diffusions score generally low in self-esteem and high in anxiety. (Marcia and Friedman, 1970; Romano, 1975; Schenkel and Marcia, 1972). Prager (1976) noted higher self-esteem scores for Identity Achievement and Foreclosure women as compared with those who are Moratoriums and Identity Diffusions. In addition, Identity Achievements and Foreclosures also tended more toward "masculinity" and androgyny, while Identity Diffusions were more "feminine." Studying married women with at least one child in the home, Amstey (1977) reported a greater frequency of women who are Identity Achievements and Moratoriums going to continuing education courses than women who are Foreclosures and Identity Diffusions. Weston and Stein (1977) found that Identity Achievement women had the highest frequency among the statuses of participation in campus activities.

Although there is no difference in intelligence test scores among the identity statuses in women, Marcia and Friedman (1970) reported that women who are Identity Achievements chose the most difficult college majors, while women who are Identity Diffusions chose the least difficult ones. Foreclosure women appeared similar to Identity Achievement women in this area, while Moratorium women resembled Identity Diffusions. Studying young women in Denmark, Matteson (1974) obtained similar findings. Fannin (1977) reported that Identity Diffusion women tended to choose atypical college majors while Foreclosure women were in more typical areas of study and also held more traditional sex-role attitudes.

Investigating cognitive dimensions underlying the statuses, Schenkel (1975) found that Identity Achievement and Foreclosure women were more field-independent than Moratorium and Identity Diffusion women. This finding complemented an earlier one by Toder and Marcia (1972) who reported greater conformity (and greater personal discomfort) in an Asch-type situation for Identity Diffusion and Moratorium women as contrasted with Identity Achievement and Foreclosure women. Howard (1975) and Miller (in progress) both reported that Identity Achievement and Foreclosure women had a more

[12]P. Lacks 1976: personal communication.

internal locus of control while Moratorium and Identity Diffusion women were more external.

In a study investigating moral reasoning in women, Poppen (1974) found that Identity Achievement women showed more sophisticated levels of moral thought than did either Foreclosure or Identity Diffusion women. Looking at general psychosocial development in married women, Miller (in progress) reported that women who are Identity Achievements and Foreclosures had more overall positive scores on the Constantinople measure than did Moratoriums and Identity Diffusions.

Marcia and Friedman (1970) noted unexpectedly high anxiety scores for Identity Achievement women. This finding was supported in a study by Howard (1975) on fear of success. Orlofsky (1978) has done the most definitive study to date on the relationships among identity status, ηachievement, and fear of success in women. In studying both college men and women, he found that Identity Achievements of both sexes had the highest ηachievement scores, and that the Identity Diffusions had the lowest scores. Women, in general, seemed more afraid of success than men; Moratorium women were the highest of all eight (status × sex) groups on this variable and Identity Achievement women were next highest. Diffusion men had a greater fear of success than men in the other identity statuses. The female pattern of high fear of success among Identity Achievements and Moratoriums and low fear among Foreclosures and Identity Diffusions was exactly reversed for men. Hence, while statuses in both sexes were similar in ηachievement, they differed dramatically on fear of success. Orlofsky's conclusions regarding these results were:

> Thus the high Fear of Success scores obtained by Achievement and especially Moratorium women are understandable as reflecting the conflicts which these more ambitious achieving women probably experience as they pursue . . . less traditional, more achievement-oriented goals. Since Foreclosure and Diffusion women are less motivated for academic/vocational achievement, they experience less conflict between achievement strivings and traditional feminine role behaviors. . . .'' [P. 60]

In addition to the separate findings of the studies reported above, there has emerged a pattern of identity status groupings for women different from that found in men. Although the status grouping on many variables for men have been Identity Achievement plus Moratorium versus Foreclosure plus Identity Diffusion, the modal pattern for women has tended to be Identity Achievement plus Foreclosure versus Moratorium plus Identity Diffusion. In other words, foreclosing an identity has seemed to have about the same positive effects for women as achieving an identity. In a research monograph (Marcia, 1976b) the author put it this way:

> Most of our research with men suggested that *chronological proximity* to Identity Achievement was a crucial factor in the grouping of the statuses. That is, Moratoriums could be expected to behave most like Identity Achievements on any measure involving general ego strength, while Foreclosures would perform most like Identity Diffusions. However, with women, the *stability* of the identity status was emerging as the important issue. Identity Achievement and Foreclosure are both fairly stable statuses; both groups have an identity, even though one is achieved and the other, foreclosed. Moratorium and Identity Diffusion are unstable statuses; neither one has a firm sense of identity, although Moratoriums are moving towards it. [P. 103]

This view of the adaptability of the foreclosure status for women finds some support in Dignan's (1965) research indicating that girls who identify strongly with their mothers are also high in ego identity. Tangential evidence on this point is furnished by sex differences obtained in the Rothman (1978) study on psychosocial crisis variables relating to identity status. Female Foreclosures scored higher on industry than did male Foreclosures; female Identity Diffusions were higher on trust than were male Identity Diffusions. This finding, especially when viewed in the light of greater social support for male identity resolution, suggests that men who do not resolve the identity issue are more developmentally handicapped than women who do not achieve an identity.

Raphael (1977) has suggested that the moratorium status may not be as nonadaptive for women as it appears, but that this notion stems from methodological defects in studies reporting this finding. He bases this partly on his own findings of superior performance on cognitive tasks by Moratorium high-school girls as compared with Foreclosures and Identity Diffusions (Raphael, 1975). Further support for this view may be drawn from research by Greenhouse (1975) who, studying the same-age girls as Raphael, reported that Moratoriums were less willing to give in to their boyfriends' wishes, better able to express dissatisfaction and anger toward them, and less traditional in life-style goals. All of this may be taken to be indicative of greater ego strength on the part of Moratorium women. However, the Moratorium/Identity Diffusion grouping for females has been reported so frequently and with such varying ages of subjects and varying methodologies that it must be accounted for in terms other than methodological. For example, studying the same age girls as Raphael, LaVoie (1976) again obtained the Identity Achievement/Foreclosure, Moratorium/Identity Diffusion grouping — this time on measures of personality integration and psychosocial maturity. Prager (1976), in the study cited previously, found the same grouping on a self-esteem measure. On the other hand, Orlofsky (1978) reported Identity Achievement/Moratorium and Foreclosure/Identity Diffusion clustering both in ηachievement and fear of success.

The central issue here is the relative adaptiveness of the Foreclosure versus the Moratorium status for women. There seems little dispute about Identity Achievement versus Identity Diffusion status. Perhaps the mixed results we see in these studies reflect fairly accurately the current social confusion. Are women to continue to function as "carriers of the culture" (a Foreclosure position) or are they to take on a more innovative, sometimes iconoclastic responsibility (a Moratorium position)? I would suggest that the relative adaptiveness of the Moratorium or Foreclosure status for women is a function both of the dependent variables used in a particular study and of the existing cultural supports for women's explorations of alternatives. However, there are still implications for personality structure of the identity formation process and the resulting identity status. Hence I think that in a situation where equal social support is given to *either* a Moratorium or a Foreclosure approach to the identity issue, Moratorium women will score higher on measures reflecting ego strength.

Psychodynamics of Women's Identity Status

Josselson (1972, 1973) constructed psychodynamic portraits of women in the various identity statuses based on extensive interview material covering biographical information, defensive structures, conflict areas, fantasy material, object relations, and so on. Her descriptive approach to women bears similarities to Donovan's (1975) work with men. She found Foreclosure women attempting to recreate their familial closeness in their current interpersonal relationships. They were firmly tied to parentally based superegos and were generally inhibited in impulse expression. The Identity Achievement women, as contrasted with the Foreclosure women, were more invested in the exercise of their own abilities toward their own goals rather than in winning the love and approval of their parents. They appeared to trust their own capacities and chose men who would be cooperative companions rather than protective parents. They were more concerned with who they might be rather than by whom they might be loved. Josselson (1972, 1973) described Moratorium women as being caught in the guilty oedipal bind of rejecting the mother and attendant dependency, while identifying with the father and striving to fulfill his ambitions. She also found them to daydream a great deal and to have an excessive need to be "right." Their interpersonal relationships were intense and ambivalent. There was a quality of "wanting everything" about this status. However, for all of their conflicts and anxiety, the Moratoriums emerged as the most sensitive, insightful, and likeable of the groups. The Identity Diffusion women were characterized by fear (of ego dissolution upon commitment), fantasy (to bolster a self-esteem insupportable in reality), and flight (rather than confrontation and mastery). Identity Diffusion women, as had Identity Diffusion men, described their parents as "not there." They seemed to sense little past to integrate, little future for which to plan; they were only what they felt in the present.

Developmental Aspects

In his Danish study, Matteson (1974) found less clear-cut evidence in women than in men for the developmental progression of Foreclosure/Identity Diffusion/Moratorium/Identity Achievement. None of the four dependent variables on which this progression was based (autonomy, impulse expression, authoritarianism, and complexity) met the criteria of significant differences in a predicted direction. Constantinople (1969) also obtained ambiguous data on female identity development. In contrast to men, the level of Identity Diffusion among college women was as great in the senior year as it had been in the freshman year.

Although there are no studies of females' families comparable to Jordan's (1970, 1971) studies on males, Matteson's (1974) work on family triads in Denmark provides some description of women's family interactions. Among Foreclosure families, the daughter was given more support and encouragement from the father than was the son, who was more often the recipient of paternal criticism. In Identity Diffusion families, Matteson found that, with sons, mothers were active and fathers passive; with daughters, this pattern was reversed — active fathers and passive mothers. He concluded that Identity Diffusion families seemed to consist of a weak passive youth and a weak passive parent of the same sex. Daughters in Moratorium families were the most active and outgoing of the statuses. In contrast to males who were encouraged to be this way, the females seemed to have attained this style on their own with a minimum of obvious support and encouragement for autonomy.[13]

Parental characteristics of the various identity statuses have been the subject of other studies with women. Morse (1973) reported that Identity Achievement college women seemed to sense a lack of acceptance from their fathers (more rejection, hostile control and detachment, enforcement, etc.) and a lack of possessiveness on the part of their mothers. There was a "pushed out of the nest" quality to their perceptions of their families. Among Foreclosures, fathers were seen as accepting, child centered, positively involved, and so on — in short, the usual Foreclosure halo. Women in this status experienced both parents as less hostilely detached than did women in the other statuses. Identity Diffusion women

---

[13]No data were available for the Identity Achievement status.

reported less positive involvement and less child centeredness from their mothers; they also experienced less withdrawal of relationships on the part of their fathers. This feeling of disconnectedness from the same-sexed parent supports Matteson's (1974) notions about Identity Diffusion families. No clear patterns were reported for Moratorium women.

Allen (1976) studied college women and their mothers. She reported the following observations. Identity Achievements seemed to have reestablished a tie with their mothers, but had an awareness of the differences between them. Moratorium women seemed to be the most critical of their mothers and saw themselves as unlike them. Foreclosures were the least aware of mother-daughter differences and seemed unable to risk criticizing their mothers. Identity Diffusion women felt so distant from their mothers that no rapprochement seemed possible. In general, Identity Achievement and Moratorium women seemed more sure of their mother's affection than did Foreclosure and Identity Diffusion women.

Supporting the general trend of findings that the same-sexed parent is the more important one for identity development, Kirsch, Shore, and Kyle (1976) stated that relationships with the mother seemed more important than those with the father for women's identity formation. In the same study, they also reported that both boys and girls who strongly endorsed equalitarian beliefs about sex-role were more advanced in identity formation than those who did not and that this was especially true for girls.

The development of identity in women beyond college age has been explored in three studies. Joyce (1970) studied Catholic teaching nuns in age ranges from 18 to 59 and reported a progressive increase in Dignan's Ego Identity Scale scores. O'Connell (1976) studied women in the age range of 30 to 58. She categorized her subjects into life-style orientations of traditional, neotraditional, and nontraditional. She also divided them according to style of identity, either reflected or personal (self-achieved). Traditional and neotraditional women seemed to have undergone a moratorium in development of personal identity during their adolescence and childrearing; in fact, with the coming of the first child, they appeared to have adopted a largely reflected identity. Only after the diminishing of childrearing duties, did they seem to begin to develop a personal identity. Nontraditional women, by contrast, showed a strong sense of personal identity throughout all portions of the life-cycle studies. For all women, the first married stage was associated with an increase in identity.

Miller (in progress) studied a group of married women with an average age of 35. The following brief characterizations are condensed from her more lengthy report. They are particularly interesting when juxtaposed with Josselson's (1972, 1973) description of college women in the same identity statuses. *Identity Achievement:* They have adopted, lived through, and partially rejected traditional social forms. They describe their previous sense of identity as "vicarious" (recall O'Connell's "reflected") and now see themselves as competent and assertive. Often, they have rearranged their family structures to meet their occupational and ideological needs. *Moratorium:* They are involved in a "yes-but" game wherein they "want to be themselves" but feel guilty, defiant, approval-seeking, and afraid. They feel ambivalent about their wife-mother roles and seem to want a guarantee of security. *Foreclosure:* Their identity is securely tied to their families. They see themselves as nurturing, loving, and devoted, but not particularly competent outside of their homes. Any unhappiness or discontent not suppressed is dismissed as part of "woman's role." *Identity Diffusion:* They doubt their adult femininity and seem preoccupied with infantile battles and fantasies. They see their mothers as nonemulatable or discouraging and their fathers as idealized but unattainable. In the company of inadequate husbands and boyfriends, they dream of Prince Charmings. Extremely afraid of being hurt or betrayed, any consistent "identity" is a negative one.

NEW DIRECTIONS IN IDENTITY RESEARCH

There are two lines along which new and productive work on identity in adolescence might proceed: research on female identity formation and the nature of the relationships among cognitive development, moral reasoning, and ego identity.

Identity Research with Women: Suggestions for a New Approach

A number of writers have been critical of the identity-status approach to research on women's identity. "Direct comparisons between male and female studies are confounded by the differences in samples used, differences in interview format, and differences in the measurement of some of the dependent variables" (Matteson, 1974, p. 276). "The attempt to extend 'identity status' research to *female* adolescents has been less successful, or, at the very least, more confusing" (Gallatin, 1975, p. 332). "Not only is the process of identity formation qualitatively different for women than men, but the very nature of female identity is not the same" (Miller, 1978, p. 52).

The need to continually vary interview areas and the presence of theoretically contradictory results in the studies themselves suggest the need for a new approach. For example, there is the issue of the apparent "adaptability" of the Foreclosure status for women. Even in research strategy, the initially circumscribed interview questions about "attitudes toward premarital intercourse" has now burgeoned into a host of questions about "life-style orientation." Investigators have reported difficulty in fitting women into the existing identity statuses (Howard, 1974; Lacks[14]) and have found it necessary to suggest new statuses to accommodate their female subjects (Donovan, 1975; Schenkel, 1975).

One source of these difficulties may lie in maintaining the original research tactics. The identity status research was undertaken as a construct validity project based on Erikson's theory. Thus at least the face validity of that theory was accepted. Erikson's theory is one that accounts largely for identity development in males.

> Like other theorists we have reviewed, Erikson is ultimately tripped up to a degree by the mysteries of feminine development. [Gallatin, 1975, p. 333]

I do not mean to disparage the valuable insights into feminine identity that Erikson has provided us, particularly those contained in "Womanhood and Inner Space" (Erikson, 1968). The problem is that the implications of these insights have not been carried through into theory and research in the same systematic way for women as for men. Both Erikson's work and the identity status research began with a theoretical model applicable to men and then extended that model to women. The results are that both Erikson's theory and the identity status approach work only more or less, when applied to women.

> Understanding of female development in adolescence is a far more complicated task than the understanding of male development. Female development is quieter, subtler. And because the end-points of female development are ambiguous, it is harder to identify significant markers along the way. . . . Because the Eriksonian stages of identity and intimacy are probably merged for girls

---

[14]P. Lacks 1976: personal communication.

. . . identity development proceeds at a deeper and less tangible level. [Josselson, Greenberger, and McConochie, 1977b, pp. 162, 164]

Perhaps it is time to take Douvan and Adelson (1966) seriously. The predominant concerns of most adolescent girls are not with occupation and ideology. Rather, they are concerned with the establishment and maintenance of interpersonal relationships. Adolescent boys are encouraged to make life decisions that will often lead to increased interpersonal conflict with both authorities and families. The experience of such conflict can be an identity-confirming event. However, if an adolescent girl, who is expected to become proficient in interpersonal relationships, creates such tension and conflict by her decisions, she may take this as a *disconfirmation* of the success of her identity formation.

If identity is an internal, self-fashioned structure, then what might be the effect on the woman's identity-formation process of being encouraged always to look outside of herself for evidence of her development as an acceptable person? At the very least, it must prolong the identity process, while the expected social forms (engagement, marriage, childbearing) are fulfilled. Some empirical support for this view may be found in a study by Hodgson (1977) who reported that men were more advanced in intrapersonal identity issues, while women were further advanced in interpersonal areas as well as being further along in the achievement of intimacy than men. Hodgson concluded that while male identity focuses on individual competence and knowledge, female identity development seems to revolve around issues of relating to others.

I would like to make two suggestions here for approaches to research on identity with women. The first is, that if an identity status approach is to be taken, the areas around which crisis and commitment are to be determined should be those around which women are expected, initially, to form an identity: the establishment and maintenance of relationships. I do not mean by this that the ''male'' concerns of occupation and ideology are not available as identity-constellating issues for women. They are. But as society is currently structured, women who go this route, particularly if they do so to the exclusion of the interpersonal one, will pay a price in the lack of extensive social support, a factor contributing to the mixed results on self-esteem and anxiety scores for Identity Achievement women as determined by ''male'' criteria. Now, of course, there is a third possibility: the exceptional woman can do both. She can ''make it'' in ''female'' terms of relationships and in ''male'' terms of occupational commitment. However, I am less concerned here with the exceptional than I am with the average. And I think that the average female adolescent has to be evaluated in identity terms according to the most widely held social expectations. (Identity is, after all, a psycho*social* concept.) So long as society maintains different expectations according to different genital configurations, one must evaluate identity development with respect to the individual's unique style of coming to terms with those expectations.

I think that the identity formation process takes longer for women than for men (just as the establishment of intimacy probably takes longer for men). My second suggestion for studying identity in women stems from this position. It might be fruitful to begin investigating identity in women retrospectively, starting with 35- to 40-year-old women one is relatively certain meet the criteria for identity attainment and asking them to reflect on the process of their own development. This should yield material about stages in female identity formation that could then be checked out on a sample of younger women of different ages. In a sense, this is similar to Erikson's psychohistorical approach to figures, such as Shaw, Luther, and Gandhi. What one hopes to obtain from such a procedure is a kind of road map of identity formation from one who has been there.

Initiation of a General Ego Developmental Approach

A second direction for identity research is the theoretical and empirical linkage of levels of cognitive development, development of moral reasoning, and identity formation. Results of research attempting to relate these three areas have thus far been tantalizingly inconclusive. Postconventional moral reasoning seems to be related to formal operations and identity achievement appears to be related to postconventional moral reasoning. The problem lies in relating identity to formal operations. Cauble (1976) found no relationship; neither did Berzonsky, Weiner, and Raphael (1975). However, there are methodological problems in both studies.

Coleman, Herzberg, and Morris (1977) studying self-concept in 12-, 14-, and 16-year-old boys, concluded that, "Concern with future self . . . shows a marked and consistent increase as a function of age" (p. 73). This statement implies a relationship between identity and formal operations. Wagner (1976) reported a progressive increase in both identity and formal operational thought as a function of age in 10 to 18-year-old males and females. She obtained a positive correlation between a combinational measure of formal operations and identity and a positive correlation between a balance measure of formal operations and identity. However, the former increased with age, while the latter decreased. Part of the difficulty in relating identity to formal operations lies in the apparent independence of different measures of formal operations from each other. For example, in the Wagner study, there were two measures of identity and two measures of formal operations. At no age level, nor in the overall analysis, were there significant correlations between the two measures of formal operations. The only significant correlations were between the two identity measures and between the identity measures and one or the other measure of formal operations.

I think that the hypothesis to be pursued in this area is that formal operations are a necessary but not sufficient condition for the achievement of identity. That is, there should be no subjects categorized as Identity Achievement who do not exhibit formal operational thought. This is a stringent requirement, particularly in view of the imperfect reliability of the identity statuses and of the imperfect validity of measures of formal operations. Because of these factors, the research should be begun with "pure types." That is, only subjects who clearly do or do not exhibit formal operational thought on several measures and who are clearly either identity achieved or not should be utilized. A beginning in this direction has been made by Rowe (in progress). In an intensive but small ($N = 26$) study with college males he found that all three Identity Achievement subjects were at postconventional levels of moral reasoning and possessed formal operations. Combining Identity Achievements and Moratoriums, six out of seven subjects were in formal operations. In other words, there were no Identity Achievements and only one Moratorium who was not at a formal operational level of thought.

Pursuing the issue a bit further, it might be speculated that formal operations are the necessary but not sufficient condition for *both* postconventional morality and identity and that identity and moral reasoning are linked together in a reciprocal way. The progression may run something like this: formal operations are necessary to identity development; a sense of identity allows one to be open to the experience of moral dilemmas in one's life — a precondition for advancement in levels of moral reasoning. For example, we have sufficient evidence for the conceptual styles of Foreclosures to suggest that they are so closed to self-disconfirming evidence that they may seldom experience moral dilemmas. We also know that they tend to operate at preconventional and conventional levels of morality. To recapitulate, the attainment of formal operational thought should increase the probability of both identity achievement and postconventional moral reasoning; and these latter two should be linked together in a reciprocally enhancing fashion.

CONCLUSION

The utility of the concept of identity in looking at personality development in adolescence has been reasonably well established. It is a construct that can be fairly reliably measured, related to concurrent variables, and to antecedent and consequent conditions. It has a place within a known theoretical structure and relates to constructs in other theoretical systems. Moreover, it is an educationally and clinically useful concept. Individuals ''do'' better and feel better about themselves and others when they ''have'' it.

I think that it is reasonable to suggest that at the same time we explore identity formation in women and search for identity's cognitive underpinnings; we should also begin to think about the design of cultural institutions within which identity is formed — particularly such general contexts as high school and college.[15] If we begin to evaluate these institutions as settings for psychosocial growth, we must take into account the fact that since such growth is continuous throughout the life cycle, we shall be dealing with intersecting and overlapping stages: industry and identity for youth; intimacy, generativity, and integrity for their teachers.

REFERENCES

Allen, J. G. Identity formation in late-adolescent women. Unpublished doctoral dissertation, City University of New York, 1976.

Amstey, F. H. The relationship between continuing education and identity in adult women. Unpublished doctoral dissertation, University of Rochester, 1977.

Andrews, J. The relationship of values to Identity Achievement status. *Journal of Youth and Adolescence,* 1973, *2* (2), 133–138.

Baker, F. Measures of ego identity: A multitrait multimethod validation. *Educational and Psychological Measurement,* 1971, *31,* 165–174.

Bauer, R. H. and Snyder, R. Ego identity and motivation: An empirical study of achievement and affiliation in Erikson's theory. *Psychological Reports,* 1972, *30,* 951–955.

Bell, N. D. The relationship of occupational choice to ego identity and self-concepts. Unpublished doctoral dissertation, Utah State University, 1969.

Berzonsky, W. M., Weiner, A. S., and Raphael, D. Interdependence of formal reasoning. *Developmental Psychology,* 1975, *11,* 258.

Blos, P. *On adolescence.* New York: Free Press, 1962.

Bob, S. An investigation of the relationship between identity status, cognitive style, and stress. Unpublished doctoral dissertation, SUNY at B, 1968.

Boyd, R. D. and Koskela, R. N. A test of Erikson's theory of ego-stage development by means of a self-report instrument. *Journal of Experimental Education,* 1970, *38,* 1–15.

---

[15]A study by Penna (1975), while not extensive, furnishes an example of this approach. He compared two styles of teaching literature — classroom discussion versus the tutorial approach — for their effects on adolescent ego identity, finding that the former was more beneficial.

Breuer, H. Ego identity status in late-adolescent college males, as measured by a group-administered incomplete sentences blank and related to inferred stance toward authority. Unpublished doctoral dissertation, New York University, 1973.

Bunt, M. Ego identity: Its relationship to the discrepancy between how an adolescent views himself and how he perceives that others view him. *Psychology,* 1968, *5*(3), 14–25.

Byrne, P. The repression-sensitization scale: Rationale, reliability, and validity. *Journal of Personality,* 1961, *29,* 334–349.

Cabin, S. Ego identity status: a laboratory study of the effects of stress and levels of reinforcement upon self and peer evaluations. Unpublished doctoral dissertation, The Ohio State University, 1966.

Cauble, M. A. Formal operations, ego identity, and principled morality: Are they related? *Developmental Psychology,* 1976, *12,* 363–364.

Chapman, J. W. and Nicholls, J. G. Occupational identity status, occupational preference, and field dependence in Maori and Pakeha boys. *Journal of Cross-Cultural Psychology,* 1976, *7*(1), 61–72.

Coleman, J., Herzberg, J., and Morris, M. Identity in adolescence: Present and future self-concepts. *Journal of Youth and Adolescence,* 1977, *6*(1), 63–75.

Constantinople, A. An Eriksonian measure of personality development in college students. *Development Psychology,* 1969, *1,* 357–372.

Côté, J. E. A dialectical model of ego identity formation and a study of the relationship between ego identity formation and selected aspects of cognitive structure. Unpublished master's thesis, Trent University, 1977.

Cross, J. H. and Allen, J. G. Ego identity status, adjustment, and academic achievement. *Journal of Consulting and Clinical Psychology,* 1970, *34,* 288.

————. Antecedents of identity status: Differences between males and females. Paper presented at the Eastern Psychological Association meeting, 1971.

Davidson, S. The level of differentiation of ego functioning in the identity-achieved and identity-foreclosed statuses. Unpublished doctoral dissertation, Boston University, 1978.

Deldin, L. S. Sex-role development and identity achievement. Unpublished doctoral dissertation. University of Florida, 1976.

Dignan, M. H. Ego identity and maternal identification. *Journal of Personality and Social Psychology,* 1965, *1,* 476–483.

Donovan, J. M. Identity status and interpersonal style. *Journal of Youth and Adolescence,* 1975, *4*(1), 37–55.

Douvan, E. and Adelson, J. *The adolescent experience.* New York: Wiley, 1966.

Dufresne, J. and Cross, J. H. Personality variables in student drug use. Unpublished master's thesis, University of Connecticut, 1972.

Erikson, E. H. Identity and the life cycle. *Psychological Issues,* 1959, *1*(Monograph No. 1).

————. *Childhood and society.* New York: Norton, 1963.

————. *Identity: Youth and crises.* New York: Norton, 1968.

Fannin, P. M. Ego identity status and sex-role attitudes, work-role salience, atypicality of college major, and self-esteem in college women. Unpublished doctoral dissertation, New York University, 1977.

Gallatin, J. E. *Adolescence and individuality.* New York: Harper & Row, 1975.

Genthner, R. W. and Neuber, K. A. Identity Achievers and their rated levels of facilitation. *Psychological Reports,* 1975, *36*(3), 754.

Gilmore, G. E. Exploration, identity development, and the sense of competency: A case study of high-school boys. Unpublished doctoral dissertation, University of Michigan, 1970.

Gombosi, P. G. Regression in the service of the ego as a function of identity status. Unpublished doctoral dissertation, Boston University, 1972.

Greenhouse, E. M. The relationship between identity status and several aspects of heterosexual relationships in college women. Unpublished doctoral dissertation, Columbia University, 1975.

Gregoire, J. C. The development of ego identity in juvenile delinquents. Unpublished doctoral dissertation, University of Michigan, 1976.

Gruen, W. Rejection of false information about oneself as an indication of ego identity. *Journal of Consulting Psychology,* 1960, *24,* 231–233.

Hauser, S. T. *Black and white identity formation.* New York: Wiley-Interscience, 1971.

Hayes, J. M. Ego identity and moral character development in male college students. Unpublished doctoral dissertation, The Catholic University of America, 1977.

Hershenson, D. B. Sense of identity, occupational fit, and enculturation in adolescence. *Journal of Counseling Psychology,* 1967, *14*(4), 319–324.

Hodgson, J. W. Sex differences in processes of identity and intimacy development. Unpublished doctoral dissertation, The Pennsylvania State University, 1977.

Hogan, R. Moral conduct and moral character: A psychological perspective. *Psychological Bulletin,* 1973, *79,* 217–232.

Hopkins, L. B. Construction and initial validation of a test of ego identity status for females. Unpublished doctoral dissertation, Temple University, 1977.

Howard, L. Identity conflicts in adolescent girls. *Smith College Studies in Social Work,* 1960, *31,* 1–21.

Howard, M. R. Ego identity status in women, fear of success, and performance in a competitive situation. Unpublished doctoral dissertation, SUNY at B, 1975.

Jacobson, S. B. The Achievement and Moratorium identity statuses: An investigation of their late-adolescent interpersonal correlates among college seniors. Unpublished doctoral dissertation, New York University, 1977.

Jegede, R. O. The identity status of Nigerian university students. *Journal of Social Psychology,* 1976, 100, 175–179.

Jordan, D. Parental antecedents of ego identity formation. Unpublished master's thesis, SUNY at B, 1970.

———. Parental antecedents and personality characteristics of ego identity statuses. Unpublished doctoral dissertation, SUNY at B, 1971.

Josselson, R. L. Identity formation in college women. Unpublished doctoral dissertation, University of Michigan, 1972.

———. Psychodynamic aspects of identity formation in college women. *Journal of Youth and Adolescence,* 1973, *2*(1), 3–52.

Josselson, R. L., Greenberger, E., and McConochie, D. Phenomenological aspects of psychosocial maturity in adolescence. Part I: Boys. *Journal of Youth and Adolescence,* 1977a, *6*(1), 25–55.

Josselson, R., Greenberger, E., and McConochie, D. Phenomenological aspects of psychosocial maturity in adolescence. Part II: Girls. *Journal of Youth and Adolescence,* 1977b, *6*(2), 145–167.

Joyce, M. U. An empirical investigation of Erikson's developmental crises of ego identity, intimacy, and generativity in religious women. Unpublished doctoral dissertation, Fordham University, 1970.

Kelly, G. A. *The psychology of personal constructs.* (2 vols.) New York: Norton, 1955.

Kinsler, P. Ego identity status and intimacy. Unpublished doctoral dissertation, SUNY at B, 1972.

Kirby, C. S. Complexity-simplicity as a dimension of identity formation. Unpublished doctoral dissertation, Michigan State University, 1977.

Kirsch, P. A., Shore, M. F., and Kyle, D. G. Ideology and personality: Aspects of identity formation in adolescents with strong attitudes toward sex-role equalitarianism. *Journal of Youth and Adolescence,* 1976, *5*(4), 387–395.

Kohlberg, L. and Kramer, R. Continuities and discontinuities in childhood and adult moral development. *Human Development,* 1969, *12,* 93–120.

LaVoie, J. C. Ego identity formation in middle adolescence. *Journal of Youth and Adolescence,* 1976, *5,* 371–385.

Mahler, C. The assessment and evaluation of the coping styles of two ego identity status groups: Moratorium and Foreclosure, two identity conflict-arousing stimuli. Unpublished master's thesis, SUNY at B, 1969.

Marcia, J. E. Development and validation of ego identity status. *Journal of Personality and Social Psychology,* 1966, *3*(5), 551–558.

———. Ego identity status: Relationship to change in self-esteem, "general maladjustment," and authoritarianism. *Journal of Personality,* 1967, *35*(1), 119–133.

———. Identity six years after: A follow-up study. *Journal of Youth and Adolescence,* 1976a, *5,* 145–160.

———. Studies in ego identity. Unpublished research monograph. Simon Fraser University, 1976b.

Marcia, J. E. and Friedman, M. L. Ego identity status in college women. *Journal of Personality, 38*(2), 1970, 249–263.

Matteson, D. R. Alienation vs. exploration and commitment: Personality and family correlaries of adolescent identity statuses. Report from the Project for Youth Research. Copenhagen: Royal Danish School of Educational Studies, 1974.

Matteson, D. R. *Adolescence today: Sex roles and the search for identity.* Homewood, Ill.: Dorsey, 1975.

———. Exploration and commitment: Sex differences and methodological problems in the use of identity status categories. *Journal of Youth and Adolescence,* 1977, *6,* 353–374.

Meilman, P. W. Crisis and commitment in adolescence: A developmental study of ego identity status. Unpublished doctoral dissertation, University of North Carolina, 1977.

Miller, J. E. Ego identity in married women. Master's thesis, Simon Fraser University, in progress.

Morse, B. Identity status in college women in relation to perceived parent-child relationships. Unpublished doctoral dissertation, The Ohio State University, 1973.

Munro, G. and Adams, G. R. Ego identity formation in college students and working youth. *Developmental Psychology,* 1977, *13,* 523–524.

Neuber, K. A. and Genthner, R. W. The relationship between ego identity, personal responsibility, and facilitative communication. *Journal of Psychology,* 1977, *95,* 45–49.

O'Connell, A. N. The relationship between life style and identity synthesis and resynthesis in traditional, neotraditional, and nontraditional women. *Journal of Personality,* 1976, *44*(4), 675–688.

Offer, D. and Offer, J. B. *From teenage to young manhood: A psychological study.* New York: Basic Books, 1975.

Offer, D., Marcus, D., and Offer, J. L. A longitudinal study of normal adolescent boys. *American Journal of Psychiatry,* 1970, *126,* 917–924.

Orlofsky, J. L. Identity formation. Achievement, and fear of success in college men and women. *Journal of Youth and Adolescence,* 1978, *7,* 49–62.

Orlofsky, J. L., Marcia, J. E. and Lesser, I. M. Ego identity status and the intimacy vs. isolation crisis of young adulthood. *Journal of Personality and Social Psychology*, 1973, *27*(2), 211–219.

Oshman, H. P. Some effects of father-absence upon the psychosocial development of male and female late adolescents: Theoretical and empirical considerations. Unpublished doctoral dissertation, University of Texas, Austin, 1975.

Oshman, H. P. and Manosevitz, M. The impact of the identity crisis on the adjustment of late-adolescent males. *Journal of Youth and Adolescence*, 1974, *3*, 207–216.

Pack, A. T., Brill, N. Q., and Christie, R. L. Quitting marijuana. *Diseases of the Nervous System*, 1976, *37*, 205–209.

Paranjpe, A. C. *In search of identity*. New York: Wiley, 1976.

Penna, R. F. The relative effectiveness of the classroom discussion approach and the tutorial approach to literature for the development of adolescent ego identity. Unpublished doctoral dissertation, Fordham University, 1975.

Perry, W. G., Jr., et al. Patterns in development in thought and values of students in a liberal arts college: A validation of a scheme. Bureau of Study Counsel, Harvard University, April 1968.

Podd, M. H. Ego identity status and morality: The relationship between two developmental constructs. *Developmental Psychology*, 1972, *6*, 497–507.

Podd, M. H., Marcia, J. E., and Rubin, B. M. The effects of ego identity and partner perception on a prisoner's dilemma game. *Journal of Social Psychology*, 1970, *82*, 117–126.

Poppen, P. J. The development of sex differences in moral judgment for college males and females. Unpublished doctoral dissertation, Cornell University, 1974.

Prager, K. J. The relationship between identity status, self-esteem, and psychological androgyny in college women. Unpublished doctoral dissertation, University of Texas, Austin, 1976.

Protter, B. S. Ego identity status: Construct validity and temporal perspective. Unpublished doctoral dissertation, Purdue University, 1973.

Raphael, D. An investigation into aspects of identity status of high-school females. Unpublished doctoral dissertation, University of Toronto, 1975.

———. Identity status in university women: A methodological note. *Journal of Youth and Adolescence*, 1977, *6*(1), 57–62.

Rasmussen, J. E. Relationship of ego identity to psychosocial effectiveness. *Psychological Reports*, 1964, *15*, 815–825.

Romano, N. C. Relationship among identity confusion and resolution, self-esteem, and sex-role perceptions in freshmen women at Rutgers University. Unpublished doctoral dissertation, Rutgers University, The State University of New Jersey, 1975.

Rosenfeld, R. U. The relationship of ego identity to similarity among self, ideal self, and probable occupational-role concept among college males. Unpublished doctoral disseration, University of Maryland, 1972.

Rothman, K. M. Multivariate analysis of the relationship of psychosocial crisis variables to ego identity status. *Journal of Youth and Adolescence*, 1978, *7*, 93–105.

Rowe, I. Ego identity status, cognitive development, and levels of moral reasoning. Master's thesis, Simon Fraser University, 1978.

Schenkel, S. Relationship among ego identity status, field-independence, and traditional femininity. *Journal of Youth and Adolescence*, 1975, *4*, 73–82.

Schenkel, S. and Marcia, J. E. Attitudes toward premarital intercourse in determining ego identity status in college women *Journal of Personality*, 1972, *3*, 472–482.

Schilling, K. L. Ego identity status: A reevaluation and extension of construct validity. Unpublished doctoral dissertation, University of Florida, 1975.

Shaffer, C. S. The ego identity status interview as a predictor of positive change in self-actualization of university-counseling-center clients participating in human-potential seminars. Unpublished doctoral dissertation, University of Virginia, 1976.

Simmons, D. D. Development of an objective measure of Identity Achievement status. *Journal of Projective Techniques and Personality Assessment,* 1970, *34,* 241–244.

————. Further psychometric correlates of the Identity Achievement Scale. *Psychological Reports,* 1973, *32, 1042.*

Stark, P. A. Diminished identity diffusion as a function of training in nonverbal communication in the counseling practicum. Unpublished doctoral dissertation, St. Louis University, 1976.

Stark, P. A. and Traxler, A. J. Empirical validation of Erikson's theory of identity crises in late adolescence. *The Journal of Psychology,* 1974, *86,* 25–33.

Tan, A. J., Kendis, R. J., Fine, J. T., and Porac, J. A short measure of Eriksonian ego identity. *Journal of Personality Assessment,* 1977, *41,* 279–284.

Toder, N. and Marcia, J. E. Ego identity status and response to conformity pressure in college women. *Journal of Personality and Social Psychology,* 1973, *26*(2), 287–294.

Tzuriel, D. and Klein, M. M. Ego identity: Effects of ethnocentrism, ethnic identification, and cognitive complexity in Israeli, Oriental, and Western ethnic groups. *Psychological Reports,* 1977, *40,* 1099–1110.

Wagner, J. A study of the relationship between formal operations and ego identity in adolescence. Unpublished doctoral dissertation, SUNY at B, 1976.

Walters, A. S. An investigation of the relationship between an Eriksonian-like construct of ego identity and classroom behavior of student teachers. Unpublished doctoral dissertation, Temple University, 1975.

Waterman, A. S. Ego identity and academic behaviors and attitudes. Unpublished manuscript, 1970. Reported in A. S. Waterman, *From adolescent to adult.* Boston: Houghton-Mifflin, in press a.

————. *From adolescent to adult.* Boston: Houghton-Mifflin, in press b.

Waterman, A. S., and Goldman, J. A. Correlates of ego identity status among a sample of male students at a liberal arts college. Unpublished manuscript, 1977. Reported in A. S. Waterman, *From adolescent to adult.* Boston: Houghton-Mifflin, in press a.

————. A longitudinal study of psychosocial maturity and evaluations of college. Unpublished manuscript, 1977. Reported in A. S. Waterman, *From adolescent to adult.* Houghton-Mifflin, in press b.

————. A longitudinal study of ego identity development at a liberal arts college. *Journal of Youth and Adolescence,* 1976, *5,* 361–369.

Waterman, A. S. and Waterman, C. K. The relationship between ego identity status and satisfaction with college. *Journal of Educational Research,* 1970, *64*(4), 165–168.

————. A longitudinal study of changes in ego identity status during the freshman year at college. *Developmental Psychology,* 1971, *5,* 167–173.

————. The relationship between freshman ego identity status and subsequent academic behavior: A test of the predictive validity of Marcia's categorization system for identity status. *Developmental Psychology,* 1972, *6,* 1, 179.

Waterman, A. S., Geary, P. S., and Waterman, C. K. A longitudinal study of changes in ego identity status from the freshman to the senior year at college. *Developmental Psychology,* 1974, *10,* 387–392.

Waterman, A. S., Kohutis, E., and Pulone, J. The role of expressive writing in ego-identity formation. *Developmental Psychology*, 1977, *13*, 286–287.

Waterman, C. K. and Nevid, J. S. Sex differences in the resolution of the identity crisis. *Journal of Youth and Adolescence*, 1977, *6*, 342.

Waterman, C. K. and Waterman, A. S. Ego identity status and decision styles. *Journal of Youth and Adolescence*, 1974, *3*, 1–6.

———. Fathers and sons: A study of ego identity across two generations. *Journal of Youth and Adolescence*, 1975, *4*, 331–338.

Waterman, C. K., Buebel, M. E., and Waterman, A. S. The relationship between resolution of the identity crisis and outcomes of previous psychosocial crises. *Proceedings of the 78th Annual Convention of the American Psychological Association*, 1970, *5*, 467–468. (Summary)

Weston, L. C. and Stein, S. L. The relationship of the identity achievement of college women and campus participation. *Journal of College Student Personnel*, 1977, *18*, 21–24.

Whitbourne, S. and Waterman, A. S. A longitudinal study of psychosocial development ten years after college. Unpublished manuscript, 1977. Reported in A. S. Waterman, *From adolescent to adult*. Boston: Houghton-Mifflin, in press.

Yufit, R. Intimacy and isolation: Some behavioral and psychodynamic correlates. Unpublished doctoral dissertation, University of Chicago, 1956.

CHAPTER 6

Ego Development in Adolescence

Ruthellen Josselson

Our understanding of ego development has undergone vast changes in the past 25 years. Essentially, we have shifted from focusing on the defensive functions of the ego to considering the work of the ego that is adaptive and autonomous from the drives. Early interest in the adolescent ego centered on how the defensive system copes with the upsurge of impulses brought on by puberty (Freud, 1936; Freud, 1958; Josselyn, 1952; Wittenberg, 1955). The theorists stated the problem this way: given that the ego uses repression to obviate the dangers of oedipal sexuality and given that this repression serves through the latency period, then the question is, How does the ego deal with the onslaught of sexual impulses unleashed at puberty? In other words, how does the asexual child become a sexual adult?

This literature, although it added enormously to our understanding of defenses, drew an extremely skewed picture of adolescents. The adolescent was seen to be desperately warding off a revival of the Oedipus complex, and the successful adolescent was one who re-resolved the Oedipus complex by choosing a "nonincestuous sexual partner." All other aspects of adolescence, such as interests, friendships, or identity, were either overlooked or treated as sublimations designed to contain oedipal dangers. The adolescent was seen to become autonomous from his parents because repudiating the incestuous (oedipal) tie also involved relinquishing all ego ties to the parents (Josselyn, 1952; Balser, 1966). This repudiation of the parents was viewed as a necessary means to avoid regression to oedipal fixations.

Predominantly clinical in nature, this early literature stressed the universality of "ego weakness" in adolescence. The ego, besieged by drives and unable to rely on the now-dangerous parental ego for support, was seen to be in "turmoil," shifting unpredictably from one state to another. Turbulence, maladjustment, even psychoticlike states were described as normal (even necessary) aspects of adolescent development.

This "turmoil" theory of ego development was so widespread that it misled a generation of adolescent researchers. Mounting evidence has, however, largely discounted this theory. Masterson (1967, 1968) demonstrated that psychopathology in adolescence was not part of the normal developmental sequence and that disturbances and symptoms in adolescence were not outgrown. Douvan and Adelson (1966), guided by traditional theory in their study of 3500 "normal" adolescents, were unable to find evidence of preoccupation with drives and their control. Similarly, the Offers (Offer, 1969; Offer & Offer, 1975), in an intensive longitudinal study of 73 "modal" adolescents, failed to find turmoil, ego weakness, or repudiation of ties to parents. These researchers made it clear that adolescence was a great deal more than the integration of sexuality, that oedipal anxieties were far from central, and that the ego was seldom weakened by drive. Their work led to the suspicion that the equation of adolescence and drive upsurge missed the real developmental significance of this period.

It was primarily the contributions of Hartmann (1958) and Erikson (1956) that led theorists to state the problem of adolescent development differently. Their emphasis on autonomous ego functions made it possible to consider systematically ego growth that does not depend on drives. Therefore, the question could be broadened: Given that the child is dependent and parent-centered, how does the ego assume the reins of an independent, fully functioning person? Hartmann laid the foundation for conceptualizing aspects of the ego that are nondefensive in origin. Thus the ego may grow in response to its own needs and energies, influenced by, but apart from, psychosexual demands. Hartmann's stress on adaptation and on the conflict-free sphere of the ego provided a model within which to understand normal developmental growth processes. The ego to Hartmann is, above all, an organizational ego, one that has as its main task the "fitting together" of internal and external experience.

The effects of Erikson's work are too numerous to treat adequately here. He revolutionized our thinking along the following lines:

1. Adolescence is intimately linked to the rest of the life cycle with its own special tasks that have been in preparation all along — the notion of ego continuity.

2. Adolescence is a psychosocial demand that will be imposed on the individual whether or not there is an internal push for it — the notion of adolescence as a maturational necessity.

3. Ego integration at adolescence is an emergent phenomenon in the sense that the organization of aspects of self is more than the sum of the parts and resides precisely in the manner in which the parts are synthesized — the notion of ego identity.

The ego to Hartmann and Erikson is extraordinarily complex and cannot be reduced to other, simpler functions without obliterating the very phenomenon one wishes to study. This conception of the ego has necessitated a holistic framework, where the ego becomes an abstraction for the organization of ego functions.

Building on this work, we now understand the ego to have two tasks in addition to its defensive functions: (1) to consolidate autonomy through individuation and internalization and (2) to integrate identity. Because most of this chapter will explore these tasks, I do no more than mention them at present.

Before turning to a discussion of *how* the ego develops in these areas, it is necessary to stress a singular pitfall that has plagued the theory of adolescence. As noted above, theory has often strayed far from the phenomenology of adolescence. Our theoretical portrait used to have adolescents racked by overwhelming forces they could barely contain, while the majority of adolescents were in fact living rather humdrum lives bounded by cars, clothes, and stereotyped relationships. So distressed were some observers by the placidity of adolescents that they condemned these adolescents for not being "real" adolescents, for "avoiding" adolescence through conformity (Grinker, 1962; Blos, 1962).

Researchers who investigate normal adolescents continue to find evidence that development during adolescence is slow, gradual, and unremarkable (Douvan & Adelson, 1966; Offer, 1969; Offer & Offer, 1975; Westley & Epstein, 1969; Rosenberg, 1965; Josselson et al., 1977a, 1977b). Maturation in adolescence most often takes place in steady, silent, and nontumultuous ways. Adolescents may appear to us to be bland, docile, or limited in vision because we expect (or want?) them to be otherwise. But our task at this point is to accept and understand the gradualness of ego growth and to respect the cataclysmic ego changes that hardly make a sound.

NEW DIRECTIONS IN THE STUDY OF EGO DEVELOPMENT

Individuation and Autonomy

The primary legacy of the ''new'' ego psychology has been its stress on internalization as the keystone of development. Through mechanisms of internalization, aspects of external reality become aspects of, and under the control of, the self. As the individual internalizes what was external, he simultaneously gains autonomy from it. The young child learns to console and reassure himself in the same way his mother had reassured him, thus reducing his anxiety. Now that he can ''take over'' this function for which he had previously depended on his mother, he experiences a measure of independence from her. At first, the mother is introjected by the child — she is ''swallowed whole,'' so that the child comforts himself by replaying his memory trace of his mother comforting him. Later, he may identify with this introject and experience the comfort as coming from a part of his own self. These processes of introjection and identification are, of course, largely unconscious and are central to the development of both the ego and the superego.

The problem of internalization is that of making distinctions between self and not-self. The child's propensity to introject the parents and the parents' ego necessitates the differentiation, at a developmentally appropriate time, among his own ego experience, his introjected parents, and his identifications. Often one hears a young child describe an experience his parents had with as much emotional intensity and detail as if he himself had had the experience. In this sense, his parents' experience has become as much a part of his own ego history as if it had happened to him, although later the child will be able to discriminate better the one from the other. Individuation encompasses such processes of differentiation as well as others that involve the crystallization of a unique self from the amalgam of shared ego experience.

The growth of object-relations theory has provided us with an approach to understanding processes of internalization and individuation central to ego development. Mahler, Pine, and Bergman (1975) have mapped the most complex of ego developmental phases, that of infancy and early childhood. It is in this period that the ego first comes to the experience of self as unique and separate, as individuated from the early mother–child ego mass, and — because it is now separate — as able to differentiate self-experience from the perceptions and demands of others.

Blos (1962) introduced the concept of individuation to the study of adolescence. He saw adolescence as a phase in which aspects of self still enmeshed in the parents were differentiated and given autonomy. Like Mahler, Blos saw as critical the sharpening of the boundaries and clarifying of the attributes of the self as distinct from others. Much of the work in this second phase of individuation takes place with respect to internalized objects — the internalizations that served to promote autonomy through childhood now hinder progressive development in adolescence. The adolescent task of individuation, then, is to gain difference and distance from internalized parents, that is, to transcend infantile object ties.

The understanding of individuation is central to a discussion of ego growth during adolescence, yet we use the term individuation as shorthand for a series of complex and subtle processes. The experience of individuation is that of a sharpened sense of one's distinctness from others, a heightening of boundaries, and a feeling of selfhood and will. Adolescents who have done "good-enough individuation" will have internalized and processed adequate resources to feel that their choices and their lives are their own. Or, as Blos (1967) puts it, "Individuation implies that the growing person takes increasing responsibility for what he does and what he is, rather than depositing this responsibility on the shoulders of those under whose influence and tutelage he has grown up" (p. 168).

The process of separation-individuation is one that runs the course of the life cycle, taking on its phase-specific character from both the current capacities of the ego and the psychosocial demands of the particular life crisis. Clearly, individuation has different dynamics in infancy when it is oriented to the formation of distinct self and object representations than in adulthood, for example, when it serves to continue the differentiation of self and object representations. Schafer (1973) objects to the broad use of the term "individuation" to describe what happens during adolescence on the grounds that it is used, in this context, to mean "the giving up of infantile objects." He recommends the use of the term "detachment" for adolescence, saving "individuation" for the prerelationship infancy phase. Although there is merit in terminological purity, the language we use to describe these phenomena greatly colors our thinking about them. Speaking of "detachment" as the adolescent struggle, Schafer goes on to state that detachment is manifested in the adolescent's totalistic "effort to 'stamp out' his parent's influence on him." The term "detached" is thereby connotative of more psychological distance from the parents than "individuated" and causes us to picture the adolescent as untying his connections to his parents. As we shall see later, this is what adolescents do not do, except to the extent that we selectively perceive them in that light.

A second argument for using the term individuation to understand the adolescent experience is that it links adolescence to a continuous process of development rather than setting it apart as an idiosyncratic phase. This eliminates the problem of defining limits for the beginning and end of adolescence; individuation has its beginning at birth and its end at death. Adolescence is the phase in which work on individuation is renewed and dominant; it ends when tasks of individuation become less central.

One problem in the theory of ego development is the theoretician's wish for development to have a beginning point, a period of struggle, and then closure. Such words as "resolved" and "consolidated" are ubiquitous in developmental literature to indicate that the process is at an end. Erikson's concept of the identity stage has been much abused in this regard. Although his stage theory proposes that certain developmental crises are prominent at certain ages, he does not see these stages as finite. The "diagonality" of the developmental chart that sets out this theory (and how often is that reproduced?) clearly indicates that each stage crisis has both antecedents and derivatives. Identity formation may be the "star" of adolescence, but it has been rehearsing and will continue to act throughout the life cycle.

Having established that individuation is an appropriate and useful concept to describe much of the ego's business during adolescence, it is also important to specify the relationship of individuation processes to other central adolescent ego concerns that are intimately tied to it. Autonomy is the other side of the individuation coin. As individuation proceeds, autonomy grows. It depends on whether we are looking at what the adolescent is moving away from (individuating) or moving towards (gaining autonomy). *Identity formation* (or ego identity) refers to the work of the ego in integrating aspects of self into a coherent whole. Aspects of the self that have become individuated and autonomous must be incorporated into identity. Therefore, there is an interdependent sequence of: individuation/autonomy/identity formation. It is also recursive in the sense that increasing identity formation leads to further individuation. As the sense of self becomes more certain and stable, the individual is prepared to review and amend other aspects of self that have been left behind. Or alternatively, gains in identity formation may demand that aspects of the self that are still tied to the past or to introjects must be freed, as in the case of a would-be musician who fears that accepting a job in another city will disappoint her mother who prefers her to live at home. Individuation, autonomy, and identity formation are discrete though indivisible phenomena: we cannot look at one without implying effects on the others.

Our difficulty in describing the process of *individuation* has been in keeping our language and concepts modulated. Just as it is easier to depict revolution than gradual social change, so we can have greater empathy for the Holden Caulfields than the mass of adolescents. It is not necessary for adolescents to overthrow either their parents or society for the adolescent task to be accomplished. Nor is it even necessary for the adolescent to be observably different in values and attitudes from his parents for individuation to have taken place. What is necessary is for the organization of experience to be sifted through the adolescent's own increasingly differentiating ego. Opposition is only important in that negativism makes clear — to the self and others — that one is autonomous and not surrendering. It is harder to say "yes" and be certain that one is deciding on one's own terms. The phenomenology of adolescence, therefore, can be dramatic, but it can also be inscrutable.

Here is a late-adolescent woman reflecting on her own experience of individuation:

> Up to a certain age, I believed everything my parents said. Then, in college, I saw all these new ideas and I said, "Okay, I'm not going to believe all that stuff you told me," and I rejected everything and said to myself, "Okay, now I'm going to make a new Debbie which has nothing to do with my mother and father. I'm going to start with a clean slate" and what I started to put on it were all new ideas. These ideas were opposite to what my parents believed. But slowly, what's happening is that I'm adding on a lot of the things which they've told me and I'm taking them as my own and I'm coming more together with them. [Josselson, 1973, p. 37]

Many observers have commented on the fluidity and instability of adolescent views of reality. What is utterly clear to the adolescent one day may be equally clear — in the opposite direction — the next. This comes largely from the free interchange between the internal and external object worlds — what feels part of the self one day may be experienced as part of someone else the next. This is confusing both to the adolescent and to those of us who try to make sense of the adolescent experience. Psychoanalytic theory has focused on the internal world, translating all adolescent experience into its internal roots. The socialization theories of adolescence transpose all internal experience into external terms. Thus far, no theory has been able to keep both internal and external aspects simultaneously in focus.[1] As Schafer points out, "I do not think we yet have a good empirical grasp of these directional, representational and behavioral differentiations from

---

[1]Erikson has done this to some extent, but his theory tends to be suggestive and connotative and no one has as yet succeeded in making it precise and operational.

the parents of infancy: we know that they occur, and something about why they occur and their consequences, but not so much about how they occur'' (1973, pp. 45–46).

In order to understand *how* adolescents go about the process of individuating, we must endeavor to be clear about the experiences that serve the ego's relations with reality and those that serve the ego's relations with internal objects. These threads are, of course, much intertwined, partly by the tendency of adolescents to obscure these boundaries by projecting internal objects and treating them as reality problems and by introjecting reality in order to control it better. With respect to parents, for example, adolescents have two tasks: (1) to separate psychologically from the reality parents and (2) to individuate from the (introjected) parents of infancy. In order to deal more effectively with the introjects, the adolescent may project them back into the reality parents and, for example, fly into a rage when his mother asks, Where are you going? For the moment, the reality mother is experienced as the controlling, overpowerful mother of early childhood. This interaction, although it takes place in reality, has its meaning vis-à-vis the internal world. Similarly, the same adolescent may tell us he wants to go to college (and may indeed experience a wish to go to college) out of fear of provoking a battle with the reality parents. Here, what seems to be internal goal-setting is rather a mechanism for keeping peace with reality.

Individuation is a primarily intrapsychic process that is nevertheless affected by and expressed in reality. Mahler, Pine, and Bergman (1975) have provided a set of concepts for understanding infantile separation-individuation that elucidate the observable developmental manifestations of this process. The authors describe four subphases of the early individuation process. The first is the differentiation subphase, the precipitation of separate self and object representations from the undifferentiated symbiotic mass. In the second subphase, the infant ''practices'' awareness of self as the autonomous ego grows in close proximity to the mother. The child concentrates on experimenting with his rapidly developing independent skills, often oblivious to his mother's presence. The awareness of his physical and psychological separateness stimulates a need to regain closeness to the mother. Thus begins the rapprochement subphase in which the toddler demands the mother's investment in his newfound autonomy. In this subphase the child has an increased need to share his new experiences as well as a great need for his mother's love. The fourth phase sees the consolidation of individuality and the beginnings of emotional object constancy.

The dynamics of adolescent individuation are strikingly parallel to the processes described by Mahler and her associates. Although the outcome of the early individuation phase is structuralization, it is not unlikely that the massive structural modification that takes place in adolescence repeats the process of the original structure formation.

During the latency phase, the psychic structures are in relative harmony. The superego is internalized and augments the ego in its control of impulse. The child, at this point, is both realistically and emotionally dependent on the parents. Self-esteem is derived through parental approval and the growth of skills, which are themselves largely tied to parental approval. The superego, composed primarily of parental introjects, and the reality parents are in harmony, although latency children are often found to be stricter about moral issues than their more ego-oriented parents. Children of latency age trust their parents' judgment above their own — they may break rules, but they do not challenge the Rightness of the rule. Belief in parental omnipotence is intact during latency; the parental ego is the child's ego ideal and much ''learning'' during this age occurs through the child's identifications with parental ego functions.

The latency child's ego is differentiated from the parental ego in the sense that the child knows that he or she is a separate person with different attributes. Yet there is a kind of symbiosis here, a participation in "we-ness," perhaps a shared narcissism in the synchrony of the child's ego functions with those of the parents.[2]

Mahler describes the second subphase of individuation as one of practicing, a time when the autonomous ego grows in close proximity to the mother. This process is much like the "practice" that recurs in latency.

It is precisely this harmony that is shattered by the instinctual demands of puberty.[3] New, exciting, and frightening feelings emerge that can only be meaningfully shared with companions — never with the more mature, steady parents. "Secrets," primarily about one's body and one's view of the opposite sex, become the core of new object ties as the adolescent seeks to regain the ego support formerly supplied by the parents. At the same time, new interests and new mobility involve the adolescent more deeply in the extrafamilial world. This does not imply, however, that the adolescent gives up dependency on the parental ego — rather, certain areas are precipitated out of the former parent-centered world. This is the beginning of adolescent autonomy.

Early adolescence maintains many of the characteristics of the practicing subphase in its lack of ambivalence. The adolescent, generally from the ages of 11 to 13, delights in his feeling of separateness and autonomy, often wants to act as though he has no parents at all, and defines himself primarily through saying "no" to the parents or anyone else who tries to intringe on his freedom. In some ways, early adolescence is a second stage of omnipotence — a young person of this age feels he can do anything, the self is all good; bad self-representations are projected onto others. The early adolescent strives to effect some, preferably visible, difference from the parents around which to organize a feeling of individuality. In large part, the early adolescent attempts to feel separate and distinct from his parents by finding ways of irritating them. This is a way of flexing the will, of proving to oneself that one is taken seriously as a separate person. Physical separation and involvement with peers buttress this embryonic independent set of self-representations.

When the early adolescent has constructed for himself enough of a sense of autonomy (in the form of separate will) to feel safe from the regressive needs of childhood, he can allow himself to experience his reliance on the parental ego and his need to participate in the parents' perceived omnipotence. More important, he wants the love of the objects from which he has been separating, as do the young children Mahler observed:

> Conflicts ensued that seemed to hinge on the desire to be separate, grand, and omnipotent on the one hand, and to have mother magically fulfill their wishes, without their having to recognize that help was actually coming from outside on the other. In more cases than not, the prevalent mood changed to that of general dissatisfaction, insatiability, a proneness to rapid swings of mood and to temper tantrums. The period was thus characterized by the rapidly alternating desire to push mother away and to cling to her. [Mahler, Pine, and Bergman, 1975, p. 95]

Although adolescent behavior is more symbolic than physical, Mahler's above description of rapprochement in the two-year-old is applicable to the middle adolescent's ambivalent wishes to rely on and to repudiate parental ego support. Much like the child in

---

[2]A. Freud (1958) reports that the adolescence of orphaned children is preceded by the search for an intensely cathected mother image from which to detach.

[3]The instinctual demands of puberty form the link between psychosexual development and ego development. Many writers, however, conceptualize ego development as an autonomous process that does not rely on psychosexual forces to unfold.

the rapprochement phase, the adolescent may come suddenly to an awareness of separateness, to a realization of the meaning of psychological detachment and of its negative aspects. With the recognition that he is functioning in areas outside of parental scrutiny, the adolescent experiences an increased desire to restore harmony. The most common plaint of the middle adolescent is, ''My parents don't understand me,'' a cry that condenses both the wish for distinctness and the wish for approval. If the parents do not understand the adolescent, that means the adolescent is separate and an individual. But if the parents do not understand him, they do not love him. The adolescent longs to share the new ego experiences, to be understood, but would lose the sense of individuation if this were to come about too completely or too rapidly. At the same time, the adolescent, like the child in the rapprochement subphase, wants his parents there as a home base to return to in times of need. This ambivalence over autonomy is what creates much of the pain — for both parent and adolescent — of this period of development.

In this second phase of individuation, the dynamics of rapprochement play themselves out over a number of years. Each gain in ego separateness is followed by efforts to reassure himself that the parents are still there, approving and loving. And with each gain in ego autonomy, the adolescent becomes less reliant on the parental ego for the very approval he seeks.

The importance of rapprochement in adolescent development bridges a chasm between theoretical and phenomenological portraits of adolescence. From traditional theory, we have understood adolescent individuation to rest on disavowal and devaluation of parents, on decathexis of them, on shattering idealizations of them, on the flight from identifications with them, and so on. Our research and phenomenological literature (e.g., Douvan and Adelson, 1966; Josselson, Greenberger, and McConochie, 1977a and b; Offer, 1969) shows, however, that most adolescents retain fundamentally positive, valuing, close, and warm relationships with their parents and that rebellion is minimal. What had appeared to be an enigmatic schism between two views of adolescence seems instead to be two complementary aspects of one process. As with the young child, individuation for the adolescent involves both some distance from the parents and compensatory efforts to reestablish connectedness. The growth of ego autonomy (for both young child *and* adolescent) takes place through gradual accretions of competence, preserving (or revising) relationships at each step. Although oedipal object ties may be loosened at adolescence, they are not severed.

Physical and emotional separation from parents does not necessarily imply intrapsychic separateness or individuation. Adolescents who attempt to cope with the individuation process by wholesale abrogation of parents, through withdrawl or physical separation, are often masking their incapacity to separate from internal objects. They act as though ''getting away'' from parents will get them away from their troublesome introjects, and such dramatic disengagement efforts seldom serve progress in individuation. Rapprochement is a necessary aspect of individuation in that it reinforces the feeling of individuality in the context of ongoing relationship. Although there are many adolescent behaviors that serve individuation and many pathways through the adolescent process, the more volcanic adolescent separation efforts probably reflect more difficulty in separating. On the other hand, there are adolescents who abdicate the necessity of individuating at all.

Mahler (1975) sees separation and individuation as interwoven but distinct tracks that are most clearly discriminable when one lags behind the other. In adolescence, individuation may fail to keep pace with separation, so that the adolescent feels compelled to make decisions without the ego resources to do so. The struggle for autonomy is, in the main, not against the parents, but against the adolescent's own wishes to deny his aloneness and his own wishes to believe that parents do know best and will always protect him. Much of this process is, surprisingly, quite conscious. Interviews with normal adolescents continually unearth fervent gratitude for parental controls and limits (e.g., Josselson Greenberger, and McConochie, 1977a and b). These young people would not, however, admit to their parents how much they look to them for rules and standards. What they seem to be expressing is a sense of their developmental status on the track of individuation. They are and can be separate, but they do not yet feel ready to assume full responsibility for their actions: "I can take care of myself, but not completely, not yet."

For the adolescent, the awareness of separateness from his reality parents is intensified by his eventual recognition of the limits of the usefulness of the parental ego in maintaining him. This is when the adolescent senses that his parents really cannot tell him what to do, no matter how much he or his parents may want it.

The growth of formal operations (Inhelder and Piaget, 1958) makes accessible to the adolescent both observational capacities and ideational systems that are in the service of the autonomous ego. The adolescent now has the cognitive capacity to construct hypotheses about how the world operates and to "see" the world more clearly. He has a need (and the emerging ability) to make sense of the social world, to resolve uncertainty and cognitive dissonance. These capacities interact with the adolescent's discovery of the limits of the parental ego. In building a history of his own life experiences, the adolescent has less need to rely on his parents' judgment and may indeed find the parents' views dysfunctional. When adolescents tell us that their parents do not understand the world as they find it, they are reporting an often accurate appraisal. More mature adolescents, those who have successfully individuated, are forgiving of their parents' inability to guide them. The generation gap usually has more to do with differences in the life history of generations than with rebellion (Conger, 1971). Examples of these tensions abound: recently, I have been particularly struck by my college students' extreme cynicism about marriage. The women students particularly (many of whom are college seniors) see marriage in a way I would have never thought of. "Look at the divorce rate," they tell me, "I don't want to get married because I don't want to get divorced." How different is their view from when I was in their place, when everyone "knew" that a woman was a "failure" if she did not marry right after college.

At the other extreme, we sometimes see somewhat pathetic examples of adolescents making use of parental ego functions that are inappropriate. One high-school boy whom I interviewed told me he had selected a career in a company on the basis of its good retirement plan. Given that his father was facing retirement and given his lack of independent ego resources, this boy was simply putting to use the "good advice" he was accustomed to taking.

Our understanding of the unfolding of gains in individuation is again limited by our language. Both middle and late adolescents are, for example, building autonomy. The differences are subtle but readily recognizable. In interviewing middle adolescents (high-school students), I have noticed that an interviewee cannot talk about himself without simultaneously talking about his parents. Any opinion or perception the interviewees offer is generally followed spontaneously and predictably by their assessment of one of their parents' corresponding observations. Late adolescents, that is, college-age young people, do less of this, unless it is an area of internal conflict for them, in which case the parents and their views will appear in a highly cathected way. Over a period of months, I had been conducting intensive interviews with college seniors. On one occasion, I was interviewing a young woman who was exceedingly involved in talking about her parents, what they thought about this and that in contrast to her own thoughts. I became extremely interested in trying to understand what aspects of her psychic development caused her to be so much more attached to the parental ego than others in the sample until I discovered that the young woman was a sophomore erroneously included. Even with just two years' difference and even in light of all the individual differences in the sample, the quality of autonomy was noticeably distinct. How can this phenomenon be described except as the slow, steady growth of individualization and psychological distance?

The individuation process will repeat itself later with respect to peers. When we discuss adolescent peer groups, we often overlook how coercive adolescents are with each other. Peers at first serve to mitigate the pull toward the parents, supporting the individuating and individuated aspects of the ego. "Do you think I did the right thing?" adolescents continually ask each other in one form or another. And because adolescents have not yet mastered adult "diplomacy," the answer is not always "yes." Therefore, learning takes place in the sharing of distinctly adolescent experiences. At the same time, adolescents find it difficult to tolerate different-ness from those on whom they depend for ego support. Variation implies more comfort with ambiguity than the adolescent ego can bear. It is easier for the adolescent to gain distance from parents by saying (and feeling) "I'm like my friends" than "I'm doing what I choose." As a result, adolescents feel a desperate need for their friends to embody their choices and independence.

Toward the middle of adolescence, late high-school age, the ego has garnered a mass of individuation experiences vis-à-vis parents and internalized these as a sense of distinctness and competence. At this point, the peers begin to seem oppressive in their insistence on sameness and conformity. The adolescent then begins looking for ways to define himself as distinct from his peers, to make some choices that are neither buttressed by parents nor determined by friends. Sometimes, adolescents may try to separate their own egos from their peers' egos through outright rejection of their friends. This probably is no more successful than total disavowal of parents. Again, individuation seems to be most well integrated when it occurs in connection with rapprochement. The experience of individuation is most clear when the adolescent is most himself *with* others on whose ego he formerly relied.

So far we have considered how the *reality* parents and peers are utilized in the process of individuation. This analysis highlights the manner in which external factors influence what happens intrapsychically and how intrapsychic factors color the reality relations of the adolescent.

The Introjects

A second front in the battle for ego autonomy takes place vis-à-vis the adolescents' introjects. The most troublesome of these reside in the archaic, prohibitive superego. During latency, the ego is dominated by the superego; hence the preoccupation with goodness and rules. Because of the sexually repressive nature of these superego introjects, the ego must struggle to free itself from their domination during adolescence. This aspect of ego autonomy is an internal one, an effort to wrest controls from the superego. To a large extent, this takes place by projecting the superego outward, where it can be dealt with as an external (and less anxiety-arousing) conflict. But the manner in which the ego deals with the superego determines the particular rhythm that adolescence will have.

The course of the ego's efforts to gain mastery of the superego in adolescence is dictated largely by the nature of the preadolescent psychic organization. This is, in part, what accounts for the extreme variation among the pathways through adolescence.

The outcome of the restructuring of the ego organization during adolescence is the capacity to internally regulate self-esteem. Previously held "bad" self-representations must be freed from their association with guilt and the self-loving function of the superego must be tempered. The ego must dissociate self-esteem from both the environmental vicissitudes personified by the parents and the valent self-representations of the superego. This involves the construction of stable, reality-tested self-representations that can withstand both archaic guilt and reality-related disapproval. Blos (1962) postulates the development of a self-critical ego at the onset of adolescence that serves to complement and eventually supplant the self-valuing aspects of the superego.

The reordering of self-representations during adolescence and their liberation from corresponding object representations takes place through the resifting and differentiation of identifications. Previous defensive identifications are reworked into usefulness as adaptive ego functions or discarded (Blos, 1962). Transient, experimental identifications are adopted to test their workability as stabilizing mechanisms. The importance of being like one's peers compensates for the loss felt through selective repudiation of identifications with parents, and the sense of shared qualities with a valued object provides a source of value for new identifications. The adolescent hunger for group participation has a defensive function in warding off the experience of inner emptiness and in preventing the adolescent from withdrawing from others in the face of the inner conflict. The adaptive function of this increased interest in the social world is to provide ego-sharing experiences and new identifications.

As the ego increases its role in directing the individual, aspects of the superego that are still troublesome and guilt-inducing are reprojected back onto real objects. These projections are maintained (and generally not reality-tested) while the ego consolidates its capacities in less conflicted and anxiety-arousing areas. A group of late-adolescent girls gives a clear instance of this process. While interviewing a group of college senior women, I asked how their parents would feel about their sexual behavior. I was struck by the extremeness of their responses. A great many of these young women spoke of how their parents would have heart attacks, disown them, commit hara-kiri, and engage in other disastrous activities. These were all women who had worked through enough of their own guilt over sexuality to have sexual relationships, but the remainder of the guilt, the more imperious part, was projected onto their parents (in highly unrealistic fashion).

The danger of too-abrupt attacks on the superego is in the potential disruption of the fragile narcissistic balance of adolescence. The resolution of the problem of infantile omnipotence is the projection of omnipotence onto the parents and a subsequent introjection of these omnipotent objects as the core of the superego. Although some authors locate the idealized introjects in the ego ideal (Blos, 1962) and some in the superego (Kohut, 1971), the necessity of pleasing these introjects is critical to preadolescent self-esteem. As these introjects are deidealized during adolescence, the ego experiences a sense of emptiness, of vulnerability in the loss of an internal protective function. The ego must strive to reconstitute the superego-ego-ideal system with more realistic content and thus mourn the loss of narcissistic omnipotence, replacing it with self-esteem.

The difficulties involved in giving up the belief in omnipotent objects are demonstrated in adolescent vulnerability to gurus, would-be messiahs, and other such leaders.

As the ego strives to take over functions previously handled by the superego, it must be prepared to give up the self-love supplied by the superego. The love of the omnipotent parent, previously structuralized in the superego, must be replaced by love of the self or the possible self.[4] Much of the adolescent fantasy and play is the enactment of the transmuted narcissism, visions of the self to replace the lost superego love. As these images grow more and more under the control of the reality ego, daydreaming gives way to planning. The transition out of narcissism is accompanied by a commitment to objective reality, where the self is experienced as an initiator of activity, capable of setting and reaching goals (Fast, 1975).

Although all of the processes involved in ego development during adolescence bear on the internal regulation of self-esteem, this movement from superego to ego sources of narcissistic gratification is perhaps the most critical. Much of the pathology of "normal" adolescence is traceable to failures in this process. Adolescent boys, low in psychosocial maturity, were found to be unable to disengage themselves from the unrealistic demands of their superegos (Josselson, Greenberger, and McConochie, 1977a). That is, through internalization of parental standards for which they lacked the talent or will to live up to, these boys face adolescence with great deficits. Because they cannot satisfy the superego's demands, they cannot mitigate successfully the superego's power. The superego's disapproval interferes with realistic goal-setting because all achievement is felt to be not good enough. As a result, many of these boys avoid goal-setting altogether, retreating to passivity or grandiosity.

Another potential outcome of difficulties in modulating the ego-superego balance in adolescence is seen in women who have foreclosed identities and bypassed adolescence (Josselson, 1973). The internal life of these women is dominated by the superego and marked by rigidity and constriction. Their self-esteem derives from being good, from avoiding guilt. Although outwardly successful, these women often lack compassion, empathy, and a capacity for rich relationships. Their lives are dominated by what they see as "good" and "bad," and they tend to be unable to take risks with the self. In such adolescents, the ego "plays it safe" by staying with a gratifying, barely modified psychic organization of childhood.

At the other extreme is the phenomenon of prolonged adolescence (Blos, 1954), characterized by an inability to close the adolescent process. The period of crisis and testing is kept open indefinitely as the adolescent strives to avoid the finality of choices. In these young people, narcissistic aggrandizement, expressed in the sense of potentiality, cannot be supplanted by reality commitments. As a result, the reality ego is kept in thrall to the omnipotent introjects.

During the course of normal adolescent development, both the content and power of introjects are reworked. But this process takes place within limits about which we understand little. Introjects are not infinitely flexible: one always remains somewhat a product of one's own history. Even in the most successful psychoanalysis, change in the character structure is circumscribed. The adolescent challenge is to modify those introjects that are flexible, to modulate those that are not, and above all to integrate the resultant internal world into a consistent and workable identity.

Adolescent self-consciousness and self-preoccupation are in the service of discovering

[4]Here I recall a patient whose parents had always told her that she was the "prettiest little girl in the world." Her adolescent development became blocked by her inability to give up the narcissistic gratification of that self-image and to value herself and not *really* be "the prettiest little girl in the world." Her disappointment in the promise of her introjects was overwhelming.

what aspects of the self are malleable. It is with a sense of shock that the adolescent recognizes that he cannot invent himself, that he has traits with which he is stuck. A 15-year-old adolescent patient of mine was trying to flee an intense oedipal attachment to her father through involvement in the peer culture. This effort was hampered, however, by her shy, fearful approach to people. She decided at this point to "become" a popular girlfriend whom she idealized, to dress like her, talk like her, and behave in all the ways her friend behaved. My patient was reasonably successful in this venture as she did make many new friends, had more dates, and so on. She was, however, very prickly on the subject of her shyness and would become enraged if any of her friends would allude to her "quietness." Loudly, she would protest any such opinion by unleashing a great torrent of words. After some months of this new personality, she began to wonder if her friends really liked her "for herself" or not, and she hesitantly admitted to a feeling of strain at having to act in a way that "just isn't me." At this point, she started to ask herself if there really was anything so bad about being shy and quiet. She was able to notice some virtues in others whom she perceived in that way and formerly rejected. Paradoxically, her ability to accept her own "quietness" coincided with a genuine decrease in shyness, which resulted from her (initially counterphobic) experiences with her new friends. This vignette may be a paradigm for much of adolescent development.

As self and object representations are reorganized, the adolescent may experience a loss of the sense of self in the form of a query: "Who am I?" There is a feeling that one has moved past previous ways of viewing self and others but lacks experience that the new self and object representations are trustworthy. As a result, the adolescent may turn to experience in affect, an intense here-and-now feeling, which is at least a reassurance that the self exists. Once the autonomous ego grows more stable and more certain of at least some aspects of self, the dangers of loss of ego continuity become less present.

Taking exception to Erikson, Kernberg (1976) does not think that the establishment of ego identity is a universal issue in normal adolescence. His view is that adolescence provides identity crises that are dealt with by a relatively stable ego identity established throughout infancy and childhood. The better integrated the ego, the more successful it will be in reworking this relationship to the psychosocial environment and in integrating total object relations. Kernberg believes that identity diffusion is a pathological rather than a normal phenomenon during adolescence. This view would appear to be in line with studies of normal adolescents that suggest that development is gradual enough to avoid the ego loss associated with identity diffusion.

Erikson's concept of the psychosocial moratorium defines the period in which ego-integrative processes are played out. Affect and fantasy are given free rein in the service of self-differentiation. In addition, practice of social and work skills are emphasized in the interest of self-confirmatory experiences. Reliable self-representations, independent of the infantile introjects, are consolidated as permanent but flexible sources of self-esteem.

Much of the reworking of internal object relations in adolescence takes place through interpersonal learning among peers. It is not so much the content of the object representations, but their valence that is worked through. Adolescents tend to have peers they "love" and peers they "hate." Often these are the same friend on different days, a friend who moves from best friend to worst enemy in a matter of hours. As adolescence progresses and affect is modulated, the young person becomes better able to experience ambivalence toward the friend, to recognize his or her positive and negative qualities simultaneously.

Similar changes take place in areas of interests and goals as the adolescent gives up the absolutism of the superego-dominated self. Rather than protesting about how things should be or experiencing intense disappointment in reality, the adolescent increasingly integrates positive and negative aspects of himself and his world. This movement from totalism to balance is a reflection of increasing ego control in areas formerly dominated by the superego.

To a large extent, the grandiose self (Kohut, 1971) is reactivated in adolescence in the form of daydreams and fantasies in order for the reality ego to come to new terms with it. The gradual recognition of realistic limitations of the self increasingly replaces grandiosity in the equilibrium of self-esteem. As the need for the gratification of the narcissistic ideal becomes less insistent, the narcissistically invested aspects of the reality parents and the internalized parent images become less highly cathected, making way for reliance on one's own activities as a source of self-esteem. In the process, the ego gains in autonomy.

The ego's work in relation to the internal world of adolescence is, then, to become the guardian of self-esteem. To do this, as we have seen, it must make peace with the introjects of childhood, rework narcissistic investments, and test the self in reality. The adolescent feels (and is) vulnerable (and finds various ways to deny this vulnerability) precisely because his reliance on ego functioning for self-esteem is so new. He is much like a gambler with limited funds who must ante all of his ego-related self-esteem on each foray of the self into reality. It is perhaps more than coincidence that adolescents understand and use the word ''ego'' to mean ''self-esteem.'' Phrases, such as ''ego trip,'' ''blow to the ego,'' ''he's got a big ego,'' all reflect the special adolescent sensitivity to the vagaries of valuing the self.

In general, the newly individuating adolescent ego cannot alone bear the weight of maintaining self-esteem. But unlike the child, adolescents, who have in part freed themselves from introjects, can choose the external sources they wish to depend on for self-esteem. Not surprisingly, adolescents will often choose an external source of self-esteem who is as much like their own superego as possible. As theorists, we have largely overlooked the importance of coaches, ministers, older siblings, and so on, as transitional objects in adolescent development. Adolescents hunger for firm, definite others against whom they can pit themselves (in emulation or defiance) and evaluate themselves. For adolescents, the worst ego experience is not failure but uncertainty.

Identity

Ego identity is a function of the synthetic capacities of the ego. Those ego elements that gain autonomy from external and superego control and that contribute to reality-oriented self-esteem are candidates for inclusion in the emerging identity. How these elements are integrated and transmuted is the problem in the understanding of ego identity. As Erikson (1956) has pointed out, a summation of identifications does not produce a fully functioning person. Identification may serve a variety of functions (Schafer, 1968), among them:

- To preserve the object, as in mourning; or to give it up, as in mastery and independence.
- To weaken object ties, by substituting the self for the object; or to enhance them, as in intimacy.
- To bolster self-esteem, where identification serves the ego-ideal; or to lower it, as in negative identification.

- To defend against fear of the object, that is, identification with the aggressor; or to express love for the object.

Identificatory components have been amassed over the life span of the adolescent. During adolescence, identification as both a defensive and an adaptive maneuver intensifies, producing an assortment of identifications that serve a variety of functions. In the process of identity formation, the array of primitive, narcissistic, and totalistic identifications as well as the more mature and recent identifications are subjected to a selection process that preserves those partial identifications that are in harmony with the reality-ego core. The work of the ego in identity formation is similar to that in artistic creativity: identificatory elements are synthesized in a unique way that integrates the parts into a unified whole. Internalized object relations are depersonified and integrated into higher-level ego structures (Kernberg, 1976), contributing to an increasingly differentiated and ego-oriented regulation of self-esteem.

Beyond the synthesis of internal experience, the ego must consolidate a harmonious set of self and object representations that is confirmed by reality experience. Such integration allows the individual to trust that his perception of himself matches the world's perception of him and makes it possible for him to resist others' appraisals of his self that do not "fit." Accumulated experience, organized into a stable sense of identity, gives the ego distance from the impact of new events (White, 1966). If one has had enough experiences to know that one is intelligent, being called stupid has little effect. At the same time, the increasing automatization of ego stability engenders a deepening interest and perception of aspects of others. Total object relations tend to replace identificatory or narcissistic relationships as other people are increasingly viewed with emotional objectivity. Integration of ego identity implies a harmonious world of internalized object relations, which provides support and enrichment of ongoing experience (Kernberg, 1976).

Furthermore, the attainment of ego identity implies a sense of meaning in relationship to the social world. The individual gains an experience of belonging in some valuable and consistent way to some ongoing reality outside of himself, a sense of commitment that enriches the self.

Erikson's concept of ego identity has been widely misused and misunderstood. For Erikson, identity subsumes Blos's (1962) concept of consolidation, integration, and ego continuity, Kernberg's (1976) stress on the capacity for total object relations, as well as a linkage between the self and the more symbolic social world. In middle adolescence, identity formation is embryonic. Autonomous ego elements are beginning to form what may be the core of a later identity. But what some researchers study and label as "identity" in 13-year-olds is really ego stability or self-esteem, and we lose the richness of the identity concept if we overgeneralize it.

Much of the process of identity formation takes place in selective repudiation of possible selves. Identity is exclusive; it is manifested in commitment and in the giving up of potentialities: "I will do (be) this *and not* that or that."

Like the process of individuation, identity formation proceeds gradually, unconsciously, and often unintentionally. It is Aristotelian in inevitability but not in drama. Identity is a result of minute, seemingly inconsequential choices: whom one chooses for friends, what school one attends, what courses one takes, what one reads or does not read, whether one learns to play tennis or fly airplanes, whether one takes drugs or robs a store. Choice and action, however transient or impulsive, become part of one's life history and part of one's meaning for society. In Erikson's view, identity ". . . is dependent on the process by which a society identifies the young individual, recognizing him as somebody who had to become the way he is and who, being the way he is, is taken for granted'' (1968, p. 159).

Identity formation, then, goes beyond the tasks of individuation and of reorganization of internal experience. It requires congruence between one's sense of inner sameness and continuity and the sameness and continuity of one's meaning for others. The ego's work on identity formation is largely reserved for late adolescence, a time when choice and action ''count.'' Middle-adolescent preoccupation with how and how much to value the self gives way to late-adolescent concern that others value the self for those attributes one has come to value in oneself. Identity resides in mutuality between self and society, in a public declaration of the self that the individual intends to be taken seriously.

Ego Development and the Life Cycle

Loevinger's (1976) search for a unitary thread underlying ego development over the life cycle has led to a description of stages of structural ego growth. The accommodations in the ego that take place with development are ways of organizing experience. As new structural accommodations are made, previous experience is reassimilated. All of the ego stages show increasing internalization, complexity, abstractness, and freedom from dependency on others. In the earliest stages of ego development, according to Loevinger's scheme, the focus in on differentiating self from non-self and experiencing rudimentary object relations.[5] The next level of ego development, Self-protective, is characterized by ''opportunistic hedonism'' in which responsibility for one's generally blameworthy actions is attributed to others. At the Conformist stage, the child (or adult) identifies his own welfare with that of others and becomes concerned with social approval. The focus of a person in this stage is on external aspects of living, on being like others in a valued group. The next stage, the Self-aware level, marks the transition from the Conformist to the Conscientious stages. The growing recognition of one's internal life leads to an awareness of individuality and initiates a replacement of group values by individual standards characteristic of the Conscientious stage. In this ego configuration, internalization of rules has taken place and the Conscientious person experiences himself as an initiator of all activity, a person who makes choices. The Autonomous stage (preceded by a transitional Individualistic stage) is characterized by ''a capacity to acknowledge and cope with inner conflict . . . to unite and integrate ideas that appear as incompatible alternatives to those at lower stages'' (Loevinger, 1976, p. 23). The person in the Autonomous stage is above conscience, values abstract ideals, and thinks in terms of psychological causation, taking a broad view of life as a whole. At the highest level of ego development, the Integrated stage, the person is seen to be self-actualizing and Loevinger suggests that this kind of ego functioning is rare.

Although the Loevinger scheme does not postulate age-specific changes in ego level, most adolescents (and, according to Loevinger, most adults) appear to be at or between the Conformist and Conscientious levels. This is consistent with developmental conceptions of adolescence, which view the ego as moving away from reliance on others toward internalization of self-evaluated standards.

In that Loevinger's model of ego development is content-bound and descriptive, questions of the impetus for and the mechanisms of ego development are not considered. Her survey of efforts to classify ego development does, however, focus the dilemma of

[5]Loevinger calls these early stages Presocial, Symbiotic, and Impulsive.

what we see as development and what is more appropriately to be seen as individual differences. The tendency of descriptive researchers to "order" observable differences and call them development is widespread. The Loevinger scheme itself, beyond the Conscientious stage, is open to this criticism in that post-Conscientious ego functioning is defined by the adoption of *particular* values rather than structural change. The Autonomous stage, for example, is marked by the capacity "not only to accept, but to cherish individuality" (Loevinger, p. 22). This definition, in its inextricable connection to current sociocultural concerns, may have more to do with values than maturation. At the same time, Loevinger's effort to come to terms with ego development of adulthood may ultimately put adolescent ego development in more judicious perspective.

The problem of confusion between content and process has been a recurring one in the psychology of adolescence. Ego development need not imply increasing virtue (see van dan Daele, 1975), but only greater structuralization and autonomy of ego functions. Politics and ideology used to be seen as the keystone of adolescent growth, so much so that Blos (1962) laments the disappearance of "real" adolescence among apolitical American youth. Anna Freud believed that asceticism à la Stephen Dedalus was typical and necessary for adolescence. Many writers in this field were greatly drawn to the "hippies" and the "radicals" because it seemed that finally adolescents were doing what they *ought* to be doing. Expectation of specific behavior or certain values from adolescents leads us nowhere; instead, we must ask what function the behavior serves. There is no necessary reason why participation in a rock music group is any less autonomy enhancing for the adolescent than joining a political group. And rebellion and acting out is often more in the service of maintaining dependency ties than severing them (Masterson, 1972).

We are generally most cognizant of the dynamics of ego development in adolescence when the process fails. Most of our theory of normal development in adolescence is deduced as the obverse of pathological development; we are better at saying what does not happen than what does. As I have tried to show, the gains in individuation-autonomy in normal adolescence are gradual, often silent, and primarily result from internal reorganization of structures and self and object representations. Adolescence is a continuation of growth processes begun in infancy and childhood, distinguished by the necessity of integrating sexual identity and behavior into the ego organization and of gaining sufficient independence from parents to make adulthood possible. What is most critical to the understanding of adolescent ego development is the conceptualization of individuation, autonomy, and identity formation as matters of degree. Our theories stress the growth of independence in adolescence; our studies find that most adolescents are not that independent. Our theories focus on the myriad potentialities for identity formation in adolescence; our research discovers that adolescents are rather constricted and unimaginative in their hopes for themselves. Perhaps the emerging interest in adult development will lead us to temper our wish for adolescence to somehow "complete" growth and we shall then be able to see adolescent ego development more clearly as a series of steps somewhere in the middle of a long and continuous staircase.

Regression and Progression

Thus far, I have considered the ego's business vis-à-vis reality and vis-à-vis the internalized self-and-object world. I have discussed the process of individuation-autonomy as paralleling in rhythm and style that of the early individuation phases. Implied in, but not encompassed by, these struggles are the twin dangers inherent in regression and progression.

Blos has greatly added to our understanding of the necessity for adolescent regression in the service of development. He points out that adolescence is the only period of life where regression is part of the maturational process. Put simply, the maturing ego through regression comes into contact with infantile drive positions, old conflicts, infantile objects, and narcissistic formations (Blos, 1968). Growth, therefore, must involve psychological risks. The dangers of such regression are, like the dangers of all regression, that one will be enmeshed or unable finally to renounce infantile gratification. Dependent needs are the most prevalent reminder to the adolescent of the dangers of regression. Through clinical experience we understand much of the phenomena of unsuccessful regression in the service of development. Efforts to reach back and re-resolve infantile conflicts can overwhelm the precarious maturing ego in laying bare previously masked ego defects. In healthier adolescents, what cannot be resolved is structuralized as character defense; in those who are less healthy, psychosis may result.

We have a far better understanding of the regressive aspects of adolescent ego development than of the progressive conflicts. In fact, conflict is itself often seen, by definition, to be regressive. In contrast, the more existential writers (e.g., Fromm, Wheelis, Erikson) have focused our attention on the inescapable conflicts of adolescence that are future oriented and inherent in growth.

At the same time as the adolescent must find ways to overcome regressive strivings, he must deny the anxiety of his growing autonomy — his existential fears of his aloneness. As the adolescent's freedom grows, so does his awareness of the terrors of such freedom — his essential capacities to choose in the absence of heroic wisdom — either his own or others'. It is at adolescence that the emerging person first has the cognitive capacities to puzzle about the meaning of life, to ponder the mysteries of existence, to recognize the arbitrariness of the universe, to experience T. S. Eliot's "fear in a handful of dust." In this sense, the adolescent becomes, of necessity, a philosopher for the first time and must, like all humans, find a way of silencing a too keen perception of man's (and his own) condition (Becker, 1973). The special sensitivity and insight of adolescents often reflects their confrontation with questions that have no answers, questions that they have not yet learned not to ask. Irony, cynicism, idealism, and alienation are efforts to find a personal response to the existential dilemma. The capacity for freedom coincides with a capacity to search for meaning; in this realm the adolescent must face anxieties about independence that are unlike any he has faced before. This is one of the reasons that identity diffusion can occur in the absence of previous ego pathology and may also account for the general identity constriction we witness among adolescents. In this sense, the progressive conflicts can be as overwhelming as the regressive ones and cause the adolescent to escape into either anomie or packaged identity.

Another existential dilemma, influenced by, but not reducible to, the childhood dependency situation, is that of finding a balance between the duality of one's nature. This duality, of Agape and Eros [or agency and communion (Bakan, 1966)], contains dangers of both isolation and merger. The adolescent experiences a human (not an infantile) need to commune with something larger than himself; hence the impassioned work for causes, gangs, or philosophies. At the same time, the adolescent must find a means of experiencing and expressing his own uniqueness, his distinctive talents, his vehicle for making his own mark on the world. These ego needs are emergent at adolescence, though they are often described as re-editions of infantile conflicts. Once infantile conflicts of dependency and individuation have been adequately resolved, the adolescent is still faced with adult editions of the same issues and may, indeed, confuse the two levels of experience. An illustration of the kind of confusion that may result comes from a clinical vignette. A 22-year-old woman, struggling to make her way in a relationship with a man, had fallen in the habit of regarding all of her needs for intimacy as ''childish dependency.'' Her adult needs for communion had been disowned as a result of her horror of her regressive dependency wishes. Similarly, we witness adolescents' uncertainty as to whether their goals are realistic or grandiose — someone, after all, does become President.

In the development of the adolescent ego, infantile dependence gives way to adult interdependence, infantile narcissism gives way to adult purposefulness and perseverance, infantile magic to adult spirituality. The adolescent is in the special position of having to counterbalance dilemmas from both regressive and progressive conflicts. Even as trite and commonplace a conflict as How much do I conform? and How much do I dare listen to a different drummer? is *both* a reworking of childhood dependency needs *and* a rehearsal for adult choices.

Stages of Ego Development in Adolescence

Recent longitudinal studies provide evidence for discontinuity of development at adolescence. These results support the psychoanalytic emphasis on the importance of regression to progressive development during this phase. Peskin and Livson (1972) found that predictions of adult psychological health at age 30 were best from preadolescent behavior. Preadolescents whose behavior indicated independence, self-confidence, and intellectual curiosity were most likely to grow into well-integrated adults. Adolescent characteristics were predictive of adult psychological health when they *reversed* preadolescent functioning. That is, movement from relative preadolescent stability to emotional disruption in adolescence was found to produce the most favorable adult outcome. A relatively high degree of preadolescent ego strength seems to be necessary to tolerate the affectivity and regression of the adolescent process. Late-maturing boys, because of their longer preadolescent period, show more flexibility of defenses in dealing with drive than their early-maturing peers who prematurely structuralize drive defenses (Peskin, 1973). A period of unrest in early adolescence has also been found to be associated with psychosocial maturity (Josselson, Greenberger, & McConochie, 1977a and b) in later stages of adolescence. Haan (1972) comments on the lack of continuity of personality trends over time. Older adolescents lack homogeneity as an age group in contrast to younger adolescents and adults.

What these data suggest is that the adolescent ego undertakes the reintegrating regression to a greater or lesser extent depending on the degree of ego strength present in the preadolescent phase. Conflicts are then worked through by the adolescent process in widely varying behaviors and durations, such that the correlation between chronological age and developmental stage is low. Hatcher (1973) found near-perfect association of adolescent-stage phenomena by ignoring chronological age.

The substages of adolescent development, therefore, are best defined by growth tasks rather than chronology. Because the tasks tend to be taken in order, it makes sense to delineate early, middle, and late phases of adolescence as long as we remain clear that a 16-year-old could well be in any of these phases.

Stage theory of adolescence is primarily focused on psychosexual development (Blos, 1962; Sullivan, 1953). The ego's role is conceptualized as mainly defensive and conflict-resolving. Characteristic of early adolescence is the decathexis of the incestuous love object that results in free-floating libido clamoring for new accommodations. Regression to preoedipal conflicts demands re-resolution of these issues. Ego expansion, in the form of skill and social mastery, is both cause and effect of increased conflict resolution.

In middle adolescence, the rise of genital sexuality predominates, reawakening oedipal conflicts and burdening the ego with renewed superego pressures. It is at this point that the ego most directly begins its challenge to the superego for control. The shift in cognitive capacity to formal operations aids the ego in its attempts to be realistic rather than dominated by feelings of guilt or shame. Interpersonal relationships in this phase tend to be largely identificatory, and identifications can serve the ego, the superego, or the ego ideal. Using Loevinger's ego-development framework, this is probably the subphase of adolescence in which those who are able begin to shift from the Conformist toward the Conscientious ego level. The increased cognitive capability allows for middle-adolescent self-consciousness: the adolescent can now take the self as an object of thought. This awareness of self allows for the gradual replacement of group values by self-determined standards. This is the forerunner of internally regulated self-esteem and the transition accounts for observable adolescent uncertainty, self-proclaimed "identity crises," and confusion. Adolescent failure in ego functioning may precipitate backward movement into early adolescent safety in numbers.

Late adolescence is marked by the theme of consolidation. The ego vacillation of middle adolescence gives way to more confident, predictable, and reliable ego functioning. Affectivity has been mastered and emotions are both tolerated and enriching. Although feelings of shame and guilt may occur, they are integrated rather than experienced as overwhelming. The ego is secure in both its reality testing and defensive functions as well as differentiated enough to provide flexibility in the character structure. Old psychosexual conflicts are absorbed into the character armor in a way that maximizes the ego's conflict-free sphere.

Because of the "stairway" aspects of adolescent ego development, the oldest group we look at always appears to be the last step. As a result, we have a research literature in which high-school seniors are described as "independent, self-reliant, and in possession of firm ego identity" in contrast to younger adolescents. We then re-encounter these same young people as college freshmen; here they are described as "dependent, parent-oriented and prematurely crystallized in identity" in contrast to their older peers. What this disparity indicates is that there are qualitative differences in the nature of the individuation-autonomy process at different stages of adolescence.

For the middle adolescent, ego development focuses primarily on sexual identity and individuation. The emphasis is on recognition of the self as a man or woman and exploration of the psychosocial capacities of the individuating self. The middle adolescent is concerned with moving away from, with taking over more and more ego functions separate from parental influence. Each step, from driving a car to holding a first job are accretions of knowledge about one's capacity to function on one's own. The sense of the future is dim as energy is expended in disconnecting from the past. "I'm not a child anymore" is the battle cry. The present is all-consuming as this is where the self is most fully realized. One adolescent athletically oriented subject I interviewed described his most pressing concern in life as "staying in shape and having a good season." As we have seen, individuation and autonomy are two sides of the same coin. But middle adolescents are looking at the individuation side, storing the autonomy. They think more about whether they have freedom or not, about what they are like than about what to do with either their freedom or themselves.

Late adolescents, by contrast, are more preoccupied with the autonomy side of the coin. Now that they have a relatively stable and integrated self, the problem is what to do with it. This is the crisis of psychosocial identity and autonomy. The sense of potentiality expands (but may be defensively avoided). The future takes on new reality. "Who am I?" gives way to "What shall I become?" In this stage, late adolescents are more concerned with "fitting" their newfound self to the object world and in forcing the world to "fit" with them. I think that Erikson's rich description of identity-crisis phenomena most clearly applies to the late adolescent struggle.[6] Where the middle adolescent works to become an individual, he remains a satellite of his parents. The late adolescent, now a satellite, must strive to find his own orbit.

In summary, ego development in adolescence focuses on the problem of internalization: of values, of controls, and of self-esteem. The task of the ego is to free itself both of its dependence on external environmental controls (such as parents and peer groups) and of its submission to the archaic superego. Mechanisms of projection and introjection are used to accomplish this second phase of individuation, so that, at the close of adolescence, the young person has consolidated the ego equipment to prepare him for the developmental crises of adulthood.

REFERENCES

Bakan, P. *The duality of human existence*. Chicago: Rand McNally, 1966.

Balser, B. H. A new recognition of adolescents. *American Journal of Psychiatry*, 1966, *122*, 1281–1282.

Becker, E. *The denial of death*. New York: Free Press, 1973.

Blos, P. Prolonged adolescence. *American Journal of Orthopsychiatry*, 1954, *24*, 733–742.

———. *On adolescence: A psychoanalytic interpretation*. New York: Free Press, 1962.

———. The second individuation process of adolescence. In R. S. Eissler et al. (Eds.), *Psychoanalytic study of the child* (Vol. 15). New York: International Universities Press, 1967.

———. Character formation in adolescence. In R. S. Eissler et al. (Eds.), *Psychoanalytic study of the child* (Vol. 23). New York: International Universities Press, 1968.

Conger, J. J. A world they never knew: The family and social change. *Daedalus*, 1971, 1105–1138.

Douvan, E. and Adelson, J. *The adolescent experience*. New York: Wiley, 1966.

Erikson, E. The problem of ego identity. *Journal of the American Psychoanalytic Association*, 1956, *4*, 56–121.

———. *Identity, youth, and crisis*. New York: Norton, 1968.

Fast, I. Aspects of work style and work difficulty in borderline personalities. *International Journal of Psychoanalysis*, 1975, *4*, 397–403.

[6]Newman and Newman (1976) discuss the period from ages 13 to 17 as a crisis of group identity versus alienation and reserve the Eriksonian crisis of identity versus role diffusion for ages 18 to 22.

Freud, A. *The ego and the mechanisms of defense*. New York: International Universities Press, 1936.

———. Adolescence. In R. S. Eissler et al. (Eds.), *Psychoanalytic study of the child* (Vol. 13). New York: International Universities Press, 1958.

Grinker, R. R. "Mentally healthy" young males, *Archives of General Psychiatry,* 1962, *6,* 405–453.

Haan, N. Personality development from adolescence to adulthood in the Oakland Growth and Guidance studies. *Seminars in Psychiatry,* 1972, *4,* 399–414.

Hartmann, H. *Ego psychology and the problem of adaptation,* New York: International Universities Press, 1958.

Hatcher, S. M. The adolescent experience of pregnancy and abortion: A developmental analysis. *Journal of Youth and Adolescence,* 1973, *2,* 53–102.

Inhelder, B. and Piaget, J. *The growth of logical thinking from childhood to adolescence.* New York: Basic Books, 1958.

Josselson, R. Psychodynamic aspects of identity formation in college women. *Journal of Youth and Adolescence,* 1973, *2,* 3–52.

Josselson, R., Greenberger, E., and McConochie, D. Phenomenological aspects of psychosocial maturity in adolescence. Part I: Boys. *Journal of Youth and Adolescence,* 1977a, *6,* 25–56.

———. Phenomenological aspects of psychosocial maturity in adolescence. Part II: Girls, *Journal of Youth and Adolescence,* 1977b, *6,* 145–167.

Josselyn, I. M. *The adolescent and his world.* New York: Family Service Association of America, 1952.

Kernberg, O. *Object-relations theory and clinical psychoanalysis.* New York: Jason Aronson, 1976.

Kohut, H. *The analysis of the self,* New York: International Universities Press, 1971.

Loevinger, J. *Ego development.* San Francisco: Jossey-Bass, 1976.

Mahler, M., Pine, F., and Bergman, A. *The psychological birth of the human infant.* New York: Basic Books, 1975.

Masterson, J. F. *The psychiatric dilemma of adolescence.* Boston: Little, Brown, 1967.

———. The psychiatric significance of adolescent turmoil, *American Journal of Psychiatry,* 1968, *124,* 1549–1554.

———. *Treatment of the borderline adolescent.* New York: Wiley, 1972.

Newman, P. R. and Newman, B. M. Early adolescence and its conflict: Group identity vs. alienation. *Adolescence,* 1976, *9,* 261–274.

Offer, D. *The psychological world of the teenager,* New York: Basic Books, 1969.

Offer, D. and Offer, J. B. *From teenage to young manhood.* New York: Basic Books, 1975.

Peskin, H. Influence of the developmental schedule of puberty on learning and ego functioning. *Journal of Youth and Adolescence,* 1973, *2,* 273–290.

Peskin, H. and Livson, N. Pre- and postpubertal personality and adult psychologic functioning. *Seminars in Psychiatry,* 1972, *4,* 343–354.

Rosenberg, M. *Society and the adolescent self-image.* Princeton, N.J.: Princeton University Press, 1965.

Schafer, R. *Aspects of internalization.* New York: International Universities Press, 1968.

———. Concepts of self and identity and the experience of separation-individuation in adolescence. *Psychoanalytic Quarterly,* 1973, *42,* 42–59.

Sullivan, H. S. *The interpersonal theory of psychiatry.* New York: Norton, 1953.

Van den Daele, L. D. Ego development and preferential judgement in life-span perspective. In N. Datan & L. H. Ginsberg (Eds.), *Life-span developmental psychology*. New York: Academic, 1975.

Westley, W. A. and Epstein, N. B. *The silent majority*. San Francisco: Jossey-Bass, 1969.

White, R. *Lives in progress*. New York: Holt, Rinehart & Winston, 1966.

Wittenberg, R. On the superego in adolescence. *Psychoanalytic Review*, 1955, *42*, 271–279.

CHAPTER 7

Thinking Processes in Adolescence

Daniel P. Keating

To ask the question, "What is the nature of adolescent thinking?" is to imply that there may be something unique or special about it, something that distinguishes it from the thinking of the child, which it succeeds, or from the thinking of the adult, which it precedes, or both. There exists a host of variables pertaining to cognitive activity, any one of which, or any combination, is potentially the basis for distinguishing child, adolescent, and adult thought. The majority of research and theory has concentrated on a small subset of these possibly relevant variables.

Certainly the most influential theory, which has also generated the bulk of the research activity, is Piaget's notion of a stage of formal operations, which employs the logical structure of thought as its principal variable. He considers the development of formal operational reasoning the signal cognitive accomplishment of the adolescent years, and much of the research in adolescent cognition has followed a Piagetian paradigm. Some of the best and most recent research, however, has been highly critical of the Piagetian position. This literature has not been extensively reviewed to date and will be included in this chapter together with the more frequently reviewed supportive literature (e.g., Ausubel & Ausubel, 1966; Neimark, 1975a). The alternative perspectives on adolescent thinking from information-processing and psychometric traditions will also be examined.

The initial assertion that there are differences of major practical significance between the cognitive activity of the child and of the adolescent seems virtually unassailable. This has of course been known for many years: implicitly in the graded instruction found in school settings and explicitly through standardized ability and achievement testing. Recently, Garfinkel and Thorndike (1976) reported an item analysis of Stanford-Binet tests given to large samples of children and adolescents in 1972. We can examine the percentage of different age groups passing each item to gain an appreciation for the magnitude of the differences in cognitive performance over this age span. For example, the age-8-year items are passed by only 67% of the 7-, 8-, and 9-year-olds, whereas the same items are done correctly by virtually all (99%) of the 14-, 15-, and 16-year-olds. Similarly, on the "average-adult" items, the younger group was unable to do much at all (less than 1% passing), but the adolescents showed signs of increased cognitive maturity, with 55% passing these items. There is thus little room for doubt that, when faced with increasingly sophisticated cognitive demands, adolescents are better able to cope than children. Viewing the theoretically vague but empirically potent collection of cognitive tasks in the Stanford-Binet, we can see readily that vocabulary knowledge, numerical reasoning, general problem-solving, and so forth, increase steadily and impressively throughout the years of childhood and adolescence.

The goal of cognitive developmental research has been first to describe better and eventually to explain the easily observed phenomenon of age-increasing cognitive performance. The appeal of the Piagetian position is precisely that it offers a comprehensive theory of how these changes come about. Because Piaget has inspired so much of the research on adolescent cognitive development, it is appropriate to begin with a brief description of (1) the kinds of changes noted by Piaget and others and (2) the theory of formal operations before proceeding to an examination of the relevant research.

DESCRIPTION OF ADOLESCENT THINKING

A point made by Piaget, but not often noted by Piagetian commentators, is that although the acquisition of formal logic by the adolescent underlies many of the observable changes in adolescent thinking, it does not account for all of them: "There is more to thinking than logic" (Inhelder & Piaget, 1958, p. 335). Before we turn our attention to the formal system and its associated research, it will be useful to have a more general description of these characteristic modes of adolescent thought, which the theory seeks to explain. There are several excellent sources that I shall draw on for these descriptions; the interested reader will want to explore these firsthand (Elkind, 1974; Flavell, 1977; Inhelder & Piaget, 1958). Numerous different selections and organizations of the topics discussed here are certainly possible and equally valid. One further caution is needed: there is no assumption at this point that these cognitive activities are "impossible" for children, merely less frequent, at least on a spontaneous basis. We shall reserve for the moment the issue of possible "true" differences in underlying cognitive competence between children and adolescents or between adolescents and adults.

Thinking about Possibilities

A major distinction often made between the typical thinking process of the child as compared to the adolescent is that the child's thinking is much more closely tied to concrete reality. Although much or even most of adolescent (and adult) thought is also concerned with the sensible here-and-now, there seems to be a capacity or inclination to consider and examine possibilities that are not immediately present. This dimension of the real versus the possible or the concrete versus the abstract is perhaps the most frequently noted and the most easily observable dimension used to categorize characteristic ways of thinking, which change with development. "There is no doubt that the most distinctive feature of formal thought stems from the role played by statements about possibility relative to statements about empirical reality" (Inhelder & Piaget, 1958, p. 245).

The developmental changes associated with greater capacity for abstraction are not the sole property of Piagetians (see Flavell, 1970), but they have been systematically observed most often and most clearly via the Piagetian approach. Whereas the child is much more at ease with what can be observed directly or inferred from direct observables with very few intermediate steps, the adolescent seems more likely to place a given problem in a context of possibilities, of which the observable reality is but a single case: "reality is now secondary to possibility" (Inhelder & Piaget, 1958, p. 251).

There is of course considerable variation in the circumstances under which adolescents (or adults) activate this mode of thinking. In many real-world circumstances, the mental operations characterized as formal are not required for competent performance. In addition, many circumstances in which such a perspective could be useful involve other components (emotional content, e.g.) that inhibit or prevent the dispassionate analysis suggested by separating the reality of the situation from the broader context of possibility. It remains the case, however, that this cognitive activity is observed far more frequently among adolescents than among children.

Thinking through Hypotheses

Closely related to the separation of the real from the possible is thinking that entails the generation and testing of hypotheses. The success of the Western scientific tradition testifies to the power and the general nature of this strategy in the pursuit of truth. Indeed, the notion of falsifiability (Popper, 1968) is intimately connected with the creation and testing of hypotheses, although they are not the only important elements in the process of scientific discovery. Again, it seems to be the case that such activity is far more characteristic of adolescent than child thought or at least far more readily observable in the contexts in which it has been studied (Inhelder & Piaget, 1958; Lovell, 1961; Lunzer, 1965, pp. 19–46; Ausubel & Ausubel, 1966; Neimark, 1975a).

A different but equally appropriate heading for this section would be "thinking about the *im*possible." An important aspect of hypothetical thinking is that it is not necessarily tied to the testing of states in the real world. In colloquial use of course the notion of a "hypothetical" assumption is often identical with the notion of a "contrary-to-fact" assumption. Although hypotheses obviously need not be contrary to fact, they are allowed to be; the acceptance of this cognitive game is greater among adolescents than among children (Elkind, 1974; Bart, 1972).

There are important implications for research to be drawn from the above discussion on the notions of possibility and hypothetical thinking. It has been the case in much research on logical thinking at all ages that a separation of the real and the abstract is presumed to be necessary in order to assess the individual's ability to deal with pure logic uninformed by experience. There is an important source of potential confounding here, however, in that an individual who may be quite capable of carrying out "real" logical operations on elements that have realistic content may be unable to do so when the elements are either entirely abstract or when they are contrary to fact. This may lead us to underestimate the logical competence of individuals who are unable, unwilling, or unpracticed with respect to abstraction. The use of logic and the use of logic with abstract content are conceptually and empirically separable, and we risk overestimating the role of logic per se in performance when we fail to make the separation. This may be especially problematic in the case of older adults for whom abstraction but not logic may be an unfamiliar and difficult process (Arenberg, 1968). Much the same may be true of children. This is not to argue that the combination of logical competence and abstraction is no more powerful than either alone, but rather that their contributions to cognitive changes are likely separable and attributions of causality to one or the other (in practice, typically to logic) in studies where they are not separated are unwarranted. Roberge and Paulus (1971), in fact, found a strong interaction of type of content with type of reasoning.

Thinking Ahead

A powerful general strategy in any problem-solving situation is planning. In some types of problems it may be essential in order to achieve a correct solution. A variety of activities may be included in the concept of planning, including foresight or anticipatory knowledge of what information will be needed and of the general form of the solution; problem definition; and algorithm or strategy selection, in which the individual seeks similarities between the current problem and similar problems for which there is a known solution. It is clear that these activities lead to a more generalized and more sophisticated problem-solving approach. Such an approach seems to be used more frequently by adolescents than by children, although certainly not all adolescents use planning even when it is necessary (Siegler & Liebert, 1975).

Pitt (1976) demonstrated the use of planning through an ingenious comparison of two structurally similar problems in chemistry: combination to produce a specified effect and qualitative analysis. The first task was the standard combination of colorless liquids experiment from Inhelder and Piaget (1958), in which the subject must find the correct combination from among four chemicals to produce the desired effect, a yellow-amber liquid. In this experiment, two of the chemicals produce the desired effect, while one of the remaining two chemicals cancels or inhibits the production of the color. In order to find the full solution, the subject must construct and test a full matrix of all possible combinations with chemicals taken one, two, three, and four at a time. The qualitative analysis problem is similar, in that it involves a matrix from which information is to be extracted. The key difference, however, is that in this problem the chemicals are already mixed and the elements from the matrix must be tested in a specific order to ascertain the presence or absence of a given chemical. In other words, this is a matrix-reduction paradigm as contrasted with a matrix-construction paradigm. An important additional condition was that half the subjects received "do" instructions (i.e., they were told to carry out the experiment) similar to the standard Inhelder and Piaget (1958) instructions. The other half of the subjects received "plan" instructions (i.e., they were told to list all the steps in the solution prior to carrying out the experiment).

There were several noteworthy findings in this study. First, Pitt (1976) analyzed the use of specific processes in the problem solution, namely problem definition, data acquisition, and interpretation. On both tasks she found a significant age by process interaction, attributable to differentially greater use of problem definition by the older subjects (20 years old) as compared to the younger subjects (15 years old). In addition to the process analysis, there was a rating of overall success on the task. In the combinations task, there was an age effect (as expected), but no condition effect (plan vs. do). In the qualitative analysis problem, however, there was both an age effect and an effect of condition, with the plan-condition subjects greatly outperforming the do-condition subjects, although this was true only of the older group (and, surprisingly, of a small control group of professional scientists, who had 100% performance in plan and 0% in do conditions!).

In summary, it can be seen that planning is an important cognitive strategy in some but not all circumstances. It is more likely to be done spontaneously by adolescents than by children, and to be more successfully employed by adults and older adolescents than by younger adolescents. It is obvious that this aspect of thinking bears important implications for both assessment of cognitive competence and for instruction, some of which will be addressed later.

Thinking about Thoughts

There are several related ways of characterizing this aspect of thinking, which seems also to be more prevalent among adolescents and adults than among children. First, there is a relatively direct and straightforward notion of metacognition advanced and described for a number of different cognitive activities (metamemory, metacommunication, metattention) by Flavell (1977). The common thread is the individual's awareness and knowledge about cognitive activity itself and about the mechanisms that can make it more or less efficient. In metamemory, for example, knowledge of specific mnemonic strategies (rehearsal, method of loci, and so on) increases with age — although quite young children have some rudimentary knowledge about how to remember things — and also serves to increase performance in the primary area, in this case memory. Certainly the adolescent shows greater metacognitive sophistication but also seems to expend considerable energy on internal cognitive regulation, occasionally to the point of elevating concern with the form of cognitive activity above the substance.

This brings us to the second way in which this aspect of thinking shows a change with adolescence; that is, the frequently remarked increase in introspection (Elkind, 1974). There seems to be a great fascination among adolescents for probing their own internal states, whether cognitive or emotional. If the area is too sensitive, the adolescent may of course retreat temporarily from introspection of any sort (Conger, 1977), but the magnet of attempting to understand one's self in many respects appears to be a strong one for most adolescents.

The third way in which we may consider this aspect of thinking is more directly related to Piagetian theory. It involves what has been called "second-order" thinking — or the performing of operations upon operations. The earliest cognitive accomplishments involve the acquisition of rules and knowledge about the real world (e.g., object permanence), and this acquisition is of course a process of life-span proportions. At some point (according to Piaget about the time of adolescence), it becomes possible to develop rules concerning the rules, to hold disparate thoughts while comparing and contrasting them, in short to perform mental operations upon the operations themselves rather than upon elements. Thus the elements upon which formal logic operates are not real-world situations directly but rather ideas about relations among those situations.

Thinking beyond Old Limits

The more sophisticated cognitive activity of the adolescent is of course not restricted to test-taking or experimental sessions. It is used across the board by the adolescent in an attempt to make sense of all aspects of experience; as indicated in a number of chapters on other topics, cognitive changes underlie many of the developments in other areas. Perhaps the best way to characterize this change is as a general broadening of horizons on all dimensions. Issues that have never or rarely been considered by the adolescent will take on enlarged significance and meaning. Topics of identity, society, existence, religion, justice, morality, friendship, and so on, are examined in detail and are contemplated with high emotion as well as increased cognitive capacity. The spark for such consideration is not purely cognitive, of course; there are many lines of development converging with special significance for the adolescent. But at least some of the motivation for this stretching and breaking of old limits is probably cognitive in the purest sense: *"Cogito ergo sum."* In addition, the cognitive skills that can be applied to the task are much sharper, which makes the enterprise all the more exciting and attractive.

Some Constants

There is an old saying about research in the social sciences that, given sufficient time and financial support, one will always find that for which one is looking. Although this probably overstates the case, it is true that by focusing our attention in one direction or another, we are more or less likely to see pertinent aspects of the situation. If our focus is on change, as it has been here, we may be likely to overlook important consistencies. Many areas could be examined, but two can be noted here since they will play a role later in our evaluation of the research on the changes in adolescent thinking.

The first involves the applications of rules in cognitive activity. Many of the changes described above are interdependent in the sense that they have much to say about the kind, extensivity, and application of rules the individual has available to deal with cognitively demanding situations. It should be remembered, however, that even young children's thinking is rule-governed (Flavell, 1977; Siegler, 1976). For young children, the demands of certain tasks often overburden the rule systems available, and there is an observed breakdown in performance. But if, as research suggests, the child possesses an orientation toward systematic extraction and processing of information from the environment from the earliest age at which we can reliably assess it, this fact should give us pause before asserting that some behavior is in some absolute sense beyond the grasp of children of a given age. Such assertions about competence are to be tested carefully, not assumed on the basis of inferior performance in a given situation.[1]

The second element of continuity is related to the first. There exists a collection of well-studied task variables that can reliably alter performance on most or all cognitive tasks. Examples from this collection are negative information versus positive information, the negative information being more difficult to evaluate; memory load in nonmemory tasks, again decreasing performance; and so on. It is noteworthy for practice and perhaps for theory that these task variables seem to operate in highly similar fashion regardless of the age of the subject. Certainly, evaluating the negative information may be relatively more difficult for a younger compared to an older subject, but it is clear that such a task variable places similar limitations on performance. The practical point for research is that these extraneous (in some cases) task variables may interact in unknown ways with primary task performance and thus need to be kept in mind when conducting or evaluating research on cognitive changes. The theoretical point is that the existence of similar limitations on the cognitive systems of children, adolescents, and adults suggests a fairly basic continuity which needs to be taken into account.

FORMAL OPERATIONS: THEORY

For a theoretical position as influential as Piaget's on formal reasoning development, it is remarkably difficult to pin down the specific elements that are crucial to it. The basic source is of course the Inhelder and Piaget (1958) volume on *The Growth of Logical Thinking from Childhood to Adolescence*.

Probably the most readable description of the Piagetian theory of formal operations is to be found in Flavell (1977). In accord with Piaget's general theory, the adolescent transition involves a basic reorganization of cognitive structures. Inhelder and Piaget (1958) characterize this particular transition in a number of related ways. Most directly, it involves an acquisition of the structures of formal propositional logic: "We must first describe the development of propositional logic, which the child at the concrete level

---

[1]A recent finding in infant research highlights the problems of concluding a certain behavior is impossible at a given age. Contrary to Piagetian (and others') expectations, Meltzoff & Moore (1977) seem to have found reliable evidence of imitation in 12- to 21-day-old human infants. Caution is warranted in assumptions about what individuals are "unable" to do.

(. . . from 7-8 to 11-12 years) cannot yet handle'' (p. 1). The key to this inability to handle propositional logic according to Piaget is the coordination and interaction of propositional statements, not the factual evaluation of single propositions. In the Piagetian scheme, children do acquire the structures by means of which a given proposition can be tested for its truth value, but they remain unable to deal with the complexity of considering more than one proposition simultaneously. In other words, intrapropositional thinking becomes available in childhood, but interpropositional thinking becomes available only during adolescence (Flavell, 1977).

It should be noted that the propositional logic system that Piaget elaborates as the underlying model for formal operational thinking is not without its critics. Parsons (1960) and Ennis (1975, 1976) have been especially critical from the logician's perspective, arguing that there are some significant inconsistencies within the logical system itself. These criticisms will be reviewed later, but a brief description of Piaget's logical system is appropriate here. There is some risk of becoming lost in logical arguments and losing sight of the goal of understanding adolescent thinking, but understanding the logic is central to evaluating much of the research presumably designed to test the theory.

The Structured Whole

Inhelder and Piaget (1958) have asserted quite explicitly in several places that the understanding of specific logical propositions is not a sign of formal operations, but rather the full integration of the elements into a "structured whole." The existence of this structured whole in the thinking of the individual requires a complete combinatorial system whereby all combinations of logical possibilities can be generated. They argue:

> The combinatorial system necessary for the formal analysis of the associations [or logical elements] is based on what can be called a "structured whole," which . . . is composed of 16 combinations [in the case of two propositions] . . . . [T]his complete combinatorial system is precisely the mark of formal thought. [P. 55]

What exactly is this combinatorial system to which Inhelder and Piaget refer? An insightful exegesis of *The Growth of Logical Thinking* by Ennis (1975) indicates that there is some confusion about the nature of this combinatorial system among Piaget interpreters, and that the confusion rests on an ambiguity in the text itself. From the above quotation, the clear indication is that the criterion of formal thought is the ability to comprehend all the relationships among logical elements.

Using standard notation, we can identify the four logical elements in the case of two propositions, p and q: p and q occur together, $(p \cdot q)$; p can occur without q, $(p \cdot \bar{q})$; q can occur without p $(\bar{p} \cdot q)$; or neither p nor q can occur, $(\bar{p} \cdot \bar{q})$. For convenience, we may label these four logical elements or statements A, B, C, and D, respectively. These can then be combined in 15 possible combinations, which becomes 16 if we add the null set (i.e., complete negation): 0, A, B, C, D, AB (i.e., A *or* B), AC, AD, BC, BD, CD, ABC, ABD, ACD, BCD, and ABCD. These 16 combinations are the operations that can be carried out on the two propositions, p and q. For clarity these combinations are rearranged and shown in Table 1 together with the constructed combination and Piaget's notation, after Ennis (1975). One of the confusions cited by Ennis is whether the ability to generate all possible combinations of x elements is a mark of formal operational thought, as suggested in Inhelder and Piaget's (1958) discussion of the combination of chemicals task, or instead whether it is the far more stringent criterion of being able to understand and/or use effectively the entire logical system indicated in Table 1. Judging from their statements cited above about the combinatorial system being the mark of formal operational thought, one would conclude the latter is the appropriate criterion, a conclusion supported by additional textual analysis (see Ennis, 1975). Judging from Inhelder and Piaget's usage in the chemicals task and from other subsequent usage of "combinatorial thinking," one might, however, conclude the former. Pitt (1976) argues that combinatorial thinking in this sense is a presupposed ability for formal reasoning to occur, but is not the criterion for it. It is certainly the case that generating all possible combinations of x elements has become a standard criterion in research tasks used to diagnose the presence or absence of formal operational thinking (e.g., Neimark, 1975b). The question of whether this or any other performance criterion can adequately serve the purpose of diagnosing formal operations will be discussed later.

The Four Group

The logical system employed by Piaget is further integrated through four group operators:

- (I)dentity
- (N)egation
- (R)eciprocal
- (C)orrelative.

Any of the 16 operations in Table 1 (i.e., the 16 possible relationships of two elements) can also be derived from the remaining operations and the INRC group. These operators specify the relationship between operations and are presumed to be a significant part of the

Table 1   Piaget's System of 16 Binary Operations

Piaget's Name and Number	Constructed Combination	Corresponding Construction from Text	Piaget's Logical Shorthand
1. Complete affirmation	$p \cdot q \vee p \cdot \bar{q} \vee \bar{p} \cdot q \vee \bar{p} \cdot \bar{q}$	ABCD	$p * q$
2. Negation of complete affirmation	nothing	O	0
3. Conjunction	$p \cdot q$	A	$p \cdot q$
4. Incompatibility	$p \cdot \bar{q} \vee \bar{p} \cdot q \vee \bar{p} \cdot \bar{q}$	BCD	p / q
5. Disjunction	$p \cdot q \vee p \cdot \bar{q} \vee \bar{p} \cdot q$	ABC	$p \vee q$
6. Conjunctive negation	$\bar{p} \cdot \bar{q}$	D	$\bar{p} \cdot \bar{q}$
7. Implication	$p \cdot q \vee \bar{p} \cdot q \vee \bar{p} \cdot \bar{q}$	ACD	$p \supset q$
8. Nonimplication	$p \cdot \bar{q}$	B	$p \cdot \bar{q}$
9. Reciprocal implication	$p \cdot q \vee p \cdot \bar{q} \vee \bar{p} \cdot \bar{q}$	ABD	$q \supset p$
10. Negation of reciprocal implication	$\bar{p} \cdot q$	C	$\bar{p} \cdot q$
11. Equivalence	$p \cdot q \vee \bar{p} \cdot \bar{q}$	AD	$p = q^a$
12. Reciprocal exclusion	$p \cdot \bar{q} \vee \bar{p} \cdot q$	BC	$p \vee\vee q$
13. Affirmation of p	$p \cdot q \vee p \cdot \bar{q}$	AB	$p [q]$
14. Negation of p	$\bar{p} \cdot q \vee \bar{p} \cdot \bar{q}$	CD	$\bar{p} [q]$
15. Affirmation of q	$p \cdot q \vee \bar{p} \cdot q$	AC	$q [p]$
16. Negation of q	$p \cdot \bar{q} \vee \bar{p} \cdot \bar{q}$	BD	$\bar{q} [p]$

Source: Ennis (1975), Table 3, p. 9.

[a]Piaget also uses "$p \supseteqq q$" for "equivalence."

structure underlying the individual's use of logic. Identity appears to be the easiest and first to appear, followed by Negation and Reciprocal and their coordination, with the Correlative the most difficult and final operator to come into use (Pitt, 1976; Stolarz, 1976). It should again be emphasized that the presence or absence of a given operation or operator is not the test of formal operational reasoning in the fullest sense, but rather the systematic coordination of all the propositional and group operations.

Other Theoretical Concerns

There are a number of corollaries to the theory of formal operations. Three of these deal with aspects of the hypothesized change to formal operations: the change is qualitative, the change is abrupt or discontinuous, the change occurs universally. Each of these needs to be examined briefly.

The notion of a qualitative change is of course central to the entire theory of stage changes. The issues involving the existence of stage changes and the utility of stage notions are numerous and complex, well beyond the scope of this chapter (see, e.g., Wohlwill, 1973). In the case of the transition in question here, the qualitative change is from an underlying structure of class logic to one of propositional logic.

How this is to be ascertained and how a decision that a qualitative change has occurred remains problematic here as elsewhere. Osherson (1975) lucidly addressed the issue in this way:

> It is possible that distinct patterns of logical abilities in children and adolescents result from similar reasoning processes. Conversely, there is the danger that superficially similar abilities may mask genuine differences in the mental structures mediating them. . . . It is also true of the present conception that whether two phenomena are considered alike or unalike depends on the state of the current theorizing. [P. 9]

Osherson proceeds to argue that the appropriate task is to construct veridical theories that account for the logical abilities of children and adolescents, and then compare them. (His attempt to execute this plan is described in a subsequent section.) There is much to be said, however, for the argument that complete and relatively unambiguous models of logical abilities, well supported by real-world data, are needed before the issue of qualitative or other change can take on much significance. In the interim, the question is somewhat diversionary from the prior task of adequately producing and verifying such models.

Whether the change in adolescent thinking is gradual or abrupt appears to be conceptually independent of whether it is qualitative. All four possibilities (abrupt or gradual; qualitative or not) are hypothetically possible, although abrupt but nonqualitative changes may be more difficult to account for theoretically. (What, for example, might trigger a rapid advance in what has been a gradual, cumulative process?) Perhaps for this reason, abrupt, discontinuous change has been viewed as concomitant with qualitative change. Neimark (1975b) argued that a pattern of discrete shifts in cognitive-strategy scores, rather than one of continuous increments, provided "extremely strong support for Piaget's stage theory" (p. 212). She argued further, with better justification, that patterns of growth that appear continuous in cross-sectional data may be misleading and that longitudinal data are needed to address this question. In any case, the theory would seem to require proof of discrete shifts less than it would require data-based comprehensive models of reasoning at the different ages.

The third problematic corollary to the formal-operations theory is the expectation that its development is universal among normal adolescents and adults. Using Inhelder and Piaget's (1958) tasks, researchers discovered early that formal operations was far from universally attained. Among college students and adults, rates of successful performance on these tasks average around 40 to 60% (see King, 1977, and Neimark, 1975a, for reviews). Ausubel and Ausubel (1966) suggested that intersituational generality ought not to be a criterion for the theory since differential familiarity with the content area and other factors might well inhibit performance. They cited the Piagetian notion of horizontal decalage to buttress the argument. Piaget (1972) has argued similarly.

This does leave attempts to disconfirm the theory in a pickle. Where formal operational reasoning is presumed to occur by the theoretical account, its failure to make a convincing appearance is attributed to extraneous task factors, such as differential familiarity and horizontal decalage. Where, however, formal operations are presumed not to exist (i.e., in children), the inability to perform is unambiguously attributed to the absence of formal operations. A contrary account that would hold "extraneous" task factors as the principal source of variance in both adolescents (or adults) and in children — but more potently in children — seems not to have been much considered or tested.

This is perhaps the best jumping-off point into the research on formal operations and adolescent thinking. Many of the themes already considered will return in the context of what we have actually learned about adolescent cognitive development.

FORMAL OPERATIONS: RESEARCH

The most fruitful method for organizing the research on formal operations is to consider the way in which the construct may be validated. Such a construct-validity approach will also provide a framework for examining the vast majority of research in adolescent thinking.

The question can be phrased in this fashion: What would we need to know in order to assert at some reasonable level of confidence that Piaget's account of formal operations is accurate? If, as widely believed, the theory can account for important aspects of adolescent (and adult) thinking, then the categories of evidence we should collect to verify it can be rather straightforwardly stated.

It is always appropriate to keep the opposite perspective firmly in mind, and this is perhaps especially true in this area. What would we have to find empirically in order to falsify or disconfirm the theory? In addition, we need to restrict such potential negative findings to the realm of the reasonable. For example, it would be generally considered disconfirmatory to find children outperforming adults or adolescents on any of the formal operations tasks. But given the widely known monotonic-age increase in performance on cognitive tasks, such a finding would be highly unlikely: the theory clearly requires more than monotonic increases with age. Thus, with an appropriately skeptical perspective, we can evaluate the variety of evidence so far collected. For convenience, we can list a number of questions to organize this evidence. The reader will note that all the questions are to a large degree interdependent.

1. How is the construct operationalized?
2. Does formal reasoning ability increase with age?
3. Is the change to formal operations stagelike?

4. Is the ability generalizable?

5. Can planned intervention provoke a transition to formal operations?

6. Is the hypothesized ability-change discriminable from other known or hypothesized changes?

7. Viewing all the evidence, can we draw supportable conclusions about the theory of formal operations?

Operationalizing the Construct

In the strictest sense, Piaget's theory of formal operations is clearly a structural competence theory. Inhelder and Piaget (1958) employed 15 different tasks for which formal-reasoning competence was presumed to be necessary and through which they attempted to illustrate the differences between formal and nonformal reasoning. The tasks can generally be divided into three classes on the basis of the expected performance manifestation of the latent formal-reasoning structure: combinatorial reasoning, isolation or separation of variables, and proportionality. We shall examine each of these briefly.

Combinatorial Reasoning

Although the ability to generate all possible combinations of a given set of elements cannot constitute a direct test of the existence of the full combinatorial logical system, as noted above, Inhelder and Piaget (1958) argue for a close correspondence between them. In other words, their assumption is that when, on the surface level, the subject is combining physical elements (in this case, in the chemical combinations task) he or she is also carrying out propositional combinatorials on a deeper level:

At the same time that the subject combines the elements or factors given in the experimental context, he also combines the propositional statements which express the results of these combinations of facts and in this way mentally organizes the system of binary operations consisting in conjunctions, disjunctions, exclusions, etc. But this coincidence is not so surprising when we realize that the two phenomena are essentially identical [P. 122]

It seems that Inhelder and Piaget here are arguing that, given the close similarity between producing combinations of facts and producing combinations of propositions and given also the simultaneous occurence of the surface combinations (i.e., combining chemicals) and what "must" be going on in the subject's thinking, one may safely assume that the successfully performing subject is demonstrating the existence of the underlying logical system. It is the status of this assumption that Ennis (1975) questioned. If the theory requires demonstration of the full combinatorial propositional system, as it seems to, then an analogous and (presumed) simultaneous demonstration of a full combinatorial of experimental facts is insufficient. In other words, it would appear to be a necessary but not sufficient demonstration.

Isolation of Variables

The ability to separate the effects of several variables in an experimental situation through the method of holding all of them constant except one is presented by Inhelder and Piaget (1958) as another clear sign of the presence of the formal operational system. One of the standard tasks in which this is assessed is the pendulum task. In this experiment, the subject must hold a number of factors constant while varying one in order to estimate the effect of each on the period of a pendulum (length of string, weight of the swinging object, height from which the object is dropped, and impetus or push given to the object). Appropriate testing reveals that length is the controlling factor, and it is the process of generating the correct (i.e., unconfounded) tests and recognizing their necessity that indicates that formal reasoning has transpired.

The logical connection between the theory and this operational definition is similar to the previous one, and has been subjected to a similar criticism by Ennis (1975). Inhelder and Piaget (1958) write with respect to the pendulum problem:

> Analyzing all the inferences accepted by a substage III-B subject [i.e., fully formal operational] and all those he rejects, one must assume that he has knowledge of the [sixteen true] combinations. . . . This knowledge itself presupposes a knowledge of the sixteen other rejected combinations. [P. 79]

The thrust of Piaget's argument is that the full combinatorial system of propositional logic can be assumed to be operating on the basis of a performance in which all appropriate "states of nature" resulting from combining experimental factors are generated, tested, and defended as necessary to any conclusion about controlling factors. This is the same assumption contested by Ennis for combinatorial reasoning.

Proportionality

It is through tasks that require a concept of proportionality that the operation of the INRC group can be inferred, according to Inhelder and Piaget (1958, p. 176). A representative task in this class is equilibrium in the balance beam. In this task, subjects are required to deduce the rule relating weight and distance from the fulcrum in a balance beam, that is, that their effects are proportional. It is somewhat more difficult to specify the logical connection between the theory (the INRC group) and the task (proportionality) in this case. It appears to rest on the subject's understanding of the necessity of multiplicative compensation or of reciprocity to account for the proportional relationships. Although it is clear that the group operators can be used to generate the solution, it is less clear that they are necessarily implied by the establishment of a proportionality concept. It is rather the subject's explanation and extensivity of the concept that is used as the basis for the assumption that the INRC group and hence the propositional logic system is in use:

> The rapidity with which the subject makes the transition from qualitative correspondence to the metrical proportion seems at first to indicate the presence of an anticipatory schema. However, the analogy that the subject [ROG] established between the balance and the game of marbles shows that this schema is taken from notions of reciprocity or of compensation. [Inhelder & Piaget, 1958, p. 174]

It is difficult to see from this argument (or similar ones elsewhere in Inhelder and Piaget's book) how performance on proportionality tasks can directly be used as evidence for the presence of formal operations. Statements by subjects going beyond the task, which imbeds the explanation in a logical system, constitute a different (perhaps useful) criterion, but one that has not been used in practice.

Siegler (1976) carried out a detailed processing analysis of performance on the balance-beam task from a somewhat different perspective. He first assessed subjects' initial knowledge on the task in terms of the sophistication of the rule systems they were using and, not surprisingly, found an increase with age in initial knowledge. He then took subjects of different ages who were similar in initial knowledge and presented them with similar conflict situations in which the subjects' predictions would be wrong. He found that older subjects made better use of this information, more often adjusting their rule system to take the new information into account. In a subsequent study, it was learned that the younger subjects were not encoding (attending to) the discrepant information. When they were instructed to attend to specific aspects of the problem, they improved their performance approximately to the level of the older subjects. This interesting piece of research illustrates the problems in drawing inferences about underlying structure from unanalyzed performance data, a general problem that we need to consider briefly.

The Competence/Performance Problem

As if it were not already abundantly clear, I should state explicitly that much of the foregoing analysis is not in the spirit of the Piagetian approach. One gets the sense in reading the literature in this area that many researchers are working at cross-purposes, with little communication among individuals who work with different sets of assumptions. There is no attempt to resolve these differences here. My purpose is to clarify these differences sufficiently so that the interpretation of the following evidence can be placed in an appropriate context. A variety of the most confusing and controversial issues seems to cluster under the handy general heading of competence/performance distinctions.

As noted earlier, Piaget's is a structural theory of logical competence. Further, the theory is about the deep structure of cognitive activity, analogous to deep-structure grammar in language. [This analogy is not original here — see Pitt (1976) and Osherson (1975).] Its claim as theory is to a logical grammar that underlies the surface structure of performance in the cognitive domain. What rule does evidence based on performance (surface structure) play in evaluating the competence (deep-structure) theory? Obviously, it can play only an indirect role, principally through a demonstration of the adequacy (or inadequacy) of a set of transformational rules linking deep to surface structure. Piaget, however, does not supply the transformational rules (see Pitt, 1976). Thus even the indirect role that evidence based on performance might play in verifying or disconfirming the theory is seriously attenuated, if not lost.

It appears to be precisely this point that Ennis (1975, 1976) has made so vigorously: "Piaget's claim that children 11–12 and under cannot handle propositional logic is either untestable or false or otherwise defective, depending on one's interpretation of the claim" (Ennis, 1975, p. 2). His major concern is that the connection from theory to data is insufficiently explicated, if at all. Hence data-based tests are probably irrelevant.

There seem to be two prominent lines of defense against this sort of criticism. First, Inhelder and Piaget (1958, pp. 103–104) analyzed one protocol [(GOU) on the invisible magnet task] that would demonstrate the presence of 16 binary operations inferrable directly from the subject's statements. Bynum, Thomas, and Weitz (1972), however, offered a convincing counterargument that only a few of the operations could in fact be derived from GOU's protocol. Even if all 16 were derivable from the protocol, it would not appear to constitute conclusive evidence since it is the interpreter rather than the subject who establishes (i.e., infers) evidence for the operations. In the absence of stated transformational rules, the confounding of the interpreter's reading and the subject's performance is unavoidable.

The second line of defense is both more general and more plausible. This argument refers back to one of Piaget's original goals, which was the elucidation of certain epistemological principles via developmental analysis rather than descriptions and explanations of cognitive performance. In this light, the analysis of performance is seen to be for illustrative purposes only, to show that a particular logical framework *could* (rather than does) account for a set of responses to certain cognitive tasks. Much of the language in *The Growth of Logical Thinking* would be interpretable in this fashion. For better or worse, this interpretation removes from the theory the onus of demonstrating its psychological reality (for example, linguistics vs. psycholinguistics), but also (lacking additional theory-building) restricts interest in the theory for those individuals concerned with cognitive activity.

The uncertain status of the connection between the tasks and the theoretical account has been exacerbated by the diversity of ways in which formal-operations tasks are administered and scored. Many observers have commented on the lack of scoring similarity among researchers, all of whom are using the same group of tasks. This variance is of course traceable to the Piagetian clinical method of collecting data. Because Piaget is aiming for a process account of cognition rather than a strictly product account, he argues the necessity of preserving a relatively open-ended observational approach. The task of the investigator is thus to be sensitive to clinical ''signs'' of the underlying reasoning process rather than to be concerned with the product outcome alone (i.e., the subject's right or wrong solution to the problem). Although this is undoubtedly a method of observing that elicits a more varied and thorough repertoire of behavior from the subject and yields (or, minimally, allows) a richer description of behavior from the observer, the interpretation of data derived by means of the clinical method is notoriously difficult (Meehl, 1954; Brainerd, 1973a).

It is possible and, according to numerous research studies, relatively easy to obtain interrater agreement, but this apparently occurs only when reasonably explicit rules are used to judge performance on the task. A little reflection reveals what has actually transpired at this step in the operational definition process. The clinical method has been abandoned, or at least seriously constrained, since the scoring rules supplant the open-ended observation. More importantly, each researcher (or rule-writer) has quite literally written his or her own set of transformational rules connecting the theory to the tasks under consideration. Very few researchers are explicit about this rule-writing step connecting logic to task (see Osherson, 1975, on the difficulty of writing such rules). Indeed, the comparison of performance across studies, usually done on the basis of similarly described formal-operations levels, is probably less instructive for theory than a comparison of researchers' transformational rule systems would be. Unfortunately, most researchers' rule-writing systems are insufficiently explicit to make such a comparison very informative (including Keating, 1975; Keating & Schaefer, 1975).

The more usual procedure is to employ formal-operations tasks (i.e., those so labeled by Inhelder & Piaget, 1958) as adequate performance tests of the presence, absence, or emergence of formal operational structures in the mind of the subject. This casts the research headlong into a variety of well-known problems in psychological measurement, few of which have been addressed empirically in any significant way (Green, Ford, & Flamer, 1971). Briefly, if we are to treat these tasks in a more general way, viewing them as reasonable tests of some holistic scientific or logical reasoning ability rather than explicit tests of a logical competence theory, then a different set of rules of evidence comes into play. This set of rules includes those that apply to psychological measurement in general, especially issues of sampling, reliability, and validity. Instead the practice has been to assume that the label ''formal-operations task'' ipso facto guarantees the validity of both the task and the presumed underlying construct. Thus, if two age groups of children differ in performance on these tasks, they are assumed to differ by virtue of differing cognitive structures (i.e., plus, minus, or in between on formal operations). A consideration of the multiplicity of factors that might contribute to the observed performance variance rapidly reveals the unfounded nature of this assumption.

The thrust of the argument being made is now clear. In the process of defining operationally a construct or theory so that it may be evaluated empirically, one cannot have it both ways. If the theory is to be tested via a logical analysis of a specific set of performance situations, the rules connecting competence to performance must be explicit and testable. If instead a general ability construct is proposed, in which evidence and construct definition serve to reinforce each other (Cronbach & Meehl, 1955), then psychometric as well as logical rules of evidence are applicable. Assertions about the validation (Inhelder & Piaget, 1958; Lovell, 1961; Ausubel & Ausubel, 1966; Neimark, 1975a) or invalidation of the structural theory of competence based on general performance data are thus inappropriate. It is more appropriate to deal with the performance data *as such,* attempting to derive some information about a general logical-ability construct, including logical-reasoning development and associated variables.

One may choose to pursue the former course of explicit theory construction as Osherson (1975) has done. It is noteworthy, however, that his hopes for success were not realized, and, by his account, for logically intrinsic and insurmountable reasons. First is the apparent fact that at least several deep-structure theories can equally well generate the same set of transformational rules. Since evidence about performance speaks only to the rules, it is not possible to discriminate among the competing theories on an evidentiary basis. This, incidentally, is not a serious problem for researchers interested in empirically uncovering the operating rules and conditions of their application to performance (e.g., Siegler, 1976). Second, Osherson argues for the primacy or at least heuristic priority of semantic (or knowledge-network) considerations above logical competence (or syntactic) considerations (Keating, 1977).

Summary and Evaluation

The patient reader has now come full circle to the original question that inspired this inquiry. What accounts for the observed major increases in performance on complex cognitive tasks at adolescence? There is a Piagetian belief that a major shift in underlying cognitive structures is primarily accountable for this increase. It is believed to account for two related aspects of adolescent cognitive development. First, the increased ability of the adolescent to handle problems requiring propositional logic are directly accounted for. Second, since whatever cognitive structures the individual has available at a given time are presumably activated any time reasonably demanding thinking is required, the shift in structures affects indirectly the adolescent's reaction to a variety of situations discussed earlier, that is, questions of identity, society, morality, and so on.

The purpose of the preceding analysis of the operational definition of the theoretical account is to cast serious doubt on the adequacy and utility of that belief system. This generation of doubt is conducted with some ambivalence, since Piaget's theory of formal operations is to be given most of the intellectual credit for initially raising the important questions that remain the focus of attention in this area. But in evaluating what we know and what we need to know, the status of the prevailing belief system needs to be addressed.

The account of formal operations offered by Inhelder and Piaget (1958) is best regarded as an organizational framework for interesting questions, as a holistic ability notion, and as a source of interesting tasks and useful descriptions of adolescent thinking. Using it to explain other behaviors, either cognitive or noncognitive, is both premature and potentially counterproductive. For example, attributing poor academic achievement or personal integration to under- or nondeveloped formal operations is no more helpful than attributing it to low intelligence. Both formal operations-task performance and IQ-test performance are behaviors in need of explanation rather than adequate sources of explanation (Keating & Bobbitt, 1978).

The most defensible interpretation of formal operational reasoning ability is as a general ability construct with all the standard validity requirements that implies (Cronbach & Meehl, 1955). Given these considerations, we can now turn to the evidence gathered using the formal-operations construct with a clear notion of its connection to psychological interpretations.

Increases in Formal Reasoning with Age

Virtually every study that has permitted an age comparison of performance on the Inhelder and Piaget (1958) tasks has revealed a significant effect of age (see Neimark, 1975a, for a partial listing — among the studies since that review are Keating, 1975; Kuhn & Angelev, 1976; Neimark, 1975b; Ronning, 1977; Siegler, 1976; and numerous others). Age effects on task performance are undoubtedly among the easiest to find, but they remain among the most difficult to interpret. Since nearly all performance factors increase with age, it is impossible to attribute changes in performance to a single hypothesized domain (i.e., logical competence) among many competitors (e.g., memory load, planning, external task structure).

An elegant series of studies on transitive inference reported by Trabasso (1975) raises the issue of competing explanations dramatically. Given a series of transitive inference problems of the class

$$A > B > C > D > E; B \lessgtr D?$$

young children are on first analysis decidedly poorer than older children and adolescents — whether the content of the inference involves concrete referents or abstract concepts makes a difference in how much poorer, with abstraction increasing the age effect (Glick & Wapner, 1968). It may seem quite reasonable, given the structure of the problem, to conclude that younger children lack the logical structures necessary to carry out the task (i.e., make the correct inference). But further analysis of the task reveals its complex nature. Before an inference can be made, the premises must be retrieved accurately. Not surprisingly, the younger children are also less accurate in retrieving the original premises. Indeed, the accuracy of recalling the original premises is highly correlated ($r = .80$) with accuracy in making inferences from the premises. Further, when younger children are trained to an increasingly strict criterion on premise recall, their performance on the inferences increased concomitantly, eventually to near ceiling.[2] As Trabasso (1975) noted, this does not entirely explain the developmental differences, but it does raise questions about unanalyzed attributions of differences to underlying logical competence.

---

[2]The series of studies reported by Trabasso (1975) was more complex than discussed here. His whole discussion of transitive inference models is of interest.

Setting aside momentarily the issue of causality in performance, we may inquire about the shape of the growth curve on formal-operations and logical-reasoning tasks. Since these are typically based on cross-sectional studies (except Neimark, 1975b) with subjects selected in many different ways, the results require cautious interpretation. Whether one looks at performance on formal-operations tasks or at logical reasoning per se (Ennis, 1976; Neimark, 1975a, 1975b; Roberge, 1976; Roberge & Paulus, 1971), the picture is reasonably consistent: performance increases with age in a smooth, gradual function; the changes appear larger in early adolescence than in late adolescence. The cumulative data are insufficient to argue strongly for an additional point that is suggested by some studies — the appearance of a positive acceleration to the curve at the transition from childhood to early adolescence (at about ages 10 to 12). If this were to be established more firmly, it would lend credence to a notion that physiological changes associated with puberty may be related to and partially account for a surge in cognitive growth during this period (Petersen, 1976; Kohen-Raz, 1974).

The transition from adolescence to adulthood and the possibly associated cognitive changes has also been a focus of recent discussion. Inhelder and Piaget (1958) argued that once formal operations were acquired, subsequent cognitive growth was a matter of gaining more experience with the real world — that is, reining in idealism produced as a result of runaway concern with possibilities to the exclusion of reality constraints and gaining a better understanding of a wide variety of areas through application of formal operational thinking to them (Piaget, 1972).

Others (Arlin, 1975, 1977; Riegel, 1973) have argued for structural development beyond formal operations. Riegel (1973) argues that to obtain a full account of cognitive development, a stage of dialectical operations needs to be posited, a stage that goes beyond propositional reasoning. This notion has not yet been subjected to empirical test. Arlin (1975, 1977) sees a fifth stage of cognitive development, also going beyond formal operations. She regards the latter as problem-solving, whereas the newly proposed stage can be described as problem-finding. Problem-finding is assessed by making a qualitative rating of the generality of the questions subjects ask when confronted with an un-categorized set of objects (wooden cubes, cardboard, clamps, etc.). She did not find any nonformal thinkers (based on a criterion of performance on tasks from Inhelder and Piaget, 1958) scoring beyond + 1 standard deviation of the distribution of problem-finding scores in a college sample (60 women). She found a significant effect on problem-finding scores of age and Piagetian operations score among 7-, 9-, and 11-year-olds. It is not entirely clear whether Arlin is proposing a structural theory or another ability dimension. In either case, the evidence is somewhat questionable since the structure-behavior connection is unspecified (first interpretation) and discriminant validity evidence is unavailable (second interpretation). The question of postadolescent cognitive development, however, remains an open one.

General performance data that indicate a smooth overall increase with age may obscure deeper underlying aspects of cognitive growth. In particular, the formal-operations ability construct implies something other than just age increases. Most explicitly, the requirement is for evidence of stages in cognitive growth. The next section is devoted to this question.

Stagelike Nature of Adolescent Cognitive Changes

The issue of stage changes in any domain, including cognitive growth, is intimately connected with the level of analysis. What appear to be qualitative shifts at one level of analysis may be quantitative at a different level. For example, colors are perceived as qualitatively different but are, at another level, quantitative variations in wavelength.[3] The specification of appropriate criteria is difficult (Pinard & Laurendeau, 1969, pp. 121–163); perhaps the most direct approach is to investigate how the concept is dealt with in practice.

Two studies that offer the most promise of establishing empirically a cognitive development progression that differs from the smooth and apparently quantitative growth described above will be considered in detail (Brainerd, 1971; Neimark, 1975b). Consider in each case the criteria specified for a stage progression and the empirical fulfillment of them.

Brainerd's Proportionality Study

Brainerd (1971) studied the development of the proportionality scheme in three tasks: (1) concept of density, (2) conservation of solid volume, and (3) conservation of liquid volume. Although admitting that the inference connecting performance on the three tasks are related through an incipient proportionality scheme is not necessarily warranted by the performance data (Brainerd, 1971, p. 473), he argued that five explicit tests of the Piagetian framework are possible:

1. Change with age.
2. Nonlinear age trends.
3. Coordinated emergence.
4. Earlier emergence of density concept relative to volume concept.
5. More rapid learning by older subjects.

Subjects were 8-, 11-, and 14-year-olds tested on all three tasks.

The results offered unsurprising and unequivocal support for a significant age effect. The search for a nonlinear component was not as successful, and Brainerd (1971) offered a qualified negative answer to the question of discrete shifts. To this point, the evidence for a stagelike change is not strong.

On the third question, Brainerd (1971) predicted significant correlations among the tasks, and, more significantly, a stronger correlation pattern among the older subjects. The results were interpreted by him as support for the predictions: three of three multiple correlations were significant for the oldest group, two of three for the middle group, and one of three for the youngest group. Several problems are evident with regard to this interpretation. First, since most kinds of performance are correlated, it would be far more convincing to demonstrate not only intercorrelation among presumably related tasks, but also lack of correlation of these tasks with others lying outside the hypothesized domain. Second, toting up the number of significant correlations by age is a weak test of the hypothesis of coordinated emergence with age. The test, rather, is whether there are significant differences between the correlations at one age versus another. The reported multiple correlations do not appear to differ significantly as a function of age.

Brainerd's (1971) affirmative answer to the fourth question, on invariant sequence, appears somewhat more solidly based. The prediction, derived from Piagetian theory, is that a density concept invariably emerges after a volume concept. Brainerd (1971) suggests a curious paradox in testing the prediction:

---

[3]I thank Mark Davison for suggesting this analogy.

For the assumption of invariant sequence to be supported, the proportions of subjects conserving density but not solid or liquid volume must be significantly smaller than the proportions of subjects evidencing the reverse. Theoretically, no subjects should evidence density conservation in the absence of volume conservation, if the invariant sequence assumption holds. [P. 474]

Brainerd resolves the paradox by arguing that imperfect task reliabilities moderate the theoretical expectation of *no* out-of-order subjects. On the other hand, a requirement only of significantly more correct than incorrect patterns seems far too weak given the theoretical prediction. On the significance test he used, between the number of in-order compared to out-of-order subjects, the prediction was strongly supported. Consider, however, that in solid volume, 11% of discrepant subjects were out of order and in liquid volume 7% were out of order. This may be either mere noise due to lack of reliability (not reported for these tasks) or reasonable counterevidence worthy of consideration. Larger samples and a broader array of tasks would seem to be needed to resolve the issue.

Brainerd's (1971) affirmative answer to the fifth question is even more open to different interpretations. On the assumption that subjects closer to acquiring the concept would be more likely to shift to a correct response in the course of testing, he compared the performance on the fourth transformation of the density problem of third and sixth graders who had at least one error on the first three transformations (i.e., the shape and size of clay in relation to its sinking). He found sixth-graders significantly more likely to answer the final question correctly. Since, however, the correct response in the first three steps was "sink," for which there was feedback, it is just as reasonable to assume the older children were more sensitive to task demand as to assume they were closer to acquiring the concept of density.

Brainerd (1971) interprets the results from this study as reasonably strong support for a stage transition in the proportionality scheme. Other plausible hypotheses at each step of the interpretation warrant caution in adopting the stage-transition interpretation.

Neimark's Longitudinal Study

The only extensive longitudinal study in the published literature on formal-reasoning development is one reported by Neimark (1975b). In that study, she claims the strongest empirical support to date, "This evidence provides extremely strong support for Piaget's stage theory" (p. 212). How strong is the evidence?

There are, of course, the standard methodological problems that plague longitudinal studies, including sample depletion with time, retention and/or change of measures, and so on. Of these, the major preliminary problem in this study is the complex calendar of task administration, for which an overriding rule is not stated and is not apparent on inspection (Neimark, 1975b, Table 2, p. 185). The effects of differences between cohorts and of differing times between sessions on the results are difficult to estimate. For example, the diagnostic problems are administered to Cohort I with the following intervals (in months) for the nine sessions: 3, 3, 3, 4, 4, 7, 5, 9; to Cohort II at intervals of 4, 4, 4, 6, 8 (six sessions); and to Cohort III with intervals of 6, 3, 4, 5, 6 (six sessions). These variations may have little effect, but they are somewhat troublesome given that the data are pooled across cohorts on the crucial tests.

Turning to the evidence directly, we see that the grouped data show the standard smooth curve of Piaget ratings, strategy ratings, and strategy score, with no marked variations (Neimark, 1975b, Figure 2, p. 189 and Figure 6, p. 199). As Neimark pointed out, grouped data are not appropriate for the detection of discrete shifts within individuals. She thus analyzed her data for cognitive-development transitions within individuals.

The first analysis concerns the degree to which there is uniform growth to higher levels of performance across testings in the qualitative ratings on the Piaget and problem-solving tasks. If regression is not found within a given problem, this is taken as moderately strong evidence of the prediction. (It is, however, hard to conceive of a different hypothesis that would actually predict regression in task performance.) The number of subjects showing regression was 5%, 21%, 3%, and 8% in different tasks. Except for the second percentage, these are reasonably low. Consider, however, that this is a percentage of all transitions, including "no-change" transitions. Since lack of any change seems to count as much for as against the prediction, we should compute a percentage of regressions relative to any change (regressions plus progressions). In this case, the number of subjects regressing was 9%, 35%, 27%, and 13%, respectively. These figures are more difficult to dismiss as measurement error residuals. Thus these results provide inconclusive support for a weak test of a strong prediction.

In addition, as Neimark (1975b) noted, detection of qualitative change on restricted qualitative-rating scales (four possible categories) would be questionable even if the data were perfectly predicted. If one were to detect discontinuous emergence of an ability measured on an objective, continuous scale, then the evidence would be more convincing. In this study, subjects in each session first performed a series of problem-solving tasks (matching a concealed pattern to a set of eight possible patterns by uncovering one binary feature on each move) for which Neimark derived a mean strategy score across a number of similar problems based on the information acquired on each move relative to the potential for acquiring information on a given move. Following the testing, each subject described the strategy he or she used, and this description was rated on a 0 to 3 scale.

Neimark then compressed the subjects into 10 groups based on the pattern of their qualitative ratings across sessions (000000, 00000X, where $X \neq 0$, etc.) and plots the mean strategy score across six sessions for each group (Figure 1). The nine sessions of

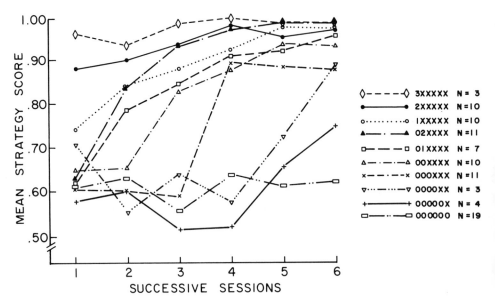

Figure 1 Changes in strategy score in successive sessions for groups differing with respect to pattern of strategy rating on successive occasions. (Source: Neimark, 1975b, Figure 9, p. 211.)

Cohort 1 are reduced to six sessions for pooling; which six sessions, however, is unspecified. She argued for evidence of discrete shifts on the basis of the patterns shown there.

It is reasonably clear from these data (with a few exceptions) that during the session in which subjects first articulate any strategy other than (apparent) random selection (level 0), their strategy scores (the continuous variable) increase. Neimark wrote that, "marked shifts to higher performance scores tend to accompany an increase in generality of S's described strategy" (1975b, p. 211).

What question is answered by these data? Minimally, they indicate that children improve in problem-solving performance with age and that, for a given task, the employment of a strategy and the articulation of that strategy tend to occur together. But how does this speak to the coordinated emergence of a formal reasoning ability? If one follows individuals' performances over time with respect to a given task, there will be a point at which they begin to get it right (i.e., performance improves). It makes sense that at this point they might also be able to say something sensible about how they are doing it. Demonstrating that these tend to emerge together for a given task does not appear to constitute strong evidence for a discontinuity in the acquisition of a general ability. Generalization of such emergence to other tasks would, however, speak to the issue. Before turning to the issue of generalizability, a few comments on transition are appropriate.

Summary

Discontinuous and/or abrupt changes in cognitive development, perhaps especially in late childhood and beyond, are difficult to demonstrate convincingly. This may be attributed to insufficiently sensitive measures of cognitive growth, to disagreements about the level of analysis, or, perhaps, to an absence of truly discontinuous processes. The cumulative evidence to date on adolescent cognitive development leaves a strong impression of continuous, quantitative, and multidimensional growth in abilities. Arguments for stage transitions must thus counteract the weight of evidence in the other direction. Current evidence for stages is deficient for a variety of reasons noted above.

What sort of evidence would be needed to establish adequately a stagelike transition? Recall that we are dealing with a holistic reasoning-ability construct. If we are to argue for a stagelike acquisition of this ability, then a coordinated pattern of discrete shifts in performance on reasoning tasks within the domain, compared with the absence of such a pattern in one or more unrelated (or less related) task domains would be a major initial step. Changes in factor structures of task performance may be helpful in revealing such a pattern, as would coordinated longitudinal changes within the ability domain compared with noncoordinated changes across domains. Fairly rigorous specific criteria could be elucidated with little difficulty. Brainerd (1973b), in fact, has subsequently argued against the possibility of detecting true cognitive stages. But strong evidence of the sort described, would, at a minimum, increase the likelihood of finding stage or stagelike changes.

One might object to these requirements on several grounds. First, Inhelder and Piaget's (1958) tasks, or others derived elsewhere to represent the same domain, have typically demonstrated moderate reliability at best. Thus factor structures or correlation patterns based on these tasks are too noisy to show the required pattern clearly. The solution here is to improve the measures, not to ascribe deviations from a reasonably predicted pattern to unreliability, since unreliability obscures either pattern (continuous or discontinuous) equally well; nor is the solution to deny the appropriateness of the analysis. Second, the presumed underlying change in ability may be so general that it affects equally performance on all conceivable cognitive tasks for which variance exists at this age; hence differential growth as reflected in factor structure changes or correlation pattern changes are inappropriate. If one holds to this interpretation of the construct, the criticism of the requirements is valid. But note that this revised construct is indistinguishable from Spearman's (1904) *g* (except that it posits a nondisconfirmable substrate explanation), a notion abandoned long ago in ability research (Horn, 1976).

A different approach would concede the validity of the requirements, observe the difficulties in meeting them, and adopt a "softer" stage notion. Such a notion might address the level of description, noting that on the whole adolescent performance on cognitive tasks looks substantially different from the performances of children (Flavell, 1977). This may be a useful idea by which to encode some of the findings on adolescent thinking, but of course it could not aspire to account for the behavior described.

Generalizability of the Construct

Over and above the obvious interdependence of all construct-validity questions, the next three sections could readily be combined under a larger question: What is the range of this construct? This section deals with the extent to which performance related to the construct is stable within individuals and across situations; the next section deals with the question of whether a specific class of situations, namely planned interventions, has an effect on the emergence of the construct; and the section following that deals with the construct's limits relative to other ability constructs. Two aspects of the generalizability question will now be considered: (1) What is the internal homogeneity of performance on formal operations and related tasks? (2) What factors have been discovered to affect performance and how are such performance factors to be interpreted?

Internal Homogeneity

The first question can be answered with some confidence: the internal consistency of such tasks is moderately high (Neimark, 1975b; Martorano, 1974; Keating, 1975; Keating & Schaefer, 1975; Bart, 1971, 1972; Stephens et al., 1972). The average intercorrelations of such tasks obviously vary, decreasing as one departs from standardized task situations (Kuhn & Brannock, 1977). But typically the intercorrelations average between .30 and .50. Depending on the number of tasks used in a given study, the formal-operations battery usually attains stepped-up reliabilities of .60 to .80. In Martorano's (1974) dissertation, 10 formal-operations tasks were administered to 80 girls in the sixth, eighth, tenth, and twelfth grades. I calculated an internal homogeneity reliability[4] for her data, based on the task intercorrelation matrix, and found it to be respectably high, .83. Of course, the expense of administering a large number of tasks is high, and reliability decreases with a reduction in the number of tasks or items.

Another piece of confirming evidence comes from factor analyses of Piagetian task performance (Bart, 1971; Stephens et al., 1972; Martorano, 1974). Such tasks have almost uniformly high loadings on the same factor, indicating again moderate-to-high

---

[4]Note that this is *not* interrater reliability. These two are frequently confused. Interrater reliability indicates the consistency in scoring in a set of tasks; internal homogeneity reliability estimates the extent to which a number of tasks or items tap common variance.

internal consistency. The reliability of a given set of formal operations tasks is thus likely to be at least adequate, if a reasonable number of them are used.

Performance Factors

Diagnosing the formal-reasoning ability of an individual is likely to be difficult, as we have already seen. There are a number of performance factors that confound the detection problem further, several of which we can now address. In particular, consider the roles of language, of task content, and of task structure.

Inhelder and Piaget (1958) contend that language is not a necessary part of formal-reasoning development, nor is verbal expression of concepts an appropriate criterion of formal reasoning. This latter stricture, however, seems to be violated by them on at least some occasions (Ennis, 1975; also see quote on p. 222). In any case, the acquisition and sophisticated use of language would seem to extend the range of reasoning processes and aid in demonstrating their presence. Furth and Youniss (1971) were able to find some evidence of formal reasoning among deaf adolescents, although their range of problem-solving and overall performance was lower than hearing adolescents. In a normal sample, Bart (1971) reported a substantial correlation of verbal knowledge and formal operations scores. Jones (1972) studied high- and low-verbal boys who were matched on Raven's Progressive Matrices and found no difference on any of three formal-reasoning scores, suggesting an independence of language and formal reasoning in development and in assessment. She did not report whether a test of the three tasks taken together also yielded a nonsignificant difference, which seems important given the reliability of a single task. The results from these and other studies indicate an important role of language skills at least in assessment and probably also in development, although overt linguistic skill is perhaps not absolutely necessary. We do not know the actual degree of difference in language knowledge between deaf and hearing adolescents (Furth & Youniss, 1971), so firm conclusions are difficult. Brainerd (1973a) has argued on the assessment issue that judgments, not explanations, are appropriate criteria for Piagetian tasks. This would minimize the verbal-sophistication problem, but this may be difficult for formal-reasoning tasks and is not common practice in any case. The serious problem for assessment is increasing false negatives, that is, subjects who can do the reasoning but not express or justify the answer. The larger theoretical issue of the role of language in later cognitive development has not been substantively addressed.

The issue in terms of task content involves differential familiarity with the problems included in a formal operations assessment. As noted earlier, Piaget (1972) has subsequently argued that individuals are more likely to display formal operational reasoning in areas they know well in terms of content, even though the logical structures (or logical ability) are conceptually independent of content. This can be especially problematic in attempting to assess reasoning level for validation purposes since one may be generating either false negatives or false positives or both. It is worth noting that Weitz et al., (1973) found 80% of their subjects correctly performing the ''magnet'' formal-operations task without any prior reasoning. Even though simply getting the right answer may be insufficient for being judged formal operational, one's chances of devising a method of solution must be greatly increased if the correct answer is known (i.e., guessed accurately) ahead of time.

The solution to this dilemma is easy conceptually but difficult practically: equate for prior content knowledge. One suggestion is to use abstract or abstruse rather than reality-based content, but this accentuates performance differences (Arenberg, 1968; Bart, 1972). Piaget (1972) suggests deriving new tasks for different content areas so that each individual is tested in his or her specialty, but the problems of equating for task difficulty across content areas are enormous. Perhaps the most defensible approach is a direct one, training subjects beyond criterion on their knowledge of a limited and specific-content domain, prior to assessing their reasoning with that content [cf. similar ideas in Trabasso (1975) and Siegler (1976)].

The final issue considered here is the role of task structure. Are the subjects evaluating logical statements per se or using logic to solve problems? If the former, are they required to accept valid arguments or reject invalid ones, or both? What are the response options? The list of questions is probably finite but nonetheless long, so I shall select two examples to demonstrate their importance. Two studies, one by Moshman (1977) the other by Knifong (1974), have been interpreted by their authors as illustrating how performance factors associated with task structure can artifactually generate results discrepant from a Piagetian model.

Moshman (1977) examined the role of negation in an instance-evaluation task, using the logical principles of implication and disjunction. There were six problems for each of four categories, negated and nonnegated implication and disjunction. He postulated a specific consolidation model (based on Flavell & Wohlwill, 1969) for the emergence of formal operations in these tasks. The model took performance factors into account. Moshman (1977) argued that within each logical operation the predictions of the consolidation model differ appreciably from both a purely structural model and a commonsense model. Compared to the structural model, the consolidation model predicts perfect performance on the nonnegated form together with less than perfect performance on the negated form, whereas the structural model (absent performance features) predicts perfect performance on both simultaneously. Compared to the commonsense model, the consolidation model predicts few cases of partial success on nonnegation combined with zero success on negation, whereas the commonsense model predicts (for unspecified reasons) partial success on nonnegation prior to any success on negation. His results showed a strong performance factor of negation and predictive superiority of the consolidation model over both the purely structural model and the commonsense model. Moshman (1977) argued further that these results provided partial support for a stagelike emergence of a structured whole in logical competence, obscured earlier by failing to take performance factors into account.

Closer inspection, however, reveals some serious drawbacks in concept and execution. First, the differentiation from the commonsense model seems weak. They differ only in the predicted number of subjects who have partial success on nonnegation prior to *any* success on negation; Moshman argues that the commonsense model predicts this group to be large. Why? It seems more commonsensical that partial success on one form is highly correlated with partial success on the other. Second, even if one accepts the differentiation above, the test is coarse-grained. Partial success is defined as getting as least one but fewer than all of the six problems in the category correct. We do not know how many subjects in the ''partial-success-on-both-forms'' category may be there due to random guessing (or better than random guessing, but less than true knowledge). Although the probability of getting any given problem correct, as Moshman (1977) noted, is only 1.6%, it is also true that, with correction for guessing, a score of 1 in a given category is in fact 0 $(1 - 5/5 = 0)$. We are assured that there was little random guessing (in fact three subjects were discarded due to substantial random guessing), but the analyses are not presented.

Finally, it is not clear how a static picture of a given age group speaks to developmental-stage emergence; some movement within the categories, it would seem, is necessary, whether cross-sectionally or longitudinally. If the same results were obtained on a group of 40-year-olds (not unlikely), would the evidence by construed as support for consolidated-stage development?

Knifong (1974) reanalyzed data that had been used to demonstrate the presence of propositional reasoning in young children. First, children may arrive at a correct conclusion in simple implication, for example, without recognizing its logical necessity. Introducing a "maybe" category negatively affects performance (O'Brien & Shapiro, 1968). Second, children may be arriving at the correct response without propositional reasoning, using instead transductive reasoning, which overgeneralizes the "and" connective. The full argument is too complex to recapitulate here; suffice it to say that children may seem to show conditional reasoning when in fact that is not what they are doing. Since data for older groups were not included, the developmental implications are not clear, except that similar detection of false positives on subjects of all ages is warranted.

There are, of course, numerous other studies that have varied one or more of these performance factors (e.g., Kuhn & Brannock, 1977, content; Keating & Caramazza, 1975, linguistic component; Ronning, 1977, modeling and instructions). There is great difficulty in integrating the results of the many studies that have demonstrated the importance of performance factors.

One integrative orientation is to use the general category of performance factors as a source of explanation for discrepancies from expectations based on the formal operational ability-construct, as, for example, by Moshman (1977) and Knifong (1974). Performance factors can be employed to account for precocious cognitive development in children or for poor performance among adolescents and adults, both of which raise doubts about the theoretical formulation. Neimark (1975a) argued for breadth of logical reasoning across situations as a criterion for attainment, but she did not define the criterion further.

The opposite orientation is to employ performance factors to discount evidence of any developmental change in underlying ability. Since performance features have typically been unsystematically added or subtracted relative to the original construct, there is as yet no conceivable overall integration (at least not by me). It is something like a merry-go-round, where each horse is a performance factor — rising here to discount discrepant evidence, rising there to discount supportive evidence; and since each researcher chooses which horse to ride and for how long, no comprehensive picture of the construct or its range is obtained. Belaboring our metaphorical horses a bit further, note that one possible solution would be to step back and follow a single factor, or a small set, long enough to understand its workings before arguing what the whole pattern looks like. Switching metaphors in midstream, we must avoid the Scylla of overspecification (Neisser, 1976; Newell, 1973) and the Charybdis of overgeneralization (Siegler, 1976; Sternberg & Rifkin, in press). In other words, we need to examine how general a model of cognitive development should be.

Intervention Studies

Deliberate training of subjects in order to advance their level of cognitive development, or at least to improve their performance, is a special case of the generalizability issue. In addition to the assessment and generalizability problems noted, training studies are notoriously difficult to interpret (see Brainerd, 1973b). Problems concerning transfer effects to other tasks are especially difficult, reminiscent of an earlier research area's (raising IQ's) concern with "teaching to the test." Two illustrative studies are considered (Siegler, Liebert, & Liebert, 1973; Kuhn & Angelev, 1976).

Siegler, Liebert, and Liebert (1973) employed a three-component training procedure on the Inhelder and Piaget (1958) pendulum problem: conceptual training, training on analogous procedures, and measurement training. This concept, analog, measurement (CAM) training proved quite effective in improving 10- and 11-year-olds' performance on this task, even though the CAM training did not directly involve experience with it. In a series of further probe studies with different subjects, the CM and AM components were as successful as the full CAM training. The level of success on this task, given modest training on related skills, raises important questions about the depth and nature of the hypothesized ability development.

Kuhn and Angelev (1976) reported a more extensive intervention study. The authors assessed fourth and fifth graders on three formal-operations tasks — pendulum, chemicals, and verbal problems. They then assigned subjects to conditions varying in amount of exposure to a problem similar to the pendulum problem (isolation of variables), but different in content, in which they could earn tokens for correct responses. One group also received demonstrations of the best strategy in four sessions; one group was a pretest-posttest control; and there was a second posttest-only control group. The intervention lasted fourteen weeks. On the pendulum problem there was no treatment-condition effect at posttest 1 (one week after training), but there was one at posttest 2 (four months later); for chemicals, there was a treatment-condition effect at both posttests; and for the verbal problems, differential sample depletion across conditions made comparison difficult, but change-score analysis indicated no overall effect of treatment condition, with only a suggestion of a significant effect on posttest 1. Kuhn and Angelev (1976) argue that this pattern is supportive of a structural developmental notion, although far from conclusive. The definitional and reliability problems are significant, however, and beyond that the equivocal nature of the results is obvious. They also emphasize that there was no direct training (except in the demonstration condition), arguing for a self-regulatory developmental mechanism (perhaps equilibration), but they did not estimate the degree of subjects' interactions with each other over a 14-week period. Such peer teaching is a real possibility. They argue against Brainerd's (1973b) conclusion that training studies cannot in principle verify stage notions, but concede that their study was not a strong test of structural theory, especially given Ennis's (1975, 1976) criticisms.

What we have learned from these studies is similar to the conclusion of the previous section, that salient performance factors, such as instruction and practice, have significant effects on performance. They do not appear to establish strong empirical support for a theory of the structure of underlying competence or of stage changes.

Discriminant Validity

Recalling again that we are dealing with a holistic, logical-reasoning ability construct, we need to examine how it relates to other ability or cognitive-competence constructs. The first part deals with IQ and general mental ability; the second with other performance constructs.

IQ or Mental Ability

A number of researchers have been concerned with the relationship between level of development assessed on Piagetian tasks compared with more traditional IQ or ability measures. One approach is the direct one, looking for correlations between abilities or significant effects of ability on Piagetian task performance. Comparing average ability to very bright (upper 2%) 11- to 12- and 13- to 14-year-olds, Keating (1975) and Keating and Schaefer (1975) found highly significant effects for ability. Webb (1974) did not find much success on formal-operations tasks with very bright younger children (6- to 11-year-olds), although sample size may have limited the opportunity of observing this. Kuhn (1976) reported a nonsignificant positive correlation of IQ and formal-operations task performance (and a significantly higher one for IQ and concrete operations), but lower reliability on the formal-operations tasks and unreported IQ range may have affected this finding. The evidence is thus mixed; the correlation between IQ and formal-operations task performance is probably significant, but they do not covary perfectly.

Two factor analytic studies (Martorano, 1974; Stephens *et al.*, 1972) make a case for a separation of formal reasoning and IQ. Both administered a battery of Piagetian tasks and standardized ability and achievement tests, and both found clearly separate factors for test scores and Piagetian "operativity."

On the face of it, this is good discriminant validity evidence. Both have the same curious discrepancy, however, and that is the factor loading pattern of chronological age: in both cases it has a high positive loading on the operativity factor virtually identical with the average loading of the Piagetian tasks on that factor, and a negative (Stephens et al., 1972) or zero (Martorano, 1974) loading on the ability/achievement factor. What can account for this result? The parsimonious explanation is that the ability and achievement tests are already corrected for age (i.e., age is partialled out), but the Piagetian tasks are not. Rather than labeling the factors Piagetian operations and psychometric ability one may label them age-graded and non-age-graded tasks.

Another potential confounding factor is method variance, highlighted in a factor analysis by Bart (1971). Four formal-operations tasks, three paper-and-pencil formal-operations tests (in biology, history, and literature), and a vocabulary test were given to 90 adolescents. When the tasks and the vocabulary test were factored together, a single factor resulted; when the formal-operations tests and the vocabulary test were factored together, a single factor resulted; and when all were factored together, two factors resulted: (1) a general ability factor and (2) a methods factor on which the tasks loaded negatively and the tests positively. In studies where Piagetian operativity is assessed only by tasks and ability or achievement only by tests, the problems in interpreting unambiguously a resulting factor analysis are insurmountable.

In summary, there is no evidence that Piagetian formal-operations tasks tap different sources of variance from standard ability and achievement measures. If one wished to establish such a discrimination, multitrait-multimethod designs (Campbell & Fiske, 1959) would be essential, as would similar controls for chronological age in both sets of measures. The value of such an analysis may justifiably be questioned. If, as argued above, formal operations is appropriately regarded as a holistic reasoning ability, then there is every reason to suspect that variance on tasks from that domain is inextricably intertwined with variance from the very broad domain of general mental ability. They both sample from the same overall domain and hence are likely highly overlapping. The earlier contention that both formal-operations task performance and IQ or general-ability test performance are phenomena in need of explanation is appropriately recalled.

Other Domains

Scores on formal-operations tasks have been found to be related to a host of other variables (e.g., to 19 of 22 "personal" variables by Cloutier & Goldschmid, 1976). The role of cognitive style, especially field independence, is unclear (Saarni, 1973; Pascual-Leone, 1970). Tomlinson-Keasey and Keasey (1974) argued on slight evidence for a connection between formal-operations reasoning and principled moral judgment. It is difficult to make much of this correlational and comparative research, other than the ability variance tapped by Piagetian tasks is nearly as pervasive as IQ variance. Given the methodological problems (noted above) when only one source of variance was age-confounded, the problems of comparing to other domains, often with tasks of unknown reliability and validity (cf. Kurtines & Greif, 1974, on moral judgment), are multiplied. Suffice it to say that adequate tests of discriminability from other ability or cognitive developmental domains have not been carried out, including particularly multitrait-multimethod approaches.

One also finds the anticipated effects of educational and cultural differences (see Neimark, 1975a, for a review), and in the expected directions. Less-schooled individuals and those from non-Western cultures typically have great difficulty with the Inhelder and Piaget (1958) tasks and their derivatives; some task variations reduce this difference. The multiplicity of assessment questions makes interpretation of these results difficult, but it would be incorrect, on the basis of present evidence, to conclude that such reasoning as required on these tasks is unavailable to these subjects.

Conclusions and Implications

Unlike earlier reviewers (Ausubel & Ausubel, 1966; Neimark, 1975a), I am led to conclude by the evidence above, first, that we know very little about how adolescents' thinking differs from children's thinking beyond the obvious (but important) performance descriptions; and, second, that Inhelder and Piaget's (1958) general theoretical model is not an accurate account of the change. Separating the insightful descriptive components of their treatment from the more central structural theory, we note that there appear to be no empirical tests of crucial elements of the latter (Brainerd, 1973a,b; Ennis, 1975, 1976; Osherson, 1975). Implicitly reducing Piaget's structural theory of competence to a holistic ability notion, most researchers have nonetheless continued to collect evidence as if a competence theory were the focus. Reassessing this corpus of research in the proper perspective as construct-validity evidence, we see that strong support can be mustered for internal homogeneity of many of the formal operations and related tasks and for age changes in performance on them. Attractive and differentiating components of this ability construct relative to other ability constructs are its claims to generalizability across situational variation (i.e., its nature as a deeply underlying ability), to stagelike emergence, and to discriminability from general mental ability, particularly IQ. These claims are found to be unsupported by evidence. Future sound evidence in support of these claims is possible, but researchers should consider seriously the problems and probabilities of obtaining adequate evidence for any of them within a narrow-Piagetian framework.

Considered from a broader perspective, we can note many positive contributions of the Piaget-inspired research in adolescent thinking. Conditional reasoning remains an interesting cognitive process and task domain, and careful analyses of specific tasks (e.g., Siegler, 1976) may be highly productive. We have much more information, not yet systematized or even fully explored, on a variety of performance factors and their effects at different ages. Finally, we have an organizational framework if not a structural theory, within which more modest theoretical accounts of performance are possible.

PSYCHOMETRIC RESEARCH

Space permits only the briefest consideration of two different approaches to cognitive development, the psychometric and the information-processing paradigms. These areas have not yet contributed greatly to our understanding of adolescent cognitive development, hence their relative de-emphasis here.

Factor Analytic Research

The most prominent methodology within psychometric research is factor analysis, and a variety of researchers over the years have attempted to address developmental issues via such analyses (Cronbach, 1967; Fitzgerald, Nesselroade, & Baltes, 1973; Very, 1967; Dye & Very, 1968; reviews by Reinert, 1970; and Horn, 1976). One attempt has been to detect qualitative shifts in performance with age by factoring longitudinal ability-test data. Cronbach (1967) demonstrated that, because of the simplex structure of age-related intercorrelations (i.e., high correlations for adjacent ages decreasing with larger age differences), one could vary the age at which apparent qualitative "shifts" occurred by changing the age range under consideration or the frequency of testing.

A more frequently researched topic is the age-differentiation hypothesis (see Reinert, 1970; Horn, 1976). According to this hypothesis, mental ability is relatively undifferentiated and global in childhood, then shows increasing differentiation and specification with age, beginning markedly in adolescence (Dye & Very, 1968). The evidence on this point is conflicting: some researchers find such evidence, others do not. Fitzgerald, Nesselroade, and Baltes (1973) argue that the adult factor structure is present no later than 12 or 13 year olds, whereas Dye and Very (1968) argue for major differentiation between 12 and 18 years. A variety of factors, from subjects' socioeconomic status to researchers' rotational strategy, affects the results. The age-differentiation hypothesis remains an unfulfilled explanatory concept (Horn, 1976).

IQ Changes with Age

The overall stability of IQ scores within this age range is well established (Bloom, 1964). Growth curves based on similar data are expectedly smooth and continuous throughout this age range. There are individual variations from this overall pattern, however, which McCall, Applebaum, and Hogarty (1973) analyzed in the Fels Longitudinal Study. Through a clustering analysis, they identified five groups of subjects who showed similar patterns of changes in IQ with age (see Figure 2). The largest group, Cluster 1, shows stability throughout. Clusters 2 and 3 decrease similarly in childhood but diverge in adolescence. Interestingly, these two clusters were also similar on the parent-behavior

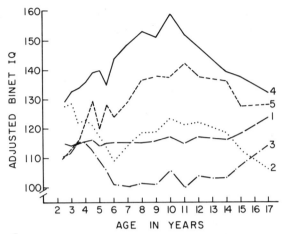

Figure 2　Mean IQ over age for the five IQ clusters based on patterns of IQ changes. (Source: McCall, Applebaum, and Hogarty, 1973, Figure 5, p. 48.)

variable of accelerative attempt (low) but differed on the variable of parental severity, with Cluster 2 the least penalized and Cluster 3 the most. A variety of intriguing hypotheses worthy of investigation are generated by this study, but no pattern connected directly with adolescence is immediately apparent.

Range of Differences

Even though psychometric research on individual differences has thus far not been especially fruitful in accounting for developmental changes, there is still a need to account for the presence of great individual differences in this age period as in others. Research by Stanley and his colleagues (Stanley, Keating, & Fox, 1974; Keating, 1976) highlights the upper range of those differences. They reported the results of several mathematics talent searches for 12- to 14-year-olds. A substantial number of these early adolescents scored above the 95th percentile of college-bound high-school seniors on mathematics ability (Scholastic Aptitude Test) and achievement (Cooperative Entrance Examination Board Mathematics Achievement, Levels I and II). Subsequently, these students were successful in challenging mathematics-related college courses, while still in early and middle adolescence. Such performances demand explanation as much as some adolescents' inability, in some circumstances, to succeed on seemingly straightforward formal-operations tasks.

INFORMATION-PROCESSING RESEARCH

The information-processing approach has only recently been directed toward the question of cognitive development, and little direct evidence for interpretation of adolescent cognitive changes is available. Several areas have potential importance for the topic and can be briefly considered.

Pascual-Leone's Neo-Piagetian Model

In an attempt to firm up certain aspects of Piagetian theory, Pascual-Leone (1970) proposed a mathematical model of cognitive growth. Its primary goal was to account for the stage transitions necessitated by a Piagetian approach. The principal addition to theory was a variable, k, which (1) described the cognitive capacity limits at a given age and (2) changed discretely as a function of age in step with Piagetian operational levels. Pascual-Leone and others have subsequently collected further evidence, using the same basic paradigm as that of 1970, and described the evidence as supportive. Trabasso and Foellinger (1978) reanalyzed Pascual-Leone's original data and added some data of their own. They argue strongly that the neo-Piagetian model is inaccurate on several grounds. In particular, Pascual-Leone's approach does not overcome the assessment problems of stage theories and it creates some additional problems of estimating specific-capacity parameters for individual subjects. Trabasso and Foellinger (1978) argue that a true test of the theory is practically impossible, since one would have to equate across subjects on strategy and effort in order to evaluate capacity. Also, goodness-of-fit tests of the data to the model's predictions have not supported the model.

Task Analysis

A more promising approach is the development of processing models that yield verifiable accounts of performance on a given task or class of tasks, as exemplified in the work of Pitt (1976), Sternberg and Rifkin (in press), and Siegler (1976). In these cases, possible sets of rules for performance, varying in ways that make different predictions about the data, are compared for goodness-of-fit and successively refined. Siegler's (1976) and Pitt's (1976) research was described earlier. Sternberg and Rifkin (in press) did a fine-grained analysis of analogical reasoning, taking both individual differences and age into account in testing the performance models. These research programs represent a promising method of getting off the performance factor merry-go-round, since they build performance factors into the model from the beginning. It is not apparent now whether models of performance on given tasks will generalize beyond those tasks. One hopes so, for parsimony's sake (Newell, 1973).

Cognitive-Processing Differences

A complementary approach to task analysis is focusing on specific cognitive-processing components that seem a priori to be of general importance across tasks and study the developmental and/or individual-difference patterns in them. Typically, these analyses employ processing parameters that have a strong theoretical basis from adult research and that can be rather precisely estimated, although this is not always true (Birch, 1976; Friedrich, 1974; Keating & Bobbitt, 1978, and references therein; Labouvie-Vief, Levin, & Urberg, 1975; Naus & Ornstein, 1977).

Keating and Bobbitt (1978) examined developmental and ability-differences (Raven's Progressive Matrices) in memory search rate, choice minus simple reaction time, and long-term memory retrieval efficiency in 9-, 13-, and 17-year-olds. They found clear age differences on the latter two, a borderline difference on the first, and clear ability differences on the first and third. Others have found varying patterns when looking at different processes. There is suggestive evidence that late childhood and very early adolescence are a prime time for maturation of the information-processing system.

This approach is necessarily more open-ended than the task-analytic approach, but one anticipates consistent patterns emerging eventually. The role of encoding and selective attention, for example, may get special attention in the future.

With both task-analytic and general-processing research increasing, there is some hope of convergence in future models that will account for some of the pervasive performance variance described by Piaget and in Piaget-inspired research.

REFERENCES

Arenberg, D. Concept problem-solving in old and young adults. *Journal of Gerontology,* 1968, *23,* 279–282.

Arlin, P. K. Cognitive development in adulthood: A fifth stage? *Developmental Psychology,* 1975, *11,* 602–606.

———. Piagetian operations in problem-finding. *Developmental Psychology,* 1977, *13*(3), 297–298.

Ausubel, D. P., and Ausubel, P. Cognitive development in adolescence. *Review of Educational Research,* 1966, *36,* 403–413.

Bart, W. M. The factor structure of formal operations. *British Journal of Educational Psychology,* 1971, *41,* 70–77.

———. A comparison of premise types in hypothetico-deductive thinking at the stage of formal operations. *Journal of Psychology,* 1972, *81,* 45–51.

Birch, L. L. Age trends in children's time-sharing performance. *Journal of Experimental Child Psychology,* 1976, *22,* 331–345.

Bloom, B. S. *Stability and change in human characteristics.* New York: Wiley, 1964.

Brainerd, C. J. The development of the proportionality scheme in children and adolescents. *Developmental Psychology,* 1971, *5,* 469–476.

———. Judgments and explanations as criteria for the presence of cognitive structures. *Psychological Bulletin,* 1973a, *79,* 172–179.

———. Neo-Piagetian training experiments revisited: Is there any support for the cognitive-developmental stage hypothesis? *Cognition,* 1973b, *2,* 349–370.

Bynum, T. W., Thomas, J. A., and Weitz, L. J. Truth-functional logic in formal operational thinking: Inhelder and Piaget's evidence. *Developmental Psychology,* 1972, *7*(2), 129–132.

Campbell, D. T., and Fiske, D. W. Convergent and discriminant validation by the multitrait-multimethod matrix. *Psychological Bulletin,* 1959, *56,* 81–105.

Cloutier, R., & Goldschmid, M. L. Individual differences in the development of formal reasoning. *Child Development,* 1976, *47,* 1097–1102.

Conger, J. J. *Adolescence and youth: Psychological development in a changing world* (2nd ed.). New York: Harper & Row, 1977.

Cronbach, L. J. Year-to-year correlations of mental tests: A review of the Hofstaetter analyses. *Child Development,* 1967, *38,* 283–289.

Cronbach, L. J., and Meehl, P. E. Construct validity in psychological test. *Psychological Bulletin,* 1955, *52,* 281–302.

Dye, N. W., and Very, P. S. Growth changes in factorial structure by age and sex. *Genetic Psychology Monographs,* 1968, *78,* 55–88.

Elkind, D. *Children and adolescents: Interpretive essays on Jean Piaget* (2nd ed.). New York: Oxford University Press, 1974.

Ennis, R. H. Children's ability to handle Piaget's propositional logic: A conceptual critique. *Review of Educational Research,* 1975, *45*(1), 1–41.

————. An alternative to Piaget's conceptualization of logical competence. *Child Development,* 1976, *47,* 903–913.

Fitzgerald, J. M., Nesselroade, J. R., and Baltes, P. B. Emergence of adult intellectual structure: Prior to or during adolescence? *Developmental Psychology,* 1973, *13,* 114–119.

Flavell, J. H. Concept development. In P. H. Mussen (Ed.), *Carmichael's manual of child psychology* (3rd ed.). New York: Wiley, 1970.

————. *Cognitive development.* Englewood Cliffs, N.J.: Prentice-Hall, 1977.

Flavell, J. H., and Wohlwill, J. F. Formal and functional aspects of cognitive development. In D. Elkind and J. Flavell (Eds.), *Studies in cognitive development: Essays in honor of Jean Piaget.* New York: Oxford University Press, 1969.

Friedrich, D. Developmental analyses of memory capacity and information-encoding strategy. *Developmental Psychology,* 1974, *10,* 559–563.

Furth, H. G., and Youniss, J. Formal operations and language: A comparison of deaf and hearing adolescents. *International Journal of Psychology,* 1971, *6,* 49–64.

Garfinkel, R., and Thorndike, R. L. Binet item difficulty then and now. *Child Development,* 1976, *47,* 959–965.

Glick, J., and Wapner, S. Development of transitivity: Some findings and problems of analysis. *Child Development,* 1968, *39,* 621–638.

Green, D. R., Ford, M. P., and Flamer, G. B. (Eds.), *Measurement and Piaget.* New York: McGraw-Hill, 1971.

Horn, J. L. Human abilities: A review of research and theory in the early 1970s. *Annual Review of Psychology,* 1976, *27,* 437–485.

Inhelder, B., and Piaget, J. *The growth of logical thinking from childhood to adolescence.* New York: Basic Books, 1958.

Jones, P. A. Formal operational reasoning and the use of tentative statements. *Cognitive Psychology,* 1972, *3,* 467–471.

Keating, D. P. Precocious cognitive development at the level of formal operations. *Child Development,* 1975, *46,* 276–280.

————. (Ed.) *Intellectual Talent: Research and Development.* Baltimore, Md.: Johns Hopkins University Press, 1976.

————. (The Review of *Logical abilities in children:* Vol. III. *Reasoning in adolescence: Destructive inference,* by D. N. Osherson). *American Journal of Psychology,* 1977, *90,* 345–347.

Keating, D. P., and Bobbitt, B. L. Individual and developmental differences in cognitive processing components of ability. *Child Development,* 1978, *49,* 155–167.

Keating, D. P., and Caramazza, A. Effects of age and ability on syllogistic reasoning in early adolescence. *Developmental Psychology,* 1975, *11,* 837–842.

Keating, D. P., and Schaefer, R. A. Ability and sex differences in the acquisition of formal operations. *Developmental Psychology,* 1975, *11,* 531–532.

King, P. Formal operations and reflective judgment in adolescence and young adulthood. Unpublished doctoral dissertation, University of Minnesota, Minneapolis, 1977.

Kohen-Raz, R. Physiological maturation and mental growth at preadolescence and puberty. *Journal of Child Psychology and Psychiatry and Allied Disciplines,* 1974, *15,* 199–213.

Knifong, J. D. Logical abilities of young children — Two styles of approach. *Child Development,* 1974, *45,* 78–83.

Kuhn, D. Relation of two Piagetian stage transitions to IQ. *Developmental Psychology*, 1976, *12*, 157–161.

Kuhn, D., and Angelev, J. An experimental study of the development of formal operational thought. *Child Development*, 1976, *47*, 697–706.

Kuhn, D., and Brannock, J. Development of the isolation of variables scheme in experimental and "natural experimental" contexts. *Developmental Psychology*, 1977, *13*(1), 9–14.

Kurtines, W., and Greif, E. B. The development of moral thought: Review and evaluation of Kohlberg's approach. *Psychological Bulletin*, 1974, *81*, 453–470.

Labouvie-Vief, G., Levin, J. R., and Urberg, K. A. The relationship between selected cognitive abilities and learning: A second look. *Journal of Educational Psychology*, 1975, *67*, 558–569.

Lovell, K. A follow-up study of Inhelder and Piaget's "The growth of logical thinking." *British Journal of Psychology*, 1961, *52*, 143–153.

Lunzer, E. A. Problems of formal reasoning in test situations. In P. Mussen (Ed.), European research in cognitive development. *Monographs of the Society for Research in Child Development*, 1965, *30*(2), Serial No. 100.

McCall, R. B., Applebaum, M. I., and Hogarty, P. S. Developmental changes in mental performance. *Monographs of the Society for Research in Child Development*, 1973, *38*(3, Serial No. 150).

Martorano, S. C. The development of formal operations thought. Doctoral dissertation, 197. *Dissertation Abstracts International*, 1974, *35*, 515B–516B. (University Microfilms No. 74-15, 486)

Meehl, P. E. *Clinical vs. statistical prediction*. Minneapolis: University of Minnesota Press, 1954.

Meltzoff, A. N., and Moore, M. K. Imitation of facial and manual gestures by human neonates. *Science*, 1977, *198*, 75–78.

Moshman, D. Consolidation and stage formation in the emergence of formal operations. *Developmental Psychology*, 1977, *13*(2), 95–100.

Naus, M. J., and Ornstein, P. A. Developmental differences in the memory search of categorized lists. *Developmental Psychology*, 1977, *13*, 60–69.

Neimark, E. D. Intellectual development during adolescence. In F. D. Horowitz (Ed.), *Review of child development research* (Vol. 4). Chicago: University of Chicago Press, 1975a.

———. Longitudinal development of formal operations thought. *Genetic Psychology Monographs*, 1975b, *91*, 171–225.

Neisser, V. *Cognition and reality*. San Francisco: Freeman, 1976.

Newell, A. You can't play 20 questions with nature and win: Projective comments on the papers of this symposium. In W. G. Chase (Ed), *Visual information processing*. New York: Academic, 1973.

O'Brien, T. C., and Shapiro, B. J. The development of logical thinking in children. *American Educational Research Journal*, 1968, *5*, 531–542.

Osherson, D. N. *Logical abilities in children: Vol. III. Reasoning in adolescence: Deductive inference*. Hillsdale, N.J.: Erlbaum, 1975.

Parsons, C. Inhelder and Piaget's "The growth of logical thinking." II: A logician's viewpoint. *British Journal of Psychology*, 1960, *51*, 75–84.

Pascual-Leone, J. A mathematical model for the transition rule in Piaget's developmental stages. *Acta Psychologica*, 1970, *32*, 301–345.

Petersen, A. C. Physical androgyny and cognitive functioning in adolescence. *Developmental Psychology*, 1976, *12*, 524–533.

Piaget, J. Intellectual evolution from adolescence to adulthood. *Human Development,* 1972, *15,* 1–12.

Pinard, A., and Laurendeau, M. "Stage" in Piaget's cognitive-developmental theory: Exegesis of a concept. In D. Elkind and J. Flavell (Eds.), *Studies in cognitive development: Essays in honor of Jean Piaget.* New York: Oxford University Press, 1969.

Pitt, R. B. Toward a comprehensive model of problem-solving: Application to solutions of chemistry problems in high-school and college students. Unpublished doctoral dissertation, University of California, San Diego, 1976.

Popper, K. R. *The logic of scientific discovery.* New York: Harper & Row, 1968.

Reinert, G. Comparative factor analytic studies of intelligence throughout the human life span. In L. R. Goulet and P. B. Baltes (Eds.), *Life-span methodology: Research and theory.* New York: Academic, 1970.

Riegel, K. F. Dialectic operations: The final period of cognitive development. *Research Bulletin RB–73–3,* Educational Testing Service, 1973.

Roberge, J. J. Developmental analyses of two formal operational structures: Combinatorial thinking and conditional reasoning. *Developmental Psychology,* 1976, *12,* 563–564.

Roberge, J. J., and Paulus, D. H. Developmental patterns for children's class and conditional reasoning abilities. *Developmental Psychology,* 1971, *4,* 191–200.

Ronning, R. R. Modeling effects and developmental changes in dealing with a formal-operations task. *American Educational Research Journal,* 1977, *14,* 213–223.

Saarni, C. I. Piagetian operations and field independence as factors in children's problem-solving performance. *Child Development,* 1973, *44,* 338–345.

Siegler, R. S. Three aspects of cognitive development. *Cognitive Psychology,* 1976, *8,* 481–520.

Siegler, R. S. and Liebert, R. M. Acquisition of formal scientific reasoning by 10- and 13-year-olds: Designing a factorial experiment. *Developmental Psychology,* 1975, *11,* 401–402.

Siegler, R. S., Liebert, D. E., and Liebert, R. M. Inhelder and Piaget's pendulum problem: Teaching preadolescents to act as scientists. *Developmental Psychology,* 1973, *9*(1), 97–101.

Spearman, C. "General intelligence" objectively determined and measured. *American Journal of Psychology,* 1904, *15,* 201–293.

Stanley, J. C., Keating, D. P., and Fox, L. H. (Eds.) Mathematical talent: Discovery, description, and developments. Baltimore, Md.: The Johns Hopkins University Press, 1974.

Stephens, B., McLaughlin, J. A., Miller, C. K., and Glass, G. V. Factorial structure of selected psychoeducational measures and Piagetian reasoning assessments. *Developmental Psychology,* 1972, *6,* 343–348.

Sternberg, R. J., and Rifkin, B. The development of analogical reasoning processes. *Journal of Experimental Child Psychology,* in press.

Stolarz, S. High-school and college students' understanding of correlation. Unpublished doctoral dissertation, University of California, San Diego, 1976.

Tomlinson-Keasey, C., and Keasey, C. B. The mediating role of cognitive development and moral judgment. *Child Development,* 1974, *45,* 291–298.

Trabasso, T. Representation, memory, and reasoning: How do we make transitive inferences? In A. Pick (Ed.), *Minnesota Symposium on Child Psychology* (Vol. 9). Minneapolis: University of Minnesota Press, 1975.

Trabasso, T., and Foellinger, D. B. Information processing capacity in children: A test of Pascual-Leone's model. *Journal of Experimental Child Psychology,* 1978, *26,* 1–17.

Very, P. S. Differential factor structures in mathematical ability. *Genetic Psychology Monographs,* 1967, *75,* 169–207.

Webb, R. A. Concrete and formal operations in very bright 6- to 11-year-olds. *Human Development,* 1974, *17,* 292–300.

Weitz, L. J., Bynum, T. W., Thomas, J. A., and Steger, J. A. Piaget's system of 16 binary operations: An empirical investigation. *Journal of Genetic Psychology,* 1973, *123,* 279–284.

Wohlwill, J. F. *The study of behavioral development.* New York: Academic, 1973.

CHAPTER 8

Values in Adolescence

Norman T. Feather

When one writes about values one becomes involved with a topic about which everyone seems to have an opinion, especially when these values concern adolescence and youth. There is a fascination with the young that, when taken to the extreme, leads to romantic and exaggerated claims on the one hand and condemnation and abuse on the other. Much of the popular commentary generalizes on the basis of inadequate and superficial evidence, and some of it tells us more about the values of the commentators themselves than about the adolescents being described. This judgment may seem harsh, but it is reasonably accurate. It is easy for those who write about youth to indulge in flights of fancy, guided by personal hopes and wishes and unconstrained by detailed analysis of present reality or by an awareness of past history.

In the present chapter we shall try to avoid these more impressionistic forms of analysis that are so often bound by situation and by time (e.g., youth in the 1960s). Instead we shall concentrate on studies that have at least made some attempt to assess values reliably and that, in total, take us beyond limited samples, such as those that involve college students. We shall attempt to construct a mosaic that has a pattern, though, given the early state of the art, it will be one with many gaps. Throughout the following presentation the focus will be on the *content* of adolescent values rather than on processes of moral development. But we shall have occasion to discuss some of the conditions that determine the development of values in adolescence and the issue of how the relationship of values to behavior might be conceptualized.

VALUES AND VALUE SYSTEMS

First, however, some clearing of the ground is necessary so that we may achieve an understanding of the concepts of value and value system. It must be admitted that the ground to be cleared is tangled and thorny. There has been a lot of discussion and debate about what values are, how they develop, and how they function at the personal and social levels. Because the concept of value has been used so widely, these discussions have come from all fields of social science — from psychology, sociology, anthropology, economics, political science, education, philosophy, and religion.

The concept has been analyzed and defined in various ways, differentiated from other concepts, and related to the broad context of social science. Certain key issues have been discussed, including the questions of the definition and classification of values; the assumed "oughtness" characteristic of values; the relationship of values to means and ends and to persons and objects; the role of values in preference and choice; the functions of values for the individual and for society; the main influences that determine the development of values; and so on. The sociological and social-psychological literature contains many thoughtful and useful discussions about the nature of values and value systems (e.g., Albert, 1968; Allport, Vernon, & Lindzey, 1960; Kluckhohn, 1951; Kluckhohn & Strodtbeck, 1961; Kohlberg, 1969; Kohn, 1969; Morris, 1956; Parsons, 1968; Rokeach, 1973; Scheibe, 1970; Scott, 1965; Smith, 1969b, 1978; Williams, 1968, 1971). These contributions are too numerous to summarize within the confines of this chapter, though they are basic sources for anyone concerned with conceptual analysis and research applications. The ensuing discussion draws mainly from two recent publications, *The Nature of Human Values* (Rokeach, 1973) and *Values in Education and Society* (Feather, 1975). Together they summarize many of the important issues.

The main aspects of Rokeach's approach to the concepts of value and value system are evident in the extended definition he provides:

> To say that a person has a value is to say that he has an enduring prescriptive or proscriptive belief that a specific mode of behavior or end-state of existence is preferred to an oppositive mode of behavior or end-state. This belief transcends attitudes toward objects and toward situations; it is a standard that guides and determines action, attitudes toward objects and situations, ideology, presentation of self to others, evaluations, judgments, justifications, comparisons of self with others, and attempts to influence others. Values serve adjustive, ego-defensive, knowledge, and self-actualizing functions. Instrumental and terminal values are related yet are separately organized into relatively enduring hierarchical organizations along a continuum of importance. [Rokeach, 1973, p. 25]

There are several features of this definition that deserve comment. It is evident that Rokeach prefers to conceive of values as general beliefs that persons have rather than in terms of the values associated with objects. In this he agrees with Williams (1968, p. 283) who argues that the more important usage of the term for purposes of analyses in social science is likely to be one in which values are defined as criteria or standards held by people that affect the evaluative acts in which they are involved. For Rokeach, values are very general, transcendental, relatively enduring beliefs wherein some means or end of action is judged to be personally or socially desirable in relation to its opposite or converse. For example, a person might believe that equality is to be preferred to inequality or that it is preferable to behave honestly rather than dishonestly.

Rokeach assumes that the number of values relating to goals or "end-states of existence" (the terminal values) is likely to be very small, while the number relating to means or "modes of conduct" (the instrumental values) is likely to be rather larger, but still much less than the many thousands of specific beliefs and attitudes that a person has at any one time. Terminal and instrumental values occupy central positions in the total system of a person's beliefs and attitudes and changes in them are likely to have widespread effects throughout the system and on behavior.

Values function as standards or criteria that guide thought and action in various ways. When organized into value systems they may function as general plans that can be used to resolve conflicts and as a basis for decision-making. Values also may satisfy a variety of motivational functions (adjustment, ego-defensive, and knowledge) but, in the final analysis, Rokeach believes that all values are in the service of the self. Thus "a person's values are conceived to maintain and enhance the master sentiment of self-regard — by helping a person adjust to his society, defend his ego against threat, and test reality" (Rokeach, 1973, p. 15).

Values and value systems may be seen as intervening variables mediating between antecedent conditions and consequent cognition and action at both personal and social levels. The antecedents can be traced to culture, society and its institutions, and personality. The consequences will be "manifested in virtually all phenomena that social scientists might consider worth investigating and understanding" (Rokeach, 1973, p. 3). Rokeach agrees with Brewster Smith (1969b, pp. 97–98) that the concept of value has been used loosely in the social-science literature and has been given too many different meanings. In an attempt to nail the concept further, he distinguishes it from other related concepts, such as attitude, social norm, need, trait, interest, and value orientation.

Our own approach to the concept of value (Feather, 1975) assumes that values are influenced both by the properties of the person who is engaged in valuing and by the characteristics of the object being valued. In the case of general values the objects are abstract concepts (for example, behaving honestly, wisdom, and so on). It is possible to weight one's research interest more to the study of values that persons are assumed to have than to the study of values that objects are said to possess. Thus, "one may be more concerned with comparing persons in the values they assign to a standard, delimited set of abstract concepts than with comparing a wide variety of objects in regard to the values assigned to them by a standard set of persons" (Feather, 1975, p. 3).

We conceive of values and value systems in terms of a general theory of abstract structures (Feather, 1971, 1975). Abstract structures are residues or summaries of past experience and they are formed as a person copes with the influx of information from both the social and physical environments. They are organized and relatively stable products of information processing and they provide continuity and meaning under changing environmental circumstances. They can change, however, as new and discrepant information is encountered that cannot readily be interpreted in terms of existing schemata. Abstract structures have a normative aspect in that they incorporate the precipitate of modal or most frequent experiences and so represent what ought to be or is usually the case.

A value may be seen as a particular kind of abstract structure, one that involves a general concept — for example, behaving responsibly (a mode of conduct) or freedom (an end-state of existence). This concept has structural properties and involves a network of associations, which may take different forms for different people. It should be possible to investigate these different structural properties of a value. For example, national security as a value may have a limited and rather undifferentiated network of associations for one person and occupy a fairly peripheral place in that person's total system of beliefs, attitudes, and values. For someone else the value may involve a complex network of associations and a much more central position. It should be clear, therefore, that individuals may differ in the structural characteristics of their values along such dimensions as degree of differentiation, integration, isolation, and centrality — to mention just a few of the dimensions of cognitive structures suggested by various authors (see Zajonc, 1968, pp. 320–338 for a review). A given value may therefore have the same verbal label attached to it (for example, equality), but the value may differ structurally across individuals with some aspects in common and other aspects that are unique, with some aspects that are primary and others that are secondary.

Not only do values involve networks of cognitive and behavioral implications and associations, but they are also tied to our feelings. The associative structures contain links with positive and negative affect. We may experience a deep emotional commitment to our important values, feel angry when others frustrate those values, disapprove of those who support values that appear to be incompatible with our own, and so on. In addition to this affective component, values also have a normative quality about them involving what is desirable or undesirable, what ought to be preferred or not preferred.

As we have seen, each value can be considered as an abstract structure when viewed in isolation. A value system may be conceptualized as a more complex type of abstract structure, one in which various general concepts that have affective and normative significance are ordered along a continuum of importance. A great deal of our research effort has been concerned with exploring the consequences that occur when the value systems held by people are discrepant with those that they attribute to particular environments. In the course of these studies of "cognitive ecology" a fair amount of information has been obtained about the values of various adolescent groups and we shall refer to these findings later in this chapter.

SOURCES OF EVIDENCE ABOUT VALUES

We have dwelt at some length on these two closely related approaches to the concept of value because it is fair to say that many studies that investigate values empirically make little attempt to define the term or to distinguish it from other concepts. As a result a lot of the research is a hodgepodge, seemingly unrelated because there is no agreement or even attempt to agree about basic terms. Many studies appear to be assessing interests, opinions, or attitudes rather than general values; others are more concerned with quite general philosophical orientations. Future research should pay more attention to conceptual clarification, otherwise studies move past one another like ships in the night with no contact or cumulative import.

When one looks at empirical studies of values it is apparent that they have drawn upon various sources of evidence. Williams (1968, p. 285) mentions *testimony* or what individuals are able to tell about their values; systematic studies of the *choices* of objects or actions that are made either in "natural" behavior or in specially designed tests, interviews, and experiments; the *directions of interest* shown by cultural products as well as by directly observed behavior; and observations of the *rewards and punishments* that follow particular lines of action — as when a child is praised for behaving honestly and punished for being dishonest. Williams also notes that indirect procedures, such as projective techniques, may have to be used when values are concealed or camouflaged by conformity to social conventions and taboos or by defenses arising from repressions. Information about values may also be obtained from content analysis of ideological materials. Each of these methods has its problems and its pitfalls. We agree with Williams (1960) that, "When used in combination, these several different approximations gain reliability in so far as they are mutually consistent" (pp. 408–409). In studying values one should attempt to use a variety of methods that converge from different directions on the same conclusion.

To fill out the picture we can provide a limited sample of some of the specific procedures that have been devised, particularly by psychologists and sociologists, while again recognizing that usage of the term "value" varies and that in many cases there is no serious attempt at definition (details about some of the tests that have been developed may be found in recent compendia (such as those by Bonjean, Hill, & McLemore, 1967; Johnson, 1976; Johnson & Bonmorito, 1971; Lake, Miles, & Earle, 1973; and Robinson & Shaver, 1969).

One of the best known procedures is the Study of Values test developed by Allport, Vernon, and Lindzey (1931, 1951, 1960) to measure the relative strength of six basic values: theoretical, economic, aesthetic, social, political, and religious [suggested by

Spranger's *Types of Men* (1928)]. The earlier research using this instrument has been reviewed by Dukes (1955). More recently, procedures involving ranking have been devised that cover a much wider range of values. Following from his conceptual analysis Rokeach (1973) has developed a Value Survey that involves a set of 18 terminal values and a set of 18 instrumental values, each accompanied by a short descriptive phrase (see Table 1). In the usual form of administration the respondent ranks the values in each set in their order of importance in regard to self. One therefore obtains both a terminal-value system and an instrumental-value system from each respondent. The Value Survey can also be used, however, to discover the value systems that respondents attribute to other individuals, groups, or social environments (Feather, 1975).

Procedures involving choice of most important values or ranking of values in order of importance have also been used by Kohn (1969) in his study of social class and parental values and by Bengtson (1975) in his investigation of generation and family effects in value socialization. Many of the items used by Kohn (1969) and Bengtson (1975) relate to the general values included in the Rokeach Value Survey although their items are more specific and, in Bengtson's study, were selected on the basis of earlier proposals suggested by Fallding (1965). Forced-choice procedures and procedures involving Q-sort methodology have been employed by Gordon and Kikuchi (1970) and by Gorlow and Noll (1967a, 1967b). Jack Block (1971) and Jeanne Block (1973) have both made creative use of Q-sorts in longitudinal and cross-cultural studies that include some variables akin to values. Triandis (1972, p. 81) classified ranking, forced-choice, and Q-sort methodology as procedures involving structured cognitive tasks. His own approach to the analysis of value structures in "subjective cultures" is one that relies on cognitive tasks and one that looks for consistent themes in the judgments that people make, thus implying the need to examine interrelationships among responses as evidence for underlying value structures. He and his colleagues have also contributed a new technique called the antecedent-

Table 1   Terminal and Instrumental Values

Terminal Values	Instrumental Values
A comfortable life (a prosperous life)	Ambitious (hard working, aspiring)
An exciting life (a stimulating, active life)	Broad-minded (open-minded)
A sense of accomplishment (lasting contribution)	Capable (competent, effective)
A world at peace (free of war and conflict)	Cheerful (lighthearted, joyful)
A world of beauty (beauty of nature and the arts)	Clean (neat, tidy)
Equality (brotherhood, equal opportunity for all)	Courageous (standing up for your beliefs)
Family security (taking care of loved ones)	Forgiving (willing to pardon others)
Freedom (independence, free choice)	Helpful (working for the welfare of others)
Happiness (contentedness)	Honest (sincere, truthful)
Inner harmony (freedom from inner conflict)	Imaginative (daring, creative)
Mature love (sexual and spiritual intimacy)	Independent (self-reliant, self-sufficient)
National security (protection from attack)	Intellectual (intelligent, reflective)
Pleasure (an enjoyable, leisurely life)	Logical (consistent, rational)
Salvation (saved, eternal life)	Loving (affectionate, tender)
Self-respect (self-esteem)	Obedient (dutiful, respectful)
Social recognition (respect, admiration)	Polite (courteous, well mannered)
True friendship (close companionship)	Responsible (dependable, reliable)
Wisdom (a mature understanding of life)	Self-controlled (restrained, self-disciplined)

Source: Rokeach (1973), Value Survey, pp. 358–361.

consequent procedure, that employs a form of sentence completion with selection of the missing item from a set of fixed choices. They believe that this procedure will prove to be useful in comparing values across cultures (Triandis, et al., 1972).

Some recent research has focussed upon the values involved in work, relating such variables as job performance and worker satisfaction to Protestant ethic values, to desired attributes of the work situation, to goodness of person–environment fit in regard to value systems, and to other value characteristics (e.g., Feather, 1979; Mirels & Garrett, 1971; Orpen, 1978; Wollack, et al., 1971). Questionnaires designed to measure Protestant ethic values (e.g., Mirels & Garrett, 1971; Wollack et al., 1971) are being increasingly used in work-related studies.

More general measures of value orientations and general philosophies of life have also been developed. Kluckhohn and Strodtbeck (1961) compared cultures in regard to five value orientations:

1. Conceptions of the character of innate human nature: evil, neutral or mixed, good; mutable or immutable.

2. Man's subjugation, harmony, or mastery over nature and supernature.

3. The temporal focus of human life, whether past, present, or future.

4. The modality of human activity: being, being-in-becoming, or doing.

5. Man's relationship to other men: linearity, collinearity, or individualism.

Morris (1956) developed 13 paragraphs, each of which describes a possible way of living; respondents are asked to rate each "Way" in regard to how much they like it. These "ways to live" are too complex to describe in detail, but each one involves patterns of values that define a coherent philosophy of life. Morris (1956, p. 1) provides the following brief indentifications for each way of living:

> *Way 1:* Preserve the best that man has attained; *Way 2:* Cultivate independence of persons and things; *Way 3:* Show sympathetic concern for others; *Way 4:* Experience festivity and solitude in alternation; *Way 5:* Act and enjoy life through group participation; *Way 6:* Constantly master changing conditions; *Way 7:* Integrate action, enjoyment, and contemplation; *Way 8:* Live with wholesome, carefree enjoyment; *Way 9:* Wait in quiet receptivity; *Way 10:* Control the self stoically; *Way 11:* Meditate on the inner life; *Way 12:* Chance adventuresome deeds; *Way 13:* Obey the cosmic purposes.

Specially designed questionnaire items are legion, particularly in survey research. Among the best-known recent attempts to monitor value-change among youth by use of survey instruments are those by Yankelovich (1973, 1974). Scott (1965) also used questionnaire measures of the following values with college students: intellectualism, kindness, social skills, loyalty, academic achievement, physical development, status, honesty, religiousness, self-control, creativity, and independence. Atkinson and Litwin (1960) have suggested that the Edwards Personal Preference Schedule (EPPS) based on Murray's (1938) classification of human needs may in fact be measuring values rather than needs, providing information about the relative value assigned by respondents to achievement, deference, order, exhibition, autonomy, affiliation, and other needs from Murray's list. Many others working in specific contexts have developed specially tailored items to assess values concerned with work, school, politics, religion, modernization, leisure, education, and so on (for example, the short review in Triandis, 1972, p. 80).

Ideographic procedures that allow one to discover unique patterns of variables by more indirect means have also been employed as opposed to nomothetic procedures that constrain responses in terms of an imposed general framework (Allport, 1963). For example, content analysis of personal and cultural products, such as letters, newspapers, folktales, movies, interview material, childrens' readers, and so on, have all been used as evidence about personality characteristics and cultural values (for example, Gillespie and Allport, 1955; Goodman, 1957; McClelland, 1961, 1971; R. K. White, 1951; R. W. White, 1966). Repertory (REP) grid procedures have also been applied to value assessment (Glossop, Roberts, & Shemilt, 1975). Zavalloni (1973, 1975) has also advocated the use of ideographic procedures for the study of subjective culture and social identity and has proposed a technique that she calls Associative Network Analysis to permit an ideographic exploration of cognitive mapping. Nor should one forget the use of depth interviews as a means of obtaining evidence about personal value systems (for example, Keniston, 1965) or, at the societal level, detailed study of the structure and functioning of a society in relation to its basic institutions and aspects (the law, polity, family, education, religion, and so on).

It can be seen, therefore, that a wide variety of tests have been devised to measure values both within and across cultures and most of these can be applied to the measurement of values in adolescence. In some cases test development has been guided by a theoretical framework but in other cases research has been at the surface and lacking in conceptual analysis. The general question of how one arrives at a set of basic values in terms of which persons, groups, or cultures can be described is a very difficult one to answer bound up with one's theoretical proclivities and with the range of phenomena that one is attempting to explain. As we noted earlier (Feather, 1975), an inquiry into the adequacy of value taxonomies would need to compare:

. . . alternative ways of classifying values with respect to how well they can be integrated into theoretical systems that enable a comprehensive account of the role of values at the personal and social level. Some value classifications may be more fertile than others, both theoretically and empirically, permitting the development of clearly stated theories that can be applied to a wide range of phenomena. New values may be added to these taxonomies contingent upon their success in improving the power of explanation. [P. 270]

Apart from the need to develop taxonomies of values that are theoretically fertile, in that they further our understanding of both the person and society, one also has to devise measurement procedures that minimize error and that enable comparative inquiry. This is no easy task. The debates concerning nomothetic versus ideographic methods at the level of personality (Allport, 1963); "emic" versus "etic" procedures at the level of cultures (Berry, 1969; Brislin, Lonner, & Thorndike, 1973); the appropriateness and equivalence of measures (Feather, 1975; Frey, 1970; Przeworski & Teune, 1970); and other issues concerned not only with ways of maximizing reliable and valid measurement, but also with the logic of comparative appraisal — all still continue and are not easily resolved. There is no doubt, however,that studies using multiple methods that converge on the same conclusion as well as cumulative investigations that add new findings, while reinforcing previous ones, are those that advance our understanding. When exploring a complex territory one must observe from many different vantage points and check the accuracy of the observations on different occasions. So it is with the study of values and especially so because the territory itself, involving as it does persons and societies, is continually changing, while at the same time retaining basic stabilities.

Let us now turn to examine values in adolescence, first as they have been discussed in the theoretical literature, then in regard to the empirical findings.

THEORETICAL VIEWS ABOUT ADOLESCENCE: IMPLICATIONS FOR VALUES

General Themes

The main characteristics of youth and adolescence in regard to biological change, psychodynamics, ego development, ego identity, moral development, and so on, have been discussed in other chapters of this book. We do not intend to cover the same ground again. Nor can any summary do justice to the many rich, subtle, and insightful discussions of adolescence that have already appeared in the literature (for example, Campbell, 1969; Coleman, et al., 1974; Douvan & Adelson, 1966; Dragastin & Elder, 1975; Erikson, 1950, 1968; Havighurst & Dreyer, 1975). Some of the general themes in these discussions do, however, have implications for value priorities in adolescence.

Among these general themes are the following: adolescence is seen as a stage of development between childhood and adulthood in which there is a "psychosocial moratorium" during which the person seeks to work out problems of identity so that he or she achieves some sort of answer to the questions Who am I? What do I stand for? How do other people see me? What is my future? In this search for identity the adolescent is assumed to experiment with a variety of roles, to use various sources of information with the peer group gaining in influence, to define personal rights and liberties, to move away from the ways and modes of childhood thinking, to develop increasing independence and autonomy, to formulate ideals and values that become integrated into an emerging philosophy of life, and to make certain important choices that concern the future. These choices allow for the opportunities that are available and in some cases involve commitments not easy to reverse, for example, choices that concern work, education, social groups, and so on. As Douvan and Adelson (1966) succinctly put it, "During this period, the youngster must synthesize earlier identifications with personal qualities and relate them to social opportunities and social ideals" (p. 15).

During this stage there is a development of cognitive capacities, so that the adolescent starts to achieve "formal operations" (Inhelder & Piaget, 1958) in contrast to the more concrete modes of thought of childhood. Thus there is increasing ability to think abstractly with propositions and general concepts, to reason with hypotheses that involve a number of variables, and to distinguish between the thinking of self and others (Bruner, 1960). This cognitive growth enables the adolescent to entertain a wider range of alternatives from which personal, occupational, sexual, and ideological commitments are made.

These general discussions about adolescence also emphasize the biological changes that occur and the consequent need for the person to cope with biological impulse and to come to terms with emerging sexuality and with growing heterosexual interests. The family, peer group, and school function as the primary socializing agents and as important reference sources as the adolescent works through different crises. Communication via the mass media is also seen as an important socializing influence. The young person is assumed to express a ripening need for independence and autonomy by moving away from parents toward the peer group, while, at the same time, retaining dependence on the family as a stable anchor point for the resolution of many important issues.

The adolescent is assumed to be involved in a search for fidelity, looking for people and ideas to have faith in and abhorring falsity and hypocrisy (Erikson, 1968). Gradually, most adolescents are assumed to develop a sense of identity that integrates the past, the present, and the future and that also provides some stability in a changing world together with a feeling of self-regulation and direction. With successful passage through adolescence, most problems of identity confusion are resolved and one sees the progressive development of increasingly mature interpersonal relationships in which the self enters into shared intimacy with others. Individuals differ in the way they cope with the adolescent experience and there are asynchronies and regressions in development that cut across the general themes that we have outlined.

What implications do these descriptive statements have for the analysis of value systems in adolescence? They suggest that certain values may be given special prominence at this stage of development. If we take Rokeach's (1973) taxonomy of values, for example, one might expect the adolescent to assign relatively high importance to such values as being honest and responsible and achieving freedom and true friendship. Later in adolescence, as shared intimacy develops, one might expect to find an increase in the degree to which being loving and the achievement of mature love are seen as important values. Thus the analysis of the shared problems that adolescents face and the ways they go about trying to solve them does have some general implications when we attempt to state hypotheses about adolescent value systems.

Sex Differences in the Adolescent Experience

The discussion so far has ignored differences in the way boys and girls move through adolescence. Douvan and Adelson (1966) argue that important sex differences exist that qualify the general themes that we have just summarized. The boy is assumed to separate the tasks of achieving identity and intimacy. For him the pressures to make a vocational choice and to prepare for an occupation are especially important in forcing a resolution of the identity crisis and this resolution is achieved by separating from others, becoming independent and autonomous, and defining the self and what it stands for. The boy then moves on to confront problems of intimacy — exploring and developing close interpersonal commitments in which love is given and received. The girl, however, is assumed to develop her identity through her relationships with other people and ultimately her identity is bound up with the traditional family roles of wife and mother. Thus the tasks of achieving identity and intimacy are not separated but are closely intertwined. As Douvan and Adelson (1966) put it:

> The key terms in adolescent development for the boy in our culture are the erotic, autonomy (assertiveness, independence, achievement), and identity. For the girl the comparable terms are the erotic, the interpersonal, and identity. . . . What the girl achieves through intimate connection with others, the boy must manage by disconnecting, by separating himself and asserting his right to be distinct. [Pp. 347–348]

More recently, Douvan (1975) notes that social change and social forces (especially increased educational expectations and attainment among women, birth control technology, and the women's movement) have had important effects on female socialization, so that the traditional view may no longer be accurate for more highly educated girls and women whose identity problem may now be more similar to that traditionally confronted by the boy. The male role may also be changing in that it may increasingly require socioemotional and supportive skills, given a general shift in job demands away from production and technical skills toward the manipulation of words, ideas, and people (Douvan, 1975, p. 40; Pleck, 1976).

The themes developed by Douvan and Adelson (1966) emerge in other writings about sex differences. In an early contribution, Parsons (1958) argued that the masculine role is essentially instrumental or task-oriented, while the feminine role tends to be expressive and person-oriented. More recent contributions have referred to the importance of affiliation and social skills in female socialization (for example, Bardwick, 1971; Block, 1973; Stein & Bailey, 1973) and of achievement, competence, and the control of feelings and expressions of affect in male socialization (for example, Block, 1973; Pleck, 1976). These discussions are only part of the dramatic increase in attention given to the whole question of sex roles, sex typing, and sex differences in socialization in recent years with a proliferation of collections of papers, literature reviews, and new journals (see, for example, Hoffman, 1977; Maccoby & Jacklin, 1974; Mischel, 1970; Ruble & Frieze, 1976; Spence and Helmreich, 1978; Mednick, Tangri, & Hoffman, 1975; Mednick & Weissman, 1975 — among others). These discussions reveal increasing sophistication in recognizing the need to relate sex roles to the wider social context and to the social changes that are occurring in the redefinition of what are deemed to be appropriate behaviors for the two sexes. But it is difficult to abstract strong predictions about male and female adolescent values on the basis of these more recent analyses some of which appear to suggest a drift away from sex typing in the direction of more androgynous sex roles. Clearly we need more evidence about the scope and permanence of any changes that may have occurred in both socialization practices and outcomes. Given the traditional analysis, however, which still probably holds for large segments of the population, one can predict that males may assign higher importance to values concerned with achievement and competence, whereas females may place more emphasis on values relating to nurturance and affiliation.

Youth and Youth Culture

Recent discussions of youth and youth culture provide another source of hypotheses about values in adolescence. To some extent these discussions overlap with those already considered. Indeed there is a certain amount of slippage in the definitions of the age-spans for adolescence and youth, the latter term often being used to encompass the years of later adolescence and young adulthood. Thus the editors of a recent yearbook on youth (Havighurst & Dreyer, 1975) take the age-span of 15 through 24 as the formal definition and, similarly, the President's advisory panel on youth defines this period as spanning the ages from 14 through 24 (Coleman et al., 1974). On the other hand, Keniston (1971) sees youth as a psychological stage of development that emerges between adolescence and adulthood and one that is not universally experienced across the population. Despite these different meanings, discussions of youth and the youth culture are of interest in suggesting hypotheses about values, especially in later adolescence.

Keniston (1971) argues that youth is a new stage of life opened up by the prolongation of education in the more affluent societies. He believes that its central characteristic is a tension between selfhood and the existing social order. In this stage one can discover the following themes among the young: a concern with actual or potential conflicts and discrepancies between what one is and what one perceives society to be; a pervasive ambivalence toward both self and society; intense and wary probing of both self and society; alternating feelings of estrangement and omnipotentiality; critical analysis of one's earlier socialization and acculturation; emergence of youth-specific identities and roles; high value placed on change, transformation, and movement; and the formation of youthful countercultures. Among the transformations that are assumed to occur at this stage are the resolution of the self-society relationship, a developing intimacy with others, a shift to mutuality in interpersonal relationships, a more complex and realistic appreciation of parents and the older generation, and futher development in the moral and cognitive spheres.

The President's panel on youth lists certain characteristics of the youth culture that recur and that are held in common among different segments of the culture (Coleman et al., 1974). The youth culture is described as inward-looking in the sense that the culture itself is the important reference source; youth is assumed to become attached psychically to others of their own age with an increasing need for close relations with others in the age group who can provide love, security, and support; there is a press toward autonomy and a respect for those who challenge adults; there is a concern for the underdog that finds its expression mainly in political support and that probably derives from the underdog or outsider position of youth in modern society; and there is an interest in change that itself relates to the outsider status of youth and the consequent pressure to achieve a stake in society by changing it. The President's panel does not see these characteristics as part of the essential ''nature of youth'' but rather as responses by youth to the rest of society. Thus they state (Coleman et al., 1974):

Youth are segregated from adults by the economic and educational institutions created by adults, they are deprived of psychic support from persons of other ages, a psychic support that once came from the family, they are subordinate and powerless in relation to adults, and outsiders to the dominant social institutions. Yet they have money, they have access to a wide range of communications media, and control of some, and they are relatively larger in number. [P. 125]

In a study of the ''seasons of a man's life,'' Levinson et al. (1978) discuss pre-adulthood as the era that includes childhood, adolescence, and the early adult transition (17 years to 22 years). This transition is seen to involve *two* major tasks. One is to:

. . . terminate the adolescent life structure and *leave the pre-adult world*. A young man has to question the nature of that world and his place in it. It is necessary to modify existing relationships with important persons and institutions, and to modify the self that formed in pre-adulthood. Numerous separations, losses and transformations are required. [P. 73]

The second task is to:

. . . *make a preliminary step into the adult world:* to explore its possibilities, to imagine oneself as a participant in it, to make and test some tentative choices before fully entering it. The first task involves a process of termination, the second a process of initiation. [P. 73]

These various discussions again suggest that among their personal values, the young may emphasize values concerned with close relationships and with independence and autonomy. They also imply, however, that the late adolescent and young adult will be concerned with values that relate to changing the existing social order in the direction of greater freedom and equality — with values that imply a less conservative stance toward social issues than that taken by their elders. Thus one might expect them to upgrade values concerning freedom and equality and to downgrade values that imply acceptance of institutionalized authority and social conventions. One must be careful to qualify these implications by indicating that they will not apply to all segments of the young age groups but more so to those who have been segregated by economic and educational forces.

Finally, we should note that these discussions have little or nothing to say about sex differences. Douvan (1975), in fact, finds Keniston's (1971) statement peculiarly feminine or at least androgynous.

Adolescent Prototypes

So far in our discussion of theoretical contributions that relate to the content of values in adolescence we have dwelt on the general and, apart from sex differences, have had nothing to say about individual or group differences in developmental outcomes. There are some discussions in the literature that point to different adolescent prototypes, to different subspecies of adolescents that may emerge on the basis of socialization experiences and other factors connected with development. Because these contributions may suggest hypotheses about value priorities they are presented here, though in very summary form.

Peck and Havighurst (1960) define five character types, which they label amoral, expedient, conforming, irrational-conscientious, and rational-altruistic. The development of these character types is explained in terms of three dimensions that closely resemble those later proposed by Hogan (1973, 1975): socialization, empathy, and autonomy. Hogan (1973) argues that moral conduct can be explained and the development of moral character can be described in terms of these three dimensions and two others: moral knowledge and a person's ethical basis (involving the ethics of conscience and/or ethics of responsibility). Moral maturity is seen by Hogan as the ideal end-point of moral development in which there is optimal placement on all five dimensions, but in practice the endpoint is usually social conformance. Different character types can be described in terms of how the individual copes with major transition points in development (socialization, empathy, and autonomy) that occur at progressively later periods in time. Hogan (1973) argues that:

> . . . the emergence of socialization, empathy, and autonomy are adaptive within the context of the social environment during maturation; they are capacities which mediate both the needs of the individual and the demands of his social group . . . all three stages are distinct developmental challenges whose outcome defines each person's unique character structure. [Pp. 230–231]

Baumrind (1975) constructs eight adolescent prototypes that correspond to the eight possible combinations of high and low scores on three dimensions of social behavior that have appeared in a number of studies: *social responsibility* (friendly versus hostile, facilitative versus disruptive, obedient versus disobedient; controlled versus uncontrolled; and so on); *active-passive* (expressive versus reserved, explosive versus calm, and so on); and *individualistic-suggestible* (ascendant versus submissive, purposive versus aimless, individualistic versus conforming, and so on). The eight prototypes are social agent (high, high, high), social victim (low, low, low), traditionalist (high, high, low), alienated (low, low, high), socialized (high, low, low), delinquent (low, high, high), humanist (high, low, high), and antihumanist (low, high, low). Each of these prototypes is discussed in terms of parent-child relationships that might underly development in that direction, the prototypes being grouped in the following pairs: social agent versus social victim, traditionalist versus alienated, socialized versus delinquent, and humanist versus antihumanist. For example, the upbringing of the traditionalist is assumed to be one in which firm discipline is emphasized accompanied by strong affectional family ties and by appeals to religious and patriotic values in order to justify adult authority. The delinquent prototype is assumed to be associated with harsh, exploitative, and arbitrary treatment by parents; middle-class delinquency is associated with a disregard or habitual violation of the norm of reciprocity by adults in authority.

Havighurst (1975) in a recent discussion of youth in relation to the social institutions of contemporary society distinguishes between three main types of youth. The first are the "forerunners" who are in the vanguard of social change, who create countercultures, and who comprise about 20% of youth — 10% in the cultural wing (for example, the "hippies") and 10% in the political wing (for example, the "new left"). The college and high-school students in this group use their formal education to criticize society rather than as a means of conforming to it. The second type, who are by far the largest group of youth, are the "practical-minded." According to Havighurst (1975):

> They are the apprentices to the leaders and maintainers of the technocratic, production-oriented, instrumental society. They maintain the stable values central to the contemporary democratic society, with special strength in productivity, achievement motivation, social responsibility, friendliness, and family solidarity. [P. 124]

Most youth from upper-middle-class families are in this group. These are the people training for professional vocations (for example, managers, scientists, doctors, lawyers, teachers, and so on). The vast majority of the "practical-minded," however, come from the families of lower-middle-class or white-collar workers and stable manual-working-class families — youth who are graduating from high school and perhaps proceeding to a community college, a technical institution, or to a business college. The "practical-minded" are assumed to comprise about 60% of youth. The final type involves the "left-outs" who comprise about 20% of youth. These are the youngsters who do not complete a high-school course; many of them are outside of the mainstream of society. Havighurst (1975) describes a subgroup of them as apathetic, without ambition or self-confidence, and dependent on others for direction. Another smaller subgroup is an alienated and hostile group consisting mainly of young men in small peer groups seeking, in a self-centered way, exciting and dangerous expressive activities. Havighurst's (1975) analysis draws on survey data by Yankelovich (1973) and Keniston's (1971) discussion of dissenting youth.

One could go on adding to the classifications that have been advanced, particularly from the literature on youth movements — see Braungart (1975, pp. 264–265) who refers to classifications by Matza (1961), Clark and Trow (1960), Peterson (1968), and Block, Haan, and Smith (1973). The latter authors provide a useful taxonomy of American college youth in the late 1960s and early 1970s in terms of six different types: politically apathetic youth, alienated youth, individualistic youth, constructivist youth, activist youth, and dissenters. They also provide evidence about family relationships and other variables that relate to their typology (see also Block, Haan, & Smith, 1969). At the more general level of personality description Jack Block (1971), in an important analysis of longitudinal data from the Institute of Human Development at Berkeley, has described various personality types in relation to development through early adolescence, late adolescence, and middle adulthood.

The examples that we have provided show that it is simplistic to conceive of adolescence and youth in a monolithic way, as a relatively homogeneous culture as far as values are concerned. It should be apparent that one can describe different subspecies of adolescents who may share some important values but differ in the priority they give to other values. Within the age range of adolescence and youth, therefore, we should be set to look for differences as well as for similarities in value systems and to develop ways of understanding how both have come about.

Other Influences on Values

The thrust of the discussion about the emergence of adolescent value systems has so far been on influences that are assumed to be endemic to the life course as youngsters grow, cope with biological changes and emergent sexuality, seek to define their identities, develop increasing independence and autonomy, make plans for the future, and take on new roles and responsibilities. Weaving through the discussion are various threads that relate to lines of development in intellectual capacities, ego processes, moral reasoning, sex roles, social relationships, and so on.

It is important not to forget that development occurs in a wider social and cultural milieu and is influenced by secular trends and events and by the impact of history and tradition. The individual has to adjust not only to changing internal conditions, but also to external influences, such as wars, economic crises, and changes in social and political institutions that may have lasting effects on developmental outcomes. These kinds of influence have been emphasized by those working in the fields of political socialization, generational analysis, and life-span developmental psychology (for example, Bengtson & Starr, 1975; Bengtson, Furlong, & Laufer, 1974; Elder, 1975; Jennings & Niemi, 1974, 1975; Riley, 1973; the series of books on life-span developmental psychology emanating from the West Virginia Conferences — Baltes & Schaie, 1973; Goulet & Baltes, 1970; Nesselroade & Reese, 1973; and the special issues on youth, generations, and social change in the *Journal of Social Issues:* Bengtson & Laufer, 1974).

Thus Bengtson and Starr (1975) argue that:

> The analysis of contemporary youth is enhanced from a perspective that allows consideration of the time-related processes of maturation (individual development or aging) and period change (cultural development); of the lineage (socialization) relationship that bonds the generations together; of the structural elements of age strata; and of generations as historically conscious aggregates. Four factors can be seen as influencing differences or similarities among contemporaneous age groups: aging (maturation) effects, lineage (socialization) effects, period (historical) effects, or generation unit (ideological) effects. [P. 236]

Similarly, Jennings and Niemi (1975) distinguish between life-cycle effects (the kinds of change endemic to the life course), generational effects (differences in the shared community of experiences that different age cohorts undergo), and period or *zeitgeist* effects (those influences that reflect important trends and events during a period of history and that have a roughly common impact on most segments of society). These different influences are assumed to interact in complex ways so as to determine continuity and discontinuity between the generations over time.

Paralleling these relatively new theoretical perspectives on development has been the emergence of more sophisticated procedures for analyzing the relative effects of the different influences. These procedures involve a combination of longitudinal and cross-sectional designs in which data are collected for different segments of society in a sequential way, starting at different points in history and following up age cohorts over long periods of time. These methodological innovations are complex and costly, but necessary if we are to advance our understanding of the basis for stability and change across the life course in regard to the characteristics of individuals and groups.

These theoretical and methodological advances will in time add to our knowledge of how and why particular values emerge in adolescence. They alert us to be cautious about generalizing about the nature of adolescent values without regard to place and time. Value priorities that are found in one culture may not occur in other cultures, nor even for all adolescents within the same society. And those adolescent values that are discovered may be relative to a particular epoch and to the mould of historical trends and events. For example, one would expect the children of parents who experienced the Great Depression in the early 1930s to have different sets of values from those who were raised in affluence

(Elder, 1974); and one would expect youth who faced the horrors and uncertainties of the Vietnam War and who actively worked through the moral implications of this war to develop value priorities differing from those of the current crop of youth who are grappling with economic uncertainties and a highly competitive job market.

Final Comment

The set of influences that affect adolescent values is obviously complex and it is not possible at our present stage of knowledge to formulate precise theories about how these influences combine to determine particular outcomes. Indeed, most discussions of factors that influence adolescent development probably should not be called theories at all but descriptive statements that note sequences of events that appear to bear some relationship to one another (for example, antecedent socialization experiences and subsequent outcomes). Moreover, many of these general discussions are culture bound, based on observations of adolescents in the more affluent, industrialized countries where young-sters are fairly well educated and have a waiting period before work and marriage. As Baumrind (1975) notes:

> Psychosocial adolescence is a luxury afforded the highly civilized and the affluent, since crises of survival preclude crises of meaning. . . . Personal autonomy and individuation are not universally accepted defining characteristics of the mature person, a fact American behavioral scientists are prone to overlook. [Pp. 117–118]

Not to be forgotten also are the biases that sometimes intrude as observers project their own personal and cultural values when interpreting the attitudes, values, and behavior of some of the more visible, vivid, and voluble young, especially those from elite college campuses. Clearly, one needs to look at different segments of the adolescent population and, where possible, across different cultures.

Thus we move like explorers in difficult territory where the ground is often shaky and where the blind sometimes leads the blind. But that is no reason for holding back. Let us now with appropriate caution look at some of the empirical evidence about values in adolescence.

EVIDENCE ABOUT VALUE SYSTEMS: DESCRIPTIVE STUDIES

Variation in Value Systems Across Adolescence

In a recent article Beech and Schoeppe (1974) refer to a number of studies of the values of high-school students and teenagers (for example, Garrison, 1966; Hallworth & Waite, 1966; Harris, 1966; McLellan, 1970; Morris, 1958; Peck, 1967; Remmers & Radler, 1957; Shepherd, 1966; Thompson, 1961) but note that generally there has been a lack of reseach that looks at changes in value systems from early through late adolescence. They obtained information from pupils in New York City public schools about their value systems, using the Value Survey (Rokeach, 1973). Children from grades 5, 7, 9, and 11 were tested (corresponding to ages 11, 13, 15, and 17 years respectively) and half of the respondents came from middle-class and half from lower-class schools. Boys and girls were represented in approximately equal numbers for each grade and the results were presented separately for each sex. The data collection occurred in the spring of 1969.

The results for the boys showed that, among the terminal values (those concerned with goals or end-states of existence), a world at peace, freedom, family security, and equality were consistently ranked among the four or five most important values on the average across all grades, whereas salvation and social recognition were consistently ranked among the four or five least important values. Among the instrumental values (those concerned with modes of conduct), being honest and loving were consistently ranked as very high in importance and being logical and imaginative as very low.

The following values increased in relative importance for the boys from the fifth grade to the eleventh grade: a sense of accomplishment, self-respect, wisdom, being ambitious, being broad-minded, being intellectual, and being responsible. In contrast, the following values decreased in relative importance: a world at peace, a world of beauty, true friendship, being cheerful, being clean, being forgiving, being helpful, and being obedient.

As far as the girls were concerned, certain values were also regularly ranked high or low in importance across all grades. Thus a world at peace and freedom were consistently among the first four terminal values and salvation was consistently ranked lowest in importance on the average. Among the instrumental values, being honest and loving consistently ranked very high in relative importance at all age levels, while being imaginative and logical were consistently ranked very low.

The following values increased in relative importance for the girls from the fifth grade: a sense of accomplishment, equality, inner harmony, self-respect, social recognition, wisdom, being ambitious, being broad-minded, being independent, being logical, and being responsible. The following values decreased in relative importance: a comfortable life, an exciting life, a world of beauty, family security, pleasure, salvation, true friendship, being cheerful, being helpful, being honest, being obedient, and being polite.

Beech and Schoeppe (1974) discuss these results in relation to a number of different themes. For our purposes, it is interesting to note that peace, freedom, honesty, and love were highly valued by both boys and girls and so was family security, whereas being imaginative and logical were consistently devalued in the relative sense. There were signs that both sexes were increasingly valuing achievement, open-mindedness, responsibility, and self-respect as they grew older and downgrading modes of behavior connoting conformity to convention and authority. These changes make sense in relation to the general theoretical discussions that we have reviewed that emphasize emerging concerns about identity, autonomy, and fidelity in adolescence and a movement away from adult authority in some matters. At the same time, the security of the family remains as an important concern. Beech and Schoeppe (1974) suggest that the emphasis on a world at peace may reflect a momentary concern (the Vietnam War was then being fought), but it may also indicate the general political philosophy of the children because they also ranked freedom and equality as high in relative importance.

We have obtained similar results in a large survey of nearly 3000 Adelaide, Australia, schoolchildren most of whom were from 15 to 17 years of age and in their last two years of high school (Feather, 1975). These children came from 19 schools in metropolitan Adelaide and the test program extended from mid-1970 to early 1971. Table 2 presents the median rankings for the terminal and instrumental values for these children and compares these medians with those obtained for the eleventh-grade schoolchildren from the Beech and Schoeppe (1974) study. The extent to which these results are similar to those of Beech and Schoeppe (1974) is quite striking considering that the comparison crosses national

Table 2 Median Rankings and Composite Rank Orders of Own Values for Boys and Girls from Adelaide (Australia) and New York City Secondary Schools (Ages 16 to 17 approximately)

Terminal Value	Adelaide Boys	Adelaide Girls	New York City Boys	New York City Girls	Instrumental Value	Adelaide Boys	Adelaide Girls	New York City Boys	New York City Girls
N	715	690	92	97		734	703	92	97
A comfortable life	9.39 (11)[a]	13.58 (16)	8.50 (7.5)	12.13 (14)	Ambitious	6.45 (3)	8.79 (10)	7.10 (3)	5.71 (1)
An exciting life	7.33 (8)	9.93 (11)	11.70 (13)	12.64 (15)	Broad-minded	7.48 (5)	6.25 (3)	8.17 (6)	8.60 (5)
A sense of accomplishment	7.31 (7)	7.44 (8)	9.50 (10)	9.00 (10)	Capable	7.88 (6)	9.94 (12)	8.79 (7)	8.71 (7)
A world at peace	6.22 (3)	4.54 (1)	3.64 (1)	3.20 (1)	Cheerful	9.02 (8)	7.53 (4)	11.21 (13)	10.96 (14)
A world of beauty	12.94 (15)	11.31 (13)	13.17 (17)	11.80 (13)	Clean	10.18 (12)	10.11 (13)	10.50 (11.5)	9.14 (9)
Equality	8.70 (10)	6.05 (4)	5.50 (3)	5.22 (2)	Courageous	10.30 (13)	9.87 (11)	7.25 (4)	8.69 (6)
Family security	7.71 (9)	7.07 (7)	6.17 (4)	7.91 (7)	Forgiving	10.64 (15)	8.71 (9)	9.50 (10)	9.63 (11)
Freedom	5.46 (2)	5.43 (3)	4.95 (2)	6.58 (3)	Helpful	10.56 (14)	7.91 (5)	9.07 (8)	9.33 (10)
Happiness	6.30 (4)	6.30 (6)	6.90 (5)	7.46 (6)	Honest	4.72 (2)	2.54 (1)	6.00 (1)	5.94 (2)
Inner harmony	10.38 (12)	8.51 (10)	10.00 (11.5)	8.81 (9)	Imaginative	13.31 (18)	14.45 (18)	12.17 (16)	13.75 (18)
Mature love	6.46 (5)	8.11 (9)	9.30 (9)	10.56 (11)	Independent	8.47 (7)	10.41 (14)	9.17 (9)	8.75 (8)
National security	13.78 (16)	13.15 (14)	12.50 (15)	14.91 (17)	Intellectual	11.48 (16)	13.95 (17)	11.50 (15)	10.13 (12)
Pleasure	10.76 (14)	13.54 (15)	11.90 (14)	13.57 (16)	Logical	9.73 (11)	12.46 (16)	12.67 (18)	12.71 (16)
Salvation	15.63 (18)	14.79 (18)	16.07 (18)	16.00 (18)	Loving	9.69 (10)	7.96 (6)	7.07 (2)	7.38 (3)
Self-respect	10.71 (13)	10.09 (12)	10.00 (11.5)	7.40 (5)	Obedient	11.97 (17)	11.36 (15)	12.33 (17)	13.20 (17)
Social recognition	13.84 (17)	14.58 (17)	12.90 (16)	11.19 (12)	Polite	9.67 (9)	8.51 (7)	11.39 (14)	10.19 (13)
True friendship	5.24 (1)	4.74 (2)	8.50 (7.5)	8.56 (8)	Responsible	4.56 (1)	4.41 (2)	7.30 (5)	7.65 (4)
Wisdom	7.30 (6)	6.27 (5)	7.50 (6)	6.75 (4)	Self-controlled	7.46 (4)	8.66 (8)	10.50 (11.5)	11.00 (15)

Source: Data are from Feather (1975) for Adelaide and from Beech and Schoeppe (1974) for New York City.

[a] Lower numbers denote higher relative value. In each column, the rank order of each median (low to high) is denoted in parentheses after the median.

263

boundaries. There are differences, to be sure, but these are outweighed by the similarities that exist. Note, for example, the high priorities given by all groups to a world at peace, freedom, and to being honest and responsible, and the low priorities assigned to salvation, social recognition, and to being logical, intellectual, and imaginative.

A measure of the degree of similarity between the average value systems can be provided in terms of the rank-order correlation coefficients. For the terminal value systems the Spearman rhos between Adelaide and New York City were .80 for the boys and .85 for the girls. For the instrumental value systems the rhos were .60 for the boys and .54 for the girls. When the average value systems of boys and girls were compared, the rhos for the terminal values were .88 for Adelaide and .84 for New York City. The between-sex correlations for the instrumental values were .65 for Adelaide and .94 for New York City. These rank-order correlations reflect both similarities and differences in the average value systems for boys and girls in the two different and widely separated cities.

In another Australian study, Connell et al. (1975) obtained a considerable amount of information from an extensive cross-sectional survey of over 9000 Sydney teenagers, aged from 12 to 20, of whom there were just over 8000 still at school and just over 1000 who had left school to enter the workforce. The survey contained a wide range of questionnaire items covering eight broad areas of teenage life: family, peers, and peer groups; activities and interests; aspects of self-concept; the school and school life; the mass media; moral values and moral judgments; politics and society; and thinking and intelligence. The items concerned with personal values were constructed following procedures described by Gorlow and Noll (1967a, 1967b) and Kerlinger (1967). These items allowed for both *value referents* (for example, persons, ideas, actions, events, or classes) representing things of value to the person and *value criteria* (for example, justifications, standards, reasons, explanations) representing the bases or criteria used to justify preferences. There were 12 value referents (for example, self; parents and family; friends; education and schooling; religion; affection, love, and sex; politics, war, and peace) and 8 value criteria (for example, self-interest and selfish satisfactions; self-autonomy and independence; conformity to other people, reciprocity with other people; humanitarian ideals). The following item, for example, refers to friends as a referent and to reciprocity as a justification: "Lending and borrowing between friends is alright because helping each other is good;" whereas the following one refers to school as a referent and self autonomy as a justification: "Staying on at school is important because it helps you to get a job and become independent" (Connell et al., 1975, p. 75). Items so constructed were presented in pairs or in triads and subjects had to choose the item preferred.

Analysis of the choices for the teenagers still at school indicated the importance of affection-love-sex when mutual and reciprocal opportunities and benefit were emphasized; social and humanitarian concerns when one's personal and self-interest were involved; and money, property, and possessions when these enabled the achievement of greater autonomy and independence. The area most universally rejected was that relating to politics, war, and peace when it was justified for reasons of conformity. The choices showed that, as far as criteria of judgment were concerned:

. . . there is an overwhelming rejection of conformity and social compliance as the basis for valuing anything, and a nearly equivalent affirmation of a principle of personal independence and autonomy. Coercive justification and narrow self-satisfaction are also relatively disfavoured, while ideals, reciprocity, and expertise are more often given a high place in the rank order of categories. [Connell et al., p. 79]

The results for the teenagers who had left school also showed the importance of affection-love-sex as a value referent with emphasis on reciprocity and personal interest and autonomy as justifications. Parents and family were seen as high in value when they promoted personal independence and freedom. As Connell et al. note (1975):

> Not only do these judgments seem to accord with the stereotype of older teenagers, more and more independent of earlier restraints and dependence, but they also imply an independence related to establishing an independent sexual and family role of one's own making. [P. 79]

Leisure and recreation were rejected as an area when self-interest was involved and both work aspirations as well as politics, war, and peace were devalued when they were justified in terms of conformity. Like the teenagers still in school, these teenagers who had left school also disfavored social conformity and narrow self-interest as bases for justification; reciprocity, ideals, and personal independence were strongly favored to justify choices.

In another part of their survey Connell et al. used sets of questions to provide information about young people's responses to some typical everyday moral issues, following the strategy employed by Eppel and Eppel (1966) and by Havighurst and Taba (1949) in studies of adolescent morality in England and the United States respectively. Analysis of items relating to responsibility, honesty, and friendship for the school sample showed that both boys and girls had a high regard for these values and that there was an overall increase toward stricter commitments to them with increasing age. The trend toward more rigorous standards was especially associated with older girls of good intellectual ability.

We have described the Connell et al. study at some length because of its scope and because it used a different methodology from that employed by Beech and Schoeppe (1974) and by Feather (1975). Despite this difference we find that their results overlap with those of the Rokeach-based investigations and show a convergence in conclusions. For example, all three lines of research indicate the importance of autonomy, responsibility, and honesty for the adolescent and the relative unimportance of values that involve conformity to authority and social convention. Both Australian studies demonstrate the importance of affiliation and friendship in the teen-age respondents. There are differences, to be sure, some of which relate to differences in the nature and range of items used and some to differences between the two cultures involved in the research. But the similarities are impressive.

One should remember that the three cities sampled in these studies are in affluent countries, that the United States and Australia are similar in other respects as well, and that comparisons across widely different cultures would be expected to indicate less similarity in value systems. It is important, therefore, to extend the range of cross-cultural comparisons. We can do this by reviewing some recent studies that mainly involve college youth.

Value Systems of College Youth in Different Cultures

Table 3 presents information about the four most important and the four least important terminal and instrumental values from the Value Survey for five samples of male students enrolled at colleges or universities in their respective countries (for details of these samples see Feather, 1970, 1975; Feather & Hutton, 1974; Rokeach, 1973). All of the data were collected at around the same time — in the late 1960s or early 1970s. We have presented more recent data for Australian student groups in *Values in Education and*

Table 3   Four Most Important and Four Least Important Values in Five Groups of Male Students

Rank of Value	United States	Canada	Australia	Israel	Papua New Guinea
			Terminal Values		
1	Freedom	Freedom	Wisdom	A world at peace	A world at peace
2	Happiness	Happiness	True friendship	National security	Equality
3	Wisdom	Mature love	Freedom	Happiness	Freedom
4	Self-respect	Self-respect	A sense of accomplishment	Freedom	True friendship
15	Pleasure	A world of beauty	A world of beauty	A comfortable life	A sense of accomplishment
16	Salvation	Social recognition	Social recognition	Social recognition	Pleasure
17	National security	National security	National security	A world of beauty	Mature love
18	A world of beauty	Salvation	Salvation	Salvation	A world of beauty
			Instrumental Values		
1	Honest	Honest	Honest	Honest	Honest
2	Responsible	Responsible	Broad-minded	Responsible	Helpful
3	Ambitious	Loving	Responsible	Logical	Responsible
4	Broad-minded	Broad-minded	Loving	Capable	Ambitious
15	Cheerful	Imaginative	Imaginative	Clean	Independent
16	Polite	Polite	Polite	Imaginative	Clean
17	Clean	Clean	Clean	Obedient	Logical
18	Obedient	Obedient	Obedient	Forgiving	Imaginative

Society (Feather, 1975) and for Papua New Guinea students at Goroka Teachers' College in Feather (1976). We have also recently reported an analysis of similarities and differences in the average value systems of young samples of Australians and Papua New Guineans, based upon data collected over a 10-year period from 1969.[1] Moore (1976) has published information about average value systems for student groups involving Israeli Jews, Israeli Arabs, German exchange students, Australians, Americans, and Canadians — see also Beech et al. (1978)[2] for comparisons involving students from the United States, Australia, New Zealand, and England.

The similarities and differences between the student groups in Table 3 have been discussed in detail before (Feather, 1975, Chapter 8; Rokeach, 1973, pp. 88–93) and we shall repeat only a few general points. The similarities between the value priorities for students from the three affluent countries are obvious and the rankings also resemble those presented in Table 2 for the high-school students. Presumably these three societies involve sets of influences that shape value systems among college students in similar ways. The fact that we are dealing with college youth compounds the similarity because students to some extent constitute an international subculture.

Closer inspection does, however, reveal differences in value priorities that are consistent with other analyses and with other information that we have about the cultures being compared. For example, in a wider comparison involving both children and adults, Americans emerged as more materialistic, more achievement-oriented, and more orthodoxly religious (salvation-minded) than did their Australian counterparts. The Australian respondents placed more emphasis on peace of mind, an active life, and a cheerful approach to life; they were more concerned with values that involved affiliation at the level of close interpersonal relationships — especially true friendship (for details see Feather, 1975, pp. 206 217). These differences can be understood in terms of historical influences and sociological forces. For example, Lipset (1963a, 1963b), using an approach in terms of pattern variables (Parsons, 1951, 1960), notes the emphasis on achievement in American society. Various commentators have discussed ''mateship'' as a value in Australian society (Clark, 1963; Ward, 1958).

More dramatic are some of the differences in the value priorities of students from the less affluent countries (Israel, Papua New Guinea) when compared with the other three. The Israeli differences have been discussed by Rokeach (1973) who comments on the relatively high concern of the Israeli students with competence, peace, and national security and the low order of importance they assign to two basic Christian values: salvation and being forgiving. He notes also that values concerned with the national interest appear to dominate those that favor personal and interpersonal concerns, a difference that probably reflects the stress under which Israelis were living at the time.

The Papua New Guinea results have been discussed in relation to the stage of national development of this new nation and to its history and culture (Feather, 1975, pp. 217–228). It is not surprising, for example, that the Papua New Guinea students ranked values such as a world at peace and national security very high given the assumption that, in a less affluent, developing country moving into nationhood, safety and security needs would be especially salient and values related to these needs would assume greater importance (see also Cantril, 1965). Nor it is surprising that these students assigned a higher priority to salvation when compared with the other groups, given the strong influence of the church and the missions in Papua New Guinea.

---

[1] N. T. Feather. Similarity of value systems within the same nation: Evidence from Australia and Papua New Guinea. Paper submitted for publication.

[2] Available from R. P. Beech, Chicago-Read Mental Health Center, Chicago, Illinois.

We have concentrated on comparisons with the Value Survey because this research is most recent and involves a number of different countries. But other tests of values have also been employed in cross-cultural comparisons with useful results. For example, the Kluckhohn value-orientation schema has been used in different cultures (Kluckhohn & Strodtbeck, 1961; see also Bachtold and Echvall, 1978; and Harrison, 1974, for two recent examples). The "ways to live" questionnaire has been administered to groups in the United States, Canada, India, China, Japan, and Norway (Morris, 1956). The "antecedents-consequents" procedure has been used by Triandis and his colleagues in America, Greece, India, and Japan (Triandis et al., 1972). The values of Indian and American adolescents have been compared by Sundberg, Rohila, and Tyler (1970) using Q-sort items. Ghei (1966a, 1966b) used the Edwards Personal Preference Schedule (EPPS) to compare the needs of college students in America and India. McClelland and his colleagues have also compared social motives in different cultures (see McClelland, 1971; McClelland, et al., 1958; McClelland & Winter, 1969). A value-hierarchy instrument was used by Peck (1967) to compare the value systems of Mexican and American youth. Kikuchi and Gordon (1966, 1970) have used the Survey of Interpersonal Values (Gordon, 1960) in cross-cultural studies with college students in the United States and Japan. Connell et al. (1975) have compared the responses of teenagers to items concerning beliefs about moral issues with those of their English (Eppel & Eppel, 1966) and American counterparts (Havighurst & Taba, 1949). Havighurst and his colleagues have also conducted a cross-national study involving Buenos Aires and Chicago adolescents (Havighurst, 1973; Havighurst et al., 1965). Garbarino and Bronfenbrenner (1976) have discussed similarities and differences in the socialization of moral judgment and behavior across cultures and refer to earlier research using a moral-dilemmas test (Bronfenbrenner, 1970). Coleman's (1961) study of the adolescent society in the United States may be compared with a similar one conducted in Sweden by Andersson (1969). Klineberg et al. (1979) have used questionnaire measures to look at attitudes and values in student groups in 11 different countries, particularly in relation to political protest and political identification.

These various studies traverse difficult ground, given the problems of developing measures of values that are appropriate to the cultures that are sampled, the need to establish equivalence of concepts and methods in cross-cultural research (Feather, 1975; Frey, 1970; International Studies of Values in Politics, 1971; Przeworski & Teune, 1970), and the demands for close analysis of the societies concerned when interpreting results. Cross-cultural research is very important, however, in that it takes us outside of our own shells and underlines the cultural forces at work in shaping our values. The important point is that adolescent values are influenced not only by life-cycle or ontogenetic factors, but also by the cultural context in which the child develops and by the particular problems that confront a given society in the historical period in which growth to adolescence occurs. One therefore needs to place the development of adolescent values within the matrix of a nation's culture and history, taking account of the nature of the present society, the legacy of its past, and the problem that it currently faces and tries to solve.

Value Change over Time

There is no shortage of studies that compare the value priorities of adolescents and youth at different times. The main contribution of these studies is to bring out the effects of secular trends and historical events that may shape different generations in different ways.

For example, 18-year-old adolescents in 1950 belong to a different generation or cohort than 18-year-old adolescents in 1970 and comparisons of the value systems of these two groups would have to take account of the effect of the social forces and historical events that have helped to shape each generation (for example, the Vietnam War, changes in economic and educational conditions, demographic changes, and so on). Some influences will be fairly constant across generations, others will alter in systematic ways, and some will be unique. Hence one can expect some continuity across different generations and also some change.

The whole topic of generational analysis has undergone considerable expansion in recent years, both in theoretical treatment and in increased methodological sophistication. We do not have space to consider the relevant literature here, but the reader is referred to recent reviews by Bengtson and his colleagues that consider some of the major developments (Bengtson and Starr, 1975; Bengtson, Furlong, & Laufer, 1974); to Baltes, Schaie, and others who discuss the life-span approach and implications for collecting data (Goulet & Baltes, 1970; Nesselroade & Reese, 1973; Schaie & Gribbin, 1975); and to Riley (1973) for a succinct account of issues concerned with interpreting differences when they are found.

We shall take the Yankelovich (1973, 1974) surveys as an illustration of this type of research and then briefly note some other studies as they relate to adolescent values. In extensive surveys of both college and noncollege youth Yankelovich has monitored changes in beliefs and values from 1967 to 1973. His results indicate that new value priorities incubated and emerged on American college campuses during the 1960s in a period when many dramatic events occurred that engaged the attention of college youth (for example, the Kennedy presidency, the rise of the Civil Rights movement, the student protest movement, the assassinations, and, above all, the Vietnam War). These new values involved moral norms dealing with sex, authority, religion, and obligations to others; social values concerned with money, work, family, and marriage; and a concern with self-fulfillment. They first appeared in a group that Yankelovich called the "forerunners" [see earlier discussion of Havighurst's (1975) typology] which, in the early 1960s, constituted a counterculture demeaning and reacting against the old values. Reaction against the Vietnam War focussed the opposition and led to a spurt in political radicalism. According to Yankelovich (1974), "Inevitably, the Vietnam-inspired political radicalism became entangled with the cluster of new life styles and social values that had their genesis in an earlier period" (p. 8). With the end of the war the cultural revolution continued, but the political revolution moved backwards. Thus "the enduring heritage of the 1960s is the new social values that grew on the nation's campuses during that same fateful period and now have grown stronger and more powerful" (Yankelovich, 1974, p. 9).

In his recent survey, Yankelovich (1974) finds that the new values have diffused more widely to other segments of the population and that there now exists a sometimes curious mixture of the new values with older, more traditional beliefs among both college and noncollege youth with some differences remaining between these two groups. These results are of considerable interest for they demonstrate changes in values occurring for different segments of the population at different times and remind us of the importance of looking at continuity and change in value systems for different segments of the same generation as well as between generations. By way of example, in the most recent Yankelovich (1974) survey both college and noncollege youth showed a decline in the percentage nominating religion; patriotism; and leading a clean, moral life as very important values (see Table 4). More than 70% of the 1973 respondents in both groups

Table 4   Percentage of College Youth and Noncollege Youth Who Endorsed Various Personal Values as Very Important in Yankelovich Surveys (1969 and 1973)

Value	Total College %		Total Noncollege %	
	1969	1973	1969	1973
Love	85	87	90	88
Friendship	84	86	90	87
Fulfilling yourself as a person	—[a]	87	—	87
Family	—	68	—	81
Privacy	62	71	74	78
Education	80	76	81	75
Doing things for others	51	56	55	64
Living a clean and moral life	46	34	78	57
Work	—	43	—	53
Being creative	—	50	—	52
Being close to nature	—	45	—	50
Having children	—	31	—	45
Religion	39	23	65	42
Patriotism	35	19	61	40
Money	18	20	40	34
Changing society	33	24	29	27

Source: Yankelovich (1974).
[a]Percentages from the 1969 survey were not available for some values.

endorsed love, friendship, fulfilling yourself as a person, privacy, and education as very important values, but 45% or less endorsed having children, religion, patriotism, money, and changing society as very important. Yankelovich also notes that, among noncollege youth, there has been a decline in beliefs supporting the puritan ethic in American life, a movement toward freer and more open attitudes toward sex, a shift in attitudes away from endorsing war as an instrument of national policy, an erosion in support for authority and conformity, and other changes in the direction of college norms of the late 1960s. Noncollege youth, however, place more emphasis on the family as a very important personal value than do college youth (81% versus 68%) and on having children (45% versus 31%).

The youth movement has, of course, been the focus of a great deal of discussion (for example, Braungart, 1975; Feather, 1975; Havighurst, 1975; Light & Laufer, 1975; Lipset, 1976; Sampson, 1967; and the 1974 issues on "Youth, Generations, and Social Change" from the *Journal of Social Issues*). Havighurst (1975) has described a movement from instrumental to expressive values in American society and draws on the Yankelovich (1973) findings in constructing the typology of youth noted earlier in this chapter. Light and Laufer (1975) have also described a shift to concern with self-fulfilment and liberation among contemporary youth that conflicts with many of the values of industry, technology, and the large research-oriented universities. Lipset (1976) has provided illuminating discussion of factors involved in the rise of the student-protest movement, drawing attention to such factors as the special responsiveness of students to political trends and the need for social change, the opportunities they have to effect protest in the unique environment of the university, the impact of an intelligentsia that helps to liberalize opinions, and the presence of a relatively large youth cohort in the 1960s compared with other generations. Other sociologists have talked about postindustrial society and the emergence of a new consciousness (Bell, 1973; Reich, 1970). We mention these works to underline the fact that adolescent values are closely intertwined with the forces and fabric of society and with the details of history.

Many other studies have mapped value-change across time for adolescent and youth groups. These will be mentioned briefly, not because they lack importance but because we lack space. Lipset (1976) has referred to other survey studies of college youth that supplement the Yankelovich (1973, 1974) surveys. Hoge and Bender (1974) found rather large changes occurring in theoretical, aesthetic, and religious values among three groups of Dartmouth College students who were tested with the Study of Values (Allport & Vernon, 1931) between 1931 and 1956 and restudied as alumni between 1952 and 1969. Their data supported a "current-experiences" model that stresses the similar impact of historical events on college graduates of all ages and also on students. But they note the importance of considering the appropriateness of "cohort" and "standard-life-cycle" models for considering change as well, and refer to earlier literature relating to the three kinds of models. Studies of changes in religious attitudes and values have also been recently reported by Hastings and Hoge (1972) in the United States and by Pilkington et al. (1976) in England — both of which show a movement away from religion among college youth in recent years.

In a unique study that spans half a century of change, Caplow and Bahr (1979) conducted a survey of the attitudes of high school students in "Middletown," the midwestern community that the Lynds began to investigate in 1924 (Lynd and Lynd, 1929). The attitude questionnaire included 20 attitude items from the questionnaire that the Lynds had administered to a comparable population 53 years earlier. On the basis of their results, Caplow and Bahr (1979) conclude that ". . . some of the religious, political, and social attitudes of the post World War I era have persisted with remarkable tenacity" (p. 15) among Middletown's adolescents. The data do not indicate ". . . any trace of the disintegration of traditional social values that is commonly described by observers who rely on their own intuitions" (p. 17). According to Caplow and Bahr (1979), it appears that the young people of Middletown in 1977 ". . . are as strongly imbued with religion, patriotism, and the Protestant ethic as their grandparents were at the same age . . ." (p. 17), but that ". . . they are also more tolerant of those who disagree with them, or who hold other values, . . ." (p. 17).

Major studies of student attitudes and values have been conducted by Astin and his colleagues (Astin, 1977a, 1977b) at UCLA during the late 1960s and the 1970s, using data obtained year by year from several hundred thousand freshmen who entered an average of 600 colleges of various types. Astin and his colleagues have also followed up about 200,000 of the students to measure changes in values and personal opinions over time so as to obtain information about the effect of college on their values and opinions. The data are too numerous to describe in detail (see Astin, 1977a, 1977b). As far as values are concerned, however, Astin (1977b) reports that in general, ". . . the freshmen responses show declining idealism and increasing cynicism and materialism, particularly during the last five years" (p. 50). For example, in the 1967 survey, "developing a meaningful philosophy of life" was one of the most popular life goals, being endorsed by 79% of the men and 88% of the women. But only 61% of the entering 1976 freshmen considered it a very important goal. And only about a third of that class reported a commitment to the idea of "influencing social values" or "keeping up with political affairs." Moreover, from 1971 to 1976 the goal of "being well-off financially" increased from 50 to 61% among men, and from 28 to 45% among women. Astin (1977b) reports that the 1976 freshmen ''. . . also showed an increasing concern for such status-oriented goals as becoming an authority in their field, gaining recognition from their peers or colleagues, and having administrative responsibility for the work of others'' (p. 50). Some of these changes are likely to be related to secular events, especially to the effect of the flagging world economy on youths' opportunities for employment in the 1970s. For example, one would expect that declining job opportunities would be associated with evidence that college youth was becoming increasingly concerned with their futures in the world of work, as expressed in their hopes for financial security linked to high-status jobs. This is a realistic response to worsening economic circumstances.

In the United Kingdom, Wright and Cox (1971) compared the answers given to questionnaire items about moral beliefs by a large group of English grammar-school sixth-formers tested in 1963 with another large group tested in 1970 (most of the boys and girls were 17 to 19 years of age). They found that the greatest change was toward increased permissiveness in attitudes toward sexual behavior, but there were changes on other issues as well. During 1969 Gorsuch and Smith (1972) administered the Crissman (1942, 1950) questionnaire about the ''wrongness'' of 50 acts to American students at the University of Wyoming and the Ohio State University. They, too, found a definite shift in the area of sexual behavior (decreases in the severity of ratings), but most other changes were fairly small, the judgments of the college students being quite similar to those of previous years. As noted previously, Yankelovich (1974) also found increasing liberalism among college youth on issues concerning sexual freedom. Astin's (1977) survey also indicates that today's college students have more liberal attitudes toward sex than those of a decade ago.

Finally, Morris and Small (1971) compared responses to the ''ways to live'' scale (Morris, 1956) from college students in the United States who were tested in 1970 with those of students tested around 1950. They found a marked drop in liking for Way 1 (''preserve the best that man has attained''), but both the 1950 and 1970 respondents were most in favor of Way 7 (''integrate action, enjoyment, and contemplation''). Overall, Morris and Small found that the 1970 American students did not differ greatly from the 1950 students and they concluded that the differences ''. . . are primarily, though not entirely, differences in strategy, in operative rather than conceived values'' (p. 260) — that is, in values manifested in conduct rather than in values assessed verbally.

Sex Differences in Adolescent Values

Given the theoretical speculations about sex differences in orientations mentioned earlier in this chapter, one might expect to find differences in value priorities between the two sexes. In a review of earlier studies dominated by use of the Study of Values (Allport & Vernon, 1931), Dukes (1955) concluded that there is ample evidence that men score higher than women on the Allport-Vernon theoretical, economic, and political values but lower on the aesthetic, religious, and social. Morris (1956) observed that men and women answering the ''ways to live'' questionnaire showed that they followed closely the same cultural patterns. But there was some suggestion that women were lower than men on a factor called ''enjoyment and progress through action,'' whereas women were higher than men on a factor called ''receptivity and sympathetic concern.'' In the United States, for example, women rated the passive, devoted, and dutiful Way 13 (''obey the cosmic purposes'') higher than did men, whereas men rated the controlled, vigilant, and rational

Way 10 ("control the self stoically") and the active, adventurous, and powerful Way 12 ("chance adventuresome deeds") higher than did women. These sex differences in ratings occurred in both the 1950 samples and in the 1970 samples (see Morris & Small, 1971, Table 1).

These various differences slot in rather well with a recent integrative analysis by Jeanne Block (1973). She has looked at conceptions of sex roles cross-culturally and also longitudinally in terms of Loevinger's (1966, 1976) model of ego development. She also employs Bakan's (1966) distinction between *agency* and *communion,* conceived of as two fundamental modalities that are characteristic of all living forms. Block (1973) describes these two modes as follows:

Agency is concerned with the organism as an individual and manifests itself in self-protection, self-assertion, and self-expansion. Communion is descriptive of the individual organism as it exists in some larger organism of which it is a part and manifests itself in the sense of being at one with other organisms. [P. 515]

For Bakan (1966), a fundamental task in the development of any individual is "to try to mitigate agency with communion" (p. 14) — that is, to balance and integrate the two modes.

Block (1973) presents evidence indicating that agency in boys is encouraged by parents in childhood socialization, though with some behavioral proscriptions, whereas for girls there is an emphasis on the interpersonal, communal aspects of being. She notes also that Barry, Bacon, and Child (1957) in a survey of ethnographic material from mostly nonliterate cultures, ". . . found a widespread pattern of greater socialization pressure toward nurturance, obedience, and responsibility in girls, while for boys socialization pressure was directed toward self-reliance and achievement strivings" (p. 518). Moreover, in a study of conceptualizations in six different countries (Norway, Sweden, Denmark, Finland, England, and the United States), using data from university students, Block (1973) found impressive cross-cultural stability in the ideal self-descriptions of males and females and differential emphases on agency and communion in the two sexes. Males in the United States, for example, put more emphasis on agentic adjectives, such as practical, assertive, dominating, competitive, critical, rational, and ambitious, when compared with females. Females in the United States put more emphasis on communal adjectives, such as loving, sympathetic, generous, sensitive, and artistic, when compared with males. In a related study Carlson (1971) also found similar results, with men representing their self-image in impersonal, individual terms and women representing their self-images in interpersonal terms. Consistent with these findings, Ahlgren and Johnson (1979), using a sample of schoolchildren from a midwestern school district, found that females showed consistently more positive attitudes toward cooperation in school, and that males showed consistently more positive attitudes toward competition. These differences in attitudes occurred over grades 2–12 but were greatest in grades 8–10.

Block (1973) has also provided developmental data in which self-descriptions that involved agentic/communal modes were related to level of moral and ego development. She has also reported longitudinal findings that present further information about sex roles and socialization. The former data supported the view that higher levels of moral and ego functioning are associated with the development of self concepts that integrate agentic and communal concerns. The latter findings led Block (1973) to the interesting conclusion that: "The sex role definitions and behavioral options for women . . . are narrowed by the socialization process, whereas, for men, the sex role definitions and behavioral options are broadened by socialization'' (pp. 525–526). That is, the socialization process for men is more likely to encourage some degree of androgyny in sex-role definitions, with some integration of agency and communion, whereas the socialization process for women tends to "reinforce the nurturant, docile, submissive and conservative aspects of the traditionally defined female role and discourages personal qualities conventionally defined as masculine'' (Block, 1973, p. 525) — for a somewhat different view that relates more to the implications of changing sex roles for males and females in contemporary society, see Douvan (1975). One should note that the results cited by Block (1973) are relative to culture, time, and generation or cohort.

Australian studies with high-school and university or college students repeat some of the findings about sex differences that we have just mentioned. In the Flinders University program, for example, boys from secondary schools ranked the following values from the Value Survey (Rokeach, 1973) as relatively more important than did girls: a comfortable life, an exciting life, mature love, pleasure, ambitious, capable, independent, intellectual, logical, and self-controlled. But girls ranked the following values as higher in importance when compared with boys: a world at peace, a world of beauty, equality, inner harmony, wisdom, cheerful, forgiving, helpful, honest, loving, and polite (Feather, 1975, Table 5–11). Many of these differences also occurred in data from extensive surveys conducted in metropolitan Adelaide in 1972 and 1973 with parents and their children (Feather, 1975, Table 6–7).

In a recent study, two different samples of undergraduate students at Flinders University answered a sex-role inventory developed by Bem (1974). Analyses of responses at the item level showed that, in both samples, males rated the following traits as significantly more true of themselves than did females: athletic, has leadership abilities, willing to take risks, masculine, acts as a leader, competitive, aggressive, makes decisions easily, and dominant. Females rated the following traits as significantly more true of themselves than did males in both samples: feminine, affectionate, sympathetic, gullible, tender, loyal, sensitive to the needs of others, understanding, sincere, eager to soothe hurt feelings, and loves children (Feather, 1978a). The similarities to Block's (1973) findings are obvious.

Finally, in the Connell et al. (1975) study of Sydney teenagers, girls tended to maintain stricter standards with age as far as moral beliefs about responsibility, honesty, and friendship were concerned. They were also more conscientious in church attendance. In English studies, girls scored higher on measures of religious belief and practice than did boys both in the early 1960s and the early 1970s, though the evidence also indicated that, over the intervening years, women students moved further away from religion than did men (Pilkington et al., 1976; Wright & Cox, 1971).

These various studies demonstrate differences in value priorities between boys and girls that are consistent with the general discussions in the literature about psychodynamic aspects of development, sex-typing, and socialization, which we mentioned earlier in this chapter. No doubt one could add other evidence to the list. It is fair to say, however, that the study of sex differences in values is still in its infancy and that there is plenty of scope for further theoretical and empirical developments. Such developments will have to take account of similarities and differences in socialization practices, both across cultures and at different times in history. That is, they should deal with cultural diversity and with social change. And they should recognize that boys and girls end up with many value priorities in common as well as differing in some of their important concerns. A focus on differences can sometimes ignore the extensive overlap that occurs between the sexes in psychological characteristics.

Subdividing the Adolescent Population

We have already discussed one subdivision of the adolescent population (males versus females) and referred to others as well (for example, college youth versus noncollege youth). It is obvious that there are many other subgroups that one can look at when comparing adolescent value systems: working-class youth versus middle-class youth, activists versus nonactivists, city youth versus rural youth, juvenile offenders versus nonoffenders, youth with different political commitments, Protestant versus Catholic youth, immigrant youth versus native-born youth, married youth versus unmarried youth, and so on. The pie can be sliced in many different ways within the one society and for the same generation so as to bring out similarities and differences in value priorities. And most of the work remains to be done.

In *Values in Education and Society* we have summarized theory and research on the value systems of student activists, juvenile offenders, and immigrant youth, and have presented new evidence using the Rokeach Value Survey (Feather, 1975, Chapter 7). We shall focus here on the former two subgroups. Activist respondents in Australia ranked the following values significantly higher in importance than did control respondents: a world at peace, a world of beauty, equality, freedom, courageous, helpful, imaginative, and loving. They ranked a comfortable life, family security, happiness, national security, salvation, ambitious, capable, cheerful, clean, obedient, polite, and responsible as less important on the average than did the controls. These results are consistent with other evidence and discussions about the youth movement that are too numerous to summarize here (see Ellerman & Feather, 1976). The juvenile offenders from two Adelaide training centers also differed from controls in their value priorities. For example, the juvenile offenders placed being clean at the top of their hierarchy of instrumental values, whereas the control respondents placed this value at the bottom.

The results for both the student activists and juvenile offenders have been compared and then discussed in relation to the classic analysis by Merton (1968, 1971) of the effects of a disjunction between dominant societal goals and the institutionalized means of attaining these goals — the activist displaying what Merton calls nonconforming behavior and the delinquent showing aberrant behavior, but both groups significantly departing from social norms. The detailed comparison of the average value systems of these two groups showed that they were very different in their priorities. The student activists were much more concerned with general social goals; with honest, imaginative, and intelligent ways of behaving; and with prosocial modes of conduct than were the delinquents. The delinquent boys put more emphasis on immediate hedonistic concerns; stimulus-seeking; material comforts; and with being ambitious, cheerful, and clean than did the student activists. But both groups were alike in giving a relatively high priority to being courageous and relatively low priorities to being responsible and self-controlled when compared with other young males tested in the Flinders University program. As we noted previously (Feather, 1975): "Although the two groups were marching to different drummers, moving toward different terminal goals, they both shared a strong commitment to action without high regard for the inhibitions of control and restraint'' (p. 193).

Other studies have investigated the value systems of different groups of adolescents in relation to their courses of study and to the vocational choices they make (Dukes, 1955; Feather, 1975; Rosenberg, 1957). The Flinders University program in particular has examined the extent to which the value systems of high-school or university students match those they attribute to the environments in which they presently work or are currently entering, and the likely effects of a mismatch. More generally, Rokeach (1973) has looked at value systems in the United States in relation to differences in sex, social class, age, race, religion, and politics — but for the population as a whole rather than for adolescents. Also, more generally, Kohn (1977) has explored the effects of social class on values in the United States arguing that:

> The higher a person's social class position, the greater is the likelihood that he will value self-direction, both for his children and for himself, and that his orientational system will be predicated on the belief that self-direction is both possible and efficacious. The lower a person's social class position, the greater the likelihood that he will value conformity to external authority and that he will believe in following the dictates of authority as the wisest, perhaps the only feasible, course of action. [P. 2]

Kohn believes that the social class-values relationship results from systematic differences in conditions of life, especially one's occupational life, and presents evidence in support of this claim. We noted earlier that Havighurst (1975) considers that the largest proportion of "practical-minded" youth have lower-middle-class and stable manual-working-class families. These are the youth who, according to Havighurst (1975), are more likely to conform to the traditional values involving instrumentalism and materialism as opposed to self-expression and idealism. Rokeach's (1973) analysis of social class differences in value priorities is not inconsistent with Kohn's (1977) thesis, although Rokeach (1973) concluded that " . . . the present data also suggest that the culture of poverty . . . and the culture of affluence differ far more extensively than Kohn's data indicate" (p. 63).

These wider studies, that map value differences across different segments of society, highlight the importance of considering where a person is located in the social structure and what influences and socioeconomic realities within that location shape his or her development and control the behavioral options that are available. It is to a consideration of the more important socializing influences that we now turn.

SOCIALIZING INFLUENCES ON ADOLESCENT VALUE SYSTEMS

The various agents of socialization that influence the adolescent have been discussed in detail in most books on adolescence (for example Adams, 1973; Coleman, 1961; Coleman et al., 1974; Douvan & Adelson, 1966; Dragastin & Elder, 1975; Grinder, 1969; Havighurst & Dreyer, 1975; Rogers, 1972); by Campbell (1969) in a chapter on adolescent socialization in Goslin's (1969) handbook; and by various authors interested in political socialization (for example, Dawson & Prewitt, 1969; Hess & Torney, 1967; Hyman, 1959; Jennings & Niemi, 1974; Sears, 1969). These discussions refer to the role of the family, the school, the peer group, and the mass media as agents by means of which the adolescent learns about his culture and subculture and acquires orientations and ways of behaving that are generally adaptive. Most analyses of socialization also refer to psychological theories about how the learning proceeds. For example, Jennings and Niemi (1974) mention observational learning, reinforcement and psychoanalytic theory, and cognitive-developmental theory as important frameworks for understanding socialization;

Baumrind (1975) adds two other processes that may be important in understanding adolescent identity, namely, reciprocal role assumption and psychological reactance.

It is trite to observe that these various agents of socialization influence adolescent values. What is needed are detailed studies of their effects on values that are both methodologically sophisticated and theoretically informative. Unfortunately there are few such studies available. In this next section we shall concentrate on some recent investigations of the school and the family as they relate to adolescent values. In so doing, we do not imply that the peer group and the mass media are unimportant influences. Far from it. They have strong effects that are generally acknowledged. But in view of the large amount that has been written about socialization, we can afford to be a bit selective and so we focus on studies that come from or relate to our own research program.

The School: Flinders Studies

There is a vast literature on the impact of school and college on the students who attend them, going back at least to the classic Bennington study (Newcomb, 1943; Newcomb et al., 1967; see also Newcomb, 1978). Feldman and Newcomb (1969) have reviewed much of the American research. They showed that freshman-to-senior changes among students occurred in several characteristics with considerable uniformity across different colleges and universities. The senior students tended to be less authoritarian, less conservative, less prejudiced, and more sensitive to aesthetic experiences than the freshmen. Senior students also demonstrated increasing intellectual interests and capacities and a declining commitment to religion, especially in its orthodox forms. In general, the overall picture was one in which the seniors became increasingly open to new experiences and displayed greater tolerance. Feldman and Newcomb (1969) suggested that the college experience may act to accentuate differences among students that were already present when the students selected their college, academic majors, and so on. They noted many methodological inadequacies and pitfalls in this area of research (for example, the lack of control groups, the need to control for attrition) and argued for future studies that ask more complex questions not only about different institutional environments, different kinds of students, and different ways of change but also about the possible interactive effects of these and other factors. One also hopes that these studies will be based on theory as well as meeting the needs of evaluation research.

The survey studies by Astin and his colleagues (Astin, 1977a, 1977b) lend more recent support to some of Feldman and Newcomb's (1969) conclusions. In his follow-up studies of freshmen entering colleges in the United States over the past decade, Astin found evidence of increasing liberalism among students during their years in college. He concluded that, ". . . in effect college seems to polarize students: those who arrive as liberals tend to become more so; many moderates turn into liberals; and the conservatives simply remain conservatives" (p. 53). Increases in political liberalism were more likely to occur among men, among younger students, among bright students, among students concentrating in the humanities, arts, and social sciences, and (when, other factors were controlled) among those who lived on campus. The largest increases in political liberalism among students tended to occur in the elite, selective four-year colleges. Astin also found substantial declines in religious belief and behavior during college, declines that occurred more often among men and most often among the brighter students (Astin, 1977b, p. 53).

In a study at Flinders University that used control groups (Feather, 1975, pp. 97–106) students tested on enrollment in 1969 were retested in 1971 using the Value Survey

(Rokeach, 1973). The analysis of results showed that the following values increased significantly in relative importance over the two-and-one-half-year interval: a world of beauty, mature love, intellectual, forgiving, and loving. The following values decreased in relative importance: a sense of accomplishment, national security, salvation, ambitious, obedient, polite, and self-controlled. Most of these differences were consistent with the general pattern of change noted by Feldman and Newcomb (1969). But these changes occurred not only in the university group, but also in the two control groups (those students who had left to study at another tertiary institution and those who were no longer in tertiary study). There was a virtual absence of changes that applied only to the Flinders students. Nor was there any evidence of accentuation of value differences from 1969 to 1971 among students enrolled in different schools within the university when more detailed analyses were conducted (see also Thistlethwaite, 1973).

Other studies in the Flinders program have provided information about how students perceive high-school or university environments. As one might expect, high-school students saw their schools as emphasizing values concerned with achievement, competence, rules of conduct, and responsibility (Feather, 1975, pp. 93–94). The more the students' own value priorities diverged from those they attributed to their schools, the more dissatisfied they were with aspects of the school environment (Feather, 1975, Chapter 4). The principle of person-environment fit also operated at the university level because incoming students were more likely to enroll in schools within the university that were perceived as promoting values congruent with their own than in schools with more divergent values (Feather, 1975, Chapter 3). These studies have been discussed within the context of both discrepancy and reinforcement theory (Feather, 1975, pp. 61–62) and demonstrate a kind of cognitive ecology in which environments are selected that, where possible, match cognitive structures.

The Family: Flinders Studies

The family has been traditionally regarded as the prime agent of socialization for preadults and a lot of evidence now exists to show children will resemble their parents in some of their social and political orientations and behaviors (for example, Acock & Bengtson, 1976; Bengtson, 1975; Bengtson & Starr, 1974; Hill, 1970; Jennings & Niemi, 1968, 1974; Feather, 1975; Feather, 1978b; Kandel & Lesser, 1972; Thomas, 1971; Troll, Neugarten, & Kraines, 1969) — though variations among studies in the degrees of resemblance obtained show that there is still a lot to be explained. Indeed some observers have preferred to focus on discontinuities between parents and their children and to interpret these in terms of intergenerational conflict and rebellion (for example, Feuer, 1969), while others have argued that both continuity and conflict influence the development of student ideology (for example, Block, 1972; Kraut & Lewis, 1975).

This debate implies the importance of looking at: (1) the family in detail as an interpersonal, interactive system within which influence can flow from children to parents as well as in the reverse order and (2) at the roles of both mother and father as influencing agents and the degree to which their separate and combined effects are moderated according to whether the child is male or female, first born or later-born, and so on. The debate also implies the need to consider the effects of the family in relation to the wider society, where the family is located in the social structure, and what sociopolitical trends and events impinge on it. All of this is to say that the causes of similarities and differences between parents and their children in their values and political and social orientations are obviously complex and that a simple lineage model is insufficient to account for them (see the excellent discussions by Bengtson, 1970; Bengtson, Furlong, & Laufer, 1974; and Bengtson & Starr, 1975, which also argue for a multivariate model).

We have conducted two extensive surveys of families in metropolitan Adelaide, one in 1972 and the other in 1973, both involving the Value Survey (Rokeach, 1973). Measures of social attitudes were also included — general conservatism (Wilson & Patterson, 1968; Wilson, 1973) in the first survey and a questionnaire about how people explain poverty (Feagin, 1972) in the second. In each survey parents were tested along with children who were 14-years-old or more. The mean age of the parents was in the 40s; the mean age of the children was around 18 years. The results have been presented and discussed in *Values in Education and Society* (Feather, 1975, Chapter 6). They will be briefly summarized here.

The results showed that there was value congruence as well as value discrepancy when the average value systems of parents were compared with those of their children — the similarity coefficients based on the aggregate data were all positive, but they varied in size. In line with the discussion by Douvan and Adelson (1966) noted earlier, daughters were closer to their parents than were sons in their average value systems. A detailed within-family comparison of conservatism scores also showed that daughters were more similar to their parents than sons were, although the resemblances were moderated by socioeconomic status, in that the similarity of daughters to fathers was reduced in lower SES families (see Feather, 1978b, for a discussion of these results and related findings).

Both parents and children ranked values, such as a world at peace, happiness, wisdom, honest, and responsible, high in importance and values, such as pleasure, social recognition, salvation, obedient, and imaginative, low in importance. As with all data based on the Value Survey, it must be remembered that terminal or instrumental values that are assigned low rankings are not necessarily unimportant to the person. Rather, they are less important relative to other values. When one examines the significant differences in value priorities between parents and their children that were replicated from the 1972 to the 1973 survey, it is clear that parents assigned relatively more importance to values concerning both family and national security, self-respect and responsibility, politeness to others and cleanliness, and competence (that is, being capable). The children assigned relatively more importance than their parents to such values as excitement and pleasure, equality and freedom, a world of beauty, close companionship with others, and a broad-minded and imaginative stance toward the world. The results also showed that parents were more conservative than their children and that they were more likely to blame poverty on the poor themselves — that is, in terms of individualistic rather than social-structural reasons.

These similarities and differences reflect sets of influences on the development of values and social attitudes that one cannot really unravel in a cross-sectional study. Some of the differences have an ontogenetic basis. We noted before that the relatively high priority assigned to true friendship by teen-age children no doubt reflects the importance of companionship and the peer group for young people coping with the problems of adolescence. And the emphasis that the older generation puts on family security (and this is an emphasis that crosses national frontiers — see Rokeach, 1973) would relate to their responsibility in raising and caring for their children and maintaining the family unit. As we have indicated previously (Feather, 1975): "These sorts of problems are universal, rooted in biology, in changing personal needs, and in the different roles and responsibilities that one assumes throughout life" (p. 143). But one should not forget the impact of unique sociocultural trends or events that are either generation-specific or common to different age cohorts and that may also have a lasting effect on producing both similarity and difference between the generations [see, for example, Elder's (1974) study of children of the Great Depression].

These results and those from other studies suggest that one should not discount the family as an important force in the socialization of adolescent values. It is noteworthy, for example, that Kohn (1977) found that both mothers and fathers from middle- and working-class families in the United States emphasized honesty, happiness, considera- tion, obedience, and dependability as highly desirable characteristics in boys and girls and that some of these values ranked high for both parents and children in the Flinders University studies, despite cultural differences. In a perceptive review of research on adolescent socialization Campbell (1969) argues that:

> Any scholarly attempt to describe and dramatize the growth of peer group influences, the power of youth culture, the adolescent's struggle for freedom, etc., must eventually come to terms with the fact that family structures endure through the entire period of adolescence — as residential, affectional, and companionship units. . . . The research literature is almost entirely compatible with the conclusions that ties between parents and children remain close throughout the adolescent years; that the positive orientation toward parents does not diminish, and may indeed increase, during adolescence; and that parents and the parent-child relationship are both important influences on the adolescent. [Pp. 829–831]

Nor should one ignore the fact that the evidence suggests that most children have generally close and friendly relationships with their parents and regard them as an important reference source (Bengtson, 1970; Campbell, 1969; Curtis, 1975; Offer & Offer, in press).

Other Studies

Not much has been done to explore the details of value similarities and differences between adolescent subgroups that have different histories of parent-child relationships (for example, the adolescent prototypes described earlier in this chapter). Smith (1969a) compared the results of Q-sorts in which respondents sorted adjectives into seven equal piles, ranging from those most saliently descriptive of the ideal self to those most saliently contrary to the ideal self. He found that undergraduate Free Speech Movement (FSM) arrestees were less likely to describe themselves in terms of Protestant ethic values (for example, ambitious, conventional, competitive, self-controlled, and so on) but were more likely to use adjectives, such as unfettered, rebellious, imaginative, creative, and free, when compared with a student control group [see also the Ellerman and Feather (1976) results described in an earlier section]. There were different adjective profiles for different subgroups labeled as inactives, conventionalists, constructivists, broad-spectrum ac- tivists, and dissenters. More research is needed on the value systems of the various adolescent typologies that have been proposed in the literature.

In recent years we have seen the application of improved methodologies, especially in studies of political socialization, that allow for multivariate effects and that, in some cases, go beyond cross-sectional designs to make comparisons over time (for a brief summary see Feather, 1975, pp. 143–146). Noteworthy here is the research into the political character of adolescence by Jennings and Niemi (1968, 1974) and their related study of continuity and change in political orientations over time in both parents and their children (Jennings & Niemi, 1975). Also important is the research by Bengtson and his colleagues on adolescent values and the factors that influence them (for example, Acock & Bengtson, 1976; Bengtson, 1975). The field is becoming far more sophisticated.

This recent research is too complex and rich to summarize here, but some general conclusions from the Jennings and Niemi (1974) monograph are worth noting. After describing some of the main findings about the impact of family and school, these authors indicate that these factors by no means provide a complete account of the political dispositions of 18-year-olds — there is much that cannot be explained by direct appeal to the principal agents of learning. They suggest that this is so for several reasons. The growing child is subject to a whole range of social conditioners; much socialization is low-key and haphazard; an adolescent's political character only partly derives from home and school and is subject to the impact of political events; and sole reliance on specific agents when accounting for political socialization is insufficient because it fails to recognize the active role of the child in working over experience and developing constructions of reality that become more sophisticated with movement through childhood and adolescence. It is to this latter point that we now turn.

ADOLESCENT VALUES AND DEVELOPMENTAL STAGES

When considering the development of adolescent values, it is important to take account of both children's emerging capacities and their active role as processors of information. Children are not passive receivers, moulded like clay by outside forces, but are actively involved in interpreting, constructing, and transforming experience in a unique way, influenced by the nature of the information that they encounter and by their level of maturity. This theme has a long history in the psychology of cognition. In more specific form it emerges as a fundamental aspect of stage theories of moral development provided by Piaget (1932) and, more recently, by Kohlberg (1969, 1976). It also appears in theories of moral character and ego development that, in line with most other developmental perspectives, emphasize that the basic task of a living organism is to adjust internal conditions to external demands. It is accepted that these adjustments are the outcomes of changes that occur both in the organism and in the environment as the individual matures and encounters new conditions (for example, Hogan, 1973; Loevinger, 1966, 1976; Loevinger & Wessler, 1970; Peck & Havighurst, 1960; Riegel, 1976).

As Adelson (1975) points out on the basis of the research that he and his colleagues have conducted, it is naive to expect a preadolescent or young adolescent to provide much in the way of answers to questions about political institutions and ideology because the capacity to manage abstract concepts or to use a set of general principles may not have developed sufficiently. It is only with increasing maturity that the adolescent becomes able to form generalized concepts, to understand the role of history and the impact of the present on the future, to get some feeling for social change and the possibility that man and social institutions may alter and be altered, to weigh up the wider costs and benefits of actions and decisions, and to develop principles and frameworks for judging particular events (Adelson, 1975; see also Connell, 1971; Walker & Richards, 1979). These considerations imply that general questionnaires, such as the Value Survey (Rokeach, 1973), may be inappropriate for young teenagers because the abstract concepts that they assume exist may not be present at that age or may be there only in rather concrete and rudimentary form, linked to specific instances.

What do we know about the relationship of particular values to stages of ego development and moral development in older adolescents? Research involving Kohlberg's theory of moral development (Kohlberg, 1969) and Loevinger's related stage theory of ego development (Loevinger, 1976) is relevant here. Kohlberg's theory distinguishes six *stages* in the development of moral reasoning and these six stages fall into three broad *levels:* a pre-moral level, a level of conventional morality, and a level of postconventional or principled morality (Kohlberg, 1969); see Chapter 9 of this handbook for more details. Loevinger's (1976) related model is more general but also involves a succession of stages. Jeanne Block (1973) found some evidence that students who were at Stage 6 in their moral reasoning, as assessed by Kohlberg's moral-dilemmas procedure (Kohlberg, 1969), and students who were at the "conscientious" level of ego development, as assessed by Loevinger's procedure (Loevinger & Wessler, 1970), were more likely to describe themselves by using adjectives that combined agency and communion (Bakan, 1966) than did students at lower levels of moral or ego development. The Block data on moral reasoning were abstracted from an earlier report by Haan, Smith, and Block (1968) that investigated a number of correlates of moral reasoning. These results are too numerous to summarize in full, but some findings reported by Smith (1969a) may be noted. At Level 2 of the Kohlberg sequence of moral reasoning (the conventional role-conformity level, involving "personal concordance" and "law-and-order" orientations), both males and females emphasized the following adjectives in Q-sorts for their "idealized selves" (presumably providing evidence about their important values): ambitious, competitive, foresightful, orderly, sociable, and responsible. Smith (1969a) describes these as the familiar values of the Protestant ethic. At Level 3 in moral reasoning (the principled or postconventional level involving "social-contract" and "individual-principles" orientations), males emphasized the following adjectives in their ideal Q-sorts: rebellious, idealistic, creative, sensitive, loving, self-controlled, perceptive, empathic, and altruistic. There were fewer items that emerged as distinctive for women at this level: rebellious, free, sensitive, and individualistic. Smith (1969a) concludes:

> At this point in history, then, conventionality in moral judgment goes with a particular, presently conventional pattern of moral values. The Morality of Self-Accepted Principles seems, rather, to be linked with the humanistic values of self-actualization. . . . [P. 338]

Again we should note that these results are relative to time (late 1960s), to sample (college students), to place (the Berkeley campus), and they may not occur at other periods in history or in other cultures for other samples of youth. Clearly we need more research.

In a study with seventh-, ninth-, and eleventh-grade male high-school students, McLellan (1970) found that two values from the Value Survey (Rokeach, 1973) — freedom and obedient — discriminated among Kohlberg's moral stages when age was held constant. Rankings of freedom were found to be highest at Stage 2 (the "instrumentalist relativist" orientation) and at Stage 5 (the "social contract" orientation). Rankings of obedient were highest at Stage 1 (the "obedience-and-punishment" orientation) and at Stage 4 (the "law-and-order" orientation).

Fishkin, Keniston, and MacKinnon (1973), in a study that involved a sample of university students from eight large United States campuses, showed that conservative ideology, as assessed by endorsement of conservative political slogans (for example, "Better dead than red" or "I fight poverty — I work"), was unequivocally associated with Stage 4 conventional reasoning as assessed by the Kohlberg procedure. Endorsement of violent radical political slogans (for example "Power to the people" or "Kill the pigs") was more typical of moral reasoning at the preconventional level. Students classified at postconventional levels were more likely to reject conservative political slogans. These findings were consistent with the behavioral evidence provided by Haan, Smith, and Block (1968). This showed that students at both extremely high and extremely low levels of moral development were overrepresented among the Free Speech movement arrestees on the Berkeley campus, whereas those at the conventional stages (the more modal stages) were very rarely involved in the sit-in.

That traditional, conventional thinking may be associated with value systems different from those associated with more radical and libertarian points of view is also suggested in our own work (Feather, 1975, 1977). Respondents from the 1972 Adelaide survey with high scores on the Wilson and Patterson (1968) Conservatism Scale had a different pattern of terminal and instrumental values than did those with low-conservatism scores. The high conservatives were more likely to stress values involving national security, orthodox religion, respect for authority, and conventional rules of conduct when compared with the low conservatives. In contrast, the low conservatives were more likely to emphasize equal opportunity, freedom, a stimulating and active life, open-mindedness, a creative stance toward the world, logic and intelligence, and sexual and spiritual intimacy when compared with the high conservatives. More recent multiple regression analyses have explored the value correlates of conservatism in much more detail (Feather, in press-a).

Some other studies relating values to development may be briefly noted. Yussen (1977) looked at the kinds of moral dilemmas that adolescents actually created when they were asked to invent one and found that these dilemmas were very different from those used by Kohlberg and his colleagues to assess moral reasoning, in that, most frequently, they focussed on interpersonal relations. Candee (1974) found that a type of political thinking that involved concepts that are internal and universal (for example, "justice," "moral rights") increased in use among college students who were at higher levels of ego development (Loevinger & Wessler, 1970). Weiner and Peter (1973) explored developing cognitions about achievement and morality from childhood through adolescence, looking at the positive or negative worth of an outcome in terms of the outcome itself, the person's intent and effort, and the person's ability (see also McKinney, Hotch, & Truhon, 1977; McMahon, 1975; Salili, Maehr, & Gillmore, 1976). This work has provided interesting new evidence about developmental sequences in the achievement and morality domains (for example, more emphasis on outcome among younger children, more emphasis on intent among older children).

Some recent research has investigated moral reasoning within the context of interpersonal interaction (Haan, 1978), distributive justice (Damon, 1977), and prosocial moral judgment (Eisenberg-Berg, 1979). These new approaches go beyond Kohlberg's (1969, 1976) research, which Eisenberg-Berg (1979, p. 128) sees as mainly concerned with the domain of prohibition-oriented reasoning, to look at other types of conflict within the moral realm. Eisenberg-Berg (1979), for example, has found evidence that older children in high school made more use of empathic understanding and judgments reflecting internalized values than younger children when responding to moral conflicts that involved prosocial dilemmas. This extension of research into moral reasoning into a wider range of content areas is to be applauded and may throw light on the interesting question of whether particular values become salient at different stages of moral development, and the degree to which any linkage between value content and stage of moral development may depend upon which moral domain is paramount at the time in the life of the individual. Does moral reasoning, generally conceived, tend to proceed at a higher level in moral domains that are reflected by a person's dominant values at the time? Or does level of moral reasoning generalize across different content areas? Does transition to a new stage of moral reasoning depend upon the emergence of particular values or do certain values emerge as important only after a particular stage of moral development has been attained? These questions await answers.

It is noteworthy that the number of studies that link value content to developmental stages is very limited. Much more research is required in this important area. Future investigations should be concerned not only with moral values that relate to modes of behavior (for example, behaving honestly, justly, and responsibly) and that involve feelings of guilt when violated, but also with other kinds of values as well (for example, those that concern competent modes of conduct and quite general personal and social goals).

ADOLESCENT VALUES AND BEHAVIOR

Throughout the foregoing presentation of evidence we have focused on some of the value-assessment procedures noted earlier in this chapter (for example, rankings, Q-sorts, questionnaire items, and so on). But it could be argued that one should look at how adolescents actually behave relative to other age groups. Is their conduct more or less honest, more or less altruistic, more or less respectful of authority and so on, than that of other age groups?

To take this approach would be to assume that behavior (for example, behaving honestly in some defined situation, giving help when needed, obeying a command) reflects one's values and nothing else. This would be absurd. A person's actions are determined by many factors and the dynamics usually involve a mixture of compatible and incompatible tendencies that are associated with different motives or values. The behavior that emerges may be assumed to reflect the tendencies that are dominant at the time. With a change in situation new tendencies may be elicited and old ones may persist from the past to influence new courses of action.

Our preference has been to conceptualize these tendencies as determined by general motives or dispositions that characterize the person, by situationally elicited expectations about the implications of the alternative responses that are possible, and by the values of the specific incentives (both positive and negative) that the situation provides. These variables combine according to theoretically stated assumptions in a fairly sophisticated motivational approach that takes both person and situation into account and that has been widely applied (for example, Atkinson & Feather, 1966; Atkinson & Raynor, 1974). Within this "expectancy-value" framework, values may be conceptualized as a particular class of motives: those tied to a normative base relating to an evaluative dimension of goodness/badness. Like motives they function to induce valences that may be positive or negative (perceived attractiveness or repulsiveness) and that may apply to particular ways of behaving and to specific outcomes or incentives (for a much fuller discussion see Feather, 1975, pp. 295–305; for some recent research findings see Feather, in press-b).

It follows from this kind of analysis that any inference from behavior must give due consideration to all of the variables involved in the dynamics of action, not just to those that define characteristics of an individual's dominant values. It is especially important to make a detailed analysis of the situation to see what values or motives it might arouse, what incentives it offers, what behaviors are possible, and what their likely consequences will be.

Of course, completing a questionnaire about values, or ranking a set of values in order of importance, or responding to any other value-assessment procedure is itself a form of behavior that can be conceptualized in expectancy-value terms (Feather, 1975, p. 294). But these procedures, at least, have the advantage that they confront respondents with reasonably standardized test situations that enable one to be on firmer ground when making inferences about individual differences in value priorities. What is important is that these instruments, along with other convergent measures, be used in research that is guided by an explicitly stated theory about how values develop and how they function. In this way, the measuring instrument becomes intertwined with the theory and one learns about its construct validity.

Similar general points that stress the need to take other variables into account — especially the situation and how it is defined — have been made in discussions about the relationship of moral reasoning to moral conduct (for example, Brown & Herrnstein, 1975, Chapter 6; Kohlberg, 1969, 1976; Mischel & Mischel, 1976) — though from rather different theoretical perspectives.

CONCLUDING COMMENTS

Our analysis of values in adolescence has taken us far afield and into territories beyond the traditional domain of developmental psychology. This is so because the concept of value is ubiquitous in social science and enters into many different disciplines. A full understanding of what values are, how they develop, and how they function, both at the individual level and within the social system, will depend on inputs from many different sources and will involve new advances in both theory and methodology. We are still at the frontier in this very important area.

We have seen that there are forces that create similarities and forces that create differences in adolescent value systems. In trying to disentangle these forces, we confront a vast array of influences that include not only the psychodynamic and psychosocial aspects of a person's life and the problems that are encountered in day-to-day living, but also the impact of cultural tradition and history. The value systems that emerge in response to internal conditions and external demands are the constructions of an active agent and they are fundamental to our understanding of human thought and action. They deserve detailed investigation in the future.

REFERENCES

Acock, A. C., and Bengtson, V. L. On the relative influence of mothers or fathers: A covariance analysis of political and religious socialization. Paper presented at the American Psychological Association Meeting, New York, August, 1976.

Adams, J. F. (Ed.). *Understanding adolescence: Current development in adolescent psychology* (2nd ed.). Boston: Allyn & Bacon, 1973.

Adelson, J. The development of ideology in adolescence. In S. E. Dragastin and G. H. Elder, Jr., (Eds.), *Adolescence in the life cycle: Psychological change and social context*. New York: Wiley, 1975.

Ahlgren, A., and Johnson, D. W. Sex differences in cooperative and competitive attitudes from the 2nd through the 12th grades. *Developmental Psychology,* 1979, *15,* 45–49.

Albert, E. M. Value systems. In D. L. Sills (Ed.), *International encyclopedia of the social sciences*. New York: Crowell Collier & Macmillan, 1968.

Allport, G. W. *Pattern and growth in personality*. New York: Holt, Rinehart & Winston, 1963.

Allport, G. W., and Vernon, P. E. *A study of values: Manual of directions*. Boston: Houghton Mifflin, 1931.

Allport, G. W., Vernon, P. E., and Lindzey, G. *A study of values: A scale for measuring the dominant interests in personality*. (Rev. ed.). Boston: Houghton Mifflin, 1951.

Allport, G. W., Vernon, P. E., and Lindzey, G. *A study of values: Manual of directions* (Rev. ed.). Boston: Houghton Mifflin, 1960.

Andersson, B. E. *Studies in adolescent behavior*. Stockholm: Almqvist & Wiksell, 1969.

Astin, A. *Four critical years*. San Francisco: Jossey-Bass, 1977a.

————. The new realists. *Psychology Today*, September 1977b, pp. 50–53; 105–107.

Atkinson, J. W., and Feather, N. T. (Eds.). *A theory of achievement motivation*. New York: Wiley, 1966.

Atkinson, J. W., and Litwin, G. H. Achievement motive and test anxiety conceived as motive to approach success and to avoid failure. *Journal of Abnormal and Social Psychology*, 1960, *60*, 52–63.

Atkinson, J. W., and Raynor, J. O. (Eds.). *Motivation and achievement*. Washington, D.C.: Winston, 1974.

Bachtold, L. M., and Echvall, K. L. Current value orientations of American Indians in northern California: The Hupa. *Journal of Cross-Cultural Psychology*, 1978, *9*, 367–375.

Bakan, D. *The duality of human existence*. Chicago: Rand McNally, 1966.

Baltes, P. B., and Schaie, K. W. (Eds.). *Life-span developmental psychology: Personality and socialization*. New York: Academic, 1973.

Bardwick, J. M. *Psychology of women: A study of biocultural conflicts*. New York: Harper & Row, 1971.

Barry, H., Bacon, M. K., and Child, I. L. A cross-cultural survey of some sex differences in socialization. *Journal of Abnormal and Social Psychology*, 1957, *55*, 327–332.

Baumrind, D. Early socialization and adolescent competence. In S. E. Dragastin and G. H. Elder Jr. (Eds.), *Adolescence in the life cycle: Psychological change and social context*. New York: Wiley, 1975.

Beech, R. P., and Schoeppe, A. Development of value systems in adolescents. *Developmental Psychology*, 1974, *10*, 644–656.

Beech, R. P., Schoeppe, A., Osman, A. C., and Minoque, W. J. D. Cross-cultural comparison of value systems of adolescents. Paper presented at 86th Annual Convention of American Psychological Association, Toronto, August, 1978.

Bell, D. *The coming of postindustrial society*. New York: Basic Books, 1973.

Bem, S. L. The measurement of psychological androgyny. *Journal of Consulting and Clinical Psychology*, 1974, *42*, 155–162.

Bengtson, V. L. The generation gap: A review and typology of social-psychological perspectives. *Youth and Society*, 1970, *2*, 7–32.

————. Generation and family effects in value socialization. *American Sociological Review*, 1975, *40*, 358–371.

Bengtson, V. L., Furlong, M. J., and Laufer, R. S. Time, aging, and the continuity of social structure: Themes and issues in generational analysis. *Journal of Social Issues*, 1974, *30*(2), 1–30.

Bengtson, V. L., and Laufer, R. S. (Eds.). Youth, generations, and social change (Parts 1 and 2). *Journal of Social Issues*, 1974, *30* (2,3).

Bengtson, V. L., and Starr, J. M. Contrast and consensus: A generational analysis of youth in the 1970s. In R. J. Havighurst and P. H. Dreyer (Eds.), *Youth*. (74th yearbook, National Society for the Study of Education.) Chicago: University of Chicago Press, 1975.

Berry, J. W. On cross-cultural comparability. *International Journal of Psychology,* 1969, *4,* 119–128.

Block, J. *Lives through time*. Berkeley, Calif.: Bancroft Books, 1971.

Block, J. H. Generational continuity and discontinuity in the understanding of societal rejection. *Journal of Personality and Social Psychology,* 1972, *22,* 333–345.

———. Conceptions of sex role: Some cross-cultural and longitudinal perspectives. *American Psychologist,* 1973, *28,* 512–526.

Block, J. H., Haan, N., and Smith, M. B. Socialization correlates of student activism. *Journal of Social Issues,* 1969, *25*(4), 143–177.

———. Activism and apathy in contemporary adolescents. In J. F. Adams (Ed.), *Understanding adolescence: Current developments in adolescent psychology* (2nd ed.). Boston: Allyn & Bacon, 1973.

Bonjean, C. N., Hill, R. J., and McLemore, S. D. *Sociological measurement: An inventory of scales and indices*. San Francisco: Chandler, 1967.

Braungart, R. G. Youth and social movements. In S. E. Dragastin and G. H. Elder, Jr. (Eds.), *Adolescence in the life cycle: Psychological change and social context*. New York: Wiley, 1975.

Brislin, R. W., Lonner, W. J., and Thorndike, R. M. *Cross-cultural research methods*. New York: Wiley, 1973.

Bronfenbrenner, U. *Two worlds of childhood*. New York: Russell Sage, 1970.

Brown, R., and Herrnstein, R. J. *Psychology*. London: Methuen, 1975.

Bruner, J. S. *The process of education*. Cambridge: Harvard University Press, 1960.

Campbell, E. Q. Adolescent socialization. In D.A. Goslin (Ed.). *Handbook of socialization theory and research*. Chicago: Rand McNally, 1969.

Candee, D. Ego developmental aspects of new left ideology. *Journal of Personality and Social Psychology,* 1974, *30,* 620–630.

Cantril, H. *The pattern of human concerns*. New Brunswick, N.J.: Rutgers University Press, 1965.

Caplow, T., and Bahr, H.M. Half a century of change in adolescent attitudes: Replication of a Middletown survey by the Lynds. *Public Opinion Quarterly,* 1979, *43,* 1–17.

Carlson, R. Sex differences in ego functioning. *Journal of Consulting and Clinical Psychology,* 1971, *37,* 267–277.

Clark, B. R., and Trow, M. Determinants of college student subculture. Unpublished manuscript, Center for the Study of Higher Education, University of California, Berkeley, 1960.

Clark, C. M. G. *A short history of Australia* (1st ed.). London: Heinemann, 1963.

Coleman, J. S. *The adolescent society*. New York: Free Press, 1961.

Coleman, J. S., Bremner, R. H., Burton, C. R., Davis, J. B., Eichorn, D. H., Griliches, Z., Kett, J. F., Ryder, N. B., Doering, Z. B., and Mays, J. M. *Youth: Transition to adulthood*. Chicago: University of Chicago Press, 1974.

Connell, R. W. *The child's construction of politics*. Melbourne: Melbourne University Press, 1971.

Connell, W. F., Stroobant, R. E., Sinclair, K. E., Connell, R. W., and Rogers, K. W. *12 to 20: Studies of city youth*. Sydney, Australia: Hicks Smith, 1975.

Crissman, P. Temporal change and sexual difference in moral judgments. *Journal of Social Psychology,* 1942, *16,* 29–38.

————. Temporal change and sexual difference in moral judgments. *University of Wyoming Publications,* 1950, *15,* 57–68.

Curtis, R. L., Jr. Adolescent orientations toward parents and peers: Variations by sex, age, and socioeconomic status. *Adolescence,* 1975, *10,* 484–494.

Damon, W. *The social world of the child.* San Francisco: Jossey-Bass, 1977.

Dawson, R. E., and Prewitt, K. *Political socialization.* Boston: Little, Brown, 1969.

Douvan, E. Sex differences in the opportunities, demands, and developments of youth. In R. J. Havighurst and P. H. Dreyer (Eds.), *Youth.* (74th yearbook, National Society for the Study of Education.) Chicago: University of Chicago Press, 1975.

Douvan. E., and Adelson, J. *The adolescent experience.* New York: Wiley, 1966.

Dragastin, S. E., and Elder, G. H., Jr. (Eds.). *Adolescence in the life cycle: Psychological change and social context.* New York: Wiley, 1975.

Dukes, W. F. Psychological studies of values. *Psychological Bulletin,* 1955, *52,* 24–50.

Eisenberg-Berg, N. Development of children's prosocial moral judgment, *Developmental Psychology,* 1979, *15,* 128–137.

Elder, G. H., Jr. *Children of the great depression.* Chicago: University of Chicago Press, 1974.

————. Adolescence in the life cycle: An introduction. In S. E. Dragastin and G. H. Elder, Jr. (Eds.), *Adolescence in the life cycle: Psychological change and social context.* New York: Wiley, 1975.

Ellerman, D. A., and Feather, N. T. The values of Australian student activists. *Australian Journal of Education,* 1976, *20,* 260–277.

Eppel, E. M., and Eppel, M. *Adolescents and morality: A study of some moral values of working adolescents in the context of a changing climate of opinion.* London: Routledge & Kegan Paul, 1966.

Erikson, E. H. *Childhood and society.* New York: Norton, 1950.

————. *Identity: Youth and crisis.* New York: Norton, 1968.

Fallding, H. A proposal for the empirical study of values. *American Sociological Review,* 1965, *30,* 223–233.

Feagin, J. R. Poverty: We still believe that God helps those who help themselves. *Psychology Today,* November 1972, pp. 101–110, 129.

Feather, N. T. Educational choice and student attitudes in relation to terminal and instrumental values. *Australian Journal of Psychology,* 1970, *22,* 127–144.

Feather, N. T. Organization and discrepancy in cognitive structures. *Psychological Review,* 1971, *78,* 355–379.

Feather, N. T. *Values in education and society.* New York: Free Press, 1975.

Feather, N. T. Value systems of self and of Australian expatriates as perceived by indigenous students in Papua New Guinea. *International Journal of Psychology,* 1976, *11,* 101–110.

Feather, N. T. Value importance, conservatism, and age. *European Journal of Social Psychology,* 1977, *7*(2), 241–245.

Feather, N. T. Factor structure of the Bem sex-role inventory: Implications for the study of masculinity, femininity, and androgyny. *Australian Journal of Psychology,* 1978a, *30,* 241–254.

Feather, N. T. Family resemblances in conservatism: Are daughters more similar to parents than sons are? *Journal of Personality,* 1978b, *46,* 260–278.

Feather, N. T. Human values and the work situation. *Australian Psychologist,* 1979, *14,* 131–141.

Feather N. T. Value correlates of conservatism. *Journal of Personality and Social Psychology,* in press. (a)

Feather, N. T. Values, expectancy, and action. *Australian Psychologist,* in press. (b)

Feather, N. T., and Hutton, M. A. Value systems of students in Papua New Guinea and Australia. *International Journal of Psychology*, 1974, *9*, 91–104.

Feldman, K. A., and Newcomb, T. M. *The impact of college on students* (2 vols.). San Francisco: Jossey-Bass, 1969.

Feuer, L. *The conflict of generations*. New York: Basic Books, 1969.

Fishkin, J., Keniston, K., and MacKinnon, C. Moral reasoning and political ideology. *Journal of Personality and Social Psychology*, 1973, *27*, 109–119.

Frey, F. W. Cross-cultural survey research in political science. In R. T. Holt and J. E. Turner (Eds.), *The methodology of comparative research*. New York: Free Press, 1970.

Garbarino, J., and Bronfenbrenner, U. The socialization of moral judgment and behavior in cross-cultural perspective. In T. Lickona (Ed.), *Moral development and behavior: Theory, research, and social issues*. New York: Holt, Rinehart & Winston, 1976.

Garrison, K. C. A study of the aspirations and concerns of ninth-grade pupils from the public schools of Georgia. *Journal of Social Psychology*, 1966, *69*, 245–252.

Ghei, S. N. A cross-cultural study of need profiles. *Journal of Personality and Social Psychology*, 1966a, *3*, 580–585.

———. Needs of Indian and American college females. *Journal of Social Psychology*, 1966b, *69*, 3–11.

Gillespie, J. M., and Allport, G. W. *Youth's outlook on the future*. New York: Random House, 1955.

Glossop, J., Roberts, C., and Shemilt, D. Value constructs: Relationships with intelligence and social background. *British Journal of Social and Clinical Psychology*, 1975, *14*, 147–153.

Goodman, M. E. Values, attitudes and social concepts of Japanese and American children. *American Anthropologist*, 1957, *59*, 979–999.

Gordon, L. V. *Survey of interpersonal values*. Chicago: Science Research Associates, 1960.

Gordon, L. V., and Kikuchi, A. The comparability of the forced-choice and Q-sort measurement approaches: An other-cultural study. *Journal of Social Psychology*, 1970, *81*, 137–144.

Gorlow, L., and Noll, G. A. A study of empirically derived values. *Journal of social psychology*, 1967a, *73*, 261–269.

Gorlow, L., and Noll, G. A. The measurement of empirically determined values. *Educational and Psychological Measurement*, 1967b, *27*, 1115–1118.

Gorsuch, R. L. and Smith, R. A. Changes in college students' evaluations of moral behavior: 1969 versus 1939, 1949, and 1958. *Journal of Personality and Social Psychology*, 1972, *24*, 381–391.

Goslin, D. A. (Ed.). *Handbook of socialization theory and research*. Chicago: Rand McNally, 1969.

Goulet, L. R. and Baltes, P. B. (Eds.). *Life-span developmental psychology: Research and theory*. New York: Academic, 1970.

Grinder, R. E. (Ed.). *Studies in adolescence: A book of readings in adolescent development* (2nd ed.). London: Collier-Macmillan, 1969.

Haan, N. Two moralities in action contexts: Relationships to thought, ego regulation, and development. *Journal of Personality and Social Psychology*, 1978, *36*, 286–305.

Haan, N., Smith, M. B., and Block, J. H. Political-social behavior, family background, and personality correlates. *Journal of Personality and Social Psychology*, 1968, *10*, 183–201.

Hallworth, H. J., and Waite, G. A comparative study of value judgments of adolescents. *British Journal of Educational Psychology*, 1966, *36*, 202–209.

Harris, L. The teenagers. *Newsweek,* March 21, 1966, pp. 57–72.

Harrison, J. D. The Kluckhohn value-orientation research instrument used in Papua New Guinea. *New Guinea Psychologist,* 1974, *6,* 3–8.

Hastings, P. K. and Hoge, D. R. Religious change among college students over two decades. In P. K. Manning and M. Truzzi (Eds.), *Youth and sociology.* Englewood Cliffs, N.J.: Prentice-Hall, 1972.

Havighurst, R. J. A cross-cultural view of adolescence. In J. F. Adams (Ed.), *Understanding adolescence: Current developments in adolescent psychology* (2nd ed.). Boston: Allyn & Bacon, 1973.

Havighurst, R. J. Youth in social institutions. In R. J. Havighurst and P. H. Dreyer (Eds.), *Youth.* (74th yearbook, National Society for the Study of Education.) Chicago: University of Chicago Press, 1975.

Havighurst, R. J. and Dreyer, P. H. (Eds.), *Youth.* (74th yearbook, National Society for the Study of Education.) Chicago: University of Chicago Press, 1975.

Havighurst, R. J., and Taba, H. *Adolescent character and personality.* New York: Wiley, 1949.

Havighurst, R. J., et al. *A cross-national study of Buenos Aires and Chicago adolescents.* New York: Karger, 1965.

Hess, R. D., and Torney, J. V. *The development of political attitudes in children.* Chicago: Aldine, 1967.

Hill, R. *Family development in three generations.* Cambridge, Mass.: Schenkman, 1970.

Hoffman, L. W. Changes in family roles, socialization, and sex differences. *American Psychologist,* 1977, *32,* 644–657.

Hogan, R. Moral conduct and moral character: A psychological perspective. *Psychological Bulletin,* 1973, *79,* 217–232.

Hogan, R. Moral development and the structure of personality. In D. DePalma and J. Foley (Eds.), *Moral development: Current theory and research.* Hillsdale, N.J.: Lawrence Erlbaum Associates, 1975.

Hoge, D. R., and Bender, I. E. Factors influencing value change among college graduates in adult life. *Journal of Personality and Social Psychology,* 1974, *29,* 572–585.

Hyman, H. H. *Political socialization.* New York: Free Press, 1959.

Inhelder, B., and Piaget, J. *The growth of logical thinking from childhood to adolescence.* New York: Basic Books, 1958.

International Studies of Values in Politics, *Values and the active community.* New York: Free Press, 1971.

Jennings, M. K., and Niemi, R. G. The transmission of political values from parent to child. *American Political Science Review,* 1968, *62,* 169–184.

———. *The political character of adolescence.* Princeton, N.J.: Princeton University Press, 1974.

———. Continuity and change in political orientations: A longitudinal study of two generations. *American Political Science Review,* 1975, *69,* 1316–1335.

Johnson, O. G. *Tests and measures in child development* (Handbook II). San Francisco: Jossey-Bass, 1976.

Johnson, O. G., and Bonmorito, J. W. *Tests and measures in child development* (Handbook I). San Francisco: Jossey-Bass, 1971.

Kandel, D., and Lesser, G. *Youth in two worlds.* San Francisco: Jossey-Bass, 1972.

Keniston, K. *The uncommitted: Alienated youth in American society.* New York: Harcourt, Brace & World, 1965.

———. *Youth and dissent: The rise of a new opposition.* New York: Harcourt Brace Jovanovich, 1971.

Kerlinger, F. N. Social attitudes and their criterial referents: A structural theory. *Psychological Review*, 1967, *74*, 110–122.

Kikuchi, A., and Gordon, L. V. Evaluation and cross-cultural application of a Japanese form of the survey of interpersonal values. *Journal of Social Psychology*, 1966, *69*, 185–195.

Kikuchi, A., and Gordon, L. V. Japanese and American personal values: Some crosscultural findings. *International Journal of Psychology*, 1970, *5*, 183–187.

Klineberg, O., Zavalloni, M., Louis-Guérin C., and BenBrika, J. *Students, values, and politics: A crosscultural comparison*. New York: Free Press, 1979.

Kluckholn, C. Values and value orientations in the theory of action. In T. Parsons and E. A. Shills (Eds.), *Toward a general theory of action*. Cambridge: Harvard University Press, 1951.

Kluckholn, F. R., and Strodtbeck, F. L. *Variations in value orientations*. Evanston, Ill.: Row, Peterson, 1961.

Kohlberg, L. Stage and sequence: The cognitive-developmental approach to socialization. In D. A. Goslin (Ed.), *Handbook of socialization theory and research*. Chicago: Rand McNally, 1969.

———. Moral stages and moralization: The cognitive-developmental approach. In T. Lickona (Ed.), *Moral development and behavior: Theory, research, and social issues*. New York: Holt, Rinehart & Winston, 1976.

Kohn, M. L. *Class and conformity: A study in values*. Homewood, Ill.: Dorsey, 1969.

———. *Class and conformity: A study in values* (2nd ed.). Chicago: University of Chicago Press, 1977.

Kraut, R. E., and Lewis, S. H. Alternate models of family influence on student political ideology. *Journal of Personality and Social Psychology*, 1975, *31*, 791–800.

Lake, D. G., Miles, M. B., and Earle, R. B. *Measuring human behavior: Tools for the assessment of social functioning*. New York: Teachers College Press, 1973.

Levinson, D. J., Darrow, C. N., Klein, E. B., Levinson, M. H., and McKee, B. *The seasons of a man's life*. New York: Knopf, 1978.

Light, D., Jr., and Laufer, R. S. College youth: Psychohistory and prospects. In R. J. Havighurst and P. H. Dreyer (Eds.), *Youth*. (74th yearbook, National Society for the Study of Education.) Chicago: University of Chicago Press, 1975.

Lipset, S. M. *The first new nation*. New York: Basic Books, 1963a.

———. The value patterns of democracy: A case study in comparative analysis. *American Sociological Review*, 1963b, *28*, 515–531.

———. *Rebellion in the university* (Phoenix ed.). Chicago: University of Chicago Press, 1976.

Loevinger, J. The meaning and measurement of ego development. *American Psychologist*. 1966, *21*, 195–206.

———. *Ego development: Conceptions and theories*. San Francisco: Jossey-Bass, 1976.

Loevinger, J., and Wessler, R. *Measuring ego development* (Vol. 1). San Francisco: Jossey-Bass, 1970.

Lynd, R. S., and Lynd, H. M. *Middletown: A study in American culture*. New York: Harcourt Brace Jovanovich, 1929.

McClelland, D. C. *The achieving society*. Princeton, N.J.: Van Nostrand, 1961.

———. *Motivational trends in society*. New York: General Learning Press, 1971.

McClelland, D. C., Sturr, J. F., Knapp, R. H., and Wendt, H. W. Obligations to self and society in the United States and Germany. *Journal of Abnormal and Social Psychology*, 1958, *56*, 145–255.

McClelland, D. C., and Winter, D. G. *Motivating economic achievement*. New York: Free Press, 1969.

Maccoby, E. E., and Jacklin, C. N. *The psychology of sex differences*. Stanford, Calif.: Stanford University Press, 1974.

McKinney, J. P., Hotch, D. F., and Truhon, S. A. The organization of behavioral values during late adolescence: Change and stability across two eras. *Developmental Psychology*, 1977, *13*, 83–84.

McLellan, D. D. Values, value systems, and the developmental structure of moral judgment. Unpublished master's thesis, Michigan State University, 1970.

McMahan, I. D. Sex and person in achievement and moral evaluation. *Developmental Psychology*, 1975, *11*, 659–660.

Matza, D. Subterranean traditions of youth. *The Annals*, November 1961, *338*, 102–108.

Mednick, M. T. S., and Weissman, H. J. The psychology of women: Selected topics. *Annual Review of Psychology*, 1975, *26*, 1–18.

Mednick, M. T. S., Tangri, S. S., and Hoffman, L. W. (Eds.), *Women and achievement: Social and motivational analyses*. New York: Wiley, 1975.

Merton, R. K. *Social theory and social structure* (Rev. ed.). New York: Free Press, 1968.

———. Social problems and sociological theory. In R. K. Merton and R. Nisbet (Eds.), *Contemporary social problems* (3rd ed.). New York: Harcourt Brace Jovanovich, 1971.

Mirels, H. L., and Garrett, J. B. The Protestant ethic as a personality variable. *Journal of Consulting and Clinical Psychology*, 1971, *36*, 40–44.

Mischel, W. Sex-typing and socialization. In P. H. Mussen (Ed.), *Carmichael's manual of child psychology* (Vol. II). New York: Wiley, 1970.

Mischel, W., and Mischel, H. N. A cognitive social-learning approach to morality and self-regulation. In T. Lickona (Ed.), *Moral development and behavior: Theory, research, and social issues*. New York: Holt, Rinehart & Winston, 1976.

Moore, M. A cross-cultural comparison of value systems. *European Journal of Social Psychology*, 1976, *6*, 249–254.

Morris, C. W. *Varieties of human value*. Chicago: University of Chicago Press, 1956.

Morris, C. W., and Small, L. Changes in conceptions of the good life by American college students from 1950 to 1970. *Journal of Personality and Social Psychology*, 1971, *20*, 254–260.

Morris, J. F. The development of adolescent value judgments. *British Journal of Educational Psychology*, 1958, *23*, 1–14.

Murray, H. *Explorations in personality*. New York: Oxford University Press, 1938.

Nesselroade, J. R., and Reese, H. W. (Eds.). *Life-span developmental psychology: Methodological issues*. New York: Academic, 1973.

Newcomb, T. M. *Personality and social change*. New York: Holt, Rinehart & Winston, 1943.

Newcomb, T. M. Youth in college and corrections: Institutional influences. *American Psychologist*, 1978, *33*, 114–124.

Newcomb, T. M., Koenig, K. E., Flacks, R., and Warwick, D. P. *Persistence and change: Bennington College and its students after 25 years*. New York: Wiley, 1967.

Offer, D., and Offer, J. Three developmental routes through normal male adolescence. In S. C. Feinstein and P. Giovacchini (Eds.), *Adolescent Psychiatry*. New York: Basic Books, in press.

Orpen, C. The work values of Western and tribal black employees. *Journal of Cross-Cultural Psychology*, 1978, *9*, 99–112.

Parsons, T. M. *The social system*. Glencoe, Ill.: Free Press, 1951.

———. Social structure and the development of personality: Freud's contribution to the integration of psychology and sociology. *Psychiatry*, 1958, *11*, 321–340.

———. Pattern variables revisited. *American Sociological Review*, 1960, *25*, 467–483.

———. On the concept of value-commitments. *Sociological Inquiry*, 1968, *38*, 135–159.

Peck, R. F. A comparison of the value systems of Mexican and American youth. *Revista Interamericana de Psicologia,* 1967, *1,* 41–50.

Peck, R. F., and Havighurst, R. J. *The psychology of character development.* New York: Wiley, 1960.

Peterson, R. E. The student left in American higher education. *Daedalus,* 1968, *97*(1), 293–317.

Piaget, J. *The moral judgment of the child.* London: Kegan Paul, 1932.

Pilkington, G. W., Poppleton, P. K., Gould, J. B., and McCourt, M. M. Changes in religious beliefs, practices and attitudes among university students over an eleven-year period in relation to sex differences, denominational differences, and differences between faculties and years of study. *British Journal of Social and Clinical Psychology,* 1976, *15,* 1–9.

Pleck, J. H. The male sex role: Definitions, problems, and sources of change. *Journal of Social Issues,* 1976, *32*(3), 155–164.

Przeworski, A. and Teune, H. *The logic of comparative social inquiry.* New York: Wiley, 1970.

Reich, C. A. *The greening of America.* New York: Random House, 1970.

Remmers, H. H. and Radler, H. A. *The American teenager.* Indianapolis, Ind.: Bobbs-Merrill, 1957.

Riegel, K. F. The dialectics of human development. *American Psychologist,* 1976, *31,* 689–700.

Riley, M. W. Aging and cohort succession: Interpretations and misinterpretations. *Public Opinion Quarterly,* 1973, *37,* 35–49.

Robinson, J. P. and Shaver, P. R. *Measures of social psychological attitudes.* Ann Arbor, Mich.: Institute for Social Research, 1969.

Rogers, D. *The psychology of adolescence* (2nd ed.), New York: Appleton-Century-Crofts, 1972.

Rokeach, M. *The nature of human values.* New York: Free Press, 1973.

Rosenberg, M. *Occupations and values.* Glencoe, Ill.: Free Press, 1957.

Ruble, D. N., and Frieze, I. H. (Eds.), Sex roles: Persistence and change. *Journal of Social Issues,* 1976, *32*(3).

Salili, F., Maehr, M. L., and Gillmore, G. Achievement and morality: A cross-cultural analysis of causal attribution and evaluation. *Journal of Personality and Social Psychology,* 1976, *33,* 327–337.

Sampson, E. E. (Ed.). Stirrings out of apathy: Student activism and the decade of protest. *Journal of Social Issues,* 1967, *23*(3).

Schaie, K. W., and Gribbin, K. Adult development and aging. *Annual Review of Psychology,* 1975, *26,* 65–96.

Scheibe, K. E. *Beliefs and values.* New York: Holt, Rinehart & Winston, 1970.

Scott, W. A. *Values and organizations.* Chicago: Rand McNally, 1965.

Sears, D. O. Political behavior. In G. Lindzey and E. Aronson (Eds.), *The handbook of social psychology* (Vol. 5). Reading, Mass.: Addison-Wesley, 1969.

Shepherd, J. The *Look* youth survey. *Look,* September 26, 1966, pp. 44–49.

Smith, M. B. Morality and student protest. In M. B. Smith, *Social psychology and human values.* Chicago: Aldine, 1969a.

———. *Social psychology and human values.* Chicago: Aldine, 1969b.

Smith, M. B. Psychology and values. *Journal of Social Issues,* 1978, *34*(4), 181–199.

Spence, J. T., and Helmreich, R. L. *Masculinity and femininity: Their psychological dimensions, correlates, and antecedents.* Austin: University of Texas Press, 1978.

Spranger, E. *Types of men.* Halle, Germany: Niemeyer, 1928.

Stein, A. H., and Bailey, M. M. The socialization of achievement orientation in females. *Psychological Bulletin,* 1973, *80,* 345–366.

Sundberg, N. D., Rohila, P. K., and Tyler, L. E. Values of Indian and American adolescents. *Journal of Personality and Social Psychology,* 1970, *16,* 374–397.

Thistlethwaite, D. L. Accentuation of differences in values and exposures to major fields of study. *Journal of Educational Psychology,* 1973, *65,* 279–293.

Thomas, L. E. Political attitude congruence between politically active parents and college-age children. *Journal of Marriage and the Family,* 1971, *33,* 375–386.

Thompson, O. E. High school students' values: Emergent or traditional. *California Journal of Educational Research,* 1961, *12,* 132–144.

Triandis, H. (Ed.). *The analysis of subjective culture.* New York: Wiley, 1972.

Triandis, H., Kilty, K. M., Shanmugam, A. V., Tanaka, Y., and Vassiliou, V. Cognitive structures and the analysis of values. In H. Triandis (Ed.), *The analysis of subjective culture.* New York: Wiley, 1972.

Troll, L., Neugarten, B. L., and Kraines, R. J. Similarities in values and other personality characteristics in college students and their parents. *Merrill-Palmer Quarterly,* 1969, *15,* 323–336.

Walker, L. J., and Richards, B. S. Stimulating transitions in moral reasoning as a function of stage of cognitive development. *Developmental Psychology,* 1979, *15,* 95–103.

Ward, R. *The Australian legend.* Melbourne: Oxford University Press, 1958.

Weiner, B., and Peter, N. A cognitive-developmental analysis of achievement and moral judgments. *Developmental Psychology,* 1973, *9,* 290–309.

White, R. K. *Value analysis: The nature and use of the method.* Glen Gardner, N.J.: Society for the Psychological Study of Social Issues, 1951.

White, R. W. *Lives in progress: A study of the natural growth of personality.* New York: Dryden, 1966.

Williams, R. M. Jr. *American society: A sociological interpretation.* (2nd ed.). New York: Knopf, 1960.

Williams, R. M. Jr. Change and stability in values and value systems. In B. Barber and A. Inkeles (Eds.), *Stability and social change.* Boston: Little, Brown, 1971.

Williams, R. M. Jr. Values. In D. L. Sills (Ed.), *International encyclopedia of the social sciences.* New York: Crowell Collier & Macmillan, 1968.

Wilson, G. D. (Ed.). *The psychology of conservatism.* New York: Academic, 1973.

Wilson, G. D., and Patterson, J. R. A new measure of conservatism. *British Journal of Social and Clinical Psychology,* 1968, *7,* 264–269.

Wollack, S., Goodale, J. G., Whiting, J. P., and Smith, P. C. The measurement of work values. *Journal of Applied Psychology,* 1971, *55,* 331–338.

Wright, D., and Cox, E. Changes in moral belief among sixth-form boys and girls over a seven-year period in relation to religious belief, age, and sex difference. *British Journal of Social and Clinical Psychology,* 1971, *10,* 332–341.

Yankelovich, D. *The changing values on campus.* New York: Washington Square Press, 1973.

——. *The new morality: A profile of American youth in the 70's.* New York: McGraw-Hill, 1974.

Yussen, S. R. Characteristics of moral dilemmas written by adolescents. *Developmental Psychology,* 1977, *13,* 162–163.

Zajonc, R. B. Cognitive theories in social psychology. In G. Lindzey and E. Aronson (Eds.), *The handbook of social psychology* (Vol. 1). Reading, Mass.: Addison-Wesley, 1968.

Zavalloni, M. Subjective culture, self-concept, and the social environment. *International Journal of Psychology,* 1973, *8,* 183–192.

——. Social identity and the recoding of reality: Its relevance for cross-cultural psychology. *International Journal of Psychology,* 1975, *10,* 197–217.

CHAPTER 9

Moral Development in Adolescence

Martin L. Hoffman

There has been considerable theorizing but surprisingly little research on adolescent moral development, probably because the predominant interest of most developmental researchers has been with infancy and early childhood. Those investigators who have obtained data on adolescents typically lack a developmental perspective and, with few exceptions, comparable data on other age groups are lacking. As a result, it is often difficult to tell those findings that are peculiar to adolescence and those that may be characteristic of other periods as well. With these limitations in mind, I shall try to summarize the main theories, pointing up their limitations and bringing in pertinent findings where available. We begin with cognitive disequilibrium and psychoanalysis, which have dominated the theoretical literature, followed by a third, newer approach that to a greater degree attempts a synthesis of cognitive and affective processes. After that, the research on the effects of socialization experiences, with parents and peers, and on sex differences in moral internalization is reviewed. The research on student activism insofar as it bears on adolescent morality is also discussed. Finally, on overall framework for viewing adolescent morality in developmental perspective is offered and some suggestions for research are made.

COGNITIVE DISEQUILIBRIUM

The cognitive-disequilibrium theorists — notably Piaget and Kohlberg — view internalization as occurring in a series of fixed, qualitatively distinct stages whose end product, which is achieved if at all in adolescence, is a universal sense of justice or concern for reciprocity among individuals. Each stage is viewed as a homogeneous type of moral reasoning strategy or conceptual framework designed to answer moral questions and evaluate issues; moral reasoning within a stage is thus consistent across different moral problems and situations. Each stage builds upon, reorganizes, and encompasses the preceding one and is, therefore, more comprehensive, providing new perspectives and criteria for making moral evaluations. The content of moral values is postulated as not playing an important role in defining a stage.

All individuals regardless of culture are viewed as going through the stages in the same order, varying only in how quickly and how far they move through the stage sequence. The stages are held to be constructed by individuals as they try to make sense out of their own experience, rather than implanted by culture through socialization.

Piaget's Model

Piaget's two stages were derived from both the attitudes expressed by children toward the origin, legitimacy, and alterability of rules in the game of marbles, as well as the responses to stories, such as the well-known one in which children are asked to judge who is naughtier, a boy who accidentally breaks 15 cups as he opens a door or a boy who breaks 1 cup while trying to sneak jam out of the cupboard (Piaget, 1932). In Piaget's first stage — referred to as moral realism, morality of constraint, or heteronomous morality — children feel an obligation to comply with rules because they are sacred and unalterable. They tend to view behaviors as totally right or wrong and think everyone views them in the same way. They judge the rightness or wrongness of an act on the basis of the magnitude of its consequences, the extent to which it conforms to established rules, and whether it is punished. They believe in "immanent justice" — that violations of social norms are followed by physical accidents or misfortunes willed by God or by some inanimate object.

Children in the more advanced stage — attained by late childhood or early adolescence and called autonomous morality, morality of cooperation, or reciprocity — view rules as established and maintained through reciprocal social agreement and thus subject to modification in response to human needs. They recognize a possible diversity in views. Their judgments of right and wrong place stress on intentions as well as consequences. They think that punishment should be reciprocally related to the misdeed (e.g., through restitution) rather than painful, arbitrary, and administered by authority. Also, duty and obligation are no longer defined in terms of obedience to authority but more in terms of conforming to peer expectations, considering their own welfare, expressing gratitude for past favors, and, above all, putting oneself in the place of others.

Piaget believes that both cognitive development and peer interaction play a role in the transformation from one stage to the next. The main threads of his argument are as follows. Young children's moral immaturity is based on: (1) two cognitive limitations, namely, egocentrism (assuming that others view events the same as they do) and "realism" (confusing subjective with objective experience, e.g., perceiving dreams as external events); and (2) their heteronomous respect for adults — a syndrome of feelings (including inferiority, dependency, affection, admiration, and fear) that produces feelings of obligation to comply with adult's commands and to view adult's rules as sacred and unchangeable. Moral growth requires that the child give up egocentrism and realism and develop a concept of self as distinct from others who have their own independent perspectives about events. This shift occurs in interactions with peers, beginning in childhood and extending into adolescence, in two ways:

1. By growing older, children attain relative equality with adults and older children, which lessens their unilateral respect for them and gives the children confidence to participate with peers in decisions about applying and changing rules on the basis of reciprocity. This new mode of interaction makes the child's initial conception of the rules no longer tenable. The rules are no longer seen as having an infinite past and a divine or adult origin but, increasingly, as products of cooperation and agreement based on the human goals they serve and amenable to change by mutual consent.

2. When one interacts with peers, there is often a need to take alternate and reciprocal roles with them. This facilitates awareness that one is coordinate with others — that one reacts to similar situations in similar ways, that the consequences of one's acts for peers and theirs for oneself are similar; yet events seem different when viewed from different vantage points. The child thus becomes sensitized to the inner states that underlie the acts of others; this contributes, among other things, to the tendency to take other's intentions into accounts.

Peer interaction also serves to stimulate and challenge the individual because it contradicts his or her expectations. The resulting cognitive disequilibrium then motivates one to utilize one's newly attained cognitive capabilities to resolve the contradiction; it is through this effort that preexisting patterns of moral thought are reorganized.

Kohlberg's Stage Schema

Kohlberg's stage schema and the research it stimulated has more direct relevance to adolescent moral thought and will be discussed in greater detail. In developing his scheme, Kohlberg attempted to retain the best of Piaget's analysis and to fit it into a more refined, comprehensive, and logically consistent framework. Kohlberg's six stages are based on extensive case analyses of boys ranging from 10 to 16 years of age (Kohlberg, 1958). The data were obtained from two-hour interviews that focused on nine hypothetical moral dilemmas in which acts of obedience to laws, rules, or commands of authority conflict with the needs or welfare of other persons. The subject was asked to choose whether one should perform the obedience-serving act or the need-serving act and to answer a series of questions probing the thinking underlying his choice. Kohlberg's interest was not in the action-choices selected by the subjects, which presumably reflect the content of their moral values, but in the quality of their judgments as indicated in the reasons given for their choices and their ways of defining the conflict situations.

Each stage was defined in terms of its position on 30 different moral issues, which the subjects brought into their thinking. The six stages were ordered into three levels of moral orientation, the basic themes and major attributes of which may be summarized as follows.

Premoral. Control of conduct is external in two senses: standards consist of outer commands and the motive is to avoid external punishment, obtain rewards, have favors returned, and so on. This level characterizes childhood.

Stage 1—Obedience and punishment orientation. Definition of good and bad is based on obedience to rules and authority. Deference to superior power or prestige exists but is not heteronomous in Piaget's sense. Instead, punishment is feared like any other aversive stimulus.

Stage 2—Naive hedonistic and instrumental orientation. Acts are defined as right that satisfy the self and occasionally others. Values are relative to each actor's needs and perspectives.

Morality of conventional rule-conformity. Morality is defined as maintaining the social order and conforming to expectations of others; adherence to established norms is the essence of moral obligation. Control of conduct is external in that standards consist of rules and expectations held by those who are significant others by virtue of personal attachment or delegated authority. Motivation is largely internal — though based on anticipation of praise or censure by significant others, the child now takes their role and respects their judgment. Thus the personal reactions of authority now serve as cues to the rightness or wrongness of an act and the moral virtue of the actor. This level is usually dominant in late childhood and early adolescence.

Stage 3—Good-boy morality of maintaining good relations. Orientation is to gain approval and to please and help others. The morally good person is one who possesses moral virtues. In judging others, intentions are considered.

Stage 4—Authority and social-order maintaining morality. Orientation is to "doing one's duty," showing respect for authority, and maintaining social order for its own sake. Takes the perspective of others who have legitimate rights and expectations in situation. Believes that virtue must be rewarded.

Morality of self-accepted moral principles. Morality is defined as conformity to shared or sharable standards, rights, duties. Possibility of conflict between two socially accepted standards is acknowledged and attempts at rational decision between them are made. There is a moral obligation to abide by established norms, but only insofar as they serve human ends. Control of conduct is internal in two senses: (1) the standards have an inner source and (2) the decision to act is based on an inner process of thought and judgment concerning right and wrong. This level characterizes adolescence, though many people never attain it.

Stage 5—Morality of contract and democratically accepted law. Norms of right and wrong are defined in terms of laws or institutionalized rules, which are seen to have a rational base, for example, they express the will of the majority, maximize social utility or welfare, or are necessary for institutional functioning. Although recognized as arbitrary, sometimes unjust, and one of many choices, the law is generally the ultimate criterion of the right. Duty and obligation are defined in terms of contract, not the needs of individuals. When conflict exists between the individual and the law or contract, though there may be sympathy for the former, the latter prevails because of its greater functional rationality for society.

Stage 6—Morality of individual principles of conscience. Orientation is not only to existing rules and standards, but also to conscience as a directing agent, to mutual respect and trust, and to principles of moral choice involving appeal to logical universality and consistency. Conduct is controlled by an internalized ideal that exerts pressure toward action that seems right, regardless of reactions of others present. If the individual acts otherwise, self-condemnation and guilt result. Though aware of the importance of law and contract, moral conflict is generally resolved in terms of broader moral principles, such as the Golden Rule, the greatest good for the greatest number, or the categorical imperative.

Kohlberg's (1958) stage descriptions are more fully developed than his conception of the processes involved in the individual's progress through the stages. His recent writings stress two processes: cognitive disequilibrium and role-taking. The first is an extension of the concepts of cognitive disequilibrium and equilibration in Piaget's theory of intellectual (rather than moral) development. The hypothesis, as formulated most clearly by Turiel (1966), is that moral growth results from exposure to levels of moral reasoning that are moderately higher than one's current level ("structural match"). The resulting cognitive conflict, or disequilibrium, is tension-producing, which results in the person's becoming motivated to make sense out of the contradiction.

The moral stages, according to Kohlberg, also reflect a sequence of successive changes in role-taking ability. The ability to take another person's perspective is seen as having special significance in the transition from premoral to conventional morality (from Stage 2 to 3). Indeed, Kohlberg at times seems to imply that role-taking is the defining characteristic of conventional morality. At other times, however, role-taking is seen as functioning primarily in the service of cognitive conflict, that is, role-taking experiences provide the individual with different perspectives and thus instigate cognitive conflict and its resolution through modification of the existing moral structure.

Kohlberg has devised a Moral Judgment Scale to determine an individual's stage of moral development. The only complete description of the scale is given in his doctoral dissertation (Kohlberg, 1958). The instrument consists of the same nine hypothetical dilemmas used initially to derive the stages. An interviewer presents the subject with one dilemma at a time, and the person must make a judgment about the situation and justify his choice. The subject is encouraged to respond freely and is asked probe questions to elicit additional responses, all of which are recorded. The scoring is based not on a subject's specific judgment in response to each moral dilemma, but rather on the reasoning that the subject gives in support of his or her judgment. The scale is complex and difficult to score. Precise scoring instructions are available only from Kohlberg personally, and extensive training is necessary in order to score protocols correctly. There are two scoring methods: (1) a global intuitive one in which the rater assigns the subject both a stage score for each dilemma (resulting in a profile) and an overall score consisting of the subject's dominant stage and (2) a highly detailed system of coding the responses in terms of a classification scheme based on the 30 moral issues, each defined by a six-point scale corresponding to the six stages. The detailed scoring system, obviously the one most potentially useful for other researchers because of its greater objectivity, recently underwent a drastic revision (Colby, Speicher, & Kohlberg, 1973; Kohlberg, 1976). The new procedure puts emphasis on fewer moral issues and places more weight on the highest stage attained by the subject on each issue. A problem created by the new scoring system is that it throws into question the findings obtained using the old procedure.

Research Review and Critique

Kohlberg's model has stimulated a great deal of research, that has been critically reviewed elsewhere (Hoffman, 1977, pp. 86–135; Kurtines & Greif, 1974). The research, by and large, provides little support for the main tenets of the theory — that the stages are homogeneous, that their postulated sequence is universal and invariant, and that moral growth results from exposure to levels of moral reasoning that are moderately higher than one's own. To illustrate the type of research stimulated by the theory, let us examine in detail the experimental study by Turiel (1966), which is still cited as basic supporting evidence for the invariant sequence of the stages.

Forty-seven adolescent (seventh-grade) boys were assigned stage scores based on their responses to six Kohlberg dilemmas. In the experimental condition, three different dilemmas were administered. In each, the subjects were instructed to take the role of the central figure and "seek advice" from the experimenter. To produce cognitive conflict without suggesting which action the central figure should take, the experimenter's advice consisted of arguments on both sides of the issue, each cast in terms of moral concepts at a level that diverged from the subject's own stage position by certain specified amounts — either one or two stages above (+1 or +2) or one stage below (−1). The subjects were retested a week later on all nine dilemmas.

The results confirmed one hypothesis: a person's existing stage of thought limits how far he can go; therefore he will be more likely to assimilate moral reasoning one stage above rather than two stages above his current level. The more interesting, crucial hypothesis was based on the assumption that (1) higher stages are reorganizations and displacements of preceding stages rather than mere additions to them and (2) there is a tendency toward forward movement through the stage sequence, that is, irreversibility. The group exposed to the + 1 treatment was therefore expected to shift in the + 1 direction to a greater degree than the − 1 group would shift in the − 1 direction. The findings were just the opposite from those expected, and furthermore the experimental groups did not shift to a significantly greater degree than the control group, which had experienced no treatment. The control group, however, for some unknown reason showed considerably more shift in the − 1 direction than in the + 1 direction. As a result, the net shift (experimental minus control) was greater for the + 1 than the − 1 group. This difference is in the hypothesized direction and of borderline significance. In other words, it is only when the action of the control group, which is inexplicably more dramatic than either experimental group, is taken into account that the findings may be interpreted as providing the slightest evidence in favor of the hypothesis. This problem together with others mentioned by Kurtines and Greif (1974) casts doubt on the support this study provides for Kohlberg's theory.

In a recent study using an improved version of Turiel's design (Tracy & Cross, 1973), seventh-grade children who initially scored at Kohlberg's lowest two moral stages (but not the higher-stage subjects) were influenced in the expected manner, that is, they shifted more in the direction of higher than of lower levels of moral judgment. These same lower-stage subjects, however, also obtained high scores on a social desirability measure; furthermore, within this group, social desirability was found to relate positively to the amount of shift. Since these subjects had an external moral orientation to begin with (the lowest two stages are external), these findings suggest that direct social-influence processes may account for their shift in judgment rather than the disequilibrium and "structural match" postulated in Kohlberg's theory.

The studies of comprehension and preference for higher moral levels, which also follow Turiel's format (e.g., Rest, 1973) and employed adolescent subjects, appear to have other problems. The findings were that comprehension was high, up to the subject's own predominant stage, and then fell off rapidly; and the highest stage comprehended was the most preferred of those comprehended. Stage-6 statements, however, were the most preferred of all, which means that the subject's predominant stage did not predict his preference. This casts doubt on the implications of the entire study. It also raises a possible question about the design of all these studies. The investigators themselves apparently constructed the statements of "advice" and despite their attempts to balance each pro/con pair for stage, attitude, and issue, it is possible that high-stage statements were inadvertently phrased more attractively than low-stage statements. This would introduce a spurious element in the subjects' choices. Perhaps a better procedure in studies like these would be to have independent persons construct the statements.

It is possible that Kohlberg (1975) is correct when he suggests that the lack of empirical verification of his theory may be due to the inadequacies of his earlier scoring procedures and that support for the theory may be expected from research using his newer, improved methods. Besides the lack of verification, however, Kohlberg's theory has been taken to task by Simpson (1974) for being a culturally biased approach that claims universality but is actually based on the style of thinking and social organization peculiar to Western culture. Stage 5, for example, makes sense only in a constitutional democracy; Stage 6 requires a level of abstract thought that may disqualify most people in the world. The theory has also been criticized from various philosophical perspectives by Alston (1971, pp. 269–284), Baier (1974), and Peters (1971, pp. 237–267). Peters has also suggested that it is important to understand the development of the motivation to be concerned for others, which is ignored in Kohlberg's theory, because this motive is presumably needed to provide direction for translating Kohlberg's abstract moral concepts of justice into actual behavior. In addition, Hogan (1975) has criticized Kohlberg's system, especially the high value it places on Stage 6, as reflecting a "romantic individualism." Hogan views this individualistic perspective with its "concomitant suspicion of the traditional mores and cultural values," as reflecting and contributing to the "general erosion of confidence in civilization." And, finally, Sampson (1978) has pointed out that Kohlberg's views reflect a pronounced masculine bias.

Whether the theory is confirmed or not, Kohlberg must be given credit for sensitizing researchers to the highly complex nature of moral development and the cognitive dimensions that may be necessary for a mature moral orientation. Both he and Piaget have also called attention to the possible importance for moral growth of the person's own direct social experience and his or her active efforts to draw meaning from its contradictions. And, despite the lack of empirical support to date, certain of the concepts in the theory continue to have appeal. Cognitive disequilibrium and structural match, for example, may help account for the developmental progression from a rudimentary moral sense that originates in early childhood (perhaps in the discipline encounter as will be discussed later) to the complex moral concepts often held by adolescents and adults. Finally, although Kohlberg's stages may not form a universal invariant sequence, as he claims, they may nevertheless provide a valid description of the changes in moral thought that occur with age in our society. His measure may thus afford the best available means of comparing adolescent morality with pre- and postadolescent morality.

Most interesting in this connection is the longitudinal study by Kohlberg and Kramer (1969), in which the results of a follow-up study of Kohlberg's original sample are reported. Moral reasoning profiles for lower- and middle-class males at 16, 20 and 24 years of age were available, and the findings in general were in accord with the expected developmental pattern. The major exception was that a fifth of the subjects who obtained Stage-4 scores at 16 years of age dropped to Stage 2 at 20 years. Most of them returned to Stage 4 (some advanced to 5) by 24 years. The drop to Stage 2 would appear to pose a problem for the cognitive-developmental view, according to which development is always forward and which makes no provision for regression. Most of the Stage-2 responses, however, apparently fit the category of "instrumental relativism," and the investigators interpreted the findings as follows. These individuals, who were all in the middle class, had been confronted, largely through the liberal-arts curriculum in the colleges they attended, with two developmental challenges. One resulted from exposure to the great diversity of moral expression and opinion and the suggestion that any given society's definition of right and wrong, however legitimate, is only one among many. The other challenge resulted from the discovery (contrary to the subjects' previous assumption that people lived by conventional moral norms and that rewards in life came to those who did so most faithfully) that frequent inconsistencies occur between moral expectations and the actual behavior of adults, individually and in institutions.

These challenges often served to undermine the individual's conventional moral orientation and to lead him to regress temporarily to a relativistic position. Furthermore, when he later returned to Stage 4, this appeared to be accomplished at a higher level of ego integration, that is, with less distorting idealization of the group and authority system in which he believed and with greater tolerance and realism about those who deviate from it or are outside of it. That is, the person returns to the same moral structure (Stage 4) but now takes a more realistic stance toward it. Kohlberg and Kramer (1969) also make the broader generalization that the integration of one's moral ideology with the facts of moral diversity and inconsistency, and its incorporation into one's growing identity may be a general developmental task of youth in an open society. And, the temporary disorganization and regression may in the long run make a constructive contribution, may indeed be necessary in some cases, for accomplishing this integration.

In a later article Kohlberg and Gilligan (1971) stress the difference between the temporary or transitional Stage-2 position of the older adolescents and the "natural" Stage-2 responses found in young children. The main difference is that transitional Stage-2 individuals understand and can use conventional moral thinking, although they now view it as arbitrary. Furthermore, at this point they lack a commitment to any principle except perhaps to "do your own thing."

Turiel (1974) has rejected Kohlberg and Kramer's (1969) hypothesis of a temporary regression in the service of movement from Stage 3 to Stage 4. Turiel suggests instead that this transition, like all cognitive transformations, involves a phase of conflict or disequilibrium during which the existing mode of thinking is reevaluated and a new mode is constructed. This process of change entails not regression but the "deformation of one structure through its formation into another structure." That is, through awareness of the contradictions and inadequacies of the existing structure, the logic of that structure is rejected and a new structure is created. Turiel suggests further that the stage being rejected by the adolescent (Stage 4) involves what Turiel calls "conventional" issues or values and the stage toward which he or she is moving involves primarily "moral" values or issues. Thus the adolescent is viewed by Turiel as moving toward a conceptualization of two distinctly different value systems: one encompasses those moral values or principles considered to be objectively valid and universalizable (e.g., the value of life, trust, honesty, responsibility, individual rights); the other includes values, such as customs and conventions, considered to be specific to a given individual or society (e.g., sexual mores, dress codes, forms of address, sex roles, national and religious rituals or customs). In short, Turiel suggests that the instrumental-relativistic responses may represent that intermediate point (which may last months or years) in which the person is protesting against and loosening his attachment to conventional Stage-4 thinking about "conventional" values, and beginning to gravitate toward an autonomous orientation in which the value content is for the first time truly moral.

These conceptions by Kohlberg and Kramer (1969), and by Turiel (1974) about moral transition in adolescence are difficult to evaluate. They seem intuitively reasonable and may indeed explain the findings. It should be noted, however, that these writers are not the first to suggest that a liberal-arts education contributes to the erosion of one's previous beliefs and to the acquisition of more liberal, humanitarian views (see review by Feldman and Newcomb, 1969). The difference here is that, in keeping with their cognitive stress, these writers are suggesting that what occurs is a change in moral structure rather than in moral value content.

Turiel (1974) provides the reader with sample protocols; it seems clear from reading them that the value content of the respondents is at least as much at issue as the harder-to-define "structure." Indeed, Turiel seems to realize this when he hypothesizes that adolescents are moving from a concern with "conventional," to a concern with truly "moral" issues. Nevertheless, he uses "structural" terminology to explain this shift, that is, he views the shift as resulting from the individual's awareness of the "inner" contradictions in his or her previous mode of thought. Examination of the sample protocols, however, reveals no evidence of awareness or concern with "inner" contradictions (though there may be an awareness of the contradiction between the professed values and people's behavior) or for the emergence of "incomplete understanding of Stage 5 concepts.'' Indeed, there is no evidence from their remarks that the subjects are in transition between stages. The responses cited do indicate that the subjects are relativistic, in that they recognize that people have different values, that they have a right to hold these values, that one should not arbitrarily impose one's values on others, and that individuals and societies with different values should be respected. Furthermore, the subjects often express the view that there are no objective criteria for validating moral standards, and they explicitly reject the idea that God and the existing social norms can provide such criteria. On the other hand, their relativism is tempered by the fact that human principles, such as the importance of human life and freedom from external constraint, are dominant concerns. (That these subjects may qualify these concerns by presenting them as expressions of their own personal bias does not alter the fact that they appear to hold these human values strongly.) Indeed, these principles are sometimes cited as the grounds for rejecting religious and other conventional institutions. In sum, it is true, as Turiel (1974) claims, that the responses lack a regressive flavor, hence do not provide support for Kohlberg and Kramer's (1969) view. The fact that humanistic or moral principles are dominant for this group, however, indicates that the relativism of these subjects may be confined to what Turiel defines as ''conventional'' values. They do not appear to be relativistic as regards ''moral'' issues.

There is additional evidence against the cognitive-disequilibrium interpretation. In a later article Turiel (1977) reports that even preschool-aged children distinguish between ''conventional'' and ''moral'' issues and, furthermore, they apparently realize that only the moral issues are beyond the bounds of conventional rule-making. A similar finding has been reported by Eisenberg-Berg (1977): elementary school children appear to be more advanced in moral reasoning pertaining to prosocial matters than in moral reasoning pertaining to prohibitions. It thus appears that the adolescent responses in question may not reflect the *beginning* of a concern with truly moral issues, as Turiel (1977) suggests, but perhaps the resurrection of earlier concerns that may have been for a time relegated to the background as the child learned the conventional norms of society. In this connection we may note an interesting set of findings by Staub (1970; 1971). Half his second-to-fourth-grade subjects left an assigned task to help a crying child in the next room. Many fewer sixth-graders did this, which Staub interprets as reflecting the interference of the older children's concerns about obedience to authority. In keeping with this interpretation, Staub also found that when a comparable group of sixth-graders had been given prior permission to enter the next room, half of them did subsequently rush to offer help when they heard the cry. And over 90% of a sample of seventh-graders did the same under similar conditions.

I have suggested elsewhere (Hoffman, 1970a) that middle-class American children have long been socialized in two directions: one stresses the importance of subordinating impulses in accordance with the requirements of conventional institutional authority, law, and order; the other highlights the importance of altruism and compassion for the less fortunate. Compliance to both sets of norms ordinarily poses little or no problem to young children since the norms seem to be applicable on different occasions. At some point in development, however, the norms are apt to be in conflict in situations requiring a choice of actions for oneself or a judgment about someone else's behavior. Perhaps in middle childhood the socialization pressures at home and school place a premium on conventional norms; human concerns are consequently often overridden. In adolescence, particularly in the 1960s, when the Kohlberg and Kramer (1969) data were collected, the reverse may have been true and human values may have become salient. Extending this idea further, and taking account of the tendency toward conservatism in adulthood, it may be that the duality of the early socialization prepares the individual to stress conventional or human concerns at different points in the life cycle, depending on circumstances.

In any case, there appears to be no evidence as yet for Kohlberg and Kramer's (1969) view of temporary regression, or for Turiel's (1974) view of structural deformation and reformation, as mediating mechanisms of moral growth in adolescence. Furthermore, there appears to be no evidence that cognitive-structural or stage concepts are needed to explain the findings. It may simply be true that if individuals are confronted both by evidence for relativism as well as the fact that their prior moral values do not fit the real world, their prior values will be undermined, thus creating a void of meaning. To fill this void they may search for new values, which, for some individuals, entails selecting from an array of available ideologies.

Kohlberg and Gilligan (1971) have advanced an interesting historical hypothesis based on an unpublished study of adolescents by Podd (1969), done in the late 1960s. The instrumental relativists in this study were reported as having a more stable, less crisis-like pattern of low moral commitment than their counterparts in the Kohlberg and Kramer (1969) study, which was done in the early 1960s. Kohlberg and Gilligan suggest that the rejection of conventional morality in the late 1960s (and presumably since then) may no longer be the result of individuals' spontaneous reflection on their own experience. Instead it may be the result of direct exposure to the prepackaged product of a "cultural industry" called the counterculture. The counterculture, that is, may have been transformed into another "moral system" available for adoption by adolescents not through spontaneous questioning, as it was formerly, but in the same nonreflective manner as has traditionally been true for the conventional moral system. Thus, Kohlberg and Gilligan (1971) suggest adolescents may now be faced with two moral systems, the conventional and the countercultural, offering alternative ideologies. Either of these may be accepted permanently on a nonreflective basis, or it may eventually be seen in principled terms, that is, with its validity resting on the extent to which it successfully embodies larger principles of justice. Unfortunately, the data for evaluating this hypothesis are inadequate. Its implications not only for adolescent moral development, but also for history and social change are obviously profound, and it clearly deserves further attention.

To conclude, it appears that the strength of theories in the Piaget and Kohlberg tradition lies in the elaboration of the development and complex nature of moral thought; these theories are limited, however, because they neglect the motivational side of the phenomenon called conscience. Even if moral thought develops (as these writers suggest) by exposure to increasingly complex and comprehensive moral structure, concepts are still needed to connect these thoughts to feelings and action. One interesting possibility, suggested by Langer (1969), is the following: a discrepancy between one's level of moral reasoning and overt behavior creates a state of disequilibrium, to reduce which the individual is compelled to lessen the discrepancy by bringing behavior and reasoning closer together. It is possible, however, that the development of moral motives proceeds along tracks that are entirely different from the development of moral thought.

We now turn to two theoretical approaches that focus on moral motivation. One, the psychoanalytic, stresses anxiety and repression; the other focuses on the role of empathy and its developmental transformations.

PSYCHOANALYTIC THEORY

Although minor variations exist, the central thrust of the psychoanalytic account of conscience development, which has been worked out primarily for males, may be reconstructed as follows. The young child is inevitably subjected to many frustrations, some of which are due to parental intervention and control and some of which, for example, illness and other physical discomforts, have nothing directly to do with the parent. All of these frustrations contribute to the development of hostility toward the parent. In addition, the child experiences urges to maximize the amount of close bodily contact with the mother because of the erotic pleasure it affords. The child's main rival for the mother's affection is of course the father, and the child's expressions of impulse toward the mother are often punished. Due to anxiety over anticipated punishment, especially loss of love and abandonment by the parent, children repress both their hostility and their erotic feeling toward the mother. To help gain mastery over their anxieties and maintain the repression, as well as elicit continuing expressions of affection from the parents, children adopt, in relatively unmodified form, the rules and prohibitions emanating from the parents, especially the father. They also develop a generalized motive to emulate the overt behavior and to adopt the inner states of the parent. Finally, they adopt the parents' capacity to punish them when they violate a prohibition or are tempted to do so — turning inward, in the course of doing this, the hostility that was originally directed toward the parent. This self-punishment is experienced as guilt feelings, which are dreaded because of their intensity and their resemblance to the earlier anxieties about punishment and abandonment. Children therefore try to avoid guilt by acting always in accordance with incorporated parental prohibitions and erecting various mechanisms of defense against the conscious awareness of impulses to act to the contrary. These basic processes of conscience-formation are accomplished by about five to six years of age and they are then worked through and solidified during the latency period — the remaining, relatively calm years of childhood.

Few psychoanalytic writers have dealt explicitly with adolescence, but the general view appears to be that the relative calm and impulse-control achieved during the latency period suffers a disruption at puberty due to the emergence of intense sexual impulses, and the child is plunged once again into an oedipal situation. Writers see different processes as resulting from this recapitulation of the oedipal situation. According to Blos (1962), for example, a "rebellion against the superego" takes place in which individuals reject their parents' standards and also the part of themselves that has unreflectively adopted their parents' morality. Jacobson (1964) and Hartmann (1960), on the other hand, contend that the superego mellows with age. According to Jacobson, the superego loses some of its "exaggerated idealism" as the result of ego maturity, particularly after the "tempest of instinctual conflicts during adolescence has subsided." With the aid of the neutralized energy then available to it, the superego can operate on the basis of more reasonable goals, more mature moral judgments, and more tolerance.

Solnit (1972) suggests that in adolescence the infantile ties to the parents are reawakened, and although the thought of relinquishing them is painful, the adolescent knows that he must do so. Furthermore, the hold of the childhood superego is loosened, and the adolescent may long for experiences that will bolster the superego's function and form a bulwark against regressive tendencies. This longing may be felt as a need to act in accord with certain lofty ideals. In addition, because of the weakened superego, the adolescent may experience an interest in joining groups, in order to borrow strength from the group's cohesiveness and identifications. Hence the importance of peers for the adolescent.

In Douvan and Adelson's (1966) interpretation, too, the Oedipus complex is recapitulated in adolescence, but there are important differences between the two situations. Mainly, there now exist substitutes for the mother, who are legitimate love objects. The child is thus relatively free to express his erotic impulses, and he can proceed to establish a set of moral values and controls on more realistic grounds. He may, for example, identify with the father, though not as a global defense against an overpowering rival since the father is no longer a rival in the same crucial way.

More recently, Settlage (1972) has argued that the superego is "re-externalized" in adolescence. That is, the values contained in the superego are made available to conscious appraisal, are reassessed, played out, tested and challenged in discussions (mainly with peers) and sometimes in action. Some of the values are seen as mythical and unreal and are discarded. Others are retained and reincorporated into the superego. As a result the superego, which formerly represented only the tradition and cultural values held by the parents, now represents the values and ideals that are unique and appropriate at the time. What triggers this reappraisal are the contradictions, duplicities, and uncertainties that abound in society and the fact that adults are less sure of their values than they were in the past. Consequently youth are deprived of the security that stems from the conviction of the older generation and feel under pressure to work out some system of guiding ideals. For those who are not exposed to the society's contradictions, that is, those who must assume adult responsibilities without participating in a moratorium, such as a college education often affords, the childhood superego may remain unchanged.

According to the most recent formulation by Blos (1976), adolescence involves not only the recapitulation of the oedipal conflict, but also the continuation of certain issues that were not resolved earlier and were suspended during latency. These issues crop up again in adolescence when they are manifested increasingly in relation to peers, and less in relation to the family. Specifically, Blos suggests that the image of the parent internalized in early childhood is a split image, entailing a totally "good" and a totally "bad" parent. This split image may account for the frequent observation that young adolescents tend to act out the "good" and "bad" parent within the peer group. And it may explain what Blos calls "adolescent totalism," the adolescent's tendency to view objects, the world, events, and even the self as dichotomies — as extremes, rarely a blend — despite intermittent recognition that this is unrealistic.

Finally, Erikson's (1970) views are worth noting here. Erikson suggests there are three broad stages of moral development: specific moral learning in childhood, ideologies experienced in adolescence, and ethical consolidation in adulthood. Erikson's main concern, of course, is with the adolescent's search for an identity, which requires a sense of purpose. If in the face of overwhelming evidence the adolescent becomes disillusioned with the moral and religious beliefs acquired in childhood, then there is a loss of purpose, a vacuum. There may then ensue a desperate search for an ideology that will provide purpose and thus facilitate identity formation. The ideology, to be acceptable, must fit both the "evidence" and the adolescent's relatively high cognitive level. And if, in addition, others share the ideology, this is to the good because it then also provides community. For Erikson, then, ideology becomes the "guardian of identity" because it provides a sense of purpose, helps tie the present to the future, and contributes meaning to action.

These formulations are all interesting and suggestive, but there has been little attempt to show the connections between them and, more importantly, they lack empirical support. The writers either give no evidence for their views, which presumably derive from their clinical and personal observations or, more typically, they bolster their case with an example or two, drawn from their case files, which provide at best a superficial level of support. Settlage (1972), for example, describes adolescents who do appear to react to their peers in terms of dichotomous extremes, as his theory predicts, but no evidence is given to show that these actions derive from split, internalized parental images. Perhaps equally important, the writers do not come to grips with certain critical issues pertaining to the presumed nature of the superego. If the superego acquired in childhood is indeed based on repression (a central concept in psychoanalytic theory), then it is not enough to state that it mellows with age and is enriched by values acquired on a more cognitive basis in adolescence. The crucial question ignored is, How can cognitively acquired values be incorporated into a mental structure that has been largely unconscious since its formation? On the other hand, to say that the repression is lifted as the result of development of the ego, which then takes over the function of the superego, appears to abandon the concept of a conscience entirely, since the ego can serve selfish and immoral as well as moral purposes. The crucial question that is begged here is, What makes the person utilize his ego capacities for moral ends rather than egoistic ends? In short, what seems to be missing in the psychoanalytic account, as in the cognitive-disequilibrium view, is a concept of a mature motive force that may underlie moral action. The theoretical approach that follows is a beginning attempt to fill this gap.

EMPATHIC AROUSAL AND TRANSFORMATION

The idea that empathy, defined as a vicarious emotional response to another person, may provide a motive base for moral action has a long history, going back at least two centuries. Writers like Hume, Rousseau, Shelley, and Adam Smith, for example, wrote extensively about this aspect of experience and its significance for human interaction and organized social life. Early psychological theorists like Stern, Scheler, and McDougall advanced the view that empathy provided the motivational base for specific prosocial acts, like helping and comforting others, taking turns, cooperating, and sharing. Some of these writers thought empathy was the basic prosocial bond making civilized life possible, though most simply assumed it to be part of human nature and that if a person responds empathically to someone he or she is more apt to behave in a benevolent manner towards them. These writers all seemed to share the conception of empathy as the basis for a moral motive rather than a skill that might serve egoistic and moral motives alike.

I have elsewhere pulled together the evidence that a neural basis for empathy exists and that it may have always been a part of man's biological makeup (Hoffman, 1979a). I have also proposed a theoretical model for the ontogenetic development of empathy, its transformations, and its implications for moral development (Hoffman, 1976a; 1978, pp. 227–256). In the model, a summary of which follows, empathy has three components; an affect arousal component, a cognitive component, and a motivational component. The focus is on the empathic response to another's distress, which is obviously relevant to the moral domain.

Affective Component

There appear to be at least five distinct modes of empathic arousal, which vary in degree of perceptual and cognitive involvement, type of eliciting stimulus (e.g., facial, situational, symbolic), and the amount and kind of past experience required. The first two modes (the cry of the newborn infant in response to the sound of another infant's cry and the conditioning of empathy that may result from the bodily transfer of the caretaker's affective state to the infant through physical handling) are not pertinent to adolescence. The last three are and will be described in some detail.

The first of these is a simple variant of the associationistic paradigm. It holds that cues of pain or pleasure from another person or from one's situation evoke associations with the observer's own past pain or pleasure, resulting in an emphatic affective reaction (Humphrey, 1922). A simple example is the child who cuts himself, feels the pain, and cries. Later, on seeing another child cut himself and cry, the sight of blood, the sound of the cry, or any other distress cue or aspect of the situation having elements in common with his own prior pain-experience can now elicit the unpleasant affect initially associated with that experience.

The second mode was advanced some time ago by Lipps (1906) who viewed empathy as the result of an isomorphic, presumably unlearned "motor mimicry" response to another person's expression of affect. According to Lipps, the observer automatically imitates the other person with slight movements in posture and facial expression ("objective motor mimicry"), thus creating in himself inner cues that contribute through afferent feedback, to his understanding and experiencing of the other person's affect. This conception has been ignored over the years but there is some recent, modest support for it. First, the evidence for motor mimicry comes from studies showing that college students engage in increased lip activity and increased frequency of eye-blink responses when observing models who stutter or blink their eyes (Berger & Hadley, 1975; Bernal & Berger, 1976). Second, there is evidence for afferent feedback: the different emotions appear to be accompanied by different degrees of tone in the skeletal muscles (e.g., the loss in muscle tone that accompanies sadness is associated with characteristic postures, which are diametrically opposed to those seen in a happy mood) and by different patterns of facial muscle activity (e.g., Gelhorn, 1964; Izard, 1971). It also appears that cues from one's facial musculature may contribute to the actual experience of an emotion. In a series of remarkable experiments by Laird (1974) college students were instructed to arrange their facial muscles, one at a time, into positions that correspond to "smiles" or "frowns," without knowing that their faces were set in smile or frown positions. This was done by asking the subject to contract various muscles. For example, the experimenter touched the subject lightly between the eyebrows with an electrode and said, "Pull your brows down and together . . . good, now hold it like that." The subjects reported feeling more angry when their faces were set in the frown position and more happy when their faces were set in the smile position even though they were unaware of frowning or smiling. They also reported that cartoons viewed when "smiling" were more humorous than cartoons viewed when "frowning."

The previous two modes are both involuntary and minimally cognitive, requiring only enough perceptual discrimination to detect the relevant cues from the other person (mimicry) or from his or her situation (association). The final mode, imaginging how it would feel if the stimuli impinging on the other person were impinging on the self, is clearly the most advanced developmentally. The pertinent research, done by Stotland, can be illustrated by two studies. In one (Mathews & Stotland, 1973), nursing students watched a training film in which a severely ill patient, followed from the time of entry into the hospital, finally dies. Those who indicated previously that they often imagine themselves in the other person's place (in the movies, for example) showed more palmer sweat if they imagined themselves in the place of the dying woman. In the second study, subjects instructed to imagine how they would feel and what sensations they would have in their hands if exposed to the same painful heat treatment being applied to another person, gave more evidence of empathic distress, both physiologically and verbally, than (1) subjects instructed to attend closely to the other person's physical movements and (2) subjects instructed to imagine how the *other* person felt when he or she was undergoing the treatment (Stotland, 1969). The last finding, in particular, suggests that imagining oneself in the other's place may produce an empathic response because it reflects processes generated from within the observer rather than from the observer's orientation to the model. These may be processes in which connections are made between the stimuli impinging on the other person and similar stimulus events in the observer's own past. That is, imagining oneself in the other's place may produce an empathic response because it has the power to evoke associations with real events in one's own past in which one actually experienced the affect in question. This process, then, may have much in common with the associationistic mode discussed earlier, the evocative stimulus in this case being the mental representation of oneself in the other's situation. Another important difference is that here the arousal is triggered by a cognitive restructuring of events (what is happening to the other is viewed as happening to the self) and is thus more subject to conscious control.

   I do not regard these five modes of empathic arousal as forming a stage sequence in the sense of each mode superceding the previous ones. The first two operate in infancy, as noted, and are superceded by the others. The remaining three, however, once operative, may continue to function throughout life and, indeed, they may all operate in the same situation.

Cognitive Transformation of Empathy

Since empathy is a response to another person's feeling or situation, mature empathizers know that the source of their own affect is something happening to another person and that person's affective response to these events, and the empathizer has a sense of what the other is feeling. The young child who lacks a self–other distinction may be empathically aroused without these cognitions. Thus how persons experience empathy depends on the level at which they cognize others, which undergoes dramatic changes developmentally (Hoffman, 1975c). Briefly, the research suggests that for most of the first year, children appear to experience a fusion of self and other. By about 12 months, they attain "person permanence" and become aware of others as physical entities distinct from the self. By two or three years of age, they acquire a rudimentary sense of others as having inner states (thoughts, perceptions, feelings) independent of their own inner states; this is the initial step in role-taking, which continues to develop into increasingly complex forms. Finally, by late childhood or early adolescence, they become aware of others as having personal identities and life experiences beyond the immediate situation.

As the child passes through these four stages the experience of empathy may be expected to include, in addition to a purely affective component, an increasing awareness of the source of the affect as lying in someone else's situation and a more veridical awareness of the other's feelings.

I shall now describe the four hypothetical levels of empathic response that result from this coalescence of empathic affect and the cognitive sense of the other, as exemplified by the empathic response to another person in distress. The first three stages, which refer to infancy and early childhood, will be mentioned briefly to provide a developmental context for the last stage.

1. For most of the first year, before children have acquired "person permanence," distress cues from others may elicit a global empathic distress response — presumably a fusion of unpleasant feelings and stimuli that come from the infant's own body (through conditioning or mimicry), from the dimly perceived "other," and from the situation. Since they cannot yet differentiate themselves from the other, they must often be unclear as to who is experiencing any distress that they witness and they may, at times, behave as though what happened to the other was happening to them.

2. With the emergence of a sense of the other as a physical entity distinct from the self, the affective portion of children's empathic distress is extended to the separate "self" and "other" that emerge. And, children become, for the first time, capable of empathic distress, while also being aware of the fact that another person, and not the self, is the victim. They cannot yet distinguish between their own and the other's inner states, however, and are apt to assume they are the same, as evidenced in their efforts to help, which may consist chiefly of giving the other what they themselves find most comforting.

3. By two to three years of age, children begin to be aware that other people's feelings and thoughts may sometimes differ from their own and that others' perspectives may be based on their own interpretations of events. Consequently, they become more cautious and tentative in their inferences and more alert and responsive to additional cues about the feelings of others besides their own responses. By about four years of age most children respond with appropriate affect and can recognize signs of happiness or sadness in others in simple situations (e.g., Borke, 1971; Feshbach & Roe, 1968). And we may assume that with further role-taking ability they can detect the cues of complex and mixed emotions as well as become capable of being empathically aroused by imagining themselves in the other's place.

4. Sometime during late childhood or early adolescence, owing to the emerging conception of self and other as continuous persons each with his or her own history and identity, children become aware that others feel pleasure and pain not only in particular situations, but also in the context of their larger pattern of life experiences. Consequently, though children may continue to react to someone's immediate situational distress, their concern is intensified when they know it reflects a chronic condition. That is, they can now empathize not only with people's transitory, situation-specific distress, but also with what they imagine to be their general condition. This fourth stage, then, consists of empathically aroused affect together with a mental representation of the general plight of others

— their typical day-to-day level of distress or deprivation, the opportunities available or denied to them, their future prospects, and the like. If this representation falls short of what the observer conceives to be a minimally acceptable standard of well-being, an empathic distress response may result, even if contradicted by the other's apparent momentary state. That is, the observer's mental representation may at times override contradictory situational or facial cues.

To summarize, individuals who progress through these four stages (which is usually accomplished by adolescence) become capable of a high level of empathic distress. They can process various types of information — that gained from their own vicarious affective reaction, from the immediate situational cues, and from their general knowledge about the other's life. They can act out in their mind the emotions and experiences suggested by this information and introspect on all of this. They may thus gain an understanding and respond affectively in terms of the circumstances, feelings, and wishes of the other — while maintaining the sense that this is a separate person from themselves.

It also seems likely that with further cognitive development persons may be able to comprehend the plight not only of an individual, but also of an entire group or class of people — such as people who are economically impoverished, politically oppressed, socially outcast, victims of war, or mentally retarded. Because of a different background, their own specific distress experiences may differ from others. All distress experiences probably have a common affective core, however, and this together with the individual's high cognitive level at this age provides the requisites for a generalized empathic distress capability. The combination of empathic affect and the perceived plight of an unfortunate group would seem to be the developmentally most advanced form of empathic distress.

Sympathetic Distress

Thus far, I have suggested that empathic distress includes both an affective component and a cognitive component derived from the observer's cognitive sense of the other and his or her awareness that the other's state is the source of the affect. Many affect theorists, notably Schachter and Singer (1962) and Mandler (1975) suggest that how a person labels or experiences an affect is heavily influenced by certain pertinent cognitions, "One labels, interprets, and identifies this stirred-up state in terms of the characteristics of the situation and one's apperceptive mass . . ." (Schachter & Singer, 1962, p. 380). These writers are explaining how we distinguish among different affects (e.g., anger, joy, fear) aroused directly. Quite apart from this issue, the cognitive sense of others appears to be so intrinsic to *empathically* aroused affect as to alter the very quality of the observer's affective experience. More specifically, once persons are aware of others as distinct from the self, their empathic distress, which is a parallel response (that is, a more or less exact replication of the victim's actual feelings of distress) may be transformed, at least in part, into a more reciprocal feeling of concern for the victim. This transformation is in keeping with how people report they feel when observing someone in distress. That is, they continue to respond in a purely empathic, quasi-egoistic manner — to feel uncomfortable and highly distressed themselves — but they also experience a feeling of compassion (or what I call sympathetic distress) for the victim along with a conscious desire to help because they feel sorry for the victim and not just to relieve their own empathic distress. The distinction between empathic and sympathetic distress is highlighted by Mathews and

Stotland's (1973) report that nurses often experience conflict between feelings of sympathy, which include an intense desire to help their severely ill patients, and their own empathic distress which makes it difficult at times even to stay in the same room with their patients.

The last three stages of empathic distress should also be viewed as stages of sympathetic distress. And, insofar as the transformation of empathic into sympathetic distress takes place, the description of the stages should be modified to stress the interaction between affective and cognitive components and the important qualitative change in feeling tone that results.

Guilt

The burgeoning literature on causal attribution suggests that people have a natural tendency to make inferences about the causes of behavior and events. Since empathic distress is a response to someone else's plight, any cues about what caused that plight, if salient enough, may therefore serve as cognitive inputs, in addition to those deriving from the observer's sense of the other, that help shape the observer's affective experience. Furthermore, once observers have the capacity to recognize the consequences of their actions for others and to be aware that they have choice and control over their own behavior, they have the necessary requisites for a self-critical or self-blaming response to their own actions. It follows that if the cues in a situation in which they respond empathically to someone in distress indicate that they are the cause of that distress, their response may then have both the affectively unpleasant and cognitive self-blaming component of the guilt experience. Thus empathic distress may be transformed by the attribution of self-blame into a feeling of guilt.

The earliest guilt experience of this type probably occurs when the child's empathic response and his or her awareness of harming another person occur together or, at least, when the awareness follows soon after the empathic response (as when the parent points out the harmful effect of the child's action after the fact) since this type of situation is the least demanding cognitively. A second type of guilt, guilt over inaction, becomes a possibility once the child acquires the additional capacity to construct a mental representation of an event that might have occurred but did not (e.g., a representation of what one might have done to help a person whose distress one did not cause). The observers' realization that they did not act to reduce the other's distress when they might have, that they may therefore be to blame for the continuation (if not the cause) of the other's distress, may then be expected to transform their empathic distress into guilt. A similar analysis can be made for anticipatory guilt, which is highly demanding cognitively since persons must have the capacity to visualize not only an act that they have not performed (but may be contemplating) but also the other person's probable distress response as well.

There is as yet no developmental research on guilt but the findings obtained in a study of 10–14-year-old children are pertinent here. The subjects were asked to give written completions to projective stories in which the central figure commits a moral transgression. Most of the subjects showed in their responses a clear capacity for feeling guilty not only over action, but also over inaction (Hoffman, 1975d). This is worthy of note since the central figure in the story has really done nothing wrong but happened to be present when someone needed help. Although children are taught to feel bad over harming someone, it is doubtful that they are often taught to feel bad over inaction. I would suggest that the guilt the subjects projected was due to their empathic response to the victim, in combination with the awareness of what the central figure (with whom they identified) might have done to help were it not for his involvement in pursuing his own goals. Guilt over inaction may thus have much in common with sympathetic distress — the difference being that in the case of guilt observers are aware of something they could have done but did not.

The human capacity to experience guilt even when one has done no wrong is illustrated still more dramatically in other situations. The well-known phenomenon of survivor guilt in natural disasters and in war is a case in point. An example from the Vietnam War is the Navy pilot whose right arm had been partially crippled by shrapnel, who said on being released after two years as a war prisoner, "Getting released, you feel a tremendous amount of guilt. You developed a relationship with the other prisoners . . . and they're still there and you're going away" *(Newsweek,* 1972, p. 27). This remark, as well as statements by the Hiroshima atomic-bomb survivors cited by Lifton (1968), suggests that despite a person's own plight, one may feel guilty if one feels he or she is far better off than others. This possibility contrasts interestingly with "social comparison processes" (e.g., Festinger, 1954; Masters, 1972, pp. 320–339), which focus on self-other comparisons in a competitive context, for example, the enhancement in one's self-esteem that may result from out-performing others.

The link to adolescent moral development becomes evident when we examine some of the responses given by the affluent social activists studied by Keniston (1968). The essence of guilt over feeling relatively advantaged is conveyed by Keniston (although he calls it indignation rather than guilt) when he describes these activists as stressing "their shock upon realizing that their own good fortune was not shared . . . and their indignation when they 'really' understood that the benefits they had experienced had not been extended to others" (pp. 131–132). One of Keniston's respondents, in discussing some poor Mexican children he had known years earlier, vividly described his realization of relative advantage in a way that also suggests its possible role in moral action.

. . . I was the one that lived in a place where there were fans and no flies, and they lived with the flies. And I was clearly destined for something, and they were destined for nothing. . . . Well, I sort of made a pact with these people that when I got to be powerful I might change some things. And I think I pursued that pact pretty consistently for a long time. [P. 50]

Something between guilt over survival and guilt over affluence is exemplified by the black student at Harvard who wrote that he and others like him,

. . . have had to wrestle with the keen sense of guilt they feel being here while their families still struggle in Black ghettoes. . . . The one sure way of easing guilt was (by demanding) 'relevance' from Harvard, which means, in effect, instruction that can be directed toward improving the quality of life for Blacks as a whole in this country . . . (and) via building takeovers, strikes, and other kinds of demonstrations. . . . [Monroe, 1973, p. 46]

Guilt over survival and over affluence differ in certain obvious respects. Survivors have shared in the other's distress and feel guilty over not continuing to suffer, or suffering less than they; their own condition may be bad but the other's condition is much worse. Affluent youths typically have not shared in the other's distress and the contrast to which they react is between their own life condition, which is extremely good, and the other's condition, which is extremely bad. What the survivor and the affluent as well as the formerly disadvantaged person have in common, however, is that they feel deeply guilty over the vast difference in well-being that they perceive to exist between themselves and relevant others.

I call this reaction existential guilt to distinguish it from true guilt since these persons have done nothing wrong but feel culpable because of circumstances of life beyond their control. Existential guilt may take on some of the qualities of true guilt, however. The activist youths in Keniston's sample, for example, appear to have concluded that their privileged position makes it possible for them to do something to alleviate the condition of the less fortunate; that if they do nothing, they become personally responsible for helping perpetuate the conditions they deplore. For some individuals existential guilt may shade still further into a sense of individual complicity or true personal guilt, should they come to view the other's plight as due to the action of people with whom they identify, for example, parents or members of their social class. An example of existential guilt shading into true guilt comes from the response given by a congressional intern to the question, Why are so many middle-class youth turned off by the very system that gave them so many advantages and opportunities?

They feel guilty because while they are enjoying this highest standard of living, American Indians are starving and black ghettoes are overrun by rats. . . . This goes on while they eat steak every day. Their sense of moral indignation can't stand this; and they realize that the blame rests on the shoulders of their class. [New Republic, November 28, 1970, p. 11]

These and other statements I have heard that explicitly point up the actor's relative advantage suggest that two conditions are necessary for existential guilt to be experienced: (1) the circumstances of the other's life must be vividly imagined and (2) there must be a lack of justification for one's relative well-being. The first, a keen sense of the other's plight, may require direct exposure to the day-to-day life experiences of the less fortunate, hence being witness to the discrepancy in well-being as well as the basic human similarities that exist. Such exposure may be gained through the kind of close personal contact that Civil Rights, Peace Corps, and Vista volunteers had a decade ago. Continued exposure through books, travel and perhaps some liberal-arts and social-science curricula also play a contributing role. Perhaps even more significant are the mass media, especially the vastly increased news coverage that instantly brings the scene home to many people.

As regards the second requisite, recent European and American history has seen the breakdown of many of the former justifications for relative advantage. Perhaps the most significant contribution to this breakdown in the past century is the emergence and rising acceptance in most developed societies of equalitarian social norms — all people have equal worth. The diminished hold of traditional religious doctrine, such as the Calvinist view of well-being as a sign of grace is another contributing factor. Of more recent importance is widespread acceptance of the scientific evidence against genetic inferiority and in favor of environmental determinism. Finally, one of the last remaining justifications in our society, the idea that one deserves what one earns, appears only now to be losing its effectiveness, owing to recent increases in the proportion of young people from affluent homes who rely on financial aid from parents and social agencies.

The statements and actions of some of the white radicals of the 1960s suggest that existential guilt may at times be a far more potent motivating force than the simpler type of true personal guilt discussed earlier. Existential guilt may require continued activity in the service of alleviating human suffering (rather than merely a discrete act of restitution) in order to afford one a continuing sense of self-worth. It also seems likely, as with true guilt, that persons who do nothing will continue to feel guilty or will cognitively restructure the situation so as to justify themselves or to deny their own relative advantage: "The other has his pleasures and enjoys living the way he does"; "He is a bad person and brought his misfortune on himself"; "I worked hard for what I have."

Another choice may be to reduce the relative advantage by renouncing one's privileges or in other ways "identifying with the lowly." This choice may take on the character of pure self-punishment and cease to be altruism. Indeed, for some individuals existential guilt may be an obstacle to the development of personal competence, achievement, and success. A study of achievement and fear-of-success motivation by Hoffman (1974) provides an interesting illustration of this phenomenon. Horner's projective story cue (1968), "John finds himself at the top of his medical-school class," drew the following response from a male college student: "John is perplexed upon hearing the news. He's mad that everything is so assured. Resents the fact that he's hereditarily good and others are not." If this response really does reflect guilt over relative competence and is at all representative, it might mean that existential guilt is contributing to the erosion of the competitive, individualistic ethic among some individuals in the affluent, highly educated group in which this ethic has traditionally been foremost.

In like manner, the search for personal fulfillment in general may be hampered by existential guilt. This would throw into question Maslow's dictum that once an individual's deficiency needs are satisfied, his or her primary motive becomes the attainment of self-actualization and peak experience. Perhaps when others in society are known to be at a deficiency level, striving for personal fulfillment and peak experiences, makes us feel guilty, unless we repress the misery of others or resort to the type of cognitive restructuring mentioned above. If so, Maslow's formulation would need to be revised as follows: given the awareness of one's relative advantage, the satisfaction of one's deficiency needs leads either to the motivation to fulfill oneself or to existential guilt. Or, some individuals may strive both for personal fulfillment and the resolution of existential guilt, for example, by entering one of the service professions with the aim of helping others.

As an aside, I should note that these views on existential guilt seem far less applicable to the youth of today than in the mid-1960s. I have interviewed young people informally and found several types of responses that might explain the change. The most prevalent responses indicate that the youth of today place a high value on success and, despite their parents' affluence, they do not feel relatively advantaged because of (1) their own worries about finding a desirable job and (2) their view that economic conditions have improved for many disadvantaged groups who now also appear to enjoy a favored position in the job market. These responses suggest that though existential guilt may be the most advanced developmentally, it may be confined historically to certain times and places.

Developmentally, these different types of guilt should be related to the levels of empathic and sympathetic distress discussed earlier. Thus at the second level of empathic distress, in which children are especially responsive to the other person's inner states in the situation, they will experience sympathetic distress when not responsible for the other's distress but when their actions have caused that distress they will experience guilt. With further cognitive development, but still within the second level of empathic distress, the transformation of empathic distress into guilt may result from the awareness of not helping when one might reasonably have been expected to help. And, with the capability of foreseeing the consequences of action and of inaction, anticipatory guilt also becomes possible. Similarly, at the highest level of empathic distress, when the observer is particularly sensitive to the other's general plight outside the immediate situation, if the focus of the observer's concern shifts from the other's plight to the contrast between it and the observer's own relatively advantaged life style, empathic distress may also be transformed into feelings of guilt. (For a fuller discussion of the developmental levels of guilt, see Hoffman, 1979b.)

Thus I am suggesting that there may be one basic prosocial affect, empathic distress, which may be transformed into sympathetic distress or guilt depending on the causal attributions made by the observer.[1]

The Motivational Component of Empathic Affect

As already noted, the idea that empathy provides a motive base for moral action is not new. Most writers, however, view empathic distress as essentially an egoistic motive, that is, it leads to moral action only because it constitutes an aversive state in the observer which can usually best be alleviated by giving help to the victim. I disagree with this view because with the partial transformation of empathic into sympathetic distress the conscious aim of the person's action is gradually changed, at least in part, from relieving his or her "own" empathic distress to relieving the distress perceived in the other. More importantly, even if empathic distress were experienced primarily as aversive to the self rather than compassion for the other, it would differ from the usual egoistic motives (e.g., sensual pleasure, material gain, social approval, economic success) in three significant ways: it is aroused by another person's misfortune, not by one's own; a major goal of the ensuing behavior is to help the other, not just oneself; and the potential for gratification in the observer is contingent on acting to reduce the other's distress. It therefore seems more appropriate to designate empathic distress as an altruistic motive — perhaps with a quasi-egoistic component — than to call it an egoistic motive. (For an extended discussion of this issue, see Hoffman, 1979a).

The Research

There is considerable evidence that people of all ages tend to respond empathically to another person in distress, unless instructed to take an observational set that fragments victims or makes them an object of intellectual scrutiny or a source of data. There are no definitive findings on the relation between age and degree of empathic affect arousal, although it is reasonable to assume that the highest levels of sympathetic distress and guilt do not appear regularly until early adolescence or later.

The evidence that empathic affect contributes to moral behavior is unclear in children, but the research on college-age subjects provides consistent support. It may be useful first to state the kind of evidence needed. If empathic or sympathetic distress motivates moral action, it should be associated with a tendency to help others, and it should diminish in intensity following a helpful act but continue at a high level in the absence of action. The

---

[1]It also seems reasonable to suppose that if the cues in the situation point to the victim's being responsible for his or her own plight, the observer's empathic distress might be transformed into a feeling of indifference or derogation of the victim. If the cues indicate a third person is to blame, the observer may feel angry at that person because he sympathizes with the victim or because he empathizes with the victim and feels attacked himself. Finally, a cultural molding of empathic responsiveness may take place whereby certain people are classified as less than human (e.g., the untouchables in India). Empathic responses to these people may also be transformed into derogatory feelings or indifference.

evidence is supportive on both counts. Thus there are at least 10 studies, all using physiological indices of arousal, showing that when persons are exposed to others in distress, they either respond empathically or with an overt helping act, whichever is being investigated; 5 studies show that when data are collected on both empathy and helping, subjects typically show both responses. There is also evidence that as the magnitude of the pain cues from the victim increases, the latency of the helping act decreases, that is, the subject acts more quickly. Finally, there is evidence that empathic effect is aroused prior to the helpful act and that it diminishes in intensity following the helpful act. This research has all been reviewed in detail elsewhere (Hoffman, 1977b), but I shall describe the results of one study by Weiss et al. (1973), which may suggest the sequence of the responses involved.

The subjects, college students, viewed a model who evidenced overt signs of stress (e.g., sweating, reflex kicking), while performing a motor task and apparently receiving continuously painful shocks. The subject's task was to make evaluations of the model's performance and record them by pressing certain buttons. Pressing the buttons also terminated the shock, as indicated by visible signs of relief from the model. There were 15 training trials. The main finding was that the subjects acquired the button-pushing response without any reinforcement other than the victim's expressions of relief. Furthermore, the learning curves closely resembled those obtained in more conventional escape-conditioning studies. For example, the speed of the button-pushing response increased at an increasing rate over the 15 trials; it also increased when the distress cues from the model were more intense; and variables like partial reinforcement and delay of reinforcement operated just as they do in conventional studies. It therefore appears that the consequences to the observer of helping someone in distress correspond closely to the consequences of conventional reinforcement. This suggests that an aversive state, such as sympathetic distress, might have been induced in the observer, and the termination of that state functioned as a reinforcer in acquiring the helping response.

Weiss et al. unfortunately did not collect systematic data on the affect aroused in the subjects. They did note anecdotally, however, that the subjects "sweated visibly and showed other physical signs of stress." From this, as well as the evidence for empathic arousal in similar experiments, we may conclude that the subjects probably did experience sympathetic distress. Weiss et al. also note that the subjects often said they wished they could do something to help the confederate. We are not told when these statements were made, but they must have been made in the early training trials before the subjects learned that there was something they could do, namely, push the bottons. This is important because the speed of the button pushing response was accelerated in the later trials. The study thus appears to provide suggestive evidence that the subjects did experience sympathetic distress, which, by and large, preceded and probably served as the motive for the helping act. It is difficult to explain the pattern of results otherwise.

Perhaps more convincing is the study by Gaertner and Dovidio (1977). The subjects, female undergraduate students, observed (through earphones) a situation in which a confederate left an experimental task in order to straighten out a stack of chairs that she thought was about to topple over on her. A moment later the confederate screamed that the chairs were falling on her, and then was silent. The main finding was that the greater the subject's cardiac responsiveness (as indexed by heart-rate acceleration), the more quickly she intervened. Furthermore, the physiological arousal was not merely the artifactual result of the subject rising from her chair, since the arousal preceded the rising. The heart-rate acceleration score was based on data obtained during the 10-second period immediately following the confederate's scream, whereas the median latency for rising was 40 seconds. Thus the speed of intervention was systematically related to the magnitude of the heart-rate acceleration just prior to the intervention.

Empathic or sympathetic distress arousal, of course, does not guarantee moral action any more than other motives can guarantee action. Other factors may operate, for example, the extent to which the situation points up the observer's responsibility to act rather than indicating that responsibility is diffused among many people (e.g., Geer & Jarmecky, 1973; Latané & Darley, 1970; Schwartz, 1970). Furthermore, in individualistic societies the motive to help will often be overriden by more powerful egoistic motives, as evidenced by the negative relationship obtained between helping others and competitiveness (Rutherford & Mussen, 1968). As I noted earlier, American middle-class children are often socialized both to help others and to respect authority and follow the rules, but in some situations one cannot do both. Perhaps the best-known instance of the way authority may serve as a deterrent to prosocial behavior is Milgram's finding (1963) that adult males will administer high levels of shock on instruction from the experimenter, despite strong feelings of compassion for the victim. It should be noted, however, that in a partial replication Tilker (1970) found that when the subject was assigned the role of observer he not only showed increasing empathic distress as the shock levels to the victim were increased but often intervened to stop the experiment, despite specific instructions to the contrary and continuing opposition from the person administering the shock.

Empathic Overarousal

Empathic affect, like other motives, may also be self-limiting. There is evidence, first of all, that moral action may require a certain amount of need fulfillment in the actors, so as to reduce their self-preoccupation and leave them open and responsive to cues signifying the needs of others in the situation. For example, the arousal of deprived need-states, such as concerns about failure, social approval, and even physical discomfort due to noise, have been found to interfere with helpful action (e.g., Mathews & Canon, 1975; Moore, Underwood & Rosenhan, 1973; Murphy, 1937; Staub & Sherk, 1970; Wine, 1975). Since empathic distress may itself be extremely aversive under certain conditions, it might be expected at times to direct the observers' attention to themselves and thus actually decrease the likelihood of a moral act. That is, there may be an optimal range of empathic arousal — determined by the individual's level of distress-tolerance — within which he or she is most responsive to others. Beyond this range, one may be too preoccupied with one's own aversive state to help anyone else. Another possibility is that once over one's threshold of distress tolerance, observers may employ certain mechanisms to reduce the level of arousal itself. They might, for example, avoid interacting with people in pain, like some of the highly empathic nursing students observed by Mathews and Stotland (1973). Or, they might employ certain empathy inhibiting perceptual and cognitive strategies. Here is an illustrative quote from a study by Bandura and Rosenthal (1966) in which college students were given a strong dose of epinephrine before observing someone being administered electric shocks:

After the first three or four shocks, I thought about the amount of pain for the other guy. Then I began to think, to minimize my own discomfort. I recall looking at my watch, looking out the window, and checking things about the room. I recall that the victim received a shock when I was thinking about the seminar, and that I didn't seem to notice the discomfort as much in this instance.'' [P. 61]

This quote illustrates at once the involuntary tendency to empathize with someone in distress, the aversive quality of empathic distress, and the use of defensive strategies to eliminate the aversive state or reduce it to a more tolerable level. The concept of empathic overarousal implies, then, that empathic distress may trigger prosocial moral action increasingly but only up to the actor's threshold of distress-tolerance. Beyond that point, it may trigger egoistic self-protective action.[2]

Guilt as a Moral Motive

Examination of young adolescents' responses to projective story-completion items involving transgressions reveals that in most cases the guilt feelings described were followed immediately by the attribution to the story character of some sort of reparative behavior, which functioned to reduce his or her guilt. When reparation was precluded by the story conditions (it was too late for anything to be done), the guilt response was typically prolonged. The central figures in the story were also often portrayed as resolving to become less selfish and more considerate of others in the future. This suggests that one mechanism by which guilt may contribute to altruistic behavior is to trigger a process of self-examination and restructuring of values that may help strengthen one's moral motives.

Experimental evidence that guilt contributes to altruism has been obtained in numerous studies in which college students who were led to believe they had harmed someone showed a heightened willingness to help others — and not just those to whom they had done harm. Thus they engaged in various altruistic deeds, such as volunteering to participate in a research project (Freedman, Wallington, & Bless, 1967), contributing to a charitable fund (Regan, 1971), or spontaneously offering to help a passerby whose grocery bag had broken (Regan, Williams, & Sparling, 1972). These studies are limited: they showed only short-run effects (the good deed immediately followed the guilt induction) and the subjects were college students. Nevertheless, together with the story-completion findings and the anecdotal evidence cited earlier that existential guilt may have been a motive base for some student activists, these findings suggest, somewhat paradoxically, that guilt, which is usually the result of immoral or at least egoistic action, may subsequently operate as an altruistic, moral motive.

The foregoing theoretical model is as yet loose and tentative. Though consistent with the available data, its confirmation or disconfirmation awaits the test of hypotheses derived specifically from it. For example, is empathic distress transformed into sympathetic distress as the child begins to acquire a sense of the other as distinct from the self? Does empathic arousal lead to an increase in guilt feelings after one has harmed another? Does the frequent use of child-rearing practices that direct the child's attention to other people's inner states contribute to sympathetic distress and prosocial behavior, or is it more likely to contribute to a tendency to be empathically overaroused and to use strategies designed to reduce the resulting aversive state?

---

[2]It seems likely that empathic overarousal may contribute to the ''burn out'' phenomenon often found among workers in the service professions.

THEORETICAL OVERVIEW

We may note that all three approaches view the morality of the child as limited or deficient in some respect. For psychoanalytic theory the early superego is rigid, primarily unconscious, and sometimes unduly harsh. For the cognitive-disequilibrium theorists young children are either not truly moral, their actions being predicated on the contingencies of punishment and reward, or they have a conventional moral orientation based on a thoughtless allegiance to certain authority figures and institutions. In the empathy-based conception young children's feelings for other persons are confined, owing to their cognitive limitations, to simple emotions experienced in the immediate situation.

In attempting to account for the advances in moral development in adolescence the three approaches take off from one or more of the inevitable physical and cognitive changes associated with that period. Psychoanalytic theory focuses on the hormonal changes at puberty and the associated drives and emotional states that disrupt the delicate impulse-control system developed in childhood. Psychoanalytic theory also stresses the anxiety associated with the loss of this control system, as well as the loss of the close, dependent relation on the parent which had provided the system's main support. And, finally, the theory views the individual as compelled either to find new, more mature grounds for a moral stance or to erect defenses as a way of warding off uncontrollable instinctual drives and maintaining the earlier control system intact.

Cognitive-disequilibrium theory derives from the fact that adolescents' thinking, formerly tied to the concrete and immediate, is freed, and they become capable for the first time of logical and deductive reasoning, of comparing the actual with the ideal, and constructing contrary-to-fact propositions. They are also cognitively able to relate themselves to the distant past and present and to understand their place in society, in history, and in the universe. And, finally, they can conceptualize their own thought and take their mental constructions as objects and reason about them. (Only by about 11 to 12 years of age, for example, do children spontaneously introduce concepts of belief, intelligence, and faith into their definitions of their religious denominations.) When children move out into the world (from the relatively homogeneous grade-school neighborhood to the more heterogeneous high-school and, eventually, college environments) they are thus ripe for recognizing contradictions between the moral concepts they have come to accept and what occurs in the real world, as well as for recognizing that their beliefs are but one of many and that they have no clear basis for deciding which is superior. They may thus begin to question and perhaps reject their former beliefs and, sometimes taking many months in the process, they may begin to construct a more viable moral system.

My own conception of an empathy-based morality stresses the importance of the integration of young adolescents' capacity for empathic arousal, which they have had all along, with their newly emerging cognitive awareness of others as well as themselves as individuals, each having their own identity, life circumstances, and inner states. In addition, the perceived contrast between the other's well-being and one's own is seen as producing a potential force toward moral action.

SOCIALIZATION AND MORAL DEVELOPMENT IN ADOLESCENCE

There is a considerable body of research on the effects of childrearing practices on moral development. Much of it has employed older children and adolescents as subjects.

Although this was done mainly for practical reasons (e.g., it is difficult to obtain moral data from young children) rather than because of a special interest in adolescence, the findings may still have a bearing on adolescence.

Parent Discipline and Moral Internalization

Most of the socialization research pertains to discipline. The rationale for assuming discipline important is, first of all, that moral internalization implies the existence of motivation to weigh one's desires against the moral requirements of the situation without regard to external sanctions. The central conflict in any moral encounter, then, must be that between the person's egoistic needs and the moral standards applicable in a given situation. It seems reasonable to assume that the key socialization experiences must therefore include children's early encounters with an analogous conflict, that between their desires and the prevailing moral standards, which are at first, of course, external to the children. These standards are embedded in many of the physical and verbal messages from the parent regarding how the child should and should not act, that is, in the parent's discipline techniques. The discipline encounter, then, has much in common with many later moral encounters. In each, there is conflict and individuals are compelled to work out a balance between behaving in accord with their desires, on the one hand, and subordinating their desires and acting in line with moral standards, on the other. The moral requirements are external in the discipline encounter and, with proper socialization, they eventually become internalized in the moral encounter. Children's experiences in the discipline encounter — the type of discipline to which they are repeatedly exposed and that determines the options available to them — must therefore weigh heavily in determining the extent to which they acquire internal resources for controlling egoistic impulses and behaving morally. Some discipline techniques, for example, may help perpetuate children's initial sense of opposition between their desires and external demands, whereas others may provide them with the inner resources — both cognitive and motivational — for changing their views about these demands and adopting them as internal guides to their own behavior.

I recently reviewed the discipline research (Hoffman, 1977a), done mainly in the 1950s and 1960s, and organized it around three broad types of discipline:

1. *Power assertion* — which includes physical force, deprivation of material objects and privileges, or the threat of these; the term is used to highlight the fact that in using these techniques parents seek to control the child by capitalizing on their physical power or control over the child's material resources.

2. *Love withdrawal* — which includes techniques whereby parents simply give direct but nonphysical expression to their anger or disapproval of the child for engaging in some undesirable behavior (e.g., ignores the child, turns one's back on the child, refuses to speak or listen to the child, explicitly states a dislike for the child, isolates or threatens to leave the child). Love withdrawal, like power assertion, has a highly punitive quality. It poses no immediate physical threat to the child, however, but rather the ultimate threat of abandonment or separation. Whereas power assertion ordinarily consists of discrete aversive acts that are quickly over and done with, love withdrawal is typically more prolonged — lasting many minutes, hours, or even days — and its duration may be variable and unpredictable.

3. *Induction* — which includes techniques in which the parents give explanations or

reasons for requiring children to change their behavior or directly appeal to conformity-inducing agents that may already exist within the children. Examples are appealing to children's pride, mastery strivings, or concern for others, and pointing out the implications of the child's behavior for others. These techniques rely less on fear and more on the children's connecting their cognitive content with his own resources for comprehending the requirements of the situation and controlling his behavior accordingly.

The moral internalization indices used represent different levels of behavior (overt, affective, cognitive). The indices most often included in the studies employing adolescent subjects are the extent to which the subject:

1. Makes cognitive judgments about the transgressions of others that are based on moral principles (e.g., "It was wrong to do that because the man trusted him.") rather than external considerations (e.g., "He'll go to jail if he's caught.").

2. Confesses and accepts responsibility for a misdeed even though no one apparently witnessed it — usually based on the parent's or teacher's reports.

3. Experiences guilt (as opposed to fear of punishment) following a transgression — usually measured in terms of responses to deviation story-completion items.

4. Resists the temptation to cheat on a test when no one is around to witness it.

It should be noted that the attempt in all these measures is to obtain an index of the subject's behavior in the absence of external surveillance. This is done in order to assess the extent to which the individual's moral orientation has an internalized component that may operate in real life regardless of the presence or absence of surveillance.

The findings support the following empirical generalizations:

1. A moral orientation characterized by independence of external sanctions and high guilt is associated with the mother's frequent use of inductive discipline — especially "other-oriented" inductions in which the implications of the child's behavior for other people are pointed out — and with her relatively frequent expression of affection in nondiscipline situations.

2. A moral orientation based on fear of external detection and punishment is associated with the mother's use of discipline techniques that have high power-assertive components.

3. There appears to be no consistent relationship between moral orientation and love withdrawal, although there is some evidence that love withdrawal, especially in its more subtle forms, may contribute to inhibition of anger.

These generalizations do not appear to be the spurious result of social class, IQ, or sex — each of which relates to discipline and to some moral indices — since sex was usually controlled and in one study all three variables were controlled with no detrimental effect on the relation (Hoffman & Saltzstein, 1967). Furthermore, the generalizations gain strength from the fact that they reflect a convergence of results from studies using a variety of measures (Campbell & Fiske, 1959).

There is also evidence for two types of internal moral orientation in adolescent subjects: (1) a "flexible-humanistic" or empathy-based type in which antimoral impulses are tolerated and guilt tends to be experienced due to awareness of the harmful effects of one's behavior on others and (2) a "rigid-conventional" or anxiety-based type that appears to be based largely on the need to control hostility, and in which guilt is often the result of one's hostile feelings rather than awareness of the harm done to others (Hoffman, 1970a). The mothers of both types express affection and use inductive discipline frequently, in keeping with the foregoing generalization. Those whose children are flexible-humanistic, however, use more varied discipline techniques, ranging from a totally permissive response to the occasional use of power assertion when the child is openly and unreasonably defiant; they cushion their handling of aggression by focusing on the precipitating issues and suggesting reparative action where possible. In contrast, the mothers of the rigid-conventional subjects rarely use power assertion, and their techniques often have a pronounced love-withdrawing component, especially in situations in which the child expresses anger. A recent study by DePalma (1974) indicates that flexible-humanistic individuals may be somewhat less dependent on the environment as a source of evaluation of their actions and thus more internalized than rigid-conventional children.

Despite the consistency of the findings, these studies have methodological shortcomings. The discipline data, for example, are usually obtained by interviewing the parents, which makes them subject to memory lapses and possible "social desirability" effects. These problems may be lessened somewhat in the studies employing the subjects' reports of the parent's discipline, but the subjects' feelings and attitudes toward the parents may color their response, and there is the further problem of a lack of independence in the data sources for discipline and moral orientation. The virtues and defects of the moral internalization indices have been discussed elsewhere (Hoffman, 1970b). Guilt and moral judgment, for example, may clearly differentiate internal and external responses, but they are far removed from overt moral action. Confession is usually measured in terms of overt behavior, but it may often be an attempt to seek approval rather than a moral act since confession is often rewarded. The resistance-to-temptation measure has the special virtue of tapping overt moral behavior in a standard situation, but here too the motivation may be external (e.g., a pervasive fear of detection despite being left alone) rather than internal (e.g., wishing not to betray the adult's trust). There is evidence that this may be more of a problem in males than in females (Hoffman, 1975d). In addition, motivation for obtaining the reward for doing well, hence degree of temptation, has not been controlled. Despite the flaws, general support for the utility of these measures comes from the consistency of the results obtained regardless of the particular measures used.

A more fundamental limitation is that this research is correlational, which raises the problem of inferring causal direction. This limitation has been highlighted recently by several investigators who cite, as evidence against the assumption of parental influence, the burgeoning research showing that children often affect their parent's behavior (see especially Bell, 1968, 1971). I cannot disagree with the general argument but I do think that although causal direction cannot automatically be assumed, there may be a greater scientific risk associated with being overly cautious and assuming nothing about causality than with making a tentative causal inference when there are reasonable grounds for doing so. And I have argued elsewhere that there are grounds for inferring that parental discipline is more likely to be an antecedent than a consequence of the child's moral internalization (Hoffman, 1975b).

The most recent attempt to interpret the discipline findings, which has been presented in parts elsewhere (Hoffman, 1963a; 1976b; 1977a) may be summarized briefly as follows:

1. Most discipline techniques have some power-assertive, love-withdrawing, and inductive properties.

2. The first two comprise the motive-arousal component, which is often necessary to get children to stop what they are doing and attend.

3. Having attended, children will often be influenced cognitively by the information contained in the inductive component and thus experience a reduced sense of opposition between their desires and external demands.

4. The information contained in the inductive component, which communicates the harm children have done to someone else, may also both elicit empathic distress and transform it into a feeling of guilt, in the sense discussed earlier.

5. Too little arousal and children may ignore the parent; too much arousal and the resulting fear or resentment may prevent effective processing of the inductive content, thus perpetuating the felt opposition between desires and demands and precluding the arousal of empathy and guilt.

Techniques having a salient inductive component ordinarily achieve the best balance and are therefore most effective in the discipline encounter. Furthermore, in keeping with recent memory research — notably the distinction between episodic and semantic memory (Tulving, 1972, pp. 381–403) — children may be expected over time to remember the ideas communicated in inductions, as well as the associated empathy and guilt, but to forget that they originated with the parent. With no external agent to whom to attribute these ideas and feelings, children may then be expected to experience them as their own.

Identification and Moral Internalization

It has been commonly held, since Freud, that parent identification is a major process in conscience development. The details of Freudian theory have by no means been accepted, but many human developmentalists still assume that by adopting the parent's evaluative orientation with respect to his or her own behavior, the child eventually stops striving only for impulse gratification. Furthermore, since the parent's orientation derives largely from his or her cultural group, identifying with the parent is a means of internalizing the standards of the culture.

The intriguing theoretical question for most writers, though neglected by researchers, is what impels children to emulate parents. Psychoanalytic writers stress two motives: first, children's anxiety over losing the parents' love, to overcome which they strive desperately to be like the parents in every way. This "anaclitic identification" leads children to adopt the parents' behavioral mannerisms, thoughts, feelings, and even the capacity to punish themselves and experience guilt when they violate a moral standard. It contributes to lasting developmental changes in children, such as the acquisition of a sex-role identity and an internalized conscience. Some reformulations — termed "developmental," "emotional," or "true" identification — stress children's love for parents rather than the threat of loss of love. The second motive, derived from Freud's notion of castration anxiety, is fear of physical attack. The resulting "identification with the aggressor" or "defensive identification" is currently viewed as a transitory defense mechanism or possibly as contributing to aggressive behavior but not to moral internalization.

Social learning theorists view children as emulating the parents to acquire the parents' power, mastery, and other resources. A self-reinforcing process is sometimes postulated in which children fantasize themselves as the model who controls or consumes the valued resources; they then act like the model, and the resulting similarity is reinforcing because it signifies that they may be able to attain the model's desired goal states.

The research relating parent identification to moral internalization is meager. Two basic approaches have been used. One predicts that if the moral attributes are acquired through identification there should be consistency among them. The other predicts that if moral internalization is the product of identification it should be related to parental discipline techniques in ways predictable from anaclitic identification theory, that is, it should relate positively to love withdrawal. The research is nonsupportive in both cases. The intercorrelations among the moral indices are generally low, and, as we have seen, moral internalization does not relate to love-withdrawal. This casts doubt on the notion of identification as an encompassing, unitary process. To see if identification plays any role in moral development requires independent assessment of children's tendency to identify and also their moral orientation. This was done in one study (Hoffman, 1971b). The identification scores of the subjects, all seventh-grade children, were based on the extent to which they consciously admired and strived to emulate their parents. Few significant relationships were obtained: father identification related positively to conformity to rules, internal moral judgments, and salience of moral values in boys, and to conformity to rules in girls. Mother identification related to conformity to rules in boys. Neither mother nor father identification related significantly to the major moral internalization indices: guilt, confession, and acceptance of blame.

These findings may reflect the fact that parents do not often express guilty, self-critical feelings openly and thus do not provide the child with an effective model for these internal moral states. In addition, the child's motive to identify may not be strong enough to overcome the natural aversion to the pain associated with a self-critical perspective. In other words, it appears that identification may contribute to the adoption of certain moral attributes that are visible and do not require self-denial [see Hoffman (1975a) for evidence that parents who place a high value on helping others often have children who help others]. These attributes may be internalized in the sense that the child uses them rather than external sanctions as the criteria for right and wrong, as in making moral judgments about others. The data do not suggest, however, that identification contributes to the use of moral standards as an evaluative perspective with which to examine one's own behavior. As indicated earlier, this internalized perspective may be fostered under certain conditions in the discipline encounter — in being criticized by another rather than in emulating another's self-criticism. The relative effectiveness of the discipline encounter may be due in part to the fact that the children's attention in the discipline encounter is directed toward their own actions and the consequences of these actions.

The Role of the Father

From discipline research it appears that the mother's but not the father's discipline may have differential effects on the child's moral internalization. Data on the father's discipline were obtained in only a fourth of the studies and, in contrast to the mother's, very few significant relationships were obtained and there was no apparent pattern among them. In the identification research, identification with the father as well as with the mother loomed as relatively unimportant in moral internalization. Nevertheless, the father is one of the child's two major socialization agents. His presence must therefore make itself felt in some way and his absence must create an enormous gap in the child's experience. The father's special role in moral development, furthermore, is suggested in both the Parsonian view that the father brings the larger society's normative standards into the home and the Freudian view that by identifying with the father, the child — at least the boy — acquires the moral standards of society as well as the motivational and control systems needed to assure adherence to them.

Though the particular discipline techniques the father uses may not make much difference, there is some evidence that fathers play an important role in moral socialization. For one thing, the father's behavior towards the mother is often one of the factors affecting the mother's discipline pattern, which in turn affects the child (Hoffman, 1963b). Furthermore, in a study of father absence, adolescent (seventh-grade) boys without fathers (for at least six months prior to the study) obtained significantly lower scores on three out of four moral internalization indices (guilt, internal moral judgment, confession) than a group of boys — controlled for IQ and social class — who had fathers (Hoffman, 1971a). The boys who had no fathers were also rated by their teachers as more aggressive than the boys who had fathers, which replicates the findings obtained in previous research with boys this age and older (Glueck and Glueck, 1950; Gregory, 1965; Miller, 1958; Siegman, 1966). No differences were obtained for girls.

Evidence was also obtained in the study of Hoffman (1971a) that the effects of father-absence on boys were similar to, but more pronounced than, the effects of not identifying with a father who is present. This suggests that some, but not all, of the negative effects of the father's absence are attributable to the lack of a paternal model. Finally, evidence was presented that suggests that the effects of father absence on boys may be partially mediated by the resulting changes in the mother's childrearing practices.

The Influence of Peers

The influence of peers is generally assumed to reach a peak in adolescence, and, as noted by Devereaux (1970), there is a body of literature that tends to support this assumption. That is, parental controls gradually weaken as children grow from childhood to early adolescence and on into adolescence proper. And the peer group appears to play an increasingly salient role as a source of values and as a controller and reinforcer of behavior (e.g., Bowerman and Kinch, 1959; Costanza and Shaw, 1966). The content of peer-group values and the directions in which peer groups pull their members have also been studied. In some instances, broad areas of concordance between peer and adult values have been found (e.g., Langworthy, 1959); in these cases the sanctioning force of the peer group would seem to be added to that of important adults in holding children to approved moral standards. Other studies provide evidence that peer groups sometimes carry values that deviate from the standards and expectations of adult society. Such deviance may represent a modest difference in emphasis and priorities, as illustrated by Coleman's (1961) finding that adolescent subcultures in high schools often stress athletic prowess or popularity at the expense of academic achievement. Under certain conditions, however, usually but not always characterized by extreme poverty, peer groups may promulgate a delinquent subculture (e.g., Cloward and Ohlin, 1960). At the other socioeconomic extreme, a "youth culture" (Parsons, 1942) may be generated, which at certain times in history contributes to radical ideology and action (e.g., Keniston, 1968) or to a turning away from any type of moral commitment (e.g., Keniston, 1965).

There are several theoretical approaches to the effects of the peer group on moral development, some of which come to the conclusion that peers generally serve a constructive purpose. Piaget (1932), as indicated earlier, has argued that informal and unsupervised play among peers fosters the kind of spontaneous, flexible rule-making and rule-enforcing that is necessary for the development of a mature moral orientation. Such peer group experiences help move the child away from moral realism, in which rules were seen as external, constraining forces arbitrarily imposed by powerful adult authority figures, and toward the notion of morality based on principles of cooperation and mutual consent. Parsons and Bales (1955), similarly, believe that, owing to the absence of the gross differentials of power that obtained in relations with adults, leadership and authority in the peer group are more apt to be based on objective criteria of merit and the willing consent of participants, which helps the child achieve a mature approach to rules. Finally, Kohlberg (1964, pp. 383–431) sees the possible differences between peer and adult norms as creating, perhaps for the first time in children's lives, a conflict or disequilibrium which may compel them to think through and question their earlier beliefs and make the kinds of moral discriminations and judgments essential to the development of autonomous moral structures. Kohlberg also makes the assumption, which is at the core of his approach to moral education (Kohlberg, 1973), that members of the peer group who initially operate at low moral levels will be positively affected by exposure to other members who function at higher moral levels. The latter will not be adversely affected by the former, however. Therefore, peer interaction should be more likely to result in an increase rather than a decrease in the moral level of most group members.

The opposed view, as stated simply by Bronfenbrenner (1970), is that "if all children have contact only with their age-mates, there is no possibility for learning culturally established patterns of cooperation and mutual concern" (p. 117). This view, illustrated dramatically in William Golding's book, *Lord of the Flies,* is also in keeping with Le Bon's (1895/1960) notion that crowds have destructive effects on the consciences of individuals. It also fits well with the findings of Sherif et al. in *The Robber's Cave Experiment* (1961), which showed how newly formed groups of preadolescent boys without adult supervision could exert a tyranny that eventually undermined the effectiveness of the moral orientation brought to the group by some individuals.

There has been no direct systematic research on the effects of the peer group on moral development, although there is some research suggesting what these effects might be. Devereaux (1970) reports a correlational study in which preadolescent children who said that they frequently associated with peers gave responses to a test of moral dilemmas indicating that they might be more ready and willing to yield to temptation and go along with the crowd in committing a deviant act. This effect was enhanced among children who preferred gangs to a small number of friends and who actually played with large groups. Such children were more likely to play in places where no adults were present, and such unsupervised groups were reported, in fact, to engage in more misconduct. Devereaux also reports that these peer-group experiences appeared to reduce both anxiety and guilt feelings, which probably originated in the home. Thus the home may have lost much of its power to motivate and control behavior among gang-oriented children. Finally, evidence is presented to indicate that as the child grows older, and the hold of the peer group increases at the expense of the family, the children apparently become more responsive to peer pressure. Devereaux concludes that peer-group experiences appear to constitute a major roadblock for moral development of children and that the path from middle childhood to middle adolescence for peer-oriented children is one of "continuous moral regression."

There is also some very different, experimental research (see reviews by Hoffman, 1970b; in press) that ends up with similar results. This research shows that children who observe a model who gets rewarded, or simply is not punished, after behaving in a physically aggressive manner, will tend to behave aggressively if given the opportunity shortly thereafter. The same has been found in the studies of resistance to temptation. Children who observe models who yield to the temptation to cheat in a game without being punished, will generally cheat if soon given opportunity to do so. There is no evidence, on the other hand, that observing models who resist the temptation to engage in deviant action increases the likelihood that the child will resist temptation. One set of findings is particularly interesting in this connection. In a study by Bandura, Grusec, and Menlove (1967), children participated in a bowling game with an adult or peer model. The scores were controlled by the experimenter. At the outset, the children and the models were given access to a large supply of candy from which they could help themselves as they wished. Under one experimental condition the model set a high standard of self-reward — rewarding himself with candy only when his performance exceeded a certain level. In another condition the model rewarded himself even when he performed at a very low level. After exposure to the model, the children played the bowling game. Their scores, which, unknown to them, were rigged, varied considerably and the level of performance for which they rewarded themselves with candy was recorded. In previous research using this paradigm, children were found to employ stringent or lenient standards of self-reward, depending on what the model did; they also tended to imitate an adult rather than a peer when the same self-reward criterion was used, (e.g., Bandura and Kupers, 1964). In the study by Bandura, Grusec, and Menlove (1967), however, the effectiveness of an adult model's stringent standards was undermined by the presence of a peer model using a more lenient standard. To the degree that we may generalize from these findings they suggest that group members who behave in a deviant, noninternalized fashion are apt to have more effect on the group than are members who behave in a more internalized fashion. In other words, there may be tendencies toward the lowest common denominator of moral action. This interpretation is consistent with the findings reported by Devereaux (1970) and exactly the opposite of what might be predicted from Piaget's (1932), Kohlberg's (1964) and Parsons' (1955) formulations.

In conclusion, it may be a mistake to think of peer groups as exerting influence apart from the influence of adults. The data that led to Piaget's (1932) perhaps overly benign view of the effects of peer interaction were based on observations of middle-class children. We cannot be certain but it seems likely that these children's parents frequently employed reasoning and used inductive discipline. This may have contributed to a positive orientation toward others, which, in turn, led to the type of role-taking in the group that impressed Piaget. It also seems likely that when conflicts among peers arose, they were discussed at home and the parents' contribution may sometimes have been, as it is in many American homes, not to give unquestioning support to their own child but to clarify the *other* child's point of view. This "coaching" by the parent may serve as a catalyst for the development of a role-taking perspective in the peer group. Something similar may operate in Kohlberg's (1973) conception of the teacher's role in the moral education classroom, which is to clarify the various views expressed by the children and to help maintain as high a level of discussion as possible. It is difficult to imagine a group of children operating in accord with Piaget's or Kohlberg's notions if there were a critical mass of members who came from highly power-assertive homes and there was an absence of adult supervision.

Sex-Role Socialization

In Freud's view, owing to anatomical differences, girls are not compelled to resolve the Oedipus complex quickly and dramatically and thus do not identify with the parent as fully as boys do. Consequently, females have less internalized moral structures than males. In Freud's (1925/1961) words:

> For women the level of what is ethically normal is different from what it is in men. Their superego is never so inexorable, so impersonal, so independent of its emotional origins . . . they have less sense of justice, less tendency to submit themselves to the great necessities of life and frequently permit themselves to be guided in their decisions by their affections or enmities. [Pp. 257–258]

Freud's followers differed in details but drew essentially the same conclusions: females are more dependent on the moral view of others; males more often internalize moral principles and act autonomously in accord with them.

Other developmental theories have ignored sex differences in moral internalization. An exception is Aronfreed's (1961) hypothesis that our society expects males to be self-reliant and to exercise control over their actions and environment and expects females to be more responsive to directions from without; consequently, the moral orientations of boys rely more on inner resources than girls.

There has been little research on sex differences in moral internalization but what there is suggests that, contrary to theory, female adolescents, and adults as well, are more internalized than males. In a national survey of 14- to 16-year-olds Douvan and Adelson (1966) asked respondents why they thought parents made rules and what would happen if there were no rules. More males than females gave responses suggesting "a high degree of impulsivity ready to make its appearance once there is a failure in external constraint." For example, the males more often stated that parents made rules to keep children out of trouble. In an experimental study based on the Milgram obedience paradigm, females resisted pressures to violate a norm against harming others to a greater extent than males (Kilham and Mann, 1974), which is the more remarkable since females typically conform to a greater degree than males in a variety of experiments having nothing to do with moral issues (e.g., Wallach and Kogan, 1959). In a field experiment by Gross (1972) females were more likely than males to return valuable items found in the street when no witnesses were present; only when others were in the vicinity did males return the items as often as females.

In a developmental study of sex differences in white, middle-class preadolescents (fifth-graders), adolescents (seventh-graders), and their parents, females gave strong evidence of having a more internalized moral orientation than males (Hoffman, 1975d). The results, in all three age groups, for example, indicate that moral transgressions are more apt to be associated with guilt in females and with fear of detection and punishment in males. On a measure of personal values, females revealed a consistently more positive orientation towards humanistic concerns, (e.g., going out of one's way to help others). Furthermore, there was evidence that the achievement values of males, which were more pronounced than those of females, probably reflect an egoistic rather than a moral (e.g., Protestant ethic) orientation.

The sex differences in adolescents may be due in part to childrearing differences: more induction and affection have been reported for females, power assertion for males (Hoffman, 1975d; Zussman, 1975). Childrearing differences cannot explain the differences between mothers and fathers in the Hoffman (1975d) study, however, unless their early childhood experiences are assumed to parallel those of their children. This may be a reasonable assumption, although the fact that the adult differences were actually more pronounced than the child differences suggests the possible influence of factors beyond childhood. A clue to these factors appears in the view by Parsons and Bales (1955) and Johnson (1963) about society's traditional sex-role division of labor. Females have been traditionally socialized into the "expressive" role — to give and receive affection and be responsive to the feelings and needs of others (thus providing the orientation necessary for maintaining the family as an intact, harmonious unit). This role is entirely consistent with the humanistic morality that the females appear to have. Males are also socialized into the expressive role and may thus acquire humanistic concerns, but as they approach adolescence they are increasingly instructed in the "instrumental" character traits and skills necessary for acting as liaison between family and society, that is, for occupational achievement and success. This instruction is done mainly by the father, who is more likely than the mother to make rewards contingent on achievement and performance. Thus the overall results might best be explained by the increasing pressures on males, especially in adolescence and adulthood, to achieve and succeed, which may often conflict with the moral concerns acquired earlier.

STUDENT ACTIVISM AND THE MORALITY OF YOUTH AND ADOLESCENCE

Student activism has been associated empirically with certain broad cultural factors, such as increasing technology; urbanization; family mobility; and, above all, with the increasing number of young people in college, which serves to disengage them from the rest of society and keep them free of adult responsibilities and concerns for a long time. Student activism is not a new phenomenon, dating at least as far back as the town-and-gown riots at Oxford in 1354 and occurring with notable frequency in every century since then. The activism of the 1960s was different, however, in that it extended beyond the confines of one or two universities and constituted a direct attack on society's dominant institutions.

Why include activism in a chapter on moral development? The main reason is that if there is a moral component to activism it may provide clues as to adolescent moral development in general. This is important because there has been little empirical work on the distinctive aspects of morality in adolescents and youth. The bulk of the research has employed adolescent or preadolescent subjects but, as already noted, the interest has been in moral-development processes in general rather than in adolescence; the methods used tap the same, highly limited moral conceptions of childhood. Writers like Erikson, who contend that adolescence, more than any other time in life, is a period in which moral issues are at the forefront of consciousness, have in mind something more complex than resisting the temptation to cheat, feeling guilty over injuring someone, or even making judgments of action in situations in which the moral issues are obvious. These writers refer, rather, to the struggle that many adolescents apparently go through in coping with the lack of obvious rationality and the outmoded nature of the moral concepts acquired in childhood, as well as the discrepancies they observe between principle and practice in adults, sometimes the very adults from whom they originally acquired the moral concepts. Many of their past role models, or idols, may thus have fallen because they do not appear to have lived up to their own moral pronouncements. Finally, the exposure to diverse points of view in teachers and peers may compel individuals to abandon the simple dualistic thinking about right and wrong, good and bad, that characterizes childhood and, at least temporarily, move them to a relativistic conception of morality and truth. This struggle, which is perhaps inevitable in a rapidly changing, open society can be heightened by such highly visible historical events as those which occurred in the 1960s.

There is evidence that many of the protestors, at least in the early phases of the highly visible activist decade of the 1960s, may have been acting morally. Haan (in press) has cautioned that while, in the broadest sense, moral protest may always be activistic, activism is not in itself necessarily moral. Haan also notes, however, that although:

. . . the claim of moral purpose seemed too easily made [by the protestors] and in the post-Freudian, older generation's view, might very well mask other phenomena, such as the melancholy outcome of several decades of permissive childrearing, youth's concern with justice for disadvantaged groups, with civil liberties, and with the war against the Vietnamese undeniably involved moral issues.

Empirically, there is some modest support for a moral component to the activism of the 1960s. Keniston (1968) conducted intensive interviews with 11 radicals, mostly males, who were leaders of the Vietnam Summer movement in the early 1960s. In Keniston's view these people did not appear to hold any coherent ideology, but they showed a strong, largely implicit belief in the basic moral principles of justice, decency, equality, responsibility, fairness, and nonviolence — this was before violence became a fairly regular feature of protest demonstrations. The quotes from Keniston's respondents, presented earlier and suggesting that some of their actions may have been motivated by "existential guilt," also support the moral underpinning of some protest action.

In a more systematic fashion and using a much larger sample, Haan, Smith and Block (1968) found that the level of moral reasoning was closely, though not linearly, related to participation in the Free Speech movement sit-in at Berkeley in 1964. Using Kohlberg's (1958) moral judgment dilemmas, these investigators found that students at both extremely high and extremely low levels of moral development were overrepresented among those arrested, while those at the modal ("conventional") stage of moral reasoning were rarely involved in the sit-in. In a later study, Fishkin, Keniston and MacKinnon (1973) hypothesized that the Free Speech movement activists were characterized by at least two traits: (1) in the realm of ideology, a generalized liberalism, leftism, or radicalism and (2) in the realm of behavior, a disposition to take action in the name of their beliefs in a situation of moral conflict. In 1970 Fishkin, Keniston, and MacKinnon administered the Kohlberg moral dilemmas along with a list of 31 political slogans, to each of which the subjects responded on a five-point scale of agreement or disagreement. A factor analysis of the responses to the slogans yielded these factors: violent radicalism, peaceful radicalism, conservatism, general radicalism, radicalism versus conservatism. The results were that the subjects who reasoned at Kohlberg's conventional moral level, especially Stage 4 ("law and order"), were politically conservative, while preconventional subjects favored violent radicalism. Principled, postconventional moral reasoning was associated with the rejection of conservative slogans but not with the acceptance of radical slogans. While not providing an exact replication, the Fishkin, Keniston, and MacKinnon (1973) findings concur in a general way with the findings obtained by Haan, Smith, and Block (1968). Thus law-and-order moral reasoning was found to relate to behavioral conservatism in one study and to ideological conservatism in the other; a more principled morality, which characterized a subgroup of the radical activists in one study, related to rejection of conservative slogans, though not to acceptance of radical slogans, in another.

We may tentatively conclude that there very likely was a moral component to the radicalism of the 1960s and that the behavior of many activists, relative to that of other youths, was guided more by ethical principles than by the precepts implied by the commonly held conventions concerning what is right and what is wrong. Three important qualifications must be made, however. First, many of the activist subjects did not exhibit moral principles. This is not surprising since people can obviously support ideologies as well as affiliate and act with protesting groups out of dispositions having nothing to do with moral principles, for example, the excitement and adventure of identifying with a mass movement. Second, even among those who did act out of explicit moral principles, there are undoubtedly some, as suggested by Keniston (1970), whose adherence to principle was accompanied by a lack of humility, compassion, empathic identification, and love for fellow persons that arise through rewarding interpersonal relationships. In such individuals the result may often be a kind of moral zealotry that leads to violence and disregard for the feelings of others. Thus the moral component of an individual's radicalism does not assure that he or she will behave in a virtuous manner. The third qualification is methodological. It seems likely that Kohlberg's (1958) moral judgment index, which was used in some of this research, confounds the level of morality with political ideology. The responses designated as "postconventional" or principled, for example, are far more likely to reflect a deep concern with the sanctity of human life than with the value of property and upholding the status quo; Stage 4 responses, by contrast, are supportive of "law and order" and the status quo. The correlation between Stage 4 and political conservatism, and between Stage 6 and left-radicalism may, therefore, indicate nothing more than consistency among different measures of ideology and may tell us very little about the relation between morality and activism. It may be necessary to remove the ideological value content from the moral indices, if this is possible, before conclusions about the relation between morality and activism can be made with confidence.

Socialization and Activism

Horn and Knott (1971) reviewed the research dealing with the socialization correlates of student activism. Activism was defined specifically by public acts and behavior, such as participating in sit-ins, marches, or similar protest actions, throughout the 1960s. The bulk of the protest actions, a dozen in all, occurred at prestigious universities across the country, and Horn and Knott estimate that the individuals actually involved in the demonstrations numbered about 15% of the student bodies at these institutions. Perhaps the most important findings, now widely known, were that the economic setting of the activists' homes was usually one of affluence. Furthermore, the evidence indicates that the activist youths were not so much rebelling against their parents as they were extending a pattern of action that characterized their parents. That is, the activist youth appeared to derive their motivations from parents with whom they had formed "solid bonds of identification." Several facts support this generalization. First, the activists selected high-school and college course work in areas in which their parents had studied (typically the social sciences and humanities); insofar as they identified with the world of work, they typically preferred a career in service to other people rather than one that ensured status or financial prominence, which is in keeping with the interest and social orientation of their fathers' occupations. The studies also indicated that the political and ethical views of the activist youths were often similar to those held by their parents. The parents were usually described as liberal rather than conservative; they tended to support the Civil Rights movement and oppose the bombing in Vietnam. In general, the social philosophies and economic orientations of the parents of the activists were similar, although less extreme, than those of their children. Horn and Knott (1971) interpret the findings as suggesting that although there were differences in orientation, the similarities were more outstanding; the activist youths were basically identified with their parents and were carrying forward programs of action which, in general principle, if not in every detail, were favored by their parents.

As regards childrearing practices, results from several of the studies reviewed by Horn and Knott suggest that the parents of activists, more than other parents of the same generation, were influenced by Freudian theory, particularly as embodied by Dr. Spock's popular manuals on child care. Their approach was thus to use inductive discipline, to give the child reasons for the kinds of behavior they wanted and for the punishment they administered, to use spanking and other forms of corporal punishment rarely, to encourage their children to express themselves openly and to take responsibility. Needless to say, not all activists are characterized by the pattern just described. At least one study (Block, Haan, & Smith, 1969) has identified a subgroup for which there are indications of rejection of parental values. This subgroup engaged in considerable protesting but, unlike other activists, showed little interest in social-service activities (e.g., tutoring, hospital volunteer work), and frequently described their relationship with their parents as involving conflict, anger, criticism, tension, and the absence of warmth, intimacy, and appreciation.

It must be noted that in virtually all these studies the description of parental behavior was obtained not from the parents but from the activists, many of whom were undoubtedly familiar with the prevailing views about childrearing practices and may have been trying to make a good impression. Also, in many cases (e.g., Keniston, 1968) the data were obtained in clinical-type interviews and the analyses were made subjectively by investigators who appear to have been sympathetic to their subjects. Nevertheless, the high degree of convergence of the findings by different investigators is impressive and it seems reasonable to conclude that, by and large, the activists were not so much rebelling against their parents — values that their parents explicitly held but for which they may not have had the courage or the opportunity to fight.

CONCLUSIONS

It seems clear that none of the theories has a monopoly on explanation, nor are there many obvious contradictions among them. Each bears mainly on a particular aspect of moral development and seems to capture a bit of the truth. My conclusion is in the form of an overall framework for adolescent moral development that attempts to integrate the findings and the most promising hypotheses, provides a developmental perspective, and also takes account of the competitive egoistic processes that are often ignored. First, there appear to be at least three types of moral-internalization processes, each with its own experiential base:

1. *Anxiety-based inhibition:* The first type refers to the general expectation that people often have, without necessarily being aware of it, that their actions are constantly under surveillance. In the extreme, this may reflect an irrational fear of ubiquitous authority figures or retribution by gods or ghosts. The result, in any case, is that the individual often behaves in the morally prescribed way, even when

alone, in order to avoid punishment. The socialization experiences contributing to this orientation very likely include a long period in which significant others have punished deviant acts, with the result that painful anxiety states become associated with them. Due to repeated punishment, for example, the kinesthetic and other cues produced by the deviant act may arouse anxiety, which may subsequently be avoided only by inhibiting the act. From the standpoint of the observer the individual is behaving in an internalized manner, because external surveillance is unnecessary. Applying a subjective criterion, however, moral action based on fear of external sanctions, whether realistic or not, cannot be considered an instance of internalization. When the anxiety over deviation is unaccompanied by conscious fears of detection, however, as sometimes happens, this may be viewed as a primitive form of internalization.

2. *Empathy-based concern for others:* The second type pertains to the integration of the human capacity for empathy and the cognitive awareness of other people's inner states and how they are affected by one's behavior. As a contributing socialization experience, I have suggested exposure to inductive discipline, which fosters the simultaneous experiencing of empathy with awareness of harming another person. Reciprocal role-taking with peers, in Piaget's (1932) sense, that is, in which the person alternately affects others and is affected by them in similar ways, may also help heighten the individual's sensitivity to the inner states aroused in others by one's own behavior. Having been in the other person's place helps one to know how the latter feels in response to one's behavior.

3. *Cognitive disequilibrium and equilibration:* The third type pertains to one's active efforts cognitively to process morally relevant information that is at variance with one's preexisting conceptions and the proclivity to adopt perspectives more comprehensive than one's own. It seems likely that a person will feel a special commitment to — and in this sense internalize — moral concepts that he or she has been actively involved in constructing. The cognitive-developmental theorists may thus be correct in stressing cognitive disequilibrium, although there is no evidence that the newly adopted perspectives follow a preordained hierarchical order. It is also problematic whether the cognitive processing is instigated by awareness of logical or ''structural'' contradictions within the individual's previous moral conceptions, or by discrepancies between his or her moral values and perceived social reality.

These three processes are best not thought of as moral stages. The first, anxiety-based process, may be the most pervasive and in one form or other may account for a good deal of moral behavior by people of all ages in many societies. Anxiety over retribution by God, for example, often provides the major motive for moral action in traditional society. This is true to some degree in our country as well, though mainly in children. Adolescents have often questioned the existence of God (e.g., Kuhlen & Arnold, 1944; Jones, 1960) and, in the absence of any other moral base, may lose their only moral motive in the process. The second, empathy-based process may also be prevalent at all ages, especially in liberal, humanistically oriented groups. If linked to religion, it is apt to be the value prescriptions (how one should behave toward one's fellow man) rather than fear of retribution by a diety. The third, highly cognitive process may be the most unique to adolescence, though perhaps only applicable to a relatively small number of those for whom intellectually attained values are of special importance. The three processes may also develop independently. And finally, they may be mutually supportive, for example, an empathy-based concern for others may provide direction for one's cognitive efforts to resolve conflicting moral concepts. Or they may interfere with each other, for example, early anxiety-based inhibitions may prevent behaviors from occurring later when their control might be acquired on the basis of an empathic response to their harmful effects on others.

It may also be useful to view the three not as alternatives but as component processes in a person's moral orientation. A mature orientation in our society, then, might be one in which the anxiety-based component is minimal, while the empathy-based and perhaps the cognitively based components are predominant. How do such moral orientations develop? I have noted that American children are socialized through empathy- or anxiety-based processes to be moral and (especially the boys) are also socialized to compete successfully against others. In later childhood and adolescence the competitive pressures usually increase and a choice between the moral and the competitive, egoistic demands must often be made. Furthermore, as children move further into adolescence they may also be confronted with other sorts of stimuli noted throughout this paper, such as the existence of different moral-ethical viewpoints, the inequities, and the inconsistencies between principles and actions of important adults and institutions — all dramatized by the mass media.

Finally, in recent decades, an increasing number of adolescents, who have not experienced early pressures toward finding an adult identity, have had the luxury of a prolonged college moratorium, in which both the curriculum and the almost exclusive interaction with peers has contributed to at least a partial undermining of the basis of their childhood morality. Keniston (1970) suggests this pattern may be a fundamental feature of adolescent moral development and that it leads to the breakdown of the conventional morality of childhood. In this formulation, Keniston seems to overlook his own evidence that the childhood morality of many of the activists in the 1960s was more humanistic than conventional. It may thus be more accurate to hypothesize that the above adolescent experiences may have not one but several possible consequences. One is that the anxiety-based component of childhood morality is undermined. This is in keeping with Keniston's hypothesis, although it seems likely that such a process is also accompanied by high levels of anxiety because of the rejection of the superego (Blos, 1962) and the rejection of the parents that it usually implies. Another possibility is that the empathy-based component is undermined, resulting in a kind of moral cynicism, and perhaps some disillusionment with the parents for having misled the child into seeing the world as more benign than it is. The activist research suggests still another consequence, one in which the empathy-based component remains firm because of the adolescents' strong and continuing identification and respect for the adults from whom they gained the empathy-related values, as well as because of sympathetic distress and perhaps the existential guilt that may be aroused because of the adolescents' relatively advantaged position in life. The salience of the empathy-based moral component may also be enhanced by exposure to professionals and political leaders who seem to provide plausible role models for implementing empathy-related values. This moral component may also take on more complex cognitive and ideological dimensions as the result of prolonged, intense discussion with peers who are in the same situation.

For some adolescents the process is much simpler. These are the ones, noted by Erikson (1970), for whom the pressure to choose the roles of breadwinner and parent and to begin working toward them are paramount. For them, the morality of childhood may continue into adolescence with little change, except perhaps to be weakened by the striving for instrumental, competitive success. The same thing may be true for others who continue to live in relatively protected, culturally homogeneous environments (e.g., those who study engineering or medicine or who live in fraternities and sororities), although in these cases the childhood morality may be cognitively elaborated into a conservative political ideology.

In sum, adolescent moral development may build on childhood morality in different ways. The experiences of adolescence may undermine or foster the cognitive elaboration of one or another component of the child's morality. Erikson (1970) has suggested that in the desperate struggle for an identity, adolescents often seek an ideology that makes them feel good morally, fits their emotional needs, and makes cognitive sense of their world. Such an ideology may help provide the necessary tie between individuals and their society and consequently may serve as the "guardian of identity."

Complex, intact moral ideologies can also be packaged and taught to children at a young age. As developmentalists we would say that young children are incapable of fully grasping an ideology so presented and can only learn it in a rote manner. In adolescence, when they have the cognitive tools for full comprehension, several things may then happen. If they are in a protected environment, they may continue to hold the ideology in the same nonreflective way. If exposed to contradictions and divergent viewpoints, however, they may be expected to examine and reevaluate the ideology in relation to the real world and to accept and reject portions of it that pass or fail the test. The implications of having an ideology to which one was committed in childhood that fails the intellectual test in adolescence, compared to not having an ideology in the first place, are interesting to contemplate. This is a problem faced by many parents who grew up with a religious or other moral ideology, only to abandon it in adolescence: Is the total belief in a moral system an important source of security in childhood, even though the moral system may have to be rejected later in life?

Clearly there are more hypotheses than facts about the distinctive aspects of adolescent moral development. Empirically, thanks mainly to the work of Kohlberg and Kramer (1969), we have some idea of how moral cognition in adolescence differs from that in childhood and adulthood. And the work of Keniston (1968), Haan (in press), and others provides evidence that at least among some adolescents there is a direct connection between moral concepts, political and social ideology, identity, and action in the real world. We know less about the affective side of adolescent morality, although there is suggestive evidence that adolescents are capable of experiencing guilt not only over the commission of a specific deviant and harmful act, over which young children may also be capable of feeling guilty, but also over not helping others when the opportunity to do so was there. Furthermore, it appears that some adolescents are capable of feeling guilty over their affluence or over being in a relatively advantaged position in life as compared to others. Aside from the obvious need for further research, especially on the affective and behavioral dimensions of adolescent morality, certain broad developmental issues, which may be amenable to research, come to mind. I shall discuss three:

1. *The transition between childhood and adolescent morality.* The theories all agree that adolescents often tend to reject their moral standards on cognitive grounds. It seems likely, however, that despite the cognitive rejection, adolescents will continue to feel guilty when they violate these standards. Though cognition

may obviously lead one to generalize and thus add new areas of guilt, it is not clear how conscious cognition (as opposed to defense mechanisms) can reduce guilt. At the affective level, then, it seems easier to account for adolescents' retaining their childhood morality than for their advancing to higher levels. It also appears that early socialization that results in guilt and anxiety over transgressions may to some extent actually pose an obstacle to moral growth in adolescence. It follows from such a life-cycle perspective that we not only need research on the relation between affect and cognition in adolescent moral growth but that we may also need to reevaluate some of the research on childhood morality. High scores on the resistance-to-temptation measures used in the study of preschool and grade-school children, for example, may need to be downgraded as indices of effective moral socialization.

2. *The implications of the disparity that may exist between the adolescents' and their parents' moral orientation.* The research has pointed up the discrepancy that sometimes exists between the adolescents' developing moral stance and that of their parents. Since in most cases the parents and adolescent children continue their relationship, the question arises, do parents continue to have an effect on the adolescents' moral development despite the parents' loss of credibility as a source of moral values? Haan (1971) makes the interesting suggestion that for many reasons, which have been cited earlier, adolescents nowadays often attain higher levels of moral development than their parents. Their morality, however, tends to be formalistic, that is, preoccupied with hypothetical and propositional matters, because it has been arrived at largely through cognitive processes (Haan accepts the Kohlberg, 1958 view). The parents' moral level, on the other hand, though less advanced, is more solidly grounded in a lifetime of experience. Adolescents who no longer regard the parents as the sole authority on moral matters and consider their own morality as superior to that of their parents may challenge the parents' moral concerns and point up the lack of objective grounding for these moral concerns. The resulting conflict is a type of disequilibrium in the family unit. Haan (1971) suggests that when such disequilibrium occurs the moral level of the family may be raised by equilibration processes triggered by open discussion between adolescents and the parents. When the process succeeds, the adolescents' moral view gains substance and the parents' moral level rises. Many of us can recall instances in the 1960s in which parents seemed to be influenced by their adolescent children. Whether the latter were also influenced, as Haan suggests, may have been less evident, at least in the short run.

3. *The potential conflict between moral and achievement socialization.* In explaining the findings on sex differences, I suggested they might be due in part to the conflict, especially pronounced in males, between pressures to compete and the moral standards acquired in childhood. This interpretation raises questions for research that might have societal as well as theoretical importance: When does achievement socialization in males begin to conflict with moral socialization? What might parents and other socialization agents be doing that often tips the balance in favor of achievement? Is this a deliberate attempt to help assure the future success of male children, and are the adults aware of the potentially negative consequences for moral socialization? An unpublished experimental study by Burton (1972) brings into bold relief the dilemma that may confront

many parents in their efforts to socialize their children in terms of both morality and achievement. It also demonstrates that under certain conditions parents may communicate to their children that when success and honesty are in conflict it is more important to succeed than to be honest.

REFERENCES

Alston, W. P. Comments on Kohlberg's "From is to ought." In T. Mischel (Ed.), *Cognitive development and epistemology*. New York: Academic, 1971.

Aronfreed, J. The nature, variety, and social patterning of moral responses to transgression. *Journal of Abnormal and Social Psychology*, 1961, *63*, 223–240.

Baier, K. Moral development. *Monist*, 1974, *58*, 601–615.

Bandura, A. Social-learning theory of identificatory processes. In D. A. Goslin and D. C. Glass (Eds.), *Handbook of socialization theory and research*. Chicago: Rand McNally, 1969.

Bandura, A., and Kupers, C. J. Transmission of patterns of self-reinforcement through modeling. *Journal of Abnormal and Social Psychology*, 1964, *69*, 1–9.

Bandura, H., and Rosenthal, L. Vicarious classical conditioning as a function of arousal level. *Journal of Personality and Social Psychology*, 1966, *3*, 54–62.

Bandura, A., Grusec, J. E., and Menlove, F. L. Some determinants of self-monitoring reinforcement systems. *Journal of Personality and Social Psychology*, 1967, *5*, 449–455.

Bell, R. Q. A reinterpretation of the direction of effects in studies of socialization. *Psychological Review*, 1968, *75*, 81–95.

———. Stimulus control of parent or caretaker behavior of offspring. *Developmental Psychology*, 1971, *4*, 63–72.

Berger, S. M., and Hadley, S. W. Some effects of a model's performance on observer electromyographic activity. *American Journal of Psychology*, 1975, *88*, 263–276.

Bernal, G., and Berger, S. M. Vicarious eyelid conditioning. *Journal of Personality and Social Psychology*, 1976, *34*, 62–68.

Block, J., Haan, N., and Smith, M. B. Socialization correlates of student activism. *Journal of Social Issues*, 1969, *25*, 143–178.

Blos, P. *On adolescence*. New York: Free Press, 1962.

———. The split parental imago in adolescent social relations. *Psychoanalytic Study of the Child*, 1976, *31*, 7–33.

Borke, H. Interpersonal perception of young children: Egocentrism or empathy. *Developmental Psychology*, 1971, *7*, 263–269.

Bowerman, C. E., and Kinch, J. W. Changes in family and peer orientation of children between the fourth and tenth grades. *Social Forces*, 1959, *37*, 206–211.

Bronfenbrenner, U. *Two worlds of childhood: US and USSR*. New York: Russell Sage Foundation, 1970.

Burton, R. V. Cheating related to maternal pressures for achievement. Unpublished manuscript, 1972.

Campbell, D. T., and Fiske, D. W. Convergent and discriminant validation by the multitrait-multimethod matrix. *Psychological Bulletin*, 1959, *56*, 81–105.

Cloward, R. A., and Ohlin, L. E. *Delinquency and opportunity*. Glencoe, Ill.: Free Press, 1960.

Colby, A., Speicher, D., and Kohlberg, L. Standard form scoring. Paper presented at the Moral Development and Education Workshop, Harvard University, 1973.

Coleman, J. S. *The Adolescent Society*. New York: Free Press, 1961.

Constanza, P. R., and Shaw, M. E. Conformity as a function of age level. *Child Development*, 1966, *37*, 967–975.

DePalma, D. J. Effects on social class, moral orientation, and severity of punishment on boy's moral responses to transgression and generosity. *Developmental Psychology*, 1974, *10*(6), 890–900.

Devereux, E. C. The role of peer-group experience in moral development. In J. P. Hill (Ed.), *Minnesota symposia on child psychology* (Vol. 4). Minneapolis: University of Minnesota Press, 1970.

Douvan, E., and Adelson, J. *The adolescent experience*. New York: Wiley, 1966.

Eisenberg-Berg, N. The development of prosocial moral reasoning and its relationship to Kohlbergian, prohibition-oriented moral reasoning. Paper presented at the Society for Research in Child Development Meeting, New Orleans, March, 1977.

Erikson, E. H. Reflections on the dissent of contemporary youth. *International Journal of Psychoanalysis*, 1970, *51*, 11–22.

Feldman, K. A., and Newcomb, T. M. *The impact of college on students* (2 vols.). San Francisco: Jossey-Bass, 1969.

Feshbach, N. D., and Roe, K. Empathy in six- and seven-year-olds. *Child Development*, 1968, *39*, 133–145.

Festinger, L. A theory of social comparison processes. *Human Relations*, 1954, *7*, 117–140.

Fishkin, J., Keniston, K., and MacKinnon, C. Moral reasoning and political ideology. *Journal of Personality and Social Psychology*, 1973, *27*, 109–119.

Freedman, J. L., Wallington, S. A., and Bless, E. Compliance without pressure: The effect of guilt. *Journal of Personality and Social Psychology*, 1967, *7*, 117–124.

Freud, S. Some psychical consequences of the anatomical distinction between the sexes. In J. Strachey (Ed. and trans.), *Standard edition of the complete psychological works of Sigmund Freud* (Vol. 19). London: Hogarth Press, 1961. (Originally published, 1925.)

Geer, J. H., and Jarmecky, L. The effect of being responsible for reducing another's pain on subject's response and arousal. *Journal of Personality and Social Psychology*, 1973, *26*, 232–237.

Gelhorn, E. Motion and emotion: The role of proprioception in the physiology and pathology of the emotions. *Psychological Review*, 1964, *71*, 457–472.

Glueck, S., and Glueck, E. *Unravelling juvenile delinquency*. New York: Commonwealth Fund, 1950.

Gregory, I. Anterospective data following childhood loss of a parent: I. Delinquency and high-school dropout. *Archives of General Psychiatry*, 1965, *13*, 99–109.

Gross, A. E. *Sex and helping: Intrinsic glow and extrinsic show*. Paper presented at American Psychological Association Meetings, Honolulu, September 1972.

Haan, N. Moral redefinition in families as the critical aspect of the generation gap. *Youth and Society*, 1971, *2*, 259–283.

———. Activism as moral protest: Moral judgments of hypothetical moral dilemmas and an actual situation of civil disobedience. In L. Kohlberg and E. Turiel (Eds.), *The development of moral judgment and action*. New York: Holt, Rinehart & Winston, in press.

Haan, N., Smith, M. B., and Block, J. Moral reasoning of young adults: Political-social behavior, family background, and personality correlates. *Journal of Personality and Social Psychology*, 1968, *10*, 183–201.

Hartmann, H. *Psychoanalysis and moral values*. New York: International Universities Press, 1960.

Hoffman, M. L. Parent discipline and the child's consideration for others. *Child Development*, 1963a, *34*, 573–588.

———. Personality, family structure, and social class as antecedents of parental power assertion. *Child Development*, 1963b, *34*, 869–884.

———. Conscience, personality, and socialization techniques. *Human Development*, 1970a, *13*, 90–126.

———. Moral development. In P. H. Mussen (Ed.), *Carmichael's handbook of child psychology* (Vol. 2). New York: Wiley, 1970b.

———. Father-absence and conscience development. *Developmental Psychology*, 1971a, *4*, 400–406.

———. Identification and conscience development. *Child Development*, 1971b, *42*, 1071–1082.

———. Altruistic behavior and the parent-child relationship. *Journal of Personality and Social Psychology*, 1975a, *31*, 937–943.

———. Developmental synthesis of affect and cognition and its implications for altruistic motivation. *Developmental Psychology*, 1975b, *11*, 607–622.

———. Moral internalization, parental power, and the nature of parent-child interaction. *Developmental Psychology*, 1975c, *11*(2), 228–239.

———. Sex differences in moral internalization. *Journal of Personality and Social Psychology*, 1975d, *32*, 720–729.

———. Empathy, role-taking, guilt, and development of altruistic motives. In T. Likona, (Ed.), *Moral development: Current theory and research*. New York: Holt, Rinehart & Winston, 1976a.

———. Parental discipline and moral internalization: A theoretical analysis, *Developmental Report No. 85*, University of Michigan, 1976b.

———. Moral internalization: Current theory and research. In L. Berkowitz (Ed.), *Advances in Experimental Social Psychology*, (Vol. 10). New York: Academic, 1977a.

———. Empathy, its development and prosocial implications. In C. Keasey (Ed.), *Nebraska Symposium on Motivation* (Vol. 25). Lincoln: University of Nebraska Press, 1977b.

———. Toward a theory of empathic arousal and development. In M. Lewis and L. Rosenblum (Eds.), *The development of affect*. New York: Plenum, 1978.

Hoffman, M. L., and Saltzstein, H. D. Parental discipline and the child's moral development. *Journal of Personality and Social Psychology*, 1967, *5*, 45–57.

Hogan, R. Theoretical egocentricism and the problem of compliance. *American Psychologist*, 1975, *30*, 533–540.

Horn, J. L. and Knott, P. D. Activist youth of the 1960s: Summary and prognosis. *Science*, 1971, *171*, 977–985.

Horner, M. Sex differences in achievement motivation and performance in competitive and noncompetitive situations. (Doctoral dissertation, University of Michigan, Ann Arbor, 1968). *Dissertation Abstracts International*, 1968, Vol. 30, No. 1 (July, 1969), Pages 1B–1423B. (University Microfilms No. 69–12, 135)

Humphrey, G. The conditioned reflex and the elementary social reaction. *Journal of Abnormal and Social Psychology*, 1922, *17*, 113–119.

Izard, C. E. *The face of emotion*. New York: Appleton-Century Crofts, 1971.

Jacobson, E. Superego formation and the period of latency. *The self and the object world* (Part II). New York: International Universities Press, 1964.

Johnson, M. J. Sex-role learning in the nuclear family. *Child Development*, 1963, *34*, 319–333.

Jones, M. L. A comparison of the attitudes and interests of ninth-grade students over two decades. *Journal of Educational Psychology,* 1960, *51,* 175–186.

Keniston, K. *The uncommitted.* New York: Harcourt, Brace and World, 1965.

———. Student activism, moral development, and morality. *American Journal of Orthopsychiatry,* 1970, *40,* 577–592.

Kilham, W., and Mann, L. Level of destructive obedience as a function of transmitter and executant roles in the Milgram obedience paradigm. *Journal of Personality and Social Psychology,* 1974, *29,* 696–702.

Kohlberg, L. The development of modes of moral thinking and choice in the years 10 to 16. Unpublished doctoral dissertation, University of Chicago, 1958.

———. Development of moral character and moral ideology. In M. L. Hoffman and L. W. Hoffman (Eds.), *Review of child development research* (Vol. 1). New York: Russell Sage Foundation, 1964.

———. The contribution of developmental psychology to education: Examples from moral education. *Educational Psychologist,* 1973, *10*(1), 2–14.

———. The cognitive-developmental approach: New developments and a response to criticism. Paper presented at the Society for Research in Child Development Meeting, Denver, March 1975.

———. Moral stages and moralization: The cognitive-developmental approach. In T. Likona (Ed.), *Moral development and behavior.* New York: Holt, 1976.

Kohlberg, L., and Gilligan, C. The adolescent as a philosopher: The discovery of the self in a postconventional world. *Daedalus,* 1971, *100,* 1051–1086.

Kohlberg, L., and Kramer, R. Continuities and discontinuities in childhood and adult moral development. *Human Development,* 1969, *12,* 93–120.

Kuhlen, R. G., and Arnold, M. Age differences in religious beliefs and problems during adolescence. *Journal of Genetic Psychology,* 1944, *65,* 291–300.

Kurtines, W., and Greif, E. B. The development of moral thought: Review and evaluation of Kohlberg's approach. *Psychological Bulletin,* 1974, *81,* 453–470.

Laird, J. D. Self-attribution of emotion: The effects of expressive behavior on the quality of emotional experience. *Journal of Personality and Social Psychology,* 1974, *29,* 475–486.

Langer, J. Disequilibrium as a source of development. In P. H. Mussen, J. Langer, and M. Covington (Eds.), *Trends and issues in developmental psychology.* New York: Holt, 1969.

Langworthy, R. L. Community status and influence in a high school. *American Sociological Review,* 1959, *24,* 537–539.

Latané, B., and Darley, J. Bystander intervention in emergencies. In J. Macaulay and L. Berkowitz (Eds.), *Altruism and helping behavior.* New York: Academic, 1970.

Le Bon, G. *The crowd: A study of the popular mind.* New York: Viking, 1960. (Originally published, 1895.)

Lifton, R. *Death in life: Survivors of Hiroshima.* New York: Random House, 1968.

Lipps, T. Das Wissen von fremden Ichen. *Psychol Untersuch.,* 1906, *1,* 694–722.

Mandler, G. *Mind and emotion.* New York: Wiley, 1975.

Masters, J. C. Social comparison by young children. In W. W. Hartup (Ed.), *The young child* (Vol. 2). Washington, D.C.: National Association for the Education of Young Children, 1972.

Mathews, K. E. and Canon, L. K. Environmental noise level as a determinant of helping behavior. *Journal of Personality and Social Psychology,* 1975, *32,* 571–577.

Mathews, K., and Stotland, E. "Empathy and nursing students' contact with patients." Mimeographed. Spokane, Wash.: University of Washington, 1973.

Miller, W. B. Lower-class culture as a generating milieu of gang delinquency. *Journal of Social Issues,* 1958, *14,* 5–19.

Monroe, S. Guest in a strange house. *Saturday Review of Books,* February 1973, pp. 45–48.

Moore, B. S., Underwood, B., and Rosenhan, D. L. Affect and altruism. *Developmental Psychology,* 1973, *8,* 99–104.

Murphy, L. B. *Social behavior and child personality.* New York: Columbia University Press, 1937.

Parsons, T. Age and sex in the social structure of the United States. *American Sociological Review,* 1942, *7,* 604–616.

Peters, R. S. Moral development: A plea for pluralism. In T. Mischel (Ed.), *Cognitive development and epistemology.* New York: Academic, 1971.

Piaget, J. *The moral judgment of the child.* New York: Harcourt, 1932.

Regan, D. T., Williams, M., and Sparling, S. Voluntary expiation of guilt: A field experiment. *Journal of Personality and Social Psychology,* 1972, *24,* 42.

Regan, J. W. Guilt, perceived injustice, and altruistic behavior. *Journal of Personality and Social Psychology,* 1971, *18,* 124–132.

Rest, J. R. The hierarchical nature of moral judgment: A study of patterns of comprehension and preference of moral stages. *Journal of Personality,* 1973, *41,* 86–109.

Rutherford, E., and Mussen, P. Generosity in nursery-school boys. *Child Development,* 1968, *39,* 755–765.

Schachter, S., and Singer, J. E. Cognitive, social, and physiological determinants of emotional state. *Psychological Review,* 1962, *69,* 379–399.

Schwartz, S. Moral decision-making and behavior. In J. Macaulay and L. Berkowitz (Eds.), *Altruism and helping behavior.* New York: Academic, 1970.

Settlage, C. F. Cultural values and the superego in late adolescence. *Psychoanalytic Study of the Child,* 1972, *27,* 57–73.

Sherif, M., Harvey, O. J., White, B. J., Hood, W. R., and Sherif, C. *Intergroup conflict and cooperation: The robber's cave experiment.* Norman, Okla.: University Book Exchange, 1961.

Siegman, A. W. Father-absence during childhood and antisocial behavior. *Journal of Abnormal Psychology,* 1966, *71,* 71–74.

Simpson, E. L. Moral development research: A case study of scientific cultural bias. *Human Development,* 1974, *17,* 81–106.

Solnit, A. J. Youth and the campus: The search for a social conscience. *Psychoanalytic Study of a Child,* 1972, *27,* 98–105.

Staub, E. A child in distress: The influence of age and number of witnesses on children's attempts to help. *Journal of Personality and Social Psychology,* 1970, *14,* 130–140.

———. Helping a person in distress: The influence of implicit and explicit "rules" of conduct on children and adults. *Journal of Personality and Social Psychology,* 1971, *17,* 137–144.

Staub, E., and Sherk, L. Need for approval, children's sharing behavior, and reciprocity in sharing. *Child Development,* 1970, *41,* 243–253.

Stotland, E. Exploratory investigations of empathy. In L. Berkowitz (Ed.), *Advances in experimental social psychology* (Vol. 4). New York: Academic, 1969.

Tilker, H. A. Socially responsible behavior as a function of observer responsibility and victim feedback. *Journal of Personality and Social Psychology,* 1970, *14,* 95–100.

Tracy, J. J., and Cross, H. J. Antecedents of shift in moral judgment. *Journal of Personality and Social Psychology,* 1973, *26,* 238–244.

Tulving, E. Episodic and semantic memory. In E. Tulving and W. Donaldson (Eds.), *Organization of memory.* New York: Academic, 1972.

Turiel, E. An experimental test of the sequentiality of developmental stages in the child's moral judgments. *Journal of Personality and Social Psychology,* 1966, *3,* 611–618.

———. Conflict and transition in adolescent moral development. *Child Development,* 1974, *45,* 14–79.

———. Social convention and the development of societal concepts. Unpublished manuscript, University of California, Santa Cruz, 1977.

Wallach, M., and Kogan, N. Sex differences and judgment processes. *Journal of Personality,* 1959, *27,* 555–564.

Weiss, R. F., Boyer, J. L., Lombardo, J. P., and Stitch, M. H. Altruistic drive and altruistic reinforcement. *Journal of Personality and Social Psychology,* 1973, *25,* 390–400.

Wine, J. D. Test anxiety and helping behavior. *Canadian Journal of Behavioral Science,* 1975, *7,* 216–222.

Zussman, J. U. Demographic factors influencing parental discipline techniques. Paper presented at the American Psychological Association Meeting, Chicago, September 1975.

CHAPTER 10

Political Thinking in Adolescence

Judith Gallatin

DEFINING POLITICAL SOCIALIZATION

The term political socialization remains somewhat vaguely defined. Most students of the field are aware of the problem (see especially Connell, 1969; Nathan & Remy, 1977; Renshon, 1977a; Sigel & Hoskin, 1977a; Torney, 1976). Greenberg (1970a) has probably put his finger on its origin when he remarks:

> For some reason every scholar feels that he must start at ground zero by defining anew the concept of socialization. As a result, the student has a myriad of descriptions from which to make his selection. While such a state of affairs is highly desirable in a restaurant, it is hardly useful in scholarly inquiry. [P. 3]

This lack of conceptual clarity has led a few researchers (Sigel & Hoskin, 1977a) to balk at even trying to define the field. However, most others do precisely what Greenberg (1970a) does — resort to a broad and all-encompassing description:

> To recognize the range of definitional treatment yet not be hampered by it, we will define political socialization quite loosely as the process by which the individual acquires attitudes, beliefs, and values relating to the political system of which he is a member and to his own role as a citizen within that political system. [P. 3]

Greenberg observes that his definition accommodates ''a wide range of conceptual approaches and theories without a commitment to any one in particular.'' He is undoubtedly correct. Fuzzy and blurred as the field of political socialization is, it has attracted investigators from a number of different disciplines — political science, sociology, and psychology. Research on political socialization, including research that involves adolescents, continues to accumulate at an impressive (if not alarming) rate. As evidence, the representative, but by no means exhaustive, list of references for this chapter contains over 200 separate citations, many of them studies carried out after 1970. A more general review by Sears (1975b) cites more than 300 sources; a recent handbook (Renshon, 1977b), boasts almost 1600 bibliographic entries.

Unfortunately, the field's great virtue is also its chief liability. Because researchers have come at it from so many different directions, it suffers from disorganization. Different investigators studying the same general population (e.g., adolescents) have made contradictory inferences. Theoretical disputes have begun to crop up. As almost always happens in any new subdivision of the social sciences, methodologists (Cutler, 1977; Weissberg & Joslyn, 1977) have started to question the validity of much current research. It is impossible to draw any conclusions about political socialization during adolescence without addressing these larger issues as well.

MODELS AND TOPICS

The first order of business is to provide some sort of framework for discussing the various research findings. A promising way to begin is to identify the major theoretical orientations. The field of political socialization may appear to be diffuse — "vulgarly empirical" as Merelman (1969) puts it — but on closer scrutiny a somewhat different picture emerges. One is reminded of David Rapaport's assertion:

> Many features of observables can be counted, rated, and measured, but the observables themselves cannot tell us which features and what method of counting or measuring them will reveal the relationship between them and the explanatory concepts: only theory can do that. [1960, p. 36]

In other words, no one actually does "purely empirical" research. Presumably, investigators always have some kind of theoretical model in mind, or some kind of preconception or "bias". Without at least a vague notion of what to look for, researchers would find it impossible to interpret their results. The underlying models may not be very well defined, but they exist nonetheless. They help to determine what problems are studied in the first place, and, equally important, *how* such problems are studied (see Connell, 1969, for an especially fine exposition of this point).

There seem to be four major approaches within the field of political socialization, and most of the research involving teenagers can be considered under one or another of these. The first three are rather closely related, while the fourth is something of a "stepchild" within the field. These four major "schools" are:

1. Social learning or behavioral
2. Sociological or "generational"
3. Psychodynamic
4. Cognitive-developmental

The Behavioral School

The social learning or behavioral orientation is probably the most popular. Although a few proponents have tried to set forth a precise set of principles (Rohter, 1975), most behavioral researchers have contented themselves with rather general statements of their underlying assumptions. Indeed, one of the leading devotees of social learning theory (Sears, 1975b) actively opposes a more precise formulation:

> Such loving care for the arid esoterica of various learning approaches is hardly required for the crude levels of explanation political socialization researchers will be dealing with in the foreseeable future (as indeed it has been of doubtful value in other applications of learning theory).

In any case, researchers who have adopted a social learning orientation — principally Easton, Hess, Torney, Dennis, Jennings, Niemi, and Langton, in addition to Sears — appear to assume that there is a stable political order into which the individual is "socialized." According to this point of view, the child begins life as a completely apolitical creature and is gradually molded by various agencies of the existing "regime" —parents, schools, churches, assorted authority figures, and to some extent peers (Easton & Dennis, 1973). As Renshon (1977a) notes, these researchers have tended to emphasize the primacy of early learning. Although there is some variation of opinion within the group, for the most part they have taken the position that political socialization is largely complete by the beginning of adolescence. Easton, Hess, and Torney are the strongest advocates for this point of view. Jennings, Niemi, and Sears (see especially, Sears, 1975c) agree that early childhood is a crucial period in political socialization but ascribe some importance to adolescence (particularly late adolescence) as well.

Not surprisingly, in view of their orientation, this group has shown a great deal of interest in tracing the development of political attitudes during childhood and adolescence (Easton & Dennis, 1965, 1967, 1969; Easton & Hess, 1961, 1962; Hess & Torney, 1967; Torney, 1971), and they have also tried to assess the actual impact of parents, teachers, peers, and the like (Jennings, 1968, 1974, 1975; Jennings, Ehman, & Niemi, 1974; Jennings & Niemi, 1968a, 1968b, 1976; Langton, 1967, 1969; Langton & Jennings, 1968; Sebert, Jennings, & Niemi, 1974). On occasion they have employed face-to-face interviews, but their chief research technique has been the large-sample, paper-and-pencil survey.

The Generational School

Members of what I call the "generational school" have also adopted a somewhat global perspective on political socialization. However, as sociologists they have been concerned chiefly with the shifts in ideology that are supposed to occur as one generation ages and another grows to maturity. These researchers (Bengston, 1970; Bengston, Furlong, & Laufer, 1974; Braungart, 1974, 1976; Cutler, 1975, 1977; Laufer & Bengston, 1974; Starr, 1974) have typically tried to identify historical factors or status forces that might account for cleavages between the older and younger generations, but they have also investigated ideological differences within the same age-cohort (Braungart, 1976; Kasschau, Ransford, and Bengston, 1974.)

The generational school merits special attention here because it has relied so heavily on the sociological and psychohistorical theories of Mannheim (1952), Eisenstadt (1963), Erikson (1968), and Bettelheim (1963) for inspiration. What is important for our purposes is that all of these theorists envision late adolescence as a particularly critical period in political socialization. All of them also argue that the special circumstances of adolescence — "status inferiority," "the need to establish a separate identity," "the desire to replace the older generation" — encourage the young to embrace ideologies that are contrary to those of their parents.

Given their theoretical orientation, it is not exactly astonishing that "generational" researchers have shown great interest in such adolescent phenomena as student activism and the so-called "generation gap." Like the behavioral group, they tend to make use of attitude surveys and paper-and-pencil measures.

The Psychodynamic School

Investigators who share a psychodynamic orientation (Greenstein, 1969; Keniston, 1968; Knutson, 1972, 1973a; 1973b; Lane, 1959, 1968, 1969, 1973; Renshon, 1974, 1975; Sigel, 1975) stress the psychological rather than the sociological. According to this point of view (one that is quite well established within psychology, see Adorno et al., 1950), people are attracted to various ideologies — democratic, conservative, authoritarian, even apathetic — because there is some kind of "fit" between a particular political philosophy and their own personal makeup. For example, an open, self-actualized, vital individual will presumably be more attracted to democratic values than someone who is insecure and distrustful (Knutson, 1972).

Researchers partial to the psychodynamic approach have tended to focus on adults. However, in recent years a number of them have begun to study adolescent populations (Keniston, 1968; Lane, 1968, 1969; Renshon, 1974; Sigel, 1975). Typically, they have attempted to find correlations between a particular psychological trait or personality type and a particular measure of political activity or ideology. In this connection, they have employed a wide variety of techniques — personality inventories, Q-sorts, Thematic Apperception Test (TAT) protocols, autobiographical accounts, intensive interviews, and paper-and-pencil surveys.

As I have indicated, there are no sharp dividing lines among these three schools. Behavioral researchers freely cite their more psychodynamically or sociologically oriented colleagues. Their areas of interest overlap. Jennings and Niemi, who are partial to social learning theory, have recently conducted several "generational" studies (Jennings and Niemi, 1975, 1976). On occasion, researchers from one school have even collaborated with those from another, for instance, Lane, who favors a psychodynamic approach, and Sears, who prefers social learning theory (Lane and Sears, 1964).

Researchers from each of these three camps get on so well, I suspect, because they share certain assumptions about the relationship between individual and environment. Although the specific tenets of the underlying model may differ, each school portrays the individual as somehow passive and vulnerable — subject to forces (e.g., agencies, historical events, status considerations, psychological needs) that are beyond his conscious control. Not so for the fourth school, a group of researchers who seem to be somewhat isolated from the rest. Indeed, in his chapter on "assumptive frameworks in political socialization theory," Renshon (1977a) does not even identify this school as a separate approach.

The Cognitive-Developmental School

Investigators who have adopted a cognitive-developmental or Piagetian orientation view the political socialization process less as a kind of passive molding and more as a kind of active involvement between the individual and his or her environment. The investigators agree that there are various agents in political socialization, but they believe that the individual interacts with them rather than being "imprinted" by them. As Connell (1969, 1971) and Rosenau (1975) describe it, the child and later the adolescent and adult gradually construct an image of the political scene. The key concepts are Piaget's (1952) principles of assimilation, accommodation, and equilibration. Persons who attempt to make a new experience conform to their old preconceptions are trying to assimilate it; those who alter their old preconceptions on the basis of a new experience have accommodated it. And the glue that binds the whole process together is equilibration. Rosenau (1975) gives the following example:

> When the young child points to a cow and says, 'dog,' he is assimilating the novel stimulus to his single existing schema for four-legged animals. Later, after accumulating experience with other varieties of four-legged animals, he incorporates variation into his cognitive structures. [P. 165]

Describing equilibration, she adds:

The goal is always assimilation, as after accommodation there exists a new schema into which similar inputs will subsequently be assimilated. But a balance is maintained between the two processes so that neither dominates, and this balancing process is equilibration. [P. 165]

Interestingly enough, Piaget himself has not devoted much attention to political socialization. He has explored the related area of moral judgment (1932/1965) and conducted one study on the development of national awareness (Piaget and Weil, 1951). Except for these, there is only his tantalizing suggestion (Inhelder and Piaget, 1958) that adolescence may be a particularly significant period for formulating ideologies. Not until adolescence, he and Inhelder explain, does the youngster acquire the capacity for formal thought.

As attractive as his model may be to its adherents (including myself), Piaget's theory places certain restrictions on researchers. Given the number of possible influences, it is difficult to imagine how one would actually measure the interaction between individuals and their political environment. Cognitive-developmental researchers have therefore usually been content to explore the growth of political thinking per se without attempting to ascertain the impact of specific agencies. As a rule, they have employed relatively small samples and studied them intensively, often with face-to-face interviews. Mindful of Inhelder and Piaget's suggestion that formal thought and political ideology are somehow linked, most cognitive-developmental researchers have concentrated on preteens and adolescents (Adelson, 1971b; Adelson & Beall, 1970; Adelson and O'Neil, 1966; Adelson, Green, & O'Neil, 1969; Bush, 1970; Crain & Crain, 1974; Gallatin, 1967, 1972, 1976; Gallatin & Adelson, 1970, 1971). Connell (1969, 1971), in fact, represents about the only major exception, having included children as young as six or seven in his studies.

Research on the development of political thinking also overlaps considerably with studies of moral development (Friedman, 1977; Hogan, 1973, 1975; Kohlberg, 1958, 1964; Kohlberg and Gilligan, 1971; Kohlberg and Kramer, 1969; Rest, 1973; Turiel, 1974) and legal socialization (Tapp, 1976; Tapp and Kohlberg, 1971; Tapp and Levine, 1970, 1972, 1974). Indeed, Sullivan (1970) aptly describes the connection between these areas when he remarks:

The relationship between moral and political development is closely intertwined in the area of ideology, moral development being more generic concerning both private and public morality. Political ideology is more specific and deals with that particular aspect of the moral domain which relates to public political institutions. [P. 101]

RESEARCH ON POLITICAL SOCIALIZATION DURING ADOLESCENCE

Having identified the major theoretical models within the field, the next challenge is to impose some semblance of order on the existing data. The key question, of course, is whether or not adolescence constitutes a particularly significant stage in the development of political orientations and attitudes. This question can be broken down into a number of subsidiary questions, and after listing them, I shall take each one up in sequence:

1. How much do teenagers know about politics?
2. What are their political attitudes and beliefs?
3. What effect do various agents — family, school, the media, and peers — apparently have on political socialization during adolescence?

4. How are variables, like sex, social class, race, nationality and intelligence, related to adolescent political thought?

5. What impact do specific experiences or events — military service, government scandal, assassination — have on teenagers?

6. What is the relationship between personality and politics during adolescence?

7. What motives and variables appear to underlie political activity during adolescence?

After reviewing the relevant research, I shall comment on various methodological problems that have become evident and outline some considerations for future study.

HOW MUCH DO TEENAGERS KNOW ABOUT POLITICS?

Is conventional wisdom correct and are adolescents largely ignorant when it comes to politics, or are they reasonably knowledgeable? As it turns out, the answers depend a good deal on whose research a reviewer examines, and here the influence of differing models and assumptions is all too clear. Behavioral researchers, for instance, tend to reach different conclusions than those who have affected a cognitive-developmental stance.

Behavioral Research

Judging from the work of behavioral investigators, teenagers do not exhibit a very firm grasp of politics. In one of the most widely cited studies in the field, Langton and Jennings (1968) administered a six-item questionnaire to approximately 2000 high-school students, asking among other things, "the number of years a U.S. Senator serves" and "whether President Franklin Roosevelt was a Republican or Democrat" (p. 855). The students were also requested to indicate which of the two leading political parties in the United States was the more conservative. Since Langton and Jennings were supposedly investigating the impact of the high-school civics curriculum on political socialization, they did not report the actual percentage of correct responses for anything but the item on political parties. But the general tone of their article nonetheless managed to convey the impression that adolescents possess little political sophistication (see Patrick, 1977). They asserted, for example, that high-school civics courses had almost no effect on students, basing their conclusion on the fact that students who had taken civics and government had no more success with the questionnaire items than those who had not. (As we shall see, the findings were a little different for black youngsters.)

However, there *is* evidence — assembled chiefly by cognitive-developmental researchers — that adolescents may not be quite so ignorant after all. They may be hazy about specific details, but a substantial proportion appear to have acquired a fair comprehension of the political process by age 18. Comparisons with younger children are particularly useful here.

Not surprisingly, most of the studies with younger children (i.e., second to fifth grade) have been carried out by behavioral researchers who assumed, a priori, that almost everything that was going to be learned had already been learned by adolescence [Connell and Greenstein, of course, represent notable exceptions]. Whatever their biases, people who have studied political thinking among younger children have ended up using one or more of the following terms to describe them: global, diffuse, personalized, and even unconscious. (See Connell, 1969, 1971; Easton and Dennis, 1965; Easton and Hess, 1962; Greenstein, 1960, 1961a, 1965; Hess and Torney, 1967; Schwartz, 1975b; Torney, 1971). Researchers agree that what might be called political awareness develops very early. Schwartz (1975b), for instance, discovered that a large number of preschoolers (ages three to six) had heard of and formed opinions about various political symbols ("the President," "America").

But younger children appear naive when confronting the realities of the political scene. In a well-known study (Hess and Torney, 1967), a large number of second-graders agreed with the statement, "The President would help me if I were in trouble." This study did include a sample of early adolescents (seventh- and eighth-graders); here the results were strikingly different. Relatively few of these youngsters believed that the President would personally extend a helping hand.

Cognitive-Developmental Research

Researchers who are partial to cognitive-developmental theory, in fact, have concluded that only during adolescence does the youngster become capable of truly comprehending the political milieu. Although he has not done much work with adolescents, Greenstein (1965) expresses much the same opinion. Indeed, he asserts that the young child's grasp of politics is largely "affective" in contrast to the teenager's more "cognitive" approach.

This distinction — affective versus cognitive — is not, in my opinion, entirely satisfactory. It implies that young children think in feelings rather than concepts. But it does begin to get at the essential difference between children and adolescents. Amending Greenstein somewhat, I would argue that the key difference has to do with the kinds of concepts children and adolescents are able to employ. Where the young child and even the preadolescent has to grapple and grope and piece together an answer to a particular question about politics, the adolescent — particularly the older adolescent — appears (relatively speaking) articulate and knowledgeable.

As an illustration, consider the following two excerpts from my own study of political thinking (Gallatin, 1972). As part of this project, youngsters of varying ages (sixth, eighth, tenth, and twelfth grade) were given an intensive interview consisting of more than 100 items. The first subject is a sixth-grader:

Interviewer: Do you think it would ever be possible to eliminate poverty?

6-grader: No.

Interviewer: Do you know what I mean by poverty?

6-grader: No

Interviewer: That means poorness, not having any money. So the question asks if it would ever be possible to make it so that nobody was poor.

6-grader: I don't, well, if they got the person to really work hard that there might not be anyone that would, uh, be poor and that, but if there was someone that would just uh would uh be retired, he could just lay around the house because he's already put in his years of work and that.

Interviewer: Do you think it would ever be that there wouldn't be any poor people?

6-grader: Maybe, in the future, if they could enforce the law that all lazy people and that should work.

I suspect that because of the child's lack of familiarity with a formal concept like "poverty," his answer seems even more garbled and confused than it really is. If we examine what he says closely, we discover that he appears to have made a rather popular political assumption, that is, that poverty exists because some people are lazy (" . . . if they got the person to really work hard that there might not be anyone that would, uh, be poor . . ."). He also seems, like a good, concrete, Piagetian 11-year-old, to be struggling to keep his categories straight. It apparently occurs to him midway through his answer that sheer laziness is not the whole story. He recognizes that there are a class of people who have a legitimate right not to work, that is, "retired people."

But because we see this sixth-grader piecing his answer together right before our eyes (rather like watching someone lurch around on a bicycle for the first time), there is an inevitable temptation to label his efforts simplistic or confused. Compare his reaction, earnest but awkward, with that of a high-school senior responding to the same question:

Interviewer: Do you think it would ever be possible to eliminate poverty?

12-grader: Yes because this is the most highly advanced, richest country in the world. And the world knows because we're putting money over here, overseas there, or we're putting money over there. Money in Africa, putting a hell of a lot of money in Asia, the Southeast. I don't see why we should be putting money there while we still have poor here. I'd say we could put in a little money but why do we have to buy airplanes. We've done a hell of a lot for the foreign countries, as they say, so I don't think we should.

Like the sixth-grader, the twelfth-grader has difficulty containing his thoughts, and his answer becomes, in part, a diatribe on American foreign policy. His proposed remedy for poverty — have the government spend money on the poor people at home rather than "wasting" it abroad — might also be described as simplistic. But the sweep and scope of his response are far broader. He does not have to have the term poverty defined. He identifies it as a national problem rather than attributing it to "lazy people," and he surveys the international scene in his attempt to suggest a solution. He exhibits, in short, what Adelson and O'Neil (1966) have aptly described as a "sense of community."

Patterns in Political Thought

The excerpts I have presented exemplify trends that have turned up regularly in cognitive-developmental research. To be sure, methodologists (notably Cutler, 1977) have criticized such studies because they are cross-sectional rather than longitudinal. But these trends have turned up so persistently with so many different groups at so many different points in time, that I believe we can be reasonably sure of their validity. Indeed, researchers who have explored closely related areas, like moral judgment and legal socialization, have obtained strikingly similar results. The pattern of political thinking that emerges from our cross-sectional investigations is a consistent one. Based on our work with subjects in Western democracies, we have concluded that the youngster's perception of the political system shifts markedly between childhood and late adolescence. Not only do youths in their late teens appear to be more knowledgeable about politics, their entire image of government is different.

Perceptions of the Political System

Prior to adolescence, the child views government and law principally as coercive agencies. If asked, children will declare that the function of political institutions is to police people — to keep them in line and make sure that they are unable to get away with any wrong-doing (Adelson & O'Neil, 1966; Adelson & Beall, 1970; Adelson, Green, & O'Neil, 1969; Tapp, 1976; Tapp & Kohlberg, 1971; Tapp & Levine, 1972). As children reach adolescence, this perception begins to alter, and by the time they have reached their late teens, a substantial proportion of youngsters have acquired a less forbidding image of the political system. The government is seen as a cooperative venture — an agency that provides services and insures that society functions smoothly rather than a glorified policeman. (The contrast between preadolescent and late adolescent is evident even in the brief excerpt given above. When asked how to eliminate poverty, the 11-year-old replies that lazy people ought to be forced to work, while the 18-year-old clearly favors increased government spending.)

The Individual and the Political System

There is an important corollary to this basic finding, and it has to do with the way in which the late adolescent characterizes the relationship between the individual and the state. As youngsters' view of government grows less coercive and authoritarian, their support of individual rights becomes increasingly evident. If asked, for instance, what sorts of laws should be permanent, preteens and younger adolescents are apt to mention rules and regulations that seem trivial by adult standards. A very impressive proportion of older adolescents, by contrast, cite laws guaranteeing individual freedoms (Gallatin & Adelson, 1971; Gallatin, 1972). Two behavioral researchers (Zellman & Sears, 1971) report comparable findings with a sample of preteens and adolescents (fifth through ninth grade). However, they claim that their subjects showed more support for civil liberties in the *abstract* (i.e., agreeing that there should be "free speech for all") than in specific instances (i.e., agreeing that Communists ought to be able to teach in the schools).

In any case, I should point out that findings like the ones I have cited are relative rather than absolute. The differences between younger and older adolescents are more marked for some issues than for others. Nonetheless, there is a definite tendency for younger subjects to have difficulty comprehending political questions, although a significant proportion of older subjects handle them with ease. On the basis of my own work and that of other researchers, I have identified three stages or levels in the growth of political thinking:

> *Level 1:* The confused, simplistic, punitive, or concretely pragmatic response.
>
> *Level 2:* Transitional responses. Answers that express the rudiments of a political concept but remain somewhat fragmentary or personalized.
>
> *Level 3:* Conceptual responses. Answers that are phrased in terms of a political principle or ideal.

As I have indicated, the precise number of preadolescents and adolescents at any of these three levels depends to some extent on the issue at hand. However, the figures in Table 1 may be used as a rough guide. (These percentages were obtained by taking responses to 100 questionnaire items, coding them into levels, and then dividing by the total number of items.) Of course, this average percentage is only a rather crude index of the conceptual shifts that occur between preadolescence and late adolescence. But Table 1 does show that younger subjects give a disproportionate number of lower-level responses and that older subjects are concentrated in the transitional and higher levels.

Table 1   Level of Response by Age (in percentages)

	Level 1	Level 2	Level 3
6th grade	59	23	11
8th grade	43	31	20
10th grade	31	33	32
12th grade	19	29	41

$N = 480$

My own taxonomy bears a striking resemblance to those described by Connell (1971) and Crain and Crain (1974). It is also similar to the levels of moral and legal thinking identified by Kohlberg (1958, 1964) and Tapp (1976); Tapp and Kohlberg (1971); Tapp and Levine (1972).

Adolescence and Ideology

This is not to say that 18-year-olds who have reached the conceptual stage (or what Connell (1971) calls the ideological stage) can hold forth like political philosophers. As Adelson (1971b) has observed, very few of these older adolescents are able to construct anything like a coherent ideology, a fact that requires further amplification.

The discussion of ideology is, as Adelson puts it, "a most complicated matter," but he offers the following useful explication:

> The root of the complication is that we may adopt a weak or a strong definition of ideology. By the latter we mean a highly structured, hierarchically ordered, internally consistent body of general principles from which specific attitudes follow. Used in this sense, the ideological capacity in adolescence is extremely rare, almost never found before the later years of high school, and even then only among the most intelligent, intellectually committed, and politically intense. In a weak definition, we construe ideology to involve the presence of attitudes *roughly* consistent with each other, and *more or less* organized in reference to a more encompassing, though perhaps tacit, set of political principles. Used in this sense, we can say that ideology is dim or absent at the beginning of adolescence, and that the criteria for achieving ideology are apparent only during the middle period. [Adelson, 1971b, pp. 120–121]

See Merelman (1969) for a somewhat different analysis of the same issues.

Comprehension of Partisan Differences

Then, too, there are areas of politics that remain curiously beyond the grasp of even older adolescents. One of these, surprisingly, is partisan politics. Although children may *call* themselves "Democrat" or "Republican" from a very early age (Hess and Torney, 1967), few of them have the foggiest idea what such labels entail, a fuzziness that persists well into late adolescence. Bush (1970), for example, discovered that preadolescents became completely confused when asked to explain why political parties came into being, and her older subjects (12-graders) were not a great deal more articulate. Langton and Jennings (1968) report similar results — roughly 30% of the high-school students in their study were of the opinion that Republicans were more conservative than Democrats, while the rest didn't know or guessed incorrectly. I have confirmed this finding in my own research (Gallatin, 1972).

All in all, however, I believe the conclusions I drew when the legal voting age was lowered from 21 to 18 are still valid:

. . . the Constitutional Amendment lowering the voting age to 18 will not, as some of its opponents have claimed, have any dire consequences for the future of the republic. On the contrary, with the exception of a few weak points, the average 18-year-old seems well equipped to assume his new civic responsibilities. [Gallatin, 1972, p. 151]

POLITICAL ATTITUDES AND BELIEFS

What teenagers know about politics — how they describe the workings of the political system — bears a close relationship to what they feel and believe about politics, their so-called political attitudes. Here too, at first glance, the research appears to be contradictory. One might infer from the data I have just presented that teenagers become more idealistic about government as they mature — more equalitarian, less inclined to see political institutions as a coercive and punitive force. Yet other researchers — principally those with a social learning or psychodynamic orientation (Easton and Dennis, 1965; Easton and Hess, 1962; Greenstein, 1960, 1961a, 1965; Hess and Torney, 1967)—have concluded that children's first impressions of government are overwhelmingly positive and benevolent, and that they become more skeptical and cynical with the onset of adolescence. How can we reconcile these two apparently opposing points of view?

To begin with, there is some evidence that young children do *not* always perceive government through rose-colored glasses. Not too surprisingly, the milieu in which they reside appears to have some impact. As an example, Jaros and his associates (Jaros, Hirsch, & Fleron, 1968) administered a political questionnaire to a group of children and adolescents living in Appalachia. Youngsters in the lower grades *already* displayed a marked lack of enthusiasm for political figures, and they simply grew more disaffected with increasing age. Other researchers have gained much the same impression of black children (Lyons, 1970; Schwartz, 1975a).

Second, even if we assume that such precocious cynicism is the exception rather than the rule, the data on the development of political attitudes are still not too difficult to interpret. I think the most reasonable explanation is that the child is simply less "realistic" about government than the adolescent — at least when judged by adult standards. Lacking the conceptual skills to comprehend politics the way adults do, the child views the political scene not so much in rose-colored pastels but in shades of black and white. Thus the President takes on the qualities of an all-powerful, all-knowing deity, and the government itself is seen as one gigantic policeman. Gradually (we are still unable to specify precisely how, see pp. 347–348), the child "corrects" his or her earlier perceptions and by midadolescence has acquired a more balanced view, neither quite as trusting nor as punitive.

Finally, several specialists have suggested that the young child's so-called diffuse loyalty may be something of an artifact. Connell argues (Connell, 1969; Connell and Goot, 1972–1973) that the research methods employed in attitude studies — large samples, paper-and-pencil surveys, forced-choice items — may be inappropriate for use with younger children:

A man walks into the classroom of a primary school. He passes some printed sheets around, checks that everyone in the class has a pencil, reads some instructions, and tells the children to start answering the questions on the sheet.

Any child knows what is going on. He is being tested. He has been in this situation often before, and knows what it is all about: he has to give, or guess, the answers to the questions which best fit the adult's notion of what are the right answers. The fact that the man has said, "this is not a test" is of little significance, for this obviously *is* a test. "Who is the Governor of Connecticut?" "What does Congress do?" "Check the names of the four most important people. . . ." [Connell, 1969, p. 58]

Thus it is perhaps not so astounding that in his search for the "right" answer, the young child ends up painting a very benevolent picture of the body politic.

There is some empirical support for Connell's position. Vaillancourt (1973) surveyed groups of children and younger adolescents (ages 9 to 15) on two different occasions several months apart. She discovered that the correlations between the two sets of answers were only moderately positive (.3 to .5), leading her to suspect that many of the subjects had simply been expressing their nonattitudes (Converse, 1964, 1970) on the issues. Similarly, a study by Blanchard and Price (1971) indicates that children may have a tendency to respond positively in *any* situation where evaluation is called for, while adolescents prefer a more balanced approach.

AGENTS IN THE POLITICAL SOCIALIZATION OF TEENAGERS

Critics like Connell and Vaillancourt help to remind us that political socialization does not occur in a vacuum. Whatever a person's eventual orientation to politics, he or she presumably does not possess one at birth (see Davies, 1977, for an attempt to identify possible prenatal factors in political socialization!). Indeed, the research I have already cited suggests that political views develop rather gradually between early childhood and late adolescence, which brings us to the problem of agents. Regardless of their specific predilection — behavioral, sociological, psychodynamic, or cognitive-developmental — all researchers assume that there *are* agents, that is, outside influences in political socialization. It appears almost self-evident that youngsters *acquire* their ideas somehow. Hence, parents, the media, schools, and peers are commonly adduced as the most likely sources.

Methodological Problems

That political socialization must proceed in this fashion seems obvious, but researchers have had a difficult time confirming it empirically. The chief stumbling block is methodological. As we have seen, researchers have encountered enough obstacles trying to determine what teenagers *themselves* know and feel about politics. When they move beyond the subjects themselves and attempt to ascertain what impact other people or agencies may have had on adolescents, the problem is severely compounded.

How is it possible to measure the impact of parents — or even more nebulous influences, like the schools and the media — on youngsters? In a recent handbook on political socialization (Renshon, 1977b), author after author attests to the difficulty (see especially Beck, 1977, on the general issue of agents in political socialization; Chaffee, 1977, on the role of the media; Gergen and Ullman, 1977, on student activism; Silberger, 1977, on the role of peers; and Weissberg and Joslyn, 1977, on research methods. See also, Dennis, 1968, and Niemi, 1973).

Chaffee, I think, provides the best exposition of the essential dilemma:

Neither communication nor political behavior can be observed in the actions of a single individual; instead, *both are relational in nature, i.e., they are concepts that refer to relationships between persons.* [italics added] Communication is a transaction of shared meanings between persons, and political behavior involves the structuring of power relationships among persons. This forces the investigator, who normally interviews or otherwise observes only one person at a time, either to attempt to impose some common context on the individuals under study, or to make unchecked *ceteris paribus* assumptions about the immediate social environment of the behavior observed. (1977, p. 230)

Furthermore, even if there were adequate measures, the statistical techniques available are largely correlational. As even a beginning student of statistics knows, "correlation does not necessarily imply causation." Multiple regression, partialling, factor analysis, and path analysis all represent additional strategies for getting at this problem, but it remains as a formidable obstacle.

Research on Agents in Political Socialization

Only cognitive-developmental researchers have been deterred by the methodological stumbling blocks mentioned above. These researchers, of course, assume that individuals acquire their political beliefs in the course of a never-ending series of relationships and interactions. The entire process is envisioned a priori as being extremely complex, and the cognitive-developmental group has generally stopped short of trying to study it directly.

Other investigators, most notably the behavioral group, have been less reticent, principally, I suspect, because of the model that underlies their work. As we have noted, researchers who are partial to social learning theory have rather set notions about the kinds of interactions that occur in political socialization. According to their account (Easton and Hess, 1961; Easton and Dennis, 1969; see also Connell's analysis, 1969), the relationships between individual and agents run largely one way. A stable political order and its representatives (already socialized adults, like parents, teachers, policemen, and TV news commentators) impress its values on passive, malleable children and adolescents. This type of theory, with its more explicit assumptions about cause and effect, can be tested more readily than cognitive-developmental theory.

The Role of Parents

Of all the possible agents available, behavioral investigators have tended to focus on parents. Since parents are the first major "outside influences" in a child's life, the choice seems logical enough. What does the actual research indicate?

Jennings and Niemi (1968b) have carried out what is unquestionably the most widely cited study. (The title, "The Transmission of Political Values from Parent to Child," is also noteworthy.) Both high-school seniors and their parents were asked to indicate their political affiliation (i.e., Republican, Democrat, or Independent). In addition, the researchers had them respond to a four-item, political-issues survey and a five-item, political-cynicism scale. In their attempt to "assay the flow of certain political values from parent to child" (p. 170), Jennings and Niemi computed a series of tau-beta coefficients.

These correlations between the adolescent subjects and their parents turned out to be positive but rather modest. Reminiscent of Hyman's pioneering study (1959), party affiliation turned out to be the strongest relationship (tau beta = .47), while the other coefficients ranged from a high of .34 (on an item regarding the federal government's role in integrating schools) to a low of .05 (on a question of whether or not people should be permitted to speak against religion). The correlation for political cynicism was an unimpressive .12, with parents appearing to register more distrust of government than their offspring. Not surprisingly, Jennings and Niemi (1968b) concluded that, "any model of socialization which rests on assumptions of pervasive currents of parent-to-child transmissions of the types examined here is in serious need of modification" (p. 183).

Although they used a less-direct measure, Hess and Torney (1967) drew similar conclusions. Their large-scale study of elementary and junior-high-school students contained a number of brothers and sisters. Hess and Torney reasoned that if parents exerted a strong influence on political attitudes, the responses of children and adolescents from the same family ought to resemble each other closely. They found that the actual correlations between siblings were positive but low, leading them to surmise that parents had played only a minor role in the transmission of political attitudes. [I should add that at least one cognitive-developmental researcher, Connell (1972) agrees with this assessment.]

The Generation Gap

Jennings and Niemi have offered relatively low-key explanations for findings like these. In one of their more recent attempts (Jennings, Ehman, & Niemi, 1974), they have suggested that the lack of correspondence between parent and child may reflect indifference more than anything else. Politics has such low salience for adults, they argue, that most parents probably just don't care what kind of views their teenagers hold on the subject.

On the other hand, members of the "generational" school have cited these parent-child comparisons as evidence for the existence of a generation gap (see especially, Bengston, 1970; Bengston, Furlong, & Laufer, 1974; Thomas, 1974). The sociological theorists on whom they rely for inspiration (Eisenstadt, 1963; Mannheim, 1952) would, of course, predict such a discrepancy. If nothing else, the parents and teenagers in Jennings and Niemi's research had been exposed to a different historical milieu. As Cutler observes:

> The basic point of these analyses is that individuals raised in different historical contexts will have been exposed to quite different sets of cultural, social, and political events. Hence the nature of their attitudes and even the essence of the processes of their socialization can be different. [1977, p. 299]

The notion of a generation gap also finds some support among psychodynamic theorists. According to psychoanalytic theory, for instance, adolescence is supposed to be a period of intense "storm and stress" (A. Freud, 1936). In response to all their internal turmoil and frustration, teenagers are supposed to rebel against their parents, opposing them politically and in every other way possible.

THE GENERATION GAP: RESEARCH

However, if we examine this so-called generation gap more closely, we discover that even Jennings and Niemi, as cautious as they are, may have overstated it. In the first place, there is little empirical evidence that anything approaching an "organized rebellion" actually takes place during adolescence. In two of the best-known studies of adolescent development, Douvan and Adelson (1966) and Offer (1969) reported that relationships between parents and teenagers were surprisingly harmonious.

Furthermore, researchers who have attempted to study the generation gap firsthand, express much the same opinion. Lerner and his associates (Lerner, 1975; Lerner et al. 1975; Lerner, Pendorf, & Emery, 1971; Lerner, et al. 1972) devised a 36-item, political-attitudes questionnaire and administered it to several groups of teenagers (e.g., high-school students, college students) and their parents. To their astonishment (they had expected to observe sizable differences), parents and children agreed rather closely. There was some disagreement, to be sure, but for the most part it did not involve a strong difference of opinion. On a number of items, teenagers tended to respond "strongly agree," while their parents checked off "somewhat agree," but only in a few cases (principally items dealing with sex and drugs) was there an actual "attitude reversal."

Other researchers (Butler & Tapper, 1970; Dodge & Uyecki, 1962) have obtained comparable results. Indeed, one group of researchers (Coopersmith, Regan, & Dick, 1975) has become so completely disenchanted with the whole notion of adolescent rebellion, that they entitled a recent book on the subject, *The Myth of the Generation Gap*. As these authors note, research on the generation gap appears to demonstrate that:

> There are indeed many differences between generations but they are apt to be differences in defining and implementing ideals, in role, in responses to change, and in personal taste, which generally occur within a context of mutual acceptance, rather than differences that bespeak hostility and disrespect. The gap is largely between the general worlds of adults and young people rather than between parents and children. [Pp. 316–317]

In short, adolescents may take issue with their parents over personal matters, like sex, drugs, clothes, and hair styles, but such disagreements do not seem to be all that intense. And there is practically no evidence that parents and teenagers routinely find themselves at odds over politics (see Adelson, 1970).

Methodologists have even raised questions about the one study (Jennings and Niemi, 1968b) that is usually cited in support of the generation gap. Weissberg and Joslyn (1977) argue that by using correlational statistics, Jennings and Niemi probably underestimated the degree of agreement between parents and teenagers. When Weissberg and Joslyn reexamined data from the Jennings and Niemi (1968b) study, they arrived at much the same conclusion as Lerner and his associates, that is, that parents and children corresponded rather closely. Even though the correlations were modest, there was a high percentage of agreement between the two groups.

Furthermore, Beck (1977) argues that the absence of a correlation between parent and child does not necessarily imply lack of influence. Parents can, after all, encourage adolescents to be independent and not meekly assume their views. Neither a correlational statistic nor a percentage would provide an adequate index of this kind of political influence.

The Parent-Child Interaction

How then can we determine what sort of role parents play in the political socialization of adolescents? Given the kind of technical problems I have outlined, it is difficult to say for sure. However, in view of the criticisms discussed above, it might be worthwhile to take a look at the way in which families interact. There is not much research on the subject, but what little exists is quite intriguing. When we examine adolescents within the context of their family, certain patterns of interaction do seem to be associated with certain patterns of political thought.

For instance, the already much-cited Jennings and Niemi (1968b) note that it makes a difference how consistent a teenager's parents are. In households where mothers and fathers tended to agree on the issues, the correlations were much higher than in households where mothers and fathers tended to disagree. Similarly, although so-called adolescent rebellion is rather rare, it does seem to be associated with a "stormy" family constellation. Middleton and Putney (1963) and Eckhardt and Schriner (1969) discovered that adolescents who diverged politically from their parents were more likely to report conflict at home than adolescents who shared their parents' views.

There is also evidence that political distrust among teenagers is correlated with overprotection at home. In a study of Belgian adolescents, Pinner (1965) surmised that those who came from overprotective families were more suspicious of government than teenagers who were not so carefully shielded. Renshon (1974) reports somewhat comparable findings. In his study of college students, lack of autonomy within the home was associated with external locus of control, which, in turn, was correlated with political distrust.

Finally, in one of the most interesting and little-known series of studies, Stone & Chaffee (1970), Steinkopf (1973), Chaffee, McLoed, and Wackman (1973), Jackson-Beeck and Chaffee (1975), and Chaffee (1977) examined four different types of family-communication patterns:

- *Laissez-faire* (homes offering no directives for political socialization).
- *Protective* (homes stressing obedience and social harmony).
- *Consensual* (homes encouraging openness but discouraging family disputes).
- *Pluralistic* (homes emphasizing free communication and discussion).

Teenagers from consensual and pluralistic families were "prepared to encounter more civic responsibility than were those from protective or laissez-faire home environments" (Chaffee, 1977, p. 245). In addition, youngsters from pluralistic households made the best showing on measures of political knowledge, and those from protective families performed the worst, even when controls for IQ were applied.

Does the family have an influence on political socialization during adolescence? The most recent findings would seem to indicate that early authorities (Hyman, 1959; Davies, 1965) overestimated its impact and that some of the researchers who followed (Hess & Torney, 1967; Jennings & Niemi, 1968b) underestimated its significance. Now the balance seems to be swinging back to a more reasonable position, somewhere between these two extremes. As an additional intriguing, if not conclusive bit of data, Chaffee (1977) observes that teenagers who rely for information on "interpersonal sources outside the home," (i.e., friends and teachers) exhibit "low levels of political knowledge" — which brings up the next point. What about extrafamilial agents? What influence do the schools, the media, and peers have on political socialization during adolescence?

The Role of Schools

Beck (1977) notes that, after parents, the next most powerful agent in political socialization is assumed to be the schools. But once again we encounter formidable methodological problems when we try to assess their actual significance. If it is difficult to determine precisely what role parents play, the obstacles are only compounded when a researcher tries to measure something as nebulous as the effects of the educational system. In the absence of more sophisticated techniques, most investigators have employed one or another of the following methods:

1. Test students before and after they have taken a specific course in government or political science.
2. Compare students who have taken courses in civics or government with those who have not.
3. Compare the political attitudes of students with those of their social studies teachers.

With one notable exception, researchers who have used any of these three designs have reached much the same conclusion: the educational system has a minimal impact on political thinking during adolescence. For example, Litt (1963) surveyed high-school students enrolled in a civics course at the beginning of the term and retested them at the end. He discovered that they were slightly more likely to support democratic ideals after having taken the course than they had been before. But he also noted that only upper-social-class adolescents seemed to have altered their attitudes about political participation. Along the same lines, Langton and Jennings (1968) compared teenagers who had completed one or more civics courses with those who had not. Although the former were a little more knowledgeable about politics than the latter, the statistical correlations were so low (e.g., .06) that the researchers describe them as "bordering on the trivial" (p. 858). Finally, Jennings, Ehman, and Niemi (1974) administered a political-attitudes questionnaire to high-school students and their social studies teachers. When they compared the responses of individual students with those of their instructors, they discovered that the degree of correspondence was considerably lower for students and teachers than it had been for students and their parents. The Jennings group cites this finding as additional evidence that the schools have little impact on political socialization (Jennings, Ehman, & Niemi, 1974).

Interestingly enough, Hess and Torney (1967) have formed just the opposite impression. As part of their study of primary- and secondary-school students, they also compared youngsters with their teachers. The attitudes of the adolescent subjects (seventh- and eighth-graders) corresponded quite closely to those of their teachers, a finding that led Hess and Torney to conclude that "the school apparently plays the largest part in teaching attitudes, conceptions, and beliefs about the operation of the political system" (p. 218). Not surprisingly, sociological researchers have used Hess and Torney's analysis to support their claims that there is a generation gap (see especially, Starr, 1974).

As with the research on parents, Hess and Torney (1967) have probably overstated the case for teachers, while other researchers have probably understated it. Although I cannot offer any definitive proof, I think Hess and Torney have probably hit closer to the mark than other researchers. My chief objection to most of the existing studies is that they define political socialization solely in terms of political attitudes or some narrowly constructed measure of political knowledge. What about political concepts and principles? Surely they too figure in political socialization. As we have seen, the youngster's overall grasp of political concepts and principles shifts dramatically during adolescence. It may be difficult to determine precisely what part the schools play in effecting this change, but I find it hard to believe that their influence is completely negligible. School is, after all, the one place where the youngster comes in contact with the formal documents of the political system (e.g., the Declaration of Independence and the Constitution).

Higher Education and Political Thinking

Studies that have uncovered a link between college-level instruction and so-called liberal attitudes are also suggestive. When researchers compare youngsters at a university with those who are not attending college, the students typically appear to be more tolerant and open-minded about political matters — more committed to the principle of free speech, more concerned about retaining procedural safeguards in criminal cases, and so forth (Kasschau, Ransford, & Bengston, 1974; Montero, 1975; Trent & Craise, 1967). Furthermore, studies that have compared freshmen with seniors (Newcomb, 1958; Selvin & Hagstrom, 1960) have turned up similar findings. There is some question as to what produces this liberalizing effect. Feldman and Newcomb (1969) assert that college represents the first opportunity for adolescents to question their values — political and otherwise. But it is also possible that adolescents who choose to attend college are more open and liberal to begin with. College students — particularly those who last for four years — are almost certainly the most intelligent segment of the demographic grouping aged 18 to 21. But whatever the cause of this liberalization, the university system appears to constitute an important element in what Connell (1971) calls the "sociopolitical context." (See Braungart, 1976, for a somewhat comparable set of conclusions.)

The Role of the Media

Connell (1969, 1970[1], 1971) maintains that television plays a significant part in political socialization, perhaps the most significant part. What influence do the media — especially TV — actually have? Chaffee (1977) provides an excellent summary of current research. For all the awesome powers attributed to television, he notes that there have not been a great many studies; the relatively few that exist are subject to the usual methodological limitations. Nonetheless, he offers the following assessment.

First of all, judging from the responses of children and adolescents themselves, TV and newspapers are both important sources of information about politics. Younger children seem to be especially influenced by TV, while for teenagers newspapers start to become significant too. Second, teenagers claim that the media affect their attitudes toward politics (Kraus & Davis, 1976; Chaffee, Ward, & Tipton, 1970). Finally, the "intergenerational differences in media use" that showed up in Jennings and Niemi's (1968b) original panel study seem to be persisting. When they first surveyed their subjects, Jennings and Niemi reported (1975), teenagers preferred TV as a source of political information and their parents preferred newspapers. Eight years later, contrary to expectation, these differences are holding up.

But mindful of his own work on family communication patterns (see pp. 358–359), Chaffee assigns the media a lesser role in shaping political participation and notes that even their impact on political attitudes may be overdrawn:

In general, we can say that mass media use is clearly not an isolated factor in the life of the developing citizen. It interacts in complex ways with one's network of primary group interpersonal communication contacts, and most fundamentally with the person's family communication background. [1977, p. 247]

[1]1970: personal communication. R. W. Connell.

The Role of Peers

Peers are also often cited as a possible influence on political socialization. Yet, as Beck observes, "For all of the attention paid to the importance of peer groups in the United States, it is surprising that so little research has been conducted on peer influence in political socialization" (1977, p. 132). If research on other aspects of political socialization is sparse, studies on the impact of peers are positively fragmentary. Indeed, in her very competent review of the literature, Silberger (1977) is forced to rely mainly on indirect evidence. But direct or indirect, the consensus seems to be that teenagers' peers make a pretty minimal contribution to their political views. Peers seem to exert an influence only in rather unusual circumstances. In his study of Jamaican adolescents, for example, Langton (1967) observed that upper-class youngsters appeared to have some political impact on lower-class friends. In addition, Sebert, Jennings, and Niemi (1974) suggest that where adolescents have a reason to be strongly involved in an issue, the opinions of friends may actually count for something. These researchers surveyed a sample of high-school students to determine their views on lowering the voting age to 18—obviously a matter of some import to teenagers. In this case, the subjects reported that they had consulted and been influenced by their classmates.

The Sebert, Jennings, and Niemi study, in fact, exemplifies a pattern that has emerged from more general investigations of peer influence. Despite claims about the monolithic power of the adolescent peer culture (Coleman, 1961), existing research indicates that adolescents are quite selective about seeking counsel from their friends. Several authors have inferred that teenagers actually have a kind of dual orientation, relying on the judgment of friends for ordinary day-to-day decisions but consulting their parents for more serious questions (Brittain, 1963; Gallatin, 1975; Kandel, 1974).

STATUS AND ASCRIPTIVE VARIABLES IN POLITICAL SOCIALIZATION

In addition to the agents commonly identified in political socialization, a number of other variables — both status and ascriptive — are frequently cited. It is widely assumed that a teenager's nationality, race, social class, IQ, and sex have some effect on his or her political thinking. Perhaps because variables like these are more global and all-encompassing than specific agents, cognitive-developmental researchers have paid at least as much attention to them as have behavioral researchers.

Cross-national Research

An example that comes readily to mind is the work of Adelson and his associates, including myself, (Adelson, 1971b; Adelson and Beall, 1970; Bush, 1970; Gallatin and Adelson, 1970, 1971; Gallatin, 1976). We administered our intensive questionnaire on political thinking to preteens and adolescents in the United States, Great Britain, and Germany. The developmental pattern that I described earlier (see pp. 350–352) emerged quite noticeably among subjects of all three countries. However, there were some significant cross-national differences as well. All in all, the American youngsters seemed to have the strongest sense of community and were also most strongly committed to upholding individual freedoms. The British subjects, by comparison, seemed rather pragmatic, envisioning government more as a provider of social services than a protector of personal liberties. And the German adolescents fell somewhere in between. At times they sounded submissive and authoritarian, but they were nonetheless more enthusiastic about safeguarding personal freedom than were the British.

Oppenheim and Torney's (1974) study is at least somewhat comparable. In their survey of three different age groups from four Western countries (America, Great Britain, Germany, and Sweden), they too observed a rise in equalitarian sentiment with increasing age. In addition, Dennis et al. (1968) report findings that are astonishingly similar to our own. They conducted a study of American, British, German and Italian youngsters aged 8 to 15. As in our own work, the older subjects in all four countries expressed considerably more support for democratic principles than did younger subjects. Equally notable, the British youngsters consistently demonstrated less enthusiasm for democracy than anyone else. Dennis et al. *also* observed the same peculiar split among German adolescents that I have described above, leading them to remark, "The German pattern of development is very mixed."

Nationality, of course is such a global variable that it is difficult to do more than speculate about the way in which it may shape political thinking. By their late teens, youngsters living in different countries have been subjected to a whole host of different socializing experiences: differences in childrearing, formal instruction, input from the media, friendship patterns, not to mention political traditions. It will require a great deal of time, contemplation, and funding to clarify the data on cross-national comparisons. But the fact that researchers from two different camps (i.e., cognitive-developmental and behavioral) report such similar findings is nonetheless very intriguing. (See Nathan and Remy, 1977, for an excellent survey of research on comparative political socialization and an extended discussion of this point.)

Racial Differences

Although specialists have expressed considerable interest in exploring the relationship between race and political socialization, comparatively few studies have included adolescents. Once again, because the model that dominates the field emphasizes the primacy of early experience, a good deal of the existing research has focused on younger children. Sears (1975b) competently summarizes much of it. Overall, the consensus is that black children resemble Jaros's disaffected Appalachian youngsters (Jaros, Hirsch, & Fleron, 1968). In most surveys, black children appear to be more cynical and less attached to the political system than white children.

Significantly, the few studies involving black adolescents paint a less gloomy picture. Summing up his research on the political socialization of black children, Greenberg (1970b) observes:

A recurring phenomenon was the cognitive and affective recovery experienced by black children during the junior high school years. The black child's image of government is seriously eroded during his elementary school years; older black children, on the other hand, seem to gain a renewed sense that national government is important, helpful, and benevolent. . . . There is a pronounced recovery for the national government . . . in the estimation of junior high school age children. Black children in these grades appear suddenly to comprehend that national government has an impact on their lives, but more importantly, it comes to be seen as rather helpful, protective, and nurturant. (Pp. 182; 184).

The work of Langton and Jennings (1968) bears out this assessment. These researchers, it may be recalled, concluded that high-school civics courses had a negligible impact on white students. However, they found that such courses seemed to be associated with an increase in feelings of political efficacy among black adolescents. Black students who had taken American government were also notably more knowledgeable about politics than those who had not.

My own research (Gallatin, 1972) provides some additional corroboration. The black adolescents in my study did seem slightly more disaffected than whites in a few respects. Their impression of the police, for example, was a little less favorable (although not markedly so). Nonetheless, the white subjects appeared overall to be the more cynical of the two. As an illustration, white adolescents were more likely to advocate bribery as a means of influencing public officials and they were less likely to believe that a group of dissidents could influence the mayor of their particular city.

If political research on black teenagers is scarce, studies of teenagers from other racial and ethnic groups within the United States is almost nonexistent (although see Maykovich, 1973, for one involving Asian college students, and Gutierrez and Hirsch, 1974, for a study of Chicano adolescents.)

Social Class

Research comparing teenagers from different social classes is almost as rare. Indeed, Adelson (1970) scores social scientists for this omission when he complains, ''Most of us have never had a serious and extended conversation with a youngster from the working or lower-middle classes'' (p. 36). What little research there is mirrors the findings on black adolescents to some extent. Of course, since many black youngsters are also lower class, this finding is not too surprising. As Torney (1971) and Hess and Torney (1967) observe, working-class youngsters seem to have reduced feelings of political efficacy. They also supposedly have a more pronounced law-and-order orientation than upper-class youngsters.

Both of these tendencies are borne out in an interesting and rather impressionistic study by Steinitz et al. (1973). A study of college-age youth by Kasschau, Ransford, and Bengston (1974) furnishes some additional support. These researchers found that blue-collar adolescents were considerably more conservative than white-collar adolescents. However, here education turned out to be a most significant variable. Only those blue-collar adolescents who were not in college fell into the typical working-class mold. Blue-collar young people who were attending college resembled their white-collar counterparts much more closely than their working-class peers. Conversely, white-collar youngsters who were not in school had more in common politically with noncollege blue-collar youngsters than their own white-collar peers. These findings, of course, lend added weight to the argument that a university education is somehow associated with liberal political views.

Sex Differences

Oddly enough, this liberalizing trend may not hold up as strongly among female adolescents. When Montero (1975) compared a sample of men and women in college, for example, he discovered that the male students were considerably more libertarian than the female students. The coeds were markedly more liberal than a comparable group of young women who were not in school but only slightly more liberal than a group of noncollege males.

Such findings may reflect the greater push toward conformity and compliance in women (Maccoby and Jacklin, 1974). They may also be associated with the political apathy or indifference thought to be characteristic of female youngsters (Greenstein, 1961b).

However, to balance the picture somewhat, I should point out that such sex differences may be in the process of disappearing. Beck and Jennings (1975) report that the female adolescents in their panel study professed almost as much interest in politics as male adolescents. Furthermore, female youngsters may be less liberal than male youngsters, but they have also traditionally been viewed as less "warlike and aggressive" (Tolley, 1977). Finally, my own intensive study of political thinking (Gallatin, 1972) did not turn up *any* striking sex differences. Girls seemed very slightly less knowledgeable about politics than boys but no less libertarian.

Intelligence and Political Socialization

There have also been a few scattered attempts to assess the impact of intelligence on political socialization during adolescence. Generally, cognitive-developmental researchers (Adelson, 1971b; Gallatin & Adelson, 1970, 1971) have concluded that intelligence exerts a rather subtle influence on political thinking. Adelson (1971b) observes that bright teenagers seem to acquire a grasp of political concepts just a bit earlier than youngsters with average skills and that they are also, typically, somewhat more articulate. But the differences are not, on the whole, very sharp.

Behavioral researchers (Torney, 1971; Hess & Torney, 1967) tend to place greater emphasis on intelligence, considering it, in fact, a far more significant variable than social class. Hess and Torney declare, "The intelligence of the child is one of the most important mediating influences in the acquisition of political behavior" (1967, p. 220). An examination of their findings, however, reveals that the difference between behavioral and cognitive-developmental researchers is merely one of degree. Hess and Torney maintain that the kind of changes that regularly show up at the beginning of adolescence — greater skepticism about political matters, a more balanced approach, a less personalized perception of government — seem to be evident a little earlier among bright youngsters. (See also Harvey & Harvey, 1970, for a study that explores the relationship between intelligence and the adoption of leftist-liberal views.)

POLITICAL CLIMATE, PERSONALITY, AND POLITICAL SOCIALIZATION

Before addressing myself to the complex issue of political activity during adolescence, I would like to take up two additional and even more nebulous elements in political socialization: (1) political climate and (2) personality. What impact do all-encompassing variables like these have on political thinking during adolescence?

Political Climate

There are, of course, many factors that affect the political climate, but among the most readily identifiable are events like assassination, war, and public scandal. How do adolescents respond to such phenomena? Existing research (undertaken largely by psychodynamically oriented and behavioral researchers) indicates that they react much the way adults do (a finding that squares quite well with cognitive-developmental studies of political thinking).

One of the most shocking political events of recent times was the assassination of President Kennedy. In the wake of the tragedy, several research teams tried to determine how it had affected children and adolescents. The two best-known studies conflict with each other on at least one point. Sigel (1965) concluded that teenagers were less upset than children or adults, and Wolfenstein (1965) concluded that adolescents were especially upset. But both investigations did demonstrate that adolescents were well aware of what had happened and that, for the most part, they experienced the same anxieties and concerns about the assassination as adults.

In their survey of adolescent males, Bachman and VanDuinen (1971) detected a similar pattern, particularly with respect to the war in Vietnam. Their study is especially notable because it was longitudinal. Beginning in the 10th grade, the subjects were questioned about their perceptions of the Vietnamese War, among other issues. In 1966, before public opinion had turned against the conflict, few teenagers (a mere 7% of the total) expressed much concern. However, by 1970, at a time when public dissatisfaction was beginning to peak, the percentage of adolescents who were worried about Vietnam had jumped dramatically to 75%. There were probably several elements in this shift — cognitive maturation, the fear of being drafted, newspaper and TV coverage of the war, the consciousness-raising effects of antiwar protests. But the extent to which the adolescent response to the Vietnam situation paralleled that of the adult population is nonetheless striking.

Interestingly enough, Jennings and Markus (1975) and Bachman and Jennings (1975) discovered that young people who had actually participated in the war and presumably needed to rationalize their involvement were only a little more supportive of the government's efforts. Using subjects from their own panel study (Jennings & Niemi, 1968b) and the Youth in Transition Project (the same group surveyed by Bachman and VanDuinen, 1971), these researchers compared young men who had served in Vietnam with those who had not. They discovered that youths who had been in the armed forces were only slightly less disillusioned with American politics than those who had never been in the service. In fact, both groups registered such a precipitous drop in support that Bachman and Jennings (1975) offered the following gloomy assessment: "Trust in government has been greatly eroded, and our findings clearly indicate that the U.S. role in Vietnam was one of the major causes" (p. 155).

And if Vietnam had disastrous effects on public morale, Watergate could only have been expected to exacerbate the situation. Here, too, teenagers appear to have responded much as adults have. Sigel and Hoskin (1977b) report that a group of high-school students interviewed early in 1974 registered only lukewarm sentiments about many aspects of government (e.g., the performance of the then current administration, the Constitution, the courts, etc.). They too relate their findings to the prevailing political climate: "This generally lukewarm stance of students, which contrasts with the high regard adolescents have been observed to hold for these institutions traditionally, appears typical of (a) larger trend . . . which Louis Harris has labelled a 'Crisis of Confidence'" (p. 131).

However, before we conclude that teenagers are about to become totally disenchanted with politics, I should point out that some researchers have not observed any marked decline in support. Perhaps regional factors play a part. Sigel and Hoskin's (1977b) adolescents resided in Pennsylvania. Lufper and Kenny (1976) interviewed high-school students in Memphis, Tennessee, surveying them several times between 1972 and 1975.

Although they were a little less enthusiastic post-Watergate than pre-Watergate, these teenagers did not appear to be particularly disillusioned with government. Indeed, their post-Watergate attitudes were actually more positive in some respects.

PERSONALITY AND POLITICS

Finally, we turn to the relationship between personality and politics during adolescence. Perhaps because they assume that personality does not crystallize fully before the end of adolescence, some of the leading proponents of the psychodynamic school (Greenstein, 1969; Knutson, 1972; Lane, 1959, 1962) have concentrated their energies on adults. (Greenstein, of course, has done extensive work with children, but generally not from a psychodynamic point of view.) However, recently, they have demonstrated more interest in adolescents, particularly older adolescents (Lane, 1968, 1969; Sigel, 1975; Renshon, 1974, 1975).

Behavioral researchers have also on occasion explored the relationship between personality and politics. Indeed, since their approach is a little less systematic, I propose to take up their work first. Even their scattered findings are interesting. Rosenberg (1965), for instance, discovered that teenagers with low self-esteem reported less concern with public affairs than those with high self-esteem. Similarly, Schwartz's (1975a) study presents evidence that certain personal qualities are associated with political cynicism during adolescence, at least during early adolescence. In a sample of eighth-graders, political cynicism correlated positively with pessimism and negatively with personal efficacy. Among older subjects the findings were less clear-cut, possibly because they were more cynical as a *group*. Nonetheless, even among twelfth graders, Schwartz observed a significant correlation between personal cynicism and political cynicism. Finally, in a study of children and adolescents (fifth through ninth grade), Zellman and Sears (1971) observed that subjects with the highest self-esteem were also most tolerant of dissent.

Psychodynamic studies are even more intriguing. Lane's work with college students (1968, 1969) is probably the most ambitious and provocative. He asked members of his seminar on political science to write a series of autobiographical essays and then proceeded to interpret their papers, applying concepts from psychoanalytic and neo-psychoanalytic theory. The resulting analysis is a fascinating tour de force.

Essentially, Lane concluded that a student's politics derived from the nature of the adolescent "life struggles" he was undergoing. Formal instruction figured in the process, but only in a highly personalized fashion. A youth drew from courses and from politics whatever he felt would help him with his current "crisis of identity" (Erikson, 1968). Lane describes the case of a young man named Demming who "was fed by personal feelings of insecurity, a sense that he was not and could not be a success in conventional terms, and an abiding loneliness" (p. 492).

In Lane's analysis, Demming "brought these feelings of inferiority to bear on political matters for the first time at Yale" and he cites the student's own autobiographical statements as evidence: "The Democratic party always represented to me the party of change and of the poorer classes. . . . The Republican party seemed to embody the group in which I wanted to be accepted and couldn't, and so I accepted the Democrats as the opposite" (Lane, 1968, p. 492).

There is a certain oppositional quality to this passage — such that a clinician might suspect that the writer was having conflicts at home. Sure enough, Lane discovered that Demming's "new-found liberalism" provided a convenient vehicle for getting back at his parents and asserting his independence. His Democratic leanings: "so opposed to the extreme conservatism of my parents, acted as a good medium both to express hostility and to show that I have a mind of my own" (p. 492). (Schiff, 1964, employs a framework somewhat similar to Lane's in his study of "conversions" to conservatism.)

Renshon (1974, 1975) and Sigel (1975) use somewhat more conventional methods to explore the link between personality and politics.[2] Both have attempted to study the relationship between psychological "locus of control" and political thinking during adolescence. Renshon administered Rotter's locus-of-control scale and a variety of other inventories and political surveys to a group of college students. He discovered that adolescents who believed their lives were dominated largely by external forces (external locus of control) tended to have a rather different image of politics than those who believed they were masters of their own fate (internal locus of control). Youngsters who placed the locus of control outside themselves displayed less trust of government and expressed more dissatisfaction with the existing political order. Sigel (1975) obtained comparable results with a sample of high school students, that is, adolescents who were externally oriented had a less favorable impression of politics than those who scored high on internal locus of control.

POLITICAL ACTIVITY DURING ADOLESCENCE

The issue of personality and politics merges quite naturally with the issue of political activity during adolescence, the last topic I shall address before offering some concluding remarks. A persistent theme throughout this paper has been the lack of research in certain areas. One might expect, just on the basis of common sense, that participation in politics during adolescence would be no exception. Ironically, specialists have devoted more attention to this subject than to any other aspect of youthful politics.

The situation is all the more paradoxical because teenagers are so inactive politically. Only about 40% of them claim to follow public matters closely (Beck & Jennings, 1975), and they vote less regularly than almost any other segment of the population. There is nothing too astounding about this state of affairs. Dependent as they are economically and psychologically, teenagers are scarcely in a position to become a political interest group. Indeed, until recently, a person had to be *out* of his teens even to enter a voting booth. How, then, do we account for the vast amount of research on adolescent excursions into politics?

The Phenomenon of Student Activism

The explanation is not very mysterious, and it probably tells us more about social scientists than anything else. During the early 1960s and 1970s, there seemed to be an enormous upsurge in student activism. According to the media and some representatives of the academic community (Aldridge, 1970; Feuer, 1969) the country was in the throes of

[2]I should point out that S. A. Renshon's (1974) book contains a brilliant attempt to apply psychodynamic and cognitive-developmental concepts to political socialization. However, this approach is somewhat less prominent in his actual research.

some great adolescent revolt. As it turned out, most of the activity occurred on a relatively few campuses (Heist, 1965, 1967; Peterson, 1966, 1968a, 1968b), and many of the participants were not even adolescents. A survey prompted by the Free Speech movement sit-in at Berkeley, for instance, revealed that 40% of the students aged 23 to 29 considered themselves "militants" versus only 25% of those between the ages of 17 and 20 (Somers, 1965).

Nonetheless, after having complained about youthful apathy during the previous decade, social scientists rushed into the field, understandably eager to study this new and unexpected phenomenon. Almost overnight, several collections of articles appeared (Graubard, 1968; Lipset, 1968; Lipset & Wolin, 1965; Miller & Gilmore, 1965), and empirical studies began to proliferate. Who were these new young radicals? What forces and personal characteristics had propelled them into the very forefront of politics? [With few exceptions, notably the work of Schiff (1964, 1966) and Westby and Braungart (1970), nobody even bothered with students toward the right of the political spectrum.]

As Gergen and Ullman (1977) observe in their extensive review of the research on student activism, the answers remain somewhat obscure. It now seems doubtful that anything like a large-scale youth movement was at work [although see Fendrich (1974), and Starr (1974) for arguments to the contrary]. In light of the new conservatism on campus (Astin, 1977) it also appears that one crucial element must have been the war in Vietnam — on all counts one of the least popular foreign conflicts in American history. But it was not clear that such was the case at the beginning.

Adelson (1971a), is no doubt correct in his assertion that much of the early research on student activism was misleading. At first glance, these campus rebels looked almost too good to be true. Although not particularly committed to any formal religion (Bruce & Sims, 1975; Flacks, 1967; Peterson, 1968b), activists were supposed to be highly altruistic and humanistic (Fishman & Solomon, 1964; Flacks, 1967; Keniston, 1968; Quarter, 1972; Solomon & Fishman, 1964). Using scores on Kohlberg's scale of moral values (1958) as an index, researchers concluded that activists were of high moral character (Block, Haan, & Smith, 1973; Haan, Smith & Block, 1968; Smith, 1968). Other investigators (Heist, 1965, 1967; Peterson, 1968b; Somers, 1965) described them as being uncommonly bright. Indeed, Keniston (1967) declared flatly: ". . . student protestors are generally outstanding students; the higher the student's grade average, the more outstanding his academic achievements, the more likely it is that he will become involved in any given political demonstration" (p. 546).

Furthermore, far from rebelling against their parents or society in general, these youngsters allegedly came from upper-class families (Flacks, 1967; Westby & Braungart, 1970) and believed that they were simply putting into practice all the humanitarian values they had acquired at home (Flacks, 1967; Keniston, 1967, 1968). They were, in short, an unusually well-adjusted and autonomous lot (Bay, 1967).

However, even in these earlier studies, there were hints of "trouble in paradise." In one of the very first surveys, Somers (1965) reported that while two-thirds of the students responding favored the aims of the Free Speech movement at Berkeley, only two-thirds approved of their tactics. Trent and Craise (1967) were generally complimentary in their description of these new young radicals, but they too seemed slightly uneasy when they remarked, ". . . the relatively small minority of student activists seems to be providing a healthy, *if sometimes extreme,* departure from commonly accepted goals and norms (p. 46, italics added)." Other researchers uncovered even more disturbing trends. Smith (1968) and Haan, Smith & Block (1968), for instance, noted that a disproportionate number of the radicals they interviewed had attained Level III on Kohlberg's scale, the level of "principled" morality. However, they also found a disproportionate number at Level I, the primitive, premoral stage.[3] Furthermore, the students' own reports of their relationships with their families suggested at least a degree of conflict at home.

As campus demonstrations became increasingly violent and, paradoxically, faddish, the uneasiness grew. Critics began to ask whether a new gymnasium (the issue that triggered the 1968 disturbances at Columbia University in New York City) or the operation of a discount bookstore (the object of a 1969 sit-in at the University of Michigan) were so terribly important, and researchers began to conclude that activists were not such a saintly lot after all. Westby and Braungart (1970) surveyed members of Students for a Democratic Society. These youngsters did *not* seem simply to be "living out their parents' ideals." Their family relationships were not particularly harmonious, and they appeared overall to be alienated and disaffected. (See also Watts & Whittaker, 1966.)

Other findings began to wash out as well. Baird (1970) inferred from his study that student activists were lacking in altruism, a finding corroborated to some extent by Kerpelman (1972), who reported no correlation between altruism and activism. Nor did radicals appear to be more intelligent than their less active counterparts (Kerpelman, 1969). Finally, it appeared, radicals were not even from upper-class families (Lewis and Kraut, 1972), a finding that was verified by two of the staunchest supporters of the New Left (Mankoff & Flacks, 1971). Not too surprisingly, Mankoff and Flacks cited their data as evidence that the student-protest movement was acquiring a broader base of support.

Even Keniston reported an unsettling discovery (Fishkin, Keniston, & MacKinnon, 1973): activists who advocated violence tended to show up as moral "primitives" on Kohlberg's scale. And Thomas whose initial research (1971) seemed to confirm the proposition that leftist students were simply acting out ideals they had acquired at home, later (1974) became reluctant to conclude that they had any "core values" in common with their parents.

Social scientists began to hear pleas for a more balanced approach. Hogan (1973), Simpson (1974), and Snodgrass (1975) all observed that "liberal" was not necessarily synonymous with "good" any more than "conservative" was necessarily synonymous with "bad." Adelson (1971a) was even more pointed in his criticisms, insisting that some of the earlier researchers had suffered a "fatal failure of distance."

The most recent crop of studies would seem to bear out this assessment. To be sure, no one would argue that all of the student radicals of the 1960s and 1970s were violent and irresponsible. Many of the youngsters who participated in demonstrations — particularly those protesting the war in Vietnam — were pointedly nonviolent and idealistic. But a growing body of data seems to indicate that it takes more than idealism to justify political activity during adolescence — especially when the great mass of teenagers seems to remain unmoved by any call to arms. What seems to be necessary in addition is a conviction that the world is somehow unjust and out of control.

Adelson hints at such a motive in his discussion of utopian ideals during adolescence. Noting that the vast majority of older adolescents are positively antiutopian and realistic when it comes to politics, he goes on to observe:

And it is no surprise either that the impulse to utopian thought in the few instances we find it, appears among inner-city adolescents, largely black but some white, who feel themselves despised

---

[3]D. A. Friedman (1977) claims that some of the activists at level I may have been "transitional" and on their way to becoming level III's. Apparently, E. Turiel is about to publish some data which point in this direction.

and rejected, and by young suburban intellectuals, morally troubled, and feeling in themselves a destiny to innovate and lead. [Adelson, 1971b, p. 131]

A number of researchers, working quite independently, have obtained findings that provide some support for this appraisal. As an example, Blumenthal (1973) interviewed students who had participated in a street disturbance during the summer of 1969. She discovered that these youngsters, who considered themselves very humanistic and loving, harbored extremely negative attitudes about the police. Significantly, the majority of them did not describe their own disruptive protest as violent but did indicate that they would apply that label to the police. Isenberg, Schnitzer, and Rothman (1977), Kleiber and Manaster (1972), Rubin and Peplau (1975), and Renshon (1974) have all obtained results that are roughly comparable.

What emerges from the more recent data on student activism is an aura of self-justification and externalization — even a kind of apocalyptic sentiment. Kleiber and Manaster (1972) report that activists are more pessimistic about the future than nonactivists. Similarly, Isenberg, Schnitzer, and Rothman (1977) found in their projective study that the typical activist was characterized by "masochistic surrender," a tendency to portray himself as "surrending to some outer force, agent, or fate to which he felt himself to be allied, subjugated, or at times fused" (p. 17). And using their "just-world scale," Rubin and Peplau (1975) report that students who describe the world as unjust are more likely to be politically active than those who consider the world a just place. Finally, Renshon (1974) observes that political activity during adolescence seems to be positively correlated with external locus of control. In his study, students who believed that their lives were subject largely to external forces were more likely to report that they had participated in a political demonstration than students who judged themselves to be in control of their own destiny.

Such findings are probably not too startling. It would be reasonable to expect youngsters who engage in protests to be dissatisfied with *something*. However, the more recent studies do, in my opinion, constitute an important corrective for the earlier work on student activism.

CONCLUSIONS

As I have emphasized throughout this chapter, given the methodological limitations of the field and the mass of semidigested data, it is difficult to reach any definitive conclusions about political socialization during adolescence. However, I am willing to cite some tentative ones. In view of the wide variety of differences that researchers have observed—cross-national, educational, sexual, intellectual, and social—political sociali-zation does indeed appear to be a complex phenomenon. As behavioral, generational, psychodynamic, and cognitive-developmental researchers have all suggested, teenagers' views on politics do seem to be colored by a large number of different influences.

But even within the present confusion and uncertainty, we can identify a few trends. First judging from research on the development of political thinking and awareness of public issues, I think we can conclude that adolescence is a significant period for political socialization. Teenagers appear to be aware of what is occurring on the political scene and they are at least reasonably knowledgeable about how the system works. Furthermore, their overall grasp of political issues and concepts seems to increase markedly between early and late adolescence. Second, it now appears that researchers were too eager to discount the role of parents in political socialization. Studies on family communication patterns and the generation gap suggest that parents do influence their youngsters' attitudes toward politics. Finally, although a substantial number of teenagers are at least casually interested in public affairs, relatively few can be described as politically active. The few that do demonstrate or protest may be idealistic and humanitarian, but they also contain among their ranks a number of individuals who seem just a bit self-justifying and externalized.

SUGGESTIONS FOR FUTURE RESEARCH

I have repeatedly emphasized the methodological problems that plague the field of political socialization, but these difficulties are common to all of the social sciences. The basic concern in studying any aspect of human development is to be able to identify cause and effect, something that none of the social sciences has been able to do very successfully. While common sense tells us that behavior is obviously the product of certain environmental influences and innate characteristics, we find it hard to demonstrate that such is the case. For various reasons — ethical, technical, monetary — the methods continue to elude us.

It is not surprising, then, that researchers, impatient with the status quo, have tended to rush into the field with whatever techniques were handy. Often (as in the case of early studies on student activism) they have seemed blithely unaware of their own biases. Just as frequently (as with research on the development of political attitudes in children), their choice of measures has been somewhat inappropriate. I agree with Sears (1975a) that the results have not been all that disastrous. As we have seen, critics are sufficiently numerous to insure that questionable findings do not remain unquestioned for very long.

Nonetheless, I think we are at the point where a more analytical and balanced approach to political socialization would be helpful. The field would rapidly become less disorganized if researchers from the various schools could get together, compare their assumptions, review the existing data, and agree on some common objectives. I also believe that specialists from the behavioral, generational, and psychodynamic "camps," could benefit from the example of cognitive-developmental investigators. (As a cognitive-developmental researcher myself, I freely admit my own biases.) It is my impression that methodologists have a tendency to advocate elaborate and elliptical strategies where simpler techniques might well be more enlightening. For instance, Weissberg and Joslyn (1977) conclude their excellent critique of research methods in political socialization with a call for more "multivariate analysis." Similarly, in his paper on generational studies, Cutler (1977) observes that an increasing number of adolescents have begun to identify themselves as "Independents," eschewing either of the two established political parties in the United States. He adduces a complicated sociological explanation to account for this phenomenon and then approvingly cites the conclusion of another researcher: "Careful empirical investigation of the interrelations, and trends in interrelations, among class, the various dimensions of liberalism-conservatism, and party support would probably throw much light on the changing character of American politics" (Glenn, 1972, cited in Cutler, 1977, p. 314).

I am reminded here of a seminar I attended in graduate school. The instructor was an expert on the use of the Minnesota Multiphasic Personality Inventory (MMPI) in clinical diagnosis, someone intimately acquainted with the most elaborate factor analytic techniques. The wonders he could perform with a simple MMPI profile were nothing short of miraculous. But he had, in addition, one infallible diagnostic procedure. "How do you determine whether or not a person is homosexual?" he would demand of an unsuspecting class. After the students had suggested various elevations or depressions of the appropriate MMPI scales, he would smile disarmingly, shake his head, pause, and reply, "No. You ask him."

I believe this is good advice for specialists in political socialization no matter which "school" they belong to. To be sure, the more direct methods are also, paradoxically, more cumbersome. The face-to-face interview does not lend itself readily to statistical analysis, and it is expensive and time-consuming. But it may also be the only way we can discover what we need to know. Cognitive-developmental researchers have already demonstrated the utility of interviews in their work with adolescents, and in her review of the literature on "the role of peers in political socialization," Silberger (1977) furnishes additional support for this approach. She notes that very few people seem to be influenced politically by their peers but adds:

Instead of the aggregate techniques we have been relying on in field studies such persons should be understood through the use of extended interviews, longitudinal followup, and other intensive approaches. It may be (and it is certainly worth discovering) that while most people, most of the time are not influenced by peers, the one time they are so influenced is with regard to a critical turning point or major commitment. [P. 189]

If a reviewer can advocate this sort of in-depth strategy for studying a relatively minor aspect of political socialization, it stands to reason that such techniques ought to be used more extensively with teenagers. In any case, the political development of young people is too vital a concern to be explored piecemeal or with anything but an intense commitment.

REFERENCES

Adelson, J. "What generation gap?" *New York Times Magazine,* January 18, 1970, pp. 101ff.

———. Inventing the young. *Commentary,* 1971a, *51,* 43–48.

———. The political imagination of the young adolescent. In J. Kagan and R. Coles (Eds.), *Twelve to sixteen: Early adolescence.* New York: Norton, 1971b.

Adelson, J., and Beall, L. Adolescent perspectives on law and government. *Law Social Review,* 1970, *4,* 495–504.

Adelson, J., Green, B., and O'Neil, R. Growth of the idea of law in adolescence. *Developmental Psychology,* 1969, *1,* 327–332.

Adelson, J., and O'Neil, R. P. Growth of political ideas in adolescence: The sense of community. *Journal of Personality and Social Psychology,* 1966, *4,* 295–306.

Adorno, T. W., Frenkel-Brunswick, E., Levinson, E. J., and Sanford, R. N. *The authoritarian personality.* New York: Harper, 1950.

Aldridge, J. M. *In the country of the young.* New York: Harper & Row, 1970.

Astin, A. The new realists. *Psychology Today,* 1977, *4,* 50–53; 105–106.

Bay, C. Political and apolitical students: Facts in search of a theory. *Journal of Social Issues,* 1967, *23,* 76–91.

Bachman, J. G., and Jennings, M. K. The impact of Vietnam on trust in government. *Journal of Social Issues,* 1975, *31,* 141–155.

Bachman, J. G., and VanDuinen, E. *Youth look at national problems.* Ann Arbor, Mich.: Institute for Social Research, 1971.

Baird, L. L. Who protests: A study of student activism. In J. Foster and D. Long (Eds.), *Protest! Student activism in America.* New York: Morrow, 1970.

Beck, P. A., and Jennings, M. K. Parents as "middlepersons" in political socialization. *Journal of Politics,* 1975, *37,* 83–107.

———. The role of agents in political socialization. In S. A. Renshon (Ed.), *Handbook of political socialization: Theory and research.* New York: Free Press, 1977.

Bengtson, V. L. The generation gap: A review and typology of social-psychological perspectives. *Youth and Society,* 1970, *2,* 7–32.

Bengtston, V. L., Furlong, M. J., and Laufer, R. S. Time, aging, and the continuity of social structure: Themes and issues in generational analysis. *Journal of Social Issues,* 1974, *30,* 1–30.

Bettelheim, B. The problem of generations. In E. H. Erikson (Ed.), *Youth: Change and challenge.* New York: Basic Books, 1963.

Blanchard, E. B., and Price, K. C. A developmental study of cognitive balance. *Developmental Psychology,* 1971, *5,* 344–348.

Blumenthal, M. D. The belief systems of protesting college students. *Journal of Youth and Adolescence,* 1973, *2,* 103–124.

Braungart, R. G. The sociology of generations and student politics: A comparison of the functionalist and generation unit models. *Journal of Social Issues,* 1974, *30,* 31–54.

———. College and noncollege youth politics in 1972: An application of Mannheim's generation unit model. *Journal of Youth and Adolescence,* 1976, *5,* 325–348.

Block, J. H., Haan, N. H., and Smith, M. B. Activism and apathy in contemporary adolescents. In J. F. Adams (Ed.), *Understanding adolescence: Current developments in adolescent psychology* (2nd ed.). Boston: Allyn & Bacon, 1973.

Brittain, C. V. Adolescent choices and parent-peer pressures. *American Sociological Review,* 1963, *28,* 385–391.

Bruce, W. E., and Sims, J. H. Religious apostasy and political radicalism. *Journal of Youth and Adolescence,* 1975, *4,* 207–214.

Bush, M. *A developmental study of adolescent political thinking.* Unpublished doctoral dissertation, University of Michigan, 1970.

Butler, D., and Tapper, E. R. Continuity and change in adolescent political party preferences. *Political Studies,* 1970, *18,* 390–394.

Chaffee, S. H. Mass communication in political socialization. In S. A. Renshon (Ed.), *Handbook of political socialization: Theory and research.* New York: Free Press, 1977.

Chaffee, S. H., McLoed, J. M., and Wackman, D. B. Family communication patterns and adolescent political participation. In J. Dennis (Ed.), *Socialization to politics.* New York: Wiley, 1973.

Chaffee, S. H., Ward, L. S., and Tipton, L. P. Mass communication and political socialization. *Journalism Quarterly,* 1970, *47,* 647–659; 666.

Coleman, J. S. *The adolescent society.* New York: Free Press, 1961.

Connell, R. W. *The child's construction of politics.* Unpublished doctoral dissertation, University of Sydney, Australia, 1969.

———. *The child's construction of politics.* Melbourne, Australia: Melbourne University Press, 1971.

———. Political socialization in the American family: The evidence re-examined. *Public Opinion Quarterly,* 1972, *36,* 323–333.

Connell, R. W., and Goot, M. Science and ideology in American "political-socialization" research. *Berkeley Journal of Sociology,* 1972–1973, *27,* 166–193.

Converse, P. E. The nature of belief systems in mass publics. In D. E. Apter (Ed.), *Ideology and discontent.* New York: Free Press, 1964.

———. Attitudes and nonattitudes: Continuation of a dialogue. In E. R. Tufte (Ed.), *The quantitative analysis of social problems.* Reading, Mass.: Addison-Wesley, 1970.

Coopersmith, S., Regan, M., and Dick, L. *The myth of the generation gap.* San Francisco: Albion, 1975.

Crain, W. C., and Crain, E. F. The growth of political ideas and their expression among young activists. *Journal of Youth and Adolescence,* 1974, *3,* 105–134.

Cutler, N. E. Toward a generational conception of political socialization. In D. C. Schwartz and S. K. Schwartz (Eds.), *New directions in political socialization.* New York: Free Press, 1975.

———. Political socialization as generational analysis: The cohort approach versus the lineage approach. In S. A. Renshon (Ed.), *Handbook of political socialization: Theory and research.* New York: Free Press, 1977.

Davies, J. C. The family's role in political socialization. *The Annals of the American Academy of Political and Social Science,* 1965, *361,* 11–19.

Davies, J. C. Political socialization from womb to childhood: In S. A. Renshon (Ed.), *Handbook of political socialization: Theory and research.* New York: Free Press, 1977.

Dennis, J. Major problems of political socialization research. *Midwest Journal of Political Science,* 1968, *12,* 85–114.

Dennis, J., Lindberg, L., McCrone, D., and Stiefbold, R. Political socialization to democratic orientations in four Western systems. *Comparative Political Studies,* 1968, *1,* 71–101.

Dodge, R. W., and Uyecki, E. S. Political affiliation and imagery across two related generations. *Midwest Journal of Political Science,* 1962, *6,* 266–276.

Douvan, E., and Adelson, J. *The adolescent experience.* New York: Wiley, 1966.

Easton, D., and Dennis, J. The child's image of government. *Annals of the American Academy of Political and Social Science,* 1965, *361,* 40–57.

———. The child's acquisition of regime norms: Political efficacy. *American Political Science Review,* 1967, *61,* 25–38.

———. *Children in the political system.* New York: McGraw-Hill, 1969.

———. A political theory of political socialization. In J. Dennis (Ed.), *Socialization to politics.* New York: Wiley, 1973.

Easton, D., and Hess, R. D. Youth and the political system. In S. M. Lipset and L. Lowenthal (Eds.), *Cultural and social character.* Glencoe, Ill.: Free Press, 1961.

———. The child's political world. *Midwest Journal of Political Science,* 1962, *6,* 229–246.

Eckhardt, K. W., and Schriner, E. C. Familial conflict, adolescent rebellion, and political expression. *Journal of Marriage and the Family,* 1969, 31, *3,* 494–499.

Eisenstadt, S. N. Archetypal patterns of youth. In E. Erikson (Ed.), *The challenge of youth.* New York: Doubleday, 1963.

Erikson, E. H. *Identity: Youth and crisis.* New York: Norton, 1968.

Feldman, K., and Newcomb, T. *The impact of college on students: An analysis of four decades of research.* San Francisco: Jossey-Bass, 1969.

Fendrich, J. M. Activists ten years later: A test of generational unit continuity. *Journal of Social Issues,* 1974, *30,* 95–118.

Feuer, L. *The conflict of generations: The character and significance of student movements.* New York: Basic Books, 1969.

Fishkin, J., Keniston, K., and MacKinnon, C. Moral reasoning and political ideology. *Journal of Personality and Social Psychology,* 1973, *27,* 109–119.

Fishman, J. R., and Solomon, F. Youth and social action: An introduction. *Journal of Social Issues,* 1964, *20,* 1–27.

Flacks, R. The liberated generation: An exploration of the roots of student protest. *Journal of Social Issues,* 1967, *23,* 52–75.

Freud, A. *The ego and mechanisms of defense.* New York: International Universities Press, 1936.

Friedman, D. A. Political socialization and models of moral development. In S. A. Renshon (Ed.), *Handbook of political socialization: Theory and research.* New York: Free Press, 1977.

Gallatin, J. *The development of the concept of rights in adolescence.* Unpublished doctoral dissertation, University of Michigan, 1967.

———. *The development of political thinking in urban adolescents.* (Final Report: Grant No. 0–0554.) National Institutes of Education. Washington, D.C.: U.S. Government Printing Office, 1972.

———. *Adolescence and individuality: A conceptual approach to adolescent psychology.* New York: Harper & Row, 1975.

———. The conceptualization of rights: Psychological development and cross-national perspectives. In R. Claude (Ed.), *Comparative human rights.* Baltimore, Md.: Johns Hopkins University Press, 1976.

Gallatin, J., and Adelson, J. Individual rights and the public good. *Comparative Political Studies,* 1970, *3,* 226–242.

———. Legal guarantees of individual freedom. *Journal of Social Issues,* 1971, *27,* 93–108.

Gergen, K. J., and Ullman, M. Socialization and characterological basis of political activism. In S. A. Renshon (Ed.), *Handbook of political socialization: Theory and research.* New York: Free Press, 1977.

Glenn, N. D., Sources of the shift to political independence: Some evidence from a cohort analysis. *Social Science Quarterly,* 1972, *53,* 494–519.

Graubard, S. R. (Ed.) Students and politics. *Daedalus,* 1968, *97.*

Greenberg, E. S. Consensus and dissent: Trends in political socialization research. In E. S. Greenberg (Ed.), *Political socialization.* New York: Atherton, 1970a.

———. The political socialization of Negro children. In E. S. Greenberg (Ed.), *Political socialization.* New York: Atherton, 1970b.

Greenstein, F. I. More on children's images of the president. *Public Opinion Quarterly.* 1961a, *25,* 648–654.

———. Sex-related political differences in childhood. *Journal of Politics,* 1961b, *23,* 353–371.

———. The benevolent leader: Children's images of political authority. *American Political Science Review,* 1960, *54,* 934–943.

———. *Children and politics.* New Haven, Conn.: Yale University Press, 1965.

———. *Personality and politics.* Chicago: Markham, 1969.

Gutierrez, A., and Hirsch, H. The militant challenge to the American ethos: "Chicanos" and "Mexican Americans." *Social Science Quarterly,* 1973, *53*(4), 830–845.

Haan, N., Smith, M., and Block, J. Moral reasoning of young adults: Political social behavior, family background, and personality correlates. *Journal of Personality and Social Psychology,* 1968, *10,* 183–201.

Harvey, S. K., and Harvey, G. Adolescent political outlooks: The effects of intelligence as an independent variable. *Midwest Journal of Political Science,* 1970, *14*(4), 565–595.

Heist, P. Intellect and commitment: The faces of discontent. In O. W. Knorr and W. J. Minter (Eds.), *Order and freedom on the campus: The rights and responsibilities of faculty and students.* Boulder, Colo.: Western Interstate Commission for Higher Education, 1965.

——. "The dynamics of student discontent and protest." Mimeographed. 1967.

Hess, R. D., and Torney, J. V. *The development of political attitudes in children.* New York: Anchor, 1967.

Hogan, R. Moral conduct and moral character: A psychological perspective. *Psychological Bulletin,* 1973, *79,* 217–231.

——. The structure of moral character and the explanation of moral action. *Journal of Youth and Adolescence,* 1975, *4,* 1–15.

Hyman, H. *Political socialization: A study in the psychology of political behavior.* Glencoe, Ill.: Free Press, 1959.

Inhelder, B., and Piaget, J. *The growth of logical thinking from childhood to adolescence.* New York: Basic Books, 1958.

Isenberg, P., Schnitzer, R., and Rothman, S. Psychological variables in student activism: The radical triad and some religious differences. *Journal of Youth and Adolescence,* 1977, *6,* 11–24.

Jackson-Beeck, M., and Chaffee, S. H. Family communication, mass communication, and differential political socialization. Paper presented at the International Communication Association Meeting, Chicago, April 1975.

Jaros, D., Hirsch, H., and Fleron, F. J., Jr. The malevolent leader: Political socialization in an American subculture. *American Political Science Review,* 1968, *62,* 564–575.

Jennings, M. K. Parental grievances and school politics. *Public Opinion Quarterly,* 1968, *32,* 363–378.

——. An aggregate analysis of home and school effects on political socialization. *Social Science Quarterly,* 1974, *38,* 394–410.

——. Discontent with schools: Some implications for political socialization and behavior. *Youth and Society,* 1975, *7,* 49–68.

Jennings, M. K., and Markus, G. B. Political participation and Vietnam-era war veterans: A longitudinal study. Paper presented at the Conference on the Social Psychology of the Military, Chicago, April 1975.

Jennings, M. K., and Niemi, R. G. Patterns of political learning. *Harvard Educational Review,* 1968a, *38,* 443–467.

——. The transmission of political values from parent to child. *American Political Science Review,* 1968b, *62,* 169–184.

——. Continuity and change in political orientations: A longitudinal study of two generations. *American Political Science Review,* 1975, *69,* 1316–1335.

——. "The persistence of political orientations: An overtime analysis of two generations." Mimeographed. 1976.

Jennings, M. K., Ehman, L. H., and Niemi, R. G. Social studies teachers and their pupils. In M. K. Jennings and R. Niemi (Eds.), *The political character of adolescence.* Princeton, N.J.: Princeton University Press, 1974.

Kandel, D. Inter- and intragenerational influences on adolescent marijuana use. *Journal of Social Issues,* 1974, *30,* 107–135.

Kasschau, P. L., Ransford, H. E., and Bengtston, V. L. Generational consciousness and youth movement participation: Contrasts in blue-collar and white-collar youth. *Journal of Social Issues,* 1974, *30,* 69–94.

Keniston, K. *Young radicals: Notes on committed youth.* New York: Harcourt Brace Jovanovich, 1968.

————. The sources of student dissent (1967). In P. H. Mussen, J. J. Conger, and J. Kagan (Eds.), *Readings in child development and personality* (2nd ed.). New York: Harper &

Kerpelman, L. C. Student political activism and ideology: Comparative characteristics of activists and nonactivists. *Journal of Consulting Psychology*, 1969, *16*, 8–13.

————. *Activists and nonactivists*. New York: Behavioral Publications, 1972.

Kleiber, D. A., and Manaster, G. J. Youths' outlooks on the future: A past-present comparison. *Journal of Youth and Adolescence*, 1972, *7*, 223–232.

Knutson, J. *The human basis of polity: A psychological study of political men*. Chicago: Aldine-Atherton, 1972.

————. The new frontier of projective techniques. In J. Knutson (Ed.), *Handbook of political psychology*. San Francisco: Jossey-Bass, 1973a.

————. Personality in the study of politics. In J. Knutson (Ed.), *Handbook of political psychology*. San Francisco: Jossey-Bass, 1973b.

Kohlberg, L. *The development of modes of moral thinking and choice in the years ten to sixteen*. Unpublished doctoral dissertation, University of Chicago, 1958.

————. Development of moral character and moral ideology. In M. L. Hoffman and L. W. Hoffman (Eds.), *Review of child development research* (Vol. I). New York: Russell Sage Foundation, 1964.

Kohlberg, L., and Gilligan, C. The adolescent as philosopher: The discovery of self in a post-conventional world. *Daedalus*, 1971, *100*, 1051–1086.

Kohlberg, L., and Kramer, R. Continuities and discontinuities in childhood and adult moral development. *Human Development*, 1969, *12*, 93–120.

Kraus, S., and Davis, D. *The effects of mass communication on political behavior*. University Park, Pa.: Pennsylvania State University Press, 1976.

Lane, R. E. *Political life*. New York: Free Press, 1959.

————. *Political ideology*. New York: Free Press, 1962.

————. Political education in the midst of life's struggles. *Harvard Educational Review*, 1968, *38*, 468–494.

————. *Political thinking and consciousness*. Chicago: Markham, 1969.

————. Patterns of political belief. In J. Knutson (Ed.), *Handbook of political psychology*. San Francisco: Jossey-Bass, 1973.

Lane, R. E., and Sears, D. O. *Public opinion*. Englewood Cliffs, N.J.: Prentice-Hall, 1964.

Langton, K. P. Peer group and school and the political socialization process. *American Political Science Review*, 1967, *61*, 751–758.

————. *Political socialization*. New York: Oxford University Press, 1969.

Langton, K. P., and Jennings, M. K. Political socialization and the high-school civics curriculum in the United States. *American Political Science Review*, 1968, *62*, 852–867.

Laufer, R. S., and Bengtston, V. L. Generations, aging, and social stratification: On the development of generational units. *Journal of Social Issues*, 1974, *30*, 181–205.

Lerner, R. M. Showdown at generation gap: Attitudes of adolescents and their parents toward contemporary issues. In H. D. Thornburg (Ed.), *Contemporary adolescence: Readings* (2nd ed.). Belmont, Calif.: Brooks/Cole, 1975.

Lerner, R. M., Pendorf, J., and Emery, A. Attitudes of adolescents and adults toward contemporary issues. *Psychological Reports*, 1971, *28*, 139–145.

Lerner, R. M., Karson, M., Meisels, M., and Knapp, J. R. Actual and perceived attitudes of late adolescents and their parents: The phenomenon of the generation gap. *Journal of Genetic Psychology*, 1975, *126*, 195–207.

Lerner, R. M., Schroeder, C., Rewitzer, M., and Weinstock, A. Attitudes of high-school students and their parents toward contemporary issues. *Psychological Reports*, 1972, *31*, 255–258.

Lewis, S. H., and Kraut, R. E. Correlates of student political activism and ideology. *Journal of Social Issues,* 1972, *28,* 151–170.

Lipset, S. M. Students and politics in comparative perspective. *Daedalus,* 1968, *97,* 1–20.

Lipset, S. M., and Wolin, S. S. (Eds.). *The Berkeley student revolt.* New York: Doubleday, 1965.

Litt, E. Civic education, community norms, and political indoctrination. *American Sociological Review,* 1963, *28,* 69–75.

Lupfer, M. B., and Kenny, C. T. The impact of Watergate on youths' views of the presidency. *Public Affairs Forum,* 1976, *5,* 1–8.

Lyons, S. R. The political socialization of ghetto children: Efficacy and cynicism. *Journal of Politics,* 1970, *32,* 288–294.

Maccoby, E., and Jacklin, C. *Psychology of sex differences.* Stanford, Calif.: Stanford University Press, 1974.

Mankoff, M., and Flacks, R. The changing social base of the American student movement. *The Annals of the American Academy of Political and Social Science,* 1971, *395,* 54–67.

Mannheim, K. The problem of generations. In P. Kleckemeti, (Ed.), *Essays on the sociology of knowledge.* London: Routledge and Kegan-Paul, 1952.

Maykovich, M. K. Political activation of Japanese-American youth. *Journal of Social Issues,* 1973, *29,* 167–186.

Merelman, R. M. The development of political ideology: A framework for the analysis of political socialization. *American Political Science Review,* 1969, *63,* 750–767.

Middleton, R., and Putney, S. Political expression of adolescent rebellion. *American Journal of Sociology,* 1963, *68,* 527–535.

Miller, M. V., and Gilmore, S. (Eds.), *Revolution at Berkeley.* New York: Dell, 1965.

Montero, D. Support for civil liberties among a cohort of high-school graduates and college students. *Journal of Social Issues,* 1975, *31,* 123–136.

Nathan, J. A., and Remy, R. C. Comparative political socialization: A theoretical perspective. In S. A. Renshon (Ed.), *Handbook of political socialization: Theory and research.* New York: Free Press, 1977.

Newcomb, T. M. Attitude development as a function of reference groups: The Bennington study. In E. E. Maccoby, T. M. Newcomb, and E. L. Hartley (Eds.), *Readings in social psychology.* New York: Holt, Rinehart, & Winston, 1958.

Niemi, R. G. Collecting information about the family: A problem in survey methodology. In J. Dennis (Ed.), *Socialization to politics.* New York: Wiley, 1973.

Offer, D. *The psychological world of the teenager.* New York: Basic Books, 1969.

Oppenheim, A. N., and Torney, J. *The measurement of children's civic attitudes in different nations.* New York: Wiley, 1974.

Patrick, J. J. Political socialization and political education in the schools. In S. A. Renshon (Ed.), *Handbook of political socialization: Theory and research.* New York: Free Press, 1977.

Peterson, R. E. *The scope of organized student protest in 1964–1965.* Princeton, N.J.: Educational Testing Service, 1966.

———. *The scope of organized student protest 1967–1968.* Princeton, N.J.: Educational Testing Service, 1968a.

———. The student left in American higher education. *Daedalus,* 1968b, *97,* 293–317.

Piaget, J. *The origins of intelligence in children.* New York: International Universities Press, 1952.

———. *The moral judgment of the child.* New York: Free Press, 1965. (Originally published, 1932.)

Piaget, J., and Weil, A. The development in children of the idea of the homeland and of relations with other countries. *International Social Science Bulletin,* 1951, *3,* 561–578.

Pinner, F. A. Parental overprotection and political distrust. *The Annals of the American Academy of Political and Social Science,* 1965, *361,* 59–70.

Quarter, J. *The student movement of the 60's.* Ontario, Canada: Ontario Institute for Studies in Education, 1972.

Rapaport, D. The structure of psychoanalytic theory: A systematic attempt. *Psychological Issues,* 1960, *6,* 1–157.

Renshon, S. A. *Psychological needs and political behavior.* New York: Free Press, 1974.

———. The role of personality development in political socialization. In D. C. Schwartz and S. K. Schwartz (Eds.), *New directions in political socialization.* New York: Free Press, 1975.

———. Assumptive frameworks in political socialization theory. In S. A. Renshon (Ed.), *Handbook of political socialization: Theory and research.* New York: Free Press, 1977a.

———, (Ed.). *Handbook of political socialization: Theory and research.* New York: Free Press, 1977b.

Rest, J. The hierarchical nature of moral judgment: A study of patterns of comprehension and preference of moral stages. *Journal of Personality,* 1973, *41,* 86–109.

Rohter, I. S. A social-learning approach to political socialization. In D. C. Schwartz and S. K. Schwartz (Eds.), *New directions in political socialization.* New York: Free Press, 1975.

Rosenau, N. The sources of children's political concepts: An application of Piaget's theory. In D. C. Schwartz and S. K. Schwartz (Eds.), *New directions in political socialization.* New York: Free Press, 1975.

Rosenberg, M. *Society and the adolescent self-image.* Princeton, N.J.: Princeton University Press, 1965.

Rubin, Z., and Peplau, L. A. Who believes in a just world? *Journal of Social Issues,* 1975, *31,* 65–89.

Schiff, L. F. The obedient rebels: A study of conversions to conservatism. *Journal of Social Issues,* 1964, *20,* 74–95.

———. Dynamic young fogies: Rebels on the right. *Trans-action,* 1966, *3,* 30–36.

Schwartz, S. K. Patterns of cynicism: Differential political socialization among adolescents. In D. C. Schwartz and S. K. Schwartz (Eds.), *New directions in political socialization.* New York: Free Press, 1975a.

———. Preschoolers and politics. In D. C. Schwartz and S. K. Schwartz (Eds.), *New directions in political socialization.* New York: Free Press, 1975b.

Sears, D. O. Current prospects in political socialization. Paper presented at the Annual Meeting of the American Psychological Association. Chicago, August 1975a.

———. Political socialization. In F. I. Greenstein and N. W. Polsby (Eds.), *Handbook of political science.* Vol. 2: *Micropolitical theory.* Reading, Mass.: Addison-Wesley, 1975b.

———. The problem of generations: A social psychologist's perspective. Paper presented at the Annual Meeting of the American Political Science Association. San Francisco, September 1975c.

Sebert, S. K., Jennings, M. K., and Niemi, R. G. The political texture of peer groups. In M. K. Jennings and R. G. Niemi (Eds.), *The political character of adolescence.* Princeton, N.J.: Princeton University Press, 1974.

Selvin, H. C., and Hagstrom (1960), W. O. Determinants of support for civil liberties. In S. M. Lipset and S. S. Wolin (Eds.), *The Berkeley student revolt.* New York: Doubleday, 1965.

Sigel, R. S. An exploration into some aspects of political socialization: School children's reactions to the death of a president. In M. Wolfenstein and G. Kliman (Eds.), *Children and the death of a president: Multidisciplinary studies.* New York: Doubleday, 1965.

———. Psychological antecedents and political involvement: The utility of the concept of locus-of-control. *Social Science Quarterly,* 1975, *39,* 315–322.

Sigel, R. S., and Hoskin, M. B. Adult political socialization. In S. A. Renshon (Ed.), *Handbook of political socialization: Theory and research.* New York, Free Press, 1977a.

———. Affect for government and its relation to policy output among adolescents. *American Journal of Political Science,* 1977b, *21,* 111–134.

Silberger, S. A. Peers in the political socialization process. In S. A. Renshon (Ed.), *Handbook of political socialization: Theory and research.* New York: Free Press, 1972.

Simpson, E. Moral development research: A case study of scientific cultural bias. *Human Development,* 1974, *17,* 81–106.

Smith, M. B. Psychology and student protest. Paper presented at the Illinois Psychological Association Meetings, Chicago, November 1968.

Snodgrass, S. R. Some relationships between sociopolitical ideology and moral character among college youth. *Journal of Youth and Adolescence,* 1975, *4,* 195–206.

Solomon, R., and Fishman, J. R. Youth and peace: A psychosocial study of student peace demonstrators in Washington, D. C. *Journal of Social Issues,* 1964, *20,* 54–83.

Somers, R. H. The mainsprings of rebellion: A survey of Berkeley students in November, 1964. In S. M. Lipset and S. S. Wolin (Eds.), *The Berkeley student revolt.* New York: Doubleday, 1965.

Starr, J. M. The peace and love generation: Changing attitudes toward sex and violence among college youth. *Journal of Social Issues,* 1974, *30,* 73–106.

Steinkopf, K. Family communication patterns and anticipatory socialization. *Journalism Quarterly,* 1973, *50,* 24–30.

Steinitz, V. A., King, P., Solomon, E. R., and Shapiro, E. D. Ideological development in working-class youth. *Harvard Educational Review,* 1973, *43,* 335–361.

Stone, V., and Chaffee, S. H. Family communication patterns and source-message orientation. *Journalism Quarterly,* 1970, *47,* 239–246.

Sullivan, E. V. Political development during the adolescent years. In E. D. Evans (Ed.), *Adolescents: Readings in behavior and development.* Hinsdale, Ill.: Dryden, 1970.

Tapp, J. L. Psychology and the law: An overture. *Annual Review of Psychology,* 1976, *27,* 359–404.

Tapp, J. L., and Kohlberg, L. Developing senses of law and legal justice. *Journal of Social Issues,* 1971, *27,* 65–93.

Tapp, J. L., and Levine, F. J. Persuasion of virtue: A preliminary statement. *Law and Society Review,* 1970, *4,* 566–582.

———. Compliance from kindergarten to college: A speculative research note. *Journal of Youth and Adolescence,* 1972, *1,* 233–249.

———. Legal socialization: Strategies for an ethical legality. *Stanford Law Review,* 1974, *27,* 1–72.

Thomas, L. E. Family correlates of student political activism. *Developmental Psychology,* 1971, *5,* 206–214.

———. Generational discontinuity in beliefs: An exploration of the generation gap. *Journal of Social Issues,* 1974, *30,* 1–22.

Tolley, H., Jr. Childhood learning about war and peace: Coming of age in the nuclear era. In S. A. Renshon (Ed.), *Handbook of political socialization: Theory and research.* New York, Free Press, 1977.

Torney, J. V. Socialization of attitudes toward the legal system. *Journal of Social Issues,* 1971, *27,* 137–154.

———. Old problems and partially new solutions. *Contemporary Psychology,* 1976, *21,* 568–569.

Trent, J. W., and Craise, J. L. Commitment and conformity in the American college, *Journal of Social Issues,* 1967, *2,* 34–51.

Turiel, E. Conflict and transition in adolescent moral development. *Child Development,* 1974, *45,* 14–29.

Vaillancourt, P. M. Stability of children's survey responses. *Public Opinion Quarterly,* 1973, *37,* 373–387.

Watts, W. A., and Whittaker, D. N. E. Free speech advocates at Berkeley. *Journal of Applied Behavioral Science,* 1966, *2,* 41–62.

Weissberg, R., and Joslyn, R. Methodological appropriateness in political socialization. In S. A. Renshon (Ed.), *Handbook of political socialization: Theory and research.* New York, Free Press, 1977.

Westby, D. L., and Braungart, R. G. The alienation of generations and status politics: Alternative explanations of student political activism. In R. S. Sigel (Ed.), *Learning about politics.* New York: Random-House, 1970.

Wolfenstein, M., and Kliman, G. (Eds.), *Children and the death of a president.* New York: Doubleday, 1965.

Zellman, G. L., and Sears, D. O. Childhood origins of tolerance for dissent. *Journal of Social Issues,* 1971, *27,* 109–136.

CHAPTER 11

*The Development of Sexuality in Adolescence**

Patricia Y. Miller and William Simon†

Contemporary industrial societies universally define adolescence as a time of transformation in social status. Within the context of other developmental goals, one is supposed to become a self-motivated sexual actor. Even so, by the beginning of adolescence, some youth have already begun sexual activity, and, for virtually all adolescents, much of what will shape their sexual careers has already occurred (Kinsey et al., 1948; 1953). Puberty, a biological event, mandates the change of status, a social event. Thus the new sexual status is attributed with far greater uniformity in time than can be ascribed to the capacity of the male to ejaculate or the onset of female menses — or the manifestation of other secondary gender developments during this period. Society responds to the diffuse and irregular biological process of puberty by linking it directly and significantly to a social event, so that which is seen from the biological perspective as process in continuity (Tanner, 1972, pp. 1–24) is seen from the social perspective as the threshold certifying the end of childhood.

What is unique in the experience of industrial societies is that young people are defined as sexually mature while simultaneously being defined as socially and psychologically immature. This incongruity of attributions — an adolescent is mature and yet somehow not mature — sets a tension between sexual activity and sexual status that focuses public concern on both individual adolescents and the cohort of adolescents. Most researchers of adolescence have examined its developmental aspect, but because adolescence in contemporary society is defined as more than puberty, it seems important to examine its metaphoric content as well.

In classic psychoanalytic theory, adolescence is seen as the end of latency, that period in which all but the pathologically disordered repress most concerns with the sexual (which had flourished earlier in expressions of infantile sexuality), so that the formal training of necessary social skills may go forward (Freud, 1962). With the onset of puberty, sexuality reawakens; a fully elaborated and rich (but primitive) sexual past must now be brought to terms with a contextual self far more mature and responsive to the external world than was the child who experienced an incipient (but profound) commitment to the primitive sexual scenario. The adolescent's sexual problem is to find ways of

*The unpublished data reported in this essay were collected under a grant from the National Institute for Child Health and Human Development (PHS HD 02257). This paper was prepared while both authors were affiliated with the University of Houston with generous support from the Office of the Dean of the College of Social Sciences. We would also like to acknowledge the editorial assistance of Penny Pickett, Georgetown University. A succession of nearly indecipherable manuscripts were wondrously transformed by Cathy Williams who typed the several versions.

†Authorship of this essay was a joint venture; authors are listed in alphabetical order.

expressing the primitively formed erotic commitments without offending the external world, while at the same time avoiding the high cost of continuing repression. The ego must carefully find its way between the conflicting demands of superego and id. In other words, psychosexual development during adolescence is seen by Freud (and others in his tradition) as essentially a stage the individual enters, with a relatively fully formed complex of erotic meanings, attempting to enact those meanings in socially and personally acceptable behavior (Offer & Simon, 1976).

Erikson (1950) and his students found markedly more continuity in the stages of development that precede adolescence. Infancy and childhood are linked to adolescence rather directly by the development of general competencies. Particular or eccentric experiences, typified by the almost accidental sources of trauma and fixation, merely sharpen or crystallize elements in an ongoing process. Sexuality is seen in terms of the degree of development of such general competencies as the capacity for intimacy and trust. In other words, the meanings of sexually related behavior are seen by Erikson (1950), and others who modify classical psychoanalytic theory the way he does, as essential properties of adolescent experience; the quality of early development and the ability to meet the more general developmental tasks specific to adolescence determine the individual's assimilation of sexual meanings and the way they are subsequently attached to behavior (Keniston, 1970).

The Offers (Offer 1969; Offer & Offer, 1975a), whose work is more like Erikson's than it is like Freud's, identify three different, fairly general strategies or styles (called continuous, surgent, and tumultuous) as characteristic of adolescent development. As categories, the styles describe not relationships between specific stages of development but alternative responses to adolescent experience. The Offers find that commitment to one or another of the three behavioral strategies is among the most important outcomes of infancy and childhood; moreover, a culminating commitment to a dominant style is more significant by adolescence than any of the specific experience or relationships that may have influenced the choice of style. The meaning of sexuality then rests largely in adolescence and the world's responses to it.

Some of the differences between Freud and revisionists such as Erikson and the Offers clearly rest in their responses to Freud's own revisions, which we might call a critical watershed between an earlier, essentially topological approach to behavior and a later, more nearly structural orientation. The topological approach was largely an attempt to understand the crucial nature of instinct as an organizing principle of human behavior; the structural expressed greater concern for ego development. A persistent physicalist bias informs much of the language of early ego-development theory in Freud and in the work of his more orthodox students. Erikson and the Offers, working in an intellectual environment that requires heightened attention to sociocultural perspectives, more easily, though not completely, abandon much of the bias of the earlier theorists. From the perspective of ego psychologists, the significance of learning during latency, particularly gender-role learning, has an importance for subsequent psychosocial development that cannot be ignored (Loevinger, 1976).

For Erikson, only the developmental pattern that gives rise to turmoil is modal. Earlier developmental stages may determine the quality of turmoil, the way it is expressed, and its consequences, but essentially it is unsettledness that is requisite in completing the developmental tasks appropriate to adolescence. The formation of a sexual identity must not only allow expression of the sexual itself but must also articulate with other aspects of identity formation, particularly the capacity for autonomy. In the literature, this can be and sometimes is linked to the resolution of the adolescent renewal of the oedipal attachment, but more as rhetoric than as explanation (see Erikson, 1959). Little that is intrinsically sexual history specifies adolescent sexual experience.

If infancy and childhood establish strong predispositions for sexual commitment, they do so in the form of competencies or adaptive styles — aspects of character that are not unique to sexuality but operate across a broad developmental spectrum. The modal child approaches adolescence with generalized competencies and meets sexual tasks that appear to be items in a complex mandate having biological and social dimension. In the social dimension, the adolescent must gain sufficient autonomy from parental figures to learn intimacy among equals and to prepare for subsequent heterosexual mate selection. The confirmation of a heterosexual and a heterosocial commitment is seen as a crucial part of adolescence.

The emerging heterosexual commitment is viewed with considerable ambivalence, however. Erikson and his followers view the failure to move into a heterosociality that expresses heterosexuality (largely dating) as symptomatic of problematic (that is, impaired) development. But they also view preoccupation with a heterosexual commitment (as reflected in too strong a commitment to heterosexual experience) as problematic, because it is too early for fully adequate pair-bonding — being informed by the narcissism appropriate to this life-cycle stage — and interferes with other tasks to be accomplished during this stage. The biological or psychobiological component makes the sexual development of the adolescent both necessary and risk-laden. In the Freudian vision, the sexual impulse may appear dangerously in the most direct of expressions, asocially seeking pleasure or even hedonism; in the Eriksonian vision, full genital maturity occurs in a benign context wherein personal pleasure, fulfillment of species necessity, and that which is defined in the West as desirable all happily coalesce (Erikson, 1959).

If adolescence represents the first restaging of childhood's primitive scenario for Freudians, for Eriksonians it is the most general expression of societal and evolutionary programming. In the Freudian view, the individual enters adolescence possessing a relatively fully articulated set of erotic meanings that seek appropriate objects and behavior. The Eriksonian view reverses this to suggest that meaning resides in the biological and social future, childhood's legacy representing basic competencies in the first genuine encounter with the sexual. For Freud, adolescence is the beginning of a quest for an appropriate interpersonal sexual script to articulate with a largely formed intrapsychic script; the quest rarely takes the individual far from the margins of the problematic. For Erikson, it is not the range of the quest but the failure to articulate the intrapsychic and interpersonal scripts that is the problematic and sometimes unexpected outcome.

Kohlberg and Piaget offer a third perspective that shares with the Freudians the idea of phylogenetically rooted constraints and, with the Eriksonians, the idea that the constraints are very general, almost abstract properties that are not specific to individual biography. It is not puberty as a changing biological event or adolescence as a changing social status that organizes adolescent experience, however; it is the level of cognitive development. For Kohlberg (1969, pp. 347–480), the experiments of adolescents are heavily conditioned, if not prompted, by recently developed or still developing capacities for formal operations. Much of what the individual brings to adolescence reflects the consequences of earlier stages of cognitive development. Little work in this perspective has focused directly on the sexual, although Kohlberg has studied gender identity and moral reasoning, two components of development generally accepted as impinging on psychosexual development in direct and powerful ways (Kohlberg, 1966).

Both Kohlberg and the classical psychoanalysts see adolescent sexual experience as hinging crucially on the integration of early infant and childhood experience and commitment, in increased expectation of more orderly, fully rationalized, and socially responsive behavior. As with Freud, for Kohlberg adolescence begins with a fairly established cast of characters and bits and pieces of scenarios. The judgments and perceptions generated during early stages, dominated by fairly primitive cognitive styles, will persist. Thus from Kohlberg's perspective, patterns of male dominance (rooted in, but not restricted to, penis envy) derive from the judgment-laden perceptions of gender-differentiated behaviors and the power relations that follow from these perceptions during the shaping of cognitive styles in early childhood. The major developmental task of adolescence and the maturational time clock fortuitously coincide. The capacity for formal operations emerges coincidentally with the specific need for a level of abstraction sufficient to allow rationalization of the conflicts between societal or interpersonal expectations and the idiocyncratic or intrapsychic. There is an acceleration in the transformation of the objects (including sounds, textures, tastes) symbolizing the erotic into suitable materials for current sexual stereotypes and scenarios (Kohlberg, 1966).

Freud, Erikson, and Kohlberg agree that whatever the outcome of sexual adolescent experience is, a significant part of what it can and cannot be has already been established in infancy and childhood, and it cannot be fully understood unless this history is first understood. Moreover, all three writers agree that the elements that determine adolescent sexuality are strikingly varied. All three recognize implicitly that however rooted in biology or however intense the drive associated with organic rootedness, adolescent sexual expression is substantially modified by layers of other experience and development remarkably remote from what is ordinarily taken for sexual.

Kinsey's (1948, 1953) essentially zoological approach affords a dramatic and possibly corrective contrast to the developmental work we have just considered. For Kinsey, sexual acts that involve genital play and at least the possibility of orgasm are more than the expression of some assumed, but rarely defined or measured, sexual drive or motivation. Sexual activity is inherently pleasurable for most people most of the time. The pleasure in sexual activity is its own motivation. The developmentalists see the sexual as a complex of motivations and meanings seeking expression in appropriate behavior; Kinsey sees sexual behavior as pleasuring with no specific or necessary meaning. An orgasm is only what it is; larger meanings and impact on sexual identity and status depend on other variables (Robinson, 1976).

For example, Kinsey sees the significant relationship between early puberty among males and homosexual adaptations not as the inevitable expression of erotic motives emanating from coercive intrafamilial relationships but as an experience that provides its own reinforcement and that articulates with psychological and social developments as best it can. Homosexuality is generated by a positive response to the sexual and it occurs in a context of high levels of gender segregation, correspondingly high levels of homosociality (where same-gender actors constitute the most critical audiences or reference groups, frequently expressing heterophobia), and virtually no access to heterosexuality, except perhaps when expressed through masturbatory imagery. Kinsey assumes either some inherent predisposition towards heterosexuality in gender selection or, as he implicitly argues in the case of early male puberty, highly contingent homosexual or masturbatory adaptations organized around the compelling attractiveness of sexual experience (Kinsey et al., 1948).

Kinsey's position is too restricting to be generally helpful in explaining either psychosexual development or its interaction with ongoing autobiography, but it can remind us that sexual activity is self-reinforcing — inasmuch as orgasm follows behavior immediately, is very specific, and is experienced almost universally as pleasurable. The concept of reinforcement may account for the impact of experience on behavior, but it doesn't explain either the initial emergence of the behavior itself or the relative lack of uniformity in age at first experience that characterizes most sexual behavior.

It seems ironic that the capacity of sexual behavior to be pleasuring or gratifying, which may be among its most universal aspects, seems only to add unsystematically to individual variation. Such behavior ultimately predicts little with reference to individual sexual careers. When sexual experience first occurs, it is clearly not in the total control of the individual. Regardless of whether an initial orgasm is a result of autoerotic activity (most nearly the universal experience of contemporary males) or of some kind of sociosexual activity (probably the most common introduction to orgasm among females), it is an outcome of developmental and contextual contingencies and, in turn, it becomes a variable contingency. Having occurred, it may or may not significantly help shape subsequent sexual behavior.

For most, adolescence is only a life-cycle stage where sexual significance in any explicit form is essentially developmental. For many individuals, sexual activity, particularly sociosexual activity, does not occur until adolescence has passed. For all individuals, adolescence no more fixes sexuality in final appearance or meaning than the earlier stages of life do. We cannot even describe this stage as one in which sexual options become fewer. To do so would be to imply that we know what all options are at some or any point in development. Nevertheless, despite its bias toward linearly sequential conceptions of causality, the developmental perspective gives the only useful coherence in a discussion of adolescent psychosexual development. We must keep in mind, however, that to adopt this perspective is to adopt its concepts but not its confusion of the shifting modal with the "normal" (Simon and Miller, 1977).

Among the psychosexual developmentalists, only Freud gives specific character to the sexual; it is something like an appetite with an approximate sense for what it hungers. But even libido rarely, if ever, appears in any guise resembling its "original" nature. In the taming of the beast on the childhood side of latency, primitive force has already become harnessed to conventionally acceptable modes of expression, some of which are at several removes from the sexual — what is called "de-eroticized" libido — (Freud, 1962). For none of the developmentalists does the sexual develop by unfolding some otherwise fixed attribute — as in the order of appearance of first and second teeth. Instead, the sexual is a process of assembly or even invention. Despite their relation to biological change, adolescent sexual commitment and activity are seen as ideological constructs that vary significantly within and across sociocultural moments. Puberty (or, more exactly, some select aspects of pubescence) initiates expression of the immediately sexual (Gagnon & Simon, 1973).

Yet we know that the manifestations of puberty and sexual activity (however these may be defined) are unevenly correlated at best. Pubescent precocity is no guarantee of precocity in social, psychological, or sexual behaviors. Moreover, the declining age of puberty — having fallen some two or more years since the beginning of the twentieth century — does not mesh with changes in either general patterns of adolescent behavior or their more specifically sexual forms. Thus the highly variable character of sexual expression, as it is seen, has immediate consequences for the kinds of conceptualization of psychosexual development that can be deemed reasonable. Even for writers who hold that the sexual expresses some innate and inherently sexual drive in its characteristic and most efficient mode of expression, the implicit model anticipates the developmental perspective where early patterns of development are modified by subsequent events in the direction of experiences, relationships, and contexts.

The major shortcoming of the developmental perspective is that all developmentalists address human development as if they were describing that which is most universal about the human. They ignore that, beyond the universality of sexual expression, there may in fact be very little that is universal about the sexual and even less that is universally necessary about its expression. It would seem that a truly effective model of psychosexual development, then, ought to include the sociocultural context as a variable. The most casual examination of the cross-cultural and historical patterns and uses of sexuality suggests how very much it has been at the service of historically specific institutions (Ford & Beach, 1951). The gender roles and sexual uses of women, for example, have frequently been described and even justified by highly ideological views on the "nature" of female sexuality, but current theories of psychosexual development do not accommodate these cultural and historical variations in female sexuality. More specifically, the capacity to experience orgasm may be constant in female sexuality, yet in very few cultures, in very few historical moments, and for relatively few women has orgasmic capacity been seen as essential, natural, or even desirable. What women are and do sexually has most often been defined by institutions charged with managing "legitimate" sexual behavior (Millett, 1970).

Similarly, definitions and expectations of adolescence surely do more to explain adolescent sexual patterns than rather abstract references to "human development" aired in some historical or cultural vacuum. The behavioral sciences can no longer blindly accept the romantic image of adolescence as the last point at which a naive, honest nature confronts and comes to terms with the rigidities and artificialities of social life. (The view is inherently sexist, deriving almost exclusively from the imagery of male experience: in the masculine drama of adolescence, the boys are "tamed," while the girls compliantly "surrender.") The significance of sexuality in adolescent development and experience has far more to do with the agenda that the surrounding society expects the adolescent to follow than with needs that the adolescent presses on society.

Thus we must try to understand not only the evolved nature of the sexual, but also the inherently complex nature of the sexual. It is complex in several ways. First there is motivation. In the post-Freudian world, the uncertain relationship between sexual behavior and sexual motives is commonplace. Much sexual behavior, particularly during adolescence, can be seen as following from largely nonsexual or nonerotic motivations; it is motivated almost entirely by response to external pressure. The world attributes a certain kind of sexual behavior to the adolescent, and the adolescent behaves with some kind of reaction to that attribution.

Further, the individual can be seen as experiencing both psychosexual development and sexual behavior on two distinct levels, not only at the inception of adolescence, but also in altering degrees through all stages of the life cycle. One level rather directly reflects the intrapsychic history and life of the individual (Simon, 1974, pp. 60–79), while the other reflects interpersonal requirements of social life (Gagnon, 1974, pp. 27–59). The intrapsychic is the source of the erotic response — psychic, neuromuscular, biochemical, and cardiovascular processes that either anticipate or lead to the psychological and physiological aspects of orgasm. Interpersonal scripts provide the structures by which the self overtly presents itself to others and responds to the behavior of others in ways that facilitate engagement with what is conventionally defined as sexual activity (including acts not necessarily approved by the same conventions). Following the distinction between the intrapsychic and the interpersonal, then, sexual activity need not necessarily be associated with erotic arousal, just as the capacity to experience erotic arousal need not necessarily accompany engagement in behavior that might conventionally be described as sexual.

It should be obvious that the individual experiences least strain when there is reciprocal facilitation between these two aspects of psychosexual development. Strain is minimized when the individual's intrapsychic and interpersonal erotic and sexual development are congruent. One of the major characteristics of adolescence is that for most individuals it is a time of dramatic flowering in both intrapsychic and interpersonal life; it is a time of increased coherence and testing, regardless of the amount of sexual activity. Intrapsychic and interpersonal sexual scripts and their articulation with other aspects of personality become for most individuals one of the most enduring and influential of the outcomes of adolescence.

In the most traditional psychoanalytic views, adolescence is seen as controlled by a set of circumstances rooted in childhood (Blos, 1962). Yet, even while it is possible that the origins of sexual commitments are in some sense located in preadolescent experience, it is very likely that the expressive mode of such commitments as well as their sequence depends on contingencies in adolescence. Childhood experience may be critical in explaining sexual outcomes; it is virtually useless in predicting sexual outcomes.

Among the contingencies that shape the interpersonal sexual scripts available to adolescents is the historical (e.g., war/peace, poverty/prosperity) and cultural (e.g., the rights and responsibilities attached to the various stages of the life cycle, the ideologies about gender differences, etc.) context specific to each maturing cohort. The norms that govern the rituals of interaction culminating in sexual activity are profoundly influenced by macrosocial factors. Moreover, just as the specific historical and cultural context defines the limited range of interpersonal scripts that organize sexual behavior, it also influences the erotic symbols and fantasy constructions through which the intrapsychic finds expression. Thus in times of war, courtship may be accelerated, a "good" woman may be licensed to provide sexual favors to a GI en route to the front, and military regalia may acquire special erotic meaning for younger boys anxious to join the fighting.

The erotic symbols that provide the raw materials for intrapsychic scripting or fantasy-construction evolve from the concrete experiences of individuals. Many of the symbols and themes of intrapsychic life tend to be highly uniform through time and across cultures because they are linked to common experiences in the microsocial world of infancy and childhood. The interpersonal scripts, however, are more heavily influenced by the sociocultural moment. Although there is considerable variation across cohorts (and across the life cycle of a given cohort) in the social strategies that facilitate actual sociosexual behavior, these are obviously common to the members of a given cohort.

Three specific influences distinguish the sexual development of contemporary adolescents from those of a generation ago. The once widely accepted ideology of inherent gender differences is being debated in high schools with an intensity equal to that found in adult arenas. As a result, distinctions between girls and boys with respect to what is acceptable or even possible behavior for the two genders are blurring. Furthermore, despite mixed messages, contemporary adolescents are expected to be more interested in sex, to become experienced earlier, and, once experienced, to approach regular sociosexual activity with greater competence than the adolescents described in the Kinsey (1948, 1953) volumes. The contemporary adolescent must fashion an interpersonal sexual script from materials provided by a society that is nearly obsessed with the sexual possibilities of adolescence. Whether sexually active or inactive, the adolescent is expected to "take a position" with reference to sexual opportunities. Finally, today's adolescents increasingly see the surrounding adult social world as itself more sexually active and sexually interested than it used to be.[1] Adults, of course, provide models for the young. In playing at being adult, children explore and rehearse the gestures — both mundane and mysterious — that symbolize adulthood. Much of the sexual activity of adolescents is disjunctive with their development, a ritual of gestures rather than an activity elicited by their intrinsic interests in sexual activity. It is behavior in search of meaning.

At puberty, adolescents experience for the first time the expectation that they will begin to experiment with and test the gestures, responses, and strategies that signal sociosexual interests. For some, this marks the occasion when a fairly well-developed fantasy life finally finds legitimate avenues for social expression. For others, expectations concerning sociosexual interests facilitate the eventual crystallization of a previously disorganized and incoherent fantasy life. Still others experience a fortuitous coincidence between the requirements of the interpersonal and the intrapsychic, a coincidence that only rarely describes an entire sexual career. Since both interpersonal and intrapsychic demands may alter as the individual moves through the life cycle, the successful synchronization of these two components of the sexual represents a recurring problem for the individual.

Typifying this is the stereotypic "teen-queen" who has internalized the "masochism" characteristic of her gender group, learned to maneuver through the rituals of romantic courtship and ultimately to experience sexual arousal in a romantic relationship. Her developmental sequence could be conceived of as optimal for the realization of conventional female goals. But the scripts that are efficient at one stage of the life cycle may be problematic at another. Following marriage, the romantic — which licensed the erotic — diminishes. As it diminishes, arousal becomes more difficult. Sexual relations may continue to be enjoyable; they most certainly will be more difficult. Sexual activity is a negotiated outcome, reflecting the partial interests of the interpersonal and the intrapsychic. The adjustment necessary to synchronize the two is not necessarily elaborate. A small gesture — a term of endearment — may be sufficient to invoke the romantic. Or the sexual may proceed on two levels, with the not uncommon "phantom lover" providing the intrapsychic arousal that complements a less than passionate performance on the interpersonal level. Most theory and research concerning the sexual assumes that comparable acts have comparable meanings. More probably, comparable

[1]Until recently, the sexual was rather successfully confined to the peripheries of social life. Although the sexual status of the never married was a matter of public concern, with marriage the social order relaxed its scrutiny. This has changed in the last decade, partly because of the increasing number of marriages terminated by divorce. The desire to remarry places large numbers of adults in the sexual marketplace. Adolescents observe numbers of adults playing the same kinds of courtship games that describe late adolescence, except that in the adult version the sexual component is more overt. Moreover, the same factors that have lowered the age of puberty (better nutrition and health care) and allowed the extension of adolescence into the twenties (diminished labor force needs, more discretionary income and leisure time) also have impacted on adults. If the young mature earlier than they used to, adults stay younger longer. Sexual attractiveness, interests and competence have all become part of the adult social agenda.

acts mean not only different things to different individuals, but also different things to the same individual.

In the complicated process of adolescent sexual development, social and intrapsychic demands are often poorly synchronized. The adolescent may satisfy social expectations without experiencing a corresponding sense of intrapsychic "success," without focusing and releasing sexual tension. Or the release of sexual tensions that satisfies the demands of the intrapsychic may require significant social failure, as the adolescents enter a role that they and/or others despise. For still others, both social and intrapyschic demands are satisfied, but this requires their consistent segregation in time and space. Individuals whose intrapsychic scriptural elements are predominantly homoerotic in character provide an excellent example of these differing adaptations to strain. Confronting social expectations that are predominately or exclusively heterosexual, they may suspend the intrapsychic in order to move through the approved rituals of adolescent sociability. Alternatively, they may risk significant disapproval and possibly rejection in the search for legitimacy. Or they may make dual investments in the rating and dating games of adolescence and the opportunities provided by the available homosexual subculture.

The relationship between interpersonal and intrapsychic demands is further complicated by the ongoing development of personality and identity during adolescence (Douvan & Adelson, 1966). These larger aspects of self constrain the individual's choices with respect to the available assortment of interpersonal scripts that organize sociosexual behavior. The specific styles of adolescence, for example, hippie, pom-pom girl, greaser, freak, each imply a set of strategies and rituals for expressing sociosexual interests (Buff, 1970). The individual's larger identity, or nonsexual sense of self, may vie with the demands of the intrapsychic for control of the social expression of sexual interests. Thus themes of sexual aggression may dominate the erotic imagery of a young man. But a larger principle, that rape is not "an appropriate act for a person such as myself," may prevent him from ever committing rape. He may "smuggle" elements suggestive of rape into his sociosexual interactions; the suggestion of rape may continue to elicit erotic arousal. But the act of rape will either anticipate or follow a profound modification of the larger, nonsexual sense of self. One might say, somewhat in the manner of Erikson, that one of the major developmental "tasks" of adolescence is the untroubled social expression of the intrapsychic in ways that do not generate conflict with the nonsexual sense of self.

The gender role is, of course, one of the major components of identity. Social expectations with reference to sexual conduct are part of a larger concern for the congruence between behavior and gender-role expectations. Sociosexual behavior is gender-significant behavior. For most adolescents, gender-role expectations provide the context within which psychosexual development and sexual experience occur since the sexual and social scenarios of the society are organized around norms for gender-appropriate behavior. The norms of gender-appropriate behavior probably represent the most powerful factor influencing sexual conduct, a factor that must be accommodated in some way by the sociosexual script. Where substantial discrepancies exist between gender identity and gender-role expectations, the creation of relatively stable strategies of accommodation is a critical problem for the adolescent.

Much sociosexual behavior in early adolescence is motivated or facilitated by expectations concerning gender-appropriate behavior rather than intrinsic interest in the sexual. "Falling in love" and "going steady" are essentially expressions of nonsexual social arrangements. These experiences potentiate sexual acts almost independently of erotic interest or sexual arousal. Light and heavy petting, for example, serve the nonsexual interests of both genders by certifying gender-role adequacy.

Undoubtedly, gender-role expectations represent the most powerful factor shaping adolescent sexual behavior. Gender roles are functional for coordinating action, they also constitute moral mandates. A violation of fundamental gender-role expectations is a violation of the moral order. Sexual behavior, then, is more than just gender-significant behavior, it is also moral behavior. Compared to the sexual, there are few other forms of behavior where the stigma attached to a flawed performance or a violation of moral standards is so enduring and encompassing.

The sex education of the adolescent is emphatically attached to moral education. Many of the specific images that form the core of the individual's earliest sense of the sexual are thoroughly imbued with vague but powerful moral tones. Not uncommonly, given the confusions of childish cognitions, some behavior that is not intrinsically sexual becomes infused with sexual meanings by being linked to seemingly common moral judgments. Moreover, judgments of the act (''that was a naughty thing to do'') extend to the actor (''you are a naughty person for doing that''). The moral definitions attached to the things we do become attached to the social and subjective definitions of who and what we are.

Although adolescence is presumed to provide the possibility of a higher level of moral development — where the capacity for formal operations transforms the quality of moral judgments — *behavior* is not necessarily correspondingly transformed. Moral postures (unlike moral judgments) continue to reflect the many accumulated layers of experience. Formal operations may guide the organization of moral judgments, but the content of moral sensibilities (the standards the individual experiences as appropriately applied to his or her own behavior) is the product of the entire life history.

For most adolescents, morality plays a significant, but supplemental or facilitative, role in their management of the sexual. Where social expectations and intrapsychic demands are congruent, morality is of relatively little significance; behavior is experienced as ''natural,'' requiring no rationalization. But where there is a conflict between the elements entering into the construction of sociosexual behavior, morality is very significant as an aid or obstacle to resolution. In such cases, morality may swing the balance in favor of social expectations. Or moral sensibilities may be revised or manipulated to legitimate intrapsychic demands. Besides facilitating the resolution of sexual conflicts, moral judgments tend to add significance to sexual activity. The sexual encounter during adolescence (or its anticipation) provides one of the few instances where ordinary people doing relatively ordinary things experience themselves as extraordinary actors in the moral universe.

In failing to recognize the complex negotiations often fundamental to sexual (or nonsexual) behavior, adolescents are sometimes characterized as shallow. They do often appear to be shallow, intensely avowing a position today they will just as intensely negate tomorrow. This rather superficial observation — that adolescent values tend to be mercurial — is sometimes posited as a necessary feature of adolescence; adolescents are thought to view the world around them in extreme terms, lacking any tolerance for ambiguity. But underlying these dramatic shifts in values is the continuous process of experimentation and adjustment through which the adolescent attempts to forge a strategy that effectively reconciles discordant mandates for behavior. These potentially conflicting mandates express not only the demands of the intrapsychic and the social, but also social expectations that incorporate mixed messages. Social expectations train adolescents to fear both sexual experience and sexual inexperience. The moral imperatives associated with each element in these dialectics will be invoked in an appeal to the larger sense of self for legitimacy in the individual's attempts to reconcile these conflicts. The experience of devising strategies to balance conflicting claims that is acquired in the course of adolescent psychosexual development may resonate into adulthood more significantly than any specific sexual experience. This implies that it is the quality rather than the amount of sexual experience that enables the individual to learn to manipulate moral postures.

Little is known about the relationship between the sexual and the moral. Our ignorance is conditioned by general societal uneasiness with the kinds of issues we have raised as well as by societal protectiveness where sexual development of the young is concerned. But we believe that intellectual positions that regard moral sensibilities as impregnable reservoirs uncontaminated by the contingencies of ongoing sexual experience are almost as defeating as ideologies that construe sexual development as the naive unfolding of the natural.

Beyond the tendency to view the sexual as something that unfolds in predetermined ways (where deviance is the outcome of the arresting or "perversion" of development), the sex act is usually seen as having a unit character that overrides all other distinctions. The major, nearly exclusive, concern of those who study adolescent psychosexual development is the initiation of coital experience, as if this act singularly transformed the individual with reference to the sexual. But as soon as we move beyond the most abstract description of coitus — a vagina accepting a penis — differences in motives, perceptions, experiences, and consequences proliferate. The socially and psychologically contingent character of such activity is obvious even in the limited data available describing adolescent sexual experience. By placing the possibility of sexual experience on the adolescent agenda, the potentially sexual encounter occasions the initial pressures to orchestrate effectively many different components of the self. The actual experience of the sex act itself does not account for the significance attached to the event by the individual or others. Similarly, coital activity per se neither generates nor certifies developmental difficulties. We must look to the social context of American adolescence and the proscription of certain kinds of sexual relations to understand the meanings of adolescent coitus:

> Both cultural norms and societal restraints, by reserving sexual experience for a later, more mature — if not marital — status, have the effect of attaching to its occurrence a variety of social-psychological meanings. Beyond the personal significance of having attained a more mature status, these may involve as well the sense of having established one's independence and autonomy, of being capable of interpersonal intimacy, of having gained peer-group respect, of being physically attractive, of having affirmed one's sexual identity, of having rejected social conventions, or of having engaged in personally and socially unacceptable behavior. [Jessor & Jessor, 1975, p. 473]

Thus adolescent motivations to engage in coitus transcend mere physiological stirrings and encompass a rich assortment of essentially symbolic goals. The attractiveness of the behavior in the face of the possibility of severe sanctions is believed to lie in the social conditions unique to adolescent status in our society. These conditions are, of course, experienced differently according to gender, race, maturity, peer climates, and aspirations for adulthood. Nevertheless, adolescent premarital coital behavior is commonly viewed as rebellious, pathological, immoral, deviant, or delinquent by the range of professionals — clinicians, social scientists, theologians, law-enforcement agents — concerned with the development of the young.

Although a substantial proportion of adolescents do have the first coital experience during their teen years, the salience of coital experience for the young is often overseen. Offer and Offer (1975b) found that heterosexual concerns are not very prominent during the high-school years for the students in their longitudinal study of "normal" males. As late as the junior year, most of these young men disapproved of sexual relations among adolescents. Very few had engaged in coital behavior and their fear was invoked to account for their inexperience. Unpublished data for a national random sample of 1177 college students in the late 1960s reinforced the point that the attractiveness of coital behavior was highly variable among youth. A substantial minority (44%) of these young men and a full majority of their female counterparts (68%) had yet to engage in their first coital experience. Among these, 48% of the females and 25% of the males said they only "rarely" or "never" had felt they wanted to have coitus. Moreover, a substantial majority (64% of the males and 78% of the females) indicated that they were *not* unhappy about their lack of coital experience.

The meanings of sexual relations for these inexperienced respondents are apparently different in some respects from those suggested by Jessor and Jessor (1975). Among both males and females, moral concerns (65%) and the fear of pregnancy (63%) were the most widely invoked reasons for avoiding premarital coitus. Then the genders diverge somewhat. A majority of females cite the control functions of significant others [fear parental disapproval (60%); fear damaging reputation (55%)], while only one other reason — the unwillingness of the partner — was claimed by a majority (55%) of the males. Compared to females, the value attached to the opinions of significant others is less critical in discouraging males from engaging in premarital coitus, but it is not a trivial factor. Fear of parental disapproval (43%) and reputational concerns (40%) are ranked fourth and sixth respectively by the males. Developmental difficulties, such as inhibitions (too shy), interpersonal problems (never met person wanted coitus with), and characterological concerns (might want coitus too often) describe but a minority of those maintaining virginity. But clearly a complex of potential motives impacts on the decisions adolescents make with respect to their sexual statuses. Premarital coitus may be attractive to the young because it signals their maturity and independence from parental authority, or it may be unattractive because it could lead to the loss of parental respect. Coital experience may certify competence and adequacy or these may be irrelevant to one's decision concerning one's sexual status. Coital experience may provide an opportunity to transcend the rules of the society, to directly experience the sanctions that follow the violation of traditional norms, or, in deferring the experience, to enjoy the sense of well being that flows from conformity. Finally, sexual status may simply be a function of the availability or unavailability of a willing partner.

Thus far we have largely ignored the role of dyadic involvement in adolescent motivations to engage in premarital coitus. The dating games of adolescence provide the context for most premarital coitus. Very few contemporary youth have their first experience with a prostitute or an "older" woman. In the national sample of college students discussed above, only 4% of the males with coital experience reported that their initial partner had been a prostitute (Simon, Berger, & Gagnon, 1972). Nevertheless, almost half (46%) of these young men were *not* emotionally involved with the initial partner. Only 31% reported they had been in love with the girl or planning to marry her. For females, however, love relationships provide an almost universal context for the first coital experience. Fully 59% of the college women planned to marry their first coital partners; an additional 22% were in love but had no plans to marry. Only 5% reported that they were not emotionally involved with the initial partner.

These gender differences in the relationship to the first coital partner imply a fundamental difference between the genders in the motivational structure that leads adolescent males and females to engage in sexual relations. For males, the rewards intrinsic to the act itself or, more probably, the recognition of the achievement by self and others appears to account for the variety of social relationships within which the first coital experience commonly occurs. If the nature of the relationship with the initial coital partner were secondary to the intrinsic rewards of the sex act, we might expect that most males would continue sexual relations with the willing partner they have succeeded in locating. But this is not the case. Among the males in our national sample of college youth, one-third (33%) have coitus with the initial partner but one time. An additional third (36%) renew sexual relations with the first partner five or fewer times (Simon, Berger, & Gagnon, 1972). Our latter hypothesis — that recognition of sociosexual "maturity" is central to the complex of motives encouraging coitus — is supported by the finding that almost one-third (30%) of the males with coital experience talk with someone other than the partner about that experience immediately afterwards; more than half (60%) discuss it within the month (Carns, 1973). Moreover, where the relationship with the first coital partner did not entail any emotional involvement, males are much *more* likely to share their experience with an audience than they were if they were in love or planning to marry.

In contrast to males, the anticipation of marriage is central to female motivations to engage in premarital coitus. According to Kinsey et al., the exact causal relationship between marital aspirations and premarital coitus is variable, ". . . it is a question whether early experience in coitus leads to early marriage, or whether the possibility of a forthcoming marriage leads, as it certainly does in some cases, to an acceptance of coitus just before marriage'' (1953, p. 287). Subsequent researchers emphasize only that females grant sexual access to serious suitors in order to secure their commitment to marriage (e.g. Gagnon and Simon, 1973). We noted earlier that the overwhelming majority of females in the sample of college students were in love or planning to marry the initial partner. More than a quarter (29%) reported that coital relations with the initial partner were continuing at the time of the interview, underscoring their sense of commitment in these relationships (Simon, Berger, & Gagnon, 1972). An additional third (34%) had coitus between 6 and 20 times with the initial partner. The percentages of males who had coitus this frequently with the initial partner (23%) or who were continuing sexual relations with her at the time of the interview (8%) is much smaller. Our conclusion that her partner, rather than her peers, provides the critical audience for her sexual activity is substantiated to some degree by data. Although almost a third of the males immediately discuss the first coital experience with someone other than their partners, only 14% of the females immediately discuss it (Carns, 1973). Within one month, 60% of the males but only about 40% of the females have shared the experience with another. Moreover, although males are more likely to seek an audience for their first coital experience where no emotional involvement with the partner existed, the decisions of females to discuss their initial coital experiences are not influenced by the nature of the relationship with the first partner.

Gender differences in the salience of the audience appear to reflect social realities. Although youth-serving professionals and scholars of adolescence may represent a universally disapproving monolith (although we doubt this is the case), attitudes toward premarital coitus in the larger society are contingent on many factors (Reiss, 1967). That generally greater premissiveness is bestowed on males is reflected in the reactions of the first person told (as these were preceived by the respondents in our sample of college students). Most of the confidants (80%) were approving (Carns, 1973). Of course, we would expect most of the respondents to favor sympathetic peers in their choices for the initial audiences. Given this bias, however, male respondents were more likely to report audience approval (86%) than females (67%). Although a substantial minority of both males and females said they received mixed reactions, virtually no males (3%) reported that the first person they had told of their premarital coital experience had been disapproving. Thus there appears to be a distinctive but hardly overwhelming tendency for others to disproportionately support the adolescent male in his premarital sexual experience. But support is conditional, diminishing as involvement with and commitment to the initial partner increases. Confidants bestowed approval on 92% of those males who had their first coital experience with a casual date or pick-up; only 77% of those intending to marry their partners received approving responses from others for their initiation into coitus. This disproportionate approval of casual liasons may reflect greater societal indulgence of male sexual experimentation where the partner is a "bad" girl, which is strongly suggested by her willingness to engage in coitus under such conditions. For females, however, approval or disapproval appears to be independent of the nature of the relationship within which the initial coital experience occurs. Based on our female college students, it appears that confidants were no more or less likely to bestow approval for coital experience where commitment characterized the relationship. Although an audience may be consoled by the rhetoric of love, love is not a mitigating factor in judgments concerning female premarital coitus as some have suggested.

For both males and females, modal experience of first coitus occurs prior to marriage. The modal male will have sexual relations with an initial partner for whom he feels neither love nor emotional attachment. The modal female, however, will be in love with her first partner and planning to marry him. The male and his partner will have coital relations a few times or perhaps never again; the female and her partner will have coitus more often and may, in fact, eventually marry. While the "scoring" ethic appears to organize much of the initial premarital coital behavior of males, the female usually enters into such relations in the service of the most conventional of goals — to secure an enduring dyadic relationship with a partner who, she hopes, will eventually make her his bride.

Of course, there are exceptions to each of these gender-linked models of adolescent sexual socialization. In addition to those who delay coital experience until after marriage, there are those "good" boys and "bad" girls who adopt the models of sexual conduct that describe the opposite sex. The "good" boy may find sexual experimentation unappealing or, in fact, impossible outside of a relationship to which he is committed. If he has premarital coitus, it will occur late in adolescence or in the early adult years within the context of an enduring love relationship. He is not the sort to "kiss and tell." The "bad" girl begins coital relations early in adolescence, casually sharing her favors with a series of boys. Her motivation may lie in the pleasure inherent in sexual relations or in the popularity that attends her sexual accessibility, providing consolation for the devalued status she quickly acquires in [or, indeed, may bring to (Reiss, 1954)] adolescent society. Or, of course, as in classic case studies of "acting out," motivation may be utterly extrinsic to both sexual pleasure and the contingencies of adolescent-status hierarchies.

American standards for sexual conduct have become more permissive in recent years. An apparent increase in the prevalance of premarital and extramarital coitus, the conventionalization of divorce, the greater visibility of "swinging" and "bisexual chic," the emergence of an institutional address for sadomasochism, and the redefinition (in some quarters) of homosexuality as a legitimate alternative life style provide some of the indicators commonly invoked to substantiate the claim that America is experiencing a "sexual revolution." Divergent opinions with respect to the specific criteria that determine an actual "sexual revolution" continue to divide the social science community. Although the data on adolescence accumulate slowly and the quality is uneven, the conclusion that sexual values and behavior are less circumspect than in the past appears to be incontrovertible. Nevertheless, there are those who hold that changes in the rates, the metric or the chronological boundaries of the normal developmental agenda with respect to the sexual are not sufficient to warrant the term "sexual revolution" in the absence of changes in the *meaning* of the sexual (Gagnon & Simon, 1970). With the exception of our data for college students, the handful of recent studies extant that evaluate change in sexual conduct focus predominately on the prevalence of behavior; the meaning of behavior has attracted less interest. Impressionistic data imply that traditional meanings continue to describe the preponderance of sexual experience.

Subsumed under the "sexual revolution" rhetoric is the concept of intergender convergence in premarital sexual behavior. The anticipation of gender convergence is usually traced to Terman (1938). Although premarital coitus was much more typical for males than females, Terman nonetheless reported a substantial increase in premarital coitus among females following World War I. Male rates were essentially stable during this period. In the following 30 years, a more or less constant gap was found in rates of male and female premarital coitus across a succession of studies. Then, another rise in the prevalence of female premarital coitus was found beginning with data collected in the late 1960s. Since there are apparent contradictions in the available data for high-school and college students, these will be treated separately in our brief review. The interested reader should consult Hopkins (1977) for an exhaustive review of the research relevant to this topic.

Coital experience continues to be exceptional among younger adolescents. Two of the three[2] available recent studies of high-school-age populations[3] find fewer than 1 in 10 boys and girls in early adolescence — the 15 birthday or the 9th grade — have engaged in coitus (Jessor & Jessor, 1975; Miller & Simon, 1974). The remaining piece of research, a study of two cohorts in a white nonmetropolitan community, reports that one in four 15-year-old boys and about half as many girls (13%) had had coital experience in 1970 (Vener & Stewart, 1974). By 1973, premarital coitus was significantly more prevalent among 15-year-olds in this same community, with 38% of the males and 24% of the females reporting an initial coital experience. Vener and Stewart concur with Zelnik and Kantner (1972) who, based on their national sample of females, predict an increase in the prevalence of coitus among younger adolescents.

By midadolescence, the percentage of youngsters with coital experience has increased substantially. For a state-wide sample of Illinois collected in 1972, Miller and Simon

---

[2] An additional study by R. C. Sorenson (1973) has been omitted because of severe methodological flaws in the sample and the reporting of the data.

[3] Not uncommonly, the usefulness of much research on sexual behavior is called into question because the data are assumed to provide a poor basis for generalization. The "volunteer effect," in its many forms, is believed to be a particularly distorting contaminant. Research by Bauman (1973) and Barker and Perlman (1975) does not support this claim. Bauman found no differences between volunteers and a random sample in sexual behavior and attitudes. The very well-designed study by Barker and Perlman reports a small number of significant relationships (to be expected by chance) in the personality traits of sex-research volunteers and those who volunteer for presumably innocuous research.

(1974) found that one in five adolescents have engaged in premarital coitus at the seventeenth birthday. Jessor and Jessor (1975) report that one-third of the twelfth-grade boys and about half (55%) of the girls living in a small western city in 1972 had full sexual relations. By 1973, Vener and Stewart (1974) found one in three 17-year-olds admitting to coital experience. Most striking is the virtual absence of any indication that the prevalence of premarital coitus is higher among contemporary adolescent males. For the 1973 high-school cohort, Vener and Stewart (1974) find a disproportionately greater number of experienced males in early adolescence; this disparity between males and females diminishes until, by 17, equal percentages of boys and girls report coital experience. This contrasts with Vener and Stewart's (1974) 1970 cohort where, expectedly, the disparity between males and females persisted across adolescence. The Illinois data also indicate a comparable prevalence of coital experience for boys and girls in each age group. In the small Rocky Mountain city studied by Jessor and Jessor (1975), consistently and substantially more females than males report coital experience throughout this four-year longitudinal study.

Several conclusions with reference to the prevalence of premarital coitus among high-school students are suggested by these studies. The percentage of contemporary adolescents who have engaged in coitus is greater than it ever has been in our society. Compared with earlier studies (e.g., Kinsey et al., 1948, 1953), a dramatic increase has occurred in the number of females with coital experience; there also appears to be a decline in the percentage of boys who have engaged in premarital coitus. In consequence, comparable levels of coital experience obtain for both genders. We might expect that females would engage in coitus a little earlier than their male agemates in the absence of a double standard for sexual experimentation. Girls tend to date boys who are somewhat older than they are and their sexual experimentation would be accelerated in their relationships with these more experienced boys. This, in fact, may be occurring. Finally, there is some suggestion that the metric of sexual development is shifting and greater numbers of youth are becoming sexually experienced earlier in the life cycle than in the past. Coupled with the earlier onset of puberty and, subsequently, fertility (Tanner, 1972) in conjunction with limited access to contraception, earlier coital experience among adolescents implies that public concern for adolescent fertility will continue to grow as the percentage of illegitimate births continues to increase (see Sklar & Berkov, 1974 for an excellent analysis of age, access to abortion, and illegitimacy).

The studies we have discussed are exceptionally competent, reflecting the lessons of the past. Nevertheless, they necessarily provide a limited basis for evaluating sexual standards among contemporary adolescents. The data do provide some support for our earlier claim that adolescents continue to hold traditional meanings where the sexual is concerned. Strong correlations between coital experience and other forms of deviant behavior (e.g., drug use, general delinquency, etc.) are reported in each study. Moreover, adolescents who have engaged in (or are about to engage in) coitus are more likely to be estranged from those institutions — the family, the church, the school — that serve to monitor and maintain commitments to conventional values. Thus sexual experimentation during adolescence apparently continues to be embedded in the social context of deviance. Furthermore, at least the vestiges of gender differences in the meaning of coitus can be inferred from the continuing disparity between boys and girls in the number of coital partners they report (Vener & Stewart, 1974). Although adolescents of both genders are about equally likely to have engaged in coitus, casual liasons continue to be preponderantly the province of males.

In the past, gender has been an important factor shaping the relationship between education and premarital coitus. Among males, the probability of premarital sexual relations declined markedly as the number of years in school increased (Kinsey et al., 1948). Since marriage was commonly deferred until the completion of schooling, coital experience (premarital or otherwise) occurred substantially later for college-educated males. Thus something of a gratification agenda more clearly organized around the sexual characterized less-educated males, where first coitus was more likely to occur early and to occur before marriage. Of course, the complications of premarital pregnancies accounted for early marriage in many instances.

For females, however, the prevalence of premarital coitus actually increased with education. But this was a spurious relationship; coital experience was not "caused" by education. Rather, the prevalence of premarital coitus was relatively stable across diverse educational groupings of women who had married at comparable ages (Kinsey et al., 1953). Premarital coitus was more prevalent among better-educated women simply because they tended to marry later than other women.

The influence of education on the sexual status of contemporary adolescents is unclear. Miller and Simon (1974) found the prevalence of coitus to be about twice as high for Illinois teenagers who did not aspire to education beyond high school. Since the school provides the sample frame for the overwhelming majority of research on adolescents, there are no extant studies treating the sexual development of contemporary youth after they have left the educational system. For this reason, we cannot comment with confidence on the stability of the relationship between education, premarital coitus, and marriage in the years since the work of Kinsey et al. (1948, 1953) was published. Our earlier discussion of gender differences in the nature of the relationship with the initial partner in conjunction with the negative association between educational aspirations and coital experience among Illinois adolescents encourages us to speculate that the effects of education and marriage continue to impact differently on the coital experience of the two genders.

Moreover, because of the reliance on school populations for data on sexual development, our consideration of coital experience in late adolescence is necessarily restricted to college students. A dozen or so studies reporting the prevalence of premarital coitus among students during the last decade are extant. The actual prevalence figures vary rather widely across these studies, suggesting that the normative climate and, hence, the experience of coitus are both highly variable in different college settings. Despite this variability, the data reported in these studies provide a reasonable basis for certain conclusions.

The prevalence of premarital coitus increases during the college experience but most dramatically in the early years, attenuating by the junior and senior years. Averaging the various studies, an estimated two females in five attending college have engaged in premarital coitus; for males, the prevalence is higher, probably averaging about three in five. These estimates, based on a number of studies (Hopkins, 1977, Table 3) indicate a substantial increase in coital experience among college girls in the past 10 years. The prevalence of coitus among college males has remained fairly stable, although they may be experiencing a modest increase as well.

As the prevalence of premarital coitus increases, the disparity between males and females may decline. The two studies finding the largest proportion of youths with coital experience also report comparable levels of male and female involvement. In their sample of college students in the Rocky Mountains, Jessor and Jessor (1975) find 85% of the females and 82% of the males have engaged in coitus by the fourth year. Baumann and Wilson (1974) report that 73% of the students of both genders have coital experience. At the other extreme, Lewis and Burr (1975) find fewer than half the students sampled in seven colleges and universities have had full sexual relations. There is a substantial disparity between the two genders in this study; 29% of the females and twice that many males (60%) have engaged in premarital coitus. Generally, the magnitude of the disparity in coital experience reported by the two genders is greater in those studies where coital experience is found to be less predominate.

Of course, those concerned with the mores of college students have largely ignored the recent transformation in both the size and, accordingly, the composition of the college population. The years following World War II brought an experiment in mass higher education that knows no historical precedent. As college enrollments increased to include about half of the population at risk, the student body became more heterogeneous. Recognizing the contextual as well as the structural effects of college attendance (and tracking for college during high school), the backgrounds, aspirations, and values of students today nevertheless correspond more closely to those of youth in general than in the past when college was the preserve of the American elite. To an unknown extent, then, the inflated prevalence of premarital coitus among college students — once among the least sexually experienced of all groups — is conditioned by their greater heterogeneity. Any comparison of contemporary college students with earlier cohorts is contaminated by this bias; it is not unique to a concern for sexual development.

Societal concern for the sexual status of the young rests on three, presumably undesirable, situations that adolescents may encounter following premarital coitus: an unwanted pregnancy; damage to reputation and, therefore, a decline in the possibility of marriage to a preferred partner; and mental health or developmental difficulties. Changes in the technology of and access to fertility control have altered the probability of pregnancy just as changes in the normative social climate have modified the role of coital experience in certifying notoriety. There are no systematic data that indicate that premarital coitus "potentiates" mental health difficulties among contemporary youth. Testing this possibility, Diament (1970) found sexual behavior independent of indicators of maladjustment in a sample of college students. Moreover, males and females who had high self-esteem also had engaged in coitus with a greater number of partners compared to those with low self-esteem at a "liberal" college in New York state (Perlman, 1974).

We noted earlier that the meanings of premarital coitus could not be understood without understanding the normative context in which it occurs. In some cases, of course, the individual can select a supportive context for his or her behavior from a number of available choices. But where behavior or values deviate sharply from a dominant single standard, the probability of a deviant self-image increases. Thus it is not surprising that Diament (1970) found significantly greater maladjustment among the college males in his sample who held very conservative sexual standards. The diversity in views of female sexual conduct implies an available support network for contemporary female adolescents whose values place them at different points on the permissiveness continuum. Among males, however, this is not the case, at least where antisexual values are concerned. Such views mark the youth as highly deviant from the gender-role expectations of both peers and the larger society. Thus his denial of the sexual rather than an enthusiastic commitment to it appears to signal more certainly developmental difficulties.

The relationship between the normative climate and the behavior and values of individuals is neither simple nor necessarily direct. Nevertheless, change in any one of these reflects or anticipates changes in the others. Values with reference to premarital coitus have become more permissive in recent years, the prevalence of premarital coital experience has increased and the context of judgment has become less monolithic, marking societal resignation if not approval.

We have marshaled evidence in support of our contention that behavioral convergence need not imply a convergence in the meanings or the motives held by the two genders. Such a convergence does, however, promise certain modifications. Elsewhere, we have argued that gender convergence in premarital coitus is both consequential and causal of the disappearance of the "bad girl" (Miller & Simon, 1974). As communities have become more homogeneous, access to girls with the devalued racial or class characteristics that mark their eligibility for this role has become more difficult. Under such conditions, male sexual experience depends to a greater extent on the willingness of a "good girl," and this implies a greater accommodation to the rhetoric of love among boys.

The increasing salience of the rhetoric of love among boys in conjunction with increasing sexual experimentation among girls suggests the possibility of gender convergence not only in sexual behavior, but also in the interpersonal scripts that organize adolescent sexual behavior. A single standard, what Reiss (1966) has called "permissiveness with affection," may eventually dominate the sexual strategies of both boys and girls as many scholars of adolescence seem to think it will. But such an outcome will not, in itself, certify a full convergence of the two genders with reference to the erotic. Recall that interpersonal scripts function, among other things, as socially accepted strategies for satisfying the requirements (or, more correctly, some of the requirements) of the intrapsychic. Full gender convergence assumes more than merely a convergence in behavior; it also assumes a convergence in the kinds of elements (or symbols) that are imbued with erotic meaning by the intrapsychic. These symbols provide the raw materials from which erotic motive and impulse are forged. The preceding discussion of gender differences in the conduct of the initial coital experience implies continuing disparities between the two genders, not only in the interpersonal scripts, but also in the intrapsychic. Our subsequent examination of the limited data available on arousal and fantasy underscores the profound gender differences in the intrapsychic scripts.

Males disproportionately experience sexual arousal in response to potentially erotic symbols. Of course, the genders do not share equal access to the pornographic materials that provide the principal celebration of explicitly sexual symbols in our culture. The consumption of sexually explicit media is gender-significant behavior; males are encouraged to seek out pornography, while females are protected from it. Gender differences in exposure to pornographic material in our national sample of college students suggest that the agents of socialization are not fully successful in this regard. While 95% of our male college students have been exposed to some form of pornography, as many as 75% of the females have also seen such material. Males learn to invest erotic meaning in the explicit symbolization of sexual acts and sexual actors, while females are trained to deny the erotic meaning of these same symbols. Parents and peers nervously contemplate the role adequacy of boys who are visibly repulsed by sexually explicit material, just as girls who exhibit an appetite for pornography elicit profound concern from significant others. Unpublished data for our college students indicate that males were about three times as likely (45%) as females (14%) to report sexual arousal[4] following exposure to pornog-

---

[4]Heiman (1974, cited in Rook and Hammen, 1978) has demonstrated that, compared to males, females have more difficulty discerning physical arousal. The greater disparity between physiological arousal and its recognition in females has profound consequences for psychosexual development. It is not particularly relevant here, however, where our concern is for the subjective meanings attached to potentially erotic symbols.

raphy (literature, drawings, or stag films). The response distribution for females is bimodal, with about equal percentages reporting "indifference" (41%) and "disgust" (37%). Fewer males report "indifference" (28%) and the rather small percentage who find pornography disgusting (15%) is comparable to the percentage of females who report arousal. Thus the agents of socialization are more effective in shaping the meaning attached to potentially erotic material by the two genders than they are in controlling access to such material.

Because of gender differences specific to pornography, the data cited above are less than conclusive with respect to our assertion that males respond sexually to potentially erotic symbols more readily than females. Somewhat more compelling are the gender differences in arousal from seeing a nude person of the opposite sex; 84% of our male college students but only about a quarter (24%) of the females said that such an experience had caused them to feel "greatly" or "somewhat" aroused. Perhaps this disparity with reference to the meaning of nudity is a condition of the training of both genders to regard female nudity as erotic and male nudity as relatively nonerotic. After all, the "sex symbols" of our culture are preponderately female. But the data suggest otherwise. Arousal at the sight of a nude person of the same gender elicited minimal levels of arousal in both females (2%) and males (1%). Thus it appears that explicitly sexual symbols articulate with the intrapsychic life of males, leading to the experience of arousal more certainly than is the case with females.

Interestingly, the gender disparity in arousal is much smaller where the erotic potential is less explicit. Among our college students, 28% of the males and 20% of the females said they were "greatly" or "somewhat" aroused by popular fiction. Similarly, 29% of the males and 23% of the females reported that they were aroused by dancing. Of course, both of these potential sources of arousal invoke interpersonal scripts. To "work," they require a capacity to infuse social behavior with erotic meaning, a capacity that is learned primarily during adolescence and the early adult years. Although the more explicitly sexual intrapsychic life of the male may give him some advantage in this regard, the magnitude of that advantage appears to be much smaller than we would have assumed.

The sources of sexual arousal are diffuse and the few we have discussed here necessarily provide a defective sample of the variety of experiences that elicit arousal. Nevertheless, our review of gender differences in the sources of arousal reinforces our thesis that marked differences characterize the intrapsychic life of the two genders. Males are much more likely to invest erotic meaning in explicitly sexual symbols. Moreover, the qualification, "explicit," is critical; where symbols are subtle, gender differences are considerably muted. Our subsequent consideration of the content of sexual fantasies suggests additional qualifications.

Sexual fantasies are the product of both cultural and idiosyncratic experience. The repertoire of erotic symbols available for fantasy construction is derived from the vagaries of autobiography as well as the shared experience of subculture and society. Thus the intrapsychic sexual life of the individual is fashioned of materials ranging from the highly idiosyncratic to the universal. With puberty and the onset of sexual activity (or the anticipation of sexual activity), a tendency towards a kind of psychic parsimony leads most individuals to abandon the more eccentric symbols. These fall to obscurity; alternatively, they may be attached to the nonsexual and/or they may be reworked or disguised to render them usable to the erotic. But the outrageously bizarre or uneconomical recede as the capacity develops to forge coherent, elaborated scripts from the hodgepodge of potentially erotic symbols the individual has accumulated. Since the coherent fantasy is an imperfect reflection of the theoretically possible, the narrative styles describing the sexual that are dominant in the society tend to dominate the intrapsychic script or fantasy construction as well. The symbols and action in fantasy are predominately sterotypic, they are products of social life.

It is the stereotyped character of fantasy rather than some property inherent in the biological organism that accounts for the crude correspondence commonly observed between reality and fantasy. Returning to our college students, the intrapsychic script most frequently cited concerned "petting or having intercourse with someone you are fond of or in love with." An overwhelming majority of males (87%) and females (79%) said that some part of the time when they were masturbating or were sexually aroused their "thoughts or daydreams" involved sexual relations within a context of affection. It appears, then, that the normatively prescribed activities of sociosexual development are rehearsed in the fantasy constructions of most adolescents. These rehearsals may entail improbable feats with improbable partners, but such improbabilities do not prevent recognition of the ways in which fantasies function for most to reinforce a commitment to the normative.

Interestingly, the genders diverge here. A parallel item — "petting or having intercourse with someone you don't know" — was the second most frequently cited item (75%) by our college males. In other words, the most common theme in male sexual fantasies concerns explicit sexual behavior; the presence or absence of emotional involvement apparently does not constrain the unfolding erotic script. Very few females (22%) indicated that they had ever had "stranger" fantasies. While the "zipless fuck" enjoys an undeniable celebrity in the popular imagination, it does not appear to be particularly salient in the imaginations of young women. Among females, emotional involvement rivals sexual behavior in significance. Indeed, the percentage of females citing "doing nonsexual things with someone you are fond of or in love with" (74%) is roughly equivalent to the percentage indicating that their fantasies included sexual behavior within a context of affection. The devalued role assigned to emotional involvement in the erotic commitments of males is underscored by the substantially smaller percentage (48%) reporting nonsexual themes in their fantasies. The explicitly sexual is not particularly devalued, repressed, or de-eroticized by females as some have argued. Rather, the investment of erotic meaning in both explicitly sexual and nonsexual symbols appears to be contingent on the emotional context. The two genders evaluate the meaning of potentially erotic symbols using distinctive sets of criteria. For males, the explicitly sexual is endowed with erotic meaning regardless of the emotional context. For females, the emotional context is endowed with erotic meaning without regard for the presence or absence of explicitly sexual symbols.

Since the emotional context forms the keystone of erotic life for females, their reactions to pornography discussed earlier can now be reinterpreted in terms of this conclusion. The "indifference" or "disgust" registered by our college females who had seen pornographic materials represent not a reaction to what is there — explicitly sexual symbols — so much as a reaction to what is not there — a sense of emotional commitment or involvement between the actors. The absence of romantic themes rather than the conjuction of genitalia depicted precludes the investment of erotic meaning in this genre of pornography for all but the exceptional female. Erotic meaning is denied because the content of pornographic material violates the norms that shape the realities (and apparently the fantasies as well) of female sexual expression.

More generally, exotic or nonnormative sexual practices have only minor constituencies. This is, of course, almost necessarily true where the referent is sexual behavior. But the freedom from normative constraints commonly presumed by those who have studied fantasy is not sustained by the available data. Among our college students, no more than about a third indicated that their fantasy constructions had ever included such themes as voyeurism, homosexuality, sadism, or masochism. Fantasies concerning "homosexual activity" are the least common, reported by 3% of both males and females. Neither do the themes of dominance and passivity that are central to male and female gender roles commonly find explicit expression in the fantasy constructions of the two genders. About a quarter of the males (24%) and substantially fewer females (6%) said their fantasies had ever included "forcing someone to do something they didn't want to do." The constituency for masochism is equally small; 21% of the females and 11% of the males reported fantasying about "being forced to do something you didn't want to do." It should be noted that while the popularity of explicitly sadistic or masochistic fantasies is limited, the directions observed in the gender differences are consonant with gender-role stereotypes. Similarly, more males (35%) than females (25%) indicated that their sexual fantasies had included "seeing other people doing sexual things," as we might have expected. But since the popular stereotype of the "peeping Tom" dictates that he be a male figure, we would not have anticipated that fully a quarter of the females would report fantasy constructions entailing voyeurism.

The relationship between the intrapsychic and the interpersonal is obviously complex. The strain towards some semblance of congruence between psychosexual and sociosexual experience is a developmental problem for many adolescents. But ample evidence of a relationship is provided by the congruence between fantasy constructions and self-reported behavior. Love and affection, the dominant themes in female fantasy constructions, find expression in what Reiss (1966) has called "permissiveness with affection." Although females continue to hold both moral and practical reservations with respect to premarital coital behavior, these reservations diminish as the intensity of dyadic involvement increases. The available data on the intrapsychic scripts of males would lead us to anticipate that the major obstacle to the initial coital experience for most was locating a willing partner. But if this were the case, love or affection should provide the context for coital activity in the overwhelming majority of cases (since the majority of girls in the pool of potential partners stipulate affection as a necessary precondition for coital behavior). But this is not what happens. A large proportion — perhaps as much as half — have their first coital experience in the context of a casual relationship. There are probably two factors accounting for this anomaly. The limited interaction skills and general sociosexual incompetence of many males during adolescence effectively precludes access, sexual or otherwise, to "good girls." Moreover, social expectations stress the virtue of "good girls." Echoes of the "Madonna complex" persist where boys are reluctant to damage the hymens, soil the reputations, or "get in trouble" the girls for whom they genuinely feel affection.

Naive conceptions of the sexual (those that view sexual behavior as having a unitary, overriding meaning) have produced a research literature almost entirely deficient in theoretical linkages. Moreover, some minimal commitment to a *verstehen* approach, which is available in the literature on virtually every other aspect of human behavior, is almost unknown in the study of human sexual behavior. In effect, these elements combine to provide a research literature that is, for the most part, both unsophisticated and inarticulate. Ironically, the poverty of behaviorism is particularly apparent with reference to a category of behavior typically viewed as especially powerful.

Although this state of affairs has generally impoverished our understanding of human sexuality, it has been particularly costly with reference to the understanding of adolescent psychosexual development. The transitional character of adolescence, where the preparation for postadolescent sexual commitments is more significant in most cases than the effects of specific adolescent sexual experiences, requires an approach that is sensitive to the underlying *processes* (expressed more often than not unevenly in behavior) particularly critical.

The uncertainty, if not "turmoil," that describes general expectations of adolescence has rarely been confirmed when reasonable samples of adolescents have been examined. It may be that we have looked for the expressions of uncertainty or turmoil in the wrong places, seeking it in the behavior of adolescents rather than in the *process* through which individual adolescents attempt to give meaning (or test the limits of meaning) in behavior. Equally critical is the attempt to make that provisional meaning articulate with his or her larger sense of self. A sense of self, it should be noted, that is itself provisional as it represents a confluence of several, unevenly scheduled dimensions of growth.

We have outlined a model of adolescent psychosexual development that, despite certain differences, shares with most other developmental perspectives a view of individual development as a continuing and dynamic process. Within this process, many forms of behavior can be productively considered as the outcome of two forces: the history of development the individual brings to the contemporary moment and the contingencies that organize the contemporary moment for the individual. The model we have attempted to describe is derived from one basic theoretical assumption, that sexual behavior is "constructed" rather than "expressive" (Berger & Luckman, 1967; Simon & Miller, 1977). However rooted in biology human sexuality may appear, it can only be understood in terms of a complex process, highly interactive with the surrounding, sometimes rapidly changing, social context. We have examined the available data on the sexual experience of contemporary adolescents. The data are consistent with the model, though clearly insufficient for its validation. We hope the model contributes to strengthening a concern for the existential experience of adolescent psychosexual development and brings us closer to a scientific literature wherein past and present adolescents can better recognize themselves and their own experiences.

REFERENCES

Barker, W. J., and Perlman, D. Volunteer bias and personality traits in sexual standards research. *Archives of Sexual Behavior*, 1975, *4*(2), 161–171.

Bauman, K. D., and Wilson, R. R. Sexual behavior of unmarried university students in 1968 and 1972. *Journal of Sex Research*, 1974, *10*, 327–333.

Bauman, K. E. Volunteer bias in a study of sexual knowledge, attitudes, and behavior. *Journal of Marriage and the Family*, 1973, *35*, 27–31.

Berger, P. L., and Luckmann, T. *The social construction of reality*. London: Penguin, 1967.

Blos, P. *On adolescence: A psychoanalytic interpretation*. Glencoe, Ill.: Free Press, 1962.

Buff, S. A. Greasers, dupers, and hippies: Three responses to the adult world. In L. K. Howe (Ed.), *The white majority: Between poverty and affluence*. New York: Random House, 1970.

Carns, D. E. Talking about sex: Notes on first coitus and the double standard. *Journal of Marriage and the Family*, 1973, *35*, 677–688.

Diament, L. Premarital sexual behavior, attitudes, and emotional adjustment. *Journal of Social Psychology,* 1970, *82,* 75–80.

Douvan, E., and Adelson, J. *The adolescent experience.* New York: Wiley, 1966.

Erikson, E. H. *Childhood and society.* New York: Norton, 1950.

———. Growth and crises of the health personality. In E. H. Erikson (Ed.), *Identity and the life cycle.* Psychological Issues, 1959 *1* (1), pp. 50–100.

Ford, C. S., and Beach, F. A. *Patterns of sexual behavior.* New York: Harper & Row, 1951.

Freud, S. Three essays on the theory of sexuality. In *Three contributions to the theory of sex.* New York: Dutton, 1962.

Gagnon, J. H. Scripts and the coordination of sexual conduct. In J. K. Cole and R. Deinstbrier (Eds.), *Nebraska Symposium on Motivation* (Vol. 21). Lincoln: University of Nebraska Press, 1974.

Gagnon, J. H., and Simon, W. Prospects for change in American sexual patterns. *Medical Aspects of Human Sexuality,* 1970, *4,* 100–117.

———. *Sexual conduct.* Chicago: Aldine, 1973.

Hopkins, J. R. Sexual behavior in adolescence. *Journal of Social Issues,* 1977, *33*(2), 67–85.

Jessor, S., and Jessor, R. Transition from virginity to nonvirginity among youth: A social-psychological study over time. *Developmental Psychology,* 1975, *11,* 473–484.

Keniston, K. Postadolescence (youth) and historical change. In J. Zubin and A. M. Freedman (Eds.), *The psychopathology of adolescence.* New York: Grune & Stratton, 1970.

Kinsey, A. C., Pomeroy, W. B., and Martin, C. E. *Sexual behavior in the human male.* Philadelphia: Saunders, 1948.

Kinsey, A. C., Pomeroy, W. B., Martin, C. E., and Gebhard, P. H. *Sexual behavior in the human female.* Philadelphia: Saunders, 1953.

Kohlberg, L. A cognitive-developmental analysis of children's sex role concepts and attitudes. In E. E. Maccoby (Ed.), *The development of sex differences.* Stanford, Calif.: Stanford University Press, 1966.

———. Stage and sequence: The cognitive development approach to socialization. In D. Goslin (Ed.), *Handbook of socialization theory and research.* Chicago: Rand McNally, 1969.

Lewis, R. A., and Burr, W. R. Premarital coitus and commitment among college students. *Archives of Sexual Behavior,* 1975, *4,* 73–79.

Loevinger, J. *Ego development.* San Francisco: Jossey-Bass, 1976.

Miller, P. Y., and Simon, W. Adolescent sexual behavior: Context and change. *Social Problems,* 1974, *22,* 58–76.

Millet, K. *Sexual politics.* Garden City, N.Y.: Doubleday, 1970.

Offer, D. *The psychological world of the teenager.* New York: Basic Books, 1969.

Offer, D., and Offer, J. *From teenage to young manhood: A psychological study,* New York: Basic Books, 1975a.

Offer, D., and Simon, W. Stages of sexual development. In B. J. Saddock, H. I. Kaplan, and A. M. Freedman (Eds.), *The sexual experience.* Baltimore, Md.: Williams & Wilkins, 1976.

Offer, J., and Offer, D. The sexual behavior and attitudes of one group of normal males (ages 13–22). Paper presented at the annual meetings of the American Sociological Association, San Francisco, 1975b.

Perlman, D. Self-esteem and sexual permissiveness. *Journal of Marriage and the Family,* 1974, *36,* 470–473.

Reiss, I. L. The double standard in premarital sexual intercourse: A neglected concept. *Social Forces,* 1954, *23,* 224–230.

————. The sexual renaissance: A summary and analysis. *Journal of Social Issues*, 1966, *22*(2), 123–137.

————. *The social context of premarital sexual permissiveness*. New York: Holt, Rinehart & Winston, 1967.

Robinson, P. *The modernization of sex*. New York: Harper & Row, 1976.

Rook, K. S., and Hammen, C. L. A cognitive perspective on the experience of sexual arousal. *Journal of Social Issues,* 1977, *33*(2), 7–29.

Simon, W. The social, the sexual, and the erotic: On the complexities of sexual scripts. In J. K. Cole and R. Deinstbrier (Eds.), *Nebraska Symposium on Motivation,* Lincoln: University of Nebraska Press, 1974.

Simon, W., and Miller, P. Y. Infant and childhood sexual experience as a substitute for God. Paper presented at the Conference on Sex and Its Psychosocial Derivatives, Stanford University, Palo Alto, Calif., 1977.

Simon, W., Berger, A. S., and Gagnon, J. S. Beyond anxiety anf fantasy: The coital experiences of college youth. *Journal of Youth and Adolescence,* 1972, *1*, 203–222.

Sklar, J., and Berkov, B. Abortion, illegitimacy and the American birth rate. *Science,* 1974, *185,* 909–915.

Sorenson, R. C. *Adolescent sexuality in contemporary America*. New York: World, 1973.

Tanner, J. M. Sequence, tempo and individual variation in growth and development of boys and girls aged twelve to sixteen. In J. Kagan and R. Coles (Eds.), *Twelve to sixteen: Early adolescence*. New York: Norton, 1972.

Terman, L. M. *Psychological factors in marital happiness*. New York and London: McGraw-Hill, 1938.

Vener, A. M., and Stewart, C. S. Adolescent sexual behavior in middle America revisited: 1970–1973. *Journal of Marriage and the Family,* 1974, *36,* 728–735.

Zelnik, M., and Kantner, J. F. The probability of premarital intercourse. *Social Science Research,* 1972, *1,* 335–341.

CHAPTER 12

Friendship and the Peer Group in Adolescence

John C. Coleman

There is little doubt that friends, companions, and others of a similar age can play an unusually important role in the development of the individual throughout the adolescent years. Textbooks of adolescence are unanimous in assigning a central place to the peer group both as a source of influence and of support, and perhaps therefore it is not surprising to find the role of the peer group featuring as an integral part of the mythology of adolescence. Where stereotypes exist, close friendships between teenagers are distrusted, customs and fashions of young people are criticized, and the negative or destructive forces abroad in society generally are perceived as emanating directly from the adolescent subculture. It will be the purpose of this chapter to examine carefully the empirical evidence that has accumulated on this subject and to attempt to answer dispassionately at least some of the major questions that have arisen concerning friendship and the peer group in adolescence.

As is frequently the case in the social sciences the literature is scattered and uncoordinated. Thus in order to create a structure it has been decided (1) to make a clear distinction between issues involving friendship and those issues concerned with the wider role of the peer group and (2) to organize the material under six separate headings. For convenience these have been expressed in terms of questions, and all are, of course, closely interrelated. As far as friendship is concerned three issues will be considered:

1. In what manner does the importance and nature of friendship change with age during adolescence?
2. Is friendship important in different ways for boys and girls?
3. What effect does family background have on patterns of friendship?

Three questions will also be discussed where the role of the peer group is concerned:

1. What factors are related to popularity?
2. What factors are most likely to produce conformity of behavior in the peer group?
3. How significant is parent-peer conflict?

Before we turn to a consideration of these questions, however, it will be as well to discuss briefly some of the reasons which underlie the assumption that the peer group is of special significance during adolescence. Of course, it should be borne in mind that friends and friendships occupy an important role throughout childhood and that in some respects the peer group has a continuous part to play in the socialization process during the whole span of school and college years. That having been said, however, there are undoubtedly special factors operating during adolescence that do elevate the peer group to a position of unusual prominence; these factors stem from the nature of the adolescent process. It has become acceptable in the last few years to use the term transitional period when describing adolescence (Lambert et al., 1972; Offer & Offer, 1976). The phrase draws attention to the fact that the individual, during this stage in the life cycle, is in transition from childhood to adulthood and thus has to cope with all the change and adaptation implicit in any such transition from one state to another. Where adolescence is concerned, three aspects of the transitional process may be mentioned, all of which serve to highlight the importance of the peer group. In the first place, during the teenage years the young person faces a marked upheaval in physical development as well as considerable reorganization in the social and emotional spheres of life. Such fundamental changes force on the individual the necessity of coping with new and unknown experiences as well as creating a major challenge to identity and self-esteem. Circumstances of this sort usually result in greatly increased dependence on support from others, especially those who are facing or have recently faced similar events in their own lives.

In the second place, an integral feature of adolescence is the gradual severance of the early emotional ties with the parents. This is a complex process, and there are significant differences not only between boys and girls, not only between those from different home backgrounds, but also between any two individuals in the way in which independence is finally achieved. Nonetheless, it is true to say that at some level all adolescents are involved in a process whereby adult standards are questioned, adult authority is challenged, and the emotional dependence on the parents formed in early childhood is gradually weakened. Thus paradoxically at a time when uncertainty and self-doubt is greatest and when support is most needed, many adolescents find themselves in an emotional position where it is difficult, if not impossible, to turn to their parents. Under such circumstances it is hardly surprising that peers play an unusually important role. Third and last, it is in the nature of transitions that they involve experimentation. A common feature of movement from one state to another is the necessity to try out new forms of behavior; this is particularly true of adolescents. Erik H. Erikson (1968) has used the term psychosocial moratorium to describe the freedom allowed to young people by the adult world for just this sort of reason. Teenagers have to learn how, as adults, their social behavior will be controlled. They have to discover what sorts of behavior are acceptable and what are not, which facets of their personality are liked and which are rejected. Above all, they have to find out how their needs and motives interact best with the social environment and which roles are compatible with their own developing identities. This process of discovery, sometimes rewarding, sometimes painful and embarrassing, is dependent on the involvement of a peer group.

For these three reasons, then, and because of the nature of the transitional period, it seems probable that the part played by friendship and the peer group can make a significant difference to adolescent development. Just how significant this difference is will be clarified as we turn to a consideration of the six questions spelled out here.

FRIENDSHIP

In What Manner Does the Importance and Nature of Friendship Change with Age during Adolescence?

In view of the reasons advanced to explain the importance of the peer group during adolescence it seems not unlikely that the nature and meaning of friendship will be determined at least to some extent by the age of those concerned. Thus the stage each individual has reached in progressing through the transitional period will undoubtedly affect the quality of his or her relationships. Writers who have been concerned with adolescent friendship have by and large been of this opinion. Anderson (1939) for example, illustrated the ways in which friendships became both more organized and more differentiated as the individuals involved grew older. In addition, his observations led him to conclude that the peer group becomes more effective in motivating behavior as well as more influential in determining attitudes and values as a function of age. A series of studies carried out by Horrocks and his colleagues (Horrocks & Thompson, 1946; Thompson & Horrocks, 1947; Horrocks & Baker, 1951) concerning the stability of friendship at different ages represents another illustration of early work in the field. These studies showed that friendship becomes increasingly more stable from the age of 5 to 18, with only minor fluctuations in a trend that is almost linear. The method used here involved asking subjects to name their three best friends and repeating the same question two weeks later. From this the authors derived a measure of friendship fluctuation based on the number of changes made during the two-week period. Horrocks makes clear that there was considerable fluctuation, even at 17 and 18, in spite of the steadily increasing stability with age. He explained this by arguing that most adolescents will have more than three good friends; thus, to a certain extent, chance factors will influence which of the three are chosen on any particular day. Douvan and Gold (1966), reviewing this work, are critical of the method used, arguing that a two-week time-span is narrowly restricted. They point out that the method gives no information at all on the nature of the relationships being studied, and provides only a limited perspective on the concept of stability.

To date the most thorough analysis of changes in friendship as a result of age is probably that of Douvan and Adelson (1966), although it is important to note that their developmental data relate only to girls. They distinguish between three phases of adolescence — early, middle, and late — and report quite distinct patterns associated with each of these stages. In the early phase (11-, 12-, and 13-year-olds) friendship appears to "center on the activity rather than on the interaction itself." Friends are people with whom things can be done, but there is as yet no notion of depth or mutuality or even of much feeling in the friendship relationship. In middle adolescence (14-, 15-, 16-year-olds) the stress is almost entirely on security. What is needed in a friend at this stage is that she should be loyal and trustworthy — someone who will not betray you behind your back. Douvan and Adelson (1966) reasonably ask the question: "Why such an emphasis on loyalty?" Their answer is twofold. First, that the girl is seeking in the other some response to or mirroring of herself, that she is in need of someone who is going through the same problems at the same time. In some senses it could be argued that the middle-adolescent girl is dealing with her problems by identification, and therefore the friend who leaves her leaves her to cope with her impulses on her own. The authors explain it by saying that: "With so much invested in the friendship, it is no wonder that the girl is so dependent on it" (1966, p. 189). Second, the authors point out that middle adolescence is the time when a girl is likely to first begin to date. Therefore she will need a friend as a source of guidance and support, as a person with whom she can share confidences and as someone who will not abandon her in favor of boys.

In contrast to all this, by late adolescence (17-year-olds and over) friendship, according to Douvan and Adelson, is a more relaxed, shared experience. "Needing friendship less, they are less haunted by fears of being abandoned and betrayed" (1966, p. 192). Although being able to share confidences is still important, by this time there is a greater emphasis on the friend's personality and interests — on what she can offer to the relationship — and a greater degree of appreciation of individual differences. Furthermore by this time more important heterosexual relationships are likely to have developed, which do of course have the effect of lessening the investment in same-sex friendships. In this outline of Douvan and Adelson's findings the emphasis has been entirely on girls. This is because their interview was used on large samples of girls between the ages of 11 and 18, and it only included a small sample of boys in the 14- to 16-year age range. Where comparisons were possible, however, they did point up some important sex differences; these will be outlined in the next section.

It is of interest to note that Douvan and Adelson's developmental findings were foreshadowed in an earlier study carried out by Powell (1955). He used a word-association technique and by comparing reaction times to neutral and stimulus words, he was able to get a measure of anxiety concerning different adolescent issues. It may be seen from Figure 1 that anxiety concerning friendship appears to be at a peak for both boys and girls in the middle-adolescent age range. It should not pass without comment that, although based on completely different methodologies, the studies of Powell (1955) and Douvan and Adelson (1966) come to identical conclusions concerning this particular aspect of friendship patterns in adolescence. Figure 2 has been included to give some measure of comparison between the amount of anxiety expressed over friendship and that felt about another salient issue. The direction of the differences may cause surprise to some readers!

More recent work has also supported Douvan and Adelson's (1966) account of the developmental process associated with friendship. In a wide-ranging study of a variety of relationships in adolescence (Coleman, 1974), the author was able to show a very similar age pattern to that described by other workers where friendship was concerned. The study involved a comparison of 11-, 13-, 15-, and 17-year-olds and the results indicated clearly that the greatest insecurity in friendship and fear of rejection occurred at 15 years of age.

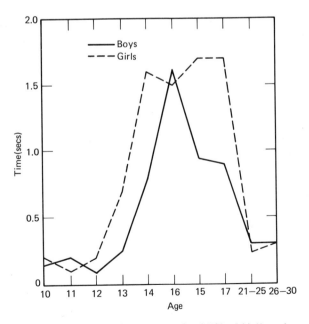

Figure 1. Mean differences in reaction times between neutral and "friendship" words on a word-association test (after Powell, 1955).

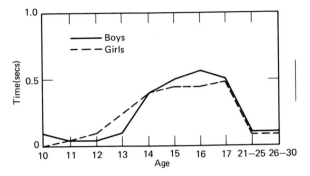

Figure 2. Mean differences in reaction times between neutral and "parent-child" words on a word-association test (after Powell, 1955).

This study will be outlined in more detail below. Finally Bigelow and La Gaipa (1975) carried out some research in which they asked children and adolescents to describe their expectations of their best friends. The results, which are illustrated in Table 1, indicate the way in which different dimensions of friendship emerge as a function of grade level. The authors draw particular attention to the late appearance of concepts, such as loyalty, intimacy, the opportunity of giving help, and so on. Such dimensions, it will be recalled, were associated by Douvan and Adelson (1966) with the stage of middle adolescence, and thus their appearance in this study at grades 7 and 8 provides satisfying corroborative evidence.

In conclusion, we need have little doubt that age is a factor that needs to be taken into account where adolescent friendship is concerned. Empirical findings are consistent with

Table 1. Percentage Incidence Distributed by Grade Levels for Friendship Expectation Dimensions

| Dimension | Onset | Grade level[a] | | | | | | | |
		1	2	3	4	5	6	7	8
Help - friend as giver	2	5	_12_	14	7	14	25	33	35
Common activities	2	3	_7_	32	52	24	40	60	60
Propinquity	3	7	5	_9_	12	12	20	38	32
Stimulation value	3	2	3	_12_	23	30	51	52	61
Organized play	3	2	0	_15_	26	9	10	17	20
Demographic similarity	3	0	3	_7_	35	15	15	10	23
Evaluation	3	2	5	_13_	13	17	33	21	30
Acceptance	4	3	0	5	_9_	9	18	18	38
Admiration	4	0	0	5	_23_	17	24	32	41
Incremental prior interaction	4	2	7	4	_10_	10	17	32	34
Loyalty and commitment	5	0	0	2	5	_10_	20	40	34
Genuineness	6	0	3	0	2	5	_12_	10	32
Help - friend as receiver	6	2	5	3	5	2	_12_	13	25
Intimacy potential	7	0	0	0	0	0	0	_8_	20
Common interests	7	0	0	5	7	0	5	_30_	18
Similarity - attitudes and values	7	0	0	0	0	2	3	_10_	8

Source: Published in B. J. Bigelow and J. J. La Gaipa (1975), p. 858. American Psychological Association.

Note. Underlined scores represent grade levels of onset.

[a]At each grade level, $n = 60$.

the expectation that young people will have different needs at different stages, needs that are reflected in the nature of the friendship relationship. In particular the results of research are cumulative in the impression they give that the middle-adolescent years are the ones of greatest stress in this respect, especially for girls, although we will be examining this issue in greater detail in the following section. For both sexes, however, this middle period represents a stage during which friendships play a particularly important role, and no doubt resulting from this, are unusually vulnerable to jealousy, insecurity, and fears of disloyalty.

Is Friendship Important in Different Ways for Boys and Girls?

Surprisingly few writers have paid much attention to this variable in considering friendship in adolescence. Horrocks and his colleagues, who were mentioned earlier, did discriminate between boys and girls but showed minimal differences between the sexes where friendship fluctuation was concerned. The work of Powell (1955) has indicated that anxiety over friendship followed much the same age course for males and females, but that the anxiety level of girls remained higher than that of boys for 2 to 3 years. This finding is consistent with the conclusions drawn by Douvan and Adelson (1966). They, it will be recalled, collected data on girls throughout the adolescent age range but on boys only between the ages of 14 and 16. Thus they were able to make comparisons between the sexes during middle adolescence. Here they found that boys differed quite considerably from girls in the expectations they had of friendship. Themes such as sensitivity and empathy were hardly mentioned by boys, while common pursuits, gang activities, and the need for help when in trouble, all feature prominently among male responses. As the authors point out, such differences are hardly surprising. For girls in our society a stronger interpersonal orientation is expected; the capacity for intimacy and dependency are not only acceptable but also highly valued, and there is little doubt that the processes of socialization all tend in this direction. For boys, however, the stress is placed on skills, achievement, and self-sufficiency. Such an orientation towards activity and autonomy clearly does not facilitate close intimate friendships in adolescence.

Evidence obtained by the author (Coleman, 1974) provides further support for this view. The study, a cross-sectional one involving a sample of over 700 adolescents, investigated the ways in which attitudes to relationships of various sorts differed between groups of both boys and girls at four age levels. Indentical tests were used at 11, 13, 15, and 17 years of age so that it was possible to compare responses of the different age and sex groups. One of the relationships investigated was that of friendship in the small group. A sentence-completion test (Coleman, 1970) was used to assess the responses to this situation. The results indicated, first, that girls undoubtedly express more anxiety about this sort of relationship at all age levels. Tensions, jealousies, and conflicts between close friends were very much more common in the girls' descriptions of friendship than in those of the boys. This difference is illustrated in Figure 3. Second, where a further analysis was carried out of the responses classified as negative (i.e., those where problems or difficulties were expressed), girls expressed a significantly greater proportion in which themes of rejection or exclusion from a friendship appeared. This was particularly striking in the 15-year-old age group and is illustrated in Figure 4. A finding that ties in well with the work of Douvan and Adelson (1966) was that where boys expressed negative themes about friendship these tended to focus on quarrels and outright disputes over property, leisure-time activities, and girlfriends. A further interesting corroboration of these results

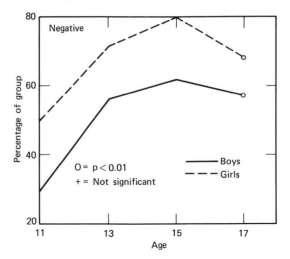

Figure 3.   Proportions of each age group expressing negative themes (anxiety, tension, etc.) on sentence-completion test items to do with friendship (after Coleman, 1974).

is reported by Sones and Feshbach (1971). They studied the reactions of 14- and 15-year-olds to the presence of a newcomer among a small group of friends and showed that girls were less welcoming and were more likely than boys to express negative or rejecting attitudes.

In summary we cannot say that friendship is more or less important for one or other of the sexes. What is clear, however, is that girls express more anxiety about this relationship, particularly in middle adolescence, and it seems probable that Douvan and Adelson (1966) are correct in pointing to the differing socialization processes as well as the high value that girls place on intimacy and dependency as the causes of this discrepancy. In addition and closely interconnected, we have seen that friendship is likely to have a somewhat different meaning for boys and girls. Although the boys lay stress on relationships that are action-oriented, for girls the satisfaction of emotional needs tends to predominate. In general, however, the evidence on sex differences is comparatively sparse, especially during early and late adolescence, and it seems likely that this is a topic that would repay further investigation.

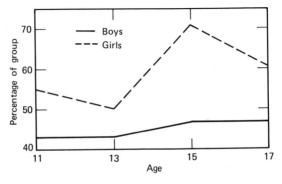

Figure 4.   Amongst those expressing negative themes regarding friendship, the proportions of boys and girls responding with items indicative of fear of rejection (after Coleman, 1976).

What Effect Does Family Background Have on Patterns of Friendship?

Although there have been few direct studies of the effect of family background on adolescent friendship, quite a considerable amount of evidence has accumulated on this topic, mainly in research projects that have had other issues as primary concerns. In the first place, it is clear that the structure of the family (presence or absence of parents as well as sex and number of siblings) has an important part to play. Numerous studies (e.g., Lynn and Sawrey, 1959; Hetherington, 1966; Biller and Bahm, 1971) have shown that paternal absence for prolonged periods of time seriously affects the sex-role development of boys, and thus, in turn, their adjustment in the peer group. The sorts of people chosen as friends, the nature of the friendship, and the types of demands made on this relationship are all affected. However, it is important to bear in mind that in their study of paternal absence McCord et al. (1962) showed that, contrary to expectation, gang and delinquent activity was not more common in families lacking a father as a result of death but was more likely to be associated with parental disruption and conflict.

In a recent study Hetherington (1972) has also investigated the effects of father-absence on adolescent girls. As did McCord et al. (1962), she distinguished between the families where the father had died and those in which the parents were divorced or separated. An elaborate series of observations of teen-age girls between the ages of 13 and 17 was carried out in a community recreation center, both the girls and their mothers were interviewed and various personality tests were administered. The effects of father-absence were, according to Hetherington, "manifested mainly in an inability to interact appropriately with males." In particular, the daughters of divorcees spent a large proportion of their time seeking out male company and engaging in sex-related behavior. Although on interview these girls showed no lack of preference for the female role, they were rarely observed in typical female activities. This was explained simply by the fact that they spent so much of their time hanging around the areas where male activities were carried out, such as the carpentry shop, basketball court, and so on. In contrast to this group, daughters of widowed women appeared much more likely to avoid contact with male peers. These girls tended to be inhibited and lacking in confidence and thus to manifest behavior that was exactly the opposite of that seen in daughters of divorced parents. As Hetherington says, "it is argued that both groups of girls were manifesting deviant behaviors in attempting to cope with their anxiety and lack of skills in relating to males" (1972, p. 324).

In addition to the structural characteristics of the family deriving from presence or absence of parents, the structure of sibling relationships also needs to be considered, for there are some indications, primarily from work with younger children, that this variable may affect both the individual's interest in peers as well as the way he or she relates to others. It was the work of Schachter (1959) that first drew attention to the role of birth order. His work appeared to show that firstborn children were more likely than those born later to seek the company of others, especially when placed in a stressful setting. Subsequent studies have failed to replicate many of Schachter's findings, and the question of the effects of birth order has become a somewhat contentious one. However, it is probably safe to say that sibling position is one variable affecting sociability but that it should not be considered in isolation from other factors, such as the number and sex of the other siblings. Although there are a number of studies that have investigated the role of these variables in friendship patterns in young children (e.g., Koch, 1957; Lewis & Rosenblum, 1975) there appear unfortunately to be very few studies of this sort with adolescents.

One exception to this rule is the study of Douvan and Adelson (1966). In their careful analysis of family structure they looked at a number of dimensions in order to see what effects these would have on adolescent adjustment. Thus family size, death, divorce, sibling position, and maternal employment were all considered in relation to a range of behaviors, including involvement with peers. First, findings showed that divorce has a differential effect on boys and girls. According to Douvan and Adelson, girls, as a result of this experience, are involved more in same-sex friendships and are more mature in their friendship relationships. This finding is not entirely in accord with that of Hetherington (1972). On the other hand, boys appear to have less self-control, to be less mature, and more easily driven to nonconforming behavior. In contrast to this, Douvan and Adelson report that teenagers who have lost a parent through death appear in most respects to be very similar to those with intact families. As far as family size is concerned, it is reported that children from large families are more oriented toward peer values, are more independent, and have more invested in the world of peers. Position in the family also appears important, since the youngest children in this study were more likely to express a strong sense of loyalty to their friends, were more likely to share leisure activities with friends rather than with family members, and were more compelled by peer pressures. Finally, maternal employment seemed to have a much greater effect on girls than on boys, for where the mother was in full-time employment, girls were more likely to spend time alone or with friends rather than with family members.

In addition to structural variables, attention also needs to be paid to processes in the family. On intuitive grounds it seems probable that attitudes and values in the home, the quality of interaction between parents and children, and parental personality all may affect in one way or another the adolescent's relationships with friends. Although there are few studies that have looked directly at this issue, some hints concerning these issues may be gained from the literature. To take one example, Peck (1958), in his study of "Prairie City" adolescents, analyzed 10 family variables and 29 personality variables in an attempt to get at the factors in the family background that determined adolescent personality. The main finding concerned a dimension Peck characterized as "ego strength" (defined by a cluster of intercorrelated items measuring the individual's capacity to react to events), a dimension that was shown to be closely related to stable consistency and mutual trust and approval between parents and children. In addition to this finding, however, he also showed that general friendliness and spontaneity in social relationships was associated with lenience and a democratic family atmosphere. Another study of a similar nature is the Berkeley Growth Study. A report by Bayley and Schaefer (1960) indicated that early maternal patterns of autonomy and control relate most closely to extraversion/introversion in adolescent boys, whereas in girls there is little relation between early maternal behavior and adolescent personality. On the other hand, concurrent maternal behavior did appear to correlate with both extraverion and popularity in adolescent girls. Mothers who were themselves socially outgoing and autonomy-granting tended to have daughters who exhibited similar traits.

Both these studies have important limitations, limitations that are typical of the early longitudinal studies. Both have designs that are dependent on correlational analyses, and both involve very small samples. Today such designs appear to be unduly simplistic. Findings of this sort, therefore, must be treated with caution, especially in view of the many intervening variables that have not been considered. A rather different example may be gleaned from a study carried out by Glen Elder (1963), in which he looked at the use of parental power in families with teen-age children. In this research, a distinction was drawn between three types of parent-child interactions — permissive, democratic, and autocratic — but a note was also made of the frequency of explanations given by parents when questioned about family rules. One of the issues studied was the reaction of adolescents when the parents developed a strong objection to their friends. Of particular interest was the finding that there were two conditions under which young people were unlikely to take much notice of parental strictures. These were the permissive and autocratic types of control, where explanations were infrequent. Thus Elder showed that the effect of particular types of parental power-assertion combined with a lack of explanation had very specific implications for the way in which adolescents handled potential clashes over friendship. Clearly, these patterns of family communication are of relevance to a wide range of adolescent behaviors, but this study is one of the few to have shown directly how attitudes to friendship will be affected by family variables.

From these few examples, therefore, it is evid ent that not only the structure, but also the processes at work within the family will have a marked effect on the way in which adolescents relate to their friends. Parental absence, especially if it is a result of separation or divorce, is likely to lead to increased demands on friends of both sexes, demands that will not always be of an appropriate nature. However, further research is needed on this topic, especially in view of the contradictory findings of Hetherington (1972) and Douvan and Adelson (1966). Family size and sibling position are also variables that are likely to play their part in determining behavior in this domain. Finally the relationship between parents and adolescents is certain to be a critical factor; here again there is obviously scope for further worthwhile research. If friendship plays an important role in adolescent development, there can be little doubt that family background determines to a large extent the use that individuals are able to make of such relationships.

THE PEER GROUP

As was mentioned earlier three questions are to be considered where the adolescent peer group is concerned. Before we turn to these issues, however, it will be as well to say something briefly about the structure of the peer group generally. It has come to be accepted in the literature that there are basically two main types of peer group, cliques and crowds, with the main determining factor being the size of the group. Cliques are generally smaller than crowds, ranging from between two to nine members, with the usual number being around five. Hollingshead (1949) suggests the following definition: "A clique comes into existence when two or more persons are related to one another in an intimate fellowship that involves going places and doing things together, a mutual exchange of ideas, and the acceptance of each personality by the other" (p. 205). Cliques tend to be of a "closed" nature, that is, they are not readily open to outsiders, and their formation results either from school or recreational activities. According to Dunphy (1963) such cliques are almost always unisexual during early adolescence but are usually transformed in nature during middle adolescence, when they become heterosexual.

Dunphy was responsible for an important study of school cliques carried out in Sydney, Australia between 1958 and 1960. He uncovered 44 cliques among a total of 303 predominantly middle-class boys and girls, ranging in age from 13 to 21. The small size of these cliques (having an average membership of 6) reflected the intimate relationships within the group, which was characterized by strong cohesiveness. As Lambert et al. (1972) point out, perhaps it is no coincidence that these cliques are not much larger than the average family, thus facilitating the transfer of allegiance from family to peer group. Cliques are generally composed of members of the same socioeconomic class and tend to be limited to those in the same grade level in school. Members usually have a common set of values, interests, tastes, and moral standards, which tend to allow for considerable intolerance and contempt of those who are different.

The average crowd is considerably larger than the normal clique. Dunphy (1963) noted that there were 12 crowds among his 303 subjects, with the size varying from 15 to 30 members, the average membership being around 20. He concluded that the crowd is basically an association of cliques, although not all cliques were connected with crowds. However clique membership appeared to be a prerequisite for membership in the crowd: in no case did an individual belong to a crowd without concurrently being a member of a clique. The large size of the crowd hinders the formation of intimate relationships, and the functions of the crowd are correspondingly different. Whereas a clique tends to be preoccupied with conversation and communication, a crowd is more concerned with organized social activities, such as parties and dances. Crowd activities tend to take place on weekends, in contrast to clique functions, which are more likely to occur during the week. According to Dunphy, however, the real significance of the crowd is that it provides a means of transition from unisexual to heterosexual social relationships by facilitating interclique activities. The early adolescent unisexual cliques come into contact with each other under the umbrella of crowd membership, thus allowing group members to practice new roles in a "protected" setting.

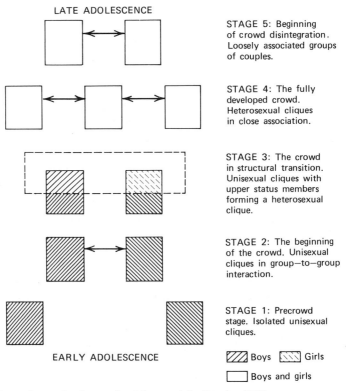

Figure 5.   Stages of group development in adolescence (after Dunphy, 1963).

The work of Dunphy has had an important impact on workers in the field, and its significance undoubtedly lies in the fact that he was able to show how the changing structure of the peer group reflected its changing function. It is now evident that different peer group structures fulfill different needs at different times; such knowledge makes it possible for us to place more clearly in perspective issues concerning popularity and the effects of the peer group on behavior. Let us now turn, therefore, to the first question.

What Factors Determine Popularity in the Peer Group?

There are in the literature a considerable number of studies that have been designed to answer this question, and on the whole there has been relatively little disagreement amongst them. Arbitrarily, the studies may be divided into those carried out pre- and post-1960, with the work of J. S. Coleman (1960, 1961) representing the dividing line between the two groups. A hallmark of all the early studies was a concern to discover the personality characteristics associated with popularity. Thus Kuhlen and Lee (1943) studied six groups of children from villages and rural areas in New York State, including over 100 boys and girls from grades 6, 9, and 12. These researchers compared the personality characteristics of the most popular 25% with the least popular 25% in each of these six groups. For students of both sexes and all grades, the traits that made for popularity were cheerfulness, friendliness, enthusiasm, enjoying jokes, and initiating games and activities.

Gronlund and Anderson (1957) carried out a similar study, using a sociometric test and asking pupils to indicate five individuals preferred as work companions, play companions, and seating companions. Subjects were in the seventh and eighth grades in schools in a small city in Illinois. These researchers distinguished between the most socially acceptable, the most socially neglected, and the most socially rejected pupils. They showed that, on the whole, similar personality traits as those mentioned by Kuhlen and Lee (1943) characterized the most accepted pupils. However in addition to these dimensions good looks were mentioned as being important by both boys and girls, with the description ''active in games'' also being of great significance for boys. It may also be noted that a trait defined as ''talkative'' was frequently mentioned as belonging to rejected individuals. As the authors point out: ''The results of this study clearly indicate that strong positive personality characteristics are associated with social acceptability among junior high school pupils'' (Gronlund & Anderson, p. 337).

Third, a study by Wheeler (1961) may be mentioned, which, although falling technically into the post-1960 era, belongs with the work of an earlier period. In Australia, Wheeler carried out almost exactly the same type of study as had his predecessors in America. He also found that there were relatively few differences between the sexes or between age groups, and that cheerfulness, good looks, physique, and sociability were the most important determinants of popularity, with the additional dimension of sporting abilities being frequently mentioned by boys.

One important sidelight on this early work came out of the California studies of early and late pubertal development. Thus Jones and Bayley (1950) reported that peers described late maturers as more restless, less reserved, less grown up, and more bossy. In a later report by Jones (1958) it was stated that the late maturers were chosen much less frequently than early maturers for positions of leadership in their school, and they were less prominent in extracurricular activities. It is not unreasonable to assume, therefore, that the dimensions we have already been considering, such as good looks, sporting ability, and so on, are connected with the individual's general rate of maturation.

The work of J. S. Coleman (1960, 1961) has marked a watershed in studies of popularity, primarily because of his shift of emphasis. The early work discussed above concentrated on attributes of popularity but did not attempt in any way to consider the implications of popularity in the wider social setting. By concentrating on the concept of status and the notion of an elite, Coleman introduced into the study of popularity a new dimension and turned attention to the impact of peer-group values on the school system as a whole. As is well known, he studied the attributes of the leading crowds in 10 different schools and argued, as a result of this work, that by and large sporting ability for boys and success in social relationships for girls were the factors that determined membership of the elite. As one part of the study, boys were asked in a questionnaire to name the best athlete, the best student, and the boy most popular with girls. As Coleman says: ''In every school, without exception, the boys named as best athletes were named more often — on average over twice as often — as members of the leading crowd than were those named as best students'' (1960, p. 339). These findings are further illustrated in Figure 6, showing how male students in the 10 schools respond to the question, ''How would you most like to be remembered in school: as an athletic star, a brilliant student, or most popular?'' Once again, athletic success is shown as being by far the most highly valued achievement.

A third question in the study was, ''What does it take to get into the leading crowd?'' For boys: sporting ability, personality, and good looks were most frequently mentioned; for girls: good looks, personality, and good clothes came at the top of the list. In all cases, good grades came relatively low down, although they were more frequently mentioned by boys than by girls.

Writers who have followed Coleman have tended to criticize him to some extent for the fact that he has overgeneralized from his findings, and it is probably fair to say that a little too much has been made of what Braham (1965) has called ''the intellectually negating

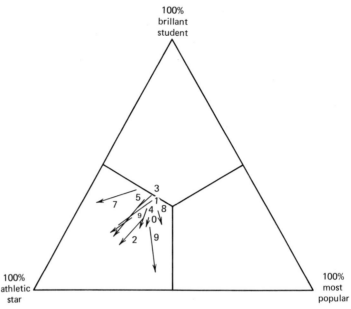

Figure 6. Positions of 10 schools and their leading crowds concerning boys relative choices: preferring to be remembered as brilliant student, athletic star, or most popular individual (after Coleman, 1960).

adolescent sub-culture.'' Many writers (e.g., Campbell, 1964; Douvan and Gold, 1966) have pointed out that Coleman found very considerable differences between schools, as well as reporting evidence that showed that a positive evaluation of academic achievment varied directly as a function of social class. In addition, although athletes were chosen as being more popular than scholars in all schools, in most cases the unusual athlete-scholars were the most popular of all, thus illustrating an interaction effect of these two attributes. It is essential, therefore, to bear in mind that although sporting ability in boys and social success for girls are undoubtedly more critical factors than achievement in school work in determining popularity and membership of the leading crowd, that fact alone does not lead to the conclusion that adolescent peer groups are anti-intellectual.

In assessing Coleman's work, it should be noted that his findings not only tie in with those of earlier studies, but also are further corroborated by subsequent research. To take one example, Horowitz (1967) collected sociometric data from eight schools across the United States, each school representing one of the eight regional areas defined by the U.S. Office of Education. He concluded that the best predictors of popularity in both sexes were scores on an English test, an interest in sports, and self-rating personality scales of sociability and leadership. He noted that a particularly important additional variable for predicting boys' popularity was their knowledge of sports. As Horowitz (1967) puts it:

> The present data delineate a pattern of interpersonal values in the adolescent world of American high schools which is similar to the one described by Coleman in his extensive study of ''The Adolescent Society.'' The present results support . . . (the findings) . . . in showing strong relationships between interest and achievement predictors from both the intellectual and athletic domains. [P. 174]

Finally we must turn our attention to a study which has served to highlight a limitation, not only of Coleman's work, but also of other studies of popularity as well. Cavior and Dokecki (1973) were interested in the relation among popularity, physical attractiveness, and attitude similarity. They concluded that physical attractiveness and attitude similarity were positively correlated both at the fifth- and eleventh-grade level and, as we would expect, that both these factors were strongly related to popularity. However the importance of this study lies in the fact that the authors, rather than looking only at the extremes of variables, such as popularity and physical attractiveness, analyzed their data by taking into account the full range of scores. Thus they were able to show, for example, that physical attractiveness determines popularity only for the most and least attractive subjects but has little effect on the large number of subjects in the averagely attractive category. In this way Cavior and Dokecki (1973) indicate that it is perfectly possible to be popular without being in the highly physically attractive group; they thereby draw attention to the fact that, by and large, studies of popularity have concentrated on the extremes of personality or achievement without paying sufficient attention to those in the middle range.

To answer the question posed at the beginning of this section, we may, with little hesitation, conclude that attractive personality characteristics, good looks, and sporting ability for boys — as well as academic success in some circumstances — are all associated with popularity. However it is important to bear in mind, as the work of Cavior and Dokecki (1973) indicates, that possession of any one of these traits or attributes is neither a necessary nor a sufficient cause for popularity. In addition this last study underlines the lack of attention that has been paid to the teenagers who do not fall at the extremes on attributes, such as sporting ability or good looks, and it is to be hoped that future studies of popularity will pay rather more attention to these groups as well as to investigating the interaction effects of the major criteria for popularity that have so far been delineated.

What Factors Are Most Likely To Produce Conformity of Behavior in the Peer Group?

As a result of the heightened importance of the peer group during adolescence, it is to be expected that pressure toward conformity will be especially strong at this stage of development. It is no doubt true that where identity and self-esteem are uncertain, there is security in being similar to the rest of the crowd; clear demarcation lines between youth and the older generation are useful when loyalties and commitments are at stake. The stereotype of "slavish conformity to fad and fashion" is frequently associated with the teenager of today, and in the minds of many people, this characteristic is an integral feature of adolescent personality. In fact, empirical studies show that the need to conform is not uniformly high during adolescence but is closely affected by age as well as being influenced by other variables, such as sex, status in the group, and a tendency to self-blame. Let us now turn to some of the studies that have provided evidence on this topic.

Costanzo and Shaw (1966) used Asch's well-known paradigm to look at the effects of group pressure. They asked subjects to make a decision about the length of a line where the illusion was given that all members of the group differed from the subject. The sample included 24 subjects at each of four age levels, each age group being equally divided between boys and girls. The authors showed that susceptibility to group pressure was significantly related to age, though not in a straightforward linear fashion. Results indicated a relatively low degree of conformity in the 7-to-9 age range, the highest level of conformity in the 11-to-13 age range, and a gradual decrease in susceptibility to group pressure from then onward. Interestingly, the level of conformity in the 19-to-21 age range appeared to be approximately the same as it had been between the 7-to-9 age range. It is noteworthy that this developmental pattern is identical for boys and girls, although the latter are somewhat more conforming.

Further studies that have provided similar evidence are those of Iscoe, Williams, and Harvey (1963) and Landsbaum and Willis (1971). In the latter study a slightly different design was used from that employed by Costanzo and Shaw (1966), in that subjects worked

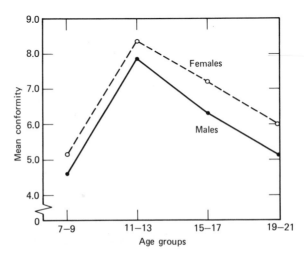

Figure 7.   Mean conformity as a function of age (after Costanzo and Shaw, 1966).

in pairs rather than in a group. This experiment demonstrated that neither intelligence nor extended contact between partners had any effect but that conformity was significantly greater between the ages of 13 and 14 than it was between 18 and 21. Although the younger adolescents did not report less self-confidence, they actually performed as if they were more uncertain since they changed their original decisions to fit with their partners' opposing judgments more often than did those in the older group.

Harvey and Rutherford (1960) were also interested in the same problem, but in their case they investigated the effect of high- and low-group status on conformity behavior. In their design, subjects first made a decision involving a preference for one of two pictures in an art-judgment test. They then received a communication indicating the choice of a high-status member of the group. The study was concerned with the proportions of each age group who altered their choice in a subsequent task to accord with the choice of the high-status member. The results showed that low-status members were more susceptible to influence than were those of high status, that girls were more susceptible to status than boys in grades 3, 6, and 9, and that, in general, status affected degree of influence at the sixth and eleventh grades but not at the third and ninth grades. These results are congruent with those of other studies mentioned, except for the performance of the ninth graders. The authors suggest that this particular result may be explicable in terms of the recent move of these teenagers from junior- to senior-high school, resulting in their being with a new largely unknown group of peers.

Costanzo (1970) added a further dimension to studies of conformity by investigating the effects of self-blame. In this study, subjects ranged in age from 7 to 21 and self-blame was assessed by including a story-completion test. In this test heroes of stories inadvertently caused some accident or disaster. The subjects were asked to complete the stories, indicating who was to blame. Conformity was measured in the same manner as in the earlier study (Costanzo & Shaw, 1966), and the results showed clearly that, although conformity followed a similar developmental pattern, its extent was strongly affected by the degree of self-blame.

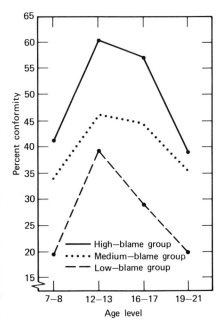

Figure 8. Percentage of conformity as a function of age at different levels of self-blame intensity (after Costanzo, 1970).

Finally, mention may be made once more of the author's own study (Coleman, 1974), one aspect of which involved a developmental investigation of the adolescent's sense of autonomy in relation to the peer group. Results derived from this element in the study might be expected therefore to cast some light, not on conformity per se, but on the opposite side of the coin. In particular, the focus here was on the interaction between increasing independence and declining conformity as a function of age. One sentence stem in the sentence-completion test that was used in the study read: "IF SOMEONE IS NOT PART OF THE GROUP, . . ." Responses were scored as being either constructive or negative. A negative response implied that to be outside the group was in some way harmful, damaging, or painful: a constructive response indicated that there were definite advantages in being independent from the group. Some examples of constructive responses are: "IF SOMEONE IS NOT PART OF THE GROUP, he enjoys it because he is not following the sheep." or "IF SOMEONE IS NOT PART OF THE GROUP, he is much respected and admired." Two examples of negative themes are "IF SOMEONE IS NOT PART OF THE GROUP, he feels inferior to them," or "IF SOMEONE IS NOT PART OF THE GROUP, he is looked upon as an outcast." The results showed that independence (constructive responses) remained at a very low level in the 11-, 13-, and 15-year-old groups but increased significantly at 17. Correspondingly conformity (negative responses) declined sharply from the age of 15 onward, although this decline was less marked for girls than it was for boys. These results are illustrated in Figure 9, and are consistent with those of Costanzo and Shaw (1966) and Landsbaum and Willis (1971).

To conclude, we can be fairly confident in saying that conformity is at its height among the early adolescent group but that it diminishes significantly from about 14 or 15 onward. Girls, under some circumstances at least, appear to be more conforming than boys, although the differences between the sexes are not unduly large. Conformity is affected by status in the peer group as well as by self-blame, and it would undoubtedly be of interest to examine its relation to other personality variables. Evidently, by middle adolescence some individuals are beginning to be able to see that there are advantages to be gained from independence, and the number taking such a view clearly increases rapidly from this stage

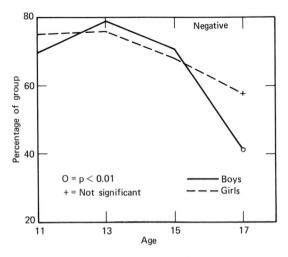

Figure 9.   Proportions of each age group expressing negative themes (anxiety, worry, etc.) on a sentence-completion test item to do with independence from the peer group (after Coleman, 1974).

onward. Further studies of conformity may well wish to concentrate on the process of disengagement from group pressure. There is surely much to be learned, not only about adolescence but about adulthood as well, from a better understanding of the way in which this autonomy is achieved.

How Significant is Parent–Peer Conflict?

The topic that has come to be known in the literature as the parent–peer issue is closely bound up not only with the notion of conformity, but also with that of the generation gap. Although much has been written about the supposed conflict in attitudes and values between parents and peers, recent evidence (e.g., Adelson, 1971; Bengtson, 1970; Coleman, 1978) has cast considerable doubt on the extent of this gap between the generations. Although there are undoubtedly differences in taste between adults and young people (e.g., in clothes, music, etc.) as well as disagreements over mundane domestic issues (see for example Douvan & Adelson, 1966; Coleman, George, & Holt, 1977), such differences do not imply major discrepancies where fundamental values are concerned. The simplistic notion of a serious divergence of attitude and belief between the generations has clouded the picture in many respects, not least with regard to the issue of adolescent reference groups. Thus, for example, it has commonly been assumed that an inevitable consequence of increased involvement with the peer group is a rejection of parental values. Clearly, however, this is not an either/or phenomenon. From the very beginning, empirical research has shown the situation to be far from straightforward.

An early study by Bowerman and Kinch (1959) illustrated this well. They were interested in the changes in family and peer orientation of children between the fourth and tenth grades. The subjects were classified on various types of orientation as well as on the extent they identified with one group or another. Thus, for example, "norm orientation" was defined as "whose ideas were most like those of the subject on a variety of topics," while in order to assess "identification," subjects were asked: whether family or friends understood them better and whether when they grew up they would rather be the kind of person their parents were or the kind they thought their friends would be. Findings showed that although "norm orientation" shifted dramatically from family to peer group over the age span, with an especially strong swing between the seventh and eighth grades, the differences between age groups on the identification measure, although in the same direction, were not nearly so marked. These results, illustrated in Table 2, indicate that

Table 2   Percentage of Children Classified as Having Family, Peer, or Neutral Orientation by Grade in School (after Bowerman & Kinch, 1959)

	4	5	6	Grade level 7	8	9	10
Normative Orientation							
Family	82.2	64.6	69.8	51.9	33.0	42.4	30.4
Peer	11.9	23.2	18.1	34.3	52.2	41.2	50.6
Neutral	5.9	12.2	12.1	13.9	14.8	16.5	19.0
Identification							
Family	81.2	79.2	77.6	72.2	57.4	62.3	51.9
Peer	5.0	2.4	4.3	9.2	18.2	13.0	26.6
Neutral	13.8	18.3	18.1	18.5	24.3	24.7	21.5

Source: Published in C. E. Bowerman and J. W. Kinch (1959).

there will be a number of different dimensions of commitment to any reference group, dimensions that do not necessarily show identical developmental patterns.

A study carried out by Brittain (1963) provided further corroboration for the view that orientation to one group or another was far from being an all-or-nothing affair. In this study, hypothetical situations involving conflict between parent-peer expectations were presented to the subjects, who were girls in grades 9, 10, and 11. In each dilemma, individuals were faced with a complex choice where one course of action was favored by parents and another by peers; the respondents were asked to indicate what the girl would probably do. The results led Brittain to the conclusion that whether the subject chose a course of action that conformed to the parents' wishes or one that was in line with peer-group pressures depended primarily on the character of the dilemma. This conclusion he later formulated in terms of a "situational hypothesis" (Brittain, 1968; 1969). This has been summarized by Larsen:

> In this case the adolescent is said to follow the wishes of his parents rather than those of his peers when the context requires decisions that have futuristic implications. Conversely when the decision involves current status and identity needs, the adolescents opt for the wishes of their peers. Brittain's research has strongly supported the assumption that adolescents perceive peers and parents as competent guides in different areas. . . . [1972a, p. 84]

Brittain's "situational hypothesis" was given additional impetus by the work of Lesser and Kandel (1969), whose findings led them to the conclusion that although for certain values peers may be more influential than parents, for other issues the reverse appears to be true. In their study, they were concerned with educational plans and future life goals; in order to assess the relative influence of parents and peers on these future-oriented decisions the authors developed a measure of concordance between both adolescent and mother and between adolescent and best friend. Results showed that where educational goals were concerned there was strong concordance between the adolescent and both mother and best friend. But this concordance was significantly greater between adolescent and mother than it was between adolescent and best friend. As a result of these data, the authors were left in little doubt that, in this domain at least, parents have a stronger influence than peers. Furthermore, the majority of adolescents appeared from this study to hold views that were in agreement with both their mothers and their friends, and those who agreed with their parents were also far more likely to agree with their peers than those who disagreed with their parents. As Lesser and Kandel put it: "We take exception to the 'hydraulic' view taken by many investigators regarding the relative influence of adults and peers which assumes that the greater the influence of the one, the less the influence of the other. Our data lead to another view: in critical areas, interactions with peers support the values of the parents" (1969, p. 222). Thus the authors not only support Brittain's hypothesis, but also carry it a step further by underlining the interactive nature of parent and peer influence.

Although it is evident that the "situational hypothesis" carries considerable weight, one writer, at least, has taken exception to it. Larsen (1972a), although using a method very similar to the one developed by Brittain, came to a somewhat different conclusion. Having carried out a major piece of research involving over 1500 subjects in the 7th, 9th, and 12th grades, Larsen reported results that appeared to show that, at best, only a very weak relation existed between the pressures of parents and peers and the type of situation. In this study, the responses of young people differed very little between situations that were oriented to the present and those that were oriented to the future. In general adolescents appeared marginally more compliant with the wishes of their parents rather than with those of their peers irrespective of the nature of the issue involved. In summarizing his work, Larsen dismissed the "situational hypothesis," and placed the blame for the contradictory findings on the methodology involved. Somewhat paradoxically, however, in a subsequent study, Larsen (1972b) once again used the method of presenting subjects with hypothetical situations, this time introducing the further variable of "parent-adolescent affect." This variable Larsen defined as, "the quality of parent-child relationships, as measured by parental interest and understanding, willingness to help, the number of family activities shared, and so on." Under these conditions he derived results of very considerable interest. He was able to show, for example, that parental influence was greatest in situations where "parent-adolescent affect" was highest. In addition, adolescents with high "parent-adolescent affect" were less likely than those with low affect to see a need to differentiate between the influences of parents and peers. Furthermore, the results indicated that "parent-adolescent affect" had greatest effect on those in grades 9 and 12, but relatively little effect on those in grade 7. There were also quite considerable sex differences, with girls, especially older girls, being more affected by this variable than boys. Some of Larsen's findings are illustrated in Figure 10.

From the foregoing it is clear that the so-called parent-peer issue is a complex one, in which a number of factors may all play an important part. It seems probable that there are no simple solutions to questions concerning the significance of parent-peer conflict, nor are there, at this stage, straightforward answers as to how adolescents resolve potential

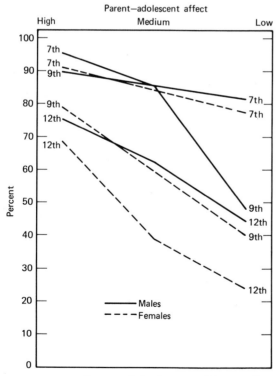

Figure 10. Orientation to parents according to grade level, parent-adolescent affect, and sex (after Larsen, 1972b).

cross-pressures. In his textbook, *Adolescence and Youth* (1977), J. Conger describes five points that should be borne in mind when considering the parent-peer issue. In the first place, Conger reminds us that there will usually be considerable overlap in values between parents and peers. In many areas there may be no conflict at all, with the values of the one group reinforcing rather than contradicting the values of the other. In this context it should perhaps be remembered that many teenagers will select precisely those friends whose values are congruent with those of their parents, a point underlined not only by Lesser and Kandel (1969), but more recently by Offer and Offer (1976). Second, Conger suggests that in some areas parents will, in any event, experience some uncertainty, and in these areas are likely to be quite willing to take their cues from the younger generation. Third, it would clearly be erroneous to assume that either peer or parental values are all-embracing, extending to every area of decision-making. In the large majority of families the opinions of parents will be of greater salience on some issues, while those of peers will be seen to be more relevant to a different set of problems. Fourth, attention is drawn to the findings of a number of research projects (e.g., Bronfenbrenner, 1970) that show that it is in situations where parental interest is lacking, or where the adolescent has no parental support to depend on, that commitment to peer-group values is at its height. Thus the role of the peer group under these conditions involves filling a vacuum rather than provoking a conflict between parents and teenagers. Finally, Conger argues that the need to conform to pressures, whether they be from parents or peers, will vary from individual to individual. Personality, maturity, family relationships, as well as other variables will all need to be considered, as the work of Larsen (1972b) has indicated. These factors seem likely to be of far greater significance than age in determining the individual's relationship with parents and peers.

CONCLUSION

In this chapter, six issues concerning friendship and the peer group in adolescence have been considered. It will be apparent to the reader that these are not the only issues that could have been discussed, but they are certainly ones that have received considerable attention in the literature. These issues have been expressed in terms of questions in the hope that the author might be encouraged to draw some conclusions from the research findings rather than simply describe experimental results. This has not always been easy, but the literature has undoubtedly provided at least some answers. Thus it has become clear that friendship is important in different ways at different stages during adolescence. Age is a significant variable in this respect. Boys and girls do differ in the meanings they ascribe to friendship relationships, and the effects of family background, while needing further investigation, evidently cannot be ignored. Attractive personality characteristics are obviously associated with popularity, although the role of the elite in determining peer-group values is still cloaked in some uncertainty. Conformity to peer-group pressures is, as we have seen, very much affected by age as well as by other variables. Lastly, although it would be erroneous to assume that there are any simple answers to the parent-peer issue, some guidelines have begun to emerge. What has become clear from this review of the literature is that friendship can and does provide support during adolescence. But it is also associated, rather more than is commonly assumed, with tension and anxiety, especially among girls. As far as influence is concerned, the general impression must be that the peer group appears to exercise less influence on teenagers than many adults believe. The common notion of outright conflict between the generations is simply not substantiated by the evidence. Thus it is undoubtedly time that the role of the peer group was seen in more realistic terms — (1) as a source of influence more often congruent with, rather than contrary to, parental values and (2) as a support and reference group only playing a major part where the family proves to be inadequate.

REFERENCES

Adelson, J. What generation gap? *New York Times Magazine*, January 18, 1970, pp. 10–14.

Anderson, J. E. The development of social behavior. *The American Journal of Sociology*, 1939, *44*, 839–857.

Bayley, N., and Schaefer, E. S. Maternal behavior and personality development data from the Berkeley Growth Study, *Psychiatric Research Reports*, 1960, *13*, 155–173.

Bengtson, V. L. The generation gap. *Youth and Society*, 1970, *2*, 7–32.

Bigelow, B. J., and La Gaipa, J. J. Children's written descriptions of friendship. *Developmental Psychology*, 1975, *11*, 857–858.

Biller, H. B., and Bahm, R. M. Father-absence, perceived maternal behavior, and masculinity of self-concept among junior-high-school boys. *Developmental Psychology*, 1971, *4*, 178–181.

Bowerman, C. E., and Kinch, J. W. Changes in family and peer orientation of children between the fourth and tenth grades. *Social Forces*, 1959, *37*, 206–211.

Braham, M. Peer group deterrence to intellectual development during adolescence. *Educational Theory*, 1965, *15*, 251–258.

Brittain, C. V. Adolescent choices and parent-peer cross pressures. *American Sociological Review*, 1963, *28*, 385–391.

———. An exploration of the bases of peer-compliance and parent-compliance in adolescence. *Adolescence*, 1968, *2*, 445–458.

———. A comparison of rural and urban adolescence with respect to peer versus parent compliance. *Adolescence*, 1969, *13*, 59–68.

Campbell, J. D. Peer relations in childhood. In M. L. Hoffman and L. W. Hoffman, (Eds.), *Review of child development* (Vol. 1) Russell Sage Foundation, 1964.

Cavior, N., and Dokecki, P. R. Physical attractiveness, perceived attitude similarity, and academic achievement as contributors to interpersonal attraction among adolescents. *Developmental Psychology*, 1973, *9*, 44–54.

Coleman, J. C. Study of adolescent development using a sentence-completion method. *British Journal of Educational Psychology*, 1970, *40*, 27–34.

———. *Relationships in adolescence*. Boston and London: Routledge and Kegan Paul, 1974.

———. Current contradictions in adolescent theory. *Journal of Youth and Adolescence*, 1978, 7, 1–11.

Coleman, J. C., George, R., and Holt, G. Adolescents and their parents: a study of attitudes. *Journal of Genetic Psychology*, 1977, 130, 239–245.

Coleman, J. S. The adolescent sub-culture and academic achievement. *American Journal of Sociology*, 1960, *65*, 337–347.

———. *The adolescent society*. New York: Free Press, 1961.

Conger, J. J. *Adolescence and youth*. New York: Harper & Row, 1977.

Costanzo, P. R. Conformity development as a function of self-blame. *Journal of Personality and Social Psychology*, 1970, *14*, 366–374.

Costanzo, P. R., and Shaw, M. E. Conformity as a function of age level. *Child Development,* 1966, *37,* 967–975.

Douvan, E., and Adelson, J. *The adolescent experience.* New York: Wiley, 1966.

Douvan, E., and Gold, H. Modal patterns in American adolescence. In M. L. Hoffman and L. W. Hoffman (Eds.), *Review of child development research* (Vol. 2). New York: Russell Sage Foundation, 1966.

Dunphy, D. C. The social structure of urban adolescent peer groups. *Sociometry,* 1963, *26,* 230–246.

Elder, G. H., Jr. Parental power legitimation and the effect on the adolescent. *Sociometry,* 1963, *26,* 50–65.

Erikson, E. H. *Identity: Youth and crisis.* London: Faber, 1968.

Gronlund, N. W., and Anderson, L. Personality characteristics of socially accepted, socially neglected, and socially rejected junior-high-school pupils. *Educational Administration and Supervision,* 1957, *43,* 329–338.

Harvey, O. J., and Rutherford, J. Status in the informal group. *Child Development,* 1960, *31,* 377–385.

Hetherington, E. M. Effects of paternal absence on sex-typed behaviors in negro and white preadolescent males. *Journal of Personality and Social Psychology,* 1966, *4,* 87–91.

———. Effects of father-absence on personality development in adolescent daughters. *Developmental Psychology,* 1972, *7,* 313–326.

Hollingshead, A. B. *Elmtown youth.* New York: Wiley, 1949.

Horowitz, H. Predictions of adolescent popularity and rejection from achievement and interest tests. *Journal of Educational Psychology,* 1967, *58,* 170–174.

Horrocks, J. E., and Baker, M. A study of the friendship fluctuations of preadolescents. *Journal of Genetic Psychology,* 1951, *78,* 131–144.

Horrocks, J. E., and Thompson, G. G. A study of the friendship fluctuations of rural boys and girls. *Journal of Genetic Psychology,* 1946, *69,* 189–198.

Iscoe, I., Williams, M., and Harvey, J. Modification of children's judgements by a simulated group technique. *Child Development,* 1963, *34,* 963–978.

Jones, M. C. The study of socialisation patterns at the high-school level. *Journal of Genetic Psychology,* 1958, *93,* 87–111.

Jones, M. C. and Bayley, N. Physical maturing among boys as related to behavior. *Journal of Educational Psychology,* 1950, *41,* 129–148.

Koch, H. L. The relation in young children between characteristics of their playmates and certain attributes of their siblings. *Child Development,* 1957, *28,* 175–202.

Kuhlen, R. G., and Lee, B. J. Personality characteristics and social acceptability in adolescence. *Journal of Educational Psychology,* 1943, *34,* 321–340.

Lambert, B. G., et al. *Adolescence: Transition from childhood to maturity.* Monterey, Calif.: Brooks/Cole, 1972.

Landsbaum, J., and Willis, R. Conformity in early and late adolescence. *Developmental Psychology,* 1971, *4,* 334–337.

Larsen, L. E. The influence of parents and peers during adolescence: The situation hypothesis revisited. *Journal of Marriage and the Family,* 1972a, *34,* 67–74.

Larsen, L. E. The relative influence of parent-adolescent affect in predicting the salience hierarchy among youth. *Pacific Sociological Review,* 1972b, *15,* 83–102.

Lesser, G. S., and Kandel, D. B. Parental and peer influences on educational plans of adolescence. *American Sociological Review,* 1969, *34,* 213–223.

Lewis, M., and Rosenblum, L. (Eds.). *Friendship and peer Relations*. New York: Wiley, 1975.

Lynn, D. B., and Sawrey, W. L. The effects of father-absence on Norwegian boys and girls. *Journal of Abnormal and Social Psychology,* 1959, *59,* 258–262.

McCord, J., McCord, W., and Thurber, E. Some effects of paternal absence on male children. *Journal of Abnormal and Social Psychology,* 1962, *54,* 361–369.

Offer, D., and Offer, J. B. *From teenage to young manhood*. New York: Basic Books, 1976.

Peck, R. F. Family patterns correlated with adolescent personality structure. *Journal of Abnormal and Social Psychology,* 1958, *47,* 347–350.

Powell, M. Age and sex differences in degree of conflict within certain areas of psychological adjustment. *Psychological Monographs,* 1955, *69,* (Whole No. 387).

Schachter, S. *The psychology of affiliation*. Stanford, Calif.: Stanford University Press, 1959.

Sones, G., and Feshbach, M. Sex differences in adolescent reactions towards newcomers. *Developmental Psychology,* 1971, *4,* 381–386.

Thompson, G. G., and Horrocks, J. E. A study of the friendship fluctuations of urban boys and girls. *Journal of Genetic Psychology,* 1947, *70,* 53–63.

Wheeler, D. K. Popularity among adolescents in Western Australia and in the United States of America. *The School Review,* 1961, *49,* 67–81.

CHAPTER 13

Strategic Interactions in Early Adolescence

David Elkind

The monumental contributions of Jean Piaget to our understanding of the development of intelligence (adaptive thought and action) have opened up many new areas of investigation. One of the most exciting of these areas is social interaction. Much of the Piaget-inspired work on this topic has focused on "perspective taking" and growth in the child's ability to see the world from other people's points of view (e.g., Flavell, 1968; Selman, 1971). Although this work is interesting and methodologically sophisticated, its conceptual base is rather narrow and limited because the Piagetian concepts are basically psychological and individual rather than sociological.

An alternative approach, the one taken by Piaget (1948, 1951, 1952) and the one taken here, does not attempt to make Piagetian concepts sociological but rather to give sociological concepts a Piagetian interpretation. That is to say, many fruitful concepts in sociology are essentially agenetic, in the sense that they are lacking a developmental dimension. What a Piagetian analysis can add to these concepts is some elucidation of when these phenomena appear in ontogeny and how they change in the course of individual growth and development.

In the present chapter I shall be particularly concerned with the sociological concept of *strategic interactions* introduced by Erving Goffman (1969). According to Goffman, strategic interactions are interpersonal encounters that have as their aim the acquisition, concealment, or revelation of information. Goffman's descriptions of strategic interactions (e.g., card players who can effectively bluff out other players with better hands) would seem, however, to require a level of mental ability that is not usually attained until early adolescence and the emergence of what Piaget calls formal operations. In addition, since early adolescence is a very self-centered period, one might expect that the strategic interactions at this period would be of a somewhat different type than they will be in older adolescents and in adults. In other words, strategic interactions might well have a developmental dimension.

Accordingly, in the present chapter I propose to do three things. I shall first review the nature of formal operations and some of the mental structures to which they give rise. In the second section, I shall describe some forms of strategic interactions that are characteristic of the early adolescent period. A final section will attempt a brief delineation of what happens to these patterns as young people mature.

FORMAL OPERATIONS

The Piagetian conception of the development of intelligence holds that cognition develops in a series of stages related to age. There are four stages in all, and each is marked by the appearance of new mental abilities that make possible intellectual achievements that surpass anything children at the preceding stage can accomplish.

Piaget's theory is well enough known so that it is not necessary to review all of the stages in detail here.[1] For our purpose, it may suffice to say that each stage of development can be depicted as concerned with constructing a particular facet of reality. The sensorimotor period (0 to 2 years) is a time devoted to constructing a world of permanent *objects*. At the next stage, the preoperational period (2 to 6 years) children are involved in constructing a world of manipulatable *symbols*. During the concrete operational period (roughly the years from 6 to 11) children are engaged in constructing a world of *rules* and of *quantities*. Finally, beginning at about the age of 11 or 12 young people attain formal operations and begin to construct a world which encompasses *thought, ideals,* and *possibilities*.

We need now to look at formal operations in somewhat more detail. In Piaget's view, the operations of intelligence are parallel to systems of logic. This is not a new idea. Both Boole (1950/1854) and Baldwin (1906–1908) advanced similar conceptions, but Piaget tied his description of the logical systems of the mind to concrete experimental demonstrations. He and Inhelder (1958) argue that the system of formal operations emerging in adolescence is to the concrete operations of the child as algebra is to arithmetic. Just as algebra can be regarded as a formalization (a separation of form from content) of arithmetic, so formal operations can be regarded as a formalization of concrete operations.

To illustrate this point, consider the following example. A child of eight or nine will, for the most part, have no difficulty with a concrete transivity problem. If the child is shown two sticks, A and B, of which A is 10 inches long and B is 8 inches long, he can easily judge A to be greater than B. Likewise, if he is shown B and C, a stick that is 6 inches long, he can also judge that B is longer than C. In addition, however, having made the foregoing comparisons he can, without comparing them directly, grasp that A is greater than C. He employed a concrete operational system of transitive inference $A > B$ and $B > C \therefore A > C$.

If, however, the same young man is asked the following question, "Helen is taller than Mary and Mary is taller than Jane. Who is the tallest of the three?" he has more difficulty. The transivity problem, by being translated to the symbolic level has been, so to speak, raised to a higher power. In a sense the young person now has to perform operations entirely in his head and without the aid of perceptual props. Under these circumstances, most children at the concrete operational stage fail to solve the problem (Inhelder & Piaget, 1958).

In addition to what they make possible symbolically, formal operations also permit more complex mental coordinations than were possible at the concrete operational stage. Basically, concrete operations permit children to coordinate two classes or two relations at a time. But formal operations permit young people to coordinate many more than two dimensions at a time. In effect, formal operations permit adolescents to use *propositional* logic, whereas concrete operations permit only the use of syllogistic logic. Propositional logic greatly expands the intellectual accomplishments of adolescents inasmuch as it makes possible the grasp of such things as experimentation, algebra, and calculus.

To illustrate the contrast between concrete and formal operational logics, a study (Elkind, Barocas, & Rosenthal, 1968) of the performance of children and adolescents on a combinatorial reasoning task is instructive. The materials consisted of four wooden chips

---

[1]Excellent summaries are provided by Flavell (1963) and by Ginsburg and Opper (1969).

that were differently colored. One was red *(R)*, one was white *(W)*, one was blue *(B)*, and the remaining chip was yellow *(Y)*. The child or adolescent was instructed to find all the possible combinations of the four chips, taking them one, two, three, and four at a time and disregarding the order. Both children and adolescents were given examples, with different colored chips, to acquaint them with the task.

The differences in performance were revealing. Concrete-operational children manipulated the chips to arrive at the various combinations and made errors of commission (repeating the same combination) and of omission (failing to report a particular combination). Many of the formal-operational children, in contrast, "read off" the combinations without manipulating the chips and without error. They said 0, *RW, RB, RY, WB, WY, YB, RWB, RWY, RBY, BWY,* and *BWRY,* often without touching the pieces at all.

As adolescents become more proficient in formal operations they can reason in a comparable way about propositions and grasp truth-functional logic. Consider the following example:

1. Be quiet in the library; be quiet outside: $p\ q$

2. Be quiet in the library; be loud outside: $p\ \overline{q}$

3. Be loud in the library; be quiet outside: $\overline{p}\ q$

4. Be loud in the library; be loud outside: $\overline{p}\ \overline{q}$

Now these four propositions can be combined in the way that the poker chips were combined, to yield a certain logical relationship. For example 2 versus 3 gives the logical relation of *incompatibility* of p and q. Likewise the coordination of $p\ q$ versus $\overline{p}\ q$ versus $\overline{p}\ \overline{q}$ indicates that p *implies* q. Again, these relations are purely formal and symbolic, in the sense that they are entirely separate from any specific content.

Propositional reasoning makes possible the attainment of many new skills and concepts. It enables the young person to engage in true experimental thinking insofar as it permits him or her to hold several variables constant while varying another. In addition, formal operations permit young people to explore many possible courses of action mentally. Formal operations also permit the understanding of such ideas as historical time, celestial space, and microscopic levels of existence. Formal operations are required to understand these because they are second-order concepts, concepts of concepts if you will. Historical time is essentially the concept of daily or yearly time raised to a higher power. Concepts of celestial space and of microscopic levels of existence are higher-order conceptualizations of the concepts of more immediate space and of normal size. In short, formal operations permit young people to comprehend concepts that are several steps removed from concrete, immediate experience.

In the realm of language, formal operations raise the young person's appreciation of the subtleties of language. Adolescents are able to understand simile and metaphor and can catch double entendres. In fiction, they can follow complex interwoven plots and appreciate characters who are multifaceted and driven by complex needs and motives. Formal operations also enable young people to appreciate fully the formal structure of the language. Only when they reach adolescence can young people really grasp and apply, in a purely formal way, the rules of grammar, even though they implicitly knew and used these rules as children.

On the interpersonal plane, the focus of concern in the present paper, formal operations make possible new achievements of a different kind. Formal operations enable adolescents to conceptualize (thought) and to think about thinking, both their own and that of other people. Two constructions grow out of this newfound ability, helping to explain some aspects of the young adolescent's interpersonal behavior. Young adolescents are preoccupied with themselves and assume that other people share that preoccupation. Young adolescents thus construct an "imaginary audience," which constantly monitors their appearance, behavior, and action. One consequence of this construction is enhanced self-consciousness (Elkind & Bowen, 1979).

A complementary construction is that of the *personal fable*. Young adolescents, because they believe that everyone is observing and monitoring their performance comes to think of the self as something special. The sense of specialness includes such notions as the belief that "others will grow old and die, but not me" and "others won't realize their ambitions, but I will." The personal fable is a story that we tell ourselves that is not true. But it does have a moral that is true, namely, that each of us has value as a human being. The fable in modified form stays with us throughout life because it is an adaptive construction. It is our salvation at times of crisis, failure, and misfortune.

Both the imaginary audience and the personal fable are powerful motivating forces for the young adolescent. Young people go to great pains to impress the audience and engage in a variety of activities to win audience approval. In the same way young people also engage in numerous activities that will enhance and support the fable of specialness. Their ability to impress the audience and to enhance the fable is aided and abetted by their ability, thanks to formal operations, to conceptualize possible courses of action and to choose, from among the many possible actions they can conceptualize, the one that best suits their purpose.

The emergence of the imaginary audience, the personal fable, and the conceptualization of possible courses of action make possible an entirely new level of interpersonal interaction. Unlike the child who is, for the most part, direct and open, adolescents become much more indirect and devious. They become much more calculating in their interpersonal relations. It is this new dimension of calculation in interpersonal relations that makes possible strategic interactions.

STRATEGIC INTERACTIONS

Erving Goffman has described a variety of human interaction patterns in an impressionistic yet consensually valid way (Goffman, 1969). One type is what he calls *strategic interactions,* interpersonal encounters that have as their aim the acquisition, concealment, or revelation of information through indirect means. In effect, strategic interactions involve calculation about the other person's thinking on the part of at least one of the people involved. Goffman quotes Chesterfield's advice to his son regarding diplomacy as an example of strategic thinking and performance:

There are some additional qualifications necessary, in the practical part of the business, which may deserve some consideration in your leisure moments — such as, an absolute command of your temper, so as not to be provoked to passion upon any account; patience to hear frivolous, impertinent and unreasonable applications; with address enough to refuse, without offending; or by your manner of granting, to double the obligation; dexterity enough to conceal a truth, without telling a lie; sagacity enough to read other people's countenance; and serenity enough not to let them discover anything by yours — a seeming frankness with a real reserve. These are the rudiments of a politician; the world must be your grammar. [Chesterfield cited in Goffman, 1969, p. 97]

Goffman's description of strategic interactions is essentially sociological and non-developmental. His description holds for adult members of the society. Looked at from the standpoint of cognitive development, however, true strategic interactions become possible only in early adolescence, thanks to the emergence of formal operations. Moreover, because the imaginary audience and the personal fable play so large a part in the young adolescent's behavior, strategic interactions have a personal, egocentric quality that is lacking in Chesterfield's description. Put differently, from a developmental standpoint one might expect the quality of these interactions to change as the individual matures.

This developmental change in the nature of strategic interactions may be explained as follows. The adolescent, much more than the child or the adult, seeks to enhance, maintain, and defend self-esteem in relation to the audience. Because he or she is breaking away from the security of parental ties, that continuing source of acceptance and self-esteem is weakened. And because the young adolescent does not yet have an occupation or supportive friendships, the usual sources of adult self-esteem and support are absent. That is why the young adolescent is so concerned with audience reactions. It is, for a brief period in life, the primary source of self-esteem enhancement.

Accordingly, strategic interactions in early adolescence have a different purpose and quality than they do in later adolescence and adulthood. In adulthood, the period Goffman (1969) writes about, strategic interactions are for the purpose of acquiring, retaining, or revealing information for some strategic purpose, such as winning a game, besting a foe, or gaining a business advantage. Although self-esteem is involved in such interactions, it is secondary to the other aims. But, in early adolescence, the prime aim of strategic interactions is the enhancement, maintenance, or defense of self-esteem.

It needs to be said, however, that some forms of strategic interaction characteristic of early adolescence are carried over to late adolescence and adulthood. But, in such instances, the interactions are clearly recognizable for what they are, egocentric interactions in the service of the imaginary audience and the personal fable. Those who are the victims of such interactions will often speak of them as "childish" or as "immature."

STRATEGIC INTERACTIONS IN EARLY ADOLESCENCE

The development of strategic interactions from early adolescence to adulthood parallels other cognitive developments, that is to say, development is usually from a stage of undifferentiation to one of differentiation and hierarchical organization (Werner, 1948). Young children, for example, do not distinguish clearly between what is physical and what is psychic; they regard dreams as physical things at the same time as they endow physical things with life. By adolescence, physical and mental are clearly differentiated and ordered in relation to one another. In the same way, young adolescents' initial efforts at strategic interactions are marked by a failure to distinguish clearly between their thoughts and those of the person being interacted with. Strategic interactions become more differentiated and more subtle with increasing age. We can now look at some of these interactions.

Phoning and Being Phoned

Among children and adults, phoning is largely a communicative activity. One calls to get or to give information. But in adolescence phoning and being phoned become indices of popularity and hence are bound up with self-esteem. Many young adolescents, therefore, engage in certain strategic interactions in order to make certain that they will receive phone calls. For example, some young people insist, at school, that they have important secret information that they will impart to a friend if the friend will call that evening.

Phoning someone else has its own strategic patterns. In calling another young person, one wants to avoid the impression that the call is made out of loneliness and a desire for friendship and companionship. If the boy or girl being phoned is not free to engage in the proposed activity, it is again necessary to avoid any show or expression of disappointment. This is what in contemporary adolescent parlance is called "cool." It means that you give no indication as to your needs or emotions and that you take whatever happens with equanimity.

Once on the phone, other strategems come into play. One of these is to stay on the phone a long, long time. Parents often assume that these long-winded discussions are solely devoted to projects or gossip. But they also have another purpose, to give other potential callers the *busy signal*. A phone in use signifies a popular person and the busy signal is a sign of popularity. Sometimes, of course, the adolescent may cut a conversation short because he or she is "expecting some other calls," which gives the caller the message that he or she is nothing special and that others are waiting to call the popular person.

These are only a few of the strategic interactions that center around phoning and being phoned in early adolescence. It is important to emphasize that this type of strategic interaction does not really persist into adulthood. Adults, for example, do not try to prove popularity by the number of calls they get. Nor do they show no emotion when friends decline to come over or to go out with them. For adults the appropriate response here is one of regret. Anything else would simply be rude.

Friendships

In early adolescence, friendship patterns often take on a strategic coloration. An attractive girl may befriend a less attractive one, in part, at least, to enhance the impression of attractiveness to the imaginary audience. But the contrast also confirms her sense of being specially, uniquely attractive. Similar motives operate for the less attractive girl, who hopes to impress the audience by the very fact of being associated with the attractive girl. And the fact of being the attractive girl's friend confirms the less attractive girl in *her* sense of specialness.

It is not surprising, then, that early adolescent friendships tend to be rather cliquish. Belonging to a special clique is impressive to an audience who admires such things (and the adolescent believes that everyone does). Likewise, belonging to the special group confirms the young person in his specialness — one would not belong unless one were special. And the adolescent who is not accepted by the clique suffers for the same reason that clique members rejoice, the audience knows he or she does not belong and the sense of being special in a negative way, the outsider, is very strong and very painful.

The foregoing paragraphs have suggested just some of the ways in which friendships are used strategically at early adolescence. Other patterns can be briefly noted. Some adolescents befriend others, again probably in part only, because the friend's parents are wealthy, well known, or both. Sometimes outsiders befriend other outsiders to demonstrate to the audience that they do have friends and to confirm their sense of specialness, in that they are the only ones to see the special qualities of the other outsider they have befriended.

It should be said, too, that the dynamics of friendship patterns can be seen within as well as between groups. This often occurs when there are three boys or girls who are rather good friends. Sociologically three is a bad number and two of the friends usually band together to ostracize the third. Here again the rejecting couple impresses the audience and confirms the fable of being special; the adolescent on the outside suffers from the public ouster and the private humiliation. Interestingly, the couples in the threesome may change so that an outsider becomes an insider and vice versa.

On Cutting and Being Cut

Recognizing another person in a public place is an important social act to both parties. By giving or withholding recognition a person can enhance or diminish self-esteem in others. This is true because to be recognized in a public place is recognition in front of an audience and a boost to self-esteem. Failure to be recognized has, of course, the opposite effect. Hence the giver or withholder of recognition has a sort of power, the use of which enhances that person's sense of specialness. But the use of that power is also seen by an audience and hence serves to impress others as well.

Young adolescents, thanks to formal operations, come to appreciate the power of recognition in public places. Nothing is so devasting to a person as to go through all the motions of public recognition — movement toward the other person, smiling, eyes clearly focused on the other person — and to have these overtures ignored by the other. On campus one day, I saw a young woman walk toward a young man, smiling and in the process of saying, "Hi, how are you?" when he turned on his heel and walked away. She was crushed, seemed to shrink into herself, looked about to see how large the audience had been and slowly walked away in a different direction from the one she had been walking in.

The power of cutting and the humiliation of being cut are largely a function of the imaginary audience that is assumed to monitor the actions of both parties involved. To be sure, cutting occurs at all later developmental periods, but it is basically an adolescent phenomena. The adult who is greeted by someone he would not prefer to meet is usually cool but polite. It is only the adult who has not matured who continues to use cutting as a strategic interaction. For most adults, cutting is a rude and immature way of dealing with difficult social interactions.

Dating

Dating involves a series of complex behavior patterns from the initial request to the final parting.

For young adolescents, dating is fraught with strategic interactions. There is, first of all, the matter of asking for a date. The problem is how to ask so as to avoid rejection. One of the first strategies young people have to learn is to ask first whether the other person is doing anything on the afternoon or evening in question. If the person *is* busy, then one has really not asked the other person out and so has not been rejected. This strategy also permits the datee to decline in advance by saying that he or she has "other plans." This strategy permits the dater to ask for a date indirectly and for the datee to refuse, equally indirectly.

Of course, not all young people are proficient in these strategies. If a young man calls up and, without preliminaries, asks a young woman to go out with him one night and she says she has other plans, he does not know if this is the truth or whether it is an evasion. This communication can be made clearer if the girl says that she would like to and would he please call again. If she does not encourage him to call again, this communication is less clear but is decidedly in the direction of rejection. Accordingly, the strategy of first asking the to-be-invited person whether they are busy offers both parties more flexibility than a direct invitation. It is a strategic interaction.

Asking for a date is, however, but one in a series of strategic interactions that will occur if the engagement is accepted. It is not necessary to discuss all of those interactions, but two are of particular interest from the standpoint of acquiring, retaining, and revealing information. These are the "pass" and the "parting gesture." We need to look at these in a little more detail.

Among older adolescents and adults, the function of a date is to bring two people together for a period of time in pleasurable circumstances and for entertainment and enjoyment. In early adolescence, however, dating is as much for the imaginary audience as it is for the pleasure of the other person. Many teenagers of the opposite sex have very little to say to one another. The idea of having a date, and of other people knowing about the date, is often more exciting than the date itself.

For the boy and for the girl as well, much of the anxiety of the date centers around the physical interaction that it entails. The boy's strategy is to try and "get" as much as he can with the girl's permission, or at least without violent protest. A usual strategy for the boy is to test the limits nonverbally with the aid of slowly moving arms and crawling fingers. The girl communicates equally nonverbally by either moving toward or away from the boy and by accepting or pushing away the troublesome hands.

How different this is from older adolescents and adults who use a variety of subtle body cues to communicate sexual attraction and willingness to engage in sexual encounter. One is reminded here of the difference, described earlier, between preadolescents and adolescents trying to solve the combinatorial problem with four chips of different colors that are to be put together in different ways. The preadolescents have to manipulate the materials themselves in order to arrive at the correct combinations. But the adolescents can do the manipulations mentally. In the same way, the early physical gropings of the young adolescent are prelude to the more subtle and covert means of communicating attraction and willingness at later stages of development.

The parting is another facet of dating that requires strategic interactions. Initiating and terminating interpersonal encounters are often the most difficult part of those encounters, and successful terminations, like successful initiations, require effective strategies. The aim of an effective termination is to leave both parties feeling good about themselves and one another and desirous of another interchange, or at least not aversive to one.

The most effective strategy for termination is to prepare for it in advance. The girl may say, as they are driving home, "My parents usually wait up for me and don't like me to ask people in at this hour." Usually, both boy and girl prepare in advance by rehearsing a few set lines such as, "Thank you very much. I had a very nice time." If either one wants to leave the door open for future engagements, one will say, "Let's do it again sometime." Often, however, young adolescents muff their lines and partings are likely to end with the boy rushing off and tossing an abrupt "See ya." into the wind.

In young adolescents, perhaps the greatest anxiety is encountered in the matter of the good-night kiss. First there are all the rules, frequently broken, about not kissing on the first date. Then there is the problem of finding out, on the boy's side, whether or not it will be permitted. What the boy has to decide is whether to ask first or simply to try it. In some ways, the verbal request invites a verbal rejection even if the girl is willing, because she may not be willing to verbalize it. On the other hand, if the boy tries to kiss the girl without asking first and she rejects the kiss, he is put in the position of being sexually aggressive and a roughneck.

Consequently, young adolescents do not usually handle terminations very well. Here again, their concern for the audience (''Hey, look at him, he kissed her!'' or ''Hey, look at him, she didn't let him kiss her!'' — in the case of the boy. And ''Hey, look at her, he really kissed her!'' or ''Look at her, she wouldn't let him kiss her!'') makes these interactions awkward in the extreme. Indeed, the young adolescent is often so concerned with the audience reaction that he or she ignores cues that would make this interaction more successful.

These are but a few of the interactions that emerge in the course of dating. I have hardly touched on the complex strategic interactions involved in petting and being petted, but here again each individual is trying to get information from the other in order to know how to proceed. Since both parties are inexperienced at this sort of communication, the interactions tend to be clumsy and unsatisfying. As young people gain in experience and practice, their strategic interactions around dating become more polished and proficient.

Forbidden Acts

Some of the most interesting and ingenious strategic interactions practiced by young adolescents have to do with the concealment or disguise of forbidden acts. Such acts include smoking, drinking, sexual intercourse, stealing from local stores, and skipping school. Because these acts are punishable to various degrees, adolescents go to great lengths to conceal or to disguise them. Many of these strategic interactions are based on the adolescent's assumptions about adult behavior patterns.

A strategic interaction engaged in by the author when he was a young teenager is illustrative of these strategems. I grew up in Detroit, where being able to drive a car was a sign of mature status. Beginners' licenses were then available at age 14. But before that, many of us at the age of 12 or 13 would ''borrow'' the family car to practice, driving it around the block. I usually tried to do this Sunday afternoons when my father was taking a nap and my mother was off visiting friends. Then I would take the keys off the dresser and a friend and I would be off for a few turns around the block.

Once, however, I failed to reckon on a party at a neighbor's house. When I returned to park the car in the spot where it had been parked before, I found the place taken! Panic quickly set in and my friend and I proceeded to push three cars back to make the correct spot open again. Tired but triumphant, I parked the car and started toward the house on my way to returning the keys to their position on the dresser. But there was my father standing on the porch! He had witnessed the whole procedure. I shall spare you the details of what followed, but I did not take the car without permission and without a permit again.

Smoking, whether it be tobacco or marijuana, is another act that young adolescents go to lengths to conceal. Finding a place to smoke that will be undiscovered presents a challenge in itself. Out of doors and in public places, of course, there is the danger of being seen and reported. Indoors there is the problem of odors, particularly if the parents do not smoke. Adolescents usually try to find a place that is not frequented by adults, such as a cellar or an attic as a place to smoke. At school, the bathroom is most often the place, but this is often policed by school officials. For young adolescents, finding a place to smoke that is free of detection is far from easy.

Concealing the fact that one has been smoking is not easy either. Breath mints are usually taken in large quantities, but they don't help the odor that attaches to clothes, hair, and skin. Some adolescents bathe and change clothes after smoking for just this reason. Obtaining new supplies is another problem that has been solved for the adolescent with the advent of cigarette machines. Store people are less cautious about selling minors cigarettes than they are about selling them beer and liquor.

Drinking presents some of the same strategic problems as smoking. It is necessary to find a place that will not be intruded on, it is necessary to get a supply of the beverage to be consumed, and it is necessary to hide or conceal the fact that any of this has taken place. The place is often someone's home that has been vacated for a known period of time. The beverage may be taken from parental reserves, but this means concealing the fact that some of those reserves are depleted. Here the adolescent's knowledge about parents comes in handy. If the parent is casual about how much beer, liquor, and wine he has on hand, it is easier for the adolescent to take some than if the parent keeps close tabs on his liquor cabinet.

A variety of strategies are employed to get supplies from stores. Fake ID cards are in great demand and some young people become quite adept at manipulating identity papers. Another strategy is to have someone who is older buy it for the younger participants. Other strategies are forging a note from parents to the effect that the vendor should sell the young person beer to take home to his parents. Still other young people dress and make themselves up to look older so that no questions will be asked.

Concealing the effects of drinking presents problems similar to those of smoking, except in the case when the young person is rather high. The strategy that is often decided on, but that often does not work, is avoidance. The young person tries to get to his or her room as quickly as possible and with as few interchanges as possible. A remark to the effect that he or she is not feeling well or has a headache, although tempting, has to be avoided because parents might become oversolicitous. A better strategy is to say that there is much homework to be done and that it has to be got at immediately.

It is interesting that in communities where alcohol is not permitted, adults have institutionalized some of the strategic interactions devised by adolescents. In Utah, for example, alcohol is sold only in state liquor stores and is not available in restaurants. But there are many private clubs where one can keep one's own liquor in a cabinet and have it served at the table. The private club is a strategy for having alcoholic beverages available in eating places when this is prohibited by law in public eating places.

One last example of strategic interactions around forbidden acts is that of skipping school. This involves a number of different strategies. One is to leave home in the morning giving no telltale signs in dress or demeanor that something is up. This is not as easy as it might appear. If the young person is too easy to awaken, dressed too quickly, and too compliant to parental requests, this could signal that something is not as it should be. Instead the adolescent has to make sure that he or she is as usual so that the parent will not suspect anything out of the ordinary. But playing one's usual self is not easy, and adolescents miscues can alert parents to the fact that something is afoot.

Finding a place to go is another problem. A movie is dark and offers concealment, but most movies do not open till mid-afternoon. In larger cities, the students can travel to another part of the city and find anonymity there. With the demise of downtown areas, many young people spend their unofficial leaves from school at shopping centers or malls. If the parents of one or another adolescent work, they can sometimes spend the day at home listening to records and watching television. It is necessary, however, to make sure that they leave no telltale signs of their full-day occupancy.

Perhaps the most difficult part of taking an unofficial day off from school comes in forging the note from parents. This is a delicate matter because the note must sound like a parent and not like a teenager. Also the notepaper must be the type that the parent would use. Trying to write neatly and to copy the style of the parental writing is still another challenge. Finally, handing the note in with the appropriate casual demeanor, when your heart is pounding against your ribs, is still another strategy that the adolescent who would engage in this type of forbidden action must master.

I hope that, in discussing the strategic interactions that surround forbidden acts, I have not given the impression of condoning these acts. I do not. For many different reasons, health, legal, and moral, I do not believe that young adolescents should smoke, or drink, or skip school. But, at the same time, I know that they do do these things and that in part, but only in part, it is because of the challenge of the strategic interactions they entail. Strategic interactions provide young people with challenge and excitement that are motivating in and of themselves, quite apart from the often dubious pleasure of the forbidden act.

That is to say, in engaging in forbidden acts and outwitting adults, adolescents are again performing for an audience. Their success impresses the audience and confirms the personal fable of uniqueness and specialness. In understanding the psychology of forbidden acts, therefore, we need to take account of the pleasure and rewards that come from successfully engaging in strategic interactions as well as the rewards associated with the forbidden acts themselves.

THE DEVELOPMENT OF STRATEGIC INTERACTIONS IN OLDER ADOLESCENTS AND ADULTS

In this chapter I have argued that strategic interactions have a developmental dimension and that some types of strategic interactions are particularly characteristic of the young adolescent. What happens to these types of interaction as young people grow older? In general, their development moves in one of several different directions: automatization, legalization, and transformation.

Automatization

Some of the interactions that young adolescents engage in with great conscious deliberation eventually become automatic. For example, as phoning and being phoned becomes a more common experience, patterns of verbal interaction over the phone become more or less automatic and do not need to be thought about. To be sure, some conscious aspects of phoning and being phoned still linger on. Being called is still an ego booster. But for the adult, such popularity usually means that he or she is successful in his or her career, not necessarily in interpersonal relations.

Dating skills also become more sophisticated and automatic with increasing age. This permits young people to be more natural with one another once the mechanics of dating becomes routine. Also, as teenagers become older they verbalize more about these interpersonal relationships and there is less need for nonverbal communication to ask and answer questions about physical interactions. And more generally, relationships in later adolescence become more comprehensive, more inclusive of the total persons involved and less focused on the sensual alone.

The automatization of some strategic interactions does not mean that all such interactions are at an end. Far from it. Young adults need to learn how best to present themselves when applying for a job, when asking for a raise, and so on. As adults we have to engage in a whole new set of strategic interactions that revolve primarily around our work, our relationships with our friends and family. Like the automatization of other skills, the automatization of strategic interactions of adolescence frees and prepares us for more complex, higher order strategic interactions that must be engaged in later in life.

Legalization

Some forms of strategic interaction, particularly those associated with some forbidden acts, are rendered unnecessary by virtue of the fact that young people have reached the age of 18 or 21. At this age it is no longer necessary to use strategems to obtain cigarettes or liquor or to find a place where they can be used without detection and to disguise the fact that they have been used.

To be sure, adults find new forms of forbidden acts to take their place. Illegal gambling, dope trafficking, and prostitution are forbidden acts that adults engage in strategic interactions to conceal. Prostitution is somewhat unique in this regard because the prostitute must reveal what it is she is vending in order to make a sale. Strategies must then be devised to avoid being picked up by the police but to enhance being picked up by a "John." Accordingly, the coming-of-age that makes some forbidden acts legal does not eliminate the phenomenon of strategic interactions about forbidden acts. There are simply new kinds of acts that are forbidden among adults and new types of strategic interactions that are substituted for those employed in adolescence.

Transformation

Some types of strategic interaction are transformed into more elaborate procedures as young people grow older. Cutting and being cut is a case in point. Adults continue to engage in cutting in public places, but it has new meaning and different consequences. Among adults cutting and being cut is often related to social and professional status. That is to say, the cutting is done to what the person represents as much as to the person himself or herself. In adolescence, cutting is always personal and lacks the social dimension.

As adults become more and more identified with occupational and social status roles, their self-esteem comes from these roles as much as it does from personal achievement. Cutting in public places for adults is often a matter of asserting one's occupational or professional role, rather than a personal slight. Administrators, for example, whether they be factory foremen or university deans, tend to be less than effusive in greeting their workers or faculty in public places. It is not that they wish to put down the particular individuals as much as it is that they wish to make clear the difference in their respective status.

Friendship patterns also undergo transformation as young people mature. Friendships tend to become much less egocentric and more based on mutual interests and compatability of temperament rather than for more exploitive purposes. Certainly, even adult friendships can have an exploitive dimension, but this is usually a secondary factor in the relationship. Strategic interactions in mature friendships often center about how best to provide support and encouragement when the friend is having a hard time and how best to rejoice in the friend's happiness and success. Mature friendships lack the egocentrism they had in early adolescence.

SUMMARY AND CONCLUSION

The aim of the present chapter was both methodological and substantive. With regard to methodology, I tried to demonstrate an alternative approach to current studies of social cognition. Rather than trying to *extend* concepts derived from developmental psychology to interpersonal phenomena, I tried to *analyze* a construct taken from sociology — namely Erving Goffman's concept of strategic interaction — from a developmental perspective. To this end, I reviewed the developmental changes coincident with formal operations to demonstrate that only when these operations are present can true strategic interactions take place.

With regard to substance, I described a number of interactions peculiar to early adolescence. These included phoning and being phoned, cutting and being cut, dating, and forbidden acts. In contrast to adults, adolescents engage in strategic interactions largely to maintain, defend, or enhance self-esteem. Many of the strategic interactions of early adolescence are modified with increasing age as a consequence of automatization, transformation, or legalization. In adulthood, new and different forms of strategic interaction come into prominence.

In his own work Piaget has always recognized the fruitfulness of borrowing from different disciplines to find problems for developmental psychology. This point has somehow been lost in contemporary studies of social cognition. I hope the present discussion has demonstrated the potential fruitfulness of starting a developmental analysis from properly sociological concepts.

REFERENCES

Baldwin, J. M. *Thought and things or genetic logic* (2 vols). New York: Macmillan, 1906–1908.

Boole, G. *The laws of thought*. New York: Dover, 1950. (Originally published, 1854.)

Elkind, D., and Bowen, R. Imaginary audience behavior in children and adolescents. *Developmental Psychology,* 1979, *15*, 38–44.

Elkind, D., Barocas, R., and Rosenthal, H. Combinatorial thinking in adolescents from graded and ungraded classrooms. *Perceptual and Motor Skills,* 1968, *27,* 1015–1018.

Flavell, J. H. *The developmental psychology of Jean Piaget*. Princeton, N.J.: Princeton University Press, 1963.

———. *The development of role-taking and communication skills in children*. New York: Wiley, 1968.

Ginsburg, H., and Opper, S. *Piaget's theory of intellectual development: An introduction*. Englewood Cliffs, N.J.: Prentice-Hall, 1969.

Goffman, E. *Strategic interaction*. Philadelphia: University of Pennsylvania Press, 1969.

Inhleder, B., and Piaget, J. *The growth of logical thinking in children and adolescents*. New York: Basic Books, 1958.

Piaget, J. *The moral judgment of the child*. New York: Free Press, 1948.

———. *The judgment and reasoning of the child*. London: Routledge & Kegan Paul, 1951.

———. *The language and thought of the child*. London: Routledge & Kegan Paul, 1952.

Selman, R. The relation of role-taking to the development of moral judgment in children. *Child Development,* 1971, *42,* 79–91.

Werner, H. *Comparative psychology of mental development*. New York: Harper & Row, 1948.

PART THREE

Variations in Adolescence

CHAPTER 14

Psychopathology in Adolescence

Irving B. Weiner

This chapter will attempt to provide a useful discussion of adolescent psychopathology (within the limited space available) by focusing on psychological disturbances that are relatively frequent among adolescents, that tend to make their first appearance during adolescence, or that bear some special relationship to the developmental tasks of the teen-age years. The first section will review some epidemiological data on adolescent psychopathology and indicate the limitations of both traditional diagnostic categories and problem-oriented classification in studying or working with this age group. Subsequent sections will address distinctively adolescent features of several patterns of disturbance that play an important role in adolescent psychopathology.

EPIDEMIOLOGY AND CLASSIFICATION

The most comprehensive epidemiological data on adolescent psychopathology currently available come from a cumulative psychiatric case register that has been maintained in Monroe County, New York, since 1960. Whereas most studies of diagnostic patterns are limited to the population of a single clinic or hospital, the Monroe County register comprises reports from both inpatient and outpatient units in a university medical center, a community mental health center, a community hospital, and a state hospital located in Rochester, New York. The national statistics published by the Department of Health, Education, and Welfare are limited to patients seen in clinics and hospitals. The Monroe County register, however, also includes the substantial segment of psychologically troubled persons who are seen in private offices. This register is sufficiently comprehensive to receive information on approximately 95% of all psychiatric contacts in the community (Gardner et al., 1963).

Table 1 indicates the distribution of traditional diagnostic categories among 1334 adolescents who constituted the total number of 12- to 18-year-olds appearing in the register during a 2-year period (from January 1, 1961 to December 31, 1962) reported by Weiner and Del Gaudio (1976). That study provides information on the relationship of diagnosis to age, sex, social class, and facility (hospital, clinic, private office) as well as on the 10-year course of adolescents initially receiving various diagnoses. Our concern here is not with the details of this epidemiological work, but rather with how much it helps to categorize adolescent psychopathology in ways that are useful for clinical and research purposes. The answer, unfortunately, appears to be not very much at all.

In particular, such broad categories of disturbance as neurosis and personality disorder are ill-suited to the formulation of incisive research or clinical strategies, such as how best

Table 1   Distribution of Traditional Diagnostic Categories in a County-wide, Two-year Sample of 12- to 18-year-old Psychiatric Patients (n = 1334)

Diagnostic Category	%
Schizophrenia	8.5
Neurosis	13.3
Personality disorder	31.4
Situational disorder	27.1
Suicide attempt	2.8
Other[a]	16.9
	100.0

Source: Based on data reported by I. B. Weiner and A. C. Del Gaudio (1976).

[a]Includes affective psychosis, organic brain syndrome, alcoholism, mental retardation, psychophysiological reaction, anorexia nervosa, special symptom disorder, behavior disorder of adolescence, diagnosis deferred, and no psychiatric diagnosis.

to study the etiology of a condition or how best to treat it. These broad categories encompass a wide variety of conditions; there is likely to be as much variation within as between kinds of neuroses and personality disorders. For example, the traditional diagnoses of hysterical neurosis and obsessive-compulsive neurosis probably involve more differences in personality structure and dynamics than do hysterical *neurosis* and hysterical *personality* (American Psychiatric Association, 1968).

The problems inherent in broad, heterogeneous diagnostic categories can be avoided by categorizing adolescent psychopathology according to the specific kinds of neuroses and personality disorders included in traditional diagnostic nomenclature. However, these subclassifications tend to be unreliable. Clinicians can agree reasonably well on whether a disturbed person is suffering from an organic, schizophrenic, neurotic, or personality disorder, but, at best, they agree poorly in assigning more specific diagnostic labels (Kendell, 1975, Chap. 3; Spitzer & Wilson, 1975; Tarter, Templer, & Hardy, 1975; Zubin, 1967). It is for this reason that the Rochester group and most other epidemiological researchers choose to work with the kinds of broad categories listed in Table 1.

Even if traditional diagnostic categories could be made reliably specific, they would not be uniformly relevant to what is salient in adolescent psychopathology. Some traditional diagnoses, such as depressive neurosis, relate closely to the kinds of concerns and pathological reactions that young people are likely to have. Others, such as obsessive-compulsive neurosis and schizoid personality, may occur in adolescents but have no special significance for them as opposed to other age groups.

Finally, the usefulness of traditional epidemiological data in identifying disturbances especially frequent among adolescents is often more apparent than real. To illustrate, the most striking difference between adolescent and adult patients suggested by Table 1 involves the category of situational disorder. Situational disorder was diagnosed for 27.1% of Weiner and Del Gaudio's adolescent cohort, whereas among adults the incidence of this diagnosis in outpatient clinics — where one might expect them to occur most frequently — is about 5 to 6% (U.S. Department of HEW, 1969). Nevertheless, it is questionable whether situational disorder is a largely adolescent pattern of psychological disturbance; rather, it seems to be a much overused term that is often invoked when clinicians are unable to recognize or unwilling to label the early stages of specific psychopathology in their adolescent patients.

Situational disorder is defined as follows in the *Diagnostic and Statistical Manual* of the American Psychiatric Association:

> This major category is reserved for more or less transient disorders . . . that occur in individuals without any apparent underlying mental disorders and that represent an acute reaction to overwhelming environmental stress. . . . If the patient has good adaptive capacity his symptoms usually recede as the stress diminishes. [P. 000]

This definition implies that situational disorders come and go in relation to external stresses alone, do not usually indicate a need for psychotherapy, and do not ordinarily progress into more serious forms of psychopathology.

These expectations were not borne out by Weiner and Del Gaudio (1976) in the 10-year follow up of the adolescents in their population. From 1962–1972, 52.4% of their original cohort reappeared in the case register for one or more periods of psychiatric service. Those originally diagnosed situational disorder were just as likely to reappear (51.9%) as those originally diagnosed neurosis (51.7%) or personality disorder (51.3%). Moreover, the situational disorder group returned for as many subsequent periods of psychiatric help over the next 10 years (mean: 3.93) as the neurosis (mean: 4.47) and personality disorder (mean: 3.22) groups. Finally, 11.2% of the situational disorder group who returned for further help for subsequently diagnosed schizophrenic as compared to 14.1% of the neurotic group and 14.4% of the personality disorder group.

Hence, despite the frequency with which situational disorder is diagnosed among adolescent patients, it seems unwise to assign it much significance in theoretical, research, or clinically oriented discussions of adolescent psychopathology. Its usage frequently masks more specific conditions that should be identified in their own right to avoid minimizing the potential seriousness of a disturbed adolescent's condition and to promote prompt and appropriate treatment planning (Masterson, 1967b, 1968; Meeks, 1973; Weiner, 1970, Chap. 2).

The shortcomings of traditional diagnostic categories can be avoided by using a problem-oriented approach to classify adolescent psychopathology. A focus on clearly observable behavior problems known to have special significance in adolescence, such as suicidal or delinquent behavior, provides categories that are both reliable and relevant. However, a behavior-problem approach also has disadvantages. Most of all, it may fail to incorporate optimally the considerable body of information available from clinical and research studies of some traditional diagnostic categories, notably schizophrenia and depression.

Hence our purposes seem best served by an eclectic perspective that draws on the following mix of traditional-diagnostic and behavior-problem categories:

1. *Schizophrenia.* Schizophrenia, the most prevalent of serious psychological disorders, is more likely to make its first appearance during the adolescent and early adult years than at any other time of life.

2. *Depression.* In its mild and transient forms, depression is probably the most commonly experienced type of psychological distress among adolescents; when relatively severe or prolonged, it contributes to a wide range of behavior problems seen in youthful patients.

3. *Suicidal behavior.* The frequency of suicide attempts is disproportionately high among adolescents as compared to other age groups; familiarity with the antecedents and consequents of such suicidal behavior is essential for clinicians and researchers who work with young people.

4. *Problems of school attendance*. Although reluctance to attend school is frequently regarded as a problem primarily of elementary-school children, adolescents are not unlikely to experience an initial onset of school phobic reactions. These reactions tend to originate in concerns that are related to developmental tasks of the teen-age years and differ from the concerns of younger children who exhibit school-attendance problems.

5. *Problems of school achievement*. Difficulties in school achievement, whether secondary to other kinds of disturbance or a primary symptom in their own right, appear to account for more referrals of adolescents for professional help than any other presenting problem.

6. *Delinquent behavior*. Illegal, antisocial, and disruptive behavior increases substantially during the adolescent years, and efforts to understand and modify such behavior early in its course are extremely important in preventing progression to adult psychopathology and social maladjustment.

This chapter deals with the first five of these categories of disturbance. Delinquent behavior is considered separately in Chapter 16. For each category, the discussion will forego a general overview of the condition or problem in favor of emphasizing its distinctive features in adolescents as opposed to other age groups. For example, schizophrenia and depression in adolescents differ from adult forms of these disturbances in the frequently equivocal, mixed, or masked forms in which they first appear, whereas they seem to have the same kinds of causes at both ages. Problems of school attendance and achievement, on the other hand, have similar manifestations in adolescents as in younger children, but their most likely causes differ in the two age groups. Hence the sections on schizophrenia and depression will pay special attention to symptomatology, whereas those on school-related problems will emphasize causation.

SCHIZOPHRENIA

Because it is a seriously disabling disturbance that frequently runs a chronic or recurrent course, schizophrenia is perhaps the major mental health problem in the United States. Approximately 2% of our population is likely to experience schizophrenia at some time during their life. Almost one-half of the beds in mental hospitals in the United States — and one-quarter of all hospital beds — are occupied by schizophrenic patients. The lack of productivity by persons with schizophrenia and the expenses of their treatment and rehabilitation are estimated to cost $11.6 to $19.5 billion each year. Despite enormous effort to develop improved methods of treating schizophrenia, the majority of persons who develop this disorder are either permanently hospitalized or pass through repeated episodes of relapse and rehospitalization; it is estimated that of those schizophrenics who are living in the community, fewer than 40% are able to achieve an average level of adjustment (Babigian, 1975; Gunderson & Mosher, 1975; National Institute of Mental Health, 1972; Yolles & Kramer, 1969).

Schizophrenia is a central topic in adolescent psychopathology for two reasons. First, it has been recognized since Bleuler's (1911/1950) monograph on schizophrenia that, "the adolescent age period seems to offer a particular predisposition to this disease" (p. 340). Subsequent research findings and clinical observations generally confirm that most forms of schizophrenic disturbance tend to appear first during or soon after adolescence (Arieti,

1974, Chap. 8; Holzman & Grinker, 1974). Second, schizophrenia is present in a substantial proportion of adolescents who come to professional attention. Approximately 25 to 30% of the adolescents admitted to psychiatric hospitals and 6 to 8% of those seen in psychiatric clinics and private offices are diagnosed schizophrenic (Rosen et al., 1965; Weiner & Del Gaudio, 1976).

Like most traditional diagnoses, schizophrenia has been conceptualized in many different ways. Some clinicians and researchers define it according to certain manifest symptoms, such as widespread delusions (Carpenter, 1976; Carpenter, Strauss, & Bartko, 1974); some according to inferred defects in certain mental functions, such as the inability to maintain segmental set (Shakow, 1962); some according to inferred personality dynamics, such as concurrently intense needs to cling to and avoid other people (Burnham, Gladstone, & Gibson, 1969); and some according to inferred biochemical or neurological abnormalities, such as a failure of cortical-subcortical integration (Venables, 1967).

These conceptual differences notwithstanding, it is generally agreed that the observable manifestations of schizophrenia in adults and adolescents alike represent impaired capacity to think coherently, logically, and at appropriate levels of abstraction; distorted perceptions of reality; diminished ability to establish and maintain comfortable and rewarding interpersonal relationships; and weakened control over ideation, affect, and impulses (Arieti, 1974; Bellak, Hurvich, & Gediman, 1973; Weiner, 1970, Chap. 4).

However, there are three aspects of schizophrenic disturbance in adolescence that merit special attention:

1. Schizophrenia beginning in adolescence is more likely than adult-onset schizophrenia to present as a mixed disturbance in which identifying features of schizophrenia are obscured by other kinds of symptoms.

2. Certain kinds of personality developments during childhood and adolescence can be identified as having a relatively high risk for subsequent schizophrenia.

3. The long-term prognosis for schizophrenia is somewhat less favorable when it becomes manifest in adolescence than when it appears in adulthood.

Presenting Picture

Only about 30 to 40% of schizophrenic adolescents present with clear indications of the kinds of cognitive, interpersonal, and integrative impairments that characterize schizophrenic breakdown. The rest tend initially to show a mixed picture in which such indications of schizophrenia as incoherent thinking, innaccurate perceptions, and inappropriate affect are peripheral or secondary to other kinds of problems or complaints. Two types of mixed picture are particularly likely to represent the early phase of a schizophrenic breakdown. In one, the young person complains primarily of depressive symptoms, including feelings of hopelessness, lack of interest in people or activities, and suicidal thoughts or attempts. In the other picture, the clinical data are colored primarily by behavior problems that suggest sociopathic tendencies, including family conflict, fighting, stealing, running away, truancy, and school failure (Masterson, 1967a, Chap. 5; Sands, 1956; Symonds & Herman, 1957; Weiner, 1970, Chap. 4).

The initial onset of schizophrenia is therefore often more difficult to detect in adolescents than in adults. Sometimes only the persistence of the schizophrenic features in a mixed picture, especially after other symptoms or behavior problems have abated, makes the presence of a schizophrenic disorder clear. In other instances, the particular intensity of a young person's disordered thinking, impaired reality testing, or interpersonal aversion, especially as revealed in psychological testing, may point to schizophrenia, despite the predominance of nonschizophrenic elements in the diagnostic picture (Cohen et al., 1970; P. Katz, 1967; Rinsley, 1972; Spotnitz, 1961; Weiner, 1970, Chap. 4; Weiner, 1977b).

Premorbid Patterns

A substantial amount of research has sought to identify personality patterns that have more than a chance predictive relationship to subsequent schizophrenia. Some of this work has concluded that young people who later become schizophrenic are relatively likely to display a "schizoid" premorbid adjustment. Bower, Shellhamer, and Daily (1960), for example, found that high-school students who later became schizophrenic had significantly less interest in social relations and group activities than their peers and could be characterized as having a shut-in, withdrawing kind of personality.

Other work has suggested that preschizophrenic young people tend to behave in a "stormy" rather than a withdrawn or unobtrusive manner. Robins (1966), for example, found that children and adolescents who became schizophrenic were more likely to display overt, antisocial behavior problems than they were to be seclusive or to pass unnoticed through the developmental years.

More recent studies indicate that such findings are complementary rather than contradictory. Depending on individual differences and variations in sampling, both withdrawn and antisocial patterns of personality development are associated with an increased risk of schizophrenic breakdown (Offord & Cross, 1969; Watt, 1972; Watt et al., 1970; Woerner et al., 1972). Research has also provided three more precise clues to what may be the early stages of a developing schizophrenic disturbance.

With respect to withdrawal, first of all, Barthell and Holmes (1968; see also Meehl, 1971) used the number of times a graduating senior's picture appeared in his or her high-school yearbook as an index of participation in peer-group activities. They found that a sample of adult schizophrenics had significantly fewer such pictures than a comparison group of their classmates. These data imply that those young people who pass relatively unnoticed through adolescence because they do not become engaged in peer-group activities — and not simply because they have a quiet nature — are the ones who are particularly likely to manifest serious psychological problems later on.

Second, the friendship patterns of adolescents seem especially significant in determining whether they are at high risk for subsequent schizophrenia. Young people who have very few friends, who see these "friends" only infrequently and share few common interests or activities with them, and who are involved in exploitative rather than mutual relationships with them are much more likely to become schizophrenic than youngsters who, even if they have a relatively inactive social life, carry on at least a few really close and mutual friendships (Kreisman, 1970; Pitt, Kornfeld, & Kolb, 1963).

Third, the direction of any antisocial behavior among adolescents appears to have implications for the nature of their subsequent adjustment. Young people who act selfishly and aggressively in the community but do not direct such behavior toward their family are more likely to develop an antisocial personality disorder as adults than they are to become schizophrenic; on the other hand, sociopathic behavior by adolescents within their own home and family environment is more likely to be a precursor of schizophrenia than of sociopathy (Nameche, Waring, & Ricks, 1964).

Finally of interest are reports by Watts (1978) and Watt and Lubensky (1976) of sex differences in the kinds of behavior that are likely to precede schizophrenic disturbance. The schizophrenic males they studied tended to become noticeably more irritable, aggressive, negativistic, and defiant of authority than other boys during their high school years. The preschizophrenic females tended to be emotionally immature and more passive than other girls as far back as elementary school; as adolescents they became less passive but grew increasingly shy, inhibited, and withdrawn from peer-group activities. Thus it may be that a premorbid, "stormy" personality pattern is especially likely to characterize boys who become schizophrenic and a premorbid, "schizoid" pattern to characterize girls who become schizophrenic.

Prognosis

It has generally been found that one-third of adults who are hospitalized with an initial schizophrenic breakdown recover, another one-third improve but suffer relapses and must re-enter the hospital from time to time, and the remaining one-third become permanently hospitalized (Mosher, 1975). When an initial schizophrenic breakdown occurs during adolescence, the prognosis is somewhat less favorable than this.

Data pooled from five follow-up studies indicate that 23% of adolescents hospitalized for schizophrenia recover, 25% improve but suffer lingering symptoms or occasional relapses, and the remaining 52% make little or no progress and remain hospitalized indefinitely (Annesley, 1961; Carter, 1942; Errara, 1957; Masterson, 1956; Warren, 1965). The long-term prospects of schizophrenic adolescents are probably not quite so grim for those who can be treated entirely on an outpatient basis, without requiring hospitalization. Unfortunately, adequate data to determine the general outlook for nonhospitalized schizophrenic adolescents or to draw comparisons with a similar adult population are not available.

DEPRESSION

Depression, like schizophrenia, has been conceptualized in many different ways. Contemporary research on depressive disorder is influenced by three formulations in particular:

1. Depression consists primarily of a cognitive set comprising negative views toward oneself, the world, and the future (Beck, 1970, 1974).

2. Depression is a state of learned helplessness revolving around the feeling of being unable to control the events in one's life (Seligman, 1974, 1975).

3. Depression represents the inability of a person to behave in ways that lead to contingent positive reinforcement (Lewinsohn, 1974a, 1974b).

Regardless of which of these or other possible ways of viewing depression is preferred, a common element in the experience of virtually all people who are depressed — and one that is especially useful in understanding the depressive reactions of adolescents — is a sense of loss.

As the author has noted elsewhere (Weiner, 1975), a sense of loss may be experienced in relation to the loss of a personal relationship through death, separation, or a broken friendship; it may involve loss of self-esteem related to guilt or failure; or it may consist of a loss of bodily integrity subsequent to illness, incapacitation, disfigurement (which may for adolescents include having to wear glasses or braces), or even normal bodily changes. These are all experiences to which adolescents are especially sensitive as a function of the developmental tasks they are facing, such as adapting to dramatic changes in their body size and functions and learning to be psychologically independent of their parents (Weiner, 1977a). It is for this reason that some psychoanalytic writers draw close parallels between some aspects of normal adolescent development and the process of mourning (Freud, 1958; Laufer, 1966).

With respect to psychopathology, however, depressive disorders are infrequently diagnosed among adolescents seen in clinics and hospitals. The data in Table 2 come from national statistics on outpatient psychiatric services, general hospital inpatient psychiatric services, and state and county mental hospitals. They show a large increase between age 10 and 19 in the percentage of youthful patients who are diagnosed depressed; nevertheless even 18- to 19-year-old patients show only an approximately 10% incidence of this disorder, which is substantially lower than the incidence in adults.

Yet there appears to be a considerable difference between the frequency with which depression is actually diagnosed in adolescents and the role it plays in their adjustment difficulties. Whereas fewer than 10% of adolescent patients are diagnosed as being primarily depressed, about half of them display such depressive symptoms as dysphoric affect, self-depreciation, crying spells, and suicidal thoughts or attempts (Masterson, 1967a). Moreover, between 35 and 40% of nonpatient samples of young people report having some feelings of sadness, worthlessness, or pessimism about the future (Albert & Beck, 1975; Murray, 1973).

Table 2   Percentage of Psychiatric Patients Diagnosed Psychoneurotic Depressive Reaction, by Age and Sex

	Age			
	10–14	15–17	18–19	25–44
Outpatient psychiatric services				
Total	1.7	3.3	7.6	14.8
Male	1.6	2.0	4.6	7.8
Female	2.1	4.8	10.4	19.7
General hospitals				
Total	5.8	11.6	15.8	15.9
Male	4.9	8.8	10.5	9.7
Female	7.2	13.8	19.8	19.6
Mental hospitals				
Total	2.3	3.5	6.6	10.0
Male	1.7	2.0	3.7	5.3
Female	3.6	5.6	11.0	16.8

Source: From Weiner (1975). Based on U.S. Public Health Service statistics on 466,102 terminated clinic patients, 380,922 discharged general-hospital patients, and 153,314 first admissions to mental hospitals.

Depression is also noteworthy among adolescents because of the frequency with which it is expressed through other than typical depressive symptoms. A wide range of behavior problems seen in young people can be understood as masked depression or depressive equivalents. Sensitivity to masked depression has proved helpful in formulating incisive treatment strategies for many kinds of disturbed adolescents whose underlying concerns might otherwise have been overlooked (Cytryn & McKnew, 1974; Glaser, 1967; Krakowski, 1970; Malmquist, 1975; Toolan, 1971). This section will focus on the reasons why younger people often express depression in masked forms and on the most common of these forms seen in early and late adolescence.

Manifestations of Depression in Early Adolescence

Prior to age 16 or 17, adolescents are unlikely to display traditional adult symptoms of depression, for two major reasons. First, the developmental tasks young people are facing at this age — including adjusting to rapid biological changes, learning to become independent of their parents, and moving into heterosexual friendship and dating relationships — pose serious challenges to their self-esteem. As a result, they find it extremely difficult to admit to themselves or others any self-critical attitudes or concerns about being a competent person, and they are accordingly relatively unlikely to experience or to display the gloom, self-depreciation, and feelings of helplessness and hopelessness that commonly characterize depression in adults. Second, like younger children, early adolescents are still at a developmental stage in which they are inclined more toward doing things than thinking about them.

For these reasons, early adolescents who experience loss and disappointment tend to express their distress through various kinds of overt behavior, rather than through the introspective preoccupations with which adults typically manifest depression. Specifically, they behave in ways that indirectly reflect the psychological toll of depression, the efforts to ward off depression, or an appeal for help.

The Psychological Toll of Depression

Early adolescents who become depressed often show the toll their psychological problems are taking on their ability to function through a triumverate of symptoms consisting of fatigue, hypochondriasis, and concentration difficulty. Each of these is often ascribed by the youngsters' family, teachers, and pediatrician to other causes: fatigue is seen as a natural effect of growing rapidly and leading an active life; hypochondriasis is seen as a normal aspect of adolescents' attention to marked changes in how their bodies look and function; and difficulty in concentrating, which most often comes to light in relation to poor school performance, is regarded either as evidence of lack of interest in school or of some form of learning disability.

Although none of these possibilities can be ignored, they fail to identify the role that underlying depression can play in producing these three symptoms. Youngsters who are persistently fatigued, even after adequate rest, may be worn out from struggling with depressive concerns that they are unable to resolve or express directly. Youngsters with extensive body preoccupations may be experiencing depressing concerns about their physical adequacy that they are unable to admit to themselves or share with others. And youngsters who have difficulty absorbing and retaining information despite working hard on their studies may simply have a large part of their sustained attention bound up with depressive concerns of which they are not fully aware. By recognizing these symptoms as indicative of masked depression in adolescents, clinicians can often plan a treatment approach — aimed at elucidating and working through the underlying depressive concerns — that works more quickly and effectively than attempts to do something directly about the fatigue, hypochondriasis, or concentration difficulty.

Efforts to Ward Off Depression

In some instances the masked forms of depression seen in early adolescence consist not so much of the toll this disorder is taking as of efforts to ward off depression and thereby avoid any such toll. Two common forms such efforts take are restlessness and a flight to or from people. Restlessness serves as a depressive equivalent by virtue of the fact that keeping busy is an effective remedy for feeling depressed. Given their strong needs to avoid depressive feelings, early adolescents are especially likely to ward off depression through a high-activity level that seems driven rather than productive and that makes them restless and easily bored. There is a constant need for new and different kinds of stimulation and a limited tolerance for anything that is familiar or routine; what may initially appear to be a lively enthusiasm for life turns out on closer inspection to be a desperate effort to keep one step ahead of having time to think.

In their relationships with people, depressed younger adolescents may exhibit a constant need for companionship and a continuous search for new and "more interesting" friends. Like restlessness, such a flight toward people helps to keep the person stimulated and occupied, so that there is little opportunity for depressive thoughts or feelings to intrude on his or her consciousness. In other instances, especially when being around others increases their fears of being rejected or abandoned, depressed youngsters may display a flight from rather than toward people. Since they may still feel a need to ward off depression through activity, these adolescents may pair their avoidance of people with increased involvement in various kinds of solitary activities or with pets, to whom they can express affection without risk of rejection (Weiner, 1975).

Appeals for Help

In some early adolescents, depression is expressed primarily through indirect appeals for help, usually in the form of problem behavior. Unsuccessful in communicating through other means that they are in psychological pain and need solace and support, these youngsters resort to temper tantrums, running away, stealing, truancy, and numerous other defiant, rebellious, antisocial, and delinquent acts. These acts compel attention from others and force on them some recognition of need for help (Anthony, 1968; Bonnard, 1961; Burks & Harrison, 1962; Spiegel, 1967).

Problem behavior that is symptomatic of underlying depression differs in three respects from the aggressive, impulsive, and inconsiderate behavior seen in sociopathic youngsters. First, such depressive equivalents are usually uncharacteristic of the young person and in contrast to an earlier history of exemplary behavior. Second, the onset of the problem behavior can usually be traced to some presumably depressing experience, such as a divorce in the family or death of a parent. Third, as might be expected from the communication purposes the misbehavior is intended to serve, it tends to be carried out in ways that guarantee the young person's being observed or caught (Keeler, 1954; Masterson, 1970; Shorr & Speed, 1963; Weiner, 1970, Chap. 5).

Manifestations of Depression in Late Adolescence

As adolescents mature, they become increasingly oriented toward ideational as well as expressive ways of dealing with their experience, and they also develop increased capacities to think about themselves critically and to share self-critical thoughts with others. Hence they become more likely than before to manifest depression in traditional adult symptoms. Nevertheless, older adolescents commonly express depression indirectly through such maladaptive behavior as drug abuse, sexual promiscuity, alienation, and suicide attempts.

Contrary to belief in some quarters, drug abuse and sexual promiscuity characterize only a small minority of adolescents and indicate serious maladjustment when they occur. Although each of these problem behaviors has multiple causes, both have certain antidepressive features that may result in their arising at least in part as depressive equivalents. These features include a measure of excitement and stimulation, a focus around which companionship can be established and maintained, and an opportunity to engage in activities that bring attention and notoriety. When depressed adolescents find themselves unable to realize a satisfying degree of excitement, companionship, or attention through more adaptive pursuits, they may turn to sex and drugs as a way of attempting to combat their depression (Kantner & Zelnik, 1972; Levy, 1968; Luckey & Nass, 1969; McGlothlin, 1975; Schofield, 1971; Simon, Berger, & Gagnon, 1972; Smart, Fejer, & White, 1970; Sorenson, 1973; Stein, Soskin, & Korchin, 1975; Tec, 1972; Vener & Stewart, 1974; Wieder & Kaplan, 1969).

Alienation may appear in late adolescents who, because of depressive concerns about their adequacy, withdraw from efforts to make a place for themselves in the world. Instead of risking failure and disappointment, they avoid concerted effort and disavow long-term aspirations. Typically this restricted personality pattern results in pronounced apathy that is justified by a cynical, "what's-the-use-of-it-all" view of the world. Adolescents who are dealing with underlying depression in this way sometimes seek each other out to form groups of young people who become visible for their unconventional, antiestablishment ideas and actions. Some members of such groups may be attracted to them for social-psychological reasons or out of deep conviction; many, however, are less concerned about the group's avowed purposes than with being able to escape from depressing feelings of being alone, unimportant, or inadequate (Cambor, 1973; Shainberg, 1966; Teicher, 1972; Unwin, 1970; Walters, 1971).

SUICIDAL BEHAVIOR

Suicidal behavior in adolescents parallels in many ways the suicidal behavior of adults. In both age groups the psychological state that poses the greatest risk of suicide is depression. In both groups males are three times more likely to commit suicide than females, whereas females are three times more likely to make suicide attempts (although since 1970 there appears to have been a trend toward an increased rate of completed suicide among females). At both ages, hanging and shooting are the preferred methods of killing oneself; ingestion of some toxic substance is the preferred method of making a suicide attempt. Finally, suicidal adolescents and adults both have an unusually high incidence of suicidal behavior among family members and friends, who have presumably provided some model for the person to follow (Corder, Shorr, & Corder, 1974; Seiden,

1969; Silver et al., 1971; Stengel, 1964; Teicher & Jacobs, 1966; Toolan, 1975; Tuckman & Connon, 1962; U.S. Department of HEW, 1975; Weissman, 1974).

For the most part, then, adolescent suicidal behavior can be understood from familiarity with clinical and research findings related to suicidal behavior in general. It should also be noted that actual suicide is relatively rare among young people. Suicide rates in the United States increase dramatically after the age of 25, and people under the age of 20 account for only 6% of known suicides per year (U.S. Department of HEW, 1975). This would appear to suggest that a focus on suicide is more appropriate to a discussion of geriatric rather than adolescent psychopathology. On the other hand, because adolescents enjoy relatively good physical health, suicide is the fourth leading cause of death among 15- to 19-year-olds (following accidents, homicide, and cancer), whereas it is the eleventh leading cause of death among the population at large (U.S. Department of HEW, 1975).

Two other aspects of suicidal behavior are of special importance among adolescents and will be discussed in this section. These are the relatively high frequency of attempted suicide in this age group and the communication purposes these attempts are typically intended to serve.

Frequency of Suicide Attempts

Although adolescents are much less likely than adults to kill themselves, they are about equally likely to make suicide attempts. It is estimated that there are approximately 6 to 10 suicide attempts for each actual suicide in the general population, whereas for adolescents the ratio of attempted to completed suicides is estimated to run as high as 50:1 or even 100:1 (Jacobinzer, 1965; Stengel, 1964). In contrast to their committing 6% of the known suicides in the United States each year, adolescents make 12% of the known suicide attempts; each year approximately 1 out of every 1000 adolescents in the United States attempts suicide (Seiden, 1969). At inpatient psychiatric units of general hospitals, a history of suicide attempts has been found in 10 to 15% of adult patients but in as many as 40% of adolescent patients (Hudgens, 1974).

As dramatic as these figures are in demonstrating the prominent role of suicidal behavior in adolescent psychopathology, most researchers in the field regard them as underestimates (Toolan, 1975; Weissman, 1974). It is not unusual for parents to deny or conceal suicide attempts of their youngsters and well-meaning professionals sometimes record them as accidents in order to ''spare'' the young person from having a suicide attempt entered on any official records.

Communication in Adolescent Suicide Attempts

A common myth about adolescent suicide attempts holds that they are shallow, histrionic, and impulsive reactions to immediate distress, such as failing an examination or breaking up with a boyfriend or girlfriend. Although current disappointments and frustrations may be the last straw in precipitating a suicide attempt, suicidal behavior has been conclusively demonstrated to have more complex origins than these.

Adolescents who attempt suicide have typically been wrestling for some time with conflicts and concerns that they cannot resolve. Usually they have experienced increasing family instability and discord during this time, so that they have felt alienated from their parents and unable to turn to them for support. Often these youngsters have sought closeness and emotional support from people outside the family, only to have these relationships also collapse for one reason or another. As a prelude to attempting suicide, most of them have tried other ways of calling attention to their needs, such as rebellious or withdrawn behavior. Unsuccessful in solving their problems through such depressive equivalents, they have finally turned to suicide attempts as a more drastic, last-ditch effort at problem-solving (Cantor, 1976; Corder, Page, & Corder, 1974; Jacobs, 1971; Levenson & Neuringer, 1971; Perlstein, 1966; Teicher, 1973; Yusin, 1973).

For these reasons, communication is a key aspect of adolescent suicidal behavior, probably more so than it is in adults — a larger percentage of whose suicidal behavior reflects a wish to die rather than to bring about changes in how others are treating them. As would be expected, then, the most important predictor of adolescent behavior subsequent to a suicide attempt is the manner in which the young person's effort at communication is responded to. When a suicide attempt elicits concern and sympathy from the young person's family and friends and a genuine effort to help him or her resolve the difficulties that have brought matters to such a pass, suicide attempts are unlikely to recur. However, when those to whom the communication is addressed respond with anger, scorn, or lack of interest, there is a high likelihood of further, more serious suicide attempts (Weiner, 1970, Chap. 5).

SCHOOL PHOBIA

School phobia, which consists of a reluctance or refusal to attend school because of intense anxiety about being there, is customarily regarded more as a problem of elementary-school children than of adolescents. However, despite a lack of reliable epidemiological data, there is reason to believe that school-phobic problems are far from uncommon among high-school and even college students (Hodgman & Braiman, 1965; Weiner, 1970, Chap. 6). In particular, many of the circumstances in which adolescents develop somatic symptoms on a psychological basis are found to involve at least in part a need to avoid attending school.

Adolescent school phobia shares most of the characteristics of the disorder that are seen in younger children. School-phobic youngsters at all ages typically convince their parents to allow them to stay home from school either by virtue of their having some physical complaint — most commonly headache, abdominal pain, or nausea — or some complaint about the school situation, such as a teacher being overly critical or demanding. The somatic complaints of these youngsters subside rapidly when they are allowed to stay home and reappear dramatically when they are faced with returning to school; their complaints about school also have a similar will-o-the-wisp quality, so that responding to one (as by arranging for a new teacher) is soon followed by another (the new classroom is too crowded). Youngsters with this condition typically are doing well in school and express a sincere wish to get over their problem, so that they can return to the classroom. Finally, school-phobic children and adolescents typically have one or both parents who are overprotective and foster their being dependent, so that retreating to the safety of the home is encouraged and reinforced as a way of coping with difficulties in the outside world (Berg et al., 1975; Kahn & Nursten, 1962; Malmquist, 1965; Waldfogel, Coolidge, & Hahn, 1957).

However, there are two important ways in which school phobia in adolescents often differs from school-phobic reactions in younger children: the condition is more likely to originate in specific distressing events occurring at school rather than in interactions with the family, and it is more likely to signal a chronic or characterological style of dealing with experience than an acute or crisis reaction.

Origins of Adolescent School Phobia

Elementary-school children who become school phobic are usually excessively fearful of being separated from their parents. Being overdependent youngsters with overprotective parents, they typically have had less opportunity than other children to get accustomed to being away from home; having to be in school makes them anxious lest something bad happen to them or their parents while they are separated. This anxiety is displaced onto the school, and the resulting school-phobic reaction provides a basis for the child's remaining at home and thereby gaining relief from his or her anxiety about separation (Berg & McGuire, 1974; Estes, Haylett, & Johnson, 1956).

Adolescents tend to have outgrown such childish separation anxiety, even if they have been overdependent children. Now, however, the school becomes a critical setting in which they must confront and work on the developmental tasks of adolescence noted earlier, including not only adjusting to changes in body function and configuration and becoming psychologically independent of their parents, but also learning to cope with dating and heterosexual relationships. Hence the school is more likely than before to be the focus of anxiety-provoking experiences that result in overdependent and overprotected young people becoming school phobic.

Certain school situations are particularly likely to play a part in precipitating adolescent school phobia. At the junior-high-school level, some youngsters are ill-prepared to cope with having to change from the protected atmosphere of elementary school (one primary classroom, one major teacher with whom to relate, and close supervision) to the freer atmosphere of junior high (several teachers, changing classes, and relatively loose supervision in the hallways and on the playground). Children who are uncomfortable in this more open environment and who look back with longing toward the sixth grade are prone to overreact to disappointing, embarrassing, or threatening experiences in the form of school-phobic anxiety.

The gym class and the locker room are an especially common locus for such experiences. The lack of privacy in most locker rooms can cause acute embarrassment for girls who are self-conscious about their sexual development, particularly if they are maturing early; competition in sports can be humiliating for boys, particularly if they are handicapped by late maturation. These kinds of embarrassments and humiliations can occur at any age, but they are especially acute among early adolescents because of their central concern about bodily growth and adequacy. Some young people who are worried about their physical appearance, whether for good cause or for imagined reasons, may even find school intolerable just because it involves their constantly being looked at by teachers and peers.

By high school the peak of bodily concern among adolescents has passed, and young people are paying increasing attention to their success in dating and heterosexual relationships. At this age, school phobia is likely to be precipitated by social rejections that make a young person feel unable to participate as a member of his or her social group. When the daily school experience becomes a constant and painful reminder of social inadequacy, adolescents who are disposed to deal with stress by clinging to the bosom of their family are at high risk for school-phobic reactions (Levenson, 1961; Leventhal & Sills, 1964; Weiner, 1970, Chap. 6).

Acute and Chronic School Phobia

Clinical observations suggest that school phobia appears as an acute crisis reaction in some cases and as a characterological "way of life" in others. Acute school phobia generally arises in younger children who have not shown previous behavior problems, and it often does not interfere with their social development outside school. Acute school phobics are commonly contented and industrious, provided they are allowed to remain at home. They continue to enjoy peer-group activities in their neighborhood, and they may even keep up with their schoolwork if their assignments are sent home.

For most adolescents who become school phobic, there is already too much water over the dam for them to have such an acute reaction. Instead, their reluctance to attend school is most often just one aspect of a chronic adjustment problem emerging from a history of previous behavior problems (including acute school phobia in some cases). Chronic school phobics tend to withdraw from intellectual and social activities. They mope around the house without accomplishing anything, and they usually break off contact with their friends (Miller, Barrett, & Hampe, 1974; Coolidge, Hahn, & Peck, 1957).

For this reason, school phobia in adolescents is ordinarily a more serious condition than it is in younger children. School-phobic adolescents sheltered at home lag behind in their studies, in their opportunities to learn social skills and self-reliance, and in the chance to consolidate a feeling of peer-group belongingness. Unlike childhood school phobias, which respond quickly to prompt intervention, adolescent school phobia is a difficult condition to treat, and it is often a prelude to poor adult adjustment in work-related situations (Pittman, Langsley, & DeYoung, 1968; Sperling, 1967).

ACADEMIC UNDERACHIEVEMENT

Academic underachievement consists of the failure to receive grades commensurate with one's intellectual abilities. Unexpectedly poor performance in school is estimated to occur in 25% of school children, and one-third to one-half of young people seen in psychiatric clinics have been referred primarily because of school-learning problems (Gardner & Sperry, 1974; Schecter, 1974; Zigmond, 1969). Among older adolescents in college, worries about studying and grades account for over 50% of student requests for counseling and psychotherapy (Blaine & McArthur, 1971). Despite the value generally placed on a high-school education in our society, moreover, 20% of adolescents in the United States fail to complete high school, and at least half of these dropouts are estimated to possess at least average intellectual ability (Havighurst, Graham, & Eberly, 1972; Lichter et al., 1962).

In some cases academic underachievement is influenced primarily by sociocultural factors and does not constitute psychological disturbance. These factors include family and neighborhood value systems that minimize the importance or utility of formal education; policies and attitudes in the schools that are insensitive or unsympathetic to the needs of minority, disadvantaged, and first-generation American youth; and peer-group attitudes that stamp scholastic success as unmanly for the boys or unfeminine for the girls (Braham, 1965; Dalsimer, 1975; Hummel & Sprinthall, 1965; I. Katz, 1967; Morrow 1970).

In other instances learning problems in school can usually be traced to two kinds of psychological difficulties: (1) attention, concentration, and specific learning handicaps associated with minimal brain dysfunction, which most commonly emerges and is detected during the elementary-school years (Heinecke, 1972; Torgesen, 1975; Wender, 1971) and (2) neurotic patterns of family interaction that produce a syndrome of passive-aggressive underachievement, which is the most salient and unique aspect of unexpected poor school performance occurring among adolescents. This section will describe three factors that usually contribute to the emergence of this syndrome:

1. Considerable hostility, usually toward parents, that cannot be directly expressed.
2. Concerns about rivalry with parents and siblings that lead to fears of failure or fears of success.
3. A preference for passive-aggressive modes of coping with difficult situations.

Hostility toward Parents

Studies of underachieving adolescents indicate that they are more likely than their achieving peers to harbor underlying aggressive feelings that they cannot express directly. Furthermore the typical source of this anger is resentment of parental demands they cannot or prefer not to meet (Davids & Hainsworth, 1967; Morrow & Wilson, 1961; Shaw & Grubb, 1958). When these parental demands include heavy academic pressure, the stage is set for poor school performance to arise as an indirect retaliation.

Parents who foster underachievement are most often found to be imposing academic goals on their youngster. Adolescents who feel they are being forced to prepare for certain colleges or careers, when they prefer to attend college elsewhere (or not at all) or to pursue some other career, may compensate for an inability to oppose their parents' wishes directly by resorting to poor school performance. Their failure to quality for the college or career of their parents' dreams defeats the parents' purposes and is an effective way of causing them distress; unfortunately, it may also prevent the young person from realizing his or her own ambitions, and hence it represents a maladaptive, neurotic solution to this family conflict.

Concerns about Rivalry

Passive-aggressive underachievers typically suffer from fears of failure or fears of success that inhibit their academic efforts. Those who fear failure have a low opinion of their abilities and believe that it will be impossible for them to match the accomplishments of their parents and siblings. They have very little tolerance for criticism, and the more their parents and teachers express disappointment in them ("You really should be getting better grades"), the more they avoid trying to achieve in school.

Fear-of-failure underachievers often set unrealistically high goals for themselves and then work only halfheartedly to achieve them. In this way they try to deny their limitations and avoid any feeling of having been a failure. Their ambitious goals give them a ready-made excuse for not succeeding, and their minimal effort allows them the often-heard rationalization, "I could have done better if I had wanted to, but I really didn't feel like working hard." In other words, these young people carefully hedge their bets. They rarely risk making a mistake, they consistently deny having exerted themselves even when they have, and they pride themselves on what they have been able to accomplish with minimal effort ("I got a C without even cracking a book").

This underachieving pattern is particularly likely to appear at certain transition points that confront young people with more difficult coursework or more demanding academic standards than they have encountered previously. The transitions from junior high school to high school, from high school to college, and from a less to a more competitive school are especially likely to exacerbate preexisting fears of failure and to precipitate this underachieving pattern, which has aptly been described as "big-league shock" (Berger, 1961; McArthur, 1971).

Adolescents who fear success, on the other hand, are usually concerned that their doing well in school will make less able members of their family envious or resentful. Consequently, they avoid accomplishment in order to avoid the criticism or rejection they fear will follow in its wake. In contrast to adolescents who fear failure, fear-of-success youngsters publicly disparage their abilities: they set limited goals that are easily within their grasp, and they make just enough effort to reach these goals and they stop ("I was lucky to do as well as I did") (Brown, Jennings, & Vanik, 1974; Grunebaum et al., 1962; Romer, 1975).

As might be expected from the underlying concerns of underachievers who fear success, their school performance typically begins to decline when they are on the verge of surpassing their parents. Most common in this regard is a pattern of "senior neurosis," in which children of high-school educated parents begin to do poorly in the latter years of high school and thereby compromise their chances of being admitted to college (Hogenson, 1974).

Passive-Aggressive Style

The underlying hostility of passive-aggressive underachievers and their concerns about rivalry may not be obvious. Often it is only in the course of intensive diagnostic study or ongoing therapy that these parameters of the disturbance can be confirmed. On the other hand, this form of underachievement is usually easy to identify from the young person's obviously passive-aggressive style of dealing with academic requirements. Passive-aggressive behavior consists of purposeful inactivity; these kinds of underachievers work hard to make sure that nothing happens to bring their grades up to their potential.

For example, passive-aggressive underachievers are often found to be concentrating their energies on extracurricular activities that leave them little time for their studies. Compared to their academically achieving peers, many of these youngsters are equally industrious in general but, when it comes to schoolwork, study less and complete assignments less promptly (Frankel, 1960; Morrow & Wilson, 1961). It is also not unusual for academic underachievers to read widely and keep themselves well informed in general, while not finding time to read material that is required in their courses or to learn about matters that are likely to appear on examinations or in class discussions (Mondani & Tutko, 1969).

Even if they do absorb information that might help them perform well in school, passive-aggressive achievers find inactivity techniques by which they assure limited utilization of their knowledge. They remain silent during class discussions, even when they have something to contribute; they "forget" to copy down or turn in assignments or they spend hours working on the wrong assignment; on examinations they "accidentally" skip a page of questions or they misinterpret the instructions in ways that substantially lower their score. When such kinds of self-defeating academic behavior emerge without conscious intent and in the face of a young person's stated wish to do better in his or her studies, the most likely explanation is a neurotic pattern of symptom formation that can be described as passive-aggressive underachievement.

FUTURE DIRECTIONS

It may be useful to conclude this chapter with some observations on future directions for the study of adolescent psychopathology. Despite a voluminous and expanding literature on developmental problems of the teen-age years, we still lack adequate answers to two key questions: (1) What precisely are the premorbid childhood indices and the adult outcomes of particular kinds of psychological disturbance that become manifest during adolescence? (2) What *definitively* are the methods of intervention capable either of averting some particular form of psychopathology or of promptly reversing its course should it appear?

The first of these questions calls for a substantial increase in both the amount and scope of longitudinal research. If we eliminate relatively short-term studies and studies limited to a relatively small number of subjects who happened to pass through some available checkpoints, we are left with a promising but painfully thin body of longitudinal research in abnormal development. We have the beginnings of broad population surveys of children believed to be at high risk for subsequent psychopathology, from which we can learn about behaviors that have predictive validity for adolescent breakdown. We are similarly beginning to learn about kinds of continuity and discontinuity that exist between adolescent and adult problem behavior. But a much greater accumulation of such data is necessary to achieve a level of reliability that can be translated into sound theories of adolescent psychopathology and effective guidelines for preventive and rehabilitative intervention.

The second question calls for much additional research on the efficacy of specific intervention techniques in avoiding or ameliorating psychological disturbance. Psychotherapy researchers have been attuned for some years to the irrelevance of asking whether psychotherapy works; rather, one must seek to learn what kind of psychotherapy helps what kind of person overcome what kind of psychopathology. This same specificity needs to be addressed to the common adolescent disturbances discussed in this chapter. For example, under what circumstances is residential care likely to prove more effective than outpatient therapy for schizophrenic adolescents? Are behavioral approaches more helpful than analytic approaches in dealing with acute school phobia? If so, what kinds of behavioral approaches can be most usefully adapted to this task? What steps can be taken to minimize suicidal risk in depressed young people?

These and a host of similar intervention issues have received extensive comment in the literature, but mainly on the basis of clinical wisdom rather than reliable empirical findings. Although cumulative clinical wisdom is not to be taken lightly — especially when it is all we have to go on in trying to be of help — the list of remedies prescribed by one generation of wise and well-meaning clinicians but proved to be worthless by a subsequent generation of clinicians runs very long. In the end, clinical work with disturbed adolescents will not proceed much farther or faster than replicated research can take it.

REFERENCES

Albert, N., and Beck, A. T. Incidence of depression in early adolescence: A preliminary study. *Journal of Youth and Adolescence,* 1975, *4,* 301–308.

American Psychiatric Association. *Diagnostic and statistical manual of mental disorders.* Washington, D.C.: American Psychiatric Association, 1968.

Annesley, P. T. Psychiatric illness in adolescence: Presentation and prognosis. *Journal of Mental Science,* 1961, *107,* 268–278.

Anthony, H. S. The association of violence and depression in a sample of young offenders. *British Journal of Criminology,* 1968, *3,* 346–365.

Arieti, S. *Interpretation of schizophrenia* (2nd ed.). New York: Basic Books, 1974.

Babigian, H. M. Schizophrenia: Epidemiology. In A. M. Freedman, H. I. Kaplan, and B. J. Sadock (Eds.), *Comprehensive textbook of psychiatry* (2nd ed.). Baltimore, Md.: Williams & Wilkins, 1975.

Barthell, C. N. and Holmes, D. S. High-school yearbooks: A nonreactive measure of social isolation in graduates who later became schizophrenic. *Journal of Abnormal Psychology,* 1968, *73,* 313–316.

Beck, A. T. *Depression: Causes and treatment.* Philadelphia: University of Pennsylvania Press, 1970.

———. The development of depression: A cognitive model. In R. J. Friedman and M. M. Katz (Eds.), *The psychology of depression.* Washington, D.C.: Winston, 1974.

Bellak, L., Hurvich, M., and Gediman, H. K. *Ego functions in schizophrenics, neurotics, and normals.* New York: Wiley, 1973.

Berg, I., and McGuire, R. Are mothers of school-phobic adolescents overprotective? *British Journal of Psychiatry,* 1974, *124,* 10–13.

Berg, I. Collins, T., McGuire, R., and O'Melia, J. Educational attainment in school phobia. *British Journal of Psychiatry,* 1975, *126,* 435–438.

Berger, E. M. Willingness to accept limitations and college achievement, *Journal of Counseling Psychology,* 1961, *8,* 140–144.

Blaine, G. B., and McArthur, C. C. Problems connected with studying. In G. B. Blaine and C. C. McArthur (Eds.), *Emotional problems of the student* (2nd ed.). New York: Appleton-Century-Crofts, 1971.

Bleuler, E. *Dementia praecox or the group of schizophrenias.* New York: International Universities Press, 1950. (Originally published, 1911.)

Bonnard, A. Truancy and pilfering associated with bereavement. In S. Lorand and H. I. Schneer (Eds.), *Adolescents: Psychoanalytic approaches to problems and therapy.* New York: Hoeber, 1961.

Bower, E. M., Shellhamer, T. A., and Daily, J. M. School characteristics of male adolescents who later become schizophrenic. *American Journal of Orthopsychiatry,* 1960, *39,* 712–729.

Braham, M. Peer group deterrents to intellectual development during adolescence. *Educational Theory,* 1965, *15,* 248–258.

Brown, M., Jennings, J., and Vanik, V. The motive to avoid success: A further examination. *Journal of Research in Personality,* 1974, *8,* 172–176.

Burnham, D. L., Gladstone, A. I., and Gibson, R. W. *Schizophrenia and the need-fear dilemma.* New York: International Universities Press, 1969.

Burks, H. L., and Harrison, S. I. Aggressive behavior as a means of avoiding depression. *American Journal of Orthopsychiatry,* 1962, *32,* 416–422.

Cambor, C. G. Adolescent alienation syndrome. In J. C. Schoolar (Ed.), *Current issues in adolescent psychiatry.* New York: Brunner/Mazel, 1973.

Cantor, P. Personality characteristics found among youthful female suicide attempters. *Journal of Abnormal Psychology,* 1976, *85,* 324–329.

Carpenter, W. T. Current diagnostic concepts in schizophrenia. *American Journal of Psychiatry,* 1976, *133,* 172–177.

Carpenter, W. T., Strauss, J. S., and Bartko, J. J. An approach to the diagnosis and understanding of schizophrenia: Part I. Use of signs and symptoms for the identification of schizophrenic patients. *Schizophrenia Bulletin,* 1974, No. 11, 37–49.

Carter, A. B. Prognostic factors of adolescent psychoses. *Journal of Mental Science,* 1942, *88,* 31–81.

Cohen, I., Fliegelman, S., Gluck, Z., and Kelman, D. Study of early differentiation between schizophrenia and psychotic manifestations in adolescence. *Israel Annals of Psychiatry,* 1970, *8,* 163–172.

Coolidge, J. C., Hahn, P. B., and Peck, A. L. School phobia: Neurotic crisis or way of life? *American Journal of Orthopsychiatry,* 1957, *27,* 296–306.

Corder, B. F., Page, P. V., and Corder, R. F. Parental history, family communication, and interaction patterns in adolescent suicide. *Family Therapy,* 1974, *1,* 285–290.

Corder, B. F., Shorr, W., and Corder, R. F. A study of social and psychological characteristics of adolescent suicide attempters in an urban, disadvantaged area. *Adolescence,* 1974, *9,* 1–6.

Cytryn, L., and McKnew, D. H. Factors influencing the changing clinical expression of the depressive process in children. *American Journal of Psychiatry,* 1974, *131,* 879–881.

Dalsimer, K. Fear of academic success in adolescent girls. *Journal of the American Academy of Child Psychiatry,* 1975, *18,* 719–730.

Davids, A., and Hainsworth, P. K. Maternal attitudes about family life and childrearing as avowed by mothers and perceived by their under-achieving and high-achieving sons. *Journal of Consulting Psychology,* 1967, *31,* 29–37.

Errara, P. A sixteen-year follow-up of schizophrenic patients seen in an outpatient clinic. *Archives of Neurology and Psychiatry,* 1957, *78,* 84–87.

Estes, H. R., Haylett, C. H., and Johnson, A. M. Separation anxiety. *American Journal of Psychotherapy,* 1956, *10,* 682–695.

Frankel, E. A comparative study of achieving and underachieving high-school boys of high intellectual ability. *Journal of Educational Research,* 1960, *53,* 172–180.

Freud, A. Adolescence. *Psychoanalytic Study of the Child,* 1958, *13,* 255–278.

Gardner, E. A., Miles, H. C., Bahn, A. K., and Romano, J. All psychiatric experience in a community: A cumulative survey. *Archives of General Psychiatry,* 1963, *9,* 369–378.

Gardner, G. E., and Sperry, B. M. School problems: Learning disabilities and school phobia. In S. Arieti (Ed.), *American handbook of psychiatry* (Vol. 2) New York: Basic Books, 1974.

Glaser, K. Masked depression in children and adolescents. *American Journal of Psychotherapy,* 1967, *21,* 565–574.

Grunebaum, M. G., Hurwitz, I., Prentice, N. M., and Sperry, B. M. Fathers of sons with primary neurotic learning inhibitions. *American Journal of Orthopsychiatry,* 1962, *32,* 462–472.

Gunderson, J. G., and Mosher, L. R. The cost of schizophrenia. *American Journal of Psychiatry,* 1975, *132,* 901–906.

Havighurst, R. J., Graham, R. A., and Eberly, D. American youth in the mid-seventies. *Bulletin of the National Association of Secondary School Principals,* 1972, *56,* 1–13.

Heinecke, C. M. Learning disturbance in childhood. In. B. B. Wolman (Ed.), *Manual of child psychopathology.* New York: McGraw-Hill, 1972.

Hodgman, C. H., and Braiman, A. "College phobia": School refusal in university students. *American Journal of Psychiatry,* 1965, *121,* 801–805.

Hogenson, D. L. Senior neurosis: Cause-effect or derivative. *School Psychologist,* 1974, *28,* 12–13.

Holzman, P. S., and Grinker, R. R. Schizophrenia in adolescence. *Journal of Youth and Adolescence,* 1974, *3,* 267–279.

Hudgens, R. W. *Psychiatric disorders in adolescents.* Baltimore, Md.: Williams & Wilkins, 1974.

Hummel, R., and Sprinthall, N. Underachievement related to interests, attitudes, and values. *Personnel and Guidance Journal,* 1965, *44,* 388–395.

Jacobinzer, H. Attempted suicides in adolescence. *Journal of the American Medical Association,* 1965, *191,* 7–11.

Jacobs, J. *Adolescent suicide.* New York: Wiley, 1971.

Kahn, J. H., and Nursten, J. P. School refusal: A comprehensive view of school phobia and other failures of school attendance. *American Journal of Orthopsychiatry,* 1962, *22,* 707–718.

Kantner, J. F., and Zelnik, M. Sexual experience of young unmarried women in the United States. *Family Planning Perspectives,* 1972, *4,* 9–18.

Katz, I. The socialization of academic motivation in minority-group children. In *Nebraska Symposium on Motivation* (Vol. 15). Lincoln: University of Nebraska Press, 1967.

Katz, P. The diagnosis and treatment of borderline schizophrenia in adolescence. *Canadian Psychiatric Association Journal,* 1967, *12,* 247–251.

Keeler, W. R. Children's reactions to the death of a parent. In P. Hoch and J. Zubin (Eds.), *Depression.* New York: Grune & Stratton, 1954.

Kendell, R. E. *The role of diagnosis in psychiatry.* London: Blackwell Scientific Publications, 1975.

Krakowski, A. J. Depressive reactions of childhood and adolescence. *Psychosomatics,* 1970, *11,* 429–433.

Kreisman, D. Social interaction and intimacy in preschizophrenic adolescence. In J. Zubin and A. M. Freedman (Eds.), *The psychopathology of adolescence.* New York: Grune & Stratton, 1970.

Laufer, M. Object loss and mourning during adolescence. *Psychoanalytic Study of the Child,* 1966, *21,* 269–293.

Levenson, E. A. The treatment of school phobia in the young adult. *American Journal of Psychotherapy,* 1961, *15,* 539–552.

Levenson, M., and Neuringer, C. Problem-solving behavior in suicidal adolescents. *Journal of Consulting and Clinical Psychology,* 1971, *37,* 433–436.

Leventhal, T., and Sills, M. Self-image in school phobia. *American Journal of Orthopsychiatry,* 1964, *34,* 685–695.

Levy, N. J. The use of drugs by teenagers for sanctuary and illusion. *American Journal of Psychoanalysis,* 1968, *28,* 48–56.

Lewinsohn, P. M. A behavioral approach to depression. In R. J. Friedman and M. M. Katz (Eds.), *The psychology of depression.* Washington, D.C.: Winston, 1974a.

———. Clinical and theoretical aspects of depression. In K. S. Calhoun, H. E. Adams, and K. M. Mitchell (Eds.), *Innovative treatment methods in psychopathology.* New York: Wiley, 1974b.

Lichter, S. O., Rapien, E. B., Siebert, F. M., and Sklansky, M. *The dropouts: A treatment study of intellectually capable students who drop out of high school.* New York: Free Press, 1962.

Luckey, E. B., and Nass, G. D. A comparison of sexual attitudes and behavior in an international sample. *Journal of Marriage and the Family,* 1969, *31,* 364–379.

McArthur, C. C. Distinguishing patterns of student neuroses. In G. R. Blaine and C. C. McArthur (Eds.), *Emotional problems of the student* (2nd ed.). New York: Appleton-Century-Crofts, 1971.

McGlothlin, W. H. Drug use and abuse. *Annual Review of Psychology,* 1975, *26,* 45–64.

Malmquist, C. P. School phobia: A problem in family neurosis. *Journal of the American Academy of Child Psychiatry,* 1965, *4,* 293–319.

———. Depression in childhood. In F. F. Flach and S. C. Draghi (Eds.), *The nature and treatment of depression.* New York: Wiley, 1975.

Masterson, J. F. Prognosis in adolescent disorders — schizophrenia. *Journal of Nervous and Mental Disease,* 1956, *124,* 219–232.

———. *The psychiatric dilemma of adolescence.* Boston: Little, Brown, 1967a.

———. The symptomatic adolescent five years later: He didn't grow out of it. *American Journal of Psychiatry,* 1967b, *123,* 1338–1345.

———. The psychiatric significance of adolescent turmoil. *American Journal of Psychiatry,* 1968, *124,* 1549–1554.

———. Depression in the adolescent character disorder. In J. Zubin and A. M. Freedman (Eds.), *The psychopathology of adolescence.* New York: Grune & Stratton, 1970.

Meehl, P. E. High-school yearbooks: A reply to Schwarz. *Journal of Abnormal Psychology,* 1971, *77,* 143–148.

Meeks, J. E. Nosology in adolescent psychiatry: An enigma wrapped in a whirlwind. In J. C. Schoolar (Ed.), *Current issues in adolescent psychiatry.* New York: Brunner/Mazel, 1973.

Miller, L. C., Barrett, C. L., and Hampe, E. Phobias of childhood in a prescientific era. In A. Davids (Ed.), *Child personality and psychopathology: Current topics.* New York: Wiley, 1974.

Mondani, M. S., and Tutko, T. A. Relationship of academic underachievement to incidental learning. *Journal of Consulting and Clinical Psychology,* 1969, *33,* 558–560.

Morrow, W. R. Academic underachievement. In C. G. Costello (Ed.), *Symptoms of psychopathology.* New York: Wiley, 1970.

Morrow, W. R., and Wilson, R. C. Family relations of bright high-achieving and underachieving high-school boys. *Child Development,* 1961, *32,* 501–510.

Mosher, L. R. Schizophrenia: Recent trends. In A. M. Freedman, H. I. Kaplan, & B. J. Sadock (Eds.), *Comprehensive textbook of psychiatry* (2nd ed.). Baltimore, Md.: Williams & Wilkins, 1975.

Murray, D. C. Suicidal and depressive feelings among college students. *Psychological Reports,* 1973, *33,* 175–181.

National Institute of Mental Health. *Schizophrenia: Is there an answer?* Department of HEW, Publications No. (HSM) 73–9086, Washington, D.C.: U.S. Government Printing Office, 1972.

Nameche, G. F., Waring, M., and Ricks, D. F. Early indicators of outcome in schizophrenia. *Journal of Nervous and Mental Disease,* 1964, *139,* 232–240.

Offord, D. R., and Cross, L. A. Behavioral antecedents of adult schizophrenia. *Archives of General Psychiatry,* 1969, *21,* 267–283.

Perlstein, A. P. Suicide in adolescence. *New York State Journal of Medicine,* 1966, *66,* 3017–3020.

Pitt, R., Kornfeld, D. S., and Kolb, L. C. Adolescent friendship patterns as prognostic indicators for schizophrenic adults. *Psychiatric Quarterly,* 1963, *37,* 499–508.

Pittman, F. S., Langsley, D. G., and DeYoung, C. D. Work and school phobias: A family approach to treatment. *American Journal of Psychiatry,* 1968, *124,* 1535–1541.

Rinsley, D. B. A contribution to the nosology and dynamics of adolescent schizophrenia. *Psychiatric Quarterly*, 1972, *46*, 159–186.

Robins, L. N. *Deviant children grown up*. Baltimore, Md.: Williams & Wilkins, 1966.

Romer, N. The motive to avoid success and its effects on performance in school-age males and females. *Developmental Psychology*, 1975, *11*, 689–699.

Rosen, B. M., Bahn, A. K., Shellow, R., and Bower, E. M. Adolescent patients served in outpatient psychiatric clinics. *American Journal of Public Health*, 1965, *55*, 1563–1577.

Sands, D. E. The psychoses of adolescence. *Journal of Mental Science*, 1956, *102*, 308–316.

Schechter, M. D. Psychiatric aspects of learning disabilities. *Child Psychiatry and Human Development*, 1974, *5*, 67–77.

Schofield, M. Normal sexuality in adolescence. In J. G. Howells (Ed.), *Modern perspectives in adolescent psychiatry*. New York: Brunner/Mazel, 1971.

Seiden, R. H. *Suicide among youth*. U.S. Department of HEW, Public Health Service Publication No. 1971. Washington, D.C.: U.S. Government Printing Office, 1969.

Seligman, M. E. P. Depression and learned helplessness. In R. J. Friedman and M. M. Katz (Eds.), *The psychology of depression*. Washington, D.C.: Winston, 1974.

———. *Helplessness: On depression, development, and death*. San Francisco: Freeman, 1975.

Shainberg, D. Personality restriction in adolescents. *Psychiatric Quarterly*, 1966, *40*, 258–270.

Shakow, D. Segmental set: A theory of the formal psychological deficit in schizophrenia. *Archives of General Psychiatry*, 1962, *6*, 1–17.

Shaw, M. C., and Grubb, J. Hostility and able high-school underachievers. *Journal of Counseling Psychology*, 1958, *5*, 263–266.

Shorr, M., & Speed, M. H. Delinquency as a manifestation of the mourning process. *Psychiatric Quarterly*, 1963, *37*, 540–558.

Silver, M. A., Bohnert, M., Beck, A. T., and Marcus, D. Relation of depression to attempted suicide and seriousness of intent. *Archives of General Psychiatry*, 1971, *25*, 573–576.

Simon, W., Berger, A. S., and Gagnon, J. H. Beyond anxiety and fantasy: The coital experiences of college youth. *Journal of Youth and Adolescence*, 1972, *1*, 81–90.

Smart, R. G., Fejer, D., and White, J. *The extent of drug use in metropolitan Toronto schools: A study of changes from 1968 to 1970*. Toronto, Canada: Addiction Research Foundation, 1970.

Sorenson, R. C. *Adolescent sexuality in contemporary America: Personal values and sexual behavior ages 13–19*. New York: World, 1973.

Sperling, M. School phobias: Classification, dynamics, and treatment. *Psychoanalytic Study of the Child*, 1967, *22*, 375–401.

Spiegel, R. Anger and acting out: Masks of depression. *American Journal of Psychotherapy*, 1967, *21*, 597–606.

Spitzer, R. L, and Wilson, P. T. Nosology and the official psychiatric nomenclature. In A. M. Freedman, H. I. Kaplan, and B. J. Sadock (Eds.), *Comprehensive textbook of psychiatry* (2nd ed.) Baltimore, Md.: Williams & Wilkins, 1975.

Spotnitz, H. Adolescence and schizophrenia: Problems in differentiation. In S. Lorand and H. I. Schneer (Eds.), *Adolescents: Psychoanalytic approaches to problems and therapy*. New York: Hoeber, 1961.

Stein, K. B., Soskin, W. F., and Korchin, S. J. Drug use among disaffected high-school youth. *Journal of Drug Education*, 1975, *5*, 193–203.

Stengel, E. *Suicide and attempted suicide*. Baltimore, Md.: Penguin, 1964.

Symonds, A., and Herman, M. The patterns of schizophrenia in adolescence. *Psychiatric Quarterly*, 1957, *31*, 521–530.

Tarter, R. E., Templer, D. I., and Hardy, C. Reliability of the psychiatric diagnosis. *Diseases of the Nervous System,* 1975, *36,* 30–31.

Tec, N. Some aspects of high-school status and differential involvement with marihuana: A study of suburban teenagers. *Adolescence,* 1972, *7,* 1–28.

Teicher, J. D. The alienated, older male adolescent. *American Journal of Psychotherapy,* 1972, *26,* 401–407.

———. A solution to the chronic problem of living: Adolescent attempted suicide. In J. C. Schooler (Ed.), *Current issues in adolescent psychiatry.* New York: Brunner/Mazel, 1973.

Teicher, J. D., and Jacobs, J. Adolescents who attempt suicide: Preliminary findings. *American Journal of Psychiatry,* 1966, *122,* 1248–1257.

Toolan, J. M. Depression in adolescents. In J. G. Howells (Ed.), *Modern perspectives in adolescent psychiatry.* New York: Brunner/Mazel, 1971.

———. Suicide in children and adolescents. *American Journal of Psychotherapy,* 1975, *29,* 339–344.

Torgesen, J. Problems and prospects in the study of learning disabilities. In E. M. Hetherington (Ed.), *Review of child development research* (Vol. 5). Chicago: University of Chicago Press, 1975.

Tuckman, J., and Connon, H. E. Attempted suicide in adolescents. *American Journal of Psychiatry,* 1962, 119, 228–232.

Unwin, J. R. Depression in alienated youth. *Canadian Psychiatric Association Journal,* 1970, *15,* 83–86.

U.S. Department of HEW. *Outpatient Psychiatric Services,* Public Health Service Publication No. 1982. Washington, D.C.: U.S. Government Printing Office, 1969.

U.S. Department of HEW. *Vital Statistics of the United States, 1971: Vol. II. Mortality.* Rockville, Md.: U.S. Department of HEW, 1975.

Venables, P. H. Partial failure of cortical-subcortical integration as a factor underlying schizophrenic behavior. In J. Romano (Ed.), *The origins of schizophrenia.* Amsterdam, The Netherlands Excerpta Medica Foundation, 1967.

Vener, A. M., and Stewart, C. S. Adolescent sexual behavior in middle America revisited: 1970–1973. *Journal of Marriage and the Family,* 1974, *36,* 728–735.

Waldfogel, S., Coolidge, J. C., and Hahn, P. B. The development, meaning, and management of school phobia. *American Journal of Orthopsychiatry,* 157, *27,* 754–780.

Walters, P. A. Student apathy. In G. R. Blaine and C. C. McArthur (Eds.), *Emotional problems of the student* (2nd ed.). New York: Appleton-Century-Crofts, 1971.

Warren, W. A study of adolescent psychiatric inpatients and the outcome six or more years later: II. The follow-up study. *Journal of Child Psychology and Psychiatry,* 1965, *6,* 141–160.

Watt, N. F. Longitudinal changes in the social behavior of children hospitalized for schizophrenia as adults. *Journal of Nervous and Mental Disease,* 1972, *155,* 42–54.

Watt, N. F. Patterns of childhood social development in adult schizophrenics. *Archives of General Psychiatry,* 1978, *35,* 160–165.

Watt, N.F., and Lubensky, A. W. Childhood roots of schizophrenia. *Journal of Consulting and Clinical Psychology,* 1976, *44,* 363–375.

Watt, N. F., Stolorow, R. D., Lubensky, A. W., and McClelland, D. C. School adjustment and behavior of children hospitalized for schizophrenia as adults. *American Journal of Orthopsychiatry,* 1970, *40,* 637–657.

Weiner, I. B. *Psychological disturbance in adolescence.* New York: Wiley, 1970.

———. Perspectives on the modern adolescent. *Psychiatry,* 1972, *35,* 20–31.

————. Depression in adolescence. In F. F. Flach and S. C. Draghi (Eds.), *The nature and treatment of depression*. New York: Wiley, 1975.

————. Adjustment to adolescence. In B. B. Wolman (Ed.), *International encyclopedia of neurology, psychiatry, psychoanalysis, and psychology*. Princeton, N.J.: Van Nostrand Reinhold, 1977a.

————. Rorschach indices of disordered thinking in patient and nonpatient adolescents. Paper presented at the 9th International Rorschach Congress, Fribourg, Switzerland, 1977b.

Weiner, I. B., and Del Gaudio, A. C. Psychopathology in adolescence: An epidemiological study. *Archives of General Psychiatry*, 1976, *33*, 187–193.

Weissman, M. M. The epidemiology of suicide attempts, 1960–1971. *Archives of General Psychiatry*, 1974, *30*, 737–746.

Wender, P. H. *Minimal brain dysfunction in children*. New York: Wiley, 1971.

Wieder, H., and Kaplan, E. H. Drug use in adolescents: Psychodynamic meaning and pharmacogenic effect. *Psychoanalytic Study of the Child*, 1969, *24*, 399–431.

Woerner, M. G., Pollack, M., Rogalski, C., Pollack, Y., and Klein, D. F. A comparison of the school records of personality disorders, schizophrenics, and their sibs. In M. Roff, L. N. Robins, and M. Pollack (Eds.), *Life history research in psychopathology* (Vol. 2). Minneapolis: University of Minnesota Press, 1972.

Yolles, S. F., and Kramer, M. Vital statistics. In L. Bellak and L. Loeb (Eds.), *The schizophrenic syndrome*. New York: Grune & Stratton, 1969.

Yusin, A. S. Attempted suicide in an adolescent: The resolution of an anxiety state. *Adolescence*, 1973, *8*, 17–28.

Zigmond, N. K. Learning patterns in children with learning disabilities. *Seminars in Psychiatry*, 1969, *1*, 344–353.

Zubin, J. Classification of the behavior disorders. *Annual Review of Psychology*, 1967, *18*, 373–406.

CHAPTER 15

Variations in Adolescent Psychohormonal Development

Eileen Higham, Ph.D.

INTRODUCTION

The most prominent feature of puberty and adolescence is sexual maturation. The development and differentiation of the body as male or female is initiated by the fetal sex hormones during prenatal life and is completed by the pubertal sex hormones at a later period. The fetal and pubertal hormones exert a direct influence on the body and on the brain; they also exert an indirect influence on the self-image and on the behavior of others. Body morphology confirms sexual identity and evokes reactions and expectations from the social environment. The purpose of this chapter is: (1) to review the dimorphism of adolescent psychohormonal development and differentiation and (2) to explore the relationship between hormonal and behavioral aspects of normal adolescence, its variations and disorders.[1]

PSYCHOSEXUAL DEVELOPMENT AND DIFFERENTIATION

The dimorphism of somatosexual development and differentiation in prenatal life is paralleled by the dimorphism of sociosexual differentiation in postnatal life. Together these processes constitute psychosexual development and differentiation, culminating in adolescence and adulthood with sexual and erotic pair-bonding and reproductive capability. The sequential process of differentiation and development from conception to maturity, as described by Money and Ehrhardt (1972), is illustrated in Figure 1. Sexual dimorphism reaches its peak in adolescence, except when gestation, parturition, and lactation occur in a later phase of feminine psychosexual functioning.

Fetal Hormones

Fetal hormones regulate the differentiation of the primary sexual characteristics, the internal and external reproductive anatomy. The testicular hormone, androgen, controls

---

[1]A detailed account of gender identity/role differentiation and development is presented in *Man and Woman, Boy and Girl* (Money & Ehrhardt, 1972). The author gratefully acknowledges the influence of John Money and other colleagues at the Psychohormonal Research Unit of The Johns Hopkins Hospital.

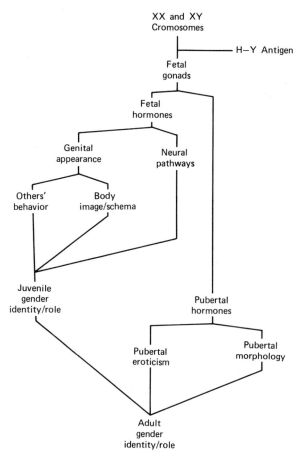

Figure 1.   Variables in the sequential differentiation of gender identity/role. (Reprinted, with permission, from Money and Ehrhardt, 1972.)

sexual dimorphism in prenatal life, influencing both the reproductive structures and the central nervous system. Without androgen, a female body morphology differentiates; with androgen, the body morphology is male. Similarly, androgen masculinizes the neurosexual pathways of the brain, which are located in the hypothalamus. The sexually dimorphic differentiation of the pathways of the brain influences social behavior in childhood and sexual behavior postpubertally.[2] Fetal ovarian hormones have no known effect on somatic or neural differentiation in prenatal life; their influence on social behavior in infancy and childhood or on sexual behavior later is not known.

Social Programming

At birth, the primary sexual characteristics, specifically the external genitalia, initiate the social programming of psychosexual differentiation as masculine or feminine. The genital appearance of the newborn infant acts as a releasing stimulus for behavior culturally and socially defined as appropriate for the male or female infant and child. The social program

[2]The sex-shared, gender-dimorphic behavior patterns that are associated with boyishness or girlishness derive from prenatal hormonal influences on the brain (see Money & Ehrhardt, 1972).

of psychosexual differentiation comprises three developmental stages:[3] infancy and early childhood, middle childhood and prepuberty, and puberty and adolescence.

Infancy and Early Childhood

In infancy and early childhood, the social models for masculinity and femininity and the daily practices of rearing establish gender identity as masculine or feminine, quite independent of chromosomes, fetal hormones, or even genital anatomy. A male infant born with a micropenis or with a hypospadias can be sex-reannounced as a female and differentiate a feminine gender identity; feminizing surgery of the genitalia provides a body-image to confirm sex of assignment. Gender identity is imprinted, as language is imprinted, in the first five years of life, as masculine or feminine. In some instances, an error in gender-identity differentiation occurs; subsequent sexual behavior may then differ from traditional, statistical, and reproductive expectations. The transpositions of gender identity and the paraphilic disorders[4] derive from errors in the psychosexual program imprinted in early life. The contribution of errors in the prenatal program that predispose a vulnerability to later sexual variations and disorders should not be overlooked (see the discussion on hormones and transpositions of gender identity, p. 490).

Variations in adult models of masculine and feminine behavior are consonant with healthy psychosexual differentiation provided that sex roles and sex-coded roles are clearly demarcated. Sex roles comprise the irreducible sex differences — menstruation, gestation, and lactation in the female, impregnation in the male. The sex-coded roles are options affected by time and place, for example, work roles, parenting roles, recreational roles, grooming styles.

Middle Childhood and Prepuberty

In childhood core-gender identity, imprinted in the first five years of life, is elaborated and consolidated. Adults continue to provide models for masculine and feminine gender roles, but peer pair-bonds become equally, or more, important. The social stimulation of peers is required for the consolidation and elaboration of gender identity/role as well as for healthy psychosocial growth. Middle childhood is a period of practice and rehearsal of present and future gender roles. Activities that are typically boyish or girlish are prominent during this period. In girls, play and fantasy activities depict romanticism, marriage, and parentalism,

---

[3]Designations for the developmental stages prior to puberty are awkward (Thomas and Chess, 1972; Sullivan, 1945). Infancy refers to the first two years of life, childhood to the years between infancy and puberty. Early childhood signifies the period prior to beginning school, and the remaining years before puberty are labeled as childhood, later childhood, or the latency period. The stages of psychosocial and psychosexual development do not readily correspond to these designations. Birth to five years constitutes the first stage of psychosexual differentiation, age five to puberty the second stage, and the pubertal growth years the third stage. For this chapter these time periods are called infancy and early childhood, middle childhood and prepuberty, and puberty or adolescence.

[4]The transpositions of gender identity include bisexualism, homosexualism, transvestism, and transexualism. The paraphilic disorders are more commonly known as the sexual deviations or perversions; these terms are judgmental and should, therefore, be avoided.

while in boys high-energy activities and competitive rivalry and assertion are emphasized. These differences are not inevitably linked with gender, but appear more frequently in one than the other and should be viewed as sex-shared, threshold-dimorphic characteristics derived from our mammalian heritage. Girls typically rehearse activities that define a stereotypic feminine gender identity, but that does not preclude the options of assertion and initiative in private or professional life. Similarly, boyhood rehearsals of the future exclude domesticity and child care, but both may, with social and cultural endorsement, be incorporated into a masculine gender identity with the goal of shared homemaking and shared parenting. Men and women with a biography of gender-shared social, family, and vocational roles respond more effectively to the personal and parental requirements occasioned by family disruptions due to death or divorce.

Puberty and Adolescence

With the advent of puberty and adolescence, the differentiation of psychosexual identity is completed. When developmental differentiation has proceeded without error, gender-dimorphic masculine or feminine erotic and pair-bonding roles emerge. Ambiguities and transpositions of gender identity constitute normal developmental phenomena that may be resolved in later years or be continued and integrated into adult life. The presence or absence of psychological distress stems from personal, familial, and sociocultural variables, not directly from variations in erotic potential. Errors in gender identity, particularly those that include unusual, bizarre, or noxious stimuli for erotic pair-bonding typically produce psychological distress, often exacerbated when the juvenile is unable to discuss sexual feelings, imagery, and functioning with adults who are nonjudgmental.

In a society that inhibits the display and practice of sexually erotic interests and activities, adolescent sexual behavior appears to issue directly from hormonal effects. Evidence from abnormalities of pubertal development (see below) and from patients with sexual disabilities indicates that the hormones act indirectly by lowering the threshold for responsiveness to both internal and external sexual and erotic stimuli. The perceptual and cognitive stimuli for pubertal eroticism are built into the adolescent's psychosexual identity in infancy, childhood, and prepuberty. Earlier rehearsals of adult sex roles and sex-coded roles are then enlisted in the gender-dimorphic behavioral and cognitive activities of the adolescent phase of development. The cognitive components include erotic imagery and fantasy stemming from the social biography as well as the perceptual stimuli from both the genitopelvic organs and the social environment; these factors jointly contribute to pubertal eroticism.

As in earlier phases of psychosexual differentiation, interaction with the social and behavioral environment as well as somatic growth are required to complete the adolescent developmental phase. Changes in the self-percept from boy or girl to a sexual being with a sexual-stimulus value depends, in part, on social interaction. The feminization or masculinization of the physique constitutes the most visible sign, to the self and to others, of sexual maturation and sexual dimorphism. Both adult and peer reactions are essential to confirm the self-percept of a new habitus. Peers provide perceptual stimuli for reciprocal and complementary social interaction, which leads, in time, to the establishment of romantic and affectional pair-bonds and eventually to sexual pair-bonding, usually in later adolescence and adulthood.

NORMAL PUBERTAL DEVELOPMENT

Timing of Pubertal Onset

The regulation of pubertal onset is a continuing subject of investigation. The central nervous system; the pituitary; the pineal and adrenal glands; the gonads; and the overall size, weight, health, and nutritional status of the body comprise a complex web of interrelationships related to adolescent growth. None of the existing theories provide an adequate explanation for normal pubertal onset, nor for precocious or delayed onset. The same applies to the progressive decline in the age of pubertal onset by 1 year, every 25 years, over the past century and a half. The correlation between body size and weight and pubertal onset suggests that improved health and nutrition may be a significant variable in earlier maturation in Western societies. Weight and size is more closely correlated with pubertal onset than chronological age, except in premature or precocious puberty, but the causal relationship remains conjectural. Critical body weight and age of pubertal onset may both reflect changes in metabolic rate stemming from activity in the limbic system, the amygdala, and the hippocampus, which, in turn, affect the hypothalamus. (Useful reviews of aspects of pubertal development are presented by Donovan, 1974; Forest, Saez, & Bertrand, 1973; Kulin, 1974; Money, in press; Root, 1973a; and Visser, 1973.)

Contemporary theory locates the mechanism for the regulation of sexual maturation in the central nervous system, specifically the hypothalamus. This part of the old brain, or limbic system, is central to the regulation of all vital functions of the body. It is connected with the cerebral cortex and the various sensory systems, especially smell and vision. Indirectly, the hypothalamus affects much of the endocrine system through its direct effect on the pituitary gland by way of neurohumoral secretions. The hypothalamic secretions instruct the pituitary gland to release hormones that activate the testes and ovaries to secrete their own hormones, androgen and estrogen, respectively.[5]

With the development of sensitive, radioimmunoassay techniques in the last decade, the interaction of the hypothalamic-pituitary-gonadal axis, which controls sexual functioning, is understood to have a negative feedback relationship which undergoes gradual maturation from prenatal life onward. The various components of the sexual system are functional from a very early stage, but remain dormant as a result of the inhibitory effect of the hypothalamus. The level of circulating hormones remains low during childhood when very small amounts of gonadal hormones inhibit hypothalamic secretion of gonadotropic releasing hormones. With increasing age and the impact of life experiences, such as health, nutritional status, psychological distress, and the influence of other internal regulatory mechanisms, the threshold for the release of hypothalamic secretions is gradually raised. As the hypothalamus becomes less sensitive to circulating gonadal hormones, the sex-hormone levels increase, and the gradual transformation to sexual maturity is set in motion. In the female, hypothalamic and pituitary secretions are released cyclically to regulate the menstrual cycle. Tonic or continuous secretions occur in the male.

Pubertal developmental status is classified according to morphologic changes — in girls, breast budding, pubic-hair development, height spurt, and age of menarche; in boys, growth of testes, pubic-hair development, penile growth, and height spurt. There are five

[5]A recent report on animals describes a new pituitary hormone, cortical androgen stimulating hormone (CASH), that may control adrenal androgen secretion. Theoretically, adrenal androgen could alter the threshold of hypothalamic sensitivity to circulating hormones and trigger the onset of puberty (Parker & Odell, 1977).

developmental stages for each of the morphological variables, ranging from prepubertal to adult (Marshall & Tanner, 1969, 1970). These changes do not occur in isolation but are accompanied by growth of the internal reproductive organs, the endocrine glands, the musculature, and possibly the brain, as well as by endocrine and metabolic changes.

Endocrinologically, childhood is not a latency period. Pubertal hormonal maturation begins at least a year in advance of the bodily changes that signal sexual development. The earliest sign of pubertal onset is the rise in gonadotropins FSH (follicular stimulating hormone) and LH (luteinizing hormone) between ages 7 and 11 in girls and 8 and 12 in boys, followed by a two- to threefold increase in blood levels of FSH and LH by the completion of puberty. The increase in FSH stimulates estrogen production and breast budding in girls, while in boys an increase in LH induces the production of testicular androgen and growth of the testicles.

There is a sixfold increase in blood levels of estrogen in girls, but the level fluctuates with the menstrual cycle; FSH and progesterone, which is produced following ovulation also fluctuate cyclically. Blood levels of androgen increase by more than twentyfold in boys between childhood and maturity. Somatic changes follow hormonal changes by approximately six months to one year in both sexes, although the relative ease of measuring breast budding in girls, as opposed to the difficulty of measuring testicular size in boys, often leads to the conclusion that the disparity in pubertal onset is two years (Tanner, 1975). The subsequent stages of pubertal development also reflect the earlier onset and more advanced developmental age in girls. The height spurt begins at the age of 9.5 to 14.5 years in girls and at the age of 10.5 to 16 years in boys; pubic hair appears at approximately 11 in girls, at 12 in boys. Boys grow for a longer period of time than girls (with the peak growth rate two years later) and are, therefore, taller than girls. Simultaneously, the internal reproductive structures enlarge and develop, the uterus in girls, the seminal vesicles and prostate in boys. With their maturation, the differentiation and development of sexual dimorphism is virtually completed. The first menstrual period, or menarche, occurs in girls between the ages of 10 and 16.5; the corresponding sign of sexual maturity in boys, the ejaculation of seminal fluid, or thoroche (Levin, 1976), occurs within the same age range. Nocturnal emissions, another indication of sexual maturity, develops more slowly but most frequently between 12 and 16 (Ramsey, 1943). Reproductive fertility lags a year or more behind menarche in girls; data regarding the onset of fertility in the male is lacking.

Pubertal development follows a typical sequence of events for girls and boys (Tanner, 1975). The age at which each stage occurs is more variable than the sequence of events, but the latter also varies. Pubic-hair development (premature adrenarche) may precede breast development and penile growth, for example.

The changes in body morphology vary, in both normal and abnormal puberty, in three different ways: timing of onset, sequence of events, and rate of passage. Each of these factors is influenced by genetic or constitutional factors and life events; in addition, the various stages of pubertal development are regulated by different hormones or hormone systems. Growth of reproductive organs and functions culminating in female menarche and male thoroche is controlled by gonadal hormones. Pubic, axillary, body, and facial hair growth (or adrenarche) is regulated by adrenal androgen secretions in both sexes. The growth spurt, which occurs two years earlier in the maturation cycle in girls, involves the synergistic action of growth hormone, adrenal androgen, and, in males, testosterone. In girls, insulin is postulated as important in statural growth. In both boys and girls, pubertal hormones seal over the epiphyses of the bones and stop statural growth.

It is an accident of scientific nomenclature that estrogen is associated with femaleness and androgen with maleness. Both hormones, as well as progesterone and prolactin, are secreted in males and females, but in differing amounts, from prepuberty onward. Androgen levels are calculated as 20 to 60% higher in males as compared to females. Estrogen levels in males compared to females vary from 2 to 30% according to the phase of the menstrual cycle. Androgen is produced by the ovary as well as the testis and also by the adrenal cortex. The source of estrogen in the male is less certain; some may come from the testis, and some may be converted from circulating androgens. The gonadal steroids are closely related chemically with progesterone-androgen-estrogen forming a production sequence.

Chronological Age, Physique Age, and Social Age

The progession of pubertal changes is such that physique age, or bone age, is a better criterion of developmental status than chronological age. Even within the range of normal development, some individuals may have virtually completed puberty, while others have scarcely begun. Developmental age is also sexually dimorphic. In girls, developmental status, measured by bone age or skeletal maturity, is more advanced than in boys from fetal life onward. It increases gradually, so that there is a two-year disparity at puberty. It is commonplace for girls to be viewed as advanced in psychosocial age as well as physique age when compared to boys of the same chronological age. Within each sex, variations in timing of puberty, its sequence, and its rate of progression also produce disparities between chronological age and physique age and between psychosocial age (or recreational age) and psychosexual age and academic age (Money and Clopper, 1974). Cultural and family customs dictate the extent to which chronological age and physique age, as opposed to psychosocial age and psychosexual age, are expected to coincide or permitted to deviate. Adolescent rebellion stems partly from pressures to conform to chronological age expectations; conversely, behavioral disabilities, psychosexual disabilities, and psychopathology may derive from unusual delays in timing, sequence, or progression. Self-awareness of body image and the reactions of peers and adults contribute to the occurrence of psychosocial and psychopathological disabilities in both normal variations and abnormalities of growth. The effects of social interaction and self-perception on psychosocial maturation are dramatically illustrated when pathology of somatosexual development occurs, as in errors of pubertal timing and rate of passage, defects of the sex organs, and endocrine disorders (see the discussion on disorders of pubertal development).

The effects of these conditions emphasize the importance of social interaction as opposed to direct hormonal influences on adolescent sociosexual behavioral development. The dramatic changes in physique and in psychosocial and psychosexual functioning, which accompany hormonal puberty, endow hormones with more power than they possess.

Hormones and Sociosexual Behavior

The relationship between hormonal status and sociosexual behavior is derived from cross-sectional studies of samples of adolescents at successive ages and from longitudinal or short-term studies of adolescents with known hormonal disorders. There are no longitudinal studies correlating hormonal with somatic status and sociosexual behavior. In both boys and girls, sexual activity, including orgasm, precedes pubertal development by many years; hormonal puberty increases the intensity of sexual drive and lowers the threshold for response to sexual and erotic stimuli.

Gender dimorphism, observable in somatic maturation, is paralleled by dimorphism in erotic functioning during puberty and adolescence. The primary difference is the lower threshold for sexual and erotic response to visual stimuli in boys and to narrative and tactile stimuli in girls (Money & Ehrhardt, 1972). In a boyhood puberty, the primacy of visual imagery is announced in nocturnal sex dreams, often accompanied by ejaculation. There is no parallel in a girl's pubertal development; sexual dreams with or without orgasm are less frequent among females of all ages (Kinsey et al., 1953). Visual imagery in masturbation fantasies is also more frequent in boys than in girls, and the evidence to date indicates that this difference remains into maturity. The masculine capacity for associating a sexual response with a wide range of stimulus events (Ramsey, 1943; Kinsey, Pomeroy, & Martin, 1948) indicates the importance of the visual or distance receptors in male sexuality.

Present evidence suggests that gender dimorphism in sexual and erotic arousal is the result of neuroendocrine differences established prenatally. Early in fetal development, the sexual centers of the brain — specifically the hypothalamus — are sexually undifferentiated or bipotential. The presence of androgen in an XY fetus with responsive tissue masculinizes the brain, producing gender differences in erotic responsiveness as well as in other behavioral characteristics (see above). Neuroanatomy of the old (or "limbic") brain is consistent with such an interpretation. The neurosexual centers of the hypothalamus are located in close proximity to — and have connections with — oral, olfactory, and visual systems. It is postulated that in primates the visual system has a comparatively greater influence on sociosexual behavior than the oral and olfactory systems (MacLean, 1973), which are of maximal importance for sexual regulation in lower animals. The way in which androgen affects neuroendocrine and neurotransmitter functions remains to be explored. The intersex syndromes of androgen excess and androgen insufficiency (see below) provide confirmatory evidence of the effect of androgen on the brain.

There is a wide range of individual variation in sexual responsiveness, however, and the effect of sociocultural inhibitions on girls versus boys is not known. The slow, gradual increase in sexual and erotic interests and activities in females, from adolescence into maturity as reported in Kinsey's studies, contrasts sharply with the sudden upsurge in sexuality in males at adolescence, as shown in Figures 2, 3, and 4.

Sociosexual behavior is influenced by cultural and educational conditions, as shown in the declining age of first intercourse and the incidence of intercourse among unmarried adolescents (Kinsey et al., 1953; Kinsey, Pomeroy, & Martin, 1948; Sorenson, 1973; Zelnik & Kantner, 1977). The Kinsey studies reported that 73% of males and 20% of females had intercourse by age 20. Sorenson's study reported 72% for males and 57% for females by age 19. The most recent survey by Zelnik and Kantner is of unmarried women only. They report that 55% of the women were sexually active by age 15 in contrast to Sorenson's figure of 30% and Kinsey's figure of 3%.

Although social and educational background exert an influence on both male and female expressions of sexuality, difference between the genders is consistent in the cultures studied (Asayama, 1975; Beach, 1974; Schofield, 1965; Schmidt & Sigusch, 1972). In Figure 3, hormonal data and behavioral data are taken from different samples of human males. The onset of sex drive (manifested in nocturnal emissions and masturba-

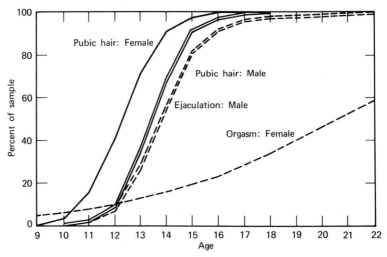

Figure 2. Cumulated percents, comparing female and male: onset of adolescence and sexual response. (Reprinted, with permission, from Kinsey et al., 1953.)

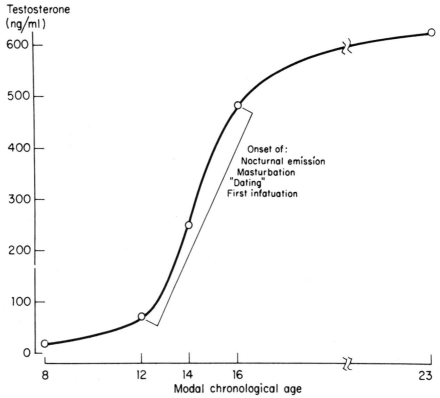

Figure 3. Levels of plasma testosterone in human males at different ages. (August et al., 1972; data referring to behavior taken from Ramsey, 1943 and Kephart, 1973. Reprinted, with permission, from Beach, 1974.)

tion) and of sociosexual behavior (dating and falling in love) correspond with the rapid rise in testosterone levels between 12 and 14. The incidence data for male American and male Japanese sexual behavior, seen in Figures 3 and 4, show a similar rapid rise with age. Hormonal data are lacking in the Japanese study, but it is reasonable to assume an increase with age, as shown in Figure 3. With the advent of hormonal puberty, males experience a desire for sexual pair-bonding, although the incidence of both proceptive (kissing, dating, etc.) and acceptive (coitus) sexual behavior is much lower, as shown in Figure 4.

The relationship between hormone levels and psychosexual functioning in females is more difficult to ascertain. The gradual increase in estrogen levels, culminating in the menarche, is paralleled by a change in interests and activities aimed at achieving attention and response from opposite-sex peers. Daydreaming (about unspecified subjects), interest in personal adornment, and in heterosexual social activities increase in the postmenarche (Stone & Barker, 1939). After menarche, female adolescents, in Kinsey's (1953) samples, experienced orgasm but far less frequently than their male counterparts in Japan or America, as shown in Figures 4 and 5. The Japanese female sample expressed a lower incidence of sex awareness, interest, and behavior as contrasted to males. Subsequent to menarche, female sexual interests, desires, and activities appear to fluctuate with hormonal variations within the menstrual cycle. Although the data are not conclusive and wide individual variations exist, erotic desire appears to be at its highest both at mid-cycle, when estrogen and gonadotropin levels are high and premenstrually when estrogen, progesterone, and gonadotropins are at the lowest levels. The reason for a premenstrual elevation in eroticism is not clear but may stem from the fact that the psychophysiologic effects of androgen levels, which fluctuate during the menstrual cycle (Persky et al., 1976), are more perceptible when estrogen and progesterone levels are low (Money & Higham, 1979). Androgen is the "libido" hormone for both sexes (see the discussion of syndromes of androgen excess and syndromes of androgen insufficiency), but much remains to be learned about the relative contributions of the sex hormones to the proceptive (attractivity and receptivity) and acceptive (coital) phases of human sexual pair-bonding (Baum et al., 1977; Rossi & Rossi, 1977).

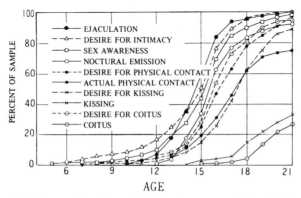

Figure 4. Japanese students' sexual development and experience: accumulative incidence. (Reprinted, with permission, from Asayama, 1975.)

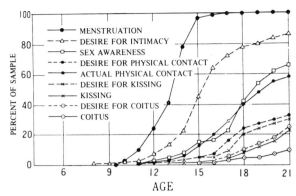

Figure 5.   Female Japanese students' sexual development and experience: accumulative incidence. (Reprinted, with permission, from Asayama, 1975.)

DISORDERS OF PUBERTAL DEVELOPMENT

The differentiation of secondary sex characteristics during pubertal development can occur too early or too late, relative to chronological age, or include incongruities or deformities. The etiology of disorders of development of sexual morphology may be unknown, or idiopathic, but also includes neurological, endocrine, and chromosomal congenital anomalies; the sequelae of tumors; systemic illness; malnutrition; or exposure to exogenous gonadal hormones (Sizonenko, 1975). The psychosexual and sociosexual consequences of disorders of morphological development derive mainly from the body image perceived by the self as well as by peers and adults, not specifically from the etiology. When there is a disorder of somatosexual development, the expected synchrony of chronological age, physique age, social age, and corresponding sociosexual maturation is disrupted.

Expectations regarding social age, recreational age, educational age, and psychosexual age derive from physique age, the most visible and customary standard for judging chronological age. Disparity of physique age and chronological age produces inappropriate expectations from peers and adults and a negative self-image. The psychological problems associated with errors of pubertal development derive from age disparities as well as from self-reactions and the reactions of others to the disparity in body image. Healthy psychosexual maturation requires social interaction as well as hormonal regulation to complete the dimorphism of adolescent eroticism; disorders of pubertal maturation disrupt the expected program of social interaction.

The most common disorders of adolescent maturation are errors in timing of pubertal onset. Whether the timing error derives from known medical abnormalities or is idiopathic or spontaneous in origin, the psychological consequences and their case management, with appropriate counseling and sex education, are similar (Money & Clopper, 1974; Ehrhardt & Meyer-Bahlburg, 1975; Watson & Money, 1975).

Precocious Puberty

Precocious puberty is diagnosed when activation of the gonads initiates sexual maturation before age 8 in girls or 9.5 in boys. It occurs more frequently in girls (Root, 1973b). The condition can be present at birth but typically begins by age 6 in girls and by age 8 in boys

(Bierich, 1975); it is completed within approximately two years. The sequence of stages and rate of progress does not differ from a normal puberty, although premature thelarche or adrenarche can occur as an isolated event. The early growth spurt places the child with precocious development two to three years in advance of his or her age-mates in stature. Girls develop pubic and axillary hair as well as breasts, and they begin to menstruate; boys also develop body and facial hair as well as growth of the penis, and they experience erections and nocturnal emissions. With the completion of sexual maturation, the epiphyses of the bones fuse as early as age 9 or 10, so that children who were once the tallest must now adjust to being among the shortest; adult height for these children is often around 5 feet. Boys also must adjust to a relative lack of strength and athletic prowess. The age-size discrepancy presents a formidable body-image problem for these children. Teasing and embarrassment regarding breasts and menses or penis size and scrotal hair are added handicaps in peer relationships and self-image.

The child with precocious puberty is generally treated as older, in accord with physique age rather than chronological age. Psychosocial development is often accelerated to permit participating with older children, thus bridging the gap between physique age and chronological age. Social and academic acceleration is beneficial for most juveniles with precocious development; the isolation and embarrassment of feeling different is thus minimized (Money & Alexander, 1969; Money & Walker, 1971).

Accelerated pubertal and psychosocial development is not to be equated with sexual precocity in either boys or girls, even though hormonal levels are normal for the pubertal stage. Gender identity is normally masculine or feminine, respectively, with appropriate interests and activities. Homosexualism, bisexualism, and sexual disabilities are unreported.

Boys experience an increase in genitopelvic aspects of sexual behavior, including erections, masturbation, and ejaculations. Erotic arousal to visual imagery (in dreams and daydreams) occurs as in normal puberty, but sociosexual activities (girlfriends, dating, and falling in love) await social interaction and the teen-age years. Precocious or promiscuous sexual behavior does not result from precocious maturation. Similarly, girls do not begin erotic and sexual activities as a result of their maturational status. As in normal girls, childhood is spent in consolidating gender identity with romantic and erotic interests emerging in the mid-teens. Girls with a negative self-image stemming from feeling isolated and different at an early age are likely to remain bashful and to delay dating and romance rather than become sexually promiscuous.

Delayed Puberty

The incidence of pubertal delay is the same for boys and girls, but boys comprise a larger proportion of children seeking diagnosis and treatment (Prader, 1975), perhaps because immaturity of stature, physique, strength, hair growth, and genitalia are difficult for a boy to conceal in his teen-age years. The diagnosis of pubertal delay is given to boys if testicular enlargement has not begun by age 13.5 and to girls if breast development has not begun by age 13 — or to either when the rate of progress from initiation to completion exceeds more than 5 years (Root, 1973b). The most common cause is constitutional delay in pubertal onset with an unknown etiology but probably familial in origin. Other disorders are secondary to hypothalamic-pituitary deficits and chromosomal disorders. These disorders, with an established etiology, include: hypogonadism resulting from testicular failure (anorchia or hyporchia) or from gonadal dysgenesis; hypogonadism secondary to hypogonadotropinism (hypothalamic-pituitary deficits), which may also include statural deficits (hypopituitary dwarfism) or anosmia (Kallmann's syndrome); hypogonadism and gonadal dysgenesis associated with a chromosome disorder (see below).

In constitutional delayed adolescence, hormonal status is in agreement with physique age or bone age, not chronological age; when puberty is initiated, the hormonal findings are normal. In all forms of hypogonadism, due either to gonadal failure (a hypothalamic-pituitary deficit) or a chromosomal disorder, testosterone and estrogen levels are low average or below average (Money & Clopper, 1974). Hormone replacement therapy, testosterone or estrogen, is required to induce pubertal development. With appropriate hormone therapy, virilization or feminization of the body is usually satisfactory, except in those males with pituitary dysfunction, for whom beard growth is deficient. The statural deficit present in dwarfism and to a lesser extent in Turner's syndrome (see below), is an additional complication in sociosexual maturation (see the discussion on chronologic age, physique age, and social age).

The disparity in physique age and chronological age is the basis of the major psychologic problems in all syndromes of delayed adolescence. Immaturity of the body image produces psychological distress, including embarrassment, shame, anxiety, and lack of self-confidence, separating the young person from peers and normal social interaction. Boys who lag behind agemates in stature and strength in early adolescence continue to feel at a competitive disadvantage in young adulthood. Girls also experience psychological distress when the body fails to feminize and increase in stature; failure to menstruate, a common form of feminine pubertal delay, is not usually a source of distress. When the signs of pubertal delay are visible, girls and boys are equally affected. Girls with a flat chest and thin torso, legs, and arms, are unable to compete in the courtship rehearsals of teenagers, just as boys are unable to compete on the playing field.

Psychosocial and psychosexual development is further hampered by adult and peer response to the juvenile appearance rather than to chronological age, educational age, social age, or mental age. The complementary psychopathology of infantilization by adults and rejection by peers, on the one hand, and withdrawal and lack of self-confidence on the other, is likely to persist even after normal adolescent maturation has been attained (Money & Clopper, 1974). Lack of self-confidence in social and sexual relationships is common both before and after hormone treatment. The pattern of withdrawal and isolation from peers, both male and female, does not yield as a result of physical maturation. Behavioral disabilities, possibly secondary to the reaction of being different, somatically, exacerbates the difficulties of social and sexual life.

Similar findings are reported for adolescents with normal variations in adolescent development. Comparisons of late- and early-maturing boys report less effective social skills, mild behavioral disabilities, and less success in work and careers in the late maturing; academic achievement may be well above average, however (Jones & Bayley, 1950; Ames, 1957; Mussen & Jones, 1957; Jones, 1958; Ehrhardt & Meyer-Bahlburg, 1975; Lewis, Money, & Bobrow, 1977). By contrast, early-maturing girls are reported as socially less successful than average and/or late-maturing girls (Jones, 1958). Whether the same conclusion pertains now, almost 20 years later, is questionable.

Psychosexual functioning is impaired, to some degree, in all males who suffer pubertal delay, of known or unknown etiology, but the degree of impairment both before and after testosterone replacement therapy is variable. In primary gonadal failure, associated with eunuchoid body proportions (in the absence of androgen the bone epiphyses do not fuse and statural growth is prolonged), the response to testosterone produces excellent virilization of the body and an increase in sexual activity, including erotic imagery, erections, masturbation, dating, petting, and intercourse. Gender identity is typically, but not exclusively, heterosexual. Cryptorchidism when surgically corrected prepubertally does not require hormone therapy for pubertal development; the condition is associated with a normal gender identity but a later than average onset and frequency of sociosexual behavior (Meyer-Bahlburg, McCauley, Schenck, Aceto, & Pinch, 1974). The cognitional component of testosterone therapy, when necessary, produces improvement in well-being and self-confidence (Money and Alexander, 1967).

When pubertal delay is secondary to hypogonadotropinism, resulting from a hypothalamic-pituitary impairment, testosterone replacement therapy is not as effective as in primary gonadal failure. Virilization of the body is incomplete, particularly with respect to facial hair. Sexual interest is low and sociosexual activity is limited, even when married. The emotional intensity of falling in love and establishing a sexual partnership, typical of normal adolescence and young adulthood, is absent. Social isolation and withdrawal is not relieved by hormone therapy; some individuals develop serious personality pathology that accentuates isolation. Statural deficits secondary to hypopituitary dysfunctions add an additional complication for the individual with pubertal delay (Bobrow, Money, & Lewis, 1971; Clopper, Adelson, & Money, 1976; Clopper & Money, 1975).

Delayed pubertal maturation occurs with the chromosome disorders of Turner's syndrome and Klinefelter's syndrome.

Turner's syndrome is produced by a 45,X0 chromosomal consititution; whether the missing chromosome is an X or a Y is not known. Affected individuals differentiate a feminine body morphology but lack ovaries. Without ovaries, the female sex hormones, which bring about maturation of the body at puberty, are not produced. Estrogen levels in Turner's syndrome are similar to those of prepubertal girls until puberty is induced by the administration of estrogen. Normal feminine development occurs, including menstruation. The psychological problem in Turner's syndrome derives from accompanying body deformities, mainly short stature. Estrogen replacement therapy is often delayed to permit further statural growth so that physique age lags behind chronologic age by several years. Although girls with Turner's syndrome are exceptionally capable of coping with stress, delayed maturation produces withdrawal, isolation, and sometimes dependency and regressive behavior. The more severe reactions occur when hormone replacement is deferred too long (Money & Mittenthal, 1970; Ehrhardt & Meyer-Bahlburg, 1975). Psychosexually, these girls are markedly feminine in orientation, displaying an interest in maternalism and childcare from an early age. Dating, romance, and marriage tend to be delayed as a result of the psychosocial lag and the special problems of finding a short-stature partner. Counseling regarding motherhood by adoption is beneficial in overcoming the disappointment of sterility (Ehrhardt, Greenberg, & Money, 1970; Ehrhardt, 1973).

The abnormality in Klinefelter's syndrome is an extra X chromosome or a 47,XXY chromosomal constitution. The body morphology is male but small external genitalia and sterility are the rule. Testicular androgen secretion is low in two-thirds of the cases and gynecomastia a frequent concomitant; virilization at puberty is inadequate. Inadequate development of secondary sex characteristics is not uniformly corrected by testosterone therapy, but such improvement as occurs is beneficial. A more convincingly masculine body image increases self-confidence and social acceptance. Hormonal therapy is of limited value, however. The XXY male is at risk for numerous forms of psychopathology, which interfere with social development. Mental disability including retardation and/or inappropriate logic, social inhibition, neurotic disorders, and varied psychosexual disabilities occur with greater than expected frequency. Hyposexuality with respect to masturbation, dating, intercourse, and marriage is typical, and transpositions of gender identity also occur. The extra chromosome is associated with a predisposition for behavioral disability, including psychosexual disability (Money, Annecillo, & Van Orman, 1974).

At present it is not possible to determine whether the somatic and behavioral deficits of any of the syndromes of delayed adolescence are produced by pathologic social interaction or by a common, underlying etiology. Interruption of the brain pathways subserving the endocrine functions of puberty may disrupt the programming of pair-bonding and mating behavior as well as predispose the development of personality disorder and behavioral disability. The failure to catch up socially when adult status is attained remains puzzling (see Money & Clopper, 1974; Lewis, Money, & Bobrow, 1977). Equally perplexing is the degree of variability in behavior traits and sexual functioning; not every individual with an endocrine, chromosomal, or developmental disorder is similarly and equally affected. The prenatal program may establish a predisposition for sexual functioning, but interaction with the social program is required to bring about psychosocial and psychosexual adequacy or disability.

Psychological counseling and sex education for the afflicted individual minimizes the adverse effects of abnormal adolescent development. Consultations with parents and the school may also be necessary.

Incongruous Puberty

Anomalies of morphology at puberty include heterotypic somatosexual development and hypo- or hyperdevelopmental conditions. Defects of the sex organs at birth, such as microphallus, cryptorchidism, anorchia, hypospadias, and enlarged clitoris produce psychologic distress and severe difficulties in psychosocial and psychosexual functioning, but the problems do not stem from pubertal hormonal development (see also the discussion on delayed adolescence as well as Money, 1973b, for a discussion of the sex errors of the body).

Heterotypic somatic development at puberty is produced by virilizing or feminizing tumors or metabolic errors; by endocrine disorders and intersex conditions; by hormone ingestion; or by ovarian abnormalities in the female. Hirsutism in girls and gynecomastia (breast growth) in boys are the most common incongruities. Although the criteria for either condition are not absolute, extremes are clearly recognizable. Family and ethnic background affects these aspects of somatic development. Any departure from normal expectations is likely to be viewed with alarm by adolescents, who, as a group, are concerned about body image.

Hirsutism can be accompanied by generalized virilizing effects, deepening of the voice, enlargement of the clitoris, and balding; menstrual failure is customary when the androgen levels are sufficient to virilize the body. Androgen levels are higher than in the normal female in these conditions. Before cortisone treatment was available, females with the adrenogenital syndrome virilized as a result of excessive androgen secretion from the adrenal cortex. In the Stein-Leventhal syndrome, abnormal ovarian function suppresses menses and causes hirsutism.

Gynecomastia to some degree is expected in one-third of adolescent boys as a normal developmental phenomenon. The condition also occurs in approximately one-third of those who have Klinefelter's syndrome (see p. 485–86). The endocrine disorder producing gynecomastia is unknown, but it is presumed to be a function of an inborn error of androgen secretion or utilization (Knorr & Bidlingmaier, 1975).

In the androgen insensitivity syndrome (see the discussion on prenatal hormones), individuals assigned and reared as male, a consequence of the presence of undescended testicles, feminize at puberty. When the body fails to respond to androgen, as in this congenital condition, the estrogen normally produced by the testes is sufficient to feminize the body, except for the absence of pubic hair, which is characteristic. To live as a boy without male genitalia and the usual pubertal signs of virilization, deep voice and beard, is a severe psychological hardship, best avoided by assigning the children as female (see the discussion on prenatal hormones and puberty).

Abnormalities of breast development in pubertal girls, hypoplasia or hyperplasia, are not well understood, except in relation to overall pubertal onset. There are wide normal variations in breast size, constitutional or familial in origin. There is some evidence that prenatal androgenization of the hypothalamic structures may affect the capacity of mammary tissue to respond to sex hormones later (Money & Ehrhardt, 1972).

Virilization in a girl or feminization in a boy is a source of anxiety, embarrassment, and mortification; the mind and the self-image are unaffected by pubertal hormones. The increased sex drive, or libido, in girls who have high levels of androgen also contributes to their sense of difference compared to agemates. Typically, the affected teenager withdraws from social participation and may also be rejected. Reconciling the incongruities with the self-image and gender identity is the major psychologic problem.

Incongruities affect both psychosocial and psychosexual development. The body image may contradict gender identity; in rare instances an ambiguity of psychosexual identity is resolved with heterotypic pubertal development and a sex-reassignment is made. Counseling, as in precocious or delayed puberty, is imperative. Relief from the more mortifying body changes can be obtained from surgery in gynecomastia and by electrolysis for excessive hirsutism.

Defects of the male genitalia, either of the testicles or the penis, are present from birth and are not the result of abnormalities of pubertal growth. Anorchia, hyporchia, and cryptorchidism are defects of testicular development; some cases of cryptorchidism correct spontaneously in the first year of life and are not associated with pathologic sequelae. Microphallus and hypospadias are defects of penile development. The etiology of these conditions is usually unknown but may include a hermaphroditic condition with other anomalies of the reproductive organs or some degree of deandrogenization. The response to pubertal hormones from the gonads, if present, or from exogenous administration is variable. The same applies to fertility in cryptorchidism or penile agenesis.

Boys with any of these developmental disorders are prone to stress and anxiety in adolescence when the genital anomaly becomes visible to others as well as to the self. Implantation of prosthetic testes is advisable to minimize adverse social reactions and improve the boys' sense of confidence and well-being. A prosthetic penis, appropriate in size and color for the chronologic age can be beneficial for boys with a microphallus if introduced early in life. Protection from embarrassment and teasing by providing privacy in the shower and toilet may also be essential. For adolescents with a defect of the sex organs, counseling as well as sex and love education, including information regarding sexual performance and what to tell the partner, should be available periodically and is essential for successful and healthy social development.

PRENATAL HORMONES AND PUBERTY

The effect of fetal hormones on sexually dimorphic behavior is difficult to assess in the human being. Experiments with animals demonstrate that feminine and masculine behavior patterns can be altered or even reversed as a function of heterotypic hormone administration (Reinisch, 1974). In the human being, where postnatal socialization and learning exert a profound influence on psychosexual differentiation, the role of prenatal hormones is not easily separated. The human clinical syndromes with a known prenatal hormonal anomaly provide evidence, which supports animal experimental findings, that the presence or absence of androgen exerts long-term developmental effects on behavior patterns in childhood, adolescence, and adulthood. The syndromes of hermaphroditism[6] in genetic males and females are experiments of nature in which the relative importance of prenatal hormones, pubertal hormones, and postnatal socialization can be examined. The hermaphroditic syndromes are produced by prenatal androgen excess in the genetic female or by prenatal androgen deficiency in the genetic male. The effects of androgen excess or deficiency are such that the anatomical criteria of sex may be ambiguous or reversed relative to genetic sex; behavior dimorphism is also altered by the effects of androgen or its absence on the neurosexual pathways of the brain.

Syndromes of Androgen Excess

The adrenogenital syndrome of male and female hermaphroditism is a genetic disorder whereby the adrenal cortex produces an androgenizing hormone instead of cortisol. The secretion of androgen occurs at a developmental stage subsequent to the differentiation of the internal reproductive organs but prior to the differentiation of the external genitalia. The female fetus is masculinized, partially or completely; the male fetus shows no effects of prenatal androgen excess, neither anatomically at birth nor behaviorally in later life. Cortisone therapy corrects the defective adrenocortical function when it is discovered at birth and surgical feminization corrects the defect of the sex organs. In rare instances, the female adrenogenital infant has been assigned and reared as male (Money, 1970) and differentiated a male gender identity. Before the discovery of cortisone therapy in 1950, affected children suffered a precocious, masculinizing puberty.

Girls with this syndrome of hermaphroditism differentiate a tomboy version of a feminine gender identity. The main features of a tomboyish femininity are a preference for vigorous, high energy-expenditure activities, utilitarian clothing styles, and lack of interest in personal adornment or in the rehearsals of maternalism with doll play and baby care. Many girls say they would prefer to have been born a boy, but they do not abhor their femininity as in female transexualism. Psychosexually, the prenatally androgenized girl is not different from other girls of her age with respect to masturbation or sex play. At puberty, however, she reaches the boyfriend stage of romantic interests, dating and falling in love somewhat later; in adulthood, marriage and motherhood also come later. The threshold for feminine erotic and sexual behavior is raised; once over the threshold, however, sexual functioning is typically feminine. The late onset of adolescent psychosexuality may also derive from the adrenogenital girl's special status medically and the difficulty in making a transition from tomboy relations with boys to romantic attachments with boyfriends. Only a few girls with the adrenogenital syndrome report

[6]For a concise summary of these syndromes see Money's (1973b) discussion of intersexual problems.

bisexual and homosexual fantasy/imagery or homosexual partnerships. In some instances, a masculine threshold for erotic arousal to visual stimuli is reported, but the content is appropriately feminine (Money & Ehrhardt, 1972; Ehrhardt & Baker, 1976; Walker & Money, 1972).

Syndromes of Androgen Insufficiency

Prenatal deandrogenization occurs in complete and partial forms in the genetic male. Deandrogenization of the genetic female is an impossibility since normal female sexual differentiation is the result of nonandrogenization; the addition of androgen in the genetic females is masculinizing (see the discussion on syndromes of androgen excess). Prenatal androgen insufficiency in the genetic male has four known etiologies: (1) complete or partial target-organ insensitivity to androgen, (2) failure to synthesize sex steroids, (3) a gonadotropin deficiency, and (4) a Y-chromosome abnormality. Only those individuals with complete and partial target-organ insensitivity have been systematically studied; the others occur very infrequently.

Complete and partial androgen-insensitivity are genetically transmitted through the mother; either is manifested only in a 46,XY chromosome constitution, that is, occurs only in the genetic male fetus. In the androgen-insensitivity syndrome (the complete form), the infant is born with female external genitalia, dysgenetic internal reproductive organs, and with undescended testicles that may be the only clue to the developmental abnormality. In partial androgen-insensitivity, Reifenstein's syndrome, the external genitalia are ambiguous: the phallus may look like an enlarged clitoris or a hypospadiac micropenis; the urinary and vaginal orifices may be fused into a single urogenital cavity; the testes may or may not be descended. Puberty is feminizing in both syndromes if the testicles are allowed to remain in place; the body responds to the estrogen that is produced in normal amounts by the testes. The normal male amounts of androgen produced by the testes fail to induce pubertal masculinization because of target-organ insensitivity. Individuals living as male must cope with breast development, which can be surgically corrected, and with a nonvirilized physique, complexion, voice, and hair distribution, which cannot be corrected by hormone therapy. Sex of assignment and rearing is almost always female in the androgen-insensitivity syndrome, but is male or female in Reifenstein's syndrome. Assignment as a girl, with appropriate surgical feminizing, is preferable since physique and sexual functioning in puberty and adulthood are more easily integrated with a feminine gender identity.

Individuals with the androgen-insensitivity syndrome, reared as female, are conventionally feminine in childhood, puberty, and adulthood. Childhood experiences include rehearsals of marriage and maternalism in fantasies and play preferences as well as in preferences for homemaking and motherhood in the future. In adulthood, androgen-insensitivity women are content with femininity and are good mothers to adopted children. Sex and eroticism are characteristically feminine, with erotic arousal mainly from touch stimuli (Masica, Money, & Ehrhardt, 1971).

Patients born with Reifenstein's syndrome differentiate a gender identity concordant with sex of rearing, either feminine, masculine, or ambiguous. Childhood play and activity preferences in the children living as boys lack the vigorous energy expenditure, assertiveness, and leadership typical in the prenatally androgenized male. Similarly, erotic arousal is more typical of femininity than masculinity. Visual imagery, as compared with touch, is less important for erotic arousal as in normal females. Sexual functioning is hampered in all of the patients by varying degrees of penile and vaginal impairment.

In both partial and complete syndromes of androgen insensitivity, erotic preferences and partner choice are heterosexual with respect to sex of rearing; chromosomal and hormonal variables are overridden by postnatal social influences. In both of these syndromes, the absence of prenatal androgenization influences childhood behavioral characteristics and pubertal eroticism. The threshold for gender-shared, nonerotic behavior is more typically feminine than masculine (Money & Ogunro, 1974).

HORMONES AND TRANSPOSITIONS OF GENDER IDENTITY

The transpositions of gender identity include bisexualism, homosexualism, transvestism, and transexualism. Homosexualism has been the focus of numerous studies aimed at discovering a correlation with hormonal functioning and transpositions of gender identity/role; few reports are available on the other transpositions. The first investigations of hormones in homosexualism were in the 1930s when it became possible to measure sex steroids in the blood stream or in the urine. Findings were inconsistent, and efforts to treat both male and female homosexuals with androgen and estrogen, respectively, were unsuccessful (see Money, 1970). In the 1960s, when radioimmunassay techniques permitted more precise measurements of blood hormone levels, there were further efforts to discover sex-hormone deficits or anomalies in homosexualism, but again, the results were inconclusive (see Money, in press). Similar negative findings are reported for male and female transexualism (see Money & Ehrhardt, 1972).

The hormonal anomaly interpretation of homosexualism and the other gender transpositions, like the early childhood/oedipal-complex-psychodynamic interpretation, is an overly simplistic approach to a complex phenomenon. Sexual/erotic preference is more likely to be the end product of a multivariable chain of events, including both prenatal and postnatal events.

Recent investigations of humans (Dörner, 1976) and of rats (Ward, 1974) suggest a prenatal neuroendocrine predisposition to homosexualism (see Money, in press). Insufficient androgenization of the hypothalamic sex-regulatory centers at a critical period of development affects later sexual/erotic behavior but not sexual anatomy. Similarly, a prenatal predisposition may be operative in the etiology of any of the sexual variations and disorders.

Postnatally, age of onset of adolescence appears to be a contributing factor in male homosexualism; the same does not apply to female homosexualism. Early-maturing boys begin all forms of sexual activity earlier than the late-maturing (Kinsey et al. 1953; Kinsey, Pomeroy, & Martin, 1948). Why some boys who mature early become homosexual is not known. Theoretically, vulnerable boys may be imprinted on male genital anatomy and male physique during childhood sex play.

Among adolescents who define themselves as homosexual, 72% of the boys begin sexual contact by age 11 to 12, and 89% of the girls begin between age 6 to 10. These figures are in marked contrast to those reported for first heterosexual intercourse, 17% of the boys and 7% of the girls by age 12 (Sorenson, 1973). First heterosexual intercourse and first homosexual contact are not necessarily comparable events, however, and the subject requires further study.

None of the syndromes of early or delayed pubertal onset nor of androgen excess or insufficiency correlate with homosexualism or other gender transpositions. Prenatal and postnatal hormones alter the threshold for sexual and erotic preferences; social biography provides the content.

REFERENCES

Asayama, S. Adolescent sex development and adult sex behavior in Japan. *Journal of Sex Research,* 1975, *11,* 91–112.

August, C., Grumbach, M., and Kaplan, S. Hormonal changes in puberty. III: Correlation of plasma testosterone, LH, FSH, testicular size, and bone age with male pubertal development. *Journal of Clinical Endocrinology and Metabolism,* 1972, *34,* 319–326.

Baum, M., Everitt, B., Herbert, J., and Keverne, E. Hormonal basis of proceptivity and receptivity in female primates. *Archives of Sexual Behavior,* 1977, *6,* 173–192.

Beach, F. Human sexuality and evolution. In W. Montagna, and W. Sadler (Eds.), *Reproductive behavior.* New York: Plenum, 1974.

Bierich, J. Sexual precocity. In J. Bierich (Ed.), *Disorders of puberty. Clinics in endocrinology and metabolism* (Vol. 4, No. 1). Philadelphia: Saunders, 1975.

Bobrow, N., Money, J., and Lewis, V. Delayed puberty, eroticism, and sense of smell: A psychological study of hypogonadotropinism, osmatic and anosmatic (Kallman's syndrome). *Archives of Sexual Behavior,* 1971, 1, 329–344.

Clopper, R., Adelson, J., and Money, J. Postpubertal psychosexual function in male hypopituitarism without hypogonadotropinism after growth hormone therapy. *Journal of Sex Research,* 1976, *12,* 14–32.

Donovan, B. The role of the hypothalamus in puberty. In D. Swaab and Schadé (Eds.), *Progress in brain research:* Vol. 41. *Integrative Hypothalamic Activity.* Amsterdam, The Netherlands: Elsevier, 1974.

Dörner, G. *Hormones and brain differentiation.* New York: Elsevier, 1976.

Ehrhardt, A. Maternalism in fetal hormonal and related syndromes. In J. Zubin and J. Money (Eds.), *Contemporary sexual behavior: Critical issues in the 1970s.* Baltimore, Md.: The Johns Hopkins University Press, 1973.

Ehrhardt, A., and Baker, S. Prenatal androgen exposure and adolescent behavior. Paper presented at the International Congress of Sexology, Montreal, Canada, October 28–31, 1976.

Ehrhardt, A., Greenberg, N., and Money, J. Female gender identity and absence of fetal hormones: Turner's syndrome. *Johns Hopkins Medical Journal,* 1970, *126,* 237–248.

Ehrhardt, A., and Meyer-Bahlburg, H. (Review of *Spätreife and bleibende unreife* by R. Corboz. Heidelberg New York: Springer-Verlag, 1967.) Psychological correlates of abnormal pubertal development. In J. Bierich (Ed.), *Disorders of puberty. Clinics in endocrinology and metabolism* (Vol. 14, No. 1). Philadelphia: Saunders, 1975.

Ehrhardt, A., and Meyer-Bahlburg, H. Psychological correlates of abnormal pubertal development. In J. Bierich (Ed.), *Disorders of puberty. Clinics in endocrinology and metabolism* (Vol. 4, No. 1). Philadelphia: Saunders, 1975.

Forest, M., Saez, J., and Bertrand, J. Assessment of gonadal function in children. *Paediatrician,* 1973, *2,* 102–128.

Jones, M. A study of socialization patterns at the high-school level. *Journal of Genetic Psychology*, 1958, *93*, 87–111.

Jones, M., and Bayley, N. Physical maturing among boys as related to behavior. *Journal of Educational Psychology*, 1950, *41*, 129–148.

Kephart, W. Evaluation of romantic love. *Medical Aspects of Human Sexuality*, 1973, *7*, 92–108.

Kinsey, A., Pomeroy, W., and Martin, C. *Sexual behavior in the human male*. Philadelphia: Saunders, 1948.

Kinsey, A., Pomeroy, W., Martin, C., and Gebhard, P. *Sexual behavior in the human female*. Philadelphia: Saunders, 1953.

Knorr, D., and Bidlingmaier, F. Gynecomastia in male adolescents. In J. Bierich (Ed.), *Disorders of Puberty. Clinics in endocrinology and metabolism*, (Vol. 4, No. 1), Philadelphia: Saunders, 1975.

Kulin, J. The physiology of adolescence in man. *Human Biology*, 1974, *46*, 133–144.

Levin, J. Thorache — a seasonal influence but no secular trend. *Journal of Sex Research*, 1976, *12*, 173–179.

Lewis, V., Money, J., and Bobrow, N. Idiopathic pubertal delay beyond age fifteen: psychologic study of twelve boys. Adolescence, 1977, 12, 1–11.

MacLean, P. New findings on brain function and sociosexual behavior. In J. Zubin and J. Money (Eds.), *Contemporary sexual behavior: Critical issues in the 1970s*. Baltimore, Md.: The Johns Hopkins University Press, 1973.

Marshall, W., and Tanner, J. Variations in pattern of pubertal changes in girls. *Archives of Disease in Childhood*, 1969, *44*, 291–303.

―――. Variations in the pattern of pubertal changes in boys. *Archives of Disease in Childhood*, 1970, *45*, 13–23.

Masica, D., Money, J., and Ehrhardt, A. Fetal feminization and female gender identity in the testicular feminizing syndrome of androgen insensitivity. *Archives of Sexual Behavior*, 1971, *1*, 131–142.

Meyer-Bahlburg, H., McCauley, E., Schenck, C., Aceto, C., and Pinch, L. Cryptorchidism, development of gender identity and sex behavior. In R. Friedman, R. Richart, and R. Van de Wiele (Eds.), *Sex differences in behavior*. New York: Wiley, 1974.

Money, J. Matched pairs of hermaphrodites: Behavioral biology of sexual differentiation from chromosomes to gender identity. *Engineering and Science*, 1970, *33*, 34–39. (California Institute of Technology, Special Issue: Biological bases of human behavior.)

―――. Effects of prenatal androgenization and deandrogenization on behavior in human beings. In W. Ganong and L. Martin (Eds.), *Frontiers in neuroendocrinology*. New York: Oxford University Press, 1973a.

―――. Intersexual problems. *Clinical Obstetrics and Gynecology*, 1973b, *16*, 169–191.

―――. Endocrine influences and psychosexual status spanning the life cycle. In H. van Praag, O. Rafaelsen, M. Lader, and E. Sachar (Eds.), *Handbook of biological psychiatry* (Vol. 3). New York: Marcel Dekker, in press.

Money, J., and Alexander, D. Eroticism and sexual function in developmental anorchia and hyporchia with pubertal failure. *Journal of Sex Research*, 1967, *3*, 31–47.

―――. Psychosexual development and absence of homosexuality in males with precocious puberty. *Journal of Nervous and Mental Diseases*, 1969, *148*, 111–123.

Money, J., and Clopper, R. Psychosocial and psychosexual aspects of errors of pubertal onset and development. *Human Biology*, 1974, *46*, 173–181.

―――. Postpubertal psychosexual function in postsurgical male hypopituitarism. *Journal of Sex Research*, 1975, *11*, 25–38.

Money, J., and Ehrhardt, A. *Man and Woman, Boy and Girl: The Differentiation and Dimorphism of Gender Identity from Conception to Maturity.* Baltimore, Md.: The Johns Hopkins University Press, 1972.

Money, J., and Higham, E. Sexual behavior and endocrinology. In G. Cahill, L. DeGroot, L. Martini, D. Nelson, W. Odell, J. Potts, E. Steinberger, and A. Winegrad (Eds.), *Metabolic basis of endocrinology.* New York: Grune & Stratton, 1979.

Money, J., and Mittenthal, S. Lack of personality pathology in Turner's syndrome: Relation to cytogenetics, hormones, and physique. *Behavior Genetics,* 1970, *1,* 43–56.

Money, J., and Ogunro, C. Behavioral sexology: Ten cases of genetic male intersexuality with impaired prenatal and pubertal androgenization. *Archives of Sexual Behavior,* 1974, *3,* 181–205.

Money, J., and Walker, P. Psychosexual development, maternalism, nonpromiscuity and body-image in 15 females with precocious puberty. *Archives of Sexual Behavior,* 1971, *1,* 45–60.

Money, J., Annecillo, C., Van Orman, B., and Borgaonkar, D. Cytogenetics, hormones and behavior disability: Comparison of XYY and XXY syndromes. *Clinical Genetics,* 1974, *6,* 370–382.

Mussen, P., and Jones, M. Self-conceptions, motivation, and interpersonal attitudes of late- and early-maturing boys. *Child Development,* 1957, *28,* 243–256.

Parker, L., and Odell, W. *Clinical Research,* 1977, *25,* 299A.

Persky, H., Lief, H., O'Brien, C., Strauss, D., and Miller, W. Dyadic relationship of personality measures and reproductive hormone levels during the menstrual cycle. Paper presented at the 2nd International Congress of Sexology, Montreal, Canada, October 1976. Audiocassette, 76–S–10. Baltimore, Md.: Hallmark Films and Recordings, 1976.

Prader, A. Delayed adolescence. In J. Bierich (Ed.), *Disorders of puberty. Clinics in endocrinology and metabolism* (Vol. 4, No. 1). Philadelphia: Saunders, 1975.

Ramsey, C. The sexual development of boys. *American Journal of Psychology,* 1943, *56,* 217–234.

Reinisch, J. Fetal hormones, the brain and human sex differences: A heuristic, integrative review of recent literature. *Archives of Sexual Behavior,* 1974, *3,* 51–90.

Root, A. Endocrinology of puberty. I: Normal sexual maturation. *Journal of Pediatrics,* 1973a, *83,* 1–19.

——. Endocrinology of puberty. II: Aberrations of sexual maturation. *Journal of Pediatrics,* 1973b, *83,* 187–200.

Rossi, A., and Rossi, P. "Body time and social time: Mood patterns are affected by menstrual cycle phase and day of week." University of Massachusetts. Unpublished manuscript, 1977.

Schmidt, G., and Sigusch, V. Changes in sexual behavior among young males and females between 1960–1970. *Archives of Sexual Behavior,* 1972, *2,* 27–45.

Schofield, M. *The sexual behavior of young people.* London. Longman's Green, 1965.

Sizonenko, P. Endocrine laboratory findings in pubertal disturbances. In J. Bierich (Ed.), *Disorders of puberty. Clinics in endocrinology and metabolism* (Vol. 4, No. 1). Philadelphia: Saunders, 1975.

Sorenson, R. *Adolescent sexuality in contemporary America.* New York: World, 1973.

Stone, C., and Barker, R. The attitudes and interests of premenarchial and postmenarchial girls. *Journal of Genetic Psychology,* 1939, *54,* 27–71.

Sullivan, H. Conceptions of modern psychiatry: The first William Alanson White Memorial Lecture, Psychiatry. *Journal of the Biology and Pathology of Interpersonal Relations,* 1945, *3.* A. Thomes and S. Chess (Eds.), Development in middle childhood. *Seminars in Psychiatry,* 1972, *4,* 331–341.

Tanner, J. Growth and endocrinology of the adolescent. In L. Gardner (Ed.), *Endocrine and genetic diseases of childhood and adolescence* (2nd ed). Philadelphia: Saunders, 1975.

Thomas, A., and Chess, S. Development in middle childhood. *Seminars in Psychiatry,* 1972, *4,* 331–341.

Visser, H. Some physiological and clinical aspects of puberty. *Archives of Diseases of Childhood,* 1973, *48,* 169–182.

Walker, P., and Money, J. Prenatal androgenization of females. *Hormones,* 1972, *3,* 119–128.

Ward, I. Sexual behavior differentiation: Prenatal hormonal and environmental control. In R. Friedman, R. Richart, and R. Van de Wiele (Eds.), *Sex Differences in Behavior.* New York: Wiley, 1974.

Watson, M., and Money, J. Behavior cytogenetics and Turner's syndrome: A new principle in counseling and psychotherapy. *American Journal of Psychotherapy,* 1975, *29,* 166–177.

Zelnik, M., and Kantner, J. Sexual contraceptive experiences of young unmarried women in the United States. *Family Perspectives,* 1977, *9,* 55–71.

CHAPTER 16

Delinquent Behavior in Adolescence

Martin Gold and Richard J. Petronio

Delinquency is presumed to be as endemic to adolescence as acne; the presumption mars the image of adolescents and shapes public responses to them. Although, in general, delinquency has remained in the forefront of social science research, the empirical base for the relationship between the *development* of *adolescence* and *delinquency* is quite inadequate. Therefore, we shall need to sift the data carefully, discriminating between those studies that examine the nature of the relationship between adolescence and delinquency in a developmental framework and those that do not. Despite the scarcity of developmental research, the relationship between adolescence and delinquency remains extremely important both theoretically and practically.

Theoretically, the investigator of juvenile delinquency has the potential for testing central hypotheses about what makes adolescents different from individuals at other developmental stages. If we can identify what it is about adolescent development that gives rise to qualitative and/or quantitative differences in delinquent behavior, we may at the same time further our understanding of the essence of adolescence generally.

Practically, a better understanding of the relationship between adolescence and delinquency will improve our ability to make two important judgments: whether or not intervention is necessary and what kind of intervention is likely to be effective. We should ultimately improve both clinical decisions and public policy.

In this review, we address ourselves to several issues concerning the relationship between adolescence and delinquency. First, we put the broad theoretical question of why one might expect adolescents to be exceptionally delinquent. We then examine the data on that relationship. This sequence may seem backward, but it makes sense in light of the conceptual and operational confusions on the subject. These confusions make it necessary to establish some guidelines to direct us to the relevant data. We need to be clear about what constitutes adolescence on the one hand and what constitutes delinquency on the other, so that we can identify the appropriate data that bear on their relationship. We pay particular attention to whether delinquency is a unitary phenomenon or whether it is more usefully conceptualized as a set of distinctive types of behavior.

After examining the question of whether and in what sense adolescence is related to delinquency, we shall consider whether adolescence conditions the relationships of other variables to delinquency. The correlates of delinquency are conceivably different at

The authors wish to thank Dr. Joseph Pleck for his helpful comments on a draft of this article; Drs. Jerald Bachman, Lloyd Johnston, and Patrick O'Malley for making data available from their study, *Youth in Transition* (1977); and Ms. Bonnie Wilde for typing the manuscript.

495

different points during adolescence; and, if this is so, the nature of these differences may illuminate the process of adolescent development.

We shall then take a broader developmental view of delinquency, reviewing the theory and data that on the one hand speak to the childhood precursors of adolescent delinquency and, on the other, to the implications of delinquency for adult development.

Literature on intervention programs will then be reviewed from the perspective of theory and field experimentation. We make no attempt to cover all these materials since so much of it is simply whistling in the dark. We shall be selective, discussing only those programs grounded in coherent theory and those programs that have been put to scientifically respectable test.

Finally, we shall summarize the materials in terms of what light the study of delinquent behavior may throw on adolescence generally — its essential nature, its importance as a condition that affects relationships among other experiences and behavior, and its place in human development. In the course of summarizing, we shall consider briefly how what may be learned from studying delinquency can help us to understand adolescent suicide and religious conversion.

THE RELATIONSHIP BETWEEN ADOLESCENCE AND DELINQUENCY

Definitions and Measures

A useful definition of adolescence will be couched in terms of those dynamics or genotypic characteristics that form the basis of a theory to explain why adolescent behavior and experience are distinctive. We assume that science has no need for the concept adolescence, unless there is some behavior or experience that in some way sets this portion of the life cycle apart from the others. We argue then that the definition of adolescence should focus our attention on the reasons for that stage distinctiveness. The definition is the beginning of theorizing. A definition that will be useful in the context of this chapter will be one that differentiates adolescence according to those characteristics that cause delinquent behavior to be different in quality or quantity at some time in the life cycle (if it is).

Such a definition will be more powerful if it serves not only to explain the distinctiveness of the delinquent behaviors at this stage, but also if it can explain other, empirically distinctive behaviors and experiences that have been identified. The more such findings whose causes flow from the defining characteristic(s), the more powerful the definition may be said to be. Such a definition may also inspire a successful search for other particular distinctively adolescent behaviors or experiences that have not up to now been identified.

Definitions of adolescence typically identify maturational or social-role characteristics or some combination of them. The psychoanalytic perspective focuses specifically on the maturation of the adult sex drive, defining adolescence as that period from puberty to the attainment of adult genital capacity; the psychoanalytic theory derives the peculiarity of adolescent experience and behavior from the introduction of this particular drive into the psyche (Spiegel, 1951). Social learning theory, as applied by McCandless (1970) to development, also selects the onset of the adult sex drive as the essential characteristic of adolescence; but this approach reasons more from the general dimensions of the drive — its novelty as a stimulus, its intensity as a drive — to adolescent behavior and experience without the psychoanalytic stress on its specifically sexual nature.

In contrast to these psychological perspectives, the sociological approach conceptualizes adolescence as a set of social roles, distinctive in respect to the rights and obligations imposed by social consensus on individuals in the age grade (Brim & Wheeler, 1966). The adolescent role-set is hypothesized: (1) to derive from the encounter of particular culture conditions — technology and ideology — with a constant, the nature and sequence of human development and (2) to generate what is distinctive about adolescent behavior and experience, both in conformity with and also in reaction against the role's requirements.

Definitions of adolescence that include both maturational and social-role elements characteristically identify rapid change as the differentiating force in adolescence. Lewin's conceptualization of adolescence in terms of marginality is one example (1951); Erikson's concept of the crisis of identity formation similarly takes both rapid maturational and social change into account (1959). These theorists derive what is distinctive about adolescence from the dynamics of change and the individual's response to it. Lewin's is the more general orientation and does not differentiate adolescents from other individuals (like immigrants), who may also be marginal because of their experience of change. On the other hand, the dynamics of Erikson's theory, rooted in psychoanalysis, applies specifically to adolescence.

This admittedly sketchy survey of definitional approaches to adolescence is intended to lay part of the basis for an inquiry into the relationship of adolescence to delinquency. In the first place, the definitions set the theoretical terms by which the two may be theoretically related. If delinquency is in some way peculiar to adolescence, then according to psychoanalytic theory, it must be a direct or indirect consequence of sexual maturation. Or according to McCandless' (1970) application of learning theory, delinquency must derive from the state of adolescents' drives — or implicated in the role-set of adolescence, or in marginality, or in attempts to resolve the crisis of identity. We shall trace these theoretical links later.

Secondly, the definitions point to the measures of adolescence by which we have selected relevant empirical studies for inclusion. These measures are direct or surrogate operations for sexual maturation, social roles, marginality, or the identity crisis. However, it is not always clear to which of these some surrogate measures refer. Chronological age, the most ubiquitous operation for adolescence, may stand in for any of these essential characteristics.

Before we plunge into the theoretical and empirical relationships of adolescence to delinquency, it is necessary to define the latter as well. For the purposes of this developmental review, we adopt a phenomenological orientation. That is, we are not so much interested in the objective fact of violative behavior as we are in the individual's consciousness of that behavior. The definition of delinquency that we employ here is *behavior by a juvenile that is in deliberate violation of the law and is believed by the juvenile to make him or her liable to adjudication if it comes to the attention of a law-enforcement agency.* We want to make explicit some of the implications of this definition and then discuss the crucial issue of measurement.

The definition is phenomenological in the sense that it identifies witting violations. An adolescent who mistakenly violates some provision of the local juvenile code is not committing a delinquent act according to this definition. (It might be worthwhile to consider such mistakes from the point of view of the marginality of adolescence, but we shall not pursue that subject in this chapter.) Similarly, adolescents who commit a technical violation that they believe is never actually enforced (like smoking tobacco) are not being delinquent.

This definition of delinquency is also social psychological. It takes into account the social consensus represented by the juvenile code and considers behaviors in those legal terms. An act is not classified as delinquent, then, because the actors believe it is morally wrong when they do not believe it is also illegal. Nor is an act that adolescents believe morally right exempted for that reason if they believe it is violative of the law. So an adolescent who feels guilty over masturbating is not being delinquent in that behavior; but an adolescent who smokes marijuana with the belief that the act should be decriminalized is being delinquent nevertheless.

It should also be clear that this definition of delinquency does not take into account whether the behavior actually comes to the attention of some authority or not. It includes undetected delinquent behavior, and it is at this point that we must consider the question of how delinquency should be measured.

Delinquent behavior has most often been measured by the self-reports of adolescents (Hardt & Bodine, 1965). Self-reports have been collected either in confidential interviews (see Farrington & West, 1977; Kulik, Stein, & Sarbin, 1968b; Gold, 1970; Gold & Reimer, 1975; Williams & Gold, 1972) or by confidential questionnaires (see Nye, 1958; Gibson, Morrison, & West, 1970; Voss, 1963; Bachman, Green, & Wirtanen, 1971). Naturally some questions have been raised as to whether adolescents will admit to their undetected delinquent behavior, especially in a face-to-face interview. But studies of the validity of the self-reports method indicate that it is adequately valid for research purposes (Berger et al., 1975; Gold, 1970). Self-reports seem to have construct validity, being related to variables such as parent-child relations (Nye, 1958; Gold, 1970; Gold & Reimer, 1975; Gold & Mann, 1972; Kulik, Stein, & Sarbin, 1968a) and scholastic achievement (Bachman, Green, & Wirtanen, 1971; Gold & Mann, 1972). The one *non*-finding that has cast perhaps the most doubt on the validity of self-reported delinquent behavior is its consistent lack of association with social status (Bachman, 1972; Empey & Erikson, 1966; Faine, 1974; Gibson, 1968; Kulik, 1967; Mann, 1976; Nye, 1958; Williams & Gold, 1971), while the official delinquency records have consistently demonstrated a strong association.

However, Hindelang, Hirschi, and Weis (in preparation) have pointed out that official records demonstrate a relationship between delinquency and social class only when the measures of both variables are aggregated over geographical areas, typically census tracts or community areas in large cities; official records and self-reported measures of delinquency show similarly negligible relationships to social class when both delinquency and social class are characteristic of individuals.

Other methods for measuring delinquent behavior include the observations of others, usually school teachers, (Farrington & West, 1977; Hackler & Lautt, 1969), and collecting the official delinquency records of those whom the subject nominates as friends (Hardt & Peterson, 1968). These measures are reliably related to self-reported delinquency and have also demonstrated construct validity.

Some students have questioned whether delinquency is a unitary concept of psychological significance. They have developed typologies of delinquency out of theories and out of empirical analyses. We shall review this literature empirically for its developmental implications.

Two methodological criteria screened the literature for inclusion in this chapter. First, because we are concerned specifically with delinquent behavior rather than official delinquency, almost all the studies we reviewed measured delinquent behavior. Compared to the volume of studies that deal with official delinquency, literature on delinquent behavior is scarce. Priority for inclusion has been given to those studies that measured delinquency by self-report. Second, because of the nature of this chapter's focus on adolescence as a stage of life, only those studies are reviewed which report developmental findings in the form of longitudinal or age-cohort data.

Theories

In one sense, adolescents are most delinquent by definition. Breaking the law before adolescence is attributed to lack of understanding rather than willful deviance; at a later age, it is considered crime. Thus delinquency is an adolescent phenomenon. To so state the obvious is not mere pedantry, for the association drawn between adolescence and delinquency has been based largely on official records, which by legal definition must indict adolescents as most delinquent. But there are almost no data that demonstrate that adolescents more often wittingly break the law than children or adults do.

The belief in the delinquent propensities of adolescents has prompted many explanations, identifying forces ranging from deeply rooted biological instincts to social movements. G. Stanley Hall (1904), who is credited with introducing the concept of adolescence into the mainstream of American thought, stressed the biological, consistent with his general thesis that individual development — ontogeny — mirrored the development of the species — phylogeny. Hall noted that: ''. . . petty theft, as nearly all statistics show, constitutes more than half the earliest crimes of youth. There is a deep instinct that things belong to those who most need or can best use them, and the finer conceptions of the sacredness of personal property come at a later stage of evolution'' (p. 364). While Hall did not disregard environment, he believed that its function was to create the inner controls over the natural and unnatural instincts that led to criminal behavior:

The power of self-control is latent and undeveloped, and its necessity must be slowly learned. If he is degenerate or of a criminal type, or if his surroundings are unfavorable, the young criminal fails to acquire this power and falls a victim to the same appetites and impulses which all normal persons feel, but repress. . . . Perhaps the animal part of his nature is abnormally and congenitally disproportionate to the intellectual, so that there is no inner opposition to the gratification of his desires. . . . Indeed, it seems very clear that much of the art of living consists in self-control, the development of which in the individual is the unconscious but perhaps primary purpose of family, church, state, laws, customs, and most social institutions. [P. 339]

The heightened criminality of adolescents that Hall noted in the official statistics was due, he thought, to the intensification of criminogenic instincts in an organism that has not yet mastered itself. ''Pubescent boys and even girls,'' he wrote, ''often feel like animals in captivity. They long intensely for the utter abandon of a wilder life, and very characteristic is the frequent discarding of foot and head dress and even garments in the blind instinct to realize again the conditions of primitive man'' (p. 348). Although he admired the vibrancy of youth and expressed confidence that under benign conditions their delinquency could be muted and would eventually pass, Hall claimed that it was in the nature of ontogeny that, ''Adolescence is the best key to the nature of crime. It is essentially antisocial, selfishness, refusing to submit to the laws of altruism'' (p. 406). And, Hall also wrote:

The dawn of puberty, although perhaps marked by a certain moral hebetude, is soon followed by a stormy period of great agitation, when the very worst and best impulses in the human soul struggle against each other for its possession, and when there is peculiar proneness to be either very good or very bad. . . . By nature, children are more or less morally blind, and statistics show that between thirteen and sixteen incorrigibility is between two and three times as great as at any other age. It is almost impossible for adults to realize the irresponsibility and even moral neurasthenia incidental to this stage of development. [P. 407]

Hall blamed the parents, educators, clergymen, and others in control of the adolescents' environment for their failure to create the benign conditions that would permit the majority of youth who were not so biologically degenerate as to be irreclaimable to negotiate this dangerous stage in the life cycle without excessive delinquency and a resultant commitment to a life of crime.

McCandless' modern textbook on adolescence (1970) echoes the biological theme that pervades Hall's work. McCandless' conceptual contribution is to link a developmental theory of adolescence with learning theory by means of the concept of *drive*. McCandless noted that the onset of adolescence is, by definition, marked by the addition of the sex drive to the organism. That the drive is sexual is not, from the perspective of learning theory, so important for explaining adolescent delinquency as that it augments the general level of drive intensity. It is this state of high drive that is at least in the first instance responsible for increased delinquent activity. McCandless wrote:

> The energizing function of drive gives an adolescent high energy to make the changes he must make if he is to become a constructive adult. But if drive is too high, behavior may become rigid, random and reckless, simplistic, and socially insensitive. The "storm and stress" theory of adolescence — a theory to which all of us must subscribe to some degree — describes such adolescent behavior characteristics. [McCandless, 1970, p. 13]

McCandless secondarily took into account the specifically sexual nature of the new drive. He pointed out that high-drive states are not so disruptive in the long run if there are available means to satisfy the drive. But adolescents' sexual needs are not easily met in our society and their frustration may lead to aggression, many forms of which are delinquent. McCandless invoked the frustration-aggression hypothesis to account not only for the greater delinquency of adolescents, but also for the commonly observed fact that adolescent boys are more delinquent than adolescent girls:

> It seems clear that frustration is an important instigator to aggression; that, when sufficiently frustrated, almost all people will *feel* aggressive; and that most people, when they feel aggressive enough, will *behave* aggressively. Thus, one can expect adolescents to be more aggressive and hostile than prepubescent children. . . . Over all, aggressiveness may increase more for boys than girls, partly because of their activity level, partly because of cultural sanctions, and partly because the frustrations they meet may be sharper and more dramatic than those that face girls. [P. 18]

McCandless did not ignore sociocultural factors. He pointed out that, "During this time of physical and social change, society tells adolescents that it is also time for them to grow up, to focus upon their futures, and to take action to make their futures good. By and large, adolescents accept these goals and tasks. But what if society denies the chance to make good?" (p. 183). McCandless then cited blocked economic and social opportunities as another source of frustration more keenly felt at adolescence than earlier, and he attributed the rise in delinquency at adolescence to this as well. (We postpone our discussion of opportunity theory and social factors generally until after further discussion of biological factors.)

Thus, in the course of creating explanations for the association between adolescence and delinquency, McCandless employed the concepts of drive and frustration to build conceptual bridges between a developmental theory of adolescence and learning theory and between developmental theory and sociological theory.

Psychoanalytic theory also attributes the impetus for adolescent delinquency mainly to biological factors. Delinquent behavior is considered to be a form of acting out internal conflicts in contemporary social relations. These classes of behaviors obviously include a great many other behaviors besides breaking the law — Blos (1962), for example, identifies a young adult's leaving home as acting out and Weiss (1942) notes that Freud considered transference also as a form of acting out — but most of the psychoanalytic concern with acting out among adolescents has been with delinquency. Blos is representative of psychoanalytic theorists in stating that, ". . . experience tells us that the incidence of acting out rises sharply when the child enters puberty. This clinical fact alone clamors for an explanation'' (1962, p. 273).

The central psychoanalytic proposition about adolescence that makes delinquency more characteristic of this stage than any other is that the onset of adult genitality requires that the adolescent withdraw his/her erotic attachments from the parents and reestablish them with extrafamilial peers. In the transition entailed by this requirement the adolescent is especially prone to act out for several reasons.

According to Spiegel (1951), diminished attachments to parents weakens the internalized social control that they have established. In psychoanalytic terms, withdrawal of cathexis from psychological representations of the parents weakens the force of the superego. This leaves the individual more free to express forbidden wishes in behavior.

According to Blos (1962), psychic disengagement from internalized objects of love and hate is experienced as a severe deprivation of stimulation: emotions are flattened and the fantasy life is impoverished. Blos submits that this "accounts for the adolescents' frantic turn to the outside world, to sensory stimulation and to activity'' (p. 273). At the same time, Blos argues, acting out satisfies the adolescent as a renunciation of childlike passivity and deference, especially insofar as it runs counter to parental strictures. Furthermore, Blos follows Freud in regarding acting out as a form of remembering, inasmuch as it expresses earlier, otherwise unremembered (repressed) conflicts and experiences. Acting out as a form of remembering is useful especially to adolescents, who are impelled at this stage to establish their own sense of individuality. This sense is promoted by the adolescents' integration of what they remember that they were in the past, what they feel they are now, and what they imagine that they will become. Acting out serves this integration by enacting the infantile and childish past in the present, often in symbolic and disguised form to be sure, and thus it enables the adolescent to bring the pieces together.

Erik H. Erikson's view of delinquency at adolescence also focuses on the theme of individuality or, in his terminology, identity. Erikson's developmental theory (1963, 1968) places the task of psychological integration primarily in the adolescent years. Sudden physical and social changes precipitate the crisis of identity; the onset of puberty is matched by changes in the social expectations laid on individuals by the family, the schools, the peer group, and other institutions. They make two kinds of integration necessary: one is the resolution of ego identity, which is the establishment of the sense of consistency over the life cycle that Blos (1962) also finds relevant; the other is the resolution of role identity, a fitting of one's motives, values, abilities, and styles with new role demands. Erikson seems to attribute delinquency primarily to the failure to resolve role aspects of an identity. Young people whose formative experiences have somehow incapacitated them for acceptable roles in their society or for whom the obligations laid on them by those closest to them are excessively demanding may choose a "negative identity'' instead, "an identity perversely based on all those identifications and roles which, at critical stages of development, had been presented to them as most undesirable or dangerous and yet also as most real'' (1968, p. 197). Some of these adolescents may choose the role of the delinquent, immersing themselves in the darkest currents of the youth culture then available to them. By organizing their lives around this identity, they create a continuity of self from one relationship and situation to another, so that they can imagine how they might react even in encounters that never occur. Not only do their own responses become predictable to themselves, but they are also then able to predict with more accuracy how others will react to them. Thus their self-image and the reflection of themselves from others fuse. And insofar as they find support for their delinquent image among their peers, who are seeking reciprocal support, and from the mass media, which are soliciting the support of this market, the image provides some degree of respect. The association between adolescence and delinquency is thus, according to Erikson, a consequence of adolescence being the critical stage in the search for an identity.

Thus far in this survey of theories of adolescent delinquency, we have moved from those that are heavily biological to those that are more biosocial. We have come now to that point in the survey where theories stress the social change at adolescence more than the biological. Inherent in such theories is that the association between adolescence and delinquency is culturally relative. If change in social roles is the primary generator of delinquency, then cultural differences in the substance and degree of that change imply differences in the degree to which delinquency increases at adolescence. Of course, this point assumes that there is wide cultural variation in the way adolescence is treated, and this assumption seems altogether warranted. Indeed historical and cultural data (Aries, 1962; Mead, 1928) raise the question of whether adolescence is a universal social phenomenon.

The cultural relativity of adolescent delinquency is most clearly asserted in the theory of Bloch and Niederhoffer (1958). They define adolescence as, ''that period of life that comes between biological and sociological maturity'' (p. 11). Bloch and Niederhoffer are explicit about the existence of cultural variations in that essential hiatus. Furthermore, they attribute the generation of adolescent problems to disparate ages of maturity: ''Observations of many societies would appear to indicate rather clearly that the wider the disparity between these two levels of maturity, the greater the area of adolescent problems and the more acute the experience of adolescent strain'' (p. 11).

Bloch and Niederhoffer's hypothesis is derived from Eisenstadt's more general theory of age-grading (1956). Eisenstadt proposes that the formation of age-specific groups in a society is a function of generational differences in access to the resources of the society. Where older generations restrict the access of younger generations, age-graded groups tend to form to facilitate collective countermeasures. Bloch and Niederhoffer submit that the adolescent gang in American society is a manifestation of this process and is furthermore responsible for the rise in delinquent behavior at that stage of life:

. . . when adolescent youths, as in our own society, find it difficult to enter the adult status, for reasons of delay, social or technical obstacles, or because of the lack of an orderly, facilitating process, they will attempt to embrace the symbolic equivalents of the adult behavior denied them. In this . . . connection, we find that the youth denied the opportunities for full marital, economic, and civic activity may be apt to affect the superficial trappings of adult privilege. Thus, the adolescent drinking, sexual escapades, wild automobile rides, immature assertiveness, violent reactions to parental restraints, protests against authority, and the other forms of intransigence which, to the youth at any rate, appear to be the prerogatives of the mature adult. [1958, pp. 29–30]

Bloch and Niederhoffer's explanation is obviously a variation on the hypothesis of blocked opportunities. It is similar to McCandless' (1970) approach in that it links opportunity theory to developmental stages by selecting out of the many features that characterize adolescence the fact that it immediately anticipates adulthood. The imminence of adult roles makes opportunities a salient issue for adolescents. But Bloch and Niederhoffer do not, like McCandless, cast delinquency into the general category of aggression and invoke the frustration-aggression hypothesis to explain it. Delinquency in their view is rather an expression of the wish to be adult. By conceptualizing delinquency in this way, Bloch and Niederhoffer make the blocked-opportunity hypothesis relevant to a developmental consideration of delinquency.

Cloward and Ohlin (1960) also invoke blocked opportunities as a pregenitor of delinquent gangs and delinquent behavior. They derive their theory from Merton's more general theory of deviant behavior (1958), a theory that identifies the unavailability of legitimate access to legitimate goals as a reason for individuals to adopt illegitimate means and/or illegitimate goals. Cloward and Ohlin hypothesize that adolescents who lack the personal skills or the social support for achieving legitimate success in their society will band together to cope with failure. Whether they will adopt illegitimate means and/or illegitimate goals—that is, the kinds of delinquent behavior that will characterize gang activities—depends upon the alternatives their communities offer them. We will discuss the developmental and other implications of Cloward and Ohlin's theory later, in the context of a discussion of delinquent typologies.

This survey of theories to explain the association between adolescence and delinquency is not exhaustive. We have selected for review examples only of those theories that fairly explicitly address themselves to this association. The association can be derived from other theories that we have not discussed. Lewin's conceptualization of adolescents as "marginal" (1939) was designed to explain in social terms the "so-called 'typical' difficulties of adolescent behavior" — "shyness, sensitivity, and aggressiveness," "emotional tension," "readiness to take extreme attitudes and action" — and lends itself to an analysis of delinquency, although delinquency is not mentioned explicitly in Lewin's brief discussion (and his phrase, "so-called 'typical' difficulties of adolescent behavior," was meant to caution everyone against "typing" anyone or any age group without taking into account the environment in which they lived).

Cohen's conceptualization of delinquency as a lower-class subcultural response to failure in the student role (1955) is obviously linked to adolescence by the same logic of blocked opportunities as Bloch and Niederhoffer (1958) employ, although Cohen does not take a developmental perspective; his speculation that middle-class boys become delinquent as an attempt to confirm a shaky sense of their masculinity is akin to Erikson's (1963) proposition regarding negative identity.

Empirical Relationships

For reasons that we have already discussed, the data that created the need for explanations of the relationship between delinquency and adolescence are quite inconclusive because official data may be misleading. If those were the only data available, we would say that the association had not been established and that attempts at explanation are premature.

The question to be addressed now is whether individuals tend wittingly to break the law more in their adolescent years than either before or after. The appropriate data to answer this question are valid counts of the offenses of children, adolescents, and adults, perhaps weighted somehow by the seriousness of the violations. We have argued that self-reports provide the most valid data we have, but their availability is severely limited.

The National Survey of Youth 1972 (see Gold & Reimer, 1975) collected self-reports of delinquent behavior from a representative sample of 1395 American youth 11- through 18-years-old. This age range was chosen in order to span adolescence, whether adolescence is defined in maturational or social terms. One might assume that many of the younger respondents, those under 13, were preadolescent and many of the older ones, postadolescents, so that these data reflect delinquency in later childhood and early adulthood as well.

The data from the National Survey of Youth 1972 demonstrate that both the frequency and seriousness of delinquent behavior rise in the adolescent years. Figure 1 shows that 18-year-old boys and girls confess to almost five times more nontrivial delinquent acts in the most recent three years than 11-year-olds do. The curves show no sign of abatement, rising fairly constantly during the adolescent years, although there is some acceleration at age 15. The acceleration at age 15 is even more marked when one takes the seriousness of offenses into account by weighting the incidents of delinquency by Sellin and Wolfgang's scales (1964); indeed, the seriousness index peaks at age 15 for boys and girls. The relationship between age and seriousness of offenses for boys and girls during adolescence is represented in Figure 2.

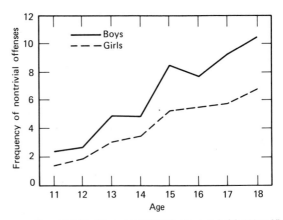

Figure 1.   Mean frequency of nontrivial incidents committed by boys and girls (11 to 18 years old).

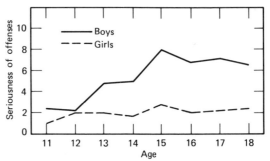

Figure 2.   Mean seriousness of delinquent offenses for boys and girls (11 to 18 years old).

Data provided by the Youth in Transition study (O'Malley, Bachman, & Johnston, 1977) extend our knowledge of the trend in delinquent behavior further into young adulthood. These data track the self-reported delinquent behavior of a representative sample of 10th-grade boys into their 23rd year. These data are most nearly comparable to those weighted by seriousness in the National Survey of Youth 1972 analysis, consisting of reports of vandalism, theft, assault and threatened assault, shoplifting, armed robbery, and joyriding. They show a decline from age 16 to age 18 as the National Survey of Youth 1972 data do, a rise at age 19, and then a decline through age 23.

These data confirm that violative behavior increases significantly from early to late adolescence. They do not indicate whether there is a decline in delinquency generally as adolescents become adults, but they do testify that commission of serious crimes is most prevalent at age 15 and begins to decline after that. So delinquent behavior is associated with adolescence. Although its frequency may or may not be higher in adolescence than adulthood, its gravity seems to be greatest at middle adolescence.

What accounts for the increase in frequency through the adolescent years and the peaking of serious offenses at age 15? What happens to individuals at this time in their lives to intensify their delinquent behavior? According to some theorists, at least part of the cause lies in puberty, but there are data that cast doubt on this hypothesis. In a subproject of the National Survey of Youth 1972, Gold and Tomlin (1975) obtained wrist X-rays of 298 boys and girls 11 through 18 year olds in the larger, representative sample of 1139. These roentgenograms were rated for skeletal age (by Dr. M. M. Maresh of the University of Colorado Medical School) using the Greulich-Pyle *Atlas* (1959) as the standard. Although skeletal age is not itself a measure of pubertal development, according to Tanner (1970), "Skeletal maturity is closely related to the age at which adolescence occurs, that is, to maturity measured by secondary sex character development. . . . Evidently the physiological processes controlling progression of skeletal development are in most instances closely linked with those that initiate the events of adolescence" (p. 107). On the basis of their skeletal age, the 298 subjects were trichotomized into slow-, normal-, and fast-maturers. The slow-growers were from 4 months to 2.6 years (median = -1.1) below the norm; the fast growers, from 7 months to 2.8 years (median = 1.2) ahead of the norm for their ages. The rate of the youths' growth was not related to the frequency of their self-reported delinquent behavior. In none of the age groups — 11 to 12, 13 to 15, or 16 to 18 — did the faster-growing boys or girls, presumably those with greater pubertal development, display more delinquent behavior. Perhaps the crucial test is among the 11 to 12-year-olds because the faster growers among them were postpubertal and the slower-growers, prepubertal. Among neither the boys nor the girls did the faster growing 11 to 12-year-olds confess to more delinquent behavior.

These maturational data obviously do not conclusively disconfirm that sexual maturation itself increases delinquent behavior. The measure of sexual maturation is indirect. Better data would be based on the hormonal content of the blood or on measures of secondary sex characteristics, like pubic-hair, penile, or breast development. But these data comprise the best available on the issue, and they suggest that role changes in adolescence rather than maturation is more determinative of delinquent behavior. This is not to rule out the effects of maturation altogether. Rather, it suggests that the effect of maturation on delinquency may depend on social reactions to adolescence.

In order to investigate the social variables in preparation for writing this article, the authors analyzed some additional data from the National Survey of Youth 1972. Our strategy was to try to reduce the amount of variance in delinquent behavior that was accounted for by chronological age by inserting other variables in an ordered, stepwise regression model.[1] The mediating variables were selected to represent the major social roles that adolescents play: son/daughter, student, and teenager, and also to reflect development of moral judgments in adolescence (Kohlberg, 1963a). We reasoned that merely growing older does not itself generate delinquency but that the correlates of growing older, particularly changes in social roles, might cause delinquency. That indeed turns out to be the case. We identified a limited set of variables that were significantly correlated both with age and with delinquent behavior; when these variables were entered into the regression equations, they reduced the relationship of age to delinquent behavior considerably.

We have already shown (see Figure 1) that the frequency of delinquent behavior is related monotonically to age. The zero order product moment correlation is .48 for boys and .41 for girls. These correlations are reduced to .12 for the boys and .05 for the girls after the effects of the other variables are partialled out (see Tables 1 and 2.) Variables that represent increasing involvement in the role of teenager (e.g., number of dates in the previous month) and increasing flexibility about the morality of deviant acts (e.g., it is not so bad to take a shortcut across someone else's property or to lie about your age to get into the movies for a cheaper price) account for the most variance in frequency. Accounting for somewhat less variance are negative attitudes toward school and poor relationships with parents (although a poorer relationship with their mothers seems to be of negligible importance among boys when the relationship with their fathers is taken into account). The data also indicate that girls, but not boys, are more frequently delinquent if they accept socio-political rationale for delinquent behavior (e.g., it is not so bad to steal from stores when you feel that stores are always cheating people or to lie to get around the many unnecessary laws and regulations). Altogether these variables account for 40% of the variance in the frequency of delinquent behavior among the boys and 41%, among the girls; the addition of age accounts for another 1% of the variance among the boys and even less among the girls. It should be noted that age remains a statistically significant correlate of the frequency of boys' delinquent behavior after the other variables are taken into account, and continues to overshadow attitudes toward school and relationships with parents in this respect.

Our finding that the flexibility about the morality of deviant acts significantly reduces the relationship between age and delinquent behavior coincides with an earlier finding by Petronio (1973). He studied 38 boys who had been on probation and under direct supervision by a county family court for two or more years. He measured a number of variables, including moral maturity using Kohlberg's (1963a, b) method of presenting vignettes. Data were also collected on the socioeconomic status (income) of the respondents' families, family size, respondents' IQ, and age. The 19 boys who were returned to court within two years of being first placed on probation proved to differ from those who were not returned to court only in their level of moral maturity, the recidivists' being higher, $p < .01$. (The protocols had been scored blind.) The recidivists on the average fell squarely within stage three; the nonrecidivist group at stage two, only bordering on stage three. Individuals in stage three typically resolve moral dilemmas by reference to conventional moral codes. Those at stage two are preconventional, resolving

---

[1]We are aware that the measures of delinquent behavior do not meet the formal assumptions for regression analysis because they are not normally distributed. But it has been demonstrated that the product moment correlation is actually quite robust even when distributions depart radically from the normal (see Havlicek & Peterson, 1977).

Table 1   Correlations with Age and Seriousness of Delinquent Behavior for Boys

Variable	Correlations[a]	
	Age (11–18)	Seriousness of Delinquent Behavior[b]
Dating[c]	.44	.30
Conflict[d]	.16	.15
School grades	−.12	−.23
Fathers' affection[e]	−.21	−.20
Mothers' affection[f]	−.24	−.19
Autonomy[g]	.24	.16
Expediency[h]	.32	.36

[a]All correlations are significant at $p < .01$; $N = 530$.
[b]Sellin-Wolfgang seriousness index.
[c]Number of dates per month.
[d]Degree of perceived conflict between adults and youth.
[e]Closeness of father and son.
[f]Closeness of mother and son.
[g]Number of rules and restrictions imposed by parents.
[h]Boys' tolerance for notion that expediency, convenience, or loyalty to a friend justifies delinquent behavior.

Table 2   Correlations with Age and Seriousness of Delinquent Behavior for Girls

Variables	Correlations[a]	
	Age (11–18)	Seriousness of Delinquent Behavior[b]
Fathers' affection[c]	−.19	−.13
Mothers' affection[d]	−.18	−.12
Revenge[e]	−.14	.20
Expediency[f]	.30	.21

[a]All correlations are significant at $p < .01$; $N = 461$.
[b]Sellin-Wolfgang seriousness index.
[c]Closeness of father and daughter.
[d]Closeness of mother and daughter.
[e]Girls' tolerance for notion that getting revenge justifies delinquent behavior.
[f]Girls' tolerance for notion that expediency, convenience, or loyalty to a friend justifies delinquent behavior.

dilemmas in order to produce optimal personal pleasure and avoid pain and punishment. Since Kohlberg's scale is developmental, these findings can only be interpreted to mean that the recidivists obtained a higher level of moral development than the nonrecidivists at the mean age for both groups of 15.

Very few of the 38 probationers had developed moral judgments beyond stage three. However, 5 did resolve dilemmas with situational ethics, making decisions about what is right and proper on the basis of contracts, both social and personal, and were thereby placed in stage five. Of those boys the average number of court appearances in a two-year period exceed two and therefore represent those youths who were the *most* ''officially'' delinquent.

Intuitively, a positive relationship between moral maturity and frequency of delinquent behavior does not seem a likely finding. Generally we tend to regard adolescents who commit more delinquent acts as less "moral." But Petronio's (1973) findings suggest that this traditional belief about repeater delinquents (we hasten to add that frequency of delinquency was based on official records) may be unwarranted. We posit two possible reasons for this relationship. One hypothesis is couched in terms of social control. Some adolescents have adopted a situational ethic that shows up in our measures as a higher level of moral development. If they are provoked to be delinquent, these adolescents are less bound to (controlled by) conventional morality. As a result of feeling less pressure to conform to normative standards, these adolescents regard delinquent behavior as less serious and therefore can use it more easily to solve personal problems. This interpretation is supported by Heise (1968), who found that 18 to 19-year-old college students were more generally condemnatory of a list of 30 deviant acts than were the students aged 20 plus. In this light, the more recidivist delinquents could be considered more mature than others.

The second interpretation is framed in a rationalization hypothesis. Instead of a situational ethic permitting more delinquent behavior, the reverse is posited. As adolescents commit more than an average amount of delinquent behavior, they find the normative mechanisms of social control inadequate for justifying their behavior. These adolescents rationalize their behavior by invoking a set of "higher" moral standards that minimizes their "badness."

In regard to the seriousness of adolescent delinquency, recall from Figure 2 that the relationship with age is not monotonic; an index of offenses weighted for their seriousness peaks at age 15, then declines through age 18, but remains higher than it is among 11- through 14-year-olds. We sought out the reasons for delinquent behavior being most grave in middle adolescence by means of multiple partial correlations. The set of independent variables included a reordered age variable that was linearly related to serious delinquency and the same six variables that represented various social roles in our investigations of the frequency of delinquency (see Tables 1 and 2).

The partial correlations between age and the seriousness of boys' delinquency was reduced from .29 ($p < .01$) to .08 ($p < .07$) and that of girls', from .11 ($p < .01$) to .03 ($p < .43$). The boys' analysis accounted for 20% of the variance; the girls' analysis accounted for 8%.

Thus we were not as successful at explaining variance in the seriousness of delinquent behavior as with the frequency of delinquent behavior. However, the reductions in correlations with age for boys and girls were still quite significant when age is entered last among a set of variables. It is interesting to note that in this set of variables, seriousness in boys is most related to those types of things that represent their concern with the youth culture (e.g., dating). For girls, their relationships with their fathers are most closely related to seriousness of their delinquent behavior. So, as we discovered with frequency of delinquent behavior, seriousness is also related to those role sets that the adolescent eventually deals with most intensely; the youth culture for boys and family for girls.

We have so far treated delinquent behavior as a unitary phenomenon, as though all behavior that fits our definition could not be usefully subdivided. But many students of delinquency have argued that *types* of delinquents can be identified whose environments, personalities, and behavior differ and who require different kinds of intervention (Ferdinand, 1966). We deal with the literature on delinquent typologies mindful of two limitations on its relevance to this review. First, here even more typically than is the general case, the data are taken from official records: the youth who are observed are adjudicated, often incarcerated delinquents, and it is conceivable that observed differences among "types" were produced by the differential treatment given them by the juvenile-justice system that classified them. The offense histories that are analyzed to discover types may have been biased initially because offenses were labeled with types in mind. Second, the literature on typologies has little developmental orientation: the intent has been to find consistencies in patterns of behavior over time, not developmental changes. So, theories and empirical research seldom include developmental variables explicitly, although they have developmental implications.

Approaches to typing delinquents may themselves be sorted into three categories: typing individuals by the nature of the delinquent acts they commit, by the structure or dynamics of their personalities, and by the social conditions that give rise to their delinquency.

Commonly used categories for typing juveniles by their offenses are status offenders, violent offenders, and thieves. The category of status offenders includes runaways, truants, drinkers of alcoholic beverages, and defiers of parental authority; violent offenders include vandals and assaulters; and thieves include burglars, shoplifters, pursesnatchers, and the like. Sometimes offenders against *property* are distinguished from offenders against *people;* then vandals are grouped with thieves instead of with assaulters. A typology by offenses assumes that a large majority of adolescents who commit one kind of offense in a category are substantially more likely to commit another in that same category than one in another category. Unless this is true, not many adolescents could be typed.

Both theoretical and empirical methods have been employed to type offenders by their personality characteristics. Types that have been generated from psychoanalytic theory include characterological, neurotic, and psychotic delinquents (Abrahamsen, 1960; Alexander & Staub, 1956; Eissler, 1949; and Friedlander, 1947). Hindelang and Weis (1972) have expanded on Eysenck's (1970) trait-theoretical hypothesis that criminals are highly extroverted and neurotic; they looked for four types of juvenile delinquents with personality patterns that cross-cut introversion/extroversion with high/low neuroticism.

Empirical methods range from clinical observations to computer-assisted exploration of personality test data. These explanations are most often guided by eclectic theory or no theory at all. Hewitt and Jenkins' observations of institutionalized children and adolescents led to categories of delinquents similar to those generated by psychoanlytic theory: the socialized delinquent and the unsocialized aggressive child (Hewitt & Jenkins, 1946; Jenkins, 1968). Other researchers have factor analyzed or otherwise searched for clusters of responses to personality inventories, such as the MMPI (Randolph, Richardson, & Johnson, 1961; Shinohara & Jenkins, 1967) or batteries of various test ratings, questionnaires, physical measurements, and case historical data (Stein, Sarbin, & Kulik, 1971).

Cloward and Ohlin (1960) derive types of delinquent subcultures and, by implication, types of delinquent offenders from the social conditions prevalent in adolescents' milieux. We pointed our earlier that Cloward and Ohlin theorize that youth are motivated to be delinquent by personal or social structural barriers to conventional status. How they adapt individually and collectively to this lack of opportunity depends, according to the theory, on the "integration of different age-levels of offenders, and integration of carriers of conventional and deviant values" (1960, p. 161). Three types are identified: criminal, conflict, and retreatist. When the age-grades in a neighborhood are integrated and the carriers of conventional and deviant values cooperate, then delinquency-prone adolescents become *criminals*. These are career-oriented, fairly well-controlled offenders who avail themselves of the opportunities to run numbers and fence stolen goods. In socially disorganized neighborhoods, where adolescents are alienated from adults and where there is little cooperation among adults generally, not to speak of cooperation between conventional and deviant adults, delinquent youth develop *conflict* patterns. They form fighting gangs; as individuals, the theory asserts, they are destructive and assaultive. The third type of delinquent is the *retreatist,* epitomized by drug-users. They are failures in any milieu: they are so disorganized personally that they are unacceptable to both organized crime and fighting gangs. So, by means of drugs, they withdraw from the awareness of their failure.

Empirical evidence for the various typologies is, at best, mixed. Attempts by Gold (1970), Hindelang (1971) and Faine (1974), to extract offense types from self-report data led to the conclusion that few adolescents specialize; but Heise (1968) and Hindelang and Weis (1972) concluded that certain offenses did cluster to characterize offenders, although their two studies identified quite different clusters. Using official records, Quay and Blumen (1963) and Empey and Lubeck (1971a) identified types of juvenile offenders, but, again, their respective types differ.

Cloward and Ohlin's (1960) typology has not stood up to the test of data. Short, Tennyson, and Howard (1963), working with streetgang workers' reports of boys' offenses, found that drug users tended not to assault or fight but that criminal activity was common among both. They write that, ''The failure to locate a criminal group, or more than one drug-using group, despite our highly motivated effort to do so, is a 'finding' of some importance, for it casts doubt on the generality of these phenomena, if not on their existence'' (p. 413). Similarly, Hindelang's (1971) attempt to isolate Cloward and Ohlin's (1960) types in self-report data led him to conclude that, ''These data are generally consistent [with Short, Tennyson, and Howard (1963)] in finding a lack of independence among different types of delinquent involvements'' (p. 533).

There is more empirical support for Hewitt and Jenkins' (1946) distinction between socialized and unsocialized delinquents. One must be cautious about some of these data because the procedures for sorting adolescent offenders into these classes relies on clinical judgments of unknown reliability; there is a large proportion of ''mixed'' types (Shinohara & Jenkins, 1967; Jenkins, 1968); and the claims for construct validity of this classification system often rest on relationships to variables, such as broken homes or parent-child relationships that were known to and probably considered by the clinical classifiers. On the other hand, Shinohara and Jenkins (1967) found different MMPI profiles for incarcerated boys of the two types, the unsocialized type scoring higher on indexes of psychopathology. Randolph, Richardson, and Johnson (1961) compared social and solitary delinquent boys on a correctional ''ranch'' and also found the MMPI profiles of the latter — solitary-ness is a hallmark of the unsocialized delinquent — showing more disturbance. Quay (1964) found Hewitt and Jenkins' (1946) types by factor analyzing probation officers' ratings based on information in the case histories of incarcerated boys. (Quay (1964) also found another type, which he called ''inadequate-immature.'') There remains the possibility that these types are found among incarcerated boys because of the differential treatment that they are given in the institutions. A more convincing and practical demonstration of the validity of the typology would be that the types responded differently to the same treatment. More on this point later, in our discussion of interventions.

The search for a typology of delinquency has up to now had no developmental orientation, although there are developmental implications. Were there reliably identifiable types, then one could ask if certain of them appeared earlier and others later in adolescence or whether the interactions of development variables with types helped to explain delinquency. Because typological theorizing has so far been largely frustrated by inconsistent or negative findings, the research has almost never got around to including developmental variables. Hindelang (1971) noted that there was no greater specialization in offenses from the early to the later years of high school; Jenkins (1968) reported in one of his studies that the socialized delinquents were older than the mostly *pre*-adolescent unsocialized delinquents. Short, Tennyson, and Howard (1963) implied that Cloward and Ohlin's (1960) "retreatists" would be older adolescents because "the development of retreatist adaptations [is] a consequence of failure in other adaptations such as conflict or crime" (p. 427).

There may be developmental reasons for the failure to find types of adolescent offenders. If one subscribes to the psychoanalytic proposition that adolescence is a time when personality patterns become fluid for a time, stabilizing only as individuals emerge from the stage (Spiegel,1951), then inconsistencies are a hallmark of adolescence. The field theory of marginality (Lewin, 1939) and the social learning theory of heightened drive (McCandless, 1970) also posit adolescent inconsistency. Moreover, if one assumes that frequent and serious delinquent behavior is symptomatic of extremely unstabilizing conditions even for adolescents, one would not expect to find consistent types. It is plausible that types of offenders appear only in adulthood, when the establishment of personality patterns, including the development of certain skills, and the acceptance into a particular criminal subculture lead to the choice of certain criminal professions.

Interactive Elements within Adolescent Stages

Some observers have found it useful to identify substages within the overall adolescent stage, like early, middle, and late adolescence (Blos, 1962). Some research has also suggested that certain variables affect delinquent behavior differently within substages of adolescence. For example Mann (1976), using the National Survey of Youth 1972 data, has shown that a pattern of consciously high but unconsciously low self-esteem is related to the delinquent behavior of 15- through 18-year-old boys, but not of 11- through 14-year-olds. Following up on the possibility that other variables might relate differently to delinquent behavior during different substages of adolescent development, the authors of this chapter conducted further analyses of data from the National Survey of Youth 1972. The sample was divided into 11- through 14-year-olds and 15- through 18-year-olds. We entered into an interactive model (Sonquist, Baker, & Morgan, 1971) those variables that had demonstrated reliable relationships to delinquent behavior in previous research (e.g., father-absence, parent-child relationships, scholastic achievement, conscious and unconscious self-esteem, anomia).

The results of our search for variables interacting with substages are diagrammed in Figure 3. This analysis "tree" suggests that it is advantageous, at least for understanding delinquency, to distinguish substages. Different variables account for the delinquent behavior of younger and older children. Specifically, we found that more of the variance in the frequency of younger boys' delinquent behavior was accounted for by their relationships with their mothers, while among older boys the relationship with their fathers was the most distinguishing variable. Among girls, the frequency of younger girls'

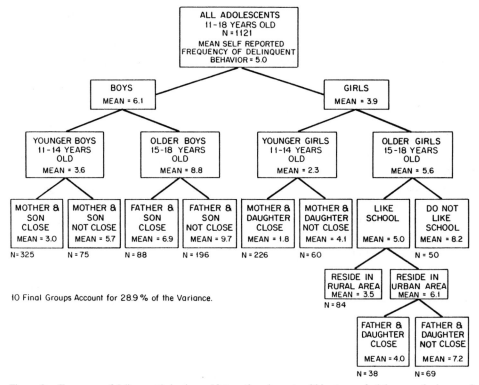

Figure 3. Frequency of delinquent behavior and interactive elements within stages of adolescence for boys and girls (11 to 14 and 15 to 18 years old).

delinquent behavior is also accounted for by their relationship with their mothers; but among older girls, attitudes towards school was the most distinguishing variable. Among older girls from urban environments, the degree of emotional warmth between fathers and daughters related significantly to delinquency.

These findings fit well into a developmental schema that recognizes change in roles as the adolescent matures. Thus the delinquent behavior of older compared to younger girls is bound more to their commitment to the roles they play in school and less to the roles they play in the family. Also of significance is the finding that the relationship with mothers accounts for more of the variance among younger boys and girls than does their relationship with their fathers. Previous analyses of the National Survey of Youth 1972 data (Gold & Reimer, 1975) had shown that relationships with fathers superceded relationships with mothers in their association with delinquent behavior among boys in the entire adolescent age range. Separating out the younger boys has perhaps uncovered the crucial control that mothers may exert over the behavior of pubertal boys.

Childhood Antecedents

Some attempts have been made to identify antecedent variables to delinquent behavior in adolescence, and with some success. Seigman (1966) found that the absence of the father for at least one year during childhood predicts reliably to adolescents' reports of relatively more delinquent behavior. Seigman's study was guided by the "masculine-protest" theory of antisocial behavior (Parsons, 1947), which implies that "all factors which tend to produce strong identification with the mother, and failure of early identification with the father, also tend to produce antisocial behavior" (p. 172). The study included 51 boys whose fathers were absent for at least one year during early childhood who were compared to 89 whose fathers were not absent during early childhood. The father-absent group scored significantly higher than the father-present group on the self-report antisocial-behavior inventory of Nye and Short (1957). Seigman concluded that "it seems reasonable to assume that father's absence from the home during the first few years of a boy's life is one such factor" (p. 71) that can predict delinquent behavior in adolescence.

It should be noted that father-absence in these studies does not imply "broken home"; for example, the fathers in Seigman's study were absent because of military commitments. This is an important distinction; official data on juvenile delinquency characteristically demonstrate a reliable association between broken homes and delinquent behavior, while the National Survey of Youth 1972 self-report data do not. Apparently early father-absence has effects on later delinquent behavior different from homes broken at other times in children's lives.

Magnusson, Duner, and Zetterblom (1975) collected data that included self-reported delinquent behavior and official delinquency of students in the sixth and then in the ninth grade. Magnusson and his coworkers found four characteristics of the sixth graders that foretold delinquent behavior in the ninth grade: disliking classmates; subjectively heavier loads of work in school; dissatisfaction with school; and low scholastic motivation. Their findings suggest that adjustment in grade school has a significant effect on adolescent adjustment. This finding in itself is not unusual; other research has also indicated that school plays an important part in the way adolescents adjust and even how delinquency can be treated (e.g., see the discussion of Bowman, 1959, in a later section of this essay). The special contribution of the Magnusson, Duner, and Zetterblom (1975) longitudinal study is that it was able successfully to identify variables predictive of later self-reported delinquent behavior.

Adolescent Delinquency as a Prodrome to Adult Development

One of the recurring controversies in the literature on adolescence is whether this developmental stage is especially marked by turmoil (Offer, 1969; Offer & Offer, 1968). And, if so, whether that turmoil is "normal," transient, and best ignored; or whether at least the more extreme forms and degrees of turmoil require some intervention lest they continue into adulthood, perhaps developmentally transformed. Delinquent behavior is surely one component of the reputed adolescent turmoil, and we have seen that it is indeed more prevalent in adolescence, especially in its more serious forms. (We hasten to say that the data show that most adolescents are not very delinquent.) Now we turn to the question of whether delinquency is predictive of the behavior and experience of adults, for better or worse.

The data on adolescent predictors of adult antisocial behavior are sparse. However, two longitudinal programs of research include data on delinquent behavior in adolescence as well as antisocial behavior in adulthood and thus shed some light on the transiency of adolescent delinquent behavior.

The first program of research, Youth in Transition, was begun in 1965 to study young males passing through high school, with the particular purpose of assessing the causes and effects of dropping out of high school (Bachman et al. 1967). This survey originally included 2213 males representative of 10th-grade boys throughout the 48 contiguous states. As many as possible were reinterviewed at ages 16 to 17, 17 to 18, 18 to 19, and 22 to 23. (The 1974 interview was eight years after the subjects were originally interviewed and five years after they had left high school.) Measures of growth and change in respondents included educational and occupational attainment, job satisfaction, self-esteem, motives, affective states, values, job attitudes and aspirations, and self-reported delinquent behavior.

Relationships between delinquent behavior in adolescence and adult development were the subject of several reports of the research staff (Johnston, 1973; Johnston, O'Malley, & Eveland, 1978; O'Malley, Bachman, Johnston, 1977). These cover the power of adolescent delinquent behaviors for predicting drug use, educational attainment, and criminality in young adulthood. Rates of delinquent behavior[2] at ages 15 to 16 were determined for five categories of later drug use, ranging from nonusers to frequent users of both "soft" and "hard" drugs. The data indicate that 18- to 19-year-old drug users were: "substantially more delinquent . . . *before they ever used drugs,* and that the more 'serious' their involvement with drugs in 1970, the more serious their prior delinquency;" and, "classifying respondents according to their 1973–74 [ages 22–23] drug use yields even more dramatic results" (Johnston, O'Malley, & Eveland, 1978, p. 154). The researchers conclude that high levels of delinquent behavior *cannot* be attributed to drug use: "Clearly the preponderance of the delinquency differences among the non-users and various drug-user groups existed before drug usage and, therefore, can hardly be attributed to drug use." [p. 154] Using cross-lagged panel correlations to address the nature of the relationships between drug use and delinquent behavior, Johnston and his co-workers found (1) a correlation of .25 (path coefficient of .111) between *theft and vandalism* at ages 18 to 19 and drug use four years later and (2) a correlation of .15 (path coefficient of .058) between *interpersonal aggression* at age 18 to 19 and later drug use. Figures 4 and 5 diagram these path analyses. In Figures 4 and 5, in parentheses are path coefficients (partial regression coefficients) in which each variable measured in 1974 is predicted from two variables measured in 1970. The other figures adjacent to the connecting lines are product moment correlations. Unfortunately no data are available for analysis of the causal relationships between delinquency at middle adolescence and later drug use because drug use was not measured until 1969–1970.

Tables 3 and 4 present the Youth in Transition data relating delinquent behavior in adolescence to criminal behavior in adulthood (Johnston, O'Malley, & Eveland, 1978). Clearly the correlations are highly significant statistically but indicate only a marginal relationship—theft and vandalism measured at ages 15 to 16 and then again at age 22 to 23 correlate at only $r = .21$; interpersonal aggression at 15 to 16 is correlated with later criminal behavior at .17. These data suggest that although some relationship exists between delinquent behavior in adolescence and criminal behavior in adulthood, the relationship is small.

A series of analyses was also done by O'Malley, Bachman, and Johnston (1977) aimed at finding those variables predictive of the level of education attained by respondents at

---

[2]Three indexes of delinquent behavior were developed in the *Youth in Transition* studies: a theft-and-vandalism index comprised of what might be called crimes against property, ranging from petty theft to arson; an interpersonal-aggression index, comprised of items that involve some physical aggression or threat thereof against other persons; and a delinquent-behavior-in-school index, comprised of items dealing with disruptive behavior in school, ranging from truancy to damaging school property.

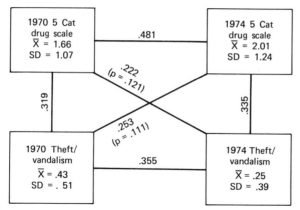

Figure 4. Cross-lagged panel correlations: index of theft and vandalism and five-category scale of drug use. (Source: L. D. Johnston, P. M. O'Malley, and L. K. Eveland, "Drugs and Delinquency: A Search for Causal Connections."

ages 22 to 23. Three indexes of adolescent delinquent behavior (see footnote 1) were correlated with later educational attainment. Delinquent behavior in school was found to be most strongly related to later educational attainment ($r = -.32$); the measure of interpersonal aggression correlated a bit less strongly than the school based measure ($r = -.25$); the theft-and-vandalism index, considerably less ($r = -.12$). All three indexes of delinquent behavior in the 10th grade were inserted in a multiple-regression analysis and accounted for 12% of the variance in educational attainment. Only delinquent behavior in school seemed to have significant predictive power; interpersonal aggression and theft and vandalism accounted for only marginal amounts of the remaining variance.

The Youth in Transition studies indicate that adolescent delinquency has some significance for adult development. However its findings also indicate that although more heavily delinquent adolescents are as young adults apt to make more illicit use of drugs, attain less formal education, and commit more crimes, many of them will be no different in these respects than their less delinquent peers.

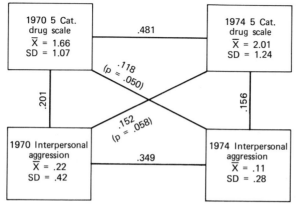

Figure 5. Cross-lagged panel correlations: index of interpersonal aggression and five-category scale of drug use. (Source: L. D. Johnston, P. M. O'Malley, and L. K. Eveland, "Drugs and Delinquency: A Search for Causal Connections," 1978)

Table 3   **Correlation Matrix Index of Theft and Vandalism Measured at 5 Time Points[a]**

	Theft/Vandalism 1966 Age: 15–16	Theft/Vandalism 1968 16–17	Theft/Vandalism 1969 17–18	Theft/Vandalism 1970 18–19	Theft/Vandalism 1974 22–23
Theft/vandalism 1968	.4702	—			
Theft/vandalism 1969	.3900	.5197	—		
Theft/vandalism 1970	.3830	.4296	.4388	—	
Theft/vandalism 1974	.2113	.2365	.2339	.3553	—
Mean Theft/vandalism score	.5100	.3708	.3740	.4252	.2514
Standard deviation	.5316	.5106	.4957	.5077	.3910

Source: L. D. Johnston, P. M. O'Malley, and L. K. Eveland (1978). Age descriptor added.

[a]The first data collection took place in the fall of 1966 when the subjects had just entered 10th grade. Subsequent interviews with subjects occured in the spring of 1968, 1969, 1970, and 1974.

Table 4   **Correlation Matrix Index of Interpersonal Aggression Measured at 5 Time Points**

	Interpersonal Aggression 1966 Age: 15–16	Interpersonal Aggression 1968 16–17	Interpersonal Aggression 1969 17–18	Interpersonal Aggression 1970 18–19	Interpersonal Aggression 1974 22–23
Interpersonal aggression 1968	.4485	—			
Interpersonal aggression 1969	.3421	.4494	—		
Interpersonal aggression 1970	.3220	.4457	.4575	—	
Interpersonal aggression 1974	.1762	.2553	.3018	.3492	—
Mean interpersonal aggression score	.5820	.2261	.2083	.2204	.1110
Standard deviation	.6312	.4206	.4205	.4186	.2802

Source: L. D. Johnston, P. M. O'Malley, and L. K. Eveland (1978). Age descriptor has been added.

A second program of research leads to the same conclusion. Robins (1966) has reported a longitudinal study that "traces the adult social and psychiatric outcomes of 524 child guidance clinic patients and compares them with the adult social and psychiatric status of 100 normal children of the same age, sex, neighborhood, race, and IQ" (preface) that were born and had resided in the St. Louis area. Each of the 524 clinic patients had been diagnosed "sociopathic personality" as a child and subsequently treated in mental-health clinics. Robins reviewed her subjects' clinic, school, police, and health records from early childhood into adulthood in search of predictors for maladjustment in adolescence and then adulthood. As adults these subjects were questioned about their marriages; relationships with children, relatives, friends, and neighbors; participation in organizations; employment and medical histories; as well as their delinquent behavior as children.

In general Robins found that only those children and adolescents who — according to official records and their own reports years later — had perpetrated an extraordinary amount of antisocial behavior were especially likely to become antisocial as adults.

If one wishes to choose the most likely candidate for later diagnosis of sociopathic personality from among children appearing in a child guidance clinic, the best choice appears to be the boy referred for theft or aggression who has shown a diversity of antisocial behavior in many episodes, at least one of which could be grounds for a juvenile court appearance, and whose antisocial behavior involves him with strangers and organizations as well as with teachers and parents. . . . Girls likely to be diagnosed sociopathic personality as adults resembled the boys except in more frequently having sexual misbehavior as a prominent part of their juvenile problems and in reporting a later onset of difficulties. [1966, p. 157]

Robins reports that only patients who exhibited at least moderately severe antisocial behavior in adolescence were diagnosed as sociopathic adults. In addition many nonsociopathic symptoms during childhood and adolescence were *not* related to adult psychiatric illness: "Children who were fearful, withdrawn or shy, had tics or mannerisms, were hypersensitive, or restless, had speech defects, insomnia or nightmares, or temper tantrums, were no more likely to be psychiatrically ill as adults than were children lacking these traits" (Robins, 1966, p. 158).

The crux of Robins' findings seems to be that a record of extremely delinquent behavior is singularly predictive of adult pathology. It is possible that it is the *record* of delinquent behavior that led to a problematic adulthood by generating a series of personal and social responses, including a deviant identity that fixes memories of extreme misbehavior. But Robins' interpretation of her findings to mean that delinquent behavior itself is an especially morbid indicator gains some credence from the results of the Youth in Transition studies.

We have reviewed the Robins' and the Youth in Transition studies in order to address the question: Is delinquency in adolescence a transient phenomenon having no relationship to adult development, or should adolescent delinquency be considered a significant prodrome to identifiable trends in adult development? These studies suggest a real but probably only marginal relationship between most adolescents' delinquent behavior and negative behavior in adulthood. The more heavily delinquent the adolescent, the more likely he is to become a deviant adult.

INTERVENTION PROGRAMS

One could fill a large book with brief descriptions of the many different kinds of attempts to reduce delinquency: individual and group psychotherapy, family therapy and family contracting, behavior modification, transactional analysis, recreation, vocational training, alternative schooling, survival camping and wilderness canoeing, incarceration and probation, "big brothers" and "big sisters," community organization, and Bible reading, to name but a few. Nevertheless, we know very little about what really works, and we suspect, from what careful research has been done, that very few methods have worked at all. Hence our purpose in this section is not to present all these modalities but rather to relate the treatment of delinquency to adolescent development and to discuss those programs that systematic assessment has proved effective.

American society has lodged the major responsibility for the treatment of delinquency in its juvenile-justice system, an institution whose very existence reflects a cultural recognition of developmental differences. (For a detailed exposition of the history, principles, and practices of the juvenile courts see the entire issue of *Crime and Delinquency* (April, 1961; Sarri & Hasenfeld, 1976). Since the turn of the century, the American legal system has defined and treated juvenile crime differently from adult crimes. Underlying the difference is the belief that children and adolescents, still in their formative stages, are not fully as responsible as adults are. So juvenile delinquency is regarded more like mental illness than like criminality; guilt is not laid on the individual, and treatment is supposed to be more curative than punitive.

In recent years, however, the belief system that takes into account developmental differences has been undergoing some significant modification. There are forces at work now to diminish the distinction between delinquency and crime. From the legal subculture have emerged objections to the lack of procedural safeguards for juveniles in the justice system comparable to those traditionally guaranteed to adults. The landmark *Gault* decision (U.S. Supreme Court, 1967) extended the right to counsel to juveniles, but more important, took formal note that the judicial consequences of juvenile crime were fully as punitive, if not more so, than the disposition of adult criminals. The juvenile-justice system has since moved slowly but surely to resemble the adult system more closely in such matters as right to counsel, rules of evidence, and self-incrimination.

At the same time, there are widespread efforts to change the definition of juvenile delinquency, so that it matches adult crime. That is, there is some movement toward removing status offenses from the jurisdiction of the juvenile-justice system, so that juveniles who run away from home, truant from school, refuse to obey the reasonable commands of their parents, frequent immoral places, or evince other behaviors that would not be criminal if committed by adults will no longer be liable to a coerced disposition of the State.

These changes in perspectives on delinquency and its treatment do not come mainly from developmental considerations; arguments about developmental differences are secondary. Arguments for change are based mainly in the belief that a system that was meant to promote child development has instead harmed children and their communities. It is charged that the liberties of too many youths have been curtailed on insufficient evidence and for insufficient reason, that treatment has been more harsh than benevolent, and that the net effect of the juvenile-justice system has been to increase rather than reduce delinquency. Developmental issues are raised only when the relative competencies of the youth and the agents of the system are debated: the youth — to remove themselves from the safety and supervision of their homes, to absent themselves from school, and to roam free; the adults — to decide where and with whom a child should live, how and for how long a child should be schooled, what in character and environment will conduce to good behavior, and how those elements may be created. The developmental evidence is clear enough on one point: there is wide variation in maturity among individuals, especially at adolescence, so that some legally defined juveniles are fully as competent as most adults and some adults not as competent as most adolescents. And no evidence can be adduced that will testify to the general effectiveness of the juvenile-justice system when compared with doing nothing at all.

It is not so much that empirical evidence testifies to the ineffectiveness of the juvenile-justice system — although there is some of that (Gold & Williams, 1969; Gold, 1970; Farrington & West, 1977) — as that there is no good evidence one way or another. Rarely has the system been systematically evaluated, but this is as true of delinquency-treatment programs aside from the justice system. History has witnessed the adoption of one fad after another, launchings of some plausible or even implausible programs when there are funds available and terminating them when the support dries up. When in rare instances the effects of a program are assessed rigorously, with reliable and valid measures applied to comparable treatment and control groups, the finding is typically that the new program is no more effective than the old one that was regarded as unsatisfactory. The use of volunteers as "big brothers" or "big sisters," as tutors or as group discussion leaders to probationers (Berger et al., 1975), guided group interaction (Empey & Lubeck, 1971b; Knight, 1971; Empey & Erickson, 1972), streetgang work (Miller, 1962; Klein, 1971; Gold & Mattick, 1974), and behavior modification (Tharp & Wetzel, 1969) have not been proved in scientifically respectable studies to be any more or less effective than cursory probationary supervision.

But it would be overly negative to assert that nothing works. Research has demonstrated (albeit in isolated instances) that some intervention efforts are effective. It is instructive to look at these programs in terms of developmental concepts. For an overview suggests that efforts that advance adolescents' movement toward independent and respectable adult status reduce their delinquency.

Bowman (1959) has reported an assessment of an alternative school program in a Quincy, Illinois, junior high school. The staff and faculty selected the 60 boys in the eighth grade who were of below average ability and doing poorly in school. Many of the boys were also behavior problems: 41% had police or court records. At random, 40 were selected to comprise two classroom groups each of 20 pupils who would experience a program different from the conventional curriculum; the remaining 20 boys continued to attend conventional classes, thus constituting a control group.

The teachers of the two alternative classes were chosen "not on the basis of any special training, but rather because of their interest in and sympathy for this kind of child" (Bowman, p. 159). The curriculum was based on individual, small-group, and classroom projects developed out of the students' interests. Classroom procedures were informal and the relationships between teachers and pupils were warm and friendly. Formal grading was abandoned and each student was instead evaluated on the basis of his own progress. Discipline was firm but not punitive and focused on solving problems for the purpose of deterrence. The students were given the opportunity to return to conventional classes at the end of the first term, only two elected to do so. One child was dropped from school because of severe emotional disturbance and one was returned to regular classes because of misbehavior.

There were marked differences favoring the experimental group by the end of the school year. It was not that the students in the alternative program demonstrated significant scholastic improvement. They performed on standard achievement tests neither better nor worse than the boys in the control group. But questionnaires revealed that the boys in the alternative program believed that they were doing better and that they liked school more. Their attendance records improved, while the controls' worsened; the behavior records of the school and the police records in the community documented that their disruptive and delinquent behavior had declined by more than one-third, while the official delinquency of the boys in the control group tripled. Furthermore, a follow-up study demonstrated that the boys in the special classes made better transitions to the world of work as indicated by their employers' ratings and the lengths of time for which they held jobs.

We find features in the Quincy program that we believe were essential to its success because they addressed peculiarly adolescent needs for autonomy and potency. We suspect that adolescent scholastic failures are under exceptional stress. Their failure not only reflects on their current competence, but it also foretells an oppressive future. Education is the gateway to a respectable adult status, and the importance of scholastic competence is impressed on youngsters as they make the transition from elementary to secondary school. Furthermore, the response of teachers and staff to the students' poor performance as well as to the often negative reactions of the students to these responses and to failure generate even heavier demands for docility and dependency on the poor students than the adequate ones. There is great potential in this situation for a deepening cycle of poor performance; poor student-teacher/student-staff relationships; feelings of derogated selves; disruptive behavior, and so on. This cycle runs counter to the social and psychological forces that impel adolescents to develop a self-image as autonomous and effective adults-to-be.

The Quincy program may have been effective because it interrupted this cycle. The alternative program offered its students special opportunities to be autonomous by permitting individual and group decision-making to direct classroom activity, and it raised students' feelings of effectiveness by avoiding deprecating comparisons with universalistic norms. Meanwhile, the informal and sympathetic interpersonal relationships with their teachers probably gave students the emotional support they needed to make the transition to the new educational mode without threatening their independence.

The program described by Massimo and Shore (1963) — see also Shore and Massimo (1973, 1979) — seems to have accomplished the same goals but in a somewhat different manner. Selected for study were 20 boys with histories of scholastic failure and delinquent and disruptive behavior, boys who were about to drop out of school. Randomly, 10 were selected who were offered the services of a social worker, initially to help them find jobs. In fact, however, the social worker provided many kinds of support in addition to job-finding by making himself available to the boys day and night throughout the following year. He not only helped the boys to find jobs, but also to keep the jobs once found and to get the additional training necessary to upgrade their employment. Some were helped to re-enrol for formal education and to cope with the schools successfully. Those who asked for it were counseled on problems with their families and their peers. Massimo and Shore (1963) have described the program as "comprehensive vocationally-oriented psychotherapy," by which they seem to mean that the program addressed the underlying psychological problems of their clients primarily through the management of quite specific problems of adjustment.

We find in this strategy, as we do in the Quincy program, a proper concern for adolescents' striving for autonomy and for their wish to attain adult respectability. The method differs from psychoanalytic psychotherapy (with its emphasis on the process of transference) and from behavior modification (with its manipulation of rewards and punishments) in that both of these encourage dependency. This program helped clear the way to immediate as well as long-term economic independence and offered its clients a relationship with a supportive adult fairly free from the emotional entanglement of family.

At the end of the year-long program, the 10 clients were clearly thriving better than the 10 boys who were not served. The frequency of their official delinquency declined, while the controls got into more frequent trouble; they were more steadily employed and at a higher level; and they more often enrolled in educational and vocational-training programs. Psychological tests showed that they harbored less aggressive feelings, were less hostile toward authority of any kind, and that basic to all these changes, the boys developed greater self-esteem. Furthermore, follow-up studies up to 15 years later demonstrated that these gains were sustained.

Gold and Mattick (1974) have reported similar results from a study of a streetgang project in Chicago. The Boys Clubs assigned streetworkers and community organizers to certain inner city neighborhoods, while comparable neighborhoods nearby were observed as controls. The program as a whole had little effect on the official delinquency rates of boys in the target areas. But the program seemed to be able to reduce delinquency when it was able through supportive services to help boys find and keep jobs or to return and to remain in school.

One well-designed study of family contracting (Alexander Barton, et al., 1973) has demonstrated that such a method can effectively reduce delinquency. The strategy of family contracting consists of creating a formal agreement between an adolescent and his parents that.governs their mutual obligations and privileges. For example, if there is disagreement between them about the time at which the adolescent should be at home at night, they are helped to contract an arrangement whereby prompt homecoming for a given number of nights is rewarded with an evening's use of the family's car. Or if the problem centers on school, then the attainment of a certain grade-point average or attendance record is rewarded with spending money.

Family contracting as a technique grew out of an operant conditioning approach to the treatment of delinquency. The cause of delinquent behavior is assumed to be that it gains greater rewards than prosocial behavior; the general principle behind treatment is to alter the contingencies by increasing the rewards for prosocial behavior and sometimes, also, by increasing the punishments for delinquency. Family contracting is a specific tool by which adolescents are assured that good behavior will be rewarded by their parents.

Alexander and his collegues compared family contracting to client-centered therapy, psychodynamic treatment, and no treatment at all, assigning these various treatment modalities to random sets of adjudicated delinquents. Family contracting proved to be the most effective by the criterion of subsequent appearance in court: only 26% of the adolescents treated that way recidivated compared to 47% of those in client-centered treatment, 73% in psychotherapy, and 50% who were not treated at all. Follow-up studies revealed not only that the superiority of family contracting was sustained for at least a year and a half, but also that the other children in the families that participated in that treatment modality appeared relatively less often in court more than two years after the program terminated (Klein, Alexander, & Parsons, 1977). Our interpretation of these results goes beyond a simple explanation in terms of the efficacy of reinforcement to specify the essence of the rewards in developmental terms. We suggest that money and the use of a car are of greater symbolic than material value; further, that the establishment of a mutual contract between parents and adolescent is crucial to the success of the technique regardless of the substance of the exchange. These are symbolic of adolescents' autonomous and equal standing vis à vis parents. Our hypothesis is that insofar as family relationships are implicated in a youth's delinquency, then family contracting will be an effective remedy when the nature of the family problem is that the adolescent's sense of autonomy is threatened. Often these teenagers complain that their parents are unreasonably strict, treat them "like babies," and deny them the privileges that their peers are given (or take). The family contract is a concrete manifestation of a change in parent-adolescent relationships that invests adolescents — perhaps, from their point of view, for the first time — with some recognized power of their own.

The poor record of psychodynamic psychotherapy in Alexander and Parsons' (1973) study is not surprising to those familiar with the literature in this area. Psychoanalysts are hesitant about treating adolescents generally and Eissler (1950) has noted their wariness about treating heavily delinquent adolescents in particular. Eissler argues that standard psychoanalysis is not suited for the treatment of delinquency without a great deal of special preliminary work. The problem, as Eissler sees it, is that heavily delinquent adolescents are typically incapable of participating in the transference relationship with their therapists, a process deemed essential to successful psychoanalysis. So Eissler prescribes an initial phase in the treatment during which the analyst induces a kind of transference neurosis; he stimulates the adolescent's identification with the analyst by creating an image of the analyst's omnipotence. Once the neurosis is established, then the adolescent is ready for standard psychoanalysis. Eissler urges that the patient at this point be treated by another analyst since the aura of omnipotence generated by the original therapist in the preliminary work will interfere with effective treatment in the second phase.

Persons (1967) conducted the only psychotherapeutic intervention with juveniles that we know of that has been proved effective by rigorous research. He randomly assigned male inmates of a juvenile correctional institution to an eclectic therapeutic program:

> Five psychotherapists participated in the study: Two psychologists and the three social workers. The social workers had no previous experience in conducting psychotherapeutic interviews, but they received supervision throughout the 20-week period. They also were taking part in a seminar on psychotherapy with delinquents taught by the two psychologists. Four of the five therapists were each responsible for one group of seven boys, and a fifth therapist had two groups, one with seven boys and one with six. Each therapist conducted both individual and group therapy sessions. In every case, a boy had the same individual and group therapist.

> One of the major objectives of the psychotherapy was to encourage in each boy the development of warm interpersonal relationships, both with the therapist and with the other boys in the group. Therapeutic procedures included exploring the boy's past behavior and attempting to teach them and have them experience living in a less self-defeating fashion than they had been. They strove for a non-threatening and nonpunitive relationship, yet attempted to prevent manipulation on the part of the boys. As the relationship developed, the therapists began to use frequent interpretation, negative reinforcement of inappropriate behavior, and approval for appropriate behavior. They also attempted to teach the boys to discriminate between acceptable and non-acceptable behavior. Role playing techniques were used during the interviews by both the therapist and the boys. During approximately the fourteenth and fifteenth weeks of group therapy, the therapists began to induce extreme amounts of anxiety and stress concerning antisocial behavior. The last three weeks were focused on the difficulties involved in returning to the community. [Persons, 1966, p. 338]

An equal number of inmates served as the control group. Persons observed the boys' experiences with the juvenile-justice system in their communities for a year after their release. He found that the treated boys violated their parole significantly less often and that significantly fewer were reincarcerated.

It is obvious to anyone familiar with the field that delinquency treatment is not now simply a matter of the skilled application of demonstrably effective methods. Rigorous assessment of programs is rare, and the handful of studies that we have just described almost exhausts the available literature on effective programs. The old saw that ''more research needs to be done'' is certainly true here. Ideally, every intervention effort should be regarded as experimental, imbedded in a rigorous research design that can demonstrate with fair assurance whether the method reduces delinquent behavior or not.

This experimental orientation to intervention offers returns beyond the identification of effective programs. If the theoretical rationale for every intervention is made explicit and its test made integral to the assessment program, then experiments in delinquency treatment will also contribute to our understanding of the causes of delinquency. For example, we have observed that two common themes may run through various effective interventions: (1) the support of warm, accepting relationships with adults and (2) the enhancement of adolescents' self-images as autonomous and effective individuals in the present and future. Evaluations of intervention efforts could test whether participant's self-concepts in fact change on these dimensions in the predicted direction and whether these changes are related to a decline in delinquent behavior. If we could thus capture the essence of effective treatment, then many different kinds of intervention efforts, adapted to their targets and to the situations in which they are operating, could incorporate that process as a central feature of the programs.

IMPLICATIONS FOR ADOLESCENCE

The relationship between adolescence and delinquent behavior may point to broader truths about adolescence. An explanation of this specific relationship may further our understanding of adolescence generally and it is to this potentiality that we turn our attention now.

First, let us gather up the apparent facts about adolescence and delinquent behavior. According to the confessions of American adolescents, the frequency of delinquent behavior accelerates from late childhood through middle adolescence, then begins to level off, although it continues to rise until early adulthood before it subsides. This is the course at least of the relatively minor delinquent acts — drinking, smoking pot, petty thefts, and such — that constitute most delinquent behavior. More serious delinquency — assault and threatened assault, acts of substantial vandalism, breaking and entering, robbery, and the like — accelerate from early adolescence, peak at middle adolescence, then decline.

Over 80% of American adolescents admit to committing one or more delinquent acts, most of these minor, in the course of a few years of adolescence, but relatively few adolescents are responsible for most of the delinquent behavior committed by the cohort. Contrary to some official statistics, the heavily delinquent adolescents are not disproportionately from the lower class or from ethnic minorities; consistent with the official data, males are markedly more delinquent than females.

An explanation of these trends in delinquent behavior in terms of the onset of puberty seems weak for at least three reasons. First, adolescents who experience puberty early are no more delinquent at that time than those who mature later. The data on this point are admittedly sparse — from one study of relatively few youth whose pubertal state was measured only indirectly by their skeletal development. Here is a serious gap in the data base inasmuch as a great deal of theory about adolescent turmoil has been spun off the experience of puberty. We need studies that relate direct measures of sexual development to direct measures of delinquent behavior.

Second, the delinquent behavior of adolescent girls increases at the same time as boys' does. Were puberty significantly responsible for delinquency, then girls' delinquency would increase at an earlier age than boys'.

Third, the relationship between age and delinquent behavior becomes negligible when variables other than sexual development are introduced into multiple-regression equations. Changes in social roles and moral judgments seem to account for the trends in adolescent delinquency. But again, the data on this issue are not nearly definitive. If reliable direct measures of sexual development were entered into the equations, they might supplant some of the other predictors, demonstrating perhaps that the social variables represented social responses to puberty. The available data suggest to us that maturation is not a significant factor in delinquency, but the state of the data is weak and should be improved.

Erikson's (1959) hypothesis of *negative identity* seems to encompass the data. It offers a coherent explanation for the trends in three dimensions of adolescent delinquency: the general increase, the shift in the incidence of certain kinds of delinquent acts at middle adolescence, and the sex difference in the frequency and seriousness of delinquent behavior. When we invoke negative identity as an explanation, we have in mind particularly *role* identity, as we distinguished that concept from *ego* identity earlier. We mean that youths commit themselves to norms that run sharply counter to the norms of those who may legitimately prescribe behavior in the youths' society, and the youths act out their opposition.

We suggest that the increasing incidence of delinquency is a function of the increasing awareness by adolescents of the adequacy with which they are playing the major roles prescribed for them in their society. Central among these roles, and most relevant to their delinquency, is their studenthood. As adolescents in American society approach that critical choice-point, college/not college, the implications for the future of their current scholastic performance become more clear and determinative. We suggest that in our culture a sense of *finality* grows on late adolescents, a feeling of crystallization of themselves and their life chances. Adolescence is, we believe, taken to be the end of the formative period. As this sense of finality deepens, the need for some identity becomes more pressing.

A negative identity requires an audience, actual or imagined. Here is the point at which Erikson's (1959) and Cohen's (1955) insights converge. A negative identity is more effective if played out for a supportive audience that shares a subculture. Delinquent subcultures coalesce and thrive on the need of certain adolescents to "repudiate, once and for all, the norms of the college-boy culture" (Cohen, 1955, p. 132). The most supportive subculture is shared by those with the same problem, who, therefore, simultaneously give and get support. But the support is not unqualified; this society has standards too. And it is in these standards that we perceive the reasons for the shift in the nature of delinquent behavior at about age 15 and for the greater delinquency of boys compared to girls.

The evidence underlying the sex difference is direct (Morris, 1965). Adolescents of both sexes are less disapproving of boys' delinquency than girls'; significantly, more adolescent girls than boys deny recorded contacts with the police. Although these data were collected more than 10 years ago and in one midwestern city, we believe that the findings would hold today and throughout our society. In our culture, delinquency seems to have a masculine character. Even delinquent sexual behavior that we associate more closely with girls, albeit falsely (Gold, 1970), is more tolerable if committed by boys. Thus girls who are heavily delinquent do not find as strong social support for that negative identity; it is a less effective alternative for them than it is for boys.

It will be helpful to advance the idea of an *optimal range of delinquent behaviors* (Gold & Reimer, 1975). All actions may be ordered on a dimension of deviancy from "super-normative" — expressing positive values, like honesty, to an extraordinary degree — to "hyper-deviant" — actions that horrify others. Focusing only on adolescent delinquent behaviors, these may be said to occupy that range of the dimension from trivial, like smoking tobacco or drinking a beer, to horrifying. Within this range there is an optimal sector: actions within this sector are deviant enough to establish a negative identity but not so deviant as to repel significant others. A 15 year old who litters or scrawls graffiti on public walls presents little evidence of his courage, independence, or skill. On the other hand, a 15 year old who burns down a barn containing live animals is likely to be regarded as terribly disturbed or vicious ("kooky") even by heavily delinquent peers. But if a 15 year old manages somehow to steal the red flasher (the "bubble gum machine") off a police scout car, that act is a genuine bid for glory.

Even stealing the red flasher seems somehow incongruous for girls, while eminently suitable for boys. In general, the optimal range of delinquent behaviors seem to be narrower and more trivial for girls than boys. We think that this is a major reason for the less frequent and less serious delinquency of girls. Delinquent behavior ordinarily fails to serve adolescent girls as it serves adolescent boys to shore up a failing sense of self-esteem. More for boys than girls in contemporary American culture, being delinquent constitutes an effective negative identity.

The concept of the optimal range of delinquent behavior was invoked by Gold and Reimer (1975) as a speculation to explain the shift from 1967 to 1972 toward increasing use of drugs, mostly marijuana, by American 13 through 16 year olds, while the incidence of other delinquent acts declined. Gold and Reimer noted that the negative correlation between the use of marijuana and close relations with parents declined considerably from 1967 to 1972, and they inferred that parents seemed to their adolescent sons and daughters in 1972 less horrified by the use of pot than they seemed in 1967. This speculation seems reasonable in light of our general impression about changing beliefs in the physical and social consequences of the use of pot. The speculation found some empirical support in two sets of data that reflected cultural differences in beliefs about marijuana. First, data from rural American adolescents — living among those whose beliefs in the heinousness of marijuana had probably not changed so much as those living in urban and suburban areas — generated higher negative correlations between pot smoking and relationships with parents and also reported markedly less increase in pot use from 1967 to 1972 (Gold & Reimer, 1975). Second, a study of Stuart, Quire, and Krell (1976) on the site of a liberal midwestern university showed that as the local penalty for possession of small amounts of marijuana was reduced to the triviality of a traffic fine, pot use declined among the community's adolescents compared to a nearby community that maintained a heavier penalty. Gold and Reimer argued that in the rural areas in 1972, smoking pot tended still to reside at the serious end of the optimal range of delinquent behaviors; in the university community it had dropped toward the trivial end of the range and perhaps out of the optimal range.

The concept of the optimal range of delinquent behavior may also help to explain the shift in the nature of delinquent behaviors that underlies the peaking of serious delinquency at middle adolescence. We suggest that some of the behaviors that count as really serious — injurious assaults, ruinous vandalism — are more creditable for 15 and 16 year olds than for older adolescents. This is reflected in the fact that the law in the various states turns juveniles into adults at about age 16. Behaviors that at age 15 might be attributed to immature judgment and the pressure of adolescence are on that account more likely within the optimal range of delinquent behavior. Later, however, they may appear more characterological and, therefore, more serious. Their perpetrators are more apt to be adjudged criminal or weird or both by other adolescents and by adults. So, late adolescents who are motivated to adopt a delinquent identity choose different acts for the purpose.

To account more fully for the increasing incidence of delinquent behavior through late adolescence, we may cite the weakness of social constraints as well as the strength of provocations. Hypotheses in terms of decathexis of the superego (Spiegel, 1951), marginality (Lewin, 1951), and social bonding (Hirschi, 1969) refer to weaker social controls over adolescents compared to the social controls over the children they once were and the adults they will become. Scholars have offered various reasons for the roles that adolescents are called on to play to exert less control over them. Developmental pressures emanating (according to psychoanalytic theory) from the recapitulation of the oedipal conflict and social pressures attendant on cultural demands for increasing autonomy in preparation for independent adulthood in contemporary American society weaken the hegemony of the role of son/daughter, this before adult roles, such as husband/wife or worker, are adopted. Meanwhile, the demands and domains of hitherto familiar roles, like male/female, student, and friend, are changing, and the consequent weakening of the consensus about them also weakens their force. These developments, which permit what Erikson has called the psychosocial moratorium, also allow the provocations to delinquency more heavily to determine the direction of adolescent behavior. Adolescence in contemporary American society may be viewed as a low point in the social controls that permit deviant behavior of all kinds.

At the same time, we recognize that adolescents also occupy a unique role that entails social controls from a new quarter, namely the role of *teenager*. Most, but by no means all, of the role prescriptions for teenagers appear to come from other teenagers and are largely enforced by them. But actually parents and the media also have their hands in this, and the stereotypes of the teenager in American culture — whether Holden Caulfield as "victim," James Dean as "rebel," or Corliss Archer as "clown" — tend to confirm themselves. In recent years, we seem to have witnessed the rise and fall of the salience of the role of teenager as the youth culture climbed to the pinnacle of Woodstock, then declined. The relevance of being a teenager to delinquency is that it seems in its several variations to allow for or even to encourage a certain amount of delinquent behavior. The teenager as "rebel" is delinquent by definition; as "victim," is pushed into it for survival; and as "clown," bumbles into it.

Insofar as the role of teenager permits the adoption of a specifically delinquent negative identity at the same time that the controlling forces of other roles are relatively weak, then it follows that the delinquent identity has a limited lifespan. As adolescents grow into young adulthood, the delinquent behavior that heretofore had found an appreciative audience among peers and a more or less patient response from the adult public and its law-enforcement agents now is neither so well appreciated nor tolerated. The optimal range of delinquent behaviors narrows to almost nothing and the delinquent identity is no longer so useful for rescuing the young adults' self-esteem. If the provocations that originally motivated the delinquency remain, then the delinquent defense no longer is adequate to channel their force into that identity. Here we believe we find the reason that Robins' "deviants grown up" are not any more often criminal than they are prey to a variety of pathologies.

One of the implications of the data on adolescent delinquent behavior is that adolescence may indeed be considered a *stage* rather than merely a phase of development. Insofar as there is a fairly rapid increase in witting violations of the law at about ages 11 to 12 and this acceleration is maintained until about age 19, the age span has stage characteristics. Is delinquent behavior the only phenomenon that distinguishes adolescence? Or are there other phenomena that support the claims of stage theory? And can we understand the peculiarly adolescent character of these phenomena in the same general terms that help to explain adolescent delinquency? We can only speculate on a few of these issues, with the hope that our speculations will inspire more rigorous theorizing and theory testing.

Apparently the suicide rate among adolescents has been climbing steeply in the last decade, almost doubling among white males from 1965 to 1974. Like delinquent behaviors, suicides have been shown to accelerate in middle adolescence (Conger, 1977). Perhaps suicide is an alternative to delinquency. There are, of course, some adolescents for whom becoming a delinquent is not a suitable identity because they are disabled — by temperament; lack of social, intellectual, or other skills; and by their close relationships with their parents — to bolster their self-esteem by delinquent performances. Nevertheless, they may experience the provocations to delinquency keenly, particularly as their future becomes clearer and darker. At about age 15, American adolescents are inducted into secondary school, where scholastic achievement begins really to count; the expectations mount for them to establish relationships with their peers. Unable to measure up, and projecting their inadequacies into an otherwise interminable future, some decide to terminate their lives.

But why should increasingly higher proportions of adolescents commit suicide in this particular historical period? It is not likely merely that the reporting of suicides has increased, while the actual incidence has not. Are the provocations increasing and the controls decreasing? Waldron and Eyer (1975) have assembled a host of correlates and potential causes that have mounted in recent years: ". . . roughly a third of the recent rise in suicide for 15-24-year olds can be predicted from the rise in parental divorce, the decline in marriage among young adults, the rise in illegitimate birthrates, the rise in childlessness among married couples, the decline in relative income and the increase in alcohol consumption" (p. 387). Clearly, there is a lot of variance left to explain and we speculate — generalizing from the concept of the optimal range of delinquent behaviors — that adolescents' attitudes toward suicide have been socialized at a time when it is becoming more tolerable than it used to be.

We note that in recent years the right to take one's own life has been more widely advocated, especially, but by no means only, for those suffering terminal illnesses. So the "Right to Die" movement may have moved suicide into the optimal range of deviant behavior for a greater number of contemporary adolescents. And how many adolescents are persuaded nowadays that suicide is not actually the end but the beginning of the nightmare that Hamlet feared? Or that suicides will be cast into the *Inferno* that Dante depicted? We are suggesting that our understanding of adolescent suicide, like our understanding of adolescent delinquent behavior, may broaden and deepen by placing the developmental phenomenon in a specified historical-cultural context.

The data on religious conversion are not even as solid as the data on suicide, but they also suggest a recent historical trend. Research at the turn of the twentieth century indicated that individuals at that time experienced religious conversion most often in the early to middle years of their adolescence (Gold & Douvan, 1969). Retrospective reports of conversion experiences pictured them as overwhelming and renewing; individuals remembered being seized, made over, and released as more whole and better. They described themselves as "saved" or "born again." The implications for identity formation are obvious; and indeed, the earliest usage of the word "identity," as Erikson has taught us to understand it, apparently was in Starbuck's (1912) interpretation of what his respondents told him of their religious conversions.

An obvious hypothesis about the function of the religious conversions of early adolescents at the turn of this century is that they helped adolescents to cope with an overwhelming sense of sinfulness that accompanied the upsurge of genital sexuality. The incidence of conversions was probably greater among youth in those religious subcultures that most severely condemned sexual pleasure (especially for women) and were particularly stern about masturbation, creating acute problems (especially for boys). These were also the religious denominations that offered the most encouragement for conversions as a solution to the problems their sexual strictures intensified. The solution for some adolescents may have been that their adoption of the role of believer lent them the ego strength to abjure sexual behavior of any kind and perhaps sexual fantasy as well. It seems more likely however that "being saved" comforted adolescents when they could not help but act on their unfamiliar sexual impulses. For being saved is constantly renewable: although one is expected to try to sin no more, faith, in any case, washes away even recurring sin. We suspect that religious conversion enabled adolescent self-respect to recover again and again as youth succumbed to what they felt was the degradation of sexual sinfulness. In this way, conversion helped those adolescents whose growing sexuality might have been experienced as an ineradicable stain to negotiate early and middle adolescence. This is not to assert that the relief from sexual sinfulness was the only or even major reason for religious conversion, but rather that it seems a likely reason for these experiences to have been more characteristic among early and middle adolescents than among other age cohorts.

Again, as in our understanding of delinquency, we have identified a problem peculiar to adolescence along with a culturally sanctioned solution in the form of a recognized role, and these combine to make certain behaviors more characteristic of adolescents than of others.

Apparently religious conversion is not so frequent among early and middle adolescents anymore. If informed observations can be trusted in the absence of any firmer evidence, the role of believer is becoming more attractive nowadays to late adolescents and young adults. These youth often adopt Pentacostal Catholicism; Orthodox Judaism; oriental creeds, like the Hare Krishna; and amalgams of East and West, like the Unification Church. Contemporary converts do not seem to come so heavily as they used to from fundamentalist Protestant backgrounds, nor is their conversion so often to Protestant fundamentalism. Adams and Fox (1978) have described one congregation of Protestant fundamentalists as a mixture of the old and new converts: (1) the younger adolescent "Jesus-boppers" looking for impulse control and (2) older adolescents and young adults emerging from the drug culture on their way to re-entering conventional society.

The decline in the conversion phenomenon of the early twentieth century seems not hard to understand. The technology and ideology of sex have changed, so the sinfulness of sex is no longer keenly felt by adolescents. Even the fundamentalist religions now recognize the legitimacy of sexual pleasure and tolerate masturbation. Contemporary culture, then, neither creates the old problem nor encourages the old solution. But why has the modal incidence of religious conversion moved somewhat later along the life cycle, or so it seems? Why is the role of believer now more often being grasped to the center of personal identities at just that life stage when formerly it was being relinquished?

It seems to us that there are differences between contemporary experiences, which might more appropriately be called religious awakenings, and the earlier experiences of religious conversions. One difference is that conversion experiences, according to reports, typically used to come on teenagers suddenly and were experienced as compelling summonses. Contemporary religious awakening seems rather to involve a more gradual and self-conscious choice. A period of only tentative commitment is apparently common. And, especially important from our point of view, recruitment and induction is carried out by peers (Heirich, 1977). In all, the contemporary phenomenon looks like a process of joining a social movement as much as, if not more than, a coming to God.

Our experience with trying to understand the data on developmental trends in delinquent behavior leads us to ask what adolescent needs may be satisfield by joining these religious sects. What psychological advantage is gained at this time? Is the modal timing a function of the developmental trend of the *motive,* so that *it* becomes most pressing at late adolescence? Or is it that at late adolescence, this *option* becomes more suitable for satisfying an *old* need? Or, as is most likely, do both the *motive* and the *option* converge developmentally at late adolescence?

Our current speculation is this: there are essentially two ways in which individuals can emerge from adolescence with some at least incipient sense of identity. First, individuals may establish continuity in their lives by assigning to one of their roles a superordinate position and allow its rights and obligations to rule their choices and chart their course. By late adolescence, an individual may, for example, become committed primarily to preparing for a career and bend his or her days to that task, anticipating that the establishment and pursuit of that career will be the thread of his or her adult life thereafter. Or the person may settle on the creation and maintenance of a family as the ruling consideration and formulate an identity around the roles of spouse and parent. Second, the sense of continuity that is the individual's identity may rest on the adoption of a more or less articulated ideology that transcends all roles, lending consistency to his or her current enactment and also making sense of the future.

Some individuals reach the end of adolescence with little or no sense of identity. They have settled neither on a dominant role nor a coherent ideology. We suspect that our culture's belief in the finality of adolescence makes these youth feel that the ground is slipping away beneath them. They are, in this respect, like the heavily delinquent older adolescents who we imagine also begin to feel desperate about what they will do next, now that the delinquent role is wearing thin. Indeed, some of them may be the same individuals: 50 of the 96 members of a Jesus Movement group observed by Simmonds (1977) reported, ''that they had had trouble with the law prior to conversion.'' One of the reasons they have got as old as they have still feeling the way they do is that none of the common roles nor any of the established ideologies fit their requirements. Perhaps they feel that their talents are not suited to successful role performance, or perhaps they feel that their talents will be wasted in the common roles. Or they may be aware, keenly or vaguely, of irreconcilable differences between their values and the accepted ideologies of their culture. Nevertheless — and this we believe is important to making the choice we are considering here — they are receptive to some sort of truth. The late adolescents and young adults we are considering are probably not a distrustful lot, nor do they cling to a rigid autonomy. Like most devout people, they tend toward dependency (Simmonds, Richardson, & Harder, 1976). When others like them say that they have found some truth and act as though they mean it, these individuals are ready to listen and believe.

The options that they are considering are within the optimal range of deviant behavior. Our American culture values religious beliefs and holds that believers are better spouses, parents, and citizens. Further, we are pluralistic in our beliefs, under Constitutional protection. Although the options that now seem popular among older adolescents and young adults are Constitutionally legitimate, they are somewhat beyond the pale of the culture. Of course, they vary in this respect. The Jesus Movement, Pentacostal Catholicism, and Orthodox Judaism are choices deviant from most of these youths' family backgrounds; but we imagine that their parents find these choices strange rather than weird or dangerous. They merely hope that their children will grow out of them. However, as one moves through the range of choices to, for example, the Children of God and the Unification Church ("Moonies"), one encounters options that dismay and outrage parents. Indeed, there is at this writing some question whether these options are even Constitutionally protected or whether parents have the right to "un-kidnap" and "de-program" offspring who make these choices.

The observations of Adams and Fox (1976) and of Heirich (1977) suggest that the new converts come to the optimal range of deviant religious behavior from two directions: from the more deviant end, particularly the drug culture; and from the ultraconventional, family-oriented religious culture. These shifts being deviant, indeed chosen in part because of their deviancy, rely heavily, like the delinquent identity, on contracultural support. We do not have in mind here young people who make a lone retreat to search their souls and ponder their place in the cosmos. Our image is rather of small groups of youths chanting in unison, talking ecstatically in tongues, preparing food together in a carefully *kosher* kitchen, or obtrusively soliciting funds in a major airport. The converts bear witness to one another acting out their identities. The crucial recognition is among them, although it is helpful when they and people like them also appear in the mass media.

Our reasoning as to why these ultrareligious options seem so attractive to those passing out of adolescence in the 1970s begins by noting that the rules governing the roles are supernormative; they are extreme expressions of eternal verities — faith, hope, charity, asceticism, obedience, and so on. It seems to us that the youth are taking up these roles to reprove their parents and their parents' generation for failing them and their generation — for having sent them or perhaps their older brothers to a bad war; for not effectively anticipating their need for jobs; for letting the energy run out and the economy run down. Whereas, the delinquents reject their parents' values because their values make them feel so low, the new believers exalt their parents' values to be better than their parents. They call attention to the fact that their elders have not lived up to certain ideals. Just as the delinquents find a modicum of tolerance in their culture's beliefs in the pressures of adolescence, the burdens of poverty, and the prerogatives of young males, so also the new believers find more than a little confirmation in their elders' self-recriminations.

The principles by which we have tried to understand the developmental trends in delinquent behavior, when applied to the two eras of twentieth-century religious conversions among adolescents and young adults, have alerted us to the importance of the roles and beliefs (the sociocultural factors) that shape adolescent experience and behavior in its concrete time and place. Only in the last generation, it seems to us, have students of adolescence begun to take society and culture seriously into account, and of course,

Margaret Mead and Erik Erikson have led the way. The reason for this neglect is not only that the developmental thinkers (such as Hall, Freud, Gesell, and Piaget) were deeply involved first in working out the genetic side of the adolescent equation, but also that the socioculturalists were not thinking in terms of individuals (leaving only Lewin really, who considered both the genetics and the social environment of adolescence too briefly to make much difference by himself). It was also true, and remains true, that adolescents do not express clearly and articulately the influences of their society and their culture. When they speak spontaneously of the roles they are supposed to play, it is characteristically to refuse to go along, and when they happen to remark on the culture their elders are trying to pass on to them, they usually express doubt if not disdain. Only in recent years, after being alerted to the possibility that sociocultural factors are decisive, have researchers systematically solicited from adolescents the beliefs and attitudes they hold but are not ordinarily moved to express. Thereby we have become aware that most adolescents are developing well within the patterns laid down by their culture. Furthermore, our considerations of delinquency have suggested that even those adolescents who seem to have broken out of their sociocultural limits are developing largely along lines that their society and culture have prearranged.

REFERENCES

Abrahamsen, D. *Psychology of crime*. New York: Columbia University Press, 1960.

Adams, R. L. and Fox, R. J. Mainlining Jesus: The new trip. *Society,* 1976, *9*(4), 50–56.

Alexander, J. F., Barton, C., Shiaro, R. S., and Parsons, B. V. Systems-behavioral intervention with families of delinquents: Therapist characteristics, family behavior, and outcome. *Journal of Consulting and Clinical Psychology,* 1976, *44*, 656–664.

Alexander, J. and Staub, H. *The criminal, the judge, and the public*. New York: Free Press, 1956.

Aries, P. *Centuries of childhood: A social history of family life*. (R. Baldick, trans.) New York: Random House, 1962.

Bachman, J. G. *Young men in high school and beyond: A summary of findings from the Youth in Transition project*. Ann Arbor, Mich.: Institute for Social Research, 1972.

Bachman, J. G., Green, S., and Wirtanen, I. *Youth in transition. Vol. III: Dropping out — Problem or symptom?* Ann Arbor, Mich.: Institute for Social Research, 1971.

Bachman, J. G., Kahn, R. L., Mednick, M. T., Davidson, T. N., and Johnston, L. D. *Youth in transition. Vol. I: Blueprint for a longitudinal study of adolescent boys*. Ann Arbor, Mich.: Institute for Social Research, 1967.

Berger, R. J., Crowley, J. E., Gold, M., and Gray, J. (with Arnold, M.). *Experiment in a juvenile court: A study of a program of volunteers working with juvenile probationers*. Ann Arbor, Mich.: Institute for Social Research, 1975.

Bloch, H. A., and Niederhoffer, A. *The gang: A study in adolescent behavior*. New York: Philosophical Library, 1958.

Blos, P. *On adolescence*. New York: Free Press, 1962.

Bowman, P. H. Effects of a revised school program on potential delinquents. *Annals,* 1959, *322*, 53–62.

Brim, O. G., and Wheeler, S. *Socialization after childhood*. New York: Wiley, 1966.

Cloward, R. A., and Ohlin, L. E. *Delinquency and opportunity*. New York: Free Press, 1960.

Cohen, A. K. *Delinquent boys*. New York: Free Press, 1955.

Conger, J. *Adolescence and youth* (2nd ed.). New York: Harper & Row, 1977.

Crime and Delinquency, April, 1961.

Eisenstadt, S. N. *From generation to generation: Age groups and social structure.* Glencoe, Ill.: Free Press, 1956.

Eissler, K. R. *Searchlights on delinquency.* New York: International Universities Press, 1949.

————. Ego-psychological implications of the psychoanalytic treatment of delinquents. In Eissler, R. S., et al. (Eds.), *Psychoanalytic study of the child* (Vol. 5). New York: International Universities Press, 1950.

Empey, L. T., and Erickson, M. L. Hidden delinquency and social status. *Social Forces,* 1966, *44,* 546–554.

Empey, L. T., and Erickson, M. L. *The Provo experiment.* Lexington, Md.: Lexington Books, 1972.

Empey, L. T. and Lubeck, S. G. (with LaPorte, R. L.) *Explaining delinquency.* Lexington, Mass.: Heath, 1971a.

Empey, L. T., and Lubeck, S. G. *The Silverlake experiment.* Chicago: Aldine, 1971b.

Erickson, M. L., and Empey, L. T. Court records, undetected delinquency, and decision-making. *Journal of Criminal Law, Criminology, and Police Science,* 1963, 456–467.

Erikson, E. H. *Identity and the life cycle.* New York: International Universities Press, 1959.

————. *Childhood and society.* New York: Norton, 1963.

————. *Identity: Youth and crisis.* New York: Norton, 1968.

Eysenck, H. *Crime and personality.* London: Granada Press, 1970.

Faine, J. R. *A multidimensional approach to understanding varieties of delinquent behavior.* Unpublished doctoral dissertation, The University of Iowa, 1974.

Farrington, D., and West, D. J. The Cambridge study of delinquent behavior. In S. A.Mednick and A. E. Baert (Eds.), *A survey of prospective longitudinal research in Europe.* Copenhagen, Denmark: World Health Organization, 1977.

Ferdinand, T. N. *Typologies of delinquency.* New York: Random House, 1966.

Friedlander, K. *The psychoanalytic approach to juvenile delinquency.* New York: International Universities Press, 1947.

Gibson, H. B. *Self-reported delinquency.* Cambridge, England: University of Cambridge Institute of Criminology, 1968.

Gibson, H. B., Morrison, S., and West, D. J. The confessions of known offenses in response to self-reported delinquency schedule. *British Journal of Criminology,* 1970, *10,* 277–280.

Gold, M. *Delinquent behavior in an American city.* Belmont, Calif.: Brooks/Cole, 1970.

Gold, M., and Douvan, E. *Adolescent development: Readings in research and theory.* New York: Allyn & Bacon, 1969.

Gold, M., and Mann, D. Delinquency as defense. *American Journal of Orthopsychiatry,* 1972, *42,* 463–479.

Gold, M., and Mattick, H. W. *Experiment in the streets: The Chicago Youth Development Project.* Ann Arbor, Mich.: Institute for Social Research, 1974.

Gold, M., and Reimer, D. J. Changing patterns of delinquent behavior among Americans 13 through 16 years old: 1967–72. *Crime and Delinquency Literature,* 1975, *7,* 483–517.

Gold, M., and Tomlin, P. "Skeletal and chronological age in adolescent development." Mimeographed. Ann Arbor, Mich.: Institute for Social Research, 1975.

Gold, M., and Williams, J. R. The effect of "getting caught": Apprehension of the juvenile offender as a cause of subsequent delinquencies. *Prospectus,* 1969, *3,* 1–12.

Greulich, W. W., and Pyle, S. I. *Radiographic atlas of skeletal development of the hand and wrist* (2nd ed.). Stanford, Calif.: Stanford University Press, 1959.

Hackler, J. C., and Lautt, M. Systematic bias in measuring self-reported delinquency. *Canadian Review of Sociology and Anthropology*, 1969, *6*, 92–106.

Hall, G. S. *Adolescence: Its psychology and its relations to physiology, anthropology, sociology, sex, crime, religion, and education* (Vol. 1). Englewood Cliffs, N.J.: Prentice-Hall, 1904.

Hardt, R. H., and Bodine, G. E. *Development of self-report instruments in delinquency research*. Syracuse, N.Y.: Youth Development Center, Syracuse University, 1965.

Hardt, R. H., and Peterson, S. J. Arrests of self and friends as indicators of delinquency involvement. *Journal of Research in Crime and Delinquency*, 1968, *5*, 44–51.

Havlicek, L. L. and Peterson, N. L. Effect of the violation of assumptions upon significance levels of the Pearson *r*. *Psychological Bulletin*, 1977, *84*, 373–377.

Heirich, M. Change of heart: A test of some widely held theories about religious conversion. *American Journal of Sociology*, 1977, *83*, 653–680.

Heise, D. Norms and individual patterns in student deviancy. *Social Problems* 1968, *16*, 78–92.

Hewitt, L. E., and Jenkins, R. L. *Fundamental patterns of maladjustment: The dynamics of their origin*. Springfield: The State of Illinois, 1946.

Hindelang, M. J. Age, sex, and the versatility of delinquent involvements *Social Problems*, 1971, *18*, 522–535.

Hindelang, M. J., Hirschi, T., and Weis, J. G., Correlates of delinquency: The illusion of discrepancy between self-report and official measures. Albany, New York: State University of New York, in preparation.

Hindelang, M. J., and Weis, J. G. Personality and self-reported delinquency. *Criminology*, 1972, *10*, 268–294.

Hirschi, T. *Causes of delinquency*. Berkeley: University of California Press, 1969.

Jenkins, R. L. The varieties of children's behavioral problems and family dynamics. *American Journal of Psychiatry*, 1968, *124*, 1440–1445.

Johnston, L. D. *Drugs and American youth*. Ann Arbor, Mich.: Institute for Social Research, 1973.

Johnston, L. D., O'Malley, P. M., and Eveland, L. K. *Drugs and delinquency: A search for causal connections*. In D. G. Kandel (Ed.), *Longitudinal research on drug use: Empirical findings and methodological issues*. Washington, D.C.: Hemisphere, 1978, 137–156.

Klein, M. W. *Street gangs and street workers*. Englewood Cliffs, N.J.: Prentice-Hall, 1971.

Klein, N. C., Alexander, J. F. and Parsons, B. V. Impact of family systems intervention on recidivism and sibling delinquency: a model of primary prevention and program evaluation. *Journal of Consulting and Clinical Psychology*, 1977, *45*, 469–474.

Knight, D. *The Marshall program II: Amenability to confrontive peer-group therapy*. Sacramento, Calif.: California Youth Authority, 1971.

Kohlberg, L. The development of children's orientations toward a moral order: I. Sequence in the developmental of moral thought. *Vita Humana*, 1963a, *6*, 11–33.

———. Moral development and identification. In H. W. Stevenson (Ed.), *Child Psychology* (Part I). (62nd Yearbook, National Society for the Study of Education.) Chicago: University of Chicago Press, 1963b.

Kulik, J. A. *Interrelationships and sources of bias in several criteria of delinquency*. Paper presented at the Eastern Psychological Association, Boston, 1967.

Kulik, J. A., Stein, K. B., and Sarbin, T. R. Dimensions and patterns of adolescent antisocial behavior. *Journal of Consulting and Clinical Psychology*, 1968a, *32*, 375–382.

———. Disclosure of delinquent behavior under conditions of anonymity and nonanonymity. *Journal of Consulting and Clinical Psychology*, 1968b, *32*, 506–509.

Lewin, K. Field theory and experiment in social psychology: Concepts and methods. *American Journal of Sociology*, 1939, *44*, 868–897.

———. *Field theory and social science*. New York: Harper & Row, 1951.

McCandless, B. R. *Adolescents: behavior and development*. Hinsdale, Ill.: Dryden Press, 1970.

Magnusson, D., Duner, A., and Zetterblom, G. *Adjustment*. New York: Wiley, 1975.

Mann, D. W. *When delinquency is defensive: Self-esteem and deviant behavior*. Unpublished doctoral dissertation, University of Michigan, Ann Arbor, 1976.

Massimo, J. L., and Shore, M. F. The effectiveness of a comprehensive, vocationally oriented psychotherapeutic program for adolescent delinquent boys. *American Journal of Orthopsychiatry*, 1963, *33*, 634–642.

Mead, M. *Coming of age in Samoa*. New York: Morrow, 1928.

Merton, R. K. Social structure and anomie. *American Sociological Review*, 1958, *3*, 672–682.

Miller, W. B. The impact of a 'total community' delinquency control project. *Social Problems*, 1962, *10*, 168–191.

Morris, R. R. Attitudes toward delinquency by delinquents, nondelinquents, and their friends. *British Journal of Criminology*, 1965, *5*, 249–256.

Nye, F. I. *Family relationships and delinquent behavior*. New York: Wiley, 1958.

Nye, F. I., and Short, J. F. Jr. Scaling delinquent behavior. *American Sociological Review*, 1957, *22*, 326–331.

Offer, D. *The psychological world of the teenager*. New York: Basic Books, 1969.

Offer, D., and Offer, J. Profiles of normal adolescent girls. *Archives of General Psychiatry*, 1968, *19*, 513–522.

O'Malley, P. M., Bachman, J. G., and Johnston, J. *Youth in Transition. Final Report: Five years beyond high school: Causes and consequences of educational attainment*. Ann Arbor, Mich.: Institute for Social Research, 1977.

Parsons, T. Certain sources and patterns of aggression in the social structure of the Western world. *Psychiatry*, 1947, *10*, 172–175.

Persons, R. W. Psychological and behavioral change in delinquents following psychotherapy. *Journal of Clinical Psychology*, 1966, *22*, 337–340.

———. The relationship between psychotherapy with institutionalized boys and subsequent community adjustment. *Journal of Consulting Psychology*, 1967, *31*, 137–141.

Petronio, R. "Self-esteem and moral attitudes as factors of recidivism in juvenile delinquent boys." Unpublished manuscript, New School for Social Research, 1973.

Quay, H. C. Dimensions of personality in delinquent boys as inferred from the factor analyses of case history data. *Child Development*, 1964, *35*, 479–484.

Quay, H. C. and Blumen, L. Factor dimensions of delinquent behavior. *Journal of Social Psychology*, 1963, *51*, 272–277.

Randolph, M. H., Richardson, H., and Johnson, R. C. A comparison of social and solitary male delinquents. *Journal of Consulting Psychology*, 1961, *25*, 293–295.

Robins, L. N. *Deviant children grown up: A sociological and psychiatric study of sociopathic personality*. Baltimore, Md.: Williams & Wilkins, 1966.

Sarri, R. and Hasenfeld, Y. *Brought to justice? Juveniles, the courts and the law*. Ann Arbor, Mich.: National Assessment of Juvenile Corrections, 1976.

Seigman, A. W. Father absence during childhood and antisocial behavior. *Journal of Abnormal Psychology,* 1966, *71,* 71–74.

Sellin, T., and Wolfgang, M. E. *The measurement of delinquency.* New York: Wiley, 1964.

Shinohara, M., and Jenkins, R. L. MMPI study of three types of delinquents. *Journal of Clinical Psychology,* 1967, *23,* 156–163.

————. After ten years: A follow-up study of comprehensive vocationally oriented psychotherapy. *American Journal of Orthopsychiatry,* 1973, *43,* 128–132.

————. Fifteen years after treatment: A follow-up study of comprehensive vocationally oriented psychotherapy. *American Journal of Orthopsychiatry,* 1979, *49,* 240–245.

Short, J. F., Jr., Tennyson, R. A., and Howard, K. I. Behavior dimensions of gang delinquency. *American Sociological Review,* 1963, *28,* 411–428.

Simmonds, R. B. Conversion or addiction. *American Behavioral Scientist,* 1977, *20,* 909–924.

Simmonds, R. B., Richardson, J. T., and Harder, M. W. A Jesus Movement group: An adjective check list assessment. *Journal for the Scientific Study of Religion,* 1976, *15* 323–337.

Sonquist, J. A., Baker, E. L., and Morgan, J. N. *Searching for structure.* Ann Arbor, Mich.: Institute for Social Research, 1971.

Spiegel, L. A. A review of contributions to a psychoanlytic theory of adolescence. *Psychoanalytic Study of the Child,* 1951, *6,* 375–393.

Starbuck, E. D. *The psychology of religion.* New York: Scribners, 1912.

Stein, K. B., Sarbin, T. R., and Kulik, J. A. Further validation of antisocial personality types. *Journal of Consulting and Clinical Psychology,* 1971, *36,* 177–182.

Stuart, R. B., Quire, K., and Krell, M. Drug use by high-school students in an environment of shifting legal penalties. JSAS Catalog of Selected Documents in Psychology, 1976 (Ms. No. 1361).

Tanner, J. M. Physical growth. In P. H. Mussen (Ed.), *Carmichael's manual of child psychology* (Vol. 2, 3rd ed.). New York: Wiley, 1970.

Tharp, R. G., and Wetzel, R. J. *Behavior modification in the natural environment.* New York: Academic, 1969.

U. S. Supreme Court, *In re Gault,* 387 U.S. 1 (1967).

Voss, H. L. Ethnic differentials in delinquency in Honolulu. *Journal of Criminal Law, Criminology, and Police Science,* 1963, *54,* 322–327.

Waldron, I., and Eyer, J. Socioeconomic causes of the recent rise in death rates for 15–24 year olds. *Social Science and Medicine,* 1975, *9,* 383–396.

Weiss, E. Emotional memories and acting out. *Psychoanalytic Quarterly,* 1942, *11,* 477–479.

Williams, J. R., and Gold, M. *Final report of the national survey of youth, 1967.* Ann Arbor, Mich.: Institute for Social Research, 1971.

————. From delinquent behavior to official delinquency. *Social Problems,* 1972, *20,* 209–229.

CHAPTER 17

The Gifted Adolescent

Robert Hogan

The study of giftedness is inextricably bound up with the study of intelligence. When these two subdisciplines are conjoined in the study of human development, the result is a prolix and factfilled literature paradoxically typified by a curious conceptual barrenness. This chapter will attempt to impose some order on that prolixity and provide a small infusion of conceptual nourishment into the existing body of facts.

The chapter is organized in six sections. The first deals with definitions of giftedness. The second presents a brief overview of the theories of intelligence. The following two sections describe the characteristics of adolescents viewed from the perspective of the standard definitions of giftedness and intelligence. The fifth section describes research concerning individual differences in intellectual style within gifted samples. The final section reviews the literature concerning how best to deal with the education of the gifted.

DEFINITIONS OF GIFTEDNESS

Scientific interest in intelligence and the gifted began in the nineteenth century, inspired by Francis Galton's book *Hereditary Genius* (1869) and the success of Alfred Binet's test designed to predict school performance. In these sources we see the two standard definitions of giftedness. The more common of these defines giftedness in terms of high scores on standardized measures of cognitive or intellectual performance; these measures are invariably descendants of Binet's original test. To so define giftedness has the twin virtues of being conventionally accepted and apparently objective. The definition suffers, however, from the twin defects of being circular and empirically unproductive. Despite a century-long fascination with the concept of intelligence, the fact is that there still exists no accepted theory of intelligence — beyond the notion that intelligence is what intelligence tests test. But if giftedness is equated with intelligence, and if intelligence is defined in terms of intelligence-test scores, then giftedness also becomes that which intelligence tests test, and the tautology is complete. A second problem with defining giftedness in terms of high test scores is that, although intelligence tests reliably predict academic achievement and certain necessary correlates of this achievement (e.g., occupational attainment), they seem generally uncorrelated with meaningful life accomplishments (see Holland and Richards, 1965).

From Galton's 1869 book we have an alternative tradition of defining giftedness in terms of actual accomplishment. Although this definition is not widely used, it has certain features to commend it. It is first of all face-valid, that is, one obvious test of giftedness is gifted performance. Second, the definition has practical consequences since the best

536

predictor of future behavior is past behavior. Thus gifted adolescents in this sense are likely to become gifted adults, a claim that cannot necessarily be made for a definition based on test scores.

Whether giftedness is defined in terms of test scores or accomplishment, there is an additional and seldom articulated component to the definition that has to do with precociousness. Giftedness somehow suggests *early* exceptional performance. That is, of course, part of what it means to define giftedness in terms of high test scores in *childhood* — that is, "gifted" children are able correctly to answer test items that ungifted children answer only at a later date. The notion of early exceptional performance gives us a clue as to which definition of giftedness is more persuasive. When we are told that a certain movie starlet or athlete is gifted — that is, has an IQ of 180 — we may find that interesting. But when we are reminded that the Dutch physicist Christian Huygens taught the six-year-old G. W. Leibniz all of seventeenth-century mathematics in a week, we see a different meaning of the term gifted. Obviously young Leibniz would have "tested well"; but so do scores of children in suburban New York and Los Angeles every year. The quality of genius probably transcends simple test scores.

THEORIES OF INTELLIGENCE

The next question concerns the conceptual models that sustain these definitions of giftedness: what theory of the nature of the mind and intelligence can be used to explain gifted performance? For reasons of space it is not possible to review in detail prior conceptions of intelligence; the interested reader may consult excellent summaries by Bouchard (1968), Gough (1974), Resnick (1976), and Tuddenham (1964). Nonetheless, even a brief review will show that these prior conceptions are only partial and incomplete, a fact also noted by prior reviewers.

One of the earliest and still most influential theories of intelligence (based on Binet's early scale for predicting school performance) was propounded by H. H. Goddard (1920), Charles Spearman (1927), and others. As is well known, Binet developed a standardized interview schedule designed to evaluate children's ability to do school work. This interview schedule was quickly and enthusiastically hailed as a measure of intelligence, despite the lack of any supporting evidence for that claim. Even the ordinarily cautious Binet titled a 1900 paper "The Development of Intelligence in Children." Various writers and educators began speculating about the processes underlying scores on Binet's test. H. H. Goddard proposed that the process was a single underlying function or faculty of intelligence, ". . . our thesis is that the chief determiner of human conduct is a unitary mental process which we call 'intelligence' " (1920, p. 1). Charles Spearman (1927) reached the same conclusion. Using a set of "mental tests" in an English country school, he provided statistical support for the idea that a single mental trait or factor underlies performance on all mental tests. This g factor combined with test-specific s factors will generate any single person's test score. Spearman spent the latter portion of his career lobbying successfully for this view. There are several points to note about Spearman's unitary or "monarchical" theory of intelligence. First, it is alive and well today; the most sophisticated modern version is Cattell's theory of fluid and crystallized intelligence (Cattell 1963). In this model, fluid intelligence is equated with latent or genotypic g; crystallized intelligence reflects phenotypic g, that is, how well it translates into actual test performance. Second, many thoughtful persons feel that Spearman's g model (in any of its contemporary forms) is still the best theory of intelligency available (see Cooley, 1976; McNemar, 1964). Third, the theory of intelligence implicitly adopted by most psychologists is in fact Binet's test combined with Spearman's g model. Finally, we see here an example of scientists making a virtue out of necessity for, as I observed above, there is a real question about what Binet's test measures other than school performance. Certainly the Binet $+ g$ model is inadequate as an explanation of giftedness defined in terms of achievement.

The most influential account of intelligence other than Spearman's g theory and its derivatives is that provided by Jean Piaget. Piaget's stage theory of cognitive development is set forth by Elkind (Chapter 13) and Keating (Chapter 7) in this handbook and there is no need to review it here. But there is an additional reason for not doing so — despite its immense popularity among developmental psychologists, the theory is of little value in understanding giftedness. That is so because Piaget is unconcerned with individual differences, which are an essential part of the study of giftedness, and also because, in my judgment, Piaget's theory is inadequate, biased, and incomplete as an account of the nature of intelligence.

It is not possible to give a properly documented critique of that theory here. Let me rather summarize my objections in terms of three points. The first has to do with Piaget's claim that representational thought is, in principle, nonsocial in origin. In contrast I would argue, following Vygotsky (1962), that a child initially acquires language (one basic exemplification of representational thought) in the context of social interaction. A child asking ''What's dat?'' is not necessarily requesting information; he is often executing a move in a game designed to promote social interaction — it is only later that the child realizes that language can be put to analytical or noninteractional purposes. In this view, then, all forms of thinking, including representational thought, have social origins. And once thought begins to be filtered through language it becomes unalterably social because language is a conventional social creation.

The concept of intelligence is closely tied to epistemological theory, and my second objection to Piaget's theory of intelligence has to do with his epistemology. Piaget's theory of knowledge can be seen in the tradition of Plato, Aristotle, Herbert Spencer, and Bertrand Russell, where knowledge of the world is knowledge of structure. For Piaget an isomorphism develops over time between the structure of the mind (e.g., formal operations) and the structure of the world, making valid knowledge possible. But this is just one view. In contrast, one might argue that: knowledge of pure structure is very difficult to attain unambiguously *because* structure and function (in both the mind and the world) are always closely intertwined *because* the relationships between them are determined by the social and economic conditions under which a society exists. In this view, then, a theory of knowledge as knowledge of structure independent of its particular social context is necessarily limited or parochial. Another way of putting this is that for Piaget and other Platonists the meaning of concepts can be found in the structure of nature, provided a sufficiently energetic effort is made. But one can argue to the contrary that the meaning of most concepts is negotiated. For a child the meaning of words is negotiated with his or her parents; for scientists the definitions of concepts are negotiated with the scientific community — witness, for example, how the meaning of mental or cognitive concepts has changed in psychology since 1960. Thus concepts have no meaning outside of specified cultural systems of reference.

My third objection to the Piagetian theory of intelligence concerns its claim that formal operational thought is the endpoint of intellectual development. It has proven extraordinarily difficult to give operational specification to the concept of formal operations, and that alone makes one wonder about its utility. More importantly, by defining mature intelligence in terms of the capacity for formal operations, intelligence is equated with a . . . cold-blooded detached quality [of mind], separate from but still monitoring action as a spectator, [emphasizing] a domain of second-order derivatives; that is, a universe of discourse . . . in which words, signs, and notations not only stand for things but can be manipulated within their own boundary system without respect for things'' (Price-Williams, 1975, p. 59). And such a habit of mind requires a very special cultural context to support it, a culture characterized by leisure, by distance from the immediate demands of physical survival, and a social system that supports and rewards this detached and rather narcissistic form of thought. Elsewhere (Hogan, 1977) I have argued that in his notion of formal operations, Piaget has reified rationalism, the defining feature of French thought from Peter Abelard to Claude Lévi-Strauss. If so, the uncritical American acceptance of Piaget's theory of cognitive development can be seen as another triumph of French culture in a civilization that seems to have lost confidence in its own intellectual standards. To put the final line on this discussion, Bruner (1959) makes the point, with which I fully agree, that formal operations cannot be the end-point in cognitive development. That end-point might better be defined as the ability to use one's intelligence intelligently.

I shall conclude this section by sketching the outline of what a more complete theory of intelligence might look like. The model is adapted from an important paper by Webb (1978). Following Tuddenham (1964), intelligence is defined not as an entity or even as a dimension in a person but rather as an evaluation that we place on that person's behavior from the point of view of its adaptive adequacy. What constitutes intelligent behavior, then, depends on the person's life circumstances (i.e., the demands to which he or she is adapting). The next question conerns the factors underlying or generating intelligent behavior. Here it is necessary to distinguish three aspects of mind that enable intelligent performance. Webb calls these power, structure, and style.

Power refers to the general efficiency of a person's neurological machinery; it is equivalent to Spearman's g, and it is largely heritable. Power is manifested primarily in the speed with which a person acquires new information (words, concepts, facts) or "catches on" to ideas, trends, and procedures. In these terms, Binet's test is largely a measure of power. Moreover, it makes sense that academic achievement should be a rough measure of power in technologically advanced societies — the speed with which a child could acquire the technology of its culture once had survival value. This analysis suggests how to assess the power in less advanced cultures (i.e., by testing children's knowledge of their culture). It also predicts that measures of power will be less relevant to intelligent behavior in adulthood, where the problem tends to be less one of acquiring new information and more one of integrating and applying information already in storage.

Structure refers to specific mental capacities. All people, for example, categorize, count, use language, make tools, and navigate. There is a recognizable set of mental capacties that operate over a wide range of culturally determined contents, and there are those who do some (as well as those who do more) of these things better than others. Thus some people have a particular aptitude for languages or music or chess. These people, along with such fascinating cases as Luria's mnemonist (Luria, 1968), suggest the presence of a finite number of innate cognitive capacities or structures, again probably genetically controlled, which factor analytic studies of test performance may be able to identify (see French, Eckstrom, & Price, 1963).

The third aspect of intelligent performance is called style. Unlike power and structure, style is learned; it reflects one's culture and/or social origins and may be the most important determinant of intelligent performance. An adequate taxonomy of intellectual styles has yet to be contemplated, much less developed; examples of style, however, come readily to mind. Thus Bernstein's (1960) distinction between the restricted speech codes of the English working class and the elaborated codes of the English middle class, each, presumably, adapted to its social contexts (where, for example, presuppositions are spelled out in conversation) is one kind of style. Luria's (1976) account of the intellectual changes that accompanied exposure to Western scientific thought among Uzbek peasants in the 1920s is an example of how style is learned. Finally, to the degree that Piaget's formal operational thought merely reflects the preferred cognitive style of members of the French Academy (Anatole France, Claude Bernard, etc.) it too is a kind of style, albeit an elegant and refined version.

The remainder of this chapter is organized around the notion that power, structure, and style are the primary aspects of intelligent performance. Giftedness defined in terms of high test scores is largely concerned with power. Giftedness defined in terms of achievement concerns both structure and style. The fifth section of this chapter will focus on stylistic aspects of giftedness.

CHARACTERISTICS OF ADOLESCENTS WITH HIGH TEST SCORES

Lewis Terman devoted his professional career to determining the characteristics of one group of gifted persons followed throughout their life cycle. Stored in his five-volume series, *Genetic Studies of Genius* (1925), is a treasure chest of information regarding the nature of adolescent giftedness as defined by high test scores. Terman was a tireless, almost obsessive, champion of intelligence testing and the welfare of gifted children. His overt goal was to determine empirically what gifted children were like; his hidden agenda was to demonstrate their superiority. Many of the conclusions of his famous study were already formulated by spring of 1921, at which point he had interviewed 121 children with tested IQ's above 140 (see Terman, 1925, p. 4). In his subsequent research, Terman set about evaluating in a more careful and formal way his conclusions based on this earlier, "pilot" work.

The subjects for Terman's study came from Los Angeles and the San Francisco Bay area of California. They were selected in a three-step screening process. Teachers in public schools in grades one through eight were asked to nominate the three brightest children in their classes. The nominees from several classrooms were assembled and given a standardized group test of intelligence. Those scoring in the top 5% of unselected children of their age were given an abbreviated version of the Stanford-Binet; those attaining an IQ score of 130 were given the full Stanford-Binet. The final sample of 642 had IQ scores of 140 or greater; these were the main and most important subjects in Terman's study. The goals of this multistage selection process were: to obtain a sample of very bright children who were "representative" of gifted children as a whole. Terman probably succeeded in assembling a representative sample of children who, in 1922, would do well on the Stanford-Binet. What were these children like?

The average age of the sample was 9.5. A full range of father's occupations was represented. About 55.2% of the group could be classified as WASP, and about 10.5% were Jewish. Blacks, Mexican-Americans, and Latins were significantly underrepresented in the sample. Terman provides an astonishingly detailed account of the characteristics of these children, including, for example, information regarding how often they were constipated, brushed their teeth, and bathed. The following are some of his more interesting findings. Compared to control children the gifted were heavier at birth, they walked about a month earlier, had fewer physical defects, and were slightly taller, broader, and heavier than children in general. As Terman (1925, p. 171) notes, "The results . . . show that the gifted group is, as a whole, physically superior to the various groups used for comparison."

Two demographic features of the group are worth noting, although Terman himself doesn't comment on them. The first is that he found a substantial negative correlation ($r = -.27$) between family size and child's IQ. This is consistent with more recent data (Zajonc, 1976) that suggests there is only a fixed amount of intellectual nutrition available in the family environment; the more children, the less nutriment available for each child. A second and related finding is that slightly over half (273 of 574) of the gifted sample were firstborns or only children. Thus the advantages that accrue to being born first appear even in this rather exotic sample.

On an imaginative set of measures of dependability and honesty, all with good-reported reliability, the gifted children notably outperformed an unselected sample. The personalities of the gifted sample were further assessed in two other ways. The first consisted of administering a psychiatric screening inventory that R. S. Woodworth had developed for the U.S. Army in the first World War. The content of this 85-item test suggests that it would overlap substantially with the first factor of the MMPI, developed much later. Thus it is useful to note that approximately 75% of the gifted scored above the average for unselected children, indicating better psychological adjustment. Terman also attempted to assess aspects of nonpathological social functioning by having the sample rated by their parents and teachers (at least two sets of ratings per child) for 25 traits selected on an ad hoc basis by Terman. These included, among others, prudence, self-confidence, willpower, sociability, leadership, and conscientiousness. Reliabilities are not reported; nonetheless a consistent pattern of results emerged, with the gifted receiving higher ratings for everything except mechanical ingenuity and sociability (fondness for large groups).

Phenomenologically speaking, that is, from the viewpoint of everyday social interaction, that which set the gifted children off from their peers was, as Terman noted, their ". . . quick understanding, insatiable curiosity, extensive information, retentive memory, early speech, unusual vocabulary, etc.," (1925, p. 287). That is, they seemed to display a quickness of apprehension in conjunction with a good memory, organized apparently in verbal terms. Missing in Terman's discussion, however, is any claim for superior reasoning on the part of the gifted sample, a point to which we shall return later.

It is interesting to see what Terman himself thought his enormous compilation of facts meant. In the summary chapter of Volume I (1925) the following issues are stressed:

1. The distribution of IQ departs from that given by the normal curve, at least at the high end. Many more cases are found than the normal curve would lead one to expect. Butcher (1968) suggests that a Pearson Type IV model of the normal curve is the best fit to the actual distribution of IQ scores.

2. The gifted are above average in physical growth and general health.

3. The gifted surpass unselected children on tests of honesty, trustworthiness, and other aspects of conventional moral conduct. Terman (p. 517) regarded this as

evidence of advanced character development; a more accurate interpretation might be that these children were better socialized and more conforming to adult values than an unselected group.

4. As reflected by their scores on a modified version of Woodworth's test of psychotic tendencies, the gifted sample seemed unusually stable and well adjusted. As a group they manifested relatively few unreasonable fears and self-doubts, substantially fewer than unselected children of the same age.

5. Gifted children exceed unselected children most in terms of intellectual traits, next in emotional and moral traits, and least in physical and social traits. In this last category there seemed to be almost no advantage to the gifted group.

Terman strikes a more ominous note in his next conclusion. Despite the fact that the sample included a full range of social classes, the majority of the gifted children came from advantaged, that is, professional and upper-middle-class homes. One child, for example, could trace his family back to George Washington, and there was an impressive array of famous Americans in the family histories of other members of the group. Terman regarded these genealogical findings as being ". . . in line with the findings of others on the social origins of superior ability'' (1925, p. 64). That is, talent leads to social ascendancy, social ascendancy is proof of talent, and talent runs in the family: ''The data set forth in this chapter are very incomplete, but fragmentary as they are, they give considerable support to Galton's theory as to the hereditary nature of genius (1925, p. 111).'' God seems to have given way to the Stanford-Binet as a means for choosing Calvin's elite. In fairness to Terman, however, it should be mentioned that IQ and social class have been repeatedly found to be associated by other research. This association between talent and social advantage is one of the most important and least analyzed findings in the literature on giftedness.

In his last conclusion, Terman is more reassuring. He states quite clearly that he doesn't expect many of his group to become eminent. In part, this is so because he sees no evidence of creative or original talent in the sample and in part because they are not sufficiently gifted.

One final observation will close this discussion of Terman's research. The research itself is empirical and descriptive, relatively uninformed by overarching theoretical goals. Nonetheless, it bears quite directly on the theory of intelligence outlined earlier in this chapter. I suggested above that it is necessary to distinguish three aspects of cognitive capacity underlying intelligent performance: power, structure, and style. I further suggested that power reflected general neurological efficiency, that it was manifested in childhood as the speed with which a child caught on to or absorbed the stored knowledge of his or her culture. Finally, I suggested that power is synonomous with Spearman's g factor and is assessed reasonably well by the Stanford-Binet. In this sense, power is a systems variable and high power should be associated with a generally efficient neuroanatomical and biophysical system. And that seems to be Terman's major finding, that is, that good things go together, that high Binet scores are associated with general mental and physical vigor and fitness. On the other hand, high scores seem much less closely related to mathematical reasoning, to leadership, and to athletic success, all of which require cognitive skills that are relatively independent of the speed with which a child acquires information through basically linguistic means.

Since Terman's initial book, there have been a large number of studies on the characteristics of adolescents with high test scores (see Gowan & Demos, 1964). Two of the more systematic of these are the Study of Mathematically Precocious Youth and the Study of Verbally Gifted Youth at Johns Hopkins University. In the first study (Stanley, Keating, & Fox, 1974; Keating, 1976), carried out between 1971 and 1976, students in the seventh, eighth, and early ninth grades who had scored at or above the 98th percentile on a standardized mathematics-achievement test were invited to participate in a mathematics talent search. In 1972, 396 students from the Baltimore/Washington area participated in the contest by taking the mathematical portion of the Scholastic Aptitude Test (SAT-M). In 1973, 953 adolescents took both SAT-M and the verbal portion of the SAT (SAT-V). Using a cutting score of 640 on SAT-M, 82 students were selected for further study. The average SAT-M score for these 14 year olds placed them above the 95th percentile for college-bound 17 year olds; as a group then, they displayed an extraordinary level of mathematical talent.

These mathematics-talent-search winners were given a rather extensive battery of noncognitive measures including:

1. CPI — the California Psychological Inventory (Gough, 1969), a well-standardized, multidimensional personality inventory designed to assess aspects of social or interpersonal behavior that underlie high-level achievement.

2. VPI — the Vocational Preference Inventory (Holland, 1973), another well-standardized personality test designed to assess six personality types defined in terms of certain underlying values and interests.

3. SVA — the Study of Values (Allport, Vernon, & Lindzey, 1970), also well standardized and also designed to assess six personality types defined in terms of underlying values, but differing from the VPI in that it is scored ipsatively.

4. ACL — the Adjective Check List (Gough & Heilbrun, 1965), a well-known measure of overt self-concept.

This battery of competently developed and extensively normed and validated personality measures afforded a superb opportunity to determine the noncognitive characteristics of adolescent giftedness defined in terms of very high SAT-M scores.

Considering first the CPI, a test designed principally for use with older groups, gifted adolescents compared favorably with adults on all the standard scales (see Keating, 1976, p. 231). They actually received higher scores than the average adult on scales for Achievement via Independence, Flexibility, and Femininity, indicating that as a group they were more openminded and intellectually motivated than the average adult. When compared with average 8th graders, these gifted youngsters received higher scores on 17 of the 18 standard CPI scales. The differences were most pronounced for the measures of academic and intellectual motivation, where the average score for the gifted group was about two standard deviations above that for unselected 8th graders. These data indicate rather clearly the advantage of the gifted sample across a broad range of traits known to be associated with social effectiveness and life accomplishment: assertiveness, ambition, self-confidence, dependability, self-control, and independence.

In terms of Holland's VPI, 67% of the mathematically gifted boys were classified as Investigative types, with the remaining members of the group spread fairly even over the other five types (see Keating, 1976, p. 236). Investigative persons, according to Holland, achieve through education, avoid social sistuations, are task-oriented, introspective, have unconventional values, and a high need for acquiring understanding and control. Their interests and preferred occupations are largely scientific and academic. Of the girls, 50%

were Investigative types, another 23% were Artistic types, who are rather similar but more original and intuitive than Investigative persons.

These findings were largely confirmed by the results obtained using the Allport-Vernon-Lindzey Study of Values. The majority of the group, boys and girls, were theoretical types; the items on the SV theoretical scale primarily reflect interest in science and mathematics, and according to the test authors, an "inclination to actively seek truth in a logical, often scientific manner" (1970, p. 4).

Finally, the ACL results rather clearly portray the dominant self-image of mathematically gifted boys. Relative to nongifted boys, the gifted group saw themselves as intelligent (96%), capable (93%), adaptable (89%), logical (87%), honest (85%), and clear-thinking (83%). They also described themselves as argumentative (67%) and sarcastic (52%), but obviously not with the same vehemence.

The overall impression one gains from these personality test data is that mathematically gifted boys are self-confident, mature, well adjusted, somewhat aggressive, and primarily oriented toward scientific and technical as opposed to social, artistic, or entrepreneurial activities. More or less, the same pattern of findings holds for mathematically gifted girls.

The Study of Verbally Gifted Youth was concerned with sociopolitical intelligence, defined as the ability to reason in a sound and defensible manner about complex moral and social issues (see Hogan et al., 1977). In 1972 and 1973 a verbal talent search was conducted. Through phone calls, letters, and newspaper and radio advertising, 12 and 13 year olds from all over Maryland and suburban Washington, D.C., were invited to take part in the contest, providing they could furnish evidence that they had scored at, or above, the 98th percentile on a standardized measure of verbal achievement. Qualified applicants ($N = 659$) then completed the verbal portion of the Scholastic Aptitude Test (SAT-V) and a personal data sheet. A total of 58 students with the highest SAT-V scores were invited back for additional testing and participation in a summer enrichment program. These 33 girls and 25 boys aged 12 and 13 had an average SAT-V score of 585, which would put them as a group at about the 90th percentile for college bound 17 and 18 year olds; in verbal ability, the sample represented perhaps the upper half of 1% of the 12 and 13 year olds in the Baltimore-Washington area.

These students subsequently completed an extensive battery of additional tests, including the CPI; a measure of Holland's types; MBTI — the Myers-Briggs Type Indicator (Myers, 1962); and CMT — the Terman Concept Mastery Test (Terman, 1956). The results obtained from these measures strongly confirm Terman's findings. The group was predominantly upper middle class; the parents were well educated (51% of the mothers and 71% of the fathers had at least a college degree) and 72% of the fathers were in professional vocations. In terms of the CPI, when the gifted sample was compared with youngsters their own age (see Lessinger & Martinson, 1961), they presented a picture of unusual personal soundness, social effectiveness, and maturity of interests. As with the mathmatically gifted, these adolescents were substantially more socially poised, mature, ambitious, intellectually motivated, and self-confident than their less gifted peers. The results based on the other personality measures largely corresponded to the findings reported for the mathematically gifted.

It is gratifying to see how these two contemporary studies provide confirmation of Terman's earlier conclusions; it also seems reasonable to expect that there would be important differences between adolescents who "win" a mathematical as opposed to a verbal talent search. Putting the point another way, the Stanford-Binet is a wide band-width test designed to assess intellectual power or g. But SAT-M and SAT-V are narrow band-width measures that perhaps might be able to tell us something about intellectual structure.

When the mathematically gifted winners were compared with the verbally gifted winners, using all the measures the two groups had in common, few interesting differences emerged (see Viernstein, Hogan, & McGinn, 1977). The mathematics group had higher scores for SAT-M; the verbal group had higher SAT-V scores. Other than these obvious differences, the personality measures indicated the two groups were composed of fundamentally the same kind of persons. For each student, however, it was possible to derive a special index by subtracting SAT-M from SAT-V; this index was called a V-M difference score and can be seen as a measure of one kind of intellectual structure. That is, it seems reasonable to assume that when the effects of g are held constant, verbal and mathematical talent may be independently disturbed in a population. Their relative dominance should have other consequences.

Viernstein, Hogan, & McGinn (1977) present correlations between V-M difference scores and a large number of other tests for a group of 85 boys taken from the mathematics and verbal samples. The correlations with SAT-V, SAT-M, and the Terman CMT are artifactual. The other correlations are interpretable and suggest that, within a gifted sample, persons with high V-M difference scores are original, initiutive, impractical, and intellectually curious with a wide range of interests. Gifted adolescents with low V-M difference scores are more focused, practical, hardheaded, and businesslike. The point to be remembered here is that within, for example, groups of engineers and literary critics there will be a range of V-M difference scores. The high scorers will share the characteristics listed above regardless of their actual vocation, and the same will be true of the low scorers. That is, there will be imaginative, intuitive engineers as well as no-nonsense, data-oriented literary critics, and vice versa.

CHARACTERISTICS OF ADOLESCENT ACHIEVERS

We turn now to an examination of the nature of giftedness defined in terms of achievement. Let us begin once again with Terman's research. Terman divided his male sample into subgroups including the 100 most and 100 least successful men, defined principally in terms of the degree to which a person "had made use of his superior intelligence in his life work" (Oden, 1968). This classification was carried out on two different occasions, apparently with good reliability. The evidence suggests the two groups were in fact quite distinct in terms of their achievement, for example, the A group (high achievers) had a median total family income in 1959 almost four times as large as the median income for the C group (low achievers). What other features were associated with Terman's A-C distinction?

Parents and teachers provided a number of trait ratings of the sample during adolescence. The A group was seen as significantly more curious, intelligent, commonsensical, persevering, ambitious, popular, leaderlike, conscientious and truthful — in a descending order. Similarly the A group as young adults were rated by Terman's staff (see Oden, 1968, p. 67) as betterlooking, more poised, friendly, alert, curious, and original than the C group. Terman interpreted the difference between the groups in terms of personality, arguing that success in life depended on persistence, originality, and "the possession in the highest degree of desire to excel" (1925, p. 180) in addition to intellectual talent.

The A group was also characterized in adolescence and even more prominently in early adulthood by satisfactory mental-health and social adjustment. Parents and teachers rated significantly more of the C group as having some, considerable, or serious difficulty with adjustment. Similarly, in adolescence the C group was much more likely than the A group to come from homes broken by either divorce or the death of a parent. More than twice as many divorces had occurred among C families by 1928.

These developmental data are very reassuring to persons with a bias toward personality theory; unfortunately the factors that most powerfully separate these two groups seem less directly related to personality dynamics than to certain factors in the subjects' educational histories. Some of these have little to do with the psychology of adolescence, but it seems important to review them to provide a proper interpretation of Terman's findings. The first of these is that during the school years the A group, although no brighter than the C group, was much more likely to be accelerated in grade placement and was involved in almost twice the number of extracurricular activities. In the long run, however, the most important factor distinguishing these two groups was whether or not they graduated from college (see Oden, 1968, p. 59, Table 26); 97% of the A group graduated, whereas only 40% of the C group did so.

When this statistic is followed up, several interesting related facts emerge. Thus among the fathers of the A group, 71% graduated from high school and 47% finished college; for the C group comparable figures are 47% and 25%. Similarly, 41% of the A fathers, but only 20% of the C fathers, were employed at a professional level. Later in their lives 86% of the A group said an adequate education contributed to their life accomplishment, 55% of the C group made this claim. Similarly 78% of the A's as compared to 22% of the C's expressed deep satisfaction and interest in their vocation in 1950. In response to a question about determinants of vocational choice, 68% of the A's, but only 23% of the C's, mentioned aptitude or interests; the ". . . most frequent influence on the vocational choice of the C's was financial necessity, reported by 44% of the C men but by only 17% of A men'' (Oden, 1968, p. 84). Not surprisingly, 91% of the A's, as compared with 28% of the C's, said they had as much schooling as they wanted; the most frequent explanation given by the C's was lack of money and/or parental support. And finally the two groups were strikingly different in terms of the direction and encouragement concerning schooling given by their parents. The A group was significantly more often encouraged to forge ahead in school, to do well, and to go to college (Oden, 1968, p. 83, Table 41).

The pattern that emerges here is that achievement in the Terman sample had clear socioeconomic correlates: it was a function of college graduation, which, in turn, was related to parental education, occupation, income, and aspirations for the child. For Terman's A group, then, life achievement seems as predictable from socioeconomic class as from "volitional" traits. These findings have important implications for interpreting the literature on giftedness defined as achievement. In virtually all these studies the socioeconomic composition of the sample is skewed to the upper end, suggesting that the giftedness literature largely describes the characteristics of upper-middle-class adolescents who also have high test scores. Interpretation of their achievement is invariably confounded by social-class considerations.

One way of evaluating the contribution of psychological factors to achievement, independent of social-class influences, might be to identify a group of high IQ working-class children and see if their life achievement approximated the achievement of Terman's group. Unfortunately, there is almost no research bearing on this issue, and what evidence there is does not help much. For example, Chambers (cited in Gowan and

Demos, 1964) followed up a group of gifted adolescents (IQ = 135) from St. Louis, paying particular attention to the 139 cases with the lowest socioeconomic status. Chambers found, as Terman did, that college graduation predicted occupational success better than IQ and that children who were able to transcend their early home environments were aided, encouraged, or stimulated by a person or agency outside the home. Chambers felt his results highlighted the importance of parental and environmental backgrounds in predicting life success.

If it is presently impossible to separate the contributions of giftedness and social advantage to adult achievement, then an alternative approach may be to inquire about the mechanisms by which social advantage is translated into individual achievement — the statistical generalization linking, for example, father's education and son's income can be alternatively analyzed. What is it that wealthy, well-educated fathers give to their sons that allows the sons to maintain their competitive edge in life's race?

Some information is provided in a study by Watley (1969), who followed up the first two groups of students selected as National Merit Scholars eight years after the first group had entered college. These students represented roughly the top 2% of all high-school students who entered the National Merit Scholar competition; their standings were determined by scores on two standardized tests — the National Merit Scholarship Qualifying Test and the SAT. Watley sorted the groups into four levels of academic achievement:

1. No BA/BS
2. BA/BS only
3. Some graduate work
4. Doctoral or professional degree

An examination of the factors predicting to differential academic progress in this uniformly talented sample is consistent with the foregoing discussion. So, for example, students who had completed graduate training had, relative to the other three groups, fathers who were better educated, in higher status occupations, and more affluent. Similarly, these students received significantly more support and encouragement at home with regard to their academic progress. Watley went beyond these socioeconomic or demographic predictors through an analysis of personality test data, in this case the CPI. The men who had made the least progress received the lowest scores in the sample for Dominance, Socialization, Self-Control, Tolerance, Achievement via Conformance, and Femininity; they received the highest scores for Flexibility. Watley (1969) interprets this as a sign of their poor emotional adjustment (this interpretation is consistent with Terman's view that his C group was also poorly adjusted). Unfortunately, Watley's interpretation is in error. The pattern of CPI results he reports indicates that his low-progress group was characterized not by feelings of neurotic distress but by alienation and disaffection, impulsiveness, narcissism, and self-indulgence. Indeed, relative to the other groups they had adequate self-esteem and were free of unreasonable self-doubts and neurotic preoccupations. Conversely, men who had finished their graduate or professional training received the highest scores for Dominance, Sociability, Achievement via Independence, and Femininity. Such persons are mature, planful, outgoing, and intellectually motivated. Their achievement seems to flow naturally from a well-integrated, amiable, and achievement-oriented personality. The CPI results for the high-achieving women indicated by contrast that they were somewhat passive, methodical, cooperative, industrious, and concerned with making a good impression. Watley's study allows three provisional conclusions. The first is that social advantage may be associated with a certain personality style. The second is that there is a certain personality style associated with achievement in gifted samples (Terman's earlier conclusion). The third is that these two styles are related. The first and third conclusions require further documentation; the second is well established, as the remainder of this section will demonstrate.

In a further study of academic attainment, Hogan and Weiss (1974) compared 54 male undergraduates at Johns Hopkins recently elected to Phi Beta Kappa with both a group of non-Phi Beta Kappas approximately matched for intellectual talent and a third group of unselected undergraduates. Most Johns Hopkins students (about 80%) major in premedical studies and the undergraduate environment is characterized by intense competition for grades; moreover, the Johns Hopkins Phi Beta Kappa chapter typically admits less than half the number of new members permitted by its charter, thereby maintaining quite rigorous admission standards. This, then, was a gifted sample defined by an exceptional level of academic performance, a level in fact attained by only a small percentage of Terman's A group. The three groups were compared using the CPI. The Phi Beta Kappa group differed from the other two by virtue of its high scores for Responsibility, Socialization, Self-Control, Achievement via Conformity, Femininity, and Empathy. In terms of general psychosocial maturity, this is an exceptionally favorable pattern of scores. Briefly, persons scoring high on these scales are responsible, mature, dependable. Perhaps they are overcontrolled at the expense of spontaneity, but they are intellectually motivated, even tempered, thoughtful, and considerate.

John Holland and his associates at the National Merit Scholarship Corporation provided an even more differentiated view of the nature of giftedness defined in terms of achievement. They carried out a series of longitudinal studies with National Merit Scholars, a group as noted above characterized by very high SAT scores. Sample sizes and test scores varied over time and across analyses, but for boys mean SAT-V scores ranged between 658 and 691. For girls they varied between 656 and 707. SAT-M scores for the boys ranged from 698 to 726; for the girls these mean scores were 635 and 673. The methodology in all these studies was the same: subjects were contacted by mail and completed a large number of scales and measures (which varied from year to year) designed to predict gifted performance in four areas — academics, art, science, and leadership. Despite the range of predictors used, the results converged nicely. Holland was unconcerned with demographic correlates of achievement; his findings with regard to the characteristics of academic achievement, however, are, as we shall see, remarkably consistent with those presented above.

There is a wealth of information in this fine series of investigations. The following summarizes the highlights. Perhaps the most important point, and certainly the dominant theme, of this research is that among gifted students academic performance is unrelated to creative achievement; as Holland (1961) observes: "Perhaps the most unequivocal finding in the present study is that, for samples of students of superior scholastic aptitude, creative performance is generally unrelated to scholastic achievement and scholastic aptitude" (p. 145). Practically, this can be interpreted as follows: if a student demonstrates creativity in science or art, then he or she probably has considerable academic potential (whether or not it is fully actualized in terms of course grades); on the other hand, if a student has high test scores, he or she may or may not be capable of creative achievement. This seems to be one of the most important generalizations to come out of research with the gifted and makes interpretable the relatively modest achievements of Terman's sample.

A second finding from Holland's research is that the best single predictor of both academic performance and creative achievement in high school, college, and beyond, is a biographical checklist. Again we see that the best predictor of future behavior is past behavior; students manifesting independent achievement in science or art in high school continued to do so in college and beyond. The incidence of creative achievement, however, was rather infrequent in the gifted sample.

A third finding is that in this gifted sample, self-ratings predicted both academic and creative performance. In particular, self-ratings for Perseverance and Self-Confidence (which also discriminated well between Terman's A and C groups) were — 35 years later — significantly correlated with both creative and academic performance in Holland's merit-scholar population. These findings suggest that adolescent achievers (academic or creative) see themselves as different from their peers, and the self-image is largely benevolent. They are neither alienated, disaffected nor ambivalent; rather they are self-confident, self-controlled, and self-directed (see also Douvan & Adelson, 1958).

Holland and Astin (1962) present concise data-based portraits of the personality styles of four types of gifted adolescent achievers, and these descriptions provide a still more differentiated view of the characteristics of giftedness. The first is called a social achiever, exemplified by outstanding performance as a leader in college. As adolescents these persons were dominant and aggressive, self-confident, sociable, enthusiastic, extroverted, responsible, and conventional. Interestingly, these student leaders gave themselves high ratings for originality and independence, but their self-ratings were not supported by any other data; rather these other data suggested the leaders were somewhat unoriginal, dependent, and lacking in self-sufficiency (p. 137).

Artistic achievers, the second type, resembled social achievers in that they were sociable, self-confident, and dominant (although less so than the leaders). In addition, they were original, complex in their outlook, and tolerant of ambiguity. They disliked practical and scientific vocations and planned artistic careers. Scientific achievers, the third type, were much less distinctive, largely because the incidence of scientific achievement was low in this otherwise gifted sample. Briefly scientific achievers were characterized by just that and by preference for scientific careers, high ratings (self and other) for originality, and mathematical aptitude.

The fourth type, called the academic achiever, was distinctive; the pattern of correlates of academic achievement in this gifted sample replicated rather closely the findings presented earlier in this chapter. Achievement was associated with self-control, ambition, perseverance, responsibility, dependability, intellectual motivation, and SAT scores. The best single predictor of college grades, not surprisingly, was high-school grades. Holland and Astin (1962) summarize their findings for academic achievement as follows:

> The academic achiever can be characterized as a person who got high grades in high school; conceives of himself as a good student; and is self-controlled, persistent, responsible . . . and passive. He comes from a family whose restrictiveness and striving attitudes may have been conducive to academic achievement with its emphasis on conformity. . . . (finally), the academic achiever has somewhat less potential for original behavior on *tests* of originality than the student who gets slightly lower grades. [P. 142]

One last study of the nature of giftedness defined as achievement should be mentioned. Following Holland's lead, Hogan et al. (1977) solicited applications for a third verbal talent search in 1975. From over 1000 applicants who were aged 13 and 14, 506 were selected on the basis of: (1) high test scores, (2) good grades, and (3) demonstrated nonacademic achievement in the arts, sciences, agriculture, neighborhood organizations, or other areas of real-life activity. These 506 completed the verbal portion of the Differential Aptitude Test (DAT); the Chapin Social Insight Test (Gough, 1965); a measure of creative potential — the Barron-Welsh Art Scale (Barron, 1965), and an accomplishments checklist. Students were then assigned scores on a regression equation that gave roughly equal weight to verbal talent (DAT), social intelligence (the Chapin test), creative potential (the art scale), and demonstrated accomplishment in leadership, mathematical/science, and art/writing. From the 506 subjects, 120 (58 boys, 62 girls) were selected for intensive counseling and study; these students completed a large battery of additional tests intended to reveal the characteristics of this group, which contained some very bright and surprisingly versatile young people.

The British might describe this group of 13- and 14-year-olds as ''all-rounders'' — they were intelligent, good students, and had demonstrated potential for nonacademic achievement. These students were compared with two other groups: (1) a sample of 58 comparably aged and gifted youngsters selected exclusively for their very high test scores and (2) an unselected group of 8th-graders. Relative to the other two student groups these student achievers were more dominant, sociable, self-confident, and autonomous but less conventional, responsible, and self-controlled. Their verbal test scores were lower than those for the group selected on the sole basis of high test scores, but they were more assertive, flamboyant, independent, and, of course, they had a record of independent, nonacademic achievement.

This discussion of giftedness defined in terms of achievement is only marginally useful for evaluating the model of intelligence presented in the third section of this chapter. The problem is that structure and style are confounded in achievement. Thus, as the Holland and Astin (1962) paper shows, scientific accomplishment depends on a combination of mathematical talent (presumably a structural variable) and originality (style again). Social achievement or leadership, given a certain level of power, seems almost entirely a matter of style. The point is, however, that due to the limitations of existing data this section has not been terribly useful as a means for evaluating theories of intelligence.

This section can be summarized as follows. Within any sample of youngsters with high test scores there will be considerable variation in life achievement. This achievement seems to be a function of social advantage and of a personality style marked by ambition, self-confidence and self-discipline, and early specialization in mathematics/science, the arts, or social participation — all reflected in biographical checklists. The relationship between social advantage and personality style is not well established and represents an important area for future research. On the other hand, the existing data are remarkably consistent in the view they present of giftedness defined in terms of precocious achievement. And these data suggest that when intellectual power and social advantage are held constant, the primary determinant of giftedness is intellectual structure (defined in terms of mathematical, verbal, or other specialized intellectual competencies) and personality style. It is to these stylistic aspects of gifted performance that we now turn.

VARIETIES OF INTELLECTUAL STYLE

In this section we are concerned not with the nature of giftedness or the characteristics of gifted achievement but with the varieties of intellectual style that can be found in gifted populations. The topic is similar to the subject of cognitive style that preoccupied personality researchers in the 1950s. Most of the research in this area has concerned creativity, and Getzels and Jackson's (1962) study was one of the first and most influential treatments of the topic. The stimulus for their research was their view that the study of giftedness had progressed very little since Terman's early work, largely because it was so closely tied to "the IQ metric." They point out that it has been a commonplace in educational psychology as far back as 1898 that, among college students, IQ and indexes of imagination and creativity are only modestly related. This suggests that the study of creativity in gifted samples would further advance our understanding of giftedness.

All students between grades 6 and 12 in a private school in the Chicago area were given a set of five face-valid measures of creativity. The average correlation between these measures and Stanford-Binet-based IQ scores was .25 ($N = 292$). Two groups were formed. The creative group ($N = 26$) were those in the top 20% on the creativity measures but below the top 20% in IQ; members of the intelligent group ($N = 28$) were in the top 20% in IQ but below the top 20% on the creativity measures.

These two groups were compared in terms of their scholastic achievement, academic motivation, public images as reported by teachers, and attitudes toward adult life. Both groups received significantly better grades than the average for their school. Surprisingly, the creative group had the best academic record, despite an average IQ (127) 5 points below the school average and 23 points below the average for the high-IQ group. The groups did not differ on a fantasy-based (TAT) measure of achievement motivation. Teachers seemed to like the high-IQ group better than the creative group, although the difference seems not to have been statistically significant. Finally, for the high-IQ group there was good agreement between the traits or qualities they valued in themselves and those that they thought would lead to success in adult life; similarly there was close agreement between the qualities they would like to see in their ideal selves and the qualities of which they thought their teachers would approve. For the creative group, however, no such good agreement obtained; although the creative group knew what qualities were required for teacher approval and for success in adult life, they did not see these qualities as desirable in or for themselves. Interestingly, one quality that the creatives valued much more highly than the high-IQ group was a sense of humor.

In the years following the publication of Getzels and Jackson's (1962) book, a considerable controversy boiled up over whether measures of creativity are in fact independent (uncorrelated) of measures of intelligence. In the course of this controversy, however, an important conclusion from their work seems to have been forgotten. This concerned the consequences of creativity as an intellectual style, that, in a gifted sample, high-creative/low-IQ children are autonomous, unconventional, playful, and achievers, despite not being well liked by teachers. Conversely, low-creative/high-IQ children are dependent, conventional, somewhat humorless achievers who are well liked by teachers. Thus, Getzels and Jackson's measures of "creativity" seemed to tap aspects of intellectual style that have important behavioral consequences.

In perhaps the most important follow-on study of Getzels and Jackson's research, Wallach and Kogan (1965) demonstrated that, with the appropriate procedural modifications, it is possible to separate measures of "creativity" from measures of intelligence. They described children who were high and low on these dimensions. Their subjects were younger than Getzels and Jackson's students, and a much larger range of scores was present in the sample. Nonetheless, certain convergences emerged. So, for example, children low on both dimensions were basically inept. The "double-highs" (high IQ/high creatives) were mature, competent, flexible, spontaneous and/or appropriately self-controlled. The low-IQ, high-creative students were conflicted, nonconforming, self-doubting, and underproductive — probably because they were not as intelligent as Getzels and Jackson's low-IQ/high-creative group. The low-creativity/high-IQ group was academically motivated, compulsive grade-getters, conforming, and dependent. On classification tasks they strongly preferred abstract, formal bases for classification. This choice was not dictated by competence; it was genuinely one of preference. This led Wallach and Kogan to conclude that preference for abstract, formal modes of classification is a kind of defense mechanism. If such classificatory preferences are also characteristic of formal operational thought in a Piagetian sense, and such a supposition seems reasonable, then this intellectual style is not the hallmark of mature intelligence; rather it may derive from darker and less rational sources in the psyche. In any case, Wallach and Kogan summarize their conclusion as follows, ". . . consideration of [a] child's *joint* status with regard to the conventional concept of general intelligence and creativity as here defined is evidently of critical importance in the search for a new knowledge concerning children's thinking" (1965, p. 303).

Welsh (1977) studied the relationship between intelligence and creativity in more than 1000 highly gifted and talented adolescents attending the Governor's School of North Carolina. Intelligence was defined by scores on Terman's (1956) Concept Mastery Test (CMT); creative potential was defined by scores on the revised art scale of the Welsh Figure Preference Test (Welsh, 1959), a well-validated measure of creative performance. The data indicate that these two measures are relatively independent, and they were in this sample. Welsh plotted test scores on two orthogonal axes and defined four groups of gifted adolescents falling into the four quadrants of the bivariate plot:

- High art scale, low CMT.
- High on both.
- Low on both.
- Low art scale, high CMT.

Actual cutting scores are presented in Welsh (1975).

Since the entire population was uniformly able, Welsh assumed the differences among the groups were largely a function of differences in intellectual style. All students completed the Adjective Check List (Gough & Heilbrun, 1965), the MMPI (Dahlstrom, Welsh & Dahlstrom, 1972), and the Strong Vocational Interest Blank (Strong, 1959). Item analyses allowed Welsh to develop a rather complete psychological interpretation of each type. Finally, two hypothetical dimensions of intellectual style (Welsh calls them personality dimensions — from the context of his article, however, he seems to mean dimensions of cognitive style) were proposed to account for the fourfold typology derived from the item analysis. With some disregard for literary style, Welsh calls these dimensions Intellectence and Origence.

Persons at the low end of the Intellectence dimension (regardless of their CMT scores) are literalistic, concrete, pragmatic, and interested in solving practical problems; such persons are also sociable and take a personal interest in others. Persons at the high end of this dimension of cognitive style are interested in figurative, abstract, and symbolic expressions of generalized principles (formal operations again?). With regard to other people, according to Welsh (1975), these people are impersonal and even unsocial.

Persons at the low end of the Origence dimension, whatever their tested intelligence, prefer orderly, structured, predictable environments where problems can be solved by conventional and well-defined methods. They do well in academic settings that stress rote memory and the mastery of a body of factual content; socially they seem persistent, planful, self-effacing, and deferential to authority. Persons at the high end often seem rebellious and nonconforming as a result of their penchant for doing things their own way. They are often interested in artistic or aesthetic problems that do not have an obviously correct answer or a practical application. They do well in academic settings requiring initiative, imagination, and independent study.

Using all the test data available to him, Welsh provides a convincing account of the consequences of variations in these two dimensions of intellectual style in a gifted sample. Persons who are high origence/low intellectence are sociable, affiliative and impulsive; they are nonconforming, and reactors rather than initiators. Their thinking tends to be diffuse, imprecise, and fantasy-based, and they gravitate toward histrionic vocations — the performing arts and sales occupations.

High origence/high intellectence persons are introverted, detached, autonomous, and self-sufficient, with unconventional and unorthodox attitudes and ideas. Their thinking tends to be synthetic, concerned with imposing order, proceeding in an intuitive, metaphorical manner, and they select intellectual occupations — careers in art, journalism, and literature.

Gifted adolescents characterized as low origence/low intellectence are, according to Welsh, indiscriminately sociable and friendly, dependent, self-effacing, conforming, prudent, and orthodox. Their thinking tends to be plodding, detailed, factual, and lacking integration, and they move toward commercial, business, and service occupations.

Finally, low origence/high intellectence students are friendly but shy and guarded in social interaction. They are inner-directed; independent, but conventional-rule followers. Their thinking tends to be logical, deliberate, analytical, tending toward specific answers and solutions with little attention to overall synthesis. Such persons choose practical, scientific, and professional careers, for example, engineering, law, medicine.

Welsh's (1977) discussion of the intellectence/origence distinction and the typologies derived from it is the end point and high watermark of the intelligence-creativity debate that lasted through the 1960s. His data strongly suggest that he has identified two important and fundamental dimensions of intellectual style that have important consequences for understanding the performance of gifted adolescents.

A review of one last research program will round out this discussion of variations in intellectual style. In an investigation of sociopolitical intelligence in gifted adolescents, Hogan et al. (1977) studied 177 winners (aged 12 to 14) of the verbal talent search described above. The total sample consisted of 57 boys and girls selected solely on the basis of high SAT-V scores and 120 boys and girls selected on the basis of a combination of high SAT-V scores *and* demonstrated accomplishment. These students completed a seven-week college-level course in either literature or social science taught by the staff of *"Study of Verbally Gifted Youth."* The students were carefully observed during class sessions; at the end of the course they were assigned ratings in accordance with the degree to which they seemed able to reach sound, defensible conclusions when discussing complex moral and political issues. Three findings emerged from this initial study of the determinants of mature sociopolitical reasoning:

1. There was considerable variation within the two subsamples, such that only a few seemed to be impressively cogent and insightful in their reasoning.

2. Ratings for mature sociopolitical reasoning were significantly correlated (on the order of about .40) with verbal intelligence scores, despite the restrictions in range inherent in these samples.

3. Ratings for socio-political reasoning were also associated with a distinctive pattern of personality characteristics, defined in terms of the CPI, which included self-confidence, responsibility, and intellectual motivation.

These findings were pursued in greater detail in two subsequent studies. Using a sociopolitical-reasoning problem developed by Adelson, Green, and O'Neil (1969), Daurio (1976) tested 38 white, middle-class, very bright youngsters, ranging in age from 8 to 14. The test problem had to do with regulating cigarette smoking on an imaginary island utopia. Specifically the problem concerned: Whether to regulate smoking? What to do if the regulation didn't work? How best to justify either regulation or nonregulation? Responses were scored in terms of predefined categories, and the scoring had good interrater reliability. These categories included:

1. A disposition to see the problem in a context broader than that immediately given.
2. A disposition to see laws not merely as restraining undesirable actions but as actually promoting human welfare.
3. A disposition to revise or repeal laws that clearly do not work.
4. A disposition to impose draconian punishment on rule violators.

Taken together the scoring categories furnished a rough index of the quality of a child's sociopolitical reasoning, so that, for example, mature responses: (1) placed the problem in the broader context of regulating by law not merely smoking but human affairs in general, (2) regarded law as a potential means of promoting human welfare, (3) indicated a willingness to revise laws that do not work, and (4) imposed punishments proportionate to the nature of the offense committed.

Four findings from Daurio's (1975) paper are important. First, his findings replicated those reported earlier by Adelson, et al. (1969), who used a slightly older and less talented sample. Second, Adelson, Green, and O'Neil (1969) found a significant transition in the quality of sociopolitical reasoning at about age 15.5, after this point most adolescents gave relatively mature responses as defined above. However, Daurio found in his very-bright sample that the transition occurred at about age 13.6. Third, four of the seven scoring categories were significantly correlated with age (average $r = .40$), nonetheless, even among the oldest and brightest students there were substantial differences in reasoning ability. This means, then, that only on-the-average do gifted children display more mature sociopolitical reasoning than same aged, nongifted peers. Finally, the three components of reasoning that were uncorrelated with age were very interesting. These components dealt with paying attention to consequences, revising laws that did not work, and the quality of punishment meted out for rule violation.

Daurio (1978) then gave this problem to 138 winners in the third verbal talent search described above (see Hogan et al., 1977); that is, 8th- and 9th-grade boys and girls selected on the basis of high test scores, academic and nonacademic achievement. Responses to the problem were scored for the same categories described earlier. These scores were intercorrelated, the resulting matrix was submitted to a principal components factor analysis, and three orthogonal items (two of which were unrelated to age in the foregoing analysis) were identified. These three aspects of sociopolitical reasoning (willingness to revise unworkable laws; willingness to compromise; willingness to evaluate a law in terms of its consequences) were combined to yield one score for sociopolitical intelligence (SPI). The seven items from the original interview protocol had an average correlation of .60 with scores for SPI. Nonetheless, these scores correlated only .15 with scores on Terman's CMT, suggesting SPI is independent of conventional IQ in gifted samples.

The reasoning style defined by scores for SPI is not uniformly present in gifted samples, but seems, like originality, to be an important dimension of individual differences. To further objectify this aspect of intellectual style, scores for sociopolitical intelligence were correlated with the CPI. The resulting correlations indicated that gifted adolescents capable of mature sociopolitical reasoning received, relative to other gifted adolescents, high scores for Dominance, Capacity for Status, Self-Acceptance, Responsibility, Achievement via Independence, Intellectual Efficiency, Femininity, Empathy, and Autonomy. This is an exceptionally favorable pattern of CPI scores, reflecting maturity, self-confidence, a wide range of interests, intellectual independence, and a judicious, even-handed interpersonal style.

Considerable work remains to be done in the analysis of sociopolitical intelligence before the concept is as well specified as Welsh's concepts of intellectence and origence. Nonetheless, Daurio's findings (which, incidentally replicated nicely a nongifted sample) seem to be an important contribution to the analysis of the varieties of intellectual style.

EDUCATING THE GIFTED

Because gifted students have unusual capabilities, it is often assumed that they should be provided unusual educational nourishment in order to allow them to develop their unique talents. If special opportunities are deemed necessary and/or desirable, the question becomes, "What form should these take?" There are basically two alternatives: acceleration or enrichment. Acceleration means moving students through the school system at a rate faster than normal. Enrichment means providing students with more educational resources than they might normally expect but not advancing them relative to their peers. What are the consequences of these forms of special education for the gifted? That is, what are the implications of enrichment and/or acceleration for the emotional and the educational development of the pupils affected?

Concerning the consequences of enrichment for the emotional adjustment of gifted students, little systematic research seems to have been conducted on the topic (see Daurio, in preparation). Martinson (1960) evaluated the effects of the special enrichment programs for the gifted in California in the 1950s. Her evaluation is largely in the form of a testimonial. Nonetheless, she concluded that gifted adolescents who were also good students, with positive attitudes toward school and popular with their peers, did not suffer socially as a result of participating in enrichment programs. Nor are there any strong theoretical grounds for assuming that enrichment per se would adversely affect students' social adjustment.

With regard to acceleration, however, there are good theoretical and empirical reasons for thinking that it would affect childrens' adjustment. For example, boys who are late maturers (i.e., young relative to their peers) seem to have characteristic problems fitting in with their peer groups (see Clausen, 1975). These problems will only be exacerbated when boys are accelerated in school. Most studies bearing on this issue report that accelerated students experience some disruption in their social relationships. Thus even so enthusiastic an advocate of acceleration as Terman reports: "The group that skipped shows, somewhat more frequently than the normal-progress group, decreased fondness for school," and ". . . the very highly accelerated are somewhat oftener rated 'below average' in social adaptability than is true of the entire group of gifted children; they are also rated somewhat oftener as playing less than the average amount" (1925, p. 629). Keys (1938) studied 348 students who were under 16.5 on their entering the University of California at Berkeley during the period from 1922 to 1930. As he notes, "more of the younger entrants at the University of California considered their undergraduate social relations as unsatisfactory" (p. 263), than did a control group of undergraduates.

It seems clear that students who are accelerated in high school and college report a relatively greater incidence of disturbed social relationships than their nonaccelerated peers. The problem is how to interpret these findings. These students are typically very bright, they excel in their studies, and their social disaffection might well be a function of the zeal with which they plunge into their studies. That is, these zealous students might have had social adjustment problems independent of their acceleration. It is presently impossible to decide on the correct interpretation.

The next question concerns the educational benefits associated with enrichment and acceleration. Here the data seem consistent with a general principle that might be described as "the more, the more," that is, the brighter and more motivated the child, the more he or she will profit from any kind of enrichment program. So, for example, Stanley and his associates (1974) have demonstrated that 4.5 years of precalculus mathematics can be taught to very able seventh and eighth graders in as few as 120 hours (see Stanley, Keating, & Fox, 1974; Fox, 1974). Similarly, Hogan and his associates (1977) conducted a college-level introduction to the social sciences during successive summers for students with very high verbal intelligence. During the first summer the students also received a course of programmed instruction in creative thinking (Covington et al., 1972). After only 14 hours of instruction, scores on Terman's CMT increased significantly in both groups, despite the fact that vocabulary building was not a deliberate or even intended part of the curriculum. On the other hand, divergent thinking, assessed by means of the Remote Associates Test (Mednick & Mednick, 1967) and the Guilford Consequences Test (Wilson, Guilford, & Christensen, 1953), improved only in the group receiving instruction in creative thinking. Along the same lines, one clearly stated curriculum goal was to improve the quality of the students' reasoning about complex social and moral issues. The consensus of the staff, however, was that the students' reasoning remained about the same despite a good deal of explicit and direct feedback on their performance; unfortunately, this observation was not supported by any quantitative data.

Perhaps the most reasonable conclusion that can be reached regarding the effects of enrichment and acceleration programs for the gifted is that such programs promote the rapid assimilation of established knowledge — as exemplified in the content of most academic courses. There is no data to suggest that such programs foster the capacity for imagination, integration, or synthesis. Nor is there much reason to believe that we educators know how to train these dispositions. It is difficult to show empirically that such programs do much good, but happily they do not seem to do much harm either. Perhaps the major single benefit to be derived from them is one that has not been investigated, indeed it has been rarely discussed, and that regards the contact with other precocious or talented peers. These contacts may serve to reduce childish egocentrism and give children perspective on the nature and limits of their talents and capabilities.

REFERENCES

Adelson, J., Green, B., and O'Neil, R. Growth of the idea of law in adolescence. *Developmental Psychology*, 1969, *1*, 327–332.

Allport, G. W., Vernon, P. E., and Lindzey, G. *Manual for the study of values*. Boston: Houghton Mifflin, 1970

Barron, F. The psychology of creativity. In T. M. Newcomb (Ed.), *New directions in psychology* (Vol. 2). New York: Holt, Rinehart & Winston, 1965.

Bernstein, B. Language and social class. *British Journal of Sociology*, 1960, *11*, 271–276.

Bouchard, T. J. Current conceptions of intelligence and their implications for assessment. In P. McReynolds (Ed.), *Advances in psychological assessment* (Vol. 1). Palo Alto, Calif.: Science and Behavior Books, 1968.

Bruner, J. Inhelder and Piaget's *The growth of logical thinking*. A psychologist's viewpoint. *British Journal of Psychology*, 1959, *50*, 363–370.

Butcher, H. J. *Human intelligence: Its nature and assessment*. London: Methuen, 1968.

Cattell, R. B. Theory of fluid and crystallized intelligence: A critical experiment. *Journal of Educational Psychology*, 1963, *54*, 1–22.

Chambers, C. P. "A follow-up study of gifted St. Louis pupils of 1920's." Unpublished doctoral dissertation, Washington University, Missouri, 1956.

Clausen, J. A. The social meaning of differentiated physical and sexual maturation. In S. E. Dragastin and G. H. Elder, Jr., (Eds.), *Adolescence in the life cycle*. Washington, D. C.: Hemisphere, 1975.

Cooley, W. W. Who needs general intelligence. In L. B. Resnick (Ed.), *The nature of intelligence*. Hillsdale, N. J.: Erlbaum, 1976.

Covington, M. V., Crutchfield, R. S., Davies, L., and Olton, R. M. *The productive thinking program*. Columbus, Ohio: Merrill, 1972.

Daurio, S. P. The development of political reasoning in verbally talented children. Paper, Eastern Psychological Association, New York, 1975.

———. The development of sociopolitical intelligence. Unpublished doctoral dissertation, The Johns Hopkins University, 1978.

———. Educational enrichment versus acceleration: A review of the literature. In W. C. George, S. J. Cohn, and J. C. Stanley (Eds.), *Acceleration and enrichment: Strategies for educating the gifted,* in preparation.

Douvan, E., and Adelson, J. The psychodynamics of social mobility in adolescent boys. *Journal of Abnormal and Social Psychology*, 1958, *56*, 31–44.

Dahlstrom, W. G., Welsh, G. S., and Dahlstrom, L. E. *An MMPI handbook, Vol. II*. Minneapolis: University of Minnesota Press, 1975.

French, J. W., Ekstrom, R. B., and Price, L. A. *Kit of reference tests for cognitive factors*. Princeton, N.J.: Educational Testing Service, 1963.

Galton, F. *Hereditary genius*. New York: Appleton, 1869.

Getzels, J. W., and Jackson, P. W. *Creativity and intelligence*. New York: Wiley, 1962.

Goddard, H. H. *Human efficiency and levels of intelligence*. Princeton, N.J.: Princeton University Press, 1920.

Gough, H. G. A validational study of the Chapin social insight test. *Psychological Reports,* 1965, *17*, 355–368.

Gough, H. G. *Manual for the California psychological inventory* (Rev. ed.). Palo Alto, Calif.: 1969.

Gough, H. G. Varieties of intellectual experience. In F. E. Aboud and R. D. Meade (Eds.), *Cultural factors in learning and education.* Bellingham: Western Washington State College, 1974.

Gough, H. G., and Heilbrun, A. B., Jr. *The adjective check list manual.* Palo Alto, Calif.: Consulting Psychologists Press, 1965.

Gowan, J. C., and Demos, G. D. *The education and guidance of the ablest.* Springfield, Ill.: Thomas, 1964.

Hogan, R. Research considerations in ethical education. Paper presented at the American Educational Research Association, New York, 1977.

Hogan, R., and Weiss, D. Personality correlates of superior academic achievement. *Journal of Counseling Psychology,* 1974, *21,* 144–149.

Hogan, R., Viernstein, M. C., McGinn, P. V., Daurio, S., and Bohannon, W. Verbal giftedness and sociopolitical intelligence. *Journal of Youth and Adolescence,* 1977, *6,* 107–116.

Holland, J. L. The prediction of college grades from the California psychological inventory and the scholastic aptitude test. *Journal of Educational Psychology,* 1959, *50,* 135–142.

———. Creative and academic performance among talented adolescents. *Journal of Educational Psychology,* 1961, *52,* 136–147.

———. *Making vocational choices.* Englewood Cliffs, N.J.: Prentice-Hall, 1973.

Holland, J. L., and Astin, A. W. The prediction of the academic, artistic, scientific, and social achievement of undergraduates of superior scholastic aptitude. *Journal of Educational Psychology,* 1962, *53,* 132–143.

Holland, J. L., and Richards, J. M. Academic and nonacademic accomplishment: Correlated or uncorrelated? *Journal of Educational Psychology,* 1965, *56,* 165–174.

Keating, D. P. (Ed.). *Intellectual talent: Research and development.* Baltimore, Md.: The Johns Hopkins University Press, 1976.

Keys, N. *The underage student in high school and college.* Berkeley: University of California Press, 1938.

Lessinger, L. M., and Martinson, R. A. The use of the California psychological inventory with gifted pupils. *Personnel and Guidance Journal,* 1961, *39,* 572–575.

Luria, A. R. *The mind of a mnemonist.* New York: Basic Books, 1968

———. *Cognitive development: Its cultural and social foundations.* Cambridge: Harvard University Press, 1976.

Martinson, R. A. The California study of programs for gifted pupils. *Exceptional Children,* 1960, *26,* 339–343.

McNemar, Q. Lost: Our intelligence. Why? *American Psychologist,* 1964, *19,* 871–882.

Mednick, S. A., and Mednick, M. T. *Examiner's manual: Remote associates test.* Boston: Houghton Mifflin, 1967.

Myers, I. B. *The Myers-Briggs type indicator manual.* Princeton, N.J.: Educational Testing Service, 1962.

Oden, M. H. The fulfillment of promise: 40-year follow-up of the Terman gifted group. *Genetic Psychology Monographs,* 1968, *77,* 3–95.

Price-Williams, D. R. *Explorations in cross-cultural psychology.* San Francisco: Chandler & Sharp, 1975.

Resnick, L. B. (Ed.). *The nature of intelligence.* Hillsdale, N.J.: Erlbaum, 1976.

Spearman, C. *The abilities of man.* New York: Macmillan, 1927.

Stanley, J. S., Keating, D. P., and Fox, L. H. (Eds.). *Mathematical talent: Discovery, description, and development.* Baltimore, Md.: The Johns Hopkins University Press, 1974.

Strong, E. K. *Manual: Strong vocational interests blanks*. Stanford, Calif.: Stanford University Press, 1959.

Terman, L. M. *Genetic studies of genius: Vol. I. Mental and physical traits of a thousand gifted children*. Stanford, Calif.: Stanford University Press, 1925.

———. *Concept mastery test manual*. New York: Psychological Corporation, 1956.

Tuddenham, R. D. The nature and measurement of intelligence. In L. Postman (Ed.), *Psychology in the making*. New York: Knopf, 1964.

Viernstein, M. C., Hogan, R., and McGinn, P. V. Personality correlates of differential verbal and mathematical ability in talented adolescents. *Journal of Youth and Adolescence, 1977, 6,* 169–178.

Vygotsky, L. S. *Thought and language*. Cambridge: M.I.T. Press, 1962.

Watley, D. J. Career progress: A longitudinal study of gifted students. *Journal of Counseling Psychology, 1969, 16,* 100–108.

Wallach, M. A., and Kogan, N. *Modes of thinking in young children*. New York: Holt, Rinehart & Winston, 1965.

Webb, R. A. (Ed.). *Social development in childhood*. Baltimore, Md.: The Johns Hopkins University Press, 1978.

Welsh, G. S. *Creativity and intelligence: A personality approach*. Chapel Hill, N.C.: Institute for Research in Social Science, 1975.

———. Personality correlates of intelligence and creativity in gifted adolescents. In J. C. Stanley, W. C. George, and C. H. Solano (Eds.), *The gifted and the creative: A fifty-year perspective*. Baltimore, Md.: The Johns Hopkins University Press, 1977.

Wilson, R. C. Guilford, J. P., and Christensen, P. L. The measurement of individual differences in originality. *Psychological Bulletin, 1953, 50,* 362–370.

Zajonc, R. B. Family configuration and intelligence. *Science, 1976, 192,* 227–236.

CHAPTER 18

Youth Movements

Richard G. Braungart

Young people have always been impatient with the traditional order, and their behavior and activities have been the focus of considerable attention throughout ancient, medieval, and modern times. Carved on a 4000-year-old tablet discovered on the site of the Biblical city of Ur is the following inscription, "Our civilization is doomed if the unheard-of actions of our younger generations are allowed to continue" (Lauer, 1973, p. 176). Over the centuries, issues surrounding the problems of children and youth have been discussed in the writings of Plato — *Laws* and the *Republic;* Aristotle — *Nicomachean Ethics* and *Politics;* Comenius — *The Great Didactic;* Locke — *Essay Concerning Human Understanding* and *Treatise on Civil Government;* Rousseau — *Emile;* Schiller — *The Robbers;* Goethe — *Sorrows of Young Werther;* and G. S. Hall —*Adolescence.*

Although the status of youth has been a constant source of strain in history, youth movements have emerged periodically as formidable agents of social and political change (Eisenstadt, 1956; Feuer, 1969, 1975; Ortega y Gasset, 1958; Westby, 1976). Most members of society in the course of their lives experience frustration and the desire for change. When established institutions fail to meet or to represent the legitimate needs of groups in society and when a significant number of people become aware of their common plight and feel something can be done to alleviate their dissatisfaction, social movements may appear. The perceived discrepancy between the individual needs or aspirations of young people and the existing social and political conditions lies at the root of youth movements (Heberle, 1951; Killian, 1966; Sherif & Sherif, 1969; Bakke & Bakke, 1971; Demerath, Marwell, & Aiken, 1971; Liebert, 1971; Oberschall, 1973; Hendin, 1975; Ash-Garner, 1977).

The Protestant Reformation provides one example of a youth movement in the early sixteenth century. Young Luther published his Ninety-five Theses at Wittenberg University in 1517. During this period, Wittenberg boasted of the youngest faculty in the history of German universities, with many of the most brilliant faculty in their early or mid-20s. These ecclesiastical rebels became Luther's followers, known as the "Wittenberg Reformers" (Moller, 1968). Aries (1965, pp. 317–318) vividly described a youth protest in 1646 at an English Jesuit college, the Prytanée of La Flèche, France, in which indiscipline and rebellion were everywhere. According to his report, youth occupied the school for two days and hoisted the red flag of rebellion. Troops with fixed bayonets were called in to suppress the uprising, whereupon the youth set fire to their books and desks and withdrew to an island that had to be taken by military force.

Gillis (1974) linked the rise of youth movements in Europe after the 1770s to the breakup of the generational continuity of the family as a result of the industrial revolution. Large numbers of young people were cut adrift from their homes and occupations as the economy moved from the traditional guild system toward a capitalist class society. Many youth were forced to migrate to cities to look for work and became a "lodger" or "boarder" population. The *Wanderjahr* tradition became established during the 1800s as youth roamed and "promenaded" aimlessly in search of a more permanent identity. In Manchester, England, youthful gang rivalries were known as "skuttling," and town and gown riots broke out throughout Europe.

In colonial America in the early 1770s, the nationalist revolutionary spirit pervaded the Harvard campus and all of the nine existing colleges either closed down or limited their operations because most of their students had joined the militia or Continental Army (Lipset, 1976). For a half century after the Revolution, college youth regularly engaged in protests, some quite violent, directed mainly against the university for various deficiencies. Samuel Eliot Morison (1936, p. 185) described the typical student of the early 1790s as an "atheist in religion, an experimentalist in morals, a rebel to authority." Throughout the nineteenth century, Lipset (1976) documented numerous youth riots at Harvard, Princeton, Yale, and the University of Virginia. Abolitionist clubs appeared on many Northern college campuses in the 1830s and 1840s and were described as "a revolt of the young" (Lauer, 1973, p. 182).

As early as 1850, antitraditionalist sentiment was leveled at Czarist Russia by dissident youth. Strikes and protests were reported to be increasing at the University of Moscow, and from 1887 onward, they became an annual campus-based ritual. Young students and free-floating intellectuals (*Freischwebende Intelligenz*) played a major part in the French Revolution, in Meiji Japan, and in the Bolshevik Revolution. Youth organizations (German *Wandervogel, Jungdeutschlandbund, Freikorps;* Italian *Avanguardia Universitaria, Gruppi Universitari Fascisti*) were also readily recruited into the European fascist movements as well as into the Indian (*Satyagraha*) and Chinese Communist revolutions (Braungart, 1969; Laqueur, 1969). Since World War II, youth have demonstrated considerable activity, contributing to the overthrow of political regimes in Africa, Asia, the Middle East, and Latin America (Lipset, 1967; Emmerson, 1968; Lipset & Altbach, 1969; Krauss, 1974).

YOUTH

Youth is defined as a biosocial age stratum in society, following childhood and adolescence and preceding adulthood. This transitional stage in the life cycle is considered to begin somewhere between the ages of 14 and 19 and to continue until approximately 22 to 25 years of age or when youth leave school and enter the labor market on a full-time basis (Flacks, 1971; Keniston, 1971; Coleman, 1974; Gordon & Gaitz, 1976). Empirical evidence is mounting that suggests that specific biosocial changes occur in each stage of the life cycle and are such that certain needs and developments are considered more important at one stage than at another (Ausubel & Sullivan, 1972; Gordon & Gaitz, 1976). The stage of the life cycle defined as youth is considered crucial for the development of:

1. Formal, critical thinking and future orientation (Piaget, 1967).

2. The evaluation of moral principles and values in society (Kohlberg, 1964; Piaget, 1965).

3. The conscious search for self-identity (Erikson, 1968).

Beginning in adolescence and continuing through the stage of youth, young people gradually expand their intellectual horizons and attempt to define their relationship to society. It is during this period that youth search for a sense of fidelity — a congruence in ideals, beliefs, and actions — within themselves, their parents, peers, and in society at large.

Eisenstadt (1956), Erikson (1959, 1963, 1968), Parsons (1963) and Keniston (1971) have all discussed the period of youth as a time and source of strain or tension between self and society. Forced to play an alienated role in society, youth interact less within the particularistic, ascriptive, diffuse spheres of the family and at the same time have not yet been included in the universalistic, personal-achievement oriented, and functionally specific occupational spheres they will someday enter. As a result, total identification with societal institutions is prolonged and problematic. However frustrating, this period of "intransigency of reality" has its positive effect — it allows youth a kind of breathing space between childhood and adulthood for the purpose of playing at or testing role alternatives required of future professional and adult commitments.

Awareness and concern with the sociopolitical world increase during youth (Connell, 1971), but the extent of this concern is determined largely through political socialization (Hyman, 1959; Block, Haan, & Smith, 1968; Orum, 1972; Jaros, 1973; Dennis, 1973a; Niemi, 1974a; Schwartz & Schwartz, 1975). Political socialization begins in early childhood and is described as a general cognitive, affective, and motivational predisposition toward politics. By the middle and upper elementary school grades, children acquire political knowledge and facts (Greenstein, 1968; Hess & Torney, 1968); during adolescence and youth, their ability to conceptualize on a higher symbolic or ideological level increases rapidly (Douvan & Gold, 1966; Adelson, 1971, 1975); and in the adult years, greater emphasis is placed on the formal aspects of politics, such as issues, candidates, and programs (Dawson & Prewitt, 1969; Sigel, 1970; Dennis, 1973b; Niemi, 1974b; Abramson, 1975; Milbrath & Goel, 1977). It is during the socialization period, somewhere between adolescence and early adulthood, that youth are drawn into radical social movements. Although the intensity of political behavior appears to result in part from their heightened psychosocial energy, the ideological direction youth follows generally remains consistent with what they have learned in the home (Flacks, 1967; Braungart & Braungart, 1975).

In recent history, the presence of large numbers of young people throughout the world appears to be related to social and political change (Moller, 1968; Gillis, 1974; Kearney & Jiggins, 1975). Demographic growth during the 1960s, both in the significant numbers of youth and the increased proportion of students attending colleges and universities across the country, provides some indication about the origin and nature of youth movements. Although the average total population increase in the United States from 1960 to 1968 for all age groups was 12%, the age group 18 to 24 experienced a 43% increase — the largest increment for all age cohorts during that time period. This rapid increase stands in sharp contrast to the population growth from 1950 to 1960. Whereas the overall growth rate during the 1950s was 19%, the growth rate for youth between the ages of 18 and 24 was −1% (Douglas, 1970). These figures provide a clue to the numerical impact this age group had on society over the last two decades. The surge in the youth population, however, is not expected to continue indefinitely. Although Ryder (1974) reported the 14- to 24-year-old age cohort grew by 52% during the 1960s, he predicts only an 11% increase in the 1970s and an 8% decline in the adolescent/youth population during the 1980s. The ratio of younger to older age groups is expected to decline, with older age groups predicted to experience dramatic increases in the coming decades (Ryder, 1974).

The earlier predictions that the World War II baby boom would have an unprecedented impact on American society were borne out. The sudden appearance of large numbers of young people in this country during the 1960s had a direct effect on higher education. For example, the number of youth per 100 persons 18 to 24 years of age enrolled in institutions of higher education in 1946 was 12.5% (2,078,000). By 1970 this figure had reached 32.1% (7,920,000) — in other words, the percentage of the youth population attending college had almost tripled in two decades. When one considers the absolute number of youth attending colleges and universities during the period 1946–1970, the figure quadrupled (U.S. Bureau of the Census, 1975).

What occurred in the United States during the 1960s was that suddenly a new class of youth appeared on the college scene, isolated from the rest of society. Statements were heard to the effect that: "You can't trust anyone over 30." and "We are alone and separate from them." This new generation developed its own culture with its unique life style, music, dress, argot, and political rhetoric (Denisoff & Peterson, 1972). The proliferation of youth placed a strain on society, especially on colleges and universities. The increased numbers of young people in the 1960s were largely absorbed by educational institutions rather than the labor market, particularly for the 16 to 19 age group (Ryder, 1974). During this period of rapid demographic change, institutions of higher education became increasingly more involved with the growth and development of the economy since they were responsible for providing the critical resources — intellectual manpower, scientific and technological knowledge — necessary to sustain the postindustrial society. As the creators and allocators of many of these resources, universities themselves became centers of power and politics. And this new political role was destined to be played out on their campuses. Although the great majority of students appeared relatively uncommitted to radical campus politics in the 1960s, a "critical mass" of students emerged who were recruited into protest activity. Although the percentage of activist youth has remained relatively small over the years (under 2 to 5%), their absolute numbers increased considerably during the 1960s. As the baby-boom cohort matures in the 1970s, the pressure for absorption has shifted from educational and military institutions to the labor market (Ryder, 1974).

YOUTH MOVEMENTS

Youth movements represent ways dissatisfied young people organize to bring about change in society (Wilson, 1973; Ash-Garner, 1977) and may be defined as those "socially shared activities and beliefs directed toward the demand for change in some aspect of the social order" (Gusfield, 1970, p. 2). Social movements appear to be reactions against major trends that threaten or "oppress" the sense of identity, self-esteem, and stability of groups in society. Out of the main drifts in contemporary society have developed countervailing forces that challenge their legitimacy. For example, Roberts and Kloss (1974) cite the three master social trends of bureaucratization, cultural imperialism (racism, sexism, colonialism, economic exploitation), and industrialization that have given rise to antibureaucratic, nativistic or nationalist, and egalitarian youth movements. The dissatisfaction among ethnic minorities, college youth, and women over the traditional forms of segregation, war, bureaucratic authority, and sex-role stereotyping has led to a desire and effort for collective change. Traditional images in these area are being replaced by a sense of personal self-development and efficacy that appear to transcend one's color, age, or sex. Among the many youth movements that have appeared in recent history are: the Civil Rights movements, Counterculture, Free Speech movement, Communalism, Peace movement, Pacifist movement, Amnesty movement, New Right, New Left, Feminist movement, Transcendentalist movements, Jesus People, Gay Liberation movement, Ecology movement, Moon movement, and the Anti-Nuclear Power movement.

Youth movements represent a worldwide phenomenon (Albornoz, 1967; Lipset, 1967; Shimbori, 1968; Emmerson, 1968; Lipset & Altbach, 1969; Flacks, 1970a; DeConde, 1971; Bakke & Bakke, 1971; Allerbeck, 1971; Liebman, Walker, & Glazer, 1972; Backman & Findlay, 1973; Yang, 1973; Brier & Tansey, 1974; Goertzel, 1974; Gella, 1975). Although the issues over which youth protest vary from country to country, certain similarities partially explain the appearance of student movements on college and university campuses. First, increasing numbers of youth attend institutions of higher learning today — although the figures are considerably higher in industrial and postindustrial societies than in modernizing nations. Second, universities share the characteristics of being "cities of youth" and centers of critical thinking and discussion over numerous domestic, national, and international issues — racism, military and economic repression, universal human rights, suffrage, conscription, citizenship, war, poverty, pollution, nuclear energy, and so on. Youth attending universities participate in these debates, and many share similar feelings over the eradication of these problems. Third, colleges and universities furnish an international medium for the rapid dissemination of new ideas and the spread of cultural and ideological values. These structural conditions the world over provide the opportunity for a vanguard of youth to emerge and lead a "carrier class" of their peers into active social and political behavior (Weinberg and Walker, 1969; President's Commission on Campus Unrest, 1970; Tygart & Holt, 1972; Meyer & Rubinson, 1972; Kearney, 1975; Kearney & Jiggins, 1975; Feuer, 1975).

The appearance of youth movements in recent history, however, cannot be explained solely in terms of large numbers of isolated college youth in close proximity to one another. Although these structural features have become more pronounced over the years, youth movements occur sporadically and usually develop in direct response to specific changes and transformations that have taken place in society. The obvious question arises: Why do youth movements appear at one particular time in history rather than another? Why in the 1930s and 1960s and not in the 1950s and 1970s? The complexity of social and historical events lies at the root of this question. No single factor can account for the sudden appearance of youth movements. Rather, the unique mix or blend of demographic conditions in combination with historical, social, cultural, and psychological factors provides some understanding into the origin of youth's behavior. If this line of thinking is correct, the youth movement in the 1960s developed as a result of a particular kind of interaction between generational, historical, social, cultural, and psychological forces in society.

Historical Factors and Youth Movements

Historical moods and fashions shift over time, and these interact with social, political, and cultural movements. The changing political *zeitgeist* has involved shifts in this country between the status quo and liberal reform since the turn of the century. The temporal location of youth in relation to decisive political events appears to be associated with the rise and fall of youth movements (see Table 1). The period 1900–1929 was characterized by economic conservatism and cultural liberalism. That is, laissez-faire capitalism,

Table 1 Temporal Location, Decisive Political Events, and Youth Movements

Temporal Location	Decisive Political Events	Youth Movements
1900–1929	Economic growth and cultural liberalism Industrialization, United States develops favorable balance of trade and becomes world industrial power World War I Isolationism Prohibition Women's suffrage "Roaring twenties"	Youth culture challenges Victorian social and sexual mores
1930–1940	The Great Depression Poverty Election of FDR—"New Deal" Government economic programs Growth of national socialism in Germany	Youth join antiwar movement Sign Oxford Pledge Campus strikes
1941–1949	World War II Truman administration Atomic bomb Returning GIs Global reconstruction, United Nations	Little youth movement activity
1950–1959	The Cold War—Eisenhower years Growth of "military-industrial complex" Dulles foreign policy Recession McCarthyism 1954 Supreme Court desegregation decision House Un-American Activities Committee	"The silent generation"
1960–1968	Kennedy-Johnson years "New Frontier" Civil rights demonstrations Peace Corps, poverty programs Vietnam escalation Assassinations of Kennedy brothers and Martin Luther King "Great Society" programs Ghetto riots and campus disruption	New Left New Right Civil rights and Black Power Protest demonstrations, strikes, violence
1969–1976	Nixon-Ford Years Emphasis on "law and order" Voting Rights Act Vietnam War ends Kissinger foreign policy Inflation, job squeeze Growth of multinational corporations Watergate OPEC and Middle East oil embargo	Women's rights Ecology movement Charismatic religious movements Quiet seventies
1977–1979	Early Carter administration Conciliatory, practical, informal mood in White House Emphasis on government reorganization National energy crisis Inflation, job squeeze continues	"No-Nuke" movement Gay liberation

imbued with the social Darwinist ethic, suddenly thrust the country into the status of an international industrial giant. At the same time, a romantic, indulgent youth culture challenged Victorian social and sexual mores and created for that generation the "roaring twenties." This historic period was followed by the Great Depression, and from 1930 to 1940, the political pendulum swung to the left with increased governmental growth and control. It was during this "liberal" historic period that many college youth signed the Oxford Pledge and pressed for international peace through noninvolvement with the impinging land war in Europe. Reports of rallies and demonstrations suggest that as many as 185,000 youth took an active part in these protests (Lipset, 1976). With the onset of World War II, the pendulum swung once again to the right; during the period 1941–1959, patriotism, global reconstruction, the Cold War, McCarthyism, and returning GIs blanketed college campuses. In the middle 1950s, anxiety over communism and alleged international subversion permeated American society. During the Eisenhower years, youth were quiescent and generally uninterested in politics, thereby earning the title the "silent generation."

The historial pendulum reversed itself once again during the 1960s, and this decade witnessed a perceptible shift toward the side of youthfulness. With the inauguration of John F. Kennedy — who symbolized the romantic vision for a fresh and idealistic generation of black and white youth — new legal and political fronts were created on civil rights and poverty. It was during this period that student movements emerged on both the political left and right, with such groups as Students for a Democratic Society (SDS), Young Americans for Freedom (YAF), Student Nonviolent Coordinating Committee (SNCC), and Congress of Racial Equality (CORE) organizing and springing up on campuses across the country. The most significant and vehemently contested issues during the early years of this decade were civil rights, university reform, and the war in Southeast Asia. By the 1970s, this priority had reversed itself, and the Vietnam-Cambodia war became the overriding national issue, closely followed by university reform and civil rights (Braungart & Braungart, 1972). During the mid 1960s, a youth movement emerged that challenged the very foundation of American society. Nurtured on college campuses, youth groups divided by a process of ideological mitosis and became increasingly revolutionary, militant, and nihilistic as the decade drew to a close.

The youth movement was made up of a minority of students in relation to the total university student population. Estimates of hardcore membership in all radical youth groups rarely exceeded 5% of the total student body in this country at any one time throughout the last decade (Block, Haan, & Smith, 1968). In fact, the largest national left-wing group, SDS, has never reported more than 10,000 dues-paying members. The right-wing YAF claimed 20,000 collegiate members on 200 campuses. Nevertheless, on occasions, such as the incidents that occurred at Berkeley, Columbia, and San Francisco State, radical youth were successful in mobilizing strong and widespread support among moderate students and faculty for student issues, especially after police and National Guard were brought on campuses (Peterson, 1966, 1968a; Peterson & Bilorusky, 1971; Gold, Christie, & Friedman, 1976). Evidence also suggested that while the youth movement was growing at a relatively moderate, albeit consistent, rate, it reflected a general campus malaise and cynicism among a much wider spectrum of college youth. Support for protest activity peaked in 1970, with 57% of the nation's colleges and universities experiencing a "significant impact" on campus operations as the result of Cambodia, Kent State, and Jackson State (Braungart & Braungart, 1972; Keniston, 1973).

As the 1960s drew to a close, the goals and objectives but not the tactics of the youth movement spread to a much larger segment of the youth population (President's Commission on Campus Unrest, 1970; Peterson & Bilorusky, 1971). This trend was demonstrated by the increasing number of youth who turned out for demonstrations and mass meetings at both the college and high-school levels. Although the majority of these youth did not define themselves as radicals or militants, they nevertheless felt the need to demonstrate when the "right" cause or issue presented itself (Braungart & Braungart, 1972). The majority of youth on college campuses remained privatists and success-oriented (Hadden, 1969); however, there developed a growing number of young people who were dissatisfied with society and the "system." Empirical evidence revealed that many of the same characteristics that described activist youth existed in their sympathetic but nondemonstrative peers (Yankelovich, 1969; Gergen, 1970[1]).

With the election of a law-and-order president in 1968, a new conservative mood began to grow throughout the country. The Nixon-Agnew strategy favored a combination of confrontation-centrist politics and appeared fairly successful especially after ending the Vietnam War, until the exposure of the Watergate affair, which revealed that the White House was administered by an overzealous, clandestine right-wing staff. The conservative wing of the youth movement was successful in reaching the White House, with former Nixon aide and past President of YAF, Tom Charles Huston, one of the principal architects of the illegal "Huston Plan," calling for bugging, break-ins, and mail-cover operations against radical youth and adult political organizations. The Nixon-appointed Ford Presidency proved uneventful and short lived. Ford was able to restore confidence in the Presidency, but lost the 1976 election to Jimmy Carter. Carter's victory resulted from his ability to galvanize and recapture the support of the old Democratic majority coalition — lost to Nixon in 1968 and 1972 — consisting of Catholics, blue-collar workers, minority groups, and organized labor. Carter also won a sizable majority of the youth vote, especially young people between the ages of 20 to 30 (Reinhold, 1976). In some ways similar to Nixon, Carter was successful in co-opting the liberal wing of the youth movement by appointing former civil-rights leader and activist, Andrew Young, Ambassador to the United Nations. Young, in turn, exported American civil-rights rhetoric and values to African and Third World nations.

Today, campuses are relatively calm, but this appears to be an uneasy calm. Numerous social problems continue to plague American society — human rights, energy, and ecology remain high on the list. Since the precedent for radical youth movements has been established, only time will determine whether the scenario of student activism will repeat itself.

What this view of history suggests is that consistent as well as opposing historical forces have been operating since the turn of the century, and these factors in combination with other conditions have influenced the form and substance of youth movements in the United States. Students attending college during the 1960s were born in the 1940s. What made this generation different from previous age cohorts was that these youth were the products of social and historical forces that developed during the 1950s and extended into the early 1960s. Youth born in the 1940s were the first generation to grow up under the specter of nuclear annihilation and mass indifference ushered in by the atomic age. These youth had never experienced the direct, personal dislocations and fears of the Depression

---

[1]K. J. Gergen. "Social background, education, attitudes, and previous experiences with activism." Personal communication to the President's Commission on Campus Unrest, August 1970.

and World War II, but instead witnessed the presence of a victorious and affluent United States playing the role of a dominant superpower — with all of its negative connotations and implications. These factors in combination with the scare tactics of the McCarthy era in the 1950s and the events of the early 1960s — the struggle by blacks to achieve legal and social equality, the violent assassinations of civil-rights workers and a young president — helped produce a generation of college youth, a large proportion of whom were cynical, strongly antiwar, and politically liberal. Youth attending college in the mid 1970s were different from those of the previous decade in that they did not experience the direct thrust of many of the historic events that took place in the late 1940s and the 1950s. They did experience, however, the dramatic events of the 1960s, in addition to the excesses of radicalism exhibited by youth groups during that period. This, coupled with the economic, consumer, and energy crises of the 1970s, may have persuaded them to tone down their own political style.

Social Structural Factors and Youth Movements

This country has experienced dramatic shifts in social and economic institutions over the last half century, which in turn have influenced the relationships and concerns of youth with society. Economic trends have revolved around the decline in the manufacturing sector and the growth of social services, especially in the areas of government, trade, finance, and utilities. The service sector now accounts for over half of national employment. The composition of the labor force has also changed, with white-collar employees now outnumbering blue-collar workers (Miles, 1971; Wattenberg, 1974). During the 1960s, the number of males 16 to 19 years of age increased by 44%, yet the number of employed males the same age grew by only 11% (Ryder, 1974). The net result of these changes is that youth have been forced out of the labor market.

Structural shifts are taking place throughout society that appear to have direct bearing on student movements. Control over local and regional institutions is being replaced by a new system of federal regulation and allocation (Fischer, 1975). In certain sectors of the economy, the family-based enterprise and the middle-size business are being taken over by national or multinational corporations. At the same time, the mobility of individuals appears to be on the increase. All of these trends increase the distance between individuals and the political and economic decision-makers in society.

Bell (1973) argues that the United States is moving toward a mass or postindustrial society. He perceives postindustrial society principally in terms of a political society wherein public mechanisms and public choice rather than markets and individual demands become the arbiter of goods and services. Postindustrial society is divided into three sectors:

1. The social structure, which encompasses the economy, science-technology, occupational, and educational systems.
2. The culture, involving the sphere of expression, symbolism, and meaning.
3. The polity, which regulates the distribution of power and adjudicates the conflicting claims and demands of individuals and groups.

Increasingly the polity is called on to resolve the strains that have grown up between the structural conditions of production, marketing, and consumption vis-à-vis the new sensate impulses of modern postbourgeois culture, articulated through its mentality of "entitlement" and idealized material life style (Bell, 1976). In order to meet the growing expectations of greater numbers of people, Janowitz (1976) notes the unprecedented growth, size, and pervasiveness of modern political regimes and of the problems they create. Contemporary societies are willing to extend the political and bureaucratic powers of the state, but at what point does this politicization weaken the fabric of competitive, representative, and parliamentary democratic societies? Youth movements on both the left and right have addressed this dilemma of the drift toward massive political control versus citizen participation and self-determination.

The growth of postindustrial society is generating additional needs for its members, along with a new type of labor force recruited primarily from institutions of higher learning. These changes have created a stratum of scientific, professional, technical, and intellectual elite who are actively promoting cultural values and demands. Whether this new labor force becomes more militant or remains in the traditional guild form will be decided over the next few decades (Bell, 1973; Ladd & Lipset, 1975). In the meantime, theoretical knowledge continues to be a major source of social and economic innovation, placing the university in the strategic position as one of the dominant institutions in society. As generators of cognitive developments and scientific-technical manpower, universities have become centers of social, structural, and cultural change.

A century ago, an elite of some 50,000 youth were enrolled in 563 institutions of higher learning. Today over 7,920,000 youth attend 2300 colleges and universities across the country (U.S. Bureau of the Census, 1975). What has occurred in the interim period has been an unprecedented transition from class-based institutions of higher learning to mass institutions, which recruit students from all class and status sectors of society. As Gusfield (1963) noted, before the Civil War education was considered a luxury and was reserved primarily for the upper-class gentry. However, since the turn of the century and with the industrialization and rapid growth of the American economy, college and university enrollment has increased substantially. Curricula have also undergone changes, with professional and occupational programs replacing the purely classical orientation. This trend has continued to the present time, particularly since the early 1960s when American universities moved into an era of mass education. In many respects, these modern multiversities are no longer the intellectual sanctuaries of a bygone era, but have become proving grounds for youth in their confrontation with themselves and with society as well. The surge of campus protest activity in the 1960s produced a voluminous literature documenting the social background characteristics of student political activists (Altbach & Kelly, 1973).

A number of studies conducted in the early and mid 1960s described activist youth as coming from middle and upper-middle class backgrounds. These were the sons and daughters of privileged, high-income families, where both parents often had four or more years of college and frequently were employed in occupations for which advanced education was a necessary prerequisite (Westby & Braungart, 1966; Flacks, 1967; Keniston, 1968, 1971; Paulus, 1968; Block, Haan, & Smith, 1968; Donovan & Shaevitz, 1973). Within more homogeneous college and university populations, such as those at Harvard, Yale, Columbia, and Stanford, where the modal income was predictably high, parents' income, education, and occupation failed to discriminate protesters from nonprotesters. As the decade of the 1960s drew to a close and the youth movement (especially the antiwar wing of the movement) became more hotly debated and diffused throughout society, family-status background was less able to differentiate activists from nonactivists (Clarke & Egan, 1969; Dunlap, 1970; Lewis, 1971; Braungart & Braungart, 1974). Participants in campus-based activist groups typically came from urban and suburban environments rather than small towns. They were more likely to live on the East or West Coasts, and were seldom the first in their families to attend college (Hodgkinson, 1970). In fact, many activists came from families in which parents had been attending college for several generations (Braungart, 1969).

The majority of activist youth were recruited from politically liberal homes with a small proportion from left-wing or radical backgrounds and even fewer who had converted or rebelled from politically conservative parents (Keniston, 1968, 1971). The bulk of empirical evidence supported the thesis that activist youth, were not rebelling against their parents' political views but were the products of privileged environments, liberal antiauthoritarian socialization experiences, and thus were acting out what they were taught in the home (Flacks, 1967, 1970b; Haan, Smith, & Block, 1968; Thomas, 1968; Watts, Lynch, & Whittaker, 1969; Wood, 1974). Although data revealed that college may have been a liberalizing experience during late adolescence and early adulthood, empirical evidence likewise suggested that many youth brought their parents' liberal political attitudes and values with them to college, especially strongly held opinions toward foreign policy, civil rights, freedom of speech, and social welfare programs. And further, when parents themselves were actively involved in politics, the probability of their progeny becoming involved was predictably high (Braungart & Braungart, 1974).

Liberal Protestant and Jewish family backgrounds were overrepresented among left-wing youth when compared with conservative Protestant and Catholic backgrounds, with a greater proportion of campus activists exhibiting nonreligious and secular attitudes than the youth population in general. Protestant denominations, such as Quaker, Unitarian, and Episcopalian, produced a disproportionately large number of youth who participated in leftist political behavior when compared with the more conservative Protestant sects (Flacks, 1967, 1970b; Braungart, 1969). While few left-wing youth came from Catholic homes, the number of students who reported coming from Jewish families was disproportionately high, higher in some instances than the combined religious affiliation of all other denominations (Gamson, Goodman, & Gurin, 1967; Auger, Barton, & Maurice, 1969; Watts, Lynch, & Whittaker, 1969; Smith, Haan, & Block, 1970; DeMartini, 1975; Isenberg, Schnitzer, & Rothman, 1977). The general trend in research indicated left-wing youth tended to be low on conventional religiosity — they were less likely to attend worship services and more readily defined themselves as agnostic or atheist. This stands in contrast to right-wing youth who were recruited from Protestant and Catholic homes with more traditional religious beliefs (Solomon & Fishman, 1964; Braungart, 1971d; Donovan & Shaevitz, 1973).

Activists more often came from homes in which democratic and equalitarian child-rearing practices were employed; there was little evidence to support the view that radical youth were reared by overpermissive or overindulgent families. Although evidence exists suggesting left-wing youth came from permissive families, permissiveness per se has never been demonstrated to be an independent cause of student activism (Keniston, 1968, 1971; Thomas, 1968; Mankoff & Flacks, 1971). It was reported that leftist parents were slightly more egalitarian than apolitical or conservative parents in allowing their offspring to express themselves and to openly experiment with life. However, parental dedication to humanitarian causes, democratic family values, and political socialization appeared to have a greater impact in explaining political activism among young people (Flacks, 1967, 1970b; Haan, Smith, & Block, 1968; Braungart, 1969, 1971a).

Members of the youth movement were recruited from the most selective and prestigious colleges and universities across the country — the highest incidence of protest occurred at private universities, private liberal arts colleges, and large public universities. The liberal traditions of schools like Reed, Swarthmore, Bennington, Antioch, and Oberlin contributed to the selective recruitment and styles of activism that took place on their campuses (Flacks, 1970b; Hodgkinson, 1970; Gergen, 1970[2]; Foster & Long, 1970; Riesman & Stadtman, 1973). Although the majority of students on these campuses were liberal and active, their total numbers remained minuscule when compared to the over 6,500,000 young people attending colleges and universities during that time. A variety of research sources suggested that large state universities were more likely to produce politicized student bodies and demonstrations than small universities and colleges (Bayer & Astin, 1969; Scott & El-Assal, 1969; Dunlap, 1970; Bayer, 1972). These multiversities, as they have been characterized, possessed both the size and heterogeneity to support nonconformist subcultures that were more likely to ignore conventional academic pursuits. Larger institutions were also under enormous competitive, organizational, and economic pressures that inhibited communication at all levels, exacerbated student-faculty rapport, and increased student alienation (Shotland, 1970; Scurrah, 1972; Braungart & Braungart, 1972). Although selective colleges and large universities were predictably centers of student unrest, this phenomenon spread throughout the country to most institutions of higher learning and filtered down to many high schools as well (Skolnick, 1969; President's Commission on Campus Unrest, 1970).

Some demographic background characteristics, such as age, year in college, and sex, indicated left-wing activists did not differ significantly from the general undergraduate student population. Activists in the Free Speech movement at Berkeley were more often than not in their late teens, drawn predominantly from the freshman and sophomore classes, and slightly overrepresented with females as compared to the general campus population (Lyonns, 1965; Whittaker & Watts, 1969; Smith, Haan, & Block, 1970; Wood, 1974). Conversely, data from SDS and other left-wing protest groups on various eastern colleges and universities revealed activists to be in their early twenties, upperclassmen, graduate students, and highly represented with females (Braungart, 1969). Because of regional differences and specific university profiles, there appeared to be few background characteristics differentiating student activists from non activists. The only demographic feature that remained consistent suggested that leftist activists were slightly more equalitarian in the sex composition of their membership than were other campus-based political groups (Auger, Barton, & Maurice, 1969; Braungart, 1969; Geller & Howard, 1969; Clarke & Egan, 1969; Kerpelman, 1972; Braungart & Braungart, 1974).

The youth movement during the 1960s reflected the power of a new adversary class reacting against a military-industrial, scientific, and technologically based society. Students (primarily recruited from the liberal arts and humanities) reacted against the deteriorating conditions in postindustrial society: especially the war in Southeast Asia, congested and polluted cities, poverty, mass education, wholesale discrimination, bureaucratic rigidity, and alienation. Although greater numbers of youth attended college, there was a decline in intellectual motivation, orientation, and performance among students. Youth enrolled in college were less interested in competition, the achievement motive, and traditional Protestant ethic values toward money and work. By the mid 1970s, however, many of these value orientations returned toward a more traditional position.

[2]Op. cit.

This leads into a discussion of the cultural changes that have taken place during recent American history and their impact on the youth movement.

Cultural Factors and Youth Movements

Another index of a changing society can be seen in the shifts in values over time. Prevailing cultural moods appeared to be associated with the growth or demise of political youth movements. For example, college students in the mid 1920s were reported to be most concerned with values centering around personal ideals, vocations, fraternity life styles, cheating on examinations, coeducation, moral choices in life and religiosity (Katz & Allport, 1931). These youth were not noted to be particularly interested in politics, and youthful political activity was relatively nonexistent during this time (Draper, 1967). In the 1930s, however, political interest heightened among youth, and the depressed economy along with the moral political consideration of war became paramount issues that triggered numerous strikes on campuses across the country. In the mid 1930s, students were reported to be concerned with the labor movement, academic freedom, university reform as well as student rights and privileges (Draper, 1967). In a national poll of college youth for *Fortune* (1936), 6% of the students reported they felt sympathetic with communism, 24% selected socialism, 45% favored liberalism, 15% chose conservatism, and 2% endorsed fascism. When compared with polls taken in the 1920s, these findings represented an unprecedented shift to the political left (Lipset, 1976). During the 1940s and through the 1950s, however, youth appeared less interested in politics and more concerned with personal goals, with the result that their political activity subsided. Goldsen et al. (1960) found not only apathy and lack of interest but extreme economic and political conservatism on campuses throughout this country in the 1950s.

An inverse relationship has appeared to exist between youth's religious values and political activity over the last 20 years (Hastings & Hoge, 1970). Among college students from 1948 to 1967, there was a reported decline in traditional religious beliefs and behavior; a greater questioning of religious precepts, especially among younger age groups; and a general liberalizing of personal values. Conversely, during this same period there was a noticeable increase in the politicization of youth that paralleled the growth of the student movement. Hastings and Hoge (1970) suggested that the history of American student political activism — which showed considerable activity during the middle 1930s and 1960s, with almost no activity in the 1940s and 1950s — is represented by a curve exactly the inverse of the curve for traditional religious commitment.

Matza (1961), Clark and Trow (1960), Peterson (1968b), and Block, Haan, and Smith (1968) constructed typologies concerning American collegiate subcultures. Each provided a profile or paradigm of the cultural styles exhibited by college youth over the last two decades. Matza studied the "spirit of rebelliousness" among nonconforming college youth in the 1950s and classified them into three groupings: delinquents, radicals, and bohemians. Clark and Trow identified and described four major types of student subcultures in the late 1950s and early 1960s: collegiate, vocational, academic, and nonconformist. The incidence of college youth falling into each of these categories was recorded by Bolton and Kammeyer (1967) in a 1964 survey of 13,000 freshmen entering 23 colleges and universities. These authors reported that 51% of the youth surveyed indicated their major interests in college centered around an active social life and carrying on the college tradition — the collegiate type. Vocational goals were given priority by

27%, while the pursuit of ideas (the academic type) was listed by 19%. Three percent of the freshmen surveyed were classified as nonconformists.

The Matza (1961) and Clark and Trow (1960) typologies stand in contrast to subcultural typologies developed by Peterson (1968b) and Block, Haan, and Smith (1968), whose typologies reflected the more politicized student subcultures of the middle and late 1960s. Peterson's paradigm consisted of eight student types distinguished by their overriding value commitments. He arranged his subcultural groups along a continuum, ranging from acceptance through neutral to the rejection of American institutions: professionalist (most accepting), vocationalist, collegiate, ritualist, academic, intellectual, left activist, and hippie (most rejecting). Another useful and comprehensive political paradigm of American college youth was constructed by Block, Haan, and Smith (1968). These authors differentiated six student subcultural types: politically apathetic, alienated, individualist, activist, constructivist, and antisocial. In comparison to Clark and Trow's (1960) model, all the categories in the Block, Haan, and Smith typology could be classified as nonconformist, with the exception of politically apathetic youth who represent the academic, collegiate, and vocational types.

What these four typologies indicate is a shift in student cultural and political styles from the late 1950s to the 1960s. Whereas political themes were not considered by Matza (1961) or Clark and Trow (1960), they became the overriding theme or core for the schemes developed by Peterson (1968b) and Block, Haan, and Smith (1968). The student subcultural paradigm developed by Block, Haan, and Smith appears especially applicable to the range of youth politics that was characteristic of the late 1960s. For example, the political styles of SDS, SNCC, and CORE were representative of activist youth, while the style of YAF strongly resembled individualist youth. The more pragmatic and less ideological youth political groups, such as Young Democrats and Young Republicans, most nearly represented the political style of constructivist youth.

National surveys of college youth in the late 1960s and 1970s undertaken by the American Council on Education (1969, 1971, 1975, 1976), Yankelovich (1972), and the Carnegie Council (Trow, 1977) indicated an association between the changing values of youth and the growth of campus-based activism. With regard to sociocultural and personal values, the following trends were cited (see Table 2). There appeared to be decline in support for traditional institutions and values, especially in the areas of family, sex, and work. During the late 1960s and early 1970s, fewer young people were interested in marriage and family, with growing approval of sexual freedom. Dramatic decreases occurred in the work ethic, with fewer youth believing that hard work always pays off, competition encourages excellence, and that the authority of a boss should be accepted. There was also a weakening of support for the institution of religion and the need to lead a moral life. Values concerning the importance of education lessened somewhat, as did interest in traditional cultural and leisure-time pursuits, such as visiting art galleries, borrowing books from a library, and playing a musical instrument. There was a marked reduction in the percentage of youth who said they planned to join a fraternity or sorority, and a sizable gain in the percentage favoring the legalization of marijuana. Regarding shifts in personal values during 1969–1971, college students reported privacy was becoming more important, but there was a sharp drop in the percentage indicating the necessity to develop a philosophy of life. At the same time, the tightening of the economy in the early 1970s appeared directly to affect young people's personal values toward jobs and money, with youth becoming more career-minded, concerned with job security, exhibiting self-doubts about making money, welcoming less emphasis on money, and with fewer taking affluence for granted.

Table 2   National Surveys of College Youth Values: 1969–1976

Surveys and Agreement over Value Issue	Year of Survey	
Yankelovich surveys	*1969*	*1971*
Marriage is obsolete	24%	34%
Extramarital sex is wrong	77	57
Favor sexual freedom	43	56
Hard work always pays off	56	39
Place emphasis on working hard	48	44
Competition encourages excellence	72	62
Accept authority of boss	49	36
Religion very important	38	31
Believe in leading clean moral life	45	34
Education very important	80	74
Privacy very important	61	64
Career minded	57	61
Concerned with job security	42	46
Self-doubts about making money	40	50
Welcome less emphasis on money	73	76
Take affluence for granted	43	39
Big business in need of reform	35	40
Patriotism important	35	27
Accept authority of police	48	45
Welcome emphasis on law and order	56	50
Carnegie Council surveys	*1969*	*1975*
Believe in a God who judges men	75%	76%
Marijuana should be legalized	46	55
Female graduate students not dedicated	21	8
Most undergraduates satisfied with their education	71	72
Satisfied with overall evaluation of college	66	71
Undergraduate education improved if grades abolished	60	32
All courses should be electives	51	35
Essential undergraduate objectives:		
Detailed grasp of a special field	62	68
Training and skills for occupation	57	67
Learn to get along with people	77	66
Formulate values and goals of life	72	62
Undergraduate grades:		
A	8	19
B	48	55
C	39	25
less than C	6	—
Relax standards and admit minorities to college	29	22
Disagree to relax requirements and appoint minority faculty	76	86
Most American universities and colleges are racist	43	27

Table 2 (continued)

Surveys and Agreement over Value Issue	Year of Survey			
Use busing to achieve racial integration in elementary schools	46	26		
No violence to achieve political goals	75	90		
Capital punishment should be abolished	60	36		
Political preference:				
Left	5	3		
Liberal	39	32		
Middle-of-the-road	37	39		
Moderate conservative	17	23		
Strongly conservative	2	3		
American Council on Education surveys	*1969*	*1971*	*1975*	*1976*
Important to raise a family	71%	60%	57%	57%
Good chance will marry within year after college	21	20	17	16
Visited art gallery during past year	71	66	—	—
Played musical instrument during past year	40	38	—	—
Checked out library book during last year	48	43	—	—
Chances good will join fraternity or sorority	23	14	15	15
Legalize marijuana	26	39	47	49
Women should get job equality	—	88	92	92
Women's activity best in home	—	42	28	28
Important to develop a philosophy of life	82	68	64	61
Can do little to change society	36	43	48	44
Important to keep up with political affairs	—	43	39	37
Current political preference:				
Far left	3	3	2	2
Liberal	30	35	29	26
Middle-of-the-road	44	46	53	56
Conservative	21	15	15	15
Far right	2	1	1	1

Source: Yankelovich, 1972; Trow, 1977; American Council on Education, 1969, 1971, 1975, 1976.

Along with changing cultural and personal values during the late 1960s and early 1970s, these national surveys suggested important shifts in political views and orientations among college youth. Although more students became concerned with the need to reform big business and gain government protection for the consumer, there was evidence of growing alienation among young people expressed in the feeling that there was little they could do to change society. Patriotism was viewed as less important, as was accepting the authority of the state and police. On the other hand, youth indicated growing support for law and order during 1969–1971.

According to the American Council on Education, the political preference of college freshmen in 1969 reflected the following ideological range: 3% identified with the far left, 30% liberal, 44% middle-of-the-road, 21% conservative, and 2% far right. Their 1971 survey of freshmen evidenced growing liberal (35%) and middle-of-the-road (46%) preferences and a decline in either conservative (15%) or far right (1%) identifications.

Although ostensibly interested in politics, youth did not care to identify with either of the two major political parties, but instead chose to classify themselves as "Independents." Ladd, Hadley, and King (1971) compared the number of political Independents under 30 years of age from 1948 to 1968 and discovered that in the 1948 presidential election, 27% of the young people under 30 classified themselves as Independents. In 1968, this percentage rose to 40%, the highest of all age groups identifying with the Independent political classification. In the Yankelovich (1972) study, 47% of the college youth surveyed in 1969 identified with the Democratic party, 25% considered themselves Republicans, and 28% did not identify with either of the two major political parties. Two years later in 1971, a similar survey revealed 36% of college youth identified with the Democratic party, 21% classified themselves as Republicans, and a sizable plurality, 43%, did not choose to identify with either major political party. These data suggest that there was a weakening of support for the traditional two-party system by youth, with growing ideological preference for liberal or middle-of-the-road politics, during the late 1960s and early 1970s.

By the mid 1970s, there was discernible movement away from the mood of the late 1960s and early 1970s, with considerably less political radicalism exhibited by young people. Although certain sociocultural values continued to liberalize, others became more conservative. The liberal trend continued in the areas of: (1) marriage and the family, with fewer youth feeling it was important to raise a family or that they would marry soon after college; (2) the legalization of marijuana; (3) the need to develop a philosophy of life; and (4) the equality of women, particularly in the areas of jobs, traditional roles, and the perceived dedication of female graduate students. During this same period, other values turned back in a more conservative or traditional direction. In the academic area, an increasing percentage of students indicated they were satisfied with college, and they did not endorse permissive higher education, such as abolishing grades or making all courses electives. A real change occurred in undergraduate objectives during 1969–1976, with students in 1976 favoring academic and vocational goals over social and personal-growth education. Youth in 1975 were more likely to report higher grades, which may indicate a shift toward improved academic performance and/or grade inflation. The work ethic regained support in the mid 1970s, with greater numbers of young people feeling more administratively responsible. However, although the women's rights issue increased its legitimacy in the 1970s, values toward race and education moved in a more conservative direction, with students disagreeing that academic standards should be relaxed to admit minorities or appoint minority faculty. Fewer students felt that American universities and colleges were racist or that busing should be used to achieve racial integration in elementary schools.

During the mid 1970s, student political orientations continued to drift away from the radical left and liberal politics of the late 1960s. Youth were strongly opposed to the use of violence to achieve political goals by 1975. Although almost half the students surveyed in 1975 by the American Council on Education reported there was little they could do to change society, their 1976 poll evidenced a decline in the percentage of alienated students. Similarly, the percentage of young people indicating that government was not protecting the consumer reached its peak in 1971 and then decreased by 1976. A sharp reversal in values occurred on the issue of capital punishment, with 60% of college students saying it should be abolished in 1969, which decreased to 36% by 1975. Political preferences had also changed by the mid 1970s. The American Council on Education and Carnegie Council surveys indicated a decline in far left and liberal identifications and increased momentum toward the center or middle-of-the-road. The trend in the growing number of political Independents under 30 years of age continued, and in the 1972 presidential election reached an all-time high of over 50% (Asher, 1976).

Yankelovich (1972) argued that an "unlinking" of cultural and political values among youth occurred in the early 1970s. That is, the continued liberalizing of cultural (or countercultural) values concerning marriage, sex, and drugs represented a distinct departure from the more conventional and middle-of-the-road political orientations that reappeared among college youth. However, this separation of cultural from political values did not take place among students who identified with the far left. For these youth, the values of the counterculture and radical politics remained highly intercorrelated. However, the vast majority of college youth — the 90 to 95% who did not identify with the revolutionary left — continued in their search for certain cultural changes, while steering clear of the more radical forms of politics. Yankelovich (1972) suggested that these shifts in values among contemporary youth reflected a new "naturalism," revolving around three major themes: emphasis on the community rather than the individual, anti-intellectualism and nonrationalism, and the search for sacredness in nature.

The 1960s witnessed a profound demographic change in American society that was unlike the 1950s and is different from the 1970s. Youth emerged as an independent source of change and interacted with historical, social, cultural, and psychological forces to produce unique forms of political behavior.

Psychological Factors and Youth Movements

A number of psychological studies were conducted during the 1960s in the attempt to explain the personal and motivational characteristics of participants in the youth movement (Altbach & Kelly, 1973; Keniston, 1973). The general thrust of much of this research focused on whether activists possessed a unique set of personality factors that differed from the general youth population. Other investigations examined personality differences of male and female activists, as well as left- versus right-wing youth.

In studies comparing activists and nonactivists, the former were typically left-wing and liberal, while the nonactivists were drawn from samples of youth not participating in protest behavior, demonstrations, or members of political organizations. A number of personality traits were remarkably consistent here, indicating a psychological profile of participants in the youth movement.

One pattern that emerged identified activist youth as having spontaneous and impulsive personalities. Empirical evidence suggested that activists lacked a certain amount of self-control; they were generally uninhibited, restless, open to new ideas, prone to be risk-takers, and adventurous (Solomon & Fishman, 1964; Heist, 1966; Gamson, Goodman, & Gurin, 1967; Astin, 1968; Sampson et al. 1969; Smith, Haan, & Block, 1970; Pierce, 1971; Lewis & Kraut, 1971; Donovan & Shaevitz, 1973; Isenberg, Schnitzer, & Rothman, 1977). A second personality trait indicated that activist youth were strong willed, assertive, highly determined, forceful, and overly concerned with dominance and power. Research supporting this personal-power orientation reported activists were rebellious toward traditional forms of authority, uncompromising on principles, nonconforming, and concerned with the manipulation of others (Astin, 1968; Cowdry, Keniston, & Cabin, 1970; Lotz, 1970; Smith, Haan, & Block, 1970; Pierce, 1971; Cherniss, 1972; Kerpelman, 1972; Donovan & Shaevitz, 1973; Isenberg, Schnitzer, & Rothman, 1977).

A third personality trait pointed out that activists felt a sense of specialness tending to be self-confident and self-centered. These youth were more likely than their nonactivist peers to be individualistic, autonomous, and at times exhibitionistic (Heist, 1966; Astin, 1968; Derber & Flacks, 1968; Doress, 1968; Keniston, 1968; Smith, Haan, & Block, 1970; Cherniss, 1972; Lewis & Kraut, 1971). A fourth set of research findings depicted activist youth as idealistic, altrustic, romantic, and nonmaterialistic. They likewise exhibited a strong desire to express and defend their ideological beliefs and practices (Flacks, 1967; Astin, 1968; Derber & Flacks, 1968; Cowdry, Keniston, & Cabin, 1970; Maidenberg & Meyer, 1970; Altbach, Laufer, & McVey, 1971). A fifth profile trait characterized activists as alienated, estranged, and distrustful, although these youth were not noted to be maladjusted psychologically. Activist youth were prone to reject conventional or traditional social institutions (religious, economic, familial, educational), and were "shocked" at social injustices and repression (Winborn & Jansen, 1967; Astin, 1968; Whittaker & Watts, 1969, 1971; Miller & Everson, 1970; Loken, 1970; Bakke & Bakke, 1971; Demerath, Marwell, & Aiken, 1971; Kerpelman, 1972).

The sixth personality characteristic, concerning scholastic aptitude and interest, identified activist youth as somewhat more intellectually oriented than nonactive college students. Typically, left- and right-wing youth were reported high on measures of intelligence and grade-point average. This has been a consistent finding in most research, especially in the early years of the youth movement. Left-wing youth scored high on verbal aptitude and low on mathematics. These youth tended to rank themselves in the upper half of their classes. Later in the 1960s, studies reported no actual difference in intellectual achievement between protesting versus nonprotesting youth. Activists did not see grades as important, nor were they as vocationally oriented as nonactivists (Gamson, Goodman, & Gurin, 1967; Keniston, 1968; Geller & Howard, 1969; Braungart, 1969; Flacks, 1967, 1970b; Watts, Lynch, & Whittaker, 1969; Miller & Everson, 1970; Kerpelman, 1972).

Seventh, leftist activist youth within American universities aspired to service and creative-expressive occupations. This stands in sharp contrast to the more success-oriented, economically motivated and rewarded professions of business, medicine, law, government, or natural science (Gamson, Goodman, & Gurin, 1967; Flacks, 1967; Whittaker & Watts, 1969; Geller & Howard, 1969; Baird, 1970; Cowdry, Keniston, & Cabin, 1970). Most research on left-wing students suggested these youth planned on becoming teachers, social scientists, entering creative-expressive occupations and becoming actively involved in community development and change. Follow-up studies a number of years later proved this to be the case (Demerath, Marwell, & Aiken, 1971; Fendrich, Simons, & Tarleau, 1972; Fendrich, 1974).

Eighth, extracurricular activities of activist youth showed them to be more involved in community-related activities, social services, and political organizations, and less involved in athletics. In general, leftist youth reached out for extra-academic experiences while attending college. They not only joined numerous campus organizations, especially those appealing to their political persuasion, but were more likely to become involved in wider community activities, such as tutorial projects, voter registration drives, and social action projects (Haan, Smith, & Block, 1968; Cowdry, Keniston, & Cabin, 1970; Demerath, Marwell, & Aiken, 1971; Kerpelman, 1972; Fendrich, 1974). Leftist youth were more prone than average college students to exhibit countercultural behavior, such as experimenting with drugs and sex, but unlike the hippie subculture, this seldom resulted in their complete withdrawal from society (Fenton & Gleason, 1969; Geller & Howard, 1969).

Ninth, youth who majored in the social sciences, humanities, and in the theoretically oriented fields of science were more politicized and active than those in the practical, applied, and experimental fields. Youth majoring in the social sciences were more likely to become knowledgeable about social problems and society's ills. Sociology, anthropology, history, and philosophy courses instilled in youth a sensitivity and a heightened consciousness toward personal, social, and political problems. Likewise, artistic and creatively inclined youth who were strongly opposed to a technologically ordered society were more likely to manifest frustrations and to be drawn into critically motivated activities (Heist, 1966; Gamson, Goodman, & Gurin, 1967; Flacks, 1967; Auger, Barton, & Maurice, 1969; Fenton & Gleason, 1969). Later in the 1960s and early 1970s, some physics and chemistry majors became politicized by the threat of impending annihilation through unleashed military power or the destruction and pollution of the environment (Dunlap, 1970; Braungart & Braungart, 1974; Lipset, 1976).

Finally, the political liberalism and religious secularism exhibited by activist youth were expressions of moral principles and underlying clusters of attitudes learned in the home. Research suggested that radical youth followed the intellectual, expressive, humanitarian, and political views of their parents. Students reported that their parents fostered independence, self-expression, and strongly encouraged socially responsible behavior in their offspring (Flacks, 1967; Thomas, 1968). Researchers reported many student activists were highly principled youth acting out a postconventional level of morality. Such findings suggested that these youth defined right and wrong in terms of universalistic criteria, as opposed to the preconventional and conventional levels of morality that were based on egocentric precepts and institutionally sanctioned norms. This is not to say that preconventional and conventional moral youth were not found among left-wing groups. In one study at least, a minority of preconventional and conventional radical youth were identified (Haan, Smith, & Block, 1968). And although no direct causal relationship has been developed, preconventional youth may have been largely responsible for campus violence and disruption that took place in the 1960s (Kohlberg, 1964, 1970; Keniston, 1968, 1971; Watts, Lynch, & Whittaker, 1969).

Several studies compared male versus female personality differences. Male activists were reported to be more adventurous, active, idealistic, spontaneous, uninhibited, open, friendly, and intensive (Astin, 1968; Pierce, 1971). Female activists were described as more impulsive, unconventional, rebellious, less friendly, nurturant-dependent (Pierce, 1971); in addition, they were more autonomous, active, assertive, feeling a sense of specialness, and highly achievement-oriented (Cherniss, 1972). There was little evidence to support the proposition that parental role-identification of sons toward their mothers was related to left-wing youth politics. Although one study suggested left-wing males identified with their mothers (Keniston, 1968, 1971), other research reported that student activists were consistent in their attitudes toward both parents. That is, the plurality of youth surveyed did not identify more with one parent at the expense of the other. Of those few who did identify with one parent over the other, both sexes appeared to identify more with mothers than with fathers, albeit this maternal relationship was found to be slightly greater for females than for males (Thomas, 1968; Fengler & Wood, 1973). Evidence also suggested that left-wing male youth identified less often with their mothers when compared with other apolitical and politically active youth groups (Braungart, 1971b).

The few studies comparing the personalities of left-wing versus right-wing activists reported the following differences. Donovan and Shaevitz (1973) characterized left-wing youth as bright, flexible, expressive, privileged, and liberal; and right-wing activists as reserved, polite, humorless, distant, with strict superegos, and a "shall-not" morality. Kerpelman (1972) described leftist students as hypersensitive, concerned for others, sociable, and independent; and rightists as conforming, valuing leadership, more "thick-skinned," and independent. Sampson et al. (1969) reported that left-wing youth often had soft-spoken fathers and dominant mothers, they opposed dominant-subordinate relationships, sought freedom, preferred unstructured situations, reacted to events more readily, were spontaneous, favored drugs, and avoided aggression. Conversely, the ROTC cadets in his study had strict fathers and submissive mothers, they supported dominant-subordinate relations, valued self-control, were practical and rational, rejected abstract-theoretical careers, and were aggressive. Schiff's (1964) study of right-wing youth described them as "conversionists" and "obedient rebels" with strong child-parent ties, while Braungart (1969, 1971c) noted a number of differences in the family background characteristics and ideological constructions of left- and right-wing activists.

In addition to the numerous studies on personality traits, family background and academic orientations, several investigations were conducted into the personal political perceptions of activist youth. Much of this research indicated that activists were likely to perceive pronounced discontinuities in society and viewed themselves as active agents of social and political change through self-assertion against the status quo (Haan, 1971; Bakke & Bakke, 1971). It is a well-known social-psychological principle that individuals are likely to perceive and interpret political situations in keeping with their own ideological positions. They have a tendency to overestimate the similarities of their views as well as those of a preferred person or political position; they tend to underevaluate the views of others (Granberg & Seidel, 1976). In comparing the attitude responses of left- and right-wing activists with members of mainstream campus political groups and apolitical youth, Braungart and Braungart (1979) found support for the notion that the more extreme the political group, the greater the distortion of attitudes in favor of that group's stand on political issues. When compared with moderate and apolitical youth groups, political extremist youth — whether left or right — endorsed a narrower latitude or range of acceptable political positions and were generally intolerant of a much wider range of viewpoints not consistent with their own. Within the ranks of extremist youth groups, there was a high degree of ideological consensus, a displacement of alternative views, a strong likelihood that attitudes and perceptions would be structured to fit their political niche, with little willingness to compromise with others over the pragmatic realities of politics (Thurber & Rogers, 1973; Braungart & Braungart, 1979).

Political activism is a means whereby youth dramatize and attempt to bring closure to their internal conflicts and belief systems (Goodwin, 1971; Feuer, 1975; Morris, 1977). Cowdry, Keniston, and Cabin (1970) referred to this phenomenon as belief-behavior consistency, arguing that activism is not merely a function of the strength of one's beliefs, but that other factors (including situational as well as psychodynamic) codetermine the likelihood that beliefs and attitudes will be translated into actions. Studies comparing youth who held similar political beliefs indicated those who took action came from more harmonious, consistent family backgrounds with social support for their views. The actions taken by youth represented an enduring pattern of behavior that was congruent with their past history and family experiences. Students not acting on their beliefs more often came from conflictful, unhappy family backgrounds where taking action represented a risk, in that they would have to move considerably further from their parents beliefs and values (Cowdry, Keniston, & Cabin, 1970; Gamson, Goodman, & Gurin, 1967). Demerath, Marwell, and Aiken (1971) reached the similar conclusion that certain social structural characteristics in combination with specific personality traits led to active political participation by youth. When compared with a random sample of college youth in their study, activist youth possessed a sense of ''specialness'' and ''duty'' that pushed them to a point where they felt they had to take action to honor their commitments. These studies all suggest that the blending or interaction of family background, personality characteristics, and situational factors propel committed young people into political activity.

THEORY CONSTRUCTION ABOUT YOUTH MOVEMENTS

A number of theories have been employed to explain youth movements. Foremost among these have been the theories of class consciousness (Mankoff & Flacks, 1971; Goertzel, 1972), status politics (Braungart, 1971b, 1971c), expressive or cultural politics (Douglas, 1970; Scott & Lyman, 1970; Bell, 1976), psychoanalytic-oedipal revolt (Bettelheim, 1963; Feuer, 1969, 1975; Hendin, 1975), family socialization (Flacks, 1967, 1971; Braungart, 1969, 1971a; Keniston, 1971), structural-functional (Eisenstadt, 1963; Parsons, 1963), existential-situational (Douglas, 1970; Goodwin, 1971), historical (Moller, 1968; Gillis, 1974), moralism (Kohlberg, 1964, 1970; Block, Haan, & Smith, 1968), and the core-periphery paradigm (Westby, 1976).

There is one comprehensive theory in sociology that appears to have the analytic capacity to explain the complex origins of youth movements, and that is Karl Mannheim's generational unit theory. Mannheim (1944, 1952) developed a theory that is capable of identifying and tracking a large number of variables over time. Although it has only begun to be formally tested (Simirenko, 1966; Zeitlin, 1966; Braungart, 1976), the popularity of this theory can be gauged by the number of discussions it has generated (Bengtson, 1970; Westby & Braungart, 1970; Brunswick, 1970; Lambert, 1970, 1971, 1972; Braungart, 1971c, 1974; Simmons, 1971; Flacks, 1971; Goertzel, 1972; Riley, Johnson, & Foner, 1972; Bengtson & Black, 1973; Cutler & Bengtson, 1974; Cutler, 1976; Lipset, 1976; Bengston & Cutler, 1976). The remaining portion of this chapter will attempt to identify and analyze the formal and emerging properties of Mannheim's generational unit theory.

Generational Unit Theory

Mannheim (1952) opens his discussion of youth movements by emphasizing the importance of biological age since this factor provides the vital base in historic, social, cultural, and psychological change. Biological location partially determines the range of human experiences, and by being ''location-bound'' one is limited to certain styles of thought and behavior. Belonging to the same age group and background endows individuals with a common location in the psychohistorical process, limiting and predisposing them to certain modes of consciousness, experience, and a characteristic type of relevant political action (Mannheim, 1952, p. 291).

Like Davis (1940), Eisenstadt (1956), Ortega y Gasset (1958), and Feuer (1969, 1975), Mannheim argues that generations play an important role in the creation of new social and historical forms. He maintains that although the phenomenon of generations is ultimately rooted in the biological rhythm of birth and death, the determining sociological fact of a generation hinges on the ''common location'' *(Lagerung)* of its members. Generations represent a particular kind of identity or location, embracing related ''age groups'' embedded in the social and historical process (Mannheim, 1952, p. 292). Feuer (1969) suggests that biological generations are not necessarily sociological generations until the shared historical experiences produce similar perceptions and understandings of reality. Lambert (1970, 1971, 1972) likewise argues that the sociological problem of generations begins where the biological problem leaves off.

Generational unit, on the other hand, represents a much stronger bond than actual generations:

> Youth experiencing the same concrete historical problems may be said to be part of the same actual generation; while those groups within the same actual generation which work up the material of their common experience in different specific ways, constitute separate generational units. [Mannheim, 1952, p. 304]

Generation units share similar location, consciousness, and common destiny. Within a generation there can exist any number of pro- or antagonistic generation units competing with one another. The units themselves respond to similar social and cultural forces and impose a parallelism of response on their members—that is, pressure to conform to partisan points of view. From the eighteenth century on, Mannheim argues, two rivaling political mentalities emerged—the romantic-conservative and the rationalist-liberal. Although both schools belonged to the same historical generation, their membership responded to social and cultural stimuli in divergent ways and thus constituted different generational units. Mannheim is explicit, however, in pointing out that not every generation produces the same number and kind of social configurations.The existence of any unit is partially determined by the unique interplay or blend of historical, social, and cultural forces. These, in turn, are selectively filtered and amplified through shared collective impulses, values, and attitudes.

Since each generation need not develop its own unique bond or consciousness, the rhythm of successive generations based on biological and sociological factors need not evolve in parallel form. Whether a particular "generational style" or *entelechy* develops every year, every 30 years, or every century depends on the "trigger action" of the combined historic, social, cultural, and psychological forces. The quantity and quality of influences within a particular historic period are important, since natural data— and Mannheim considers the concept of biological rhythm natural data — remain constant in history, and as such possess little explanatory power. The understanding of generational phenomena results when these natural data are viewed as having been influenced by the dynamic factors that play or "seize" upon the different characteristics and potentialities inherent in the natural datum. That is, according to Mannheim natural data receive their shape and form from the emerging social, cultural, and historical processes. And although the natural data of age, class, status, and values provide the range of "ingredients" that constitute the substance of society, it is the special features and transformations that occur within certain historical periods that give these natural factors their unique character and form.

Mannheim suggests, however, that historical factors alone are too idiographic and monistic to explain adequately the totality of social and cultural change. Certain entelechies, which reflect social and intellectual forces, provide the underlying currents that evolve into basic attitudes and behavior within generations. Youth movements are heavily influenced or molded by these intellectual trends, and the particular style of the period itself — whether it is liberal or conservative, static or dynamic — is expressed in the dominant force or *zeitgeist*. However, this relationship is not asymmetrical; while history or the *zeitgeist* influences generational entelechies, generation units influence the structure of society, culture, and the course of history. By selecting and amplifying certain entelechies and not others, generational units create both the genesis and dynamics for new social and historical order.

Although members must be born in the same historic period to constitute a generation, they must also experience the interplay of social and cultural forces to become a part of the same generational unit. While age similarity and historical themes influence generations and generational units, another factor in Mannheim's theory involves the actual participation in a common social and cultural destiny. Membership in a particular social-historical community is a crucial ingredient for generational location and solidarity. A generation unit exists only when a concrete bond is created among its members as a result of their exposure to similar social and intellectual forces in the process of "dynamic destabilization." Youth must be drawn into the "vortex" of social change to become members of the same actual generation, and at this point Mannheim distinguishes between the "actual" versus "potential" generation units. Isolated youth, that is, peasant or rural youth, who have the potential for experiencing generational solidarity, rarely become involved in generational movements. Membership requires participation in the social and intellectual currents of the day, which typically occur in urban centers experiencing rapid change.

Social and cultural change accelerates the "stratification of experience" *(Erlebnisschichtung)* of each successive generation. During periods of rapid social and historical change, attitudes take on new meaning and quickly become differentiated from traditional patterns of experiences. As these emerging patterns consolidate, they form fresh impulses and cores for generational configuration, which result in unique generational styles. The importance of the acceleration of social change for the realization of potentialities inherent in generations is absent in slowly changing communities. Static or slowly changing societies: (1) display no such generational units sharply set off from preceding generations; (2) articulate no unique collective entelechy; and (3) since the tempo of change is gradual, new generations evolve out of old generations without visible cleavage — there remains a strong homogeneity between generations. Periods characterized by war, natural catastrophe, and total political mobilization rarely develop generational differentiation due to the homogenization of values resulting from fear and/or national solidarity. However, during times of relative security and protracted institutional growth, the quicker the tempo of social and cultural change (due to science, technology, nationalism, overpopulation), the higher the probability that successive generations will develop their own entelechies.

Generation units likewise participate in the transmission of culture. Each successive generation experiences a "fresh contact" with traditional values and principles, and this "fresh contact" introduces new psychosocial units to the cultural and historical process. Inherent in this "fresh contact" is a radical revitalization process that forces youth to make novel interpretations and adjustments to the cultural heritage. The transmission of cultural data usually occurs through formal teaching, and these conscious forms often become the older stratum of consciousness. Around age 17 or so, youth begin to reflect on problematical issues and begin to live "in the present." As they struggle to clarify the issues of the day, they are prone to transform the uppermost stratum of consciousness into serious reflection, whereas the deeper stratum (habits) remains untouched. Youth appear to be "up to date" and close to the "present" problems by virtue of their "fresh contact" and in the fact that they are "dramatically aware of a process of destabilization and take sides on it" (Mannheim, 1952, p. 301). But their consciousness appears more substantive than formal, and although contemporary and timely, somewhat superficial.

Perhaps the most critical factor in Mannheim's generational unit formula involves the psychological structuring of consciousness, or what he terms the "stratification of experience." Merely being born during the same period in history does not guarantee similarity of consciousness within a generational unit. The sharing in the same "inner-dialectic" provides the critical experience — with its perceptions, gestalt, linguistic expressions that structure and modify environmental and sensory data — "partly simplifying and abbreviating it, partly elaborating and filling it out" (Mannheim, 1952, p. 306). The perceptions of generation units are formed in a particular way, and the structure and content of these psychological configurations depend on the collective values and goals to which their members subscribe. The importance of these formative and interpretive principles is that they provide the link between spatially separated individuals who may never have come into contact with one another. Whereas the common location in the generation cycle is of potential importance, the generational unit emerges when similarly located contemporaries share ideas, values, and participate in a common destiny.

Formalizing the Generation Unit Theory

Although few studies have attempted to measure the generational unit theory (Simirenko, 1966; Zeitlin, 1966; Braungart, 1976), considerable bivariate empirical support exists for this argument. As referred to previously, Eisenstadt (1956, 1963), Ortega y Gasset (1958), Erikson (1963, 1968), Feuer (1969, 1975), Dawson and Prewitt (1969), Keniston (1971), Ausubel and Sullivan (1972), Moynihan (1973), Ryder (1974), and Milbrath and Goel (1977) discussed biological factors inherent in the generational cycle that affect student political behavior. All suggested that the period of youth, with its search for fidelity, identity, meaning, and strong peer-group identification has important political implications.

Holzner (1962), Mills (1963), Lipset (1967, 1976), Emmerson (1968), Laqueur (1969), Lipset and Altbach (1969), Miles (1971), DeConde (1971), Lipset and Ladd (1971), Moller (1968), Altbach (1974), Gillis (1974), Unger (1974), and Vickers (1975) discussed the historical significance of youth movements, both in advanced and developing countries. They maintained that different historical configurations have influenced the form and substance of student movements around the world.

Perhaps more than any single area of research numerous empirical studies exist describing the social and demographic characteristics of youth movements. Important among these have been the works by Lyonns (1965), Somers (1965), Flacks (1967, 1971), Bayer and Astin (1969), Scott and El-Assal (1969), Kahn and Bowers (1970), Altbach and Kelly (1973), Wood (1974), and Kearney (1975), and a number of case studies (Foster & Long, 1970; Riesman & Stadtman, 1973; Taft, 1976).

Katz and Allport (1931), Laing (1967), Draper (1967), Roszak (1969), Denisoff and Levine (1970), Slater (1970), Reich (1970), Berger (1971), Revel (1971), Gottlieb (1973), and Bell (1976) investigated the influence of traditional and emerging cultural forces and their effect on the counterculture and youth politics.

Finally, Gamson, Goodman and Gurin (1967), Flacks (1967, 1971), Keniston (1968, 1971, 1973), Haan, Smith, and Block (1968), Block, Haan, and Smith (1968), Whittaker and Watts (1969), Liebert (1971), Meyer (1971, 1973), Hendin (1975), and Gold, Christie, and Friedman (1976) studied the psychological and ideological characteristics of activist youth.

What has not been undertaken to date has been a multivariate, sequential treatment of these bivariate relationships explaining the political characteristics of generational units. To formalize the general theory originally outlined by Mannheim, the following features and relationships are presented as suggestive: *generational unit* is defined as the dependent variable; the *psychological structuring* of *consciousness* the intervening variable, which is both influenced by and monitors select *historical, social, cultural,* and *biological* factors, the independent variables (see Figure 1). The generational unit model predicts that cohort membership alone will not determine generational behavior in a direct sense, but that age acting indirectly through exposure to select historical, social, and cultural factors in combination with a new psychological consciousness and common destiny will explain generation units. Mannheim also argued that generational units are able to act as influences on the historical, social, and cultural processes over time. There appears to be a feedback effect in operation whereby the political behavior of the generation units themselves can partially determine the course of social and historical change.

Discussion

The generational unit theory assumes the progression of society toward higher and more sophisticated forms of social and political organization (Braungart, 1974). What is significant about Mannheim's theory is that he does not attribute youth movements to any single cause but to youth's reactions to the major issues and contradictions that exist in society at a particular period in time. Youth groups take sides and mobilize over issues like their parents before them, but, unlike the adult population, they are more attuned to the current issues that confront their generation due to their "fresh contact" with society. When the contradictions appear historically "new" (women's rights, human rights, ecology) and when they cut across old conflicts of interest, youth movements have a greater probability of occurring.

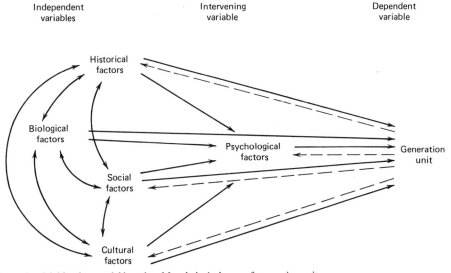

Figure 1.   Multivariate model based on Mannheim's theory of generation units.

The generational unit theory has the capacity to examine generational units both in terms of *intergenerational* and *intragenerational* behavior. In this respect, the theory can differentiate and evaluate political behavior both between and within generations. For example, Zeitlin (1966) observed differential responses to the Cuban revolution by workers in Cuba in 1962, which he attributed to their different historical experiences of being part of a particular political generation. Members of the "Castro generation," the age cohort 28 to 35, were most likely to have favorable attitudes toward the revolution — probably due to the "common frame of reference" developed during the anti-Batista struggle. Weakest support for the revolution was given by the 21- to 27-year-old age group (the youngest age group surveyed), or those workers who were too young to remember working conditions in prerevolutionary Cuba.

The theory also has the flexibility to explain differential political behavior within the same generation. Why individuals born into a particular generation display divergent political orientations appears to be due partially to the fact that groups or units within the same generation may be further differentiated by social structural factors. When Zeitlin (1966) looked at "within" generational differences in attitudes toward the Cuban revolution, he found that prerevolutionary employment status had a significant impact on attitudes toward the revolution for each of the generations studied. Workers who were unemployed or underemployed prior to the revolution tended to be strongly pro-Communist and more supportive of the revolution than workers who were regularly employed before the revolution.

Mannheim's generational unit theory appears particularly applicable in accounting for the radically divergent student political styles exhibited by youth in Canada and the United States during the late 1960s. Denisoff and Levine (1970) surveyed youth and adults in Vancouver, British Columbia, and presented evidence suggesting that generation units differentiated themselves along political and cultural lines. Opposing political orientations among members of the same age cohort were illustrated in another study of the left-wing SDS and right-wing YAF (Westby & Braungart, 1970). Both groups rejected status quo politics, and in its place constructed utopias that transcended the present and were oriented toward the future. SDS youth supported the goals of "participatory democracy," military disengagement in Vietnam, humanitarianism, and an idyllic communal order, whereas the members of YAF favored the dominance of the free enterprise system, nationalism, militarism, and rugged individualism.

These activist youth were asked to write "the history of the United States from the present to the year 2000," and the essays were classified according to their major organizing themes (Westby & Braungart, 1970). Five utopian-dystopian conceptions of the future were identified:

1. Progressive utopia (steady improvement).

2. Revolutionary utopia (overthrow of existing structure).

3. Conversionist utopia (downward drift followed by a "rapid awakening").

4. Linear decline dystopia (steady decline).

5. Eschatological dystopia (sudden cataclysm).

SDS tended to be more dystopian than utopian; YAF youth favored utopian themes. Their conceptions of the future were not determined solely by opposing political styles but appear partially the result of divergent social background experiences. When comparing the status characteristics of SDS versus YAF, members of the left-wing group tended to come from upper-middle-class, low ethnic status, and Jewish or nonreligious backgrounds. Members of the right-wing group, on the other hand, were often from the lower-middle and working-class, high ethnic status, and predominantly Protestant or Catholic backgrounds (Braungart, 1969, 1971a, 1971d). It appears that youth groups or units "within" the same generation who exhibit different structural locations experience and interpret the sociopolitical world differently. In this study, two types of status strains may be related to the origin of radical youth groups: (1) a high social-class position in conjunction with low social-status positions, and (2) low social class in conjunction with high social-status positions. SDS members, with their high achieved status albeit low ascribed status, favor the reorganization of society, while YAF, who experience low achieved status and high ascribed status, likewise repudiate contemporary society. In the first instance, when mobility and achievement in occupation and education are not matched by comparable religious and ethnic position, one might expect a rejection of the status quo in place of more universalistic, equalitarian standards. In the second instance, when groups experience social rewards on the basis of membership in established American status groupings but lack comparable class security and insulation, there is likely to be a rejection of the status quo in favor of a return to traditional principles and values. This hypothesis may partially explain the radical departure from conventional politics exhibited by SDS and YAF groups in the 1960s (Braungart, 1971d).

In a more recent series of articles devoted to youth and generations (Bengtson & Laufer, 1974), Kandel (1974) investigated inter- and intragenerational influences on adolescent marijuana use in a New York State survey. This study documented the significant impact members within the same generation had on adolescent drug users — however, the highest rate of marijuana use among youth resulted from the interaction effect when both their parents *and* best friends used drugs. In the same series, Fendrich (1974) reported the results of his research, tracking members of a generation unit over time. A group of former civil rights activists from the early 1960s retained their distinctive political characteristics a decade later in the early 1970s. The activist generation unit, when compared to student government leaders and nonactivists from that same age cohort, did not become more moderate or disillusioned with society as many critics had predicted. To the contrary, this group maintained strong political commitments, especially toward perceived economic changes within the United States. In the follow-up study, many former activists were employed in knowledge and service industries, remained active in change-oriented voluntary organizations, and participated in institutional and noninstitutional politics — all highly consistent with their earlier ideological views and political objectives.

Testing a truncated version of Mannheim's theory of generation units, Braungart (1976) constructed a multivariate model comparing sets of social location and consciousness factors explaining political behavior among two random samples of college and noncollege youth. Prior to the 1972 presidential election, both youth groups were surveyed to determine their presidential candidate support and urge to participate in a demonstration. Path analysis was used to examine the direct, indirect, and total effects of the variables in the model. Results indicated that the relationships predicting youth politics differed within and between the two youth groups. Family status and personal political attitudes differentiated candidate support and urge to demonstrate among college students, whereas demographic characteristics, family status, and institutional confidence explained considerable variance in politics among noncollege youth. The form of the generation unit theory provided a useful tool for comparing the political behavior of these two youth groups within the same generation.

The generational unit theory is not concerned with social statics, but with emerging forces and creative syntheses that continually give rise to new patterns of behavior over time. Unlike the functionalist theory of generational conflict (Eisenstadt, 1956, 1963; Bettelheim, 1963; Parsons, 1963), the generational unit theory suggests that youth are not rebelling against society but instead are creating new forms of consciousness that are partially the result of generational and social structural forces. What makes the generational unit theory different from the homeostatic or functionalist theory is that youth movements in the former represent *destabilizing* forces within history. The newer units represent the vanguard or "cutting edge" of specific entelechy that interact and compete for the definition and control of reality.

Since youth movements are not constant throughout history but occur at different times and places, their explanation cannot be attributed solely to generic social and historic forces. Although historical, cultural, social, and psychological factors add to the unfolding drama of human behavior, these factors alone cannot explain the unique "system of coordinates" or the "space between evolving events" that precipitate youth movements. Although these forces are necessary, they do not appear sufficient to explain the sporadic or unique conditions that produce change at certain periods in time. Mannheim (1940) calls the unique blends of social and psychological factors *principia media* — the underlying principles or interactions that represent "transmission belts" of human behavior. Principia media are described as temporary sets of general factors so closely intertwined that they operate as a single causal factor. As products of universal forces in a concrete setting, they become integrated out of the various factors at work in a given place at a given time — a particular combination of circumstances that may never be repeated in history. Generations are not dominated by single principium medium but by a series of them, which interact in a multidimensional way. Reality consists of the mutual relationships between economic, political, and ideological spheres and of the concrete principia media operating among them. In Mannheim's (1940) view, a large number of mutually related principia media form a structure or social psychological pattern, while interdependent change in a number of principia media constitutes structural change.

The present discussion of generational unit theory and principia media has important implications for the study of youth movements. The generational unit theory provides a model specifying formal properties that interact in a certain way, while principia media reflect the unique substantive interconnections among and between components of the theory over time. Only when we are able to understand the structural and emerging properties of historical, social, cultural, and psychological forces will we be in a better position to measure and explain the complicated interrelationships that produce youth movements.

REFERENCES

Abramson, P. R. *Generational change in American politics.* Lexington, Mass.: Heath, 1975.

Adelson, J. The political imagination of the young adolescent. *Daedalus,* 1971, *100*(4), 1013–1049.

———. The development of ideology in adolescence. In S. E. Dragastin and G. H. Elder, Jr., (Eds.), *Adolescence in the life cycle.* New York: Wiley, 1975.

Albornoz, O. *Estudiantes norteamericanos: Perfiles politicos.* Caracas, Venezuela: Instituto Societas, 1967.

Allerbeck, K. R. Soziale bedingungen für Studentischen radikalismus. Inaugural-dissertation zur erlangung des Doktorgrades der Philosophischen fakultät der Universität zu Köln, West Germany, 1971.

Altbach, P. G. *Student politics in America*. New York: McGraw-Hill, 1974.

Altbach, P. G., and Kelly, D. H. *American students*. Lexington, Mass.: Heath, 1973.

Altbach, P. G., Laufer, R. S., and McVey, S. (Eds.). *Academic supermarkets*. San Francisco: Jossey-Bass, 1971.

American Council on Education. National norms for entering college freshmen — Fall 1969. *ACE Research Reports*, 1969, *4*(7).

——. The American freshman: National norms for Fall 1971. *ACE Research Reports*, 1971, *6*(6).

——. *The American freshman: National norms for Fall 1975*. Los Angeles: University of California Graduate School of Education, 1975.

——. *The American freshman: National norms for Fall 1976*. Los Angeles: University of California Graduate School of Education, 1976.

Aries, P. *Centuries of childhood*. New York: Random House, 1965.

Asher, H. *Presidential elections and American politics*. Homewood, Ill.: Dorsey, 1976.

Ash-Garner, R. *Social movements in America*. Chicago: Rand McNally, 1977.

Astin, A. W. Personal and environmental determinants of student activism. *Measurement and Evaluation in Guidance*, 1968, *1*(3), 149–162.

Auger, C., Barton, A., and Maurice, R. The nature of the student movement and radical proposals for change at Columbia University. *The Human Factor*, 1969 *9*(1), 18–40.

Ausubel, D. P., and Sullivan, E. V. *Theory and problem of child development*. New York: Grune & Stratton, 1972.

Backman, E. L., and Findlay, D. J. Student protest: A cross-national study. *Youth and Society*, 1973, *5*(1), 3–46.

Baird, L. L. Who protests: A study of student activists. In J. Foster and D. Long (Eds.), *Protest! Student activism in Ameria*. New York: Morrow, 1970.

Bakke, E. W., and Bakke, M. S. *Campus challenge*. Hamden, Conn.: Archon, 1971.

Bayer, A. E. Institutional correlates of faculty support of campus unrest. *Sociology of Education*, 1972, *45*(1), 76–94.

Bayer, A. E., and Astin, A. W. Violence and disruption on the U.S. campus, 1968–1969. *Educational Record*, Fall 1969, pp. 337–350.

Bell, D. *The coming of postindustrial society*. New York: Basic Books, 1973.

——. *The cultural contradictions of capitalism*. New York: Basic Books, 1976.

Bengtson, V. L. The generation gap: A review and typology of social-psychological perspectives. *Youth and Society*, 1970, *2*(1), 7–32.

Bengtson, V. L., and Black, K. D. Intergenerational relations and continuities in socialization. In P. Baltes and W. Schaie (Eds.), *Life-span developmental psychology: Personality and socialization*. New York: Academic, 1973.

Bengtson, V. L., and Cutler, N. E. Generations and intergenerational relations: Perspectives on age groups and social change. In R. H. Binstock and E. Shanas (Eds.), *Handbook of aging and the social sciences*. New York: Van Nostrand Reinhold, 1976.

Bengtson, V. L., and Laufer, R. S. (Eds.). Youth, generations, and social change: Part I. *Journal of Social Issues*, 1974, *30*(2); Part II. *Journal of Social Issues*, 1974, *30*(3).

Berger, B. M. *Looking for America*. Englewood Cliffs, N.J.: Prentice-Hall, 1971.

Bettelheim, B. The problem of generations. In E. Erikson (Ed.), *Youth: Change and challenge*. New York: Basic Books, 1963.

Block, J., Haan, N., and Smith, M. B. Activism and apathy in contemporary adolescents. In J. F. Adams (Ed.), *Understanding adolescence*. Boston: Allyn & Bacon, 1968.

Bolton, C. D., and Kammeyer, K. C. *The university student*. New Haven, Conn.: College & University Press, 1967.

Braungart, R. G. Family status, socialization and student politics: A multivariate analysis. Unpublished doctoral dissertation, Pennsylvania State University, 1969.

————. Family status, socialization, and student politics: A multivariate analysis. *American Journal of Sociology*, 1971a, *77*(1), 108–130.

————. Parental identification and student politics. *Sociology of Education*, 1971b, *44*(4), 463–473.

————. SDS and YAF: A comparison of two student radical groups in the mid 1960s. *Youth and Society*, 1971c, *2*(4), 441–457.

————. Status politics and student politics. *Youth and Society*, 1971d, *3*(2), 195–209.

————. The sociology of generations and student politics: A comparison of the functionalist and generational unit models. *Journal of Social Issues*, 1974, *30*(2), 31–54.

————. College and noncollege youth politics in 1972: An application of Mannheim's generation unit model. *Journal of Youth and Adolescence*, 1976, *5*(4), 325–347.

Braungart, R. G., and Braungart, M. M. Administration, faculty, and student reactions to campus unrest. *Journal of College Student Personnel*, 1972, *13*(2), 112–119.

————. Protest attitudes and behavior among college youth: A case study. *Youth and Society*, 1974, *6*(2), 219–248.

————. Family, school, and personal political factors in student politics: A case study of the 1972 presidential election. *Journal of Marriage and the Family*, 1975, *37*, 823–839.

————. Reference group, social judgments and student politics. *Adolescence*, 1979, *14*(53), 135–157.

Brier, A., and Tansey, S. Ethnic diversity and political attitudes in a Nigerian university. *Youth and Society*, 1974, *6*(2), 151–178.

Brunswick, A. F. What generation gap? *Social Problems*, 1970, *17*(3), 358–371.

Cherniss, C. Personality and ideology: A personological study of women's liberation. *Psychiatry*, 1972, *35*(2), 109–125.

Clark, B. R., and Trow, M. "Determinants of college student subculture." Center for the Study of Higher Education, University of California, Berkeley, 1960.

Clarke, J. W., and Egan, J. "Social and political dimensions of campus protest activity." Center for Policy Analysis, Institute for Social Research, Florida State University, 1969.

Coleman, J. S. *Youth: Transition to adulthood*. Chicago: University of Chicago Press, 1974.

Connell, R. W. *The child's construction of politics*. Melbourne, Australia: Melbourne University Press, 1971.

Cowdry, R., Keniston, K., and Cabin, S. The war and military obligation: Private attitudes and public actions. *Journal of Personality*, 1970, *38*(4), 525–549.

Cutler, N. E. Generational approaches to political socialization. *Youth and Society*, 1976, *8*(2), 175–207.

Cutler, N. E., and Bengtson, V. L. Age and political alienation: Maturation, generation, and period effects. *The Annals*, 1974, *415*, 160–175.

Davis, K. The sociology of parent-youth conflict. *American Sociological Review*, 1940, *5*(4), 523–535.

Dawson, R., and Prewitt, K. *Political socialization*. Boston: Little, Brown, 1969.

DeConde, A. (Ed.). *Student activism*. New York: Scribner's, 1971.

DeMartini, J. R. Student activists of the 1930s and 1960s. *Youth and Society*, 1975, *6*(4), 395–422.

Demerath, N. J., Marwell, G., and Aiken, M. T. *Dynamics of idealism*. San Francisco: Jossey-Bass, 1971.

Denisoff, R. S., and Levine, M. H. Generations and counterculture. *Youth and Society,* 1970, *2*(1), 33–58.

Denisoff, R. S., and Peterson, R. A. *The sounds of social change*. Chicago: Rand McNally, 1972.

Dennis, J. *Political socialization research: A bibliography*. Beverly Hills, Calif.: Sage, 1973a.

———. (Ed.). *Socialization to politics*. New York: Wiley, 1973b.

Derber, C., and Flacks, R. An exploration of the value system of radical student activists and their parents. Paper presented at the annual meetings of the American Sociological Association, San Francisco, August 1968.

Donovan, J. M., and Shaevitz, M. H. Student political activists: A typology. *Youth and Society,* 1973, *4*(3), 379–411.

Doress, I. A study of a sampling of Boston University student activists. Unpublished doctoral dissertation, Boston University, 1968.

Douglas, J. D. *Youth in turmoil*. Washington, D.C.: U.S. Government Printing Office, 1970.

Douvan, E., and Gold, M. Modal patterns in American adolescence. In L. W. Hoffman and M. L. Hoffman (Eds.), *Review of child development research* (Vol. 2). New York: Russell Sage Foundation, 1966.

Draper, H. The student movement of the thirties: A political history. In R. J. Simon (Ed.), *As we saw the thirties*. Urbana: University of Illinois Press, 1967.

Dunlap, R. Radical and conservative student activists: A comparison of family backgrounds. *Pacific Sociological Review,* 1970, *13*(3), 171–181.

Eisenstadt, S. N. *From generation to generation*. Glencoe, Ill.: Free Press, 1956.

———. Archetypal patterns of youth. In E. H. Erikson (Ed.), *Youth: Change and challenge*. New York: Basic Books, 1963.

Emmerson, D. K. (Ed.). *Students and politics in developing nations*. New York: Praeger, 1968.

Erikson, E. H. *Identity and the life cycle*. New York: International Universities Press, 1959.

———. Youth: Fidelity and diversity. In E. H. Erikson (Ed.), *Youth: Change and challenge*. New York: Basic Books, 1963.

———. *Identity: Youth and crises*. New York: Norton, 1968.

Fendrich, J. M. Activists ten years later: A test of generational unit continuity. *Journal of Social Issues,* 1974, *30*(3), 95–118.

Fendrich, J. M., Simons, R., and Tarleau, A. Activists ten years later: A study of life styles and politics. Paper presented at the annual meetings of the American Sociological Association, New Orleans, August 1972.

Fengler, A. P., and Wood, V. Continuity between the generations: Differential influence of mothers and fathers. *Youth and Society,* 1973, *4*(3), 359–372.

Fenton, J. H., and Gleason, G. Student power at the University of Massachusetts: A case study. Amherst: Bureau of Government Research, University of Massachusetts, 1969.

Feuer, L. S. *The conflict of generations*. New York: Basic Books, 1969.

———. *Ideology and ideologists*. New York: Harper & Row, 1975.

Fischer, J. *Vital signs, U.S.A.* New York: Harper & Row, 1975.

Flacks, R. The liberated generation: Explorations of the roots of student protest. *Journal of Social Issues,* 1967, *23*(3), 52–75.

———. Social and cultural meanings of student revolt: Some informal comparative observations. *Social Problems,* 1970a, *17*(3), 340–357.

————. Who protests: The social bases of the student movement. In J. Foster and D. Long (Eds.), *Protest! Student activism in America*. New York: Morrow, 1970b.

————. *Youth and social change*. Chicago: Markham, 1971.

Fortune. Youth in college. *Fortune*, 1936, *13*, 99–102, 155–162.

Foster, J., and Long, D. (Eds.). *Protest! Student activism in America*. New York: Morrow, 1970.

Gamson, Z. F., Goodman, J., and Gurin, G. Radicals, moderates and bystanders during a university protest. Paper presented at the annual meetings of the American Sociological Association, San Francisco, August 1967.

Gella, A. Student youth in Poland: Four generations 1945–1970. *Youth and Society*, 1975, *6*(3), 309–343.

Geller, J. D., and Howard, G. "Student activism and the war in Vietnam." Department of Psychiatry, Yale University School of Medicine, 1969.

Gillis, J. R. *Youth and history*. New York: Academic, 1974.

Goertzel, T. Generation conflict and social change. *Youth and Society*, 1972, *3*(3), 327–352.

————. American imperialism and the Brazilian student movement. *Youth and Society*, 1974, *6*(2), 123–150.

Gold, A. R., Christie, R., and Friedman, L. N. *Fists and flowers: A social psychological interpretation of student dissent*. New York: Academic, 1976.

Goldsen, R., Rosenberg, M., Williams, R., and Suchman, E. *What college students think*. Princeton, N.J.: Van Nostrand, 1960.

Goodwin, G. A. On transcending the absurd: An inquiry in the sociology of meaning. *American Journal of Sociology*, 1971, *76*(5), 831–846.

Gordon, C., and Gaitz, C. M. Leisure and lives: Personal expressivity across the life span. In R. H. Binstock and E. Shanas (Eds.), *Handbook of aging and the social sciences*. New York: Van Nostrand Reinhold, 1976.

Gottlieb, D. "Youth and the meaning of work." University Park: College of Human Development, Pennsylvania State University, 1973.

Granberg, D., and Seidel, J. Social judgments of the urban and Vietnam issues in 1968 and 1972. *Social Forces*, 1976, *55*(1), 1–15.

Greenstein, F. I. *Children and politics*. New Haven, Conn.: Yale University Press, 1968.

Gusfield, J. R. Intellectual character and American universities. *Journal of General Education*, January 1963, *14*, 230–247.

————. (Ed.) *Protest, reform, and revolt*. New York: Wiley, 1970.

Haan, N. Moral redefinition in families as a critical aspect of the generation gap. *Youth and Society*, 1971, *2*(3), 259–283.

Haan, N., Smith, M. B., and Block, J. Moral reasoning of young adults: Political-social behavior, family background, and personality correlates. *Journal of Personality and Social Psychology*, 1968, *10*(3), 183–201.

Hadden, J. K. The private generation. *Psychology Today*, 1969, *3*(5), 32–35, 68–69.

Hastings, P. K., and Hoge, D. R. Religious change among college students over two decades. *Social Forces*, 1970, *49*(1), 16–28.

Heberle, R. *Social movements*. New York: Appleton-Century-Crofts, 1951.

Heist, P. "Intellect and commitment: The faces of discontent." Center for the Study of Higher Education, University of California, Berkeley, 1966.

Hendin, H. *The age of sensation*. New York: Norton, 1975.

Hess, R. D., and Torney, J. V. *The development of political attitudes in children*. Garden City, N.Y.: Doubleday, 1968.

Hodgkinson, H. Student protest — An institutional and national profile. *The Record,* 1970, *71*(4), 337–355.

Holzner, B. Institutional change, social stratification and the direction of youth movements. *Journal of Educational Sociology,* 1962, *36*(2), 49–56.

Hyman, H. H. *Political socialization.* New York: Free Press, 1959.

Isenberg, P., Schnitzer, R., and Rothman, S. Psychological variables in student activism: The radical triad and some religious differences. *Journal of Youth and Adolescence,* 1977, *6*(1), 11–24.

Janowitz, M. *Social control of the welfare state.* New York: Elsevier, 1976.

Jaros, D. *Socialization to politics.* New York: Praeger, 1973.

Kahn, R. M., and Bowers, W. J. The social context of the rank-and-file student activist: A test of four hypotheses. *Sociology of Education,* 1970, *43*(1), 39–47.

Kandel, D. Inter- and intragenerational influences on adolescent marijuana use. *Journal of Social Issues,* 1974, *30*(2), 107–135.

Katz, D., and Allport, F. H. *Students' attitudes.* Syracuse, N.Y.: Craftsman, 1931.

Kearney, R. N. Educational expansion and volatility in Sri Lanka: The 1971 insurrection. *Asian Survey,* 1975, *15*(9), 727–744.

Kearney, R. N., and Jiggins, J. The Ceylon insurrection of 1971. *Journal of Commonwealth and Comparative Politics,* 1975, *13*(1), 40–64.

Keniston, K. *Young radicals.* New York: Harcourt, Brace and World, 1968.

———. *Youth and dissent.* New York: Harcourt Brace Jovanovich, 1971.

———. *Radicals and militants.* Lexington, Mass.: Heath, 1973.

Kerpelman, L. C. *Activists and nonactivists: A psychological study of American college students.* New York: Behavioral Publications, 1972.

Killian, L. M. Social movements. In R. L. Faris (Ed.), *Handbook of modern sociology.* Chicago: Rand McNally, 1966.

Kohlberg, L. Development of moral character and moral ideology. In M. L. Hoffman and L. W. Hoffman (Eds.), *Review of child development research* (Vol. 1). New York: Russell Sage Foundation, 1964.

———. Moral development and the education of adolescents. In E. D. Evans (Ed.), *Adolescent readings in behavior and development.* Hinsdale, Ill.: Dryden, 1970.

Krauss, E. S. *Japanese radicals revisited.* Berkeley: University of California Press, 1974.

Ladd, E. C., and Lipset, S. M. *The divided academy.* New York: Norton, 1975.

Ladd, E. C., Hadley, C., and King, L. A new political realignment? *The Public Interest,* 1971, *32,* 46–63.

Laing, R. D. *The politics of experience.* New York: Ballantine, 1967.

Lambert, T. A. Karl Mannheim and the sociology of generations. Paper presented at the annual meetings of the Eastern Sociological Society, New York, April 1970.

———. Generational factors in political-cultural consciousness. Paper presented at the annual meetings of the American Political Science Association, Chicago, September 1971.

———. Generations and change: Toward a theory of generations as a force in historical process. *Youth and Society,* 1972, *4*(1), 21–45.

Laqueur, W. Student revolts. *Commentary,* 1969, *47,* 33–41.

Lauer, R. H. *Perspectives on social change.* Boston: Allyn & Bacon, 1973.

Lewis, R. A. Socialization into national violence: Familial correlates of hawkish attitudes toward war. *Journal of Marriage and the Family,* 1971, *33,* 699–708.

Lewis, S. H., and Kraut, R. E. "Correlates of student political activism and ideology." Department of Psychology, Yale University, 1971.

Liebert, R. *Radical and militant youth*. New York: Praeger, 1971.

Liebman, A., Walker, K. N., and Glazer, M. *Latin American university students: A six-nation study*. Cambridge: Harvard University Press, 1972.

Lipset, S. M. (Ed.). *Student politics*. New York: Basic Books, 1967.

————. *Rebellion in the university*. Chicago: University of Chicago Press, 1976.

Lipset, S. M. and Altbach, P. G. (Eds.). *Students in revolt*. Boston: Houghton Mifflin, 1969.

Lipset, S. M., and Ladd, E. C. College generations — From the 1930s to the 1960s. *The Public Interest*, 1971, *25*, 99–113.

Loken, J. O. A multivariate analysis of student activism at the University of Alberta. Unpublished doctoral dissertation, University of Alberta, 1970.

Lotz, R. E. An interpretation of student radicalism in the United States during the sixties. Unpublished masters thesis, University of Washington, 1970.

Lyonns, G. The police car demonstration: A survey of participants. In S. M. Lipset and S. S. Wolin (Eds.), *The Berkeley student revolt*. Garden City, N.Y.: Doubleday, 1965.

Maidenberg, M., and Meyer, P. The Berkeley rebels: Five years later. *Public Opinion Quarterly*, 1970, *34*, 477–478.

Mankoff, M., and Flacks, R. The changing social base of the American student movement. *The Annals*, 1971, *395*, 54–67.

Mannheim, K. *Man and society in an age of reconstruction*. New York: Harcourt, Brace and World, 1940.

————. The problem of youth in modern society. In K. Mannheim, *Diagnosis of our time*. New York: Oxford University Press, 1944.

————. The problem of generations. In K. Mannheim, *Essays on the sociology of knowledge*. London: Routledge and Kegan Paul, 1952.

Matza, D. Subterranean traditions of youth. *The Annals*, 1961, *338*, 102–108.

Meyer, J. M., and Rubinson, R. Structural determinants of student political activity: A comparative interpretation. *Sociology of Education*, 1972, *45*(1), 23–46.

Meyer, M. W. Harvard students in the midst of crisis. *Sociology of Education*, 1971, *44*(3), 245–269.

————. Harvard students in the midst of crisis: A note on the sources of leftism. *Sociology of Education*, 1973, *46*(2), 203–218.

Milbrath, L. W., and Goel, M. L. *Political participation*. Chicago: Rand McNally, 1977.

Miles, M. W. *The radical probe: The logic of student rebellion*. New York: Atheneum, 1971.

Miller, R. E., and Everson, D. H. Personality and ideology: The case of student power. Paper presented at the annual meetings of the Midwest Political Science Association, Southern Illinois University, April–May 1970.

Mills, C. W. The new left. In I. L. Horowitz (Ed.), *Power, politics and people*. New York: Ballantine, 1963.

Moller, H. Youth as a force in the modern world. *Comparative Studies in Society and History*, April 1968, pp. 237–260.

Morison, S. E. *Three centuries of Harvard*. Cambridge: Harvard University Press, 1936.

Morris, M. B. *An excursion into creative sociology*. New York: Columbia University Press, 1977.

Moynihan, D. Peace — Some thoughts on the 1960s and 1970s. *The Public Interest*, 1973, *32*, 3–12.

Niemi, R. G. *How family members perceive each other*. New Haven, Conn.: Yale University Press, 1974a.

————. (Ed.). *The politics of future citizens*. San Francisco: Jossey-Bass, 1974b.

Oberschall, A. *Social conflict and social movements*. Englewood Cliffs, N.J.: Prentice-Hall, 1973.

Ortega y Gasset, J. *Man and crisis*. New York: Norton, 1958.

Orum, A. M. (Ed.). *The seeds of politics*. Englewood Cliffs, N.J.: Prentice-Hall, 1972.

Parsons, T. Youth in the context of American society. In E. H. Erikson (Ed.), *Youth: Change and challenge*. New York: Basic Books, 1963.

Paulus, G. A multivariate analysis study of student activist leaders, student government leaders, and nonactivists. Unpublished doctoral dissertation, Michigan State University, 1968.

Peterson, R. E. *The scope of organized student protest in 1964–1965*. Princeton, N.J.: Educational Testing Service, 1966.

————. *The scope of organized student protest in 1967–1968*. Princeton, N.J.: Educational Testing Service, 1968a.

————. The student left in American higher education. *Daedalus,* 1968b, *97*(1), 293–317.

Peterson, R. E., and Bilorusky, J. A. *May 1970: The campus aftermath of Cambodia and Kent State*. Berkeley, Calif.: Carnegie Commission on Higher Education, 1971.

Piaget, J. *The moral judgment of the child*. New York: Free Press, 1965.

————. *Six psychological studies*. New York: Random House, 1967.

Pierce, R. A. "Personality styles of student activists." University Health Service, University of Rochester, 1971.

President's Commission on Campus Unrest. *The report of the president's commission on campus unrest*. Washington, D.C.: U.S. Government Printing Office, 1970.

Reich, C. A. *The greening of America*. New York: Random House, 1970.

Reinhold, R. Carter victory laid to Democrats back in fold, plus Independents. *The New York Times,* November 4, 1976, p. 25.

Revel, J. F. *Without Marx or Jesus: The new American revolution has begun*. Garden City, N.Y.: Doubleday, 1971.

Riesman, D., and Stadtman, V. A. (Eds.). *Academic transformation*. New York: McGraw-Hill, 1973.

Riley, M. W., Johnson, M., and Foner, A. (Eds.). *Aging and society: A sociology of age stratification* (Vol. 3). New York: Russell Sage Foundation, 1972.

Roberts, R. E., and Kloss, R. M. *Social movements*. St. Louis: Mosby, 1974.

Roszak, T. *The making of a counter culture*. Garden City, N.Y.: Doubleday, 1969.

Ryder, N. B. The demography of youth. In J. S. Coleman (Ed.), *Youth: Transition to adulthood*. Chicago: University of Chicago Press, 1974.

Sampson, E. E., Fisher, L., Angel, A., Mulman, A., and Sullins, C. "Two profiles: The draft resister and the ROTC cadet." University of California, Berkeley, 1969.

Schiff, L. F. The conservative movement on American college campuses. Unpublished doctoral dissertation, Harvard University, 1964.

Schwartz, D. C., and Schwartz, S. K. (Eds.). *New directions in political socialization*. New York: Free Press, 1975.

Scott, J. W., and El-Assal, M. Multiversity, university size, university quality, and student protest: An empirical study. *American Sociological Review,* 1969, *34*(5), 202–209.

Scott, M. B., and Lyman, S. M. *The revolt of the students*. Columbus, Ohio: Merrill, 1970.

Scurrah, M. J. Some organizational structural determinants of student protest in U.S. universities and colleges. Unpublished doctoral dissertation, Cornell University, 1972.

Sherif, M., and Sherif, C. *Social psychology*. New York: Harper & Row, 1969.

Shimbori, M. The sociology of a student movement: A Japanese case study. *Daedalus,* 1968, *97*(1), 204–228.

Shotland, R. L. "The communication patterns and the structure of social relationships at a large university." Unpublished manuscript, Graduate Center, City University of New York, 1970.

Sigel, R. S. (Ed.). *Learning about politics.* New York: Random House, 1970.

Simirenko, A. Mannheim's generational analysis and acculturation. *British Journal of Sociology,* 1966, *17*(3), 292–299.

Simmons, L. R. The real generation gap: A speculation on the meaning and implications of the generation gap. *Youth and Society,* 1971, *3*(1), 119–135.

Skolnick, J. H. *The politics of protest.* New York: Simon & Schuster, 1969.

Slater, P. *The pursuit of loneliness: American culture at the breaking point.* Boston: Beacon, 1970.

Smith, M. B., Haan, N., and Block, J. Social-psychological aspects of student activism. *Youth and Society,* 1970, *1*(3), 261–288.

Solomon, F., and Fishman, J. R. Youth and peace: A psycho-social study of student peace demonstrators in Washington, D.C. *Journal of Social Issues,* 1964, *20*(4), 54–73.

Somers, R. The mainsprings of rebellion: A survey of Berkeley students in November 1964. In S. M. Lipset and S. S. Wolin (Eds.), *The Berkeley student revolt.* Garden City, N.Y.: Doubleday, 1965.

Taft, J. *Mayday at Yale.* Boulder, Colo.: Westview, 1976.

Thomas, L. E. Family congruence on political orientations of politically active parents and their college-age children. Unpublished doctoral dissertation, University of Chicago, 1968.

Thurber, J. A., and Rogers, E. D. Some causes and consequences of student political participation. *Youth and Society,* 1973, *5*(2), 242–256.

Trow, M. *Aspects of American higher education 1969–1975.* Berkeley, Calif.: Carnegie Council on Policy Studies in Higher Education, 1977.

Tygart, C. E., and Holt, N. Examining the Weinberg and Walker typology of student activists. *American Journal of Sociology,* 1972, *77*(5), 957–966.

Unger, I. *The movement: A history of the American new left 1959–1972.* New York: Dodd, Mead, 1974.

U.S. Bureau of the Census. *Historical statistics of the United States, Colonial times to 1970* (Part 2). Washington, D.C.: U.S. Government Printing Office, 1975. (Bicentennial Edition)

Vickers, G. R. *The formation of the new left.* Lexington, Mass.: Heath, 1975.

Wattenberg, B. J. *The real America.* Garden City, N.Y.: Doubleday, 1974.

Watts, W. A., Lynch, S., and Whittaker, D. Alienation and activism in today's college-age youth: Socialization patterns and current family relationships. *Journal of Counseling Psychology,* 1969, *16*(1), 1–7.

Weinberg, I., and Walker, K. Student politics and political systems: Toward a typology. *American Journal of Sociology,* 1969, *75*(1), 77–96.

Westby, D. L. *The clouded vision: The student movement in the United States in the 1960s.* Lewisburg, Pa.: Bucknell University Press, 1976.

Westby, D. L., and Braungart, R. G. Class and politics in the family backgrounds of student political activists. *American Sociological Review,* 1966, *31*(5), 690–692.

———. Activists and the history of the future. In J. Foster and D. Long (Eds.), *Protest! Student activism in America.* New York: Morrow, 1970.

Whittaker, D., and Watts, W. A. Personality characteristics of a nonconformist youth subculture: A study of the Berkeley nonstudent. *Journal of Social Issues,* 1969, *25*(2), 65–89.

————. Personality characteristics associated with activism and disaffiliation in today's college-age youth. *Journal of Counseling Psychology,* 1971, *18*(3), 200–206.

Wilson, J. *Introduction to social movements.* New York: Basic Books, 1973.

Winborn, B. B., and Jansen, D. G. Personality characteristics of campus social-political action leaders. *Journal of Counseling Psychology,* 1967, *14*(6), 509–513.

Wood, J. L. *The sources of American student activism.* Lexington, Mass.: Heath, 1974.

Yang, S. C. Student political activism: The case of the 1960 April revolution in South Korea. *Youth and Society,* 1973, *5*(1), 47–60.

Yankelovich, D. *Generations apart.* New York: Columbia Broadcasting System, 1969.

————. *The changing values on campus.* New York: Washington Square Press, 1972.

Zeitlin, M. Political generations in the Cuban working class. *American Journal of Sociology,* 1966, *71*(5), 493–508.

Name Index

Abhammer, I. M., 58
Abrahamsen, D., 509, 531
Abramowitz, S., 45
Abrams, P., 40
Abramson, P. R., 562, 588
Acock, A. C., 278, 281
Adams, G. R., 170, 184
Adams, J. F., 276, 590
Adams, R. L., 528, 530, 531
Adelson, J., 18, 41, 86, 99,
   113, 115, 161, 179, 182,
   188, 195, 254, 255, 276,
   279, 281, 306, 329, 339,
   348, 351, 352, 353, 358,
   362, 364, 365, 369, 370,
   371, 391, 406, 410, 411,
   412, 413, 414, 416, 417,
   425, 429, 430, 554, 562, 588
Adorno, T. W., 347
Agnew, S., 567
Ahlgren, A., 273
Aiken, M. T., 560, 578, 580,
   591
Ainsworth, M., 112, 115
Albert, E. M., 248
Albert, N., 454
Albornoz, O., 564, 588
Aldridge, J. M., 368
Alexander, J., 509, 531
Alexander, J. F., 521, 531, 533
Alexander, R. A., 91
Allen, J. G., 165, 172, 177, 181
Allen, L., 48
Allerbeck, K., 18, 43
Allerbecl, K. R., 564, 589
Allmendinger, D. F., Jr., 10, 40
Allport, F. H., 572, 584, 593
Allport G., 543, 544
Allport, G. W., 248, 250, 253,
   271, 272
Alston, W. P., 300, 338
Altbach, P. G., 561, 564,
   569, 577, 578, 584, 589, 594
Ames, R., 51, 64, 70
Amstey, F. H., 173, 181
Anderson, J. E., 410, 429
Anderson, L., 419, 430

Andersson, B. E., 21, 40, 268
Andrews, J., 164, 181
Angel, A., 595
Angelev, J., 226, 236
Annesley, P. T., 453
Anthony, E. J., 64, 83
Anthony, H. S., 456
Applebaum, M. I., 239, 240
Apter, D., 123, 124, 125, 126
Arenberg, D., 213, 234
Ariés, P., 9, 40, 502, 531,
   560, 589
Arieti, S., 450, 451
Aristotle, 538, 560
Arlin, P. K., 227
Aronold, M., 334, 341, 498,
   519, 531
Aronfreed, J., 329, 338
Asher, H., 577, 589
Ash-Garner, R., 560, 563, 589
Astin, A., 271, 272, 277, 369,
   549, 550
Astin, A. W., 571, 577, 578,
   579, 584, 589
Atkinson, J. W., 252, 284
Attanasio, A., 122
Auden, W. H., 99
Auger, C., 570, 571, 579, 589
Ausubel, D. P., 211, 213, 220,
   225, 238, 561, 584, 589
Ausubel, P., 211, 213, 220,
   225, 238

Babigian, H. M., 450
Bachman, J., 64, 67
Bachman, J. G., 366, 498,
   505, 513, 514, 531, 534
Bachtold, L. M., 268
Backman, E. L., 564, 589
Bacon, M. K., 273
Bahm, R. M., 415, 429
Bahr, H. M., 271
Baier, K., 300, 338
Bailey, M. M., 256
Bailyn, B., 9, 40

Baird, L. L., 370, 578, 589
Bakan, D., 273, 282
Bakan, P., 205
Baker, E., 64
Baker, E. L., 511, 535
Baker, F., 166, 181
Baker, M., 410, 430
Bakke, E. W., 560, 564, 578,
   580, 589
Bakke, M. S., 560, 564, 578,
   580, 589
Baldwin, A. L., 48
Baldwin, J. M., 433
Balser, B. H., 188
Baltes, P. B., 3, 4, 5, 9, 21, 40,
   42, 43, 44, 58, 59, 60, 64,
   83, 239, 260, 269, 589
Bandura, A., 328, 338
Bandura, H., 318, 338
Bardin, C. W., 119
Bardwick, J. M., 256
Barker, G., 17, 24, 40
Barker, R., 24, 40
Barker, W. J., 397, 405
Barocas, R., 433
Barrett, C L., 461
Barron, F., 550
Barry, H., 273
Bart, W. M., 213, 232, 233,
   234, 237
Barthell, C. N., 452
Bartko, J. J., 451
Bartlett, E., 57
Barton, A., 570, 571, 579,
   589
Barton, C., 521, 531
Bartsch, W., 118, 119, 123
Battle, E., 65
Bauer, R. H., 169, 181
Bauman, K. D., 400, 405
Bauman, K. E., 141, 397, 405
Baumrind, D., 258, 261, 277
Bay, C., 369
Bayer, A. E., 571, 584, 589
Bayley, N., 43, 48, 55, 63, 64,
   70, 132, 143, 416, 419, 429,
   430

Beach, F. A., 133, 138, 140, 388, 406
Beck, A. T., 453, 454
Beck, P. A., 355, 358, 359, 362, 365, 368
Becker, E., 205
Beech, R. P., 261, 262, 263, 265, 267
Bell, D., 271, 568, 569, 581, 584, 589
Bell, N. D., 169, 181
Bell, R. Q., 58, 88, 323, 338
Bellak, L., 451
Bem, D. J., 137
Bem, S. L., 274
Bender, I. E., 271
Bengtson, V. L., 5, 9, 20, 21, 22, 23, 40, 251, 260, 269, 278, 279, 280, 281, 346, 357, 361, 364, 425, 429, 581, 587, 589, 590
Berg, I., 459, 460
Berger, A. S., 394, 395, 407
Berger, B. M., 11, 40, 584, 589
Berger, E. M., 457, 463
Berger, P. L., 405
Berger, R. J., 498, 519, 531
Berger, S. M., 308, 338
Berman, A., 190, 193, 194
Berkov, B., 398, 407
Bernal, G., 308, 338
Bernard, C., 540
Bernstein, B., 540
Berry, J. W., 253
Bertrand, J., 121, 123, 124
Berzonsky, W. M., 180, 181
Bettelheim, B., 346, 581, 588, 589
Bigelow, B. J., 412, 429
Biller, H. B., 415, 429
Bilorusky, J. A., 566, 567, 595
Binet, A., 536, 537
Binet, T., 211
Binstock, R. H., 589, 592
Birch, L. L., 241
Black, K. D., 581, 589
Blaine, G. B., 461
Blanchard, E. B., 355
Blehar, M., 112, 115
Bless, E., 319, 339
Bleuler, E., 450
Bloch, H. A., 502, 503, 531
Block, J., 55, 64, 67, 69, 79, 85, 113, 115, 251, 259, 331, 333, 338, 339, 562, 566, 569, 570, 571, 572, 573, 577, 578, 579, 581, 584, 590, 592, 596
Block, J. H., 251, 256, 259, 273, 274, 278, 282, 283, 369

Bloom, B. S., 88, 239
Bloomberg, S. H., 9, 29, 30, 40
Blos, P., 101, 102, 108, 110-112, 115, 117, 131, 132, 137, 161, 181, 189, 190, 191, 198, 199, 202, 204, 205, 207, 305, 306, 335, 338, 389, 405, 501, 511, 531
Blumen, L., 510, 534
Blumenthal, M. D., 371
Blyth, D., 64, 78
Blyth, D. A., 17, 41
Bobbitt, B. L., 226, 241
Bobrow, S. B., 45
Bock, R. D., 128
Bodine, G. E., 498, 533
Bolton, C. D., 572, 590
Bonjean, C. N., 250
Bonmorito, J. W., 250
Bonnard, A., 456
Boole, G., 433
Borke, H., 310, 338
Bouchard, T., 537
Boutourline Young, H., 64, 76
Bowen, R., 435
Bower, E., 64
Bower, E. M., 452
Bowerman, C. E., 18, 41, 326, 338, 425, 429
Bowers, K. S., 90
Bowers, W. J., 584, 593
Bowman, P. H., 513, 519, 531
Boyar, R. M., 121, 125
Boyd, R. D., 170, 181
Boyer, J. L., 343
Braham, M., 420, 429, 461
Braiman, A., 459
Brainerd, C. J., 224, 228, 229, 231, 233, 236, 238
Brannock, J., 232, 235
Braungart, M. M., 562, 566, 567, 569, 570, 571, 579, 580, 590
Braungart, R. G., 5, 8, 13, 41, 259, 270, 346, 361, 369, 370, 561, 562, 566, 567, 569, 570, 571, 578, 579, 580, 581, 584, 585, 586, 587, 590, 596
Bremner, R., 9, 41
Bremner, R. H., 254, 256, 257, 276
Breuer, H., 135, 163, 182
Brier, A., 564, 590
Brill, N. Q., 165, 185
Brim, O., 83, 86
Brim, O. G., 497, 531
Brislin, R. W., 253

Brittain, C. V., 362, 426, 429
Brodie, H. K. H., 119
Bronfenbrenner, U., 3, 41, 268, 327, 338, 428, 429
Bronson, W. C., 53, 65, 76
Brown, M., 463
Brown, R., 285
Bruce, W. E., 369
Bruch, H., 137, 144
Brunner, J., 539
Bruner, J. S., 254
Brunswick, A. F., 581, 590
Brunswik, E., 49
Buebel, M. E., 164, 170, 187
Buff, S. A., 391, 405
Bühler, C., 5, 41
Bunt, M., 163, 182
Burks, H. L., 456
Burnham, D. L., 457
Burr, W. R., 400, 406
Burton, C. R., 254, 256, 257, 276
Burton, R. V., 337, 338
Bush, D., 17, 41, 64, 78
Bush, M., 348, 353, 362
Butler, D., 358
Bynum, T. W., 223, 233
Byrne, D., 162, 182

Cabin, S., 163, 182, 577, 578, 580, 590
Cambor, C. G., 457
Campbell, D. T., 237, 322, 338
Campbell, E. Q., 254, 276, 280
Campbell, J. D., 421, 429
Candee, D., 283
Canon, L. K., 318, 341
Canter, P., 459
Cantril, H., 267
Caplow, T., 271
Caramazza, A., 235
Carlsmith, L., 8, 20, 41
Carlson, R., 273
Carns, D. E., 395, 396, 405
Carpenter, G., 141
Carpenter, W. T., 451
Carter, A. B., 453
Carter, J., 567
Cattell, R. B., 537
Cauble, M. A., 163, 180, 182
Canier, N., 421, 429
Chaffee, S. H., 355, 356, 359, 361
Chambers, C., 546, 547
Chapman, J. W., 164, 182

Chavre, V. J., 119
Cheek, D. B., 129
Cherniss, C., 577, 578, 579, 590
Chess, S., 75
Child, I. L., 273
Chiriboga, D., 64, 81, 82, 86
Chown, S. M., 88
Christensen, P., 556
Christiansen, H. T., 141, 143
Christie, R., 566, 584, 592
Christie, R. L., 165, 186
Clark, B. R., 259, 572,
    573, 575, 590
Clark, C. M. G., 267
Clarke, J. W., 569, 571, 590
Clausen, J. 64, 555
Clausen, J. A., 5, 41, 132,
    137, 143, 144, 145
Clautour, S., 64
Clifford, E., 144
Cloutier, R., 238
Cloward, R. A., 326, 328,
    503, 509, 510, 511, 531
Cohen, A. K., 17, 41, 503,
    524, 531
Cohen, I., 452
Cohen, S. H., 88
Colby, A., 299, 338
Cole, J. K., 406, 407
Coleman, J., 180, 182
Coleman, J. C., 411, 413, 424,
    425, 429
Coleman, J. S., 12, 16, 18, 20,
    41, 254, 256, 257, 268, 276,
    326, 339, 362, 419, 420,
    421, 429, 561, 590, 595
Coles, R., 407
Collu, R., 121, 123, 124
Comenius, 560
Conger, J., 527, 532
Conger, J. J., 196, 215, 428,
    429
Connell, R. W., 264, 265, 268,
    274, 281, 344, 345, 347,
    348, 349, 350, 353, 354,
    355, 356, 357, 361, 562, 590
Connell, W. F., 264, 265, 268,
    274
Connon, H. E., 458
Constantinople, A., 64, 163, 166,
    167, 169, 170, 174, 176, 182
Constanza, P. R., 326, 339
Converse, P. E., 355
Cooley, W., 538
Coolidge, J. C., 457, 461
Coopersmith, S., 358
Corder, B. F., 457, 459
Cornelius, S. W., 9, 40, 58, 59, 60

Costanzo, P. R., 422, 423,
    424, 429, 430
Cote, J. E., 165, 182
Cottle, T., 84
Cottrell, L. S., 5, 41
Coulter, J. B., 57
Covington, M., 556
Cowdry, R., 577, 578, 580, 590
Cox, E., 272, 274
Crain, E. F., 348, 353
Crain, W. C., 348, 353
Craise, J. L., 361, 369
Crandall, V, , 65
Crissman, P., 272
Cronbach, L. J., 225, 226, 239
Cross, H. J., 300, 343
Cross, J. H., 164, 165, 172, 182
Cross, L. A., 452
Crowley, J. E., 498, 519, 531
Curran, F. J., 145
Curtis, R. L., Jr., 280
Cutler, N. E., 344, 346, 351,
    357, 372, 581, 589, 590
Cytryn, L., 455

Dahlstrom, G., 552
Dahlstrom, L., 552
Daily, J. M., 452
Dalsimer, K., 461
Damon, W., 283
Darley, J., 318, 341
Darrow, C. N., 257
Daurio, S., 554, 555
Davey, I. F., 29, 30, 31, 43
Davids, A., 462
Davidson, S., 164, 182
Davidson, T. N., 513, 531
Davies, J. C., 355, 359
Davis, D., 361
Davis, J. B., 254, 256, 257, 276
Davis, K., 4, 11, 14, 21, 22,
    23, 41, 581, 590
Davis, N. Z., 9, 41
Davison, M., 228
Dawson, R., 562, 584, 590
Dawson, R. E., 276
Day, D., 62, 64, 79
DeConde, A., 564, 584, 590
Dufdsne, J., 165, 182
Deinstbrier, R., 406, 407
Deldin, L. S., 172, 182
Del Gaudio, A. C., 447, 448,
    451
DeMartini, J. R., 570, 590
Demerath, N. J., 560, 578,
    580, 591
Demos, G. D., 542, 547

Demos, J., 9, 10, 41
Demos, V., 10, 41
Denisoff, R. S., 563, 584,
    586, 591
Denney, R., 45
Dennis, J., 345, 346, 350,
    354, 355, 356, 363, 562,
    591
Dennis, W., 41
DePalma, D. J., 323, 339
de Peretti, E., 121, 123, 124
Derber, C., 578, 591
Deutsch, H., 65, 66
Devereux, E. C., 326, 327,
    328, 339
De Young, C. D., 461
Diament, L., 400, 406
Dick, L., 358
Dignan, M. H., 166, 167, 174,
    177, 182
Dirksen-Thedens, I., 118, 119,
    123
Dodge, R. W., 358
Doering, C. H., 119, 134
Doering, Z. B., 254, 256, 257,
    276
Dollard, J., 5, 14, 41
Donovan, B. T., 122
Donovan, J. M., 167-168, 169,
    171, 175, 178, 182, 569,
    570, 577, 579, 591
Doob, L. W., 41
Doress, E., 578, 591
Dotiecti, P. R., 421, 429
Douglas, J. D., 562, 581, 591
Douvan, E., 18, 41, 86, 113,
    115, 161, 179, 182, 188,
    189, 254, 255, 257, 274,
    276, 279, 306, 329, 339,
    358, 391, 406, 410, 411,
    412, 413, 414, 416, 417,
    421, 425, 430, 528, 532,
    562, 591
Dragastin, S. E., 40, 41, 254,
    276, 588
Draper, H., 572, 584, 591
Dreyer, P. H., 254, 256, 276
Duchame, H. R., 121, 123, 124
Dukes, W. F., 251, 272, 276
Duner, A., 513, 534
Dunlap, R., 569, 571, 579, 591
Dunphy, D., 417, 418, 419,
    430
Dye, N. W., 239

Earl, R. B., 250
Easton, D., 344, 345, 346,
    350, 354, 356

Eberly, D., 461
Echvall, K. L., 268
Eckhardt, K. W., 359
Egan, J., 569, 571, 590
Ehman, L. H., 346, 357, 360
Ehrhardt, A. A., 134
Eichorn, D., 76, 88
Eichorn, D. H., 254, 256, 257, 276
Eik-Nes, K. B., 119
Eisenberg-Berg, N., 283, 303, 339
Eisenhower, D., 566
Eisenstadt, S. N., 5, 10, 16, 17, 41, 346, 357, 502, 532, 560, 562, 581, 584, 588, 591
Eissler, K. R., 509, 522, 532
Ekstrom, R., 539
El-Assal, M., 23, 45, 571, 584, 595
Elder, Glen H., 3, 4, 8, 12, 16, 22, 24, 28, 29, 34, 37, 40, 41, 42
Elder, G. H., 416, 417, 430, 588
Elder, G. H., Jr., 60, 64, 82, 83, 254, 260, 261, 276, 280
Elkin, F., 113, 115
Elkind, D., 112, 212, 213, 215, 433, 435, 538
Ellerman, D. A., 275, 280
Emery, A., 358
Emmerich, W., 88
Emmerson, D. K., 561, 564, 584, 591
Empey, L. T., 498, 510, 519, 532
Ennis, R. H., 217, 218, 221, 222, 223, 227, 233, 236, 238
Eppel, E. M., 265, 268
Epstein, N. B., 189
Erickson, M. L., 498, 519, 532
Erikson, E., 109, 115, 189, 200, 201, 561, 562, 584, 589, 591, 595
Erikson, E. H., 7, 11, 42, 77, 159, 161, 166, 170, 178, 179, 182, 254, 306, 330, 335, 336, 339, 346, 367, 409, 430, 497, 501, 502, 503, 524, 528, 531, 532
Errara, P., 453
Escalona, S., 112
Estes, H. R., 460
Evans, E. D., 593
Eveland, L. K., 514, 515, 516, 533
Everson, D. H., 578, 594
Eyer, J., 527, 535

Eysenck, H., 509, 532
Ezekiel, R., 86

Fabrega, H., 138
Faiman, C., 119, 120, 123, 124, 125
Faine, J. R., 498, 510, 532
Fallding, H., 251
Fannin, P. M., 173, 182
Faris, R. L., 593
Farrington, D., 498, 519, 532
Fast, I., 199
Faust, M. S., 129, 130, 143, 144
Feagin, J. R., 279
Feather, N. T., 248, 249, 251, 252, 253, 262, 263, 265, 267, 268, 270, 274, 275, 276, 277, 278, 279, 280, 283, 284, 285
Feigelson, C., 65
Fejer, D., 457
Feldman, K., 361
Feldman, K. A., 277, 278, 302, 339
Fendrich, J. M., 25, 42, 369, 578, 587, 591
Fengler, A. P., 579, 591
Fenton, J. H., 578, 579, 591
Ferdinand, T. N., 508, 532
Feshbach, M., 414, 431
Feshbach, N. D., 310, 339
Festinger, L., 313, 339
Feuer, L., 278, 368
Feuer, L. S., 560, 564, 580, 581, 582, 584, 591
Findlay, D. J., 564, 589
Fine, J. T., 186
Finestone, H., 11, 12, 42
Finkelstein, J. W., 121
Fischer, J., 568, 591
Fisher, L., 595
Fishkin, J., 282, 331, 339, 370
Fishman, J. R., 369, 570, 577, 596
Fiske, D. W., 237, 322, 338
Fitzgerald, J. M., 239
Flacks, R., 24, 42, 277, 369, 370, 561, 562, 564, 569, 570, 571, 578, 579, 581, 584, 591, 592, 594
Flamer, G. B., 224
Flavell, J. H., 84, 212, 215, 216, 217, 232, 234, 432, 433
Fleron, F. J., Jr., 354, 363
Foellinger, D. B., 241

Foner, A., 3, 4, 5, 45, 581, 595
Ford, C., 138, 140
Ford, C. S., 388, 406
Ford, J., 567
Ford, M. P., 224
Forer, R. A., 86
Forest, M., 121, 123, 124
Foster, J., 571, 584, 589, 592, 596
Fountain, G., 113, 115
Fox, L., 543, 556
Fox, L. H., 240
Fox, R. J., 528, 530, 531
Fraiberg, S., 112
France, A., 540
Frankel, E., 463
Frasier, S. D., 121, 125
Frazier, A., 144
Freedman, A. M., 406
Freedman, J. L., 319, 339
French, J., 539
Frenkel-Brunswik, E., 64
Freud, A., 66, 81, 99, 103-104, 108, 113, 115, 117, 131, 132, 133, 145, 188, 194, 357, 454
Freud, S., 99, 117, 131, 132, 324, 328, 329, 339, 383, 384, 385, 386, 387, 406, 501, 531
Frey, F. W., 253, 268
Friedlander, K., 509, 532
Friedman, D. A., 348, 370n
Friedman, L. N., 566, 584, 592
Friedman, M., 163, 164, 173, 174, 184
Friedrich, D., 241
Frieze, I. H., 256
Frisch, R. E., 122
Frosch, J., 145
Furlong, M. J., 260, 269, 279, 346, 357
Furstenberg, F. F., Jr., 5, 7, 9, 10, 26, 29, 32, 33, 42, 44
Furth, H. G., 233

Gagnon, J. H., 140, 141, 387, 388, 394, 395, 397, 406, 407, 457
Gaitz, C. M., 561, 592
Gallatin, J., 112, 178, 182, 345, 350, 352, 353, 354, 362, 364, 365
Galton, F., 536, 540
Gamson, Z. F., 570, 577, 578, 579, 580, 584, 592
Garbarino, J., 17, 42, 268

Gardner, G. E., 447, 461
Garfinkle, R., 211
Garrett, J. B., 252
Garrison, K. C., 261
Geary, P. S., 170, 186
Gebhard, P. H., 406
Gediman, H. K., 451
Gedo, J., 109, 110, 116
Gelhorn, E., 308, 339
Gella, A., 564. 592
Geller, J. D., 571, 578, 592
Genther, R. W., 164, 167,
    182, 184
George, R., 425, 429
Gergen, K. J., 88, 90, 355,
    369, 567, 571
Gessell, A. L., 531
Getzels, J., 551
Ghei, S. N., 268
Gibson, H. B., 498, 532
Gigy, L., 84
Gillespie, J. M., 253
Gilligan, C., 302, 304, 341, 348
Gillis, J. R., 4, 5, 6, 9, 10, 13,
    24, 25, 38, 42, 560, 562,
    581, 584, 592
Gillmore, G., 283
Gilmore, G. E., 169, 182
Gilmore, S., 369
Ginsburg, H., 433
Giovacchini, P., 109, 116
Glass, G. V., 232
Glaser, K., 455
Glazer, M., 564, 594
Glazer, N., 45
Gleason, G., 578, 579, 591
Glenn, N. D., 372
Glick, J., 226
Glossop, J., 253
Glueck, E., 326, 339
Glueck, S., 326, 339
Goddard, H., 537
Goel, M. L., 562, 584, 594
Goertzel, T., 564, 581, 592
Goethals, G. W., 139
Goethe, 560
Goffman, E., 432, 435, 436, 444
Gold, A. R., 566, 584, 592
Gold, M., 410, 420, 421, 495F,
    498, 504, 505, 510, 512,
    519, 521, 525, 528, 531,
    532, 535, 562, 591
Goldberg, A., 109, 116
Goldman, J. A., 164, 165,
    170, 186
Goldschmid, M. L., 238
Goldsen, R., 572, 592
Goldstein, J., 26, 42

Goldstein, M., 64
Gombosi, 165, 183
Goodale, J. G., 252
Goode, W. J., 6, 42
Goodman, J., 570, 577, 578,
    579, 580, 584, 592
Goodman, M, E., 253
Goodwin, G. A., 580, 581, 592
Goot, M., 354
Gordon, A., 44
Gordon, C., 17, 42, 561, 592
Gordon, L. V., 251, 268
Gorlow, L., 251, 164
Gorsuch, R. L., 272
Goslin, D., 406
Goslin, D. A., 276
Gottieb, D., 584, 592
Gough, H. G., 537, 543, 550,
    552
Gould, J. B., 271, 274
Goulet, L. R., 5, 42, 260, 269
Gowan, J., 542, 546
Granberg, D., 580, 592
Granlund, N. W., 419, 430
Graubard, S., 369
Grave, G. D., 120, 149
Gray, J., 498, 519, 531
Green, B., 348, 352, 554
Green, D. R., 224
Green, S., 498, 531
Greenberg, E. S., 344, 363
Greenberger, E., 169, 178-
    179, 183, 195, 196, 199, 206
Greenhouse, E. M., 175, 183
Greenstein, F. I., 346, 349,
    350, 354, 365, 367, 562, 592
Greer, J. H., 318, 339
Gregg, C. F., 143
Gregoire, J. C., 166, 183
Gregory, I., 326, 339
Greif, E. B., 238, 299, 300, 341
Greulich, W. W., 505, 533
Greven, P. J., Jr., 9, 28, 33, 42
Gribbin, K., 269
Grilliches, Z., 254, 256, 257, 276
Grinder, R. E., 10, 42, 276
Grinker, R. R., 189
Gross, A. E., 329, 339
Gruen, W., 163, 183
Grumbach, M. M., 120, 121
Grunebaum, M. G., 463
Grusec, J. E., 328, 338
Guilford, J., 556
Gump, V., 17, 40
Gunderson, J. G., 450
Gupta, D., 122, 123, 124
Gurin, G., 570, 577, 578, 579,
    580, 584, 592

Gusfield, J. R., 563, 569, 592
Gutierrez, A., 364
Gutmann, D., 85

Haan, N., 52, 55, 56, 64, 67,
    69, 71, 79, 80, 81, 83, 85,
    102, 116, 206, 259, 282,
    283, 331, 333, 336, 337,
    338, 339, 562, 566, 569,
    570, 571, 572, 573, 577,
    578, 579, 580, 581, 584,
    590, 592, 596
Haan, N. H., 369
Hackler, J. C., 498, 533
Hadden, J. K., 567, 592
Hadley, C., 576, 593
Hadley, S. W., 308, 338
Hafner, A., 64, 67, 68
Hagstrom, W. O., 361
Hall, G. S., 10, 11, 42, 113,
    499, 500, 531, 533, 560
Hallworth, H. J., 261
Hamburg, B., 131, 144
Hamburg, D. A., 119, 134,
    135
Hammen, C. L., 401n, 407
Hampden-Turner, C., 24, 42
Hanley, C., 70, 77
Hansen, S. W., 125
Hantover, J. P., 31, 42
Harder, M. W., 530, 535
Hardt, R. H., 498, 533
Hareven, T. K., 9, 42
Harris, L., 261
Harrison, J. D., 268
Hartmann, H., 189, 305, 339
Harvey, G., 365
Harvey, J., 422, 430
Harvey, O. J., 342, 423, 430
Harvey, S. K., 365
Hasenfeld, Y., 518, 534
Hastings, P. K., 271, 572, 592
Hatcher, S., 102, 116
Hatcher, S. M., 206
Hauser, S., 64
Hauser, S. T., 166, 169, 183
Havighurst, R., 64
Havighurst, R. J., 254, 256,
    258, 259, 265, 268, 269,
    270, 276, 281, 461
Havlicek, L. L., 506n, 533
Hayes, A., 125
Hayes, J. M., 163-164, 183
Heberle, R., 560, 592
Heilbrun, A., 543, 552
Heiman, J., 401n
Heinecke, C. M., 462
Heirich, M., 529, 530, 533

Heise, D., 508, 510, 533
Heist, P., 369, 577, 578, 579, 592
Hellman, L., 121, 125
Helmreich, R. L., 256
Hendin, H., 560, 581, 584, 592
Herrnstein, R. J., 285
Hershberg, T., 5, 7, 9, 29, 32, 33, 44
Hershenson, D. B., 165, 183
Hertz, M. R., 64
Herzberg, J., 180, 182
Hess, R. D., 276, 345, 346, 350, 353, 354, 356, 357, 359, 360, 364, 365, 562, 592
Hetherington, E. M., 415, 416, 417, 430
Hewitt, L. E., 509, 510, 533
Heyneman, S. P., 13, 42
Hill, J. P., 8, 28, 42
Hill, R., 42, 278
Hill, R. J., 250
Hindelang, M. J., 498, 509, 510, 511, 533
Hindus, M. S., 28, 45
Hirsch, H., 354, 363, 364
Hirschi, T., 498, 526, 533
Hodgkinson, H., 570, 571, 593
Hodgman, C. H., 459
Hodgson, J. W., 179, 183
Hoffman, H. J., 125
Hoffman, L. W., 256, 591, 593
Hoffman, M., 99, 112
Hoffman, M. L., 299, 303, 307, 309, 312, 315, 316, 317, 321, 322, 323, 325, 326, 327, 329, 591, 593
Hogan, D. P., 33, 42
Hogan, M., 164, 183
Hogan, R., 258, 281, 300, 301, 340, 348, 539, 544, 545, 548, 549, 553, 554, 556
Hogarty, P. S., 239, 240
Hoge, D. R., 271, 572, 592
Hogenson, D. L., 463
Holland, J. L., 536, 543, 544, 548, 549, 550
Hollingshead, A., 12, 14, 15, 42
Hollingshead, A. B., 417, 430
Hollingsworth, L. S., 11, 43
Holt, G., 425, 429
Holt, N., 564, 596
Holzman, P. S., 451
Holzner, B., 584, 593
Honzik, M. P., 43, 48
Hood, W. R., 342
Hopkins, J. R., 397, 399, 406
Hopkins, L. B., 173, 183

Hopper, B. R., 124
Horn, J. L., 232, 239, 332, 333, 340
Horner, M., 315, 340
Horowitz, H., 421, 430
Horowitz, I. L., 594
Horrocks, J. E., 410, 413, 430, 431
Horst, H. J., 118, 119, 123
Hoskin, M. B., 344, 366
Hotch, D. F., 283
Hotelling, H., 90
Howard, G., 571, 578, 592
Howard, K. I., 510, 511, 535
Howard, L., 170, 183
Howard, M. R., 173, 174, 178, 183
Howe, L. K., 405
Humphrey, G., 308, 340
Huston, T. C., 567
Huston-Stien, A., 5, 43
Hutton, M. A., 265
Huygens, C., 537
Hyman, H., 357, 359
Hyman, H. H., 276, 562, 593

Ikeda, K., 6, 44
Inglehart, R., 24, 43
Inhelder, B., 196, 212, 213, 214, 216, 217, 218, 220, 221, 222, 223, 224, 225, 226, 227, 231, 233, 236, 238, 254, 348, 433
Iscoe, I., 88, 422, 430
Isenberg, P., 371, 570, 577, 593
Izard, C. E., 308, 340
Jacklin, C., 365
Jacklin, C. N., 256
Jackson, P., 551
Jackson-Beeck, M., 359
Jacobs, J., 458, 459
Jacobson, E., 145, 305, 340
Jacobson, S. B., 169, 183
Jaffe, R. B., 124
Janowitz, M., 569, 593
Jansen, D. G., 578, 597
Jarmecky, L., 318, 339
Jaros, D., 354, 363, 562, 593
Jegede, R. O., 166, 183
Jenkins, R. L., 509, 510, 511, 533, 534
Jennings, K. M., 18, 43
Jennings, M. K., 260, 276, 278, 280, 281, 345, 346, 347, 349, 353, 356, 357, 358, 359, 360, 361, 362, 363, 365, 366, 368
Jensen, A., 64

Jersild, A. I., 144
Jessor, R., 51, 64, 132, 142, 393, 394, 397, 398, 399, 406
Jessor, S., 51, 64, 393, 394, 397, 398, 399, 406
Jessor, S. L., 132, 142
Jiggins, J., 562, 564, 593
Johanson, A., 125
Johnson, D. W., 273
Johnson, M., 581, 595
Johnson, M. E., 3, 4, 5, 45
Johnson, M. J., 330, 340
Johnson, O. G., 250
Johnson, R. C., 509, 510, 534
Johnston, J., 64, 67, 505, 514, 534
Johnston, L. D., 513, 514, 515, 516, 531, 533
Jones, F., 64
Jones, H. E., 10, 14, 34, 43, 64, 71, 74
Jones, M. C., 43, 48, 64, 70, 71, 132, 137, 143, 144, 419, 430
Jones, M. L., 334, 341
Jones, O. W., 120
Jones, P. A., 233
Jordaan, J., 64
Jordan, P., 164, 169, 171-172, 176, 183
Jordan, W. D., 26, 43
Joslyn, R., 344, 355, 358, 372
Josselson, R., 167, 168, 173, 175-176, 177, 179, 183, 189, 192, 195, 196, 199, 206
Josselyn, I. M., 188
Joyce, M. U., 177, 183
Judd, H. L., 120, 121
Jung, C., 85

Kaestle, C. F., 9, 43
Kagan, J., 10, 43, 63, 65, 88, 89, 407
Kahn, J. F., 459
Kahn, R. L., 513, 531
Kahn, R. M., 584, 593
Kammeyer, K. C., 572, 590
Kandel, D., 64, 278, 362, 587, 593
Kandel, D. B., 18, 21, 43, 426, 428, 430
Kantner, J. F., 132, 141, 142, 397, 407, 457
Kapen, S., 121, 125
Kaplan, H. I., 406
Kaplan, S. L., 121

Kasschaw, P. L., 346, 361, 364
Katz, D., 572, 584, 593
Katz, I., 461
Katz, M. B., 28, 29, 30, 31, 43
Katz, P., 452
Kearney, R. N., 562, 564, 584, 593
Keasey, C. B., 238
Keating, D., 112, 538, 543, 556
Keating, D. P., 224, 225, 226, 232, 235, 237, 240, 241
Keeler, W. R., 456
Kelch, R. P., 121
Kelly, D. H., 569, 577, 584, 589
Kelly, G. A., 165, 183
Kelly, J., 64, 82
Kendell, R. E., 448
Kendis, R. J., 186
Keniston, K., 7, 10, 11, 43, 253, 256, 257, 259, 282, 313, 314, 326, 331, 332, 333, 335, 336, 346, 347, 369, 384, 406, 561, 562, 566, 569, 570, 577, 578, 579, 580, 581, 584, 590, 593
Kennedy, J. F., 566
Kenny, C. T., 366
Kenny, F. M., 123
Kerlinger, F. N., 264
Kernberg, O., 200, 202
Kerpelman, L. C., 370, 571, 577, 578, 580, 593
Kestenberg, J., 131, 132, 137, 144
Kett, J. F., 4, 9, 29, 30, 32, 38, 43, 254, 256, 257, 276
Keys, N., 556
Kiernan, K., 76
Kikuchi, A., 251, 268
Kilham, W., 329, 341
Killian, L. M., 560, 593
Kilty, K. M., 268
Kinch, J. W., 18, 41, 326, 338, 425, 429
King, L., 576, 593
King, P., 220
Kinsey, A. C., 141, 383, 386, 390, 395, 398, 399, 406
Kirby, C. S., 165, 184
Kirsch, P. A., 136, 177, 184
Kleiber, D. A., 371
Klein, E. B., 257
Klein, M. M., 163, 164, 186
Klein, M. W., 519, 533

Klein, N. C., 521, 533
Klineberg, S., 84
Kloss, R. M., 563, 595
Kluckhohn, C., 248, 252, 268
Kneapp, R. H., 268
Knifong, J. D., 234, 235
Knight, D., 519, 533
Knott, P. D., 332, 333, 340
Knutson, J., 346, 347, 367
Koch, H. L., 415, 430
Kodlin, D., 47
Koenig, K. E., 277
Kogan, N., 329, 343, 551, 552
Kohen-Raz, R., 227
Kohlberg, L., 170, 184, 248, 281, 282, 283, 285, 295, 297, 298, 299, 300, 301, 302, 303, 304, 327, 328, 331, 332, 336, 337, 338, 341, 348, 352, 353, 369, 370, 506, 507, 533, 561, 579, 581, 593
Kohlberg, L. A., 385, 386, 406
Kohn, M. L., 248, 251, 276, 280
Kohut, H., 109-110, 116, 198, 201
Kohutis, E., 165, 187
Korenman, S. G., 118, 119
Korth-Schultz, S., 121
Koskela, R. N., 170, 181
Kraemer, H. C., 119
Kraines, R. J., 278
Krakowski, A. J., 455
Kramer, R., 170, 184, 301, 302, 303, 304, 336, 341, 348
Kraus, S., 361
Krauss, E. S., 561, 593
Kraut, R. E., 278, 370, 577, 578, 594
Kreisman, D., 452
Krell, M., 525, 535
Kuhlen, R. G., 3, 43, 88, 334, 341, 419, 430
Kuhn, D., 226, 232, 235, 236, 237
Kulik, J. A., 498, 509, 533, 534, 535
Kupers, C. J., 328, 338
Kurtines, W., 238, 299, 300, 341
Kyle, D. G., 177, 184

Labouvie-Vief, G., 241
Lacks, P., 173, 178

Ladd, E. C., 569, 576, 584, 593, 594
La Gaipa, J. J., 412, 429
Laing, R. D., 584, 593
Laird, J. D., 308, 341
Lake, D. G., 250
Lambert, B. G., 409, 417, 430
Lambert, T. A., 581, 582, 593
Landsbaum, J., 422, 424, 430
Lane, R. E., 346, 347, 367, 368
Langer, J., 304, 341
Langton, K. P., 345, 346, 349, 353, 360, 362, 363
Langworthy, R. L., 326, 341
La Porte, R. L., 510, 532
Laqueur, W., 561, 584, 593
Larsen, L. E., 426, 427, 428, 430
Laslett, B., 30, 43
Laslett, P., 14, 43
Latané, B., 318, 341
Lauer, R. H., 560, 561, 593
Laufer, M., 454
Laufer, R. S., 5, 20, 21, 28, 40, 260, 269, 270, 279, 346, 357, 578, 587, 589
Laurendeau, M., 228
Lautt, M., 498, 533
La Voie, J. C., 169, 170, 172, 175, 184
Le Bon, G., 327, 341
Lee, B. J., 419, 430
Lee, P. A., 124
Leibniz, G. W., 537
Lerner, R. M., 137, 145, 358
Lesser, G., 278
Lesser, G. S., 18, 21, 43, 426, 428, 430
Lesser, I., 164, 167, 172, 185
Lessing, E., 86
Lessinger, L. M., 544
Levenson, E. A., 460
Leventhal, T., 460
Levin, J. R., 241
Levine, F. J., 348, 352, 353
Levine, L. S., 123, 124
Levine, M. H., 584, 586, 591
Levine, R., 138, 140, 141
Levinson, D., 85
Levinson, D. J., 257
Levinson, M., 85, 86
Levinson, M. H., 257
Levi-Strass, C., 539
Levy, D. M., 145
Levy, N. J., 457
Lewin, K., 497, 503, 511, 526, 531, 534
Lewinsohn, P. M., 453

Lewis, M., 415, 431
Lewis, R. A., 400, 406, 569, 593
Lewis, S. H., 278, 370, 577, 578, 584
Lichter, S. O., 461
Liebert, D. E., 236
Liebert, R., 560, 584, 594
Liebert, R. M., 214, 236
Liebman, A., 564, 594
Lief, H., 64, 68
Lifton, R., 313, 341
Light, D., Jr., 270
Lindzey, G., 248, 250, 543, 544
Linton, R., 43
Lipps, T., 308, 341
Lipschutz, M. R., 28, 43
Lipset, S. M., 17, 22, 24, 43, 267, 270, 271, 369, 561, 564, 566, 569, 572, 579, 581, 584, 593, 594, 596
Lipsitz, J., 14, 43, 145, 148
Lisonbee, L. K., 144
Litt, E., 360
Little, M., 30, 43
Litwin, G. H., 252
Livson, F., 64, 85
Livson, M., 132, 143
Livson, N., 52, 53, 62, 65, 66, 76, 84, 86, 88, 89, 90, 102, 206
Loevinger, J., 203, 204, 273, 281, 282, 283, 384, 406
Loewenberg, P., 8, 43
Loken, J. O., 578, 594
Lombardo, J. P., 343
London, H., 137
Long, D., 571, 584, 589, 592. 596
Lonner, W. J., 253
Lotz, R. E., 577, 594
Lovejoy, M. C., 22, 23, 40
Lovell, K., 213, 225
Lowe, J. C., 6, 44
Lowenthal, L., 17, 43
Lowenthal, M., 64, 81, 82, 86
Lubeck, S. G., 510, 519, 532
Lubensky, A., 64
Luckey, E. B., 457
Luckman, T., 405
Lunzer, E. A., 213
Lupfer, M. B., 366
Luria, A. R., 539, 540
Lüscher, K., 10, 43
Lyman, S. M., 581, 595
Lynch, S., 570, 578, 579, 596
Lynd, H. M., 12, 44, 271

Lynd, R. S., 44, 271
Lynn, D. B., 415, 431
Lyonns, G., 571, 584, 594
Lyons, S. R., 354

McArthur, C., 64, 67
McCall, R. B., 239, 240
McCandless, B. R., 496, 497, 500, 502, 503, 511, 534
McCarthy, J., 566, 568
McClelland, D. C., 253, 268
Maccoby, E. E., 20, 44, 256, 365, 406
McConochie, D., 169, 179, 183, 195, 196, 199, 206
McCord, J., 415, 431
McCord, W., 415, 431
McCourt, M. M., 271, 274
Macfarlane, J. W., 37, 38, 43, 44, 48
McGinn, P., 545
McKee, B., 257
McKinney, J. P., 283
MacKinnon, C., 282, 331, 339, 370
McLawghlin, J. A., 232
McLellan, D., 261, 282
McLemore, S. D., 250
McLoed, J. M., 359
McMahan, I. D., 283
McNemar, Q., 538
McVey, S., 578, 589
Maehr, M. L., 283
Magee, E. S., 16, 44
Magnusson, D., 513, 534
Mahajan, D. K., 119
Mahler, C., 162, 184
Mahler, M., 112, 190, 193, 194, 195
Maidenberg, M., 578, 594
Malmquist, C. P., 455, 459
Manaster, G. J., 371
Mandler, G., 311, 341
Mankoff, M., 370, 570, 581, 594
Mann, D. W., 498, 511, 532, 534
Mann, L., 329, 341
Mannheim, K., 5, 8, 20, 24, 44, 346, 357, 581, 582, 583, 584, 585, 588, 594
Manosevitz, M., 162, 172, 185
Marcia, J., 99, 112, 162, 163, 164, 166, 167, 172, 173, 174, 184, 185, 186
Marcus, D., 168, 184
Marcus, R., 118, 119
Maresh, M. M., 505
Markus, G. B., 366

Marohn, R., 109, 116
Marshall, W. A., 126, 143
Martin, C. E., 141, 406
Martinson, R. A., 544, 555
Martorano, S. C., 232, 237
Marwell, G., 560, 578, 580, 591
Massimo, J. L., 520, 534
Masters, J. C., 313, 341
Masterson, J., 64, 67, 68
Masterson, J. F., 188, 204, 448, 451, 453, 454, 456
Mathews, K., 309, 311, 318, 342
Mathews, K. E., 318, 341
Matteson, D., 163, 164, 165, 168, 169, 170, 171, 172, 173, 176, 177, 178, 184
Mattick, H. W., 519, 521, 532
Matza, D., 5, 25, 44, 259, 572, 573, 594
Maurice, R., 570, 571, 579, 589
Mayer, F. E., 120
Maykovich, M. K., 364
Mays, J. M., 254, 256, 257, 276
Mead, M., 11, 14, 44, 138, 141, 502, 531, 534
Mednick, M., 556
Mednick, M. T. S., 256, 513, 531
Mednick, S., 556
Mednick, S. A., 57
Medsker, L., 64, 81
Meehl, P. E., 224, 225, 226, 452
Meeks, J. E., 448
Meilman, P. W., 168, 169, 184
Melges, F. T., 134, 135
Meltzoff, A. N., 216
Menlove, F. L., 328, 338
Merelman, R. M., 345, 353
Merkl, P. H., 8, 44
Merton, K., 275, 503, 534
Meyer, J. M., 564, 594
Meyer, J. W., 10, 44
Meyer, M. W., 584, 594
Meyer, P., 578, 594
Middleton, R., 359
Midgley, A. R., Jr., 124
Migeon, C. J., 124
Milbrath, L. W., 562, 584, 594
Miles, M. B., 250
Miles, M. W., 568, 584, 594
Miller, C. K., 232
Miller, E., 166, 174, 175, 177, 178, 184

Miller, L. C., 461
Miller, M. V., 369
Miller, N. E., 41
Miller, P. Y., 387, 397, 399,
  401, 405, 406, 407
Miller, R. E., 578, 594
Miller, W. B., 326, 342, 519, 534
Millett, K., 388, 406
Mills, C. W., 584, 594
Milner, E., 64
Minoque, W. J. D., 267
Mirels, H. L., 252
Mischel, H. N., 285
Mischel, W., 256, 285
Modell, J., 5, 7, 9, 10, 26, 29,
  32, 33, 38, 44
Moller, H., 8, 23, 44, 560,
  562, 581, 584, 594
Mondani, M. S., 463
Money, J., 134
Mönks, F. J., 28, 42, 59
Monroe, S., 313, 342
Montero, D., 361, 364
Moore, B. S. 318, 342
Moore, J. W., 6, 44
Moore, M., 267
Moore, M. K., 216
Moore, T., 64
More, D. M., 64
Morgan, J. N., 511, 535
Moriarty, A., 63, 75
Morison, S. E., 561, 594
Morris, C. W., 248, 252, 268,
  272, 273
Morris, J. F., 261
Morris, M., 180, 182
Morris, M. B., 580, 594
Morris, N. M., 141
Morris, R. R., 524, 534
Morrison, S., 498, 532
Morron, W. R., 461, 462, 463
Morse, B., 173, 176, 184
Mosher, L. R., 450
Moshman, D., 234, 235
Moss, H., 63, 65, 88, 89
Mowrer, O. H., 41
Moynihan, D., 584, 594
Mulman, A., 595
Munro, G., 170, 184
Murdak, G. P., 139
Murphey, E., 64, 81
Murphy, L., 63, 75
Murphy, L. B., 318, 342
Murray, D. C., 454
Murray, H., 252
Murray, J., 128
Musgrove, F., 23, 44
Mussen, P., 318, 342

Mussen, P. H., 64, 70, 132,
  137, 143, 144, 145
Muus, R., 4, 44
Myers, I. B., 544

Nabors, C. J., 119
Nagel, J., 44
Nameche, G., 64
Nameche, G. F., 452
Nankin, H. R., 123
Nathan, J. A., 344, 363
National Commission on Re-
  sources for Youth, 13, 44
National Society for the Study
  of Education (NSSE), 14, 44
Naus, M. J., 241
Nawas, M., 64
Neimark, E. D., 211, 213,
  218, 219, 220, 225, 226,
  227, 228, 229, 230, 231,
  232, 235, 238
Neisser, V., 235
Nelson, E. A., 20, 44
Nesselroade, J. R., 4, 9, 40,
  44, 58, 59, 60, 64, 83, 239,
  260, 269
Neuber, K. A., 164, 167, 182,
  184
Neugarten, D. L., 5, 44, 85,
  88, 278
Nevid, J. S., 173, 187
New, M. I., 123, 124
Newcomb, T., 361
Newcomb, T. M., 277, 278,
  302, 339
Newell, A., 235, 241
Newman, B. M., 208
Newman, P. R., 208
Nicholls, J. G., 164, 182
Nicolson, A. B., 70, 77
Nederhoffer, A., 502, 503,
  531
Niemi, R. G., 260, 276, 278,
  280, 281, 345, 346, 347,
  355, 356, 357, 358, 359,
  360, 361, 362, 366, 562,
  594, 595
Nisbett, R. E., 137
Nixon, R., 567
Noll, G. A., 251, 264
Nye, F. I., 498, 513, 534

Oberschall, A., 560, 595
O'Brien, T. C., 235
O'Connell, A. N., 177, 184
Oden, M. H., 545, 546
Offer, D., 64, 66, 81, 112,
  113, 116, 142, 161, 168, 184,

188, 189, 195, 280, 358,
  384, 394, 406, 409, 428,
  431, 513, 534
Offer, J., 64, 66, 81, 112, 113,
  116, 280, 384, 394, 406,
  513, 534
Offer, J. B., 161, 168, 184,
  188, 189, 409, 428, 431
Ohlin, L. E., 326, 338, 503,
  509, 510, 511, 531
Olanbiwonnu, N. O., 121, 125
O'Malley, P. M., 505, 514,
  515, 516, 533, 534
O'Malley, P. S., 64, 67
O'Neil, R., 554
O'Neil, R. P., 348, 351, 352
Onqué, G., 88
Oppenheim, A. N., 363
Opper, S., 433
Orlofsky, J., 164, 167, 172,
  174, 175, 184, 185
Ornstein, P. A., 241
Orpen, C., 252
Ortega y Gasset, J., 560, 581,
  584, 595
Orun, A. M., 562, 595
Osherson, D. N., 219, 223
  224, 225, 238
Oshman, H. P., 162, 169,
  172, 186
Osman, A. C., 267

Pack, A. T., 168, 185
Paranjpe, A. C., 170, 185
Parker, D. C., 121
Parlee, M. B., 134
Parson, C., 217, 244
Parsons, B. V., 521, 522, 531
Parsons, B. W., 521, 533
Parsons, T., 13, 16, 44, 327,
  328, 330, 342, 513, 534,
  562, 581, 588, 595
Parsons, T. M., 248, 255, 267
Pascal, A., 45
Pascual-Leone, J., 238, 241
Patrick, J. J., 349
Patterson, J. R., 279, 283
Paulus, D. H., 213, 227
Paulus, G. A., 569, 595
Pearlin, L., 86
Pearson, K., 541
Peck, R., 64
Peck, R. F., 258, 261, 268,
  281, 416, 431
Pendorf, J., 358
Penna, R. F., 181, 185
Penny, R., 121, 125
Peplau, L. A., 371

Perlman, D., 397, 400, 405, 406
Perlstein, A. P., 459
Perry, W. G., Jr., 170, 185
Persons, R. W., 522, 534
Peskin, H., 52, 65, 66, 72, 74, 75, 76, 78, 81, 84, 85, 86, 87, 102, 132, 143, 144, 206
Peter, N. W., 283
Peters, R. S., 300, 342
Petersen, A., 99, 128, 130, 117-155
Petersen, A. C., 227
Peterson, N. L., 506n, 533
Peterson, R. A., 563, 591
Peterson, R. E., 259, 369, 566, 567, 572, 573, 595
Peterson, S. J., 498, 533
Petronio, R., 506, 508, 534
Piaget, J., 64, 84, 196, 211, 212, 213, 214, 215, 216, 217, 218, 219, 220, 221, 222, 223, 224, 225, 226, 227, 229, 230, 231, 233, 234, 236, 238, 239, 242, 254, 281, 295, 296, 297, 298, 301, 304, 326, 328, 334, 342, 347, 348, 385, 432, 433, 444, 531, 538, 539, 540, 542, 561, 595
Pierce, R. A., 577, 579, 595
Pilkington, G. W., 271, 274
Pinard, A., 228
Pine, F., 190, 193, 194
Pinner, F. A., 359
Pitt, R., 452
Pitt, R. B., 214, 218, 219, 223, 241
Pittman, F. S., 461
Plath, D. W., 6, 44
Plato, 538, 560
Platt, A., 13, 45
Platt, G. M., 9, 44
Pleck, J. H., 255, 256
Podd, M., 162, 163, 166, 172, 185
Pomeroy, W. B., 141, 406
Poppen, P. J., 163, 173, 174, 185
Popper, K. R., 213
Poppleton, P. K., 271, 274
Porac, J., 186
Powell, M., 411, 413, 431
Prager, K. J., 173, 175, 185
Presidential Science Advisory Commission, Panel on youth, 608, 12, 13, 45
Prewitt, K., 276, 562, 584, 590

Price, K. C., 355
Price, L., 539
Price-Williams, D. R., 539
Protter, B. S., 164, 185
Provence, S., 112
Przeworski, A., 253, 268
Pulone, J., 165, 187
Putney, S., 359
Pyle, S. I., 505, 533

Quarter, J., 369
Quast, W., 64, 67, 68
Quay, H. C., 510, 534
Quire, K., 525, 535

Raaf, S., 122
Radler, H. A., 261
Randolph, M. H., 509, 510, 534
Ransford, H. E., 346, 361, 364
Rapaport, D., 344
Raphael, D., 175, 180, 181, 185
Rasmussen, J. E., 163, 166, 169, 185
Rayonor, J. O., 284
Reese, H. W., 260, 269
Regan, D. T., 319, 342
Regan, J. W., 319, 342
Regan, M., 358
Reich, C. A., 271, 584, 595
Reichlin, S., 119
Reimer, D. J., 498, 504, 512, 525, 532
Reinert, G., 239
Reinhold, R., 567, 595
Reiss, I. L., 395, 396, 401, 404, 406
Remmers, H. H., 261
Remy, R. C., 344, 363
Renshon, S. A., 344, 346, 347, 355, 359, 367, 368, 371
Resko, J. A., 119
Resnick, L. B., 537
Rest, J., 348
Rest, J. R., 300, 342
Revel, J. F., 584, 595
Revelle, Q., 122
Reyes, F. I., 120
Richards, B. S., 281
Richards, J., 536
Richardson, H., 509, 510, 534
Richardson, J. T., 530, 535
Ricks, D., 64
Riegel, K. F., 227, 281
Riesman, D., 17, 18, 45, 571, 584, 595

Rfkin, B., 235, 241
Riley, M. W., 3, 4, 5, 45, 260, 269, 581, 595
Rinsley, D. B., 452
Roberge, J. J., 213, 227
Roberts, C., 253
Roberts, R. E., 563, 595
Robins, L., 64, 67, 68
Robins, L. N., 452, 517, 527, 534
Robinson, B., 64
Robinson, J. D., 120
Robinson, J. P., 250
Robinson, P., 386, 407
Roche, A. F., 128
Rockwell, R. W., 29, 37, 42, 60, 82, 83
Roe, K., 310, 339
Roffwarg, H., 121, 125
Rogers, D., 276
Rogers, E. D., 580, 596
Rogers, K. W., 264, 265, 268, 274
Rohil, P. K., 268
Rohter, I. S., 344
Rokeach, M., 248, 249, 251, 255, 261, 265, 267, 274, 276, 278, 279, 281, 282
Romano, N. C., 173, 185
Romer, N., 463
Ronning, R. R., 226, 235
Rook, K. S., 401, 407
Rosen, B. M., 451
Rosenau, N., 347, 348
Rosenberg, M., 189, 276, 367, 371, 592
Rosenblum, L., 415, 431
Rosenfeld, R. U., 163, 185
Rosenmayr, L., 18, 43
Rosenthal, H., 433
Rosenthal, I., 57, 64
Rosenthal, L., 318, 338
Ross, D., 10, 45
Ross, G. T., 125
Roth, J. C., 121
Roszak, T., 584, 595
Rothman, D. J., 10, 45
Rothman, K. M., 165, 169, 175, 185
Rothman, S., 570, 577, 593
Rotter, J. B., 368
Rowe, I., 163, 180, 185
Rubin, B., 162, 166, 172, 185
Rubin, Z., 371
Rubinson, R., 564, 594
Ruble, D. N., 256
Russell, B., 538
Rutherford, E., 318, 342

Rutherford, J., 423, 430
Ryder, N. B., 3, 5, 8, 45,
    254, 256, 257, 276, 562,
    563, 568, 584, 595
Ryser, P. E., 142

Saarni, C. I., 238
Saddock, H. I., 406
Salili, F., 283
Saltzstein, H. D., 322, 340
Sampson, E. E., 270, 577,
    580, 595
Sands, D. E., 451
Santen, R. J., 119
Sarbin, T. R., 498, 509, 534,
    535
Sarri, R., 518, 534
Savin-Williams, R., 64
Sawrey, W. L., 415, 431
Schachter, S., 137, 311, 342,
    415, 431
Schaefer, E. S., 55, 63, 416, 431
Schaefer, R. A., 224, 232, 237
Schafer, R., 109, 116, 191,
    201
Schaie, K. W., 3, 5, 20, 40, 45,
    58, 59, 83, 260, 269
Schaie, W., 589
Schecter, M. D., 461
Scheibe, K. E., 248
Schenkel, S., 163, 164, 172,
    173, 178, 185
Schiff, L. F., 368, 369, 580,
    595
Schilling, K. L., 171, 186
Schelossman, S. L., 10, 45
Schmidt, M., 64, 76
Schintzer, R., 371, 570, 577,
    593
Schoeppe, A., 261, 262, 263,
    265, 267
Schofield, M., 457
Schonfeld, W., 132, 137, 138,
    144
Schriner, E. C., 359
Schwartz, D. C., 562, 595
Schwartz, S., 318, 342
Schwartz, S. K., 350, 354,
    367, 562, 595
Scott, J. W., 23, 45, 571, 584,
    595
Scott, M. B., 581, 595
Scott, W. A., 248, 252
Scully, M. G., 8, 45
Scurrah, M. J., 571, 595
Sears, D. O., 276, 344, 345,
    347, 352, 363, 367, 372
Sears, R. R., 11, 41, 45

Sebert, S. K., 346, 362
Seeley, J. R., 20, 39, 45
Seidel, J., 580, 592
Seiden, R. H., 457
Seigman, A. W., 512, 513, 535
Seligman, M. E. P., 453
Sellin, T., 504, 507, 535
Selman, R., 432
Selvin, H. C., 361
Sempé, M., 121, 123, 124
Settlage, C. F., 306, 307, 342
Seyler, L. E., 119
Shaevitz, M. H., 569, 570,
    577, 579, 591
Shanas, E., 589, 592
Shanmugam, A. V., 268
Shapiro, B. J., 235
Shaver, P. R., 250
Shea, M., 64, 67, 68
Shaffer, B. P., 57
Shaffer, C. S., 167, 186
Shainberg, D., 457
Shakow, D., 457
Shaw, M. C., 462
Shaw, M. E. 326, 339, 422,
    423, 424, 430
Shellhamer, T., 64
Shemilt, D., 253
Shepherd, J., 261
Sherif, C., 342, 560, 595
Sherif, M., 327, 342, 560, 595
Sherk, L., 318, 342
Shiaro, R. S., 521, 531
Shimbori, M., 564, 596
Shinohara, M., 509, 510, 535
Shore, M. F., 177, 184, 520,
    534
Shorr, M., 456, 457
Short, J. F., Jr., 510, 511,
    513, 534, 535
Shotland, R. L., 571, 596
Siegler, R. S., 214, 216, 222,
    225, 226, 234, 235, 236,
    239, 241
Siegman, A. W., 326, 342
Sigel, R. S., 344, 346, 347,
    366, 367, 368, 562, 596
Silberger, S. A., 355, 362, 373
Silver, M. A., 458
Simirenko, A., 581, 584, 596
Simmonds, R. B., 529, 530, 535
Simmons, L. R., 581, 596
Simmons, P. D., 166, 186
Simmons, R., 64, 78, 79
Simmons, R. G., 17, 41
Simon, R. J., 591
Simon, W., 140, 141, 384,
    387, 388, 394, 395, 397,

399, 401, 405, 406, 407,
    457
Simons, R., 578, 591
Simpson, E., 370
Simpson, E. L., 300, 342
Sims, J. H., 369
Sinclair, K. E., 264, 265, 268,
    274
Singer, J. E., 137, 311, 342
Sizonenko, P. C., 121, 123,
    124
Skelar, J., 398, 407
Skolnick, A., 10, 45, 64
Skolnick, J. H., 571, 596
Slater, P., 584, 596
Small, L., 272, 273
Smart, R. G., 457
Smith, D. S., 9, 28, 45
Smith, M. B., 248, 249, 259,
    280, 282, 283, 331, 333,
    338, 339, 369, 562, 566,
    569, 570, 571, 572, 573,
    577, 578, 579, 581, 584,
    590, 592, 596
Smith, P. C., 252
Smith, R. A., 272
Smith, R. S., 68
Snodgrass, S. R., 370
Snyder, R., 169, 181
Social Science Research
    Council Committee on the
    Life Course, 6
Solnit, A., 114, 116
Solnit, A. J., 305, 342
Solomon, F., 570, 577, 596
Solomon, R., 369
Somers, R., 584, 596
Somers, R. H., 369
Sommer, B., 149
Sones, G., 414, 431
Sonquist, J. A., 511, 535
Sorenson, R. C., 132, 142,
    397, 407, 457
Soskin, W. F., 457
Sparling, S., 319, 342
Spearman, C., 232, 537, 539,
    542
Speed, M. H., 456
Speicher, D., 299, 338
Spence, J. T., 256
Spencer, H., 538
Sperling, M., 461
Spiegel, L., 65
Spiegel, L. A., 496, 501, 511,
    526, 535
Spiegel, R., 456
Spiro, M. E., 141
Spitzer, R. L., 448

Spotnitz, H., 452
Spranger, E., 251
Stadtman, V. A., 571, 584, 595
Staffieri, J. R., 137, 145
Stanley, J., 543, 556
Stanley, J. C., 240
Starbuck, E. D., 528, 535
Stark, P. A., 163, 167, 168, 186
Starr, J. M., 9, 40, 260, 269, 278, 279, 346, 360, 369
Staub, E., 303, 318, 342
Staub, H., 509, 531
Steger, J. A., 233
Stein, A. H., 256
Stein, K. B., 457, 498, 509, 534, 535
Stein, S. L., 173, 187
Steinberg, L., 64, 76
Steinitz, V. A., 364
Steinkopf, K., 359
Stengel, E., 458
Stephens, B., 232, 237
Sternberg, R. J., 235, 241
Sterns, H. L., 91
Stevenson, H. W., 88
Stewart, C. S., 141, 142, 397, 398, 407
Stewart, L. H., 64, 69
Stinchcombe, A. L., 12, 45
Stitch, M. H., 343
Stolarz, S., 219
Stolz, H. R., 70, 144, 145
Stolz, L., 19, 45
Stolz, L. M., 70, 144, 145
Stone, A., 88
Stone, V., 359
Stotland, E., 309, 312, 318, 342
Strodtbeck, F. L., 248, 252, 268
Strong, D., 10, 26, 44
Strong, E., 552
Stroobant, R. E., 264, 265, 268, 274
Stuart, R. B., 525, 535
Sturr, J. F., 268
Suchman, E., 592
Sullins, C., 595
Sullivan, E. V., 348, 561, 584, 589
Sullivan, H. S., 77, 207
Sundberg, N. D., 268
Super, D., 64
Symonds, A., 451
Symonds, P., 64, 68

Taba, H., 265, 268
Taft, J., 584, 596
Tan, A. J., 166, 186
Tanaka, Y., 268

Tangri, S. S., 256
Tanner, J., 70, 76
Tanner, J. M., 14, 45, 118, 122, 124, 126, 127, 128, 129, 383, 398, 407, 505, 535
Tansey, S., 564, 590
Tapp, J. L., 348, 352, 353
Tapper, E. R., 358
Tarleau, A., 578, 591
Tarter, R. E., 448
Taylor, A. B., 117-155
Taylor, B., 99
Taylor, F. H., 123
Tec, N., 457
Teicher, J. D., 457, 458, 459
Tennyson, R. A., 510, 511, 535
Termar, D., 109, 110
Terman, L., 540, 541, 542, 544, 545, 546, 547, 548, 549, 552, 555
Terman, L. M., 397, 407
Teune, H., 253, 268
Tharp, R. G., 519, 535
Thernstrom, S., 4, 45
Thissen, D., 128
Thistlethwaite, D. L., 278
Thomas, A., 75
Thomas, J. A., 223, 233
Thomas, L. E., 278, 357, 370, 570, 579, 596
Thomas, W. I., 3, 24, 45
Thompson, D. J., 47
Thompson, G. G., 410, 431
Thompson, J., 64, 68
Thompson, O. E., 261
Thorndike, R. L., 211
Thorndike, R. M., 253
Thurber, J. A., 580, 596
Thurnher, M., 64, 81, 82, 86
Tilker, H. A., 318, 343
Timpane, M., 13, 45
Tindall, R. H., 64
Tipton, L. P., 361
Toder, N., 173, 186
Tolley, H., Jr., 365
Tomlin, P., 505, 532
Tomlinson-Keasey, C., 238
Toolan, J. M., 455, 458
Torgesen, J., 462
Torney, J. V., 276, 344, 345, 346, 350, 353, 354, 357, 359, 360, 363, 364, 365, 562, 592
Toussieng, P., 63
Trabasso, T., 226, 234, 241
Tracy, J. J., 300, 343
Traxler, A. J., 163, 168, 186

Trent, J., 64, 81
Trent, J. W., 361, 369
Triandis, H., 251, 252, 268
Troll, L., 278
Trow, M., 12, 17, 45, 259, 572, 573, 575, 590, 596
Truhon, S. A., 283
Tryon, C., 64
Tuckman, J., 458
Tuddenham, R., 537, 539
Tuddenham, R. D., 64
Tulving, E., 324, 343
Turiel, E., 298, 299, 300, 302, 303, 304, 343, 348, 370n
Turner, R. H., 17, 45
Tyack, D., 9, 44, 46
Tygart, C. E., 564, 596
Tyler, F. H., 119
Tyler, L. E., 268
Tzuriel, D., 163, 164, 186

Udry, J. R., 141
Ullman, M., 355, 369
Unger, I., 584, 596
U. S. Supreme Court, 518, 535
Unwin, J. R., 457
Urberg, K. A., 241
Uyecki, E. S., 358

Vaillancourt, P. M., 355
Vaillant, G., 64, 67, 113, 116
Van den Daele, L. D., 204
Van Duinen, E., 366
Vassiliou, V., 268
Venables, P. H., 451
Vener, A. M., 141, 142, 397, 398, 407, 457
Vernon, P., 543, 544
Vernon, P. E., 248, 250, 271, 272
Very, P. S., 239
Vickers, G. R., 584, 596
Viernstein, M., 545
Vinko, R., 123, 124, 125, 126
Vinovskis, M. A., 9, 43
Vlach, W., 64
Voss, H. L., 498, 535
Vygotsky, L., 538

Wackman, D. G., 359
Wagner, J., 168, 180, 186
Wainer, H., 128
Waite, G. A., 261
Waldfogel, S., 459
Waldron, I., 527, 535
Waldrop, M. F., 88
Walker, K., 564, 596

Walker, K. N., 564, 594
Walker, L. J., 281
Wall, S., 112, 115
Wallach, M., 329, 343, 551, 552
Waller, W., 5, 12, 46
Wallerstein, J., 64, 82
Wallington, S. A., 319, 339
Walters, E., 112, 115
Walters, P. A., 457
Walters, S. A., 167, 186
Wapner, S., 226
Ward, L. S., 361
Ward, R., 267
Waring, M., 64
Warne, G. L., 120
Warren, W., 453
Warwick, D. P., 277
Waterman, A. S., 161, 164, 165, 168, 170, 172, 186, 187
Waterman, C., 164, 165, 170, 172, 173, 186, 187
Watley, D., 547, 548
Watt, N., 64, 69, 81
Watt, N. F., 452, 453
Wattenberg, B. J., 568, 596
Watts, W. A., 370, 570, 571, 578, 579, 584, 596, 597
Webb, R., 539
Webb, R. A., 237
Weil, A., 348
Weinberg, I., 564, 596
Weiner, A. S., 180, 181
Weiner, B., 283
Weiner, I., 99
Weiner, I. B., 447, 448, 451, 452, 453, 454, 456, 459, 460
Weinstock, A., 82, 83
Weis, J. G., 498, 509, 510, 533
Weiss, D., 548
Weiss, E., 501, 535
Weiss, R. F., 317, 343
Weissberg, R., 344, 355, 358, 372
Weissman, H. J., 256
Weissman, M. M., 458
Weitz, L. J., 223, 233

Weitzman, E. D., 121, 125
Weller, G. M., 88
Welsh, G., 552, 553, 555
Wenar, C., 57
Wender, P. H., 462
Wendt, H. W., 268
Werner, E. E., 68
Werner, H., 438
Wessles, R., 281, 282, 283
West, C. D., 119
West, D. J., 498, 519, 532
Westby, D. L., 369, 370, 560, 569, 581, 586, 596
Westley, W., 113, 115
Westley, W. A., 189
Weston, L. C., 173, 187
Wetzel, R. J., 519, 535
Wheeler, D. K., 419, 431
Wheeler, S., 497, 531
White House Conference on Child Health and Protection, 12, 46
Whitbourne, S., 170, 187
White, B. J., 327, 342
White, R., 202
White, R. K., 253
White, R. W., 253
Whiting, J. P., 252
Whiting, J. W., 139, 141
Whittaker, D., 570, 571, 578, 579, 584, 596, 597
Whittaker, D. N. E., 370
Widdowson, E., 76
Wieder, H., 457
Williams, J. R., 498, 519, 532, 535
Williams, M., 319, 342, 422, 430
Williams, R., 592
Williams, R. M., Jr., 248, 250
Willis, R., 422, 424, 430
Wilson, G. D., 279, 283
Wilson, J., 563, 597
Wilson, R., 556
Wilson, R. R., 400, 405
Winborn, B. B., 578, 597
Wine, J. D., 318, 343
Winsborough, H. H., 33, 46
Winter, D. G., 268
Winter, J. S. D., 119, 120, 123, 124, 125

Wirtanen, I., 498, 531
Wittenberg, R., 188
Woerner, M. G., 452
Wohlwill, J. F., 452, 219, 234
Woltt, E., 109, 110, 116
Wolfenstein, M., 366
Wolfgang, M. E., 504, 507, 535
Wolin, S. S., 369, 594, 596
Wollack, S., 252
Wood, J. L., 570, 571, 584, 597
Wood, V., 579, 591
Woodworth, R., 541, 542
Wright, D., 272, 274
Wu, R. H. K., 125

Yang, S. C., 564, 597
Yankelovich, D., 25, 46, 252, 259, 269, 270, 271, 272, 567, 573, 574, 575, 576, 577, 597
Yarrow, L. J., 57, 88
Yarrow, M. R., 57, 88
Yen, S. S. C., 120, 121, 124
Yolles, S. F., 450
Young, A., 567
Young, H. B., 129, 145
Young, P. E., 120
Youniss, J., 233
Yusin, A. S., 459
Yusit, R., 166, 187
Yussen, S. R., 283

Zachry, C., 26, 46
Zajonc, R. B., 249
Zavalloni, M., 253
Zeitlin, M., 581, 584, 586, 597
Zellman, G. L., 352, 367
Zelnik, M., 132, 141, 142, 397, 407
Zetterblom, G., 513, 534
Zigmond, N. K., 461
Znaniecki, F., 3, 45
Zubin, J., 406, 448
Zussman, J. U., 329, 343

Subject Index

Academic underachievement, 461-463
  fears of failure and success in, 462
  hostility in, 462
  nature of, 461-462
  passive-aggressive sytle in, 463
  rivalry in, 462
Accommodation, 347
Achievement, 60
Achievement imagery, 169
Acting out, delinquent behavior as, 501
Activism, 330-332
  effects of socialization, 332-333
Acts, forbidden, 440, 441, 442, 443, 444
Adjective check list, 543, 544, 552
Adolescent rebellion, 359, 369
Adolescent storm and stress, 357
Adrenarche, 483
Adult adjustment, predicting from adolescence, 517
Adult psychological health, 66, 78, 80, 81, 84, 85, 86, 87
Age
  norms, 4-6, 15, 25-26
  patterns, 4-7
  segregation, 12-13, 15, 17
  study of, 10, 21
  and time, 4, 21, 25, 39
Age concepts
  chronological, 4
  developmental, 4-5, 10-11, 14, 21
  historical, 4-5, 11, 21
  social, 4-5, 10-11, 14, 21
Age differentiation hypothesis, 239
Age grade
  and delinquent behavior, 497, 502

and types of delinquents, 509-510
Agency and communion, Bakan's distinction, 273, 274, 282
Aging
  process of, 4
  trend, 13
Altruism, 499
American Council on Education, 573, 575, 576, 589
Amnesty movement, 564
Andrenogenital syndrome, 488
Androgen-insensitivity syndrome, 489-490
Anorchia, 487
Antecedent-consequent procedure, 251-252, 268
Anti-Nuclear Power movement, 564
Anxiety, 162-163, 173-174
Asceticism, 108
Asch's paradigm, 422
Assimilation, 347
Associative network analysis, 253
Astin surveys of attitudes and values, 271-272, 277
Attitudes toward sex, 270, 272
Audience, imaginary, 435, 437, 438, 440
Authoritarianism, 163
Automatization, 442, 443, 444
Autonomy, 106, 164, 169, 190-197, 208
  see also Independence
Avanguardia universitaria, 561

Baby boom, 563
"Bad" girls, 396, 401
Barron-Welsh Art Scale, 550
Behavior modification, in delinquency treatment, 519, 520

Behavior settings, overmanned and undermanned, 23, 24
Bem Sex-Role Inventory, 274
Bennington study, 277
Berkeley Growth Study, 34, 416
Berkeley Guidance Study, 34
"Big Brother," as delinquency treatment, 519
"Big Sisters," as delinquency treatment, 519
Birth order, *see* Sibling position
Bisexualism, 474, 489, 490
Black adolescents, political attitudes, 363, 364
Boarding as semi-independence, 30
Boys Club, 31
Boy Scouts, 31
Breast abnormalities, 487-489
Broken homes
  and delinquent behavior, 512-513
  and suicide, 527
  and types of delinquents, 510

California Psychological Inventory (CPI), 543, 544, 547, 548, 555
Campus activities, participation in, 173
Canonical correlation, 90
Careers, multiple, 5-6
  asynchrony, 5, 27
  management of, 6, 27
Carnegie Council, 573, 574, 576
Chapin Social Insight Test, 550
Child development, as new scientific field of inquiry, 11

Childlessness and suicide, 527
Child saving ideology, 9
Chromosomes, 473-483
  androgen-insensitivity syn-
    drome, 489
  delayed puberty, 483, 484-486
  Klinefelter's syndrome, 485-
    486
  Turner's syndrome, 485
Civil liberties, support for, 361,
    364
  during adolescence, 352
  during childhood, 352
Civil rights, 566, 570
Civil Rights movements, 564
Classification, of psychological
    disorders, 447-450
Cliques, 417, 418
Cognitive complexity, 164-165
Cognitive development, 180
  age changes, 226-227, 239,
    240
  competence-performance
    distinction in, 223
  information-processing com-
    ponents in, 240-242
  stages in, 219, 227, 228-232
Cognitive performance, 164-165,
    175
Cognitive styles, 164, 173-174
Cohort
  comparisons, 8, 36-37
  differentiation and succession,
    5, 7-9
  as historical perspective, 3
  as indexed by birth year, 4-5
  mentalities of, 5, 24
  size and composition, 7, 13
  and social structure, 10, 24-25
  subgroups of, 8, 34
Cohorts, youth
  large or expanding, 8, 17,
    19, 23
  small or declining, 8, 19
  size of, and deviance, 26
  and social change, 8, 17,
    23
Coital partners, 394-395, 398,
    400, 403-404
Coitus, 393-394, 403
  premarital (prevalence), 394-
    400
College
  Antioch, 571
  Bennington, 571
  Oberlin, 571
  Prytanée, 560

Reed, 571
  San Francisco State, 566
  Swarthmore, 571
College, versus work, 170
College behavior patterns, 165,
    173-175
College major
  atypicality, 173
  change of, 165
  difficulty of, 173
College satisfaction, 165
College students
  activities and changing values,
    572-577
  as minority in youth move-
    ment, 563
  and social movements, 563-
    564
  subcultures, 572-573
College youth surveys
  American Council on Educa-
    tion, 573-577
  Carnegie Council, 573-577
  Yankelovich, 573-577
Committee on the Life Course,
    Social Science Research
    Council, 6
Communalism, 564, 586
Communication training, non-
    verbal, 167
Concept Mastery Test, 544,
    545, 552, 555, 556
Concrete operations, 433, 434
Conformity, 173, 408, 422ff
Congress of Racial Equality
    (CORE), 566, 573
Conservatism Scale, and value
    priorities, 279, 283
Continuing education, 173
Convergent validation, need for
    in value studies, 250,
    253, 285
Cooperation and competition,
    166
Counseling, 167
Counterculture, 564, 578
Criminality, predicting adult,
    510, 511, 513-517
Critical weight, 94
Crowds, 417, 418
Cryptorchidism, 487
Cultural sophistication, 165
Culture, and delinquent
    behavior, 502
Cultures and youth movements,
    572-577
Cutting, 438, 444

Dating, 438, 439
  and delinquent behavior, 506
    508
Defense mechanisms, 101, 102,
    103-105, 108
Delinquency, see Delinquent
    behavior
Delinquent behavior, 496-535
  definition, 497-498
  frequency, 504ff, 523
  measures, 498
  optimal range of, 525-526
  prediction, 512-513
  prevention, 500
  religious conversion, 529
  rural-urban differences in,
    525
  seriousness, 504ff, 523
  theories of, 499-503
  treatment, 517-523
  typology, 508-511, 514fn
Democratic Party, 576
Demographic change, 7-8, 13,
    17, 19, 26
Demographic characteristics,
    youth activists, 562-563,
    566, 569-572
Depression, 453-547
  as appeal for help, 456
  conceptions of, 453-454
  in early adolescence, 455-456
  efforts to ward off, 456
  frequency of, 454-455
  in late adolescence, 457
  psychological toll of, 455-456
Deprivation, economic
  in households, 16, 34-35
  psychosocial effects, 35-38
  timing of, in life course, 35
Destabilization, dynamic, and
    generational unit, 583,
    588
Developmental dimensions, 89-
    91
Developmental discontinuities,
    69
Developmental model, 384-388,
    391, 405
Differential Aptitude Test (DAT),
    550
Drive, 496, 500
Drives, 102-103, 104, 108
Dropouts, and delinquent beha-
    vior, 520-521
Drug use, 165, 510, 514, 525
  and religious conversion, 528,
    530

Ecology movement, 564
Education, 398-399
  age patterns, 29-33
  see also Schools
Educational attainment, and
    delinquent behavior,
    514-515
Edwards Personal Preference
    Schedule, 252, 268
Ego, 103-105, 108, 110
Ego development, 188-208
  Loevinger's model, 273, 281,
    282
  and value content, 282, 283
Ego ideals, 103, 108, 109, 110
Ego identity
  alternative measures, 166
  competence versus intimacy,
    179
  description, 159-161
  development, 18-21 year old,
    168-170
    during college, 169-171
    beyond college, 172-177
  ego developmental approach,
    180-181
  formal operations and moral
    reasoning, 180
  formation in late adolescence,
    160-161, 168-170
  interpersonal relationships,
    importance to women's
    identity, 178-179
  longitudinal development,
    168-169
  reflected versus personal, 177
  structural description, 159-
    160, 180-181
  "the move away from home"
    (Matteson), 170
  women, development in, 172-
    178
    new approaches to research
      with, 178-179
Ego Identity Incomplete Sen-
    tences Blank, 166, 172
Ego strength, 416
Elite, 420
Elmtown's Youth, 12, 14-15
  in timeless realm, 16
Emotions, 102-103, 105
Empathy
  development of, 309-311
  motive for moral action,
    316-319
  role in moral development,
    307-319

Employment
  age patterns, 29-33
  worklife, 35, 37
Employment (unemployment,
    jobs)
  and delinquency treatment,
    520-521
  and delinquent behavior, 520
Entelechies and generational
    units, 582-583
Epidemiology, of psychological
    disorders, 447-450
Epistemology, 538
Equilibration, 347, 348
Erotic arousal, 389-390, 392,
    401-404
Establishment of independent
    domicile, 32-33
Ethnocentricity, 163
Expectancy-value theories of
    action, 284-285
Explanations, frequency of, 417
Exploratory behavior, 169
Extracurricular activities and
    youth movements, 569,
    572-577

Family, 105-107
  parental power, 416, 417
  paternal absence, 415, 417
  prediction of, 61-62
  size, 416, 417
  structure of, 415, 416
Family change
  evolutionary perspective on,
    12, 16, 28
  parental control in, 28-29
  in 1930s, 35, 37
  see also Transition to adult-
    hood; Socialization
Family contracting, in delin-
    quency treatment, 521-
    522
Family communication patterns,
    359
Fantasy, 501
Father absence, and delinquent
    behavior, 512-513
Fear of failure, 463
Fear of success, 174, 463
Feminist movement, 564
Field dependence, independence,
    164, 173
Field theory, 503
Foreclosure
  adaptiveness of (women), 174-
    175, 178

anxiety in, 162, 173
authoritarianism, 163
autonomy, 164
Black students, 169
cognitive performance (women),
    175
cognitive simplicity, 165
cognitive style, 164-165
college major (women), diffi-
    culty of, 173
college satisfaction, 165
concept attainment under
    stress, 164
conformity (women), 173
criteria for, 161-162
cultural sophistication, 165
description in married women,
    177
development in college, 170
drug use, 165
fear of success, 174
field-dependence-independence,
    164, 173
impulse expression, 165
impulsivity-reflectivity, 164
industry (men versus women),
    175
interpersonal style, 167-168
intimacy, 167
leaving school, 165
locus of control, 128, 164,
    173-174
longitudinal development,
    168-169
moral reasoning, 134, 163,
    174, 180-181
mothers, women's relationship
    to, 177
object-relatedness, 167-168
parental patterns, 171, 176-
    177
psychodynamics, 167-175
psychosocial maturity (women),
    175
self-esteem, 128, 129, 163,
    173, 175
sex role stereotypy, 173
social approval, need for, 164
temporal perspective, 164
Formal operations, 180-181,
    386, 432, 433, 434,
    436, 444
  assessment of, 223-224, 232-233
  construct validity of, 220-221,
    226, 236-239
  research, 211-212, 216-220,
    220-239

Fortune, 572, 592
Free Speech movement (FSM),
564
Freikorps, 561
Freischwebende Intelligenz, 561
Friends, and delinquent behavior, 498
Friendship, 105-107, 109, 437,
444
age differences in, 408, 409ff
best friends, 412
effects of family background,
408, 415ff
fluctuations in, 410, 413
intimacy in, 413, 414
jealousy in, 413
rejection in, 413, 414
sex differences in, 408, 413ff
Frustration-aggression hypothesis, and delinquent
behavior, 500, 503

"*g*", 537, 538, 542
Gangs
and delinquency treatment,
519, 521
and delinquent behavior, 502,
503
and types of delinquents,
510
Gault decision, 518
Gay Liberation movement, 564
Gender identity role, 384, 386,
388-389, 391-392, 395-
397, 401, 404, 473-75
adult models for, 474
body image, 474
childhood rehearsals of, 474-
475
delayed puberty, 483-486
errors in, 474-475
in hermaphroditism, 487-490
imprinting, 474
incongruous puberty, 486-487
peers and, 474-475
precocious puberty, 482-483
social interaction, 474-475
transpositions of, 474, 488-490
Generation
"Castro generation," 586
cohorts, 23
conflicts, 4, 11, 21
limitations of, perspective,
21-22
new generation, 563
perspective and analysis, 20-
22, 25

Generation gap, 346, 357, 358,
361, 372, 425
research on, 357, 358
Generation unit, 5
Generation Unit theory
biological age, 581
consciousness, 581-585, 588
cultural factors, 582-585
"dynamic destabilization,"
583, 588
Erlebnisschichtung (stratification of experience), 583
formalizing the theory, 584
"fresh contact," 583, 585
historical factors, 582
"inner dialectic," 584
intergenerational and intragenerational behavior,
586-587
Lagerung ("common location"),
581
psychological factors, 581-585
social structural factors, 584-
585, 587
Genital defects, *see* Breast abnormalities; Hermaphrodi-
tism; Sex organ defects
Genotypic continuity, 89-91
Giftedness, 536-559
Great Depression, 566, 567
adolescent roles in, 35
class variations in, 34-38
economic deprivation in,
34-38
youth in, 16, 34-38
Group therapy, in delinquency
treatment, 519, 522
Gruppi Universitari Fascisti,
561
Guided group interaction, as
delinquency treatment,
519
Guilford Consequences Test, 556
Guilt
"existential," 313-316
over harming others, 312-316
as motive for moral action,
319
Gynecomastia, 485, 487

Hermaphroditism, 487-90
adrenogenital syndrome, 488-
490
androgen excess, 488-489
androgen-insensitivity syndrome, 489-490
androgen insufficiency, 489-490

Klinefelter's syndrome, 485-
486
Reifenstein's syndrome, 489-
490
Turner's syndrome, 485
Heterosexual interests (boys),
169
Heterosexuality, 385-386, 391,
394, 404
History, social
demographic data in, 9, 33
folk literature in, 33
and life history, 3, 11, 20, 39
the "new", 9
record linkage, 29
History, and youth movements,
564-568
Homosexualism, 474, 489, 490
Homosexuality, 386, 391, 397
Hormones
androgen, 472-491
brain pathways, 472-473, 488,
490
delayed puberty, 486-487
estrogen, 472-491
fetal, *see* Prenatal hormones
FSH, 477
gonadotropins, 477, 481, 489
growth hormone, 477
homosexualism, 490
incongruous puberty, 486-487
LH, 477
ovarian, 473, 486
pituitary hormone, 476
precocious puberty, 482-483
prenatal, 473, 488-490
progesterone, 478, 481
prolactin, 478
and puberty, 472-491
sexual behavior and, 478-481
social behavior and, 478-479
testosterone, 472-491
threshold effect, 475, 488-
490
transexualism, 490
transpositions of gender iden-
tity/role, 490
Human potential seminars, 167
"Huston Plan," 567
Hyporchia, 487
Hypospadias, 474, 487

Identity, 103, 108, 109, 201-
203, 384-386, 391,
393
Identity (ego identity; role
identity), 497, 529

and delinquent behavior, 501-502, 517, 524-525
and religious conversion, 528-530
Identity achievement
anxiety in, 163
autonomy, 164
cognitive complexity, 165
cognitive performance, 164
cognitive style, 164-165
college activities, participation in (women), 173
college major, difficulty of, 173
conformity (women), 173
counseling styles, 167
criteria for, 161-162
cultural sophistication, 165
description in married women, 177
development in college, 169-171
drug use, 168
fathers, relationship to, 171-172
fear of success, 174
field dependence-independence, 164-173
formal operations, 180-181
in human potential seminars, 167
impulse expression, 165
impulsivity-reflectivity, 164
influence on development, college versus work, 170
intellectual performance in college, 165
interpersonal style, 168
intimacy, 167
leaving school, 165
locus of control, 164, 173-174
longitudinal development, 168-169
moral reasoning, 163, 174, 180-181
mothers, women's relationship to, 176-177
n Achievement, 174
object-relatedness, 168
parental patterns, 131, 171-172, 176-177
poetry writing, 165
psychodynamics, 167-168, 175-176
psychosocial maturity (women), 175

self-esteem, 163, 173
sex role sterotypy, 173
study habits, 165
temporal perspective, 164
Identity Achievement Scale (IAS), 166
Identity diffusion
anxiety in, 163, 173
autonomy, 164
cognitive complexity, 165
cognitive performance (women), 175
college major (women), difficulty of, 173
conformity (women), 173
criteria for, 161-162
cultural sophistication, 165
description in married women, 177-178
development in college, 170
drug use, 165
fear of success, 174
field of dependence, independence, 173
impulse expression, 165
impulsivity-reflectivity, 164
interpersonal style, 167
intimacy, 166-167
leaving school, 165
locus of control, 164, 174
longitudinal development, 168-169
moral reasoning, 163, 174, 180-181
mothers, women's relationship to, 176-177
n achievement, 174
object relatedness, 167
parental patterns, 171, 176-177
psychodynamics, 167, 176
psychosocial maturity (women), 175
self-esteem, 163, 173
sex role stereotypy, 173
trust (men vs. women), 175
Identity Statuses
achievement-foreclosure, moratorium-diffusion grouping for women, 174-175
advantages of, 161-162
cognitive development, 180-181
college behavior patterns, 165, 173-175
consequences, 172

counseling and teaching settings, 167
criteria for, 161-162
criteria for women, 172-173, 178-179
description in married women, 177-178
developmental aspects, 168-172, 176-178
developmental sequence, men vs. women, 176
father's importance, 172
follow-up research, 172
intelligence, 164, 173
interobserver reliability, 162
interpersonal style, 167-168
intimacy statuses and, 166-167
"life style orientation" as criterion for women, 173, 178
object-relatedness, 167-168
parental patterns, 171-172, 176-178
patterns of interactions, 166-168
personality characteristics, 162-166, 173-175
quasi-longitudinal studies, 168-169
sexual attitudes, importance in women, 132, 172-173, 178-179
women, criticism of application to, 178-179
women's psychodynamics, 175-176
Identity status interview components, analysis by, 165, 170
Ideographic-nomothetic distinction, 252-253
Ideological commitment, 161-162
Ideological thinking during adolescence, 353
Ideology, definition of, 353
Illegitimate pregnancy (illegitimate births), and suicide, 527
Impulse control, 53, 499, 501
Impulse expression, 165
Impulsivity-reflecivity, 164
Independence, 60, 409, 424
Individual differences in adolescence, adolescent prototypes, 258-259

Individuation, 190-197, 208
Industry, 160, 169, 175
Inferences, problematic
  from structural level to beha-
    vior, 18
Instincts, 499
Institute of Human Develop-
  ment, 14, 34
Instrumental values, 248, 251,
  263, 266
Intellectual competence, 61-62
Intelligence, 536-559
Interactions, strategic, 432, 435,
  440, 441, 442, 444
Interpersonal style, 167
Intimacy, 160, 166-167, 179
Intimacy statuses, 167

Japan, Meiji, 561
Jesus People, 564
Jungdeutschlandbund, 561
Juvenile court, 9, 10
Juvenile delinquent, 11-12
Juvenile-justice system (juvenile
  courts), 518-519

Klinefelter's syndrome, 485-
  486
Kohlberg's moral development
  theory, review and
  critique of, 299-304

Labeling as a delinquent, 517
Leadership qualities, 51
Leading crowd, 420, 421
Leaving home, 29-30, 32-33
Legalization, 443, 444
Life course
  best and worst periods of,
    36-37
  historical change in, 4, 26,
    29-38
  multi-dimensional concept
    of, 7
  normative model of, 6
  as perspective, 3-7, 10, 20
  see also Age; Life events; Life
    stage
Life events
  occurrence, spread, and over-
    lap of, 32-33
  timing and order of, 5-7, 26-
    27, 29-33
  see also Life course; Age
Life histories, see life course
Life span
  development, 5-6

developmental approach,
  adolescent values, 260-
    261, 269, 271
developmental asynchronies,
  14
developmental psychology, 3,
  5, 21
Life stage
  early adolescence, 10, 14
  semi-independence, 13, 19, 29-
    30
  "studentry", 13
  "youth," 10, 13
Locus of control, 68, 164, 174
Longitudinal research
  alternative methods, 58-59
  generality across cohorts,
    60-62
  history of, 47-48
  methods of perspectives, 47-
    48
  politics of, 49-50
  problems of, 50-62
Love, 394-396, 401, 404

Marginality, 497, 503, 511, 526
Marriage, 394-396, 399, 400
  age norms on, 6
  change in marital timing, 26,
    32-33
  suicide and, 527
  time of, 6, 30, 30-33
"Masculine anxiety," 31
Masculine protest
  and delinquent behavior,
    503, 512-513
Mass media
  and delinquent behavior,
    502, 526
Masturbation, 386-387
  and religious conversion,
    528-529
Maternal identification (women),
  174, 177
Maturation rate, 51, 52, 53, 55,
  70-77
Maturation
  and delinquent behavior,
    497, 505
  early and late, 143-144
  rate of, 523
Menarche, 98, 477, 481, 482
Mental development, 48, 51,
  52, 55
Mental health (and sexual behavior), 394, 400, 401
Metacognition, 214-215

Microphallus, 474, 487
Middletown study of attitudes
  and values, 271
Military service
  conscription for, 9, 16, 35
  and development, 37
  and life chances, 16
  as life event, 9
Minnesota Multiphasic Personality Inventory (MMP
  I), 372, 373, 541, 552
  and delinquency, 509
  and types of deliquents, 510
Moon movement, 564
Moral behavior, 392-393, 404
Moral development, 295-304
  and achievement motivation,
    33, 337-338
  and activism, 330-332
  compared with political
    development, 348, 353
  delinquent behavior and, 499-
    500, 506-508, 524
  effect of sex-role socializa-
    tion, 328-329
  effect of socialization, 320-
    330, 332-333
  and parent discipline, 321-
    324
  and parent identification,
    324-325
  peer influences, 326-328
  and religion, 334
  role of father, 325-326
  sex differences, 328-329
  theories of, 320
Moral internalization, types
  of, 333-338
Moral judgment stages, 296-
  298
Moral reasoning, 163, 174,
  181
  and moral conduct, 258,
    285
  and value content, 273,
    282-285
Moratorium
  adaptiveness of (women),
    174-175
  anxiety in, 162-173
  autonomy, 164-175
  cognitive complexity, 165
  cognitive performance
    (women), 175
  cognitive style, 164-165
  college major
    change of, 165

difficulty of 173
college satisfaction, 165
conformity (women),
 173
cooperation and competi-
 tion, 166
criteria for, 161-162
cultural sophistication, 165
description in married
 women, 177
development in college, 170
drug use, 165
fathers, relationship to, 169
fear of success (women),
 174
field dependence, independ-
 dence, 173
formal operations, 180
in human potential semi-
 nars, 167
impulse expression, 165
impulsivity-reflectivity,
 164
interpersonal style, 168
intimacy, 167
locus of control, 164-174
longitudinal development,
 169
moral reasoning, 163
mothers, women's relationship to, 177
object-relatedness, 168
Oedipal involvement, 168,
 169, 171, 176
parental patterns, 171, 176-177
psychodynamics, 168, 176
psychosocial maturity (women)
 175
self-esteem, 163, 173, 175
Motivation, scholastic and delinquent behavior, 513
Multiversities and youth movement, 571
Myers-Briggs Type Indicator,
 544

n Achievement, 129
Narcissism, 103, 110
National Commission on Re-
 sources for Youth, 13
National Guard, 566
National Merit Scholars, 547
National Survey of Youth,
 504ff
Negative identity, deliquent
 behavior and, 501-503,
 517, 524

New Left, 564
New Right, 564
Nocturnal emissions, 477

Oakland Growth Study, 34
Object-attachment, 103,
 106, 110
Object-relatedness, 167-168
Occupational commitment,
 161-162, 169
Occupational success, 51
Oedipal conflict
 and deliquent behavior,
 526
Oedipal influences, 75-77
Oedipal involvement, 168,
 169, 171, 176
Oedipus complex, 101, 102,
 106, 490
Ontogeny, 499
Opportunities
 class differences in access to,
 12, 15
 declining, 8
Oxford Pledge, 566

Pacifist movement, 564
Pair bonding, 475-481
Parent-adolescent affect,
 427
Parent-adolescent relations
 and deliquent behavior,
 501, 506-508, 511-
 517, 521-522,
 525-526
 and types of deliquents,
 510
 and religion, 530
Parental discipline, 52
Parental patterns, 171-
 172, 176-177
Parent-child relationships,
 358, 359
Parent-peer conflict, 408,
 425ff
Parenthood
 age at first child, 26
 adolescent, 7, 26-27
 baby boom, 13
 delay of, 26
Participatory democracy,
 586
Partisan differences,
 comprehension of,
 353
Passive-aggressive under-
 achievement, 463

Peace movement, 564
Peer group, 17-19, 408, 471ff
 structure of, 417
Peers, relations with
 and deliquent behavior, 502,
 513, 524
 and religious conversion,
 529
Personality structure, 107-110
Personal fable, 435, 438
Perspective taking, 432
Phi Beta Kappa, 548
Phoning, 436, 437, 444
Phylogeny, 499
Physical growth, 14
 and lag on social status,
 14, 39
 in relation to social
 environment, 14-15
"Plateau" view of adult
 development, 83-86
Poetry writing, 165
Political activity, during
 adolescence, 368, 369,
 370, 371
Political attitudes, 350, 354,
 360, 373
 development of, 354
Political cynicism, 354, 367
Political efficacy, 364
Political events and youth
 movements, 564-
 568, 573
Political ideologies, 346, 348,
 353
Political interests, and youth
 activism, 563-564,
 572-581
Political opinions, and
 delinquent behavior,
 506-508
Political socialization, 344,
 345, 355, 359, 363,
 364, 365, 372, 373
 adolescent values, 280-281
 age cohorts in, 346
 agents in, 355, 356, 358,
 359, 360, 361, 362
 basic assumptions in, 347
 behavioral school of, 345,
 349, 356, 362, 367,
 372
 cognitive-developmental
 school of, 345, 347, 348
 348, 349, 350, 356,
 362, 372
 comparative, 363

cross-national differences in,
363
definition of, 344
during adolescence, 346
during childhood, 346
generational school of, 345,
346, 357, 372
see also Sociological school
IQ differences in, 365
personality and, 365, 369, 370
political climate and, 365, 366
psychodynamic school of, 345,
346, 357, 367, 372
racial differences in, 363, 364
relationships between schools
of, 347
research on, 344, 345, 346, 347,
354, 356, 360, 372, 373
role of media in, 361
role of newspapers in, 361
role of parents in, 356, 357,
359, 369, 370
role of peers in, 362, 373
role of schools in, 359, 360,
363, 364
role of television in, 361
schools of, 345, 347
sex differences in, 364, 365
significance of adolescence
for, 371
social class differences in,
364
social learning school of, 345
see also Behavioral school
sociological school of, 345
see also Generational school
suggestions for future
research in, 372
variables in, 362
Political socialization research
methodological problems in,
344, 351, 354, 355, 358,
359, 370, 371, 372
Political system, perceptions of,
351
Political thinking, 348, 361, 362,
364, 367
among college students, 361,
364, 367, 370, 371
cross-national differences,
362
development of, 348, 349,
350, 351, 352, 353
among black adolescents,
363, 364
levels of, 352, 353
locus of control, 368, 371

patterns of, 351
personality and, 367
research on, 348
Politics
and changing values, college
students, 572-581
knowledge of, during
adolescence, 349
parents, and youth activists,
569-572
Popularity, 408, 419ff
Pornographic (utilization), 401-
404
Preoedipal attachment, 106,
110, 111
Pregnancy, 398, 399, 400
Presidential Science Advisory
Commission, 13
President Kennedy's assassina-
tion
impact on adolescents, 366
impact on children, 366
President's Commission on
Campus Unrest, 564,
567, 571, 595
Principia media, 588
Problem foci on adolescence
by decade, 11-12
in postwar era, 12, 14, 17, 19
Progeressive era, 9
Protestant Ethic Scale, 252
Protestant ethic values, 252,
270, 271, 280, 282
Protestant Reformation, 560
Prototypes
Baumrind's classification,
258
Block, Haan, and Smith
classification, 259
Havighurst's classification,
258-259, 269, 276
Hogan's analysis, 258
Peck and Havighurst's
classification, 258
Psychoanalytic theory, 357,
383-386, 389
of delinquent behavior, 500-
503, 511, 526
of delinquency treatment,
522
and types of delinquents,
509
Psychological factors and youth
movements
ideological differences, 579-
580
male/female differences, 579

moderate and extremist
differences, 577-581
personality traits, 577-581
psychological profile, 577-581
Psychopathology (mental illness,
mental health)
and delinquent behavior, 517
and types of delinquents, 510
Psychosexual development and
differentiation, 472
hormones, 472
social program, 473
stages of, 474
infancy and childhood, 474
middle childhood and pre-
puberty, 474
prenatal, 474
puberty and adolescence, 474
Psychosocial maturity, 169, 175
Psychosocial moratorium, 409
and delinquent behavior, 526
Psychosocial transitions, 77-82
Psychosomatic synptoms, 69
Psychotherapy
and delinquency treatment,
520, 521-522
Pubertal development, 419
Pubertal growth spurt, 99
Puberty, 390, 398, 402
adolescent sexual behavior and,
139-142
androgen and, 476-478
body image and, 144-145,
483-484, 486-487
body satisfaction, 144-145
and parental attitudes, 144
and personality variables,
144-145
and sociocultural factors,
145
conceptual models of
psychological adaptation,
132-136
cultural beliefs and attitudes,
138, 145
delayed, 483-486
developmental stages, 476-
478
in boys, 476-478, 484-485
in girls, 476-478, 484-485
direct effects on psychological
development, 132-134
disorders of, 482-487
early and late maturation, 135,
143-144
psychological correlations,
143-144

theoretical perspectives, 143
endocrine changes, 96-98
estrogen and, 476-478
females, 98
incongruous, 486-487
mediated effects on psychological development,
132, 134-141
onset, 94-96, 472-476
body status and, 476
central nervous system and,
476
hormones and, 472, 476-478
maturing, early and late, 484-
485, 490
physique age, 478
in precocious puberty, 482-
483
in delayed puberty, 483-486
precocious, 482-483
process of, 93-94
progression of, 478
psychoanalytic perspectives,
117, 131-132, 137
psychological adaptation to,
131-149
psychosocial age, 478
in precocious puberty, 482-
483
in delayed puberty, 483-
486
somatic development, 98-100
sex differences in, 100
variables affecting psychological
adaptation to, 135-141
childhood patterns of
thought and feeling,
137
cultural beliefs and
attitudes, 138
peer and parental attributions, 137-138, 144
social controls, 139-141

Rapprochement, 193-195
Rationalism, 539
Reasoning
combinatorial, 221
effects of intervention on,
235-236
formal logical, 212, 216-220,
235
matrix, 214
proportional, 222-223, 228-
229
scientific, 221-222, 224
Rebelliousness, 52, 91

Reference group, 425, 426
Regression, 80-81, 100-102,
103, 105, 106, 111
Reifensteins' syndrome, see
Androgen-insensitivity
syndrome
Religion and youth movements,
570, 572
Religious conversion, 527-530
and delinquent behavior, 529
Repertory Grid Test, 253
Republican Party, 576
Remote Associates Test, 556
Research techniques, 348
Retrospective reports, validity
of, 57-58
Revolutions
Bolshevik, 561
Chinese Communist, 561
Cuban, 586
French, 561
Indian, 561
Rokeach Value Survey, 251,
261, 262, 263, 265,
267, 268, 274, 275,
276, 277, 279, 281,
282, 283
Role (social role)
and delinquent behavior,
496-497, 501, 502, 505-
506, 524
ROTC, 580
Rule assessment, 222-223, 230
Russia, Czarist, 561

Sample attrition, 55-56
Satyagraha, 561
Schizophrenia, 452-453
conceptions of, 451
frequency of, 450-451
premorbid patterns in, 452-
453
presenting picture in, 451-
452
prognosis in, 453
Scholastic achievement
(academic achievement),
and delinquent behavior,
503, 519, 524
Scholastic aptitude and youth
movements, 578
Scholastic Aptitude Test (SAT),
543, 544, 545, 547,
548, 549, 553
School
age segregation in, 10, 12-13
attitudes toward

and delinquent behavior,
506-508, 513, 519-
520
alternative, in delinquency
treatment, 519-520
emergence of junior high, 17
increasing size of, 16-17
mass attendance, 9, 15
upward trends on enrollment,
12-13, 30
variations in secondary level
attendance by sex, 30-
31
School phobia, 459-461
acute, 461
chronic, 461
nature of, 459-460
origins of, 460
Secondary sex characteristics,
98
Self, the, 108, 109, 110
Self-blame, 423
Self-concept, 502
Self-esteem, 163, 173, 199-201,
436, 437
and delinquent behavior, 511,
520-521, 523
Sense of community, 351
Sentence-Completion Test,
413, 424
Sex-coded roles, 474
Sex differences, 255-256, 272-
275
in attitudes toward delinquency,
524-525
in delinquent behavior, 500,
511-512
Sex disorders, 474-490
paraphilic, 474-490
Sex hormones, 93
Sex organ defects, 486-490
Sex roles, 80-81, 85-87, 474
effects of social forces, 255
expressive versus instrumental
distinction, 255-256,
270
implications for adolescent
values, 256
male and female socialization,
255-256, 273-274
Sex role stereotypy, 173
Sexual behavior, 139-142
cohort effects, 141
consistancy of norms, 139-140
psychological correlates, 140-
141, 142
social organization and, 139

Sexual/erotic behavior, 478-481
  adrenogenital syndrome, 488-
    489
  androgen-insensitivity syn-
    drome, 489-490
  in boys, 478-481, 488-489
  counseling, 485-487
  dating, 480, 485, 488-489
  delayed puberty, 483-486
  in girls, 478-481, 488-489
  hermophroditism, 487-489
  hormones and, 478-481, 488-
    489
  intercourse, 481, 485, 490
  Klinefelter's syndrome, 485-486
  masturbation, 479-481, 485-
    486
  orgasm, 479-481
  petting, 481
  precocious puberty, 482-483
  prenatal hormones and, 479,
    488-490
  sex-play, 481, 488-90
  tactile stimuli and, 479, 488-
    490
  Turner's syndrome, 485
  visual stimuli and, 479, 488-
    490
Sexual fantasy, 389-390, 402-
    404
Sexual functioning, 93
Sexual identity, 169
  and delinquent behavior, 513
  and father absence, 513
Sexual maturation (puberty)
  and delinquent behavior, 505
  measures of, 505
  and religious conversion, 528
Sexual motivation, 388, 394-
    396, 401
Sexual permissiveness (attitudes),
    394-397, 400-401, 404
Sexual revolution, 397
Sexual status, 383, 386, 388,
    394, 397
Shaw, Clifford, 11
Sibling position, 415, 416, 417
Siblings, and delinquent beha-
    vior, 521
"Silent generation," 566
Situational disorder, 448
"Situational hypothesis," 426,
    427
Skeletal age, 505
"Sleeper effect," 65, 69
Social and cultural effects, on
    adolescent values, 260,

    268, 269, 271, 272, 274,
    275-280, 281
Social approval, 164
Social bonding (social control,
    anomie)
  and delinquent behavior, 526
Social change
  and age expectations, 26
  and parent-youth conflict, 21
  and student activism, 22
Social class
  and delinquent behavior, 498,
    523
  status and youth movements,
    569-572
Socialization
  burden of, 13
  family's changing role in, 16,
    17
  process of, 5, 8
  and youth movements
    family, 569-570
    political, 570-571
Socializing influences
  on adolescent values, 276-281
  family effects on adolescent
    values, 278-280
  school effects on adolescent
    values, 277-278
Social learning theory (learning
    theory)
  of delinquent behavior, 496-
    497, 500, 511
Social movements
  background, 560-563
  definition of, 560
  and youth, 561, 563-564
Social structure, and youth
    movements, 568-572
Society
  post-industrial, and youth
    movements, 568-569,
    571
Socioeconomic status, 68-69,
    83
Stanford-Binet, 536, 537, 538,
    540, 542
Stanford-Binet intelligence
    test, 211
Status
  backgrounds of SDS versus
    YAF members, 586-587
  in peer group, 423
Status deprivation
  and delinquent behavior, 500,
    502-503
  and types of delinquents,

    509-510
Status offenses, 518
Stein-Leventhal syndrome, 486
"Storm and stress" (Sturm und
    Drang; adolescent tur-
    moil), 499, 500
  and delinquent behavior, 513,
    523-524
Story-completion test, 423
Stratification of experience
    (Erlebnisschichtung),
    583
Strong Vocational Interest
    Blank, 552
Student activism, 346, 368, 369,
    370, 371
  and intelligence, 369, 370
  and student activism, 369, 370
Student activists
  parents of, 369, 370
  personality characteristics of,
    369, 370
  protest movement, 268, 269,
    270-271, 275, 280, 283
Student
  college, 563, 569, 572-577
  "critical mass," 563
  radical, 563-588
Student Nonviolent Coordin-
    ating Committee (SNCC),
    566, 573
Students for a Democratic Society
    (SDS), 566, 571, 573,
    586-587
Study habits, 165
Study of values, 543
Study of Values Test, 250-251,
    271, 272
Subculture, college student
    typologies, 572-573
Suicidal behavior, 457-459
  basic facts about, 457-458
  communication in, 458-459
  frequency of, 458
Suicide, 527
Superego, 103, 104, 110, 111
  and delinquent behavior, 501,
    526
Superego development, 305-307,
    328-329
Superego strength, 60
Survey of Interpersonal Values,
    268

Teacher
  in delinquency treatment, 519-
    520

observations of delinquent
behavior, 498
Teacher performance (student),
167
Temporal perspective, 164
Terminal values, 248, 251, 263,
266
Thelarche, 483
Theories of adolescence
culture bound nature of, 261
general themes, 254-255
implications for values, 254-
261
implications of general themes
for adolescent values,
255
sex differences, 255-256
youth and youth culture,
256-258
Theory construction about youth
movements
class consciousness, 581
core-periphery, 581
existential-situational, 581
expressive or cultural politics,
581
family socialization, 581
generation uni[, 581-589
historical, 581
moralism, 581
psychoanalytic-oedipal revolt,
581
status politics, 581
structural-functional, 581,
587
Thinking
adolescent characteristics,
212-215
foresight, 213-214
hypothetical, 213, 216, 220,
233-235
self-reflective, 214-215
Thorarche, 477
Time
historical, 3-5, 7, 9, 39
life, 4-5, 7, 39
social, 4-5, 39
tables or schedules, 6, 10, 29,
32, 38
Tomboyism, 488
Transcendentalist movements,
564
Transexualism, 474, 490
Transformation, 443, 444
Transitional period or Transition, 409, 418
Transition to adulthood, 10, 13

multiple events in, 5-7, 27
in Great Depression, and
World War II, 16
discontinuities in, 16, 23
change in, during 30s and 40s,
26
during early industrialization,
29-31
impact of Depression hardship on, 35-37
and social change from 1880
to 1970, 32-33
see also Education; Employment; Life Events;
Marriage; Parenthood
Transvestism, 474, 490
Trust, 169, 175
Turner's syndrome, 485

U.S. Bureau of the Census, 563,
569, 596
Universality (cultural relativity),
502
University
Berkeley, 566
Columbia, 566, 569
Harvard, 561, 569
Jackson State, 566
Kent State, 566
Moscow, 561
Princeton, 561
reform, 566
Stanford, 569
Virginia, 561
Yale, 561, 569
Ur, 560
Utopia and dystopia, 586

Valence, as perceived attractiveness or repulsive-
ness, 284
Value(s), 247-285
as abstract structure, 249-250
of adults, 24
antecedents and consequents,
248-249
behavior and, 284-285
change, interpretation of, 268-
269
change over time, studies of,
268-271, 277-278
definitions of, 247-250
functions of, 248
of generations, 22
as inducing valences, 284
as motives, 284
as multidisciplinary concept,

247-248
parent/child differences, 279-
280
person-environment fit, 250,
276, 278
religious attitudes and, 271,
274, 277
Rokeach's definition, 248
social class and, 276, 280
sources of evidence, 250-253
of youth, 25
Value assessment
antecedent-consequents procedure, 251-252, 268
associative network analysis,
253
Value criteria, 264
Value fit, effects of person-
environment discre-
pancy, 250, 276, 278
Value orientations, 252, 268
Value referents, 264
Value systems
achievement and morality
domains, 283
Australian vs. U.S. comparison,
262-265
college youth, 265-272
concept of, 248-251
conservatism and, 282, 283
cross-cultural comparisons,
265-268, 273
developmental stages and,
281-284
early versus late adolescence,
261-262, 281
effects of family and, 278-280
effects of school and, 277-278
ego-development and, 273,
281, 282
juvenile offenders, 275
Value Systems
intergenerational differences,
279-280
moral development and, 273,
281, 282, 283
parent-child differences,, 279
sex differences, 272-275
sex differences in families and,
279
socializing influences, 254, 274,
277-281
student activists, 275
Viet Nam War
impact on adolescent political
thought, 366, 370
Virginity, see Sexual status, coitus

VPI, 543

Wanderjahr, 561
Wandervogel, 561
War
  Cambodia, 566
  Civil War, 569
  in Southeast Asia, 571
  Vietnam, 567, 586
  Vietnam-Cambodia, 566
  World War II, 563, 568
    adolescence in, 16, 36
    father-absence during, 8,
      19-20
Watergate, 567
  impact on adolescent political
    thought, 367, 377
Ways to Live Test, 252, 268,
  272
Welsh Figure Preference Test,
  552
White House, 567
White House Conference, 1930,
  on Child Health and
  Protection, 12
"Wittenberg Reformers," 560
Word Association technique,
  411

Yankelovich surveys, 252, 269-
  272
Young Americans for Freedom
  (YAF), 566, 567, 573,
  586-587
Young Democrats, 573

Young Mens Christian Association, 31
Young Republicans, 573
Youth
  as actors, 24
  "carrier class," 564
  "cities of youth," 564
  demographic growth, 562-
    563, 568-569
  general historical works on,
    9
  "idle," 30
  left-wing, 566
  related agencies, institutions, 3,
    15, 16
  right-wing, 566
  and social movements, 563-
    564
  as stage in life cycle, 561-562
  "traditions of," 5, 25
  unrest, protest, 5, 13, 24,
    26
Youth activism, 6
Youth and youth culture
  characteristics of, 257
  cross-cultural comparisons in
    values, 265-268
  and delinquent behavior, 508,
    526
  implications for adolescent
    values, 257
  President's panel, 256-257
  as stage of life, 256-257
  values on campus, 259, 268-
    272

Youth movements, 259, 268,
  269, 270-271, 275, 280,
  283
  college students as minority
    in, 566, 571
  cultural factors, 572-577
  definition of, 563-564
  demographic characteristics of
    activists, 571
  as destabilizing force, 583,
    588
  extracurricular activities, 578-
    579
  generational unit theory, 581-
    585
  historical factors, 564-568
  intellectual orientation, 578
  issues and values, 567, 570-
    579
  majors of youth activists in,
    578
  morality, 579
  multiversities, 571
  occupational aspirations of
    youth in, 576-579
  psychological and personality
    factors, 577-581
  social structural factors, 568-
    572
  spread of goals and objectives,
    566-567
Youth in transition, 505, 513-
  517

Zeitgeist, 564, 582-583